CRUSADING, SOCIETY, AND POLITICS
IN THE EASTERN MEDITERRANEAN IN
THE AGE OF KING PETER I OF CYPRUS

MEDITERRANEAN NEXUS
1100-1700
CONFLICT, INFLUENCE AND INSPIRATION IN THE MEDITERRANEAN AREA

VOLUME 10

Editorial Coordinator
Evelien CHAYES

Editorial Board
Lorenzo CALVELLI
Christopher CELENZA
Evelien CHAYES
Gilles GRIVAUD
Martin HINTERBERGER
Michalis OLYMPIOS

Crusading, Society, and Politics in the Eastern Mediterranean in the Age of King Peter I of Cyprus

Edited by

ALEXANDER D. BEIHAMMER

and

ANGEL NICOLAOU-KONNARI

BREPOLS

© 2022, Brepols Publishers n. v., Turnhout, Belgium.

All rights reserved. No part of this publication may be reproduced, stored in a retrieval system, or transmitted, in any form or by any means, electronic, mechanical, photocopying, recording, or otherwise without the prior permission of the publisher.

D/2022/0095/150
ISBN 978-2-503-59856-7
eISBN 978-2-503-59857-4
DOI 10.1484/M.MEDNEX-EB.5.128507

ISSN 2565-8549
eISSN 2565-9774

Printed in the EU on acid-free paper.

Dedicated to the memory of Michalis Pieris, whose literary studies and dramatic adaptation of Leontios Makhairas's chronicle revived «ρὲ Πιὲρ τὸν μέγαν» and his era.

Table of Contents

Preface   11
Alexander D. BEIHAMMER and Angel NICOLAOU-KONNARI

**The Life and Reign of Peter I of Lusignan
(1329–69, crowned 1359). Chronology**   13
Angel NICOLAOU-KONNARI

Introduction
The Sources and the Context

**Peter I of Lusignan (1329–69, 1359) in Historical Sources and Modern
Popular Culture**   31
Angel NICOLAOU-KONNARI

**Appendix A: The Life and Reign of Peter I of Lusignan (1329–69,
1359) according to Leontios Makhairas and William of Machaut: A
Thematic Comparison**   69
Angel NICOLAOU-KONNARI

**Appendix B: (Tentative) Psychiatric Assessment of Peter I of
Lusignan (1329-69)**   75
Kakia NIKOLAOU

**The Sack of Alexandria (1365), the Crusading Movement, and the
Eastern Mediterranean in the First Half of the Fourteenth Century**   77
Alexander D. BEIHAMMER

Part I
From Acre to Alexandria – The Politics and Ecology of Crusading

**Cyprus and the Crusades between the Fall of Acre and the Reign of
Peter I**   109
Mike CARR

Crete, 1357–67: A Stronghold for Venetian Diplomacy and Crusading in the Eastern Mediterranean   121
Charalambos GASPARIS

A Climate for Crusading? Environmental Factors in the History of the Eastern Mediterranean during the Life and Reign of Peter I of Cyprus (1329–1369)   135
Johannes PREISER-KAPELLER

Angevin and Lusignan Visual Claims to the Crown of Jerusalem: Parallel Lives?   157
Michalis OLYMPIOS

Part II
Peter I's Alexandrian Crusade (1365) – Event and Context

The Papacy and King Peter I of Cyprus   177
Peter EDBURY and Chris SCHABEL

Appendix A: Pope Innocent VI's Letters Concerning the Succession of King Peter I of Cyprus   206
Chris SCHABEL

Appendix B: Pope Urban V's Letters Concerning King Peter I of Cyprus and the Crusade   211
Chris SCHABEL

European Military Development and the Eastern Mediterranean in the Age of Peter I of Cyprus (1359–69)   241
John FRANCE

Peter I of Lusignan's Crusade and the Reaction of the Mamluk Sultanate   251
Clément ONIMUS

'Le roy de Chippre de renon': The Depiction of Peter I of Lusignan in French Literature and Historiography   273
Angel NICOLAOU-KONNARI

Part III
A Crusader Kingdom – Cypriot Society before and after Peter I

Stability or Chaos? Power Elites in Lusignan Cyprus between the 1360s and 1390s   323
Miriam Rachel SALZMANN

Le roi Pierre 1er et son conseil   345
Gilles GRIVAUD

The *Suriani* in Lusignan Cyprus until Peter I (1369). Terminology, Legal Status, and the *Curia Surianorum*   361
Johannes PAHLITZSCH

Part IV
The Rise of a New Power – Muslim-Turkish Anatolia

The Long Prose 'Epic' of Sarı Saltuk Dede (fl. *c.* 1260 to 1298) as a Source for Understanding the Style and Context of Crusading Warfare in the Late Thirteenth-Century Near and Middle East   385
Rhoads MURPHEY

'Wolves and Sheep Drank and Grazed Together': A Case Study on the Formation of the Anatolian Beyliks   417
Romain THURIN

Italian Vernaculars as Diplomatic Languages in the Medieval Levant   443
Daniele BAGLIONI

Part V
The Schismatic Ally – Byzantium between Islam and Unionism

Crusade, Civil Strife, and Byzantine-Turkish Coalitions in the Time of Emperor John VI Kantakouzenos (1341–54)   457
Alexander D. BEIHAMMER

John V Palaiologos in Rome   489
Rethinking an Imperial Visit and 'Conversion'
Sebastian KOLDITZ

Anti-Palamism, Unionism, and the 'Crisis of Faith' of the Fourteenth Century 517
Charles C. Yost

Cyprus in the Late Byzantine Theological Landscape, with Special Reference to the Palamite Controversy[*] 551
Alexis Torrance

Maps 567

List of Figures 571

Index 575

List of Contributors 627

ALEXANDER D. BEIHAMMER
ANGEL NICOLAOU-KONNARI

Preface

The completion of 650 years since the sack of Alexandria in 2015 prompted the editors of this volume to put together the international conference *Knighthood, Crusades, and Diplomacy in the Eastern Mediterranean at the Time of King Peter I of Cyprus*, generously sponsored by the Institute for Scholarship in the Liberal Arts and the Medieval Institute of the University of Notre Dame and graciously hosted by the Notre Dame Global Gateway in the heart of Rome on 14–16 October 2016. We, thus, foremost express our gratitude and thanks to the then interim director of the Medieval Institute, Prof. John Van Engen, and the committee of the Byzantine Studies program of the Medieval Institute as well as to Prof. Ted Cachey and all those who helped with the conference at the Rome Global Gateway of the University of Notre Dame.

We hoped that the conference and the ensuing publication of its proceedings would go some way towards filling the bibliographical void on King Peter I of Lusignan, the Alexandrian Crusade, and its broader Mediterranean context. The outcome certainly met all our expectations. In Rome, twenty-three participants presented their research and had fruitful discussions on various aspects of the Cypriot king's life and personality and the larger political and social framework of his reign. For several reasons, Nicholas Coureas, Laura Minervini, Sara Nur Yıldız, and David Wrisley were unable to submit their papers for publication in the present volume while Kakia Nikolaou and Romain Thurin joined the rest of the authorial team at a later stage. We wish to extend our thanks to all the participants in the Rome conference as well as to the contributors to this volume for their chapters and their patience with the editorial work. We are particularly grateful to Chris Schabel (University of Cyprus) for providing linguistic advice.

Romain Thurin and Skevi Sykopetritou deserve our gratitude for the creation of the maps and the composition of the index respectively. Special thanks go to the University of Cyprus for sponsoring the present volume. And, last but not least, we would like to thank Brepols and the editorial board of the Mediterranean Nexus series, especially Evelien Chayes, for their help. Working with them has been a great pleasure as always. We also express sincere thanks to the anonymous reviewers for their valuable comments. King Peter's figure may still remain somehow elusive but the contextual analysis of his works and days this volume provides most certainly opens up new vistas of understanding and interpretation and will hopefully incite further research.

ANGEL NICOLAOU-KONNARI

The Life and Reign of Peter I of Lusignan (1329–69, crowned 1359). Chronology

For the composition of this chronology, a great number of primary and secondary sources have been consulted, in particular: Louis de Mas Latrie, *Histoire de l'île de Chypre sous le règne des princes de la maison de Lusignan*, 3 vols (Paris: Imprimerie impériale, 1852–1861); *Bullarium Cyprium III: Lettres papales relatives à Chypre 1316–1378*, ed. by Charles Perrat and Jean Richard, with the collaboration of Christopher Schabel, Sources et études de l'histoire de Chypre, 68 (Nicosia: Centre de Recherche Scientifique, 2012); Sophie Hardy, *Édition critique de la Prise d'Alixandrie de Guillaume de Machaut* (thèse doctorale de Lettres modernes, Université d'Orléans, 2011); Philippe de Mézières, *The Life of Saint Peter Thomas*, ed. by Joachim Smet, O. Carm. (Rome: Institutum carmelitanum, 1954); *Chroniques de J. Froissart*, ed. by Siméon Luce et al., 15 vols, Société de l'histoire de France (Paris: Mme Ve. Jules Renouard et al., 1869–1975); Leontios Makhairas, Χρονικό της Κύπρου. Παράλληλη διπλωματική έκδοση των χειρογράφων, ed. by Michalis Pieris and Angel Nicolaou-Konnari, Texts and Studies in the History of Cyprus, 48 (Nicosia: Cyprus Research Centre, 2003); Nicolas Jorga, *Philippe de Mézières (1327–1405) et la croisade au XIVe siècle* (Paris: École Pratique des Hautes Études, 1896; repr. London: Variorum Reprints, 1973); Sir George Hill, *A History of Cyprus*, 4 vols (Cambridge: Cambridge University Press, 1940–52); Wipertus H. Rudt de Collenberg, *Les Lusignan de Chypre*, Επετηρίς Κέντρου Επιστημονικών Ερευνών (Κύπρου), 10 (1979–80), 85–319; Peter W. Edbury, *The Kingdom of Cyprus and the Crusades 1191–1374* (Cambridge: Cambridge University Press, 1991); and all the contributions to the present volume.

The order of events and a number of dates are occasionally uncertain or inferred from narrative sources. Such cases are often indicated by a question mark ?. The following particularly problematic cases are placed in square brackets [ ], which indicates that they are considered incorrect:
1. The older recension of Leontios Makhairas's chronicle (= Venice, Biblioteca nazionale Marciana, MS gr. VII, 16, 1080) provides two alternative dates for Peter's coronation: the chronicler first claims that Hugh IV had his son crowned

Angel Nicolaou-Konnari • University of Cyprus

on 24 November 1358, a Saturday, in his lifetime but a few lines later he adds that 'I have found it written elsewhere [in the royal archives]' that the coronation took place soon after Hugh's death, on 'Sunday 24 November 1359', which was indeed a Sunday (Leontios Makhairas, Χρονικό της Κύπρου, pp. 111–12). Recent scholarship and most of the contributors to this volume consider the year 1359 to be more likely.

2. The order of events and the chronology concerning a first (authorized to inform the pope of Peter's coronation and of the actions of the legate Peter Thomas against the Greek clergy) and a second (authorized to deal with Hugh of Lusignan's claims to the throne) Cypriot embassy to the *curia* are confused in Leontios Makhairas's chronicle. For the departure of the first embassy only the day is given (18 September), but the fact that it is placed right after the attempts of Peter Thomas (said to have come to Cyprus on 8 December 1359) to confirm the Greek clergy suggests that the year is 1360. The departure of the second embassy is placed on 9 April 1360 (Leontios Makhairas, Χρονικό της Κύπρου, pp. 117–22). However, since we know from the papal registers that the first Cypriot embassy was at the *curia* by 11 June 1360 (*Bullarium Cyprium III*, nos u-228–46, esp. u-230–34, 236–38, 240) and the second one by mid-November 1361 (*Bullarium Cyprium III*, nos u-260–88, esp. u-276–77, 281, 287), the 9 April 1360 date given for the second embassy works well for the first one and the 18 September date given for the first embassy for the second one, if we place it in the year 1361.

3. Peter's route after his sojourn at the papal court in Avignon (29 March–31 May 1363) poses many problems because of the various itineraries proposed by both major and minor sources. John Froissart has Peter travel through Germany to Prague (where he stayed for three weeks) and then return to France through Juliers, Brabant (Bruxelles), Flanders (Bruges), and Hainaut (*Chroniques de J. Froissart*, VI, § 504, pp. 85–86). Minor sources mention Peter's presence in Savoy, Basel, Strasbourg, Mainz, and Cologne in July 1363 (Jorga, *Philippe de Mézières*, pp. 173–75). William of Machaut and other sources place the journey to Germany after the coronation of Charles V on 19 May 1364 and consider it to be the beginning of a long tour that continued with sojourns in Prague and Cracow and ended in Venice (Hardy, *Édition critique de la* Prise d'Alixandrie, ll. 839–1610).

As it is unlikely that the Cypriot king made two journeys to Germany, the itinerary proposed by Machaut, who may have accompanied Peter, seems more plausible in terms of geographical sequence and time demands and agrees with documentary evidence about Peter's presence in 1363 and 1364, despite difficulties in identifying some of the place-names he gives. Although his account is at times confusing, Nicolae Iorga discusses all itineraries and also believes that Machaut's is more reliable, suggesting that Peter visited Brabant and Flanders in 1364 on his way to Germany (Jorga, *Philippe de Mézières*, pp. 173–201).

4. Leontios Makhairas (Χρονικό της Κύπρου, p. 220) and all later Cypriot narrative sources place Peter's murder on Wednesday 17 January 1369. However, the prologue to the 1369 recension of John of Ibelin's legal treatise, which describes the meeting of the Cypriot High Court right after the murder and is thus a very

reliable source (John of Ibelin, *Le Livre des Assises*, ed. by Peter W. Edbury, The Medieval Mediterranean, 50 (Leiden – Boston: Brill, 2003), p. 733), a marginal note found in a Cypriot manuscript (Costas N. Constantinides and Robert Browning, *Dated Greek Manuscripts from Cyprus to the Year 1570*, Dumbarton Oaks Studies, 30 – Texts and Studies in the History of Cyprus, 18 (Nicosia: Dumbarton Oaks Research Library and Collection – Cyprus Research Centre, 1993), pp. 62–63), and William of Machaut (Hardy, *Édition critique de la Prise d'Alixandrie*, ll. 7993–8010) give 16 January 1369 (discussion in Peter W. Edbury, 'The Murder of King Peter I of Cyprus (1359–1369)', *Journal of Medieval History*, 6 (1980), 219–33 (at pp. 223–24)). Recent scholarship and the contributors to this volume consider 16 January to be more likely.

For reasons of convenience, hereafter P. stands for Peter I of Lusignan.

9 October 1329 (Feast of St Denis)
P.'s birth in Nicosia, first son of Hugh IV of Lusignan, king of Cyprus, by his second wife, Alice of Ibelin.

3 September 1339
Pope Benedict XII refuses to grant a dispensation for the marriage of one of Hugh IV's sons to his niece Eschiva of Montfort on the grounds of age difference and consanguinity.

28 June 1342
Pope Clement VI grants a dispensation for P.'s marriage to his first cousin Eschiva of Montfort, ratified on 8 August 1342.

Summer 1343
Death of Guy of Lusignan, P.'s elder brother from a different mother and heir to the throne of Cyprus.

1344
The Christian league, in which Cyprus participates, captures Smyrna.

Count of Tripoli – *heir apparent* (*c.* 1346–59)

Before 24 November 1346
King Hugh IV makes P. count of Tripoli.

24 November 1346
P., described as count of Tripoli for the first time, attends the consecration of Bishop Francis of Arezzo of Limassol.

***c.* 1346–48?**
Philip of Mézières visits Cyprus and forms a lifelong friendship with P., with whom he will share the same crusader goals.

Mid-1340s
P. receives his calling to be a crusader after having a vision in a monastery near Famagusta hosting a piece of the cross of the Good Thief.

Before 1347? (Or late 1350s?)
P. founds the Order of the Sword.

Spring 1347
Philip of Mézières visits Jerusalem. A mass is celebrated at the Church of the Holy Sepulchre on P.'s behalf.
11 July 1347
Pope Clement VI grants P. a plenary indulgence *in articulo mortis*.
End of summer 1347–48
Black Death attacks Cyprus.
Before 13 September 1349
P.'s failed escapade to the West with his brother, Prince John of Antioch, and friends.
13 September 1349
Pope Clement VI promises Hugh IV to ask his sons to return to Cyprus if they come to Rome.
Before 12 August 1350
Hugh IV brings his sons P. and John back to Cyprus and imprisons them.
12 August 1350
Pope Clement VI intervenes for P.'s liberation.
12 July 1351
Pope Clement VI grants P. and his brother, Prince John of Antioch, a plenary indulgence *in articulo mortis*.
2 September 1351
Pope Clement VI thanks Hugh IV for having liberated P.
Before 1353
P.'s wife, Eschiva of Montfort, dies. She may have given birth to a daughter also named Eschiva, who died at a young age.
1 February 1353
P.'s gets engaged to Eleanor of Aragon.
21 August 1353
Eleanor of Aragon leaves Barcelona.
September 1353
P.'s marries Eleanor of Aragon in Nicosia.
2 August 1354
Pope Innocent VI absolves P. from his vow to visit St James of Compostela and also grants him other dispensations.
2 August 1354
P. intercedes with Pope Innocent VI for the grant of ecclesiastical benefices.
End of 1357
Birth of Peter II, son of P. and Eleanor of Aragon.

King of Cyprus (1359–69), Jerusalem (1360–69), and Armenia (1368–69)

[24 November 1358?
Hugh IV has P. crowned king of Cyprus in Nicosia.]
10 October 1359
Death of Hugh IV.

24 November 1359
P. is crowned king of Cyprus in Nicosia by Bishop Guy of Ibelin of Limassol.
Late 1350s? (Or before 1347?)
P. founds the Order of the Sword.
8 December 1359
Arrival of Peter Thomas, papal legate, in Cyprus (Paphos or Kyrenia port).
Late 1359–63
P.'s dispute with Hugh of Lusignan, son of his late half-brother Guy, as to who is the rightful heir to the throne.
January 1360
The inhabitants of Gorhigos place themselves and their land under P.'s rule.
18 February 1360
Robert of Taranto, Hugh of Lusignan's stepfather, writes to Niccolò Acciaiuoli, Grand Seneschal of the Kingdom of Naples, complaining about what he regarded as P.'s illicit accession to the throne of Cyprus.
28 March 1360
P. makes appointments to offices of the Kingdom of Jerusalem.
Easter Sunday 5 April 1360
P. is crowned king of Jerusalem in Famagusta by the papal legate Peter Thomas.
Before 9 April 1360 [rather than 18 September 1360?]
P. defends the Greek clergy against the attempts of the legate Peter Thomas to confirm the Greek clergy.
9 April 1360 [rather than 18 September 1360?]
P. sends envoys to the pope to inform him of his coronation and of the actions of the legate Peter Thomas against the Greek clergy.
16 April 1360
Earliest papal letter addressed to Peter I as king of Cyprus.
22 April 1360
Upheaval in Famagusta.
24 May 1360
Pope Innocent VI writes to P. with regards to Hugh of Lusignan's claims to the throne of Cyprus and the dowry of his mother, Empress Maria of Constantinople.
17 June 1360
Pope Innocent VI grants P. authorisation to trade with the sultan's lands for two years with only two galleys.
28 June 1360
Pope Innocent VI expresses his condolences to P. for the death of his father, exhorts him to rule well, and asks him to do justice to Hugh of Lusignan.
16 August 1360
Renewal and updating of Venetian privileges.
c. 1360
Birth of Margaret, daughter of P. and Eleanor of Aragon.
17 October 1360
P. makes appointments to offices of the Kingdom of Cyprus.

Late 1360 / Early 1361–69
Philip of Mézières serves as P.'s chancellor.
1361–62
Pestilence outbreaks in Cyprus. Processions and prayers with the participation of the royal family.
c. 1361–62 and 1367
In order to finance his expeditions, P. allows the *perpyriarioi* to buy their enfranchisement.
31 March 1361
Pope Innocent VI grants P. a plenary indulgence *in articulo mortis* and the right to have his own portable altar.
12 July 1361
P.'s fleet leaves Famagusta.
24 August 1361
P. captures Antalya (Satalia/Adalia).
8 September 1361
The emir of Alaya (Candelore, today Alanya) surrenders to P.
18 September 1361 [rather than 9 April 1360?]
P. envoys leave for the *curia* to ask Pope Innocent VI for the settlement of the dispute with Hugh of Lusignan; they are authorized to propose a pay-off, comprising an annual income of 50,000 Cypriot white bezants.
22 September 1361
P. returns to Kyrenia.
1362, 1363, 1368
P. intercedes with the Holy See for the grant of ecclesiastical benefices.
1362
P.'s envoys recruit men at arms in Lombardy.
13 April 1362
The emir of Antalya attempts to recapture the city but is repulsed. He will unsuccessfully repeat his attempts.
9 May 1362
Supplies and men at arms under a new captain are sent to Antalya from Cyprus.
After 9 May 1362
The new captain of Antalya, Admiral John of Tyre, captures the castle of Myra.
15 June 1362
P. writes to the government of Florence, asking their assistance for the recovery of Jerusalem.
15 September 1362
P. writes to Niccolò Acciaiuoli, Grand Seneschal of the Kingdom of Naples, thanking him for the offer of galleys that will be used in the war against the infidels.
24 October 1362–Autumn 1365
P.'s first journey to Western Europe for the promotion of a crusade.
24 October 1362
P. sails from Paphos, accompanied by his chancellor Philip of Mézières and the legate Peter Thomas. He stops at Rhodes.

19 November 1362
Pope Urban V extends the imposition of an ecclesiastical tithe on Cyprus, which is to be used for the kingdom's defence against the Turks, for another three years.
22 November 1362
Pope Urban V intercedes with P. on behalf of the city of Montpellier for lower customs duties.
29 November 1362
Pope Urban V intercedes with P. for the satisfaction of requests by Hugh of Lusignan and his mother Maria, Empress of Constantinople.
5 December 1362–2 January 1363
P. is in Venice.
January 1363
P. visits Mestre, Marghera, Oriago, Padua, Vicenza, Verona.
21 January 1363
P. is received by Bernabò Visconti in Milan.
After 21 January 1363–Before 1 February 1363
P. is received by Galeazzo II Visconti in Pavia.
1 February 1363
P. visits Voghera.
2 February 1363
P. visits Tortona.
End of January? / 4 February–Middle of March 1363
P. is in Genoa.
5 March 1363
P. renews the Genoese privileges.
13 March 1363
P. attends a banquet at the house of Pietro Marocello, where Doge Simon Boccanegra is allegedly poisoned (he dies on 14 March).
1363
Pestilence outbreak in Cyprus.
1363
Turkish raids against Cyprus and Cypriot retaliatory raids against the coast of Anatolia.
Holy Wednesday 29 March–31 May 1363
P. is at the papal court in Avignon, where the dispute with Hugh of Lusignan is settled.
Good Friday 31 March 1363
Proclamation of the crusade by Pope Urban V in Avignon. P. and King John II of France take the cross. The pope sends letters to King John II, P., and French prelates, announcing that the *passagium generale* is to start on 1 March 1365 under the leadership of the king of France and that P. is to set off before on a *passagium particulare*.
12 April 1363
Pope Urban V preaches the crusade. Cardinal Hélie de Talleyrand is appointed apostolic legate.

Before 1 May 1363
King John II of France and P. offer to mediate between Pope Urban V and Duke Bernabò Visconti of Milan, as peace will serve the purpose of the *passagium*. French and Cypriot (Philip of Mézières and Peter Thomas) embassies go to Milan.

25 May 1363
Pope Urban V exhorts Emperor Charles IV, the kings of England and Hungary, the marquis of Moravia, the dukes of Luxembourg, Austria, Saxony, and Bavaria, the doges of Genoa and Venice, and others to join the crusade.

25 May 1363
Pope Urban V addresses a letter on the recovery of the Holy Land to P., similar to the one of 31 March 1363.

25 May 1363 and 17 April 1364
Pope Urban V invites the Free Companies to join the crusade.

[June–July 1363?
P. travels through Germany to Prague (where he stays for three weeks with Emperor Charles IV of Luxembourg) and returns to France through Juliers/Jülich, Brabant (Brussels), Flanders (Bruges, where he is joined by the King of Denmark), and Hainaut.]

[June–July 1363?
P. leaves France for Savoy, Basel (beginning of July), Strasbourg (*c.* 4 July), Mainz (*c.* 25 July), Cologne.]

8 August 1363
Outbreak of the revolt of St Titus in Crete.

August–Beginning of November 1363
After a stay in Paris, P. visits Normandy (Rouen, Caen, Cherbourg), where he is received by the Duke of Normandy, future Charles V, arriving at Calais before 20 October.

26 September 1363
Pope Urban V grants P., his wife Eleanor of Aragon, and their son Peter II a plenary indulgence *in articulo mortis*.

11 October and 29 November 1363
The doge informs P. of the revolt of St Titus in Crete and expresses his fear that it may affect the Venetian crusader contribution.

20 October 1363
From Calais, P. informs the Venetians of his intention to depart from Venice for the East the following March.

***c.* 2 November 1363**
P. arrives at Dover.

6 November–Late November 1363
P. is in London, where he is entertained by King Edward III and Sir Henry Picard, former Lord Mayor of London (Feast of the five kings). Edward gives P. a ship called *Katherine/Catelinne*.

Shortly after 11 November 1363
P. takes part in a tournament in Smithfield.

28 November 1363
Pope Urban V invites Peter to return to Cyprus in view of Turkish threats against Antalya and promises financial help.

Beginning of December 1363
P. is robbed by highwaymen on his way back to the English coast.
Beginning of December 1363
P. visits Boulogne-sur-Mer and Amiens, where he meets King John II of France and his sons, the Duke of Normandy, future Charles V, and Philip the Bold.
Christmas 1363
P. is in Paris, where he probably meets William of Machaut.
27 February 1364
The Hospitallers of Rhodes inform Pope Urban V of the Turkish threats against the Christians of Outremer.
27 February–2 March 1364
P. attends the Parliament of Paris, in particular the discussion of the dispute between Bertrand Du Guesclin and the seneschal of Poitou William of Felton (27–29 February).
1364
Cypriot pillaging in Turkey and Turkish retaliation raids against Cyprus.
13 March 1364
Bologna peace treaty between Pope Urban V and Duke Bernabò Visconti of Milan through the mediation of Peter Thomas.
March–End of April 1364
P. visits Plantagenet-controlled areas in Western France (Poitou, Saintonge, Gascony, and Aquitaine), in particular Angoulême, where he is entertained by Edward the Black Prince, and La Rochelle.
1 April 1364
Pope Urban V sends letters concerning the *passagium* of Count Amadeo VI of Savoy, who, like P., is to set off before the main body of troups.
1 April 1364
Pope Urban V addresses a letter concerning the crusade to P., discussing at length financial matters. The letter suggests that P. visited Avignon again at the time.
End of April 1364
P. returns to Paris.
5–7 May 1364
P. attends the funeral in Paris and burial in Saint-Denis of King John II of France (died on 8 April in London).
10 May 1364
End of the revolt of St Titus in Crete.
19 May 1364
P. attends the coronation of King Charles V of France in Reims.
28 May–5/11 June 1364
P. is in Paris, where he takes part in a tournament held in the court of the royal palace on the Île de la Cité.
3 June 1364
Pope Urban V invites Peter to return to Cyprus in view of upsetting news from Outremer that he received from the Master of the Hospital.

Before 19 June 1364
Violent affray between Genoese and Cypriots in Famagusta, followed by papal mediation (letters dated 19 and 25 June and 17 July 1364, 20 and 27 February, 4, 22, and 26 March 1365) and Venetian and Cypriot embassies to Genoa.

30 June 1364
Pope Urban V informs P. that Peter Thomas has been named the new legate for the crusade, following the death of Cardinal Hélie de Talleyrand on 17 January.

Late June–August 1364
P. visits Cologne (perhaps in the company of William of Machaut) and crosses Germany through Franconia and Thuringia (Esslingen, Erfurt, Meissen) and Saxony (Lübeck) to reach Prague, where he meets the Emperor Charles IV of Luxembourg.

10 July 1364
Pope Urban V informs the legate Peter Thomas that P. plans to return to Outremer shortly in order to assist the faithful and rebuff the efforts of the infidels.

Beginning of September–10 November 1364
In the company of Emperor Charles IV of Luxembourg, P. travels through Bohemia and Silesia, with stops in Schweidnitz, Liegnitz, Breslau (11–14 September), Glogau, Kosten, Posen, Neustadt Kalisch, Baranow, Oppeln (17 September), Beuthen. He arrives in Cracow on *c.* 22 September and meets the Kings of Poland, Casimir III the Great, and Hungary, Louis I. He then proceeds to Vienna, where he meets Duke Rudolf.

11 November 1364–27 June 1365
Travelling through Carinthia, Aquileia, Treviso, and Mestre, P. arrives in Venice, where he stays for more than seven months.

18 March 1365
Pope Urban V grants the Cypriots authorisation to outfit six galleys (three the first year and three the second) for trade of non-prohibited commodities with Alexandria and other lands under the sultan's control.

18 April 1365
Pope Urban V informs Emperor John V Palaiologos of Constantinople that, in the place of the general passage of the Christians of the West, a smaller expedition against the Turks is planned as soon as P. and Genoa come to an agreement.

18 April 1365
Peace agreement between Cyprus and Genoa with extension of the Genoese privileges.

26 April 1365
Pope Urban V informs P. of the success of the negotiations with Genoa, conducted by the papal legate Peter Thomas, adding that a great number of warriors have come from Germany and other regions to join the king on his expedition.

22 June 1365
P.'s chancellor, Philip of Mézières, is granted the citizenship of Venice.

25 June 1365
Cypriot forces sail from Famagusta.

27 June 1365
P.'s crusade sails from Venice.

19 July 1365
Pope Urban V rejoices at the news of P.'s departure for the East.

August 1365
After a stop in Smyrna and Crete, P.'s crusade meets Cypriot forces in Rhodes.
Late summer / September 1365
At the behest of the Grand Master of the Hospitallers, Peter makes peace with the Emirates of Menteshe and Aydin.
4–9 October 1365
P.'s crusade sails from Rhodes and arrives in Alexandria.
10 October 1365
Capture of Alexandria.
16 October 1365
P. abandons Alexandria and returns to Cyprus. The Mamluk vanguard enters Alexandria without fighting.
Second half of 1365
P. grants new privileges to Montpellier
1366
On several occasions, Pope Urban V grants the Venetians licenses to trade with the Muslims (last one dated 23 June). He informs P. on 1 July.
6 January 1366
Death of papal legate Peter Thomas in Famagusta.
25 January 1366
Pope Urban V recommends Count Amadeo VI of Savoy to Emperor John V Palaiologos of Constantinople, comparing his expedition to P.'s triumphant wars against the Saracens.
March–June 1366
Venetian envoys, later joined by the Catalans, go to Cairo and engage in peace negotiations.
25 April 1366
P. orders his fleet to take Beirut but is prevented by the Venetians from attacking the sultan's lands.
Beginning of June 1366
The Cypriot fleet attacks Alaya.
July 1366
A Genoese embassy, hostile to the Cypriots, goes to Cairo.
Summer 1366
Mamluk envoys go to Nicosia and engage in peace negotiations.
End of June 1366
P.'s chancellor, Philip of Mézières, leaves Cyprus, carrying P.'s letters that announce the king's intention to sail against the infidels.
July–August 1366
Philip of Mézières presents P.'s position before the Venetian Senate and the doge and then proceeds to the papal court in Avignon.
17 August 1366
At the request of P.'s envoy, Philip of Mézières, Pope Urban V withdraws the license to trade with the Muslims from the Venetians, the Genoese, and the Catalans.

22 and 25 August 1366
Venice bans the export of arms and horses to Cyprus and forbids its subjects to participate in an expedition organized by P.

6 October 1366
Pope Urban V invites the kings of France and England and other princes to send military assistance to P. and the Hospitallers, threatened by the Turks after the capture of Alexandria, and authorizes the proclamation of indulgence for those who will do so.

23 October 1366
Pope Urban V congratulates P. on the capture of Alexandria and regrets the retreat that was imposed on him, urging him to work for a truce with the sultan.

October 1366
Cypriot envoys deliver captives taken in Alexandria to the authorities in Cairo.

November 1366
P.'s envoys go to Cairo with Catalan traders but fail to reach an agreement with the sultan.

c. 1366 (or earlier?)–1367 (and later?)
P. lives in adultery with Joanna L'Aleman, whom he impregnates (she is eight months with child when P. leaves for the West in autumn 1367).

End of 1366–Beginning of 1367
P. falls ill while in Famagusta.

7 January 1367
A Cypriot fleet under P. sails from Famagusta to attack the Syrian coast, but it is wrecked by a storm. Raid on Tripoli.

26 February–14 March 1367
Expedition led by Prince John of Antioch for the relief of Gorhigos from an attack by the Grand Karaman.

February 1367
Resumption of negotiations with Egypt at the instigation of Genoa, later joined by Venice and the Catalans. An Egyptian embassy arrives in Nicosia and reaches an agreement with P.

14 March 1367
Cypriot envoys leave Famagusta for Alexandria and thence proceed to Cairo for the ratification of the agreement.

26 May 1367
P. leads his fleet to Antalya, where he suppresses the mutiny of the Cypriot garrison.

June 1367
P. proceeds to Rhodes.

End of June 1367
Egyptian envoys bring new terms to P. in Rhodes, but these are rejected.

4 August 1367
In Rhodes, the lord of Rochefort and Florimond of Lesparre challenge Peter to a duel.

After 4 August 1367
P. sails from Rhodes to Antalya again, where he receives the homage of the local emirs.

Late August / First half of September 1367
P. returns to Cyprus and lands at Kiti. He falls ill and retires to Nicosia.

15 September 1367
P. returns to Kiti, where he accepts Florimond of Lesparre's challenge to a duel a year from Michaelmas (29 September) 1367.
27 September–5 October 1367
P. raids Tripoli, Tortosa, Valania/Baniyas, Lattakia, Malo, Ayas.
Autumn 1367
Cypriot galleys raid Sidon and Jaffa (?).
6 November 1367
Pope Urban V grants P. the right to have his own portable altar and to celebrate mass before sunrise.
Late autumn 1367–October 1368
P.'s second journey to Western Europe.
Late autumn 1367
P. sails from Paphos escorted by his son, Peter II, and Philip of Mézières for Western Europe. Short stop in Rhodes.
2 and 4 December 1367
Urban V forbids P. to go through with the duel with Florimond of Lesparre and instructs the archbishop of Nicosia to excommunicate P. if necessary.
2 and 5 December 1367
Urban V rebukes P. for having abandoned his wife and for living in open adultery with another lady and instructs the archbishop of Nicosia to excommunicate P. if necessary.
c. 1367 (or earlier?)–his death
P. keeps Eschiva of Scandelion as his mistress.
1367/1368
The Church of Corpus Christi is erected in Nicosia at P.'s order.
Late 1367 / Early 1368
P. arrives in Naples, where he spends a few days because of his son's illness, entertained by Queen Joanna.
Late 1367 / Early 1368
In Naples, P. receives envoys from the doge of Venice and accepts Venetian mediation for the release of merchants imprisoned by the sultan of Egypt.
Late 1367–Early 1368
Eleanor of Aragon tortures pregnant Joanna L'Aleman with the intention of inducing a miscarriage. When the child is born, Eleonor disposes of it and sends Joanna to prison.
Before 16 March–End of May 1368
P. is at the papal court in Rome, where Queen Joanna of Naples joins him on 17 March.
Holy Saturday 8 April 1368
Reconciliation with Florimond of Lesparre in Rome. The lord of Rochefort fails to appear.
Easter Sunday 9 April 1368
P. attends Easter Sunday mass at St Peter's Basilica.
1368
Riots between Venetians and Genoese in Famagusta
1368
Cypriot and Genoese privateering. An Egyptian raid on Famagusta is repulsed.

Before 19 May 1368
P. visits Florence.
19–20 May 1368
In Rome, P. authorizes Venetian and Genoese envoys to negotiate peace with the sultan on his behalf.
20 May 1368
In Rome, P. and Empress Maria of Constantinople sign a settlement of dower, according to which P. will pay Maria 5,000 florins annually.
29 May 1368
Pope Urban V grants P. the right to have Mass celebrated in places under interdict.
29 May 1368
Pope Urban V grants P. and his subjects the authorisation to outfit twenty vessels for trade of non-prohibited commodities with Alexandria and other lands under the sultan's control once only.
June–November 1368
Resumption at the instigation of Genoa, Venice, and the papacy and collapse of peace negotiations with the sultan.
1368
P. accepts the crown of Cilician Armenia.
June–10 July 1368
Siena, Pisa (he arrives on 14 June), Lucca, Pistoia, Prato, Florence, and Bologna, where P. meets John Froissart, who accompanies him to Ferrara and probably Venice.
10 July–After 4 August 1368
Ferrara, Milan, San Felice, and Mantua, where he meets Emperor Charles IV, whom he accompanies back to Ferrara and then to Modena, where he arrives on 4 August.
After 4 August–23 September 1368
P. is in Venice, where he learns of the queen's treatment of Joanna L'Aleman and of the rumours that his wife has taken a lover, John of Morphou. He orders the queen to release Joanna, who enters St Clare's convent.
***c.* 21 August–Before 6 September 1368**
P. visits Treviso.
23 September 1368
P. sails from Venice for Cyprus, putting in at Modon, where he visits his second cousin, the Despotissa Isabella/Margaret/Maria of Morea.
October 1368
P. fetches Joanna out of the convent but he is falsely advised by his High Court not to punish the queen and her lover, which renders him 'full of ill will and anger'.
23 November 1368
Pope Urban V imposes a three-year tithe to be levied in France, England, Spain, and elsewhere for the maintenance of papal galleys for the defence of Cyprus.
Autumn 1368
P.'s behaviour becomes brutal, he violates the law and customs of the kingdom, and dishonours noble women, thus alienating his brothers and the feudal nobility.

Autumn 1368
P. orders the building of the Church of Misericordia in the upper part of a tower and a prison called Margarita in its basement.
Tuesday 16 January [Wednesday 17 January] 1369 at dawn
P. is assassinated in his palace in Nicosia by a group of his barons (John of Gaurelle, Henry of Giblet, John Gorap, Philip of Ibelin lord of Arsur, and James of Nores), probably with the involvement of both his brothers, Prince John of Antioch and James, constable of Jerusalem. His body is mutilated and decapitated.
16 January 1369
The High Court of Cyprus is convened to make provisions for the regency occasioned by the minority of Peter II and to remedy P.'s abuses. The regency is offered to Prince John of Antioch.
7 April 1369
Pope Urban V expresses his grief for P.'s death and his concern for the Christian lands in Outremer.
6 January 1372
Peter II is crowned king of Cyprus in Nicosia.
10 October 1372
Peter II is crowned king of Jerusalem in Famagusta.

INTRODUCTION

The Sources and the Context

ANGEL NICOLAOU-KONNARI

Peter I of Lusignan (1329–69, 1359) in Historical Sources and Modern Popular Culture

Peter I is undoubtedly the most famous Lusignan king of Cyprus. His crusader politics, military exploits, chivalric valour, ceaseless travelling, scandalous private life, and murder by his peers (with, perhaps, the complicity of his own brothers) rendered him a popular hero of international standing, his legend seizing upon the imagination of European and Arab-Mamluk writers of the time. Nevertheless, his presence in modern scholarly literature does not correspond to his popularity during his lifetime, even though a recent study compares his reign with that of the most famous Cypriot king from Antiquity, Evagoras I of Salamis.[1] Indeed, there is no monograph, collective volume, conference, exhibition, or event of any kind dedicated to or inspired by him; the modern scholar, student, and interested reader still has to rely on general histories of Cyprus or of the crusades for his biography[2] and on a relatively small number of more or less specialized studies for the examination of specific aspects of his life and reign. One may debate at length about the reasons for this neglect, but it certainly cannot be attributed to either the lack of primary sources or Peter's dull life and unalluring personality; in fact, one may argue that it

---

1   Matteo Campagnolo, 'The Parallel Lives of Evagoras I of Salamis and Peter I de Lusignan', in *From Aphrodite to Melusine. Reflections on the Archaeology and the History of Cyprus*, ed. by Matteo Campagnolo and Marielle Martiniani-Rebe (Geneva: La Pomme d'or, 2007), pp. 49–62.
2   Nicolas Jorga, *Philippe de Mézières (1327–1405) et la croisade au XIVe siècle* (Paris: École Pratique des Hautes Études, 1896; repr. London: Variorum Reprints, 1973); Sir George Hill, *A History of Cyprus*, 4 vols (Cambridge: Cambridge University Press, 1940–52; repr. 2010), II, pp. 308–69 and passim; Kenneth M. Setton, *The Papacy and the Levant, 1204–1571*, 4 vols (Philadelphia: American Philosophical Society, 1976–1984), I, *The Thirteenth and Fourteenth Centuries*, pp. 224–84 and passim; Wipertus H. Rudt de Collenberg, *Les Lusignan de Chypre, Επετηρίς Κέντρου Επιστημονικών Ερευνών (Κύπρου)*, 10 (1979–80), 85–319 (esp. no. B,17, pp. 125–29); Peter W. Edbury, *The Kingdom of Cyprus and the Crusades 1191–1374* (Cambridge: Cambridge University Press, 1991), pp. 141–79; Peter W. Edbury, ''Η πολιτική ιστορία τοῦ μεσαιωνικοῦ βασιλείου ἀπὸ τὴ βασιλεία τοῦ Οὔγου Δ΄ μέχρι τὴ βασιλεία τοῦ Ἰανοῦ (1324–1432)', in *Ἱστορία τῆς Κύπρου*, ed. by Theodoros Papadopoullos, 6 vols (Nicosia: Archbishop Makarios III Foundation, 1995–2011), IV, *Μεσαιωνικὸν βασίλειον – Ἑνετοκρατία*, pp. 51–158 (esp. 51–108). Also see the *Chronology* of Peter's life and reign in this volume.

Angel Nicolaou-Konnari • University of Cyprus

Crusading, Society, and Politics in the Eastern Mediterranean in the Age of King Peter I of Cyprus, ed. by Alexander Beihammer and Angel Nicolaou-Konnari, MEDNEX, 10 (Turnhout, 2022), pp. 31–76
© BREPOLS ❧ PUBLISHERS   10.1484/M.MEDNEX-EB.5.128459

was his positively or negatively biased portrayal in contemporary sources as well as his extraordinary life, complex character, incongruous politics, and erratic behaviour that render his personal assessment and historical evaluation difficult.

Sources

Peter's life and exploits are narrated at length, mentioned, or simply evoked in an impressive number and variety of contemporary or near contemporary written sources. These sources diverge significantly in form, style, language, and content and include documents (papal letters, letters emanating from European rulers or the Cypriot chancery, trade or diplomatic treaties, administrative deeds and charters), literary texts in verse or prose (epic and other poems, romances, biographies, political allegories, didactic and epistolary literature, works of religious inspiration), and historiography (chronicles, annals, and other narrative works) in Medieval Greek, the Greek Cypriot dialect, Latin, various Italian dialects, Middle French, Occitan, Middle English, and Arabic. Most of these sources are used and studied exhaustively in the chapters of the present volume. Nevertheless, despite their number and variety, they prove to be insufficient or inadequate to clarify contradictory information and confusing evidence about Peter's life and actions and to provide a comprehensive understanding of his complex character.

Unfortunately, the state archives of the Lusignans have not been preserved and researchers rely on only a small number of documents that have accidentally survived and on copies of a small part of their correspondence in papal, French, Italian, and other European archives and libraries. Louis de Mas Latrie was the first to publish some of these documents in a corpus in 1852, 1855, and 1873.[3] Fortunately, archival research is still yielding results and documents, which may have been undetected, underestimated and ignored, or simply badly edited, still surface. Papal registers remain the richest source and, in 2012, volume three of the *Bullarium Cyprium* provided summaries of almost all the Cyprus-related letters of Pope Innocent VI (1352–62) and his successor, Urban V (1362–70), whose pontificate coincided with Peter's reign.[4] Some letters, though, were omitted while the summaries do not provide all the information contained in the letters and may be misleading as shown in the paper jointly produced by Peter W. Edbury and Chris Schabel in this volume. The latter has provided transcriptions of twenty-four letters previously ignored or

---

3 For Peter, see: Louis de Mas Latrie, *Histoire de l'île de Chypre sous le règne des princes de la maison de Lusignan*, 3 vols (Paris: Imprimerie impériale, 1852–1861), II, p. 206 n. 2, pp. 228–345, III, pp. 741–58; Louis de Mas Latrie, 'Nouvelles preuves de l'histoire de Chypre sous le règne des princes de la maison de Lusignan', *Bibliothèque de l'École des Chartes*, 34 (1873), 47–87, repr. with other documents as vol. IV of Louis de Mas Latrie, *Histoire de l'île de Chypre sous le règne des princes de la maison de Lusignan* (Famagusta: L'Oiseau, 1970), pp. 1–79 (60–69).

4 *Bullarium Cyprium III: Lettres papales relatives à Chypre 1316–1378*, ed. by Charles Perrat and Jean Richard with the collaboration of Christopher Schabel, Sources et études de l'histoire de Chypre, 68 (Nicosia: Centre de Recherche Scientifique, 2012).

not published in full, which allow a new examination of some aspects of the popes' relations with Peter.

The space attributed to Peter in literary and historical texts, the historicity of his portrayal, and the nature of this portrayal, be it ethical or political, vary from one work to another in accordance with the intentions of the authors and the stylistic conventions of the literary genre they serve. Interestingly, the longest work and the only one that is entirely dedicated to the Cypriot king comes from France, his ancestral home, but not from the pen of the man who knew Peter closely and had firsthand knowledge of almost all the events of his adult life, his chancellor Philip of Mézières (1327–1405). William of Machaut's (c. 1300–77) *La Prise d'Alixandre* (1369), an epic, complete biography in 8885 verses, is based on eyewitnesses' accounts and the author's personal relationship with the Cypriot king while from Mézières's works, in which Peter is a key figure but not the protagonist, one can piece together only a fragmentary picture. Although Machaut's and Mézières's depiction of Peter's person and reign may not be entirely fabricated, it is deliberately one-sided, with meaningful omissions and partial interpretation of historical events, an idealized portrayal of the king's works and days.[5] Most importantly, they influenced an important number of contemporary or near contemporary French authors, thanks to whom Peter enjoyed a prolific literary afterlife in France, by far more important than that in any other country.

In her contribution to this volume, this author analyses at length Peter's idealistic portrayal in French literature and historiography until the middle of the fifteenth century. She demonstrates the extent to which his person had seized upon the imagination of French authors and how, endowed with legendary proportions, became a model of chivalric ethos and royal power, serving their vision for a better future for France and Europe within the context of the Hundred Years' War (1337–1453), the problems faced by the French monarchy, and the Great Schism (1378–1417). As a result, with the exception of Machaut and to a lesser extent Mézières and John Froissart (c. 1337–c. 1404), the rest of the writers (an impressive list that includes authors of the calibre of Cuvelier, Honorat Bovet, Eustache Deschamps, Étienne de Conty, William of Nangis, Christine de Pizan, and François Villon as well as anonymous chroniclers) do not provide much factual information, even though Bovet and Froissart had met Peter personally; they mainly refer to his journeys in Western Europe, the taking of Alexandria, and his murder.

Not many contemporary sources survive from the Cypriot king's homeland. Out of a great number of historical marginal notes found in Cypriot manuscripts only one concerns Peter: the owner/reader of a collection of apocryphal works and

---

5 Angel Nicolaou-Konnari, 'Apologists or Critics? The Reign of Peter I of Lusignan (1359–1369) Viewed by Philippe de Mézières (1327–1405) and Leontios Makhairas (c. 1360/80–after 1432)', in *Philippe de Mézières and His Age: Piety and Politics in the Fourteenth Century*, ed. by Renate Blumenfeld-Kosinski and Kiril Petkov, The Medieval Mediterranean, 91 (Leiden – Boston: Brill, 2012), pp. 359–401; Angel Nicolaou-Konnari, 'A Neglected Relationship: Leontios Makhairas's Debt to Latin Eastern and French Historiography', in *The French of Outremer. Communities and Communications in the Crusading Mediterranean*, ed. by Laura K. Morreale and Nicholas L. Paul, Fordham Series in Medieval Studies (New York: Fordham University Press, 2018), pp. 110–49 (120–24).

homilies on the Virgin Mary (a manuscript probably copied in Cyprus in 1080) was duly impressed by the king's murder to record it: 'On 16 January 1369 the king was killed'.[6] This dating, provided by a person who lived in Cyprus at the time of the murder, refutes the dating of later narrative sources (17 January 1369)[7] and is corroborated by another contemporary and undoubtedly reliable Cypriot source, the prologue to the 1369 recension of John of Ibelin's legal treatise, which describes the meeting of the Cypriot High Court right after the murder.[8]

However, the most realistic account of Peter's life and reign and the only one with intimate information does come from Cyprus: the *Recital of the Sweet Land of Cyprus*, datable to the second quarter of the fifteenth century, attributed to Leontios Makhairas (*c.* 1360/80–after 1432), and written in the local Greek vernacular. Although he had only a second-hand knowledge of the events, often depending on archival sources, eye- or earwitnesses, and stories still circulating during his time, Makhairas may evaluate them with the benefit of hindsight in a detached and sober way. He embellishes his narrative with information of Cypriot interest and he is more detailed about local affairs, political matters taking place before 1362, logistics and royal administration, and Peter's private life. Naturally, he ignores passages narrated at length in Machaut's poem that concern European royal or princely houses and political affairs and omits the names of French knights participating in Cypriot expeditions. Moreover, stories to which Machaut devotes many verses, such as the king's journeys to Western Europe or his exploits outside Cyprus, are either entirely omitted or given in a very brief and fragmentary way by Makhairas. While Machaut considers Peter's knightly values and crusader goals to enhance his personal honour, for the Cypriot chronicler the king's deeds have a larger political meaning that influences the destiny of Cyprus. This does not mean that Peter's heroic side as a defender of the Christians is underrated. On the contrary, Makhairas attributes Peter the epithet 'the Great' («ρὲ Πιὲρ τοῦ μεγάλου») and portrays him as a charismatic, indefatigable ruler and soldier, who worked zealously for the Holy Church.[9]

---

6 Paris, Bibliothèque nationale de France (henceforth BnF), MS Paris. gr. 1215, fol. 210ᵛ, see Costas N. Constantinides and Robert Browning, *Dated Greek Manuscripts from Cyprus to the Year 1570*, Dumbarton Oaks Studies, 30 – Texts and Studies in the History of Cyprus, 18 (Nicosia: Dumbarton Oaks Research Library and Collection – Cyprus Research Centre, 1993), pp. 62–63.

7 Leontios Makhairas, *Χρονικό της Κύπρου. Παράλληλη διπλωματική έκδοση των χειρογράφων*, ed. by Michalis Pieris and Angel Nicolaou-Konnari, Texts and Studies in the History of Cyprus, 48 (Nicosia: Cyprus Research Centre, 2003), p. 220; *Chroniques d'Amadi et de Strambaldi, première partie: Chronique d'Amadi*, ed. by René de Mas Latrie (Paris: Imprimerie nationale, 1891), p. 425.

8 Vatican City, Biblioteca Apostolica Vaticana, MS Vat. lat. 4789, fols 19ʳ–22ʳ, see John of Ibelin, *Le Livre des Assises*, ed. by Peter W. Edbury, The Medieval Mediterranean, 50 (Leiden – Boston: Brill, 2003), pp. 732–37 (733). See discussion in Peter W. Edbury, 'The Murder of King Peter I of Cyprus (1359–1369)', *Journal of Medieval History*, 6 (1980), 219–33 (pp. 223–24) (repr. in Peter W. Edbury, *Kingdoms of the Crusaders. From Jerusalem to Cyprus*, Variorum Collected Studies, 653 (Aldershot: Ashgate, 1999), study no. XIII), and the *Chronology* in this volume.

9 Leontios Makhairas, *Χρονικό της Κύπρου*, p. 88; the epithet might equally indicate Peter's seniority in relation to Peter II. See Angel Nicolaou-Konnari, '"A poor island and an orphaned realm…, built upon a rock in the midst of the sea…, surrounded by the infidel Turks and Saracens": The Crusader Ideology in Leontios Makhairas's Greek *Chronicle* of Cyprus', *Crusades*, 10 (2011), 119–45.

Nevertheless, in the Cypriot chronicle the order of events is occasionally uncertain and confused and quite a few dates are inferred or wrong, as the example of the dating of Peter's murder discussed above shows. Consequently, one cannot automatically presume that Makhairas is more reliable about Peter's reign than Machaut is. If the French writer deliberately omitted unpleasant facts about Peter's conduct, the Cypriot chronicler most probably avoided directly accusing the king's brothers of fratricide and regicide, as he and members of his family were in the service of Janus (1398–1432), son of Peter's brother James I (1382/85–98).[10] Two sixteenth-century Cypriot narrative sources written in Italian, the anonymous compilation known as *Chronique d'Amadi* and Florio Bustron's *Historia*, give a shorter account that, however, follows closely Makhairas's text in structure, content, and outlook; it remains, however, unclear whether the later works used Makhairas or all three a common lost source.[11]

Despite their late date, one would be remiss if one did not include in this survey two works written by Cypriots of the post-1570/71 diaspora. Writing in the 1570s in France, Étienne de Lusignan (1537–90), a scion of the non-reigning branch of the dynasty, gives an account of the works and days of the Lusignan king who 'obtint le surnom de Grand' that both resembles and differs from that of Makhairas. Lusignan narrates Peter's military exploits and travels in more detail than Makhairas but not always agreeing with Machaut's account; he avoids mentioning Peter's marital indiscretions, although he accepts that the king insulted noblewomen and violated the laws; he mentions Eleanor's infidelity but reverses the roles of the characters in Makhairas's account, making the Viscount of Nicosia Eleanor's lover and the Count of Rouchas the person who informed Peter; he claims that Eleanor was 'favoured' by the king's two brothers and admits that they were the leaders of the conspiracy to murder him. The most valuable contribution of Étienne's account are two pieces of information of topographical and material interest, dated to his time, that will be discussed below.[12]

---

10   For a thematic comparison of the two works, see Appendix A to this introduction; for a critical comparison, Guillaume de Machaut, *The Capture of Alexandria*, English trans. by Janet Shirley, introduction and notes by Peter W. Edbury, Crusade Texts in Translation, 8 (Aldershot: Ashgate, 2001), 'Introduction', pp. 8–16 and Nicolaou-Konnari, 'A Neglected Relationship', pp. 121–24.

11   *Chronique d'Amadi*; Florio Bustron, *Chronique de l'île de Chypre*, ed. by René de Mas Latrie, Collection de documents inédits sur l'histoire de France, Mélanges historiques, 5 (Paris: Imprimerie nationale, 1886). For the complex relationship amongst the three narratives, see: Gilles Grivaud, *Entrelacs chiprois. Essai sur les lettres et la vie intellectuelle dans le royaume de Chypre (1191–1570)* (Nicosia: Moufflon, 2009), pp. 248–69; Peter W. Edbury, 'Machaut, Mézières, Makhairas and *Amadi*: Constructing the Reign of Peter I (1359–1369)', in *Philippe de Mézières and His Age*, pp. 349–58; *The Chronicle of Amadi*, trans. by Nicholas Coureas and Peter Edbury, Texts and Studies in the History of Cyprus, 74 (Nicosia: Cyprus Research Centre, 2015), 'Introduction', pp. xxv–xxvi; Ioannis Harkas, Η Ιστορία της Κύπρου του Φλώριου Βουστρωνίου: πηγές και επιδράσεις της ουμανιστικής ιστοριογραφίας (unpublished doctoral thesis, University of Cyprus, 2020).

12   Steffano Lusignano, *Chorograffia e breve historia universale dell'isola de Cipro principiando al tempo di Noè per in sino al 1572* (Bologna: Alessandro Benaccio, 1573; repr. Famagusta: L'Oiseau, 1973; repr. Nicosia: The Bank of Cyprus Cultural Foundation, 2004), fols 56^v–57^v; Estienne de Lusignan, *Histoire contenant une sommaire description des genealogies, Alliances, & gestes de tous les Princes [...] qui ont iadis commandé és Royaumes de Hierusalem, Cypre, Armenie, & lieux circonvoisins* (Paris: Guillaume Chaudière, 1579),

Giorgio de Nores (1618–38), a descendant of one of the oldest and most important Cypriot noble families, dedicated his short life to the cause of the liberation of the 'antica patria' from the tyranny of the Ottomans. These thoughts are reflected in a short treatise he wrote in Rome, which concerns the various claimants to the throne of the Kingdom of Cyprus and in which Peter's reign is treated accordingly. Giorgio refutes the rights of the sultan of Cairo because his claim that he extracted tribute from King Janus in retaliation for the injustice done to him by 'Pietro Lusignano re di Gerusalemme et di Cipri, cognominato Il Forte' is unfounded: Peter attempted to reconquer former Christian lands, usurped by the sultan, in his capacity as both the King of Jerusalem and a Christian prince, on behalf of the Christian Commonwealth, and with the approval of the Roman Pontiff. Giorgio admits, though, that Peter was killed by his subjects because he treated them cruelly.[13]

Byzantine narrative sources remain silent about Peter's person. The only mention is found in a letter Demetrios Kydones (c. 1324–98) sent to Bishop Simon Atumano of Gerace in Calabria (in office from 1348 to 1366) in 1364. Consistent with his Latinophile attitude of cooperation with the western powers in order to face the Muslim threat, Kydones praises 'the king of Cyprus' ('τὸν ῥῆγα τῆς Κύπρου') for seeking in person and without the intermediary of envoys the alliance of the people of his own faith and race, regretting the fact that his efforts and travels were not crowned with success; Kydones's words suggest that the letter was written in the second half of 1364, after the crusade failed to depart in the spring of the same year as originally planned.[14] Nevertheless, Peter's conspicuous absence from Byzantine sources does not indicate that he, in particular, was deliberately ignored;[15] a meaningful lack of interest in the Lusignan Kingdom had been the general attitude of Byzantine historiographers and it must be viewed within the context of Byzantine claims on Cyprus and a perennial indecision between a pro-Latin or a pro-Ottoman policy, as Alexander Beihammer points out in his chapter. The only notable exception was Peter's father, Hugh IV (1324–59), whose court maintained links with intellectual circles in Constantinople,

---

fols 19ᵛ–20ᵛ; Estienne de Lusignan, *Description de toute l'isle de Cypre* (Paris: Guillaume Chaudière, 1580; repr. Famagusta: L'Oiseau, 1968; repr. Nicosia: The Bank of Cyprus Cultural Foundation, 2004), chapter 21, fols 144ʳ–148ʳ.

13 Giorgio Denores, *Discorso sopra l'isola di Cipri con le ragioni della vera successione in quel Regno – A Discourse on the Island of Cyprus and on the Reasons of the True Succession in that Kingdom*, ed. by Paschalis M. Kitromilides, Graecolatinitas nostra, Sources, 7 (Venice: Hellenic Institute of Byzantine and Post-Byzantine Studies, 2006), pp. 56–57, 78–79, 82–83. On Giorgio, see: Angel Nicolaou-Konnari, 'L'identité dans la diaspora: travaux et jours de Pierre (avant 1570 (?) – après 1646) et Georges de Nores (1619-1638)', in *Identités croisées en un milieu méditerranéen: le cas de Chypre (Antiquité – Moyen Âge)*, ed. by Sabine Fourrier and Gilles Grivaud (Mont Saint-Aignan: Presses universitaires de Rouen et du Havre, 2006), pp. 329–53 (esp. 342–44); Angel Nicolaou-Konnari, 'Affinità elettive nei circoli letterari italiani del Cinquecento: Torquato Tasso, Pietro de Nores e gli altri', *Studi Tassiani*, 67 (2019), 111–65 (pp. 137, 147–51).

14 Démétrius Cydonès, *Correspondance*, ed. by Raymond-Joseph Loenertz, 2 vols, Studi e Testi, 186, 208 (Vatican City: Biblioteca Apostolica Vaticana, 1956, 1960), I, no. 93, ll. 60–65, p. 127.

15 Pope Urban V recommended Peter to John V Palaiologos (1341–91) with a letter carried by Count Amadeus VI of Savoy (1343–83) and dated 25 January 1366, *Bullarium Cyprium III*, no. v–133.

Italy, and the Arab world and who allowed Cyprus to be a refuge for anti-Palamite exiles, as shown in the chapters of Alexis Torrence and Charles Yost, thus earning the praise of Nikephoros Gregoras.[16]

The Arabic-Mamluk sources, which are valuable for the reconstruction of the events surrounding the 1365 Alexandria crusade, were belatedly used for the first time in 1938 by Aziz Suryal Atiya, who also carried out an in situ investigation of the scenes of the attack on the city by Peter; George Hill would use Atiya's work from a Cypriologist's point of view for his account of Peter's reign while Tahar Mansouri would publish a useful anthology of extracts of Cypriot interest from these sources, translated into French.[17] In his contribution to this volume, Clément Onimus discusses extensively Arabic narrative sources. The main Arabic contemporary source concerning the Alexandrian crusade is al-Nuwayrī's *Kitāb al-Ilmām*.[18] Nevertheless, although al-Nuwayrī, a citizen of Alexandria and an eyewitness of the events, gives a most detailed and precise description of the crusade and its context, he is also very partial to his compatriots and this renders his narrative unreliable at times.[19] Onimus compares al-Nuwayrī's narrative with later Arabic sources, such as al-Maqrīzī's and al-ʿAynī's works,[20] written in Cairo in the first half of the fifteenth century, or Ibn Qāḍī Šuhba's and Ṣāliḥ ibn Yaḥyā's works,[21] which give a Syrian point of view of the events as they were written in Damascus at the beginning of the fifteenth century and in Lebanon in the first third of the fifteenth century respectively. In view of the absence of Mamluk diplomatic documents, these narratives provide the only available Mamluk perspective on the Alexandrian crusade and its aftermath and shed light on issues that the Christian chronicles of William of Machaut and Leontios Makhairas neglect or misinterpret.

The papal chronicles known as Lives of Urban V, attributed to Peter of Herentals (1322-90/91) and others, provide only brief information about Peter, said to be the good,

---

16 Nikephoros Gregoras, *Historiae Byzantinae libri postremi*, ed. by Immanuel Bekker, Corpus Scriptorum Historiae Byzantinae, 48 (Bonn: Weber, 1855), pp. 27–39 (esp. 27); Pietro Luigi M. Leone, 'L'encomio di Niceforo Gregora per il re di Cipro (Ugo IV di Lusignano)', *Byzantion*, 51 (1981), 211–24 (esp. pp. 220–24); Nikephoros Gregoras, *Epistulae*, ed. by Pietro Luigi M. Leone, 2 vols (Matino: Tipografia di Matino, 1982–83), II, no. 87, p. 236.

17 Aziz Suryal Atiya, *The Crusades in the Later Middle Ages* (London: Methuen and Co, 1938; repr. New York: Kraus Reprint, 1965), pp. 319–78; Hill, *A History of Cyprus*, II, passim; *Chypre dans les sources arabes médiévales*, selected and translated into French by M. Tahar Mansouri, Sources et études de l'histoire de Chypre, 38 (Nicosia: Centre de Recherche Scientifique, 2001).

18 Al-Nuwayrī, *Kitāb al-Ilmām aw mirāt al-ʿağāʾib*, ed. by Etienne Combe and ʿAzīz Suryāl ʿAṭiya, 7 vols (Hyderabad: Dāʾirat al-Maʿārif al-ʿUṯmāniyya, 1973–96).

19 Jo Van Steenbergen, 'The Alexandrian Crusade (1365) and the Mamlūk Sources: Reassessment of the Kitāb al-Ilmām of an-Nuwayrī al-Iskandaranī (d. A.D. 1372)', in *East and West in the Crusader States. Context – Contacts – Confrontations*, III, Acta of the Congress Held at Hernen Castle in September 2000, ed. by Krijnie Ciggaar and Herman G. B. Teule (Leuven: Peeters, 2003), pp. 123–37.

20 Al-Maqrīzī, *Kitāb al-Sulūk li-Maʿrifa Duwal al-Mulūk*, ed. by Saʿīd ʿAbd al-Fattāḥ ʿĀšūr, III/1 (Cairo: Maṭbaʿa dār al-kutub, 1970); Badr al-Dīn al-ʿAyni, *ʿIqd a-Ğumān fī taʾrīḫ ahl al-zamān*, Sultan Ahmet III Library, MSS A 2911 B2.

21 Ibn Qāḍī Šuhba, *Taʾrīḫ Ibn Qāḍī Šuhba*, ed. by ʿAdnān Darwīš, III (Damascus: PIFD, 1994); Ṣāliḥ ibn Yaḥyā, *Taʾrīḫ Bayrūt*, ed. by Francis Hours and Kamāl Sulaymān al-Ṣalībī (Beirut: Dār al-Mašraq, 1969).

virtuous, and brave king, who aspired more than any other prince to the liberation of the Holy Land. As Peter Edbury and Chris Schabel say in their chapter, they 'were written with hindsight and need to be treated with caution'. They mention Peter's arrival in Avignon and the proclamation of the crusade by the pope, the capture of Alexandria, and his murder by his noblemen and brothers like Abel.[22]

Italian civic chroniclers mention Peter's visit to their cities during both of his journeys as a memorable event, most of them associating it with his crusading goals but without much elaboration, while some of them also refer to his murder; he is routinely depicted as a noble and virtuous king and knight. The Milanese Donato Bossi (1436–c. 1500) records Peter's arrival in Milan on 21 January 1363, where he stayed for twelve days as a guest of the Visconti.[23] The Genoese official historian Giorgio Stella (1365–1420) briefly mentions Peter's arrival in Genoa at the end of January 1363 (he rather arrived at the beginning of February) and his presence at the banquet given by the nobleman Pietro Malocello at his house, where Doge Simon Boccanegra was allegedly poisoned (he died on 14 March).[24]

Not all Venetian historians mention Peter.[25] Most of those who do refer briefly to his first visit to the *Serenissima* and his crusading plans in relation to the suppression of the 1363 Cretan revolt of St Titus.[26] Lorenzo de Monacis (c. 1351–1428), a Venetian diplomat and Chancellor of Crete (elected in 1389), also describes Peter's disappointment at his failure to obtain real support from the European princes for the launching of a crusade.[27] In his *Vita* of Carlo Zeno (1333–1418), the Bishop of Padua Iacopo Zeno (1418–81) associates his hero with the crusader king, specifying

---

22 *Vitae Paparum Avenionensium* [...], ed. by Étienne Baluze, 2 vols (Paris: F. Muguet, 1693), new ed. by Guillaume Mollat, 4 vols (Paris: Letouzey et Ané, 1914–1922), I, pp. 349–414, 'Prima Vita Urbani V', pp. 352–53, 357, 366, 371, 'Secunda Vita Urbani V', pp. 384–86, 389, 390, 'Tertia Vita Urbani V', p. 396, 'Quarta Vita Urbani V', p. 400.

23 Donato Bossi, *Chronica Bossiana* [...] *Gestorum dictorumque memorabilium & temporum ac conditionum & mutationum humanarum, ab orbis initio, usque ad ejus tempora* (Milan: Antonius Zarotus, 1492), fol. 126ᵛ, cited in Mas Latrie, *Histoire de l'île de Chypre*, II, p. 239 n. 1 (at p. 240).

24 Giorgio Stella, *Annales Genuenses ab anno MCCXCVIII usque ad finem anni MCCCCIX*, ed. by Ludovico Antonio Muratori, Rerum Italicarum Scriptores (ser. I), XVII/2 (Milan: Typographia Societatis Palatinae in Regia Curia, 1730), cols 945–1318 (1096); I have not been able to consult the modern edition: Giorgio Stella, Giovanni Stella, *Annales Genuenses*, ed. by Giovanna Petti Balbi, Rerum Italicarum Scriptores n.s., XVII/2 (Bologna: Zanichelli, 1975).

25 No references in: Raphayni de Caresinis, *Venetiarum Chronica: aa. 1343–1388*, ed. by Ester Pastorello, Rerum Italicarum Scriptores (ser. II), XII/2 (Bologna: Zanichelli, 1922); *Il Codice Morosini: il mondo visto da Venezia (1094–1433)*, ed. by Andrea Nanetti, 4 vols (Spoleto: Fondazione CISAM, 2010) (I thank Andrea Nanetti for his help); Marin Sanudo, *Le vite dei dogi*, ed. by Giovanni Monticolo, Rerum Italicarum Scriptores (ser. II), XXII/4, 5 vols (Città di Castello: S. Lapi, 1900–11) (I thank Daniele Baglioni for his help).

26 Andrea Navagero (1483–1529) simply says that, in 1364, the king of Cyprus was informed of the Republic's intention to send its forces against the Cretan rebels, *Historia Veneta italico sermone scripta ab origine urbis usque ad annum MCDXCVIII*, ed. by Ludovico Antonio Muratori, Rerum Italicarum Scriptores (ser. I), XIII (Milan: Typographia Societatis Palatinae in Regia Curia, 1733), cols 919–1216 (1047).

27 Laurentius de Monacis, *Chronicon de rebus venetis ab U. C. ad annum 1354*, ed. by Flaminius Corner, Rerum Italicarum Scriptores (ser. I), XVIII Appendix (Venice: Typographia Remondiniana, 1758), p. 92.

that they met in 1362 in Venice.[28] The first Venetian public historian, Marcantonio Coccio Sabellico (1436–1506), mentions Peter's first stay in Venice and the capture of Alexandria.[29] Although Gian Giacomo Caroldo's (*c.* 1480–1538/39) *Historie venete dal principio della citta fino all'anno 1382* is a later work, written between 1520 and 1532, it is a detailed and valuable testimony for Peter's first stay in Venice because, for the period 1280–1382, Caroldo used archival records, many of which were lost in a fire in 1577. Peter is said to have arrived in Venice at the beginning of December 1362 in three galleys, escorted by many noblemen. The Doge Lorenzo Celsi (*c.* 1310–18 July 1365, in office from 1361 until his death), sailed on the Bucentaur, the state barge used only on very important occasions, to welcome the Cypriot king at the monastery of San Nicolò in Lido. Peter put up at Ca' Corner in San Luca, a palace facing the Grand Canal. He was offered many gifts and attended splendid festivities, including the knighting of the Podestà of Treviso, Andrea Zane, at the ducal chapel of San Marco (today St Mark's Basilica). Caroldo then describes at length the rest of Peter's journey, probably following Froissart's itinerary, and cites a now lost letter of 16 February 1364 addressed by Peter to the Venetian authorities in relation to a passage of 2000 knights for June 1364.[30]

In Donato di Neri's (early 1300s–1371/72) *Sienese Chronicle*, the visit of the king of Cyprus, escorted by his ten-year old son and a retinue of 300 knights, in June 1368, is described as one of the most important events ever witnessed by Siena. Peter is said to have piously visited the convent of San Domenico in Camporegio (founded in 1226) and to have received and given many presents. He then travelled to Pisa and Florence, where he was also honourably received. His wish to see the pope and the emperor, his relative (*sic*), is given as the reason of his journey.[31] An anonymous Pisan chronicle mentions Peter's arrival at the city from Siena on 14 June 1368, his ceremonial reception ('Entrò sotto un palio di seta'), and the banquets and exchange of presents. The chronicle also describes Peter's murder in his chambers with a knife by one of his brothers, who was then made king by the Genoese, thus alluding to James I.[32] In the *Cronaca fiorentina di Marchionne di Coppo Stefani*, a history of Florence from ancient times up to 1385, Baldassarre Bonaiuti (1336–85) mentions

---

28 Iacobus Zenus, *Vita Caroli Zeni*, ed. by Gasparo Zonta, Rerum Italicarum Scriptores (ser. II), XIX/6 (Bologna: Zanichelli, 1940), p. 10 ('Cyprius [...] Rex, cui Petrus nomen erat, ingentis, ut fama est, virtutis et praeclari animi').

29 Marcantonio Coccio Sabellico, *Historiae rerum venetarum ab urbe condita* (Basel: Johannis Konig, 1670), pp. 247, 253–54.

30 Mas Latrie, 'Nouvelles preuves', pp. 60–64; I have not been able to consult Giovanni Giacomo Caroldo, *Istorii venețiene*, ed. by Șerban V. Marin, 5 vols (Bucharest: Arhivele Naționale ale României, 2008–12), IV, *Dogatele lui Lorenzo Celsi, Marco Cornaro și prima parte a dogatului lui Andrea Contarini (1361–1373)*. For the *palazzo* Corner, see below.

31 Donato di Neri, *Cronaca senese*, ed. by Alessandro Lisini and Fabio Iacometti, Rerum Italicarum Scriptores (ser. II), XV/6 (Bologna: Zanichelli, 1931–39), pp. 567–685 (616).

32 *Cronica di Pisa dal ms. Roncioni dell'Archivio di Stato di Pisa*, ed. by Cecilia Iannella, Antiquitates, 22 (Rome: Istituto Storico Italiano per il Medioevo, 2005), chapter 243, p. 210. Ranieri Sardo, *Cronaca di Pisa*, ed. by Ottavio Banti, Fonti per la storia d'Italia, 99 (Rome: Istituto Storico Italiano, 1963) does not mention Peter's visit. I thank Cecilia Iannella for the information from the Pisan chronicles.

very briefly the visit of Peter and his son to the city in 1368, although he does provide interesting details about the extravagant reception the king was given (gifts, feasts, and jousts, in which he competed successfully); the failure of Peter's crusading cause is blamed on Bernabò Visconti of Milan and the latter's politics in northern Italy and his murder on his barons.[33]

The renowned scholar, poet, and diplomat Francesco Petrarca (1304-74) was in a better position to assess Peter's crusading plans vis-à-vis European politics than Italian chroniclers. Petrarca spent his early childhood and much of his early adulthood at the papal court in Avignon and studied law in Montpellier, but then moved to northern Italy and retired in Venice in 1362, where he befriended the Doge Lorenzo Celsi. He met Peter in Venice during the king's second, seven-month long stay from 11 November 1364 to the end of June 1365, knew and corresponded with the king's chancellor Philip of Mézières,[34] and was a friend of the king's doctor and counsellor Guido da Bagnolo, one of the four recipients of his *De sui ipsius et aliorum ignorantia* (1368/71).[35] Petrarca refers explicitly to Peter in two letters that belong to the collection *Seniles (Letters of Old Age)*. In a letter addressed to Boccaccio (20 July 1367), Petrarca describes the capture of Alexandria as an illustrious enterprise and a memorable achievement for the consolidation of Christendom and blames the withdrawal of the Christians from the city on Peter's French troops, who were only interested in looting. A letter to Philip of Mézières (4 November 1369), 'the king's soldier', is a lament for the death in 1369 of the Lombard knight Giacomo dei Rossi, who served Peter during the taking of Alexandria and later. Petrarca duly remembers the unworthy and undignified death of the famous Cypriot king, Peter, and wishes that both Peter and Giacomo were alive so that the Christian empire could expand.[36]

---

33 *Cronaca fiorentina di Marchionne di Coppo Stefani*, ed. by Niccolò Rodolico, Rerum Italicarum Scriptores (ser. II), XXX/1 (Città di Castello: S. Lapi, 1903), p. 402.
34 Philippe de Mézières, *Letter to King Richard II. A plea made in 1395 for peace between England and France*, ed. and English trans. G. W. Coopland (Liverpool: Liverpool University Press, 1975), p. 42 ('le solempnel docteur et souverain poete, maistre François Petrac'), 115; Philippe de Mézières, *Le Livre de la Vertu du Sacrement de Mariage*, ed. Joan B. Williamson (Washington, D.C.: The Catholic University of America Press, 1993), p. 358 ('les gracieuses escriptures du vaillant et solepnel docteur-poète, maistre Fransoys Patrac, jadis mon [Philip's] espécial ami'); Nicolas Jorga, 'Une collection de lettres de Philippe de Maizières (Notice sur le ms. 499 de la bibl. de l'Arsenal)', *Revue historique*, 49 (May-August 1892), 306-22 (p. 314); Jorga, *Philippe de Mézières*, pp. 26, 144 n. 1, p. 192 n. 4, pp. 253-54, 305, 392, 417; Ernest H. Wilkins, 'Petrarch and Giacomo de' Rossi', *Speculum*, 25/3 (1950), 374-78; Evelien Chayes, 'Trois lettres pour la posterité: la correspondance entre Philippe de Mézières, Boniface Lupi et François Pétrarque (MS. Arsenal 499)', in *Philippe de Mézières and His Age*, pp. 83-117.
35 Rifoldo Livi, 'Guido da Bagnolo, medico del re di Cipro', *Atti e memorie della R. Deputazione di storia patria per le provincie modenesi*, ser. 5, 11 (1918), 45-91; Franco Bacchelli, 'Guido da Bagnolo', in *Dizionario biografico degli Italiani*, 61 (Rome: Treccani, 2004), pp. 388-90; Chayes, 'Trois lettres pour la posterité', p. 95; Gilles Grivaud's chapter in this volume.
36 Pétrarque, *Lettres de la viellesse / Rerum senilium*, III-IV, ed. by Elvira Nota, introduction and notes by Ugo Dotti (Paris: Les Belles Lettres, 2004-06), III, *Livres VIII-XI*, French trans. by Claude Laurens, Book VIII, letter 8, pp. 100-05 (102-03), cf. letter 4 (allusion to Alexandria), IV, *Livres XII-XV*, French trans. by Jean-Yves Boriaud, Book XIII, letter 2, pp. 136-45 (140-43), cf. letter 1 (allusion to Alexandria). I thank Evelien Chayes for providing me with copies of the letters.

Italian literary works are even less eloquent than historical works and, although they do express praise for Peter's heroic deeds, the king's person does not receive the ideological appropriation attested in French literature.[37] In his didactic poem *Dittamondo*, written in a mixture of French and Provençal, the Florentine Fazio degli Uberti (1305/09–after 1368) mentions the visit of the brave and wise Cypriot king ('Le reis de Cipre, qu'es mout pros et satge') to Avignon, expressing scepticism about the success of a new crusade.[38] A poem in eight stanzas of eighteen lines each, found in a manuscript that contains Giovanni Boccaccio's *Genealogia deorum gentilium* and was copied and illustrated in Venice in 1388 for Giovanni Morosini, is no exception as it provides no historical or ideological elaboration despite its length. Entitled 'Cantilena extensa Nicolai de Scachis de morte illustrissimi regis Cypri ac Yerusalem', the poem is a moralistic complaint for the murder of 'Pietro di Cypro', composed in the Venetian dialect with affectations of the Tuscan by the Veronese Nicolò di Scacchi soon after the event. The poet deplores the fact the Peter's death was fratricide, laments the loss of a staunch defender of the faith, the champion of Christ, and invites Cyprus and Jerusalem to mourn.[39] In Gasparino Barzizza's (*c.* 1360-1431) panegyric written in praise of Peter's nephew, King Janus, in the first quarter of the fifteenth century and in the Venetian Leonardo Giustiniani's (*c.* 1383- 1446) dedication to Janus's brother, Prince Henry of Galilee (1380/85?-1426), of his Latin translation of Plutarch's *Lives of Cimon and Lucullus* in 1416, Peter is celebrated, in true humanist style, as one of the glorious members of the *lusignana domus*, who, following Charlemagne's example, triumphed over the Greeks, the Turks, and the Egyptians.[40]

---

37 Although Mas Latrie, *Histoire de l'île de Chypre*, II, p. 245, seems to think that the verses 'Il successor di Carlo, che la chioma | co la corona del suo antiquo adorna, | prese à gia l'arme per fiaccar le corna | a Babilonia et echi da lei si noma', from Petrarca's poem 27, refer to Peter, modern scholarship identifies 'Charles's successor' with Philip VI of France (1328–50), heir of Charles IV (1322–28) and, ultimately, of Charlemagne, on the basis of the poem's composition date, see *Petrarch's Lyric Poems: The Rime Sparse and Other Lyrics*, ed. and English trans. by Robert M. Durling (Cambridge, Mass.: Harvard University Press, 1976), no. 27, p. 73.

38 Fazio degli Uberti, Fiorentino, *Il Dittamondo*, ed. by Cav. Vincenzo Monti (Milan: Giovanni Silvestri, 1826), IV, xxi, p. 345.

39 British Library, Egerton MS 1865, fol. 12^{r-v} (new foliation); edited by H. N. MacCracken, 'An Italian Complaint for the Death of Pierre de Lusignan', *The Romanic Review*, 2/1 (January-March 1911), pp. 89–95. See Antonio Medin, 'Canzone storico-morale di Nicolò de' Scacchi, poeta veronese del secolo XIV', in *Raccolta di studii critici dedicata ad Alessandro d'Ancona festeggiandosi il XL anniversario del suo insegnamento* (Firenze: G. Barbera, 1901), pp. 572–75.

40 For Barzizza's *Oratio ad regem Cypri*, which remains unpublished, see Clémence Revest, 'La rhétorique humaniste au service des élites chypriotes dans l'Italie septentrionale de la première moitié du XVe siècle', in *Poésie et musique à l'âge de l'Ars subtilior. Autour du manuscrit Torino, BNU, J.II. 9*, ed. by Gisèle Clément, Isabelle Fabre, Gilles Polizzi, and Fañch Thoraval, Centre d'études supérieures de la Renaissance, Collection 'Épitome musical' (Turnhout: Brepols, 2021), pp. 41-60 (48); for the preface of Giustiniani's *Cimonis et Luculli vitas*, see Marianne Pade, *The Reception of Plutarch's Lives in Fifteenth-Century Italy*, 2 vols (Cophenhagen: Museum Tusculanum Press, 2007), I, pp. 205-09, II, pp. 119-23 (121) and Gilles Grivaud, 'Résonances humanistes à la cour de Nicosie (1411-1423)', in *Poésie et musique à l'âge de l'Ars subtilior*, pp. 27-39 (36).

Peter's visit to England at the end of 1363 was quite a remarkable event and contemporary and near contemporary English narratives do not fail to record it, albeit very briefly as a memorable glamorous occasion. Only two of them mention the Cypriot king's crusader intentions, an early continuation of Ranulph Higden's *Polychronicon* (a universal history ending in *c.* 1352)[41] and Henry Knighton's chronicle (composed from *c.* 1378 until his death *c.* 1396),[42] specifying that he came to England in order to ask for the help of King Edward III (1327–77) in the liberation of his ancestral Kingdom of Jerusalem from the hands of the Saracens. Peter is not even named (always referred to as 'rex Cypriae') and he certainly does not receive the idealized depiction attested in French literature and historiography. In fact, the most detailed account of Peter's visit to England is given by a Frenchman, John Froissart.[43] The *Polychronicon* and the universal chronicle entitled *Eulogium historiarum* state that Peter arrived in London on 6 November 1363. All sources agree that the king of Cyprus was in London at the same time as the kings of France and Scotland and were all received lavishly by the English king.[44] Documentary sources inform us that Peter was present at and probably participated in a tournament in Smithfield (today a district in central London) shortly after St Martin's Day (11 November 1363).[45] Thomas Walsingham's (*c.* 1340–1422) mention of Cypriot and Armenian knights, who participated in the Smithfield tournament in 1362 and asked for the English king's help against the infidels, probably refers to Peter's visit.[46] The same chronicler and John of Reading, in his continuation of Roger of Wendover's *Flores Historiarum* (written *c.* 1366–67), add the interesting piece of information that, on his way back to the English coast, Peter was robbed of all his goods by highwaymen, who were caught and brought to justice in London.[47]

On the other hand, Geoffrey Chaucer (1340/45–1400) mentions Peter in his *Canterbury Tales*, in the Prologue and in 'The Monkes Tale', in a way that recalls

---

41 Ranulph Higden, *Polychronicon Ranulphi Higden monachi Cestrensis, together with the English translations of John Trevisa and of an unknown writer of the fifteenth century*, VIII, ed. by Rev. Joseph Rawson Lumby, Rolls Series, 41 (London: Longman & Co et al., 1882), p. 362.
42 Henry Knighton, *Chronicon Henrici Knighton, vel Cnitthon, monachi Leycestrensis*, ed. by Rev. Joseph Rawson Lumby, 2 vols, Rolls Series, 92 (London: Eyre and Spottiswoode, 1889–95), II, p. 118.
43 *Chroniques de J. Froissart*, ed. by Siméon Luce et al., 15 vols, Société de l'histoire de France (Paris: Mme Vᵉ Jules Renouard et al., 1869–1975), VI, § 507, pp. 90–92 and 280–84.
44 Ranulph Higden, *Polychronicon*, p. 362; *Eulogium (historiarum sive temporis): Chronicon ab orbe condito usque ad Annum Domini M.CCC.LXVI., A monacho quodam Malmesburiensi exaratum*, ed. by Frank Scott Haydon, 3 vols, Rolls Series, 9 (London: Longman et al., 1858–63), III, p. 233. John of Reading claims that Peter left London around All Saints' Day (1 November), which cannot be correct, *Chronica Johannis de Reading et Anonymi Cantuariensis 1346–1367*, ed. by James Tait (Manchester: At the University Press, 1914), p. 158. Further discussion below.
45 Public Record Office, Exchequer Accounts (K.R.), Wardrobe and Household, 37–38, Edward III, Roll of liveries by Henry de Snayth, keeper of the Great Wardrobe, E. 101/394/16, m. 17 and Exchequer L.T.R 4, m. 9. Further discussion below.
46 Thomas Walsingham, *Chronica Monasterii S. Albani […] Historia Anglicana*, ed. by Henry Thomas Riley, 2 vols, Rolls Series, 28 (London: Longman et al., 1863–64), I, pp. 296–97.
47 Thomas Walsingham, *Historia Anglicana*, I, p. 299 and *Chronicon Angliae*, ed. by Edward Maunde. Thompson, Rolls Series, 64 (London: Longman et al.,1874), p. 54; John of Reading, *Chronica*, p. 158.

the king's portrayal in French literature; he places his Knight, a character whose mission is to broaden Christendom with his sword, in three specific campaigns with Peter (in Alexandria, Ayas, and Antalya), praises Peter's military achievement in Alexandria, explains his murder in terms of his liegemen's envy of his chivalric prowess, and associates his fate with the theme of the fickle Fortune: 'O worthy Petro, king of Cypre also, | That Alisaundre wan by heigh maistrye, | Ful many hethen wroghtestow ful wo, | Of which thyn owene liges hadde envye, | And, for no thing but for thy chivalrye, | They in thy bedde han slayn thee by the morwe. | Thus can fortune his wheel governe and guye, | And out of Ioye bringe men to sorwe'.[48]

Polish chronicles mention briefly Peter's visit to Cracow in September 1364, in the company of Charles IV of Luxembourg, Holy Roman Emperor (1355–78) and King of Bohemia (1346–78), and the King of Denmark Waldemar IV (1340–75), where he meets the Kings of Poland, Casimir III the Great (1333–70), and Hungary, Louis I the Great (1342–82). However, they erroneously associate it with the emperor's wedding with Casimir's granddaughter Elizabeth, which took place on 21 May 1363 when Peter was in Avignon, and not with his crusade intentions; in fact, William of Machaut gives a longer and far more detailed account of Peter's visit.[49] These sources include three contemporary narratives (the chronicle by Janko of Czarnków (*c.* 1320–87), a diplomat in Avignon (1362–66) and a crown deputy chancellor of the Treasury of Poland (1366–71); the anonymous *Chronica principum Poloniae*, written in 1382–86; the *Annales Sanctae Crucis Polonici*, written in 1399/1400) and the fifteenth-century *Annales seu cronicae incliti Regni Poloniae* written by Jan Długosz (1415–80) in 1455–80.[50] Later chronicles are quite unreliable, making Peter reach Cracow from Cyprus, through the Black Sea and Russia, in order to attend the wedding.[51]

---

48 Geoffrey Chaucer, *The Canterbury Tales*, 'Prologue', ll. 43–78, esp. 51, 58, and 'The Monkes Tale', ll. 3581–88, in *The Complete Works of Geoffrey Chaucer*, ed. by Walter W. Skeat, 7 vols (Oxford: Clarendon Press, 1899²), I, pp. 2–3, IV, p. 256. See Haldeen Braddy, 'The Two Petros in the "Monkes Tale" ', *Publications of the Modern Language Association*, 50 (1935), 69–80; John H. Pratt, 'Was Chaucer's Knight Really a Mercenary?', *The Chaucer Review*, 22/1 (1987), 8–27; Derek S. Brewer, 'Chaucer's Knight as Hero, and Machaut's *Prise d'Alexandrie*', in *Heroes and Heroines in Medieval English Literature: A Festschrift to André Crépin on the Occasion of his Sixty-fifth Birthday*, ed. by Leo Carruthers (Cambridge: D. S. Brewer, 1994), pp. 81–96.

49 Sophie Hardy, *Édition critique de la* Prise d'Alixandrie *de Guillaume de Machaut* (unpublished doctoral thesis, Université d'Orléans, 2011): ftp://ftp.univ-orleans.fr/theses/sophie.hardy_1730.pdf [accessed 4 June 2016], pp. 30–41, ll. 977–1379; further discussion below.

50 Janko of Czarnków, *Kronika*, ed. by August Bielowski, in *Monumenta Poloniae Historica*, II (Warsaw: Państwowe Wydaw. Naukowe, 1961), pp. 630–31; *Kronika ksiazat polskich*, ed. by August Bielowski, in *Monumenta Poloniae Historica*, III (Warsaw: Państwowe Wydaw. Naukowe, 1961), p. 526; *Rocznik swietokrzyski*, ed. by August Bielowski, in *Monumenta Poloniae Historica*, III, p. 80; Ioannis Dlugossi (Jan Długosz), *Annales seu cronicae incliti Regni Poloniae*, ed. by Zofia Kozłowska-Budkowa (Warsaw: Państwowe Wydaw. Naukowe, 1978), Liber IX, pp. 318–21.

51 See Jorga, *Philippe de Mézières*, p. 195 and Łukasz Burkiewicz, 'Σχέσεις Κύπρου - Πολωνίας κατά το μεσαίωνα και την Αναγέννηση, ΙΔ΄ - ΙΣΤ΄ αι.', in *Πολωνία - Κύπρος. Από τη χώρα του Σοπέν στο νησί της Αφροδίτης: Σχέσεις Ιστορίας και Πολιτισμού*, ed. by Giorgos Georgis and Giorgos Kazamias (Nicosia: En Typois, 2011), pp. 18–47 (26).

Unlike written sources, contemporary archaeological and material evidence is only rarely associated specifically with Peter with the exception of coins[52] and the beautiful illustrations in manuscripts containing Machaut's poems, Froissart's chronicles, and fifteenth-century works.[53] In 1367 or early 1368, a church dedicated to Corpus Christi ('ecclesiam ad honorem precipue Sacratissimi Corporis Domini nostri Jesu Christi necnon et sancti Bartholomei apostoli et sancti Sabastiani martiris') was erected in Nicosia at Peter's order but does not survive today.[54] Sometime in autumn 1368, he is said to have ordered the building of the church of Misericordia in the upper part of a tower and a prison called Margarita in its basement, which do not survive either.[55] The church of St Catherine in Nicosia and the Nestorian church of Sts Peter and Paul in Famagusta were most probably built during Hugh IV's or Peter I's reign.[56]

Similarly, the insignia (a sword) with the motto of Peter's Order of the Sword (*Pour loyauté maintenir*) are attested adorning a very small number of contemporary items: a shield found in Antalya, where it was probably lost during the city's capture by Peter in 1361, the façade of the *palazzo* Corner Piscopia - Loredan in Venice, and a seal used by Peter in 1365, of which only the description survives.[57] The fact that

---

52 David Michael Metcalf, *Coinage of the Crusades and the Latin East in the Ashmolean Museum Oxford* (London: Royal Numismatic Society – Society for the Study of the Crusades and the Latin East, 1995²), pp. 207–10; David Michael Metcalf and Andreas G. Pitsillides, *Corpus of Lusignan Coinage*, II, *The Silver Coinage of Cyprus, 1285–1382*, Texts and Studies in the History of Cyprus, 21 (Nicosia: Cyprus Research Centre, 1996), pp. 14–16, 81–94. The Museum of the History of Cypriot Coinage of the Bank of Cyprus Cultural Foundation owns eleven coins issued by Peter I [Fig. 8 in this author's contribution to this volume].

53 Guillaume de Machaut, *Oeuvres*, BnF, MSS Fr. 1584, fols 213ᵛ, 309ʳ, Fr. 9221, fols 213ʳ, 235ᵛ, Fr. 22546, fol. 1ʳ; Jean Froissart, *Chroniques*, BnF, MSS Fr. 2643, fol. 284ᵛ, Fr. 2645, fol. 79ʳ; John of Wavrin, *Chroniques d'Angleterre*, BnF, MSS Fr. 77, fol. 259ᵛ, Fr. 87, fol. 212ᵛ [Figs. 9.1–6, 13–15].

54 *Bullarium Cyprium III*, no. v-189 (29 May 1368).

55 Hardy, *Édition critique de la* Prise d'Alixandrie, p. 244, ll. 8357–62; Leontios Makhairas, Χρονικό της Κύπρου, pp. 205–06, 410.

56 For St Catherine, see Philippe Plagnieux and Thierry Soulard, 'Nicosie. L'église Sainte-Catherine', in *L'art gothique en Chypre*, ed. by Jean-Bernard de Vaivre and Philippe Plagnieux, Mémoires de l'Académie des Inscriptions et Belles-lettres, 34 (Paris: De Boccard, 2006), pp. 160–69 and Michalis Olympios, *Building the Sacred in a Crusader Kingdom: Gothic Church Architecture in Lusignan Cyprus, c. 1209–c. 1373*, Architectura Medii Aevi, 11 (Turnhout: Brepols, 2018), pp. 284–94. For Sts Peter and Paul, see Michalis Olympios, 'The Shifting Mantle of Jerusalem: Ecclesiastical Architecture in Lusignan Famagusta', in *Famagusta, Volume I, Art and Architecture*, ed. by Annemarie Weyl Carr, Mediterranean Nexus 1100–1700, Conflict, Influence and Inspiration in the Mediterranean Area, 2 (Turnhout: Brepols, 2014), pp. 75–142 (110–13), who believes that part of the church's construction may be associated with Peter's brother, John of Antioch, and Michele Bacci, 'Patterns of Church Decoration in Famagusta', in the same volume, pp. 203–76 (227–32).

57 Evangelia Skoufari, 'L'Ordine della spada. Istituzioni e cerimonie cavallereche nel Regno di Cipro (secoli XIV–XV)', *Archivio Veneto*, 204 (2007), 5–25 (p. 21); Philippe Trélat, 'L'ordre de l'Épée à Chypre: mémoire de la croisade et instrument du pouvoir des Lusignan', in *Autour de la Toison d'or. Ordres de chevalerie et confréries nobles aux XIVᵉ–XVIᵉ siècles*, Rencontres de Vienne (24–27 septembre 2018), ed. by Alain Marchandisse and Gilles Docquier, Publications du Centre Européen d'Études bourguignonnes, 59 (Neuchâtel: Éditeurs divers suisses, 2019), pp. 317–36 (321–22, 333). Later items decorated with the Order's insignia include the *c.* 1487 depiction of Famagusta in Conrad Grünemberg's (*c.* 1415–94) illustrated travelogue (Karlsruhe, Badische Landesbibliothek, Cod. St Peter pap. 32, fol. 27ʳ [Fig. 1]) and a relief

Peter's coins show him holding a sword drawn out of its sheath instead of a sceptre may constitute an allusion to the Order.[58] The *palazzo* commonly known today as *palazzo* Loredan, house of the municipal government of Venice, was the mansion where Peter was lodged during his first stay in Venice in December 1362. At the time, it belonged to Andrea Zane, Podestà of Treviso, whose knighting Peter attended; it was soon afterwards acquired by the Corner and became known as the *palazzo* Corner Piscopia. Among the decorations on the façade, datable to 1363, one can see the Lusignan arms and, as already said, the insignia and motto of the Order of the Sword.[59]

Peter's gifts to European kings, princes, and prelates and the gifts he received are known only from written sources. For example, in 1363, while visiting Boulogne-sur-Mer, he gave a relic of the True Cross to the local church of Notre-Dame; a silver statuette of a knight bearing the Lusignan arms was his gift to the cathedral of Tréguier in Brittany; Pope Urban V received a silver lantern.[60] In 1368, Peter gave the Dominican convent of Santa Maria Novella in Florence his lance and royal cloak, embroidered with his and his son's portraits.[61] Notes of payments from the king's Keeper of the Great Wardrobe show that Edward III of England presented Peter with a pair of gauntlets and a steel aventail for his helmet and suggest that the Cypriot king actually took part in the tournament in Smithfield in November 1363.[62] One

---

datable to the sixteenth century and possibly coming from Nicosia, *Lacrimae Cypriae. Les larmes de Chypre ou Recueil des inscriptions lapidaires pour la plupart funéraires de la période franque et vénitienne de l'île de Chypre*, ed. by Brunehilde Imhaus, 2 vols (Nicosia: Department of Antiquities, 2004), I, no. 710. In the first third of the fifteenth century, the motto is used as the refrain of ballad 11 in the manuscript Torino, Biblioteca Nazionale Universitaria, J.II.9, fol. 102ʳ, see Virginia Newes, 'Raison contre Fortune: ordering and structure in the first ballade gathering of the manuscript Torino J.II.9', in *Poésie et musique à l'âge de l'Ars subtilior*, pp. 125–41 (131–32).

58 Metcalf, *Coinage of the Crusades and the Latin East*, p. 207.
59 See Giulio Lorenzetti, *Venice and Its Lagoon. Historical - Artistic Guide* (Rome: Lint, 1961), pp. 494–96 and Setton, *Papacy*, I, p. 242. The Loredan family acquired the residence in the eighteenth century; Hugh Honour, *The Companion Guide to Venice*, Companion Guides (Woodbridge: Boydell & Brewer, 2001), p. 236, wrongly believes that Peter 'in return for financial aid allowed the Loredans to use the rampant lion of Lusignan on their arms – it appears among the decoration of the frieze'.
60 Philippe Trélat, 'Le goût pour Chypre. Objets d'art et tissus précieux importés de Chypre en Occident (xiiiᵉ–xvᵉ siècles)', *Cahiers du Centre d'Études Chypriotes*, 43 (2013), 455–72 (pp. 467–68); more examples in Michalis Olympios, 'Τοτθική τέχνη στη Λευκωσία των Λουζινιανών', in Demetra Papanikola-Bakirtzis (ed.), *Μεσαιωνική Λευκωσία. Πρωτεύουσα ώσμωσης Ανατολής και Δύσης*, Catalogue of the exhibition Nicosia: *The Birth and Growth of a Capital. Byzantine - Medieval Period* (The Leventis Municipal Museum of Nicosia, 24 May 2018–27 January 2019) (Nicosia: The Leventis Municipal Museum of Nicosia, 2020), pp. 120–35 (127).
61 *Catalogus codicum latinorum Bibliothecae Mediceae Laurentianae [...], Tomus III, in quo medici, chirurgici, philosophi, politici nomici tam veteris quam recentioris aevi accuratissime recensentur operum singulorum notitia datur [...]*, ed. by Angelo Maria Bandini (Florence: Typis Caesareis, 1774), pp. 373–74; Mas Latrie, *Histoire de l'île de Chypre*, II, p. 313 n. 3.
62 Public Record Office, Exchequer Accounts (K.R.), Wardrobe and Household, 37–38, Edward III, Roll of liveries by Henry de Snayth, keeper of the Great Wardrobe, E. 101/394/16, m. 17, published by Mas Latrie, *Histoire de l'île de Chypre*, II, p. 247: 'pro coopertura unius paris plattarum datarum domino regi Cipriorum per regem pro hastiludiis factis in Smethfeld post festum Omnium sanctorum, nec non pro

notable exception may be one of the so-called reliquary scenes in the Chapel of the Virgin Mary, the *capella regia* in the Minor Tower of the Karlstein/Karlštejn Castle, located about thirty kilometres southwest of Prague and built between 1348 and 1365 by Emperor Charles IV; the fresco, painted by the emperor's court painter Mikuláš Wurmser, depicts the presentation of the relics of the True Cross to the emperor by a ruler, who might be Peter.[63]

Probably relying on stories that he heard from members of his family, Étienne de Lusignan explains in 1580 that the meeting place of the conspirators against Peter was the house of Prince John of Antioch and claims that this was the house where he was born less than two centuries later. He adds that when the Dominican church in Nicosia, where Peter was buried, was demolished by the Venetians in 1567 for the reconstruction of the city's walls, Peter's tomb was found to contain his gilded, ceremonial spurs that were inscribed with the names of the three Magi.[64]

Peter I of Lusignan: The Knight, the Crusader, the King, the Man

There survives no detailed written description or material testimony of Peter I of Lusignan's physical appearance. The information we have from writers who knew him personally is romanticized in accordance with contemporary literary conventions, Philip of Mézières describing Peter as a 'young oriental king, energetic, magnanimous, and elegant of his person' and William of Machaut portraying him as 'handsome, slender, tall, and well built, brave and strong'; a few decades later, Leontios Makhairas calls him 'vigorous'.[65] On the other hand, modern scholarship can provide only a tentative assessment of Peter's character and conduct, taking into consideration the conventions and norms of the social and cultural context of his time. Almost

---

diversis cappis pro rege circumligandis per diversas vices'; Public Record Office, Exchequer Accounts (K.R.), Wardrobe and Household, 37–38, Edward III, Exchequer L.T.R 4, m. 9, published in Charles Lethbridge Kingsford, 'The Feast of the Five Kings', *Archaeologia*, 67 (1916), 119–26 (p. 125 n. 2): 'Regi de Cipre pro hastiludio facto in Smethefeld post festum sancti Martini anno xxxvij° de dono Regis Anglie j Auentaill de acere per breve Regis de privato sigillo dato primo die Novembris eodem anno: per quod Rex mandat dicto custodi quod prefato Regi de Cipre j auentaill de acere pro hastiludio in Smythfeld de dono Regis liberari faciat'. See Hill, *A History of Cyprus*, II, pp. 325–26.

63 Other candidates include King Louis I of Hungary and the ruler of Mantua Ludovico I Gonzaga (1328–60), see Łukasz Burkiewicz, 'Sceny relikwiowe (Ostatkové sceny) i cypryjski ślad w kaplicy Najświętszej Marii Panny w zamku Karlštejn', in *Kościół w Czechach i w Polsce w średniowieczu i wczesnej epoce nowożytnej*, ed. by Wojciech Iwańczak, Agnieszka Januszek-Sieradzka, Janusz Smołucha (Kraków: Wydawnictwo Naukowe Akademii Ignatianum w Krakowie, 2020), pp. 507–20.

64 Estienne de Lusignan, *Description*, chapter 21, fol. 147ʳ. Olympios, 'The Shifting Mantle', p. 98, suggests that Peter may have seen the relics of the Three Kings at Cologne Cathedral, when he visited the city in 1364.

65 Philippe de Mézières, *Oratio tragedica*, ed. and French trans. by Joël Blanchard and Antoine Calvet, Cahiers d'Humanisme et Renaissance, 156 (Geneva: Droz, 2019), pp. 418–19 ('quemdam regem orientalem juvenem scilicet strenuum, magnanimum et in persona elegantem'); Hardy, *Édition critique de la Prise d'Alixandrie*, p. 26, ll. 861–62 ('tant estoit gens, joins, lons et droits, | hardis, puissans en tous endroits'); Leontios Makhairas, *Χρονικό τῆς Κύπρου*, p. 196 ('παιδίος').

all available sources speak very briefly of Peter the man, focusing on his deeds as a crusader, a knight, and a king and providing a monolithic depiction of his person that obeys specific ideological intentions. His idealized portrayal in the firsthand, long accounts of Machaut and Mézières is in fact a *laudatio*, with only scattered personal information and deliberate omissions of character traits, behavioural patterns, and emotional states that do not comply with the intended image. Makhairas is the only near contemporary chronicler who provides personal, intimate, and often denigrating information. Rich though it may be, his account was probably self-censored, as he was in the service of Peter's successors, and the real Peter may have been an even more complex person to assess.

It is thus necessary to evaluate Peter in his capacity as a knight, a crusader, and a king in order to understand the man. To this end, it is also important to take into account the fact that all medieval narrative and literary sources obey to some extent the codes of conduct of the courtly romance tradition. Extreme emotions are a regular feature in medieval romance, be they the pain of romantic love or the grief of death. However, there are certain constraints on masculine behaviour. The expression of grief is permitted only in a domestic setting and not publicly, while royal anger cannot be uncontrollable. Similarly, happiness is not the result of divine grace but of fate, while erotic joy is the reward of a knight at the end of long pursuit.[66] Machaut and Mézières certainly follow faithfully these conventions, but Makhairas's portrayal is more realistic, echoing the attitude of the Cypriot society of his time.

Peter's father, Hugh IV, seems to have been quite an authoritarian figure. In their chapter, Peter Edbury and Chris Schabel discuss his attitude towards his daughter-in-law Maria of Bourbon (1318–87), widow of his son from his first marriage, Guy (1315/16–43), and her son Hugh (c. 1335-85/86); the king was reluctant to give his authorization for her departure from Cyprus with her son Hugh after Guy's death in 1343, while he seems to have systematically neglected the payment of the annual amount his daughter-in-law was entitled to as her dower or the grant of any subvention to his grandson. Moreover, his ugly quarrel with his son-in-law Ferrand of Majorca (1317–45/47), who married his daughter Eschiva (c. 1325–63) in 1340, reveals a violent, vindictive man, who hated the Franciscans and was prone to bouts of anger, swearing, and shouting, no matter how treacherous Ferrand's behaviour was.[67]

The way Hugh treated his sons, Peter and John, and the knights who went with them to the West without his permission in 1349 also demonstrates his intolerance and ruthlessness. Machaut does not hesitate to state that, because Peter feared

---

66 See indicatively: Frank Brandsma, Carolyne Larrington, and Corinne Saunders (eds.), *Emotions in Medieval Arthurian Literature: Body, Mind, Voice* (Cambridge, Boydell & Brewer, 2015); *Literature Compass*, 13/6 (2016), special issue: *Emotions and Feelings in the Middle Ages*.

67 Hill, *A History of Cyprus*, II, pp. 295–97; Edbury, *Kingdom of Cyprus*, pp. 144–45; Chris Schabel, 'Hugh the Just: The Further Rehabilitation of King Hugh IV Lusignan of Cyprus', *Επετηρίδα Κέντρου Επιστημονικών Ερευνών (Κύπρου)*, 30 (2004), 139–51; Angel Nicolaou-Konnari, 'Women in Medieval Famagusta: Law, Family, and Society', in *Famagusta, Volume II, History and Society*, ed. by Gilles Grivaud, Angel Nicolaou-Konnari, and Chris Schabel, Mediterranean Nexus 1110–1700. Conflict, Influence and Inspiration in the Mediterranean Area, 8 (Turnhout: Brepols, 2020), pp. 509–633 (574).

his father very much, he kept his crusading plans secret. In a letter to the king dated 13 September 1349, Pope Clement VI (1342–52) expresses his grief for the disobedience showed by his sons and promises to ask them to return to Cyprus if they come to Rome. Machaut and Makhairas say that Hugh punished his sons imprisoning them in the castle of Kyrenia for two months and nine days and for only three days respectively. Papal letters, however, suggest that the imprisonment lasted longer. On 12 August 1350, Clement VI intervened for Peter's liberation and only on 2 September 1351 did he thank Hugh for having freed his son and heir; on 12 July 1351, the pope granted Peter and John a plenary indulgence *in articulo mortis* without specifying if they had already been liberated or not. Machaut also adds that, after his liberation, Peter was kept under tight control by his father and was deprived of any revenues. Nevertheless, Hugh's attitude does not necessarily mean he was a loveless father. Both Machaut and Makhairas underline that the episode caused the king much pain, the latter adding that Hugh waited outside the prison during the three days of imprisonment; moreover, Hugh is known to have made the meaningful donation of 300 ducats for the edification of the tomb of St Peter Martyr in the Basilica of St Eustorgius in Milan (completed in 1339).[68]

Peter seems to have inherited his father's quarrelsome and explosive character as well as the family feuds, which he carried on. The one with Hugh, the son of his elder half-brother Guy, had considerable political repercussions. Hugh disputed Peter's right to the throne of Cyprus and had the support of John II, King of France (1350-64), his mother Maria of Bourbon, Empress of Constantinople, being related to the French royal family. Peter Edbury and Chris Schabel give the political and legal background of the dispute, using, among other sources, two hitherto unpublished letters sent by Pope Innocent VI to Peter and Maria, dated 24 May and 13 June 1360 respectively, which clearly indicate that Hugh presented his case to the pope soon after Hugh IV's death and Peter's enthronement. Even as late as 24 August 1368, a long time after the settlement of the dispute at the Avignon papal court in 1363 and a period when he was in Peter's service, Hugh needed Urban V's mediation in order to be granted a licence to leave Cyprus and travel to France.[69]

Peter's quarrel with Philip of Ibelin, lord of Arsur, was more vicious; although he had been in the king's favour until 1361, Philip fell out with him for unspecified reasons and was banned from Cyprus for more than seven years. Moreover, Peter forbade

---

68 Hardy, *Édition critique de la Prise d'Alixandrie*, pp. 12–13, 18–19, ll. 381–400, 570–96; *Bullarium Cyprium III*, nos t-448, 519, 619; Leontios Makhairas, Χρονικό της Κύπρου, pp. 108–11. See: Giuseppe Gerola, *Le effigi dei reali di Cipro in S. Eustorgio di Milano* (Ravenna: Nozze Fantini-Castellucci, 1930), pp. 5–6; Hill, *A History of Cyprus*, II, pp. 302–04; Edbury, *Kingdom of Cyprus*, pp. 146–47; Chris Schabel, 'Hugh the Just', pp. 134–39; also, see below. I thank Chris Schabel for the information regarding the letter of 12 July 1351.

69 The 1360 letters together with another one (29 November 1362), which also raises the issue of Peter's unresolved relations with his nephew and sister-in-law, and the pope's official condolences to Peter for the death of his father (28 June 1360) are edited by Chris Schabel at the end of his joint paper with Peter Edbury, Appendices A.1–4 and B.2; *Bullarium*, III, no. v-210. Also see Laura Balletto, 'Nuovi dati su un'ambasceria cipriota in Occidente durante il regno di Pietro I di Lusignano', Επετηρίδα του Κέντρου Επιστημονικών Ερευνών (Κύπρου), 31 (2005), 91–108.

his niece Alice of Majorca, the aforementioned Ferrand's daughter and Philip's wife, to join her husband abroad without being deprived of her property; Peter may of course have acted according to his niece's wishes, since Alice had a lover at the time. As Peter Edbury and Chris Schabel show in their chapter, Urban V had to intervene on behalf of Philip and Alice on several occasions in 1365 and 1366. By January 1367, Philip was back in Cyprus and apparently reconciled with the king, accompanying him on his second visit to the West in 1367–68. However, the animosity must have been smouldering since, in January 1369, Philip was one of Peter's murderers. In 1373, Alice conspired with her second lover, the Genoese Admiral Peter of Campofregoso (1330–1404), to have her husband beheaded in Famagusta.[70]

On the other hand, Peter seems to have approved of his mother's second marriage or simply chose to avoid the scandal! In 1368, Alice of Ibelin (c. 1304/06–after 1386) married Philip of Brunswick (1332–69), many years her junior and prospective husband of her daughter Margaret (c. 1329–after 1347) in 1339; the archbishop of Nicosia excommunicated the couple on the grounds that they proceeded with the marriage although they were aware of the multiple impediments. On 29 May 1368, at Peter's request, Urban V absolved the couple of the excommunication, imposing minor penalties on them. Interestingly, Machaut accuses Alice of having been involved in the conspiracy that led to her son's murder.[71]

Peter's dispute with the Breton John of Rochefort and the Gascon Florimond of Lesparre, two lords who entered the king's service after the Alexandria expedition, is another episode that showcases his irritability and his inability to control his emotions. In early August 1367, while he was in Rhodes after the successful suppression of the mutiny of the Cypriot garrison of Antalya, a heated argument between Rochefort and the Cypriot John of Moustry, in which Lesparre sided with the former and Peter with the latter, ended with the Breton knight challenging Peter to meet before the pope. Lesparre, who had been nursing his own grievances against the king, challenged Peter to a duel at the court of the king of France. According to Machaut, Peter accepted the challenges in a very noble and chivalric manner; reading between the lines, though, one can detect Peter's incapacity to manage differences between the Cypriot aristocracy and the newcomers and the very fact that the French poet dedicates 577 lines to the episode indicates its importance. Pope Urban V forbade Peter from going through with the duel and instructed the archbishop of Nicosia to excommunicate the king if necessary. One of the reasons for his second journey to Europe was the need to satisfy his honour. The reconciliation with Lesparre took place before the pope in Rome on Holy Saturday 8 April 1368; Rochefort failed to appear and was declared a coward. Interestingly, both Machaut and Makhairas describe how, at the

---

70 Leontios Makhairas, Χρονικό της Κύπρου, pp. 222–23, 303; Nicolaou-Konnari, 'Women in Medieval Famagusta', pp. 574–75.
71 *Bullarium Cyprium III*, nos s-53, v-188; Hardy, *Édition critique de la* Prise d'Alixandrie, p. 240, ll. 8211–14; Wipertus Hugo Rudt de Collenberg, 'Les Ibelin au XIIIe et XIVe siècles. Généalogie compilée principalement selon les registres du Vatican', *Επετηρίς Κέντρου Επιστημονικών Ερευνών (Κύπρου)*, 9 (1977–79), 117–265 (no. C,21, pp. 186–89) (repr. in Wipertus Hugo Rudt de Collenberg, *Familles de l'Orient latin XIIe–XIVe siècles*, Variorum Collected Studies, 176 (London: Variorum Reprints, 1983), no. IV).

dinner offered to the two men by the pope after the formal reconciliation, Lesparre humbly served the sweets to the pope and the king.[72]

Peter's crusading aspirations, what Sir George Hill termed in 1948 'his ruling passion' and what we could describe today as his obsession, appeared very early in his life and demonstrate how fixated he could be on an idea or a person. His crusader vocation was entangled with his duty as a king to liberate his ancestral Kingdom of Jerusalem. It was also associated with displays of piety; according to Machaut, Peter received his calling to be a crusader after having a vision in the church of the cross of the Good Thief in Famagusta, probably in the mid-1340s.[73] At about the same time, he met Philip of Mézières, whose influence on the formation of his crusader goals was paramount. For Machaut, the destination of Peter's flight to the West with his younger brother John in secret without their father's leave, sometime before September 1349, was France and the aim the recruitment of men for his crusade; in the letter of 12 August 1350, Clement VI stressed to Hugh IV that his quarrel with his son because of the latter's flight to the West could only profit the Turks, which suggests that Peter had already formulated his crusader goals. Makhairas, though, describes the episode as simply a young men's escapade, prompted by the 'desire [that] came into their hearts to go overseas to the West to see the world and [...] strange lands' after they had met 'the men who came from the West' (perhaps an allusion to Mézières). Before or soon after the attempt to visit Western Europe, Peter founded the Order of the Sword, a common way for medieval rulers to promote a cause, appealing to the chivalric values of their men.[74]

Makhairas and the *Chronique d'Amadi* seem to believe that Peter's first journey to Western Europe in 1362–65 was motivated by the challenge to his rule from his nephew Hugh of Lusignan rather than by his crusading plans, but contemporary papal letters examined by Peter Edbury and Chris Schabel leave no doubt that the purpose of the journey was to raise support and troops for a crusade. In fact, Peter's military successes against the Muslims before his journey, his crusading plans, and the sensitive role of Cyprus as the outpost of Christianity seem to have predisposed Urban V in his favour regarding Hugh's claims while his personality and his enthusiasm about a new crusade had a great impact on the pope soon after his arrival at the *curia*

---

72 *Bullarium Cyprium III*, nos v-183–84, 187; Guillaume de Machaut, *Oeuvres*, BnF, MS Fr. 9221, fol. 235ᵛ, 'comment l'acort fu du roy de chyppre et de lesparre' [Fig. 2]; Hardy, *Édition critique de la* Prise d'Alixandrie, pp. 136, 211–32, ll. 4697–10, 4717–19, 7355–7932 and passim ('le confit', l. 7908); Leontios Makhairas, Χρονικό της Κύπρου, pp. 175–76, 180, 181–82 («το κουφέττον», p. 182). See Hill, *A History of Cyprus*, II, pp. 335 n. 7, pp. 344, 348–51, 354–56 and Edbury, *Kingdom of Cyprus*, pp. 170, 177.

73 Hill, *A History of Cyprus*, II, p. 354; Hardy, *Édition critique de la* Prise d'Alixandrie, pp. 10–11, ll. 291–327; Angel Nicolaou-Konnari's chapter in this volume for Machaut misplacing the cross from the monastery of Stavrovouni to Famagusta. In 1354, Pope Innocent VI absolved him from vows to visit the tomb of St James of Compostela in far-away Galicia, to consume only bread and water on Saturdays, and to abstain from eating meat, see *Bullarium Cyprium III*, nos u-46, 48–49 and passim for other examples of piety.

74 *Bullarium Cyprium III*, no. t-519; Hardy, *Édition critique de la* Prise d'Alixandrie, pp. 11–16, ll. 329–506 (Order), pp. 16–19, ll. 507–96 (escapade); Leontios Makhairas, *Recital concerning the Sweet Land of Cyprus, entitled 'Chronicle'*, ed. by Richard M. Dawkins, 2 vols (Oxford: Clarendon Press, 1932), I, § 79; Trélat, 'L'ordre de l'Épée à Chypre'.

on 29 March 1363 (as shown by letter dated 31 March).[75] For the same reasons, the pope could not but side with Peter in the dispute with the Neapolitan Angevins concerning his rights to the throne of Jerusalem. In his paper, Michalis Olympios reviews the major material evidence for the official, ceremonial, and ideological use of the title of Jerusalem by both the Angevins and Lusignans in the half-century or so following the loss of the crusader mainland in 1291. By examining the two dynasties' attitudes towards the title and the political ramifications of their claim in the Eastern Mediterranean and Europe, Olympios demonstrates that the two royal houses sought the legitimization of their rights to the title in diverging ways and with a completely different set of goals. However, neither the Angevin nor the Lusignan agenda had much to do with regaining control over the territories of the former Latin kingdom and reestablishing Latin Christian rule in the Levant until the reign of Peter I.

The scope of Peter's efforts to launch a crusade is amazing and involved long journeys, skillful diplomacy in counterbalancing each ruler's and each country's conflicting interests, logistics negotiated with the pope and secular leaders, and military expeditions led by himself.[76] Peter's first journey was a long diplomatic campaign to royal, princely, and ecclesiastical European courts for the promotion of a crusade. As Joël Blanchard aptly remarks, Queen Truth's allegorical journey in Mézières's *Songe du Vieux Pèlerin* is strikingly similar to Peter's real journey.[77] In terms of political geography, in three years' time (24 October 1362–autumn 1365) the Cypriot king visited almost the entire modern Europe (the Greek islands of Rhodes and Crete, Italy, France, England, Belgium, Germany, Bohemia, Poland, Austria, Switzerland, Slovenia) and met the most powerful rulers of the time (the pope, the emperor, the kings of France and England, the Black Prince, the dukes of Orleans, Berry, and Bourbon, and the doges of Venice and Genoa). The itinerary suggests a lot of planning and organisation beforehand and costly logistics [Map 1].

Peter's efforts for the promotion of a crusade are closely connected with his masculine, chivalric image, Machaut pointedly noting that his goal in life was not even distracted by hunting or pretty women.[78] All the sources discussed above

---

75 Edited by Chris Schabel at the end of his joint paper with Peter Edbury, Appendix B.3.
76 Peter W. Edbury, 'The Crusading Policy of King Peter I of Cyprus, 1359–1369', in *The Eastern Mediterranean Lands in the Period of the Crusades*, ed. by Peter M. Holt (Warminster: By Aris & Philips ltd., 1977), pp. 90–105; Svetlana Bliznyuk, 'A Crusader of the Later Middle Ages: King Peter I of Cyprus', in *The Crusades and the Military Orders: Expanding the Frontiers of Medieval Latin Christianity. In Memoriam Sir Stephen Runciman (1903–2000)*, ed. by Zsolt Hunyadi and József Laszlovszky (Budapest: Central European University Press, 2001), pp. 51–57; Łukasz Burkiewicz, 'Podróż króla Cypru Piotra I z Lusignan po Europie w latach 1362–1365 i jego plany krucjatowe', *Studia Historyczne*, R.L. Z. 1, 197 (2007), 3–29; Łukasz Burkiewicz, 'The Crusading Policy of the Rulers of the Kingdom of Cyprus after the Fall of Acre (1291)', in *Holy War in Late Medieval and Early Modern East-Central Europe*, ed. by Janusz Smołucha, John Jefferson, and Andrzej Wadas (Cracow: Wydawnictwo Akademii Ignatianum w Krakowie, Wydawnictwo WAM, 2017), pp. 185–99.
77 Philippe de Mézières, *Songe du Vieux Pèlerin*, Modern French trans. by Joël Blanchard (Paris: Pocket, 2008), p. 14.
78 Hardy, *Édition critique de la* Prise d'Alixandrie, p. 19, l. 620, p. 125, ll. 4339–40; Leontios Makhairas, Χρονικό της Κύπρου, pp. 175, 206, though, mentions hunting expeditions in Rhodes and Cyprus. See generally: Matthew M. Mesley, 'Chivalry, Masculinity, and Sexuality', in *The Cambridge Companion to the Literature*

agree that, during both his European tours, Peter, escorted by a large suite of knights, was everywhere lavishly received and provide ample information about his participation in Western European cultural and court life, revealing at the same time the pleasure-seeking aspects of his character:[79] sumptuous banquets with expensive food and wine and other extravagant festivities were given in his honour, Machaut often describing the dishes served to the king; he received and gave many precious presents (sacred relics, jewels, golden and silver vessels and statuettes, horses, wine), many of Cypriot craftsmanship;[80] an indefatigable jouster, he attended or took part in numerous tournaments, some of which he won. Most importantly, Peter's prolonged stay in European cities gave him the opportunity to get closely acquainted with and reveal his appreciation of contemporary western music, probably thanks to Mézières's influence.

Peter's entourage included cantors and organists from various European dioceses; on 28 April 1363, while he was in Avignon, Peter addressed to Urban V a long list of requests for the grant of benefices to, among others, his cantor and organist, Henry of Mosa of the diocese of Liège, and the cantor of Paphos, William Galioti. Minstrels accompanied the Cypriot king in his travel throughout Europe, to whom King Charles V (1364–80) of France made a gift of eighty gold francs in 1364. William of Machaut, whose capacity as a musician makes his testimony valuable and who may have composed some, now lost, pieces for Peter, bears ample witness to the king's love for music, describing at length a concert given in his honour by Emperor Charles IV in Prague in 1364, which made a huge impression on him ('li roys de ce moult se merveille, | et dit qu'onques mais en sa vie | ne vit si tresgrant melodie'); although this was not exceptional, Machaut also mentions the use of trumpets and other instruments during the king's military campaigns.[81] The Florentine humanist and historian Filippo Villani (*c.* 1330–*c.* 1405) claims that, in Venice, 'the most illustrious and noble king of Cyprus' bestowed a laurel wreath on the blind composer Francesco Landini (*c.* 1325/35–97) for his organ playing; Landini's coronation, however, most probably took place three months before Peter's

---

    of the Crusades, ed. by Anthony Bale (Cambridge: Cambridge University Press, 2018), pp. 146–64; Natasha R. Hodgson, Katherine L. Lewis, and Matthew M. Mesley (eds.), *Crusading and Masculinities* (London – New York: Routledge, 2019).

79 Mas Latrie, *Histoire de l'île de Chypre*, II, 237–48, 309–31 (esp. 239–41 n. 1); Hill, *A History of Cyprus*, pp. 324–29, 355–59; Jorga, *Philippe de Mézières*, pp. 142–201, 370–81.

80 Trélat, 'Le goût pour Chypre', pp. 467–68 suggests that, with his gifts, Peter promoted the trade of Cypriot luxury products.

81 *Bullarium Cyprium III*, nos u-55, v-20; Jorga, *Philippe de Mézières*, p. 189 n. 6; Hardy, *Édition critique de la Prise d'Alixandrie*, pp. cxvii, 34–35, 53–54, 61, 82, 143, 156, 157, 295–96, ll. 1139–76 (citation: 1174–76), 1817–19, 2101–04, 2111–12, 2816–18, 4967–69, 5425–27, 5466. See: Richard H. Hoppin, 'The Cypriot-French Repertory of the Manuscript Torino, Biblioteca Nazionale, J.Ii.9', *Musica disciplina*, 11 (1957), 79–125 (pp. 83–85, 90); Richard H. Hoppin and Karl Kuegle, 'Cyprus: medieval polyphony', in *The New Grove Dictionary of Music and Musicians*, Second Edition, ed. by Stanley Sadie and John Tyrrell, 29 vols (London – New York: Macmillan Publishers Limited, 2001), VI, pp. 805–07; Guillaume de Machaut, *La Prise d'Alixandre (The Taking of Alexandria)*, ed. and English trans. by R. Barton Palmer (New York – London: Routledge, 2002), 'Introduction', p. 9; Grivaud, 'Résonances humanistes', pp. 38, 39.

arrival in Venice on 11 November 1364 and Villani's claim was apparently intended to enhance his fellow citizen's triumph.[82]

However, neither the extended tour nor Peter's efforts managed to achieve the goal of the journey; despite the support of the pope and King John II of France, the European leaders did not take the cross although they did offer financial aid.[83] The Order of the Sword seems to have had limited success as well. William of Machaut does speak vaguely of knights who were honourably received in the Order but Philip of Mézières mentions it only once and no records of the Order survive; after Peter's death, membership was mainly bestowed upon noble pilgrims to the Holy Land.[84] Peter's visits to the king of England and the emperor, in particular, bear many analogies and demonstrate both how splendidly he was received and how little he gained.

Peter visited England at the end of 1363 and was entertained by King Edward III at the palace of Westminster in London. According to contemporary English sources, while he was in London a number of other kings also visited Edward, usually said to be John II of France, David II of Scotland (1329-71), and Waldemar IV of Denmark, although the kings of France and Denmark were most probably not in London at the time.[85] The *Eulogium historiarum* is the only narrative that claims that Peter came to London in the company of two pagan kings, his prisoner the King of 'Lecto/Lecco' (a Muslim prince of Asia Minor?) and the 'Lord of Jerusalem' (a Cypriot lord bearing a Jerusalemite title?); the king of Scotland arrived a few days later 'so before the end of the Parliament there were five kings present in London [...] Such a thing had never been since the time of King Arthur [...]'.[86]

This happy coincidence gave rise to many tournaments and festivities, the most renowned one being the 'Feast of the Five Kings', which was allegedly arranged by Sir Henry Picard, a vintner and former Lord Mayor of London, and hosted by the Worshipful Company of Vintners at their hall in the City of London in winter 1363. There are very few early records for the Worshipful Company of Vintners and they do not make contemporary reference to the event. All the extant sources postdate the event by more than a century and, as it must have left a huge impression on London

---

82 Filippo Villani, *Liber de Civitatis Florentiae Famosis Civibus* [...], ed. by Gustavus Camillus Galletti (Florence: Joannes Mazzoni, 1847), p. 35. See Kurt von Fischer (rev. by Gianluca D'Agostino), 'Landini, Francesco', in *The New Grove Dictionary*, XIV, pp. 212–21.

83 The pope authorised Peter to use the money collected by several countries for his crusade, provided he submitted annual accounts to the Holy See, *Bullarium Cyprium III*, nos v-84–85.

84 Jorga, *Philippe de Mézières*, p. 76 n. 2, p. 83 n. 2, p. 120 n. 3; Trélat, 'L'ordre de l'Épée à Chypre', pp. 321, 324–28; Grivaud, 'Résonances humanistes', pp. 32–33.

85 See discussion in Jorga, *Philippe de Mézières*, pp. 163–64, 179–80, Kingsford, 'The Feast of the Five Kings', pp. 125–26, and Roland Delachenal, *Histoire de Charles V*, 5 vols (Paris: Alphonse Picard & fils, 1909–31), II, p. 184 n. 3. For Waldemar's contribution to Peter's crusade, see Janus Møller Jensen, *Denmark and the Crusades, 1400-1650* (Leiden and Boston: Brill, 2007), pp. 42–50.

86 *Eulogium (historiarum sive temporis)*, III, pp. xlvi, 233, 238. Jorga, *Philippe de Mézières*, p. 178 and after him Kingsford, 'The Feast of the Five Kings', p. 124 suggest unconvincingly that Lecto may stand for Lithuania, its king's son having been given to Peter by the Teutons.

society, the story was embroidered over time.[87] The feast is first mentioned in the *Liber Niger*, one of the medieval cartularies of Westminster Abbey compiled before 1485.[88] In his *Annales of England*, first published in 1580, John Stow (*c*. 1525–1605) records a story, which, notwithstanding its reliability, is consistent with other testimonies about Peter's character; according to Stow, after the feast Peter lost fifty marks gambling with his host, who, seeing his annoyance, graciously returned the money to him together with many rich gifts.[89] The episode echoes the story related by Makhairas that Peter and his company played the dice at the house of the rich merchant Lakha in Famagusta and suggests that Peter indulged in gambling.[90]

During Peter's stay in England, King Edward III paid for all his expenses, including the gear for his participation in a tournament in Smithfield, and gave him a ship named *Katherine/Catelinne*, which Froissart saw in Sandwich harbour two years later. Although England was at the time rich and powerful after the victories in Crécy and Poitiers against the French, Edward declined Peter's invitation, saying he was too old to go on the crusade.[91] A French chronicle even claims that the English king asked Peter for the return of the Kingdom of Cyprus, 'which my ancestor King Richard entrusted long ago to one of your predecessors', in the event of the recapture of Jerusalem.[92]

In the summer of 1364 Peter went to Prague, where he met with the Holy Roman Emperor Charles IV. According to Machaut, a crowd of 20,000 people welcomed the Cypriot king, who gave a speech before the emperor and other princes in order to rally support for his crusade. In the company of the emperor and the King of Denmark Waldemar IV, Peter made for Cracow via Silesian towns, an itinerary described in detail by Machaut. In late September 1364, Peter arrived in Cracow, where he met the Kings of Poland, Casimir III, and Hungary, Louis I, and other German and Polish princes and attended the so-called Cracow Congress as the emperor's guest; the Congress had been convened by Casimir and was intended to settle the dispute between Charles and Louis. All Polish chroniclers emphasize the splendour of the

---

87 The records of the Worshipful Company of Vintners from 1253 to 2005 are located at the Guildhall Library and administered by the London Metropolitan Archives, I thank Charlotte Hopkins, London Metropolitan Archives, for the information. Kingsford, 'The Feast of the Five Kings', gives a thorough discussion of the sources and the available information. For the feast in popular culture, see below.

88 WAM Muniment Book I, fol. 78ʳ: 'De Henrico Pycard vinetar. London. qui splendide ac honorifice conviviavit Regem cum aliis Regibus'.

89 See John Stow, *The Annales of England, faithfully collected out of the most autenticall authors, records and other monuments of antiquitie, lately collected, from the first habitation untill this present yeare 1605* [1605], p. 415: <https://archive.org/stream/annalsofenglandtoostow?ref = ol#page/n. 439/mode/2up> , who places the event in 1357 (the year of Picard's mayoralty) and does not include the king of Denmark in the group of kings. In his 1598 work *A Survey of London. Reprinted From the Text of 1603*, ed. by Charles Lethbridge Kingsford, 2 vols (Oxford: Clarendon, 1908), I, pp. 106, 240, John Stow corrected the year of Peter's visit to 1363. The story is repeated in Joshua Barnes, *The History of the Most Victorious Monarch Edward III, King of England and France and Lord of Ireland […]* (Cambridge: John Hayes, 1688), p. 635, who adds the king of Denmark.

90 Leontios Makhairas, *Χρονικό της Κύπρου*, pp. 112–15.

91 *Chroniques de J. Froissart*, VI, § 507, pp. 90–92 and 280–84; n. 62 above.

92 *Chronique des quatre premiers Valois (1327–1393)*, ed. by Siméon Luce, Société de l'histoire de France (Paris: Mᵐᵉ Vᵉ Jules Renouard, 1862), p. 128.

events surrounding the presence of these eminent guests in Cracow. Following the example of the London ostentatious 'Feast of the Five Kings', Mikołaj Wierzynek, a rich burgess, gave a feast in honour of the Cracow five kings, probably on behalf of the town authorities, a dazzling event with exquisite dishes and the exchange of expensive gifts. The news of the festivities reached Machaut who describes in detail the composition of the menu and the tournament Peter won. Peter gave another speech in support of his crusade plans and the kings gave an oath to join the crusade or help but whatever promises they gave did not materialize.[93]

Peter's conduct gave Pope Urban V good cause for viewing him with increasing exasperation. The pope obviously did not approve of Peter's three–year tour of European courts in 1362–65 and would have preferred him to be in Cyprus preparing the crusade; in two letters, dated 28 November 1363 and 3 June 1364, Urban eagerly invited Peter to return to Cyprus in view of Turkish threats against Satalia and promised financial help. Neither was the pope pleased with the quarrel between Cyprus and Genoa.[94] Moreover, Peter's efforts to launch a crusade also involved a huge personal cost, both political and emotional. Philip of Mézières and Lorenzo de Monacis refer to Peter's disillusionment at the empty promises of European rulers; Mézières and Machaut also describe his frustration when a retreat was imposed on him by the other crusaders and he had to abandon Alexandria.[95] Inevitably, his prolonged absences and his military expeditions emptied the royal treasury,[96] made him neglect his royal duties and depend more on his high officers, and alienated his brothers and some of his barons.

However, three contributions to this volume show that Peter did not attempt to introduce changes to the government system he had inherited or change the distribution of power, contrary to claims that he favoured a new nobility of non-Latin Cypriots (Greeks and Syrians of various religious denomination) and foreigners in his service to the detriment of the old Frankish aristocracy. Gilles Grivaud studies the role and composition of the royal council, a body of advisors on whom the king relied for making foreign policy decisions. Although this was not a formally institutionalized organ, it appears to have been quite influential and efficient with the exception of the last months of Peter's reign, when his aberrant behaviour alienated his counsellors. The presence of foreigners in the king's entourage, to whom he bestowed fiefs and offices, does not seem to have minimized the power of the royal council, mainly composed

---

93   Hardy, *Édition critique de* la Prise d'Alixandrie, pp. 30–41, ll. 977–1379; Philippe de Mézières, *The Life of Saint Peter Thomas*, ed. by Joachim Smet, O. Carm. (Rome: Institutum carmelitanum, 1954), p. 106; n. 50 above for Polish sources. See: Malgorzata Dabrowska, 'Peter of Cyprus and Casimir the Great in Cracow', Βυζαντιακά, 14 (1994), 257–67; Łukasz Burkiewicz, 'Podróż króla Cypru Piotra I z Lusignan po Europie w latach 1362–1365 i jego plany krucjatowe', Studia Historyczne, R.L., Z. 1 (197) (2007), pp. 3–29 (22–25); Łukasz Burkiewicz, 'Σχέσεις Κύπρου - Πολωνίας'.
94   *Bullarium Cyprium III*, nos v-84, 93 (prolonged tour), v-94–95, 102, 107, 109, 111, 113–14 (Genoa); nos v-84, 93 are edited by Chris Schabel at the end of his joint paper with Peter Edbury, Appendix B.6, 8.
95   Philippe de Mézières, *The Life of Saint Peter Thomas*, pp. 120–21, 133–34; Hardy, *Édition critique de la* Prise d'Alixandrie, p. 104, ll. 3573–3606; Laurentius de Monacis, *Chronicon*, p. 92.
96   *Bullarium Cyprium III*, nos v-215 (25,000 florins lent to the merchant Jacopo Grillo), v-238, w-3, 26, 49, 52, 59 and 100 (debts to the Apostolic Chamber and the Cornaro brothers paid after his death).

of members of the old Frankish families closely related to each other. However, as Petrarca's *Cypriot* connections discussed above show, these newcomers, together with Cypriot men of letters, contributed to what this author terms in her chapter as the 'literary rehabilitation' of Cyprus, attested during the reigns of Hugh IV and Peter I.

Using a prosopographical approach, Miriam Rachel Salzmann examines how stable Cypriot power elites were between the 1360s and the 1390s and how easy it was for non-noble Cypriots to ascend the social ranks and take positions of power. She concludes that although a strong power elite, coming from both Cyprus and abroad, dominated politics under Peter I, eventually the Cypriots defended their rights against the foreigners arbitrarily incorporated into their ranks by the king. Collectively conspiring to murder him, this same elite, led by Peter's brother John of Lusignan, held the reins of power for several years, until they were ousted by Peter's widow and the Genoese. However, under James I the power elite was again dominated by men belonging to old Frankish nobility. Whatever social mobility occurred under Peter I was short-lived and in the next decades no newcomers appear in government circles. Johannes Pahlitzsch argues that only after the murder of Peter I and the Cypriot-Genoese war did the ethnic name *Suriani* become inclusive to designate all Oriental Christians and not merely the Melkites. The process was related with the extent of the competence of the *Cour des Syriens* (a court that probably assumed many of the functions of the Jerusalemite *Cour de la Fonde*) and of its jurisdiction over other ethnic groups. These phenomena facilitated the rise of wealthy Oriental Christians to high offices in the next decades.[97]

Prioritising his crusader ambitions took its toll on Peter's family life as well. Peter was apparently very fond of women, albeit in a more physical than chivalric way. His first marriage to his first cousin, Eschiva of Montfort, was arranged by his father, who wanted his niece's important estate to remain in the royal domain, despite the considerable age difference and the close consanguinity. On 3 September 1339, when Peter had not yet reached his tenth year of age, Pope Benedict XII (1334–42) refused the dispensation on the grounds that Peter was under the age of marriage while Eschiva well above ('habet plurimos annos ultra nubilem aetatem'), but, three years later, on 28 June 1342, Clement VI obligingly issued the necessary dispensation (ratified on 8 August 1342). Eschiva of Montfort died sometime before Peter's engagement to Eleanor of Aragon (d. 1417) in February 1353. She may have given birth to a daughter also called Eschiva, who died at a young age.[98]

---

[97] T. Devaney, 'Spectacle, Community and Holy War in Fourteenth-Century Cyprus', *Medieval Encounters*, 19 (2013), 300-41 examines rhetoric and performance as ways used by Peter to mobilize support from the Frankish aristocracy and his Greek subjects, but evidence is meagre; K. Scott Parker, 'Peter I de Lusignan, the Crusade of 1365, and the Oriental Christians of Cyprus and the Mamluk Sultanate', in *Medieval Cyprus. A Place of Cultural Encounter*, ed. by Sabine Rogge and Michael Grünbart, Schriften des Instituts für Interdisziplinäre Zypern-Studien, 11 (Münster – New York: Waxmann, 2015), pp. 53–71 believes that the Oriental Christians in Cyprus suffered negative effects from Peter's crusade similarly to those in Egypt and Syria.

[98] Her age is not known but she must have been born before 1314; in 1334 she was old enough to visit the Holy Land escorted by twenty men; see *Bullarium Cyprium III*, nos r-521, s-47, 54, t-3, 12. Estienne de Lusignan, *Histoire*, fols 19^v, 20^v does not mention Peter's first marriage and considers Eschiva to be Eleanor's daughter.

Peter's second marriage to Eleanor of Aragon in September 1353 seems to have been happier; it was certainly more intense. Makhairas claims that Peter was passionately in love with his wife, to the extent that he always slept with her shirt when he was away from her, a story mentioned four times in the chronicle! His love for the queen did not prevent the king from having two mistresses, Joanna L'Aleman and Eschiva de Scandelion; he left Joanna pregnant before his second trip to the West in 1367–68, the chronicler providing a long and colourful description of Eleanor's attempts to induce a miscarriage. He also makes a point of reminding his reader of the shirt on the occasion of Peter's 1367 visit to Queen Joanna of Naples (1324/26–82), who 'received him with heartfelt kindness and there he stayed for many days', a reassurance of the king's attachment to his wife that makes one speculate about the romantic encounters he had during his long journeys. Makhairas justifies Peter's marital indiscretions in a half-approving, gendered way, blaming 'the demon of fornication' ('ὁ δαίμων τῆς πορνείας'), who 'beguiled the king', and the king's 'great sensuality' ('λουξουρία'), as he was a 'vigorous young man' ('παιδίος ἄνθρωπος').[99] Makhairas also reports rumors about the queen having a lover, John of Morphou, a humiliating and demeaning affair for the king. Machaut refers to Eleanor's infidelity, underlining that he does not believe the story, but carefully avoids mentioning Peter's extramarital affairs.[100] As a father, Peter is said to have loved and spoiled his son, Peter II (1357–82, crowned 1369), excessively, taking him with him on his second journey to Europe in 1367–68 and ill-treating the Giblet family for a pair of greyhounds the prince coveted.[101]

Peter's notorious marital indiscretions drew the pope's attention; in two letters dated 2 and 5 December 1367, when Peter was most probably in Naples, Urban V rebuked him for having abandoned his wife, a lady 'of illustrious origin and endowed with elegant manners', to live shamelessly in open adultery with another woman, appealed to Peter's moral responsibility as a king and a crusader, and instructed the archbishop of Nicosia to excommunicate him if necessary.[102] When in 1368 Peter again visited the pope in Rome, Urban unambiguously bestowed the Golden Rose – an award granted to the most noble man present at the *curia* – to Joanna of Naples,

---

99 Leontios Makhairas, *Χρονικό τῆς Κύπρου*, pp. 132, 181, and 195–96 (shift), 132, 181, and 191–94 (mistresses); Leontios Makhairas, *Recital*, I, §§ 234, 242 for the translation. See Nicolaou-Konnari, 'Apologists or Critics?', pp. 393–96.
100 Leontios Makhairas, *Χρονικό τῆς Κύπρου*, pp. 194–99, 200–205; Hardy, *Édition critique de la* Prise d'Alixandrie, pp. 235–36, ll. 8053–68. See Nicolaou-Konnari, 'Women in Medieval Famagusta', pp. 570–71 on Eleanor. The name *Linora* was quite popular on the island among Greek female serfs in the middle of the sixteenth century; see Marina Ilia, *Socioeconomic Aspects of Rural Life in Venetian Cyprus*, 2 vols (unpublished doctoral thesis, University of Cyprus, Nicosia, 2021), I, pp. 98, 181, 109, 110, II, pp. 74, 94, 114, 115, 117, 118, 123, 132, 165, 198, 169, 204, 260, 268.
101 Hardy, *Édition critique de la* Prise d'Alixandrie, pp. 241–45, ll. 8255–8375; Leontios Makhairas, *Χρονικό τῆς Κύπρου*, pp. 206–09.
102 *Bullarium Cyprium III*, nos v-182 ('tu, propria abiecta consorte, illustri genere ac morum elegantia decorata, non erubescis quandam adulteram publice retinere') and 184 (mistress). The pope probably did not know about Eschiva de Scandelion; she was granted a plenary indulgence *in articulo mortis* on 29 May 1368, *Bullarium Cyprium III*, no. v-195. I thank Chris Schabel for the transcription of the two letters that concern Peter's adultery.

said to be the first woman to receive that honour; Peter Edbury and Chris Schabel consider the event to be an indication of the decline of the high prestige the Cypriot king had enjoyed in the eyes of the pope.[103]

Makhairas builds up adroitly the drama of Peter's personality change during the last months of his life, providing details that endow his account with verisimilitude and describing in a climactic way the king's moral degradation and abuse of power that led to his murder. He offers as an explanation for Peter's deviant behaviour only the queen's affair, a 'matter [that] is very heavy and hard to endure, and shameful and unseemly' and had a destructive effect on his behavior; falsely advised by his barons not to punish the queen and her lover, Peter was 'full of ill will and anger', violated the law and customs of the kingdom, behaved 'arrogantly', and dishonoured noble women.[104] Machaut also presents Peter's murder as the climax of a series of events but he underplays his hero's deplorable conduct, presenting the king as a martyr, the victim of his brothers, his liegemen, and even his own mother. Interestingly, Machaut places at the beginning of the last period of Peter's life a serious illness that kept him in bed for seven weeks and could perhaps have accounted for his personality change; Makhairas mentions Peter falling ill twice, but in the summer of 1367.[105] Philip of Mézières remains silent about Peter's behaviour, explaining his murder in terms of the Cypriot barons' resentment at the harmful effect Peter's wars had on their interests and at his favours to foreigners in his service.[106]

Peter's murder aroused the fear and horror of Western Christendom as few assassinations of kings have. Papal correspondence, historiography, and literature deplore his death and express the indignation it provoked for the undignified, undeserved loss of a valiant defender of the faith. Western public opinion seems to have almost unanimously accepted the complicity of Peter's brothers in the regicide while Cypriot sources carefully avoid implicating them in the conspiracy.[107] The way Makhairas describes this final act of the drama bears distinct sexual connotations: it is set in the bedroom of the king, who is found in an undignified situation, naked in bed with his mistress, and it climaxes with James de Nores symbolically mutilating the decapitated, breechless body with the words 'these cost you your life'.[108]

---

103 *Vitae Paparum Avenionensium*, I, 'Prima Vita Urbani V', p. 366, 'Secunda Vita Urbani V', p. 389. Estienne de Lusignan, *Histoire*, fol. 20[r-v] claims the pope made Peter senator of Rome.
104 Leontios Makhairas, *Recital*, I, §§ 251, 272.
105 Hardy, *Édition critique de la* Prise d'Alixandrie, p. 241, ll. 8243–54; cf. Leontios Makhairas, Χρονικό της Κύπρου, pp. 176–77, 189.
106 Philippe de Mézières, *Oratio tragedica*, pp. 22–23, 66–67, 460–65.
107 Mas Latrie, *Histoire de l'île de Chypre*, II, pp. 342–45; Jorga, *Philippe de Mézières*, pp. 386–94; Hill, *A History of Cyprus*, II, pp. 363–68; Jean Richard, 'La révolution de 1369 dans le royaume de Chypre', *Bibliothèque de l'École des Chartes*, 110 (1952), 108–23; Edbury, 'The Murder of King Peter I'; Edbury, *Kingdom of Cyprus*, pp. 172–77; Nicolaou-Konnari, 'Apologists or Critics?', pp. 396–99.
108 Leontios Makhairas, Χρονικό της Κύπρου, pp. 220–22. The illustration of the murder in Jean Froissart, *Chroniques*, BnF, MS Fr. 2645, fol. 79[r] [Fig. 13 in this author's contribution to this volume], is not very flattering either, presenting the king in a vulnerable position, attacked by his barons while he is naked in bed, and with a frightened look.

Who was Peter then? A hero or a failed crusader? An accomplished knight or a dishonoured man? A fair king or a tyrant? A loving husband or a philanderer? Peter is depicted in contemporary sources as an attractive personality and a restless spirit, a headstrong, obstinate, and adventurous man able to inspire both loyalty and hatred, an extraordinary person with often arbitrary and extreme behaviour who indulged in recreations such as jousting, hunting, gambling, and banqueting or in fighting duels. The political impact of his reign on the history of Cyprus can and has been evaluated in retrospect. But how accurately can the modern reader assess Peter's character and conduct through this elusive portrayal, which conforms to the social and literary conventions of the time? Dr Kakia Nikolaou has kindly provided a tentative psychiatric assessment of Peter's personality in Appendix B to this introduction, which may answer some of these questions.

Peter's Depiction in Modern Popular Culture

Surprisingly, Peter's figure did not attract the imagination of the Enlightenment or of nineteenth- and twentieth-century literature, performing arts (theatre, dance, cinematography), visual arts (painting, sculpture), or music (opera). History used as a source of artistic inspiration in a form of popular culture serves its popularisation, often according to specific ideological and artistic ends. Unlike the reasons for his limited presence in modern scholarly works discussed above, Peter's absence from literature and the arts may be attributed to the fact that Cypriot retromedievalism thrives when the historical person or event inspiring the author or the artist can be exploited for political, ideological, or aesthetic purposes that go beyond the limited scope of Cyprus; this is what the example of opera shows, Richard I the Lionheart's conquest of Cyprus inspiring two operas and Caterina Cornaro's reign five.[109]

Accordingly, there are no Cypriot thematical elements in Giuseppe Verdi's *Simon Boccanegra*, set to a libretto based on Antonio García Gutiérrez's play *Simón Bocanegra* (1843) by Francesco Maria Piave (and Giuseppe Montanelli) and first performed at the Teatro La Fenice in Venice on 12 March 1857, although Peter was present when the doge died in Genoa on 14 March 1363.[110] Gabriele D'Annunzio's (1863–1938) verse-play *Pisanella* uses elements from Makhairas's chronicle and the popular song of *Arodaphnoussa*, discussed below, but situates the story in the thirteenth century, the hero being young King Hugh II of Lusignan (1253–67).[111] On the other hand, Peter

---

109 Angel Nicolaou-Konnari, 'Melodramatic Perceptions of History: Caterina Cornaro Goes to the Opera', in *Caterina Cornaro. Last Queen of Cyprus and Daughter of Venice – Ultima regina di Cipro e figlia di Venezia*, ed. by Candida Syndikus and Sabine Rogge, Schriften des Instituts fur Interdisziplinare Zypern-Studien, 9 (Münster – Munich – Berlin – New York: Waxmann, 2013), pp. 385–447 and plates 27–30.
110 Nicolaou-Konnari, 'Melodramatic Perceptions of History', p. 387 n. 7.
111 Gabriele D'Annunzio, *La Pisanella*, Commedia in tre atti e un prologo, volta in verso italiano da Ettore Janni (Milan: Fratelli Treves, 1914) (originally written in French in 1913). See Bruno Lavagnini, *Alle fonti della Pisanella, ovvero D'Annunzio e la Grecia moderna* (Palermo: G. B. Palumbo, 1942), chapter V, appendices III–IV.

is one of the characters in the play *Noc na Karlštejně* (*A Night at Karlstein*), written by the Czech writer Jaroslav Vrchlický (1853–1912) in 1883 and first produced at the Royal National Theatre in Prague in 1884, but only a secondary one. The play is a romantic comedy of errors based on the legend that Emperor Charles IV banned women from Karlstein Castle; his much younger wife Elizabeth has to disguise herself as a young man in order to enter the castle and meet her husband, who is in the company of Peter (who did visit Prague and Charles IV in August 1364) and other princes. The play has been quite successful and has stayed in the repertoire of Czech theatres without any long breaks ever since.[112] Similarly, the painting *The Five Kings* by Albert Chevallier Tayler (1862–1925) was inspired by a civic legend born out of a memorable event of the history of London, the presence of several kings in the city, and not solely out of Peter's merits. This large panel commemorates the banquet allegedly offered to the kings of England, Scotland, France, Denmark, and Cyprus by the Vintners' Company at their hall in the City of London in winter 1363; commissioned from Tayler by the Vintners' Company, it was presented to the Royal Exchange in 1903 [Fig. 3].[113]

The king's person would gain some topicality only in historical or pseudo-historical literature produced in Cyprus and Greece from the late nineteenth century to our days. This new-found interest may have been incited by the popularity of the chronicle of Leontios Makhairas, first edited by Constantinos N. Sathas in 1873 and then by Richard M. Dawkins in 1932.[114] As early as 1874, Theodoulos Constantinides, a man of letters from Larnaca, wrote a play in three acts inspired by Peter's life.[115] Sathas was also the first to suggest that Peter's affair with Joanna L'Aleman and the brutal treatment she received in Eleanor of Aragon's hands may have inspired the Greek Cypriot popular song of *Arodaphnoussa*. The song has been orally transmitted throughout the centuries, has survived in various versions, and was first published in 1868;[116] its characters clearly belong to the Frankish period but their identification with Peter I, his queen, and his mistress remains only an attractive theory.[117] The

---

112 Jaroslav Vrchlický, *Noc na Karlštejně*, comedy in three acts (Prague: Jos R. Vilímek, 1885).
113 Kingsford, 'The Feast of the Five Kings'. The London Metropolitan Archives hold a print of Tayler's painting, shelf mark SC/PZ/CT/01/1074. On the Company, see Anna Crawford, *A History of the Vintner's Company* (London: Constable, 1977).
114 Λεοντίου Μαχαιρᾶ, *Χρονικὸν Κύπρου*, in *Bibliotheca Graeca Medii Aevi – Μεσαιωνικὴ Βιβλιοθήκη*, ed. by Constantinos N. Sathas, vols I–III (Venice: Chronos, 1872–73), vols IV–VII (Paris: Maisonneuve, 1874–94), vol. II, pp. 51–409; Leontios Makhairas, *Recital*.
115 Theodoulos Constantinides, *Πέτρος ὁ Α΄, βασιλεύς τῆς Κύπρου καί Ἱερουσαλήμ, ἤ ἡ Ἐκδίκησις τοῦ Κιαρίωνος. Δρᾶμα εἰς πράξεις τρεῖς* (Cairo, 1874).
116 Athanasios Sakellarios, *Τὰ Κυπριακά*, vols I, III (Athens: A. Aggelopoulos, 1855–68), vol. III, «Κυπριακὰ ᾄσματα», nos 15–16, 2nd ed. in 2 vols (Athens: P. D. Sakellariou, 1890-91), vol. II, «Δημώδη κυπριακὰ ᾄσματα», nos 10–11, pp. 46–52; Sathas, 'Introduction', in *Bibliotheca Graeca Medii Aevi*, vol. II, p. ʾἡς΄.
117 Angel Nicolaou, *La Chanson d'Arodaphnoussa, des origines franques à la tradition populaire actuelle* (unpublished Maîtrise de Lettres Modernes, Université Paul Valéry, Montpellier III, 1982); Angel Nicolaou, «Αροδαφνούσα», in *Μεγάλη Κυπριακή Εγκυκλοπαίδεια*, 14 vols (Nicosia: Philokypros, 1984–91), vol. II, pp. 322–24; Nicolaou-Konnari, 'Apologists or Critics?', pp. 393–99; Michalis Pieris, 'Cronaca e poesia popolare: Arodafnusa e Zuana l'Aleman. Interrogativi e problemi', in *La presenza femminile nella letteratura neogreca, Atti del VI Convegno Nazionale di Studi Neogreci, Roma, 19–21 novembre 2001*, ed. by Alkistis

chronicle and the song, together or separately, would inspire many literary works (poems, short stories, novels, and plays) but very few musical or artistic creations.[118]

Under the influence of Greco-centered, nationalistic approaches to the island's Frankish domination,[119] the literary works depict Peter as both an exotically romantic knight and an oppressive ruler, mainly using his military exploits, his scandalous love life, and his murder.[120] His and the other Frankish Cypriots' alterity with relation to the Greek Cypriots is outlined in various ways. In Costis Palamas's poetry, Eleanor is demonized and Arodaphnoussa becomes the symbol of enslaved Cyprus under foreign rule.[121] In Panos Ioannides's play *Peter I*, the Frankish royalty and aristocracy speak in standard Greek and the lower classes of the Greeks in the Cypriot dialect, a stylistic device intended to show the social and cultural divide between the ruling Franks and the oppressed Greeks, which oddly identifies the *Other* with the Greeks from the mainland; this linguistic convention was also adopted for the play's stage production (Cyprus Theatre Organisation / THOC, December 1990–January 1991) and televised series version (director Andreas Constantinides, Cyprus Broadcasting

---

Proiou and Angela Armati (Rome: Università di Roma 'La Sapienza', 2003), pp. 49–62; Michalis Pieris, «Λογοτεχνία και λογοτεχνικότητα κατά το πέρασμα της Κύπρου από τον Μεσαίωνα στην Αναγέννηση», in *La Serenissima and* la *Nobilissima. Venice in Cyprus and Cyprus in Venice*, ed. by Angel Nicolaou-Konnari (Nicosia: The Bank of Cyprus Cultural Foundation, 2009), pp. 120–44 (120–27, 137–39).

118 Michalis Christodoulides wrote the music for the televised series *Peter I* (Cyprus Broadcasting Corporation, 1994); Evagoras Karagiorgis composed the music for the songs and Psarantonis wrote additional music for Michalis Pieris's dramatic adaptation of the chronicle of Leontios Makhairas for TH.E.PA.K. (Nicosia, 1998); some of the works for small ensembles, composed by Nicos Vichas, Evagoras Karagiorgis, and Giorgos Karvellos and presented at the 20th Cultural Festival of the University of Cyprus (26 June 2017) were inspired by the popular song; two engravings by Hambis Tsangaris were also inspired by the song [Figs 6a-b].

119 For the historical and ideological context of the origin and use of the term *Frankokratia*, see Gilles Grivaud and Angel Nicolaou-Konnari, 'Aux origines de la «frankokratia». Genèse, péripéties idéologiques et apologie d'un néologisme de l'historiographie néo-hellénique (en deux parties)', *Frankokratia*, 1 (2020), 3–55 and 2 (2021), 1–30.

120 See in chronological order (the list is not exhaustive): Glafkos Alithersis's one-act tragedy in verse Ἀροδαφνοῦσα, published in Κυπριακὰ Γράμματα, 1 (1935), pp. 451–463 and in 1939 in Alexandria; two poems by the Nobel laureate George Seferis, ''Ο δαίμων τῆς πορνείας' and 'Τρεῖς μοῦλες', both published for the first time in 1955 in the collection Κύπρον, οὗ μ' ἐθέσπισεν ... , George Seferis, *Collected Poems, 1924–1955. Bilingual Edition*, ed. and trans. by Edmund Keeley and Philip Shephard (New Jersey: Princeton University Press, 1976), pp. 367–75; Thanasis Petsalis-Diomidis's short story Ἔξαρσις τῆς γλυκείας χώρας Κύπρου. Χρονικὸ τοῦ ΙΒ΄ αἰ. (Athens: Petros Sergiadis, 1956), which received the first State Prize for Literature (Short Story) in 1957; Panos Ioannides's collection of short stories Κρόνακα, 2 vols (Nicosia, 1970, 1972); Costas Charalambides's play Αροδαφνούσα, staged by the Laiki Skini Kyprou in Kaimakli in January 1982; Alexis Alexandrou's short story Η Φραγκοκρατία στην Κύπρο, ιστορικό αφήγημα (Nicosia: Holy Archbishopric of Cyprus, 1991); Andreas Iacovides's novel Αροδαφνούσα, Ιστορία μιας αγάπης (Larnaca, 1991); Maria Mantaka's novel Αίμα στην αυλή των Λουζινιανών (Athens: Kedros, 2005); Pantelis Mitsis's novel Η Κυρά της Χούλου (Nicosia: K. Epiphaniou, 2020).

121 Costis Palamas, 'Κύπρος', first published in Ἐφημερὶς τῶν Κυριῶν (15 April 1901), p. 2, and then in the collection Ἡ πολιτεία καὶ ἡ μοναξιά (Athens: I. N. Sideris, 1912²), pp. 53–56; Costis Palamas, ''Εκατὸ φωνές', in Ἀσάλευτη ζωή (Athens: Estia, 1904), pp. 102–35 (130).

Corporation, 1994) [Fig. 4].[122] In 1998, Michalis Pieris adapted for the stage Makhairas's chronicle and directed it for the University of Cyprus Theatre Workshop, using solely extracts from the text, most of which concern Peter's reign, without any stylistic or linguistic changes; the performance has been very successful and has known many revivals in Cyprus and abroad [Figs 5a-b].[123]

The lavish banquets given in Peter's honour during his first journey to Western Europe have found their way into twentieth-century commercial culture. The Vintners' Company's Swan feast of 1934 (finally held on 15 May 1935), known as the 'Feast of the Five Princes', was intended to commemorate that of 1363. In 1935, the five princes entertained were the Prince of Wales, the Dukes of York, Gloucester, and Kent, and Prince Arthur of Connaught.[124] In the second quarter of the twentieth century, when the island was under British rule, the Cypriot beverage company KEO, founded in 1927 in Limassol, created a still produced very old reserve brandy named *Five Kings*; the legend was enhanced with the claim that a similar spirit was served to the kings in London, especially shipped from Cyprus! A copy of Tayler's painting of the banquet is displayed at the Cyprus Wine Museum in Erimi village near Limassol, founded in 2004. The memory of the splendid feast given in Peter's honour by Mikołaj Wierzynek, Cracow's wealthy burgess, is still alive in Cracow. A well-known restaurant named *At Wierzynek's* is located in the old city's main market square; it serves traditional Polish dishes, occupies four floors in a fourteenth-century building, and has been visited by many world leaders and celebrities.[125]

Paradoxically, although Peter's figure and life provide the most fitting material for a film hero, they have failed so far to draw the attention of a script writer or director. To the best of our knowledge, the only exception is *Noc na Karlštejně* (*A Night at Karlstein*), a 1973 Czech historical musical film directed by Zdeněk Podskalský (1923–93). Based on the 1884 play by Jaroslav Vrchlický, Podskalský wrote his own script and worked with composer Karel Svoboda and lyricist Jiří Štaidl; the result was a veritable cult hit, but the main character was not Peter, a role played by the singer Waldemar Matuška (1932–2009). We hope that this book will constitute a compelling invitation for cinematographers to plunge into the ocean of Cypriot medieval history with source material well suited to the swim!

---

122   Panos Ioannides, *Πέτρος ο Πρώτος* (Nicosia: PKI, 1991).
123   *Λεόντιος Μαχαιράς, Χρονικό της Κύπρου*, Program, TH.E.PA.K. (Nicosia, 1998), pp. 125–66.
124   Records of the Worshipful Company of Vintners, CLC/L/VA/F/037C/MS36750, Papers relating to the Swan feast of 1934 (held in May 1935) and including menu, photograph, booklets, and historical notes; Corporation of London Records, COL/AC/13/001/039, Printed historical record of the 'Feast of the Five Kings' (1363), compiled on the occasion of a commemoration 'Feast of the Five Princes' at a Swan feast (15 May 1935). I thank Charlotte Hopkins, London Metropolitan Archives.
125   Dabrowska, 'Peter of Cyprus and Casimir the Great in Cracow', p. 263 n. 29; Restaurant's website: http://wierzynek.pl/en/nasza-legenda/.

PETER I OF LUSIGNAN (1329–69, 1359) 63

Fig. 1: Conrad Grünemberg, *Beschreibung der Reise von Konstanz nach Jerusalem*, Karlsruhe, Badische Landesbibliothek, Cod. St. Peter pap. 32, fol. 27ʳ, View of Famagusta.

Fig. 2: Guillaume de Machaut, *Oeuvres narratives et lyriques*, Paris, Bibliothèque nationale de France, MS Fr. 9221, fol. 235ᵛ, 'comment l'acort fu du roy de chyppre et de lesparre'.

Fig. 3: Albert Chevallier Tayler, *The Entertainment of the Five Kings by the Vintners' Company* (1903). From: Sir Harry C. Luke, *A Portrait and an Appreciation. Cyprus* (London: Harrap, 1965²), p. 65.

Fig. 4: Panos Ioannides, *Πέτρος ο Πρώτος*, televised series, director Andreas Constantinides (Cyprus Broadcasting Corporation, 1994).

Figs 5a-b: Michalis Pieris, dramatic adaptation of the chronicle of Leontios Makhairas (TH.E.PA.K., Nicosia, 1998).

Figs 6a-b: Hambis Tsangaris, engravings inspired by the tragic story of Arodaphnoussa.

Appendix A
The Life and Reign of Peter I of Lusignan (1329–69, 1359) according to Leontios Makhairas and William of Machaut: A Thematic Comparison

Leontios Makhairas
Recital concerning the Sweet Land of Cyprus entitled 'Chronicle'

Guillaume de Machaut
La Prise d'Alixandre

[ed. and English trans. Richard M. Dawkins, 2 vols (Oxford: The Clarendon Press, 1932), I)]

[ed. and English trans. R. Barton Palmer (New York – London: Routledge, 2002)]

Prooimion: the chronicler states his intention to write a didactic and entertaining narrative (§§ 1–2).
Peter of Lusignan's family (§ 78).

Prologue: Peter's mythological origins (ll. 1–258).
Peter of Lusignan's early years as a lover, a knight, and a devout Christian (ll. 259–90).
Peter's calling to be a crusader after a vision in a church (ll. 291–328).
The foundation of the Order of the Sword (ll. 329–506).

Peter's escapade to the West with his brother John in search of new experiences; the efforts of their father Hugh IV to bring them back and their imprisonment (§§ 79–85).
Peter's coronation as king of Cyprus in Nicosia in 1358 before his father's death (§ 86).
Offices and titles of the kingdom of Cyprus (§§ 87–89).

Peter's journey to France in an attempt to recruit men for his crusade; the efforts of his father Hugh IV to bring him back and his imprisonment (ll. 507–96).

Angel Nicolaou-Konnari • University of Cyprus

Alternatively, Peter's coronation may have taken place in 1359 after his father's death (§ 90).
The wealth of the Famagustans thanks to trade; the example of the Lakha brothers (§§ 91–96).
Acts of James I (1382–98) (§§ 97–98).
Offices conferred by Peter. His marriage to Eleanor of Aragon (§ 100).
The papal legate Peter Thomas's attempt to confirm the Greek clergy of Cyprus in 1360 (§§ 101–02).
Raids by Catalan privateers in 1360 (§ 103).
Peter's coronation as king of Jerusalem in Famagusta in 1360 (§ 104).
The claims of Hugh of Lusignan, Prince of Galilee, to the throne of Cyprus and the settlement of the dispute by the pope (§§ 105–08).
Peter's envoys to the West (§§ 109–10).
Upheaval in Famagusta in 1360 (§ 111).
The inhabitants of Gorhigos place themselves and their land under the rule of the Cypriot king in 1360 (§§ 112–15).
Peter's expedition against Satalia and the capture of the city in 1361 (§§ 116–25).
Attempt of Emir of Takka on Satalia in 1362 (§ 126).
The Cypriot army takes Myra in 1362 (§§ 127–28).
Peter leaves for Western Europe in 1362 (§ 129).
Peter's love for his wife (§ 130).
Peter's journey to Western Europe, 1362–1365: Rhodes, Venice, Avignon (§ 131).

Various military affairs concerning Satalia (§§ 132–35).
Plague in Cyprus (§ 135).
Peter's journey to Western Europe, 1362–1365: Avignon, France, the court of the German emperor, Genoa (§ 136).

Peter's coronation as king of Cyprus after his father's death in 1359 (ll. 597–618).

Peter captures Gorhigos by force in 1360 (ll. 619–40).

Peter's expedition against Satalia and the capture of the city in 1361 (ll. 641–60).

Peter's journey to Western Europe, 1362–1365: Avignon, Paris, Gascony, Flanders, England, Germany, Prague, Bohemia, Cracow, Vienna, Venice, Crete (ll. 661–1622).

Turkish raids against Cyprus and Cypriot retaliation raids along the coast of Anatolia (§§ 137–44).
Quarrel in Famagusta with the Genoese (§§ 145–9).
Cypriot pillaging in Turkey and Turkish retaliation raids against Cyprus (§§ 150–52).
Peace with Genoa (§§ 153–56).
Taxes (§ 157).
Languages used in Cyprus (§ 158).

The Cypriot fleet joins Peter in Rhodes in 1365. List of the Cypriot noblemen participating (§§ 159–64).

Peter sails to Rhodes in 1365. He is ill on board but he miraculously recovers ashore. He sends for provisions to Cyprus and the Cypriot fleet joins him in Rhodes. List of the ships (ll. 1623–920).

Peace with Genoa (§ 165).
At the bequest of the Grand Master, Peter makes peace with Ephesus and Miletus (§ 166).

Alexandria expedition (1365): number of ships, the Famagusta merchants do not favour the war (§§ 167–70).

Alexandria expedition (1365): last preparations, Peter receives the advice of Perceval de Coulonges who knows Egypt (ll. 1921–2082).

The taking of Alexandria (§§ 171–73).
The news of the Alexandria exploits reach the West (§§ 174–76).

The taking of Alexandria (ll. 2083–3660).

Raids against Turkey, including the failed expedition of 1367 and the sack of Tripoli, and negotiations with the sultan (1366–1367). The role of Venice (§§ 177–93).

Raids against Turkey, including the failed expedition of 1367, and negotiations with the sultan (1366–1367). The role of Venice (ll. 3661–4452).

The relief of Gorhigos in 1367 (§§ 194–95).

The relief of Gorhigos in 1367. List of the Western noblemen participating (ll. 4453–5675).

More negotiations with the sultan (1367) (§§ 196–98).

More negotiations with the sultan ending in failure (1367) (ll. 5676–6720).

Mutiny of the Cypriot contigent in Satalia in 1367 (§§ 199–201).
Failure of the negotiations with the sultan (1367) (§§ 202–05).
Dispute between Peter and some of his noblemen, notably Florimond of Lesparre. The Grand Master returns to Rhodes (§§ 206–07).
Peter in Satalia (§ 208).
Peter's illness in Cyprus (§ 209).

Peter attacks Tripoli, Tortosa, Baniyas, Latakia, Malo, Ayas, and Sidon in 1367 (§§ 210–13).
The quarrel with Lesparre and preparations for the second visit to the West, 1367 (§ 214).
Taxes (§ 215).
The quarrel with Lesparre and the second visit to the West, 1367–1368: Rhodes, Naples, Rome, Florence, Milan (§§ 216–18).
Cypriot and Genoese privateering and Arab raid on Famagusta in 1368 (§§ 219–22).
Genoese and Venetian envoys negotiate unsuccessfully on Peter's behalf with the sultan (§§ 223–30).

Peter attacks Tripoli, Ayas, Tortosa, Baniyas, and Latakia in 1367 (ll. 6721–7194).
The second visit to the West, 1367–1368: Rome (ll. 7195–311).

Envoys from trade cities negotiate successfully on Peter's behalf with the sultan (ll. 7273–311).
Peter receives the crown of Armenia in 1368 (ll. 7313–42).
The second visit to the West: Venice (ll. 7343–56).
The quarrel with Florimond of Lesparre settled before the pope (ll. 7357–934).

Queen Eleanor of Aragon and Peter's pregnant mistress Joanna L'Aleman (§§ 234–37).
Peter's second mistress, Eschiva of Scandelion (§ 238).
The affair of Queen Eleanor of Aragon with John of Morphou. John Visconti informs Peter (§§ 239–43).
Peter returns to Cyprus in 1368 (§ 244).

Peter returns to Cyprus in 1368 (ll. 7935–54).

John of Morphou bribes Peter's mistresses and they do not tell the king about his affair with the queen (§§ 245–49).
Quarrel between the Genoese and the Venetians in Famagusta in 1368 (§ 250).

Peter's brothers and liegemen put the blame on Visconti for the queen's affair (§§ 251–58).

The king's murder on 16 January 1369 at dawn (ll. 7955–8028).
The conspirators included Peter's brothers and liegemen and even the king's mother. They accused John Visconti, who informed

Peter's insulting behaviour towards his brothers, liegemen, and noble ladies (§§ 259–60).
The incident with the dogs of Henry Giblet and the marriage of Maria of Giblet (§§ 261–67).
Peter's brothers and liegemen are angry at the king for violating the laws of the *Assises* (§§ 268–77).
The knights decide to kill Peter (§ 278).

The king's murder on 17 January 1369 at dawn (§§ 278–81).

Peter II, the dead king's son, enters upon the rule of the kingdom (§ 282).

the king of Queen Eleanor's affair and of the conspiracy, of lying to the king (ll. 8029–244).
The incident with the dogs of Henry Giblet and the marriage of Maria of Giblet (ll. 8245–492).

The king's brothers and knights decide to kill him (ll. 8493–630).
The king's murder (ll. 8631–768).
The king's burial (ll. 8769–806).
The regency violates the laws of the kingdom (ll. 8807–32).

Peter's encomium (l. 8833–87).

Appendix B
(Tentative) Psychiatric Assessment of Peter I of Lusignan (1329-69)

Despite the lapse of 652 years, Peter's psychiatric assessment might have been relatively accurate had testimonies provided by the subject or his close milieu been available to us. In view of the limited, mostly non-contemporary and indirect, and potentially biased (positively or negatively) extant evidence, it is scientifically hazardous to attempt anything more than a tentative assessment, which is based on a synthesis of the sparse information and can yield only a speculative and precarious clinical diagnosis. This assessment follows the Diagnostic and Statistical Manual of Mental Disorders, 5th Edition (DSM-5, 2013), American Psychiatric Association (APA), and the International Statistical Classification of Diseases and Related Health Problems, 10th Edition (ICD-10, 1983), World Health Organization (WHO).

1. Premorbid Personality

One must take into consideration the fact that, in Peter's specific social and cultural context, erratic attitudes, arbitrary decisions, and extreme or even brutal reactions similar to his were the norm and were accepted if not expected by a ruler. Despite some excesses and inconsistencies for modern perceptions, the portrayal of Peter's personality until his return to Cyprus in October 1368 does not deviate much from the standard depiction of a medieval king.

2. Psychiatric History

A clear change in Peter's demeanour occurred at the age of 39, after his return to Cyprus in October 1368. The change escalated relatively fast, within weeks, lasting until his death in January 1369, i.e., a period of three to four months. The symptoms may be described as persecutory ideation, suspiciousness, ideas of reference, feelings of threat, and violent behaviour and are all out of character. These may have been delusions, but since they were plausible and well grounded, they probably represented firm beliefs, something very common for his social position and justified by the

Kakia Nikolaou • Thessaloniki General Hospital 'G. Papanikolaou' - Thessaloniki Psychiatric Hospital

circumstances. Moreover, he does not seem to have completely lost contact with reality; on the contrary, he appears to have had adequate insight and reality control left.

3. Differential Diagnosis

This ideation may have occurred in the context of psychotic symptoms (paranoid ideas) as a result of severe stressors in a personality with narcissistic and paranoid traits. The ideas are plausible, non-bizarre, shared by a large portion of those belonging to the subject's social, cultural, and religious background, of short duration and mild delusional intensity, while a certain degree of reality control remains intact. Such a psychological response could be classified as an adjustment disorder.

A persecutory type of delusional disorder is less likely as, in such a case, the delusions must have been expressed with profound conviction and unusual persistence or force and must have been well constructed and consistent, longer standing, and out of the patient's social, cultural and religious background.[1] Similarly, there is little evidence of depressive mood, feelings of helplessness and hopelessness, loss of interest in daily activities, significant weight loss or weight gain, sleep changes, loss of energy, strong feelings of worthlessness or guilt, concentration and attention problems, signs that could be accounted for depression with psychotic symptoms.

Paranoid personality disorder and paranoid schizophrenia may be ruled out, mainly on the basis of the age of onset and the absence of extremely disorganized behaviour, formal thought disorder, bizarre delusions, and perception disorders (hallucinations). Moreover, there is no concrete evidence of potential medical etiologies (neurodegenerative disorders, infectious diseases, metabolic disorders, endocrinopathies, vitamin deficiencies, alcoholism, toxins), which may present similar symptoms, even though, given the prevalence of some of these conditions at the time, it cannot be completely ruled out.[2]

---

1 I do not agree with Dr Panayiotis Vengos's assessment (in Matteo Campagnolo, 'The Parallel Lives of Evagoras I of Salamis and Peter I de Lusignan', in *From Aphrodite to Melusine. Reflections on the Archaeology and the History of Cyprus*, ed. by Matteo Campagnolo and Marielle Martiniani-Rebe (Geneva: La Pomme d'or, 2007), pp. 49–62, at p. 59 n. 26) that Peter's behaviour could be defined as delusions of grandeur in the context of a delusional disorder.

2 See Angel Nicolaou-Konnari's introductory chapter in this volume, n. 105, for mentions of Peter falling ill by William of Machaut and Leontios Makhairas.

ALEXANDER D. BEIHAMMER

The Sack of Alexandria (1365), the Crusading Movement, and the Eastern Mediterranean in the First Half of the Fourteenth Century

The attack on the Egyptian port and trade centre of Alexandria, which a joint force of Cypriot and Hospitaller naval contingents headed by King Peter I of Cyprus carried out on 9–16 October 1365 and modern historians usually refer to as 'the sack of Alexandria',[1] is both a logical culmination of and an unexpected deviation from the development of the Latin-Christian crusading movement in the decades following the Mamluk conquest of Acre in 1291. The end of the political and territorial existence of the Kingdom of Jerusalem in Syria and Palestine had ushered in a new phase of Muslim-Christian relations in the Levant. The Mamluk sultanate—which specialists discuss whether it should be labelled 'empire' or not—had rid itself of the crusaders' military presence in the Syro-Palestinian littoral and had successfully fought back the Mongol invasions. Having thus averted the two most dangerous threats to the sultanate's predominance and territorial integrity in Syria and Egypt, the ruling elite of Cairo henceforth excelled as the single major centralized power in the Muslim world of the time, assumed a leadership role in the defence of Islam, and was able to

---

1 Aziz Suryal Atiya, *The Crusade in the Later Middle Ages* (London: Methuen, 1938), pp. 319–78; Sir George Hill, *A History of Cyprus*, 4 vols (Cambridge: Cambridge University Press, 1940–52; repr. 2010), II, pp. 317–60; Frederíck J. Boehlke, *Pierre de Thomas: Scholar, Diplomat, and Crusader* (Philadelphia: University of Pennsylvania Press, 1966), pp. 267–94; Kenneth M. Setton, *The Papacy and the Levant (1204–1571)*, 4 vols (Philadelphia: American Philosophical Society, 1976–84), I, pp. 258–72; Eliyahu Ashtor, *Levant Trade in the Middle Ages* (Princeton: Princeton University Press, 1983), pp. 88–102; Peter W. Edbury, *The Kingdom of Cyprus and the Crusades, 1191–1374* (Cambridge: Cambridge University Press, 1991), pp. 166–71; Norman Housley, *The Later Crusades: From Lyon to Alcazar, 1274–1580* (Oxford: Oxford University Press, 1992), pp. 39–43, 66–69, 192–94; Nicholas Coureas, 'The Lusignan Kingdom of Cyprus and the Sea, 13th–15th Centuries', in *The Sea in History – The Medieval World*, ed. by Michel Balard and Christian Buchet (Woodbridge: The Boydell Press, 2017), pp. 369–81 (pp. 373–75 on the size of Peter's fleet).

Alexander D. Beihammer • University of Notre Dame

Crusading, Society, and Politics in the Eastern Mediterranean in the Age of King Peter I of Cyprus, ed. by Alexander Beihammer and Angel Nicolaou-Konnari, MEDNEX, 10 (Turnhout, 2022), pp. 77–106
© BREPOLS 🕮 PUBLISHERS   10.1484/M.MEDNEX-EB.5.128460

benefit from its advantageous position at the intersection between Mediterranean and Asian trade zones.[2]

In Christian Europe, after overcoming the first shock and confusion caused by the harrowing reports of the Mamluk victory, the papal curia, theoreticians and preachers of the crusade, as well as the political leaders of the Latin East engaged in a process of ideological and strategic reorientation. The focus of their discussions about future crusading projects shifted from defence to recovery of the Holy Land.[3] In addition, the pertinent discourse quickly came to include more pragmatic approaches and more immediate objectives. The protection of the remaining Christian outposts in the region, such as the kingdom of Cyprus, the kingdom of Cilician Armenia, and from 1307 onwards the lordship of the Knights Hospitaller in Rhodes, as well as the maintenance of fleet squadrons policing the waters of the Eastern Mediterranean so as to enforce the papal prohibition of trade with the Mamluk sultanate were the most pressing issues.[4] Before long, it became manifest that the emergence of a new Christian-Muslim conflict zone in western Asia Minor and the Aegean Sea was in the offing.[5]

In the decades of the so-called Nicaean Empire (1204–61) and the reign of Michael VIII Palaiologos (1259–82), the Byzantine-Turkish borderland, which in Muslim sources is frequently called 'uc', i.e., 'extremity, fringe', had witnessed an extended period of relative tranquillity and prosperity based on peaceful relations between Byzantine and Seljuk rulers.[6] However, the disintegration of the Seljuk sultanate of Rūm in the wake of the Mongol-Ilkhānid occupation of large parts of Asia Minor, intra-dynastic rivalries, and the ensuing influx of growing numbers of Turkmen pastoralists into Anatolia caused a gradual breakdown of the Byzantine administration and defensive system.[7] Turkish warlords carved out independent

---

2 Jo Van Steenbergen, 'Revisiting the Mamlūk Empire: Political Action, Relationships of Power, Entangled Networks, and the Sultanate of Cairo in Late Medieval Syro-Egypt', in *The Mamluk Sultanate from the Perspective of Regional and World History: Economic, Social and Cultural Development in an Era of Increasing International Interaction and Competition*, ed. by Reuven Amitai and Stephan Conermann (Bonn: Bonn University Press, 2019), pp. 75–106 (esp. pp. 75–77 on the sultanate around 1300 and pp. 77–85 on the notion of empire).

3 Luca Mantelli, 'De recuperatione terrae sanctae: Dalla Perdita di Acri a Celestino V', *Rivista di storia della Chiesa in Italia*, 67 (2013), pp. 397–440; Constantinos Georgiou, *Preaching the Crusades to the Eastern Mediterranean: Propaganda, Liturgy and Diplomacy, 1305–1352* (Abington and New York: Routledge, 2018), pp. 20–21, 36–49.

4 Josep Trenchs Odena, '«De Alexandrinis»: el comercio prohibido con los Musulmanes y el papado de Aviñon durante la primera mitad del siglo XIV', *Anuario de estudios medievales*, 10 (1980), 237–318; Norman Housley, *The Avignon Papacy and the Crusades, 1305–1378* (Oxford: Clarendon Press, 1986), pp. 9–49, 82–123; Jonathan Riley-Smith, *The Knights Hospitaller in the Levant, c. 1070–1309* (Hampshire and New York: Palgrave Macmillan, 2012), pp. 223–28.

5 Mike Carr, *Merchant Crusaders in the Aegean 1291–1352* (Woodbridge: The Boydell Press, 2015), pp. 39–49.

6 Andrew C. S. Peacock, 'The Seljuk Sultanate of Rum and the Turkmen of the Byzantine Frontier, 1206–1278', *al-Masāq: Journal of the Medieval Mediterranean*, 26 (2014), 267–87.

7 Claude Cahen, *The Formation of Turkey: The Seljukid Sultanate of Rūm: Eleventh to Fourteenth Century*, trans. and ed. by Peter M. Holt (Harlow: Longman, 2001), pp. 196–233; Dimitri Korobeinikov, *Byzantium and the Turks in the Thirteenth Century* (Oxford: Oxford University Press, 2014), pp. 217–97.

emirates or 'beyliks', as they are labelled in modern Turkish historiography, and after gaining access to the major ports of western Asia Minor they engaged in seaborne raids against Byzantine and Frankish domains in the Aegean Sea and along the shores of the Greek mainland.[8] A new phenomenon, the naval *ghazā* or Holy War, came into being.[9] The Byzantines, the Italian maritime republics, and various Latin local lords were facing a hitherto unknown threat emanating from the Muslim Turks of Anatolia.

Fighting the Turks in the Aegean became a new objective of western crusading initiatives, which from the 1320s onwards gained prominence over the traditional goals regarding the Holy Land.[10] Certainly, the dream of a *passagium generale*, a general campaign of Christendom aiming at the reconquest of Jerusalem under the umbrella of a Franco-papal alliance and the leadership of the French king, lingered on and was repeatedly voiced in diplomatic documents, papal bulls, programmatic treatises, and crusader sermons.[11] At the level of day-to-day business and decision making, however, all parties involved tacitly acknowledged the post-1291 state of affairs and aligned themselves with the strategic considerations and commercial interests of the local and supra-regional powers operating in the Eastern Mediterranean. The fall of Acre as 'the gate to the Muslim Levant' covering increasing European demands for Oriental luxury commodities and granting access to markets for the export of European textiles initially had been a heavy blow for European-Muslim commercial relations.[12] The political and economic consolidation of the Mamluk sultanate

---

8 Paul Wittek, *Das Fürstentum Mentesche. Studie zur Geschichte Westkleinasiens im 13.–15. Jh.*, Istanbuler Mitteilungen 2 (Istanbul: Archäologisches Institut des Deutschen Reiches, 1934); Elizabeth A. Zachariadou, *Trade and Crusade: Venetian Crete and the Emirates of Menteshe and Aydin (1300–1415)*, Library of the Hellenic Institute of Byzantine and Post-Byzantine Studies, 11 (Venice: Istituto Ellenico di Studi Bizantini e Postbizantini di Venezia, 1983), pp. 3–20; Muharrem Kesik, *Anadolu Türk Beylikleri* (Istanbul: Bilge Kültür Sanat, 2018), p. 32: 'Selçukluların hakimiyetinde topraklarda kurulmuş olan bu beyliklere eski kaynaklarda "Tavâif-i Mülûk" adı verilir. Modern tarih literatüründe ise Anadolu Beylikleri olarak adlandırılan bu Türk beyliklerin büyük bir kısmı […]'.
9 Halil İnalcik, 'The Rise of the Turcoman Maritime Principalities in Anatolia, Byzantium, and the Crusades', *Byzantinische Forschungen*, 9 (1985), 179–217 (p. 180: 'The crucial development in the new period of struggle between Islam and Christendom was […] the rise of Turkish navies manned by sea ghazis').
10 Zachariadou, *Trade and Crusade*, p. 15: The first Venetian initiatives to organize an anti-Turkish league date to the period 1325–27, when the Turks of Aydın stood in alliance with the Catalans and attacked Negroponte, Naxos, and other targets. For the origins of the idea of naval leagues against the Turks, see Carr, *Merchant Crusaders*, pp. 66–70, who points to the coalitions of the Knights Hospitaller with Genoese privateers during the conquest of Rhodes 1306–10 and with the rulers of Chios and Phocaea, Martino and Benedetto II Zaccaria, before 1319, as well as to a note in the crusader treatise *Liber secretorum fidelium crucis* by Marino Sanudo Torsello from 1322/23.
11 Norman J. Housley, 'The Franco-Papal Crusade Negotiations of 1322–3', *Papers of the British School at Rome*, 48 (1980), 166–85; Norman J. Housley, 'Pope Clement V and the Crusades of 1309–10', *Journal of Medieval History*, 8 (1982), 29–43; Christopher J. Tyerman, 'Marino Sanudo Torsello and the Lost Crusade: The Alexander Prize Essay', *Transactions of the Royal Historical Society*, 32 (1982), 57–73; Christopher J. Tyerman, 'Philip VI and the Recovery of the Holy Land', *The English Historical Review*, 100 (1985), 25–52; Georgiou, *Preaching the Crusades*, pp. 67–96; for a recent summary, see Christopher Tyerman, *The World of the Crusades* (Yale: Yale University Press, 2019), pp. 375–90.
12 Ashtor, *Levant Trade*, pp. 3–17.

offered new opportunities. The maritime republics of Genoa and Venice, as well as Catalan, French, and other European merchant communities were keen to gain a share in the east-west long-distance trade of Asiatic commodities reaching the ports of the Levant, such as Famagusta in Cyprus, Ayas in Cilicia, Beirut, or Alexandria. Peaceful relations with the Mamluk sultanate were an indispensable prerequisite for engaging in this profitable business. While the papal trade embargo formally stayed in force and was partly implemented, the papacy acquiesced to these activities by granting exemptions through licenses.[13] When the Apostolic See in the years 1323–44 imposed stricter prohibitions of commercial activities in Egypt and Syria, the ports of Cyprus and Cilician Armenia gained in importance as hubs of Levantine trade, but the trade routes with the Mamluks were by no means severed and new routes to Persia and Southern Russia were opened.[14] In 1345 Pope Clement VI returned to a more liberal policy in issuing trade licenses and thus brought about a significant surge in the commercial exchanges between the western trading nations and the Mamluks while Cyprus continued to play an important role in this network.[15] In order to protect its interests, the Lusignan government sought to curb both Muslim and Christian piracy, uphold the trade embargo as an effective means of precluding undesired competition, and respond to specific threats when need arose.[16] Crusader propaganda still served various purposes, be it in projecting the universal leadership role of the papacy and its rights to ecclesiastical tithes or in soliciting help from or buttressing the expansionist ambitions of the kings of France, the Angevins of Naples, and the crown of Aragon.[17] Yet launching new wars would not only have jeopardized the fragile stability of eastern Mediterranean trade networks but would also have damaged profitable businesses. It was only in response to the growing pressure in the Aegean Sea that the anti-Turkish league came into being in 1334.[18]

Against this background, King Peter I's 1365 expedition was certainly in line with chivalric ideals and theoretical claims brought forward in crusader treatises and

---

13 Jean Richard, 'Le royaume de Chypre et l'embargo sur le commerce avec l'Égypte (fin XIIIe–début XIVᵉ siècle)', *Comptes rendus des séances de l'Académie des Inscriptions des Belles-Lettres*, 1 (1984), 120–34; Ashtor, *Levant Trade*, pp. 17–44.
14 Ashtor, *Levant Trade*, pp. 44–63.
15 Ashtor, *Levant Trade*, pp. 64–88; Mike Carr, 'Crossing Boundaries in the Mediterranean: Papal Trade licenses from the *Registra supplicationum* of Pope Clement VI (1342–52)', *Journal of Medieval History*, 41 (2015), 107–29.
16 Edbury, *Kingdom of Cyprus*, pp. 103–04, 111, 133–35, 137–38, 151–52.
17 For a broader discussion of this topic, see Christopher Tyerman, '"New Wine in Old Skins?" Crusade Literature and Crusading in the Eastern Mediterranean in the Later Middle Ages', in *Byzantines, Latins, and Turks in the Eastern Mediterranean World after 1150*, ed. by Jonathan Harris, Catherine Holmes and Eugenia Russell (Oxford: Oxford University Press, 2012), pp. 265–89; for Aragon, see Donald J. Kagay, 'The Theory and Practice of Just War in the Late-Medieval Crown of Aragon', *The Catholic Historical Review*, 91 (2005), 591–609; for the Angevins, see Norman J. Housley, 'Angevin Naples and the Defence of the Latin East: Robert the Wise and the Naval League of 1334', *Byzantion*, 51 (1981), 548–56; Norman J. Housley, 'Charles II of Naples and the Kingdom of Jerusalem', *Byzantion*, 54 (1984), 527–35; for the French kings, see the bibliography cited above, n. 11.
18 Setton, *Papacy*, I, pp. 179–92; Zachariadou, *Trade and Crusade*, pp. 21–24, 29–37, 41–45, 49–54; Carr, *Merchant Crusaders*, pp. 70–76.

Franco-papal agreements regarding the future recovery of the Holy Land. In terms of *realpolitik*, however, it appears as a reckless enterprise running counter to the strategic considerations, military priorities, and economic interests of the majority of the Christian powers operating in the Eastern Mediterranean at the time. In quest for the deeper causes and motives, one comes across a bewildering mixture of high hopes, hazy aspirations, and pragmatic needs. Accordingly, in modern scholarship King Peter's crusade is presented either in a romanticizing manner as feat of valour of a champion of Christian knighthood or more critically as ill-fated endeavour of a dreamer led by outmoded concepts. Aziz Suryal Atiya and George Hill adopted Peter's idealizing representation in William of Machaut's verse chronicle on the seizure of Alexandria and some papal letters as a true 'athlete of Christ' replete with religious zeal and enthusiasm of fighting the infidels.[19] Frederick Boehlke and Kenneth Setton draw the image of a tragic hero, who along with his likeminded comrades-in-arms, the papal legate Peter Thomas and the chancellor Philip of Mézières, took action without the pope's knowledge and against the explicit wishes of Venice. They were capable military commanders and had no share in the soldiers' ransacking, but their efforts were doomed to failure because of adverse circumstances.[20] Contrarily, Eliyahu Ashtor characterizes King Peter 'a romantically minded knight whose ideas did not fit the political circumstances of his time'.[21] Peter Edbury tries to rationalize King Peter's course of action by ascribing it to economic considerations. In his view, the king must have been aware of the difficulties of recovering the Holy Land and used these references merely as a propaganda tool. His actual objective was to re-strengthen Famagusta as emporium of Levantine trade, which had begun to lose its position to the Mamluk ports in Syria and Egypt.[22]

The outcome of the abortive campaign fell nothing short of a disaster. The crusaders looted Alexandria, yet in view of the city's indefensibility against the approaching Mamluk army the fleet hastily abandoned the gained position and withdrew.[23] Thereafter, western merchants were incarcerated; trade routes and commercial activities between Egypt and Europe were disrupted; Cyprus was drawn into an exhausting war, which drained the kingdom's economic and military resources. While King Peter sought to keep up some military pressure by mounting attacks on Syrian coastal cities, Venice, Genoa, and the papacy urged him to make concessions in the peace negotiations with the Mamluk sultanate. The treaty which was reached after King Peter's assassination brought no gains. In sum, the Alexandrian crusade

---

19 Atiya, *Crusade*, p. 319: 'Young, virile, chivalrous, pious and full of enthusiasm for the cause, he had an additional incentive [...] in the condition of affairs in his island-kingdom'; p. 321: 'The young prince was a great lover of adventure.' Hill, *A History of Cyprus*, II, p. 319: 'In another aspect, the way in which the whole adventure centres on a single individual, as in the intensity of the religious enthusiasm which inspired that leader, it has its nearest parallel in the Crusades of St Louis [...] He believed that he had a mission, directly confided to him in a vision [...].'
20 Boehlke, *Pierre de Thomas*, pp. 277–94; Setton, *Papacy*, I, pp. 266–72.
21 Ashtor, *Levant Trade*, p. 88.
22 Edbury, *Kingdom of Cyprus*, p. 171; Tyerman, 'New Wine', p. 269, shares the same view.
23 Atiya, *Crusade*, pp. 345–69; Hill, *A History of Cyprus*, II, pp. 329–34; Setton, *Papacy*, I, pp. 271–72.

and its consequences weakened the kingdom of Cyprus economically, militarily, and diplomatically.[24] The Mamluk sultanate, while desisting from any acts of retaliation, was keen to restore the previous state of affairs and to re-open its trade routes with the Italian maritime republics and other European trading nations.[25] Cyprus was more isolated than ever and the decay of the port of Famagusta was further precipitated.[26] Contemporary witnesses and modern historians arrived at the conclusion that King Peter's crusade achieved nothing but distracting resources and manpower from the war against the Turks in the Aegean Sea.[27]

All too often modern scholars are stunned by the short-sightedness of historical figures. So many disasters could have been avoided had they only known better. At all events, this kind of reasoning hardly leads us to a better understanding of the precise circumstances of a given historical event or the expectations, motives, and incentives of its protagonists. Moreover, as most studies on the period focus on specific agents, entities, or regions, we easily run into danger to make misleading generalizations or to overemphasize one factor over another. The papacy, the Italian maritime republics, and the major western powers of the time have left the greatest amount of primary source material and thus their viewpoints figure most prominently in the modern bibliography. However, in order to gain a more holistic view of the Eastern Mediterranean and Muslim-Christian conflicts in the first half of the fourteenth century, it is imperative to attach equal importance to regional developments and the standpoints of local entities. This volume wants to contextualize the reign and crusading policy of King Peter I of Cyprus within the political, structural, and intellectual developments in the Latin East, Byzantium, Muslim Anatolia, and the Mamluk sultanate. By juxtaposing and comparing simultaneous events, structures, and behavioural patterns in the Latin, Byzantine, and Muslim realms of the Eastern Mediterranean, it seeks to go beyond the traditional analysis of political and economic antagonisms and the pros and cons of King Peter's military efforts. It wants to approach King Peter's policy and mindset under the light of and in connection with political, religious, and ideological attitudes in the adjacent spheres of Byzantium and the Muslim powers.

The scholarly discussion of Byzantium's limited involvement in fourteenth-century crusade alliances mostly focuses on Venetian and Genoese hegemonial politics, French-Angevin ambitions to restore the Latin Empire of Constantinople, and the tensions resulting from the schism between the Greek and the Latin Churches. A number of crucial aspects, however, such as the internal disputes in the time of the Hesychast controversy, the nature of the Byzantine unionist movement and its approaches to the papal church and the idea of conversion, as well as the peculiarities of Byzantium's experience of the Muslim Turks, are equally important and enable us to grasp the deeper cultural and intellectual links between Byzantium, the Greek

---

24 Atiya, *Crusade*, pp. 370–78; Hill, *A History of Cyprus*, II, pp. 334–60; Setton, *Papacy*, I, pp. 272–84; Edbury, *Kingdom of Cyprus*, pp. 168–71.
25 Hill, *A History of Cyprus*, II, pp. 372–76; Setton, *Papacy*, I, pp. 275–76, 279–80, 283.
26 See the characteristic conclusion of Setton, *Papacy*, I, p. 272: 'One of the chief results of the crusaders' destruction of Alexandria was the eventual destruction of the crusaders' own kingdom of Cyprus.'
27 Coureas, 'Kingdom of Cyprus and the Sea', p. 373 with bibliographical references, n. 7.

population of Cyprus, and the Frankish ruling elite of the island. Likewise, the scholarly literature discusses the Turks of Asia Minor mostly from the viewpoint of western sources as dangerous enemies or trade partners in the commercial relations with Venetian Crete.[28] Much less effort has been made to understand the internal structures or ideological attitudes of the Anatolian beyliks and their implications for Muslim-Christian relations and conflicts.

The same holds true for the internal developments of the Mamluk sultanate during the period in question, which shed more light on the deeper causes for the moderate and, at times, indecisive reactions of the sultanate to King Peter's aggression. As Clément Onimus points out in his chapter, apart from a general reluctance to pursue expansionist goals, Mamluk foreign policy was influenced by conflict-ridden domestic affairs and the infighting of Mamluk emirs and their slave households. In the time of King Peter's attack, the central government of Cairo was dominated by Yalbughā al-Khāṣṣakī, an emir of Sultan al-Nāṣir Ḥasan (1354–61), who in early 1366 was overthrown and then assassinated by a group of opponents backed by Sultan al-Ashraf Shaʿbān (1363–77).[29] This event triggered a new phase of internal turmoil and rebellions. Against this background it becomes understandable why the initial efforts to strengthen the defensive structures in the coastland of Egypt and Syria and to construct a sizable naval force never resulted in a large-scale counterattack on Cyprus. Despite the eagerness of Venice, Genoa, the Catalans, and the papacy to restore peace, the negotiations of the years 1366–70 went through a diplomatic gridlock, which was dominated by a playing for time strategy, a roundabout diplomacy, and mutual suspicions before the necessities of commercial interests eventually prevailed.

Important, though hitherto widely neglected, factors which to some extent set the framework and determined the radius of action of fourteenth-century crusading, are climate and environmental conditions. For all the pitfalls of misleading causal links and over-deterministic assumptions, there is no doubt that the interrelations and reciprocities between climatic-ecological phenomena and human decision-making in the sphere of Muslim-Christian warfare in the Eastern Mediterranean need to be analysed in the light of recent methodological advancements. In this volume, Johannes Preiser-Kapeller examines possible connections between the period's historical evidence and environmental data provided by the 'archives of nature'. A sequence of floods and droughts hitting different regions of the Eastern Mediterranean (a low flood and famine in Egypt in 1295–97; a flood in Nicosia in 1330; extreme dryness in Syria and southern Anatolia in the 1360s), the Black Death of 1348, and a locust plague affecting Cyprus in 1351 are some of the climatic and ecological phenomena known from this period. The famine in Egypt induced the Byzantine emperor and merchants in Rhodes and Sicily to export grain to the Mamluk sultanate despite

---

28 Zachariadou, *Trade and Crusade*; Carr, *Merchant Crusaders*.
29 For a fresh assessment of this personality in historiography and Mamluk politics and society, see Jo Van Steenbergen, 'The Amir Yalbughā al-Khāṣṣakī, the Qalāwūnid Sultanate, and the Cultural Matrix of Mamlūk Society: A Reassessment of Mamlūk Politics in the 1360s', *Journal of the American Oriental Society*, 131 (2011), 423–43.

the papal ban and caused western propagandists to assert that the famine was a sign of God's wrath. Extreme heat and dryness in Asia Minor may in part account for the Turks' failure to expel the Cypriot garrisons. The short period in which the canal connecting Alexandria and the river Nile was navigable may have determined the time of King Peter's attack. It remains questionable whether signs of erosion and landscape degradation on Cyprus are actually due to the overexploitation of a water-intensive plantation culture supported by the Lusignan rulers, the Knights Hospitaller, and the Venetians.

Another crucial aspect pertaining to the nature of fourteenth-century crusading is the change of military techniques in the later Middle Ages. Reviewing battle tactics and behavioural patterns of cavalry units, infantry men, and archers between the twelfth and fourteenth century, John France sees no signs of a proper 'military revolution' in the time of Peter I. Nevertheless, there was a conspicuous trend towards professionalization, which led to the emergence of well-trained professional soldiers and mercenary companies in Italy and other regions of Europe. The Catalan Grand Company is but one well-known example for the activities of such a group in the realm of Byzantium and the Latin East. A high degree of coherence among these soldiers facilitated the development of new battle tactics. The accounts of King Peter's wars document that the Cypriots were familiar with these changes and used professional soldiers alongside knights and zealots of the Holy War. This warfare, however, was also very expensive and created enormous economic pressure which a successful conquest of Alexandria would have substantially mitigated.

In what follows we will briefly recall some key aspects of the Lusignan kingdom's involvement in western crusading activities, of the formation of the Turkish beyliks in western Asia Minor, and of Byzantium's relations with both the Muslim Turks and Frankish crusaders in the years between 1291 and 1365. These topics will be discussed in connection with the results and findings of the contributions gathered in this volume in order to present an overview of the new arguments and interpretations the following chapters are able to offer.

The Papacy and Franco-Papal Alliances

As has already been pointed out, the papal curia continued to exert its spiritual, propagandistic, and political leadership role in the crusading movement of the post-1291 period, albeit within a different set of power relations in Europe and the Levant and apparently with less impact on decision-making procedures at European courts. In their joint analysis of the papacy's role in the Alexandrian crusade, Peter Edbury and Chris Schabel broach a crucial question: Why did King Peter I, with his personal leadership claims and the destination of his crusade, act against the pope's explicit intentions and strategic considerations?

Apart from the specific constellations in the year 1365 and the king's personal choices, the answer to this question partly lies in the overall inefficiency of Franco-papal crusading projects in the post-1291 period. Since the election of the Frenchman Raymond Bertrand de Got as Pope Clement V (1305–14), the papal curia stood under the heavy influence of King Philip IV of France (1285–1314) and in 1309 it took up residence in Avignon.[30] Henceforth, the papal policy regarding the remnants of the crusader states and the organization of new crusades was more closely than ever before aligned with the wishes of the French crown, as the abolition of the Templar Order vividly illustrates.[31] Besides, the papacy was facing numerous challenges in enforcing its trade embargo and in organizing financial and military aid for the kingdoms of Cyprus and Cilician Armenia as the most exposed outposts of Latin Christianity. As long as the antagonism between the Mongol Ilkhānids of Persia and the Mamluk sultanate lingered on prospects of forging a Christian-Mongol alliance against the Mamluks induced the papal curia to establish diplomatic contacts with the Ilkhānid court.[32] All these initiatives, however, hardly brought any tangible results for the Christians in the Levant in terms of reducing Muslim military pressure in Asia Minor and northern Syria.

The papacy kept calling for a general crusade but found little resonance. The projects either failed to take off or developed into different directions from what was originally intended. Soon after the fall of Acre, Pope Nicholas IV (1288–92) set the summer of 1293 as date for the departure of a crusade to re-conquer the Holy Land but found hardly any response.[33] On ratifying his alliance with the French crown and the Angevins of Naples in the summer of 1307 at Poitiers, Pope Clement V in August 1308 announced a crusade which was to be under the command of the papal legate Peter of Pleine Chassagne and the Hospitallers and aimed at securing the survival of the kingdoms of Cyprus and Cilician Armenia. The expedition took eventually place but never reached the shores of the Eastern Mediterranean, instead supporting the Hospitallers' efforts to complete the conquest of Rhodes and the surrounding islands.[34] The island may at times have been threatened by naval raids from the Menteşe Turks, who held sway over the opposite coastland of Asia Minor.[35] Rather than fighting the Muslim foe, however, the campaign resulted in the consolidation of Hospitaller rule over a former Byzantine province with a mostly Orthodox Greek-speaking population.[36] A side effect of the abolishment of the Templar Order at the Council of Vienne in 1311–12 was the proclamation of a new crusade that was to

---

30 Setton, *Papacy*, I, p. 163; Housley, *Avignon Papacy*, pp. 1–7.
31 For the weakness of the papacy's position, see, for instance, Julien Théry-Astruc, 'The Flight of the Master of Lombardy (13 February 1308) and Clement V's Strategy in the Templar Affair: A Slap in the Pope's Face', *Rivista di storia della Chiesa in Italia*, 70 (2016), 35–44.
32 James Muldoon, 'The Avignon Papacy and the Frontiers of Christendom: The Evidence of Vatican Register 62', *Archivium Historiae Pontificiae*, 17 (1979), 125–95 (pp. 171–82); James Daniel Ryan, 'Nicholas IV and the Evolution of the Eastern Missionary Effort', *Archivum Historiae Pontificiae*, 19 (1981), 79–96; Edbury, *Kingdom of Cyprus*, pp. 104–06.
33 Edbury, *Kingdom of Cyprus*, p. 102; for Acre, see now the articles collected in *Acre and Its Fall: Studies in the History of a Crusader City*, ed. by John France (Leiden: Brill, 2018).
34 Housley, 'Pope Clement V', pp. 30–33, 35, 37–38.
35 Zachariadou, *Trade and Crusade*, pp. 9–10.
36 Zachariadou, *Trade and Crusade*, pp. 11–12, assumes that after an initial commercial agreement with the Turks of Menteşe in 1311 relations quickly deteriorated and the Hospitallers faced joint Genoese-Turkish naval raids until 1313.

be headed by King Philip IV but once again never materialized.[37] Attempts of his successors Philip V (1317–22) and Charles IV (1322–28) to organize a naval force and bring the plans to fruition were of no avail. In view of mounting Mamluk military pressure on Cilician Armenia and open threats against Cyprus and after a series of preliminary negotiations with the French crown since 1317, Pope John XXII (1316–34) authorized the preaching of the crusade in late 1322, but again the commitments of the French king were rather lukewarm. Charles IV may have been genuinely interested in launching a crusade, but the question of raising the necessary revenues proved to be a serious obstacle and the Franco-papal alliance had lost its efficacy.[38] Hence, in 1323 the Armenians agreed on a new truce with the Mamluk sultanate.[39]

The plans announced by King Philip VI (1328–50) regarding the recovery of Jerusalem caused the papacy in 1331 to issue a new authorization for the preaching of the crusade in France, but like all previous initiatives the enthusiasm quickly evaporated in the absence of sufficient financial resources and the imminent conflict with Edward III of England so that Pope Benedict XII (1334–42) in March 1336 requested him to postpone the project.[40] At about the same time, the Mamluks mounted attacks against Cilician Armenia and in 1337 conquered the port of Ayas. The pope therefore was forced to suspend the preaching of the crusade in Cyprus in order to avert the danger of provoking the Mamluks.[41]

Considering this long sequel of abortive Franco-papal crusading initiatives, it can be assumed that Pope Urban V's plans for a new *passagium generale* that was to be headed by King John II of France (1350–64) were received with some suspicion and disenchantment in the Latin East. Moreover, his morale-boosting victories in the southern Anatolian coastland may have encouraged King Peter to pursue independent goals based on his own and his regional allies' resources. Edbury's and Schabel's analysis of pertinent papal letters demonstrates that Pope Urban V combined the traditional concept of a French-led crusade with the new objectives defined by the anti-Turkish league established in 1333/34 and the recent contacts with the Byzantine Empire. Defending Smyrna and the Aegean, fending off the Turks of Anatolia, and backing Byzantium on condition of its submission to the Roman Church were the principle aims of the planned expedition.[42] The Holy Land would benefit on the long run from such achievements. In the time span 1363–65, Pope Urban V had to deal with various unexpected obstacles, such as King John II's death, a revolt in Venetian Crete, and Lusignan-Genoese frictions, but the commercial links with the Mamluk sultanate remained largely undisturbed. The existing alliances

---

37 Setton, *Papacy*, I, pp. 169–70.
38 Housley, 'Franco-papal Crusade Negotiations', pp. 166–85, esp. p. 166: 'Franco-papal cooperation was no longer fruitful, that it hampered rather than forwarded the cause of the crusade, and that crusading in the eastern Mediterranean could only revive when the initiative passed elsewhere.'
39 Edbury, *Kingdom of Cyprus*, p. 135.
40 Setton, *Papacy*, I, 178–79; Tyerman, 'Philip VI', pp. 25–52; Edbury, *Kingdom of Cyprus*, pp. 144, 157; Mike Carr, 'Benedict XII and the Crusades', in *Pope Benedict XII (1334–1342): The Guardian of Orthodoxy*, ed. by Irene Bueno (Amsterdam: Amsterdam University Press, 2018), pp. 217–40 (pp. 219–23).
41 Edbury, *Kingdom of Cyprus*, pp. 157, 161.
42 For the details, goals, and historical context of this league, see below, pp. 93–94.

between the beyliks in southern Anatolia and the Mamluks suggest that a new war in Asia Minor would inevitably have led to an involvement of Cairo, something that the lords and commanders in the Latin East may have known much better than the papal curia. Hence, there were a number of reasons why King Peter and his counsellors at some point took the initiative and decided to go beyond the strategic and political framework set by the Avignon papacy and its European supporters.

Cyprus, The Crown of Jerusalem, and Aragonese-Angevin Antagonism

Another salient factor in the evolution of the crusading movement in the post-1291 period was the cluster of claims to the legacy of the kingdom of Jerusalem. This issue was closely intertwined with Mediterranean power politics in the first half of the fourteenth century, in particular with the antagonism between the French-Angevin coalition and the crown of Aragon along with its various junior branches over Sicily, influence in Italy, and alliances in the Eastern Mediterranean. French and Angevin titular claims to the Latin Empire of Constantinople and relations of intermarriage and feudal suzerainty with the Italian and Frankish lords in the duchy of Athens, the principality of Achaea, and the coastland of the Ionian Sea persisted and at times caused estrangement or open conflicts with the Despotate of Epirus and the Palaiologan elite in Byzantium. Cyprus was in this respect only a minor player among a large number of independent local lordships in the Eastern Mediterranean, but it had a major strategic and ideological significance due to its exposed geographic position and its long-standing dynastic and institutional claims to the crown of Jerusalem.

It was already with the establishment of the Lusignan kingdom in 1196–97 through the conferral of a royal crown by the German Emperor Henry VI that numerous institutions, feudal customs, and legal traditions had been transplanted from Jerusalem to Cyprus, although the demographic, religious, and cultural substrate emanating from the island's Byzantine past had also a strong impact on the kingdom's structure and identity.[43] After 1291, Cyprus appeared in many ways as the immediate heir of the kingdom of Jerusalem and the other crusader states. Members of the leading noble families, Frankish burgesses of Catholic denomination, and indigenous Arabic-speaking Christians adhering to the Monophysite churches relocated to Cyprus. The military Orders established their new headquarters on the island. With the abolishment of the Templars, the knights Hospitaller became one of the richest landowners on the island despite the fact that their headquarters was transferred to Rhodes. The Lusignan dynasty, the royal court of Nicosia, and the Cypriot nobility were deeply imbued with the political concepts, the ceremonial language, titles, and hierarchical structures of the kingdom of Jerusalem. Members of the Cypriot aristocracy were

---

43 Edbury, *Kingdom of Cyprus*, pp. 29–34; see the contributions collected in *Cyprus: Society and Culture 1191–1374*, ed. by Angel Nicolaou-Konnari and Chris Schabel, The Medieval Mediterranean, 58 (Leiden and Boston: Brill, 2005).

granted the traditional court dignities of Jerusalem, and princes of the Lusignan family assumed the honorific titles of the major lordships, such as count of Tripoli, prince of Antioch, prince of Galilee, count of Jaffa, etc.[44] Most importantly, the royal title of Jerusalem was united with that of Cyprus in personal union. The official title of Henry II in the letters and royal charters issued by his chancery referred to the crowns of both Cyprus and Jerusalem, and his successors performed two separate coronation ceremonies in Nicosia and Famagusta.[45] Mike Carr's contribution to this volume brings further details about the political and ideological role the kingdom of Cyprus played in the crusading movement in the post-1291 period.

Considering the rival claims of supra-regional powers and the neutral attitude the papacy adopted in order not to be drawn into these conflicts, it becomes understandable that Cyprus made serious efforts to forge links with the house of Aragon so as to contain the ambitions of the Angevins of Naples and their network of supporters within the French nobility. King Peter III (1276–85) and his son James II (1285/1291–1327) had built up a cluster of Aragonese domains and royal dynasties stretching from the Iberian Peninsula to mainland Greece. It comprised the kingdom of Majorca, which came to be ruled by Peter's brother James II and his successors, and the kingdom of Sicily, where Peter III in the wake of the Sicilian Vespers in 1282 was proclaimed king and after a series of violent engagements with the Angevins of Naples and the treaty of Caltabellotta in 1302 the rights to the throne devolved to Peter's third son Frederick III (1295–1337) and his offspring.[46] To these domains, the crown of Aragon later added a formal suzerainty over the Catalan duchy of Athens and the kingdom of Sardinia in 1324.[47] This conglomeration of power formed a strong counterweight to the Angevin kings of Naples, who as a result of the expansionist policy of Charles I of Anjou (1266–85) and his son Charles II (1285–1309) not only seized a large portion of the Hohenstaufen legacy in southern Italy but also acquired territories in Frankish Romania, at times spearheading efforts to restore the Latin Empire of Constantinople.[48] Despite the loss of Sicily in 1282, the Angevins maintained

---

44 Edbury, *Kingdom of Cyprus*, pp. 101–02, 107–09.
45 Edbury, *Kingdom of Cyprus*, pp. 109, 141, 148.
46 Joseph F. O'Callaghan, *A History of Medieval Spain* (Cornell: Cornell University Press, 1975), pp. 382–406, esp. pp. 382–91, 394–96, 398–401, 404–06; Thomas N. Bisson, *The Medieval Crown of Aragon: A Short History* (Oxford: Clarendon Press, 1986), pp. 86–96; David Abulafia, 'The Rise of Aragon Catalonia' in *The New Cambridge Medieval* History, V: *c. 1198–c. 1300*, ed. by David Abulafia (Cambridge: Cambridge University Press, 1999), pp. 661–67; Alan Forey, 'The Crown of Aragon' in *The New Cambridge Medieval History*, VI: *c. 1300–c. 1415*, ed. by Michael Jones (Cambridge: Cambridge University Press, 2000), pp. 595–96; Alessandra Cioppi and Sebastiana Nocco, 'Islands and the Control of the Mediterranean Space', in *The Crown of Aragon: A Singular Mediterranean Empire*, ed. by Flocel Sabaté, linguistic correction by Chris Boswell (Leiden: Brill, 2017), pp. 337–60.
47 Kenneth M. Setton, *Catalan Domination of Athens 1311–1388* revised edn (London: Variorum, 1975), p. 37.
48 Jean Dunbabin, *Charles I of Anjou: Power, Kingship and State-Making in Thirteenth-Century Europe* (London and New York: Routledge, 1998), pp. 83–113; David Abulafia, 'The Kingdom of Sicily under the Hohenstaufen and Angevins', in *The New Cambridge Medieval* History, V: *c. 1198–c. 1300*, ed. by David Abulafia (Cambridge: Cambridge University Press, 1999), pp. 510–21; see also David Abulafia, 'The State of Research: Charles of Anjou Reassessed', *Journal of Medieval History*, 26 (2001), 93–114.

a powerful position in Italy as close allies of the papacy and exerted suzerainty over Albania, the coastland of the Ionian Sea, and the principality of Achaea. Moreover, Charles II and his successor Robert the Wise (1309–43) made efforts to take the initiative in the crusading movement and antagonized the Lusignan kings in their rights to the crown of Jerusalem.[49]

Michalis Olympios examines the ideological expressions of these rival claims as they are reflected in monuments and works of art commissioned by the two dynasties. While Charles I's successors abandoned their ancestor's ambitious military projects, they continued to refer to his expansionist dynastic concepts as the fundament of Angevin royal identity. The genealogical representations on the painted panel of Charles II's saintly son Louis of Toulouse crowning Robert I (after 1317), the double frontispiece of the Anjou/Mechelen Bible dating to the 1340s, and the sarcophagus in Robert the Wise's tomb in Santa Chiara (Naples) constitute impressive pieces of visual propaganda, which employ the arms of the kingdom of Jerusalem alongside other heraldic references to Angevin, Capetian, and Hungarian connections so as to project the idea of orderly succession and royal sacredness within a *beata stirps* related to the most powerful families of Christian Europe. In Lusignan Cyprus, the arms of Jerusalem began to appear on coins from the reign of Amaury, lord of Tyre (1306–10), onwards. Stylistic references in the form of Gothic revisions of twelfth-century crusader churches can be found in the Bellapais Abbey commissioned by King Hugh IV and, above all, in the monumental edifices of Famagusta from the time prior to the Genoese takeover of 1373. The urban space where the Lusignan kings received the crown of Jerusalem had visually to be presented as true heir of Acre's symbols and traditions.

The Cypriot royal house's main tool of strengthening their alliances during the reigns of Henry II, Hugh IV, and Peter I was to negotiate marriages with various branches of the Aragonese dynasty. In the absence of a direct male descendant, Henry II even contemplated the possibility to place his kingdom under Aragonese protection by wedding his sister Maria to King James II of Majorca in 1315.[50] In the event of Henry's death, the rights to the throne of Cyprus would devolve to Maria, her husband, and their common offspring. The plan eventually foundered because of Maria's premature death in 1322 without giving birth to a child. In addition, Isabella of Ibelin, the daughter of Philip the Seneschal, married Ferrand, the younger son of James I of Majorca and former commandant of the Catalan Grand Company in Greece (1316), and King Henry II himself married Constance, the daughter of Frederick III

---

49 Norman J. Housley, 'Angevin Naples and the Defence of the Latin East: Robert the Wise and the Naval League of 1334', *Byzantion*, 51 (1981), 548–56; Norman J. Housley, 'Charles II of Naples and the Kingdom of Jerusalem', *Byzantion*, 54 (1984), 527–35; Peter Lock, *The Franks in the Aegean 1204–1500* (New York and London: Routledge, 1995), pp. 92–95; Andreas Kiesewetter, *Die Anfänge der Regierung König Karls II. von Anjou (1278–1295): das Königreich Neapel, die Grafschaft Provence und der Mittelmeerraum zu Ausgang des 13. Jahrhunderts* (Husum: Matthiesen Verlag, 1999); Nikolaos G. Chrissis, 'Crusades and Crusaders in Medieval Greece', in *A Companion to Latin Greece*, ed. by Nickiphoros I. Tsougarakis and Peter Lock, Brill's Companions to European History, 6 (Leiden and Boston: Brill, 2015), pp. 23–72.
50 Hill, *A History of Cyprus*, II, p. 282; Edbury, *Kingdom of Cyprus*, p. 138.

of Sicily (1317). As a result, Aragonese influence in Cyprus grew significantly over these years.[51]

Henry II's nephew and successor, Hugh IV (1324–59), pursued a dynastic policy along the same lines by wedding children of his second wife Alice of Ibelin to members of the Aragonese royal house. In 1340 he married his daughter Eschiva to Ferrand, the son of Ferrand (son of James I of Majorca) and Isabella of Ibelin, in 1343 his son John to Henry II's former wife Constance of Sicily, and in 1353 his second son Peter to Eleanor, daughter of the Infante Peter of Ribargoza, the fourth son of King James II. Only the last marriage was to last, for Ferrand after a falling-out with his father-in-law left Cyprus as soon as 1342 and Constance died in about 1350.[52]

An exception to this practice was the marriage of Hugh IV's first-born son Guy from his first wife. In 1330, Guy married Maria, the daughter of Louis of Clermont, the duke of Bourbon and second cousin of the king of France.[53] This marriage forged links with the French nobility and has to be seen in conjunction with the crusading plans of the French crown. After the outbreak of war with England in 1337 and the premature death of Guy in 1343 these plans, too, came to grief. A serious problem for the Lusignan royal house accrued from Guy's and Maria of Bourbon's son Hugh of Lusignan, who after the death of Hugh IV claimed to be the rightful heir of the kingdom and contested the succession of King Peter I. The fact that Maria of Bourbon in 1347 married Robert of Taranto, prince of Achaea and titular Latin emperor (1332/43–64), and enjoyed some backing from the French royal house and the Angevins of Naples—Robert was Charles II's grandson—made the papacy well-disposed towards Hugh and his ambitions and put additional pressure on King Peter.

Edbury and Schabel re-examine the papal letters and other documents referring to the conflict between Peter and his nephew Hugh, especially in the time between Hugh's first complaint to the curia in May 1360, just a few weeks after Peter's coronation to king of Jerusalem by the papal legate Peter Thomas, and March 1363, when Peter about five months after the accession of Pope Urban V (1362–70) came to Avignon in person. They demonstrate that for all the sympathy Pope Innocent VI may have harboured for Hugh's claims, King Peter's adroit diplomatic moves were overall successful and induced the new pope to accept Peter's succession as fait-accompli. Hugh was to receive some compensation, but Peter's early feats of war against the Turks recommended him as a capable military commander. It may be assumed that King Peter's trip to Avignon was primarily motivated by his crusading plans rather than the succession dispute with his nephew.

Apparently, with the shift of the crusading movement's main focus to the Aegean Sea both the kingdom of Cyprus and the royal title of Jerusalem lost much of their attractiveness for western claimants. Ever since the establishment of the Holy League

---

51 Hill, *A History of Cyprus*, II, pp. 282–83; Edbury, *Kingdom of Cyprus*, pp. 138–39.
52 Hill, *A History of Cyprus*, II, pp. 295–97 (Ferrand affair), p. 308 (marriage to Eleanor); Edbury, *Kingdom of Cyprus*, pp. 144–46.
53 Edbury, *Kingdom of Cyprus*, pp. 143–44.

in 1333/34, western ambitions regarding the island mostly concentrated on harnessing the kingdom's economic and military resources for the struggle against the Turks of Asia Minor. Nevertheless, the pope's initial support of Peter's French-backed nephew attests to the fact that the old expansionist tendencies vis-à-vis the kingdom of Cyprus were still smouldering and that the papacy had a certain propensity to buttress such efforts. Irrespective of the preponderant purpose of Peter's visit to Avignon, the whole affair about Hugh's claims must have brought home to King Peter and his entourage that utmost caution was at order with respect to Franco-papal cunning.

The Rise of the Anatolian Beyliks

By the 1320s the westward expansion and seaborne raids of the Turkish beyliks had become a serious problem for the Christian regional powers, the Italian maritime republics, and the proponents of the western crusading movement. This leads us to the question as to the nature of these nascent principalities and the sources of their military power and expansionist thrust. What made Turkish warriors of nomadic background, who had prevailed in the power struggles of the decaying Seljuk sultanate, successful state builders, political entrepreneurs, and military commanders spreading fear and terror among the Christians of the Levant and Europe?

The contributions of Rhoads Murphey and Romain Thurin to this volume deal with some of the key aspects of the formation period of the Turkish beyliks in the second half of the thirteenth century. Only a proper understanding of this prehistory and its cultural-ideological foundations enables us to accurately assess the role and position of the beyliks in the fourteenth-century crusades and Mediterranean history more broadly. Murphey focuses on the living conditions and thought world of the Turkish nomadic warriors, the core element of the new ruling elites, as is reflected in the Saltuk-nāme, an epic tale narrating the feats of the hero Sarı Saltuk (d. 1297) and his brothers-in-arm, which was compiled from various oral sources in the 1470s and came down to us in sixteenth-century manuscripts. In contrast to the court-based dynastic chronicles of the late Seljuk period, this compilation is reflective of the traditions, mentalities, and value systems of Turkmen tribesmen and war bands and grants us insights into their political and social structures. They formed self-governing groups based on the loyalties of kinship-based groups (*obuk*) and herding units (*ayil*) with horizontal command structures. Characteristic features of their worldview were concepts of chivalric bravery, military comradeship, booty raiding as a basic pattern of steppe warfare, a strict code of honour, as well as a preparedness to conclude alliances across ethnic and religious boundaries and to seek accommodation in a highly volatile and unstable political environment.

Thurin examines the genesis of two of the most powerful fourteenth-century beyliks, the Germiyānids and the Karāmānids, from their modest origins as Turkmen tribal groups up to their crystallization into powerful confederations meddling in the power struggles of various Seljuk rival factions. From a widely dispersed range of frequently sparse and elusive shreds of evidence, he reconstructs the migratory movements and politico-military activities of these groups. Turkmen pastoralists settling in the region of Garmiān near Malatya in the Upper Euphrates region in about

1260–65 moved westwards to the region of Değirmençayı near Sivrihisar. There, the Germiyānid chiefs lent active support to Sultan Ghiyāth al-Dīn Kaykāwūs II (1246–62) and, after the execution of their leader, switched side to the Mongol-backed faction of Sultan Kılıç Arslan IV (1246–65). The Karāmānids made their first appearance in the 1230s as pastoralists settling near Ermenek in the Taurus Mountains of Cilicia. During a large-scale Turkmen rebellion in 1261–63, Karāmān Bey, a former charcoal dealer, emerged as powerful chief but was eventually killed in a battle against the Armenians. After a period of suppression, in 1265 the Seljuk vizier Muʿīn al-Dīn Pervāneh won the Karāmānids over and restored their land grants in the region of Ermenek. A decisive factor in the development of Turkmen confederations in Anatolia were the two Mongol invasions of 1243 and 1256, which apart from extensive devastation brought about a serious economic crisis, starvation, and the occupation of nomadic pasturelands by Mongol troops. In response, Turkmen groups were forced to form larger military coalitions, became actively involved in the power struggles of the Seljuk elite, and eventually carved out their own lordships in the fringe areas of the sultanate.

In the early 1300s, the Germiyānid beylik under the leadership of Yaʿqūb ibn ʿAlīshīr significantly consolidated its position in a vast swathe of land extending from Kütahya in Phrygia to Laodikeia (Denizli) in the Lykos valley and exerted a strong influence over Turkmen groups in the Byzantine borderland.[54] This, in turn, generated a strong impetus for the Turkish westward expansion.

The coastland of Caria in southwestern Asia Minor had been the first region to slip away from Byzantine control in the 1260s.[55] In 1282 the Turks of Menteşe Beg had taken hold of the estuary area of the Maeander River and thence had extended their sway along the river valley, seizing places like Tralleis (Güzelhisar) and Nyssa (Sultanhisar).[56] In the wake of the Germiyānid consolidation, Sasa Beg, probably a subordinate commander of the Menteşe Turks,[57] and Mehmed Beg ibn Aydın, a Germiyānid vassal, advanced farther north into the Kaystros (Küçük Menderes) valley, seizing important places on their way, such as Ephesus (Ayasuluk), Pyrgion (Birgi), and Thyraion (Tire).[58] During the ensuing rivalries among the Turkish chiefs, Mehmed Beg prevailed, seized Ayasuluk, and in 1307/1308 established his chief residence in Birgi.[59] In the 1310s, Saruhan Beg, another Turkmen commander

---

54 Kesik, *Anadolu Türk Beylikleri*, pp. 224–27.
55 Wittek, *Fürstentum Mentesche*, pp. 23–26.
56 Wittek, *Fürstentum Mentesche*, pp. 26–27, 41.
57 George Pachymeres, *Relations historiques, livres I–VI*, ed. by Albert Failler, trans. by Vitalien Laurent, Corpus Fontium Historiae Byzantinae, 24/1–2, 2 vols (Paris: Belles Lettres, 1984), *livres VII–XIII*, ed. and trans. by Albert Failler, Corpus Fontium Historiae Byzantinae, 24/3–5, 3 vols (Paris: Institut Français d'Études Byzantines, 1999–2000), IV, p. 647 (book XIII, chapter 13): 'Κατείληπται Ἔφεσος παρὰ τοῦ Περσάρχου Σασᾶν, ὅς, γαμβρὸς ἅμα καὶ θεράπων τοῦ Περσάρχου Καρμανοῦ Μανταχίου ὤν'.
58 Wittek, *Fürstentum Mentesche*, pp. 41–44; see also Albert Failler, 'Éphèse fut-elle prise en 1304 par les Turcs de Sasan?', *Revue des Études Byzantines*, 54 (1996), 245–48, who argues against the commonly accepted date provided by a colophon of the scribe Michael Loulloudes in MS Venet. Marcianus 292, fol. 327ᵛ, that Ephesus was conquered on 24 October 1305.
59 Paul Lemerle, *L'émirat d'Aydin, Byzance et l'Occident: recherches sur la "Geste d'Umur pacha"* (Paris: Presses Universitaires de France, 1957), pp. 19–26.

from the uc region with links to the Germiyānids, managed to seize Magnesia (Manisa) at Mount Sipylus, Nymphaion (Kemalpaşa), the plain of Menemen at the northern shores of the Gulf of Smyrna, as well as various places along the Hermos (Gediz) valley.[60] In the years 1302–06, the Turks of Karasi established themselves in Balıkesir, Pergamon, and the coastland of Mysia.[61] This is the same period in which the Ottoman Turks made a decisive step towards becoming the predominant power in Bithynia and north-western Asia Minor by gaining a victory over Byzantine forces in the battle of Bapheus near Nicomedia in July 1301 or 1302.[62] From the vantage point of Constantinople, this was just one of a whole series of abortive attempts to stem the tide of the Turkish westward advance, among them expeditions led by Michael VIII in person, his brother Despot John, his son Andronikos II, the general Alexios Philanthropenos, and Andronikos II's son Michael IX.[63] Under these circumstances, the Byzantine administration gradually broke down, defensive structures vanished, regional insurgencies occurred, indigenous groups were displaced, and the remaining rural and urban population sought to survive by way of local arrangements and agreements with the Turkish chiefs. In short, by the early 1300s various Turkish begs held sway over the entire western littoral of Asia Minor while the presence of Christian political entities was confined to some isolated Byzantine and Genoese outposts. The ill-fated campaign of the Catalan Grand Company under Roger de Flor in 1304 quickly derailed into looting and ransacking and failed to restore Byzantine control over the region. This marked the definitive end of any large-scale attempts to regain territories in western Asia Minor.[64]

---

60 Wittek, *Fürstentum Mentesche*, pp. 20–21; Lemerle, *L'émirat d'Aydin*, pp. 63–64; Feridun M. Emecen, *XVI. Asırda Manisa Kazâsı*, Türk Tarih Kurumu Yayınları, XIV. Dizi, 6¹, 2nd ed. (Ankara, 2013), pp. 17–19; Kesik, *Anadolu Türk Beylikleri*, pp. 243–45.
61 Elisabeth Zachariadou, 'The Emirate of Karasi and That of the Ottomans: Two Rival States', in *The Ottoman Emirate (1300–1389): Halcyon Days in Crete I, A Symposium Held in Rethymnon, 11–13 January 1991*, ed. by Elisabeth Zachariadou (Rethymnon: Crete University Press, 1993), pp. 225–36 (pp. 225–26); Michael IX withdrew from Pergamon via Kyzikos to Pegai on the Propontis coast in the summer of 1303: Pachymeres, IV, p. 426 (book XI, chapter 10); Donald M. Nicol, *The Last Centuries of Byzantium, 1261–1453*, 2nd edn (Cambridge: Cambridge University Press, 1993), p. 128; for the succession of rulers in this dynasty, see Johannes Mordtmann, 'Über das türkische Fürstengeschlecht der Karasi in Mysien', in *Sitzungsberichte der königlich-preußischen Akademie der Wissenschaften* (Berlin: Verlag der Preussischen Akademie der Wissenschaften, 1911), pp. 1–7.
62 Halil İnalcik, 'Osmān Ghāzī's Siege of Nicaea and the Battle of Bapheus', in *The Ottoman Emirate (1300–1389): Halcyon Days in Crete I, A Symposium Held in Rethymnon, 11–13 January 1991*, ed. by Elisabeth Zachariadou (Rethymnon: Crete University Press, 1993), pp. 77–99, argues for 27 July 1301 and locates the otherwise unknown site of Bapheus to the area of Yalak Ova at a distance of *c.* 30 km from Nicomedia. Rudi P. Lindner, 'Bapheus and Pelekanon', in *Identity and Identity Formation in the Ottoman World: A Volume of Essays in Honor of Norman Itzkowitz*, ed. by Baki Tezcan and Karl K. Barbir (Madison: University of Wisconsin Press, 2007), pp. 17–26, rejects İnalcik's dating on account of the chronological data mentioned by Pachymeres and wants the battle to have taken place in a location closer to the walls of Nicomedia.
63 Wittek, *Fürstentum Mentesche*, pp. 24–27; Nicol, *Last Centuries*, pp. 84–86, 123–24. For a detailed analysis of Philanthropenos's campaigns, see Angeliki Laiou, 'Some Observations on Alexios Philanthropenos and Maximos Planoudes', *Byzantine and Modern Greek Studies*, 4 (1978), 89–99.
64 Wittek, *Fürstentum Mentesche*, pp. 43–47; Nicol, *Last Centuries*, pp. 128–31.

Before long, the emirs of Aydın and Menteşe engaged in naval activities that threatened Byzantine and Latin domains in the Aegean and the Greek mainland. In about 1302/1303 they started attacking Rhodes and other islands off the shores of Asia Minor, such as Chios, Samos, and Karpathos.[65] This newly emerging menace caused Emperor Andronikos II in about 1308 to entrust the Genoese Zaccaria family of Phocaea with the protection of Chios.[66] Members of the same family increased their hold over the region by seizing Adramyttion and the port of Smyrna in 1326. The family's expansionism caused new conflicts with the Turks of Aydın and Saruhan.[67] Turkish naval raids were curbed by the conquest of Rhodes by the Knights Hospitaller and peaceful commercial relations between Italian merchants and the emirate of Menteşe, as seem to have been in place in 1311.[68] Yet in 1318 the alliance between Alfonso Fadrique, vicar general of the Catalan Duchy of Athens, and the Turks of Aydın and Menteşe ignited a new wave of military clashes in the region. Angevin-Catalan rivalries, Venetian diplomatic manoeuvres vacillating between Catalan and Turkish alliances in order to protect Venice's interests in the Duca di Candia, Negroponte, and other Aegean colonies, and Turkish threats to the Knights Hospitaller of Rhodes created an explosive mixture fuelling incessant piracy and warfare. The fleets of Aydın and Menteşe threatened or actually attacked places of crucial significance, such as Crete, Rhodes, Negroponte, Naxos, and raided numerous smaller islands.[69]

As we have seen, the political constellations in the Byzantine-Turkish frontier underwent profound changes in the period 1260–1320. The disintegration of the Seljuk sultanate under Mongol suzerainty led to an erosion of the bipolar axis Constantinople–Konya. It gave way to a multicentred network of localized small-size entities holding sway over a limited number of cities and their hinterland. By combining the habits of nomadic war bands, the political vocabulary and institutional tools of the Seljuk administration, religious traditions of Orthodox and popular Islam, and efficient mechanisms of accommodation and integration vis-à-vis the indigenous Christian population, the nascent lordships gained access to resources, created cohesion, and engaged in profitable political and commercial activities.

A remarkable side effect of these developments is the intensification of Christian-Muslim diplomacy. Ever since the early thirteenth century, the Seljuk sultanate of Rum, the Venetians, and Frankish entities in Latin Romania employed the Greek language and Byzantine chancery practices in their official communication.[70] In this volume, Daniele Baglioni discusses the use of Italian as a 'diplomatic and commercial

---

65 Pachymeres, IV, 377 (book X, chapter 29): 'τὸ Περσικὸν ὅσον ἦν ἐνδοτέρω ναυπηγησάμενον ταῖς Κυκλάσιν ἐπέχραον καὶ κακῶς ἐποίουν, καὶ τοῦτο μὲν Χίῳ, τοῦτο δὲ Σάμῳ καὶ Καρπάθῳ καὶ αὐτῇ Ῥόδῳ καὶ πολλαῖς σὺν αὐταῖς ἑτέραις οὐκ ὀλίγαις προσβάλλοντες ταῖς ναυσί, τὰς τέως ἐνῳκισμένας σχεδὸν ἀοικήτους εἰργάζοντο'. Zachariadou, *Trade and Crusade*, p. 6.
66 Zachariadou, *Trade and Crusade*, pp. 7–8, with an extensive discussion of chronological issues in n. 24.
67 Zachariadou, *Trade and Crusade*, pp. 8–9.
68 Zachariadou, *Trade and Crusade*, pp. 9–12.
69 Zachariadou, *Trade and Crusade*, pp. 13–16.
70 Alexander Beihammer, 'Multilingual Literacy and the Lusignan Court: the Cypriot Royal Chancery and its Byzantine Heritage', *Byzantine and Modern Greek Studies*, 35 (2011), 149–69.

lingua franca'. In the thirteenth and fourteenth century, Venice, Genoa, and Pisa increasingly employed Italian translations of letters and treaty documents in their diplomatic contacts with Muslim rulers in the Levant, North Africa, Persia, and the Crimea. Linguistic phenomena and formulaic patterns that made their first appearance in these documents paved the way for the development of an Italian language of diplomacy, which was widely used in the communication with the Ottoman Empire.

The Holy League and the Crusades in the Aegean

From 1325–27 onwards Venice made increasing efforts to forge an anti-Turkish league by approaching the papacy and King Philip VI and by entering negotiations with various regional powers, such as Byzantium, the Knights Hospitaller of Rhodes, Niccolò Sanudo of Naxos, and Bartolomeo Ghisi of Tenos and Mykonos.[71] The parties involved initially conceptualized the anti-Turkish coalition in the Aegean Sea as a preliminary operation to King Philip's crusade to Jerusalem. In late 1333, the allies began mounting their first attacks and, after co-opting King Hugh IV of Cyprus, they assembled their naval forces of about 40 galleys in May 1334 in Negroponte. While conducting operations along the coastal strip between Smyrna and Adramyttion they destroyed a fleet of the emirate of Karasi.[72] Just as in the case of Christian-Mamluk relations, however, warfare was by no means the only way to handle affairs in the Aegean. The Venetian Duca di Candia in Crete took pains to maintain its commercial links with the coastland of Anatolia and thus in 1331 signed a treaty with Emir Orhan of Menteşe, which most probably renewed and supplemented an earlier treaty dating to 1318.[73] Niccolò Sanudo of Naxos seems to have reached a separate treaty with the principalities of Aydın and Menteşe in March 1332, and similar agreements including the payment of tribute may be assumed for Negroponte and Bartolomeo Ghisi.[74]

In the 1340s and 1350s, western crusading efforts focused almost exclusively on the war against the Turkish emirates, culminating in the so-called crusade of Smyrna. In October 1344, a joint naval force supported by the papacy, Cyprus, the Hospitallers, and Venice seized the harbour of Smyrna from the legendary sea ghazi Umur Pasha, son of Mehmed ibn Aydın.[75] While the fighting with the Aydın Turks, who entrenched themselves in the upper town and citadel on Mount Pagos, dragged on, Humbert II, Dauphin of Viennois, launched a second campaign against the Turks of Smyrna in the summer of 1346. Although he failed to expel the Turks from the city, he helped solidify the league's position in the harbour district.[76] This and other achievements brought growing pressure on the Turks of Aydın so that after Umur's death in battle

---

71   Zachariadou, *Trade and Crusade*, p. 15 (first thoughts about an anti-Turkish league in 1325), pp. 21–22.
72   Zachariadou, *Trade and Crusade*, pp. 29–33.
73   Zachariadou, *Trade and Crusade*, pp. 18–20 and 187–89 (text of the treaty dated 13 April 1331).
74   Freddy Thiriet, *Régestes des délibérations du sénat de Venise concernant la Romanie*, 3 vols (Paris: Mouton, 1958–1961), I, pp. 24–25 (no. 11); Zachariadou, *Trade and Crusade*, pp. 22 and 25 with n. 93.
75   Zachariadou, *Trade and Crusade*, pp. 49–51; Carr, *Merchant Crusaders*, pp. 74–76.
76   Zachariadou, *Trade and Crusade*, pp. 51–53; Carr, *Merchant Crusaders*, pp. 76–77.

his brother and successor, Hızır of Ephesus, in August 1348 was ready to sign a disadvantageous peace treaty with the papacy and the Holy League.[77]

The Black Death, dwindling financial resources, the outbreak of a new war between Venice and Genoa, and frictions between Venice and the Hospital resulting from the latter's support for Genoese operations were factors that prevented Pope Clement VI and his allies from capitalizing on the gains of the period 1344–48.[78] Nevertheless, both he and his successor Innocent VI (1352–62) were eager to keep the league alive and to secure the financial and military resources required for the defence of Smyrna. The negotiations which the papal curia in Avignon conducted with the emissaries of King Hugh IV of Cyprus, the doge of Venice, and the master of the Hospital in the spring of 1350 came to the conclusion that they would not accept Hızır Beg's proposals for a definitive peace treaty, and in August of the same year the league was extended for another ten years with all parties being committed to assemble armed galleys in Negroponte.[79] Despite all obstacles, the papacy kept struggling for some level of naval presence in the Aegean and for the defence of Smyrna, be it by reminding the allies of their obligation to pay their annual subventions, by securing free passage for their ships, or by soliciting support from other powers, such as the Western Emperor Charles IV (1346/1355–78).[80] Meanwhile in 1354, Emir Orhan's son Süleyman and a number of ghazi chiefs subject to the Ottoman Turks gained a permanent foothold on the Gallipoli Peninsula and began to expand into Thrace.

In his case study of diplomatic relations between the Venetian Duca di Candia and the beyliks of Aydın and Menteşe in the period 1357–67, Charalampos Gasparis offers valuable insights into the procedures of one of the key members of the Holy League and a major stronghold of Venetian diplomacy in the Eastern Mediterranean. The surviving proceedings of the decisions of the Cretan Senate, which were made in consultation with the duke, his councillors, and a committee of elected *sapientes*, illustrate the local authorities' intricate manoeuvring vis-à-vis its multiple involvements in protecting commercial interests in the ports of Ayasuluk/Theologo and Miletus/Palatia, taking defensive measures against Turkish piracy, and partaking in the Holy League's crusading activities. The challenging period 1357–58, which preceded the renewal of the treaties with the emirates of Aydın and Menteşe in the summer and fall of 1358 respectively, provides rich evidence for Crete's strong position and the wide range of issues the Cretan officials were discussing with the emirates. The Cretan authorities successfully forced Menteşe to make concessions with regard to indemnities and the release of captives and included additional territories in the new treaty. When in August 1360 the fleet of the Holy League was dissolved, Venetian Crete kept maintaining two galleys for defensive purposes. The Revolt of St Titus (1363–67), however, brought about some radical changes in the relations between the island and the metropolitan city of Venice, and the role of Crete in local affairs was henceforth diminished.

---

77 Setton, *Papacy*, I, 216–17; Zachariadou, *Trade and Crusade*, pp. 54–56, 201–05 (text of Latin translation).
78 Setton, *Papacy*, I, pp. 218–20; Edbury, *Kingdom of Cyprus*, p. 159.
79 Setton, *Papacy*, I, p. 220.
80 Setton, *Papacy*, I, pp. 220–22, 227, 229–31.

By the early 1360s, the western and southern littoral of Asia Minor had become the key area of the Christian-Muslim contact and conflict zone in the Levant. The military operations in the first years of King Peter I's reign tally with the general strategic objective to bolster Christian military presence along the shores of Asia Minor. After King Constantine V (1344–62) of Cilician Armenia had ceded the coastal fortress of Korykos/Gorigos to King Peter in early 1360, Cypriot forces in August 1361 seized the Lycian port of Satalia (Antalya), which had been a major outlet and hub of trade of the Seljuk sultanate ever since the early thirteenth century, and threatened other strongholds farther east, such as 'Alā'iyya (Alanya), Monovgat, and later Anemourion.[81] While holding firm in Antalya until 1373, Cypriot troops engaged in conflicts with the former ruler of the city and emir of Tekke, Mübāriz al-Dīn Mehmed Bey, and the neighbouring emirates of Ḥāmid, Karāmān, and 'Alā'iyya.[82] Interestingly, this period saw not only a number of abortive attempts to expel the Cypriots from their recently gained foothold but also a joint Turkish naval attack on the northern shores of Cyprus and a Mamluk intervention calling for jihad against Cyprus.[83] Although this campaign did not materialize it is still noteworthy that the war in the southern Anatolian coastland led to the establishment of a supra-regional Muslim alliance encompassing all beyliks of the region and the Mamluk sultanate. Apparently, the Muslim lords attached outstanding commercial, political, and strategic significance to the ports of the region. Unlike the piracy in the Aegean, this was a war fought for securing spheres of influence and access to vital hubs and strongholds. On top of that, it offered an opportunity to the Mamluks to claim some sort of supreme leadership over the Muslim emirates in the Eastern Mediterranean, as their call for jihad clearly implies.

Byzantium, the Union of the Churches, and the Crusading Movement

Byzantium was barely affected by the fall of Acre in 1291. A decade earlier in 1281–82, Emperor Michael VIII had a diplomatic exchange with the Mamluk Sultan Qalāwūn (1279–90) about a peace treaty, which provided for the safety of ambassadors, trade licenses for merchants, and measures against piracy.[84] Considering the threat the emperor was facing at that time from the west, the Byzantine emperor also proposed

---

81 Atiya, *Crusade*, pp. 323–24 (Gorigos), pp. 325–27 (Adalia), p. 327 (submission but no occupation of Alaya and Monovgat); Hill, *A History of Cyprus*, II, pp. 320–22, 323 (Anamur); Housley, *Later Crusades*, p. 182; Kesik, *Anadolu Türk Beylikleri*, pp. 293–94 (significance of Antalya), p. 295.
82 Atiya, *Crusade*, pp. 327–30; Hill, *A History of Cyprus*, II, pp. 322–23; Kesik, *Anadolu Türk Beylikleri*, pp. 295–96; for Mehmed Beg's allies, see pp. 281–82 (Ḥāmid in the region of İsparta, Burdur, Eğridir), p. 276 (beylik of 'Alā'iyya/Alanya), pp. 352–53 (Karāmān).
83 Atiya, *Crusade*, p. 329; Hill, *A History of Cyprus*, II, p. 323; Kesik, *Anadolu Türk Beylikleri*, p. 296.
84 Franz Dölger, 'Der Vertrag des Sultans Qalā'ūn von Ägypten mit dem Kaiser Michael VIII. Palaiologos (1281)', in *Serta Monacensia F. Babinger zum 15. Januar 1961 als Festgruß dargebracht* (Leiden: Brill, 1952), pp. 60–79, reprinted in Franz Dölger, *Byzantinische Diplomatik: 20 Aufsätze zum Urkundenwesen der Byzantiner* (Speyer: Buch-Kunstverlag Ettal, 1956), pp. 225–44.

a military alliance against Charles of Anjou.[85] Although this collaboration did not materialize, Byzantine relations with the Mamluk sultanate were generally stable and peaceful, and any acts of aggression against Mamluk interests were out of the question for Constantinople. For the reign of Andronikos II (1282–1328) alone, the available sources attest to sixteen Byzantine embassies that were dispatched to Cairo for purposes that are not always documented but were certainly related to the assertion of amicable intentions, as loads of precious gifts insinuate, or to the protection of the churches and Christian communities of Jerusalem and Egypt.[86] Nevertheless, Byzantium was the main victim of the Turkish westward advance and from the 1290s onwards suffered great losses in territories, tax revenues, economic resources, and population. Byzantium, therefore, shared the concerns of the local Latin lords and the western powers operating in the Aegean and could be regarded a natural partner for leagues and joint military action.

At any rate, the disbandment of the Byzantine fleet, the decay of the armed forces, the economic depression, and the dwindling revenues from taxes and other sources of wealth significantly reduced the empire's potential to play an active role in such efforts.[87] On top of that, the Constantinopolitan government had serious reasons to be suspicious about the possibility of forging coalitions with western powers. The French-Angevin schemes aiming at a restoration of the Latin Empire of Constantinople were backed by Pope Clement V, who in the years 1306–10 excommunicated Emperor Andronikos II, declared the planned expedition a crusade rescuing Constantinople from an imminent Muslim threat, and secured the participation of Venice. The disastrous campaigns of the Catalan Grand Company in Asia Minor and mainland Greece in the years 1304–11 wrought havoc to the empire's provinces.[88] The situation was further aggravated by the two civil wars of the years 1321–28 and 1341–47 respectively. In these troublesome times of internecine feuding, the cohesion of the ruling dynasty and the aristocracy was heavily shattered, the economic and social structures of the provinces suffered severe damage, and vast territories in Macedonia, Thessaly, and Epirus were eventually seized by the Serbian Empire of Stephan Dušan (1331–55).[89]

Additional friction accrued from the schism between the Latin and the Greek Churches. The renunciation by Emperor Andronikos II of the ecclesiastical union which Michael VIII had proclaimed at the Council of Lyon (1274) and the subsequent ouster and condemnation of Patriarch John XI Bekkos (1275–82) and other pro-union dignitaries signalled a sharp turn in imperial politics towards a reconciliation with

---

85 Dölger, 'Vertrag', pp. 234–35.
86 Franz Dölger, *Regesten der Kaiserurkunden des oströmischen Reiches von 565–1453*, IV: *Regesten von 1282–1341* (Munich and Berlin: C. H. Beck, 1960), nos 2111 (1285, c. fall), 2240 (1302), 2289 (before 1305, July 24–1306, July 12), 2311 (1308, before April 5), 2317 (c. 1310), 2326 (1311–13), 2343 (before 1312, December 10), 2354 (1314, before April 13), 2368 (late 1315), 2377 (1316, March 26–1317, March), 2395 (1317, before November), 2413 (1319, February 22–1320, February 11), 2442 (1320, before May 4), 2536 (1325, before August 26), 2542 (1325, December 8–1326, November 26), 2563 (1327, before April 15).
87 Nicol, *Last Centuries*, pp. 107–10.
88 Setton, *Papacy*, I, pp. 163–69; Nicol, *Last Centuries*, pp. 116–17, 128–36, 137–38.
89 Nicol, *Last Centuries*, pp. 152–61, 185–208, 218–19 (territorial losses).

the Arsenite and Josephite factions in Byzantium and put a temporary end to all attempts of reunification.[90] This change of course had serious implications for the domestic situation of the Byzantine Church. Andronikos II was called to resolve highly contentious issues of canonical lawfulness and ecclesiastical leadership within the patriarchate of Constantinople and to placate the dissent of opposing factions that had resulted from his father's policy. Interestingly, the historian George Pachymeres establishes a direct link between the breakdown of the Byzantine administration in Asia Minor and the ecclesiastical affairs in the time of Michael VIII by having the emperor ascribe the reasons for the political decay to the overall lack of loyalty and cohesion caused by the ecclesiastical conflicts.[91]

It was not before 1326–27, amidst the turmoil of the first civil war, that Andronikos II and his Grand Logothete Theodore Metochites resumed contacts with the papal curia in Avignon and the French king Charles V.[92] The surviving documents—among them two original letters written in the Latin language by the imperial chancery, which are nowadays preserved in the National Archive of Paris—make plain that the Byzantine side was interested in improving its relations with the papacy and the French crown by resuming talks about the ecclesiastical union but was also concerned about the practical impediments resulting from the rejective stance of the empire's subjects and the unrest of the civil war. Pope John XXII dispatched the Dominican friar Benedict of Cumae to initiate negotiations about the union, but the fear of an anti-unionist backlash seems to have prevailed in Constantinople. The papacy wanted Byzantium to be part of the anti-Turkish league that began to take shape by that time, but it considered the union of the churches a necessary precondition for that.[93] Things were further complicated by the unbridgeable gap separating the standpoints held by the two sides. In the pope's eyes, the union was to be achieved by the Greek Church's renouncing its heretical doctrines and by returning to the fold of the Church of Rome. According to the views prevailing in Byzantium at that time the union could only materialize through an ecumenical council that was to find a solution for all issues separating the two sides. Moreover, the harsh reactions to Michael VIII's policy had made plain that the union could not be imposed by force.

Another important factor that came to bear in this period was the fact that the Byzantine imperial government began to engage in a policy of peaceful relations and stabilization with the recently established Muslim-Turkish principalities of western Asia Minor. Soon after Andronikos III's (1328–41) coup against his grandfather Andronikos II, the new emperor and his Grand Domestikos John Kantakouzenos in June 1329 had their first direct, yet inconclusive, encounter with the Ottoman Turks in the battle of Pelekanon at the southern shores of the Gulf of Nicomedia (near modern Bayramoğlu and Gebze) in a bid to regain Bursa, which had been seized

---

90 Nicol, *Last Centuries*, pp. 94–100.
91 Pachymeres, II, pp. 632–35 (book VI, chapter 29).
92 Dölger, *Regesten*, IV, nos 2556–57 (1326, before August 20), 2564–66 (1327, c. May); Nicol, *Last Centuries*, p. 173.
93 Nicol, *Last Centuries*, pp. 173–74.

by the Ottomans in 1326, and to assist Nicaea.[94] Apparently in order to solidify his strategic position in western Asia Minor, Andronikos III at about the same time reached a peace agreement with Demirhan of Karasi.[95] This course of action paralleled the simultaneous efforts of Italian local lords in the Aegean to negotiate their own agreements with the Turks and was by no means a Byzantine peculiarity.

Despite these efforts, the Ottomans in the following year increased their pressure on the remaining Byzantine possessions in Bithynia by putting Nicomedia under siege. With the aid of his fleet, Andronikos III in 1330 and 1331 was still able to reach the city and the surrounding villages in person with his troops and to reinforce the local population with grain supplies. Yet he was cautious in engaging in a new battle with the Ottomans and opted for a peace agreement with their leader Orhan, which was publicly celebrated through an exchange of ambassadors, gifts, and mutual gestures of respect.[96] This event epitomizes a change of attitude which appeared within the Byzantine ruling elite perhaps in the wake of the 1328 coup. Efforts of ousting the Turks from the western coastland by military means gave way to a strategy of accommodation. The imperial government came to acknowledge the Turkish rulers exerting political authority over former Byzantine provinces as an irreversible fait accompli and expected to have some benefits from the new state of affairs.

While the papacy, Venice, and their allies were negotiating the details of the anti-Turkish league, the Byzantine government was preoccupied with military operations against the Genoese Zaccaria and Cattaneo families so as to restore its rule over the islands of Chios and Lesbos and to extend its influence in the region of Phocaea on the opposite mainland.[97] In 1329 the Zaccaria lords suffered a heavy blow: they lost Chios to the Byzantines and were expelled from the port of Smyrna by the Turks of Aydın. Subsequently, Andronikos III was acknowledged as overlord of Phocaea, but he had to ward off Genoese attempts to regain the islands of Chios and Lesbos.[98] As a result, just at the time when the Holy League scored its first

---

94 Nicol, *Last Centuries*, pp. 159–61 (final phase of the first civil war) and pp. 169–70; Lindner, 'Bapheus and Pelekanon', pp. 21–26, who interprets the battle as a 'tactical victory for Andronicus', which did not bring him any advantages in terms of his military goals, and 'a defeat for nomadic warfare'.
95 Dölger, *Regesten*, IV, no. 2727; John Kantakouzenos, *Historiarum libri IV*, ed. Ludwig Schopen, Corpus Scriptorum Historiae Byzantinae, 23–25, 3 vols (Bonn, 1828–1832), I, p. 339 (book II, chapter 5): 'τὸ δ' ἔτι τούτων αἰτιώτερον, ἵνα τὸν Φρυγίας ἄρχοντα Ταμηρχάνην τὸν τοῦ Γιαξῆ ταῖς κατὰ τὸν Ἑλλήσποντον ἐφαις πόλεσιν ἐπικείμενον οὔσαις ὑπηκόοις βασιλεῖ, πρὸς συμβάσεις πείσῃ χωρῆσαι'.
96 Kantakouzenos, I, pp. 446–47 (book II, chapter 24), pp. 459–60 (book II, chapter 26): 'συνέβησάν τε καὶ ἔθεντο σπονδὰς εἰρηνικάς, ὥστε Ὀρχάνην βασιλέως εἶναι φίλον καὶ τὰς τὴν ἕω πόλεις, ὅσαι ἔτι ἦσαν ὑπήκοοι Ῥωμαίοις, ἀδικεῖν μηδέν'; Dölger, *Regesten*, IV, nos 2762–63 (autumn of 1330); a short chronicle written in about 1352 dates the treaty with Orhan to August 1333 and mentions a tribute of 12,000 *hyperpyra* in exchange for the cities of Mesothynia between Nicomedia and Constantinople: *Die byzantinischen Kleinchroniken*, I: *Einleitung und Text*, ed. by Peter Schreiner, Corpus Fontium Historiae Byzantinae 12/1 (Vienna: Österreichische Akademie der Wissenschaften, 1975), p. 80 (Chron. 8. 27); Nicol, *Last Centuries*, p. 170.
97 Nicol, *Last Centuries*, pp. 171–72 and pp. 172–74 (the anti-Turkish league); see also Dölger, *Regesten*, IV, no. 2792, mentioning a message of Andronikos III conveyed in about 1333 by two Dominican friars to Pope John XXII in Avignon concerning possible negotiations about the union of the churches.
98 Zachariadou, p. 16; Nicol, *Last Centuries*, pp. 171–72.

victory off the shores of Asia Minor Byzantium intensified its rapprochement policy towards the Turks by means of new peace agreements. In the fall of 1335 Andronikos III arrived in Phocaea to fend off Domenico Cattaneo's attack on Lesbos and concluded a treaty with Saruhan Beg. On this occasion, the sons of Mehmed of Aydın, Hızır, Süleymanshāh, and Umur, joined the agreement while the latter had a four-day meeting with John Kantakouzenos at Kara Burun. This encounter, an unprecedented act of intimacy in Byzantine-Turkish diplomacy at the time, prepared the ground for an unwavering brotherhood of arms between the two political leaders and had lasting consequences for Byzantine-Turkish relations in the Aegean up to 1354.[99]

Despite the fact that both Andronikos II and his grandson Andronikos III were married to princesses of respected Italian noble families, Yolanda-Eirene of Montferrat and Anna of Savoy respectively, the two emperors had no special sympathy for the cause of the union.[100] While the time of the civil war 1341–47 hardly allowed any consistent policy in this respect, John VI Kantakouzenos (1347–54) was equally reluctant to make any concessions to the papacy.[101] As a result, the period 1324–54 can be considered a time of stagnation in Byzantine-papal relations, in which both sides merely entrenched themselves in their traditional positions. Andronikos III was slightly more willing than his grandfather to resume the negotiations, and his military successes in the Aegean Sea and mainland Greece made him an attractive partner. Since 1332 the papacy sought to include him into the anti-Turkish league, yet the imperial government handled these contacts with the utmost reticence and secrecy, as is illustrated, for instance, by the messages conveyed to the pope by Dominican missionaries in 1333, the Venetian Stephan Dandolo in early 1337, or by the secret mission of Barlaam of Calabria to Pope Benedict XII in 1339.[102]

During the civil war, Anna of Savoy solicited help from potential western allies and was ready to denounce her opponent John Kantakouzenos for having Turkish mercenaries in his employ. In the summer of 1343, she also declared her submission to Pope Clement VI on behalf of the other members of the Constantinopolitan regency for her underage son John V.[103] While the Holy League achieved its greatest victories

---

99 Kantakouzenos, I, pp. 479–80 (book II, chapter 29): 'βασιλεὺς δὲ πρεσβείαν πρὸς Σαρχάνην πέμψας, ὃς ἦρχε τῆς ἕω τῆς κατὰ τὴν Φώκαιαν, σπονδὰς ἔθετο πρὸς αὐτὸν καὶ συμμαχίαν, ὥστε Σαρχάνην μὲν ἐπικουρίαν βασιλεῖ παρασχεῖν πεζήν τε καὶ ναυτικὴν πρὸς τὴν τῆς Φωκαίας καὶ Μιτυλήνης πολιορκίαν. Kantakouzenos, I, p. 481 (book II, chapter 29): διατρίβοντί τε κατὰ τὴν Φώκαιαν βασιλεῖ οἱ τοῦ Ἀϊτίνη παῖδες, ὃς ἦν σατράπης Ἰωνίας, Χετὴρ καὶ Ἀμοὺρ [...] καὶ τρίτος Σουλαϊμάσας ὠνομασμένος, προσῆλθόν τε κατὰ φιλίαν καὶ προσεκύνησαν ἐπηγγείλαντο εὖνοι ἔσεσθαι καὶ φίλοι βασιλεῖ'; Nikephoros Gregoras, Byzantina Historia, ed. by Ludwig Schopen, Corpus Scriptorum Historiae Byzantinae, 38–39, 2 vols (Bonn: Weber, 1829–1830), I, p. 538 (book XI, chapter 4). For the events and their political background, see Lemerle, L'émirat d'Aydin, pp. 106–15; Dölger, Regesten, IV, nos 2820–21; Nicol, Last Centuries, pp. 174–75; Christopher Wright, The Gattilusio Lordships and the Aegean World 1355–1463, The Medieval Mediterranean, 100 (Leiden and Boston: Brill, 2014), pp. 36–37.
100 Nicol, Last Centuries, pp. 151–52, 167.
101 Nicol, Last Centuries, pp. 234–35.
102 Dölger, Regesten, IV, nos 2792 (1333, to Pope John XXII), 2830 (before 1337 January 17, to Pope Benedict XII); Nicol, Last Centuries, pp. 174, 211.
103 Nicol, Last Centuries, pp. 198–99.

by conquering Smyrna and strengthening its position in the western coastland of Asia Minor, the papacy was certainly keen to have Byzantium on its side, but John Kantakouzenos pursued his own goals by relying on Turkish mercenaries in his domestic conflict with the Constantinopolitan regency and by maintaining his alliances with the Turks of Aydın and the Ottomans.[104] Like his predecessors, he insisted on the idea of discussing all differences in an ecumenical council. The emperor had frequent diplomatic contacts with Pope Clement VI and after the latter's death even with his successor Innocent VI, but he never went beyond expressing his interest in the union and his good will for negotiations in very general terms.[105]

The situation radically changed with the rise to power of John V in late 1354. He and a faction of pro-Latin dignitaries adopted a different approach to the issue of the ecclesiastical union and initiated a policy that aimed at securing the greatest possible support of western military forces and a potential crusade in exchange for the submission of the Byzantine emperor to the pope. The negotiations went through different stages until John V's journey to Rome and conversion in October 1369.[106] Irrespective of John V's personal convictions regarding the Latin Church, there were a number of factors that made this change of attitude possible. With the Ottoman advance from the Gallipoli Peninsula into Thrace and the Marica Valley, Constantinople was at risk to be encircled by the Turks and to lose its independence.[107] The Hesychast controversy and the fact that the Church of Constantinople in 1351 fully adopted the Athonite views of Hesychasm and its theological foundation laid by Gregory Palamas as official doctrine marginalized or forced into exile numerous anti-Palamite intellectuals and aristocrats.[108] This, in turn, brought about a merging with originally separate pro-Latin tendencies and an overall strengthening of pro-western and pro-unionist attitudes among Byzantine dissidents in Constantinople but also in some Latin-held regions, which served them as places of refuge. The kingdom of Cyprus with its Greek majority population and a Greek ecclesiastical organization recognizing the supreme authority and jurisdiction of the Latin hierarchs provided an ideal environment for a certain amount of Greek-Latin theological cross-fertilization and pro-Latin sympathies of intellectuals adhering to the Byzantine tradition. The Byzantine historian Nikephoros Gregoras's report on the island's affairs, which the author ascribed to the semi-fictional character of his student Agathangelos, and Gregoras's letter to King Hugh IV of Cyprus, which praises the manifold possibilities

---

104 Nicol, *Last Centuries*, pp. 202–04.
105 Franz Dölger, *Regesten der Kaiserurkunden des oströmischen Reiches von 565–1453*, V: (Schluss) *Regesten von 1341–1453*, unter verantwortlicher Mitarbeit von Peter Wirth (Munich and Berlin: C. H. Beck, 1965), nos 2930 (1347, September 22), 2937 (1348, spring), 2942–43 (1349, c. spring), 2957 (late 1349–before 1350, February 13), 2961 (1350, spring), 2965 (1350, late summer), 3007 (late 1352, Pope Clement VI died before receiving the letter, which was responded by his successor Innocent VI on 1353, March 15), 3010 (1353, summer); Nicol, *Last Centuries*, p. 235.
106 Oskar Halecki, *Un empereur de Byzance à Rome. Vingt ans de travail pour l'union des églises et pour la defense de l'empire d'Orient 1355–1375*, Travaux historiques de la société des sciences et des lettres de Varsovie, 8 (Warsaw: Wydane z Zasiłku Wydziału Nauki, 1930; repr. London: Variorum, 1972), pp. 31–212.
107 Nicol, *Last Centuries*, pp. 241–42, 261–63.
108 Nicol, *Last Centuries*, pp. 231–34.

of unhinged intellectual exchange and the multicultural character of the royal court, are an immediate expression of these experiences.[109]

As Alexis Torrence points out, in the years between the 1340s and the 1370s the island of Cyprus was considered from the viewpoint of Byzantine theology an outpost of anti-Palamite opposition. This is not to say that the Greek church of Cyprus unanimously adopted anti-Palamite views. There were some renowned representatives of the Hesychast movement of Cypriot origin, such as Gregory of Sinai (d. 1346), and the surviving documents insinuate that the majority of the Greek clergy was rather confused by the intricacies of the theological argumentation. On the other hand, there certainly was a strong anti-Palamite network which consisted of Cypriot theologians, prominent exiles, and Constantinopolitan dignitaries maintaining correspondence with the former. Torrence aptly characterizes the situation on the island as a 'microcosm of a larger intellectual tug-of-war'. A number of pro-Palamite letters, like that of Joseph Kalothetos to Cypriot monks (1346–47), of Patriarch Kallistos I to the Cypriot clergy and nobility (1361–62), and of John Kantakouzenos to Bishop John of Karpasia (1370–71), exemplify various ways in which representatives of the Church of Constantinople reacted to and sought to come to terms with the spread of anti-Palamite theological thought on the island.

What were the consequences of the prevalence of the hesychast dogma for anti-Palamite intellectuals and their relations with the Church of Constantinople? Charles Yost spots the contours of a profound spiritual crisis which proponents of the anti-hesychast position went through in the years after the synod of 1351. Specifically, he discusses the case of John Kyparissiotes, who after a protracted period of exile in Cyprus ended his life as member of the retinue of Pope Gregory XI (1371–78) in 1378, and that of Manuel Kalekas, who died in 1410 as a Dominican friar on the island of Lesbos. Their opposition to Palamism led both personalities to adopt pro-Latin attitudes with Kalekas making even a step further to full conversion. Yost sees a key feature of their intellectual development in their ecclesiological approaches towards the Church of Constantinople and distinguishes between a pre-crisis mentality of John Kyparissiotes and a crisis mentality in Manuel Kalekas's reasoning. The former rejects the legality of the Palamites and criticizes the Constantinopolitan hierarchy but refrains from separating the Church of Constantinople from the universal Church of God. As a result, he does not deny his ancestral church, as long as a few people

---

109 Agathangelos's report: Nikephoros Gregoras, *Historiae Byzantinae libri postremi*, ed. by Immanuel Bekker, Corpus Scriptorum Historiae Byzantinae, 48 (Bonn: Weber, 1855), pp. 27–39. Gregoras's letter: Pietro L. M. Leone, 'L'encomio di Niceforo Gregora per il re di Cipro (Ugo IV di Lusignano)', *Byzantion*, 51 (1981), 211–24. Recent English translations of both texts: George Boustronios, *A Narrative of the Chronicle of Cyprus 1459–1489*, trans. by Nicholas Coureas, together with an Anthology of Greek Texts of the Fourteenth and Fifteenth Centuries Relating to Cyprus, trans. by. Hans Pohlsanders, Texts and Studies in the History of Cyprus, 51 (Nicosia: Cyprus Research Centre, 2005), pp. 231–38; for the character of Agathangelos and his function in Gregoras's work, see Foteini Kolovou, *Der gefangene Gelehrte und sein nächtlicher Gast. Geschichtskonzeption und Phantasie in Nikephoros Gregoras' Rhomaike Historia*, Sitzungsberichte der Sächsischen Akademie der Wissenschaften zu Leipzig, Philologisch-historische Klasse, Bd. 141/4 (Leipzig - Stuttgart: Verlag der Sächsischen Akademie der Wissenschaften zu Leipzig/Steiner, 2016).

within this church uphold the true apostolic and patristic tradition. Kalekas, instead, argues that the adoption of the Palamite heresy makes plain that the Church of Constantinople has lost its magisterial inerrancy and thus can no longer be identified with the catholic church. Kalekas saw himself forced to leave his church so as to find the true Church of Christ in the Church of Rome. In sum, while western efforts to organize a new crusade and Byzantine needs for western military aid generated a considerable amount of pressure on the Byzantine ruling elite to adopt pro-Latin views and to make concessions to the Church of Rome, the repression of dissidents in the wake of the victory of hesychasm brought even more Latinophile attitudes to the foreground. A considerable group of influential theologians began to rethink their relations with Rome and developed new ecclesiological concepts in their definitions of the true church.

With John V's takeover, previously marginalized dignitaries gained more influence and were ready to collaborate with Latin hierarchs in articulating a new pro-union policy in order to gain the support of the papacy. In the late 1350s and 1360s this trend coincided with fresh efforts made by the popes Innocent VI and Urban V to revive the Holy League, secure the previously gained strongholds, and organize a new crusade against the Muslim threat. The earliest explicit manifestation of this new policy is John V's famous *horkōmotikon chrysoboullon*, i.e., 'chrysobull accompanied by an oath', to Pope Innocent VI dating from 15 December 1355.[110] Elusive prospects of a Byzantine-Latin cooperation within a common crusade project had finally given way to an unvarnished call for western military support. In exchange, the imperial government was ready to offer unprecedented concessions, propositions, and guarantees regarding the emperor's and his family's submission to the papacy as well as a gradual Latinization of all Byzantine subjects. In the course of the ensuing diplomatic contacts, which went on until late 1357, high-ranking representatives of the Church of Rome, such as the Carmelite friar Peter Thomas, the Dominican William Conti, and Archbishop Paul of Smyrna, sought to propagate the ecclesiastical union and to promote the emperor's conversion, but John V and his proponents were not yet strong enough to make their viewpoints public and lacked the consent of the ecclesiastical leadership.[111] Pope Innocent VI, on his part, focused his efforts on reconstituting the anti-Turkish league and consolidating the Christian position in Smyrna and other places of western Asia Minor, as Peter Thomas's activities as apostolic legate in the East or the attack on Lampsakos in 1359 illustrate.[112]

Constantinople resumed the negotiations with the papal curia when Urban V's preparations for the planned crusade came to a head in 1363–64.[113] An important side effect of these endeavours, which had an immediate impact on the Byzantine attitudes towards the papal plans, was the fact that the 'Green Count' Amadeus VI

---

110 Halecki, pp. 31–52; Franz Dölger, *Regesten*, V, no. 3052; Setton, *Papacy*, I, pp. 225–26; Nicol, *Last Centuries*, pp. 258–60.
111 Nicol, *Last Centuries*, pp. 260–61.
112 Nicol, *Last Centuries*, p. 261.
113 Nicol, *Last Centuries*, p. 263.

of Savoy (1343–83), the son of a half-brother of Empress Anna and thus a cousin of John V, took the cross and sought to direct the main thrust of the planned campaign against the Turks of Asia Minor.[114] Demetrios Kydones, who after a period of exile had resumed a leading position at the imperial court, and other pro-Latin dignitaries in Constantinople worked towards the same direction. King Peter I's abortive attack on Alexandria and John V's trip to King Louis the Great of Hungary (1342–82) in 1366, which brought no results in terms of military aid and ended with the emperor being trapped in the border fortress of Vidin, must have had disenchanting effects on the Constantinopolitan government.[115] However, the conquest of Gallipoli by the joint forces of Amadeus of Savoy and Francesco Gattilusio of Lesbos on 23 August 1366 caused the proponents of a Latinophile policy among the ruling elite to entertain fresh hopes.[116] As his speech to the senate of Constantinople regarding Amadeus's conquest of Gallipoli demonstrates, by that time Demetrios Kydones had developed a full-blown strategy of cooperation with western powers. It relied upon the premises of cultural and religious affinities and shared interests in fighting back the Muslim threat. Thus, he persuaded the Constantinopolitan leadership to openly side with Amadeus by opening the city gates to his fleet on 2 September 1366.[117] Nevertheless, the content and context of Kydones's speech also indicates that there must have been a strong opposition to this view, voicing serious concerns about the prospects of obtaining western help and opting instead for an appeasement policy towards the Ottoman Sultan Murād I and the ghazi chiefs in Thrace. After all, seeking alliances with the Turks, using them as mercenaries against internal and external foes, and securing some degree of stability by paying tribute to the Turkish rulers was a well-established practice since the early days of Andronikos III and his Grand Domestikos John Kantakouzenos and was one of the factors leading to Kantakouzenos's victory in the civil war of 1341–47, as Alexander Beihammer points out in his chapter. Just as in the question of the union of the churches, with respect to the Turkish threat, too, the Byzantine ruling elite had developed different attitudes and in the years prior to and following the Alexandrian crusade it was by no means foreseeable whether a pro-Latin or a pro-Ottoman approach was the right way to move forward. A significant difference between Byzantine and Latin attitudes towards the Muslim threat lies in the fact that Byzantium looked back on a long tradition of interacting and living side-by-side with the Turks of Asia Minor. Many preferred the prospects of a peaceful coexistence on the basis of treaties and mutual recognition over a costly and risky life-and-death struggle with uncertain results.

---

114   Halecki, pp. 138–45; Nicol, *Last Centuries*, pp. 263, 265.
115   Halecki, pp. 111–37.
116   Halecki, 145–51; Eugene L. Cox, *The Green Count of Savoy: Amedeus VI and the Transalpine Savoy in the Fourteenth Century* (Princeton: Princeton University Press, 1967), pp. 206–21.
117   Demetrios Kydones, 'Oratio pro subsidio Latinorum, Ῥωμαίοις συμβουλευτικός, ἐγράφη δὲ ἀποδημήσαντος ἐν Ῥώμῃ τοῦ κυροῦ Ἰωάννου τοῦ Παλαιολόγου ἐπὶ τῆς πατριαρχίας τοῦ κυροῦ Φιλοθέου', in *Patrologia Graeca* 154, ed. by Jacques Paul Migne (Paris, 1866), coll. 961–1003. For a recent analysis of the speech, see Judith R. Ryder, *The Career and Writings of Demetrios Kydones: A Study of Fourteenth-Century Byzantine Politics, Religion and Society*, The Medieval Mediterranean, 85 (Leiden: Brill, 2010), pp. 57–81.

Sebastian Kolditz's analysis of John V's visit to Rome elucidates the manifold challenges the imperial government was facing in its attempt to find a middle ground between its efforts to forge a firm alliance with the papacy and the need to come to terms with the aforementioned opposition groups within Byzantium. The commonly held opinion that John's 'conversion' has to be seen as private act of an individual following his own conscience is quite anachronistic and runs counter to the fact that John V continued to be revered by both his contemporaries and later historical memory as a purely Orthodox emperor. Kolditz draws a clear distinction between the original intentions of the imperial government and the plans the pope and his representatives sought to implement in this matter. While John from 1355 onwards was apparently prepared to show obedience to the papacy in exchange for western military aid, Pope Urban V persistently rejected the Byzantine proposal of an ecumenical synod and insisted instead on the emperor's personal conversion by inviting him to Rome (April 1365) and demanding a profession of faith (July 1366). The compromise solution achieved in October 1369 during John V's stay in Rome was a two-step procedure consisting of a public ceremony of subordination, in which John was led at the pope's hand into the Lateran Church, and a confidential declaration of conversion. The emperor complied with the core elements of the pope's demand on the basis of the formulae agreed with Demetrios Kydones, but the act was carried out in the seclusion of a cardinal's private chamber and in the presence of low-ranking Byzantine witnesses. Furthermore, the emperor refused to abjure the errors of the Greeks, as a proper conversion would have required. Apparently, 'binary concepts of exclusive belonging' do not apply in this case, and John V made his declaration without terminating his adherence to his ancestral church.

No doubt, the Eastern Mediterranean in the years 1291–1365 was a highly complex world. The papacy, the Italian maritime republics, and the leading dynasties of Latin Europe dominated it only partially. They may have exerted strong spiritual, political, and economic influence and they may have called the tune in matters of war and crusading. Yet, there also was a cluster of local powers, among them Byzantium and the Lusignan kingdom of Cyprus, which despite all dependencies and allegiances asserted some degree of autonomy and insisted on their cultural, religious and political particularities. They were forced to withstand western expansionist tendencies, and their proximity to the Anatolian beyliks and the Mamluk sultanate often prompted them to take a different stance from their European coreligionists. A strong faction within the Byzantine elite opted for ecclesiastical independence and a policy of accommodation vis-à-vis the Turks, whereas the papacy, western powers, and their domestic supporters urged for union and a Greek-Latin coalition against the common foe. Contrarily, when a majority of western powers preferred the maintenance of a peaceful status quo, King Peter I mounted a foolhardy attack on Egypt's main port. It is these multifaceted tensions and interdependencies between supra-regional and local factors that make the region's historical development so diverse and unpredictable.

Part I

From Acre to Alexandria – The Politics and Ecology of Crusading

MIKE CARR

Cyprus and the Crusades between the Fall of Acre and the Reign of Peter I

The fall of Acre to the Mamluks in 1291 had enormous repercussions for the kingdom of Cyprus.[1] The island became the only Latin-ruled territory in the south-eastern Mediterranean, which meant that it was both a safe-haven for refugees fleeing from the crusader states and also an important launch pad for new crusading campaigns. As a consequence, the Lusignan kings were once again placed at the forefront of the crusading movement and thus became embroiled in the increasingly complex economic, religious and political conflicts of the Aegean and the Eastern Mediterranean. This chapter will focus on the relations of the kings of Cyprus with the main Latin crusading powers, that is the papacy, France, Venice, Genoa and the Hospitallers, as well as with the main Muslim targets of the crusades during this period, namely the Turkish beyliks of Anatolia and the Mamluks of Egypt and Greater Syria. Particular attention will be paid to the relationship between Cyprus and the crusading projects to recover the Holy Land, as well as to the campaigns waged against the Turks in the Aegean, such as the contributions of King Hugh IV to the naval leagues of 1332–34 and 1343–52, as well as to his victories against the Turkish beyliks of Hamid and Karaman in the 1330s and 1340s.[2] The importance of Cypriot agents at the papal court will also be discussed. They petitioned the pope for support in forming a new crusade, sometimes in league with the Venetians and Hospitallers, and also for other privileges ranging from indulgences to trade licences.[3]

---

1 Anne Gilmore Bryson, 'The Fall of Acre, 1291, and Its Effect on Cyprus', in *Acre and Its Falls: Studies in the History of a Crusader City*, ed. by John France (Leiden: Brill, 2018), pp. 116–29.
2 For these events, see Mike Carr, *Merchant Crusaders in the Aegean, 1291–1352* (Woodbridge: Boydell & Brewer, 2015), esp. chapters 3–4; Nicholas Coureas, *The Latin Church in Cyprus: 1313–1378* (Nicosia: Cyprus Research Centre, 2010), esp. chapter 2; Peter W. Edbury, *The Kingdom of Cyprus and the Crusades, 1191–1374* (Cambridge: Cambridge University Press, 1991), esp. chapters 6–7.
3 For more on trade licences in this context, see Mike Carr, 'Between the Papal Court and the Islamic World: Famagusta and Cypriot Merchants in the Fourteenth Century', in *Famagusta Maritima: Mariners, Merchants, Pilgrims and Mercenaries*, ed. by Michael J. K. Walsh (Leiden: Brill, 2019), pp. 113–27.

Mike Carr • University of Edinburgh

Crusading, Society, and Politics in the Eastern Mediterranean in the Age of King Peter I of Cyprus, ed. by Alexander Beihammer and Angel Nicolaou-Konnari, MEDNEX, 10 (Turnhout, 2022), pp. 109–119
© BREPOLS PUBLISHERS   10.1484/M.MEDNEX-EB.5.128461

The fall of Acre in 1291, and subsequent collapse of Latin-Christian territories in the Levant, signified a major milestone in the history of the crusades. From this moment very few great campaigns led by the kings of Western Europe would materialise, and the Crusader States would never be recovered. In fact, the fall of Acre did more than signify the end of the great crusades to the Holy Land; it signified a complete reordering of the geo-political situation in the Eastern Mediterranean. By the 1290s the Mamluks were the undisputed masters of the seaboards of Syria and Egypt, while further north, the Turkish beyliks had begun to expand towards the western Anatolian coast at the expense of the Byzantines. By the turn of the fourteenth century the only Christian outpost on the Eastern Mediterranean coast was the embattled state of Cilician Armenia, hemmed in by the Mamluks to the south and the Karaman Turks to the north. Cyprus, which lay less than 100 miles from the coasts of Syria, Turkish-held regions of Anatolia and Cilician Armenia thus became an important bastion of Catholic Christendom in the East and integral for any future crusade. Even in the last days of the Crusader States, the importance of Cyprus had been evident, both as a base from which to supply the beleaguered garrisons on the Levantine coast, and as a refuge for refugees fleeing the Mamluk advances. These included Frankish nobles and Arabic-speaking Christians from *Outremer*, as well as members of the military orders and other religious communities who set up their headquarters on the island.[4] Cyprus also had symbolic importance for the crusading movement, especially as the Lusignan monarchs remained titular kings of Jerusalem and many honorific titles pertaining to the Crusader States were preserved amongst the members of their family and other prominent nobles on the island.[5]

Immediately after the fall of Acre, Pope Nicholas IV called upon the churchmen, rulers and tacticians of Latin Christendom to formulate plans for the successful recovery of the Holy Land. This resulted in a number of treatises written by the so-called crusade theorists in the last decade of the thirteenth and the first decades of the fourteenth century. As is to be expected, Cyprus featured heavily in the works of the theorists, who recognised its importance for a forthcoming crusade. In particular, many advocated a commercial blockade against Mamluk Egypt, which would be used as a precursor to a major military assault.[6] The aim was to starve the Mamluks of war materials, especially metal, pitch and timber for ships, as well as slave boys, who would be used as soldiers in the Mamluk army.[7] Because of the position of Cyprus on

---

4   David Jacoby, 'Refugees from Acre in Famagusta around 1300', in *The Harbour of all this Sea and Realm: Crusader to Venetian Famagusta*, ed. by Michael J. K. Walsh, Tamás Kiss, and Nicholas Coureas (Budapest: Central European University Press, 2014), pp. 51–67.
5   Edbury, *Kingdom of Cyprus*, pp. 107–9.
6   Antony Leopold, *How to Recover the Holy Land: The Crusade Proposals of the Late Thirteenth and Early Fourteenth Centuries* (Aldershot: Ashgate, 2000), pp. 105–36; Mike Carr, 'Policing the Sea: Enforcing the Papal Embargo on Trade with "Infidels"', in *Merchants, Pirates, and Smugglers. Criminalization, Economics and the Transformation of the Maritime World (1200–1600)*, ed. Philipp Höhn et al. (Frankfurt: Campus Verlag, 2019), pp. 329–41.
7   For the sale of slaves to the Mamluks, see Hannah Barker, *That Most Precious Merchandise: The Mediterranean Trade in Black Sea Slaves, 1260–1500* (University of Pennsylvania Press, 2019). For war materials, see David Jacoby, 'The supply of war materials to Egypt in the crusader period', in David Jacoby, *Commercial Exchange Across the Mediterranean* (Aldershot: Ashgate, 2005), no. 2, pp. 102–32.

the shipping routes between Egypt and the Black Sea, from where most slaves were brought, and between Egypt and Western Europe, from where most ship-building materials and arms were exported, the Lusignan kings of the island were considered as the most suitable people to intercept illicit trade with the Mamluks, such as was argued by two of the best-informed crusade theorists of the fourteenth century: the Hospitaller Grand Master Fulk de Villaret, writing in c. 1306, and Marino Sanudo in a copy of his *Liber Secretorum* written in 1321.[8] Others went even further and suggested that Cyprus should be the base from where a new crusade would be launched, such as the king of Cyprus himself, Henry II (r. 1285–1306, 1310–24), who suggested this in his treatise of 1311–12.[9]

As well as being considered as an important base for upholding the embargo, crusade strategists also recognised that Cyprus, along with Cilician Armenia, was seriously threatened by the Mamluks and thus several campaigns were proposed with the joint aim of enforcing the papal blockade while at the same time defending Cyprus and Armenia. These two objectives would become closely intertwined in the form of a *passagium particulare*, which was conceived as a small-scale preliminary campaign that would pave the way for a larger expedition, or *passagium generale*, to liberate the Holy Land. One naval expedition which had elements of a *passagium particulare* sailed to the Eastern Mediterranean in 1292 under the command of the Genoese Manuel Zaccaria. It was designed to enforce the embargo and bring aid to Cyprus and was joined by fifteen galleys provided by Henry II. The combined fleet attacked Alanya on the south-eastern coast of Asia Minor, where it captured a tower by the sea but was unable to take the town, and then sailed to Egypt for an unsuccessful assault on Alexandria.[10] In addition to this, King Henry, along with the papacy and other crusading powers, entered into negotiations with the Mongol Ilkhans over joint operations against the Mamluks in Syria. In some instances the Cypriots took advantage of Mongol successes by launching raids on the Levantine coast, such as one in 1300, which consisted of sixteen galleys captained by Henry II in person, but these did little damage to the Mamluks.[11] A reoccurring feature of

---

8   *Documents on the Later Crusades, 1274–1580*, ed. and trans. by Norman Housley (Basingstoke: MacMillan, 1996), pp. 40–47; Marino Sanudo Torsello, *The Book of the Secrets of the Faithful of the Cross*, trans. by Peter Lock (Farnham: Ashgate, 2011), pp. 26–27, 62–3.

9   Louis de Mas Latrie, *Histoire de l'île de Chypre sous le regne des princes de la maison de Lusignan*, 3 vols (Paris: Imprimerie Nationale, 1852–61), II, pp. 118–25; Leopold, pp. 152–54. Interestingly Marino Sanudo argued that a crusade should sail directly to Egypt instead of using Cyprus as a base: Marino Sanudo Torsello, *The Book of the Secrets*, p. 75.

10 *Annali genovesi di Caffaro e de suoi continuatori*, ed. by Luigi Tommaso Belgrano et al., 5 vols (Rome: Instituto Storico Italiano, 1890–1929), V, pp. 143–44; *The 'Templar of Tyre': Part III of the 'Deeds of the Cypriots'*, trans. by Paul F. Crawford, Crusade Texts in Translation (Abingdon: Routledge, 2016), pp. 121–22 (§ § 524–25); Marino Sanudo Torsello, *The Book of the Secrets*, p. 370; Edbury, *Kingdom of Cyprus*, p. 102; Jean Richard, 'Le royaume de Chypre et l'embargo sur le commerce avec l'Egypte (fin XIIIe–début XIVe siècle)', *Comptes rendus des séances de l'Académie des Inscriptions et Belles-Lettres*, 128 (1984), 120–34 (p. 123).

11 Edbury, *Kingdom of Cyprus*, pp. 104–06; Sylvia Schein, 'Gesta Dei per Mongolos 1300: The Genesis of a Non-Event', *The English Historical Review*, 94 (1979), 805–19.

this period is that although some smaller expeditions were launched to the Eastern Mediterranean, no major campaign was successfully organised in coordination with either the Mongols or the great crusading powers of the West.

Although the failure to organise a major crusade in these years was mostly because of the conflicts within Europe, internal disputes on Cyprus also hampered the ability of Henry II to enact an effective crusading strategy. His policies brought him into conflict with the Templars and the Genoese, and his inability to deal effectively with the enemies of the kingdom provoked such dissatisfaction amongst the nobility that his brother Amaury (r. 1306–10) was able to usurp power from him in a bloodless coup in April 1306.[12] Amaury was a more capable military leader than Henry and he actively assisted the Hospitallers in the initial stages of their conquest of Rhodes, which began in 1306. The exact details of the campaign remain obscure, but along with allowing the Hospitallers to use Cyprus as a base of operations, Amaury also dispatched galleys to help the Order in early 1307 and impounded a Genoese vessel, which had been sent from Constantinople to aid the Byzantines. As the conquest of Rhodes dragged on, the Hospitallers began planning a crusade to cement their control of the island, which had the ostensible aim of bringing aid to Cyprus and Armenia and enforcing the papal blockade.[13] By this point Amaury's rule had become increasingly unpopular and his relations with the Hospitallers, as well as many western powers, had soured, leading him to fear that a crusade from the West would force him from power and reinstate his brother as the ruler of the island. The Hospitaller crusade set sail from Italy in November 1309 but in the end it was only used to finalise the conquest of Rhodes in the following summer.[14] The threat to Amaury actually lay far closer to home as on 5 June 1310 he was assassinated in the royal palace at Nicosia and his brother was reinstated as king.

Although the conquest of Rhodes strained Hospitaller-Cypriot relations, in the long term it presented the Lusignan kings with the opportunity to form a union with a powerful new Latin state in the East. By the second decade of the fourteenth century, the target of a crusade in the East had begun to subtly change. The recovery of the Holy Land and Jerusalem was still the ultimate objective of the Latin powers, but events in the West since the fall of Acre had made this seem increasingly difficult to achieve. The power-struggle between Philip IV of France and Pope Clement V had hindered any great crusade by relegating it below other matters, such as the trial of the Templars, while a vacancy in the papacy from 1314–16 and other problems in Europe,

---

12 Peter Edbury, 'Knights, Nobles and the Rule of Amaury of Tyre, 1306–1310', Επετηρίδα του Κέντρου Επιστημονικών Ερευνών 38 (2016), 9–93; Chris Schabel and Constantinos Georgiou, 'Neither at Peace Nor at War: the Non-Implementation of the Armenia-Cyprus Agreements of 1310', Επετηρίδα του Κέντρου Επιστημονικών Ερευνών 38 (2016), 95–116.
13 Constantinos Georgiou, *Preaching the Crusades to the Eastern Mediterranean: Propaganda, Liturgy and Diplomacy, 1305–1352* (London: Routledge, 2018), pp. 25–32.
14 Anthony T. Luttrell, 'Hospitallers at Rhodes, 1306–1421', in *A History of the Crusades*, ed. by Kenneth M. Setton, 6 vols (Philadelphia: University of Pennsylvania Press, 1955–89), III, pp. 283–84; Norman Housley, 'Pope Clement V and the Crusades of 1309–10', *Journal of Medieval History*, 8 (1982), 29–43; Edbury, *Kingdom of Cyprus*, pp. 118, 123–25.

such as the Great Famine of 1315–22 and the escalation of conflicts between England and France, further distracted the western powers from the Eastern Mediterranean.[15] To add to this, in the Aegean and Asia Minor the Anatolian Turks had emerged as a powerful opponent of the Latin Christians in the region. By this point the Turks had captured almost all of Anatolia from the Byzantines and the former Seljuk-Mongol lords, and had formed a patchwork of beyliks stretching from the Karamanids in the southeast to the Ottomans in the northwest.[16]

The beylik that posed the greatest threat to the Christians of the Aegean was Aydın, which ruled the coastal lands between the Hermos and Maeander rivers, and included the important port-cities of Ephesos and Smyrna. The emirs of Aydın had launched many raids against neighbouring Byzantine regions, and since 1318 they also began to make attacks against Latin Christian territories, including Hospitaller Rhodes, Genoese Chios (ruled by the Zaccaria family), Venetian Negroponte and the archipelago, and also some Frankish lands in Greece. The primary instigator of these raids was the lord of Smyrna, Umur Pasha, the son of Emir Mehmed of Aydın (d. 1334), and the younger brother of Hızır, the lord of Ephesos and emir from 1334 to c. 1360. Umur's exploits were so renowned, or notorious depending on the point of view, that they attracted attention from several writers at the time, including the Turkish poet-chronicler Enverī, who based part of his *Düstūrnāme* (c. 1465) on a lost contemporary account of Umur's deeds, as well as several Italian writers such as Boccaccio, Giovanni Villani and the Anonimo Romano.[17] By the late 1320s Umur's depredations had become so great that the Latin powers in the Aegean, along with the Byzantines, began to discuss the possibility of organising a joint military campaign against the beylik of Aydın. This would form the foundation of the naval league, or *Sancta Unio*, of 1332–34, to which Cyprus would contribute galleys.[18]

Cyprus was, however, a relative latecomer to the Aegean anti-Turkish coalitions. By the early 1320s papal crusading strategy in the Eastern Mediterranean focussed on two separate, but interconnected, objectives. The first was the continuation of support for a great crusade to the Holy Land, led by the kings of France, which the papacy supported through preaching and the awarding of generous crusade privileges,

---

15 Georgiou, *Preaching the Crusade*, pp. 35–6.
16 For this, see Dimitri Korobeinikov, *Byzantium and the Turks in the Thirteenth Century* (Oxford: Oxford University Press, 2014), esp. pp. 217–88.
17 For example: Enveri, *Le destān d'Umūr Pacha (Düstūrnāme-i Enverī)*, trans. by Irene Mélikoff-Sayar (Paris, 1954); Giovanni Boccaccio, *The Decameron*, trans. by Guido Waldman, ed. by Jonathan Usher (Oxford: Oxford University Press, 1993), pp. 124–5 (II.7); Giovanni Villani, *Nuova cronica*, ed. by Giuseppe Porta, 3 vols (Parma: Fondazione Pietro Bembo, 1990–1), III, book 13, chapter 39, pp. 390–1; Anonimo Romano, *Cronica*, ed. by Giuseppe Porta, 2nd edition (Milan: Adelphi, 1981), pp. 84–5; Carr, *Merchant Crusaders*, pp. 51–5.
18 Carr, *Merchant Crusaders*, pp. 44–55; Elizabeth A. Zachariadou, *Trade and Crusade: Venetian Crete and the Emirates of Menteshe and Aydin (1300–1415)*, Library of the Hellenic Institute of Byzantine and Post-Byzantine Studies, 11 (Venice: Istituto Ellenico di Studi Bizantini e Postbizantini di Venezia, 1983), pp. 13–62; Paul Lemerle, *L'Émirat d'Aydin, Byzance et l'occident: Recherches sur "La gesta d'Umur Pacha"* (Paris: Presses Universitaires de France, 1957).

such as full crusade indulgences and church tithes.[19] The second was the granting of limited support to those Latin states in the Aegean and Greece which were combating the Turks and other infidels on their borders, namely the Hospitallers on Rhodes, the Zaccaria on Chios and the Franks in the Peloponnese. Although the papacy supported the defence of these territories through the granting of indulgences, these were indulgences *in articulo mortis*, which were lesser spiritual rewards than those granted for fighting in the Holy Land. Indeed, no formal preaching, tithes, or other financial contributions were made in support of these campaigns, which meant that the overall contribution of the papacy was fairly minimal.[20]

For most of the early 1320s Cyprus remained strongly connected to the Franco-papal plans to liberate Jerusalem, rather than to the campaigns in the Aegean. However, the position of the island in close proximity to the Anatolian and Syrian coasts meant that it was regarded as at the forefront of the defence against the Turks as well as playing an important role in any forthcoming crusade to the Holy Land, thus straddling the two strands of crusading operations. Evidence of this is given in 1322 when Pope John XXII granted plenary indulgences 'as for the Holy Land' to all those who would travel overseas and fight in support of Cyprus and Cilician Armenia against the Mamluks and 'other infidels', among whom the Karaman Turks were specifically named.[21] The Karamanids occupied substantial territories on the southern coast of Asia Minor and although little is known of their contacts with Cyprus in these years, presumably news had reached the papal curia of the threat they were posing to both the island and Cilician Armenia. This crusade bull was connected to the ongoing French crusading plans for the Holy Land and thus represents one of the first instances when Cyprus's conflicts with the Turks became connected to a larger crusading mission. By 1323 these plans had advanced to the point where Charles IV of France agreed to send a fleet to the Eastern Mediterranean to enforce the trade embargo and bring support to the Christians of the region, in advance of a major expedition to the Holy Land.[22] But despite the enthusiasm of the French, wrangling over who should finance the expedition and the death of Charles in 1325 meant that neither the fleet nor a larger crusading campaign materialised.

The collapse of the papal-Franco projects, added to the fact that the Cypriots lacked the strength to take the fight to the Mamluks on their own, provides an explanation for why the next king of Cyprus, Hugh IV (r. 1324–58), sought to involve his kingdom in the

---

19 For more on these papal-Franco crusade projects, see Georgiou, *Preaching the Crusade*, passim.
20 Carr, *Merchant Crusaders*, pp. 109–14.
21 The document refers to the emir of Karaman, 'Haramanus Turcomanorum': *Lettres secrètes et curiales du pape Jean XXII, 1316–1334, relatives à la France*, ed. by Auguste Coulon, 4 vols (Paris: Fontemoing, 1900–72), II, no. 1572; Carr, *Merchant Crusaders*, p. 110.
22 *Lettres secrètes et curiales du pape Jean XXII, 1316–1334, relatives à la France*, nos 1683–5. For more on this, see Georgiou, *Preaching the Crusade*, 41–4; Christopher J. Tyerman, 'Sed nihil fecit? The Last Capetians and the Recovery of the Holy Land', in *War and Government in the Middle Ages: Essays in Honour of J. O. Prestwich*, ed. by John Gillingham and James C. Holt (Woodbridge: Boydell, 1984), pp. 170–81; Idem, 'Marino Sanudo Torsello and the Lost Crusade: Lobbying in the Fourteenth Century: The Alexander Prize Essay', *Transactions of the Royal Historical Society*, 32 (1982), 57–73; Norman Housley, 'The Franco-papal crusade negotiations in 1322–3', *Papers of the British School at Rome*, 48 (1980), 166–85.

anti-Turkish naval leagues in the Aegean which were gaining momentum by the mid-1320s. The first iteration of this league was formally agreed on Rhodes in September 1332 and was to consist of 20 galleys provided by the Venetians, Hospitallers and Byzantines.[23] Cyprus was not a formal contributor to this venture, but it was nevertheless considered as an important future participant and over the next year Hugh IV sent embassies to the West, along with representatives from Venice, Armenia and the influential Marino Sanudo, to promote the league to Philip VI of France, who was planning his own crusade to the Holy Land.[24] In November 1333 Hugh IV, who must have already been considered as a *de facto* member of the league, was formally invited by the Venetians to contribute.[25] At that point Pierre Roger, the Archbishop of Rouen and future Pope Clement VI, preached a sermon to Philip VI where he exhorted the French to aid their brothers in Cyprus, Armenia and Rhodes against Turkish attacks, thus explicitly linking French crusading plans to the aid of Cyprus.[26] In the end the league consisted of 34 galleys: ten from Venice, ten from the Hospitallers, eight from the papacy and France together, plus six from Cyprus.[27] As with previous campaigns against the Turks, the participants received indulgences *in articulo mortis* from the pope.[28] The fleet attacked the beyliks of Aydın, Karası and Saruhan along the north-western coast of Asia Minor, and in September 1334 it won several important victories near the Gulf of Adramyttion, opposite Lesbos, against the emir of Karası.[29] News of these events reached the West where Giovanni Villani in Florence wrote that the crusaders had killed 500 Turks and destroyed fifteen of their ships in one encounter.[30]

The late 1330s and early 1340s mark the next stage in Cypriot contributions to crusading when Hugh IV seems to have taken a leading role in the fight against the Turks and also in petitioning the papacy for support for a new naval league. This, however, proved to be difficult as the new pope, Benedict XII (1334–42), was less enthusiastic about eastern affairs than his predecessor.[31] Unfortunately, our sources for

---

23 *Diplomatarium Veneto-Levantinum: sive acta et diplomata res Venetas Graecas atque Levantis illustrantia a. 1300–1454*, ed. George M. Thomas, 2 vols (Venice: Deputazione veneta di storia patria, 1880–89; reprinted New York: B. Franklin, 1966), I, nos 116–17.
24 Christopher J. Tyerman, 'Philip VI and the recovery of the Holy Land', *English Historical Review* 100 (1985), 25–52, at 35. Sanudo had advocated Cypriot involvement in the league for some years up to this point: *The Book of the Secrets*, p. 62.
25 Coureas, *The Latin Church in Cyprus*, p. 98.
26 Georgiou, *Preaching the Crusade*, pp. 47, 162–3 and text at pp. 246–7.
27 *Diplomatarium Veneto-Levantinum*, I, no. 126. For recent discussions on the formation of the league, see V. Ivanov, 'Sancta Unio or the Holy League 1332–36/7 as a political factor in the eastern Mediterranean and the Aegean', *Études Balkaniques* 48 (2012), 142–76; Carr, *Merchant Crusaders*, pp. 70–3.
28 Carr, *Merchant Crusaders*, pp. 111–12.
29 Friedrich Kunstmann, 'Studien über Marino Sanudo Torsello den Aelteren', *Abhandlungen der Historischen Classe der Königlich Bayerischen Akademie der Wissenschaften* 7 (Munich, 1855), 695–819, at 811–12 (letter 7); Carr, *Merchant Crusaders*, p. 73.
30 Giovanni Villani, *Nuova cronica*, III, p. 58. A number of other western chroniclers also mentioned this battle, but with few details: Carr, *Merchant Crusaders*, p. 73.
31 On Benedict XII, see Mike Carr, 'Pope Benedict XII and the Crusades', in *Pope Benedict XII (1334–1342): The Guardian of Orthodoxy*, ed. by Irene Bueno (Amsterdam: Arc Humanities Press, 2018), pp. 217–40; Georgiou, *Preaching the Crusade*, pp. 67–73.

Hugh's activities against the Turks in these years are quite vague and the information about his role in crusade negotiations is obscured somewhat by the papal letters, which only provide one side of the correspondence. Nevertheless, according to a sixteenth-century continuation of the *Liber Pontificalis*, in 1336 the king sent twelve galleys and twelve armed *pamphillae* against the Karaman Turks 'which caused much damage and killed many'. Then in the following July he sent another fleet of 21 galleys and many more other vessels, which 'captured a lord of the Turks amongst others'.[32] Another victory, or possibly the same one, was also reported in a papal letter of February 1338, where Hugh was praised for a 'glorious victory against the Turks, the blasphemers of the Christian name'.[33] At around the same time the pilgrim Ludolf of Sudheim claimed that 'all the coastal places in Turkey pay tribute to the king of Cyprus' including the important ports of Antalya (Adalia) and Alanya (Candelore) in the beyliks of Hamid and Karaman.[34]

Despite Hugh's military feats against the Turks, papal support for Cyprus was not forthcoming. This led the king to renew ties with the Latins in the Aegean by dispatching his ambassador, Lamberto Baldwin della Cecca, the bishop of Limassol, to Rhodes and Venice in 1341. Lamberto informed the Venetians and Hospitallers that his king had unsuccessfully petitioned the pope for aid against the Turks, who were 'destroying, looting, despoiling and molesting' the Christians of the region, and he urged them to add their voices to those of his king in beseeching the pope to act in order to preserve their lands. It transpired that the Hospitallers had also unsuccessfully appealed to the pope on the same grounds, and that the Venetians were willing to add their weight to a coalition and to make petitions at the curia.[35] The response of Benedict XII to the combined entreaties is unknown as he died in April 1342, but we do know that Cypriot representatives were present at the curia in the summer of 1343 when the next pontiff, Clement VI (1342–52), set plans in motion for a new crusade.[36] In fact Clement, who had previously warned of the Turkish threat when delivering a sermon to Philip VI in 1333 when he was archbishop of Rouen, proved to be one of the most ardent supporters of a new campaign against the Turks. This is signified by his issuing in September 1343 of the bull *Insurgentibus contra fidem* in which he ordered prelates to begin preaching a new crusade against the Turks, in the form of a naval league, and decreed that the full crusade indulgence be granted to participants and that church tithes be allocated to help finance the campaign.[37]

---

32   *Le Liber pontificalis: Texte, introduction et commentaire*, ed. Louis Duchesne, 3 vols (Paris: E. de Boccard, 1886–92), II, p. 527.

33   *Benoît XII (1334–1342), Lettres closes et patentes intéressant les pays autres que la France*, ed. by Guillaume Mollat and Jean-Marie Vidal (Paris: E. de Boccard, 1913–50), no. 1673.

34   Ludolf of Sudheim, *Description of the Holy Land, and of the Way Thither*, trans. by Aubrey Stewart (London: Library of the Palestine Pilgrims' Text Society, 1895), p. 44; Carr, *Merchant Crusaders*, pp. 102–03.

35   Giorgio Fedalto, *La chiesa latina in Oriente*, 3 vols (Verona: Casa Editrice Mazziana, 1981), III, p. 51; Mas Latrie, *Histoire*, II, pp. 180–81.

36   *Lettres closes, patentes et curiales du pape Clément VI se rapportant à la France*, ed. by Eugène Depréz, Guillaume Mollat, and J. Glénnison, 3 vols (Paris: E. de Boccard, 1901–61), I, no. 311.

37   Clement VI, *Lettres closes, patentes et curiales*, I, no. 433–34; *Documents on the Later Crusades*, pp. 78–80.

This league consisted of twenty galleys: six from Venice, six from the Hospitallers, four from the papacy and four from Cyprus.[38] Although this fleet was slightly smaller than the previous league, it was more successful. In May 1344, the crusader galleys won a notable victory against the Turks at Longos, a harbour on the western promontory of the Chalkidike peninsula, where they ambushed and burned a fleet of some sixty vessels and captured a close relative of a Turkish emir.[39] In October this was followed by an even more impressive feat when the crusaders launched a surprise attack on Smyrna, where they managed to capture the harbour and harbour fortress of the city from Umur Pasha, but not the acropolis overlooking the harbour, which remained in his hands.[40] From 1345–7 a second wave of the crusade sailed to the Aegean under the command of the Dauphin Humbert II of Viennois, but this was unable to expel the Turks from Smyrna and the crusade remained a stalemate.[41] Nevertheless, in the summer of 1347 the galleys of the league won a notable victory against the Turks of Aydın and Saruhan off the island of Imbros, and in the spring of 1348 the crusaders enjoyed another victory when Umur was killed at Smyrna, apparently shot by an arrow when leading an unsuccessful assault against the walls of the harbour fortress.[42]

Unfortunately, there is no detailed narrative source for the Crusade of Smyrna and most of our information derives from a smattering of documents from the papal, Venetian and the Hospitaller archives, along with a handful of Italian and Byzantine chronicles. Therefore, we do not know the exact role of the Cypriot forces in the different encounters during the Crusade, only that the Cypriot galleys seem to have fought alongside the others of the league. Nevertheless, there is evidence that contemporaries considered the role of Cyprus to be important. This is suggested by a spurious Latin letter purporting to be written by Hugh IV to Queen Joanna of Sicily, which circulated in parts of Italy and France during the crusade. The letter, which was incorporated into a contemporary Pistoian chronicle and also survives in a French version, describes an exaggerated victory of 200,000 *crucesignati* over a force of 1,200,000 Turks on a plain between Smyrna and Ephesos in June 1345. During the encounter the crusaders, who in the Pistoian version were led by Peter, the son of the

---

38 *Clément VI (1342–1352): lettres closes, patentes et curiales se rapportant à la France*, ed. by Eugène Depréz, Guillaume Mollat, & J. Glénnison, 3 vols, Bibliothèque des Écoles françaises d'Athènes et de Rome (Paris: E. de Boccard, 1901–61), I, no. 341; Carr, *Merchant Crusaders*, p. 74.
39 John Kantakouzenos, *Ioannis Cantacuzeni eximperatoris Historiarum libri IV*, ed. by Ludwig Schopen and Barthold Georg Niebuhr, 3 vols (Bonn, 1828–32), II, book 3, chapter 69, pp. 422–3.
40 For the papal letters congratulating the crusaders, see *Clément VI (1342–1352): lettres closes, patentes et curiales se rapportant à la France*, I, nos 1350–1, 1395, 1397, 1462, 1464. Several Byzantine and Turkish sources also mention this event, see Carr, *Merchant Crusaders*, p. 75.
41 The crusade of Humbert of Viennois has been discussed recently by Georgiou, *Preaching the Crusade*, pp. 75–82; Idem, 'Ordinavi armatam sancte unionis, Clement VI's Sermon on the Dauphin Humbert II of Viennois' Leadership of the Christian Armada Against the Turks, 1345', *Crusades* 15 (2016), 157–75; Mike Carr, 'Humbert of Viennois and the Crusade of Smyrna: A Reconsideration', *Crusades* 13 (2014), 237–51.
42 *Clément VI (1342–1352): lettres closes, patentes et curiales se rapportant à la France*, II, nos 3336–7; Nikephoros Gregoras, *Byzantina Historia*, ed. L. Schopen and I. Bekker, 3 vols (Bonn, 1829–55), II, book 16, chapter 7, pp. 834–5; Carr, *Merchant Crusaders*, pp. 75–77.

King Hugh, were on the brink of defeat until the figure of John the Baptist appeared above them and reassured them of divine assistance and the promise of eternal life to those who died. After this the crusaders rose afresh and fought so fiercely that they vanquished the Turks, killing 70,000 of them.[43] The emphasis this story gives to the promise of eternal reward suggests that it was used as a recruitment aid for preachers, a factor that further emphasises Hugh IV's connection to the Crusade. The numbers of recruits for the Smyrna campaign are difficult to gauge, but it is possible that around 15,000 men fought in some capacity, which was a sizeable force for the Aegean region at this time.[44] In 1350 the league was renewed but its numbers were reduced to eight galleys, with three each provided by Venice and the Hospitallers, and two provided by Cyprus. But by this time other events, most notably the Black Death, had begun to compromise the coherence of the league and in 1351 it was disbanded. Nevertheless, Hugh IV was asked to contribute to the defence of Smyrna, usually through an annual payment of 3,000 florins, which he seems to have maintained for the rest of his reign. In 1357 the smaller league of 1350 was reformed, this time for five years, with Hugh IV again contributing galleys, although little is known about its activities.[45]

As Peter Edbury has commented, it is difficult to know how effective these later leagues were, but it is nevertheless clear that Hugh IV took his crusading responsibilities against the Turks seriously.[46] Given that Cyprus lay some way from the main actions of the leagues in the northern Aegean, the motives for the king's participation in them were not a simple matter of defence. Instead they were reflective of a more general change in the justification of crusading and in the perceptions of Muslim groups of the Eastern Mediterranean in these years. At the turn of the fourteenth century, the enforcement of the papal embargo and support of Cyprus and Armenia as part of a precursor to a major crusade against the Mamluks took precedent, and was reflected in the policies of Henry II and Amaury, but during the second and third decades of the century, the Anatolian Turks emerged as a more pressing danger to the Latins of the Aegean. Cyprus, although outside of the Aegean, was under threat from the Karaman Turks and, more importantly, was connected to Europe and the Black Sea by the shipping routes which passed through the Aegean and were being disrupted by the Turkish raids there. The naval leagues thus offered Hugh IV the chance to form alliances with powerful Latin neighbours, to combat the Turks nearer to home, and to protect the shipping routes which ran to his island.

This change in perception of the Turks went hand-in-hand with a relaxation of attitudes towards the Mamluks, especially within the context of trade. In the 1320s John XXII issued trade licences to the Zaccaria of Chios who were at the forefront

---

43 Nicolae Jorga, 'Une lettre apocryphe sur la bataille de Smyrne', *Revue d'Orient Latin*, 3 (1895), 27–31; *Storie pistoresi (1300–1348)*, ed. S. A. Barbi, RISNS 11.5 (Bologna, 1927), pp. 215–6; Kenneth M. Setton, *The Papacy and the Levant: 1204–1571*, 4 vols (Philadelphia: American Philosophical Society, 1976–84), I, pp. 201–2; Carr, *Merchant Crusaders*, p. 116; Georgiou, *Preaching the Crusade*, pp. 118–20.
44 Carr, *Merchant Crusaders*, pp. 85–7.
45 Edbury, *Kingdom of Cyprus*, p. 160.
46 Edbury, *Kingdom of Cyprus*, pp. 160–61.

of crusading against the Turks. These permits allowed them to ship mastic to the Mamluk sultanate without incurring the usual punishments for breaking the trade embargo.[47] This policy was expanded significantly by Clement VI who granted over ninety known licences during his pontificate, many of which allowed trade with the Mamluks specifically on the condition that the recipients use the proceeds to help finance the crusade against the Turks.[48] King Hugh was himself a recipient of two licences in 1349 and 1350, both of which allowed him to send two galleys to Mamluk Egypt. In the records of his petitions the scribes specifically stated that Hugh had been maintaining four galleys in the Aegean 'for the defence of the Christian faith against the Turks'.[49] This is a clear reflection of the change in crusade strategy during his reign, one where a great campaign to liberate the Holy Land from the Mamluks was replaced by maritime action against the Turks. In fact, the king himself had even asked the pope to cease preaching a crusade to the Holy Land on Cyprus in 1336, 1346 and 1351 because he feared antagonising the Mamluks.[50] Considering these factors, the crusading policies of Peter I are even more interesting. In some senses he continued the strategies of his father, such as by raiding Korikos and Antalya on the Anatolian coast in 1360–61 and re-imposing the tributes owed by the Karamanids. But in many other ways his policies were a stark contrast to his predecessors. This is what makes his famous attack on Alexandria even the more intriguing.

---

47 Mike Carr, 'Trade or Crusade? The Zaccaria of Chios and Crusades Against the Turks', in *Contact and Conflict in Frankish Greece and the Aegean, 1204–1453: Crusade, Religion and Trade between Latins, Greeks and Turks*, ed. Mike Carr and Nikolaos Chrissis (Farnham: Ashgate, 2014), pp. 115–34, esp. 125–27; Edbury, *Kingdom of Cyprus*, pp. 150–51.
48 Carr, *Merchant Crusaders*, 132–42; Mike Carr, 'Crossing Boundaries in the Mediterranean: Papal Trade Licences from the *Registra Supplicationum* of Pope Clement VI (1342–1352)', *Journal of Medieval History*, 41 (2015), 107–29.
49 Carr, 'Crossing Boundaries', p. 117; Idem, 'Between the Papal Court and the Islamic World', pp. 118-19.
50 Edbury, *Kingdom of Cyprus*, p. 161.

CHARALAMBOS GASPARIS

Crete, 1357–67: A Stronghold for Venetian Diplomacy and Crusading in the Eastern Mediterranean

The years of the reign of King Peter I of Cyprus (1359–69) coincide with an interesting period of the Venetian history, during which Crete, the largest Venetian colony in the Eastern Mediterranean, played a leading role in the area. In 1357, just two years after the third Venetian-Genoese War (1351–55), the hitherto close diplomatic and trade relations between Crete and the Turkish emirates of Palatia/Miletus/Menteshe (Menteşe) and Theologo/Ayasuluk (Aydin) in Asia Minor were almost severed. That same year the new Holy League assembled a fleet for another crusade against the 'infidel' Muslims, the third one during the fourteenth century. Ten years later, in 1367, the great Cretan Revolt of St Titus (1363–67) definitively came to an end. The revolt not only shocked the mother city but also adversely affected Venice's international relations at a time when its allies sought its help.[1] Moreover, by the end of the revolt the political context in Crete changed partially, due to the weakening of the local Venetians and the reinforcement of the central metropolitan power. At the same time, the focus of Venetian foreign policy gradually shifted to the Ottoman threat, as the Turkish emirates in Asia Minor began to weaken. In the intervening years, especially between 1357 and 1363, Crete became a stronghold for Venetian diplomacy and crusading in the region.

The Venetian colony of Crete had been organized as 'another' Venice in the Eastern Mediterranean since the first half of the thirteenth century. The political and administrative system was in fact that of the metropolis in miniature, facilitating Venice's employment of the island, whenever necessary, in various ways through familiar processes that had proven effective. The island had its own government (*regimen* or *dominium*), consisting

---

1 For the Revolt of St Titus and its consequences, see: Sally McKee, 'The Revolt of St Tito in Fourteenth-Century Crete: A Reassessment', *Mediterranean Historical Review*, 9/2 (1994), 173–204; Sally McKee, *Uncommon Dominion. Venetian Crete and the Myth of Ethnic Purity* (Philadelphia: University of Pennsylvania Press, 2000), pp. 133–51; Nicholas Coureas, 'King Peter I of Cyprus and the Rebellion of 1363 on Crete', in Πρακτικά του Τρίτου Διεθνούς Κυπρολογικού Συνεδρίου (Λευκωσία, 16–20 Απριλίου 1996), II: Μεσαιωνικό τμήμα, ed. by Athanasios Papageorgiou (Nicosia: Imprinta Ltd, 2001), pp. 519–26.

Charalambos Gasparis • National Hellenic Research Foundation

of the duke of Crete and his two councillors, all three coming from the metropolis. There were also several administrative councils, namely the Great Council and the Senate in the capital city of Candia and four feudal councils, one in the main city of each of the four departments of the island, including Candia. All the members of these councils were Venetians of Crete.[2] Therefore the island's political and administrative structures were divided between two centres of authority, the metropolitan (represented by the duke and his councillors) and the local one (represented by the various councils); as early as the thirteenth century, these two centres would often come into conflict, even though the metropolis ensured that it always maintained control over policy.

By the early fourteenth century Crete's political role was enhanced both through Venice's diplomatic contacts with the Turkish emirates of Asia Minor and via the crusading movements in the Eastern Mediterranean in the same period. During the period 1357–63, however, the island's prominence was reinforced by the political circumstances: local officials and councils discussed various matters of significance not only to the colony but also to Venice itself, making decisions without any direct intervention from the metropolis. Indeed, at this time the metropolitan councils did not deliberate or decide on these issues. As a result, the upper stratum of local Venetians, through the Senate and in cooperation with the local government, temporarily had the capacity to make political decisions on issues that were not solely of local import. Furthermore, the Venetians of the colony were given the opportunity to occupy positions that were normally reserved to the Venetians of the metropolis.

In his paper at the International Congress of Byzantine Studies in 1961, Freddy Thiriet first noted Crete's prominent political role in the Eastern Mediterranean in the fourteenth century. Some two decades later, in 1983, Elizabeth Zachariadou published her book with the revealing title *Trade and Crusade. Venetian Crete and the Emirates of Menteshe and Aydin (1300–1415)*, providing a detailed analysis of the relations, both diplomatic and commercial, between the two parties, as well as the texts of the treaties signed.[3] Thus this present paper will not examine the diplomatic relations between Crete and the Turkish emirates or the crusading activity of the Holy League against the Turks in the Aegean, since both topics have been studied sufficiently.[4] It

---

2 On the Cretan councils and their role in local administration, see: McKee, *Uncommon Dominion*, pp. 19–56; Anastasia Papadia-Lala, *Ο θεσμός των αστικών κοινοτήτων στον ελληνικό χώρο κατά την περίοδο της βενετοκρατίας (13ος-18ος αι.). Μια συνθετική προσέγγιση* (Venice: Istituto ellenico di studi bizantini e postbizantini di Venezia, 2004), pp. 52–72.

3 Freddy Thiriet, 'Les relations entre la Crète et les émirats turcs d'Asie Mineure au XIVe siècle (vers 1348–1360)', in *Actes du XIIe Congrès International d'Études byzantines (Ohride, 10–16 septembre 1961)*, 3 vols (Belgrade: Comité Yougoslave des Études byzantines, 1963–1964), II, pp. 213–21 (repr. in Freddy Thiriet, *Études sur la Romanie gréco-vénitienne (x[e]-xve siècles)* (London: Variorum, 1977), no. VII); Elizabeth Zachariadou, *Trade and Crusade. Venetian Crete and the Emirates of Menteshe and Aydin (1300–1415)* (Venice: Istituto ellenico di studi bizantini e postbizantini di Venezia, 1983). For Crete's role in the same period, see also Mike Carr, *Motivations and Response to Crusades in the Aegean: c. 1300–1350* (unpublished doctoral thesis, Royal Holloway, University of London, 2011), pp. 105–07, 144–45, 175–83 and passim.

4 Zachariadou, *Trade and Crusade*; Carr, *Motivations and Response*. For the events in the Aegean and the Eastern Mediterranean during the first half of the fourteenth century, see Mike Carr, *Merchant Crusaders in the Aegean. 1291–1352* (Suffolk - New York, 2015) and Mike Carr, 'Trade or Crusade? The Zaccaria of

will focus instead on the institutional procedures involved in Venetian diplomatic activity with the Turkish emirates, the political climate in Crete between 1357 and 1367, and, most importantly, the specific roles played by both the local government and the Venetians of Crete within this context.

Venetian trade in Asia Minor became more intense with the establishment of Venice's maritime state during the first half of the thirteenth century. The Venetians continued their intense commercial activity even after the collapse of the Seljuk state and the formation of the two Turkish emirates in the second half of the thirteenth century. During the same period, Venice conquered and organized the colony of Crete, which became the main centre for its trade with the Turkish emirates. The important commercial interests of Venetian merchants in Asia Minor as well as Crete's need for certain products (such as cereals and horses) inevitably led to the development of diplomatic relations. As early as the first decades of the fourteenth century, the metropolis assigned the responsibility for fostering these links to the duke of Crete and his councillors. The diplomatic and, mainly, commercial relations between Crete and the Turkish emirates were defined in a series of fourteenth-century treaties signed by the duke of Crete and the two emirs, in which as good neighbours the emirates agreed not to host pirates in their ports and on their shores. Piracy against Crete and other Venetian colonies or trading posts as well as against Venetian citizens travelling in the Aegean had long been a major problem. In order to achieve these goals, Venice established a consul's office in each of the two emirates.[5] The first treaty was signed in 1331 between the duke of Crete and the emir of Menteshe, to be followed in 1337 by another with the emir of Menteshe and one with the emir of Aydin. These first treaties laid the groundwork for all subsequent ones until the conquest of the two emirates by the Ottomans in 1424.[6]

The negotiations for the agreements were conducted through ambassadors from both sides, who travelled to the emirates or Crete respectively, while the Venetian consuls in Palatia and Theologo also played a key role as long as these positions were occupied. In the fourteenth century, piracy and political events often tested the good commercial and diplomatic relations established by the treaties between Venice and the emirates. The years immediately following the third Venetian-Genoese War until the end of the Revolt of St Titus were a difficult period and constitute the object of the present study.

The stabilization of relations with the Turkish emirates through trade and, at the same time, the devastating attacks of the same Turks against Venetian colonies and commercial vessels were among Venice's primary concerns at that time. Using

---

Chios and Crusades against the Turks', in *Contact and Conflict in Frankish Greece and the Aegean, 1204–1453. Crusade, Religion and Trade between Latins, Greeks and Turks*, ed. by Nikolaos G. Chrissis and Mike Carr (Farnham: Ashgate, 2014), pp. 115–34.

5 In Palatia, the office was established before 1331, or even earlier, while in Theologo by the treaty of 1337. See Zachariadou, *Trade and Crusade*, pp. 18–19, 137–38.

6 Apart from the first three treaties, five more were signed between the duke of Crete and the Turkish emirs: in 1353 with the emir of Aydin, in 1358, 1375, 1403, and 1407 with the emir of Menteshe. See the text of all treaties in Zachariadou, *Trade and Crusades*, pp. 187–237.

every means, the *Serenissima* tried to reconcile these two conflicting issues with great diplomatic skill in order to maintain the coveted equilibrium. In Crete, the diplomatic affairs with the Turkish emirates as well as the affairs related to the activity of the Holy League naturally passed into the hands of the local Senate in close cooperation with the local government, i.e. the duke and the two councillors, who in any case convened the Senate. The surviving proceedings of the decisions of the Cretan Senate for this specific period often contain the different proposals of the members of the government and the *sapientes* and record the debate during the sessions as well as the relevant voting, enabling us to understand the various tendencies within the council or amongst the members of the committee of *sapientes* and, in some cases, even disagreements between the members of the local government and the members of the Senate.[7]

For an entire year (from December 1357 to December 1358), all the meetings of the Cretan Senate, with just one exception, concerned the Turkish emirates and the Holy League. The usual procedure for the discussion, whenever a problem arose on the part of either the emirs or the Venetian consuls in the emirates, was as follows: first, a committee of *sapientes* was appointed from among the Senate members to examine the problem and express their opinion along with the duke and the two councillors; then, the proposal was submitted to a plenary session of the Senate for discussion and voting. As this paper intends to show, although the meetings of the Cretan Senate took place within the political context of a colony, they were not just standard procedures ending with the adoption of a policy suggested by the metropolitan authorities, but genuine discussions leading to original decisions.

The negotiations between the Cretan authorities and the two emirs between 1356 and 1358 perfectly demonstrate the significant political role of Crete in this period. About a year after the end of the war with Genoa, Venice began to negotiate with the emirs of Asia Minor for new treaties. On 10 April 1356, three *sapientes* were elected in the Cretan Senate to study the letters received from Giuliano Zeno, the Venetian ambassador in Palatia, and to submit a proposal for discussion. The main issues were the debt owed by the emir of Menteshe and the indemnity for damages to the *griparia* of Leo Marmaras. A week later, on 17 April, the Senate authorized Giuliano Zeno to ask the emir to pay – under certain terms – the debt and the indemnity. If the emir agreed to those terms, the ambassador could proceed with the signing of the agreement; if, on the other hand, the emir refused, the ambassador should return immediately to Candia. The Cretan Senate gave the ambassador further instructions in case the emir asked him to sign a new treaty: he should respond that he was not authorized to do so and that there was no need for a new treaty since the previous one of 1337 was still valid according to its clauses.[8] The negotiations ended without success.

---

7 *Duca di Candia. Quaternus Consiliorum (1350–1363)*, ed. by Paola Ratti-Vidulich (Venice: Comitato per la pubblicazione delle fonti relative alla storia di Venezia, 2007).
8 *Duca di Candia. Quaternus Consiliorum*, nos 177–78. According to the instructions given to Zeno, if the emir of Menteshe invoked the new treaty signed with the emir of Aydin in 1353, he should respond that this happened because the previous emir had died and a new treaty had to be signed; since the emir of Menteshe was still the same person, there was no need for a new treaty.

Towards the end of 1356, Turkish ships were in the Aegean and the Senate in Candia decided to take specific defensive measures in eastern Crete, which was quite vulnerable to attacks by sea.[9] In January 1357, the Venetian consul in Palatia sought instructions concerning the negotiations with the emir. On 25 January, the Senate elected five *sapientes* to present the matter to the body. On 31 January, the Senate gave the consul instructions on how to argue and negotiate with the emir according to the proposal made by the duke of Crete Goffredo Morosini and the councillor Vittore Trevisan. The main issue remained the debt to the Venetian state and the indemnity to Leo Marmaras as well as piracy originating mainly from the Emirate of Menteshe. If the emir accepted the Venetian terms, the consul should travel to Candia with the treaty to be signed.[10] At the same time, negotiations with the emir of Aydin were also underway.

The fact that all discussion in the Cretan Senate between 1357 and 1358 concerned the emirate of Menteshe indicates that negotiations with Aydin were rather smooth or at least did not involve any serious obstacles that had to be removed before the conclusion of a new treaty. During the talks with both Menteshe and Aydin, trade between Crete and the Turkish emirates continued as usual.[11] In late 1357, the Venetians, driven by their patriotic pride and the illusion that they were able to exercise pressure on the emirs, devoted much time to lengthy negotiations. The sessions and the relevant decisions of the Cretan Senate in this period are characteristic of the political climate and highlight the pivotal role of the Cretan authorities and councils. On 5 December 1357, the Cretan Senate appointed a committee of five *sapientes* with the task of making proposals concerning the new negotiations with the emirate of Menteshe ('negocium ambaxate [ad] Palatiam').[12] The negotiations still concerned the debt of the emir of Menteshe to the Venetian state and the indemnity owed to Leo Marmaras, but a new matter appeared in the documents: Turkish vessels had captured and plundered the boat of Nicola Mazamordi, while other ships had attacked the northeastern coast of Crete, in the area of Sitia, and had captured many inhabitants. The duke of Crete demanded not only indemnities for the damages and losses that Nicola Mazamordi had suffered, but also the return of the captured Cretans, who had been sold as slaves. The emir agreed to the first set of terms concerning the old matters, but refused to satisfy the second set because, as he claimed, the ships involved in the raids did not come from his emirate.

Next day, 6 December 1357, during a plenary session, the members of the Cretan Senate discussed and voted on four different proposals, submitted respectively by the duke and three *sapientes*, one of the two councillors, the other councillor, and the remaining two *sapientes*. Although the ultimate goal of all proposals was the same, i.e. the emir's acceptance of all the above-mentioned terms, the proposed methods

---

9   On 31 December 1356, five *sapientes* were elected to propose defensive measures and on 2 January 1357 these measures were taken: *Duca di Candia. Quaternus Consiliorum*, nos 200–01.
10 *Duca di Candia. Quaternus Consiliorum*, nos 203–04.
11 On 24 February 1357, for example, the Great Council of Crete approved an extension of time for the importation of horses from the emirates: *Duca di Candia. Quaternus Consiliorum*, no. 206.
12 The five *sapientes* elected were Ruggiero Querini, Giorgio da Molin, Giacomo Mudazzo, Alessio Corner, and Marco Fradello: *Duca di Candia. Quaternus Consiliorum*, no. 223.

and the procedure of the negotiations as well as the force of the arguments and the pressure to be put on the other side varied. The negotiations took place in Candia between the government and the ambassadors sent by the emir of Menteshe.[13] The emir had already agreed to pay the debt owed to the Venetian state and the indemnity owed to Leo Marmaras, but the issues of the indemnities owed to Nicola Mazamordi and of the return of the Cretan captives remained open; thus, the main question posed to the Turkish ambassadors was whether they would accept this specific term.

The duke and the three *sapientes* declared that the treaty would be signed only if the Turkish ambassadors accepted all the terms. If the ambassadors argued that they had not been authorized to negotiate concerning the indemnities to Nicola Mazamordi and the return of the captured Cretans, then it was inevitable that a Venetian envoy should be sent along with the Turkish ambassadors to Palatia to negotiate with the emir. This envoy should argue that the latest attacks were quite serious and contrary to the still valid clauses of the last treaty. If the emir accepted the terms, the Venetian ambassador could sign the treaty. Otherwise, the ambassador should return to Candia and all Venetians, i.e. the consul, the merchants and the citizens, should abandon Palatia within two months.

The councillor Lorenzo Zane suggested that, in case the Turkish ambassadors were indeed not authorized to negotiate on these issues, they should write to the emir and ask permission, or one of them should travel back to Palatia and receive instructions; in fact, the Cretan government could even offer a ship for his travel. If the ambassadors refused this solution as well, then the Cretan government should ask the Venetian consul in Palatia to find an appropriate person who could negotiate with the emir. If this was not possible, then the consul should seek instructions from the duke of Crete. Zane also proposed that the treaty should be signed in Crete, as had been the practice, and not in Palatia. Furthermore, given that the emir was in a very difficult position because of his war with the Hospitallers and the fleet of the Holy League, he had to realize that, if he still wished to continue enjoying the profits from the Venetian trade, he should accept the terms; according to the councillor's proposal, 'the emirates need Venice and not the opposite'.

In his turn, the councillor Geronimo Cavatorta proposed that a Venetian ambassador should be sent immediately, along with the Turkish ambassadors, to Palatia to negotiate and, if he failed to persuade the emir, he should return to Candia.

Finally, the two other *sapientes*, Pietro Querini and Giacomo Mudazzo, proposed that, if the Turkish ambassadors refused to negotiate because they were not authorized, they should write to the emir for further instructions. If the emir did not accept the terms, then the negotiations should be interrupted, and each side should 'manage its own household'.[14]

---

13 Although the ambassadors were sent by the emir of Menteshe, the Cretan senators sometimes speak of the 'emirs', also including the emir of Aydin. This happens not only because negotiations with the emir of Aydin were taking place at the same time, but mainly because the latter was involved in the capture of the boat of Nicola Mazamordi and of the Cretan inhabitants.

14 *Duca di Candia. Quaternus Consiliorum*, no. 224.

The proposal approved by a relatively large majority (thirty-four out of fifty-one voters) was that of the Duke and the three *sapientes*. This was a rather conciliatory proposal, based on 'the old and true friendship' ('antiqua et vera amicitia') of the two parties and advising further discussion and exchange of ambassadors between the two sides until reaching an agreement 'for the benefit of both Venice and Crete' ('unde tam comune Veneciarum quam ista insula solet sentire comodum'). At the same time, it adhered to a very strict course of political action, suggesting that, if the emir continued to reject the terms, the Venetians should withdraw from Palatia. This last term, which highlights the combination of Venetian pride and efforts for an agreement, was probably what made the difference between this and the other proposals. It is no coincidence that the proposal of the councillor Lorenzo Zane, which received the considerable number of twelve votes, was also in favour of continuing the talks and the preservation of Venetian dominance over the emirate. According to the other two proposals (receiving only three and two votes respectively), much effort should be invested in order to reach an agreement, but, in the event of a negative outcome, the negotiations should most certainly be interrupted.

Three months later, in March 1358, there had been no progress in the negotiations and it was more than obvious that the emir of Menteshe was unwilling to satisfy the requests of the Venetians; on the contrary, his fleet was moving menacingly towards Crete. The *sapientes* appointed to study the situation unanimously proposed that it was absolutely necessary to take defensive measures in eastern Crete,[15] but they disagreed amongst themselves on how the Venetians should behave with regard to the negotiations. In the context of insecurity and war, the moderate proposal to try again to reach a settlement by sending a letter to the emir of Menteshe was rejected, although by a very narrow margin.[16] On the contrary, the most rigorous proposal was approved, which provided for the immediate suspension of all commercial and diplomatic contacts with the Turkish emirate of Menteshe. On the other hand, for the 'benefit of the *comune* and the merchants', it was decided that trade between Crete and the emirate of Aydin should be intensified and that a consul should be appointed in Theologo to this end. This decision made it clear that Venetian disagreement was with the emir of Menteshe and not with that of Aydin.

A few days later, between 22 and 24 March 1358, a new discussion took place, regarding the necessary defensive measures. Although both the Cretan government and the three *sapientes* elected had proposed specific measures for the area of Sitia on the northeastern coast, the *sapientes* additionally proposed the same measures even for the area of Ierapetra in southeastern Crete. Thus, two proposals were put to a vote. The duke and the two councillors fought for their opinion, but failed to win

---

15 On 9 March 1358, five *sapientes* were elected from among the members of the Senate: Francesco Marcello, Giacomo Mudazzo, Alessio Corner, Marco Borgognono, and Pietro Lando, *Duca di Candia. Quaternus Consiliorum*, no. 234. The plenary session of the body for the discussion and the decision was held on 13 March 1358: *Duca di Candia. Quaternus Consiliorum*, no. 235.
16 The proposal received twenty-two positive, twenty-eight negative, and three neutral votes. See *Duca di Candia. Quaternus Consiliorum*, no. 235.

in four consecutive ballots. Instead, it was the proposal of the committee of the three *sapientes* – members of the Cretan Senate – that was finally adopted.[17]

The negotiations with the emir of Menteshe continued despite the fear that diplomatic efforts would fail and notwithstanding the military preparations for possible Turkish attacks. On 28 April 1358, the Venetian consul in Palatia informed the Cretan government that, following an investigation, the emir of Menteshe managed to locate 'eight or nine' of the Cretans captured in the area of Sitia; he intended to return them and he was willing to pay the indemnities to both the Venetian state and Leo Marmaras. On 28 May, the Senate drew up its answer to the consul, focusing exclusively on the issue of the captive Cretans.[18] The senators expressed their perplexity concerning the number of the captives: although they were initially estimated to be thirty-four, a few months earlier the emir claimed to have located nineteen, and now only nine. But even so, the Senate, showing goodwill, decided to accept the emir's proposal under the condition that, if more captives were located after the signing of the treaty, they should be returned immediately. If the emir agreed to this last term, he should dispatch an ambassador to Crete to sign the treaty.

It is characteristic of the tension between the two sides that the consul of Palatia was then living on Rhodes, where he carried out his duties. This is why he had asked the Senate to send with its response instructions whether he would have to travel to Palatia or not. The Senate replied that, if the emir eventually accepted the terms, it was up to the consul to decide whether it was necessary to travel there or not. If he finally decided to travel to Palatia, he could stay while the emir prepared his answer, except that under no circumstances should he wait there for more than a month. If, on the contrary, the emir decided to proceed with the signing of a treaty, sending for this reason an ambassador to Crete, then the consul could stay in Palatia as long as he wanted. The above instructions prove that at that time not only were commercial relations disrupted, but diplomatic ties were also much reduced.

While negotiations between the duke of Crete and the emir of Menteshe continued, a new treaty was signed with the emir of Aydin in the early summer of 1358. As a result, the Venetian Senate this time decided, on 14 June 1358, that a consul in Theologo would be helpful for Venetian trade and that his salary should derive from a duty on the commercial activity between Crete and Aydin.[19] The Venetian Senate's decision entailed that a person be elected to a vacant post, since the 'office' of consul in Theologo had been already established by the treaty of 1337.[20] The election of the new consul was entrusted once more to the Cretan authorities and, on 24 August 1358,

---

17 *Duca di Candia. Quaternus Consiliorum*, nos 236–38.
18 *Duca di Candia. Quaternus Consiliorum*, no. 252.
19 According to the decision: 'Quia utilimum esse decernitur pro mercatoribus nostris habere unum ydoneum consulem in partibus Theologi [...] quod salarium exigi debeat de mercacionibus et rebus viagii Theologi, videlicet que conducentur de Theologo in Candiam et que de Candia in Theologum portabuntur, imponendo talem impositionem dictis mercacionibus quod nil ultra dictum salarium exigatur'. See *Venezia - Senato. Deliberazioni miste. Registro XXVIII (1357–1359)*, ed. by Ermanno Orlando (Venice: Istituto Veneto di Scienze Lettere ed Arti, 2009), no. 453.
20 Zachariadou, *Trade and Crusade*, pp. 36, 61.

the Senate in Candia appointed Giovanni Moro for a period of one year. At the same time, three *sapientes* were also elected to make suggestions on how the consul's salary would be collected in Crete.[21] Three days later, the Candiote Senate decided on the collection of the duty, but specifying that this duty was imposed on trade not only from the port of Candia, but also from the ports of Chania, Rethymno, and Sitia. It seems that there had already been voices of protest from the other cities and there was fear that the measures would not be properly implemented.[22] Thus, it was also decided that, if the rectors of the other three cities refused to collect the duty, the consul in Theologo would undertake the task of collecting it on exports and imports between these three ports and Aydin.[23]

The negotiations with the emir of Menteshe finally came to an end a few months later. Having accepted the Venetian terms, the emir dispatched an ambassador to Candia for the final discussion. On 19 September 1358, the Senate, according to the proposal of the five *sapientes* who had negotiated with the Turkish ambassador the previous day, decided in favour of the signing of a new treaty that would repeat all the clauses of that of 1337 between the duke of Crete Giovanni Sanudo and the father of the present emir. In the new treaty, the island of Amorgos was included as well as any future possessions of Venice. A Venetian ambassador would be dispatched from Candia to Palatia, before whom the emir of Menteshe would take the oath and sign the treaty. On 20 September, it was decided that the duke of Crete would swear allegiance to the clauses of the treaty before the Turkish ambassador.[24] Finally, on 13 October 1358, the emir of Menteshe also signed the treaty and took the oath of allegiance.[25]

The long negotiations leading to the signing of the treaties of 1358 by the emirs of Menteshe and Aydin constitute good examples of how the government and the Senate of Crete acted as the main interlocutor with the emirates in the name of '… …..'. Afterwards, until 1367, the Cretan authorities consistently assumed the same role each time a new problem arose with Menteshe and Aydin.

There is no doubt that in the period 1356–58 diplomatic and commercial relations between Venice and the emirate of Menteshe were strained. On the contrary, exchanges with the emirate of Aydin, although not without problems, were much smoother. The signing of the treaty with the emir of Menteshe in 1358 was a decisive

---

21 *Duca di Candia. Quaternus Consiliorum*, no. 257.
22 There were probably complaints by the merchants in Chania in western Crete, since Candia was the main port of Crete that was in direct contact with the emirates. Thus, the rector of Chania asked the duke of Crete, and then the latter asked the doge of Venice, whether the citizens of Chania were obliged to pay for the salary of the consul in Theologo; on 20 November 1358, the doge of Venice Giovanni Delfino answered that all Cretan subjects should pay their share for the salary ('dicta impositio debet extendi ad omnes subditos insule nostre Crete'). See *Duca di Candia. Ducali e lettere ricevute (1358–1360; 1401–1405)*, ed. by Freddy Thiriet (Venice: Comitato per la Pubblicazione delle Fonti relative alla Storia di Venezia, 1978), no. 1.
23 *Duca di Candia. Quaternus Consiliorum*, no. 258.
24 *Duca di Candia. Quaternus Consiliorum*, nos 261–63.
25 On the events that had preceded the signature of the new treaty, the negotiations, and the text of the treaty, see Zachariadou, *Trade and Crusade*, pp. 60–62, 217–18.

step towards the full re-establishment of relations between the two sides. The treaty certainly did not solve all the problems and negotiations continued over the next few years, not only because outstanding issues were left unresolved, but also because new ones arose from time to time. Nevertheless, the fact that this treaty remained valid for seventeen years means that it had been founded on solid ground. In fact, thanks to these two treaties, gradually the relations between Crete and the two Turkish emirates were fully restored.

After 1358, the duke of Crete and his two councillors, having acquired more experience in such matters, slightly modified some of the relevant procedures in order to enhance their role as executive members of metropolitan policy, weakened by the powerful local Senate. As a result, in July 1361, when the need arose to elect a committee of six *sapientes* who would deal with a serious matter regarding the emirates, the Senate decided that, for the first time, three of these *sapientes* would be appointed by the government and only three would be elected by the local body of the Senate, and not the entire committee as was the custom until then.[26] Thus, the gap between the two centres of authority in Crete became more evident from 1360 onwards, although at the same time the possibility for a strong, local political front was reduced. In other words, it was no longer easy for the committee of *sapientes* to introduce for discussion proposals opposing those of the local government. Two months later, two proposals were submitted for debate and, coincidentally or not, the one approved was the proposal of the three *sapientes* chosen by the government.[27] About a year later, during the process for the election of a similar committee, a quota of one person per Venetian family was established.[28] In this way the Cretan government believed that factions against metropolitan policy could be avoided. Moreover, the procedure for the election of such committees and for debates in plenary sessions became stricter: all Senate members should be present in the sessions in order to reach decisions on urgent and very serious problems, and a tight schedule should be observed. For this reason it was required that the elected *sapientes* be present in Candia or return immediately to the city to avoid losing valuable time. It is possible that these measures to implement new political procedures that were easier to manipulate indicate that the government had already perceived a gradually increasing indifference to important state problems or even active opposition and efforts to undermine central policy on the part of some of the local Venetians.[29] It is worth noting that all these measures to strengthen the Cretan government's position vis-à-vis the local Venetians and,

---

26 Duca di Candia. Quaternus Consiliorum, no. 405.
27 Duca di Candia. Quaternus Consiliorum, no. 410.
28 On 29 May 1362, because of a new problem with the emir of Aydin, the Senate decreed that each of the five *sapientes* should come from a different family ('quinque sapientes unus pro domo'). See Duca di Candia. Quaternus Consiliorum, no. 447.
29 According to a decree dated 8 September 1361, some of the elected *sapientes* were not in Candia and, consequently, the council did not meet in time for the discussion of a matter concerning the emirate of Aydin; as a result, new letters were sent from the emir of Aydin and the Venetian consul in Palatia, seeking a response. On this occasion, the Senate decided that, because of the seriousness of the matter, all members of the Senate should participate in the session and every absent member should pay a fine

at the same time, to develop more flexible diplomatic procedures were taken a few years before the outbreak of the great Revolt of St Titus by the Venetians of Crete. It is thus certain that reactions of local Venetians against metropolitan policies were already apparent long before the outbreak of the revolt of 1363.

The office of the consul in Palatia and Theologo constituted another important matter for the local Venetians. Customarily, both consuls played a key role not only in Venetian commercial activities, but also in the negotiations and the diplomatic contacts before and after the treaties of 1358. Both were elected by the Cretan Senate and usually came from the Venetians of Crete who belonged to the upper stratum of the island's feudatories.[30] Between 1358 and 1362, five consuls were elected for Theologo.[31] The first two, although they lived in Crete, came from Venice, as the designation 'de Veneciis' indicates, while the other three were Cretans.[32] The five consuls were elected annually for Theologo, and while there is documentary evidence for elections for Palatia during the period, archival sources mention as consuls in Palatia Nicolo Pisani from April 1356 until May 1358 and Domenico Querini in September 1361.[33] Perhaps these two consuls covered the entire period; if so, they definitely remained in office longer than the consuls in Theologo, who served for only a year. What is certain from the extant documentation is that, during the period in question, letters from Palatia arrived in Crete, although it is not always clear who sent them. All things considered, one cannot exclude the possibility that the office remained vacant for a number of years, especially during periods of tense relations with the emir of Aydin, with the consul of Theologo acting for Palatia as well.

The consuls in Palatia and Theologo were sent to the emirates as representatives of all Venetians and not only of those in Crete. Nevertheless, since the great commercial interests of the Turkish emirates were directly linked to Crete, the salary of these consuls, as already mentioned, derived from a special duty on local trade paid by the island's merchants, who were active in the emirates.

---

of six *grossi*; furthermore, all *sapientes* were obliged to stay in the city until the final decision was taken and dispatched or else they should pay a fine of twenty-five *hyperpyra*. See *Duca di Candia. Quaternus Consiliorum*, no. 409.

30 In the treaties of 1337 with the emirs of Aydin and Menteshe, the clause about the election and the appointment of the consuls is quite clear: 'Et quod habeamus ibi unum consulem de nostris, quem voluerimus, qui gentem nostram et Venetos ac fideles omnes dicti domini ducis et omnes predictos regat et gubernet [...]' / 'Item quod dominatio Cretae habere possit supra omnes Cretenses et Venetos et fideles comunis Venetiarum consulem, quem constituere voluerit per suas litteras'. In the treaty of 1353 with the emir of Aydin, the same clause is again included: 'Item dominatio Cretae habeat unum consulem de suis, quem voluerit'. See Zachariadou, *Trade and Crusade*, pp. 191, 197, 214.

31 The first consul of Theologo after the treaty of 1358 was Giovanni Moro (elected on 24 August 1358). A year later, on 30 August 1359, the elected Ermolao Minotto refused the office and Nicola Morosini was elected in his place. Seven months later, Morosini resigned and Nicola Zorzi was elected on 18 March 1360. On 9 July 1361, Marino Morosini was elected and, finally, on 22 July 1362, Giovanni Mudazzo. See *Duca di Candia. Quaternus Consiliorum*, nos 257, 306–07, 342, 407, 460.

32 The designation 'de Veneciis' after the name usually means that the person lived in Crete, but was born and raised in Venice and had recently arrived in the island.

33 *Duca di Candia. Quaternus Consiliorum*, nos 178, 204, 224, 252, 410.

Apart from the office of consul, the Venetians of Crete had yet another opportunity to be involved in metropolitan politics via appointment to the prestigious office of ambassador (*ambaxator* or *nuncius*). The ambassador was the person who negotiated directly with the emir according to the instructions of the Senate; he sometimes used the assistance of the consul or of a person who lived in the emirate and had knowledge of the issues at hand. Furthermore, it was the Venetian ambassador who swore before the emir after the signing of a treaty, the same way the Turkish ambassador swore before the duke of Crete. This is why the ambassador should be an 'eminent, discreet, and capable person', usually a nobleman.[34] Depending on the circumstances, however, the ambassador could also be a qualified and experienced notary of the ducal chancery of Candia. This is the case of the notary Bentivegna Traversario, who was sent to Palatia to negotiate with the emir concerning the trade of alum between December 1359 and February 1360.[35] In fact, public notaries often served as auxiliary staff to the consul or the ambassador.[36]

In addition to commercial relations and diplomatic contacts with the Turkish emirates, the crusading movement in the Eastern Mediterranean in the mid-fourteenth century also enhanced the political significance of Crete. At the end of the war with Genoa in 1355, Venice joined the Holy League for a crusade against the Muslims in the region. The events and the ambiguous attitude of Venice, dictated by the possibility that the league might attack the Turkish emirates, are well known. Crete played a leading role in the coalition: Venice committed the colony to equip two or three galleys for the crusader fleet and to elect the corresponding *sopracomiti* in the Senate. Undoubtedly, these obligations further elevated the position of the Venetians of Crete, making them active members of the wider foreign policy of their mother city. At the same time, however, they were burdened by the high cost of these obligations, which very soon gave rise to the outbreak of the revolt of 1363. Even so, the diplomatic and military activity inside and outside the island offered the opportunity to a number of local Venetians to occupy salaried offices, which enhanced their financial, social, and political status.

---

34 On 15 August 1352, for example, the Cretan Senate decided to dispatch an ambassador to Theologo, authorized to negotiate with the emir. According to the decision: 'mittatur per dominium unus ambaxator qui sit providus, discretus et sufficiens', see *Duca di Candia. Quaternus Consiliorum*, no. 64. On 20 September 1358, the duke of Crete and the emir of Menteshe reached an agreement and the Senate decided that: 'dominus ducha iuret in presentia ambaxatoris Palatie concordium pacis [...]. Item quod predictum iuramentum fiat per nostrum nuncium iturum Palatiam coram domino Palatie', see *Duca di Candia. Quaternus Consiliorum*, no. 263.
35 On 5 December 1359, it was decided that a notary of the ducal chancery ('unus de notariis curie maioris') be dispatched to Palatia and, on 2 February 1360, a letter was sent to the notary Bentivegna Traversario, who was already in Palatia. See *Duca di Candia. Quaternus Consiliorum*, nos 330, 332.
36 For example, during the disarmament of the galleys of the Holy League, it was decided on 31 August 1360 that a notary be sent from Crete to Rhodes to deliver a letter from the Cretan government to the papal legate, and, on 12 September 1361, that an ambassador be dispatched to the emir of Menteshe together with a notary and his assistant ('prefatus ambaxator [...] teneatur conducere et habere secum ad suas expensas duos famulos et unum notarium cum eius famulo'). See *Duca di Candia. Quaternus Consiliorum*, nos 356, 410.

Venice joined the Holy League in 1357 and promised to contribute a number of galleys. About the activity, if there was any, of the Christian fleet we know almost nothing.[37] The crusader fleet was finally dissolved in August 1360, but Venice maintained two galleys to patrol the Aegean and face Turkish attacks.[38] Despite the formal dissolution of the crusader fleet, Venice continued to call these two galleys 'crusading' ('galee unionis'), emphasizing their mission and maybe hoping for a revival of the crusading efforts. Nevertheless, keeping 'crusading' galleys was actually a defensive measure that concerned almost exclusively Venice and its possessions in the Eastern Mediterranean. This is why the *sopracomiti* of these galleys were elected by the Cretan Great Council and not by the Senate, as the custom had been in previous years within the framework of the Holy League.[39] Furthermore, in the absence of the captain of the Gulf, the *sopracomitus* elected with the highest number of votes would take the title and office of the 'captain of the galleys' ('capitaneus galearum') and would coordinate the rest of the *sopracomiti*.[40]

The intense diplomatic and crusading activity between 1357 and 1363, which turned Crete into a stronghold for Venetian diplomacy, was violently interrupted by the outbreak of the Revolt of St Titus in August 1363. Four years later, in 1367, after the suppression of the revolt, the political context on the island was no longer the same. The two local councils representing the Venetians of Crete, the Senate and the Great Council, had disappeared, while the tripartite government was reinforced by a fourth member, also sent from Venice, the so-called 'captain of Crete' (*capitaneus Crete*), who was responsible for the military organization and the control of the local defence system.[41] Although the duke of Crete continued to be the person implementing Venetian foreign policy concerning the emirates and any crusading effort in the Aegean and the Eastern Mediterranean, the relevant mandates now came directly

---

37 Kenneth M. Setton, *The Papacy and the Levant, 1204–1571*, 4 vols (Philadelphia: American Philosophical Society, 1976–84), I: *The Thirteenth and Fourteenth Centuries*, pp. 224–57; Zachariadou, *Trade and Crusade*, 60–67.

38 According to a decree of the Cretan Senate, on 31 August 1360 the papal legate left Smyrna, the city's captain being the *sopracomito* Matteo Mudazzo of Crete, and went to the island of Rhodes, where the Hospitallers' galleys were going to be disarmed; the same decree further informs us that the Lusignan galleys also returned to Cyprus to be disarmed. On Crete, the Senate decided to send a small galley ('galedellum') to Rhodes with a notary carrying a letter from the duke of Crete for the papal legate, probably concerning the crusading fleet. See *Duca di Candia. Quaternus Consiliorum*, no. 356.

39 See, for example, the elections of *sopracomiti* by the Senate in 1358–60 (*Duca di Candia. Quaternus Consiliorum*, nos 231, 278, 286, 333) and those by the Great Council in 1361–62 (*Duca di Candia. Quaternus Consiliorum*, nos 389, 390, 400, 439).

40 On 25 April 1361, Leonardo Gradenigo and Pietro Grimani were elected 'sopracomiti' by the Cretan Great Council and the former, who had received the highest number of votes, was appointed 'capitaneus' in order to exercise the 'capitanariam' of the galleys 'quandocumque essent sine capitaneo Culphi secundum mandatum ducale', see *Duca di Candia. Quaternus Consiliorum*, no. 400. On 8 February 1362, three, instead of two, 'sopracomiti' were elected; according to the same decision, in this case the 'capitaneus' should be the one who had received the votes of at least half the members of the council: see *Duca di Candia. Quaternus Consiliorum*, no. 428.

41 On the office of *capitaneus Crete*, see Charalambos Gasparis, 'Μητροπολιτική εξουσία και αξιωματούχοι των αποικιών. Ο καπιτάνος Κρήτης', *Σύμμεικτα*, 12 (1998), 171–214.

from Venice and the metropolitan Senate. During the years of the Revolt of St Titus, diplomatic exchanges between Crete and the Turkish emirates were not a priority, although the five *provisores* dispatched from Venice to Crete were commissioned to negotiate, if necessary, with the emirates.[42] Talks with the emirates restarted after 1367, when normality had returned to the island. In early 1368, the Venetian Senate received a letter from the duke of Crete regarding the negotiations with the emir of Aydin. On 2 March 1368, the members of the Venetian Senate commissioned the duke of Crete to send an ambassador to Theologo to discuss a number of issues; precise instructions about the negotiations were given, the same way the Cretan Senate used to do before 1363. The Venetian Senate also informed the duke of Crete that, in the event the embassy failed, 'after we are fully informed about the negotiations, we will make sure to let you know what can be done'.[43] The voice of the Venetians of Crete was silenced and the political role of Crete was thenceforth greatly diminished.

---

42 On 12 September 1363, the doge of Venice dispatched five *provisores* to Crete, authorized to negotiate with the rebels and to act as a temporary government; according to their mandate, they could also discuss, if necessary, any urgent problem with any ruler or person, including the Turks, i.e. the emirs of Aydin and Menteshe ('Item volumus quod possitis in casu necessitatis, mittere, tractare et componere cum quibuscumque dominis et personis, etiam Turchis, si necessitas pur urgeret'). In March 1364, Venice sent Angelo Michiel to the emirates to secure provisions for the Venetian army fighting in Crete; at the same time, the new *provisores* of Crete were commissioned to give him the necessary money for these provisions. See Freddy Thiriet, *Délibérations des assemblées vénitiennes concernant la Romanie*, I: *(1160–1363)* (Paris - La Haye: Mouton et Cie, 1966), no. 702 and p. 325; Johannes Jegerlehner, 'Der Aufstand der Kandiotischen Ritterschaft gegen das Mutterland Venedig. 1363–1365', *Byzantinische Zeitschrift*, 12 (1903), 78–125 (pp. 124–25).

43 According to the Venetian Senate, 'Et quod propterea rescribant nobis omnia que sequuntur in predictis, ut similiter informati ad plenum, et superinde sicut opus fuerit providere possimus', Archivio di Stato di Venezia, *Senato Misti*, Reg. 32, fol. 107^r. The issues that the ambassador from Crete had to discuss with the emir of Aydin were the Venetian prisoners in Theologo, the indemnity of 2.000 ducats to Nicolo Morosini, and the illegal minting of Venetian ducats in the emirate.

JOHANNES PREISER-KAPELLER

A Climate for Crusading? Environmental Factors in the History of the Eastern Mediterranean during the Life and Reign of Peter I of Cyprus (1329–1369)[*]

In Leontios Makhairas's chronicle, Cyprus's Christian history starts with a severe long-lasting drought, resulting in famine and the abandonment of the island. Only St Helen, the mother of Emperor Constantine, who restores precipitation and settlement, ends this state of emergency.[1] Interestingly, such a prolonged drought around this period is also mentioned in the Life of St Spyridon, but here that saint miraculously brings about rainfall. Despite the clearly hagiographic background, in their systematic catalogues both Ioannis Telelis as well as Dennis Stathakopoulos list this exceptional drought among the extreme events of the early fourth century CE, since other sources equally confirm dry conditions for this period.[2]

For our topic, the awareness of the ecological vulnerability of the island, especially due to a lack of precipitation, as reflected in this passage, is of interest. This

---

[*] I would like to thank the editors of this volume for the organisation of the wonderful conference on Peter I of Cyprus at the Notre Dame Global Gateway in Rome in October 2016 and the generous invitation to present a paper and to publish it. The study was finished within the framework of the project 'Moving Byzantium: Mobility, Microstructures and Personal Agency' (FWF-Z 288 Wittgenstein-Preis; PI: Prof. Claudia Rapp; <http://rapp.univie.ac.at/>) funded by the Austrian Science Fund FWF at the Institute for Medieval Research/Division for Byzantine Research of the Austrian Academy of Sciences.

[1] Leontios Makhairas, *Recital Concerning the Sweet Land of Cyprus Entitled 'Chronicle'*, ed. by Richard M. Dawkins (Oxford: Clarendon Press, 1932), I, § 3, pp. 2–5: 'Constantine the Great, after he was baptized, saw that our land of Cyprus had been without any inhabitants for thirty-six years, because there was a great famine from lack of rain and all the tillage was spoiled. And the famine became great, and all the waters of the springs failed, and men were going from place to place with their flocks to find water that they might live, they and their flocks. And everything dried up, both cisterns and springs; and they deserted our most admirable Cyprus, and crossed over to this place and to that, wheresoever each one of them found a resting place. And the island remained without inhabitants for thirty-six years.'

[2] Ioannis G. Telelis, Μετεωρολογικά φαινόμενα και κλίμα στο Βυζάντιο, 2 vols (Athens: Akademia Athenon, 2004), no. 6; Dionysios Stathakopoulos, *Famine and Pestilence in the Late Roman and Early Byzantine Empire: A Systematic Survey of Subsistence Crises and Epidemics* (Aldershot: Ashgate, 2004), no. 2.

Johannes Preiser-Kapeller • Austrian Academy of Sciences, Austria

vulnerability is of course also significant today, when Cyprus is facing a decreasing amount of precipitation and a dramatically increasing water demand; thus, the island is more and more dependent on cost- and energy-intensive desalination plants.[3] This paper, however, will focus on the fourteenth century. First, it presents the range and sources for environmental history by contextualising another extreme weather event of the lifetime of Peter I within the climatic conditions of the time. Secondly, the paper discusses aspects of the vulnerability and ecology of Cyprus in the fourteenth century Cyprus more generally. Finally, some interplays between changing environmental conditions and crusading at that time are analysed. It will become evident that these interplays are complex, demand a well-balanced combination of socio-economic and paleo-environmental evidence and elude any climatic deterministic interpretations.[4]

The environmental history as well as all other aspects of the historical study of the Mediterranean have profited enormously from the defining opus magnum of Fernand Braudel, *La Méditerranée et le monde méditerranéen à l'époque de Philippe II*, first published in 1949. Braudel located environmental factors mainly in the relatively stable sphere of the 'longue durée', which provided the long term parameters for the 'medium term' dynamics of social and economic history and the more rapid sequence of the 'history of events'.[5] In later works, however, Braudel adopted new findings from climate history research and also recognized the importance of short-term fluctuations in climatic parameters.[6] A new perspective highlighting the actual multitude of 'micro-regions' within the Mediterranean, characterised in each case by specific geological, hydrological and atmospheric conditions, was introduced by Peregrine Horden and Nicholas Purcell in their ground-breaking volume *The Corrupting Sea: A Study of Mediterranean History* in 2000. They equally illustrated how this fragmentation in turn necessitated and stimulated connectivity and the exchange of goods, peoples and ideas between these areas.[7] While Horden und Purcell thereby challenged the idea of one spatially coherent Mediterranean,

---

3 Christina Papadaskalopoulou and others, 'Review and Assessment of the Adaptive Capacity of the Water Sector in Cyprus against Climate Change Impacts on Water Availability', *Resources, Conservation and Recycling*, 105 (2015), pp. 95–112; Theodoros Zachariadis, *Climate Change in Cyprus: Review of the Impacts and Outline of an Adaptation Strategy* (Heidelberg: Springer, 2016).

4 Cf. also Bruce M. S. Campbell, 'Nature as Historical Protagonist: Environment and Society in Pre-industrial England', *Economic History Review*, 63/2 (2010), pp. 281–314; Ioannis G. Telelis, 'Environmental History and Byzantine Studies. A Survey of Topics and Results', in *Aureus. Volume dedicated to Professor Evangelos K. Chrysos*, ed. by Taxiarchis Kolias and Konstantinos Pitsakis (Athens: National Hellenic Research Foundation, 2014), pp. 737–60.

5 See the expanded new edition Fernand Braudel, *La méditerranée et le monde méditerranéen à l'époque de Philippe II* (Paris: Armand Colin, 1966).

6 On the development of Braudel's perspective see Franz Mauelshagen, *Klimageschichte der Neuzeit* (Darmstadt: Wissenschaftliche Buchgesellschaft, 2010), pp. 30–31; Dominik Collet, *Die doppelte Katastrophe. Klima und Kultur in der europäischen Hungerkrise 1770–1772* (Göttingen: Vandenhoeck & Ruprecht, 2019), p. 7.

7 Peregrine Horden and Nicholas Purcell, *The Corrupting Sea: A Study of Mediterranean History* (Oxford and Malden: Wiley-Blackwell, 2000).

recent studies using both historical as well as natural scientific data (see below) even more emphasised the temporal dynamics of climatic and environmental conditions below the level of the 'longue durée' in various macro-regions at large as well as in specific smaller areas.[8] The present study uses these latest findings and trends in scholarships in order to integrate the environmental aspects of the history of Cyprus and of the reign of King Peter I within the wider debate on the 'Great Transition' of the fourteenth century (see below).[9]

Later in his chronicle, Makhairas reports another extreme event; this time the opposite of drought took place early in the lifetime of Peter I. The flood of November 1330 in Nicosia occurred during the prime time of autumn-winter precipitation, but was so devastating that a procession in remembrance was held still one century later.[10] New annual paleo-environmental reconstructions of summer wetness and dryness across Europe and the Mediterranean for the last 2,000 years – the so-called 'Old World Drought Atlas' (OWDA) of Edward R. Cook and his colleagues – enable us to contextualize this extreme event within the general climatic conditions of the year 1330, which according to this reconstruction was especially humid across most of the Eastern Mediterranean [Fig. 3.1].[11] The data of the 'Old World Drought Atlas' equally allows for an annual reconstruction of wetness or dryness in time series across longer durations; we can see that for the area of Nicosia the early 1330s were the wettest in the entire fourteenth century [Fig. 3.2]. Beyond the regional level, this data also provides a general perspective on the diversity of weather conditions in the various areas and cities with which Cyprus was connected through the networks of trade as reconstructed on the basis of the 'pratica della mercatura' of Francesco Pegolotti,

---

8   See especially the overview in Jürg Luterbacher and others, 'A Review of 2000 Years of Paleoclimatic Evidence in the Mediterranean', in *The Climate of the Mediterranean Region: from the Past to the Future*, ed. by Piero Lionello (Amsterdam: Elsevier, 2012), pp. 87–185, and the new massive volume *Das Mittelmeer: Geschichte und Zukunft eines ökologisch sensiblen Raums*, ed. by Robert Hofrichter (Berlin: Springer, 2020). As the subtitle of David Abulafia, *The Great Sea: A Human History of the Mediterranean* (Oxford: Oxford University Press, 2011), indicates, his study focuses primarily on human agency and is less relevant for the environmental history of the Mediterranean. Cyprian Broodbank, *The Making of the Middle Sea: A History of the Mediterranean from the Beginning to the Emergence of the Classical World* (Oxford: Oxford University Press, 2013), in turn, provides valuable insights on the interplay between environmental factors and human communities in the early history of the Mediterranean.
9   Bruce M. S. Campbell, *The Great Transition: Climate, Disease and Society in the Late-Medieval World* (Cambridge: Cambridge University Press, 2016).
10 Makhairas, *Recital*, I, § 65, pp. 60–61: '(On the tenth of November) 1330 after Christ (there was a great storm of rain, and in the night) the river in the capital came down with such violence that it rooted up many trees and brought them down and carried them to the town, and blocked up the Seneschal's Bridge: and the river made a way round in the town, and destroyed many houses and drowned many people. And the height of the water is marked (for remembrance) by a nail of St George of the Halfcastes (and by another nail in the house of the Count of Tripolis over against the castle. And because of those souls and for a remembrance a procession is held even to this day on the tenth of November).' On the precipitation regime of Cyprus cf. also Adrianos Retalis and others, 'Precipitation Climatology over the Mediterranean Basin – Validation over Cyprus', *Atmospheric Research*, 169 (2016), pp. 449–58.
11 Edward R. Cook and others, 'Old World Megadroughts and Pluvials during the Common Era', *Science Advances* 1, No. 10 (November 2015), pp. 1–9.

who spent some time in Famagusta during the 1320s [Fig. 3.3].[12] The exceptional humidity of the early 1330s affected not only Cyprus in a catastrophic way: severe floods occurred in parts of southern France during the same winter. Aragon was plagued by floods in September 1331; and in November 1333, the Arno submerged large parts of Florence. Equally, floods and other catastrophes in the 1330s contributed to the crisis of the faltering rule of the Mongol Yuan dynasty in China, illustrating the 'global' dimension of this period of weather extremes as one result of the general change of climatic conditions during the fourteenth century.[13]

The background to this increasing amount of data, which enables us to connect our historical evidence with more and more detailed and reliable natural scientific data, needs to be shortly discussed. In most parts of the Mediterranean, systematic instrumental measurements of precipitation, temperature or air pressure only began in the later nineteenth and early twentieth century.[14] For periods before that time, we have to rely on a combination of 'archives of society', especially written sources on weather conditions, and of 'archives of nature', that is data based on various phenomena such as tree rings or lake sediments whose past quantity or chemical composition depended on climatic parameters at that earlier times. A pioneer of this 'multi-archival' approach is the Swiss historian Christian Pfister. Two important types of archives of nature, which provide data in annual resolution, are tree rings and speleothems (meaning dripstones, whose rate of growth and chemical composition depends on precipitation and temperature conditions). This data then is compared and calibrated against modern-day precipitation or temperature measurements in order to project back reconstructions of past conditions as in the case of the 'Old World Drought Atlas'.[15] On this basis, three significant periods of transition have

---

12 Francesco Pegolotti, *La pratica della mercatura: Book of Descriptions of Countries and Measures of Merchandise*, ed. by Allan Evans, The Medieval Academy of America 24 (Cambridge, Mass.: Medieval Academy of America, 1936).
13 Campbell, *The Great Transition*; John L. Brooke, *Climate Change and the Course of Global History: A Rough Journey* (Cambridge: Cambridge University Press, 2014); Elena Xoplaki and others, 'The Medieval Climate Anomaly and Byzantium: A Review of the Evidence on Climatic Fluctuations, Economic Performance and Societal Change', *Quaternary Science Reviews*, 136 (2016), pp. 229–52; Johannes Preiser-Kapeller and Ekaterini Mitsiou, 'The Little Ice Age and Byzantium within the Eastern Mediterranean, ca. 1200–1350 CE: An Essay on Old Debates and New Scenarios', in *The Crisis of the 14th Century: 'Teleconnections' between Environmental and Societal Change?*, ed. by Martin Bauch and Gerrit J. Schenk, Das Mittelalter: Perspektiven mediävistischer Forschung, Beihefte, 13 (Berlin: De Gruyter, 2019), pp. 190–220. On the 'global context' of Peter's reign cf. also John France, 'Philippe de Mézières and the Military History of the Fourteenth Century', in *Philippe de Mézières and His Age. Piety and Politics in the Fourteenth Century*, ed. by Renate Blumenfeld-Kosinski and Kiril Petkov (Leiden, Boston: Brill, 2012), pp. 283–94.
14 For Cyprus, early systematic measures were undertaken between 1834 and 1839 by the American missionary Lorenzo Warriner Pease, see: *The Diaries of Lorenzo Warriner Pease, 1834–1839. An American Missionary in Cyprus and his Travels in the Holy Land, Asia Minor and Greece*, ed. by Rita Severis (Ashgate: Nicosia 2002). I thank Christopher David Schabel for this reference.
15 Rudolf Brázdil, Christian Pfister, Heinz Wanner, Hans von Storch, and Jürg Luterbacher, 'Historical Climatology in Europe – the State of the Art', *Climatic Change*, 70 (2005), pp. 363–430; Rüdiger Glaser, *Klimageschichte Mitteleuropas: 1200 Jahre Wetter, Klima, Katastrophen* (Darmstadt: Wissenschaftliche Buchgesellschaft, 2008); Christian-Dietrich Schönwiese, *Klimatologie* (Stuttgart: UTB, 2008); Franz

been identified in the global climate history of the Middle Ages: from the 'Roman Climate Optimum' towards cooler conditions in Late Antiquity (with one especially cold period recently identified as 'Late Antique Little Ice Age'), towards warmer conditions of the 'Medieval Climate Anomaly' in the ninth century CE and again towards colder conditions of the 'Little Ice Age' in the late thirteenth and fourteenth century.[16]

These global trends, however, had regionally diverse impacts, depending on respective interplays between local ecologies, patterns of land use and socio-economic organisation, as also the example of Cyprus demonstrates. Clearly, the 'sweet land of Cyprus' (as Makhairas calls it) experienced some significant environmentally induced challenges similar to other polities of the time. Immediately after the description of the flood of 1330, Makhairas describes three more catastrophes which took place during the lifetime of Peter I: two waves of the plague pandemic of the Black Death in 1348 and 1363 and a plague of locusts in 1351.[17] Especially the later phenomenon has attracted several studies during the last decades, not the least since locusts remained a problem for the island until the nineteenth century. In all of these studies up to the most recent one of Irene Dietzel, the beginning of the damaging presence of these insects on Cyprus has been identified with the plague of locusts recorded by Makhairas for 1351.[18] Sara Kate Raphael however, has called our attention to a letter of Bishop Godfrey of Hebron to King Edward I of England from 1280, in which the 'high price of food' in the Holy Land is traced back to 'the

---

Mauelshagen, *Klimageschichte der Neuzeit* (Darmstadt: Wissenschaftliche Buchgesellschaft, 2010); Ozan Mert Göktürk, *Climate in the Eastern Mediterranean through the Holocene Inferred from Turkish Stalagmites* (unpublished doctoral thesis, University of Bern, 2011); Luterbacher and others, 'A Review of 2000 Years of Paleoclimatic Evidence in the Mediterranean'; Raymond S. Bradley, *Paleoclimatology. Reconstructing Climates of the Quaternary* (Amsterdam: Academic Press, 2014).

16 Luterbacher and others, 'A Review of 2000 Years of Paleoclimatic Evidence'; Xoplaki and others, 'The Medieval Climate Anomaly and Byzantium'; Preiser-Kapeller and Mitsiou, 'The Little Ice Age and Byzantium'; Johannes Preiser-Kapeller, 'A Collapse of the Eastern Mediterranean? New Results and Theories on the Interplay between Climate and Societies in Byzantium and the Near East, ca. 1000–1200 AD', *Jahrbuch der Österreichischen Byzantinistik*, 65 (2015), pp. 195–242.

17 Makhairas, *Recital*, § 66, pp. 60–61: 'And in the year 1348 God sent a plague for our sins, and the half of the island died. And in 1351 the locust, with God's blessing, began to come to Cyprus (and did great damage). And in 1363 another plague came upon the children, and (the greater part of) the island was destroyed.' On the interpretation of the plague and other vicissitudes as signs of God's wrath, cf. also Angel Nicolaou-Konnari, 'Apologists or Critics? The Reign of Peter I of Lusignan (1359–1369) Viewed by Philippe de Mézières (1327–1405) and Leontios Makhairas (ca. 1360/80–after 1432)', in *Philippe de Mézières and His Age. Piety and Politics in the Fourteenth Century*, ed. by Renate Blumenfeld-Kosinski and Kiril Petkov (Leiden, Boston: Brill, 2012), pp. 359–402, and in general, Christian Rohr, *Extreme Naturereignisse im Ostalpenraum: Naturerfahrung im Spätmittelalter und am Beginn der Neuzeit* (Cologne: Böhlau, 2007). On Makhairas' narrative of Peter's rule in general cf. Peter W. Edbury, 'Machaut, Mézières, Makhairas and Amadi: Constructing the Reign of Peter I (1359–1369)', in *Philippe de Mézières and His Age. Piety and Politics in the Fourteenth Century*, ed. by Renate Blumenfeld-Kosinski and Kiril Petkov (Leiden, Boston: Brill, 2012), pp. 349–58.

18 Ronald C. Jennings, 'The Locust Problem in Cyprus', *Bulletin of the School of Oriental and African Studies*, 51/2 (1988), 279–313; Irene Dietzel, *The Ecology of Coexistence and Conflict in Cyprus: Exploring the Religion, Nature, and Culture of a Mediterranean Island* (Berlin: De Gruyter, 2014).

locusts that hit Armenia [meaning Cilicia] and Cyprus' in that year, thus already 70 years before the plague of 1351.[19] Only for the later plague of locusts, however, we learn about possible remedies for this problem as advised by the Patriarch Ignatios II of Antioch (c. 1341/42–1363), who was in Cyprus at that time; this ecclesiastical tradition equally continued until the period of Makhairas.[20] Modern scholarship has tried to identify other chains of causation for the appearance of the locusts during the Lusignan period. As Jennings pointed out, increasing deforestation has been identified 'as an important factor in making Cyprus hospitable to locusts', caused 'by the introduction [...] by the Latin (Venetian and French) elite of a 'full-blown plantation agriculture' for the cultivation of sugar in order to meet the increasing demand of 'Latin Europe'.[21] Similarly, deforestation is regarded as causal for processes of erosion, aggravating both the effects of floods and droughts and leading to landscape degradation.[22] As a matter of fact and as reported by Marino Sanudo Torsello for instance, the production of sugar very much expanded in fourteenth century Cyprus;[23] as Mohamed Ouerfelli has described, investment in the cultivation and refinement of sugar intensified especially after the loss of the last territories in Syria to the Mamluks in 1291. The most important agents in this business were the royal house of Lusignan, the Knights Hospitaller (after the 1310s) and especially (since the reign of Peter I) the Venetian family of Corner. Due to its demand for water, areas of sugar production were centred in the southwest of the island, around ancient Paphos and along the river Kouris, where the Lusignan kings, the Hospitallers and the Corner were active [Fig. 3.4].[24] In the same areas,

---

19 Sarah Kate Raphael, *Climate and Political Climate: Environmental Disasters in the Medieval Levant* (Leiden: Brill, 2013), pp. 39–40 (with further references) and pp. 168–83 (on the frequency of plagues of locusts in the late medieval Levant).
20 Makhairas, *Recital*, I, § 40, pp. 40–41: 'Also Ignatios, the Patriarch of Antioch, hearing of the great damage done by the locusts [in 1351] told King Hugh to give orders for a picture to be painted of St Christopher the Martyr and St Tarasios, Patriarch of Constantinople, and St Tryphon the Martyr, and the said patriarch consecrated it; and they sent it to Palokythro, where the (plague of locusts) was. And he told them that when the locust hatched they should carry the picture in procession and say mass, and the Lord will protect the crops. (And they were delivered from the locust).' On the life and career of Patriarch Ignatios II of Antioch cf. *Prosopographische Lexikon der Palaiologenzeit*, ed. by Erich Trapp and others, CD-ROM-Version (Vienna: Verlag der Österreichischen Akademie der Wissenschaften, 2001), no. 8073.
21 Jennings, 'The Locust Problem in Cyprus', pp. 312–13.
22 Dietzel, *The Ecology of Coexistence*; Zachariadis, *Climate Change in Cyprus*; N. Cleridou and others, 'Water Resources of Cyprus under Changing Climatic Conditions: Modelling Approach, Validation and Limitations', *Environmental Modelling & Software*, 60 (2014), 202–18; Patricia L. Fall and others, 'Long-term Agrarian Landscapes in the Troodos Foothills, Cyprus', *Journal of Archaeological Science*, 39 (2012), 2335–47.
23 Marino Sanudo Torsello, *Liber Secretorum Fidelium Crucis*, trans. by Peter Lock (Farnham: Ashgate, 2011), pp. 51–52: 'In Cyprus great quantities of sugar are produced from which Christians can be adequately supplied.'
24 Mohamed Ouerfelli, *Le Sucre: Production, commercialisation et usages dans la Méditerranée médiévale* (Leiden: Brill, 2008), pp. 103–21; Jean Richard, 'Une économie coloniale? Chypre et ses ressources agricoles au Moyen Age', *Byzantinische Forschungen*, 5 (1977), 331–52; Marie-Louise von Wartburg, 'The Archaeology of Sugar Cane Production: A Survey of Twenty Years of Research in Cyprus', *The Antiquaries Journal*, 81 (2001), 305–35; Richard Jones, *Sweet Waste: Medieval Sugar Production in the Mediterranean Viewed from*

also another water-demanding crop—cotton—was cultivated by the same actors, but never reached the importance of sugar.[25] Since the Hospitallers and the Corner had to share the same waters of the river Kouris for the irrigation of their plantations, conflicts as we encounter them in the sources may seem 'natural', especially from the late fourteenth century onwards, when precipitation conditions on Cyprus changed for the worse (see also below).[26] Accordingly, it may seem plausible that these competing enterprises contributed to an overexploitation of water and forest resources with its medium- and long-term impacts on the island's ecology as described by Jennings, for instance. But as Sarah Harris or Irene Dietzel have pointed out in their recent studies, this narrative of landscape degradation on Cyprus due to foreign, 'colonial' rule can actually been traced back to the time of the British occupation in 1878. The British claimed to have 'found a severely degraded landscape, ruined by years of mistreatment by foreign rulers and a population of ignorant natives.' Blame was assigned in ascending order to the Lusignan, the Venetians and of course to the Ottomans, while British rule was also legitimized as a regime of landscape recovery and especially forest restoration.[27] Recent geo-archaeological research, however, has put into question this narrative of 'linear and progressive' degradation and highlights the resilience of local ecologies, allowing for the reconstitution of landscapes when land use abated. Most data for this research so far stems from sites in and around the Troodos Mountains [Fig. 3.4]; we would need similar studies for the areas of intensified sugar plantation for instance to determine its actual impact on the hydrological and ecological balance. So far at least, results compel us to re-evaluate more generally the notion of increased vulnerability of the island to environmental change due to 'colonial' rule.[28]

---

the 2002 *Excavation at Tawahin es-Sukkar, Safi, Jordan* (Glasgow: Potingair Press, 2017), pp. 23, 46–50, 70–72. To what extent sugar was cultivated and processed already before the late thirteenth century, perhaps since the time of Arab occupation, which ended in the tenth century, is unclear, see Sidney M. Greenfield, 'Cyprus and the beginnings of modern sugar cane plantations and plantation slavery', in Jace Andrew Stukey, ed., *The Eastern Mediterranean frontier of Latin Christendom* (Farnham: Ashgate, 2014), pp. 135–54.

25 Marino Sanudo Torsello, *Liber Secretorum Fidelium Crucis*, pp. 51–52: 'Indeed, cotton grows in Apulia, Sicily, Crete, Romania and Cyprus in good quantities.' Cf. also Jong-Kuk Nam, *Le commerce du coton en Méditerranée à la fin du Moyen Age* (Leiden: Brill, 2007), pp. 173–83.

26 von Wartburg, 'The archaeology of sugar cane production'; Ouerfelli, *Le Sucre*, pp. 122–26; Jones, *Sweet Waste*, pp. 46–50.

27 Dietzel, *The Ecology of Coexistence*; Sarah E. Harris, *Colonial Forestry and Environmental History: British Policies in Cyprus, 1878–1960* (unpublished doctoral thesis, The University of Texas, Austin, 2007); Sarah E. Harris, 'Cyprus as a degraded landscape or resilient environment in the wake of colonial intrusion', *Proceedings of the National Academy of Sciences*, 109 (2012), pp. 3670–75 (for the citation). Cf. also Aleksander G. Pluskowski, Adrian J. Boas, and Christopher Gerrard, 'The Ecology of Crusading: Investigating the Environmental Impact of Holy War and Colonisation at the Frontiers of Medieval Europe', *Medieval Archaeology*, 55 (2011), pp. 192–225.

28 Karl W. Butzer and Sarah E. Harris, 'Geoarchaeological Approaches to the Environmental History of Cyprus: Explication and Critical Evaluation', *Journal of Archaeological Science*, 34 (2007), pp. 1932–52: 'The tentative evidence for partial biotic recovery and pedogenic renewal supports the notion that the Mediterranean biota of Cyprus were sufficiently resilient, so that environmental transformation was

Without doubt, the theoreticians of crusade in the fourteenth century, such as Marino Sanudo Torsello, also established their own narratives on the ecologies of their desired theatre of operations in order to support their strategic planning. Thus we read in the same work that 'Cyprus abounds in much corn, wine and beasts or animals both larger and small for sending to the army' of an intended crusade, while the island is rated worse than Egypt when Sanudo wishes to reject those who argue for an assemblage of the crusade on Cyprus.[29]

As we learn from the treatise of William of Adam, planning for the crusade also included the hope to take advantage of environmentally induced calamities of the enemy. The low flood of the Nile and the following famine, which affected Egypt in 1295 to 1297, is explained by William of Adam as divine punishment for the ejection of the Christians from the Holy Land a few years earlier. This interpretation according to him was shared by the 'Saracens', who even 'considered returning the Holy Land to the Christians' until the 'perfidious' Byzantine Emperor (Andronikos II) brought relief to the Egyptians.[30] This drought and famine, which afflicted Syria in that time, are as well described in detail by al-Maqrīzī and by al-Nuwayrī.[31] In addition, Sanudo Torsello mentions it as God's punishment for the Egyptians.[32] According to the Chronicle of Amadi, though, the Byzantines were not the only ones to provide relief to Egypt; grain was also sent from Sicily and Rhodes (then still under Byzantine

---

cyclical, rather than linear and progressive. Landscapes can deteriorate, especially after agricultural abandonment, but they may also be reconstituted'. Cf. also P. L. Fall, 'Modern Vegetation, Pollen and Climate Relationships on the Mediterranean Island of Cyprus', *Review of Palaeobotany and Palynology*, 185 (2012), pp. 79–92; Christopher S. Galletti and others, 'Maxent Modeling of Ancient and Modern Agricultural Terraces in the Troodos Foothills, Cyprus', *Applied Geography*, 39 (2013), pp. 46–56.

29 Marino Sanudo Torsello, *Liber Secretorum Fidelium Crucis*, pp. 75–76 and 117.

30 Guillelmus Ade, *Tractatus quomodo Sarraceni sunt expugnandi*, ed. and trans. by Giles Constable, (Washington, D. C.: Dumbarton Oaks, 2012), chapter III, pp. 40–43: 'When also Egypt suffers from famine he [the Byzantine Emperor Andronikos II, r. 1282–1328] sends grain and whatever other necessities of life he can. When the Christians lost Acre [in 1291] and its surroundings it happened that the Lord afflicted Egypt with a great plague of famine (*tanta ... plaga famis*), for the river Nile had not flooded for three years, so that the Saracens collapsed, wild with hunger, dead on every side, lacking the means to survive. The famine was so great that grain could not be found I do not say for food but not even for seed. The Saracens indeed attributed this plague to a miracle because through a miracle the Lord thus had afflicted Egypt because the Christians had been expelled from the Holy Land, and they therefore considered returning the Holy Land to the Christians. This emperor, however, the persecutor and ancient enemy of the Roman church, made one of the largest ships in the world and sent it loaded with grain to Alexandria. This ship carried 14,000 mule loads of grain in addition to arms and many other things. Thus, the emperor, the perfidious friend and ally of the Saracens and enemy and torment of the Romans, relieved the neediness of the Babylonians.'

31 Aḥmad ibn 'Alī al-Maqrīzī, *Mamluk Economics: A Study and Translation of al-Maqrīzī's Ighāthah*, trans. by Adel Allouche (Salt Lake City: University of Utah, 1994), pp. 43–48; Šihāb ad-Dīn Aḥmad b. 'Abd al-Wahhāb b. Muḥammad an-Nuwairī, *The Ultimate Ambition in the Arts of Erudition*, trans. by Elias Muhanna (London: Penguin, 2016), pp. 258–59. Cf. also Raphael, *Climate and Political Climate*, pp. 90–94; Kristine Chalyan-Daffner, *Natural Disasters in Mamlūk Egypt (1250–1517): Perceptions, Interpretations and Human Responses* (unpublished doctoral thesis, University of Heidelberg, 2013), pp. 566–78.

32 Marino Sanudo Torsello, *Liber Secretorum Fidelium Crucis*, pp. 370–71.

rule, but soon to be conquered by the Knights Hospitaller).³³ All these authors understood the dependence of Egypt on the quantity of the Nile flood, which, as we know now in detail, in turn depended on the amount of precipitation in the upper East African catchment area of the Nile and was connected to the monsoon systems of the Indian Ocean. Since antiquity, measurements of the minima and maxima of the Nile flood were transmitted (from the Nilometer in Cairo, for instance), and from 622 CE onwards we possess more or less continuous data.³⁴ Recent analyses of these time series indicate a significant transition from a period of relatively low floods towards a major high in the mid-fourteenth century, again as one aspect of the general change of global climate conditions in this period [Fig. 3.5].³⁵ This did not necessarily improve the parameters for agriculture in Egypt, since frequent extremely high floods could have as catastrophic consequences as low ones.³⁶ Moreover, low Nile floods still occurred as reported by al-Maqrīzī for the year 1373–1374, when the Nile 'did not attain 16 cubits'; prices rose, resulting in famine, which was aggravated by a plague. This time, we also learn about measures of the state authorities to lessen the suffering of the poor.³⁷ Stuart Borsch in his monograph "The Black Death in Egypt and England" provides fourteenth century data, which illustrates the dramatic differences in grain prices during 'good' and 'bad' years [Fig. 3.6].³⁸ As the armchair strategists of the crusade may have hoped, such supply shortfalls could perturb the

---

33 *Chroniques d'Amadi et de Strambaldi, première partie: Chronique d'Amadi*, ed. by René de Mas-Latrie (Paris: Imprimerie nationale, 1891), p. 233. On the trade between Cyprus and Mamluk Egypt, see David Jacoby, 'Western Merchants, Pilgrims, and Travellers in Alexandria in the Time of Philippe de Mézières (ca. 1327–1405)', in *Philippe de Mézières and His Age. Piety and Politics in the Fourteenth Century*, ed. by Renate Blumenfeld-Kosinski and Kiril Petkov (Leiden, Boston: Brill, 2012), pp. 403–25; Mike Carr, *Merchant Crusaders in the Aegean 1291–1352* (Woodbridge: Boydell & Brewer, 2015), pp. 135–36.
34 William Popper, *The Cairo Nilometer: Studies in Ibn Taghri Birdi's Chronicle of Egypt* (Berkeley: University of California Press, 1951).
35 Elfatih A. B. Eltahir and Guiling Wang, 'Nilometers, El Niño, and Climate Variability', *Geophysical Research Letters* 26/4 (1999), pp. 489–92; Fekri A. Hassan, 'Extreme Nile Floods and Famines in Medieval Egypt (AD 930–1500) and their Climatic Implications', *Quaternary International*, 173/74 (2007), pp. 101–12; Fekri A. Hassan, 'Nile Flood Discharge during the Medieval Climate Anomaly', PAGES news, 19/1 (2011), pp. 30–31. Cf. also Stuart J. Borsch, 'Nile Floods and the Irrigation System in Fifteenth-Century Egypt', *Mamluk Studies Review*, 4 (2000), pp. 131–45.
36 Chalyan-Daffner, *Natural Disasters in Mamlūk Egypt*; Alan Mikhail, *Nature and Empire in Ottoman Egypt: An Environmental History* (Cambridge: Cambridge University Press, 2011).
37 al-Maqrīzī, *Mamluk Economics*, p. 49: 'A famine occurred during the reign of al-Ashraf Shaʿbān (764–78/1363–1376). It was caused by the failure of the Nile to reach its plenitude in the year 776/1374 [should be corrected to 1373–1374]: indeed, it did not attain 16 cubits. The canal was opened, [causing] the water level to drop and prices to increase. […] Foodstuffs became scarce and were rarely available. So many people died of hunger that they filled the streets. This was followed by an epidemic that caused further deaths. […] The sultan gave orders to collect the poor, whom he distributed among the commanders and the wealthy merchants. The famine lasted approximately two years; the God send succour to mankind and caused the Nile to flow, quenching the land's thirst.' Cf. also Raphael, *Climate and Political Climate*, pp. 22–23.
38 Stuart J. Borsch, *The Black Death in Egypt and England: A Comparative Study* (Austin: University of Texas Press, 2005). Cf. also Johan Söderberg, 'Grain Prices in Cairo and Europe in the Middle Ages', *Research in Economic History*, 24 (2007), pp. 189–216.

stability of political regimes in Egypt or even reduce its military capacities, especially in combination with other calamities such as an epizootic of horses as reported by an-Nuwairī for Syria in 1303/04. He tells us that the 'stables of amirs and soldiery were empty'.[39] Nevertheless, environmental vicissitudes alone were not sufficient to bring about the polity's collapse, and a well-organized regime may have been able to reduce the population's distress and thereby even increase its legitimation, as al-Maqrīzī reports for the year 1373–74.[40] For Egypt in the 1360s, we also cannot see that Peter I may have profited from any environmentally induced weakening of the Mamluks; and the plague epidemic of 1362–63 affected both Cyprus and Egypt.

Another aspect of the Nile's environmental history, though, may have played a role in the planning and timing of Peter's most spectacular endeavour, the attack on Alexandria in October 1365. As Eric Cooper has analysed recently in detail, Alexandria provided the best port along the entire coast of Egypt. Yet, 'throughout the medieval period, the city had no natural connection to the Nile and the rest of the country anymore, even through Lake Mareotis, which had dwindled to marshland as a result of the silting up of the Canopic branch of the Nile'. Only very laboriously, the canal of Alexandria could be kept operational in order to provide connectivity with Cairo and irrigation for the city's hinterland. Sultan an-Nāṣir Muḥammad ibn Qalāwūn in 1310 invested a considerable amount of money and work force to upgrade this vital canal, but still its navigability especially for larger ships was only guaranteed during the high-water level of the Nile between September and January. Thus, as Cooper illustrates, there was also only a small overlap with the main sailing season in the Mediterranean from September until early November.[41] Anyone intending to use Alexandria as basis for a possible further advance into Egypt by ship had to take this window of time into consideration, as the army of Peter I presumably did in October 1365. Of course, at the same time, even without the threat of an advancing Mamluk army, the approaching end of the sailing season forced the crusaders either to risk a several month-long stay in Egypt or to return to their bases very quickly – as they eventually did.[42] A few years later, the relatively beneficial navigation conditions on the Alexandria canal created by the works of Ibn Qalāwūn ended; after high floods of the Nile in 1368/69, sand blocked the mouth of the Lake Abu Qir and the canal.[43]

---

39 an-Nuwairī, *The Ultimate Ambition*, pp. 276–77. Cf. also Raphael, *Climate and Political Climate*, p. 47; David Joseph Wrisley, 'Historical Narration and Digression in al-Nuwairī al-Iskandarānī's Kitāb al-Ilmām', in *Philippe de Mézières and His Age: Piety and Politics in the Fourteenth Century*, ed. by Renate Blumenfeld-Kosinski and Kiril Petkov (Leiden: Brill, 2012), pp. 451–76.
40 Eric Chaney, 'Revolt on the Nile: Economic Shocks, Religion, and Political Power', *Econometrica* 81/5 (September 2013), pp. 2033–53; Jo Van Steenbergen, *Order out of Chaos: Patronage, Conflict and Mamluk Socio-Political Culture, 1341–1382*, The Medieval Mediterranean, 40 (Leiden: Brill, 2006).
41 John P. Cooper, *The Medieval Nile. Route, Navigation, and Landscape in Islamic Egypt* (New York: The American University in Cairo Press, 2014), pp. 52–68, 117–23, 132–37, 162–83.
42 Cf. Jo Van Steenbergen, 'The Alexandrian Crusade (1365) and the Mamluk Sources: Reassessment of the kitab al-ilmam of an-Nuwayri al-Iskandarani', *East and West in the Crusader States: Context, Contacts, Confrontations*, 3 (2003), pp. 123–37.
43 Cooper, *The Medieval Nile*, pp. 66–67.

Climatic trends, however, may have played a more decisive role for the operations of Peter's fleet along the coasts of *Turchia* and Syria during the 1360s, with the occupations of Korykos and of Antalya as the most significant achievements.[44] The data of the 'Old World Drought Atlas' indicates extremely dry conditions for most of Asia Minor and parts of coastal Syria for several years, such as in 1362 for instance, when the emir of Antalya unsuccessfully attempted to re-conquer his city. During the entire reign of Peter I, repeatedly droughts affected the territories of the Turkish emirates [Fig. 3.7].[45] A view on the reconstructed time series for the Antalya region identifies the 1360s as the driest decade in the entire period from 1250 to 1450 [Fig. 3.8]; a similar picture emerges for the Konya area, one core of the emirate of Karaman, the most powerful among the Turkish polities of the region [Fig. 3.9]. The same is true for the area of Lebanon in the Mamluk Sultanate [Fig. 3.10].[46] Cyprus, on the contrast, did not experience such extremely dry conditions during these years [Fig. 3.2]. Interestingly, we observe similar spatial and temporal patterns of long-lasting droughts in twentieth-century data from Turkey; the areas with an already delicate balance of precipitation in the interior of Anatolia of course were affected most.[47] In the 1360s, however, also the usually more humid coastal regions frequently suffered from drought. As Nükhet Varlık demonstrates in her ground-breaking monograph based on written sources, another plague epidemic in the years 1362–63 aggravated these hydrological shortfalls in Anatolia.[48] We could therefore assume that this ongoing environmental stress reduced the power of resistance of the Turkish potentates to the benefit of Lusignan crusading. Explicitly, however, such a causal link is only drawn the other way round by Makhairas for the Turks attacking Cyprus in 1363 when they

---

44 Barbara H. Flemming, *Landschaftsgeschichte von Pamphylien, Pisidien und Lykien im Spätmittelalter* (Wiesbaden: Franz Steiner GmbH, 1964), pp. 83–88; Elizabeth A. Zachariadou, *Trade and Crusade: Venetian Crete and the Emirates of Menteshe and Aydin (1300–1415)* (Venice: Hellenic Institute of Byzantine and Post-Byzantine Studies, 1983), pp. 66–67; Hansgerd Hellenkemper and Friedrich Hild, *Lykien und Pamphylien*, Tabula Imperii Byzantini, 8 (Vienna: Verlag der Österreichischen Akademie der Wissenschaften, 2004), pp. 135–36, 312–14, 588–89.
45 Cook and others, 'Old World Megadroughts'; Hellenkemper and Hild, *Lykien und Pamphylien*, pp. 312–14. Cf. also Ramzi Touchan and others, 'May–June Precipitation Reconstruction of Southwestern Anatolia, Turkey during the Last 900 Years from Tree Rings', *Quaternary Research*, 68 (2007), pp. 196–202; Ingo Heinrich and others, 'Winter-to-spring Temperature Dynamics in Turkey Derived from Tree Rings since AD 1125', *Climate Dynamics*, 41 (2013), pp. 1685–1701; John F. Haldon and others, 'The Climate and Environment of Byzantine Anatolia: Integrating Science, History, and Archaeology', *Journal of Interdisciplinary History*, 45/2 (2014), pp. 113–61; Hai Cheng and others, 'The Climate Variability in Northern Levant over the Past 20,000 Years', *Geophysical Research Letters*, 42 (October 2015), pp. 8641–50.
46 Cf. also David Kaniewski and others, 'The Medieval Climate Anomaly and the Little Ice Age in Coastal Syria Inferred from Pollen-derived Palaeoclimatic Patterns', *Global and Planetary Change*, 78 (2011), pp. 178–87.
47 Wolf-Dieter Hütteroth, *Türkei*, Wissenschaftliche Länderkunden (Darmstadt: Wissenschaftliche Buchgesellschaft, 1982), pp. 123–27.
48 Nükhet Varlık, *Plague and Empire in the Early Modern Mediterranean World: The Ottoman Experience, 1347–1600* (Cambridge: Cambridge University Press, 2015). Cf. also Michael W. Dols, 'The Second Plague Pandemic and Its Recurrences in the Middle East: 1347–1894', *Journal of the Economic and Social History of the Orient*, 22/2 (1979), pp. 162–89; Ole J. Benedictow, *The Black Death 1346–1353: The Complete History* (Woodbridge: Boydell & Brewer, 2004), pp. 60–74.

learned about the outbreak of the plague there and the king's absence in Europe.[49] Again, the one-to-one equation of environmentally induced relative gains or losses into strategic advantages cannot be solved that easily as it is often done also in recent studies on climatic effects on history.[50]

To sum up: we can identify the impacts of the global 'Great Transition' of the fourteenth century as recently impressively described by Bruce Campbell[51] in the Eastern Mediterranean during the life and reign of Peter I of Cyprus, both in the increasing frequency of meteorological extremes and the occurrence of accompanying plagues of locusts or of the Black Death. Variations in the severity and spatial extent as well as of timing and duration of these phenomena interacted with differences in regional ecologies, patterns of land use and socio-economic organisation as well as levels of political stability of regimes; together, they created very diverse impacts on the short- and long-term balances of powers between Christian and Muslim polities around Cyprus.

We need more detailed studies and further data to do justice to the complexity of these processes. For the island of Cyprus itself, the assassination of Peter I on 16 January 1369 not only marked a turning point in the fate of the kingdom towards the worse in the interpretation of his friends, such as Philip of Mézières,[52] but also in Cyprus's climate history: around that time, a long-term upwards trend in summer precipitation was replaced by a long-term downwards one for one century until the death of the last Lusignan King James III in 1474 [Fig. 3.2]. A medieval observer, if he or she had become aware of this fact, would have maybe regarded it as an impact of the Divine; the modern-day reader may connect it to the global impact of oscillations of solar irradiance.[53]

---

49 Makhairas, *Recital*, I, § 137, pp. 120–21: 'When the Turks heard that the plague [in 1363] had wiped out the men of Cyprus, and the king was in France, all the Turks together fitted out twelve galleys and appointed a captain called Chamout Raïs, and came to Cyprus and landed at Pentagia and raided many people; and he carried them off prisoners and went away (to Turkey).' Cf. also Aysu Dincer, 'Disease in a Sunny Climate: Effects of the Plague on Family and Wealth in Cyprus in the 1360s', in: *Economic and Biological Interactions in Preindustrial Europe, from the 13th to the 18th Century* (Florence: Firenze University Press, 2010), pp. 531–40; Nicolaou-Konnari, 'Apologists or Critics', pp. 373–74.

50 Cf. for instance David D. Zhang and others, 'Global Climate Change, War, and Population Decline in Recent Human History', *Proceedings of the National Academy of Sciences*, 104/79 (2007), pp. 19214–19; Solomon M. Hsiang, Marshall Burke and Edward Miguel, 'Quantifying the Influence of Climate on Human Conflict', *Science* 341, 1235367 (2013) doi: 10.1126/science.1235367.

51 Campbell, *The Great Transition*.

52 For this interpretation cf. Kevin Brownlee, 'The Figure of Peter I and the Status of Cyprus in *Le songe du vieil pelerin*: Crusade Ideology, Salvation History, and Authorial Self-Representation', in: *Philippe de Mézières and His Age: Piety and Politics in the Fourteenth Century*, ed. by Renate Blumenfeld-Kosinski and Kiril Petkov (Leiden, Boston: Brill, 2012), pp. 165–88.

53 For the actual validity of biblical models for the interpretation of extreme events in the middle ages see however Rohr, *Extreme Naturereignisse im Ostalpenraum*, and Thomas Wozniak, *Naturereignisse im frühen Mittelalter. Das Zeugnis der Geschichtsschreibung vom 6. bis 11. Jahrhundert* (Berlin, Boston: de Gruyter, 2020).

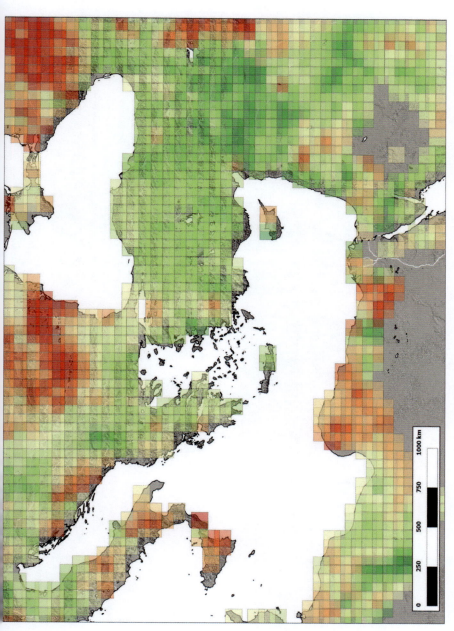

Fig. 3.1: Reconstruction of summer wetness and dryness across the Eastern Mediterranean for the year 1330; the colour scale from red to green shows the Palmer Drought Severity index, ranging from -4 or less (extreme drought) to +4 or above (extremely moist) (data: Cook and others, 'Old World Megadroughts'; map: J. Preiser-Kapeller, 2017).

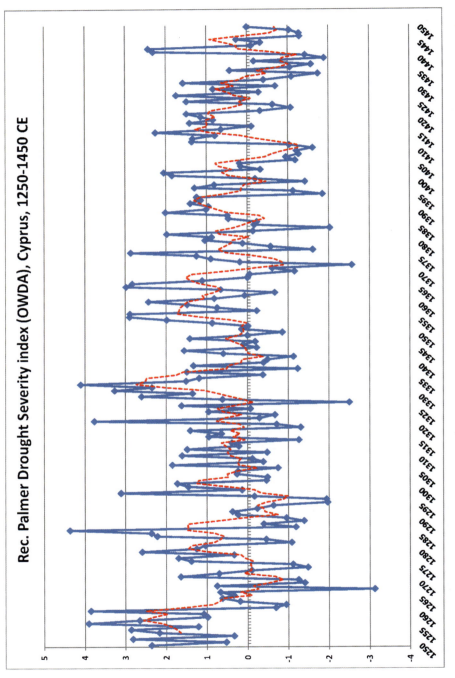

Fig. 3.2: Reconstruction of summer wetness and dryness in Cyprus for the years 1250–1450 (Palmer Drought Severity index) (data: Cook and others, 'Old World Megadroughts'; graph: J. Preiser-Kapeller, 2017).

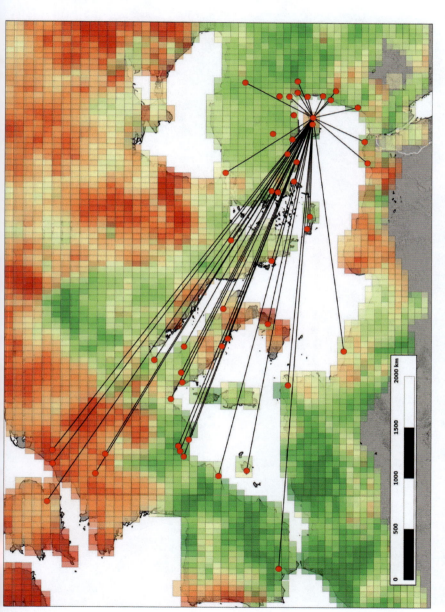

Fig. 3.3: Reconstruction of summer wetness and dryness across Europe and the Mediterranean for the year 1330; the colour scale from red to green shows the Palmer Drought Severity index, ranging from -4 or less (extreme drought) to +4 or above (extremely moist) (data: Cook and others, 'Old World Megadroughts') and network of trade connections of Famagusta according to Pegolotti, *La pratica della mercatura; map*: J. Preiser-Kapeller, 2017).

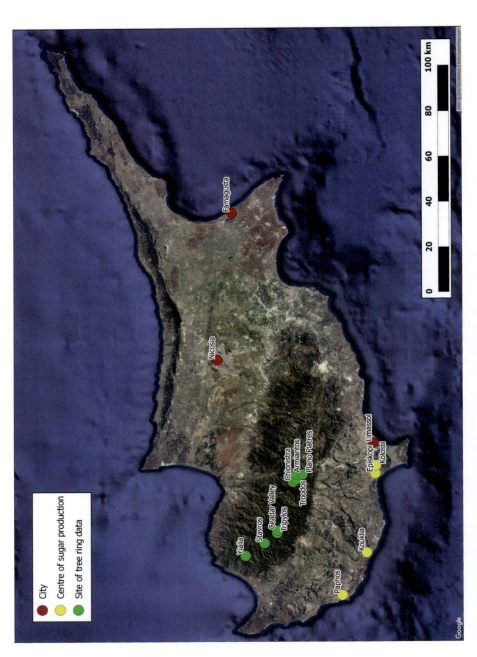

Fig. 3.4: Map of important cities and centres of sugar production on fourteenth century Cyprus (data: Ouerfelli, *Le Sucre*) and sites of tree ring data (cf. https://www.ncdc.noaa.gov/data-access/paleoclimatology-data/datasets/tree-ring; map: J. Preiser-Kapeller, 2017).

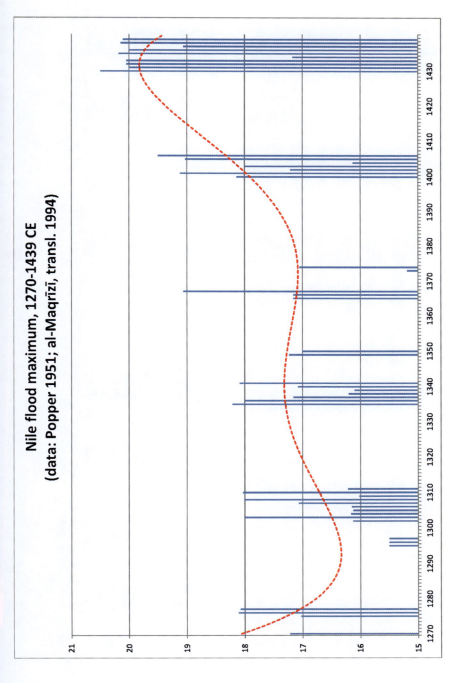

Fig. 3.5: Nile flood maxima data for the years 1270 to 1439 (data: Popper, *The Cairo Nilometer*; al-Maqrīzī, *Mamluk Economics*; graph: J. Preiser-Kapeller, 2017).

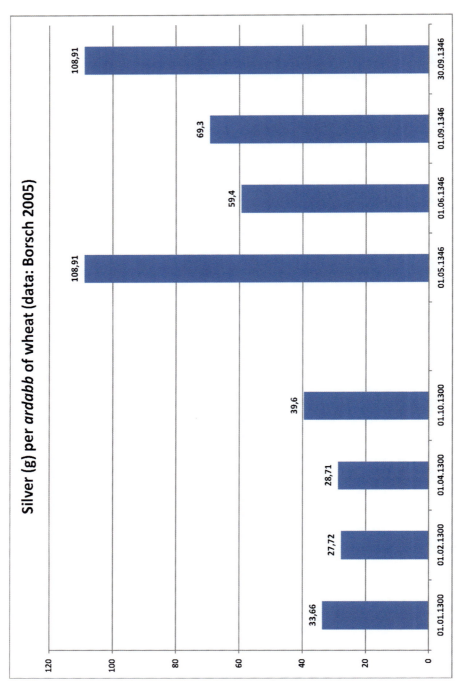

Fig. 3.6: Differences in wheat prices in Egypt across a year with a sufficient Nile flood level and a year with an insufficient Nile flood level in the fourteenth century (data: Borsch, *The Black Death*; graph: J. Preiser-Kapeller, 2017).

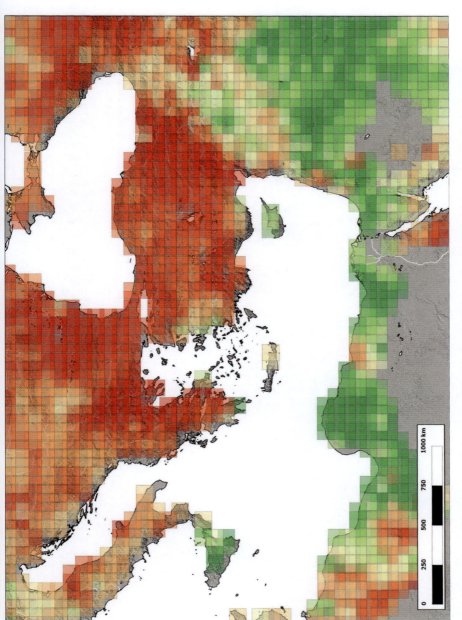

Fig. 3.7: Reconstruction of summer wetness and dryness across the Eastern Mediterranean for the year 1362; the colour scale from red to green shows the Palmer Drought Severity index, ranging from -4 or less (extreme drought) to +4 or above (extremely moist) (data: Cook and others, 'Old World Megadroughts'; map: J. Preiser-Kapeller, 2017).

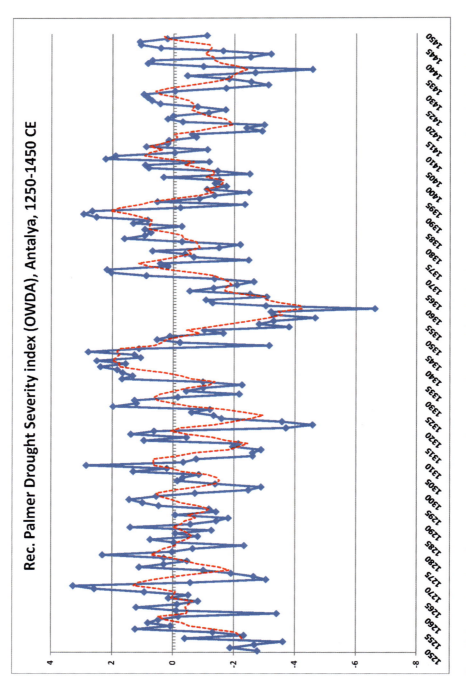

Fig. 3.8: Reconstruction of summer wetness and dryness for the area of Antalya for the years 1250–1450 (Palmer Drought Severity index) (data: Cook and others, 'Old World Megadroughts'; graph: J. Preiser-Kapeller, 2017).

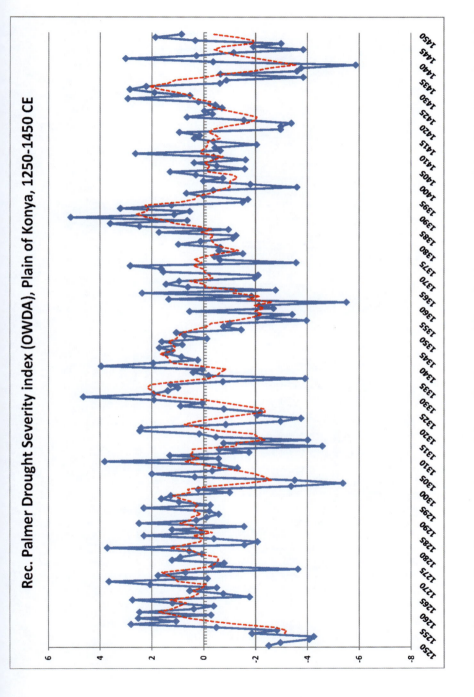

Fig. 3.9: Reconstruction of summer wetness and dryness for the area of Konya for the years 1250–1450 (Palmer Drought Severity index) (data: Cook and others, 'Old World Megadroughts'; graph: J. Preiser-Kapeller, 2017).

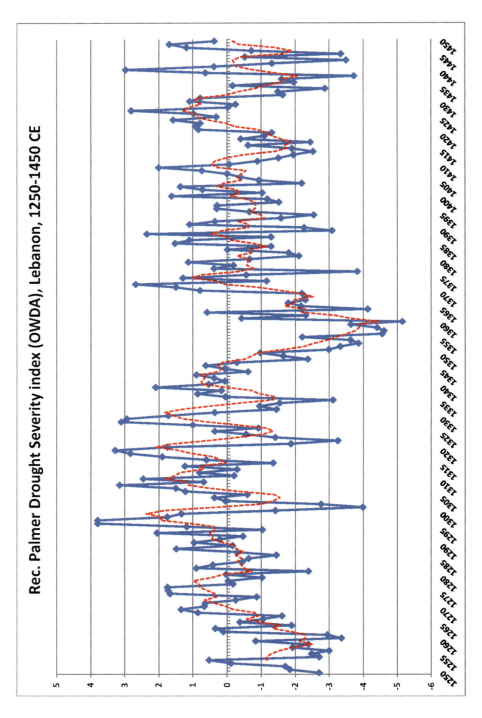

Fig. 3.10: Reconstruction of summer wetness and dryness for the area of Lebanon for the years 1250–1450 (Palmer Drought Severity index) (data: Cook and others, 'Old World Megadroughts'; graph: J. Preiser-Kapeller, 2017).

MICHALIS OLYMPIOS

Angevin and Lusignan Visual Claims to the Crown of Jerusalem: Parallel Lives?

The loss of the town of Acre to Latin Christendom in 1291 could only be described as a profoundly cataclysmic event. The outcome of decades of armed struggle against Mamluk military prowess, it sealed the irrevocable collapse of Frankish power in Latin Syria and the decisive reshuffling of the demographic, social, economic, and political map of the late medieval Mediterranean. Nevertheless, despite the wholesale eradication of what once were the Principality of Antioch (1268), the County of Tripoli (1289), and the Latin Kingdom of Jerusalem, the eminently prestigious royal title in the land where Christ had worn the Crown of Thorns carried on being claimed by the rival dynasties of the Angevins of Naples and the Lusignans of Cyprus for as long as the latter sat on their respective thrones, and by their successors thereafter.[1]

Historians have long queried the documentary sources in an effort to probe the legitimacy of each claimant's rights and discuss the plausible incentives that prompted such an enduring obsession with the title of a – for all intents and purposes – defunct polity; they have also attempted to gauge the degree of involvement of successive sovereigns on both camps with the affairs of the Holy Land, in order to evaluate their willingness to devote time and resources to the reinstatement of Christian rule in the Levant and, thus, the lengths to which they

---

1 Steven Runciman, 'The Crown of Jerusalem', *Palestine Exploration Quarterly*, 92 (1960), 8–18. On the events surrounding the fall of Acre, see generally: Jean Richard, *The Crusades, c. 1071–c. 1291*, trans. by Jean Birrell, Cambridge Medieval Textbooks (Cambridge: Cambridge University Press, 1999), pp. 460–69; Peter W. Edbury, 'The Crusader States', in *The New Cambridge Medieval History*, 7 vols (Cambridge: Cambridge University Press, 1995–2006), V (ed. by David Abulafia), pp. 590–606 (606); Jonathan Riley-Smith, *The Crusades: A History* (New Haven - London: Yale University Press, 2005²), pp. 241–44; Michel Balard, *Les Latins en Orient (XIe–XVe siècle)*, Nouvelle Clio: L'histoire et ses problèmes (Paris: Presses Universitaires de France, 2006), pp. 209–12; Thomas Asbridge, *The Crusades: The War for the Holy Land* (London: Simon and Schuster, 2010), pp. 651–58; the second half of the essays in *Acre and Its Falls: Studies in the History of a Crusader City*, ed. by John France, History of Warfare, 116 (Leiden - Boston: Brill, 2018).

Michalis Olympios • University of Cyprus

Crusading, Society, and Politics in the Eastern Mediterranean in the Age of King Peter I of Cyprus, ed. by Alexander Beihammer and Angel Nicolaou-Konnari, MEDNEX, 10 (Turnhout, 2022), pp. 157–173
© BREPOLS PUBLISHERS 10.1484/M.MEDNEX-EB.5.128464

would go to justify their claim. Conversely, what has hitherto been comparatively little studied in connection with these issues is the visual evidence furnished by works of art commissioned by and for the ruling houses of Naples and Cyprus, or by individuals in their employ and their immediate environment. When not preoccupied with essential questions of style, date, and attribution, art historians have contributed cogent insights into the ways in which particular buildings and objects produced for the court responded to the contemporary need for political and dynastic self-promotion. In this short paper, I will venture to review the major material evidence for the official, ceremonial, and ideological use of the title of Jerusalem by both the Angevins and Lusignans in the half-century or so following the obliteration of the crusader mainland. By examining the two dynasties' attitudes towards the title and its potential ramifications on the political scene of the Eastern Mediterranean and Europe, I shall attempt to demonstrate that the two royal houses wished to bank on their claim in vastly diverging ways with a view to achieving a completely different set of goals.

Charles I (1266–85), a brother of Louis IX of France and the first Angevin king of Sicily, appears to have staked his claim to the throne of Jerusalem almost from his reign's very beginning. Charles's conquest of southern Italy and Sicily having resulted in the execution of Conradin, the last king of Jerusalem of the Hohenstaufen line, in 1268, rights to the title were subsequently proclaimed by Hugh of Antioch-Lusignan, who had succeeded Hugh II (1253–67) as king of Cyprus the previous year, and his aunt, Maria of Antioch. Although the latter presented a legally sounder case, being a closer relative of the deceased sovereign, in the end the barons of the High Court of Jerusalem opted for Hugh, probably due to his being already in charge of the ailing kingdom's affairs and due to his ability to mobilize his Cypriot troops for its defence. At the time Hugh was crowned king of Jerusalem at Tyre in 1269, Charles of Anjou was making his first move towards securing a foothold in the Holy Land. It has recently been shown that Charles's interest in the Latin kingdom's affairs went as far back as the eve of Louis IX's Tunis crusade (1270), which marked both the beginning of his generous provisioning of the Latin Levant and the earliest extant testimonies of his acquaintance with Maria of Antioch. The salutary supply of foodstuffs and military equipment to the East, mainly via the military orders, continued unabated through the 1270s, while Maria was campaigning at the papal court for the recognition of her rights to the Jerusalem crown and negotiating their sale to Charles. The latter's purchase of the title in 1277 marked a turning point in his eastern policy, which could now lead to more concrete action in favour of the Holy Land.[2] His new acquisition

---

2 For these developments, see: Peter W. Edbury, *The Kingdom of Cyprus and the Crusades, 1191–1374* (Cambridge: Cambridge University Press, 1991), pp. 35–36, 93–96; David Abulafia, *The Western Mediterranean Kingdoms 1200–1500: The Struggle for Dominion*, The Medieval World (London - New York: Longman, 1997), pp. 62–66; Jean Dunbabin, *Charles I of Anjou: Power, Kingship and State-Making in Thirteenth-Century Europe*, The Medieval World (London - New York: Longman, 1998), pp. 96–97, 227; Gian Luca Borghese, *Carlo I d'Angiò e il Mediterraneo: politica, diplomazia e commercio internazionale prima dei Vespri*, Collection de l'École française de Rome, 411 (Rome: École française de Rome, 2008), pp. 181–85, 190, 220–27; Philip B. Baldwin, 'Charles of Anjou, Pope Gregory X and the Crown of Jerusalem', *Journal of Medieval*

was celebrated with the minting of gold and silver *carlini* the following year, which displayed the arms of Anjou impaled with those of Jerusalem on the obverse.[3]

In spite of his grand eastern ambitions, Charles sought to deal with the Mamluks at the diplomatic level, without putting into motion any serious plan for direct military action.[4] Of his successors, Charles II (1289–1309) and Robert I (1309–43), who also styled themselves 'kings of Jerusalem and Sicily' even after the fall of Acre, only the latter is known to have gone beyond training a watchful eye on the East, by maintaining correspondence with local rulers and establishing, together with his wife, Sancia of Mallorca, a Franciscan convent on Mount Zion in the 1330s and 1340s.[5] Robert's latest biography highlights the king's minimal martial involvement in ventures concerned with the defence of the Latin East, which seems to have paralleled his distaste for large-scale military campaigns in general, except for those dedicated to recovering Sicily from the Aragonese – a perennial entry in the Angevin political agenda.[6] The reluctance of Charles I's immediate descendants to commit to any substantial military project in the region is perhaps reflected in the excision of the arms of Jerusalem from the reverse of the silver *gigliati* issued under Charles II and Robert after the monetary reform of 1303.[7] In other words, although the Angevins

---

History, 38 (2012), 424–42; Philip B. Baldwin, *Gregory X and the Crusades* (Woodbridge: The Boydell Press, 2014), pp. 104–36; ; Georges Jehel, *Les Angevins de Naples: une dynastie européenne 1246-1266–1442*, Biographies et Mythes historiques (Paris: Ellipses, 2014), pp. 109–12.

3 Philip Grierson and Lucia Travaini, *Medieval European Coinage, with a Catalogue of the Coins in the Fitzwilliam Museum, Cambridge, 14 Italy (III) (South Italy, Sicily, Sardinia)* (Cambridge: Cambridge University Press, 1998), pp. 195–97, 205. The Jerusalem arms also appeared, at about the same time, on the tomb of Charles' son, Philip of Anjou (d. 1277), in Trani Cathedral: Lorenz Enderlein, *Die Grablegen des Hauses Anjou in Unteritalien: Totenkult und Monumente 1266–1343*, Römische Studien des Bibliotheca Hertziana, 12 (Worms am Rhein: Wernersche Verlagsgesellschaft, 1997), pp. 32–33; Tanja Michalsky, *Memoria und Repräsentation: Die Grabmäler des Königshauses Anjou in Italien*, Veröffentlichungen des Max-Planck-Instituts für Geschichte, 157 (Göttingen: Vandenhoeck & Ruprecht, 2000), pp. 251–52; Francesco Aceto, 'La sculpture, de Charles Ier d'Anjou à la mort de Jeanne Ire (1266–1382)', in *L'Europe des Anjou: aventure des princes angevins du XIIIe au XVe siècle* (Paris: Somogy éditions d'art, 2001), pp. 74–87 (77).

4 Dunbabin, *Charles I of Anjou*, pp. 96–97, 227; Borghese, *Carlo I d'Angiò*, pp. 184–85.

5 Abulafia, *The Western Mediterranean Kingdoms*, pp. 112–13; Borghese, *Carlo I d'Angiò*, p. 261. On Charles II, see also: Norman Housley, 'Charles II of Naples and the Kingdom of Jerusalem', *Byzantion*, 54 (1984), 527–35; Andreas Kiesewetter, *Die Anfänge der Regierung König Karls II. von Anjou (1278–1295): Das Königreich Neapel, die Grafschaft Provence und der Mittelmeerraum zu Ausgang des 13. Jahrhunderts*, Historische Studien, 451 (Husum: Matthiesen Verlag, 1999), pp. 364–70; Jehel, *Les Angevins de Naples*, pp. 161–62.

6 Samantha Kelly, *The New Solomon: Robert of Naples (1309–1343) and Fourteenth-Century Kingship*, The Medieval Mediterranean, 48 (Leiden - Boston: Brill, 2003), pp. 209–13. On Robert and Sancia's installation of the friars on Mount Zion, see also Denys Pringle, *The Churches of the Crusader Kingdom of Jerusalem: A Corpus*, 4 vols (Cambridge: Cambridge University Press, 1993–2009), III, pp. 261–87, esp. 269–71. See also Jehel, *Les Angevins de Naples*, pp. 201–03.

7 Grierson and Travaini, *Medieval European Coinage*, pp. 207, 210, 213–25. The arms of Jerusalem do not resurface on Angevin coinage until the old-fashioned *carlini* issued during the reign of Joanna I and Louis of Taranto (1352–62), for which see pp. 232–33. Joanna's and Louis' artistic patronage respected dynastic tradition in pairing the Angevin arms with those of Jerusalem: Alessandra Perriccioli Saggese, 'Gli *Statuti dell'Ordine dello Spirito Santo o del Nodo*. Immagine e ideologia del potere regio a Napoli alla metà del

fastidiously held on to the title of the lost kingdom, they appear not to have been prepared to lavish precious resources on its recovery, when those could be employed more usefully elsewhere.

The Angevins' overall rather lukewarm stance vis-à-vis the situation in the East during the first half of the fourteenth century, as glimpsed through the fragmentary textual record, is belied by the available visual evidence. Even a cursory survey would reveal that the arms of the Kingdom of Jerusalem featured quite prominently in works of art more or less closely linked to the patronage of the Neapolitan royalty and their entourage. Arguably the most celebrated example would be the painted panel of *St Louis of Toulouse crowning Robert I* by the Sienese painter Simone Martini (Fig. 1).[8] Scholars tend to date this work to immediately after the canonization of St Louis in 1317 and to concur on its function as an altarpiece, yet individual authors have located it in widely varied contexts, ranging from the high altar (or the transept) of the Franciscan church of San Lorenzo Maggiore, to chapels dedicated to St Louis

---

Trecento', in *Medioevo: immagini e ideologie*, ed. by Arturo Carlo Quintavalle, I Convegni di Parma, 5 (Milan: Università di Parma – Mondadori Electa, 2005), pp. 519–24; Andreas Bräm, *Neapolitanische Bilderbibeln des Trecento: Anjou-Buchmalerei von Robert dem Weisen bis zu Johanna I.*, 2 vols (Wiesbaden: Reichert Verlag, 2007), I, pp. 128–44, 180–84; Paola Vitolo, 'Royauté et modèles culturels entre Naples, France et Europe. Les années de Robert et de Jeanne Ire d'Anjou (1309–1382)', in *Identités angevines: entre Provence et Naples XIIIe-XVe siècle*, ed. by Jean-Paul Boyer, Anne Mailloux, and Laure Verdon, Le temps de l'histoire (Aix-en-Provence: Presses Universitaires de Provence, Aix-Marseille Université, 2016), pp. 247–66 (249–50).

8   On this visually stunning work, as well as the views summarized in this and the following paragraph, consult Julian Gardner, 'Saint Louis of Toulouse, Robert of Anjou and Simone Martini', *Zeitschrift für Kunstgeschichte*, 39 (1976), 12–33 (repr. in Julian Gardner, *Patrons, Painters and Saints: Studies in Medieval Italian Painting*, Variorum Collected Studies (Aldershot: Ashgate, 1993), no. VIII); Andrew Martindale, *Simone Martini* (Oxford: Phaidon, 1988), pp. 18, 192–94; Lorenz Enderlein, 'Zur Entstehung der Ludwigstafel des Simone Martini in Neapel', *Römisches Jahrbuch der Bibliotheca Hertziana*, 30 (1995), 135–49; Adrian S. Hoch, 'The Franciscan Provenance of Simone Martini's Angevin St Louis in Naples', *Zeitschrift für Kunstgeschichte*, 58 (1995), 22–38; Klaus Krüger, 'A deo solo et a te regnum teneo. Simone Martinis "Ludwig von Toulouse" in Neapel', in *Medien der Macht: Kunst zur Zeit der Anjous in Italien*, ed. by Tanja Michalsky (Berlin: Dietrich Reimer Verlag, 2001), pp. 79–119; Pierluigi Leone de Castris, *Simone Martini* (Milan: Federico Motta Editore, 2003), pp. 136–54; Francesco Aceto, 'Spazio ecclesiale e pale di "primitivi" in San Lorenzo Maggiore a Napoli: dal "San Ludovico" di Simone Martini al "San Girolamo" di Colantonio, I', *Prospettiva*, 137 (2010), 2–50; Diana Norman, 'Politics and Piety: Locating Simone Martini's *Saint Louis of Toulouse* Altarpiece', *Art History*, 33/4 (2010), 596–619; Mario Gaglione, 'Il San Ludovico di Simone Martini, manifesto della santità regale angioina', *Rassegna storica salernitana*, 58 (2012), 9–125; Diana Norman, 'The Sicilian Connection: Imperial Themes in Simone Martini's *St Louis of Toulouse Altarpiece*', *Gesta*, 53 (2014), 25–45; Sarah K. Kozlowski, 'Circulation, Convergence, and the Worlds of Trecento Painting: Simone Martini in Naples', *Zeitschrift für Kunstgeschichte*, 78 (2015), 205–38; Francesco Aceto, 'Per Simone Martini pittore: ancora sull'iconografia del "San Ludovico" del Museo di Capodimonte a Napoli', in *Da Ludovico d'Angiò a San Ludovico di Tolosa: i testi e le immagini*, ed. by Teresa d'Urso, Alessandra Perriccioli Saggese, and Daniele Solvi, Collana della Società internazionale di studi francescani, 34 / Figure e temi francescani, 7 (Spoleto: Fondazione Centro Italiano di Studi sull'Alto Medioevo, 2017), pp. 33–50. Mirko Vagnoni, 'L'iconografia di S. Ludovico di Tolosa e la dinastia angioina', *Memorie Valdarnesi*, 9th series, 186/10 (2020), 115–30 and Mirko Vagnoni, 'Roberto d'Angiò nella gloria della Morte: il "San Ludovico di Tolosa" di Simone Martini', *Eikón Imago* 10 (2021), 241–57 emphasize the painting's religious function over its propagandistic / political message.

in the Clarissan church of Santa Chiara or the cathedral at Naples. Mild divergence of opinion is also to be noted on the subject of the work's patron. Even though most everyone would agree that King Robert, who is depicted kneeling in supplication before the saint, must have been involved in some capacity, some historians would also wish to implicate Sancia, Robert's queen, Philip of Taranto, Robert's brother, Mary of Hungary, mother to Louis, Robert, and Philip, or even Robert's grandson-in-law, Andrew of Hungary. Be this as it may, the message at the heart of this complex piece of visual propaganda is striking in its straightforwardness: St Louis, Franciscan friar, bishop of Toulouse, and second son to Charles II and Mary, receives a celestial crown in confirmation of his newly acquired saintly status, while, at the same time, he is seen transferring his rights to the earthly crown of Sicily to his younger brother, Robert.

After the death of Charles Martel, Charles II's firstborn, in 1295, Louis, who was now heir apparent, gave up his rights in favour of Robert in order to be able to enter his beloved Franciscan Order. Given the somewhat unorthodox way in which Robert acquired the crown, his position remained vulnerable to rival claims, such as those of Carobert, son of Charles Martel, who had been spurned and effectively banned from succeeding his father by Charles II. Robert's fervent artistic attempts to legitimize his rule were couched in thickly applied dynastic rhetoric. Historians have long suspected that the St Louis coronation scene was patterned after the splendid coronation mosaics of the Norman kings and the Angevins' Aragonese rivals in Palermo and Monreale, probably with a view to cementing the family's rights to the crown of Sicily. Furthermore, the panel is awash with heraldry referring to the Angevin branch of the French royal family, the Kingdom of Hungary, and the Latin Kingdom of Jerusalem. These visual cues, in conjunction with the iconography of the double coronation, were meant to associate Robert with his Angevin, Capetian, and Hungarian forebears through the mediation of his saintly sibling. The arms of the defunct Levantine kingdom, impaled with the *fleurs-de-lys* of the Capetians, adorn the relief morse clasped in front of Louis's chest, while also appearing on Robert's vestments (Fig. 2).[9] The conspicuous evocation of the dynasty's rights to the Jerusalem crown was apparently subsumed within a wider Angevin legitimizing agenda, which aspired not only to promote the family's dynastic prerogatives, but to also correlate Angevin political assets and ambitions with those of their predecessors, namely the Norman kings of Sicily and the Hohenstaufen emperors, who had either claimed or indeed possessed the crown of the crusader kingdom.[10]

King Robert's infatuation with family history colours a number of further artistic commissions, placed either by him or his close relatives. The sumptuous Anjou or

---

9 On the heraldic motifs adorning the figures' dress, see (in addition to the pertinent literature already cited) Lisa Monnas, 'Dress and Textiles in the St Louis Altarpiece: New Light on Simone Martini's Working Practice', *Apollo*, 137 (1993), 166–75 (pp. 168–69); Lisa Monnas, *Merchants, Princes and Painters: Silk Fabrics in Italian and Northern Paintings 1300–1550* (New Haven - London: Yale University Press, 2008), pp. 232–34.

10 On Angevin emulation of their Norman and Hohenstaufen predecessors, see also the comments in Abulafia, *The Western Mediterranean Kingdoms*, p. 151 and Dunbabin, *Charles of Anjou*, pp. 114–15.

Mechelen Bible, now in Leuven, is such an object.[11] Made in the 1340s, probably at Robert's behest, to be given as a gift to Andrew of Hungary, husband to his granddaughter and designated heir, Joanna, the book passed into the hands of Niccolò Alunno d'Alife, royal secretary and notary, upon Andrew's murder on the eve of his royal coronation in 1345. This luxury manuscript, one of a series of richly-adorned late medieval Neapolitan Bibles, contains a number of extraordinarily lavish illustrations, executed by Cristoforo Orimina, a local painter. Its double frontispiece consists of two miniatures set into a rectangular frame, at the corners of which are appended the arms of Jerusalem. The image of the first frontispiece presents Robert seated in majesty on a throne speckled with gold Angevin lilies on a blue ground, and surrounded by a series of Virtues trampling Vices and the Devil underfoot. The second frontispiece carries a condensed genealogy of the Neapolitan Angevins, with particular emphasis on the regularity of dynastic succession (Fig. 3). In the upper register, Charles I and his queen, Beatrice of Provence, are seen enthroned in majesty, with the king crowning a kneeling Charles II; the latter occupies the second register, in the company of Mary of Hungary and the couples' offspring, including Charles Martel, Louis, and Robert himself, who appears to be taking his granddaughters, Joanna and Maria, under his protection; Robert also puts in an appearance, this time as sovereign on the side of Sancia, both of whom are accompanied by their son, Charles, Duke of Calabria, and his wife, Mary of Valois, and once again Joanna and Maria, whose importance in dynastic matters had increased considerably after the premature death of their father, Duke Charles (in 1328). The three royal couples are projected against repeating heraldic patterns, where the Angevin arms alternate with those of Jerusalem (in the case of Charles I), Hungary (for Charles II) and Aragon (for Robert). This intriguing series of dynastic portraits, complemented by a potent heraldic component and a set of eloquent gestures indicative of the favoured scenario for royal succession, served to underline the unbroken continuity of Angevin rule in the kingdom, both before and after Robert's reign.

An analogous genealogical scheme brands yet another work of the 1340s with intimate ties to Robert's vision of canonical royal succession in the Angevin Kingdom. This sovereign's tomb in Santa Chiara, Naples, assumed the form of a majestic five-storied canopied funerary structure carved in marble by the Florentine sculptors Giovanni and Pacio Bertini.[12] The monument's sarcophagus, raised on

---

11 Bräm, *Neapolitanische Bilderbibeln des Trecento*, I, pp. 15, 111–50, 169–77, 404–05; *The Anjou Bible: A Royal Manuscript Revealed, Naples 1340*, ed. by Lieve Watteeuw and Jan Van der Stock, Corpus of Illuminated Manuscripts, 18 - Low Countries Series, 13 (Paris - Leuven - Walpole, MA: Peeters, 2010).

12 Enderlein, *Die Grablegen des Hauses Anjou*, pp. 167–88; Michalsky, *Memoria und Repräsentation*, pp. 169–73, 325–41; Brendan Cassidy, *Politics, Civic Ideals and Sculpture in Italy c. 1240–1400* (London - Turnhout: Harvey Miller Publishers, 2007), pp. 68–85; Nicolas Bock, 'A Kingdom in Stone: Angevin Sculpture in Naples', in *The Anjou Bible: A Royal Manuscript Revealed*, pp. 94–111 (102); Vinni Lucherini, 'Le tombe angioine nel presbiterio di Santa Chiara a Napoli e la politica funeraria di Roberto d'Angiò', in *Medioevo: i committenti*, ed. by Arturo Carlo Quintavalle, I Convegni di Parma, 13 (Milan: Electa, 2011), pp. 477–504 (482–85 and passim); Stefano d'Ovidio, 'Osservazioni sulla struttura e l'iconografia della tomba di re Roberto d'Angiò in Santa Chiara a Napoli', *Hortus Artium Medievalium*, 21 (2015), 9–112.

stout columns boxed in by figures of Virtues, had its front face decorated with elegant Gothic arcading framing a series of enthroned figures (Fig. 4). The latter represent Robert in the centre, flanked by his two wives (Yolande of Aragon and Sancia of Mallorca) and his children, all carefully labeled and marked by heraldry as in the Anjou Bible miniature, in a conscious effort to avoid any possible misidentification. This genealogy in stone, modelled after the same subject in the tomb of the king's mother, Mary of Hungary, in the church of Santa Maria Donnaregina, aimed, once again, to canonize Robert's stated preferences regarding who would succeed him. Here, the arms of Jerusalem appear on either side of the figure of Robert, superimposed on a pattern of Angevin lilies.

From the foregoing discussion, it becomes clear that any reference to the Angevin claim to the title of king of Jerusalem in the artistic production emanating from Robert's court was inextricably bound up with the burning issues of dynastic genealogy and orderly succession to the throne of Naples. On several occasions, André Vauchez, Tanja Michalsky, Klaus Krüger, Samantha Kelly, Jean Dunbabin, and other scholars have broached the concept of the *beata stirps* (i.e. 'blessed lineage'), which encouraged Angevin exceptionalism on the basis of the great number of family saints inherited from the intermarriage between the royal houses of France and Hungary, as well as the promotion of Louis of Toulouse as a saintly figure having emerged from the ranks of the Neapolitan Anjou themselves.[13] This prodigious familial assembly of saints ensured the legitimacy of Robert's and his descendants' accession to the crown, in parallel with the long-established notion of Capetian sacral kingship. Lisa Monnas has convincingly shown that the garments worn by Robert and his predecessors in the aforementioned royal portraits represented the Angevin ceremonial coronation robes, which were made to resemble clerical vestments.[14] According to what is known about the coronations of Charles II and Robert, royal candidates received unction as both kings and priests, during a papal ceremony rife with imperial undertones and including elements explicitly contrived to recall the *sacre* of the French monarchy.[15] In all of this, the role of the arms and title of Jerusalem was undoubtedly significant, if perhaps secondary. The evidence of the coinage and the Anjou Bible frontispiece suggests that the title of the Levantine polity was first and foremost associated with Charles I, who had held it for more than a decade before the Latin kingdom's

---

13 André Vauchez, '"Beata stirps": sainteté et lignage en Occident aux XIIIe et XIVe siècles', in *Famille et parenté dans l'Occident médiéval*, ed. by Georges Duby and Jacques Le Goff, Collection de l'École française de Rome, 30 (Rome: École française de Rome - Palais Farnèse, 1977), pp. 397–406; Michalsky, *Memoria und Repräsentation*, pp. 38–40, 61–73, 86; Krüger, 'A deo solo', 86; Kelly, *A New Solomon*, pp. 119–29; Jean Dunbabin, *The French in the Kingdom of Sicily, 1266–1305* (Cambridge: Cambridge University Press, 2011), pp. 19–98. On further uses of art in Angevin dynastic politics, see, for instance, Catherine Léglu, 'Ambivalent Visual Representations of Robert "the Wise" in Occitan Illustrated Texts', *Italian Studies*, 72/2 (2017), 192–204.

14 Monnas, 'Dress and Textiles', pp. 168–69.

15 Bernhard Schimmelpfennig, *Die Zeremonienbücher der römischen Kurie im Mittelalter*, Bibliothek des Deutschen Historischen Instituts in Rom, 40 (Tübingen: Max Niemeyer Verlag, 1973), pp. 50–51, 94, 176–86; Jean-Paul Boyer, 'Sacre et théocratie: le cas des rois de Sicile Charles II (1289) et Robert (1309)', *Revue des sciences philosophiques et théologiques*, 81 (1997), 561–607.

ultimate demise. In Martini's altarpiece, the Anjou Bible, and his tomb in Santa Chiara, Robert appears to be evoking his claim to Jerusalem primarily as a means of linking himself back to his grandfather, the dynasty's founder, through his father and canonized brother. More generally, it could be argued that the idea and memory of the Kingdom of Jerusalem post-1291 held a fairly abstract ideological meaning for the Neapolitan royalty and their entourage, which was informed by recourse to biblical imagery. Charles II and his 'wise' son, Robert, were routinely and favourably compared to Solomon in contemporary rhetoric, while the title of Jerusalem was frequently interpreted allegorically to refer to the kings' distinct virtues – for instance, the Dominican preacher Federico Franconi translated 'Jerusalem' from the Hebrew to mean 'vision of peace', in order to extoll Charles II's pacific nature.[16]

The Angevins' rivals for the crown of Jerusalem, the Lusignans of Cyprus, seem to have taken an altogether different approach. The acceptance of Hugh III's candidature by the Jerusalem barons against that of Maria of Antioch led to no less long-lived a claim on the title than that of the Neapolitan dynasty. To judge by the heraldic ornament once featured on the lid of the heart tomb of Theobald V, king of Navarre and count of Champagne, in the Dominican church of Provins (now in Mont-Sainte-Catherine-lès-Provins), Hugh employed the arms of Jerusalem alongside those of the Lusignan house as early as the 1270s.[17] Furthermore, as Pagona Papadopoulou has shown, by the early fourteenth century, Amaury, lord of Tyre and usurper of the throne of Cyprus (1306–10) from his brother, Henry II (1285–1324), impaled the Lusignan arms with those of the Kingdom of Jerusalem on his coins; he was followed soon thereafter by Henry himself, upon his reinstatement in 1310.[18] The Jerusalem arms became a permanent fixture of the coinage minted in the Kingdom of Cyprus down to the end of Lusignan rule, and came to accompany the arms of the ruling house on many a monumental building (Fig. 5).[19] In the realm of *Realpolitik*,

---

16 David L. D'Avray, *Death and the Prince: Memorial Preaching before 1350* (Oxford: Clarendon, 1994), pp. 95–99; Kelly, *A New Solomon*, pp. 242–86; Cathleen A. Fleck, 'Art of an Emblematic King: Robert I of Naples as King of Jerusalem in the Fourteenth Century', in *New Horizons in Trecento Italian Art*, ed. by Bryan C. Keene and Karl Whittington, Trecento Forum, 2 (Turnhout: Brepols, 2020), pp. 247–61. On the preaching activity of Robert, who often discoursed on royal virtues and duties by allusion to biblical kingship, see Darleen Pryds, '*Rex Praedicans*: Robert d'Anjou and the Politics of Preaching', in *De l'homélie au sermon: histoire de la prédication médiévale*, ed. by Jacqueline Hamesse and Xavier Hermand, Université catholique de Louvain - Publications de l'Institut d'Études médiévales, Textes, Études, Congrès, 14 (Louvain-la-Neuve: Brepols, 1993), pp. 239–62 (esp. 248–50); see also Darleen N. Pryds, *The King Embodies the Word: Robert d'Anjou and the Politics of Preaching*, Studies in the History of Christian Thought, 93 (Leiden - Boston - Cologne: Brill, 2000), pp. 51–62 for a more in-depth account.

17 Xavier Dectot, 'Les tombeaux des comtes de Champagne (1151–1284): un manifeste politique', *Bulletin monumental*, 162 (2004), 3–62 (pp. 7, 10, 13, 17–18, 45–48); Arnaud Baudin, *Emblématique et pouvoir en Champagne: les sceaux des comtes de Champagne et de leur entourage (fin XIe - début XIVe siècle)* (Langres: Éditions Dominique Guéniot, 2012), p. 255 and n. 73 (for the heraldry).

18 Pagona Papadopoulou, 'Betwixt Greeks, Saracens and Crusaders: Lusignan Coinage and Its Place in the Eastern Mediterranean (1192–1324)', *Cahiers du Centre d'Études Chypriotes*, 43 (2013), 473–92 (pp. 482–86).

19 David M. Metcalf, *Coinage of the Crusades and the Latin East in the Ashmolean Museum Oxford* (London: Royal Numismatic Society - Society for the Study of the Crusades and the Latin East, 1995), pp. 202–24. For the most recent discussion of Lusignan heraldry in architecture, see Jean-Bernard de Vaivre, 'Le décor

possession of the Levantine crown and a position at the eastern frontier of Latin Christendom meant a more or less active involvement in military campaigns geared towards the recapture of the Holy Land and the protection and welfare of Christians in the East, even though Peter I (1359–69) was the only Cypriot monarch to have pursued such plans to fruition in the 1360s, securing for himself a prolific literary afterlife as the quintessential crusader hero.[20]

In the sphere of political and dynastic ideology, however, the Lusignans went several steps further than their Neapolitan counterparts. By decision of the royal court and the Latin bishops, the town of Famagusta, the kingdom's main port from the second half of the thirteenth century, was designated as the legal heir to the Latin Kingdom of Jerusalem on Cypriot soil. From the fall of Acre to the town's occupation by the Genoese (1373–1464), the kings of Cyprus were bestowed the crown of Jerusalem in a separate ceremony held at the Latin cathedral of St Nicholas the Confessor, which had been institutionally merged with the Syrian bishopric of Tortosa by papal mandate.[21] From the reign of Hugh IV onwards, the obsolete seigneurial titles of the old crusader mainland were revived and distributed to the nobility on the day of the kings' coronation at Famagusta. Vacuous titles, such as 'count of Tripoli' and 'prince of Antioch', were even passed on to the monarch's offspring. Even though such titulature does not seem to have implied any tangible benefits or responsibilities beyond the purely ceremonial, the resplendent prestige with which it was invested

---

héraldique sur les monuments médiévaux', in *L'art gothique en Chypre*, ed. by Jean-Bernard de Vaivre and Philippe Plagnieux, Mémoires de l'Académie des Inscriptions et Belles-lettres, 34 (Paris: De Boccard, 2006), pp. 425–72 (429–32 and passim).

20 Edbury, *Kingdom of Cyprus*, pp. 156–79; Peter W. Edbury, 'Ἡ πολιτικὴ ἱστορία τοῦ μεσαιωνικοῦ βασιλείου ἀπὸ τὴ βασιλεία τοῦ Οὕγου Δ΄ μέχρι τὴ βασιλεία τοῦ Ἰανοῦ (1324–1432)', in *Ἱστορία τῆς Κύπρου*, ed. by Theodoros Papadopoullos, 6 vols (Nicosia: Archbishop Makarios III Foundation, 1995–2011), IV, *Μεσαιωνικὸν βασίλειον - Ἑνετοκρατία*, pp. 51–158 (52–87). For recent assessments of the propagandistic literature that attempted to mould Peter I's posthumous image into that of a paradigmatic crusader king, see Daisy Delogu, *Theorizing the Ideal Sovereign: The Rise of the French Vernacular Royal Biography* (Toronto - Buffalo - London: University of Toronto Press, 2008), pp. 92–123; Angel Nicolaou-Konnari, '"A poor island and an orphaned realm..., built upon a rock in the midst of the sea..., surrounded by the infidel Turks and Saracens": The Crusader Ideology in Leontios Makhairas's Greek *Chronicle of Cyprus*', *Crusades*, 10 (2011), 119–45; Peter W. Edbury, 'Machaut, Mézières, Makhairas and *Amadi*: Constructing the Reign of Peter I (1359–1369)' and Angel Nicolaou-Konnari, 'Apologists or Critics? The Reign of Peter I of Lusignan (1359–1369) Viewed by Philippe de Mézières (1327–1405) and Leontios Makhairas (ca. 1360/80-after 1432)', both in *Philippe de Mézières and His Age: Piety and Politics in the Fourteenth Century*, ed. by Renate Blumenfeld-Kosinski and Kiril Petkov, The Medieval Mediterranean, 91 (Leiden - Boston: Brill, 2012), pp. 349–58 and 359–401 respectively (all with earlier bibliography); Angel Nicolaou-Konnari's chapter in this volume.

21 Jean Richard, 'La situation juridique de Famagouste dans le royaume des Lusignan', in *Πρακτικὰ τοῦ Πρώτου Διεθνοῦς Κυπρολογικοῦ Συνεδρίου*, ed. by Theodoros Papadopoullos, 3 vols (Nicosia: Society of Cypriot Studies, 1972–73), II, *Μεσαιωνικὸν Τμῆμα*, pp. 221–29 (repr. in Jean Richard, *Orient et Occident au Moyen-Âge: Contacts et relations (XIIe-XVe siècles)*, Variorum Collected Studies (London: Variorum, 1976), no. XVII); Philippe Trélat, 'Nicosia and Famagusta in the Frankish Period (1192–1474): Two Capitals for a Kingdom?', in *The Harbour of All This Sea and Realm. Crusader to Venetian Famagusta*, ed. by Michael J. K. Walsh, Tamás Kiss, and Nicholas S. H. Coureas, CEU Medievalia, 17 (Budapest: Central European University Press, 2014), pp. 21–39 (25–28).

would have helped form a tight-knit caste around the king, whose social privileges accrued from their participation in this meticulous staging of Latin Syria in exile, in the Kingdom of Cyprus.[22]

Architecture and the built environment were of paramount importance in conveying the Cypriot court's calculated nostalgia for the former Crusader states. While Angevin patronage in southern Italy progressed from largely French-inspired solutions in the reign of Charles I to more locally circumscribed designs under Charles II and Robert I, the new trends in Cyprus under Hugh IV and Peter I embraced a decidedly retrospective aesthetic.[23] The monastic buildings of Bellapais Abbey, a royal Premonstratensian house located at the foot of the Kyrenia mountain range, were commissioned by Hugh IV himself in a mid-fourteenth-century Nicosian Gothic style. Nevertheless, a number of conspicuous features gracing the refectory, such as its main portal, were inspired by Romanesque buildings in the Syro-Palestinian littoral. Unsurprisingly, the most blatant use of these outdated models is encountered in Famagusta in the second and third quarters of the fourteenth century. Grandiose edifices, such as the Greek and Nestorian cathedrals, along with a host of smaller-scale oratories belonging to various rites, were conceived as Gothic revisions of twelfth-century crusader churches, such as the cathedrals of Gibelet or Beirut (Fig. 6). The arms of the king and members of his family, coupled with those of Jerusalem, pepper the largest and most visible buildings of the period, implying royal involvement in, encouragement of, or acquiescence with their construction. In other words, the stylistic revival of obsolete twelfth-century architectural forms had its roots in courtly patronage, and could be achieved via the relatively unobstructed circulation of craftsmen between mainland and island in the fourteenth century. What is more, it was certainly ideologically motivated, in an attempt to recreate a 'Holy Land ambiance' in the town where the Lusignans received the crown of Jerusalem

---

22 Jean Richard, 'Pairie d'Orient latin: les quatre baronnies des royaumes de Jérusalem et de Chypre', *Revue historique de droit français et étranger*, s. 4, 28 (1950), 67–88 (pp. 84–85) (repr. in Richard, *Orient et Occident au Moyen-Âge*, no. XV); Chris Schabel, 'Hugh the Just: The Further Rehabilitation of King Hugh IV Lusignan of Cyprus', Επετηρίδα Κέντρου Επιστημονικών Ερευνών (Κύπρου), 30 (2004), 123–52 (pp. 147–50) (repr. in Christopher D. Schabel, *Greeks, Latins, and the Church in Early Frankish Cyprus*, Variorum Collected Studies (Farnham - Burlington, VT: Ashgate, 2010), no. X); Peter W. Edbury, 'Franks', in *Cyprus: Society and Culture 1191–1374*, ed. by Angel Nicolaou-Konnari and Chris Schabel, The Medieval Mediterranean, 58 (Leiden - Boston: Brill, 2005), pp. 63–101 (70–71, 84–85).

23 Caroline Bruzelius, 'Charles I, Charles II, and the Development of an Angevin Style in the Kingdom of Sicily', in *L'état angevin: pouvoir, culture et société entre XIIIe et XIVe siècle*, Collection de l'École française de Rome, 245 / Istituto storico italiano per il Medio Evo, Nuovi studi storici, 45 (Rome: École française de Rome - Palais Farnèse / Nella sede dell'Istituto - Palazzo Borromini, 1998), pp. 99–114; Caroline Bruzelius, '"Il gran rifiuto": French Gothic in Central and Southern Italy in the Last Quarter of the Thirteenth Century', in *Architecture and Language: Constructing Identity in European Architecture c. 1000–c. 1650*, ed. by Georgia Clarke and Paul Crossley (Cambridge: Cambridge University Press, 2000), pp. 36–45, 176–78; Caroline Bruzelius, *The Stones of Naples: Church Building in Angevin Italy, 1266–1343* (New Haven - London: Yale University Press, 2004), esp. pp. 75–131, 201–02. Alexander Harper, 'Pierre d'Angicourt and Angevin Construction', *Journal of the Society of Architectural Historians*, 75 (2016), 140–57 (pp. 145–51) argues that the 'local' character of much Angevin architecture derived from the nature of the workforce employed at construction sites, rather than grand ideological designs.

and substantial numbers of refugees from the mainland had settled in the wake of the Mamluk military advances. Consequently, public ceremonial and architectural design were closely coordinated to convert Famagusta into a 'new Jerusalem' or a 'new Acre'. The principal goal of this transformation was to retroactively visualize Lusignan sovereignty over the former mainland Latin territories, for the benefit of both the locals and foreign visitors, in a bid to preserve the title of Jerusalem for the Cypriot ruling dynasty.[24]

Ultimately, in the post-1291 Eastern Mediterranean, both the Angevins of Naples and the Lusignans of Cyprus exploited their claim to the title of Jerusalem to further agendas having little to do with regaining control over the territories of the former Latin kingdom and reestablishing Latin Christian rule in the Levant. The court of Naples employed heraldic insignia in visually explicit genealogical portraits as a vehicle for enhancing the legitimacy of royal succession; in such contexts, the arms of Jerusalem served as linkage with Charles I of Anjou, founder of the dynasty and sovereign of the Levantine kingdom prior to its dissolution, and quite possibly the Hohenstaufen before them. Nevertheless, the Angevins were far more invested in reacquiring Sicily, of which they were also titular kings without *de facto* jurisdiction, than challenging the Lusignans for retention of the Syrian title. The house of Cyprus, on the other hand, moulded Famagusta into a showpiece for projecting the Lusignan version of the story. As the site where the kings of Cyprus received the much-sought-after Jerusalemite crown, and where titular officials for the mainland kingdom were appointed, the town was repackaged to exude a distinctly Levantine flavour meant to enhance visual and ideological allusions to the glorious era of the Crusader states. It may be noted that, in the first half of the fourteenth century, evocations of the Latin Kingdom of Jerusalem in the courtly arts of both Naples and Cyprus had often assumed a learned, intellectual quality, probably predicated on the idiosyncracy, wishes, and ambitions of their primary *moteurs*, namely the erudite *connoisseurs* Robert I and Hugh IV. Even after crusader Jerusalem had faded from the geopolitical map of the Mediterranean, its memory continued to excite, entrance, and shape the visual policies of its ideological successors down to the era of Peter I of Cyprus – its most proactive fourteenth-century adherent – and beyond.

---

24 On Hugh IV's patronage and the emergence of a historicist architectural style in the second quarter of the fourteenth century, see Michalis Olympios, 'The Shifting Mantle of Jerusalem: Ecclesiastical Architecture in Lusignan Famagusta', in *Famagusta, Volume I, Art and Architecture*, ed. by Annemarie Weyl Carr, Mediterranean Nexus 1100–1700, Conflict, Influence and Inspiration in the Mediterranean Area, 2 (Turnhout: Brepols, 2014), pp. 75–142 (101–20); Michalis Olympios, 'Courtly Splendours: Hugh IV's Bellapais Abbey and the English Decorated Style', in *Decorated Revisited: English Architectural Style in Context, 1250–1400*, ed. by John Munns, Architectura Medii Aevi, 9 (Turnhout: Brepols, 2017), pp. 173–96 (177–84).

Fig. 1: Simone Martini, *St Louis of Toulouse crowning Robert I of Anjou*, c. 1317–19 (Museo di Capodimonte, Naples). Photo: Reproduced with the permission of the Ministero per i Beni e le Attività Culturali / Alinari Archives, Florence.

Fig. 2: Simone Martini, *St Louis of Toulouse crowning Robert I of Anjou*, detail.

Fig. 3: Cristoforo Orimina, *Angevin Genealogy*, in the Anjou Bible, fol. 4r (frontispiece), 1340s. Photo: Reproduced with the permission of KU Leuven, Maurits Sabbe Library.

ANGEVIN AND LUSIGNAN VISUAL CLAIMS TO THE CROWN OF JERUSALEM: PARALLEL LIVES? 171

Fig. 4: Giovanni Bertini and Pacio Bertini, Tomb of Robert I of Anjou, 1343–46 (Santa Chiara, Naples). Photo: Alinari Archives, Florence.

Fig. 5: Bellapais Abbey, tympanum and lintel of main refectory portal, 1340s/50s. Photo: Michalis Olympios.

ANGEVIN AND LUSIGNAN VISUAL CLAIMS TO THE CROWN OF JERUSALEM: PARALLEL LIVES? 173

Fig. 6: Famagusta, Ss Peter and Paul of the Nestorians, view of the east end, third quarter of fourteenth century. Photo: Michalis Olympios.

Part II

Peter I's Alexandrian Crusade (1365) – Event and Context

PETER EDBURY and CHRIS SCHABEL

The Papacy and King Peter I of Cyprus

The papal registers comprise the largest assemblage of documentary material for the history of Cyprus in the medieval period, and the appearance in 2012 of volume three of the *Bullarium Cyprium*, which provides a calendar of all—or, rather, most of—the papal letters relating to Cyprus between 1316 and 1378, offers a sufficient excuse for re-examining some aspects of the popes' relations with King Peter I. Peter's reign coincided with the last years of the pontificate of Innocent VI (1352–62) and most of that of his successor, Urban V (1362–70). For the period between the death of King Hugh IV on 10 October 1359 and Peter's own death in January 1369, the *Bullarium* has a total of 301 entries, many of them summarized in print for the first time. The older project of the Bibliothèque des Écoles Françaises d'Athènes et de Rome to publish all the correspondence of these two popes in full or in summary form was never completed. The *Bullarium* therefore provides a valuable tool for researchers with much new material, but it should be stressed that the *Bullarium* is incomplete, the summaries can mislead, and an examination of the full text of the letters often reveals fresh information or significant nuances that can seriously alter our perceptions.[1]

At the risk of stating the obvious, it took time for correspondence to pass between Cyprus and the papal court. For much of Peter's reign the popes were based at Avignon, but even when from mid-1367 to mid-1370 Urban V was residing in or near Rome, the lines of communication were long, and in any case the popes and the chancery officials might well take their time before responding to the information or the requests laid before them. Thus, for example, Pope Urban's earliest reaction to the news of Peter's murder

---

1 At the Rome conference held in October 2016 the authors read separate papers: Peter Edbury spoke about the challenge from Hugh of Lusignan, and Chris Schabel considered the pope's plans for Peter's crusade that took place in 1365. The appendices with editions of pertinent papal letters are by Chris Schabel.

Peter Edbury • Cardiff University
Chris Schabel • University of Cyprus

on 16 January 1369 is dated 7 April—almost three months later.[2] One consequence of the distances involved was that the popes are not known to have made any attempt to influence Peter's military policies while he was in the East, presumably on the grounds that they knew that events would long since have overtaken any intervention on their part. Another was that a sizable proportion of the papal letters addressed to people in Cyprus was generated in the context of embassies to the *curia*, or, as in the case of Peter's reign, in the context of his own two visits. It is evident that, as soon as it was known that an embassy was being prepared, a wide variety of people would persuade the ambassadors to submit petitions to the pope on their behalf for indults such as dispensations for marriage within the prohibited degree or expectations to benefices.

There are two major questions relating to Peter's reign that deserve to be revisited. First, to what extent was his departure for the papal court in 1362 motivated by the need to deal with the challenge to his rule from his nephew, Hugh of Lusignan, rather than by Peter's crusading aspirations? Second, given that Peter's journey to the West resulted in the calling of a crusade, how did Pope Urban V see King Peter's role vis-à-vis the *passagium generale* that was planned for 1365 and did his view change over time? This second question leads on naturally to a further topic that can be dealt with far more briefly: what was Urban's attitude towards Peter in the years following his assault on Alexandria in October 1365?

Hugh of Lusignan's Claim to the Throne

Two Cypriot chronicles, the one attributed to Leontios Makhairas and the other known as the *Chronique d'Amadi*, are in no doubt: Peter's visit to the papal court in 1363 was intended to solve the problem of his nephew's claim to the throne and came about in answer to a direct summons to appear in person.[3] Makhairas provides a coherent account of the background, even though his chronology requires some adjustments. After his father's death, Peter sent an embassy headed by a knight named Raymond Babin to the pope to report his coronation.[4] From the papal registers it is clear that Raymond and his co-ambassador, John Carmain, were at the *curia* by 11 June 1360, so the date incorrectly given in the chronicles for the departure of a later embassy from Famagusta, 9 April 1360, may apply to this first embassy, since this was five days after Peter's coronation as king of Jerusalem.[5] According to Makhairas, at this juncture

---

2   *Bullarium Cyprium, III: Lettres papales relatives à Chypre 1316–1378*, ed. by Charles Perrat and Jean Richard, with the collaboration of Christopher Schabel, Sources et études de l'histoire de Chypre, 68 (Nicosia: Centre de Recherche Scientifique, 2012), nos v-218–19.

3   Leontios Makhairas, *Recital concerning the Sweet Land of Cyprus entitled 'Chronicle'*, ed. by Richard M. Dawkins, 2 vols (Oxford: Clarendon Press, 1932), I, pp. 112–15 (§ 129); *Chroniques d'Amadi et de Strambaldi, première partie: Chronique d'Amadi*, ed. by René de Mas Latrie (Paris: Imprimerie nationale, 1891), p. 412.

4   For the first embassy, Makhairas, *Recital*, I, pp. 90–91 (§ 102). Makhairas's date, 18 September, is clearly wrong.

5   *Bullarium Cyprium III*, nos u-228–46. Raymond and John are named in nos u-230–34, 236–38, 240. For the 9 April 1360 date mistakenly applied to the second embassy, Makhairas, *Recital*, I, pp. 92–97 (§ § 105–08), and *Chronique d'Amadi*, p. 410.

Hugh of Lusignan came before the pope armed with letters from his kinsman, the king of France, and asserted his right to the throne of Cyprus as the heir of the late king, Hugh IV; Hugh claimed that his parents' marriage contract had specifically envisaged the situation in which he now found himself: should his father, Guy of Lusignan, predecease the king, Guy's heir, and not a surviving son of the old king, was to inherit the throne. Raymond Babin, so we are told, made the best defence he could, lecturing the pope on Cypriot succession law, but to no avail: the pope was unsympathetic and gave Peter a year to make his defence.[6]

As we shall see, letters of Innocent VI omitted from the *Bullarium Cyprium* but printed below allow us to correct Makhairas in the details. Hugh of Lusignan in fact presented his case to the pope before the arrival of Raymond Babin in Avignon, for on 24 May 1360 Pope Innocent addressed two letters to King Peter on the matter, a long, stern one on behalf of Hugh and a briefer one concerning the dowry of Hugh's mother, the Empress Maria of Constantinople, with no mention of the embassy [Appendix A.1-2]. Innocent sent a soldier of his household, Angelo of Lucca, to Cyprus with these letters, probably just missing Peter's ambassadors, for on 13 June Pope Innocent wrote to the Empress Maria informing her that the embassy had arrived [Appendix A.3]. Two weeks later, on 28 June, Innocent wrote again to King Peter, expressing his official condolences for the death of Peter's father, King Hugh IV. Although the pope explains that he had already learned of Hugh's death, now he has heard the news from Peter's ambassadors, Raymond Babin, the butler of the Kingdom of Cyprus, and John Carmain [Appendix A.4].

Raymond and John left Avignon at the end of June or early in July, giving the letter to the king, who had presumably already received the earlier letter from Angelo of Lucca. According to Makhairas, Peter consulted his vassals and decided that Hugh's claim would have to be bought off with an annual pension of 50,000 white bezants, and he then sent two senior vassals, John of Morphou and Thomas of Montolif, to the pope to negotiate.[7] The papal registers show that that these envoys had arrived in Avignon by mid-November 1361.[8] It would seem from the narrative accounts that they returned to Cyprus under the impression that they had concluded the negotiations successfully; however, Hugh of Lusignan subsequently reappeared in Avignon with letters from the king of France, insisting that he was rightfully king and rejecting the deal agreed with the envoys. It was at this point, so both Makhairas and the *Amadi*-author inform us, that the pope summoned Peter to the *curia*.

We now have to confront a serious problem. The registers containing Pope Innocent VI's diplomatic correspondence, the *litterae secretae*, for the sixth, ninth and tenth years of his reign are missing from the Vatican Archives. The registers for the sixth and tenth years—that is, for 1358 and for the period from January to 12 September 1362,

---

6   Makhairas, *Recital*, I, pp. 92–95 (§ § 105–07); *Chronique d'Amadi*, p. 410.
7   Makhairas, *Recital*, I, pp. 95–97 (§ 108); *Chronique d'Amadi*, p. 410.
8   *Bullarium Cyprium* III, nos u-260–88. John and Thomas are named in nos u-266, 276–77, 281, 287. As mentioned above, Makhairas and Amadi both give the date of the departure of the second embassy as April 1360.

which is the day the pope died—are lost.[9] The register for the ninth year, 1361, does survive and is now in the possession of the Archivio di Stato di Roma. The 250 letters that it contains were published as far back as 1717.[10] However, this register contains no references either to John of Morphou's embassy or to Peter's conquest of Antalya in August 1361, which we might imagine could have elicited the pope's congratulations; the fact that only twenty of the letters in this register date from the period from September to December raises the possibility that a significant proportion of the correspondence from these months was either omitted altogether or perhaps found its way into the missing volume for 1362. On the other hand, the registers containing the *litterae communes*—the various types of papal privilege granted in response to petitions—do survive from these years, and the material from these registers relating to Cyprus is duly calendared in the *Bullarium Cyprium*. Even so, for the crucial period January–September 1362 there is a major gap in the evidence.

Before examining what light the papal registers can shed on the negotiations between the start of Peter's reign and his arrival in Avignon, however, the background to Hugh of Lusignan's claim to the throne requires some consideration. The story begins as far back as the rule of Amaury of Tyre in 1306–10, when the king, Henry II, was suspended from the exercise of royal authority.[11] At that time Henry had taken on the responsibility for bringing up his nephew, the future Hugh IV, whose father, Henry's younger brother, had died a few years earlier. Towards the end of his rule, Amaury had the youthful Hugh taken away from his uncle and, so it would seem, married to Maria of Ibelin, the sister of Philip count of Jaffa. When King Henry returned to power in 1310, Philip was imprisoned in Kerynia Castle, and he remained there until his death in 1316. Whereas Maria was clearly of sufficient social standing to marry into the royal family, the support that her brother had given Amaury of Tyre and his brother Aimery and his subsequent incarceration and death would have cast a shadow over the union. She herself had evidently died by 1318, when Hugh received a papal dispensation legitimizing his second marriage.

It may be unwise to attach too much significance to the fact that Maria receives not a single mention in the *Chronique d'Amadi*'s detailed narrative of the events of these years, although it is possible that she was deliberately 'air-brushed' out of the record. But in any case, it could well be that the memory of this union and the circumstances in which it was contrived left an unhappy legacy, especially once Hugh was married

---

9 Innocent became pope on 30 December 1352, and so his pontifical year coincides with the calendar year.
10 Archivio di Stato di Roma: Collezione acquisti e doni b. 23, n. 4, printed in Edmond Martène and Ursin Durand, *Thesaurus novus anecdotorum*, 5 vols (Paris, 1717), II, cols 843–1072. Especial thanks are due to Dr Karl Borchardt who has checked the manuscript against the printed edition and has confirmed that the printed edition is complete. For the missing registers, see *Innocent VI (1352–1362), Lettres secrètes et curiales publiées ou analysées d'après les registres des archives vaticanes*, ed. by Pierre Gasnault, Marie-Hyacinthe Laurent, Nicole Gotteri, Bibliothèque des Écoles Françaises d'Athènes et de Rome, 3ᵉ Série, 5 vols (Paris: De Boccard and École française de Rome, 1959–2006), V, p. vi, and Pierre Gasnault, 'Innocenzo VI', in *Enciclopedia dei Papi* <http://www.treccani.it/enciclopedia> [accessed 6 May 2016].
11 For this paragraph see Peter W. Edbury, 'Knights, Nobles and the Rule of Amaury of Tyre, 1306–1310', Επετηρίδα Κέντρου Επιστημονικών Ερευνών (Κύπρου), 38 (2016), 9–93 (pp. 36–37).

to Alice of Ibelin, his second wife. Guy, King Hugh's first-born son and the father of Hugh the claimant in the early 1360s, was seemingly the child of the earlier marriage. In 1328, when the contract was drawn up for Guy to marry Maria, the daughter of Louis duke of Bourbon, it was stated that he was already of an age to marry, something that could not have been true had he been born to Alice.[12] Guy's bride was a great granddaughter of King Louis IX and a second cousin of the then king of France, Philip VI. She arrived in Cyprus in 1330,[13] and the marriage lasted until Guy's death, which occurred at some point before September 1343.[14] Hugh was apparently their only child. Contrary to his later assertion, the marriage contract says nothing about the rights of their children to claim the throne in the event of Guy dying before his father. What it does stipulate is that in the event of Guy's death, Maria would be at liberty to return to the West and was not to be constrained to re-marry in Cyprus.[15] King Hugh, however, was slow to permit her departure. Maria's brother, who by now had succeeded to the duchy of Bourbon, had already contacted the pope by May 1344 about arranging her return, but in April 1346, when the duke was sending envoys to Cyprus to escort the young Hugh and his mother to the West, the king had still not granted his authorisation.[16] It is worth recalling here that a contemporary visitor to Cyprus, Niccolò di Poggibonsi, noted that everyone needed a licence to leave the island.[17]

In 1347 Maria married Robert of Taranto, the titular emperor of Constantinople and, as a grandson of King Charles II of Anjou, a member of the Angevin dynasty in Naples.[18] It would appear that henceforth she and her son normally resided in southern Italy. The fact that the Neapolitan Angevins were the Lusignans' rival claimants to the title of 'king of Jerusalem' would have had the effect of alienating Maria and her son from Hugh IV and his court. In 1354 Innocent VI wrote to King Hugh inviting him to treat his grandson generously so that he might live as befitted his royal standing. A similar letter followed in April 1356 and then in September of that year the pope wrote again, reminding King Hugh that he frequently had cause to write on his grandson's behalf; the pope explained that Hugh has reached adulthood and King John of France was taking an interest because, thanks to 'the wretched state of the kingdom of Sicily', Hugh's mother, the empress, could not support him adequately; John was sending an envoy to solicit King Hugh's subvention, and Maria was alleging that she was owed 2,000 florins annually from Cyprus as her dower and

---

12 Louis de Mas Latrie, *Histoire de l'île de Chypre sous le règne des princes de la maison de Lusignan*, 3 vols (Paris: Imprimerie Nationale, 1852–61), II, p. 145.
13 *Chronique d'Amadi*, pp. 403–04.
14 *Bullarium Cyprium III*, nos t-90–91.
15 Mas Latrie, *Histoire*, II, p. 148.
16 *Clément VI (1342–1352), Lettres closes, patentes et curiales se rapportant à la France*, ed. by Eugène Déprez, Jean Glénisson, Guillaume Mollat, Bibliothèque des Écoles Françaises d'Athènes et de Rome, 4 vols (Paris: De Boccard, 1901–61), no. 2458; *Bullarium Cyprium III*, nos t-107, 118, 185.
17 Girolamo Golubovich, *Biblioteca bio-bibliografica della Terra Santa et dell'Oriente francescano*, 5 vols (Quaracchi: Collegio di Bonaventura, 1906–27), V, p. 18. On licences to leave Cyprus, see also Mas Latrie, *Histoire*, II, pp. 231 and n. 4, 234–35.
18 *Bullarium Cyprium III*, no. t-228.

had received nothing since her husband died.[19] What came of this papal intervention is not known: there is no more on Hugh's financial needs during his grandfather's reign, and a settlement of Maria's claim had to wait until 1368.[20] There is nothing in the sources to suggest that either Maria or Hugh ever re-visited Cyprus during Hugh IV's reign, but it may be significant that in 1351, the first occasion when the papal archives record Hugh bringing a petition to the pope, he was careful to describe himself as the son of the king's eldest son (*filius primogeniti*).[21]

According to William of Machaut, the future Peter I was born on the feast of St Denis, 9 October 1329.[22] Although William is generally ill-informed about Peter's career before his first visit to the West, other evidence suggests that this date could well be correct. In September 1339 Pope Benedict XII wrote to Hugh IV about the king's niece, Eschiva of Montfort, the daughter of his uterine half-brother. Eschiva's interests had been taken up by a kinsman of hers who was a cardinal, and it is clear that she had good reason to feel aggrieved. She had inherited the Cypriot estates of the lords of Beirut, and, as her father had died as far back as 1313,[23] she would by now have been well past the age at which she would have expected to marry. It would seem that Hugh, arguing that he had to find a husband for her who would match her social status, was keeping her unwed until such time as one of his sons should reach the age of puberty. What this would mean in practice was that, although there would be a considerable age difference, the king would be able to endow whichever son she was given at no cost to the royal domain. In 1339 the pope was unimpressed: the sons were still too young, and in any case he could see no grounds for granting a dispensation.[24] (Although the papacy frequently gave dispensations for second or third cousins to marry each other, permission for first cousins to marry was still at that time something of a rarity.) But if Peter, who at the time was not yet the heir to the throne, was not considered old enough to marry in 1339, in 1342 the new pope, Clement VI, thought otherwise and issued the necessary dispensation.[25] The idea that he was born in 1329, just a year before the marriage of his elder half-brother to Maria of Bourbon, is therefore distinctly plausible.

---

19 Innocent VI, *Lettres secrètes*, nos 863, 2014, 2458; *Bullarium Cyprium III*, nos u-38, 93, 119.
20 Mas Latrie, *Histoire*, II, pp. 289–91. The fact that in 1368 Peter agreed to pay Maria 5,000 florins annually rather than the 2,000 she was claiming in 1356 suggests that indeed the dowry had not been paid and that the higher figure represents compensation for the arrears.
21 *Bullarium Cyprium III*, no. t-614.
22 Sophie Hardy, *Edition critique de la* Prise d'Alexandrie *de Guillaume de Machaut* (unpublished doctoral thesis, Université d'Orléans, 2011): <ftp://ftp.univ-orleans.fr/theses/sophie.hardy_1730.pdf> [accessed 8 April 2016], p. 5, ll. 133–36
23 *Chronique d'Amadi*, p. 395.
24 *Benoît XII (1334–1342), Lettres closes et patentes intéressant les pays autres que la France publiées ou analysées d'après les registres du Vatican*, ed. by Jean-Marie Vidal and Guillaume Mollat, Bibliothèque des Écoles Françaises d'Athènes et de Rome, 3 Série, 2 vols (Paris: Fontemoing et Cie and De Boccard, 1913–50), no. 2500; *Bullarium Cyprium III*, no. s-54, cf. no. s-47.
25 Abraham Bzovius, *Annalium Ecclesiasticorum post illustrissimum et reverendissimum Dominum Caesarem Baronum S. R. E. Cardinalem Bibliothecarium*, 8 vols (Cologne, 1621–40), 1342, § 23; *Bullarium Cyprium III*, nos t-3, 12.

Peter was therefore significantly younger than Guy, and, as Hugh of Lusignan was old enough to petition the pope in 1351, perhaps not that much older than Guy's son. It is hard to know how King Hugh would have viewed his daughter-in-law and grandson following Guy's death, but it could well be that Maria of Bourbon was left isolated in a court dominated by the king, his second wife and their growing family. There were certainly serious tensions at Hugh's court that cannot now be fully understood.[26] The treatment of Eschiva of Montfort would suggest a certain ruthlessness on the king's part when it came to family matters, while the report on his treatment of his son-in-law, Ferrand of Majorca, raises more questions than it answers. The fact that Hugh's quarrel with Ferrand also led to a rupture with Hugh count of Jaffa probably has more to do with Count Hugh's position as Ferrand's stepfather than with his role as the king's first wife's brother and hence Guy's maternal uncle, but the possibility that that consideration may have played some part cannot be ruled out altogether. Whether the delay in Maria of Bourbon's return to the West owed more to the practicalities of her move than to the reluctance of the king to allow it remains unclear. However, with Maria and her son out of the way, the interests of Hugh's children by his second wife could now come to the fore, so much so that on the king's death there is no hint in the sources that Hugh of Lusignan's claims to the throne had any support within Cyprus itself. By 1359 he would have been a little-known absentee whose ambition to become king would have alienated him from the rest of the royal family. His connections with the Angevins and their rival claim to the throne of Jerusalem would have made him even less acceptable.

It may be possible to go further and suggest that King Hugh deliberately promoted Peter as his heir almost as soon as Guy was dead. As Jean Richard long ago established, the later assertion that Hugh made Guy prince of Galilee appears to be incorrect,[27] although by the late 1330s he had appointed him constable of Cyprus.[28] On the other hand, his younger half-brothers, Peter and John, had been designated count of Tripoli and prince of Antioch respectively before 24 September 1346 when they are named as having been present at the consecration of the new bishop of Limassol.[29] Their appearance with these titles not long after Guy's death raises the unanswerable question of why Guy seems not to have been honoured in the same way, and it

---

26 For a recent discussion, see Christopher Schabel, 'Hugh the Just: The Further Rehabilitation of King Hugh IV Lusignan of Cyprus', Επετηρίδα Κέντρου Επιστημονικών Ερευνών (Κύπρου), 30 (2004), 123–52 (repr. in Christopher Schabel, *Greeks, Latins, and the Church in Early Frankish Cyprus*, Variorum Collected Studies, 949 (Farnham: Ashgate, 2010), no. X).

27 Jean Richard, 'Pairie d'Orient latin: les quatre baronnies des royaumes de Jérusalem et de Chypre', *Revue historique de droit français et étranger*, ser. 4, 28 (1950), 67–88 (p. 85 n. 1).

28 Mas Latrie, *Histoire*, II, p. 178; *Chronique d'Amadi*, p. 404. A Venetian document from c. 1336 names him as marshal of Cyprus, but it is not known whether this is an error or means that he had been promoted. *I libri commemoriali della repubblica di Venezia regesti (1293–1778)*, ed. by Riccardo Predelli and Pietro Bosmin, 8 vols (Venice: a spese della Società, 1876–1914), II, p. 69.

29 In Archivio Apostolico Vaticano (henceforth AAV), *Instrumenta Miscellanea* 1717, edited in Christopher Schabel, '*Ab hac hora in antea*: Oaths to the Roman Church in Frankish Cyprus (and Greece)', in *Crusader Landscapes in the Medieval Levant: The Archaeology and History of the Latin East*, ed. by Micaela Sinibaldi and others (Cardiff: University of Wales Press, 2016), pp. 361–72 (371).

may also be wondered whether it is purely coincidental that their earliest known use followed closely on the departure of Maria of Bourbon and her son. The titles themselves are suggestive. In the aristocratic scale of values, as Leontios Makhairas explicitly states, a prince would outrank a count;[30] yet here it is the younger brother who is given the more senior title. The obvious explanation is that while it would have been envisaged that John would continue to use his title of prince for the rest of his life, Peter would discard his once he came to the throne.

The *Chronique d'Amadi* and Makhairas report that on 24 November 1358 Hugh IV had Peter crowned king of Cyprus in his own lifetime.[31] It has often been suggested that this was a move intended to pre-empt any claim that Hugh of Lusignan might try to make.[32] When one re-examines Makhairas's account, it is less certain that this interpretation is correct. In the Venice manuscript, which is more surely linked to Makhairas himself, he goes on to say that he had 'found it written elsewhere' that Peter was crowned on Sunday 24 November 1359.[33] In 1359 24 November did indeed fall on a Sunday, the normal day for medieval coronations, whereas 24 November 1358 fell on a Saturday, a strange day for a coronation if legitimacy were an issue. Moreover, having the king crowned about six weeks after his father's death is eminently plausible, and a late-1359 coronation fits well with the fact that the first evidence that news of the coronation reached the West is from Naples, 18 February 1360, three months after the coronation, not fifteen. It would also mean that when by May 1360 Hugh of Lusignan complained to the pope about Peter's coronation, he was responding quickly once news had reached the West; the 1358 date would imply that he had been far more dilatory.[34] Finally, the last letter Innocent wrote to Hugh IV, on 20 August 1359, and the first he wrote to Peter I, on 16 April 1360, concern the same matter, a dispute over the course of the Pediaios and the *casale* of Psimolophou, and yet in the first the pope does not hint that Peter is also king, whereas in the second Innocent makes a point of saying that he had written the late Hugh on the same matter, with no hint that the succession was other than normal.[35] In any case, some of the other statements in Makhairas's paragraph that speaks of the coronation occurring in 1358 are demonstrably wrong: in particular, James of Lusignan's appointments as constable of Jerusalem and seneschal of Cyprus date from well into Peter's reign and

---

30   Makhairas, *Recital*, I, pp. 78–79 (§§ 87, 89).
31   Makhairas, *Recital*, I, pp. 76–79 (§ 86). Cf. *Chronique d'Amadi*, p. 408.
32   For example, Peter W. Edbury, *The Kingdom of Cyprus and the Crusades, 1191–1374* (Cambridge: Cambridge University Press, 1991), p. 147.
33   Makhairas, *Recital*, I, pp. 80–81 (§ 90); Leontios Makhairas, Χρονικό της Κύπρου. Παράλληλη διπλωματική έκδοση των χειρογράφων, ed. by Michalis Pieris and Angel Nicolaou-Konnari (Nicosia: Cyprus Research Centre, 2003), p. 112 (on p. 111 all three mss have the 1358 report).
34   News of Peter's accession had evidently reached Naples by 18 February 1360, when Hugh of Lusignan's stepfather, Robert of Taranto, wrote to Niccolò Acciaiuoli, complaining about what he regarded as Peter's illicit accession and coronation. Jean Alexandre C. Buchon, *Nouvelles recherches historiques sur la principauté française de Morée et ses hautes baronnies*, 2 vols (Paris: Imprimeurs unis, 1843), II, pp. 131–34.
35   *Bullarium Cyprium III*, nos 11-216 and 226. The documents are edited in Chris Schabel, 'The *Casale* of Psimolophou, Property of the Latin Patriarchs of Jerusalem During the Avignon Papacy, 1309–1376', *Perspectives on Culture*, 4/35 (2021), 29-56 (pp. 46-52).

not from the time of Hugh IV.[36] In the absence of the archbishop of Nicosia, who had been in the West since 1357,[37] the ceremony was conducted by Guy of Ibelin, the aristocratic bishop of Limassol and brother of Philip of Ibelin, the lord of Arsur.

What was much more remarkable was Peter's coronation as king of Jerusalem in Famagusta on Easter Day, 5 April 1360, by the papal legate, Peter Thomas.[38] Since the 1270s, when the disputed succession between the Lusignans and the Sicilian Angevins over the throne of Jerusalem had arisen, the popes had normally maintained a deliberate neutrality, declining to address either claimant with that title.[39] It is inconceivable that the papal legate would have been unaware of their conflicting claims, and yet he gave Peter a decisive and highly public endorsement. It is also hard to believe that Peter Thomas was unaware of Hugh of Lusignan's claim to be Hugh IV's heir. As Philip of Mézières records, the legate later had cause to fear Maria of Bourbon's wrath.[40] However, there is no evidence for him being rebuked by the pope, and any papal displeasure may have been soon evaporated: in March 1363 Urban V promoted him to archbishop of Crete and then, in July 1364, to the patriarchate of Constantinople.[41]

As mentioned, the earliest papal letter addressed to Peter I as king of Cyprus is dated 16 April 1360, repeating a call addressed to Hugh IV the previous year to intervene and do justice in a dispute over irrigation rights between the patriarch of Jerusalem and James of Norès, the turcopolier.[42] It would appear that it was at this point that Hugh of Lusignan arrived in Avignon and made his case to the pope. On 24 May Innocent, writing to 'his dearest son in Christ, Peter illustrious king of Cyprus', set out at length Hugh's complaint [Appendix A.1]. Hugh claimed that his right to succeed as the representative heir of his father was safeguarded in his parents' marriage contract, and he contended that the king's second-born son, Peter, had unjustly taken the title of king and usurped the rule. The pope, clearly sympathetic to Hugh's claim, took the line that in turning to him Hugh had rightly sought justice while seeking to maintain peace; Peter is to be given the chance to explain himself, but the pope's language is severe and it looks as if he was expecting Peter to abdicate in Hugh's favour if indeed the facts of the case were as stated. What would seem to have happened was that almost immediately, and certainly well before the pope's letter could have reached Cyprus, Raymond Babin and his party arrived at the papal court to announce Peter's accession. As explained already, they were present some

---

36 These posts were held by Philip of Brunswick and Philip of Ibelin, lord of Arsur, respectively in the early part of the reign.
37 Nicholas Coureas, *The Latin Church in Cyprus, 1313–1378* (Nicosia: Cyprus Research Centre, 2010), pp. 190–91.
38 Makhairas, *Recital*, I, pp. 92–93 (§ 104); Philippe de Mézières, *The Life of Saint Peter Thomas*, ed. by Joachim Smet (Rome: Institutum Carmelitanum, 1954), pp. 91–92.
39 For a letter of October 1361 in which the pope exceptionally addressed Queen Joanna as 'queen of Sicily and Jerusalem', see Martène and Durand, *Thesaurus novus anecdotorum*, II, col. 1058. For a letter of 1368 referring to Peter as king of both Cyprus and Jerusalem, see *Bullarium Cyprium III*, no. v-207. It is to be assumed that in both cases the form of the title came about as the result of carelessness on the part of a papal clerk who was adapting the phraseology of a petition.
40 Philippe de Mézières, *The Life of Saint Peter Thomas*, p. 94.
41 Conrad Eubel, *Hierarchia catholica medii aevi*, 6 vols (Münster, 1913–67), I, pp. 206, 215.
42 *Bullarium Cyprium III*, no. u-226, cf. no. u-216.

time before 11 June when the pope gave his approval to a number of supplications that Raymond had submitted,[43] and on 28 June Innocent wrote again to Peter, mentioning the embassy and this time taking a far less hostile stance [Appendix A.4]. Perhaps the gentle tone was because in the letter the pope offered Peter his condolences on the death of his father and exhorted him to rule well; it is only at the end that he instructed the king to do justice to his nephew. He also accorded Peter a licence to send galleys to Alexandria.[44] There is nothing in either letter to confirm Makhairas's claim that the pope gave Peter a year in which to make his defence.

It has to be assumed that Raymond Babin had done well in setting out the justification for Peter's rule. No doubt, as Leontios Makhairas reported, Raymond had argued that Cypriot custom going back to the beginning of Latin rule in Cyprus favoured the succession of a younger son over the claims of a grandson. That, as is well known, is set out clearly in the thirteenth-century legal treatises from the Latin East by both the anonymous author of the *Livre au Roi* and John of Ibelin.[45] Whether a version of Hugh's parents' marriage contract was produced at the *curia* at this point is unclear, but, as mentioned above, the surviving version does not support Hugh's claim that his succession was guaranteed. What Raymond would have been able to tell the pope was that at Easter Peter had been crowned king of Jerusalem by the papal legate—news which quite possibly had not reached Avignon until now and which would seriously cut the ground from under the pope's feet—and he could also explain that the late king had been grooming Peter as his successor for many years before his death, while Hugh, so far as is known, had stayed in the West and had no following in Cyprus.

The gap in the papal archives makes it difficult to know for certain how Innocent's relations with King Peter developed. As mentioned already, the view in Cyprus was that Hugh of Lusignan's claim would have to be bought off and John of Morphou and Thomas of Montolif's embassy duly arrived in Avignon in the autumn of 1361. Its task was twofold: to persuade the pope that there was no point in continuing to back Hugh, and then, with papal assistance, to induce Hugh to accept the pay-off comprising, so Leontios informed his readers, an annual income of 50,000 Cypriot white bezants.[46] The existing arguments for Peter's rule—Cypriot inheritance custom, coronation by the papal legate, and the new king's popularity within Cyprus—were now augmented by a considerable military achievement: Peter's capture of the port of Antalya in August 1361, a success at Turkish expense that would have rivalled the capture of Smyrna in 1344. Under the circumstances it would have been difficult for Innocent to continue supporting Hugh of Lusignan's claim to the throne, even though Hugh apparently stood high in the pope's estimation. In August 1360 Innocent had

---

43 *Bullarium Cyprium III*, nos u-230–40, cf. nos u-228–29, 241–46.
44 *Bullarium Cyprium III*, no. u-245. It is impossible to know whether the fact that this privilege is dated six days after almost all the others is of any significance.
45 *Livre au Roi*, ed. by Myriam Greilsammer (Paris: L'Académie des Inscriptions et Belles-Lettres, 1995), pp. 233–34; John of Ibelin, *Le Livre des Assises*, ed. by Peter W. Edbury, The Medieval Mediterranean, 50 (Leiden and Boston: Brill, 2003), pp. 159–61, 619.
46 Makhairas, *Recital*, I, pp. 94–97 (§ 108).

appointed him senator of Rome, a demanding position that required considerable political skill. It is, however, unclear how much time Hugh actually spent in Rome as senator or indeed whether his tenure proved satisfactory to the pope; in any case he had relinquished his office by October 1361.[47] According to Makhairas, John of Morphou's embassy initially met with little success, but then the deal was struck and John of Morphou arranged for Hugh of Lusignan to be betrothed to his own daughter. It was only later that Hugh attempted to revoke the agreement and reassert his claims.

But although we do not have any papal diplomatic correspondence relating to the Cypriot embassy's presence at Avignon at the end of 1361, a large number of papal indults were issued at that time.[48] John of Morphou then travelled on from Avignon; in January he met King John of France and performed homage, and in early February he was in Paris.[49] Presumably one purpose of this visit was to secure the French king's backing for the proposed deal with Hugh. The existence of a small group of papal indults issued at the end of March 1362, including two in favour of King Peter, could well signify that John and his party had then revisited the papal court on their way home to Cyprus.[50] Whether in the light of the embassy Innocent wrote any further letters to the king regarding his nephew's claim is open to doubt. Certainly none survive.

With the accession of Urban V in November 1362, the situation immediately becomes clearer. By then, assuming that Makhairas's chronology is correct, Peter was already on his way to Avignon, although his arrival at the papal court was delayed until March 1363. On 29 November [Appendix B.2] the pope wrote to Peter raising the subject of his still unresolved relations with his nephew and sister-in-law, while giving no indication that he was aware that the king was *en route* for the West; Peter is upbraided for not responding to the earlier letter from Innocent VI, perhaps that of 24 May 1360 [Appendix A.1], but once again there is no suggestion in this letter that the king had been summoned to appear in person. On the other hand, the importance that the new pope accorded this issue was underlined by the fact that on the same day he wrote to the king's brother, John of Antioch, and to Peter Thomas, the papal legate, evidently expecting them to put pressure on Peter to act.[51]

So to return to the original question: to what extent was Peter's visit to the papal court motivated by the need to deal with the challenge to his rule presented by his nephew,

---

47 Ferdinand Gregorovius, *History of the City of Rome in the Middle Ages*, trans. by Annie Hamilton, 8 vols (London: George Bell and Sons, 1894–1902), VI, ii, p. 401. For papal letters referring to Hugh's position, see *Thesaurus novus anecdotorum*, II, cols 846–847, 929–302 (nos 5, 6, 98).
48 *Bullarium Cyprium III*, nos u-260–88.
49 Mas Latrie, *Histoire*, III, p. 741.
50 *Bullarium Cyprium III*, nos u-291–301. The idea that they were in Avignon in March is commensurate with evidence that at the end of April the ambassadors were arranging for Genoese galleys to collect them from Aigues-Mortes for the start of their return journey to Cyprus: Laura Balletto, 'Nuovi dati su un'ambasceria cipriota in Occidente durante il regno di Pietro I di Lusignano', Επετηρίδα Κέντρου Επιστημονικών Ερευνών (Κύπρου), 31 (2005), 91–108 (pp. 99–102).
51 *Lettres secrètes et curiales du pape Urbain V (1362–1370) se rapportant à la France extraites des registres d'Avignon et du Vatican*, ed. by Paul Lecacheux and Guillaume Mollat, Bibliothèque des Écoles Françaises d'Athènes et de Rome, 3 Série (Paris: De Boccard, 1902–55), nos 120–21; *Bullarium Cyprium III*, nos v-11–12.

Hugh of Lusignan? The reference in Urban's letter to correspondence from Innocent VI serves to highlight the frustration arising from the loss of the registers—Urban may have been alluding to letters sent *apropos* John of Morphou's embassy that are no longer extant—but on the other hand, Peter's failure to respond might suggest that concluding a deal with Hugh of Lusignan was not high on his list of priorities.[52] His position as king was secure, and, although Hugh was certainly able to make a nuisance of himself, he cannot have posed much of a threat. The idea that Peter may have been in no hurry to settle affairs with his nephew finds further support in what we know of the chronology of John of Morphou and Thomas of Montolif's embassy. It would seem that the envoys left Cyprus in April. By 3 June they were in Venice. In 1360 Peter had renewed the Venetians' commercial privileges, but there were some unresolved issues, and these the envoys were now endeavouring to settle.[53] Precisely when they reached Avignon is not known, but the fact that the many of the indults issued in response to their petitions date from the middle of November suggests that they may not have arrived until towards the end of October.[54] The point is that the envoys had clearly taken their time to make their way to the papal court, and that too might suggest that from the Cypriot point of view the affair did not have any particular urgency.

But if his conflict with his nephew was not uppermost in the king's mind, the only plausible alternative explanation for Peter's visit has to be that he was looking for support for further military action against the Muslim powers. The problem here is that it is easy to be misled by hindsight, in particular through the writings of Philip of Mézières and William of Machaut, both of whom, albeit from widely different perspectives, needed to present Peter as the dedicated crusader and the 1365 Alexandria campaign as intended to lead to the recovery of the Holy Land.[55] Leontios Makhairas, who by contrast gives little attention to the king's crusading ambitions, mentions Peter's representative recruiting mercenaries in Italy in 1362, and this can be seen as confirming that the available manpower in Cyprus itself was inadequate for the king's needs.[56]

Two letters written by Peter, in all probability drafted by his chancellor Philip of Mézières, survive from 1362 and would appear to indicate that the idea of him leading

---

52 The letter of 29 November [Appendix B.2] states (with surprise) that Peter had never responded in writing to Innocent, who had written to him 'iam sunt longa tempora retroacta'. If Urban is referring to Innocent's extant letters from 1360, it is hard to understand why he should complain given that John of Morphou's embassy would itself have constituted a response. On the other hand, if the pope is alluding to the king's failure to respond to non-extant letters written at the time of the embassy, they could scarcely be described as dating from long past. If Peter had never responded to Innocent's letters from 1360, perhaps the pope did not write further on the matter.

53 Mas Latrie, *Histoire*, II, pp. 229–32, 233–35.

54 *Bullarium Cyprium III*, nos u-260-88. Perhaps they also petitioned for the isolated indult issued on 29 October, *Bullarium Cyprium III*, no. u-259.

55 This is a large subject in its own right. See Peter W. Edbury, 'Machaut, Mézières, Makhairas and *Amadi*: Constructing the Reign of Peter I (1359–1369)', in *Philippe de Mézières and His Age: Piety and Politics in the Fourteenth Century*, ed. by Renate Blumenfeld-Kosinski and Kiril Petkov (Leiden and Boston: Brill, 2012), pp. 349–58.

56 Makhairas, *Recital*, I, pp. 96–97 (§ 109), cf. I, 96–97 (§ 111), where presumably the 1360 date is an error (22 April 1360 was not a Sunday, but neither was 22 April 1362).

a crusade was indeed in his mind. In June he wrote to the government of Florence, recalling that the kingdom of Jerusalem had fallen to the Muslims in the days of his great uncle, Henry II, and asserting that since his childhood he had the desire to recover the Holy Land, which was his inheritance; he was therefore appealing to them for aid in a campaign timed to commence on 1 March 1364.[57] The second letter, dated 15 September—in other words shortly before Peter's departure for the West—is addressed to Niccolò Acciaiuoli, a leading figure in the major Florentine banking house of that name and grand seneschal of Sicily; it says nothing of Jerusalem but thanks him for the 'magnificent offer of galleys' that will be used 'in honour of the Christian name and the destruction of the infidels'. The letter mentions Peter's ambassadors—quite probably John of Morphou and Thomas of Montolif—and taken in isolation might seem to imply that Peter was holding out the prospect of co-operation with the Neapolitans in shoring up the Christian position in the Aegean and Frankish Greece against the Turks. Quite what Peter had been proposing is not stated, but the fact that he seems to have been working in cooperation with Niccolò Acciaiuoli suggests that he had had some success in ensuring the political isolation of Hugh of Lusignan.[58] The Florentine letter is more problematic. Perhaps it should be taken at face value, but the absence of any papally sanctioned crusade at the time, and especially a crusade with the ambition to recover the Holy Land, makes one wonder if it was largely a matter of window dressing. Peter is both emphasizing his right to the title 'king of Jerusalem' and claiming the moral high ground. Was this a further attempt to eliminate potential support for Hugh of Lusignan? Was Peter doing no more than trying to create an environment in which the Florentine authorities would be sympathetic to his attempts to raise mercenary troops? Part of the problem is that we have no way of knowing whether he sent similar letters to other rulers or whether and in what ways John of Morphou and his colleague's remit included sounding out the prospects of western support for further military action. They certainly met King John II of France, but what they discussed is lost to view. All that can be said is that the letter to Niccolò Acciaiuoli is possibly an indication that they—if indeed they are the ambassadors mentioned—had been authorized to discuss further military action.

The available evidence does not therefore admit a simple answer. That Peter wanted to settle Hugh of Lusignan's claim to the throne is certain, but, on the other hand, it may not have been top of his agenda. Even if the Florentine letter was little more than a propagandist ploy designed to influence a potential source of military support, it does at least imply that getting recruits in the West was one of his goals.

---

57 Mas Latrie, *Histoire*, II, pp. 236–37. Also published in Giuseppe Müller, *Documenti sulle relazioni delle città Toscane coll'Oriente Cristiano e coi Turchi fino all'anno MDXXXI* (Florence, 1879), p. 119. For the idea that the letter was composed by Philip, see Kenneth M. Setton, *The Papacy and the Levant (1204–1571)*, 4 vols (Philadelphia: American Philosophical Society 1976–84), I, p. 242; Philippe Contamine, 'Entre Occident et Orient. Philippe de Mézières (vers 1327–1405): itinéraires maritimes et spirituels', in *Philippe de Mézières and His Age: Piety and Politics in the Fourteenth Century*, ed. by Renate Blumenfeld-Kosinski and Kiril Petkov (Leiden and Boston: Brill, 2012), pp. 19–40 (25).
58 Buchon, *Nouvelles recherches*, II, pp. 134–35.

Whether Peter could have anticipated King John II's espousal of the crusading ideal and, with it, the crusading rhetoric of his forebears is another question that allows no easy solution. At very least it looks as if Peter was setting out to raise support and troops in the West: getting the pope to proclaim a crusade with himself as the leader of what was supposed to be the advanced party ahead of the French king's *passagium generale* may mean that, when eventually he did arrive at Avignon, he was far more successful than he could have reasonably hoped.

Pope Urban's Plans for King Peter and the Crusade of 1365

We come now to the question of the role that Urban envisaged for Peter in his crusade.[59] Two letters that have apparently not previously attracted attention sparked our interest, because they suggest that Urban did not expect the king to participate in the main expedition that was then planned, the *passagium generale*.[60] By the time he arrived in Avignon at the end of March 1363, almost six months had passed since he had left his kingdom. While Peter was staying at the papal curia in April and May, the pope warned him to return home as soon as possible, and he repeated his admonition in late November and again in early June 1364. Yet by then the leader of the crusade, King John II of France, had died, and Urban had to focus on Peter's activities and a serious obstacle to their successful realization: the threat of Genoese hostilities.

On 7 November 1362, the day after his election, the new pope informed the secular rulers of his assumption of the papacy; he made no mention of the recovery of the Holy Land, and his letter to Peter contained nothing directly concerning the king or his kingdom.[61] Twelve days later, on 19 November [Appendix B.1], Urban addressed a somewhat lengthy letter to the archbishop and bishops of Cyprus concerning the Turkish naval threat to Romania and nearby islands and areas, to which his predecessors Clement VI and Innocent VI had responded by imposing an ecclesiastical tithe on Cyprus and other places. The Turkish threat was continuing, however, and Urban considered maintaining the city of Smyrna, captured from the Turks in 1344, to be, along with other measures, key to the defence of the Christians of Cyprus and other regions against the Turks. The apostolic camera was supposed to pay for these efforts with the incomes from the tithe, but the expenses of defending and recovering Church lands in Italy from 'powerful tyrants'—mainly Bernabò Visconti—were too

---

59 The lives of Urban V in Etienne Baluze, *Vitae Paparum Avenionensium hoc est historia pontificum Romanorum qui in Gallia sederunt ab anno Christi MCCCV usque annum MCCCXCIV*, new edition by Guillaume Mollat, 4 vols (Paris: Letouzey et Ane, 1914–27), I, pp. 349–414, were written with hindsight and need to be treated with caution.

60 They were not summarized by Lecacheux, but Setton, *Papacy*, I, p. 246b, n. 108, transcribed the first of the letters [Appendix B.6] in a footnote and told the reader to compare it to the second [Appendix B.8], but did not make much of them. In general, Setton's detailed coverage of the build-up to the 1365 expedition in Urban V's (pp. 243a–263b) reign is quite exhaustive, employing other unpublished sources, but our present goals are more limited.

61 Urban V, *Lettres secrètes et curiales*, no. 41; *Bullarium Cyprium III*, no. v-1.

burdensome, and Urban was reluctantly forced to extend the tithe another three years. At the time Urban's crusading focus was thus squarely on the Aegean and the Turks in Anatolia, in addition to Italy. When on 29 November he wrote his first letter specifically to King Peter, the topic was, as we have seen, not the crusade, but Peter's unresolved relations with his nephew Hugh and his sister-in-law the Empress Maria [Appendix B.2]. Although the pope would have been aware of Peter's capture of Antalya in 1361, his only mention of 'the enemies of Christ' was to underline the point that discord between those who live among the infidels is especially dangerous. In any case, as already noted, it is clear from this letter that the pope was unaware that King Peter was on his way to Avignon.

It was only when Peter arrived at the curia in Avignon on 29 March 1363[62] that the pope became fully appraised of the king's further ambitions against the infidels. Almost immediately, on 31 March, Urban wrote enthusiastic letters to French prelates and King John II of France concerning the crusade, but it has gone almost unnoticed that Urban also addressed a parallel letter to Peter himself [Appendix B.3]. In these letters, Urban relates how the 'Hagarenes' long ago occupied the Holy Land and how the Turks have advanced against the Christians in the East. The danger inspired King Peter to make the perilous journey to the Apostolic See in person to explain the situation in the East to the pope and the cardinals. According to Peter, whose capture of Antalya 'and several other castles and localities' Urban praises, the time is right to drive out the 'Hagarenes' and Turks and to recapture the Holy Land, because they are decimated by the plague, divided by internal discord, and weakened—even frightened—by their losses to Peter himself. Urban reports that for this reason, King John II, King Peter, and many other nobles took the sign of the cross from the pope's hands and promised to go personally for the recovery of the Holy Land. Thus the pope proclaims a crusade, a *passagium generale*, to the Holy Land and other infidel parts in the East, granting the customary indulgences, appointing King John II as rector and captain general of the crusade, announcing the preaching of the crusade in the Kingdom of France, ordering various ecclesiastical incomes in France converted to the cause, and fixing 1 March 1365 as the deadline for setting off on the venture.[63]

In the letter to Peter Pope Urban added that King John could not depart on his campaign until around the fixed deadline, but that 'you, as an athlete of Christ and intrepid precursor, who are at present at the [Apostolic] See, propose to cross over, as you asserted to us, considerably before (*satis ante*) said deadline with supporting forces from the faithful on this side of the sea'. The pope therefore outlined in great detail how the Church would help finance King Peter's efforts and under what conditions, largely with donations, bequests, and fines paid to the Church in areas

---

62 *Vitae Paparum Avenionensium*, I, p. 384, n. 10.
63 For the parallel letters to King John and the French prelates (not in the *Bullarium*), see *Caesaris S. R. E. Card. Baronii, Odorici Raynaldi et Jacobi Laderchii Annales Ecclesiastici*, tomus XXVI, 1356–1396 (Bar-le-Duc: Guerin, 1872) (= *Annales Ecclesiastici*, XXVI), pp. 81–84 (1363, nos 14–19); Maurice Prou, *Étude sur les relations politiques du pape Urbain V avec les rois de France Jean II et Charles V (1362–1370)* (Paris: E. Bouillon et E. Vieweg, 1888), pp. 91–94, doc. 14; Urban V, *Lettres secrètes et curiales*, nos 346–347 (letters not in *Bullarium*).

from Hungary through the Balkans to Crete and Cyprus, other eastern outposts such as Caffa, as well as Sicily and certain Italian provinces [Appendix B.3].

At this point the destination of the crusade was unspecified and unclear, for alongside the Holy Land, long occupied by the Muslims, Urban also mentions the Turks, closer to Christian populations, and Peter's victory in Antalya and other places on the coast of Asia Minor.[64] Moreover, Urban was perhaps echoing Peter's own propaganda, intended to persuade the pope, who had already made clear his intention of making the defence of Smyrna a priority in his eastern policy. Yet Urban was also preoccupied with a military confrontation with Bernabò Visconti, 'the enemy of God and His holy Church', an impediment to any crusading activity. From the pope's letter of 1 May to Cardinal Gil Álvarez de Albornoz of Santa Sabina, we learn that, likely at Urban's request, King John II and King Peter had sent ambassadors to Bernabò to persuade him to relinquish papal castles and come to terms with the Church, 'both in support of this *passagium* and for the peace and quiet of the Roman Church and parts of Lombardy'.[65] On 25 May, the same day that Urban wrote similar letters to the Emperor Charles IV, the kings of England and Hungary, the marquis of Moravia, the dukes of Luxembourg, Austria, Saxony, and Bavaria, the doges of Venice and Genoa, and many others, urging them to join and contribute in various ways to the planned crusade,[66] Urban addressed Peter himself a letter of which two versions survive in the papal registers, the second and shorter of which is mostly included in the first [Appendix B.4-5: § §3, 9, 4, 10]. In the arenga of the longer letter, the pope expands on his focus on the recovery of the Holy Land in letter of 31 March, not in vague terms, but specifically as the land of the Lord's birth. In contrast to the occupation of the Holy Land by the 'Hagarenes, the treacherous enemy of the Saviour and His orthodox faith', the advances of the cruel Turks, closer to the faithful, are again only mentioned secondarily, although they present an immediate danger.

Much of the body of the longer letter of 25 May follows the lines of the earlier one of 31 March [Appendix B.3-4: § §1-4]. Urban repeats that King John will have difficulty departing much before the deadline, but that Peter, as a fearless athlete of Christ, who is still at the curia, the pope remarks, plans to set off well before the deadline, on what we might call a *passagium particulare*. Urban now specifies [Appendix B.4-5: § 4] that Peter can take with him 200 mounted nobles from the Kingdom of France and, from areas other than France, 2000 horsemen and 6000 infantry with their familiars, 'and any men at arms from any companies, wherever they may be', a reference to the numerous mercenary armies active at the time, who otherwise

---

64 In the *Vitae Paparum Avenionensium*, I, pp. 352, 384, the crusade is simply called 'contra Turcos'.
65 Urban V, *Lettres secrètes et curiales*, no. 387; *Bullarium Cyprium III*, no. v-22. Bernabò was eventually bought off on 13 March 1364: Setton, *Papacy*, I, p. 247a.
66 *Annales Ecclesiastici*, XXVI, pp. 84–86 (1363, nos 20–22); *Diplomatarium Veneto-Levantinum*, ed. by Georg M. Thomas and Riccardo Predelli, 2 vols (Venice, 1880–99), II, pp. 92–95; Urban V, *Lettres secrètes et curiales*, nos 476–489; *Bullarium Cyprium III*, nos v-38–39. On 15 April Urban had urged the king of Navarre to support the crusade: Urban V, *Lettres secrètes et curiales*, no. 354.

presented an obstacle to the success of the *passagium generale*.[67] In addition, he can accept anyone from the provinces of Aquileia, Grado, and Salzburg, the Kingdoms of Hungary and Cyprus, the region of Sclavonia, Sicily and nearby islands, as well as Romania and other areas of Outremer, in other words most of the areas mentioned in the previous letter from which the funding would be derived. They will have the same graces and privileges they would have if they were to set off with the king of France. On 31 May Peter set off to gather support for his expedition.[68]

So when did Urban expect Peter to go on his expedition and where was he to go? On 28 November 1363 [Appendix B.6], almost six months to the day after Peter had left the Apostolic See, Urban V wrote to the king as follows:

> A while ago (*dudum*), carefully considering the many and great dangers that could befall your kingdom and the areas of Outremer on account of your serenity's long absence from your kingdom and those parts, with fatherly affection we urged you, who were then at the Apostolic See, to take care to return as soon as you comfortably could to your kingdom, situated between the jaws of the enemies of the faith, once you had visited the kings and princes that you had decided to visit. Recently (*nuper*), however, having learned that the treacherous Turks are trying to harm said kingdom and have a large army around your city of Antalya, because of which you should instead return to those parts quickly, with much concern we urge and beseech you not to delay your return to said parts any further, with God assisting.

Thus when Peter was still in Avignon, Urban had exhorted the king to return to Cyprus as soon as possible after making the rounds that he had planned, because his prolonged absence presented a danger to Cyprus and to Outremer in general.[69] Given that Urban had granted him permission to take an army of over 8000 men and their retinues in advance, and given the weather patterns, it is reasonable to assume that in November 1363 Urban anticipated a departure in the spring of 1364. In a letter dated Calais, 20 October 1363, Peter I informed the Venetians of his intention to depart from Venice the following March.[70] Long beforehand Peter had written to the Florentines concerning some sort of expedition that he planned for 1 March 1364, and it may not be coincidental that this date ended up being exactly a year before the deadline Urban set for the *passagium generale*. One can further infer that, for the pope, the intended goal was on the western and/or the southern coast of Asia Minor, beating back the

---

67 Norman Housley, 'The Mercenary Companies, the Papacy, and the Crusades, 1356–1378', *Traditio*, 38 (1982), 253–80 (pp. 271–72) (repr. in Norman Housley, *Crusading and Warfare in Medieval and Renaissance Europe*, Variorum Collected Studies, 712 (Aldershot: Ashgate, 2001), no. XV), sees the problem with the mercenaries, the *routiers*, as an even more important cause of the eventual failure of the general passage than King John II's death in 1364.
68 *Vitae Paparum Avenionensium*, I, pp. 384–85.
69 For the threat to Antalya, see Makhairas, *Recital*, I, pp. 116–19 (§ § 132–34) (shortly after Peter's departure for the West); for threats to Cyprus and the Cypriot response, see Makhairas, *Recital*, I, pp. 120–25 (§ § 137, 139–43).
70 Mas Latrie, *Histoire*, III, p. 743.

Turks while expanding the territory under Christian control around Smyrna and/ or around Antalya and nearby areas. It does not seem likely that Palestine or Egypt would have been Urban's intended target for Peter, because those areas did not seem to present an imminent danger to the Christian territories in Cyprus, Armenia, and Romania, and what danger there was required Peter's presence more for defensive than for offensive purposes.

The context of the letter of 28 November 1363 [Appendix B.6] reinforces this idea. The Turks were threatening Cyprus from the north and apparently laying siege to Antalya. Urban now urges Peter to return right away. It would not have been easy for Peter to sail safely with a large force during the winter, so either the pope wanted him to return immediately with his own retinue or wait for the spring and take whatever troops he could gather. Peter was therefore not to be a participant in King John II's *passagium generale*,[71] wherever that was going, at least not from the time of its departure, but rather he would lead a sizeable advance party, probably to western and/or southern Asia Minor. In granting a license to visit the Holy Sepulchre on 7 November, however, while Urban stipulated that the recipient should not go except with the king of Cyprus *or* wait for the *passagium generale*, explicitly separating King Peter from the main event, the pope apparently (inadvertently?) leaves open the possibility that Peter could also end up in Palestine.[72]

In the event, King Peter returned neither immediately nor in the early spring. The main reason for Peter's delay was the revolt on Venetian Crete that had broken out in the summer of 1363, which was not quelled until the late spring of 1364. While Peter was writing his letter of 20 October 1363 from Calais, a letter from the doge of Venice dated 11 October was making its way to him, bearing news of the revolt. On 29 November, the day after Urban's letter to the king, in response to Peter the doge announced that the revolt might affect their crusade contribution.[73] Urban first reacted in a letter of 15 October, but although he was concerned about the rebellion and the possible effect on the general passage, he does not seem to have connected it to King Peter in his pertinent correspondence.[74]

On 1 April 1364, a year after the initial proclamation of the crusade, Pope Urban sent a series of ten letters concerning the *passagium* of Count Amadeo VI of Savoy, who, like Peter (who is mentioned in eight of these letters), was expected to set off before the main body of troops under King John of France. These letters are well

---

71 Urban's letter to French prelates on crusade funding, dated 31 March 1364, thus makes no mention of King Peter: Urban V, *Lettres secrètes et curiales*, no. 868.
72 AAV, Reg. Suppl. 41, fol. 2ᵛ, summarized on Brepols's online database *Ut per litteras apostolicas...*, ed. by Anne-Marie Hayez and others; this is not a transcription, however, and we have not seen the original.
73 Mas Latrie, *Histoire*, III, pp. 742–43; Setton, *Papacy*, I, p. 251a–b, and pp. 249a–257b on the revolt in general; and, for Peter I, Nicholas Coureas, 'King Peter I of Cyprus and the Rebellion of 1363 on Crete', in Πρακτικά του Τρίτου Διεθνούς Κυπρολογικού Συνεδρίου (Nicosia, 16–20 April 1996), II, Μεσαιωνικό Τμήμα, ed. by Athanasios Papageorghiou, II (Nicosia: Society of Cypriot Studies, 2001), pp. 519–26.
74 Most of the letter of 15 October is in Setton, *Papacy*, I, p. 251a, n. 131; see also pp. 251b–252a, n. 135, for Urban's continuing hopes for Peter's spring departure as of 5 December 1363.

known, but those that have been printed were misdated 1 April 1363 in the editions.[75] More important, the letter preceding these bulls, indeed the very first letter of Reg. Vat. 253, is addressed to King Peter of Cyprus himself, although as far as we know this has gone unnoticed [Appendix B.7]. This letter reminds Peter of the situation, repeating much of what had been said before [Appendix B.3, 7: § §1-4, 5-8], and adding 'Pera near Constantinople' to the many places from which Peter would receive crusade subsidies, as opposed to Amadeo's reliance on his own lands. The main difference between the letter addressed to Peter on 31 March 1363 and the one sent on 1 April 1364 is in the lengthy discussion of the financing of the crusade.

In the letter of 1 April 1364, Urban states that Peter is now at the papal curia, but since the same clause is found in the 31 March 1363 letter and in the same context [§ 4], one wonders whether it was copied by mistake.[76] Nevertheless, the letter of 1 April 1364 does exhibit minor modifications by the chancery in the sections repeated from the 31 March 1363 bull, for example the change to '*dudum*' to describe what happened a year before, as opposed to what had just occurred '*nuper*' in 1363 [§ 2]. So the chancery was conscious that not everything could be repeated verbatim. Since we know that Peter was in the area in 1364, it seems that we can say that he probably visited Avignon again, but this is less than certain.

Two weeks later, on 17 April 1364, Urban wrote the captain and company of the English in Italy, i.e., John Hawkwood and the mercenary White Company, urging them to join the fight against the infidels along with 'our beloved sons in Christ the illustrious Kings John II of France and Peter of Cyprus, or one of them'.[77] Urban learned soon afterward that King John II had died on 8 April 1364, but that did not mean that he automatically replaced John with Peter as leader of the general passage. On 3 June 1364 [Appendix B.8], two months after John II's death, Urban wrote a brief letter to Peter, explaining that two agents of the master of the Hospital, Roger de Pins, had recently (*nuper*) showed him a letter that the master had sent them, dated Rhodes, 28 February,

---

75 See Setton, *Papacy*, I, p. 285, nn. 2–3. F.E. Bollati di Saint-Pierre, *Illustrazioni della spedizione in Oriente di Amedeo VI (il Conte Verde)* (Turin: Bocca, 1900), docs. VI–XII, pp. 344–67, are seven bulls of 1 April 1364 concerning Amadeo of Savoy's *passagium*, but misdated 1 April 1363, perhaps taken from other copies. Setton notes that the same dating error is in the earlier Pietro Datta, *Spedizione in Oriente di Amedeo VI conte di Savoia, provota con inediti documenti* (Turin: per Alliana e Paravia, 1826), pp. 225–241, which is the text in letter number 3 listed below. See parallel discussion on Amadeo's goal in Setton, *Papacy*, I, p. 286b, since the bulls talk both of the Holy Land and of the closer Turks. The following in AAV, Vat. Reg. 253, mention or discuss Peter I of Cyprus, all from 1 April 1364: no. 2, fols 2ᵛ–5ʳ: Archiepiscopo Collocensi [Kalosca, in Hungary] eiusque suffraganeis: *Et si cunctorum*; no. 3, fols 5ʳ–7ʳ: Amedeo: *Et si cunctorum*; no. 4, fols 7ʳ–9ᵛ: Prelates subject to Amedeo: *Et si cunctorum*; no. 5, fols 9ᵛ–12ʳ: To the same: *Beatitudinis eterne bravium*; no. 6, fol. 12ʳ⁻ᵛ: Amedeo: *Gerentes dudum prout*; no. 7, fols 12ᵛ–13ʳ: Prelates as above: *Gerentes dudum prout*; no. 8, fols 13ʳ–14ʳ: Amedeo: *Calamitosa miseria opprobriosaque*; no. 9, fol. 14ʳ–16ʳ: Prelates as above: *Calamitosa miseria opprobriosaque* (also same day, not mentioning Peter of Cyprus: no. 10, fol. 16ʳ⁻ᵛ: Amedeo: *Fidei orthodoxe super*; no. 11, fols 16ᵛ–17ʳ: Prelates as above: *Fidei orthodoxe super*).

76 Indeed, the text of the 1 April 1364 letter parallels that of a separate one that had been sent to King John and others on 31 March 1363, and among these in the papal register there is the beginning of the corresponding one to Peter, which is cancelled with the marginal note: 'This was written in the second year', that is, 1364.

77 Urban V, *Lettres secrètes et curiales*, no. 891; *Bullarium Cyprium III*, no. v-90.

which contained upsetting news for the pope from Outremer, besides business of the Hospital. The pope sent King Peter a copy, but unfortunately this does not survive in the papal registers, although it may survive in the order's archives. Perhaps it contained the first news of the violence between Genoese and Cypriots discussed below, but whatever the specifics of the letter, it convinced Urban that Peter's delay in returning to his kingdom 'or other parts overseas' was very dangerous unless he cut short his western sojourn quickly. Moreover, it appeared to the pope that those who wished to accompany Peter, seeing that the king was staying a very long time in France, might get tired of waiting, giving rise to further dangers. In stronger terms than before, therefore, Urban incited, requested, and urged Peter to hurry back to his kingdom and Outremer without any delay. Unless Urban had already abandoned hope of a general passage departing in early 1365, he still considered Peter the leader of a first wave of warriors defending Cyprus and nearby Christian holdings, rather than King John II's replacement, and he continued to advise Peter to leave as soon as possible.

Even if in Urban's eyes Peter's role was still limited, the appearance of a new obstacle must have brought home to the pope the king's increased significance in the project. On 19 June 1364 [Appendix B.9], Pope Urban wrote to King Peter a short note, reporting that he had recently heard that a brawl (*rixa seu tumultuosa discordia*) had occurred in Cyprus between the locals and some Genoese citizens,[78] concerning which the pope had written to Doge Gabriel Adorno and the council and commune of Genoa. Without mentioning the cause or assigning any blame, Urban pleaded with Peter to make satisfaction to those citizens for their injuries and damages and otherwise show them justice so that Genoa would be content, to avoid escalating the quarrel. Urban included a copy of his letter to the Genoese, which also survives in the Vatican Archives. Blaming the Devil for the discord, Urban remarks that he has heard that the doge and council have ordered the Genoese to cease residing in Cyprus from now on. As a result, the pope fears not only a decisive break in relations between the Cypriots and the Genoese, but also a dangerous escalation (*periculosa novitas*) in the dispute. Urban informs the Genoese that he is quite displeased with what has happened and afraid for greater evils in the future. Reminding the Genoese that King Peter was in the West at the time of the tumult, as he still is, the pope maintains that this prudent and just prince, a friend of the Genoese, will surely make satisfaction and show justice, adding that he is urging Peter in writing to do so. Being devout Christians and soldiers of the Lord, the Genoese have been supporting the planned crusade, for which Peter himself has laboured continually. Since the discord between the Genoese and the Cypriots puts the entire general passage in jeopardy, 'for the reverence of God's holy faith, the Apostolic See, and ours', Pope Urban asks the doge and council to avoid any escalation and to maintain their support for the crusade. The pope concludes by assuring the Genoese that he will strive for the satisfaction for the injuries and damages in any way he can, writing King Peter presently on the matter, and he hopes to hear their positive response.

---

78 Makhairas, *Recital*, I, pp. 126–31 (§§ 145–49), describes the events, not always without chronological confusion.

Six days later, however, on 25 June 1364, Urban wrote again to Doge Gabriel Adorno and the council and commune, relating that he had heard that very day, with sorrow, that the Genoese were arming a number of galleys to carry their ambassadors to threaten (*diffidare*) the king and kingdom. Urban emphasizes that King Peter is fighting for Christ and the Christian faith on the orders and at the pleasure of the pope himself, reiterating that Peter is in the West dealing with the business of the general passage. The pope now asserts that such escalation could thus cause irreparable damage not only to the king and the crusade, but also to the Genoese themselves, for whom starting new wars is very risky. In strong terms Urban exhorts the Genoese to back off, at least for the time being, and even offers to assist directly in satisfying the Genoese or their citizens in Cyprus for their injuries and damages, completing what the king or his subjects cannot fulfil. In order to deal with the matter directly, that same day the pope sent back to Genoa with instructions the Genoese provost (*prepositum*) Filippo de Varesio, who was at the curia on Genoese business.

Urban's quick response was at least temporarily successful. On 17 July the pope wrote to King Peter that the diplomatic efforts of the Apostolic See had persuaded the Genoese to wait for the king's 'processes and sentences, both against the delinquents and against those who neglected justice', in the business of the violence between the Cypriots and the Genoese, which Urban now specifies as having occurred in Famagusta. The pope therefore urged the king to consider the patience and the good will of the Genoese in his administering of justice, in order to erase all matter of scandal, 'especially at this time of the general passage'.[79]

Nevertheless, Urban apparently still thought that King Peter would leave soon as part of an advance party and did not consider him leader of or perhaps even participant in the general passage. The original legate for King John II's crusade was to be Cardinal Hélie de Talleyrand, who had many connections with Outremer, but Talleyrand had died on 17 January 1364. On 30 June the pope informed the king of Cyprus that, as the king must have already learned, Peter Thomas, patriarch of Constantinople and former papal legate in Outremer, had been named the new legate for the general passage. Although the pope noted that it was surely unnecessary to persuade the king, he urged King Peter to treat the legate fittingly. On 10 July, after relating to Peter Thomas the background to the crusade as he had described the previous year, Urban prefaced his description of the legate's new assignment as follows:

> The king of France and Bishop [Talleyrand] have gone the way of all flesh, as pleased the Lord, and said king of Cyprus, like an athlete of Christ and fearless vanguard, plans to cross over shortly with auxiliaries for the faithful of Outremer in order to assist those faithful and to rebuff the efforts of the infidels.[80]

---

79   Urban V, *Lettres secrètes et curiales*, no. 1102; *Bullarium Cyprium III*, no. v-102.
80   Urban V, *Lettres secrètes et curiales*, no. 1080 (*Bullarium Cyprium III*, no. v-99): 'Cum autem idem rex Francie et episcopus, sicut Domino placuit, sint viam universe carnis ingressi et dictus rex Cypri ad succurrendum eisdem fidelibus et conatus eorundem infidelium reprimendum, velut athleta Christi et precursor intrepidus, proponat in brevi cum auxiliis citramarinorum fidelium transfretare'.

Among the numerous letters Urban sent the same day is another, much longer, unpublished one to Peter Thomas, covering the same ground but adding details on areas of recruitment and preaching, repeating the regions outlined the previous year, but being more specific. In order to drum up support, Urban mentions that it would be 'in eiusdem Terre Sancte succursum', but the overall emphasis is on the Turkish menace. Urban associates King Peter explicitly with a *passagium*, but does not characterize it as a *passagium generale*, in contrast to how King John II's original venture is labelled in describing the history of the plans.[81]

For unknown reasons, after 17 July the *Bullarium Cyprium* records no further papal correspondence on the matter over the next seven months. Either the letters have been lost, Perrat and Richard did not find them, or there was no reason for Urban to write. Indeed, once the Genoese had been placated, for the time being, and once Peter had again missed the opportunity to sail East, perhaps delayed this time by his quarrel with the Genoese, there was little point in Urban's writing to Peter before late winter, when preparations would ideally have been underway to meet the original 1365 deadline for the crusade's departure. Still, as late as 16 October 1364, in a letter to Emperor John V Palaiologos responding to his offer to assist the *passagium generale*, Urban closed by relating that, after the death of King John II of France, he had not yet deliberated about the matter of John's replacement as captain general.[82]

For the time being, however, Peter was the main 'crusader'. Thus Urban began his letter to the doge, council, and commune of Genoa, dated 20 February 1365, as follows:

> Last summer, while our dear son in Christ Peter, the illustrious king of Cyprus, serving our Saviour and His most holy faith like a busy bee, to promote the support of the general passage, on our mandate and at our pleasure, toured certain kingdoms of the faithful and then, especially, regions of Germany [...].

Urban then reiterated what had happened the previous summer, before filling in the blanks about what ensued, hoping that Peter's return to Italy would allow easier negotiations. After Peter did arrive in Italy, on 11 November 1364,[83] the pope learned that Doge Lorenzo Celsi of Venice, where Peter was supposedly staying at the time that Urban composed his letter, sent ambassadors to the Genoese to work for an agreement between them and King Peter, since it would be easier than going all the way to Avignon. As Urban noted in a shorter letter to Peter on the same day, 20 February,[84] in which the pope adds that the tumult in Famagusta involved officials of the kingdom, despite his many prayers and exhortations asking the Genoese to refrain from reprisals, he had just found out with much bitterness that the ambassadors had returned to Venice without having achieved anything. In Urban's letter to the Genoese,

---

81 AAV, Reg. Vat. 253, fols 31ʳ–33ᵛ, noted also in Setton, *Papacy*, I, p. 258ᵃ⁻ᵇ and n. 2.
82 Urban V, *Lettres secrètes et curiales*, no. 1305; *Annales Ecclesiastici*, XXVI, p. 104 (1364, no. 27).
83 As B.14 states, the pope knew that Peter had returned to Italy, contrary to the summary in *Bullarium Cyprium III*, no. v-106. For the date of Peter's return, see Hardy, *Edition critique de la* Prise d'Alexandrie, pp. 45–46, ll. 1535–39.
84 Urban V, *Lettres secrètes et curiales*, no. 1602; *Bullarium Cyprium III*, no. v-107.

we are told that they were disposed to war against King Peter and his subjects. The pope therefore resolved to send Peter Thomas, patriarch and legate, to Genoa.

Urban's first justification for his concern is to avoid 'a manifest obstacle to and the subversion of the [general] passage'. In February 1365 Urban must have known that any fighting against the infidels that would take place that year, as originally intended, would now be under the leadership of King Peter I of Cyprus, even if the pope still avoided associating Peter with the general passage as captain or participant. To persuade the Genoese to stand down, however, the pope warns them of the evils that would otherwise befall not only the Genoese and the Cypriots, both groups being great warriors against Christ's enemies and for His faith, but also all of Christianity because of the impediment to the general passage. Not only that, but it would result in a great 'stain of infamy' on the good name of the Genoese and they would greatly offend the Saviour, not to mention the princes and other leaders who are assisting King Peter in the business of the crusade. Indeed, if the Genoese impeded the crusade they could perhaps face other wars and enemies because of their actions. The pope urges and warns the Genoese to listen to Peter Thomas and to make peace or at least agree to a truce of long duration with the Cypriots and their king. If the legate's intercession did not work, Urban asks the Genoese to send ambassadors to Avignon so that the pope could work directly for peace with both sides, since the pope also wrote to King Peter on the same matter. In his letter to Peter, Urban asked the king to do satisfaction for the Genoese damages and injuries, so that 'you do not make the *culpa* of others your own'.

The pope did not wait for the Genoese response before taking other action. On 27 February 1365, revealing that the main motivation was the crusade, Urban told Master Roger de Pins and the Hospitallers to remain neutral in the dispute between Genoa and Cyprus, so as not to exacerbate the situation.[85] On 4 March Urban addressed Peter a letter in which he explains why he had written to the Knights of St John: after 20 February Peter had informed the pope that he feared that the Hospitallers were against him; Urban told the king that he had written to the Hospitallers on the matter and he asked Peter to let him know if there was anything else the Apostolic See could do to help.[86]

Urban was right to be concerned. Even without the Genoese problem, the crusade had lost its leader, the advance passage had never materialized, and the original deadline for the general passage had come and gone. Despite the efforts of every single pope of the era, nearly a century had passed since the last general passage had set off for Muslim territory, and it must have appeared to Urban that his plans too would not come to fruition. On 22 March 1365 Urban wrote again to the Genoese, beginning by saying that it was no longer necessary to tell them how important he considered concord between Genoa and Cyprus. Now the pope complained that the delay in reaching an agreement was in turn delaying the crusade. Peter Thomas had gone to Genoa and then left for Venice, where King Peter was still staying, and afterwards the legate was expected to return to Genoa. This was perhaps understandable, but the process was taking so

---

85   Urban V, *Lettres secrètes et curiales*, no. 1609; *Bullarium Cyprium III*, no. v-108.
86   Urban V, *Lettres secrètes et curiales*, no. 1619; *Bullarium Cyprium III*, no. v-109.

long that it would probably harm the affairs of Outremer seriously. The pope was very upset that King Peter and the noble crusaders were still in the West, and he beseeched the Genoese to come to an agreement quickly, with the guidance of the legate, so that Peter of Cyprus would not depart from the West with the affair weighing on his mind.[87]

Four days later, on 26 March 1365 [Appendix B.16–17], Urban wrote the Genoese, King Peter, and Peter Thomas, pushing for a quick agreement upon the legate's impending return to Genoa, but, failing that, God forbid, the pope urged the two sides to send nuncios to Avignon after all, so that the pope could deal directly with the problem. In his letter to Peter Thomas, Urban referred vaguely to a 'nova causa' of the Genoese, while in writing to King Peter the pope also mentioned negotiations concerning the 'union between [the king] and many other faithful', in progress at the curia, referring, it seems, to the delayed military expedition of the advance party.[88]

In the end the negotiations in Genoa were successful (a treaty was signed on 18 April)[89] and Urban did not have to deal with the issue directly in Avignon. On 26 April the pope wrote the king, expressing his joy at the outcome, which he had learned from Peter Thomas's letter. Urban also heard that a great number of nobles and other warriors had come from Germany and other regions to join the king on his expedition. With hope rekindled for an attack on the infidels, the pope urged King Peter to depart quickly, lest further delay result in the dissolution of the army, with the potential warriors returning home.[90] Finally, on 19 July, the pope was able to write the king again, happy and obviously relieved to have learned from Peter of Lusignan's letter that he had finally left Venice for the East: 'Age, igitur, fili carissime, bellum Dominicum magnanimiter et devote!'

Where did Urban think King Peter was headed? Various letters from 1365 suggest that it was not Alexandria, unless it was all a grand papal conspiracy. First, on 18 March, responding to their petitions, Urban wrote to the *universitates* of the cities, castles, and other places of the Kingdom of Cyprus, granting them the right to outfit six galleys, 'three one year and three the other', for trade with Alexandria and other areas of Outremer under the control of the Sultan of Babylon, as long as the cargos did not include any of the prohibited merchandise. As late as 25 August, Urban granted a similar license to the Venetians, who according to a document of as late as 3 July 1365 were under the impression that Peter would take his army to 'parts of Turkey'.[91]

---

87 Urban V, *Lettres secrètes et curiales*, no. 1649; *Bullarium Cyprium III*, no. v-111.
88 Urban V, *Lettres secrètes et curiales*, no. 1650; *Bullarium Cyprium III*, nos v-113, 115; Urban V, *Acta Urbani PP. V (1362–1370) e regestis Vaticanis aliisque fontibus*, ed. by Aloysius L. Tăutu, Pontificia commissio ad redigendum codicem iuris canonici orientalis, Fontes, Series III (Rome: Typis Pontificiae Universitatis Gregorianae, 1964), no. 73. On 17 April Urban wrote again to King Peter, relating that, probably for this other affair, the king had sent Pietro Malocello as his nuncio, who was the bearer of the present letter to the king: Urban V, *Lettres secrètes et curiales*, no. 1700; *Bullarium Cyprium III*, no. v-116.
89 The text is in Mas Latrie, *Histoire*, II, pp. 254–66. The Cypriots seem to have conceded all the Genoese demands. See also Makhairas, *Recital*, I, pp. 134–41 (§ § 153–56).
90 Urban V, *Lettres secrètes et curiales*, no. 1724; *Bullarium Cyprium III*, no. v-120.
91 Urban V, *Lettres communes*, ed. by Michel and Anne-Marie Hayez and others, Bibliothèque des Écoles Françaises d'Athènes et de Rome (Paris: De Boccard, 1954–89), no. 15175; Mas Latrie, *Histoire*, III, pp. 752–53. Thus, the 25 August 1365 document led Setton, *Papacy*, I, pp. 261b–262b, to remark, 'one wonders whether Urban V did not know that Alexandria was to be the crusaders' target'.

Second, on 18 April, Urban wrote to Emperor John V Palaiologos. After a rather extraordinary arenga concerning the Greeks being damned but nevertheless sons of the Church, Urban relates that he often thinks about how to defend John's empire, which the infidels, especially the abominable Turks, have destroyed and occupied almost completely. Then he continues:

> Because due to certain obstacles the general passage of the Christians of the West cannot succeed at present, we mention with sorrow, we have arranged to form a certain union of some faithful with the apparatus of galleys and armed men [...] for the expulsion of those Turks from said empire.

Urban expresses the hope that, once King Peter and Genoa come to an agreement, this union will succeed. The pope urges the emperor to rejoin the Church, in which case the pope will redouble his efforts for the good of empire and emperor.[92] Finally, a few days earlier, on 14 April, Urban had sent letters to a number of Hospitallers in the West concerning the danger the Turks posed to the Hospital on Rhodes if aid did not arrive soon: 'Because the business of the general passage—which we report with sorrow—is not advancing happily at present', the pope announces that 'we have arranged to form soon a certain union in order to have a number of men at arms and galleys for the defense of said island and areas, and to attack the Turks'.[93]

If we are to take these letters at face value, two things are clear. First, the dream of a *passagium generale* was over so far as Urban was concerned. After the reconciliation between King Peter and Genoa of 18 April, the Genoese apparently intended to ask Urban to appoint Peter as captain of the crusade,[94] but it would have been too late, even if Urban had wanted to do so. For Urban, the king of Cyprus was to lead an advance party, although in the end it departed after the general passage itself was supposed to have begun and so it no longer served as a vanguard for any real crusade.[95] Second, Urban never intended for Peter to go to Alexandria or anywhere else controlled by the Sultan of Babylon, but instead to fight the Turks, thereby defending Cyprus, Smyrna, Armenia, and the Greek Empire and building on Peter's recent victories and conquest of Antalya. We might view Urban's plan for King Peter

---

92 Urban V, *Lettres secrètes et curiales*, no. 1703; Urban V, *Acta*, no. 74 (not in *Bullarium*): 'Et quia ex certis impedimentis generale passagium occidentis christianorum non potest moderno tempore, quod dolenter referimus, prosperari, certam unionem quorundam fidelium cum apparatibus galearum et armigerarum gencium, presertim ad informationem et supplicationem dilectorum filiorum .. magistri et conventus hospitalis Sancti Johannis Jerosolimitani ac nobilium virorum .. marchionis Montisferrati, et .. ducis et communis civitatis Januensis, ad expellendum eosdem Turchos de dicto imperio providimus faciendam'.
93 AAV, Reg. Vat. 254, fol. 119ʳ (summaries in Urban V, *Lettres secrètes et curiales*, nos 14779–14991): 'Propter quod nos, cupientes de possibili et celeri in hac parte remedio providere, cum negotium generalis passagii—quod dolenter referimus—non procedat feliciter de presenti, et congruens necessitas exigat quod dictis partibus de fidelium subsidio congruo succurratur, per dictos magistrum et conventum ac quosdam magnates et potentes populos, certam unionem ad habendum quarundam gentium armigerarum et galearum numeros ad defensionem dictarum insule ac partium impugnationemque dictorum Turchorum providimus de proximo faciendam'.
94 Setton, *Papacy*, I, p. 261a and n. 10.
95 This is also the view in *Vitae Paparum Avenionensium*, I, p. 357.

as a more ambitious version of Humbert of Viennois's expedition to Smyrna in 1345. Urban may have wanted King John II and the crusade proper to aim for Jerusalem, but not Peter of Lusignan.

After Alexandria

What Pope Urban really thought about the Alexandria campaign he was careful not to put into writing. As we have seen, he would have preferred the expedition to have been put to use to bolster the position of the Byzantine Empire, which was now becoming ever more precarious as the Turks continued to make inroads into the Balkans. The earliest allusion to the events of October 1365 comes in a letter of January 1366 addressed to Emperor John V Palaiologos. In it the pope was concerned to encourage moves towards Church union, and he reminded the emperor of Western efforts against the Muslims led by King Louis of Hungary on land and King Peter of Cyprus, of whose 'marvellous triumph over the enemy' the emperor is aware, by sea.[96] It is easy to imagine that John V would have been far more impressed if either king had actually achieved something that had directly helped his own situation.

The following day the pope wrote to the doge of Venice complaining that the Venetians were already trying to patch up their relations with the Mamluk sultanate after King Peter's assault and that that entailed preventing shipping from being placed at the disposal of the king and others of the faithful who wished to join him.[97] Urban was now finding himself caught between Peter's ambitions and his need to recruit warriors in the West and bring them to Cyprus to supplement his forces, on the one hand, and the demands of the Italian mercantile republics, who were well placed to lobby for their interests, on the other. What the Italians wanted was to be allowed to make peace and so gain the release of their nationals who had been interned, secure the recovery of the merchandise that had be confiscated, and resume trading. Thus on 1 July the pope wrote to the king explaining that the doge of Venice had made representations and that he had granted him licences to trade with the Mamluks.[98] However, on 17 August, following representations from the king's envoys, all such licences held by the Venetians were cancelled until such time as the king of Cyprus and the Hospitallers could make a truce with the sultan.[99] Then on 6 October, prompted by the presence of Peter's envoys at the papal court, Urban wrote to King Charles V of France and a number of other western rulers mentioning the capture of Alexandria, 'which as we sorrowfully relate' was only held for a few days, and calling on them to allow warriors to make their way to the East to aid the king of Cyprus and the Hospitallers. At the same time he authorized the proclamation of indulgences

---

96 Urban V, *Acta*, no. 90. Cf. *Bullarium Cyprium III*, no. v-133.
97 *Annales Ecclesiastici*, XXVI, p. 127 (1366, no. 12) (not in *Bullarium*).
98 *Bullarium Cyprium III*, no. v-147.
99 *Diplomatarium Veneto-Levantinum*, II, nos 69–70; *Bullarium Cyprium III*, nos v-150–51.

for those aiding the war against the Mamluks.[100] He followed this with a letter to the doge of Venice, calling on him to stop obstructing the war effort and facilitate the transport of men and war materials to the combatants.[101] However, writing to King Peter on 23 October, he expressed fears for the security of Cyprus and, taking into consideration the interests of the Venetians and Genoese, urged the king to work for a truce with the Mamluks.[102]

Pope Urban was clearly in a dilemma. On the one hand, he had to be seen to be supporting the Holy War against the Infidel; on the other, political realities meant that he could see that the best way forward was for King Peter to extricate himself as best he might from an unwinnable war that ran counter to the interests of the powerful Italian trading republics. Norman Housley has written that in the 1360s papal policy with regard to crusading 'was in fact confused and unsure of itself'.[103] That may be so, but it looks as if by the end of 1366 Urban was coming to regard Peter's war as something of an embarrassment. It is noticeable that in the 1366 correspondence the war is consistently spoken of as being the joint effort of Cyprus and the Hospitallers, and so in a subtle way Urban was denying Peter the credit for his success in launching the crusade. It is also true that after October 1366 Urban is not known to have taken any positive steps to promote Peter's war, a war which in any case had lost all momentum by late 1367. At the end of 1367 Peter again set off for Europe, apparently in the vain hope of reviving support for his military endeavours. Instead, he found himself under pressure to make peace with the Mamluks—something he himself had already begun. He was now required to allow the Venetians and Genoese to negotiate on his behalf. In effect he had been sidelined—something that would have been galling—although in fact nothing had been achieved before his death in January 1369.

It is likely that, quite apart from the king's action in taking the crusade to Egypt and its inglorious denouement, Urban had good cause for viewing Peter with increasing exasperation. As we have seen, neither his extended tour of Europe nor the quarrel with the Genoese would have endeared him to the pope. Among the more minor irritants there was the case of Philip of Ibelin, lord of Arsur. Philip, the leading member of a distinguished branch of the Ibelin family, was Peter's third cousin.[104] In 1355 he had received a dispensation to marry Alice of Majorca, King Hugh's granddaughter.[105] With Peter's accession everything seems to have begun well, and, according to an admittedly garbled report by Leontios Makhairas, Peter was said to have appointed Philip seneschal of Cyprus. In 1360 he and his wife were among the beneficiaries of papal indults requested by Raymond Babin, and in 1361 he commanded a ship in Peter's fleet that captured Antalya.[106] But then, for reasons that are unknown,

---

100 *Annales Ecclesiastici*, XXVI, pp. 128–29 (1366, no. 15); *Bullarium Cyprium III*, nos v-154–56.
101 Mas Latrie, *Histoire*, II, pp. 288–89 (not in *Bullarium*; wrongly dated by the editor to 1367 instead of 1366).
102 *Annales Ecclesiastici*, XXVI, pp. 127–28 (1366, no. 13); *Bullarium Cyprium III*, no. v-158.
103 Norman Housley, *The Avignon Papacy and the Crusades, 1305–1378* (Oxford: Clarendon Press, 1986), p. 41.
104 They had a common ancestor in Guy of Ibelin, constable of Cyprus in the mid-thirteenth century.
105 *Bullarium Cyprium III*, no. u-74. Philip had previously been married to Hugh's niece, Eschiva of Dampierre: *Bullarium Cyprium III*, nos s-60, t-44.
106 Makhairas, *Recital*, I, pp. 88–89, § 100 and n. 1, pp. 102–05, § 119; *Bullarium Cyprium III*, nos u-239, 244.

he and the king quarrelled.[107] There are no echoes of this episode in the narrative sources, and we only know of it thanks to the series of letters Pope Urban wrote in an attempt to effect a reconciliation. Peter challenged the validity of the earlier marriage dispensation, although it is not clear whether the marriage itself was a source of the dispute or if Peter's challenge was simply a piece of vindictiveness on his part. Philip was sentenced to a seven-year exile, and he evidently made use of his absence from Cyprus to lobby the pope in Avignon. The earliest hint that anything was wrong dates to May 1364 when the pope reissued the 1355 dispensation.[108] Further letters followed in June 1365, September 1365 [Appendix B.19–20], and April 1366 in which the pope called on Peter to set aside his antagonism—letters that seem to imply that Urban was sympathetic to Philip's plight.[109] Philip was of course not present on the Alexandria campaign when the post of seneschal that may or may not have been his was conferred on the king's brother James.[110] However, by January 1367 he was back in Cyprus and henceforth played a full part in Peter's military activities before accompanying him on his second visit to the West in 1367–68.[111] Outwardly it might appear that the two men were indeed reconciled. But then in January 1369 Philip was one of Peter's murderers.

In December 1367 Urban addressed two letters to Peter, both of which can be taken as showing that his patience with the king was wearing thin. In the first he upbraided him for his adultery, a matter on which Leontios Makhairas provides considerable lurid detail.[112] In the second he ordered the king to put a stop to his preparations to fight a duel with Florimond of Lesparre, backing up his prohibition with an instruction to the archbishop of Nicosia to excommunicate the king if he persisted.[113] Florimond was a French nobleman who had been attracted to Cyprus in the aftermath of the Alexandria campaign, and it would seem that a dispute involving one of Peter's officers escalated to the stage where the king would lose face in the eyes of all the other western volunteers if he failed to react. The dispute, which attracted

---

[107] There is no evidence whatsoever to support Rudt de Collenberg's claim that Philip had sided with Peter's nephew, Hugh of Lusignan. Wipertus Hugo Rudt de Collenberg, 'Les Ibelin au XIIIe et XIVe siècles. Généalogie compilée principalement selon les registres du Vatican', Επετηρίς Κέντρου Επιστημονικών Ερευνών (Κύπρου), 9 (1977–79), 117–265 (p. 148) (repr. in Wipertus Hugo Rudt de Collenberg, Familles de l'Orient latin XIIe-XIVe siècles, Variorum Collected Studies, 176 (London: Variorum Reprints, 1983), no. IV).

[108] Bullarium Cyprium III, no. V-91. It might be noted that, according to the summaries in the Bullarium, the dispensations issued in 1355 and 1364 wrongly state that Alice was Hugh's niece when in fact he was her maternal grandfather.

[109] Bullarium Cyprium III, nos V-122, 129–30, 141–42, 144; cf. nos V-168–69.

[110] Makhairas, Recital, I, pp. 172–73 (§ 172).

[111] Mas Latrie, Histoire, II, p. 291; Makhairas, Recital, I, pp. 168–71, 174–75 (§ § 190, 194); Chronique d'Amadi, p. 416.

[112] Annales Ecclesiastici, XXVI, p. 147 (1367, no. 13); Bullarium Cyprium III, no. V-182. Cf. Makhairas, Recital, I, § § 234–38, 245, 248–49, 280. Makhairas tells of the king's two mistresses; the pope was evidently only aware of one.

[113] Urban V, Lettres secrètes et curiales, no. 2567; Bullarium Cyprium III, nos V-183–84.

considerable interest from the chroniclers, was resolved thanks to papal mediation when Peter arrived at the *curia* early in 1368.[114]

Peter's own aims and ambitions, which, as argued many years ago, may have centred on restoring Cyprus as the hub for sea-borne trade in the Eastern Mediterranean, did not coincide with those of the successive popes.[115] If Peter managed to outflank Pope Innocent VI's evident support for Hugh of Lusignan and his claims, it is also clear that Urban V's endorsement of Peter as a leader of the crusade against the Infidel had totally evaporated by the time of his second visit to the West. Other irritants served to lessen Peter's standing in papal eyes still further and, when in 1368 Peter returned to the papal court, Pope Urban pointedly declined to confer on him the Golden Rose—an accolade for the most noble man then at the *curia*—and gave it instead to Queen Joanna of Naples, who, as one biographer of the pope put it, was 'tanquam nobilior', and who, so it is said, had the distinction of being the first woman to receive that honour.[116]

---

114 *Bullarium Cyprium III*, no. v-187. See Edbury, *Kingdom of Cyprus*, pp. 170, 177.

115 Peter W. Edbury, 'The Crusading Policy of King Peter I of Cyprus, 1359–1369', in *The Eastern Mediterranean Lands in the Period of the Crusades*, ed. by Peter M. Holt (Warminster: Aris and Phillips, 1977), pp. 90–105 (repr. in Peter W. Edbury, *Kingdoms of the Crusaders: From Jerusalem to Cyprus*, Variorum Collected Studies, 653 (Aldershot: Ashgate, 1999), no. XII); see also Edbury, *Kingdom of Cyprus*, pp. 161–63, 171.

116 *Vitae Paparum Avenionensium*, I, pp. 366, 389; Franz X. Glassschröder, 'Notizen über Urbans V Romreise 1367–1370 aus dem Klosterarchiv von S. Victor zu Marseilles', *Römische Quartalschrift für christliche Altertumskunde und für Kirchengeschichte*, 3 (1889), 299–302 (p. 300).

Appendix A
Pope Innocent VI's Letters Concerning the Succession of King Peter I of Cyprus

A.1

Villeneuve-lès-Avignon, 24 May 1360: Innocent VI to King Peter I

Manuscript: AAV, Reg. Vat. 240, part 2, fols 68^v-70^v (V).
Summary: omitted in *BEFAR* and *Bullarium Cyprium III*.
Edition: *Annales Ecclesiastici*, XXVI, pp. 53b–55a (1360, nos 15–16) (omitting arenga).

Carissimo in Christo filio Petro regi Cipri illustri, salutem.
 In summi apostolatus specula ut vigilis pastoris exerceamus officium per Eum Cuius in terris vices – licet immeriti – gerimus constituti, ad ea [V 69r] que singulorum Christi fidelium pacem et quietem respiciant libenter intendimus et illis dampnis et scandalis que, autore discordiarum procurante, nequitia exoriri verisimiliter formidantur – quantum cum Deo possumus – paternis remediis obviamus. Ad quod circa personas excellentes tanto diligentius debemus attendere quanto ex illorum discordia plura possent incomoda et graviora tam animarum quam corporum pericula Christi fidelibus provenire.
 Sane nuper dilectus filius nobilis vir Hugo de Lisignano, primogenitus quondam Guidonis de Lisignano, primogeniti clare memorie Hugonis regis Cipri, patri<s> tui, nobis exposuit cum querela quod, licet in regno Cipri fuerit observatione continua hactenus consuetum quod primogenitus regis eiusdem regni qui est pro tempore eidem regi debeat in ipso regno succedere, ac preter hoc tempore tractatus matrimonii inter <dictum Guidonem et> carissimam in Christo filiam nostram Mariam, nunc imperatricem Constantinopolitanam et tunc dicti Guidonis consortem ac prefati Hugonis de Lisignano matrem, contrahendi pro parte et nomine dicti regis conventum fuerit solemniter et firmatum quod primogenitus ex ipsis Guidone et Maria nasciturus in regno succederet prelibato, et propterea dicti regni successio ad ipsum conquerentem, qui dicti sui patris noscitur representare personam et primogenitus dicti Guidonis existit, pertinere noscatur, tu tamen, secundo genitus regis eiusdem, regnum ipsum iniuste occupas, regie dignitatis titulum et regni ipsius administrationem et regimen indebite usurpando, asserens quod huiusmodi ius suum intendit prosequi per omnem viam quam sibi noverit melius valituram, quodque ad illius consecutionem magis optaret per apostolice interpositionis remedium quam per quemcumque modum alium devenire. [V 69v] Quare nobis humiliter supplicavit quod, cum ipse paratus sit de iustitia sua nostram suffi<ci>enter informare

conscientiam et plenarie facere nobis de illa constare, super hiis prout videremus expediens partes nostras interponere et paterne provisionis adhibere remedium ab ipso huiusmodi negotii principio dignaremur.

Nos igitur, qui paterne dilectionis affectum, quem ad prefatum tuum genitorem tanquam ad nostrum et Romane Ecclesie filium predilectum et inclitum in suo regno fidei catholice defensorem et Ecclesie militantis athletam habuimus, libenter in suos posteros derivamus, tuique ac prefati Hugonis et dicti regni pacem et quietem ac prosperitatis augmentum tanto cordialius affectamus quanto hiis regnum ipsum inter hostes Christiane fidei situm et eis quasi continuis oppugnatoribus quodam modo circumseptum magis noscitur indigere. Considerantes quod idem Hugo generosis et potentibus vallatum se invenit consanguineis et amicis qui ad prosequendum eius iura tam favorabiliter quam potenter sua eidem prestare valerent auxilia et favores; quodque si inter te et ipsum – quod absit – oriretur s<c>intilla discordie in dampnosum nimium crescere posset incendium quod neque pro tuo neque pro illius arbitrio sopiretur, cum facile sit initium dare discordiis, sed sepe ultra quam difficile illas fine laudabili terminare, ac proinde personarum strages, dampna rerum, multorum turbationes fidelium, guerrarum discrimina, ac plurimorum scandala, cedes, incendia, et hiis peiora, quibus arma commota versantur, et bellici furoris incitatus ardor insanit; quodque magis timendum est, animarum pericula, non solum eidem regno, sed multis Christi fidelium populis, ex huiusmodi proventura fore discordia verisimiliter formidantes, cum tantis malis [V 70r] et scandalis nostris obviare remediis prius quam eis detur aditus ex iniuncto nobis summi apostolatus officio cura vigili debeamus et inter cunctos Christi fideles, presertim principes et potentes et sanguinis unitate coniunctos, quorum sicut pluribus concordia proficit, ita eorum dissidia in dampna derivantur plurium, pacis et unitatis vinculum conservare, magnificentiam tuam rogamus et in paterne caritatis affectu attentius exhortamur quatinus, non quid velis, sed quid velle te deceat, quid dictet ratio, quid iustitia suadeat, quid honestas exposcat, tanquilla mente discutiens – si est ita ut idem Hugo proposuit coram nobis – benignus tui ipsius censor existas et veritati que singulorum sine forensi querela conscientiam indicat mansuetudinis tue colla submittas, et animo humili iustitie debitum privatis affectibus preferendo.

Neque tibi per nos, carissime fili, suaderi rem factu difficilem videatur. In hoc enim paterna consilia maiori debes devotione suscipere, si id agere conamur, ut per occupationem indebitam – si est ita – temporalis regni et vanam huius mundi gloriam, que est ad instar puncti, veram ac solidam et duraturam perpetuo eterni regni gloriam non amittas. Illud quoque circumspecte considerans quod, cum tu prefati Hugonis patruus existas, ac propterea ipse caro et sanguis tuus fore protinus censeatur, si in regno predicto sibi faveat iustitia, tu non immerito sui honoris et status ac dignitatis eiusdem fore particeps dicereris. Et si – quod absit – ius quod ei debetur dictum regnum violenter occupando surriperes, preter offensam Dei, qui iustus est Iudex et vult unicuique tribui quod est suum, non regis titulum meruisse apud homines, sed occupatoris nomen, quod utique esse [V 70v] debet a tui generositate sanguinis alienum, potius videreris, ac per hoc illam quam querere debes gloriam non haberes, necnon et regnum ipsum multis exponeres periculis et iacturis.

Sed de uno loquendo tacere forte de iure alterius videamur, cum Illius debeamus imitatores esse apud Quem non est acceptio personarum, et Qui singulis suam vult iustitiam ministrare, exhortatione simili te rogamus quatinus, ad obviandum malis huiusmodi que ex tua et dicti Hugonis discordia possent verisimiliter exoriri, de iure tuo per personas sollempnes nostram non differas conscientiam plenarie informare.

Nos enim, inter te et Hugonem eundem non personis sed iustitie potius deferentes, cum Sedis Apostolice consulta maturitas non personas accipere sed honorare debeat in singulis veritatem pro utriusque iure cognoscendo et declarando ac debita stabilitate firmando, necnon commodis et honoribus promovendis – quantum nobis suadere iustitia, in qua debitores sumus omnibus, videatur – libenter laborare proponimus, et usque ad premissorum terminationem, quam cum favore divine gratie speramus futuram esse prosperam et votivam, indesinentibus studiis interponere partes nostras.

Super premissis autem per dilectum filium Angelum de Luca, servientem armorum[a] et familiarem nostrum, latorem presentium, expectamus tue magnitudinis litteras responsales.

Datum apud Villamnovam, Avinionensis diocesis, VIIII Kalendas Junii, anno octavo.

a) armorum] amorum *a.c. s.l.* V

A.2

Villeneuve-lès-Avignon, 24 May 1360: Innocent VI to King Peter I

Manuscript: AAV, Reg. Vat. 240, part 2, fols 70^v-71^v (V).
Summary: omitted in *BEFAR* and *Bullarium Cyprium III*.

Carissimo in Christo filio Petro regi Cipri illustri, salutem *etc.*

Pro parte carissime in Christo filie nostre Marie imperatricis Constantino[V 71r]politane fuit propositum coram nobis quod olim, tempore tractatus matrimonii tunc contrahendi inter ipsam et quondam Guidonem de Lisignano, clare memorie Hugonis regis Cipri, patris tui, primogenitum et fratrem tuum, nonnulla promissiones, conventiones, et pacta de dotario eiusdem imperatricis intervenerunt et celebrata solenniter extiterunt. Cum autem post dicti Guidonis obitum eidem imperatrici non fuerit iuxta predicta conventiones et pacta de dicto suo dotario satisfactum, nobis pro parte ipsius fuit humiliter supplicatum ut super hoc partes nostras interponere et pro satisfactione per te sibi de dicto dotario[a] facienda, prout teneris et debes, apostolicis intervenire persuasionibus dignaremur.

Attendentes itaque quod huiusmodi dotaria precipuis initum presidiis confoventur, quodque excellentiam tuam decet ea que in dicto tractatu intervenerunt post dictorum patris et fratris obitum efficaciter adimplere et illam in te ipso observare iustitiam quam faceres per tuos fideles et subditos personis singulis observari, dictamque imperatricem propter sui claritatem generis a quo exorta esse dinoscitur paterne caritatis affectu et singulari benivolentia in Domino prosequentes, serenitatem tuam rogamus et hortamur attente quatinus, diligenter considerans quod dicta imperatrix generosis exorta parentibus – ut prefertur – prolem tue regie domui de tui fratris semine procreavit, quodque excellentie tue convenit eidem imperatrici non tantum de sua respondere iustitia, sed illam que cum fratre tuo olim viro suo una caro extitit prosequi fraterne caritatis affectu, pro honoris tui debito et observatione ipsius iustitie ac pro nostra et dicte sedis reverentis nostrorumque precaminum [V 71v] interventu, prefate imperatrici de dotario predicto tam pro tempore preterito quam futuro modo et terminis ad illum solvendum in dicti tractatus contractibus celebratis facias plenarie satisfieri, predicta executioni debite sic prompte ac efficaciter mandaturus quod, preter divine retributionis premia, exinde tibi apud nos et sedem predictam laudum proveniant incrementa.

Ceterum, super premissis dilectus filius Angelus de Luca, serviens armorum et familiaris noster, lator presentium, serenitatem tuam poterit vive vocis oraculo plenius informare.

Datum apud Villamnovam, Avinionensis diocesis, VIIII Kalendas Junii, anno octavo.
a) dotario] dotorio V

A.3

Villeneuve-lès-Avignon, 13 June 1360: Innocent VI to Empress Maria of Constantinople

Manuscript: AAV, Reg. Vat. 240, part 2, fol. 85^v (V).
Summary: omitted in *BEFAR* and *Bullarium Cyprium III*.

Carissime in Christo filie Marie imperatrici Constantinopolitane, salutem.

Nuper pro parte carissimi in Christo filii nostri Petri regi<s> Cipri illustris nonnulli circumspecti et providi viri ad nostram presentiam accedentes, quedam per eundem regem eis commissa nobis exponere curaverunt. Post quorum expositionem nos, cause dilecti filii nobilis viri Hugonis de Lisignano,[a] nati tui, de questione successionis regni Cipri non immemores, tui et dicti Hugonis consideratione, ad quos paterne caritatis affectum precipue gerimus, longa sermonis serie super causa ipsa multa contulimus cum eisdem, qui, prout ab eis accepimus, nullam a rege prefato commissionem receperant de predictis.

Hec itaque serenitati tue intimanda providimus ut super eis que in materia ipsa agenda forent Hugoni prefato valeas consultius et cautius providere. Nos enim super predictis, quantum suadere videbitur iustitia, tam tibi quam dicto Hugoni libenter curabimus – prout cum Deo poterimus – complacere. De quibus omnibus venerabilis frater noster Bertrandus archiepiscopus Neapolitanus, lator presentium, serenitatem eandem valebit vive vocis oraculo plenius informare.

Datum *ut supra* <apud Villamnovam, Avinionensis diocesis, Idus Junii anno octavo>.
a) lisignano] lisignario V

A.4

Villeneuve-lès-Avignon, 28 June 1360: Innocent VI to King Peter I

Manuscript: AAV, Reg. Vat. 240, part 2, fols 90^r-91^r (V).
Summary: omitted in *BEFAR* and *Bullarium Cyprium III*.
Edition: *Annales Ecclesiastici*, XXVI, p. 53a-b (1360, nos 13–14).

Carissimo in Christo filio Petro regi Cipri illustri, salutem *etc.*

Licet prius ad nostram pervenisset audientiam de morte clare memorie Hugonis regis Cipri, patris tui, tuarum tamen litterarum series [V 90v] et dilectorum filiorum nobilium virorum Raymundi Babini bucilerii regni Cipri et Johannis de Carmayno, ambassiatorum tuorum, latorum presentium, pia ac diligens expositio, mortem regis eiusdem nostri carissimi filii et tui patris affirmans, compassionis materiam nostris sensibus renovavit. Non enim non turbari de tam catholici principis et nobis et Sedi Apostolice ac Romane Ecclesie specialis filii morte patris precordia potuerunt, quoniam inter ceteros orbis terre reges et principes propter grandis sue devotionis et fidei quam ad nos et dictam gerebat Ecclesiam et alias sonorum clare sue fame preconium hunc non immerito singularem et carissimum habebamus, tibi quoque, carissime fili, affectione paterna compatimur, tuisque doloribus condolemus.

Verum, ex hoc materiam consolationis assumimus et te consolari ex eo similiter affectamus quod, licet patrem benivolum amiseris, rex ipse tamen, ut pote princeps Christianissimus, in dierum longitudine senuit et tandem, receptis – ut catholicum decet principem – salutaribus sacramentis, finivit, prout leti didicimus, in bonorum cursu operum dies suos eterne benedictionis gaudiis – sicut speramus – in Domino cum supernis principibus potiturus.

Ceterum, de eo quod tam per dictos ambassiatores quam litteras easdem te ad omnem reverentiam Sancte Romane Ecclesie atque nostram liberaliter obtulisti, serenitatem tuam dignis laudum preconiis attollimus, ipsamque exinde multipliciter in Domino commendantes, propositum tuum huiusmodi tuis cotidie magis inherere precordiis affectamus.

Paternis itaque exho<r>tationibus excellentiam regiam rogamus et hortamur attente quatinus, considerans diligenter quod in hoc regie dignitatis exordio qualis evasurus sis princeps imposterum [V 91r] maxime colligetur in timore Domini et reverentia dicte Ecclesie vite tue stabilitas fundamentum, ecclesias quoque et ecclesiasticas personas ob Dei honorem et sponse sue dicte Ecclesie reverentiam commendatas sub tui culminis potestate suscipias et tuis confoveas favoribus et defendas, ac per laudabiles tui patris bonorum operum semitas eius sequendo famosa vestigia gradiaris. Iustitiam, sine qua facile magna depereunt et cum qua minima prosperantur et crescunt, in regno tuo studeas personis singulis ministrare. Sicut namque scire te convenit, ubi sub equitate regnantium vivitur rerum publicarum status, tronus regius solidatur. Utique, carissime fili, per hec et alia virtutum opera preter divine retributionis premia felicium tibi successuum continue provenient incrementa. Nos quoque, sperantes te predictis aliisque salutaribus consiliis tanquam benedictionis filium cum operum efficacia diligenter intendere, libenter curabimus excellentie tue votis – quantum cum Deo poterimus – complacere.

Postremo hoc exhortationibus nostris addicimus quod, iustitiam quam faceres per tuos subditos personis singulis observari in te ipso observare procurens, in causa dilecti filii nobilis viri Hugonis de Lisignano, nepotis tui, benignus tui censor existas, prout requirere videatur ipsa iustitia, que in singulis semper est humanis negotiis preferenda, prout pro parte nostra prefatis tuis ambassiatoribus, cum quibus nostra constitutis presentia latius super materia ista contulimus, informationem recipere poterit eadem tua serenitas pleniorem.

Datum apud Villamnovam, Avinionensis diocesis, IIII Kalendas Julii, anno octavo.

Appendix B
Pope Urban V's Letters Concerning King Peter I of Cyprus and the Crusade

B.1

Avignon, 19 November 1362: Urban V to archbishop of Nicosia and suffragans

Manuscript: AAV, Reg. Vat. 245, fols 31^v-32^v (V).
Summaries: Urban V, *Lettres secrètes et curiales*, no. 113; *Bullarium Cyprium III*, no. v-7.

Venerabilibus fratribus.. archiepiscopo Nicosiensi eiusque suffraganeis, salutem *etc*.
   Dudum felicis recordationis Clemens VI primo et subsequenter Innocentius VI Romani pontifices, predecessores nostri, multorum relatibus intellecto quod gentes illorum infidelium paganorum qui 'Turchi' vulgariter nuncupantur, sitientes sanguinem populi Christiani et ad ipsius exterminum fideique catholice anhelantes, collectis sue viribus nationis, cum multitudine lignorum navalium armatorum in partibus Romanie et aliis locis fidelium convicinis eisdem Christianorum fines per mare fuerant aggressi et in Christianos ac loca et insulas fidelium partium earundem, ipsaque incendio miserabili supponentes, et – quod erat crudelius – fideles eosdem adducebant in predam ipsosque subiciebant horribili et perpetue servituti, vendendo eos ut animalia ipsosque ad abnegandum fidem catholicam compellendo, vias exquirentes et modos per quos statui dictorum Christianorum sic opresso possent utiliter providere, quia tam arduum tamque onerosum negotium magnis expensarum proflumis indigebat, decimam omnium ecclesiasticorum proventuum et reddituum in regno Cipri et nonnullis aliis mundi partibus usque ad certos annos ex tunc inantea computandos auctoritate apostolica de fratrum suorum consilio imposuerunt et impositionem huiusmodi necessitate imminente predicta ad diversos successive annos etiam extenderunt, prout in diversis dictorum predecessorum litteris exinde confectis, quarum ultime dicti Innocentii predecessoris ad vos – ut audivimus – minime pervenerunt, plenius continetur.
   Cum autem huiusmodi predictorum Turchorum persecutio et hostilitas peccatis exigentibus nondum cessaverint neque cessent, sed continue augeantur, et ad ipsorum repres[V 32r]sionem ac defensionem fidelium regni Cipri et aliarum partium predictarum multum expedire noscatur quod civitas nostra Smirnensis custodiatur attente per stipendarios providos et fideles et alias contra Turchos eosdem adhibeantur remedia oportuna, que fieri nequeunt absque magnarum oneribus expensarum, et pro dicte civitatis custodia facta retroacto tempore nonnulle pecunie

debeantur, que de huiusmodi decima debuerunt et debent persolvi, nos, plenis desiderantes affectibus in premissis oportunum remedium adhibere, cum camera nostra propter gravissimarum expensarum onera que pro defensione et recuperatione terrarum Romane Ecclesie in partibus Italie consistentium, quarum alias quorundam potentum tirannorum seva crudelitas occupat, alias vero guerrarum incursibus molestat crudeliter et affligit, necessario subire cogitur, sit nimium agravata, super hiis vestrum et nonnullorum aliorum prelatorum et ecclesiasticarum personarum subsidium – licet inviti – cogimur implorare.

Et propterea, dictorum predecessorum vestigia imitantes, decimam omnium proventuum et reddituum ecclesiasticorum in dicto regno consistentium seu proventurorum – proventibus magistri et fratrum Hospitalis Sancti Johannis Jerosolimitani, qui pro defensione dicte fidei et presertim contra Turchos eosdem exponunt iugiter se et sua, et aliis personis que in eisdem litteris dictorum predecessorum excipiebantur exceptis – convertendam in custodiam dicte civitatis Smirnensis et alias contra Turchos eosdem usque ad tres annos continuos, inchoandos in festo Omnium Sanctorum proxime preterito, de dictorum fratrum consilio duximus imponendum, cum aliis exceptionibus, modificationibus, condicionibus, modis, et formis, ac compulsionibus et sententiis in forma predictarum litterarum dictorum predecessorum vobis directarum super impositione et exactione decime [V 32v] antedicte per eosdem predecessores imposite, ut prefertur, contentis, quos in presentibus haberi volumus pro expressis. Quam quidem decimam per vos ceterasque personas ecclesiasticas exemptas et non exempta<s> regni prefati in dictis prefatorum predecessorum litteris non exceptas quolibet anno dicti trienni in terminis infrascriptis, videlicet medietatem pro primo anno in Kalendis Martii proxime secuturis et alteram medietatem in nativitatis Sancti Johannis Baptiste ex tunc immediate sequente, in aliis vero annis singulis medietatem dicte decime in nativitatis Domini et alteram medietatem in Sanctorum Petri et Pauli festivitatibus solvi volumus et mandamus.

Quocirca fraternitati vestre per apostolica committimus et mandamus quatinus vos et singuli vestrum huiusmodi decimam prout vos contingit pro[a] vestris seu vestrarum ecclesiarum proventibus integre persolvatis ac in vestris civitatibus et diocesibus per vos vel alium seu alios quos ad hoc ydoneos esse noveritis ad collectionem et exactionem ipsius decime in predictis terminis anno quolibet ipsius triennii persolvende procedatis, auctoritate nostra, iuxta tenorem dictarum litterarum eorundem predecessorum super exactione et collectione decime predicte imposite per predecessores eosdem alias vobis, ut premittitur, directarum, ac pecunias ipsius decime per vos colligendas dilecto filio Petro Demandi archidiacono Nimociensi, Apostolice Sedis nuncio, vel alii seu aliis ad hoc deputatis ab eo assignare curetis.

Porro, quia presentes littere nequirent forsan propter viarum discrimina vel alia impedimenta legitima vestrum singulis commode presentari, volumus quod per te, frater archiepiscope, vel tuum vicarium, dictarum litterarum transumptum, manu publica scriptum, tuoque communitum sigillo, vobis suffraganei<s> transmittatur, cui adhiberi per vos volumus velut originalibus plenam fidem.

Datum Avinione, XIII Kalendas Decembris, anno primo.

a) pro] per *V*

APPENDIX B: POPE URBAN V'S LETTERS   213

B.2

Avignon, 29 November 1362, Urban V to King Peter I

Manuscript: AAV, Reg. Vat. 245, fol. 16^v-17^r (V).
Summaries: Urban V, *Lettres secrètes et curiales*, no. 119; *Bullarium Cyprium III*, v-10.

Eidem <Carissimo in Christo filio Petro regi Cipri illustri, salutem *etc*.>
   Dilecti filii . . ambaxiatores carissime in Christo filie nostre Marie imperatricis Constantinopolitane ac dilecti filii nobilis viri Hugonis de Lisignano, eius filii, nepotis tui, nuper ad nostram presentiam accedentes, nobis pro parte ipsorum imperatricis ac Hugonis quasdam supplicationes, quarum tenorem presentibus interclusum regie serenitati transmittimus, presentarunt, super contentis in eis instantes multiplicibus rationibus ac precibus humilibus et devotis. Nos autem, quibus – licet indignis – cura universorum Christi fidelium a Rege regum et dominantium Domino est commissa, votis desiderantes ferventibus quod inter fideles eosdem, presertim personas sublimes ac consanguinitate et affinitate coniunctas ac positas iuxta$^{a)}$ fauces hostium Ihesu Christi, quarum discordia maiora posset pericula generare, pax vigeat, amor crescat, et unoquoque obtinente quod suum est cuiuslibet materia iurgii precidatur, magnitudinem tuam paterna caritate hortamur et rogamus attente quatinus, pro honore tui culminis ac nostrorum interventione peccaminum, et ut consan[V 17r]guineos et affines dictorum imperatricis et Hugonis tibi reddas benivolos, illa que debes imperatrici prefate regia liberalitate sibi facias exhiberi, cum dictoque Hugone, qui est os ex ossibus tuis et caro ex carne tua, et quem debes velut filium reputare, sic pie ac benivole agere studeas quod debito sanguinis satisfacias, tuisque honori et quieti consulas, nosque proinde regalem providentiam et pietatem munificam dignis laudibus attollere valeamus. Quod si forte tue magnitudini redderetur acceptum quod nos de hiis que continentur in dictis supplicationibus per viam amicabilem cognoscamus pro bono ac pace utriusque partis cum earum tractatoribus et procuratoribus, si eos informatos de suis iuribus et intentione ad nostram presentiam destinare voluerint, nos paratos offerimus paterne solicitudinis studio laborare.
   Et cum – prout audivimus – felicis recordationis Innocentius papa VI, predecessor noster, tibi super hiis provide scripserit iam sunt longa tempora retroacta, tuaque sublimitas sibi non miserit – quod vix credere possumus – responsivam, decet prudentiam regiam ut nobis responsum devotum ac rationabile transmittere non postponas.
   Datum Avinione, III Kalendas Decembris, anno primo.
a) iuxta] iuxtas V

B.3

Avignon, 31 March 1363: Urban V to King Peter I

Manuscripts: AAV, Reg. Aven. 153, fols 618^r-620^v (A); Reg. Vat. 252, fol. 31^v-33^v, no. 58 (V)

Summary: omitted in *BEFAR* and *Bullarium Cyprium III*; the paragraph beginning 'Verum, quia idem rex Francie' is quoted in *Annales Ecclesiastici*, XXVI, p. 84a (1363, no. 19).

Edition: previously unpublished, but see partial edition of parallel letter to King John II of France in *Annales Ecclesiastici*, XXVI, p. 82a-b (1363, no. 15) (omitting arenga) (summarized in Urban V, *Lettres secrètes et curiales*, no. 3210, from AAV, Reg. Aven. 153, fols 598^r-599^r; another copy is in Reg. Vat. 252, fols 16^r-17^r).

Carissimo in Christo filio Petro regi Cipri illustri, salutem etc.

Calamitosa miseria opprobriosaque servitus, quibus Terra Sancta, Salvatoris nostri Domini Ihesu Christi hereditas specialis, a nephandis Agarenis, Dei et sacre fidei hostibus, longis – proch dolor – temporibus inmaniter[a] fuit oppressa, prout indesinenter opprimitur, gravis doloris[b] aculeo viscera penetrant apostolice pietatis, ac remedia liberationis exposcunt ut, de impiis suorum inimicorum manibus liberata, eidem Salvatori, Qui in ea pro nostra redemptione dignatus est nasci et mortis subire supplicium, in sanctitate et iustitia[c] iugiter et libere a suis fidelibus serviatur.

[1] Sane dolenter referimus quod olim, peccatis exigentibus, dictam terram prefatorum Agarenorum gens perfida, eiusdem Salvatoris et sue orthodoxe fidei inimica, a longis retro temporibus, non absque dampnosa negligentia Christiani populi, occupavit, prout detinet occupatam, eam polluendo abhominandorum patratione scelerum[d] ac pro ancilla tenendo, que domina gentium debet esse. Accedit quoque ad huiusmodi infelicitatis augmentum illa erumpnosa calamitas quam ex oppressione Turchorum crudelium patitur Christianus populus Orientis et que tanto gravior redditur quanto iidem Turchi viciniores fidelibus existentes grassantur[e] sevius et facilius in eosdem, quantoque ipsorum rabies semper excrescens et cruorem Christianum aspirans effundere maius potest Christianitati generare periculum, nisi eorum qui in sua feritate confidunt presumptuosa temeritas per ipsorum fidelium potentiam reprimatur.

[2] Que omnia nuper,[f] divino spiritu – ut pie credimus – inspirante, tu prudenter considerans, et hiis maiora pericula toti Christianitati si oportunum in premissis non[g] apponatur remedium probabiliter proventura formidans, de statu dictorum infidelium, quem ex ipsorum mortalitatibus et discordiis debilitatum et prostrationi asseruisti dispositum, presertim ex captione civitatis Satalie ac nonnullorum castrorum et locorum que tu tuis providentia personalibusque laboribus et expensis de manibus infidelium predictorum eripuisti, ex quo infideles ipsos multus – ut asseritur – timor invasit, plenarie informatus, sicut princeps magnanimus et devotus, non vitatis pro Dei servicio itinerum longorum periculis, ad Sedem Apostolicam accessisti, nobis et fratribus nostris Sancte Romane Ecclesie cardinalibus et catholicis principibus et magnatibus aliisque fidelibus populis vias et modos vive tue vocis oraculo prudenter ostendens per quos istis temporibus potest faciliter eorundem Agarenorum et Turchorum[h] elidi potentia et fieri recuperatio dicte terre.

[3] Hec siquidem carissimus in Christo filius noster Johannes rex Francie illustris gaudenter accipiens, desiderium transfretandi, quod diutius – ut asseruit – gessit in corde, nuper produxit in lucem. Nam ipse et tua devota magnificentia aliique multi nobiles cum eorum potentia pro recuperatione Terre Sancte predicte promiserunt

personaliter transfretare ac receperunt de nostris manibus venerabile signum Crucis. Nosque, premissa cum ingenti considerantes letitia, cupientesque magnitudinem tuam et prefatum regem Francie et alios fervore huiusmodi devotionis accensos in tanto Salvatoris nostri predicti promovendo negotio spiritualibus et temporalibus auxiliis confovere, matura super hiis deliberatione prehabita, de dictorum fratrum consilio indiximus ad dictam Terram Sanctam et alias partes infidelium Orientis passagium generale, omnibus ad hec transfretaturis indulgentiam et privilegia transfretantibus in dicte terre subsidium consueta concedi auctoritate apostolica concedentes, ac dictum regem Francie ipsius passagii et totius exercitus [A 618v] Christiani qui transfretabit in illo rectorem constituimus et capitaneum generalem. Ac nichilominus per alias nostras inde confectas litteras verbum Crucis cum certis gratiis et indulgentiis in nonnullis partibus mandavimus predicari, ac eidem regi Francie et ceteris Crucesignatis et Crucesignandis Kalendas Martii anni nativitatis Domini millesimi trecentesimi sexagesimi quinti proxime secuturi pro termino ad transfretandum in dicto passagio duximus assignandas. Ipseque rex Francie, capitaneatum huiusmodi reverenter [V 32r] acceptans, personaliter in eisdem nostris manibus ad sancta Dei evangelia iuravit quod in eisdem Kalendis vel ante dicti passagii iter arripiet, illudque deinde, iusto et legitimo impedimento cessante, sub certis tamen condicionibus, modis, et formis in aliis nostris super hec confectis litteris seriosius annotatis, realiter et personaliter prosequetur.

[4] Verum, quia idem rex Francie – prout nobis asseruit – commode nequit nisi circa prefatum terminum versus dictas terras et partes arripere iter suum, et tu, qui es ad presens apud sedem constitutus eandem, ad succurrendum eisdem fidelibus et conatus eorundem infidelium reprimendum velut athleta Christi ac precursor intrepidus proponis[i)] – prout nobis asseruisti – satis ante dictum terminum cum auxiliis citramarinorum fidelium transfretare, nos tibi certa subsidia fidelium in Gradensi, Salzeburgensi, Strigoniensi, Collocensi, Jadrensi, Spalatensi, Ragusina,[j)] Antibarensi, Duracensi, Patracensi, Corinthiensi, Atheniensi, Thebanensi, Constantinopolitana,[k)] Neopatrensi, Pariensi, Collocensi dicta Rodo, Cretensi, Corfiensi, et Nicosiensi, ac[l)] Panormitana, Messanensi, et Montisregalis civitatibus, diocesibus, et provinciis, ac etiam in Aquilegensi, Concordiensi, Tergestina, Justinopolitana, Polensi, Parentina, Emonensi, ac Petenensi, et Caffensi[m)] civitatibus et diocesibus, ceterisque partibus ultramarinis duximus concedenda, prout in aliis nostris inde confectis litteris plenius continetur.

Et quia pro supportanda ingentium sarcina expensarum quas[n)] tanti negotii assumptio et prosecutio de necessitate requirunt ulteriori subsidio nosceris[o)] indigere, nos, considerantes summum tue devotionis affectum quem ad prosecutionem et consumationem huiusmodi per te assumpti passagii – Deo annuente – felicem habere dinosceris, et propterea dignum, quinymmo dignissimum, reputantes ut eadem tua devotio per eiusdem sedis consultam providentiam in huiusmodi sancto negotio maioribus presidiis adiuvetur, tuis supplicationibus inclinati, omnia legata ac donata inter vivos seu in ultima voluntate, ac penas, condempnationes, penitentias impositas seu iniunctas, et quecumque alia ex voto, stipulatione, pacto, vel promissione passagio generali aut in dicte Terre Sancte[p)] subsidium seu succursum in dictis civitatibus, diocesibus, et provinciis ac partibus facta seu debita – hiis tamen que per sedem eandem pro aliis certis necessitatibus concessa vel per eam pro variis urgentibus negotiis que sibi periculose nimium preteritis occurrerint^{q)} temporibus expensa fuerint,^{r)} super quibus quidem concessis, ut premittitur, et expensis stari ordinamus^{s)} et volumus simplici verbo nostro, et illis etiam de quibus per legantes vel donantes extitit ordinatum quod certis personis assignari deberent dumtaxat exceptis – necnon omnia et singula per sex annos a datis presentium numerandos in dictis civitatibus, diocesibus,^{t)} provinciis, ac partibus pro dicto passagio et Terre Sancte subsidio seu succursu leganda, donanda, penas et penitentias imponendas seu iniungendas, et alia ex voto, stipulatione, pacto, vel promissione pro^{u)} [A 619r] eiusdem passagii succursu seu subsidio disponenda in subsidium expensarum que tue serenitati ex tanti^{v)} prosecutione negotii dinoscuntur incumbere, auctoritate presentium tibi concedimus exigenda, colligenda, et levanda per diocesanos locorum, civitatum, diocesium, provinciarum, et partium earundem, et alios quos iidem diocesani ad hoc duxerint assumendos sub modis et formis, modificationibus et declarationibus infrascriptis, et personis quas tu ad receptionem huiusmodi legatorum et subsidiorum deputabis integraliter assignanda et in istius sancti passagii seu Terre Sancte succursum seu subsidium expendenda.

Ordinamus quoque omnes habentes aut detinentes species, quantitates, vel corpora seu legata que per dictam sedem concessa vel expressa aut per donantes certis personis assignari mandata non forent, ut prefertur, ad ea tradenda diocesanis seu deputandis prefatis per censuram ecclesiasticam compellantur ab ipsis. Et nichilominus ut premissa legata, donata, et alia supradicta tam pro preterito tempore quam in futurum per sex annos predictos leganda, donanda, et alias pro eiusdem passagio et subsidio seu succursu, ut premittitur, disponenda in publicam veniant [V 32v] notionem, mandamus et volumus quod diocesani predicti, singuli videlicet eorum in singulis suis civitatibus et diocesibus eorundem, tabelliones et notarios publicos civitatum et diocesium eorundem per iuramentum per ipsos diocesanos ab eorundem tabellionum et notariorum singulis exigendum, vel per excommunicationis sententiam, prout magis expedire viderint, compellere procurent ut ipsi de clausulis testamentorum vel prothocollorum ab ipsis vel ab aliis scriptorum, si aliquorum aliorum testamenta vel prothocolla forent penes eos, ad ipsius Terre Sancte negotium dumtaxat pertinentibus, de testamentis seu prothocollis eisdem canonice extractis in forma publica copiam faciant diocesanis eisdem, per quos etiam hoc idem mandamus et volumus fieri circa testatorum heredes. Et nichilominus ordinamus quod per diocesanos predictos in suis civitatibus et diocesibus fiat monitio generalis ut quicumque sciant aliqua donata vel relicta seu quovis modo alio debita in succursum seu subsidium dicte Terre Sancte vel passagii generalis, quo ad illa que superius sunt expressa, infra certum competentem terminum super hoc statuendum, ipsis diocesanis vel deputandis ab eis illa debeant revelare, quodque, lapso eodem termino, possint ipsi diocesani contra contumaces procedere ad promulgandas excommunicationis, suspensionis, et interdicti sententias, si et prout viderint^{w)} expedire.

Insuper, si diocesanis ipsis vel eorum alicui casus aliquis super hiis forsitan occurrerit qui sub verbis predictis, videlicet legata, donata, tam inter vivos quam in ultima voluntate, penas, condempnationes, penitentias impositas^{x)} seu iniunctas, debita ex voto, stipulatione, pacto, vel promissione non viderentur inclusi, volumus quod ipsi diocesani casus eosdem prefate sedi intimare debeant ut circa illos per eam ordinari valeat quod ad honorem Dei et utilitatem dicti passagii expediens videatur.

Rursus, ut hoc sanctum negotium eo felicius et efficacius finem sorciatur optatum quo maiorum subsidiorum foret fulcimento munitum, tuis devotis precibus annuentes, universa legata indistincta seu incerta, a quibuscumque personis in dictis civitatibus et diocesibus ac provinciis et partibus facta et que fient in eis[y] imposterum per sex annos predictos, quorum incertitudo seu indistinctio [A 619v] non esset talis quod vitiaret ipsa legata, tibi in subsidium concedimus premissorum, per diocesanos predictos seu succollectores deputandos ab eis, ut de aliis premittitur, colligenda, eisdemque personis per te ad hec deputandis assignanda, consumenda et distribuenda sub modis et formis ac declarationibus superius circa legata, donata, et alia supradicta et inferius etiam annotata, et in ipsius sancti passagii et Terre Sancte utilitatem sicut premissa alia integraliter convertenda.

Ad omnem siquidem circa hoc dubitationis materiam amputandam, quantum ad presentem spectat articulum, illa non reputamus incerta seu indistincta legata que possent ex post facto reduci ad certitudinem ex dispositione ordinantis vel legis aut que, licet incerta forent ex legatariorum personis, non tamen ex causa pro qua vel ob quam relicta forent, ut pote <si> pro maritandis puellis, celebrandisve missis, construendis capellis, seu constituendis capellaniis aut aliis similibus aliqua forent relicta. Et ideo legata huiusmodi et similia sub concessione non venirent predicta. Illa vero legata quo ad hec indistincta dicimus et incerta que haberent incertitudinem tam ex legatariorum personis quam ex causa pro qua forent facta, utpote cum testator legat sine determinatione aliqua pro anima sua centum, aut cum simpliciter hoc vel illud in pios usus precipit erogari. Licet enim per ordinarium forsitan iuris auctoritate vel per executorem ultime voluntatis defuncti de incertis seu indistinctis legatis huiusmodi valeat ordinari, in eis tamen et similibus concessionem locum habere volumus supradictam,[z] nisi forsan per eos ad quos hoc pertineret, antequam ad eorum notitiam concessio iam dicta perveniret aut pervenire posset, legata huiusmodi existerent distributa.

Et ne ipsi calumpniose possent concessionis eiusdem ignorantiam allegare, ordinamus et etiam declaramus quod notitiam huiusmodi concessionis ad eos censeatur potuisse venire post mensem computandum ab ipsius concessionis publicatione, que per diocesanos vel de [V 33r] mandato eorum in civitatibus aut per ecclesiarum parrochialium rectores de suorum diocesanorum, archidiaconorum, archipresbyterorum, seu decanorum mandato in ecclesiis suis parrochialibus civitatum et diocesium eorumdem facta publice foret, diebus dominicis et festivis, nisi forsan aliqua justa causa eorum ignorantiam excusaret. Et si etiam de legatis huiusmodi ad certam personam pars aliqua provenire deberet ex ordinatione disponentis vel legis, volumus quod pars ipsa in huiusmodi nostra concessione non veniat, sed ipsi persone assignari vel penes eam debetur integraliter remanere. Declaramus quoque sub concessione huiusmodi non venire legata illa incerta que reperirentur per illum ad quem pertinerent[aa] certis concessa personis vel ad usum alium deputata.

[5] Postremo, volumus quod de singulis que de premissis tue celsitudini seu aliis per te ad hoc deputatis fuerint assignata et de expensis inde factis legato Apostolice Sedis in dictis ultramarinis partibus deputato, vel alii seu aliis quos dicta sedes duxerit deputandos, tenearis reddi facere plenarie rationem.

[6] Si vero – quod absit – contingeret te infra dictos[ab)] sex annos de medio submoveri aut impedimento perpetuo impediri, cum legata, donata, et alia subsidia supradicta per nos tue sublimitati concessa in favorem dicti passagii, quod alius princeps loco tui – prestante Domino – prosequetur, tibi duxerimus concedenda, volu[A 620r]mus et mandamus quod iidem prelati ad exactionem, levationem, et receptionem legatorum et subsidiorum huiusmodi nichilominus procedant eaque fideliter conservent seu conservari faciant, donec super ipsis aliud a nobis receperint in mandatis. Et omnia que de subsidiis supradictis penes te, si vita fuerit tibi comes et – ut prefertur – impeditus extiteris, et in casu dicti tui obitus penes heredes et successores seu gentes tuos restarent, et in eiusdem passagii preparationibus aut pro eo de mandato tuo non essent expensa, necnon galee et alia quecumque facta, empta, vel predicto passagio seu pro eo de dictis subsidiis in civitatibus, diocesibus, provinciis, et partibus prelibatis quomodolibet acquisita, eidem legato vel alii seu personis de quibus sedes duxerit ordinandum per te, si, ut premittitur, vixeris et fueris impeditus, et per heredes tuos in casum dicti tui obitus, integraliter sine difficultate qualibet assignentur secundum dispositionem dicte sedis pro dicto passagio expendenda.

[7] Porro, circa illa que de tua excellentia de predictorum subsidiorum pecunia forsitan assignabit seu faciet assignari nobilibus seu quibuslibet aliis tecum transfretare volentibus, forsan ad procuranda seu emenda aliqua sibi pro passagio necessaria vel etiam oportuna, vel alias pro supportandis expensis quas[ac)] essent facturi in prosecutione passagii sepefati, pro serenitate tue conscientie ac dicti securitate negotii habeas inter alia precavere quod illi quibus facies illa tradi proprio firmare debeant iuramento quod ea que sic sibi tradentur fideliter conservabunt et illa quando commodius et utilius poterunt[ad)] in utilitatem dicti passagii seu preparatoriorum ipsius et non in alios usus convertent; et quod nichilominus in casum tui obitus seu perpetui impedimenti predicti iidem nobiles sue alii quibus de tuo mandato pecunie dictorum subsidiorum essent forsitan assignate illas seu res emptas ex eis dicto legato vel aliis personis a sede prefata, ut premittitur, deputandis debeant fideliter assignare, nisi forsan ipsi qui pecunias huiusmodi recepissent vellent[ae)] per se vel alium seu alios prosequi passagium supradictum; et quod de huiusmodi eorum prosecutione ipsis legato seu personis aliis, ut premittitur, deputandis fidem facere teneantur; et quod ad hec sub firmis et validis obligationibus se,[af)] heredes suos, et bona sua astringant; ita quod dicto passagio non possit malitiose aliquid subtrahi de predictis, et nichilominus possint tales ad premissa compelli per censuram ecclesiasticam, si visum fuerit expedire; quod si excellentia tua tales obligari non provident, ut prefertur, tu et tui heredes ac successores ad restitutionem premissam dictis faciendam prelatis remaneatis efficaciter obligati, semper tamen ratione habita rationabilium expensarum, si que forte ab illis quibus premissa fuerint tradita facte fuerint, sine fraude in emendis seu procurandis ex dicta pecunia vel etiam conservandis hiis que pro dicto passagio esse poterant oportuna, prout fuerit rationis, et habita etiam ratione aliorum que de iure [V 33v] in hec fuerint attendenda que dicti legati seu aliorum ad hoc per dictam sedem deputandorum duximus arbitrio committenda. Eo vero casu quo tua circumspectio dictam recipientes pecuniam obligati providerit, ut prefertur, non tenearis ad restitutionem huiusmodi, sed dumtaxat ad instrumenta ac litteras confecta super hiis dictis assignanda legato [A 620v] seu personis a prefata

sede, ut premittitur, deputandis et ad ipsos super huiusmodi obligationum executione iuvandos[ag] efficaciter per ministros tue iustitie temporalis, si talia recipientes eidem magnitudini tue subsint.

[8] Insuper, de illis que per receptores predictos vel alios de mandato tuo mercatoribus vel aliis quibuscumque tradentur ad faciendas provisiones quaslibet dicto passagio necessarias seu etiam oportunas, ordinamus quod tenearis in casu huiusmodi ad illa seu acquisita ex eis restituendum seu restitui faciendum legato[ah] seu personis deputatis predictis, habita tamen ut in alio casu premittitur ratione rationabilium expensarum et aliorum que in ratione reddenda fuerint attendenda, et ad hoc inquantum per rationem reddendam legato et personis eisdem apparuerit te teneri.

Nulli ergo *etc.* nostre indicionis, concessionis, constitutionis, ordinationis,[ai] reputationis, dationis, declarationis, et voluntatis infringere *etc.*

Datum Avinione, II Kalendas Aprilis, anno primo.

a) inmaniter] inhumaniter V b) doloris] doloras A c) iustitia] iustitie A d) patratione scelerum] patrocinio celerum A; patrocinio scelarum V e) grassantur] crissantur AV f) nuper] *om.* V g) non] *om.* V h) et turchorum] *om.* V i) proponis] proponit AV j) ragusina] ragusinensi V k) thebanensi constantinopolitana] *om.* V l) nicosiensi ac] nycosiensi V m) caffensi] in *add.* V n) quas] quos *a.c.* A, V o) nosceris] nostris A*V p) sancte] *om.* A q) occurrerint] occurrerunt A r) fuerint] fuerunt A s) ordinamus] ordinavimus V t) diocesibus] et *add.* V u) pro] *iter.* A (*after folio change*); *om.* V v) ex tanti] *om.* V w) viderint] viderit A x) seu] se A y) eis] et *add.* A z) supradictam] supradictum V aa) pertinerent] pertineret V ab) dictos] dicto A ac) quas] quos V ad) poterunt] potuerint V ae) vellent] vellem A af) se] seu V ag) iuvandos] et *add.* V ah) legato] legatos *a.c.* A, V ai) ordinationis] concessionis *add.* AV

B.4

Avignon, 25 May 1363, Urban V to King Peter I

Manuscript: AAV, Reg. Vat. 245, fols 170^v-173^r (V).
Summaries: some lines quoted in *Annales Ecclesiastici*, XXVI, p. 84b (1363, no. 19); Urban V, *Lettres secrètes et curiales*, no. 488; *Bullarium Cyprium III*, no. v-40.

Carissimo in Christo filio Petro regi Cipri illustri, salutem *etc.*

Misericors Dominus, et si quandoque in suum populum, quem colonum terre sue nativitatis elegit et quem tanto decet accuratius abstinere a nectitis quanto sanctior et venerabilior locus ipsius habitationis existit, ob eius forsan culpas permiserit a possessione proprie hereditatis excludi, imperpetuum tamen nequaquam irascitur nec est eius comminatio in eternum, sed, cum iratus fuerit, misericordie memorans miserationis gratiam elargitur, mentesque fidelium gratia sua preveniens et lumine [V 171r] superne claritatis illustrans corda preparat, temporaque aptitudine competentiori disponit, quibus ipsius admisse dudum terre recuperatio possit cum ipsius auxilio facilius obtineri. Hec Dominum suo fecisse Israelitico populo, in cuius locum plebs Christiana succedit, sacrarum scripturarum testimonia manifestant. Hec eadem plebs etiam suis temporibus est experta ut discant fideles ultionum non offendere

Dominum et post offensas et penas ad Eum Qui est prestabilis super omnem malitiam redire in humilitatis spiritu non formident, repetituri hereditatem Dominicam et cum Ipsius auxilio possessuri.

[1] Sane dolenter referimus quod olim, peccatis exigentibus, terram illam, quam Salvator noster Dei Filius Dominus Ihesus Christus sue presentia conversationis illuminans, in ipsa pro nostra redemptione mortem nostram moriendo destruxit et vitam sue resurrectionis gloria reparavit, Agarenorum gens perfida, eiusdem Salvatoris et sue orthodoxe fidei inimica, a longis retro temporibus, non absque dampnosa negligentia Christiani populi, occupavit, prout detinet occupatam, eam polluendo abhominandorum patratione scelerum ac pro ancilla tenendo, que domina gentium solet esse. Accedit quoque ad huiusmodi infelicitatis augmentum illa erumpnosa calamitas quam ex oppressione Turchorum crudelium patitur Christianus populus Orientis, que tanto gravior redditur quanto iidem Turchi viciniores fidelibus existentes grassantur[a)] sevius et facilius in eosdem, quantoque ipsorum rabies semper excrescens et ad cruorem Christianum aspirans effundere maius potest Christianitati generare periculum, nisi eorum qui in sua feritate confidunt presumptuosa temeritas per ipsorum fidelium potentiam reprimatur.

[2] Que nuper, divino spiritu inspirante, tu, fili carissime, [V 171v] cuius regnum est in ipsorum infidelium faucibus constitutum, prudenter considerans, et maiora pericula toti Christianitati si oportunum in hiis non aponatur remedium probabiliter proventura formidans, de statu dictorum infidelium, quem ex ipsorum mortalitatibus et discordiis debilitatum et prostrationi dispositum asseris, presertim ex captione civitatis Satalie ac nonnullorum castrorum et locorum que, licet admodum fortia, tua magnificentia tuis providentia personalibusque laboribus et expensis de manibus infidelium predictorum eripuit, ex quo infideles ipsos multus – ut asseritur – timor invasit, plenarie informatus, sicut princeps magnanimus et devotus, non vitatis pro Dei servicio itinerum longorum periculis, ad partes occidentales et demum ad Sedem Apostolicam accessisti, nobis ac fratribus nostris sancte Romane Ecclesie cardinalibus et catholicis principibus ac magnatibus aliisque fidelibus populis vias et modos prudenter ostendens per quos istis temporibus potest faciliter eorum Agarenorum et Turchorum elidi potentia et fieri recuperatio terre predicte.

[3] Hec siquidem carissimus in Christo filius noster Johannes rex Francie illustris gratanter accipiens, desiderium transfretandi, quod diutius – ut asseruit – gessit in corde, perduxit in lucem. Nam ipse ac tu aliique multi nobiles cum tua et eorum potentia pro recuperatione dicte terre promisistis personaliter transfretare ac recepistis de nostris manibus venerabile signum Crucis, quod multi magnates et nobiles ad sedem venientes eandem cum devotionis plenitudine cotidie postulant et recipiunt reverenter. Nosque, premissa cum ingenti letitia intuentes, et cupientes tantum Salvatoris nostri predicti negotium spiritualibus et temporalibus auxiliis [V 172r] confovere, matura super hiis deliberatione prehabita, ad honorem omnipotentis Dei, exaltationem et dilatationem catholice fidei, cunctorum fidelium animarum profectum, liberationem Terre Sancte predicte, ac exterminium hostium predictorum, de dictorum fratrum consilio indiximus ad dictam Terram Sanctam et alias partes infidelium Orientis passagium generale inchoandum Kalendis Martii anni nativitatis Domini millesimi trecentesimi sexagesimi quinti proxime secuturi. Considerantesque

devotionem eximiam ac compassionis affectum dicti regis Francie quem habet ad statum miserabilem dicte terre, et ipsius regis generis claritatem ac magnanimitatem et potentiam, provida super hiis cum eisdem fratribus nostris deliberatione prehabita, dictum regem Francie prefati passagii et omnium qui transfretare voluerint capitaneum constituimus generalem.

[9] Et ut cuncti fideles tanto libentius et efficacius premissa prosequi studeant quanto ex suis laboribus potiorem gratiam se noverint percepturos, nos, de omnipotentis Dei misericordia et beatorum Petri et Pauli apostolorum eius auctoritate confisi, ac illa quam nobis Deus – licet immeritis – ligandi atque solvendi contulit potestate, omnibus Christi fidelibus qui dicto rege Francie huiusmodi passagium personaliter prosequente ad recuperationem dicte terre et impugnationem hostium ac defensionem fidelium predictorum transfretaverint, et laborem huiusmodi in personis propriis et expensis subierint, plenam suorum peccaminum de quibus forent veraciter corde contriti et ore confessi veniam induximus eis in retributionem iustorum salutis eterne policentes augmentum, ipsisque alia privilegia concessimus consueta concedi transfretantibus in subsidium [V 172v] dicte terre, prout in nostris litteris exinde confectis plenius continetur.

[4] Verum, quia idem rex Francie – prout nobis asseruit – commode nequit nisi circa prefatum terminum versus dictas terram et partes arripere iter suum, et tu, qui es ad presens apud Sedem Apostolicam constitutus, ad succurrendum eisdem fidelibus et conatus eorundem infidelium reprimendum velut athleta Christi et precursor intrepidus proponis – ut nobis asseruisti – satis ante dictum terminum transfretare, tibi concedimus quod ducentos nobiles equites armatos de dicto regno Francie, ac duo milia equitum et sex milia peditum cum eorum continuis familiaribus commensalibus de quibuscumque mundi partibus, excepto regno Francie, et quascumque gentes armigeras de quibuscumque societatibus ubilibet constitutas, necnon universos et singulos de Aquilegensi, Gradensi, et Salzburgensi provinciis, ac Ungarie et Cipri regnis, et partibus Sclavonie, ac insula Sicilie et insulis ei adiacentibus, necnon Romanie et ceteris aliis partibus ultramarinis ducere seu mittere et tenere valeas etiam ante terminum memoratum, volentes et concedentes quod omnes transfretantes huiusmodi plenam suorum peccaminum de quibus, ut prefertur, fuerint veraciter corde contricti ac ore confessi veniam consequantur acsi post dictum terminum cum eodem rege Francie transfretarent, et quod gaudere valeant omnibus gratiis et privilegiis per nos generaliter concessis omnibus qui post dictum terminum transfretabunt.

[10] Ceterum, singulis locorum ordinariis presentium tenore committimus quod eisdem ducentis nobilibus ac duobus milibus equitis et sex milibus peditibus ac aliis personis dictorum Ungarie et Cipri regnorum ac provinciarum et partium qui ante [V 173r] dictum terminum voluerint transfretare venerabile signum Crucis devote volentibus, quos ad id utiles fore crediderint, concedant ac imponant humeris eorundem.

Datum Avinione, VIII Kalendas Junii, anno primo.

a) grassantur] crassantur V

B.5

Avignon, 25 May 1363, Urban V to King Peter I

Manuscript: AAV, Reg. Vat. 245, fols 173^r-174^r (V).
Summaries: Urban V, *Lettres secrètes et curiales*, no. 489; *Bullarium Cyprium III*, no. v-41.

Eidem <Carissimo in Christo filio Petro regi Cipri illustri, salutem *etc.*>
   [3] Ad recuperationem Terre Sancte ac defensionem fidelium et repressionem hostium partium Orientis plenis desideriis anhelantes, nuper generale passagium inchoandum Kalendis Martii anni nativitatis Dominice millesimi trecentesimi sexagesimi quinti ad dictam Terram Sanctam et alias partes eorundem hostium de fratrum nostrorum consilio duximus indicendum ac, provida in hac parte deliberatione prehabita, carissimum in Christo filium nostrum Johannem regem Francie illustrem dicti passagii et omnium qui transfretare voluerint capitaneum constituimus generalem.
   [9] Et ut cuncti fideles tanto libentius et efficacius premissa prosequi studeant quanto ex suis laboribus potiorem gratiam se noverint percepturos, nos, de omnipotentis Dei misericordia et beatorum Petri et Pauli apostolorum eius auctoritate confisi, ac illa quam nobis Deus – licet immeritis – ligandi atque solvendi contulit potestate, omnibus Christi fidelibus qui dicto rege Francie huiusmodi passagium personaliter prosequente ad recuperationem dicte terre et impugnationem dictorum hostium ac defensionem fidelium predictorum transfretaverint et laborem huiusmodi in personis propriis et expensis subierint plenam suorum peccaminum de quibus forent veraciter corde contriti et ore confessi veniam indulximus eis in retributionem iustorum salutis eterne pollicentes augmentum, ipsisque alia privilegia concessimus consueta concedi transfretantibus in [V 173v] subsidium dicte terre, prout in nostris litteris exinde confectis plenius continetur.
   [4] Verum, quia idem rex Francie – prout nobis asseruit – commode nequit nisi circa prefatum terminum versus dictas terram et partes arripere iter suum, et tu, qui es ad presens apud Sedem Apostolicam constitutus, ad succurrendum eisdem fidelibus et conatus eorundem infidelium reprimendum velut athleta Christi et precursor intrepidus proponis – ut nobis asseruisti – satis ante dictum terminum transfretare, tibi concedimus quod ducentos nobiles equites armatos de dicto regno Francie, ac duo milia equitum et sex milia peditum cum eorum continuis familiaribus commensalibus de quibuscumque mundi partibus, excepto regno Francie, et quascumque gentes armigeras de quibuscumque societatibus ubilibet constitutis, necnon universos et singulos de Aquilegensi, Gradensi, et Salzburgensi provinciis, ac Ungarie et Cipri regnis, et partibus Sclavonie, ac insula Sicilie et insulis eis adiacentibus, necnon Romanie et ceteris aliis partibus ultramarinis ducere seu mittere et tenere valeas etiam ante terminum memoratum, volentes ac concedentes quod omnes transfretantes huiusmodi plenam suorum peccaminum de quibus, ut prefertur, fuerint veraciter corde contricti ac ore confessi veniam consequantur asci post dictum terminum cum eodem rege Francie transfretarent, et quod gaudere valeant omnibus gratiis et privilegiis per nos generaliter concessis omnibus qui post dictum terminum tranfretabunt.

[10] Ceterum, singulis locorum ordinariis presentium tenore committimus quod eisdem ducentis nobilibus ac duobus milibus equitibus et sex milibus peditibus ac aliis personis [V 174r] dictorum Ungarie et Cipri regnorum ac provinciarum et partium qui ante dictum terminum voluerint transfretare venerabile signum Crucis devote volentibus, quos ad id utiles fore crediderint, concedant ac imponant humeris eorundem.

Datum Avinione, VIII Kalendas Junii, anno primo.

B.6

Avignon, 28 November 1363, Urban V to King Peter I

Manuscript: AAV, Reg. Vat. 246, fols 13^v-14^r (V).
Summary: *Bullarium Cyprium III*, no. v-84.
Edition: Setton, *Papacy*, I, p. 246b, n. 108.

Carissimo in Christo filio Petro regi Cipri illustri, salutem *etc.*

Dudum, considerantes attente multa magnaque pericula que ob tue serenitatis a tuo regno et ultramarinis partibus absentiam diuturnam possent eisdem regno et partibus probabiliter evenire, serenitatem eandem, [V 14r] tunc apud Sedem Apostolicam existentem, fuimus exhortati paternis[a)] affectibus ut, visitatis regibus et principibus quos decreveras visitandos, quam cito commode posses, ad dictum tuum regnum inter fauces hostium fidei constitutum remeare curares.

Nuper autem, intellecto quod perfidi Turchi dictum regnum conantur offendere et circa civitatem tuam Sataliensem tenent exercitum numerosum, propter que magis oportet quod ad illas partes celeriter revertaris, excellentiam regiam hortamur attentius et precamur quatinus regressum tuum Deo auxiliante felicem ad dictas partes ulterius non retardes. Nos enim litteras apostolicas super subsidiis que tibi concessimus – quantum potest fieri – facimus expediri, prout venerabilis frater noster Antonius episcopus Melfiensis, confessor tuus, lator presentium, qui expeditionem litterarum ipsarum et alia que sibi commisit regia celsitudo diligenter prosecutus extitit, tue magnitudini referet oraculo vive vocis.

Datum Avinione, IIII Kalendas Decembris, anno secundo.

a) paternis] patenis *a.c. s.l.* V

B.7

Avignon, 1 April 1364, Urban V to King Peter I

Manuscripts: AAV, Reg. Vat. 253, fols 1^r-2^v, no. 1 (V). The beginning of a cancelled version among the letters of 31 March 1363 (see just below) is in Reg. Vat. 252, fol. 31^{r-v} (B), with a marginal note: *Scripta est in anno secundo*.

Summary: omitted in *BEFAR* and *Bullarium Cyprium III* (parallel to letters to King John II of France and others dated 31 March 1363, summarized in Urban V, *Lettres secrètes et curiales*, no. 3211-3213, from AAV, Reg. Aven. 153, fol. 599^r-602^r; another copy is in Reg. Vat. 252, fols 17^r-20^r).

Edition: previously unpublished, but see edition of parallel letter to Amedeo of Savoy in Datta, *Spedizione in Oriente di Amedeo VI*, pp. 225-241, and of that and other parallel letters regarding Amedeo in Bollati di Saint-Pierre, *Illustrazioni della spedizione in Oriente di Amedeo VI*, pp. 344-367.

Urbanus episcopus servus servorum Dei, carissimo in Christo filio Petro regi Cipri illustri, salutem *etc*.

Et si cunctorum Christi fidelium precioso Domini Nostri Ihesu Christi sanguine redemptorum persone temporalesque facultates que ab Ipso Cuius est orbis terre debent Domino recognosci pro recuperatione Terre Sancte, in qua idem Dominus a summo celo ex sua ineffabili caritate descendens, eamque presentia sue conversationis illustrans, dignatus est mortalem carnem suscipere et salutem humani generis per suam passionem sacratissimam misericorditer reparare, promptis sint affectibus exponende, ecclesiasticorum tamen bonorum subsidia tanto ad hoc sunt offerenda libentius et promptius exhibenda quanto ipsa piis operibus sunt specialius dedicata, ut nostri Redemptoris iniurie, que in dicta terra fedata canum spurcitia irrogantur eidem, operatione fidelium propulsetur, tollatur Christianorum opprobium ex detentione dicte terre iam proch dolor antiquatum, ac exaltetur fides catholica, per quam crescat salvandorum numerus et infidelitas confundatur.

[1] Sane dolenter referimus quod olim, peccatis exigentibus, dictam terram prefatorum Agarenorum gens perfida, eiusdem Salvatoris et sue orthodoxe fidei inimica, a longis retro temporibus, non absque dampnosa negligentia Christiani[a] populi, occupavit, prout detinet occupatam, eam polluendo abhominandorum patratione scelerum ac pro ancilla tenendo, que domina gentium debet esse. Accedit quoque ad huiusmodi infelicitatis augmentum illa erumpnosa calamitas quam ex oppressione Turchorum crudelium patitur Christianus populus Orientis et que tanto gravior redditur quanto iidem Turchi viciniores fidelibus existentes grassantur sevius et facilius in eosdem, quantoque ipsorum rabies semper excrescens et cruorem Christianum aspirans effundere maius potest Christianitati generare periculum, nisi eorum qui in sua feritate confidunt presumptuosa temeritas per ipsorum fidelium potentiam reprimatur.

[2] Que omnia, divino spiritu – ut pie credimus – inspirante, dudum[b] tu prudenter considerans, et hiis maiora pericula toti Christianitati si oportunum in premissis non apponatur remedium probabiliter proventura formidans, de statu dictorum infidelium, quem ex ipsorum mortalitatibus et discordiis debilitatum et dispositum prostrationi asseruisti, presertim ex captione civitatis Satalie ac nonnullorum castrorum et locorum que tu tuis[c] providentia personalibusque laboribus et expensis de manibus infidelium predictorum eripuisti, ex quo infideles ipsos multus – ut asseritur – timor invasit, plenarie informatus, sicut princeps magnanimus et devotus, non vitatis pro Dei servicio itinerum longorum periculis, ad Sedem Apostolicam accessisti, nobis et fratribus nostris Sancte Romane Ecclesie cardinalibus ac[d] catholicis principibus et

magnatibus aliique fidelibus populis vias et modos vive tue vocis oraculo prudenter ostendens per quos istis temporibus potest faciliter eorundem Agarenorum et Turchorum elidi potentia et fieri recuperatio[e]) dicte terre.

[3] Hec siquidem carissimus in Christo filius noster Johannes rex Francie illustris gaudenter accipiens, desiderium transfretandi, quod diutius – ut asseruit – gessit in corde, nuper produxit in lucem. Nam ipse et tua devota magnificentia aliique [B 31v] multi nobiles cum eorum potentia pro recuperatione[f]) Terre Sancte predicte promiserunt personaliter transfretare et receperunt de nostris manibus venerabile signum Crucis. Nosque, premissa cum ingenti considerantes letitia, cupientesque magnitudinem[g]) tuam et prefatum regem Francie et alios fervore huiusmodi devotionis accensos in tanto Salvatoris nostri predicti promovendo negotio spiritualibus et temporalibus auxiliis confovere, matura super hiis deliberatione prehabita, de dictorum fratrum consilio indiximus ad dictam Terram Sanctam et alias partes infidelium Orientis passagium generale, omnibus ad hoc transfretaturis indulgentiam et privilegia transfreta<n>tibus in dicte terre subsidium consueta concedi auctoritate apostolica concedentes, ac dictum regem Francie ipsius passagii et totius exercitus Christiani qui transfretabit in illo rectorem constituimus et capitaneum generalem. Ac nichilominus per alias nostras inde confectas litteras verbum Crucis cum certis gratiis et indulgentiis in nonnullis partibus mandavimus predicari, ac eidem regi Francie et ceteris Crucesignatis et Crucesignandis Kalendas[h]) Martii anni nativitatis Domini millesimi trecentesimi sexagesimi quinti proxime secuturi pro termino ad transfretandum in dicto passagio duximus assignandas. Ipseque rex Francie, capitaneatum huiusmodi reverenter acceptans, personaliter in eisdem nostris manibus ad sancta Dei evangelia iuravit quod in eisdem Kalendis vel ante dicti passagii iter arriperet, illudque, iusto et legitimo impedimento cessante, sub certis tamen condicionibus, modis, et formis in aliis nostris super hoc confectis litteris seriosius annotatis, realiter et personaliter prosequetur.

[4] Verum, quia idem rex Francie – prout nobis asseruit – commode nequit nisi circa prefatum terminum versus dictas terras et partes arripere iter suum, et tu, qui es ad presens apud sedem constitutus eandem, ad succurrendum eisdem fidelibus et conatus eorundem infidelium reprimendum velud athleta Christi ac precursor intrepidus proponis – prout nobis asseruisti – satis ante dictum terminum cum auxiliis citramarinorum fidelium transfretare, nos tibi certa subsidia fidelium in Gradensi, Salzeburgensi, Strigoniensi, Collocensi, Jadrensi,[i]) [V 1v] Spalatensi, Ragusina, Antibarensi, Duracensi, Patracensi,[j]) Corinthiensi, Atheniensi, Thebana, Constantinopolitana, Neopat<r>ensi, Pariensi, Collocensi dicta Rodo, Cretensi, Corfiensi, et Nicosiensi, et Panormitana, Messanensi, et Montisregalis civitatibus,[k]) diocesibus, et provinciis, ac etiam in Aquilegensi, Concordiensi, Tergestina, Justinopolitana, Polensi, ac Palentina, Emonensi, Petenensi, ac Caffensi civitatibus[k]) comitatibus et diocesibus ac terra Pere prope Constantinopolim, ceterisque partibus ultramarinis duximus concedenda, prout in aliis nostris inde confectis litteris plenius continetur.

Attendentes igitur quod tam arduum atque onerosum negotium innumeris egebit expensis, ac volentes ad honorem Illius Qui terram ipsam dum genus humanum redemit proprio sanguine consecravit ad subventionem expensarum huiusmodi apponere solicitis studiis manum apostolice potestatis, premissis omnibus digna consideratione pensatis ac pluribus et diversis tractatibus et declarationibus cum eisdem nostris fratribus habitis super illis, impositionem ac exactionem et levationem decime triennalis ecclesiasticorum reddituum et proventuum per nos dudum, videlicet III Kalendas Februarii pontificatus nostri anno primo, pro nostris et Ecclesie Romane oneribus supportandis, in civitatibus et diocesibus ac provinciis et terra predictis imposite huic ad III Kalendas Februarii proxime futuras dumtaxat volumus perdurare; et exnunc prout extunc dictam impositionem eiusdem decime, si interim – ut speramus – insistetur persecutione dicti passagii generalis et non alias, tenore presentium revocamus; et ab ipsius decime que pro futuro extunc tempore deberetur exactione seu levatione volumus et precipimus locorum ordinarios ad hoc a nobis deputatos totaliter abstineri; ac decimam ipsam eorundem reddituum et proventuum ecclesiasticorum dictarum civitatum et diocesium, provinciarum, et terre ab universis ecclesiarum et monasteriorum prelatis aliisque personis ecclesiasticis ipsarum civitatum et diocesium, provinciarum, et terre (preterquam ab eisdem fratribus nostris Sancte Romane Ecclesie cardinalibus, quecumque dignitates, personatus, officia, prioratus, administrationes, canonicatus, prebendas, et alia beneficia, cum cura vel sine, in dictis civitatibus et diocesibus obtinentibus, et usque ad sex annos ab huiusmodi die, videlicet III Kalendas Februarii proxime futuro, computandos extunc secuturos obtenturis, qui in apostolice solicitudinis partem assumpti nobiscum universalis Ecclesie onera sortiuntur, necnon a dilectis filiis magistris, prioribus, preceptoribus, et fratribus Hospitalis Sancti Johannis Jerosolimitani aliisque personis aliorum militarium ordinum, necnon personis ecclesiasticis que, obtenta licentia debita, in isto sancto passagio personaliter transfretabunt, quos quidem cardinales, magistros, priores, preceptores, et fratres hospitalium eorundem ac personas ecclesiasticas transfretaturas ab huiusmodi prestatione decime exemptos esse volumus et immunes), de dictorum fratrum nostrorum consilio, usque ad dictos sex annos insisteret prosecutionem dicti passagii prelibati – super quo nostre vel successorum nostrorum Romanorum pontificum canonice intrantium declarationi stari volumus et, nisi nos aut iidem successores aliud duxerimus seu duxerint ordinandum, super quibus nobis et ipsis successoribus potestatem plenariam reservamus – auctoritate apostolica imponimus singulis annis dicti sexenni in duobus terminis, medietatem videlicet in Sanctorum Apostolorum Petri et Pauli et alteram medietatem in Nativitatis Domini Nostri Ihesu Christi festivitatibus solvendam, exigendam, et colligendam.

In quibus solutione, exactione, et collectione modificationes adhiberi volumus infrascriptas, videlicet:

Quod in eisdem civitatibus et diocesibus, provinciis, et terra in aliquo casu ipsius decime duplex exactio non concurrat et interim ab omni subsidio ecclesiasticarum personarum earundem civitatum et diocesium, provinciarum, et terre ac omni exactione et alio quocumque principis seu domini in eisdem civitatibus et diocesibus, provinciis, et terra temporale dominium obtinentis eisdem personis ecclesiasticis impositis et imponendis cessetur omnino.

Et quod hii quorum facultates ad integram solutionem huiusmodi decime supportatis aliis consuetis oneribus non suppetunt ultraquam iuxta suarum huiusmodi facultatum exigentiam commode possunt. Illi vero qui de ipsa decima nichil solvere possunt – super cuiusmodi ipsorum impotentia eorundem ordinariorum quibus exactionem dicte decime per alias nostras litteras committimus conscientias intendimus onerare – ad solvendum aliquid pretextu impositionis et mandati huiusmodi nullatenus compellantur.

Quodque ille persone ecclesiastice que cum licentia debita, ut premittitur, transfretaverint a prestatione decime suorum ecclesiasticorum reddituum et proventuum modo qui sequitur sint exempte, videlicet quod decima primi biennii per personas ipsas tam exemptas <quam non exemptas> preter diocesanos debita penes diocesanos earum, diocesanorum vero penes ecclesiarum suarum cathedralium capitula, deponantur in usus eorum si transfretaverint, vel in dicte terre subsidium et alias contra infideles et inimicos fidei si non transfretaverint, convertenda. Volumus tamen quod illi penes quos dicta decima deponetur illis a quibus ipsam recipient promittere debeant quod eis dum transfretabunt decimam ipsam reddent, ipseque persone collectoribus dicte decime cavere ydonee teneantur quod in casu quo transfretare non contingat easdem tertii anni decimam exclusa cunctatione qualibet collectoribus ipsis solvent.

Quia vero, considerato [V 2r] tue magnanimitatis affectu quem ad prosecutionem et consummationem Deo annuente felicem ipsius sancti negotii habere dinosceris, firmam spem gerimus quod idem negotium prosperum et votivum sortietur effectum, per quod nedum super gratiis et subsidiis tibi propterea concessis nostra quietatur non immerito conscientia, sed ad ea promptius concedenda multipliciter incitatur; considerato quoque quod, civitatibus et locis aliis que fideles Christi olim in dicte terre partibus obtinebant per ipsorum hostium rabiem truculentam[l] vastatis, locus ibidem aliquis ad recipiendum propugnatores fidei, proch dolor, non remansit, propter quod huiusmodi prosecutio passagii maioribus indiget expensarum profluviis quam hactenus indigeret dum, civitatibus et locis predictis in statu prosperitatis manentibus et tam ad recreationem utilem quam munitionem necessariam recipientibus catholicos bellatores, quidam principes Christiani in eiusdem terre subsidium transfretarunt; dictam sexannalem, decimam videlicet ecclesiasticorum reddituum et proventuum in civitatibus et diocesibus, provinciis, et terra prefatis consistentium, de quibus retro actibus temporibus solvi decima consuevit (eisdem fratribus nostris Sancte Romane Ecclesiae cardinalibus, ac personis et bonis dicti Hospitalis Sancti Johannis Jerosolimitani et aliorum ordinum militarium, ac personis aliis ecclesiasticis que dictam decimam non poterunt in totum vel in partem solvere, ut prefertur, et aliis que, obtenta debita licentia, in hoc[m] passagio personaliter transfretabunt dumtaxat exceptis), dummodo in eisdem civitatibus et diocesibus, provinciis, et terra duplex exactio decime non concurrat, et ab omni alio subsidio exactione et gravamine dictarum personarum abstineatur omnino, prout superius continetur, usque ad finem sexennii prelibati, sublimitati tue, te huiusmodi negotium personaliter prosequente, in auxilium expensarum negotii huiusmodi presentium auctoritate concedimus in utilitatem predicti passagi predicteque Terre Sancte subsidium seu succursum in modum qui sequitur colligendam ac etiam convertendam:

Videlicet quod eadem decima auctoritate sedis prefate per ordinarios locorum dictarum civitatum, diocesium, provinciarum, et terre et collectores ab eis auctoritate apostolica deputandos colligi debeat iuxta modum in aliis nostris litteris super hoc ordinariis eisdem directis contentum; quodque pecunia colligenda de dicta decima et aliis subsidiis pro dicto passagio dicteque Terre Sancte subsidio seu succursu procuratoribus ad hoc deputatis integraliter assignetur.

[5] Postremo, volumus quod de singulis que de premissis tue celsitudini seu aliis per te ad hoc deputatis fuerint assignata et de expensis inde factis legato Apostolice Sedis in dictis ultramarinis partibus deputato, vel alii seu aliis quos ad hoc dicta sedes duxerit deputandos, tenearis reddi facere plenariam rationem.

[6] Si vero – quod absit – contingeret te infra dictos sex annos de medio submoveri aut impedimento perpetuo impediri, cum huiusmodi decime et alia subsidia per nos tue sublimitati concessa in favorem dicti passagii, quod eo casu alius princeps loco tui – prestante Domino – prosequetur, tibi duxerimus concedenda, volumus et mandamus quod iidem prelati seu ordinarii ad exactionem, levationem, et receptionem predicte decime nichilominus procedant eaque fideliter conservent seu conservari faciant, donec super ipsis aliud a nobis receperint in mandatis. Et omnia que de subsidiis supradictis penes te, si vita fuerit tibi comes et, ut prefertur, impeditus extiteris, et in casu dicti tui obitus penes heredes et successores seu gentes tuos restarent, et in eiusdem passagii preparationibus aut pro eo de mandato tuo <non> essent expensa, necnon galee et alia quecumque facta, empta, vel predicto passagio seu pro eo de dictis subsidiis in civitatibus et diocesibus, provinciis, et terra prelibatis quomodolibet acquisita, eidem legato vel alii seu personis de quibus dicta sedes duxerit ordinandum per te, si, ut premittitur, vixeris et fueris impeditus, et per heredes tuos in casum dicti tui obitus, integraliter sine difficultate qualibet assignetur secundum dispositionem dicte sedis pro dicto passagio expendenda.

[7] Porro, circa illa que dicta tua sublimitas de predictorum decime et subsidiorum pecunia forsitan assignabit seu faciet assignari nobilibus seu quibuslibet aliis secum transfretare volentibus, forsan ad procuranda seu emenda aliqua sibi pro passagio necessaria seu etiam oportuna, vel alias pro supportandis expensis quas essent facturi in prosecutione passagii sepefati, pro serenitate tue conscientie ac dicti securitate negotii habeat inter alia precavere quod illi quibus faciet illa tradi proprio firmare debeant iuramento quod ea que sibi tradentur fideliter conservabunt et illa quanto commodius et utilius poterunt in utilitatem dicti passagii seu preparatoriorum ipsius et non in alios usus convertent; et quod nicholominus [2v] in casu in quo te contingeret taliter impediri quod pecunie dictorum decime et subsidiorum et alia supradicta iuxta ordinationem premissam eisdem personis a dicta sede deputandis assignari deberent, predictam pecuniam et aliam ex illa pro passagio acquisita bona fide personis resistueri<n>t memoratis; et quod etiam ad hoc sub formis et validis obligationibus et sub cohercione camerarii nostri et iurisdictionis tue in tuo regno se et heredes suos et bona eorum astringant, prout per illos qui se obligant iurisidictioni dicti camerarii est fieri consuetum, sic quid non restet in casu predicto nisi sola executio quam tu in dicto tuo regno per ministros tue temporalis iustitie, prout tales in tua iurisdictione consistent, facere tenearis; ita quod dicto passagio non possit malitiose subtrahi aliquid de predictis, et nichilominus possint tales ad predicta compelli per dictum camerarium et alias per censuram ecclesiasticam, si visum fuerit expedire; quod si dicta tua nobilitas tales obligari providerit, ut prefertur, tu et tui heredes ac successores ad restitutionem premissam dictis personis ad hoc, ut premittitur, deputandis faciendam remaneatis efficaciter obligati, semper tamen

ratione habita rationabilium excusationum, sique forte ab illis quibus premissa fuerint tradita facte fuerint, sine fraude in emendis seu procurandis ex dicta pecunia vel etiam conservandis hiis que predicto passagio esse poterant oportuna, prout fuerit rationis, et habita etiam ratione illorum que de iure super hoc fuerint attendenda. Eo vero casu quo tua circumspectio dictam recipientes pecuniam obligari providerit, ut prefertur, non tenearis ad restitutionem huiusmodi, sed dumtaxat ad instrumenta et litteras confecta super hiis dictis assignanda personis et ad ipsas super huiusmodi excusatione iuvandas efficaciter, prout poteris, per ministros tue iustitie temporales.

[8] Insuper, de illis que de mandato tuo mercatoribus et aliis quibuscumque tradentur ad faciendas provisiones quaslibet dicto passagio necessarias seu etiam oportunas, ordinamus quod tenearis in casu huiusmodi ad illa seu acquisita ex eis restituendum seu restitui faciendum personis predictis, habita tamen ut in alio casu, ut premittitur, ratione rationabilium expensarum et aliorum que in ratione reddenda fuerint attendenda, et ad hoc inquantum per rationem reddendam personis eisdem apparuerit te teneri.

De illis autem que ab aliis dicto passagio seu pro terre predicte subsidio seu succursu forsitan deberentur vel que forte detinerentur a personis aliis quibuscumque, non tamen ex facto vel mandato tuo seu deputandorum a te super hoc, ordinamus quod ad restitutionem talium que ad te vel ad tuos non pervenerint nullatenus tenearis. Nostre tamen intentionis existit quod ad colligenda omnia alia in quibus ceteri tenebuntur illos qui ad hoc per dictam sedem deputati fuerint debeas in tuo regno favorabiliter adiuvare, qui quidem deputandi omnia sibi, ut predicitur, assignanda nomine Sedis Apostolice recipere et conservare debebunt in locis congruis et securis distribuenda et convertenda per sedem eandem in dicte terre subsidium prout melius et commodius dicta sedes viderit expedire.

Ceterum, ordinamus et volumus quod tu et heredes ac gentes tui ad hoc deputate de hiis que receperitis de huiusmodi pecunia et aliis subsidiis per dictam sedem tibi concessis et imposterum – dante Domino – concedendis pro passagio prelibato, et de expensis per te seu de tuo mandato exinde factis de quibus liquere poterit, teneamini eidem sibi reddere rationem quandocumque super hoc fueritis requisiti, et ad hoc compelli per censuram ecclesiasticam valeatis.

Denique, licet proponamus quantum convenientier poterimus in colligenda dicta decima, ut prefertur, imposita, ac in utilitatem dicte terre et alias contra infideles et inimicos fidei convertenda facere diligentiam adhiberi per monitiones, sententias, et processus et alias prout fuerit oportunum, non tamen intendimus, si forsan in ea levanda, habenda, seu, ut premittitur, convertenda impedimentum aliquod eveniret quod ex hoc nobis et successoribus nostris aliquid imputetur vel passagium tuum occasione huiusmodi retardetur, nec ad probationem impedimenti huiusmodi, cum ex hoc possent alia passagii impedimenta causari, nos vel successores nostros quomodolibet obligari.

Nulli ergo *et cetera* nostre concessionis, mandati, ordinationis, intentionis, et voluntatis infringere *et cetera*.

Datum Avinione, Kalendis Aprilis, anno secundo.

a) christiani] christia + *blank V*   b) dudum] *om. B*   c) tuis] tua *V*   d) ac] et *V*.   e) recuperatio] recuperatione *V*   f. recuperatione] dicte *add. B*   g) magnitudinem] *cessat B*   h) kalendas] kalendis *V*   i) Jadrensi] spa *add. V*   j) patracensis] petracensi *V*   k) civitatibus] comitabitus *V*   l) truculentam] traculentam *V*   m) hoc] hos *a.c. V*

B.8

Avignon, 3 June 1364, Urban V to King Peter I

Manuscript: AAV, Reg. Vat. 246, fol. 208[r-v] (V).
Summary: *Bullarium Cyprium III*, no. v-93.

Carissimo in Christo filio Petro regi Cipri illustri, salutem *etc.*

Nuper dilecti filii Arnaldus Bernardieberardi, preceptor domus Burdegalensis hospitalis Sancti Johannis Jerosolimitani, et nobilis vir Bernardus de Marcrinio, miles, dominus de Planis, procuratores in partibus cismarinis dilecti filii Rogerii de Pinibus, magistri hospitalis eiusdem, quasdam litteras magistri prefati, datas Rodi die penultima Februarii proximi preteriti eisque transmissas, quedam nova de ultramarinis partibus nobis displicibilia et nonnulla hospitalis eiusdem negotia continentes, nobis exhibere curarunt, quorum novorum copiam tue serenitati transmittimus [V 208v] presentibus interclusam. Ex novis igitur huiusmodi et verisimili coniectura credentes quod tua mora redeundi ad tuum regnum seu partes alias transmarinas periculosa sit nimium nisi celeriter brevietur, et illi qui tecum volunt transfretare, sentientes te in Gallicanis partibus nimis longo tempore immorari – prout audivimus, et verisimiliter credendum existit – expectationis tedio pregraventur, et ex tali dilatione multa possent oriri periculosa quibus non posset de facili obviari, circumspectam magnitudinem regiam paternis affectibus solicitamus ac rogamus et hortamur attente quatenus tuum regressum ad prefata regnum et partes ultramarinas omni mora postposita studeas festinare.

Datum Avinione, III Nonas Junii, anno secundo.

B.9

Avignon, 19 June 1364, Urban V to King Peter I

Manuscript: AAV, Reg. Vat. 246, fol. 219[r] (V).
Summaries: Urban V, *Lettres secrètes et curiales*, no. 1027; *Bullarium Cyprium III*, no. v-94.

Carissimo in Christo filio Petro regi Cipri illustri, salutem *etc.*

Nuper ad nostram audientiam molesta plurimum assertione perducto quod inter dilectos filios incolas regni tui Cipri ac quosdam cives Januenses in dicto regno degentes esse quedam rixa seu tumultuosa discordia suscitata, scripsimus dilectis filiis nobili viro Gabrieli Adorno duci ac consilio et communi civitatis Januensis secundum tenorem presentibus interclusum. Quare serenitatem tuam rogamus et hortamur attente quatenus de iniuriis et dampnis civibus illatis eisdem sati<s>factionem fieri facias et alias taliter in hac parte ministres iustitiam quod iidem dux ac consilium et commune possint et valeant merito contentari et huiusmodi – quod absit – discordia non procedat.

Datum Avinione, XIII Kalendas Julii, anno secundo.

B.10

Avignon, 19 June 1364, Urban V to Doge Gabriel Adorno, the council, and the commune of Genoa

Manuscript: AAV, Reg. Vat. 246, fol. 220^{r-v} (V).
Summary: omitted in *BEFAR* and *Bullarium Cyprium III*.

Eisdem <Dilectis filiis nobili viro Gabrieli Adorno duci ac consilio et communi civitatis Januensis, salutem *etc.*>
Molesta plurimum nuper ad nos perduxit assertio quod, illo cuius proprium est seminare zizaniam et ponere discordiam inter fratres ac omni bono negotio exhibere se obicem – ut credimus – operante, inter quosdam cives vestros in regno Cipri degentes et incolas eiusdem regni gravis tumultuosaque fuit discordia suscitata, ex qua vos, indignati pro civibus eisdem, ut in eodem regno non morentur de cetero dicimini destinasse, quodque propterea timetur probabiliter ne non solum a mutua communione cessetur imposterum, sed inter vos et eosdem incolas periculosa novitas oriatur.
Nos igitur, de huiusmodi malis iam preteritis displicentiam habentes non modicam, et de futuris maioribus non immerito formidantes, discretionem vestram rogamus et hortamur attente quatenus, provide considerantes quod carissimus in Christo filius noster Petrus rex Cipri illustris in cismarinis partibus tempore dicte discordie erat, prout esse dinoscitur, constitutus, et quod tanquam princeps prudens et iustus vesterque amicus de iniuriis et da<m>pnis civibus illatis eisdem satisfactionem fieri faciet et alias in hac parte debitam ministrabit iustitiam, ut verisimiliter est credendum, super quibus nos eidem regi scripta nostra dirigimus, quodque vos sicut devoti Christiani et pugiles Christi prosperitatem passagii generalis, pro quo dicto regi, ut olim audivimus, vos obtulistis magnifice et quod ipse rex laboribus continuatis prosequitur, affectatis et affectare debetis, quodque per discordiam huiusmodi, si – quod absit – [V 220v] procederet, totaliter impediretur passagium memoratum, pro Dei sacre fidei ac Apostolice Sedis et nostra reverentia, ab omni novitate propter premissa vel similia facienda omnino abstinere curetis, promissum per vos pro dicto passagio exhibere subsidium non cessantes. Nos enim pro satisfactione huiusmodi vobis seu eisdem civibus facienda tam apud dictum regem, cui ad presens scribimus, ut prefertur, quam alias – prout oportunum fuerit – offerimus paternis affectibus et – prout in nobis fuerit – efficacibus effectibus interponere partes nostras. Super quibus, ut de hiis mens nostra quiescat, veletis nobis filiali et expectata obedientia respondere.
Datum Avinione, XIII Kalendas Julii, anno secundo.

B.11

Avignon, 25 June 1364, Urban V to Doge Gabriel Adorno, the council, and the commune of Genoa

Manuscript: AAV, Reg. Vat. 246, fols 219^r-220^r (V).
Summaries: Urban V, *Lettres secrètes et curiales*, no. 1034 ('219v'); *Bullarium Cyprium III*, no. v-95.

Dilectis filiis nobili viro Gabrieli Adorno duci ac consilio et communi civitatis Januensis, salutem *etc.*
  Hiis diebus, cum ad nostram notitiam pervenisset quod inter quosdam cives vestros in regno Cipri morantes et incolas ipsius regni gravis [V 219v] fuisset rixa et discordia suscitata, propter quam verisimiliter timebatur ne maior discordia oriretur, nos, futuris malis – presertim impedimento generalis passagii – que exinde verisimiliter possent accidere festinanter occurere paterna providentia cupientes, discretionem vestram precati fuimus et hortati quod, pro Dei ac sacre fidei necnon Apostolice Sedis et nostra reverentia, ab omni novitate propter premissa curaretis penitus abstinere, offerentes nos pro satisfactione dampnorum et iniuriarum vestrarum apud carissimum in Christo filium nostrum Petrum, regem Cipri illustrem, cui super hiis iam scripsimus, et alias prout oportunum existeret affectuose ac efficaciter interponere partes nostras, prout in nostris litteris exinde confectis plenius continetur.
  Quia vero hodie admodum dolenter audivimus quod armari facitis certum numerum galearum ad mittendum ambaxiatores vestros qui dictos regem et regnum debeant diffidare, nos, considerantes ex tali novitate non solum dicto regi, qui, sicut pugil Christi et Christiane fidei propugnator de nostro beneplacito et mandato, sicut nostis, in citramarinis partibus prosequitur negotium passagii generalis, sed ipsi passagio, in quo agitur de statu fidei Christiane, et etiam vobis ipsis, quibus periculosum est valde incipere nova bella, irreparabilia possent scandala provenire, vos, ut dilectos filios nostros et Christianos devotos, monemus[a)] ac requirimus et rogamus necnon in Domino obsecramus quatenus nullam pro premissis, saltem pro moderno tempore, curetis facere novitatem. Nos enim offerimus nos paratos facere vobis seu vestris civibus congrue satisfieri de dampnis et iniuriis prelibatis, et ubi hoc per dictum regem seu subditos suos non fieret, [V 220r] promittimus per nos ipsos taliter hoc efficere quod poteritis merito contentari.
  Datum Avinione, VII Kalendas Julii, anno secundo.

a) monemus] menemus *V*

B.12

Avignon, 25 June 1364, Urban V to Doge Gabriel Adorno, the council, and the commune of Genoa

Manuscript: AAV, Reg. Vat. 246, fol. 228^{r-v} (V).
Summaries: Urban V, *Lettres secrètes et curiales*, no. 1035; *Bullarium Cyprium III*, no. v-96.

Dilectis filiis nobili viro Gabrieli Adorno duci ac consilio et communi civitatis Januensis, salutem.

Super novitate inter quosdam cives vestros et incolas regni Cipri exorta diebus nuper elapsis direximus et nunc iterato discretioni vestre exhortatoria scripta nostra dirigimus quid in hac parte agere debeatis. Et quia istud negotium, quod maximum ad se posset afferre periculum, plurimum insidet cordi nostro, ad exhortationem huiusmodi vobis plenius vive vocis oraculo suadendum, dilectum filium Philippum de Varesio, [V 228v] prepositum Januensem, latorem presentium, per vos super certis negotiis ad nostram presentiam destinatum, ad vos duximus celeriter remittendum, cui super hiis que vobis ex parte nostra narraverit de premissis fidem plenariam adhibete. Negotia vero ipsa pro quibus idem Philippus ad curiam Romanam accessit habere intendimus efficaciter commendata.

Datum Avinione, VII Kalendas Julii, anno secundo.

B.13

Avignon, 30 June 1364, Urban V to King Peter I

Manuscript: Reg. Vat. 246, fol. 241^v (V).
Summaries: Urban V, *Lettres secrètes et curiales*, no. 1051 ('241r'); *Bullarium Cyprium III*, no. v-98.

Carissimo in Christo filio Petro, regi Cipri illustri, salutem *etc*.

Sicut ad serenitatem regiam iam pervenisse putamus, dudum nos, considerantes zelim fidei, scientie donum, et circumspectionis industriam, aliaque multiplicia virtutum merita venerabilis fratris nostri Petri patriarche Constantinopolitani, Apostolice Sedis legati olim in ultramarinis partibus laudabiliter comprobata, eum, de negotiis et statu earundem partium in quibus dicte sedis legatus extitit plenarie informatum et, prout per experientiam novimus, tue sublimitati acceptum, ad partes ipsas in favorem et fulcimentum generalis passagii providimus remittendum, commisso sibi de novo legationis officio in eisdem, prout in litteris nostris inde confectis plenius continetur.

Quocirca celsitudinem tuam – licet expedire non credamus – rogamus et hortamur attente quatenus eundem legatum, pro nostra et Apostolice Sedis reverentia, regiis favoribus et honoribus prosequaris.

Datum Avinione, II Kalendas Julii, anno secundo.

B.14

Avignon, 20 February 1365, Urban V to Doge Gabriel Adorno, the council, and the commune of of Genoa

Manuscript: AAV, Reg. Vat. 247, fols 51^r-52^v (V).
Summary: *Bullarium Cyprium III*, no. v-106.

Dilectis filiis nobili viro Gabrieli Adurno ac consilio et communi civitatis Januensis.

In estate nuper elapsa, dum carissimus in Christo filius noster Petrus rex Cipri illustris, Salvatori nostro et eius sacratissime fidei velut apis argumentosa deserviens, pro promotione subsidii passagii generalis de nostro beneplacito et mandato certa regna fidelium et tunc presertim partes Alamannie peragraret, ad aures nostras amara [V 51v] nimis relatione perducto quod, operante satore zizanie, inter quosdam cives vestros[a)] in regno Cipri degentes et incolas eiusdem regni gravis tumultuosaque fuerit discordia suscitata, ex qua vos, multa indignatione commoti, pro civibus eisdem ut in eodem regno non morarentur ulterius dicebamini destinasse, quodque propterea timebatur probabiliter ne non solum a communione mutua cessaretur imposterum, sed inter vos et eosdem incolas periculosa novitas oriretur, nos discretionem vestram attente rogavimus ac paterne fuimus exhortati ut, considerantes mature quod idem rex tempore dicte discordie erat in cismarinis partibus et quod tanquam princeps prudens et iustus vesterque amicus de iniuriis et dampnis civibus illatis eisdem – prout verisimilis credulitas suggerebat – satisfactionem fieri faceret ac debitam iustitiam ministraret, et quod vos sicut devoti Christiani et pugiles Christi prosperitatem dicti passagii, pro quo vos magnifice obtulistis, optare merito debebatis, quodque per discordiam huiusmodi, si procederet, totaliter impediretur passagium memoratum, pro Dei ac sacre fidei ac Apostolice Sedis et nostra reverentia, ab omni novitate propter premissa vel similia facienda abstineretis omnino, promissum per vos pro dicto passagio exhibere subsidium non cessantes. Nosque pro satisfactione huiusmodi vobis sive eisdem civibus facienda tam apud dictum regem, cui tunc scripsimus, quam alias – prout oportunum foret – obtulimus paternis affectibus et – prout in nobis foret – efficacibus effectibus interponere partes nostras.

Deinde, diebus illis, quod nostro versabatur in corde oportunis et ferventibus studiis prosequentes ne causa ista vulnus novitatis recipiet, cui non posset de facili sanativum remedium adhiberi, ac sperantes quod in reditu dicti regis ad partes Italie, ubi vicinitatis interveniret commoditas inter vos et ipsum, reformaretur sperata concordia[b)] satis cito, vos tam per litteras quam per fideles personas solicitare curavimus quod premissorum occasione nullam faceretis noxiam novitatem, obtulimusque nos paratos vobis seu vestris civibus facere congrue satisfieri de dampnis et iniuriis prelibatis, et ubi hoc per dictum regem seu subditos suos non fieret, promisimus per nos ipsos taliter hoc efficere quod possetis merito contentari. Vosque ut devoti filii nostris huiusmodi exhortationibus hucusque acquiescere curavistis.

Postmodum vero, prefato rege reverso ad [V 52r] dictas partes Italie, grata auditione percepimus quod dilectus filius Laurencius Celsi, dux Veneciarum, ubi prefatus rex asseritur presentialiter permanere, pro tractanda inter vos et ipsum regem concordia solennes ad vos ambaxiatores destinare curavit, de quo, considerato quod propter locorum vicinitatem negotium dicte concordie commodius in partibus illis quam apud Apostolicam Sedem tractari et perfici poterat, fuimus valde leti.

Sed novissime cum displicentia multa percepimus quod iidem ambaxiatores Venecias vacui redierunt, vobis dispositis ad guerram eidem regi et suis regnicolis inferendam.

Nos igitur, ex hiis tanquam ex impedimento et subversione manifestis dicti passagii merito suspirantes abintimis, et ad obviandum tanto malo quo maius extimare nescimus valituris remediis cogitantes, venerabilem fratrem nostrum Petrum patriarcham Constantinopolitanum, Apostolice Sedis legatum, virum utique circumspectum, scientia preditum, zelatorem pacis, et de ultramarinis negotiis informatum, in partibus Italie nunc degentem, quem notum vestrum et benivolum reputamus, ad vestram presentiam pro informatione huiusmodi concordie providimus accessurum, sibique per apostolica scripta precipiendo mandamus quod propter hoc ad vos veniat incunctanter.[c)]

Quare circunspectam devotionem vestram paterne caritatis affectu monemus, hortamur, et obsecramus in Domino quatenus, provide considerantes quot et quanta mala non solum vobis ac ipsi regi et regnicolis, qui omnes estis impugnatores hostium Christi et magnifici pugilles ac defensores fidei prelibate, sed toti Christianitati procul dubio resultaret, quantaque infamie macula apud omnes fideles poneretur in vestri nominis claritate ac quantam offensam inferretis ex hoc Salvatori nostro ac nonnullis principibus et magnatibus in tam pio negotio dicti passagii adiuvantibus dictum regem, et quod, si forsan impediretis Crucis negotium, Ille suscitaret vobis alia bella et hostes qui est Dominus ultionum, animos vestros ad rationabilem abilitare concordiam studeatis, eiusdem patriarche suasionibus et monitis que vobis pro parte nostra fecerit acquiescentes fideliter et devote. Nos enim sibi super huiusmodi pace firmanda vel saltem treugis longi temporis indicendis [V 52v] plenam concedimus per alias nostras litteras facultatem.

Quod si per interpositionem dicti patriarche et aliorum non possetis ad huiusmodi concordiam devenire – quod Actor pacis avertat – cum nos parati sumus in premisso negotio personaliter laborare, vos requirimus et rogamus instantius ut ambaxiatores vestros cum pleno mandato super hiis ad nostram velitis presentiam destinare, qui – ut speramus in Deo – felicis pacis commoda reportabunt. Nos enim super hiis prefato regi oportuna scripta nostra dirigimus per presentium portitorem.

Datum Avinione, X Kalendas Martii, anno tertio.

a) vestros] vestro *a.c. s.l.* V   b) sperata concordia] *inv. a.c.* V   c) incunctanter] incunctanter *a.c. s.l.* V

B.15

Avignon, 18 March 1365, Urban V to the cities, castles, and other places of Cyprus

Manuscripts: AAV, Reg. Aven. 159, fol. 426^v (A); Reg. Vat. 254, fol. 8^{r-v}, no. 68 (V)
Summaries: Urban V, *Lettres communes*, ed. Hayez and Hayez et al., no. 14427; *Bullarium Cyprium III*, no. v-110.

Dilectis filiis universitatibus civitatum, castrorum, et aliorum quorumcumque locorum regni Cipri, salutem *etc.*

Sincere devotionis affectus quem ad nos et Romanam Ecclesiam geritis promeretur ut petitionibus vestras[a)] – quantum [V 8v] cum Deo possumus – ad exauditionis gratiam admittamus.

Hinc est quod nos, vestris in hac parte supplicationibus inclinati, vobis duci faciendi semel dumtaxat sex galeas, tres videlicet uno et alias tres in alio anno, ad Alexandrie et alias partes et terras infidelium[b)] ultramarinas que per Soldanum Babilonie detinentur, cum nautis et aliis personis ad regimen galearum huiusmodi oportunis, vestris mercimoniis oneratas, et cum mercatoribus dictorum mercimoniorum, exceptis armis, ferro, lignaminibus, et aliis prohibitis, constitutionibus et processibus Apostolice Sedis spiritualibus et temporalibus penas et sententias prolatas in transfretantes cum mercibus ad partes et terras predictas continentibus nequaquam obstantibus, auctoritate apostolica plenam et liberam licentiam elargimur. Volumus quod huiusmodi gratiam nulli vendatis, sed easdem galeas de vestris rebus et mercimoniis oneretis, quodque illi qui dictas galeas principaliter conducent ac mercimoniis onerabunt in manibus diocesani loci in quo eedem galee onerabuntur quod premissa vel aliquod eorundem in fraudem non facient prestent corporaliter iuramentum, quodque idem diocesanus, quando dicte galee onerabuntur, per se vel alium seu alios se diligenter informet quod in fraudem huiusmodi nichil fiet, et si fieri repererit, dictam licentiam pronuntiet non tenere. Alioquin, nisi iuramentum huiusmodi prestiterint et idem diocesanus informationem huiusmodi omnino fecerit, ut prefertur, presentem concessionem haberi volumus pro non facta. Super cuius iuramenti prestatione et informatione predicta prefatus diocesanus duo consimilia[c)] confici faciat publica instrumenta, quorum alterum camere nostre studeat destinare, penes se reliquo reservato.

Nulli ergo *etc.* nostre concessionis et voluntatis infringere *etc.*

Datum Avinione, XV Kalendas Aprilis, anno tertio.

a) vestras] vestris V   b) infidelium] *om.* A   c) consimilia] similia V

B.16

Avignon, 26 March 1365, Urban V to King Peter I

Manuscript: AAV, Reg. Vat. 247, fol. 67^v (V).
Summary: *Bullarium Cyprium III*, no. v-114.

Carissimo in Christo filio Petro regi Cipri illustri, salutem *etc.*

Hiis diebus scripsimus et nunc iterato scribimus dilectis filiis Gabrieli Adurno duci ac consilio et communi civitatis Januensis sub formis presentibus interclusis, ac scribimus etiam venerabili fratri nostro Petro patriarche Constantinopolitano, Apostolice Sedis legato, ut, si in civitate predicta inter serenitatem tuam ac eosdem ducem et commune non sit facta vel cito fieri non possit concordia, cuius tractatum et consumationem sibi dudum commisimus, una cum tuis nuntiis et procuratoribus ad hoc sufficiens mandatum habentibus ad Sedem Apostolicam dirigat gressus suos.

Quare celsitudinem regiam paterne requirimus et rogamus quatenus, attendens utilitatem non solum tui regni sed etiam totius Christianitatis ex huiusmodi discordia dependere, ad illam congruis modis habendam cordialiter inclineris et predicto casu quo dicta concordia non sit facta – quod absit – nuncios tuos cum pleno mandato tam super ipsa concordia quam super unione tue magnitudinis et nonnullorum aliorum fidelium, de quibus apud dictam sedem agitur, sicut nosti, ad nostram presentiam non differas destinare.

Datum Avinione, VII Kalendas Aprilis, anno tertio.

B.17

Avignon, 26 March 1365, Urban V to Doge Gabriel Adorno, the council, and the commune of Genoa

Manuscript: AAV, Reg. Vat. 247, fols 67ᵛ-68ʳ (V).
Summary: omitted in *BEFAR* and *Bullarium Cyprium III*.

Dilectis filiis nobili viro Gabrieli Adorno duci ac consilio et communi civitatis Januensis, salutem. [V 68r]

Dilectos filios ambaxiatores vestros nuper ad nostram presentiam destinatos gratanter recepimus et super hiis que nobis ex parte vestra curaverunt exponere audivimus diligenter, incepimusque tractare de ultramarino negotio, pro quo principaliter eos ad nostram presentiam destinastis. Sed ipso negotio examinato plenarie, reperimus in illo non posse provida et utili deliberatione concludi donec inter vos et carissimum in Christo filium nostrum Petrum Cipri regem illustrem concordia, pro qua sepe vobis scripsimus, reformetur.

Quare devotionem et prudentiam vestram paterne requirimus, rogamus, ac in Domino exhortamur quatenus, ne impediatur tantum bonum dicti ultramarini negotii, quod vos provide atque devote principaliter promovetis, si dicta concordia, quam per venerabilem fratrem nostrum Petrum patriarcham Constantinopolitanum, Apostolice Sedis legatum, tractari mandavimus et, Deo auxiliante, firmari, nondum forsitan sit firmata, eam mediante dicto patriarcha vel alio celeriter facere – in quantum in vobis fuerit – studeatis, aut, si forsitan magis vobis placeat, cum nos, prout alias vobis obtulimus, parati sumus in dicto negotio personaliter laborare, aut dictis ambaxiatoribus aut aliis per vos ad Apostolicam Sedem mittendis detis plenum mandatum super eadem concordia facienda, in qua – quantum cum Deo poterimus – vestram iustitiam habebimus commendatam, ipsamque concordiam celeriter expedire speramus, deinde ad expeditionem dicti ultramarini negotii, cum auxilio divine gratie, sublato more dispendio, processuri. Nos enim prefato regi preces et exhortationes similes destinamus et hic apud nos sunt aliqui pro eodem, nichilominusque unus ambaxiator eius propter hoc specialiter ad nostram presentiam asseritur de proximo accessurus.

Datum Avinione, VII Kalendas Aprilis, anno tertio.

B.18

Avignon, 19 July 1365, Urban V to King Peter I

Manuscripts: AAV, Reg. Vat. 247, fol. 131ᵛ (V); Reg. Vat. 244E, fol. 70ʳᵇ, no. 156 (E).
Summaries: Urban V, *Lettres secrètes et curiales*, no. 1887; *Bullarium Cyprium III*, no. v-125.

Carissimo in Christo filio Petro regi Cipri illustri, salutem *etc.*

Recessum tuum de Venetiis[a)] cum copiosa – ut scripsisti – comitiva pro Christi servicio bellatorum,[b)] Illo pro Quo militas favente, felicem letitia percepimus expectata,

Deumque rogamus suppliciter ut iter et actus tuos ac bellatorum huiusmodi sic dirigat et in salutis prosperitate disponat[c)] ac optatos successus illis adiciat quod inde universalis letetur Ecclesia et gemat infidelitas perfidorum,[d)] multisque[e)] Christi fidelibus tuam sequendi devotam magnificentiam desiderium ingeratur. Age igitur, fili carissime, bellum Dominicum magnanimiter et devote, tuosque[f)] commilitones, quos ad hoc de diversis nationibus fidelium congregasti, ex parte nostra instantius exhorteris. Nos[g)] enim, ut huiusmodi prosperari possit negotium,[h)] favorem apostolicum in hiis que poterimus paternis affectibus impendemus.

Datum Avinione, XIIII Kalendas Augusti, anno tertio.

a) venetiis] c *add. sed del.* E   b) bellatorum] ut speramus domino *add. sed del.* E   c) disponat] quod de *add. sed del.* E   d) et gemat infidelitas perfidorum] *mg.* E   e) multisque] et multis *a.c. s.l.* E   f) tuosque] commiliones *add. sed del.* E   g) nos] tibi *add. sed del.* E   h) negotium] omnem *add. sed. del.* E   i) apostolicum in hiis que poterimus] quem nobis possibilem *a.c. mg.* E

B.19

Avignon, 17 September 1365, Urban V to King Peter I

Manuscript: AAV, Reg. Vat. 247, fol. 150[v] (V).
Summaries: Urban V, *Lettres secrètes et curiales*, no. 1968; *Bullarium Cyprium III*, no. v-129.

Carissimo in Christo filio Petro regi Cipri illustri, salutem *etc.*

Audivimus, fili carissime, quod dilectus filius nobilis vir Philippus de Iubilino, miles, dominus de Azoto, consanquineus tuus, quadam inter te et ipsum simultate suborta, tua dilectione privatus, non audet in regia presentia comparere. Cum itaque magnificentiam tuam dedeceat contra Christianos, maxime tuos propinquos, habere rancorem, eo presertim tempore quo contra infideles nostri prosequeris negotium Salvatoris, serenitatem tuam rogamus attente quatenus eundem Philippum, ob reverentiam[a)] Dei ac Apostolice Sedis et nostram, ad tuam revocare gratiam non omittas.

Datum Avinione, XV Kalendas Octobris, anno tertio.

a) reverentiam] reventiam *a.c.* V

B.20

Avignon, 17 September 1365, Urban V to Archbishop Raymond of Nicosia

Manuscript: AAV, Reg. Vat. 247, fol. 150[v] (V).
Summaries: Urban V, *Lettres secrètes et curiales*, no. 1969; *Bullarium Cyprium III*, no. v-130.

Venerabili fratri Raymundo archiepiscopo Nicosiensi, salutem *etc.*

Scribimus carissimo in Christo filio nostro Petro regi Cipri illustri ut dilectum filium nobilem virum Philippum de Iubilino, militem, dominum de Azoto, eiusdem regis consanguineum, zizanie procurante satore, a regie benivolentie gratia – prout audivimus – alienum, ad eandem velit gratiam revocare. Tuam itaque fraternitatem, quam decet discordes, presertim magnates quorum est periculosa multum dissensio, ad concordiam revocare, rogamus et hortamur attente quatenus super huiusmodi reconciliatione eiusdem Philippi apud eundem regem studeas interponere partes tuas.

Datum *ut supra* <Avinione, XV Kalendas Octobris, anno tertio.>

JOHN FRANCE

European Military Development and the Eastern Mediterranean in the Age of Peter I of Cyprus (1359–69)

Military history has often been ignored by 'mainstream' historians as something fit only for the professional instruction of trainee soldiers. But one of its products has been widely accepted, and that is the notion of a 'Military Revolution' in the early modern period, originated by Roberts and developed by Parker.[1] The basis of this idea is that in the sixteenth-century military change became so rapid and so far-reaching that it was transformative, profoundly influencing all the institutions of contemporary society. It has been welcomed especially because it seems to offer a partial but substantial explanation for the wider phenomenon of the rise of the nation state. In the same way medievalists were for long happy to accept the idea that the Carolingians invented the knight because it offered a ready-made explanation for the rise of the Frankish empire. In fact, the notion of turning points, of sudden and dramatic moments producing radical changes, is deeply ingrained and much reinforced amongst professional historians by the hope of professional kudos. It is also a great convenience, in that whole eras can be encapsulated in a neat phrase, and this tends to produce imitation. In this way Jacob Burkhardt's 'Renaissance'[2] ultimately provoked the 'Carolingian', 'Tenth-Century' and 'Twelfth-Century' Renaissances; such a plethora that one wonders quite what died and needed to be reborn so often! Inevitably the striking success of the ideas of Roberts and Parker

---

1 Michael Roberts, 'The Military Revolution, 1560–1660', An Inaugural Lecture Delivered Before the Queen's University of Belfast, 1955 (1956) (repr. in *The Military Revolution Debate: Readings on the Military Transformation of Early Modern Europe*, ed. by Clifford J. Rogers (Boulder: Westview Press, 1995), pp. 13–36); Geoffrey Parker, *The Military Revolution: Military Innovation and the Rise of the West, 1500–1800* (Cambridge: Cambridge University Press, 1988, 1996). On the historiography of this idea, see the excellent introduction by Clifford J. Rogers, 'The Military Revolution in History and Historiography', to the collection, *The Military Revolution Debate*, pp. 1–10.

2 Jacob Burkhardt, *Die Cultur der Renaissance in Italien* (Basel: Schweighauser, 1860).

John France • Swansea University

has inspired the idea of a 'Medieval Military Revolution'.[3] We even have the idea of a 'Punctuated Equilibrium Evolution', which I take to mean either two revolutions or no revolution at all.[4]

The notion of a 'Medieval Military Revolution' has become part of the wider discussion of military trends in Europe, because, if the developments hitherto seen as unique to the early modern period can be discerned in previous centuries, the whole notion of 'revolution' is undermined. It has also been argued that the changes in armies and weapons in the eighteenth century are far more deserving of the title revolutionary.[5] The whole debate has become complicated by the introduction of the notion of a 'Revolution in Military Affairs' (RMA), which signifies abrupt change confined to the military sphere without influencing the wider society. In addition, the Euro-centric nature of the discussion has been widely challenged.[6] This is not the place to examine such a free-wheeling concept. Suffice it to say that amongst medievalists there is common ground that substantial military changes occurred in the first half of the fourteenth century and continued thereafter. In the words of a leading authority: 'There was no single military revolution, but there was experiment and change, and considerable sophistication'.[7] This was really the very period of Peter's formative years. In 1349 he and his brother, John, went to Europe without consulting their father Hugh IV (1324–59) only to be dragged home and confined, while Peter spent the years 1362–65 in the West raising support for his crusade, which, famously, managed to sack Alexandria. In 1368 he tried to revive the crusade, without success.[8] France, the focus of his efforts, was at the very centre of military development at this time, so if there were radical changes he could hardly have been unaware of them.

One of the problems with all these theories of revolution, or at least radical change, is that they tend to assume a homogeneity in warfare, which simply did not exist. Cyprus was the point of collision of two worlds of war. Land warfare in the Eastern Mediterranean was dominated by the Mamluks. They were a standing force

---

3 Andrew Ayton and J. L. Price, *The Medieval Military Revolution: State, Society and Military Change in Medieval and Early Modern Europe* (London: I. B. Tauris, 1995).
4 Clifford J. Rogers, 'The Military Revolutions of the Hundred Years' War', *Journal of Military History*, 57 (1993), 241–78 (pp. 275–78); Clifford J. Rogers, '"As If a New Sun Had Arisen": England's Fourteenth-Century RMA', in *The Dynamics of Military Revolution*, ed. by MacGregor Knox and Williamson Murray (Cambridge: Cambridge University Press, 2001), pp. 15–34; Clifford J. Rogers, 'The Idea of Military Revolutions in Eighteenth and Nineteenth Century Texts', *Revista de História das Ideias*, 30 (2009), 395–415.
5 Jeremy Black, *A Military Revolution. Military Change and European Society 1550–1800* (London: Macmillan, 1991). Black's ideas have subsequently been elaborated in a large number of books and articles.
6 Lisa Blaydes and Eric Chaney, 'The Feudal Revolution and Europe's Rise: Political Divergences of the Christian West and the Muslim World before 1500 CE', *American Political Science Review*, 107/1 (2013), 16–34; Frank Jacob and Gilmar Visoni-Alonzo, 'The Theory of a Military Revolution: Global, Numerous, Endless?', *Revista Universitaria de Historia Militar*, 6/3 (2014), 189–204.
7 Michael Prestwich, *Armies and Warfare in the Middle Ages. The English Experience* (New Haven: Yale University Press, 1996), p. 345. See Rogers, '"As If a New Sun Had Arisen"'.
8 Peter W. Edbury, *The Kingdom of Cyprus and the Crusades 1191–1374* (Cambridge: Cambridge University Press, 1991), pp. 147, 161–62, 170.

of heavily equipped cavalrymen, supported by short-term levies of fast-moving light cavalry, pre-eminently horse-archers. This had proved a winning combination against crusaders and Mongols alike. But this created a battlefield unimaginable in Europe. Even more importantly, Cyprus, the last western bastion in the Eastern Mediterranean, was an island, and naval warfare to some degree imposed its own special conditions.

So what was this 'military revolution' or, at least, the critical changes which had come about by the mid-fourteenth century? It was not the development of gunpowder. Our first certain knowledge of the use of guns dates from 1326 though Roger Bacon recorded a good recipe for gunpowder about 1257. Although ship-mounted guns were used at Arnemuiden in 1338 and were present at Crécy in 1346, they remained very limited weapons.[9] Kelly DeVries and Clifford Rogers suggested that the key development of the early fourteenth century was the rise of infantry and a whole host of others have agreed with them.[10] The mass use of the longbow by the English meant that compact formations of dismounted men-at-arms could not be picked off by enemy archers and attacks against them on horseback or foot could be depleted by arrow-fire. This system of cooperation between the men-at-arms and the bowmen was developed in England and underpinned her successes in the Hundred Years' War. By the time Peter came to the West in 1362, the English appeared to have terminated this conflict by partially dismantling the Kingdom of France.

Other victories by footsoldiers, at Courtrai (1302), Halmyros (1311), Bannockburn (1314), Morgarten (1315), and Laupen (1339), have led historians to posit the eclipse of heavily armed cavalry. In this view Crécy in 1346 was the culmination of a new infantry supremacy. This, it has been suggested, constituted an "Infantry Revolution", and Clifford Rogers thinks that the higher casualties at this time were a result of the ruthlessness of the lower class, who did not share in the consensus over ransom amongst their betters. I take a different view of this apparent infantry resurgence. War leaders were perfectly well aware of the problem posed by their short-term, essentially part-time armies. This affected infantry very severely because their whole effect depended on mass and cohesion, but it also made the coherent use of cavalry difficult because individuals and small groups were unused to working together. Early in his reign Henry II of England (1154–89) tried to systematize the recruitment of infantry by demanding that his great lords should bring fixed quotas when called to war, but this was firmly resisted. Richard I of England (1189–99) conceived of raising a permanent body of 300 knights, to be paid for by remitting military service for taxes. The resistance of the high nobility scuppered the idea, and Richard could not pay for it out of his own resources because it would have cost over half the normal annual income of the crown.[11] The consequence of these failures was that both resorted to the time-honoured solution, which was to hire

---

9   Bert S. Hall, *Weapons and Warfare in Renaissance Europe: Gunpowder, Technology, and Tactics* (Baltimore: Johns Hopkins University Press, 1997), pp. 41–66.
10 Rogers, 'The Military Revolutions of the Hundred Years' War'; Kelly DeVries, *Infantry Warfare in the Early Fourteenth Century: Discipline, Tactics, and Technology* (Rochester, N.Y.: Boydell, 1996).
11 John France, *Western Warfare in the Age of the Crusades 1000–1300* (London: UCL Press, 1999), pp. 67–68, 58.

mercenaries.[12] These were expensive and could be supported only in limited numbers and, like all other soldiers, for short periods. So armies were composites; they might consist of the war-leader's personal followings augmented by mercenaries, those of his landed followers and whoever they could bring with them, along with allies.

In Italy, the second half of the thirteenth century was a period of almost continuous warfare, which was so intense that it overwhelmed the traditional attachment of the city-states to citizen forces. The result was the rise not merely of mercenaries, but of mercenary companies, within which infantry and cavalry had a role to play.[13] The power and success of such longstanding groups of professional soldiers was exemplified by the Grand Catalan Company, which moved on to extraordinary victories in Byzantium and Frankish Greece.[14] In Britain the long wars between England and Scotland produced a parallel effect, the rise of semi-professional warriors who saw profit in war even if they were not precisely mercenaries. In European armies the aristocracy remained in command, but the distinction between those who served as subjects and paid men was eroded and armies were made up more and more of professionals, though they remained short-lived entities. The English experience threw up archers using the longbow which was deadly in the hands of experienced users working in combination with men-at-arms. This combination which arose from the circumstances of war in northern England was the basis of the more sophisticated tactics of Edward III (1327–77) in the fourteenth century discussed by Rogers and others. It should always be remembered, however, that the Hundred Years' War was largely a traditional conflict conducted by the traditional means of bullying peasants. *Chevauchée* actually only means raid and attacking the economic base of your enemy is the most traditional of strategies. Vegetius, a late Roman writer much honoured at this time, had remarked in his famous rules:

> It is preferable to subdue an enemy by famine, raids, and terror, than in battle where fortune tends to have more influence than bravery.[15]

The increasing employment of professional soldiers who were taught their trade in companies made new tactics possible by the coherence that they developed. Their arrival on the scene was not a revolution but the result of a long and fairly complex development, which came to fruition in the early fourteenth century.

Peter I was perfectly familiar with such professional warriors who had a very long history in the crusading states of the eastern Mediterranean.[16] In addition, the western

---

12 David Crouch, 'William Marshal and the Mercenariat', in *Mercenaries and Paid Men. The Mercenary Identity in the Middle Ages*, ed. by John France (Leiden: Brill, 2008), pp. 33–42; John Hosler, *Henry II, a Medieval Soldier at War, 1147–89* (Leiden: Brill, 2007).

13 Michael Mallett, *Mercenaries and their Masters. Warfare in Renaissance Italy* (Totowa, N.J.: Rowman and Littlefield, 1974), especially pp. 6–25.

14 A member, Ramon Muntaner, wrote a history of its rise: *Chronicle*, trans. by Lady Goodenough (Cambridge, Ontario: In parentheses Publications, 2000).

15 Publius Flavius Vegetius Renatus, *Epitoma Rei Militaris / Epitome of Military Science*, trans. by N. P. Milner (Liverpool: Liverpool University Press, 1993), III. 26. p. 108.

16 Nic Morton, *The Crusader States and their Neighbours. A Military History, 1099–1187* (Oxford: Oxford University Press, 2020), pp. 143–53.

settlers had Turcopoles, who seem to have been light cavalry, and the likelihood is that they were paid men. They were certainly an element in the Cypriot armies.[17] Peter understood the value and the ready availability of professionals, especially in Italy. Leontios Makhairas tells us that Peter had sent envoys to Italy in 1360. They were charged with arguing his case for the Cypriot succession against the claims of his nephew, Hugh, before the pope:

> And when they were returning to Cyprus, they fell in with John of Verona whom the king had sent to recruit men at arms at a monthly wage. And at once they landed in Lombardy and recruited many men at arms, and came back together to Cyprus in company with the said John of Verona.[18]

Unfortunately, when these troops arrived in Cyprus trouble arose:

> And on 22 April 1360 after Christ, when King Peter was at Famagusta there arose a great stir and strife among the men at arms, the new recruits (who had been brought from abroad) against the older ones (of the country), Cypriots and Syrians, and two of the strangers were killed.[19]

The king imposed peace with difficulty and hanged the troublemakers. The identity of these Syrians is a puzzle, but it may relate to local Christian Arabs settled in Cyprus.[20] Alternatively Peter may have been casting his net widely and recruiting from Syria itself.

In 1363, while Peter was absent in Europe, the Turks raided Cyprus. The regent sent 'men on foot and men at arms and knights' to the area.[21] The distinction between men-at-arms and knights is important and occurs more than once, notably in 1365 when Peter sent 'knights [...] and many men at arms' for the relief of Gorhigos.[22] The careful distinction reveals that some of these were hired men. And indeed such fellows would have been essential for the ruler of an island with very limited reserves of usable military manpower.

In 1360 Peter was asked for aid against the Turks by the people of Gorhigos (ancient Corycus), a port on the Anatolian coast. The king sent galleys and on them was a certain Robert of Lusa (perhaps Lusignan) with four companies of archers; given the date and the fact that Makhairas says that Robert was English, these could well have been English, though we know nothing else of the man.[23] Gorhigos continued

---

17 Yuval Harari, 'The Military Role of the Frankish Turcopoles: A Reassessment', *Mediterranean Historical Review*, 12 (1997), 75–116.
18 Leontios Makhairas, *Recital concerning the Sweet Land of Cyprus entitled 'Chronicle'*, ed. by Richard M. Dawkins, 2 vols (Oxford: Clarendon Press, 1933), I, § 109.
19 Leontios Makhairas, *Recital*, I, § 111.
20 See Johannes Pahlitzsch's chapter in this volume.
21 Leontios Makhairas, *Recital*, I, § 137.
22 Leontios Makhairas, *Recital*, I, § 194.
23 Leontios Makhairas, *Recital*, I, § 114, II, pp. 98–99, n. 3, with the editor suggesting that he was French. All three manuscripts preserving Makhairas' chronicle give 'ρομπέρτο τε λουζά', with versions V and R specifying that he was English, see Leontios Makhairas, *Χρονικό της Κύπρου. Παράλληλη διπλωματική έκδοση των χειρογράφων*, ed. by Michalis Pieris and Angel Nicolaou-Konnari (Nicosia: Cyprus Research Centre, 2003), p. 123. The form of the name bears no similarity to the way the text delivers the name of the

to be held against the Turks with supplies, galleys, and men from Cyprus. In 1361, Peter seized Adalia (then called Satalia) from the Turks and his *Turcopolier* was left in charge 'with knights, turcopoles and *archers with cross bows* as garrison'; shortly after a Turkish counterattack was repelled by crossbows and longbows.[24] In 1366, Maria of Bourbon of Achaea and Morea recruited mercenaries from Cyprus, suggesting that the island was a known haunt of such men.[25]

These ports of southern Anatolia were important to Cyprus because its wealth depended heavily upon trade. Ships in this period liked to hug coastlines, partly because methods of navigation were very crude, and partly because small ports offered shelter against bad weather and could provide supplies of food and water. Gorhigos and Adalia were remnants of the Christian Armenian Kingdom of Cilicia, and it certainly was important for Cyprus to assist them in their struggle against Turkish attack. Anatolia had broken up into a large number of petty Turkish principalities or *beyliks*.[26] These were states on much the same scale as Cyprus, and by establishing bases on the mainland Peter could threaten them and demand tribute.[27] However, the *beyliks* in combination could be formidable and they controlled ships well able to attack Cyprus itself.[28]

But a war of tit for tat, while it might appear trivial, was actually very expensive. Troops had to be paid and ships built and maintained. Even before the famous expedition against Alexandria in 1365, Makhairas remarks that the wealth garnered by Peter's father, King Hugh IV (1324–58) had been used up by Peter in the expeditions against the Turkish *beyliks*. As a result, his government allowed rich poll-tax payers to buy lifetime exemption with a lump sum, so freeing themselves from taxation in the long run. Measures of this kind were repeated later causing serious damage to the crown's income.[29] Cyprus was not a great power. Its sugar and other exports were limited and taking a profit from foreign traders using its ports, especially Famagusta, was essential. So this kind of aggression against the *beyliks* of Turkey, which was really defensive, was probably justified in terms of protecting trade routes. Even so the cost seems to have been crippling. After Alexandria, the garrison of Adalia mutinied for lack of pay, forcing the king to come with a great fleet to overawe and buy them off.[30]

War with the *beyliks* was expensive, and the more so in that changes in the pattern of trade in the Mediterranean appear to have been damaging the prosperity of

---

Lusignans in Greek and no other source gives Lusignan; it is thus surprising that the Italian translation of the R recension, attributed to Diomedes Strambali, which in almost all cases follows closely its Greek original, gives 'Ruberto de Lusugnan', see Biblioteca Apostolica Vaticana, MS Vat. Lat. 3941, fol. 38ᵛ and *Chronique de Strambaldi*, in *Chroniques d'Amadi et de Strambaldi*, ed. by René de Mas Latrie, 2 vols (Paris: Imprimerie nationale, 1891–93), II, p. 44.

24 Leontios Makhairas, *Recital*, I, §§ 123, 133.
25 Eugene L. Cox, *The Green Count of Savoy. Amadeus VI and Transalpine Savoy in the Fourteenth Century* (Princeton: Princeton University Press, 1967), p. 214.
26 Mehmet Fuat Köprülü, *The Origins of the Ottoman Empire*, trans. by Gary Leiser (New York: State University of New York Press, 1992).
27 Leontios Makhairas, *Recital*, I, § 124.
28 Leontios Makhairas, *Recital*, I, § 116.
29 Leontios Makhairas, *Recital*, I, § 157.
30 Leontios Makhairas, *Recital*, I, §§ 199–201.

Cyprus. Famagusta had, since the fall of Acre in 1291, acted as the key port for trade with the Muslim lands, where merchants of East and West could meet. Taxes on that trade were essential to the wealth of the royal house of Lusignan. But Venice seems to have taken to trading directly with Alexandria, and the land routes for eastern luxury goods through Cilicia and Syria were disrupted by political instability.[31] In addition, Cyprus, like so much of the world, was ravaged by the Black Death. In these circumstances the costs of simply maintaining the kingdom, isolated in a hostile environment, were escalating.

This may well be the real reason why King Peter became so anxious to organize a grand crusade, efforts for which kept him in Europe from 1362 to 1365. The great expedition, which Peter organized and led in 1365, was the act of a gambler 'doubling up' in an effort to reverse a losing streak. The strife with the *beyliks* of Anatolia was costly, but it was inevitable because they were aggressive and capable at times of combining. Picking a quarrel with the local superpower, Mamluk Egypt, was dangerous, but if gains were to be made this was also inevitable. And it was somewhat tempting because the Lusignans would have been aware of the instability of Mamluk Egypt. After 1341, there was a series of violent coups and short-lived sultans, which attended the final collapse of the Bahrī regime in 1367.[32] In 1368, Cyprus and the Mamluk sultan were trying to bring an end to the war which Peter had begun. Makhairas reports in detail how factions at the Mamluk court undermined the negotiations.[33]

A pause in the Hundred Years' War with the Treaty of Brétigny of 1360 seemed to offer the possibility of a major western expedition against the Mamluk regime at a time when it was suffering from this internal instability. However, the death of the French king, John II (1350–64), ruined this prospect. It is unlikely that Peter thought he could recapture Jerusalem with the very limited help that he managed to raise in Europe. Cyprus certainly made a maximum effort to support the king's great business, with 108 ships sailing to Rhodes to meet Peter's fleet coming from Europe.[34] The combined fleet, however, could muster only 165 ships, though how many soldiers this held is a matter of guesswork.[35]

This was, however, a formidable force. We know nothing of the decision-making process in the fleet, but the Cypriots most certainly knew about the problems at the Mamluk court. The success at Alexandria must have owed much to these raging divisions in Cairo. Perhaps also the Mamluk regime had become complaisant. They must have known about the gathering of the Christian fleet, but failed to take precautions. After all, Egypt had not been attacked since the defeat of Louis IX (1226–70) in 1250. And in 1260, they had defeated the Mongols at Ain Jalut and gone on to seize control of Syria.

---

31 Edbury, *Kingdom of Cyprus*, pp. 150–55.
32 Linda S. Northrup, 'The Bahrī Mamluk Sultanate, 1250–1390', in *The Cambridge History of Egypt*, gen. ed. M. W. Daly, 2 vols (Cambridge: Cambridge University Press, 1998), I: *Islamic Egypt 640–1517*, ed. by Carl F. Petry, pp. 242–89.
33 Leontios Makhairas, *Recital*, I, § 225.
34 Leontios Makhairas, *Recital*, I, §§ 161–63.
35 Leontios Makhairas, *Recital*, I, § 167.

Certainly the Christian fleet surprised Alexandria and captured it very quickly. Peter wanted to hold the city and this perhaps reflects his true purpose in launching his expedition, to seize a hostage of such value to the Mamluks as to bring them to terms. He would later try the same thing at Tripoli, which, despite its evident vulnerability, managed to resist.[36] But his men did enormous damage to Alexandria, including firing the land gates, making the city indefensible. They then enjoyed a ferocious period of looting and took 5000 slaves.[37] But when a Mamluk army approached, they refused to fight and the king was forced to retreat back to the ships.

If we consider the make-up of his force we can see why things turned out in this way. The force at Peter's command was fairly typical of fourteenth-century armies except for one of its three elements, being made up of:
a. The king's personal following and his paid men.
b. Noblemen with whom the King had delicate political relations.
c. Professionals contracted to the great nobles.
d. A smattering of genuinely ideologically motivated zealots.

The Cypriot lords were under enormous economic pressure. Peter's aggressive policies were very burdensome, and the rich city of Alexandria offered an opportunity for them and their own men to recover something of what they had spent. The crusaders from the West were there for the short run and had their own followings to satisfy. The contracted soldiers knew from experience that all too often their wages would be late or even unpaid and wanted to assure themselves of loot.

The circumstances under which the army had come together offered little prospect of creating a cohesive fighting force. When the army gathered at Rhodes on 25 August there were tensions which exploded in fighting between some of the ships' crews. They reached Alexandria on 9 October.[38] This was a very short time for Peter to impose himself on the army in the manner of Edward III, whose forces were in any case much less variegated. In this era command was personal: charismatic leadership was essential and this took time to impose itself. The process was not helped when the men were dispersed on ships. The sheer speed of events after the landing and the flight of the Mamluk garrison meant that events went out of control. There was nothing novel in this. Mixed contract armies were as difficult to control as their predecessors, largely because payment was limited and often delayed. Edward III imposed his authority over his armies when they were together, but that was not often, for they frequently spread out to plunder and loot. This kind of beheaviour proved very difficult to restrain even when it was in English interests after the Peace of Brétigny in 1360. In the circumstances, Peter had little choice but to flee the city as the Mamluk army approached.

In the Anglo-French wars the rise of professional soldiers made new tactical developments possible but they were evolved to suit the Franco-English conflict. The Kingdom of Cyprus formed part of a fragmented world extending really from the

---

36 Leontios Makhairas, *Recital*, I, § § 210–12.
37 Leontios Makhairas, *Recital*, I, § § 171–73.
38 Leontios Makhairas, *Recital*, I, § § 164–71.

borders of Ming China, which itself had only been established in the 1340s, through the competing remnants of the Mongol Empire, Rus uneasy under the Golden Horde, Poland-Lithuania enmeshed in its quarrel with the Teutonic Order's *Ordenstaat*, and quarrelling *beyliks* of Anatolia, amongst which the Ottomans had not yet quite become the menace, to the Habsburg lands and the shambles which was late medieval Germany. The Mamluks of Egypt were a superpower, but they were exhausted by their bitter and prolonged war with the Il-Khanids of Iran and wracked by internal tensions. Moreover, as long as they lacked a fleet, the creation of which would be enormously expensive, their reach was limited. It was this situation that had so favoured Hugh IV and Peter early in his reign, in their dealing with the Turkish principalities of Anatolia.

If a real crusade, as envisaged by Peter, had materialized, it is doubtful whether the new methods of the English would have been adopted or even whether they would have been appropriate against the steppe armies of the Mamluks and the Turks of Anatolia. The fiasco of Nicopolis in 1396 and the long run of failures in the face of the Ottomans which followed suggests not. There was no military revolution or indeed any military development in fourteenth-century Europe, which could alter the balance of military advantage between steppe armies like that of the Ottomans and those of the western powers.

Peter's army, a combination of traditional vassals and contracted professional troops, was very much the norm in western Europe. The English, largely through the Scottish wars, had generated powerful forces of archers but replicating them was almost impossible for states with no training facilities and no standing armies, and in any case they operated in a very different environment and only in specific conditions. Peter was fighting a traditional kind of war such as had dominated Europe for centuries and was, in fact, still going on in France, ravaging and destruction. Of course, the particular twist here was that raids had to be carried out by sea, and once more in a traditional way largely using galleys and adapted merchantmen. It would be another century before a safe method of deploying gunpowder weapons on ships was worked out. And Peter lived more than a generation before the Ottoman reforms of the 1380s created a new and more 'balanced' kind of standing army, which would threaten Europe for nearly three centuries.

The key change in European warfare in the early fourteenth century was the professionalisation of fighting men made possible by the frequent and long-lasting wars, which wracked the continent from the late thirteenth century. In particular circumstances this gave rise to the new tactics of Edward III in the Anglo-French wars, which have sometimes been heralded as ushering in a 'Military Revolution'. But the reality was that war remained largely a matter of sieges, ravaging, and destruction. The new factor was that this was carried out by more dedicated and ruthless soldiers, who, when controlled properly, were highly efficient fighters. In particular places at particular times they could operate in new and fairly complex ways, but, for example, there was no way any king of Cyprus could have created a large body of longbowmen. In the absence of standing forces this was not a transferable skill. The value of this study of war in the reign of Peter I is that it reveals the precise nature of the most important change in European warfare, its professionalisation. Whatever charges may be levied against Peter, it cannot be said that he was outdated in his military methods.

CLÉMENT ONIMUS

Peter I of Lusignan's Crusade and the Reaction of the Mamluk Sultanate

On 9 October 1365,[1] the army led by the king of Cyprus Peter I of Lusignan (r. 1359–69) arrived within sight of Alexandria, the main port of Egypt under the rule of the Mamluk Sultan al-Ashraf Shaʿbān (r. 1363–76). The crusaders conquered and plundered the city and left one week later while Mamluk relief forces were approaching.

This event had great repercussions in the Christian West as well as in the Muslim Eastern Mediterranean. Its background and consequences are well known thanks to the works of George Hill, Aziz Suryal Atiya, and Peter Edbury.[2] Yet, most of our knowledge concerning the crusade relates to Cyprus and Peter I's foreign policy. In this article, I propose to change the heuristic perspective and to look at the event with Mamluk eyes in order to understand the surprisingly moderate reaction of the sultanate.

Even prior to George Hill's exhaustive work on the history of Cyprus (1948),[3] Aziz Suryal Atiya (1938) was the first to deal extensively with the Arabic source material,[4] as he himself, along with Étienne Combe, later edited the principal Arabic text concerning the Alexandrian crusade, al-Nuwayrī's *Kitāb al-ilmām*.[5] Nevertheless, Jo Van Steenbergen has recently demonstrated that al-Nuwayrī's work, although the most precise description of the crusade and its context, is actually not the most accurate: al-Nuwayrī was an Alexandrian citizen and eyewitness to the events but

---

1 I shall give exclusively the Julian dates and not the hijra ones.
2 Peter W. Edbury, 'The Crusading Policy of King Peter I of Cyprus, 1359–1369', in *The Eastern Mediterranean Lands in the Period of the Crusades*, ed. by Peter M. Holt (Warminster: By Aris & Philips, 1977), pp. 90–105; Peter W. Edbury, *The Kingdom of Cyprus and the Crusades, 1191–1374* (Cambridge: Cambridge University Press, 1991).
3 Sir George Hill, *A History of Cyprus*, 4 vols (Cambridge: Cambridge University Press, 1940–52; repr. 2010), II: *The Frankish Period, 1192–1432*.
4 Aziz Suryal Atiya, *The Crusades in the Later Middle Ages* (London: Methuen, 1938; repr. 1965), pp. 319–78.
5 Al-Nuwayrī, *Kitāb al-ilmām aw mirʾāt al-ʿajāʾib*, ed. by Etienne Combe and ʿAzīz Suryāl ʿAṭiya, 7 vols (Hyderabad: Dāʾirat al-Maʿārif al-ʿUthmāniyya, 1973/1996).

Clément Onimus • University of Paris 8 – Vincennes-Saint Denis

he was also partial. Consequently, his narrative is not entirely reliable.[6] Therefore, it must be compared with the other Arabic sources, which give a Cairene or a Syrian point of view, such as al-Maqrīzī's and al-ʿAynī's works,[7] written in the sultan's capital, Cairo, during the first half of the fifteenth century, or Ibn Qāḍī Shuhba's and Ṣāliḥ ibn Yaḥyā's works,[8] which both represent Syrian views of the events, the former written in Damascus at the beginning of the fifteenth century and the latter in Lebanon in the first third of the fifteenth century. These sources, which, in the absence of Mamluk diplomatic documents,[9] constitute the only available Mamluk discourse on that topic, should shed some new light on a major question that the Christian chronicles of William of Machaut and Leontios Makhairas neglect:[10] Why did the Mamluks react so moderately to the sack of one of their main cities?

My hypothesis, in this article, is that Mamluk foreign policy was contingent upon the conflict-ridden state of affairs in the sultanate's internal political sphere. This made the Mamluks incapable of reacting militarily and caused them to make the Venetians and Genoese part of the diplomatic game, in which suspicion played a key role. The diplomatic procedure ended with a peace treaty that left unsatisfied both the sultanate and its Cypriot enemy.

The Main Military Power in the Eastern Mediterranean

On 16 October 1365, the Mamluk vanguard led by Amir Quṭlūbughā al-Manṣūrī reconquered Alexandria without battle.[11] It did not go further. The sultanate's moderate military reaction is surprising in two respects, namely its ideology and its supremacy.

---

6   Jo Van Steenbergen considers him a fanatic and a storyteller: Jo Van Steenbergen, 'The Alexandrian Crusade (1365) and the Mamlūk Sources: Reassessment of the Kitāb al-Ilmām of an-Nuwayrī al-Iskandaranī (d. AD 1372)', in *East and West in the Crusader States. Context – Contacts – Confrontations*, III: *Acta of the Congress Held at Hernen Castle in September 2000*, ed. by Krijna Ciggaar and Herman G. B. Teule, Orientalia Lovaniensa Analecta 125 (Leuven: Peeters, 2003), pp. 123–37.
7   Al-Maqrīzī, *Kitāb al-sulūk li-maʿrifat duwal al-mulūk*, ed. by Saʿīd ʿAbd al-Fattāḥ ʿĀshūr, III/1 (Cairo: Maṭbaʿat dār al-kutub, 1970); Badr al-Dīn al-ʿAyni, *ʿIqd al-jumān fī taʾrīkh ahl al-zamān*, Istanbul, Sultan Ahmet III Library, MS A 2911 B2.
8   Ibn Qāḍī Shuhba, *Taʾrīkh Ibn Qāḍī Shuhba*, ed. by ʿAdnān Darwīsh, III (Damascus: PIFD, 1994); Ṣāliḥ ibn Yaḥyā, *Taʾrīkh Bayrūt*, ed. by Francis Hours and Kamāl Sulaymān al-Ṣalībī (Beirut: Dār al-Mashraq, 1969).
9   A research in al-Qalqashandī's chancery manual was fruitless.
10 Leontios Makhairas, *Recital concerning the Sweet Land of Cyprus entitled 'Chronicle'*, ed. by Richard M. Dawkins, 2 vols (Oxford: Clarendon Press, 1932); Leontios Makhairas, Χρονικό της Κύπρου. Παράλληλη διπλωματική έκδοση των χειρογράφων, ed. by Michalis Pieris and Angel Nicolaou-Konnari, Texts and Studies in the History of Cyprus, 48 (Nicosia: Cyprus Research Centre, 2003). Sophie Hardy, *Édition critique de la Prise d'Alixandrie de Guillaume de Machaut* (unpublished doctoral thesis, Université d'Orléans, 2011): ftp://ftp.univ-orleans.fr/theses/sophie.hardy_1730.pdf [accessed 21 June 2021], William of Machaut, *The Capture of Alexandria*, trans. by Janet Shirley, introduction and notes by Peter W. Edbury (Aldershot: Ashgate, 2001).
11 Badr al-Dīn al-ʿAyni, *ʿIqd al-jumān fī taʾrīkh ahl al-zamān*, Istanbul, Sultan Ahmet III Library, MS A 2911 B2, fols 50^v–49^r.

As regards the ideological point of view, we have to recall that the Mamluk sultanate established itself in the mid-thirteenth century after the usurpation of the throne by the emirs, i.e., the officers of the regiment of slave soldiers recruited by Sultan al-Ṣāliḥ Ayyūb (r. 1240–49). During this usurpation, they killed his son Tūrān Shāh, the last sultan of the Ayyubid dynasty founded by Saladin eighty years earlier, and elected one of their own sultan. A major problem of the new regime was that they lacked legitimacy not only because they had assassinated the sultan but also because they had the status of freed slaves. According to Leontios Makhairas, Peter I alluded to this lack of legitimacy in his correspondence with Sultan Shaʿbān, whom he accused of being sultan merely by chance and not thanks to the nobility of his lineage.[12] The illegitimacy of the slaves' kingship is a classical theme in anti-Mamluk propaganda.[13] Nevertheless, Peter I could not be more wrong given that Sultan Shaʿbān was actually the son and grandson of sultans – which shows that this discourse had become a *topos* in the conflict-ridden diplomatic relations of that time.

The Mamluks asserted their claims to be the legitimate rulers of Egypt and Syria through their successful leadership in the defence of Islam. As soon as their regime was established, they defeated the Seventh Crusade led by King Louis IX of France in 1249 in the battle of al-Manṣūra. Moreover, they took advantage of this victory and seized power while concealing the sultan's death, which had occurred just before the battle. Over the following 250 years, the Mamluks' legitimacy relied on their presenting themselves as the sword of the faith, the protectors of the Holy Places, and the saviour of Islam against the Franks and the Mongols.[14] This regime developed an ideology emphasizing the martial virtues of the Turkish military slaves who were imported from the Kipchak plain into Egypt and Syria. This ideology was put into practice during the first decades of the sultanate, when the Mamluks, under the rule of the sultans Baybars, Qalawūn, and Khalīl, held the Mongol Ilkhāns of Persia in check and annihilated what remained of the Latin Crusader States in mainland Syria until the fall of Acre in 1291. The role of this ideology in the legitimation of the regime and its implementation in the struggle against the Franks during the founding period of the Mamluk sultanate are in contrast to the sultanate's renunciation of any violent reaction to the attack of the kingdom of Cyprus.

During the time in question the sultanate exerted a geopolitical hegemony over the Near East. Since the first quarter of the fourteenth century, after Ilkhān Ghazan's death (r. 1295–1304) and the disintegration of the Mongol empire of Persia in 1335, the Mamluks had dominated the Near East. As the Mongols were contained and the crusaders expelled from the Syrian mainland, the Mamluk sultanate became a hegemonic regional power. It claimed a sort of suzerainty over the whole Muslim world and exerted political patronage over most of its neighbouring states.[15]

---

12 Leontios Makhairas, *Recital*, I, § 230, pp. 212–13.
13 Anne F. Broadbridge, 'Mamluk Legitimacy and the Mongols: The Reigns of Baybars and Qalāwūn', *Mamlūk Studies Review*, 5 (2001), 105–07; Anne F. Broadbridge, *Kingship and Ideology in the Islamic and Mongol Worlds* (Cambridge: Cambridge University Press, 2008), pp. 12–13, 29, 170.
14 Broadbridge, *Kingship and Ideology*.
15 Broadbridge, *Kingship and Ideology*, pp. 100–67.

Anatolia (called al-Rūm in Arabic sources) was divided into numerous Turkish emirates or 'beyliks'. Mesopotamia was under the rule of the weak Jalā'irid sultanate, which ruled Baghdad from 1336 to 1412. Upper Mesopotamia and eastern Anatolia were dominated by Turcoman and Kurdish tribes. The Hejaz (western Arabia) stood under Mamluk suzerainty, although the local *sharīf*s exerted direct rule over the region. Even the Golden Horde, which was an ally of the Mamluk sultanate, entered a phase of disintegration during the second half of the fourteenth century.

As a result, the Mamluk sultanate was an unrivalled hegemonic power until the last quarter of the fourteenth century and the expansion of the Timurid empire under Tamerlane (r. 1370–1405). Nevertheless, the Mamluk sultanate no longer pursued an imperialistic policy. Before the invasion of Armenia in 1375 (which was a consequence of Peter I's crusade) it never attempted to expand beyond its borders despite the weakness of its neighbours. The Cypriots were aware of Mamluk military superiority, as becomes clear from the accounts of William of Machaut[16] and Leontios Makhairas,[17] who frequently mention the power of the sultan and the impossibility of resisting his armies if the western crusaders abandoned Cyprus. Although Mamluk foreign policy did not prioritize external conquests during these decades, al-Nuwayrī's personal statements make clear that the author had little doubt of the military strength of the sultanate and that he hoped its army would invade the kingdom of Cyprus.[18] There is not sufficient evidence to evaluate the size of the Mamluk army[19] but despite its diminution caused by the impoverishment of the country after the Black Death, there is no doubt that it remained a powerful force capable of provoking the retreat of Tamerlane's army at the end of the fourteenth century.[20] For all these reasons, the moderate reaction of the Mamluks seems to contradict the sultanate's ideology and notion of supremacy.

The Mamluk Military Reaction: The Defence of the Coastland

Actually, the Mamluks did try to launch a counter-attack. As some Arab authors give very accurate information about various European events, we may assume that the Mamluks had access to intelligence the source of which is unknown. Italian merchants

---

16 For example, William of Machaut denounces the cowardice of the viscount de Turenne who feared that the sultan would come with 25 million soldiers. Later, William explains that the Cypriot army was not strong enough to fight the Mamluk army on its own: 'Ses gens de Chipre ne porroient / Rien encontre euls, s'il y venoient', Hardy, *Édition critique de la* Prise d'Alixandrie, pp. 98, 174, ll. 3367–76, 6047–48.
17 The same idea can be found in Leontios Makhairas, *Recital*, I, § 192, pp. 172–73.
18 Al-Nuwayrī, *Ilmām*, III, pp. 202–03, 207–09, V, p. 277.
19 Mounira Chapoutot-Remadi, *Liens et relations au sein de l'élite mamlouke sous les premiers sultans baḥrides, 648/1250–741/1340* (unpublished doctoral thesis, Université de Provence, 1993), p. 283, proposes a total of 65,000 soldiers during the fifteenth century but this might be an overestimated number.
20 In 1396, Sultan Barqūq led the Mamluk army to Syria and provoked the retreat of Tamerlane without a fight. Tamerlane, however, came back in 1401 and managed to rout the Mamluk army.

may have had a hand in that. They were well informed, for instance, about the activities of the pope[21] or the gathering of a fleet by Peter I.[22] For this reason, a *ribāṭ* ('fort') had been built on the coast of Alexandria one year before the crusade.[23] Apparently, the Mamluks made themselves ready for a war against Cyprus.

More important than gathering intelligence was improving the defensive structures of the shores against a possible new attack by the Cypriots. As soon as the Mamluk army entered Alexandria, orders were given to fortify the city, dig a moat, and restore the destroyed walls and gates,[24] which Sultan Shaʿbān later inspected while making his royal entry into Alexandria in fear of another attack.[25] Several times, the sultan or the *atābak al-ʿasākir*, i.e., the commander in chief of the army, sent reinforcements from Cairo, where most of the Egyptian army was garrisoned, in order to protect the city. In February 1366, Alexandria, which had already a peculiar administrative status as *thaghr* ('march'),[26] was upgraded in the administrative hierarchy: the city's new governor, *sharīf* Baktamur, the *atābak's* right-hand man and former prefect of Cairo, was no longer merely a *wālī* ('prefect') but a *nāʾib al-salṭana* ('viceroy') with the exceptional honorific title of *malik al-umarāʾ* ('king of the emirs'),[27] which was generally reserved for the viceroy of Damascus and sometimes the viceroy of Aleppo.[28] This administrative change had important consequences: the new governor was an emir of 100 and commander of 1000, which means that he was in charge of 100 Mamluks and 1000 cavalrymen of the *ḥalqa*, a division of the Mamluk army. Since he arrived with an emir of 40 as well as an emir of 10 and 500 cavalrymen, he had 1650 soldiers in total. Later, on 7 December 1367, a new governor arrived in Alexandria with an army of twenty emirs of 40 and 10 and three chamberlains, so the relief forces amounted to about 1700 cavalrymen.[29] Once again, in July 1369, twenty-three emirs were sent from Cairo to Alexandria in order to defend the city against John of Morphou.[30] These stable numbers (twenty-three emirs and about 1700 cavalrymen) show the consistency of Mamluk policy concerning the defence of Alexandria in contrast to other aspects of the Mamluk military reaction, as we shall see below. The efficiency (or incompetence) of these governors in protecting

---

21 Al-Nuwayrī, *Ilmām*, V, pp. 283, 286, VI, p. 403.
22 Al-Nuwayrī, *Ilmām*, II, pp. 110–11. Peter of Lusignan is designated with a double French-Greek name by al-Nuwayrī as *Ribiyar ibn Riyūk*, that is in French '*roi Pierre fils de roi Hugues*', and *Buṭrus*, that is in Greek *Petros*.
23 Al-Nuwayrī, *Ilmām*, p. 150.
24 The sultan feared that the news of Peter I's death was a ruse. Al-Nuwayrī, *Ilmām*, III, pp. 212–15.
25 15–17 December 1368. Al-Nuwayrī, *Ilmām*, V, p. 380; VI, pp. 1–31.
26 Francesco Apellaniz, 'Alexandrie, l'évolution d'une ville-port (1360–1450)' in *Alexandrie médiévale 4*, ed. by Christian Décobert, Jean-Yves Empereur, and Christophe Picard (Alexandria: Centre d'études alexandrines, 2011), p. 210.
27 The new governor arrives on 15 Jumādā II 767: al-Maqrīzī, *Sulūk*, III, pp. 114–15.
28 Maurice Gaudefroy-Demombynes, *La Syrie à l'époque des Mamelouks d'après les auteurs arabes* (Paris: Geuthner, 1923), pp. 141–44.
29 The data are not precise: the rank of the chamberlains is not clear and it is said that 20 emirs join the viceroy although the list that follows has only 19 names. Al-Nuwayrī, *Ilmām*, V, pp. 193–94.
30 Al-Nuwayrī, *Ilmām*, VI, pp. 384–91.

the city must have been frequently discussed among the Alexandrian population, for al-Nuwayrī's work contains a number of positive or negative personal judgments about them and sometimes digresses to a sort of panegyric of viceroy Ibn 'Arrām.

One of the defensive strategies against naval attacks consisted in arming the shoreline with troops. That is what Emir Janghara did when Peter I's fleet arrived in Alexandria: he ordered most of his soldiers to make a sortie so as to prevent the Franks at all costs from disembarking, even if the battle was to take place in the foreshore.[31] Although this strategy failed in Alexandria, the Mamluks adopted it several times on the Syrian coast against Cypriot invasions: in vain in Tripoli in September 1367,[32] but successfully in Latakia in October 1367,[33] and in Beirut and Jubail in June 1369.[34]

The defence of the Syrian coast required huge armies and efficient means of communication.[35] When the Mamluks conquered the coastland from the Crusader States, they destroyed most of the coastal fortifications in order to prevent the use of any stronghold as a base by a potential new crusade.[36] The armies were garrisoned in the provincial capitals (ruled by viceroys), which were not located on the coast, with the exception of Tripoli. Most of the emirs were in Damascus and Aleppo but also in Safed, Hamāh, and Kerak.[37] In order to defend the littoral, the Mamluks had constructed roads leading from the capitals to the coastal cities. Peter I tried to take advantage of this situation in January 1367 by attacking Tripoli during the winter, as he was informed that the governor and his retinue were absent and he hoped that the roads were blocked by snow.[38] To prevent such a surprise attack, the Mamluks, beginning with Sultan Baybars (r. 1260–77), had established an efficient postal network and had built postal stations with horses and pigeons as well as fires lit on mountain summits in the event of danger, as happened in September 1367 when the Cypriot fleet left Tripoli in the direction of Ayās.[39] When the alarm was raised, the viceroy of Damascus, chief emir in Syria, and the other viceroys summoned the provincial armies and led them to fight. That is what happened in Ayās, where the viceroys of Aleppo and Tripoli met and defeated Peter I's army.

The Mamluks also entrusted local emirs with the protection of the coastland. After an expedition against non-Muslim populations in 1305, which ended with the sack of

---

31 Al-Nuwayrī, *Ilmām*, II, pp. 143–49.
32 Hardy, *Édition critique de la Prise d'Alixandrie*, pp. 194–99; Leontios Makhairas, *Recital*, I, § 210, pp. 190–93; Ibn Qāḍī Shuhba, *Ta'rīḫ*, III, pp. 308–09; al-Maqrīzī, *Sulūk*, III, pp. 149–50; al-Nuwayrī, *Ilmām*, V, pp. 104–07, 123–25.
33 Leontios Makhairas, *Recital*, I, § 212, pp. 192–93; Ibn Qāḍī Shuhba, *Ta'rīḫ*, III, p. 390; al-Nuwayrī, *Ilmām*, V, pp. 161–89.
34 Leontios Makhairas, *Recital*, I, § 285, pp. 274–75; al-Maqrīzī, *Sulūk*, III, pp. 173–75; al-Nuwayrī, *Ilmām*, VI, pp. 384–91.
35 On Mamluk Syria, see Gaudefroy-Demombynes, *Syrie*; Anne Troadec, *Les Mamelouks dans l'espace syrien: stratégies de domination et résistances (658/1260–741/1341)* (unpublished doctoral thesis, EPHE, Paris, 2014).
36 Sultan Saladin pursued the same policy at the end of the twelfth century.
37 Ghazza is sometimes added to this list.
38 Al-Nuwayrī, *Ilmām*, V, p. 186.
39 Al-Nuwayrī, *Ilmām*, V, p. 182.

the Kasrawān region in the northern Lebanon Mountain, this territory was granted to Turcoman tribal chiefs along with the duty to defend it. In the south, the coastal area around Beirut stood under the responsibility of the emirs of the Gharb, a local Arab dynasty called Buḥtur, whose history was written by one of its members in the fifteenth century, Ṣāliḥ ibn Yaḥyā. Most of Ṣāliḥ's narrative concerning these events focuses on a quarrel between his family[40] and the Turcoman chieftains who obtained from *Atābak* Yalbughā, the regent of the kingdom during the sultan's minority, the fiscal grant[41] that used to be allotted to the Buḥtur, because they promised to provide 1000 men to conquer Cyprus. Eventually, the Lebanese dynasty was given back its grant thanks to the intercession of a qadi. Although this event may be considered an isolated incident, it shows how internal quarrels linked to the institutional structure of the Mamluk regime could influence foreign policy and thus could be used as a pretext or an argument for far-reaching decisions. According to Ṣāliḥ ibn Yaḥyā the event had serious implications for the history of the coastland, as the Turcoman tribes had to flee to Anatolia because they were unable to muster the troops they had promised.[42]

In short, the Mamluk sultanate efficiently organized the defence of its littoral and managed to repel several Frankish attacks: Muslim sources mention that in September 1367 an expeditionary corps from Damascus and Hamāh led by Emir Jirjī arrived in Tripoli along with Turcoman tribes. Their dust warned the Franks of their coming and provoked their retreat. Although William of Machaut presents the battle as a Cypriot victory, all other sources agree that it was a Mamluk victory.[43] Other attacks occurred in October 1367 in Latakia and Ayās[44], in May and June 1369 in Sayda, Beirut, Jubail and Ayās.[45]

The Fleet

As David Ayalon has explained, the Mamluks' most vulnerable point was their fleet. Although his interpretation is questionable—a result of the scornful comments uttered by Mamluk cavalrymen about the navy—there is no doubt that the Mamluks had no permanent navy.[46] Despite their hegemony on land they possessed no naval power.

---

40 Among whom was his own father.
41 The Mamluk military organization is based on the allotment of fiscal grants (*iqṭāʿ*) to a military officer (*emir*), which provides him with the necessary revenue to buy and train slave-soldiers (*mamlūk*) and their horses and to maintain a household (*bayt*).
42 Ṣāliḥ ibn Yaḥyā, *Taʾrīkh Bayrūt*, pp. 178–80.
43 Hardy, *Édition critique de la* Prise d'Alixandrie, pp. 194–99; Leontios Makhairas, *Recital*, I, § 210, pp. 190–93; Ibn Qāḍī Shuhba, *Taʾrīkh*, III, pp. 308–09; al-Maqrīzī, *Sulūk*, III, pp. 149–50; Al-Nuwayrī, *Ilmām*, V, pp. 79, 104–07, 123–25.
44 Hardy, *Édition critique de la* Prise d'Alixandrie, pp. 200–05; Leontios Makhairas, *Recital*, I, § 212, pp. 192–95; Ibn Qāḍī Shuhba, *Taʾrīkh*, III, p. 390; al-Nuwayrī, *Ilmām*, V, pp. 161–89.
45 Leontios Makhairas, *Recital*, I, § § 285–86, pp. 274–75; al-Maqrīzī, *Sulūk*, III, pp. 173–75; al-Nuwayrī, *Ilmām*, VI, pp. 384–91.
46 David Ayalon, 'Les Mamelouks et la puissance navale', in *Le phénomène mamelouk dans l'Orient islamique*, ed. by David Ayalon (Paris: PUF, 1996), pp. 109–24.

Nevertheless, Mamluk sovereigns ordered the building of ships for specific objectives like the conquest of Cyprus under Sultan Baybars in 1270, which failed, and under Sultan Barsbāy in 1426, which was successful.[47] Thus, it comes as no surprise that according to Ibn Qāḍī Shuhba *Atābak* Yalbughā ordered his men to build ships in the Syrian coastland as early as November 1365,[48] one month after the aggression had occurred. In April–May 1366, the *Atābak* entrusted Emir Baydamur with the construction of ships in Beirut, close to the forests of Lebanon, but the masts, yards and oars as well as skilled labour had to be imported from elsewhere.[49] The building site was located in the interior in order to avoid its destruction by the Cypriots.[50] In January–February 1366, *Atābak* Yalbughā issued the same order in Cairo: he instructed Vizier Mājid ibn al-Qazwīna to gather wood, iron, tools, and carpenters, and entrusted Emir Ṭaybughā and Bahā' al-Dīn ibn al-Mufassar with the construction of an Egyptian fleet. As the Mamluk army had no specialists in naval warfare, he had to summon Maghrebin sailors who helped build the ships as well as Turcoman tribesmen and people from Upper Egypt.[51] Ten months later the construction was completed and on 28 November 1366 the fleet was able to cast off on the Nile River. A great ceremony took place in presence of Catalan envoys.[52] This fleet is supposed to have numbered 100[53] or 200[54] boats, each of which was entrusted to an emir.[55] In a very short time the Mamluk sultanate managed to compensate for its naval inferiority. Moreover, in May 1366 Yalbughā had received an Ottoman embassy that proposed to send 100 ships as reinforcement for the war against Cyprus. Despite this generosity Yalbughā postponed the acceptance of the offer in order to prepare his own fleet, which was not yet ready.[56]

Indeed, some of these ships participated in the naval expeditions against corsairs, but not before March 1368.[57] Sultan Shaʿbān summoned the Maghrebin captain of

---

47 The island became tributary to the sultan, see Albrecht Fuess, 'Was Cyprus a Mamluk Protectorate? Mamluk Policies toward Cyprus between 1426 and 1517', *Journal of Cyprus Studies*, 11 (2005), 11–28 (p. 11).
48 The Syrian historian Ibn Qāḍī Shuhba says the order arrived during the months of November–December 1365 in the Syrian coastal cities (Ibn Qāḍī Shuhba, *Ta'rīkh*, III, p. 272). But the Cairene al-Maqrīzī mentions the Syrian order at the same date as the Egyptian order, that is in January–February 1366 (al-Maqrīzī, *Sulūk*, III, p. 113).
49 Ṣāliḥ ibn Yaḥyā in another passage (*Ta'rīkh Bayrūt*, pp. 190–91) says that Emir Shihāb al-Dīn had been ordered to cut the cypresses of the Lebanese mountain to make arrows.
50 Ṣāliḥ ibn Yaḥyā, *Ta'rīkh Bayrūt*, pp. 29–30.
51 Al-Maqrīzī, *Sulūk*, III, pp. 113, 129–30.
52 Al-Nuwayrī, *Ilmām*, III, pp. 232–33. I note that the Catalan ambassadors are supposed to have seen the crusader fleet in Cyprus on 26 November 1366, two days earlier. There may be a mistake concerning the date, either in al-Nuwayrī or in Leontios Makhairas. See Leontios Makhairas, *Recital*, I, §§ 189–90, pp. 168–71.
53 Al-Maqrīzī, *Sulūk*, III, pp. 113, 129–30; al-Nuwayrī, *Ilmām*, III, p. 231.
54 Hardy, *Édition critique de la Prise d'Alixandrie*, p. 174, l. 6054.
55 Al-Maqrīzī, *Sulūk*, III, pp. 129–30.
56 Al-Maqrīzī, *Sulūk*, III, p. 121.
57 There are some inconsistencies concerning the dates but we can assume that the captain was summoned in mid-March 1368, left Alexandria at the end of the month and came back in mid-April or at the beginning of May.

the Alexandrian arsenal, Ibrāhīm al-Tāzī, to Cairo to congratulate him for his firm response to John and Peter of Grimante's raid on the port of Alexandria a few days earlier. The sultan proposed that al-Tāzī command his navy, which was moored in Būlāq, the river port of Cairo, in an invasion of Cyprus. Captain Ibrāhīm al-Tāzī asked only for one or two of these ships,[58] as he wanted first to inspect the sea and the coastland of Cyprus. Al-Nuwayrī praises the quick success of the captain, who managed to send a little boat with spoils as soon as 30 March and seized one or two other boats near Cyprus before the Genoese galleys of the Lusignan king gave chase to them.[59] Despite the laudatory terms used by the Muslim authors to speak about Captain Ibrāhīm, it is noteworthy that this naval counterattack took place with much delay, two and a half years after the crusade, although the fleet had been ready ten months after the crusade, and furthermore that it did not last more than a month.[60] There is no other occurrence of Mamluk naval warfare, if we except the Maghrebin and Turcoman assault on Frankish ships that were attacking other boats in the western harbour of Alexandria in July 1369.[61] On the whole, the enormous war effort of the Mamluks to build a navy was in vain.

The Causes of the Military Failure

Why did such a powerful fleet fail to engage in a naval war against the Cypriots? The only sources that try to give an explanation for this failure refer to the death of Atābak Yalbughā.[62] Yet, this does not explain why his successors deployed neither the large fleet that was ready to fight on the Nile River nor the fleet that had been built on the Lebanese shore. Likewise, nothing is said about the Ottoman proposal. Moreover, should we agree with William of Machaut's statement that Yalbughā's death was provoked by his willingness to make peace,[63] which is most doubtful, his successors and murderers would have proceeded to an instant military counter-strike. Be that as it may, the hawkish policy was abandoned after Yalbughā's assassination, and various explanations can be given for that.

First, the construction of the Syrian fleet was hampered not only by the looting and destruction of the naval material during the sacks of Tartūs and Bāniyās in September 1367 by the Cypriot fleet[64] but also by the misappropriation of funds

---

58 Al-Nuwayrī states that he took two ships but al-Maqrīzī is more accurate and says that he took one ship from among the Nile fleet and took the other one from the harbour of Alexandria.
59 Leontios Makhairas, *Recital*, I, § 219, pp. 200–01; al-Maqrīzī, *Sulūk*, III, p. 159; al-Nuwayrī, *Ilmām*, V, pp. 277–83.
60 Leontios Makhairas, *Recital*, I, § 219, pp. 200–01; al-Maqrīzī, *Sulūk*, III, p. 159; al-Nuwayrī, *Ilmām*, V, pp. 283–86.
61 Al-Maqrīzī, *Sulūk*, III, p. 176.
62 Ṣāliḥ ibn Yaḥyā, *Ta'rīkh Bayrūt*, pp. 29–30.
63 Hardy, *Édition critique de la* Prise d'Alixandrie, pp. 175–78, ll. 6095–6184.
64 Hardy, *Édition critique de la* Prise d'Alixandrie, pp. 200–05; Leontios Makhairas, *Recital*, I, § § 210–13, pp. 190–95; Ibn Qāḍī Shuhba, *Ta'rīkh*, III, p. 390; Nuwayrī, *Ilmām*, V, pp. 161–89.

by the emirs who were in charge. One of these emirs, Baydamur, was eventually arrested in January 1368 and replaced by a team consisting of another emir, a qadi, and a scribe.[65] Despite the significant amounts of taxes levied for the Syrian fleet, the sources do not mention any activity of these ships. Actually, Ṣāliḥ ibn Yaḥyā relates that only two transport ships, which were destined for transferring masts for other ships, were made ready to set sail but eventually were left rotting in the harbour of Beirut. The rest of the fleet rotted on the shore and the inhabitants looted the iron.[66]

But the main cause of the naval failure was political instability. Besides the lack of a permanent navy, internal conflicts (*fitna*) were the second major weakness of the Mamluk sultanate. The power struggle between emirs, Mamluks, and sultans was an extremely frequent phenomenon in Mamluk history. As Jo Van Steenbergen has explained, the Mamluk regime was only temporarily stable when the regime was united under a strong man, the sultan, or a powerful emir, who managed to keep this coalition of officers under his patronage. Periodically, the state disintegrated when the officers' households opposed each other like autonomous political entities. During these conflict periods, the chief emirs exerted patronage in order to extend their network over the whole Mamluk elite.[67]

After Sultan al-Nāṣir Muḥammad's death in 1341, several periods of turmoil and political chaos passed until his son, Sultan Ḥasan, restored sultanic authority in 1358. But three years later he was overthrown by one of his own Mamluks, who became the ruler of the kingdom, Emir Yalbughā al-Khāṣṣakī.[68]

During his five-year rule, Yalbughā's position was not entirely safe, as Emir Ṭaybughā al-Ṭawīl competed with him. Therefore, when, in October 1365, a homing pigeon brought him the news that the Cypriot fleet was within sight of Alexandria, he believed that this was a ruse of his rival to lure him away from Cairo and take power in his absence. Instead of raising the army, he took refuge in his dwelling outside Cairo to deal with a rebellion. He took action only four days later when he finally realized that the message was true.[69]

The conflict broke out in February 1366 and Yalbughā overcame Ṭaybughā al-Ṭawīl.[70] As the only leading emir, he initiated the construction of the fleet, but in November 1366 his Mamluks revolted against his cruelty. The young Sultan al-Ashraf Shaʿbān took advantage of the situation and supported the rebels. The navy on the Nile River engaged in the fighting in the midst of the battle and became one of the

---

65 Ibn Qāḍī Shuhba, *Ta'rīkh*, III, pp. 312–13.
66 These boats were named after the names of two emirs, probably the ones that they were entrusted to: Ṣāliḥ ibn Yaḥyā, *Ta'rīkh Bayrūt*, pp. 29–30.
67 Concerning the Mamluk *fitna*, see Jo Van Steenbergen, *Order out of Chaos: Patronage, Conflict and Socio-Political Culture, 1341–1382*, The Medieval Mediterranean, 40 (Leiden: Brill, 2006); Winslow W. Clifford, *State Formation and the Structure of Politics in Mamluk Syro-Egypt, 648–741 A.H./1250–1340 C.E.* (Bonn: V&R Unipress, 2013); Clément Onimus, *Les maîtres du jeu : Pouvoir et violence politique à l'aube du sultanat mamlouk circassien (784–815/1382–1412)*, Bibliothèque historique des pays d'Islam, 13 (Paris: Éditions de la Sorbonne, 2019).
68 Van Steenbergen, *Order out of Chaos*, pp. 158–60.
69 Al-Maqrīzī, *Sulūk*, III, p. 104.
70 Al-Maqrīzī, *Sulūk*, III, pp. 116–17.

major stakes in this conflict because the belligerents wanted to control the artillery aboard the ships and the crossing of the Nile. Nothing is said about what happened afterwards with these ships, but it is most likely that a portion of the vessels sunk or were disarmed. After the battle, Yalbughā had to acknowledge his defeat, surrendered to the sultan, and was assassinated by one of his Mamluks on 9 December 1366.[71]

The young sultan did not reap the benefits from the great emir's death. Within several months, the political life of the sultanate turned into chaos. Frankish envoys noticed the smouldering tensions while mentioning the stormy debates between the emirs.[72] On 18 March 1367, for example, a violent quarrel broke out, then another one on 6 June. In the wake of the former conflict Emir Asandamur assumed power and became ruler of the state.[73] He was overthrown during a new conflict that erupted on 2 October 1367, despite the fact that at that precise moment Peter I's fleet was attacking the Syrian coast[74].

From that time onwards, Sultan Shaʿbān was effectively in control and gave the order for taxes to be collected to build a new fleet in Syria.[75] Nevertheless, Arabic sources suggest that the young sultan's authority (he was barely 15 years old) was not yet strong enough to compel the emirs to go on a military expedition. For two years, he tirelessly extended his client network within the Mamluk elite by granting offices and honours to the leading emirs and repressing others, as happened in February 1368 in the midst of war while Peter and John of Grimante were attacking Sayda.[76] No doubt, the sultanate's internal affairs were far more important than the war and the negotiations with Cyprus. The sultan feared a rebellion of the emirs and he was right: Emir Uljay tried to overthrow him in 1373.[77] The sultan was probably aware of the fact that while the political tensions dragged on he was unable to send any emirs on military expeditions: they would have refused to leave, fearing that meanwhile a rival would seize the opportunity to take power in Cairo. In this period, the chroniclers' attention focused on events in Cairo. They do not say a word about the negotiations of June–August 1368. Only the Alexandrian al-Nuwayrī gives a long report concerning the Genoese and Venetian embassy, which is corroborated by the accounts of Leontios Makhairas and William of Machaut. Only Ibn Qāḍī Shuhba's Syrian chronicle informs us that several prisoners were released after a peace treaty.[78] Generally speaking, although the sack of Alexandria itself is described at length in

---

71 Al-Maqrīzī, Sulūk, III, pp. 130–36. Concerning Yalbughā and the way his biographies were written, see Jo Van Steenbergen, 'On the Brink of a New Era? Yalbughā al-Khāṣṣakī (d. 1366) and the Yalbughāwīya', Mamluk Studies Review, 15 (2011), 118–52.
72 Hardy, Édition critique de la Prise d'Alixandrie, pp. 177, 189–90, ll. 6163–70, 6567–6618.
73 Ibn Taghrī Birdī, al-Nujūm al-zāhira fī mulūk Miṣr wa al-Qāhira, ed. by Muḥammad Ḥusayn Šams al-Dīn, 16 vols (Beirut: Dār al-Kutub al-ʿIlmiyya, 1992), XI, pp. 35–36.
74 Ibn Taghrī Birdī, Nujūm, XI, pp. 38–39; al-Nuwayrī, Ilmām, VI, p. 18.
75 Ibn Qāḍī Shuhba, Taʾrīḫ, III, pp. 321–13.
76 Leontios Makhairas, Recital, I, § 213, pp. 194–95.
77 Van Steenbergen, Order out of Chaos, p. 162.
78 Hardy, Édition critique de la Prise d'Alixandrie, pp. 208–11, ll. 7241–7340; Leontios Makhairas, Recital, I, §§ 218–24, pp. 198–205; Ibn Qāḍī Shuhba, Taʾrīḫ, III, p. 345; al-Nuwayrī, Ilmām, V, pp. 283, 366–80.

Arabic sources, all Cairene and Syrian authors, unlike the Alexandrian al-Nuwayrī,[79] consider the military and diplomatic sequels of the Alexandrian crusade as events of secondary importance compared with the sultanate's internal struggles.

It thus becomes clear that the Mamluk system, confronted with this permanent state of insecurity, was more concerned with internal problems than the challenges posed by external enemies. A similar situation had occurred in 1293 when Sultan Khalīl ordered that a fleet be constructed to conquer Cyprus, but he was assassinated for internal reasons.[80] The same problem was far more pressing forty years after the Alexandrian crusade, in 1401, when some emirs rose up against the sultan while the Mongol conqueror Tamerlane was invading Syria. Mamluk power struggles caused the rout of the army and the sultanate had to surrender.[81]

The political instability not only caused the destruction of a part of the fleet but also brought about an inability to define a policy. All political actors, sultans and emirs, as well as the chroniclers observing their actions focused on internal tensions. And indeed, they feared that leaving Cairo to wage war elsewhere would put them on the side lines of power. This inhibition in foreign affairs is one of the main reasons why the Mamluk sultanate failed to pursue an imperialistic policy.

Mamluk Diplomatic Activities

As war was no option, the Mamluks developed diplomatic activities that went through several stages during the five years between the crusade and the peace treaty. One can distinguish alternating phases of war and negotiations as follows:

- **15 October 1365:** Negotiations in the harbour of Alexandria, which brought no result.
- **16 October 1365–14 March 1366:** No diplomatic activity mentioned, war preparations in the Mamluk Sultanate.
- **March–June 1366:** Negotiations initiated at the instigation of Venice, joined by the Catalans.
- **July 1366:** Genoese embassy to Cairo, hostile to the Cypriots.
- **November–December 1366:** Negotiations with Great Emir Yalbughā, which ended in failure probably after his death.
- **January 1367:** War and Cypriot attack on Tripoli.
- **February–June 1367:** Negotiations initiated at the instigation of Genoa, later joined by Venice and the Catalans.
- **September 1367–June 1368:** Attacks on Tripoli, Sayda, Alexandria, and Ṣarafand, and Mamluk naval operations.

---

79 More than 170 pages in the printed edition deal with this topic.
80 Albrecht Fuess, 'Was Cyprus a Mamluk Protectorate? Mamluk Policies toward Cyprus between 1426 and 1517', *Journal of Cyprus Studies*, 11 (2005), 11–28 (p. 13).
81 Ibn Taghrī Birdī, *Nujūm*, XII, p. 175; al-Maqrīzī, III/3, p. 1045.

- **June–November 1368:** Negotiations initiated at the instigation of Genoa, Venice, and the papacy.
- **About January–April 1369:** Embassy sent by the regent of Cyprus, resumption of negotiations with Genoa and Venice.
- **May–August 1369:** Attacks on the Syrian coast and Alexandria, and Mamluk operations.
- **October 1369–September 1370:** Negotiations initiated at the instigation of Genoa, Venice, and the papacy.

Just after the crusade, an ill-fated round of negotiations inside the harbour of Alexandria, which involved an exchange of prisoners, failed because the crusaders fled when the Cairene army approached.[82] But the first stage of this diplomatic *procedure* began with a Venetian attempt to arrange a peace agreement: they presented themselves to the sultan as 'mediators' (*musā'iduhū*) on behalf of the king of Cyprus, stating that they had not been aware of the attack.[83] A series of embassies between Egypt and Cyprus followed, which raised the question of the liberation of the prisoners, both Christians and Muslims, the opening of the Holy Sepulchre, and the renewal of trade relations.[84] At the same time, the Venetians announced in Europe that a peace treaty had been reached in order to discourage potential crusaders. Just like the Venetians in March 1366, the Genoese, who had freed their Muslim prisoners and had proposed an alliance against Cyprus, and the Catalans sent embassies to Cairo in July and November respectively in order to dissociate themselves from the Cypriots and to negotiate a separate treaty that would allow their merchants to resume trade with the sultanate.[85] Each historian provides his own explanation for the failure of the negotiations: Leontios Makhairas says that it was caused by a protocol mistake linked to the status of the Cypriot ambassador, who was imprisoned (he was no lord, only a notary, because the lord, Sir William of Ras, had fallen sick). According to William of Machaut King Peter claimed the kingdom of Jerusalem as his 'heritage', something that in Mamluk eyes must certainly have been excessive. And Ibn Qāḍī Shuhba states that Yalbughā refused to make peace because the other side reneged on its promise to free all Muslim prisoners (after an initial release of 50 persons). In fact, both belligerents were preparing for war and were able to present their navy

---

82 The prefect of Alexandria, Ibn 'Arrām, came back in emergency from the pilgrimage to the Holy Places. When he arrived at Cairo, *Atābak* Yalbughā sent him to the army so that he started the negotiations as soon as he arrived in Alexandria on 12 October 1365. He sent a man named Ya'qūb, a Jew according to the only available piece of information, who proposed to free the Frankish merchants who had been arrested on the crusaders' arrival in exchange for the Alexandrian prisoners. But Peter I's fleet fled before an agreement was achieved as the Frankish prisoners had already been sent to Damanhūr. Al-Nuwayrī, *Ilmām*, III, pp. 208–09.

83 Actually, fifteen Venetian ships took part in the crusade, but Peter had concealed his objective and made them think that they were sailing to Anatolia: Atiya, *Crusades*, pp. 343–47.

84 Hardy, *Édition critique de la* Prise d'Alixandrie, pp. 110–21; Leontios Makhairas, *Recital*, I, §§ 184–85, pp. 162–65; al-Maqrīzī, *Sulūk*, III, pp. 118–20. See Hill, *A History of Cyprus*, II, pp. 337–43.

85 Ibn Qāḍī Shuhba, *Ta'rīkh*, III, p. 277; al-Maqrīzī, *Sulūk*, III, pp. 122–23.

to the Catalan envoys in November 1366.[86] The pretext was given by Yalbughā, who for some reason gave the order to attack the boat of the Cypriot ambassador[87] and to arrest the Turcopole James of Norès.[88] Leontios's statement that Yalbughā was in favour of peace is thus most doubtful and we may rather believe William of Machaut, who accuses him of double-dealing. To sum up, the only ones who wanted peace were the merchants: the envoys of Venice, Genoa, and Catalonia. The king of Cyprus and the sultan of Egypt and Syria used these negotiations to gain time in order to prepare for war.

Yalbughā's assassination on 9 December 1366 did not change anything in this hidden warpath: The Cypriots attacked Tripoli on 7 January 1367.[89] What changed was the internal political situation of the sultanate, which prevented the Mamluks from waging war on Cyprus.

From January to March 1367, two peace treaties were signed: the first, with Genoa, granted Genoese merchants access to Alexandria[90] while the second, with Cyprus, stipulated that prisoners should be exchanged, trade taxes should be cut by half, the tax on the pilgrims should be abolished, and the Holy Cross should be sent to Cyprus.[91] The Cypriots, nevertheless, postponed the implementation of this treaty because they were attacked in the fortress of Korykos by the Karamanids, who at that time were consolidating their influence over the southern littoral of Asia Minor. The implementation was probably postponed by the Mamluks as well because nobody had enough authority to make such a decision. As soon as the Cypriots had defeated the Karamanids, the Genoese requested that the treaty be implemented, but the Mamluks refused to ratify it as long as there was no peace with Cyprus. Apparently, this argument was only a pretext as there was already an agreement. What had changed is that upon the Genoese envoy's arrival Emir Asandamur had just seized power as a result of an internal power struggle in Cairo.[92] Negotiations with Cyprus were resumed: King Peter sent the Turcopole James of Norès back to Cairo along with a large number of Muslim prisoners, and Emir Asandamur dispatched Emir Nāṣir

---

86 Leontios Makhairas, *Recital*, I, § § 189–90, pp. 168–71; al-Nuwayrī, *Ilmām*, III, pp. 232–33; George Hill explains that a letter from Peter to Venice, carried by Philip of Mézière in June, demonstrates his intention to attack.

87 Leontios Makhairas says that the emir was angry because of the ambassador's status. Ibn Qāḍī Shuhba relates a very doubtful version according to which Emir Yalbughā ordered the assault because he had been informed that King Peter was aboard the ship.

88 Hardy, *Édition critique de la* Prise d'Alixandrie, pp. 175–78, ll. 6095–6184.

89 This attack was only partly successful as a storm dispersed the Cypriot fleet (116 ships) and only 15 ships led by Sir Florimond of Lesparre reached Tripoli but retreated because of a Mamluk counterattack. Leontios Makhairas, *Recital*, I, § 191, pp. 170–73; Ibn Qāḍī Shuhba, *Taʾrīkh*, III, p. 293; al-Nuwayrī, *Ilmām*, V, pp. 77–78.

90 On 20 January 1367: Ibn Qāḍī Shuhba, *Taʾrīkh*, III, p. 294; al-Maqrīzī, *Sulūk*, III, p. 141.

91 Hardy, *Édition critique de la* Prise d'Alixandrie, pp. 126–29, 164–66, ll. 4351–4452, 5683–5772; Leontios Makhairas, *Recital*, I, § 193, pp. 172–75.

92 Asandamur seized power on 18 March 1367 according to al-Maqrīzī and Ibn Taghrī Birdī. Leontios Makhairas states that the Genoese embassy arrived on 14 March but the text is inaccurate in matters of chronology, so we must assume that there is a mistake regarding the date. Leontios Makhairas, *Recital*, I, § § 197–98, pp. 178–79; al-Maqrīzī, *Sulūk*, III, pp. 141–42; Ibn Taghrī Birdī, *Nujūm*, XI, pp. 35–36.

al-Dīn Muḥammad ibn Qarājā al-Sharīfī and Emir Sayf al-Dīn al-Jūbānī to Cyprus. According to our Christian authors, however, King Peter became convinced that the Mamluks once again sought to postpone the conclusion of a peace treaty in order to pursue war preparations, although there is no evidence that Asandamur made efforts to rebuild the fleet.[93] The fact that King Peter arrested the Mamluk envoys and ordered his navy twice to be readied (in April and in June) may suggest that, once again, both sides were trying to gain time in order to prepare a naval campaign for the summer months. Since the Mamluk navy might have been partly destroyed during Yalbughā's power struggle and since another conflict broke out in Cairo in June 1367, Peter I had the opportunity to attack first and sent his fleet against Tripoli, Ayās and several Syrian ports, where material of the local naval contingents was destroyed. This was probably one of the objectives of the Cypriot king. In other words, as soon as Asandamur seized power, he probably sought to resume Yalbughā's policy, namely gaining time in order to prepare for war. His downfall on 2 October 1367 following another power struggle in Cairo sparked a change in Mamluk policy.

Yalbughā's policy had another aspect as well. Besides his hawkish intentions, he immediately tried to shift diplomatically the balance of power. As he had no hold over the Cypriots, he took steps to put pressure on other Frankish communities. Basically, he ordered the Italian merchants to be arrested and their goods to be seized.[94] As soon as the Alexandrian crusade began, fifty Franks who used to reside in the city were captured and sent to Damanhūr, a city in the Delta. The gold and silver coins of the treasury of Alexandria were sent to Damanhūr along with these prisoners.[95] There is no doubt that his goal was to take them as hostages. In November 1366, while the negotiations broke down, Yalbughā ordered the arrest of all Frankish merchants in Alexandria,[96] as well as of the Venetian merchants who had come back to Beirut and Alexandria because they thought that a peace agreement had been achieved.[97] The seizure of hostages cannot be understood without considering Yalbughā's decision to reject any separate peace agreement with the Frankish powers:[98] the pressure he put on the Italian merchants and the Catalans forced them to intercede with the Cypriots for peace. The peril their merchants were facing in the sultanate

---

[93] The Mamluk double game can be proven by the fact that the Mamluk sources do not say a word about these negotiations, except that King Peter arrested their ambassador (although William of Machaut says the contrary!); Hardy, *Édition critique de la Prise d'Alixandrie*, pp. 166–68, 172–73, 178–79, 182–93, ll. 5773–5828, 5980–6009, 6185–6215, 6317–6718; Leontios Makhairas, *Recital*, I, §§ 198–203, pp. 178–87; al-Nuwayrī, *Ilmām*, V, p. 77.

[94] For the consequences of Peter of Lusignan's crusade on the Frankish merchant community of Alexandria, see Apellaniz, 'Alixandrie', pp. 195–212. The author explains that the community used to be well integrated in the city before 1365 and consisted partly of Greek-Venetian merchants. This situation changed radically after 1365.

[95] Atiya, *Crusades*, p. 358.

[96] Ibn Qāḍī Shuhba, *Taʾrīkh*, III, pp. 291–92.

[97] This happened around November 1366, at about the same time as the arrest of ambassador James of Norès: Leontios Makhairas, *Recital*, I, § 186–89, pp. 166–69.

[98] Hardy, *Édition critique de la Prise d'Alixandrie*, pp. 111–13, ll. 3839–96.

and the commercial losses explain why all the negotiations were undertaken at the instigation of the Italians and the Catalans.

Yalbughā's death caused the suspension of this strategy for almost a year and Asandamur did not resume it. Two weeks after his downfall, however, Sultan Sha'bān did resume this 'roundabout diplomacy' on the alleged pretext that the Genoese and Venetian galleys that were trading in the harbour of Alexandria had a Muslim prisoner on board. The sultan decreed the arrest of all Frankish consuls and merchants in Alexandria (150 to 200 persons) and the seizure of their goods; two months later, seven other merchants who were not aware of this decree disembarked in Alexandria and were arrested as well.[99] The presence of Frankish consuls and numerous merchants in Alexandria in October 1367 is surprising: this indicates that after the negotiations of January–June 1367, the sultanate respected the peace treaty with Genoa[100] although the negotiations had failed[101] and the emirs officially confirmed that there would be no separate peace![102]

In June 1368, the Venetian Nicola Giustiniani and the Genoese Cassan Cigala[103] were sent to Egypt to negotiate the cessation of hostilities.[104] The question of the exchange of prisoners was fundamental as it was the main diplomatic tool of each party. Thus, the Mamluks did not hesitate to capture merchants through trickery, for example in the autumn of 1368, under the pretext that the ambassadors had not brought all the Alexandrian prisoners,[105] and twice in the winter of 1369: the first time because Cassan Cigala came back with just twenty Muslim prisoners, alleging that the others had converted to Christianity,[106] and the second as a consequence of the renewal of hostilities.[107] Only two Christian prisoners were freed in November 1369. They were entrusted with the mission of encouraging the Frankish communities to make peace with the sultanate and were ordered to come back to Cairo, which they did ten months later after they had fulfilled their task successfully.[108]

In sum, it is clear that, after Asandamur's fall and Ibrāhīm al-Tāzī's return from his naval campaign, the Mamluks acknowledged the failure of their military operations.

---

99 Al-Maqrīzī, *Sulūk*, III, p. 156; al-Nuwayrī, *Ilmām*, V, pp. 190, 195.
100 The peace with Genoa is mentioned in al-Maqrīzī, *Sulūk*, III, p. 141 and Ibn Qāḍī Shuhba, *Ta'rīkh*, III, p. 294.
101 Hardy, *Édition critique de la* Prise d'Alixandrie, pp. 192–93, ll. 6670–6718; Leontios Makhairas, *Recital*, I, §§ 202–03, pp. 182--87.
102 Leontios Makhairas, *Recital*, I, § 196, pp. 178–79.
103 Qāzān in the Arabic sources.
104 Hardy, *Édition critique de la* Prise d'Alixandrie, pp. 208–11, ll. 7241–7340; Leontios Makhairas, *Recital*, I, §§ 218–24, pp. 198–205; al-Nuwayrī, *Ilmām*, V, pp. 283, 366–80.
105 Al-Nuwayrī, *Ilmām*, V, pp. 373–75.
106 Al-Nuwayrī, *Ilmām*, VI, pp. 378–82.
107 The Christian sources say that the capture of a Muslim boat was the consequence of the sultan's prevarication (see Hill, *A History of Cyprus*, II, p. 372), although the Muslim sources tell that the breakdown of the negotiations was a consequence of this attack (al-Nuwayrī, *Ilmām*, V, pp. 383–84).
108 George Hill says that four prisoners were released because the first ones did not come back: Hill, *A History of Cyprus*, II, p. 343. Concerning these negotiations: Leontios Makhairas, *Recital*, I, §§ 297–309, pp. 282–97; al-Maqrīzī, *Sulūk*, III, pp. 185–91; al-Nuwayrī, *Ilmām*, VI, pp. 404–06.

They created a solidarity of fate between the Italian cities and the Cypriot kingdom and responded to the threat to their shores by threatening the merchants' lives and trade.

Nevertheless, this new strategy did not prove very effective, because no peace agreement was ratified in the three years following Asandamur's fall, although King Peter's demands became gradually more reasonable. In May 1366, besides free pilgrimage and freedom for the Christian prisoners, he asked for an exemption on customs duties and put claim to Jerusalem.[109] In February 1367, he insisted on the two first demands (exchange of prisoners and abolition of the pilgrim tax) but he forsook the claim to total exemption of customs duties, requesting instead that taxes be cut by half (from 20% to 10%), as well as his claim to Jerusalem, contenting himself with the Holy Cross being sent to Cyprus.[110] The claim to Jerusalem was of course unacceptable, be it a false claim, as proposed by Peter Edbury, or be it an important aspect of crusader propaganda, as suggested by Christopher Schabel and Peter Edbury himself in this volume.[111] It was actually a real provocation, since the king of Cyprus was preparing for war. In July 1368, King Peter's demands, which were communicated to the Mamluks by Venetian and Genoese envoys, were largely the same: exchange of prisoners, reduction of customs duties by half and free pilgrimage; he gave up his claims to the Holy Cross and Jerusalem but demanded a piece of land near Jerusalem and asked for his name to be written on the Holy Sepulchre.[112] From the Mamluk point of view, these claims were still excessive.

These negotiations were the first after Asandamur's downfall and were marked by the resumption by the Mamluks of the hostage strategy, and thus the Frankish ambassadors and sailors became progressively more suspicious when arriving in Alexandria. Even more important were the suspicions of the other side. From the summer of 1368 onwards, the Mamluk interlocutors became increasingly suspicious and postponed the conclusion of the peace treaty several times because they feared that the foreign ambassadors negotiated with the secret goal of helping the Christian prisoners escape. Mamluk historians considered the fact that the ambassadors never brought all the Alexandrian prisoners with them as a proof of their slyness.[113] Actually, the silence of the Christian sources concerning some negotiations[114] might be an indication that the Franks did not always aim at reaching a fair agreement. Moreover, the Alexandrian governors were in constant fear of attacks that the Frankish ships carrying envoys might mount on the harbour and its ships.[115] Not without reason,

---

[109] Hardy, *Édition critique de la* Prise d'Alixandre, pp. 118–21, ll. 4063–4170; Leontios Makhairas, *Recital*, I, §§ 181–82, pp. 160–63; al-Maqrīzī, *Sulūk*, III, p. 120. See Hill, *A History of Cyprus*, II, p. 340.

[110] Hardy, *Édition critique de la* Prise d'Alixandre, pp. 126–29, 163–64, ll. 4351–4452, 5673–5712; Leontios Makhairas, *Recital*, I, §§ 191–92, pp. 170–73; see Hill, *A History of Cyprus*, II, p. 345.

[111] Edbury, 'Crusading Policy', pp. 90–105; Edbury, *Kingdom of Cyprus*, p. 171.

[112] Al-Nuwayrī, *Ilmām*, V, pp. 366–80.

[113] In July–August 1368, in November 1368, during the winter of 1369 and in November 1369: Al-Nuwayrī, *Ilmām*, V, pp. 367, 376–77, VI, pp. 380–82, 383, 398–400.

[114] For example, Christian sources do not mention the negotiations of the winter of 1369.

[115] For example, in November 1368, the Mamluks prepared for war when Cassan Cigala's ships arrived in Alexandria: Al-Nuwayrī, *Ilmām*, VI, pp. 376–77.

Arabic sources frequently depicted the Franks and the Cypriots in particular as thieves or pirates (*luṣūṣ baḥr*)[116] and condemned their aggressiveness.[117]

The Necessity of Peace

Nevertheless, both sides repeatedly agreed to re-enter the negotiations. When Peter I eventually returned from Western Europe without any crusaders in the autumn of 1368, he sent envoys to Cairo to make peace. Sultan Shaʿbān replied that he expected guarantees of the king's sincerity so that no reinforcements would come to wage a new crusade on his territories. This response caused an instant breakdown of the negotiations.[118] Peter's assassination on 17 January 1369 and the good will of John of Antioch,[119] the kingdom's regent, who instantly informed the sultan of the news and released some prisoners,[120] did not completely change the geopolitical constellation: mutual mistrust and aggression continued to be a problem. The king's death, however, was probably one of the reasons why the sultan agreed to put an end to the state of war.

Surely, economic interests also converged with the necessity to make peace. The crusade itself, as Peter Edbury has proposed, might have had economic objectives.[121] Each stage of the negotiation was initiated either by Venice, Genoa or by both of them and was supported by the papacy with the objective of reopening the trade with Egypt and Syria. As we have seen, the Mamluks hoped to suffocate the Italian trade in order to force the republics to put pressure on Peter I and impose peace on their terms. The emirs did not hesitate to arrest merchants and pilgrims, to confiscate their goods, to loot the holy places in Jerusalem, to impose a tax on the Patriarch of Alexandria and an extraordinary tax of 25% on the value of goods of all Christians in the kingdom and other vexations. Hence, the *dhimmī*s, the Christian subjects of the sultan, were the main victims of the Mamluk reaction.[122]

Nevertheless, it seems that the blockade played against the economic and military interests of the sultanate itself. The Arabic sources are unfortunately too reticent on that matter, but Leontios Makhairas explains the problems the emirs in Cairo were facing: the goods remained unsold, there was a shortage of coins, and the customs duties decreased.[123] Moreover, it is well known that the Mamluk sultanate needed to import slave soldiers and lacked the materials, such as iron or wood, necessary

---

116 *Luṣūṣ* (thieves) is common (for example: al-Nuwayrī, *Ilmām*, III, pp. 64–68, 209, V, pp. 123–25, 282). Sometimes we find the expression *luṣūṣ baḥr*, i.e., 'pirate', but al-Nuwayrī also uses *karāsila*, which is an Arabization of the word *corsair*: al-Nuwayrī, *Ilmām*, II, p. 97.
117 For example, when the ambassador's ship attacked a Syrian boat that was arriving in Alexandria: Al-Nuwayrī, *Ilmām*, VI, p. 382.
118 Leontios Makhairas, *Recital*, I, § § 226–30, pp. 208–13; al-Nuwayrī, *Ilmām*, V, pp. 376–77.
119 Named '*al-brinz*' in the Arabic texts, from French, '*le prince*' because of his title: 'Prince of Antioch'.
120 Ibn Qāḍī Shuhba, *Taʾrīkh*, III, p. 348.
121 Edbury, 'Crusading Policy', pp. 90–105.
122 These anti-Christian persecutions were legitimized by the allegation that they had called on the king of Cyprus to come: Al-Nuwayrī, *Ilmām*, V, pp. 187–88.
123 Leontios Makhairas, *Recital*, I, § § 218–23, pp. 198–205.

to build a new fleet. Therefore, blocking trade prevented the sultanate from waging war on Cyprus. The fact that the final condition for the peace treaty was that the goods looted in Alexandria were to be given back, otherwise the sultan would not restore what he had confiscated, may indicate that the treaty had become a financial necessity to the sultanate.[124]

Peace, thus, became a necessity for everybody. A long process of negotiations began in October 1369 at the instigation of the Genoese and the Venetians. The first embassy failed, but ten emissaries from Venice, Genoa, Rhodes, and Cyprus arrived in November and were authorized to come to Cairo. As a consequence, in February 1370 Sultan Shaʿbān released two Italian merchants and sent them to Cyprus. They came back in July with other ambassadors. At first, the sultan refused to meet the envoys from Rhodes and Cyprus but finally an agreement was reached and oaths were taken in Cairo on 25 August 1370. Emir Ṭaqbughā Khāzindār al-ʿAlāʾī was then sent to Cyprus on 29 September, where the two sides swore another mutual oath (after the Mamluk emissaries had been imprisoned a few days).

What is striking about this agreement is that no chronicler, Christian or Muslim, wrote about its content. George Hill suggests that the peace treaty may have had the same clauses as the treaty signed in 1403: access for pilgrims to the Holy Sepulchre, St Catherine's on Mount Sinai, and other holy places; payment of dues to be agreed; the fixing of customs duties at various Mamluk ports; the punishment of merchants dealing in contraband; and a three-month notification period prior to the commencement of hostilities following the denunciation of the treaty by either the Muslims or the Christians.[125] But the fact that the authors do not mention the clauses of the treaty seems to be no coincidence.

The Mamluk chronicles give some bits of information that confirm Hill's suggestion and add a few elements:
- The treaty was supposed to be a twenty-year truce.
- An exchange of prisoners was organized on condition that looted goods would be returned to the Alexandrians. In January 1371, Frankish prisoners in Damascus were released and Muslim prisoners came back to Damascus and Alexandria.
- In January 1371, too, the Holy Sepulchre was opened.[126]

There may be a good reason that explains why Mamluk chroniclers were silent on this matter: Sultan Shaʿbān had forfeited the ambition to have all Alexandrian prisoners released. In early 1369, the Frankish ambassador Cassan's justification that most of the prisoners could not be released because they had converted to Christianity was considered by the Mamluks as a false pretext in violation of the agreements and thus constituted the main cause for the failure of the negotiations.[127] Indeed, the Cypriots may have been unable to gather all the prisoners despite the list of names

---

124 Leontios Makhairas, *Recital*, I, §§ 302–09, pp. 286–97; al-Maqrīzī, *Sulūk*, III, pp. 185–91.
125 Hill, *A History of Cyprus*, II, p. 370. I replaced 'Saracen' with 'Mamluk'.
126 Ibn Qāḍī Shuhba, *Taʾrīkh*, III, pp. 380–82; al-Maqrīzī, *Sulūk*, III, p. 190.
127 Al-Nuwayrī, *Ilmām*, VI, pp. 378–82.

that had been given to them[128] because some of them may have already been sold.[129] But in September 1370, the Mamluk ambassador Ṭaqbughā accepted the very same argument without further discussion.[130] In short, it seems that the Mamluks gave in with respect to the release of all prisoners. This might perhaps explain why the Arab authors do not detail the treaty.

At the same time, according to al-Nuwayrī, when John of Antioch, regent of Cyprus, asked for peace following his brother's assassination in the winter of 1369, he released two prisoners and presented himself as the slave and servant (*mamlūk*) of the sultan.[131] The Arabic phrase al-Nuwayrī put into John of Antioch's mouth, tough most probably fictional, aptly illustrates the fact that the Cypriot ruler acknowledged the sultan's sovereignty and stresses the idea of Mamluk ascendancy. The statement tallies with the general principles of the sultanate's foreign policy and its non-imperialistic ambition to exert regional suzerainty in the Middle East. Moreover, the fact that Sultan Barsbāy made Cyprus a Mamluk protectorate under Mamluk overlordship (1426–1517)[132] tends to confirm that such a policy might have been envisaged a few decades earlier. Indeed, there is some faint evidence corroborating that Cyprus had become a more or less loose protectorate even before 1426.[133] It is not implausible that the Mamluks may have claimed a kind of nominal suzerainty over Cyprus. If the regent accepted such a status, it would partly explain why Christian chronicles refrain from mentioning the treaty.[134] Thus, it may be suggested that both parties made concessions and that the peace treaty satisfied neither the Christian nor the Muslim chroniclers.

Conclusions

No topic requires more precise comparison between Christian and Muslim sources than a crusade. In this paper, the representation of the 'other' is omnipresent. In particular, al-Nuwayrī stresses the Mamluks' suspicious attitudes towards western Europeans (the *Faranj* or 'Franks'). It is always a tricky task to disentangle the interpretations the available primary sources give for historical facts, especially when authors alter or

---

128 A list has been given to Venetian and Genoese ambassadors in August 1368: Al-Nuwayrī, *Ilmām*, V, pp. 367–68.
129 An obscure passage of al-Nuwayrī tells us that Muslim prisoners were found on a Frankish ship in a Maghrebin harbour. As al-Nuwayrī mentions this episode, we may suggest that he regarded these prisoners as Alexandrians: Al-Nuwayrī, *Ilmām*, V, pp. 377–79.
130 Al-Nuwayrī, *Ilmām*, VI, pp. 404–06.
131 Al-Nuwayrī, *Ilmām*, VI, p. 382.
132 Fuess, 'Mamluk Protectorate?', pp. 11–24.
133 For example, when Tamerlane invaded Syria, the Cypriots asked for the sultan's permission to prepare their fleet against the conqueror; a few years later, a Mamluk emir was banished to Cyprus: Al-Maqrīzī, *Sulūk*, III, pp. 1039–40; Ibn Taghrī Birdī, *Nujūm*, XII, p. 230.
134 The Annals of Genoa, for instance, could have elaborated on such an event but they were mostly interested in domestic affairs and do not even mention Cyprus in the report sub anno 1370. See Giorgio Stella, *Annales Genuenses*, ed. Giovanna Petti Balbi (Bologna, 1975), pp. 16–24.

conceal facts under their pen. Nevertheless, sifting through all independent sources and scrutinizing the Arabic sources in order to decipher the Mamluk point of view allows us to clarify the sultanate's foreign policy towards the Franks from 1365 to 1371.

It appears that this foreign policy was contingent upon domestic policy and depended on ideological representations and social interactions that determined the Mamluk political sphere. Its conflict-ridden structure explains the sultanate's recurring incapacity to define a firm foreign policy and to lead a war against Cyprus. As the Mamluks were unable to tip the balance of power vis-à-vis the kingdom of Cyprus to their own favour, their diplomacy prevaricated. Being suspicious of the alleged Frankish deceitfulness and aggressiveness and unable to attack Cyprus, they successfully created an interdependence between Italian and Cypriot interests. As a consequence, Venice and Genoa instigated negotiations that resulted in a peace treaty the exact clauses of which are unknown. Most likely, it imposed important concessions on both treaty partners so that the chroniclers are mostly silent on this topic.

ANGEL NICOLAOU-KONNARI

'Le roy de Chippre de renon': The Depiction of Peter I of Lusignan in French Literature and Historiography

As a literary *locus* for medieval authors, the Frankish Kingdom of Cyprus often provided a negative exemplum of 'superfluity of luxury, gluttony, softness, and all kinds of voluptuousness', sins said to be committed by both its Lusignan kings and its people and considered to be the cause of divine punishment in the form of political turmoil and natural disasters;[1] these sins are frequently attributed to the combination of heat and wine and the survival of the ancient cult of Venus, *topoi* used in medieval and early modern literature to describe the Levant as well.[2] This ethical use of the island's history witnessed a spectacular reversal in the middle of the fourteenth century thanks to King Peter I (1329–69, crowned 1359); literary rehabilitation had

---

1 Benvenuto de Rambaldis da Imola, *Comentum super Dantis Aldigherij Comoediam*, ed. by William Warner Vernon and Sir James Philip Lacaita, 5 vols (Florence: G. Barbèra, 1887), V, p. 252; the 'beast' of Nicosia and Famagusta (*Paradiso*, 19.145–48) is usually identified with Henry II (before 1285–1324), whose reign witnessed much political turmoil, see Edward Peters, 'Henry II of Cyprus, *Rex inutilis*: A Footnote to *Decameron* 1.9', *Speculum*, 72/3 (1997), 763–75. The dedication by Thomas Aquinas of his treatise *De Regno* to a Cypriot king, most probably Hugh II (1253–67), echoes another period of political instability, see Gilles Grivaud, *Entrelacs chiprois. Essai sur les lettres et la vie intellectuelle dans le royaume de Chypre (1191–1570)* (Nicosia: Moufflon, 2009), pp. 52–53, 118–21. The international conference *La Culture du Locus. De l'Espace géographique à l'Espace utopique (1200–1650)*, organized by Evelien Chayes, Angel Nicolaou-Konnari, Sonia Gentili, and Rafaella Anconetani (University of Cyprus, Nicosia, May 2011), examined the various uses of Cyprus as a geographical and utopian location in medieval and Renaissance literature.

2 For literary commonplaces about *cyprios mores*, see Lorenzo Calvelli, *Cipro e la memoria dell'antico fra Medioevo e Rinascimento: la percezione del passato romano dell'isola nel mondo occidentale*, Memorie Classe di Scienze Morali, Lettere ed Arti, 133 (Venice: Istituto Veneto di Scienze, Lettere ed Arti, 2009), chapters 1.2.2, 4, and passim and Angel Nicolaou-Konnari, 'Women in Medieval Famagusta: Law, Family, and Society', in *Famagusta, Volume II, History and Society*, ed. by Gilles Grivaud, Angel Nicolaou-Konnari, and Chris Schabel, Mediterranean Nexus 1110–1700. Conflict, Influence and Inspiration in the Mediterranean Area, 8 (Turnhout: Brepols, 2020), pp. 509–633 (610–12, 618–20). For the Levant, see Catherine Gaullier-Bougassas, *La Tentation de l'Orient dans le roman médiéval. Sur l'imaginaire médiéval de l'Autre*, Nouvelle bibliothèque du Moyen Âge, 67 (Paris: Champion, 2003).

Angel Nicolaou-Konnari • University of Cyprus

Crusading, Society, and Politics in the Eastern Mediterranean in the Age of King Peter I of Cyprus, ed. by Alexander Beihammer and Angel Nicolaou-Konnari, MEDNEX, 10 (Turnhout, 2022), pp. 273–319
© BREPOLS PUBLISHERS
10.1484/M.MEDNEX-EB.5.128468

started under his father Hugh IV (1324–59), whose politics and court culture had a distinct 'pan-Mediterranean' air, as he maintained links with intellectual circles in Constantinople, Italy, and the Arab world, but the Lusignan Kingdom's literary image would undeservedly regress to its former negative status after Peter's murder.[3]

The extent of Peter's presence in French literature, in particular, easily surpasses that of any other Lusignan king or queen, even of the founder of the dynasty and ex-king of Jerusalem, the Poitevin Guy of Lusignan (1192–94).[4] In addition to his military achievements, Peter's popularity has been attributed to his attractive personality and his prolonged presence at European courts, the Cypriot king pursuing a crusading and chivalric style of kingship. Modern scholarship, however, may legitimately interpret the Cypriot king's portrayal as the ideal knight and the perfect crusader king, in quest of the defeat of the infidel and the recovery of his ancestral Kingdom of Jerusalem, in terms of a clever marketing strategy intended to promote the political and ideological intentions of French authors and their patrons. Indeed, it is quite remarkable that, despite the ultimate failure of Peter's crusader goals and his demystification as a knight and a king caused by his murder, this idealized image continued to serve as a model of chivalric ethos and royal power within the context of the Hundred Years' War (1337–1453), the problems faced by the French monarchy, and the Great Schism (1378–1417) until the middle of the fifteenth century.

The depiction or evocation of Peter and his exploits may be found in a variety of works composed by an impressive array of French authors, Peter's contemporaries or near contemporaries, as well as in the works of Italian and English writers of the

---

3 Giovanni Boccaccio (1313–75) dedicated his *Genealogia Deorum* to Hugh IV: Ioannis Boccatii de Certaldo, *Genealogiae deorum gentilium* (Venice: per Vindelinum de Spira, 1472), fol. [a]1ʳ, [b]1ʳ ('ad Ugonem inclytum Hierusalem & Cypri regem'), [D]7ʳ ('ad illustrem principem Hugonem hierusalem et sipri regem'). See: Vittore Branca, *Giovanni Boccaccio, profilo biografico* (Florence: Sansoni, 1977), pp. 24, 83, 157, for Boccaccio's Lusignan connections; Chris Schabel, 'Hugh the Just: The Further Rehabilitation of King Hugh IV Lusignan of Cyprus', Επετηρίδα Κέντρου Επιστημονικών Ερευνών (Κύπρου), 30 (2004), 123–52; Grivaud, *Entrelacs chiprois*, pp. 53–54, 65–66, 68–71, 86, 90–91, 219–20, for literary exchanges during Hugh's reign; and Sharon Kinoshita, '"Noi siamo mercatanti Cipriani": How to Do Things in the Medieval Mediterranean', in *Philippe de Mézières and His Age: Piety and Politics in the Fourteenth Century*, ed. by Renate Blumenfeld-Kosinski and Kiril Petkov, The Medieval Mediterranean, 91 (Leiden – Boston: Brill, 2012), pp. 41–60. Cf. Gilles Grivaud, 'Résonances humanistes à la cour de Nicosie (1411-1423)', in *Poésie et musique à l'âge de l'Ars subtilior. Autour du manuscrit Torino, BNU, J.II. 9*, ed. by Gisèle Clément, Isabelle Fabre, Gilles Polizzi, and Fañch Thoraval, Centre d'études supérieures de la Renaissance, Collection 'Épitome musical' (Turnhout: Brepols, 2021), pp. 27-39 (esp. 34, 39).

4 Guy is presented disparagingly in contemporary historiography, see R. C. Smail, 'The Predicaments of Guy of Lusignan, 1183–1187', in *Outremer. Studies in the History of the Crusading Kingdom of Jerusalem Presented to Joshua Prawer*, ed. by Benjamin Z. Kedar, Hans E. Mayer, and R. C. Smail (Jerusalem: Yad Izhak Ben-Zvi Institute, 1982), pp. 159–76. In later literature, he may be identified with the 'primo re di Cipri', the main character in Giovanni Boccaccio's *Decameron*, ed. by Vittore Branca, in *Tutte le opere di Giovanni Boccaccio*, IV (Milan: Mondadori, 1976), 'Giornata prima, novella nova', pp. 81–82, a politically and morally inadequate and weak king, converted through the censure of a gentlewoman from Gascony to a king with a noble character; see Peters, 'Henry II of Cyprus, Rex inutilis' and Pier Massimo Forni, 'The Tale of the King of Cyprus and the Lady of Gascony', in *The Decameron First Day in Perspective. Volume I of the Lectura Boccaccii*, ed. by Elissa B. Weaver (Toronto – Buffalo – London: University of Toronto Press, 2004), pp. 207–21.

calibre of Francesco Petrarca (1304–74)[5] and Geoffrey Chaucer (1340/45–1400),[6] which, however, will not be discussed here.[7] The French works diverge significantly in form, style, language, and content and include texts in verse or prose, Latin, French, or Occitan, which may be defined as poetry (epic poems, ballades, *dits, complaintes*), romances, biographies, political allegories, didactic and epistolary literature, works of religious inspiration, and historiography (chronicles, annals, and other historical works). The literary nature of these texts complies with the intentions of their authors and, inversely, their historicity is submitted to the stylistic conventions of the literary genre they serve. Thus, the space attributed to Peter's portrayal varies in each work, but the qualities that define it are, in fact, very similar, demonstrating the fascinating interpenetration of literature and history. Although recurrent themes in earlier French literature for the depiction of the ideal crusader are used in these works (e.g. individual salvation and development; lineage and ancestry; praise of a crusader's patron; prefiguration of a crusade by the depiction of earlier expeditions; use of the First Crusade as the archetypal crusade; vocabulary adapted from the domains of feudalism, chivalry, and religion),[8] new themes are introduced that serve the political intentions of French authors writing within the historical context of the Hundred Years' War. It would be remiss not to begin this investigation with the two French masters, William of Machaut (*c.* 1300–77) and Philip of Mézières

---

5 Pétrarque, *Lettres de la viellesse / Rerum senilium*, III–IV, ed. by Elvira Nota, introduction and notes by Ugo Dotti (Paris: Les Belles Lettres, 2004–06), III, *Livres VIII–XI*, French trans. by Claude Laurens, Book VIII, letter 8, pp. 100–05 (102–03) (letter to Boccaccio, 20 July 1367), IV, *Livres XII–XV*, French trans. by Jean-Yves Boriaud, Book XIII, letter 2, pp. 136–45 (140–43) (letter to Philip of Mézières, 18 November 1369); *Petrarch's Lyric Poems: The Rime Sparse and Other Lyrics*, ed. and English trans. by Robert M. Durling (Cambridge, Mass.: Harvard University Press, 1976), no. 27, p. 73; see discussion in this author's introductory chapter to this volume. Although in another letter Petrarca repeats the stereotypical negative image of Cyprus, he refers to the situation prior to Peter's reign since the letter is dated late November or December 1359: 'Cyprus armato hoste carens, inermi mollique otio voluptate luxuria, malis hostibus, oppugnatur, viro forti sedes inhabilis' / 'Cyprus, with no armed enemy, is beset by soft and unarmed idleness, by voluptuousness, and by luxury, evil enemies indeed, and has become a place where no strong man would live', Francesco Petrarca, *Le familiari*, ed. by Vittorio Rossi and Umberto Bosco, 4 vols (Florence: Sansoni, 1933–42), III, Book XV, 7, p. 151.
6 Geoffrey Chaucer, *The Canterbury Tales*, 'Prologue', ll. 43–78, esp. 51, 58, and 'The Monkes Tale', ll. 3581–88, in *The Complete Works of Geoffrey Chaucer*, ed. by Walter W. Skeat, 7 vols (Oxford: Clarendon Press, 1899²), I, pp. 2–3, IV, p. 256.
7 For a discussion of Peter's presence in western literature, see: Louis de Mas Latrie, *Histoire de l'île de Chypre sous le règne des princes de la maison de Lusignan*, 3 vols (Paris: Imprimerie impériale, 1852–61), II, pp. 245–46, 337 n. 2, 343; Nicolas Jorga, *Philippe de Mézières (1327–1405) et la croisade au XIVᵉ siècle* (Paris: École Pratique des Hautes Études, 1896; repr. London: Variorum Reprints, 1973), pp. 80–82, 306, 378–79, 392–94, and passim; Sir George Hill, *A History of Cyprus*, 4 vols (Cambridge: Cambridge University Press, 1940–52), II, pp. 327 n. 2, 335 n. 3, 368; Guillaume de Machaut, *La Prise d'Alixandre (The Taking of Alexandria)*, ed. and English trans. by R. Barton Palmer (New York – London: Routledge, 2002), 'Introduction', pp. 11–33; Guillaume de Machaut, *The Capture of Alexandria*, English trans. by Janet Shirley, introduction and notes by Peter W. Edbury, Crusade Texts in Translation, 8 (Aldershot: Ashgate, 2001), pp. 8–16; this author's introductory chapter to this volume.
8 See David A. Trotter, *Medieval French Literature and the Crusades (1100–1300)*, Histoire des idées et critique littéraire, 256 (Geneva: Droz, 1987).

(1327–1405), whose lives and careers are closely linked with Peter's and who exerted a great influence on the rest of the writers.

William of Machaut's *La Prise d'Alixandre*, a long and detailed chivalric biography in verse of the Cypriot king, was the last major work of the prolific poet, musician, historian, and courtier, composed within two or three years of its hero's death in 1369.[9] The work was probably ordered by King Charles V (1364–80) of France, who may have wanted to imitate the court of England, John Froissart (*c.* 1337–*c.* 1404) serving as a secretary to Queen Philippa of Hainault (1310/15–69), wife of King Edward III (1327–77) of England, in the 1360s [Fig. 1].[10] Although Machaut may have used Mézières's *Vita* of Peter Thomas (1305? –66) and was probably influenced by the chancellor's idealistic depiction of the Cypriot king as a fervent crusader,[11] his information mainly derived from his personal relationship with Peter and from the testimonies of French crusaders who participated in the latter's military campaigns.[12] Peter and Machaut met during the former's first visit to the West (1362–65), probably in Paris at the end of 1363 and at the coronation of Charles V in Reims on 19 May 1364; the poet's account in the *Prise* becomes more detailed beginning with the coronation and it is likely that he accompanied the Cypriot king on his ensuing travels in Central Europe as alluded in his works.[13] Machaut's epic poem celebrates knightly values and religious zeal and may be considered to have launched what has been described

---

9   For the work, see Sophie Hardy, *Édition critique de la* Prise d'Alixandrie *de Guillaume de Machaut* (unpublished doctoral thesis, Université d'Orléans, 2011): ftp://ftp.univ-orleans.fr/theses/sophie. hardy_1730.pdf [accessed 4 June 2016], with all the previous bibliography; a Modern Greek translation is now available, see *Η κατάληψη της Αλεξάνδρειας*, trans. Andreas Hadjisavvas (Besançon: Praxandre, 2011). Generally on Machaut: Lawrence Earp, *Guillaume de Machaut: A Guide to Research*, Garland Composer Research Manuals, 36 (New York – London: Garland, 1995); Barton Palmer's introduction to Guillaume de Machaut, *La Prise d'Alixandre*, pp. 1–27; Jacqueline Cerquiglini-Toulet and Nigel E. Wilkins (eds), *Guillaume de Machaut, 1300–2000* (Paris: Presses Paris Sorbonne, 2002); Elizabeth Eva Leach, *Guillaume de Machaut: Secretary, Poet, Musician* (Ithaca, NY: Cornell University Press, 2011); Deborah McGrady and Jennifer Bain (eds), *A Companion to Guillaume de Machaut* (Leiden: Brill, 2012).
10 Eleanor Roach, in her edition of Coudrette, *Le Roman de Mélusine ou l'histoire de Lusignan* (Paris: Klincksieck, 1982), 'Introduction', p. 23, and Hardy, *Édition critique de la* Prise d'Alixandrie, pp. lxxxi, lxxxv, suggest Duke John of Berry, as another candidate for the patronage of the work.
11 Interestingly, though, Machaut ignores completely Mézières in his work, see Guillaume de Machaut, *La Prise d'Alixandre*, 'Introduction', pp. 16–20. On the *Vita*, see below.
12 For both his historical and literary sources, see: Guillaume de Machaut, *La Prise d'Alixandre*, 'Introduction', pp. 8–10, 27–33; Guillaume de Machaut, *The Capture of Alexandria*, 'Introduction', pp. 10–11; Hardy, *Édition critique de la* Prise d'Alixandrie, pp. cxx–cxxvi; Peter W. Edbury, 'Machaut, Mézières, Makhairas and Amadi: Constructing the Reign of Peter I (1359–1369)', in *Philippe de Mézières and His Age*, pp. 349–58, esp. 350–51; Angel Nicolaou-Konnari, 'A Neglected Relationship: Leontios Makhairas's Debt to Latin Eastern and French Historiography', in *The French of Outremer. Communities and Communications in the Crusading Mediterranean*, ed. by Laura K. Morreale and Nicholas L. Paul, Fordham Series in Medieval Studies (New York: Fordham University Press, 2018), pp. 110–49 (121–22 and 141 n. 63 for the misunderstanding regarding the presence of members of Machaut's family in Cyprus).
13 Hardy, *Édition critique de la* Prise d'Alixandrie, pp. 27, 26–48, ll. 873–74 (allusion to the fact that the poet had met Peter), 839–1610 (Peter's travels in Europe from the coronation to his departure from Venice). For Peter's journeys, see Earp, *Guillaume de Machaut*, pp. 46–48 and this author's introductory chapter to this volume.

as 'a chivalric revival' embedded in real history, or what we might term a crusader revival embellished with chivalric ethos, since Peter's *Gesta* are clearly inscribed within the tradition of the crusader cycle [Fig. 2]. Combining traits from two very similar genres of dynastic history, the knightly chronicle and the royal/aristocratic biography, it is a panegyric that aims to celebrate its hero's actions, not to explain their causality.[14] It is also a very accurate account, despite some fictitious elements and the occasional erroneous dating.

The narrative follows a thematically and chronologically linear structure, with the exception of Peter's murder, which is placed *in medias res*, preceding the conspiracy that led to it. Machaut even toys with an element of suspense in accordance with the Arthurian model, as the identity of the mysterious hero is not revealed until verse 1393. In the prologue, Peter's birth is given mythological dimensions: the assembly of Gods implored Nature to fashion a most gifted man of the likes of the Nine Worthies or 'les .ix. preus' (three pagan: Hector, Alexander the Great, Julius Caesar; three Jews: David, Joshua, Judas Maccabeus; and three Christian: Arthur, Charlemagne, Godfrey of Bouillon), who would 'restore his land to noble Godfrey' of Bouillon as his true heir and 'le disiemes [preu]' [Figs 3–4];[15] Nature effected a 'conjuction' between Venus and Mars, who endowed this man with prowess in battle and charm with ladies, in other words, with the chivalric passions for war and love.[16] Despite a number of references to the Boethian figure of fickle Fortune in the poem, a theme also associated with Peter by Geoffrey Chaucer, Christine de Pizan, and François Villon, the power that activates Peter's actions depends on the extent to which they are dictated by Christian or base motives and, accordingly, his knightly values and crusader goals are directed toward his personal honour.[17] Thus, Machaut associates the story of the miraculously hanging cross of the Good Thief, erroneously misplaced

---

14 Guillaume de Machaut, *La Prise d'Alixandre*, 'Introduction', p. 2; Elizabeth Gaucher, *La biographie chevaleresque: Typologie d'un genre (XIIIe–XVe siècle)* (Paris: H. Champion, 1994), who, however, does not discuss Machaut; Daisy Delogu, *Theorizing the Ideal Sovereign. The Rise of the French Vernacular Royal Biography* (Toronto – Buffalo – London: University of Toronto Press, 2008), esp. chapter 3 on Machaut; Catherine Gaullier-Bougassas, 'Images littéraires de Chypre et évolution de l'esprit de croisade au XIVe siècle', in *Progrès, réaction, décadence dans l'Occident médiéval*, ed. by Emmanuèle Baumgartner and Laurence Harf-Lancner (Geneva: Droz, 2003), pp. 123–35; Hardy, *Édition critique de la Prise d'Alixandrie*, pp. lxxxviii–cxix.

15 Hardy, *Édition critique de la Prise d'Alixandrie*, pp. cxxiv, 3, 10, 206, 258, ll. 47–66, 307–10, 7173–88, 8848–51. See: Catherine Gaullier-Bougassas, 'Le Chevalier au Cygne à la fin du Moyen Âge. Renouvellements, en vers et en prose, de l'épopée romanesque des origines de Godefroy de Bouillon', *Cahiers de Recherches Médiévales et Humanistes*, 12 (2005), 115–46 (pp. 115–16); *Encyclopedia of the Medieval Chronicle*, gen. ed. Graeme Dunphy (Leiden – Boston: Brill, 2010), pp. 1150–52; Craig Taylor, *Chivalry and the Ideals of Knighthood in France during the Hundred Years War* (Cambridge: Cambridge University Press, 2013), p. 62. Mézières does not associate Alexander with Peter, see Catherine Gaullier-Bougassas, 'Une exemplarité déconstruite: la polémique sur Alexandre et le procès de la littérature de fiction dans *Le songe du vieil pelerin*', in *Philippe de Mézières and His Age*, pp. 207–23.

16 Hardy, *Édition critique de la Prise d'Alixandrie*, pp. 2–9, ll. 1–258.

17 Guillaume de Machaut, *La Prise d'Alixandre*, 'Introduction', pp. 24–25; Guillaume de Machaut, *The Capture of Alexandria*, 'Introduction', p. 10; Hardy, *Édition critique de la Prise d'Alixandrie*, p. cxxv, 23, ll. 731–34, 753–56; n. 6 above for Chaucer and below for Pizan and Villon.

from the monastery of Stavrovouni to Famagusta, with Peter's visionary calling to be a crusader.[18]

In general, Machaut devotes many verses to stories that constitute sensational material for a narrative, such as the king's exploits outside Cyprus in the East and the West, but he is a lot less detailed on local Cypriot affairs, especially before 1362. Significantly, he considers France to be the destination of Peter's flight to the West with his younger brother Prince John of Antioch in secret without their father's leave, sometime before September 1349, and emphasizes the special bonds Peter had with the King of France John II (1350–64), 'more powerful than other monarchs'.[19] And, naturally, he presents Peter as an accomplished champion, 'the foreign king' winning one tournament after another 'because he was the best versed' in jousting, and a music lover, who marvelled at the music produced by an orchestra composed of all possible musical instruments during a concert given in his honour by Emperor Charles IV (1355–78) of Luxembourg in Prague, 'declaring that he had never heard such exquisite melody in his entire life'.[20]

At the same time, Machaut remains meaningfully silent about Peter's scandalous private life, although his is a somehow more flawed hero than Mézières's perfect prince. He stresses that the king regretted whatever vile actions he committed, such as his behaviour towards the Giblet family and particularly the torture of Maria of Giblet, and does not hesitate to admit that, in his youth, 'all his thoughts, all his desires | were directed toward what would afford pleasure | to ladies and young women. | These he found very appealing and attractive', always, however, within the chivalric moral code.[21] His account of the events that led to Peter's murder is constructed in a highly dramatic style, but several of the unpleasant details, recounted at length

---

18 Hardy, Édition critique de la Prise d'Alixandrie, pp. 10–11, ll. 291–327. Hardy (p. cxxv) believes that Machaut borrowed the story from Jean de Mandeville, Le Livre des Merveilles du Monde, ed. by Christiane Deluz (Paris: CRNS, 2000), pp. 100, 122; the story, however, circulated long before the mid-fourteenth century, rendering the monastery a major tourist attraction, see Angel Nicolaou-Konnari and Chris Schabel (eds), Lemesos. A History of Limassol in Cyprus from Antiquity to the Ottoman Conquest (Newcastle upon Tyne: Cambridge Scholars Publishing, 2015), pp. 213, 271–72, 316–18. Leontios Makhairas, Χρονικό της Κύπρου. Παράλληλη διπλωματική έκδοση των χειρογράφων, ed. by Michalis Pieris and Angel Nicolaou-Konnari, Texts and Studies in the History of Cyprus, 48 (Nicosia: Cyprus Research Centre, 2003), pp. 65–69, does not associate Stavrovouni with Peter but considers the visit of St Helen to Cyprus after the invention of the Holy Cross to be the foundation legend of Christian Cyprus, placing the story at the beginning of his chronicle; see Nicolaou-Konnari, 'A Neglected Relationship', p. 123.
19 Hardy, Édition critique de la Prise d'Alixandrie, pp. 16-19, 22–23, ll. 507-96, 729–56.
20 Hardy, Édition critique de la Prise d'Alixandrie, pp. 26, 29, 38, 40–41, 44, 121, 34–35, ll. 842–46, 969, 1260–66, 1356–64 (quotation at 1363–64: 'mais l' estrange roy ot le pris, | com des armes li mieus apris'), 1467–88, and 4172–74 ('joustes et tournois'), 1139–76 (concert, quotation at 1174–76: 'li roys de ce moult se merveille, | et dit qu'onques mais en sa vie | ne vit si tresgrant melodie'); Barton Palmer in Guillaume de Machaut, La Prise d'Alixandre, 'Introduction', p. 9 believes that Machaut may have been engaged to compose some pieces in Peter's honour. See this author's introductory chapter to this volume for further discussion on Peter's association with jousting, minstrels, and music.
21 Hardy, Édition critique de la Prise d'Alixandrie, pp. 9, 241–48, ll. 267–73, 8257–490 (8469–71: 'Li roys moult fort se repenti, | quant onques il se consenti | a faire ce quil avoit fait'); Guillaume de Machaut, La Prise d'Alixandre, p. 51 (for the translation).

in the fifteenth-century Cypriot chronicle attributed to Leontios Makhairas,[22] are omitted or adjusted, the king presented as a martyr. Machaut considers the cause of Peter's murder by a group of his vassals to be their blasphemous opposition to both his crusader plans and his love of France, thus subtly highlighting Peter's French links. Moreover, he introduces Anglo-French rivalry to Cypriot politics by making the Cypriot knight John Visconti English; apart from the queen's infidelities, Visconti also informed the king about the conspiracy of his brothers and knights, to which Peter protested accusing Visconti of being 'a dishonorable Englishman, | False, traitorous, malicious'. The night of the murder the king was lying naked in bed with his wife and he received more than sixty wounds. Machaut stresses the active involvement of the king's brothers in both the conspiracy and the regicide, blaming their envy of 'The wisdom, the honor, and the virtue, | The courage, the great valor, | The grand enterprises, the prudence, | The generosity, the nobility, | Of the king of Cyprus'; he even accuses their mother, Alice of Ibelin (1304/06–after 1386), to have plotted against her son, thus endowing his narrative with a touch of Greek tragedy.[23]

Another two works by Machaut may have been inspired by Peter's image as the ideal courtly lover and wandering knight during his first European tour. The first sixteen verses of the *complainte*, *Mon cuer, m'amour, ma dame souvereinne*, which was probably written after the coronation of Charles V in 1364, form the acrostic 'MARGVERITE - PIERRE':[24]

> **M**on cuer, m'amour, ma dame souvereinne,
> **A**rbres de vie, estoile tresmonteinne,
> **R**ose de may de toute douceur pleinne,
> **G**ente et jolie,
> **V**ous estes fleur de toute fleur mondeinne
> **E**t li conduis qui toute joie ameinne,
> **R**uissiaus de grace et la droite fonteinne,
> **I**e n'en doubt mie.
> **T**oute biauté est en vous assevie
> **E**t vo bonté nuit et jour mouteplie;
> **P**our ce plaisence ha dedens moy norrie

---

22 For Leontios Makhairas's colourful portrait of Peter, see his Χρονικό της Κύπρου, pp. 108–222 and Angel Nicolaou-Konnari, 'Apologists or Critics? The Reign of Peter I of Lusignan (1359–1369) Viewed by Philippe de Mézières (1327–1405) and Leontios Makhairas (c. 1360/80–after 1432)', in *Philippe de Mézières and His Age*, pp. 359–401, esp. 393–96, 398–400. Generally, Angel Nicolaou-Konnari, '"A poor island and an orphaned realm…, built upon a rock in the midst of the sea…, surrounded by the infidel Turks and Saracens": The Crusader Ideology in Leontios Makhairas's Greek *Chronicle* of Cyprus', *Crusades*, 10 (2011), 119–45 and Nicolaou-Konnari, 'A Neglected Relationship'.

23 Hardy, *Édition critique de la* Prise d'Alixandrie, pp. 233–56, ll. 7953–8766; Guillaume de Machaut, *La Prise d'Alixandre*, pp. 379, 385 (for the translation).

24 Guillaume de Machaut, *Poésies lyriques*, ed., introduction, and glossary by Vladimir Chichmaref, 2 vols (Paris: H. Champion, 1909), I, no. VI, p. 256; a list of manuscript sources for the *complainte* was put together by the University of Exeter project *The Works of Guillaume de Machaut: Music, Image, Text in the Middle Ages*, <http://machaut.exeter.ac.uk/?q = node/2064> [accessed 1 September 2019].

Ioie sans peinne,
Et si m'a tout en vostre signourie
Rendu et mis, et par noble maistrie
Ravi mon cuer qui usera sa vie
En vo demeinne.

In the *Dit de la Marguerite*, dated to 1364/66 or later, the ardent lover may be identified with Peter, as suggested by verses 27 ('Indeed, from Outremer it [this flower] has healed me of my pain') and 202 ('This flower, which I chose among all flowers, has been my delight, and when I am in Cyprus or Egypt, my heart very tenderly makes it its dwelling').[25] An illumination of a crowned man kneeling before a lady, which accompanies the poem in 'the most authoritative of the Machaut omnibus manuscripts', is generally considered to represent Peter [Fig. 5].[26] Scholars have speculated that perhaps both works were inspired by the king's romance with a French lady named Marguerite or, more likely, that they constitute 'an allegory of love', a court encomium intended to serve as chivalrous compliments to a grand lady who was in a position to help the Cypriot king gain support for his crusader projects; Margaret III of Flanders (1350–1405) has been suggested as the lady for whom the poems used the praise of a flower as a subtle political allegory and for whose wedding to Philip the Bold (1342–1404), Duke of Burgundy and King Charles V's brother, in 1369 a second *marguerite* poem may have been written.[27] Machaut's *Dit de la Marguerite*, in particular, began a long tradition of *marguerite* poems in French and English, influencing, among others, Eustache Deschamps and John Froissart.[28] Whatever the connection might be, it is worth mentioning that the name of Peter's sister and daughter was Margaret while, according to Makhairas, he had a prison-tower built in the palace complex of

---

25 Edited in: *Les Oeuvres de Guillaume de Machaut* by Prosper Tarbé (Reims – Paris: Techener, 1849; repr. Geneva: Slatkine Reprints, 1977), pp. 123–29, esp. 124, 129; Jean Froissart, *'Dits' et 'Débats'*, avec en appendice quelques poèmes de Guillaume de Machaut, ed. by Anthime Fourrier (Geneva: Droz, 1979), pp. 277–84, esp. 278 ('Car elle m'a gari d'outre la mer | De ma dolour'), 284 ('Trop me delite | En ceste fleur qu'ay seur toutes eslite, | Car quant je sui en Chipre ou en Egypte | Mes cuers en li tresdoucement habite'); Guillaume de Machaut, *Quatre Dits*, Modern French trans. Isabelle Bétemps, Traductions des classiques français du Moyen Âge, 82 (Paris: H. Champion, 2008), pp. 103–20, esp. 106, 119.

26 Paris, Bibliothèque nationale de France (henceforth BnF), MS Fr. 1584, fol. 448ʳ; see Guillaume de Machaut, *La Prise d'Alixandre*, 'Introduction', pp. 8–9.

27 Guillaume de Machaut, *Le Dit de la Fleur de lis et de la Marguerite*, in Jean Froissart, *'Dits' et 'Débats'*, pp. 289–301; Guillaume de Machaut, *Quatre Dits*, pp. 129–54.

28 C. S. Lewis, *The Allegory of Love: A Study in Medieval Tradition* (Oxford: Clarendon Press, 1936); James Irving Wimsatt, *The Marguerite Poetry of Guillaume de Machaut* (Chapel Hill: North Carolina University Press, 1970), pp. 47, 49, 50; Earp, *Guillaume de Machaut*, pp. 47, 190, 193, 194, 196, 231–32, 266, 269–70; Anthime Fourrier in his edition of Jean Froissart, *'Dits' et 'Débats'*, pp. 46–52, 72–75, 75–76; Alice Spencer, *Dialogues of Love and Government: A Study of the Erotic Dialogue Form in Some Texts from the Courtly Love Tradition* (Newcastle: Cambridge Scholars Publishing, 2007), chapter 3; Jennifer G. Wollock, *Rethinking Chivalry and Courtly Love* (Santa Barbara, Ca.: ABC-CLIO, 2011), pp. 163–64; Guillaume de Machaut, *The Capture of Alexandria*, p. 9; William Calin, *The Lily and the Thistle: The French Tradition and the Older Literature of Scotland* (Toronto: University of Toronto Press, 2014), p. 63 for poems in praise of flowers by Machaut, Froissart, and Christine de Pizan; Nicolaou-Konnari, 'A Neglected Relationship', pp. 121–22; below for Deschamps and Froissart.

Nicosia in 1368, which he named Margarita; Machaut euphemistically describes it as 'an entirely new dwelling | that was to be attractive and handsome'.[29]

In Machaut's *Le Dit dou Lion*, datable to 1342, and *Le Confort d'Ami*, written in 1357, the depiction of the ideal knight and prince (including the places he visits) agrees perfectly with the one provided for Peter some fifteen years later in the *Prise* and suggests that the Cypriot king's portrayal was submitted to or conformed with Machaut's views and his society's norms. In *Le Dit dou Lion*, the poet/narrator crosses to an island and, guided by a friendly Lion, the protagonist and title figure who represents the courtly lover [Fig. 6], receives advice on matters of love from a Lady and intercedes with her on the Lion's behalf. An old knight describes the different kinds of lovers, with special emphasis on the wanderer, who always leaves seeking adventure in Europe and the Eastern Mediterranean, of whom women should be cautious, but to whose chivalric charms they usually succumb. *Le Confort d'Ami* is a *consolatio*, designed to give solace to all who have suffered from political injustice, and a *regimen principum*, an educational treatise on morals, ethics, love, politics, war, and affairs of state.[30]

Philip of Mézières's encomiastic account of Peter's reign was based on his first-hand knowledge of persons and events, since he held the office of the king's chancellor for about eight years and was in Peter's service for another seven years before he became king [Fig. 7]. For the loyal chancellor, Cyprus was the ideal Christian kingdom under the rule of 'the most serene king of Jerusalem and Cyprus', his beloved lord,[31] whose portrayal was intended to promote the single inspiration and goal of his life, the project of a crusade for the liberation of the Holy Land, an 'ardent desire' that was to govern his worldview and direct his actions throughout his life.[32] As early as 1346

---

29   For the two Margarets, see Wipertus H. Rudt de Collenberg, 'Les Lusignan de Chypre', Επετηρίς Κέντρου Επιστημονικών Ερευνών (Κύπρου), 10 (1979–80), 85–319 (nos B, 23 and 27, pp. 137-39, 145-46) and n. 62 below. For the prison, see: Hardy, *Édition critique de la* Prise d'Alixandrie, p. 244, ll. 8357–2 ('une maison toute nouvelle | que devoit estre bonne et belle'); Guillaume de Machaut, *La Prise d'Alixandre*, p. 395 (for the translation); Leontios Makhairas, Χρονικό της Κύπρου, pp. 205–06, 410.

30   Edited in: *Les Oeuvres de Guillaume de Machaut*, pp. 40–44, 94–122; Guillaume de Machaut, *The Complete Poetry and Music, Volume 2: The Boethian Poems*, Le Remede de Fortune *and* Le Confort d'Ami, ed. and English trans. by R. Barton Palmer, music ed. by Uri Smilansky, and art historical commentary by Domenic Leo (Kalamazoo, Mich.: Medieval Institute Publications, 2019). For the dating, see Earp, *Guillaume de Machaut*, pp. 189–94 and Douglas Kelly, *Machaut and the Medieval Apprenticeship Tradition: Truth, Fiction and Poetic Craft* (Cambridge: D. S. Brewer, 2014), p. 18; generally, Didier Lechat, *Dire par fiction. Métamorphoses du je chez Guillaume de Machaut, Jean Froissart et Christine de Pizan*, Études christiniennes, 7 (Paris: H. Champion, 2005), chapter 2 passim, Wollock, *Rethinking Chivalry and Courtly Love*, pp. 162–63, and William Calin, *A Poet at the Fountain: Essays on the Narrative Verse of Guillaume de Machaut* (Lexington: The University Press of Kentucky, 2015), pp. 75–91, 130–45.

31   Philippe de Mézières, *The Life of Saint Peter Thomas*, ed. by Joachim Smet, O. Carm. (Rome: Institutum carmelitanum, 1954), p. 167 ('serenissimo regi meo Ierusalem et Cypri amantissimo domino meo').

32   It was in the church of the Holy Sepulchre in 1347 that he first conceived the idea of forming the Order of the Passion of Christ for the recovery of the Holy Land. See generally: Jorga, *Philippe de Mézières*, pp. 69–77; Joan B. Williamson, 'The *Chevallerie de la Passion Jhesu Christ*: Philippe de Mézières' Utopia', in *Gesellschaftutopien im Mittelalter / Discours et figures de l'Utopie au Moyen Âge, V. Jahrestagung der Reineke-Gesellschaft / 5ᵉ Congrès annuel de la Société Reineke*, ed. by Danielle Buschinger and Wolfgang

or 1347, Mézières visited Cyprus and formed a lifelong friendship with young Peter, then Count of Tripoli and heir to the throne, two years his junior, in whose person he found more than a sympathetic ear for his crusader projects and with whom he embarked on a campaign in the West for the promotion of their plans.[33]

Philip's writings belong to a wide range of literary genres and include hagiography, moral literature, religious treatises of the *Ars moriendi* type, epistles, drama, and allegorical poetry;[34] they were all, however, intended to serve as crusading propaganda and to find remedies for the ills of Christendom in Western Europe, a major prerequisite for a successful campaign. Even in his *Epistre lamentable*, written at the age of seventy in 1397, Mézières expresses with force and eloquence the passionate desire of his youth to organize a Christian campaign against the Muslims in view of the defeat in Nicopolis (1396).[35] In most of these works, Peter is a key figure and he is presented accordingly. The longest portrayal may be found in two works: the hagiographical *Vita* of Peter Thomas, Apostolic Legate in the East since 1359, Latin Archbishop of Crete in 1363, and Latin Patriarch of Constantinople in 1364, which was composed in Cyprus during Lent of 1366 with the intention to mobilize support for Peter's planned crusade and is thus Philip's only work amongst those discussed in this paper that was written before the king's murder and does not advocate a French cause; and the *Songe du Vieil Pelerin*, a vernacular advice book in the form of a dream vision, dedicated to King Charles VI of France (1380–1422) in 1389, a year after his declaration of personal rule.[36]

Thematically, almost all the references to Peter concern his plans for a crusade and, stylistically, conventional crusader rhetoric is used to describe him. King of Jerusalem

---

Spiewok, *Jahrbücher der Reineke-Gesellschaft / Annales de la Société Reineke* 5 (Greifswald: Reineke-Verlag, 1994), pp. 165–73; Joan B. Williamson, 'Philippe de Mézières and the Idea of Crusade', in *The Military Orders: Fighting for the Faith and Caring for the Sick*, ed. by Malcolm Barber (Aldershot: Ashgate, 1994), pp. 358–64; Blumenfeld-Kosinski and Petkov, *Philippe de Mézières and His Age*, with rich bibliography.

33   For what follows on Mézières, see more examples and discussion in Nicolaou-Konnari, 'Apologists or Critics?' and 'A Neglected Relationship', pp. 120–21.

34   For a list of Philip's works, see: Jorga, *Philippe de Mézières*, pp. vii–viii; Philippe de Mézières, *Songe du Vieux Pèlerin*, Modern French trans. by Joël Blanchard (Paris: Pocket, 2008), pp. 54–55; Blumenfeld-Kosinski and Petkov, *Philippe de Mézières and His Age*, p. 497.

35   See generally the collections of essays in Blumenfeld-Kosinski and Petkov, *Philippe de Mézières and His Age* and Joël Blanchard and Renate Blumenfeld-Kosinski (eds), *Philippe de Mézières et l'Europe. Nouvelle histoire, nouveaux espaces, nouveaux langages* (Geneva: Droz, 2017).

36   Charles VI began suffering from intermittent periods of mental illness from 1392 until his death. Besides Mézières' *Songe*, another three vernacular advice books or 'mirrors for princes' were dedicated to him during his reign: Honorat Bovet's *L'Arbre des batailles* (1389), Christine de Pizan's *Chemin de long estude* (1402–03), and Pierre Salmon's *Dialogues* (1409, with a second version in 1412–15), see n. 64 and 78 below and Brigitte Roux, *Les dialogues de Salmon et Charles VI*, Cahiers d'Humanisme et Renaissance, 52 (Geneva: Droz, 1998). The books' textual contents and their manuscript images, layout, and circulation demonstrate the importance of the dedication to the construction of their messages. The books' intended audiences included the king as well as other members of his government and in particular his relatives. See Renate Blumenfeld-Kosinski, *Poets, Saints, and Visionaries of the Great Schism, 1378–1417* (University Park: The Pennsylvania State University Press, 2006), chapters 4–5 and Kristin Leigh Erika Bourassa, *Counselling Charles VI of France: Christine de Pizan, Honorat Bovet, Philippe de Mézières, and Pierre Salmon* (unpublished doctoral thesis, University of York, 2014).

and Cyprus, Peter was the most valiant Christian ruler of his time, fighting the enemies of the faith and not his fellow Christians, a great king of the East, God-fearing and devout, whose noble intention of liberating his ancestral Kingdom of Jerusalem did not involve any trace of base motives. Although his was only a very small kingdom, as a worthy lion king[37] he made the Muslim rulers tremble with fear and brought Turkish lands into subjection.[38] His deeds equalled those of biblical kings, such as the brave king of the Maccabees of the Old Testament who had recaptured Jerusalem or the king of the vineyards of Engadi in the *Song of Solomon*.[39] Surprisingly, though, Philip mentions Peter's Order of the Sword only once, in the rule of his own Order of the Passion and this perhaps indicates the limited scope of the Cypriot Order.[40]

In the *Songe*, Philip makes only passing references to Peter's heroic exploits against the Turks in southern Anatolia, but in the *Life* the 1361 capture of Antalya (Satalia / Adalia) is described at length in crusading terms, the king's intention being

---

37 Philippe de Mézières, *Le Songe du Vieil Pelerin*, ed. by George W. Coopland, 2 vols (Cambridge: Cambridge University Press, 1969), I, pp. 109, 259, 280, and 297–99 ('vaillant roy Lyon', 'noble roy Lyon'), 280 ('petit Lyonnel' for Peter's son); Nicolas Jorga, 'L'épître de Philippe de Mézières à son neveu', *Bulletin de l'Institut pour l'étude de l'Europe sud-orientale* 8 (1921), 27–40 (p. 38) ('leo fortissimus'); n. 47 below. The image of a lion may be associated with the Lusignan coat of arms, which represents a *lion rampant*, cf. Philippe de Mézières, *Life*, p. 128.

38 Philippe de Mézières, *Songe*, I, pp. 94, 96, 128, 163, and 167 (valiant king), 135 ('illustrissimus princeps Petrus rex Ierusalem et Cypri'), 97 ('devotus, Catholicus, et Deum timens'), 102 (liberation of Jerusalem); Philippe de Mézières, *Le Livre de la Vertu du Sacrement de Mariage*, ed. by Joan B. Williamson (Washington, D.C.: The Catholic University of America Press, 1993), pp. 279–80 (valiant king); Philippe de Mézières, *Le Songe du vieil pelerin*, ed. by George W. Coopland, 2 vols (Cambridge: Cambridge University Press, 1969), I, pp. 223 ('un grant roy d'orient'), 258 ('ung petit roy'), II, pp. 220, 419, and 436 (valiant king); Philippe de Mèzières, *Une epistre lamentable et consolatoire. Adressée en 1397 à Philippe le Hardi, duc de Bourgogne, sur la défaite de Nicopolis (1396)*, ed. by Philippe Contamine and Jacques Paviot with the collaboration of Céline Van Hoorebeeck (Paris: Droz, 2008), pp. 102 ('roy de Jherusalem et de Chipre, le plus vaillant roy des crestiens en son temps contre les ennemis de la foy'), 182, 211, and 212 (valiant king); Philippe de Mézières, *La Sustance de la Chevalerie de la Passion de Jhesu Crist en francois*, ed. by Abdel Hamid Hamdy, 'Philippe de Mézières and the New Order of the Passion. Part III (Transcription of the Ashmole MS 813)', *Bulletin of the Faculty of Arts* (Alexandria University) 18 (1964), 43–104 (p. 54: valiant "petit roy catholique"); Jorga, *Philippe de Mézières*, p. 511 n. 5 ('vaillant roy' of 'grande prouesse' in the inscription on Philip's tombstone).

39 Philippe de Mézières, *Campaign for the Feast of Mary's Presentation*, ed. by William E. Coleman (Toronto: The University of Toronto Press, 1981), 'Letter', p. 44 (king of the Maccabees); Philippe de Mézières, *Songe*, I, 259 ("le roy des vignes de l'Angady [...] comme le preux Judas Machabeus, le tres preu Jonathas, et le vaillant Eleazarus'), 260 and 295 (Engadi used for Cyprus); Jorga, 'L'épître', pp. 33, 38 (victorious king of the Maccabees). See Nicolaou-Konnari, 'Apologists or Critics?', pp. 373–74 for Engadi situated in or identified with Cyprus.

40 Philippe de Mézières, *De la Chevallerie de la Passion de Jhesu Crist*, Paris, Bibliothèque nationale de France, Bibliothèque de l'Arsenal, MS 2251, fol. 15ᵛ, quoted in Jorga, *Philippe de Mézières*, pp. 76 n. 2, 83 n. 2, 120 n. 3. On Peter's Order, see Sergio Baldan, *Il reale Ordine dei cavalieri di Cipro detto della Spada e del Silenzio* (Venice: Marsilio, 1990) and Philippe Trélat, 'L'ordre de l'Épée à Chypre: mémoire de la croisade et instrument du pouvoir des Lusignan', in *Autour de la Toison d'or. Ordres de chevalerie et confréries nobles aux XIVᵉ–XVIᵉ siècles*, Rencontres de Vienne (24–27 septembre 2018), ed. by Alain Marchandisse and Gilles Docquier, Publications du Centre Européen d'Études bourguignonnes, 59 (Neuchâtel: Éditeurs divers suisses, 2019), pp. 317–36.

to destroy the enemies of the faith.[41] Similarly, in the *Life* Peter's first journey to Europe is presented as a quest to rally the support of western rulers for his planned expedition, an expedition that conformed to all the criteria defining a crusade: it had a just cause and pure intentions ('sancta et devota intentione'), Peter described as a 'faithful champion defending the Christians of the East' ('athletam fidelem Christianos orientis defensurum') who launched a holy war ('passagium sanctum') against the enemies of the faith for the liberation of Jerusalem, was declared by the pope, the text providing a detailed account of Peter taking the cross in Avignon on 31 March 1363, and was preached by the legate.[42] In both works, the capture of Alexandria on Friday 10 October 1365 is described in crusading epic style as a campaign for the glory of the name of God; in the *Life*, in particular, Cypriots, French, Germans, and English are said to be all united in their common cause under Peter's leadership, aspiring to the victory against the enemies of the faith that would open the door of Paradise for them, charging against the unfaithful Saracens with the cry 'Long live Peter, our King of Jerusalem and Cyprus!'.[43] Despite the bitter lesson taught by the futile Alexandria expedition, Philip refuses to acknowledge that political and economic considerations also governed the policies of the leaders of the West; he expresses his bitter disappointment about the infamous treaty with the Mamluks imposed on Peter by the pope, commenting ironically that this was the pope's wish and his lord the king could not act against it, and blames the lack of unity and the failure of the princes to respond to the call of the Christians of the East for the loss of the capital city of the Kingdom of Christians ('maistre cite du royaume general des crestiens').[44]

Peter's less monolithic portrayal in the *Songe*, a work that may have been influenced by Machaut's *Prise*,[45] deserves further discussion. In this long allegorical poem of life as a pilgrimage, Philip of Mézières suggests solutions to problems posed by the minority and later mental illness of Charles VI of France as well as to other political concerns, such as the papal schism, the Anglo-French wars, and the conflicts between

---

41 Philippe de Mézières, *Songe*, I, p. 295, II, pp. 227, 419; Philippe de Mézières, *Life*, pp. 96–97; Jorga, 'L'épître', p. 38; Philippe de Mézières, *Epistre lamentable*, p. 217; Philippe de Mézières, *Sustance de la Chevalerie*, p. 54.

42 Philippe de Mézières, *Life*, pp. 102–06 (102, 105, 106 for the quotations). See Nicolaou-Konnari, 'Apologists or Critics?', p. 391 for Philip's crusading style.

43 Philippe de Mézières, *Life*, pp. 125–41 (128 for the quotation: 'Vivat, vivat Petrus Ierusalem et Cypri rex noster! Contra Saracenos infideles'); Philippe de Mézières, *Songe*, I, pp. 280, 295, 297–98, II, pp. 227, 419, 436. The events are also mentioned in Philip's following works: *Chevallerie de la Passion*, fols 17[r], 52[r]–53[r], 72[r]–73[r], 89[r], quoted in Jorga, *Philippe de Mézières*, pp. 299–300; *Sustance de la Chevalerie de la Passion*, p. 54; Jorga, 'L'épître', p. 33.

44 Philippe de Mézières, Letter dated 25 September 1368, Paris, Bibliothèque de l'Arsenal, MS 499, fols 154[v]–155[r], quoted in Jorga, "Une collection de lettres', p. 315; *Letter to King Richard II. A plea made in 1395 for peace between England and France*, ed. and English trans. by George W. Coopland (Liverpool: Liverpool University Press, 1975), pp. 99–100.

45 For the identical terminology used for vessels in Machaut, Mézières, and Makhairas, which, however does not necessarily indicate direct borrowings, see: Gilles Rogues, 'Les noms des bâteaux dans la *Prise d'Alexandrie* de Guillaume de Machaut', *Textes et Langages* (Université de Nantes), 13 (1986), 269–79; Hardy, *Édition critique de la* Prise d'Alixandre, p. cxxvii; Nicolaou-Konnari, 'Apologists or Critics?', pp. 384–85; Nicolaou-Konnari, 'A Neglected Relationship', pp. 121, 122.

the king's relatives that eventually descended into civil war. The old pilgrim, escorted by the Good Hope and the Virtues, seeks concrete solutions to the crises in France, providing condemnation, consolation, and advice and adapting familiar discussions of kingship to urge Charles's brothers to stop fighting amongst themselves and support their king. Naturally, in this context Peter serves as the model of the perfect crusader and the ideal, divinely chosen monarch and the French king is repeatedly advised to imitate the Cypriot's example. Accordingly, Cyprus under Peter's rule is said to have witnessed a Golden Age in terms of wealth, peace, and justice and is presented as the ideal Christian kingdom. Thanks to its commerce, protected by the wise king, the island prospered in population and resources and Peter could thus finance his expeditions against the infidel [Fig. 8]. Queen Truth's allegorical journey is strikingly similar to the Cypriot king's first journey to Europe and the Alexandria crusade is used to teach the French king how to organize a successful crusade, including practical matters and logistics. Through the triumphs of Peter's crusades in the East, the island became 'the frontier of Catholic Christendom, on which the banner of the Cross was raised against the enemies of the Faith', a powerful kingdom feared by the Infidel, a refuge for the soldiers of God and the pilgrims. After his murder and the destructive Genoese invasion, disasters had befallen Cyprus and the islands of the Greek Archipelago. Using biblical metaphors, Mézières considers the repentance of the murderers to be the only way for the regeneration of the fallen Kingdom of Cyprus.[46]

The image of Peter as 'the most illustrious of the princes of Christendom [...] a king worthy of all praise' is used by Philip in a very similar way in his *Oratio tragedica*, a devotional text in Latin written simultaneously with the *Songe*. Assuming the role of the old Orator, Philip dedicates the fourth part of his work to the recovery of the Holy Land, presenting 'Peter of Lusignan, King of Cyprus and Jerusalem' as the prince 'who won the most victories against the Infidel' although he did not receive any concrete help from the princes of the West. Philip claims that Peter's valour was for ever remembered by the Muslims with the saying 'the sword of Lion King Peter will strike you' when they wanted to scare someone. He also recounts at length and repeatedly how Peter's barons treacherously made him abandon Alexandria, a feat for which the Cypriot king deserves to be called 'the new Moses'; the fact that throughout the *Songe*, it is Charles VI, the 'roy des Frans', who is compared with young Moses, leading the French (the new Israelites) out of bondage, promotes Peter's kingship to a privileged status that equals the prestigious French one.[47]

---

46 Philippe de Mézières, *Songe*, I, pp. 109, 257–60, 295–300, 486–87, II, pp. 419, 436, and passim. See Gaullier-Bougassas, 'Images littéraires de Chypre' and Kevin Brownlee, 'The Figure of Peter I and the Status of Cyprus in *Le Songe du vieil pelerin*: Crusade Ideology, Salvation History, and Authorial Self-Representation', in *Philippe de Mézières and His Age*, pp. 165–88. Joël Blanchard has already noted the similarity between Queen Truth's and Peter's journey, see Philippe de Mézières, *Songe du Vieux Pèlerin*, 'Introduction', p. 14.

47 Philippe de Mézières, *Oratio tragedica*, ed. and French trans. by Joël Blanchard and Antoine Calvet, Cahiers d'Humanisme et Renaissance, 156 (Geneva: Droz, 2019), pp. 20–21, 62–67, 418–27, 442–61, esp. 458–61 (Moses), 466–67 ('gladius leonis Petri regis te percussiat'); Philippe de Mézières, *Songe*, I,

The way Philip presents Peter's private life corresponds in the main to the way the loyal chancellor constructs his lord's public image as a king and a crusader and accords with his authorial intentions. The few instances where Philip reveals a more human side to the king's character are again related to the crusader cause: they concern Peter's despair of having failed to secure the aid of the princes of the West for his crusade, the consolation offered by Peter Thomas in Venice in late 1364, and the king's deep sorrow when in tears he implored his allies not to abandon Alexandria. A rare exception is a passage in the *Oratio tragedica* where Philip becomes more personal, calling Peter a 'young oriental king, energetic, magnanimous, and elegant of his person'.[48] Faithful to his intention not to blemish the picture of the perfect crusader, Philip chooses to omit the deplorable events that were caused by Peter's notorious conduct and led to his murder; although he had left Cyprus in June 1366 never to return, Philip must have known of Peter's erratic behaviour, recorded in Makhairas's chronicle.[49] The chancellor does not describe in detail the events of the murder either; compared to Jesus, the king is said to have been treacherously killed by his barons in bed while sleeping and not in battle against the enemies of the faith, as would have been worthy of him. Philip offers no explanation for the murderers' motives, the only exception being a passage in the *Oratio tragedica* where he explains that the Cypriot barons, used to a life of luxury and idleness, considered Peter's wars to have had a harmful effect on their interests and were envious of his favors to the foreigners in his service. Most importantly, he does not hesitate to accuse the king's two brothers of complicity in the regicide, something that was generally accepted in the West; he even places one of them at the scene of the crime like another Cain.[50]

Philip's depiction of Peter's person and reign may thus not be entirely fabricated but it is deliberately one-sided, with meaningful omissions and partial interpretations of historical events, an idealized portrayal of the king's works and days. He presents only the image of the perfect prince, a man of heroic stature whose life was governed by the crusader ethos, ignoring all other sides to the Cypriot king's character or parameters of his policy. In other words, as Peter's apologist in works the majority of which were written after the king's death, Philip also writes the apology of his own life, justifying a lifetime's labours and goals; in his *Oratio tragedica* he characteristically

---

pp. 99–100, II, pp. 4–7, 127–30, 135–36, 455, 484, 497, 504. See Daisy Delogu, 'How to Become the 'Roy des Frans'': The Performance of Kingship in Philippe de Mézières's *Le songe du vieil pelerin*', in *Philippe de Mézières and His Age*, pp. 147–64 and Brownlee, 'The Figure of Peter I and the Status of Cyprus in *Le Songe du vieil pelerin*', pp. 179–84.

48 Philippe de Mézières, *Life*, pp. 120–21, 133–34 and *Oratio tragedica*, pp. 418–19 ('quemdam regem orientalem juvenem scilicet strenuum, magnanimum et in persona elegantem').

49 See n. 22 above.

50 Philippe de Mézières, *Campaign*, 'Letter', pp. 43–44, *Epistre Lamentable*, p. 102, *Oratio tragedica*, pp. 22–23, 66–67, 460–65, and *Songe*, I, pp. 259–60, 295–96, 299, II, p. 220; Jorga, 'L'épître', pp. 38–39. For a discussion of the events, the extent of the king's brothers' complicity, and contemporary opinions, see: Mas Latrie, *Histoire de l'île de Chypre*, II, pp. 342–45; Jorga, *Philippe de Mézières*, pp. 386–94; Hill, *A History of Cyprus*, II, pp. 363–68; Jean Richard, 'La Révolution de 1369 dans le royaume de Chypre', *Bibliothèque de l'École des Chartes*, 110 (1952), 108–23; Peter W. Edbury, 'The Murder of King Peter I of Cyprus (1359–1369)', *Journal of Medieval History*, 6 (1980), 219–33.

says that, in his quest for the 'pearl' (the liberation of the Holy Land, the Latin word 'margarita' constituting an interesting association with the *marguerite* poetry), he found in the person of Peter a king burning with the same desire.[51] Most importantly, if as a diplomat he failed to secure the concrete support of the European courts for his king's crusades,[52] as an image-maker Mézières succeeded in influencing certain literary circles.

Indeed, Peter's portrayal by both Mézières and Machaut as a heroic knight errant and a charismatic king, a devout Christian and an ardent crusader derived from a rather late medieval chivalric concept and exerted a considerable influence on a number of French authors, who were all united in their wish for peace with England and within France. Acknowledging Mézières's political and intellectual impact, Michael Hanly has termed this group a 'peace movement', a 'coalition of French and English writers and diplomats who [at the end of the fourteenth century] opposed their countries' wars on grounds both philosophical and pragmatic' and whose travels and connections might have served the transmission of these themes. Peace between the two realms would help end the schism and serve as a prelude to a crusade for the destruction of the menacing Saracens.[53] At the same time, as R. Barton Palmer suggests, the cornerstone of the literary movement of the 'chivalric revival' launched by the *Prise d'Alixandre* was the 'aristocratic code steeped in the Christian zeal', in other words the identification of the crusading revival with moral and spiritual progress. Peter's idealized literary image perfectly embodied these themes as the expression of the wishes of French writers for the improvement of the political and social life in France; the symbolism was most probably enhanced by his French ancestry even though he was not *nationalized* or *Francicized* by any of the writers, who appropriated him in a universal way.[54] The fact that, similarly to William of Machaut and Philip of Mézières, all the authors mentioned in this paper but one, Honorat Bovet, also believed in the king's brothers' complicity in his murder is hardly surprising, since a regicide that was also a fratricide threatened the very essence of chivalric ethos and legitimate succession and could serve as a negative example for French politics in view of the dynastic conflict between the Orleans and the Burgundy parties.

The epic poem on the life of Bertrand Du Guesclin (c. 1320–80), composed by the trouvère Cuvelier (fl. late fourteenth century) in the 1380s after the constable's

---

51 Philippe de Mézières, *Oratio tragedica*, pp. 62–69, 417–87, esp. 418–19, and *Epistre lamentable*, pp. 211–12.

52 It seems, though, that he did use his position in order to promote less idealistic causes, see indicatively *Bullarium Cyprium III: Lettres papales relatives à Chypre 1316–1378*, ed. by Charles Perrat and Jean Richard, with the collaboration of Christopher Schabel, Sources et études de l'histoire de Chypre, 68 (Nicosia: Centre de Recherche Scientifique, 2012), nos v-28, 36, 128, 164, cf. nos w-102, 106–07, 187, 317–18.

53 For the intellectual connections amongst Mézières, Machaut, Chaucer, Petrarch, Bovet, and Deschamps, see: Michael Hanly, 'Philippe de Mézières and the Peace Movement', in *Philippe de Mézières and His Age*, pp. 61–82; Derek S. Brewer, 'Chaucer's Knight as Hero, and Machaut's Prise d'Alexandrie', in *Heroes and Heroines in Medieval English Literature: A Festschrift to André Crépin on the Occasion of his Sixty-fifth Birthday*, ed. by Leo Carruthers (Cambridge: D. S. Brewer, 1994), pp. 81–96.

54 Guillaume de Machaut, *La Prise d'Alixandre*, 'Introduction', p. 2; Gaullier-Bougassas, 'Images littéraires de Chypre'.

death, is, like Machaut's *Prise*, a typical example of chivalric biography in verse.[55] Despite the condescending way he speaks about Cuvelier in his *Songe*, Mézières actually agrees with him on a number of issues, Peter's portrayal included.[56] On six different occasions, Cuvelier repeats in almost identical words how the worthy Bertrand (this writer's *dixième preux*), expressed his wish to take the cross and assist the valiant Christian king of Cyprus, the conqueror of Antalya and Alexandria, against the Saracens, inviting at the same time the Companies to join him. But he had to give up his plans because the king's brother, begotten by the devil, treacherously murdered him: 'En l'année, seigneur, que Bertran se croiza | Pour aler guerrier Sarrazins par delà, | Avint une merveille, telle n'avint piéçà. | Car cilz bons rois de Chippre, qui loialment régna, | Ot .I. frère germain ; déables l'engendra, | Car son frère le roy tua et dévoura'.[57]

Du Guesclin was already fairly well known and esteemed by the then dauphin Charles when Peter was in France. Peter attended the discussion at the Parliament of Paris of the dispute between Du Guesclin and the seneschal of Poitou William of Felton on 27–29 February 1364.[58] Another historical coincidence that further associated the two men was the fact that the constable took the town of Lusignan, ancestral seat of the Lusignan family in Poitou, from the English in 1374 on behalf of Duke John of Berry (1340–1416), brother of King Charles V; the king reinvested his brother with the title of Count of Poitou.[59] It is interesting to note that, according to John Froissart, Peter visited Poitou in 1364, at the time in the hands of the

---

55 Claude Tixier, *Portrait littéraire de Bertrand Du Guesclin: le héros Bertrand, son entrée sur la scène épique. Étude sur l'œuvre de Charles Cuvelier, trouvère du XIV*[e] *siècle* (Paris: Nizet, 1981); Gaucher, *La biographie chevaleresque*, passim; Micheline Dupuy, *Bertrand Du Guesclin: capitaine d'aventure, connétable de France* (Paris: Perrin, 1999); Richard Vernier, *The Flower of Chivalry: Bertrand du Guesclin and the Hundred Years War* (Woodbridge: Boydell Press, 2003); Bernard Guenée, *Du Guesclin et Froissart: la fabrication de la renommée* (Paris: Tallandier, 2008); Taylor, *Chivalry and the Ideals of Knighthood*, pp. 54–90 passim.

56 Philippe de Mézières, *Songe*, I, pp. 20, 26–28, 65, II, p. 243 ('le pauvre homme appelle Cuveliers').

57 *Chronique de Bertrand du Guesclin, par Cuvelier, trouvère du XIV*[e] *siècle*, ed. Ernest Charrière, 2 vols (Paris: Firmin-Didot, 1839), I, ll. 1732–49, 6553–59 ('Et adont dit li preux Bertran et li courtois | Qu'il yroit voluntiers prendre la sainte crois, | Et iroit dedens Chippre, pour les Sarrasinois, | Aidier le roy de Chippre, qui fu crestiens à droit, | Bons, loiaux et hardiz estoit en tous endroiz'), 7148–89, 7266–68, 7438–64 (quotation), 7549–53. I have not been able to use: *La Chanson de Bertrand du Guesclin de Cuvelier*, ed. by Jean-Claude Faucon, 3 vols (Toulouse: Éditions universitaires du Sud, 1990–91); Delphine Demelas, *Sur un air épique, sur un air lyrique: célébrer le bon connétable. Édition critique et commentaires du manuscrit 428/(306) de la bibliothèque municipale d'Aix-en-Provence contenant 'La chanson de Bertrand du Guesclin' de Cuvelier suivie de pièces lyriques*, 3 vols (thèse de doctorat, Université d'Aix-Marseille, 2016); Cuvelier, *The Song of Bertrand du Guesclin*, English trans. by Nigel Bryant (Woodbridge: Boydell Press, 2019). See Taylor, *Chivalry and the Ideals of Knighthood*, p. 62.

58 Siméon Luce, *Histoire de Bertrand Du Guesclin: la jeunesse de Bertrand (1320–1364)* (Paris: Hachette, 1876), pp. 401–06 for the affair, 405 for Peter ('presentibus illustri principe rege Chipri, consanguineo nostro'); Jorga, *Philippe de Mézières*, pp. 183–84; cf. Bertrand Du Guesclin (comte de Longueville), *Letters, Orders and Musters of Bertrand Du Guesclin, 1357–1380*, ed. by Michael C. E. Jones (Woodbridge: Boydell Press, 2004), no. 39, pp. 12–13.

59 *Chronique de Bertrand du Guesclin*, II, ll. 21979, 22038, 22505; Guyard de Berville, *Histoire de Bertrand Du Guesclin, comte de Longueville, connétable de France*, 2 vols (Paris: de Hansy le jeune, 1772), II, pp. 380–81.

English.⁶⁰ The appreciation in a popular work of the Cypriot crusader king by the French national hero, the knight *par excellence* and an outstanding military leader, is indicative of the prestige in which Peter was held and the fascination he exerted on French literary circles.

Honorat Bovet (*c.* 1345/50–*c.* 1410), a Provençal Benedictine monk and doctor of canon law, a courtier and writer who was an authority on the legal technicalities of the papal schism,⁶¹ refers to Peter in one of his works, the 1394 *Somnium super materia scismatis*.⁶² A Latin prose dream allegory intended to serve as a plea against those who supported the forced abdication of the pope of Rome through military means, the *Somnium* records several encounters of the narrator, who stands for Bovet himself, with most of the period's Christian leaders, including King Charles VI of France and King James I (1382/85–98) of Cyprus, Peter's brother. At the beginning of the Cypriot passage, the narrator observes that he had met another Cypriot king, Peter I, while in Rome during the pontificate of Urban V (1362–70) ('quondam regem Petrum Chipri alias videram, tempore Urbani justi pape, in Roma'), which clearly suggests that Bovet was in Rome when Peter visited the pope in March-May 1368. James I of Lusignan recounts then the calamities that had befallen his kingdom. Citing the Genoese occupation of Cypriot territory and the Muslim threat as causes for the island's ill fate is expected, but adding to these the fact that James was unduly accused of Peter's murder ('de morte regis Petri, venerabilis fratris sui, indebite fuerat

---

60   *Chroniques de J. Froissart*, ed. by Siméon Luce et al., 15 vols, Société de l'histoire de France (Paris: Mᵐᵉ Vᵉ Jules Renouard et al., 1869–1975), VI, § 510, p. 97; Jorga, *Philippe de Mézières*, p. 185 n. 1, claims that Peter visited Lusignan, citing Froissart who, however, does not mention the town.

61   Michael Hanly and Hélène Millet, 'Les batailles d'Honorat Bovet. Essai de biographie', *Romania*, 114 (1996), 135–81; Hélène Biu, 'Honorat Bovet', in *Histoire littéraire de la France* (Paris: de Boccard, 2005), XLII/1, pp. 83–128; Blumenfeld-Kosinski, *Poets, Saints, and Visionaries*, pp. 133–49 and passim; Michael Hanly, 'Witness to the Schism: The Writings of Honorat Bovet', in *A Companion to the Great Western Schism (1378–1417)*, ed. by Joelle Rollo-Koster and Thomas M. Izbicki (Leiden – Boston: Brill, 2009), pp. 159–96.

62   An indirect association of Bovet with the Lusignans is the presentation of a manuscript of his *Apparicion maistre Jehan de Meun* (BnF, MS Fr. 811), with a rhymed dedication at the end, to the Duchess of Orleans Valentina Visconti (1371–1408), wife of Louis I, brother of King Charles VI, and daughter of Giangaleazzo Visconti (1351–1402), who overthrew his unpopular uncle Bernabò (1323–85) in 1385 to become the first duke of Milan. See *Medieval Muslims, Christians, and Jews in Dialogue: The* Apparicion maistre Jehan de Meun *of Honorat Bovet*, ed. and English trans. by Michael Hanly, Medieval and Renaissance texts and studies, 283 (Tempe, Arizona: Arizona Centre for Medieval and Renaissance Studies, 2005), pp. 1, 3, 8 n. 22, 15–17, 20–22, 25, 30, 58–59, 160, 170, 184, 187, 190, 192, 206–07, 231–32 and figs 2, 7 (BnF, MS Fr. 811, fols 1ᵛ, 8ʳ). Bernabò's tragic ending follows that of Peter in Geoffrey Chaucer, *The Canterbury Tales*, 'The Monkes Tale', ll. 3589–96, in *The Complete Works of Geoffrey Chaucer*, IV, p. 257. Bernabò's daughter was another Valentina Visconti (1360/62–82), who married Peter I's son, Peter II (1369–82), in 1378; his son, Charles of Parma, was engaged to Peter I's daughter, Margaret, on the day of Valentina's engagement to Peter II (2 April 1376), but the marriage never materialized; his second daughter, Anglesia (1371/72 or 1377–1439), married King Janus of Cyprus (1398–1432) by proxy in Milan in 1400, but the bride never came to Cyprus and the marriage was annulled in 1407–09. See Christina Kaoulla, *The Quest for a Royal Bride. The Marriage of King Janus of Cyprus and Anglesia Visconti of Milan* (unpublished doctoral thesis, University of Cyprus, 2016). Cf. n. 65, 76, and 81 below for connections of the Visconti family with the French writers discussed in this paper.

diffamatus') is surprising and renders Bovet the only French writer who explicitly does not accept the involvement of Peter's brothers in the regicide.[63]

James's absolution should be understood in relation to his inclusion in the poem's group of illustrious contemporary princes, which, in turn, should be viewed within the context of Bovet's political thoughts expressed in the *Arbre des batailles*. Like Mézières's *Songe*, this treatise is another advice book dedicated to Charles VI in 1389. It deals with the laws of war in the middle of the Hundred Years' War; Bovet considers just war to be beneficial for society and he opposes solitary chivalric heroism, as attested in socially condoned behaviours such as the duel and the vengeance, to discipline, loyalty to one's king, and service to the common good. In compliance with these ideas, Bovet chooses to present James as loyal but unjustly discredited.[64]

A courtier who served Charles V as a diplomat on missions to several European countries,[65] Eustache Deschamps (*c.* 1340–*c.* 1406) was Machaut's pupil and perhaps nephew and his work is recommended by Mézières in the *Songe*.[66] Although Deschamps

---

63 Honoré Bonet (Honorat Bovet), *L'apparicion maistre Jehan de Meun et le Somnium super materia scismatis*, ed. by Ivor Arnold, Publications de la Faculté des lettres de l'Université de Strasbourg, 28 (Paris: Les Belles Lettres, 1926), pp. 76–78; Patsy Diane Glatt, *Somnium prioris de Sallono super materia scismatis* (unpublished doctoral thesis, Washington State University, Department of English, 2005), pp. 124–31, cf. pp. 8, 53, 256–57, 275–76, 299 (I thank Chris Schabel for bringing this work to my attention). See: Noël Valois, 'Un ouvrage inédit d'Honoré Bonet, prieur de Salon', *Annuaire-bulletin de la Société de l'histoire de France*, 26/2 (1892), 193–228; *Medieval Muslims, Christians, and Jews in Dialogue*, p. 9 n. 26; Blumenfeld-Kosinski, *Poets, Saints, and Visionaries*, pp. 140–49 (esp. 143); Hanly, 'Philippe de Mézières and the Peace Movement', pp. 75–76.

64 Honoré Bonet (Honorat Bovet), *L'Arbre des batailles*, ed. by Ernest Nys (Brussels – Leipzig: Muquardt, 1883); Hélène Biu, *L'Arbre des batailles d'Honorat Bovet, étude de l'œuvre et édition critique des textes français et occitans*, 4 vols (thèse de doctorat, Université Paris IV, 2004); *The Tree of Battles of Honoré Bouet*, English trans. by George W. Coopland, with a hitherto unpublished historical interpolation (Cambridge, MA: Harvard University Press, 1949). See: Ernest Nys, 'Honoré Bonet et Christine de Pizan', *Revue de droit international et de législation comparée*, 14 (1882), 451–72 (repr. in Ernest Nys, *Études de droit international et de droit politique* (Brussels: Castaigne – Paris: Fontemoing, 1896), pp. 145–62); Raymond L. Kilgour, 'Honoré Bonet: A Fourteenth-Century Critic of Chivalry', *Publications of the Modern Language Association of America*, 50/2 (1935), 352–61; Philippe Contamine, 'L'idée de guerre à la fin du Moyen Âge: aspects juridiques et éthiques', *Comptes rendus des séances de l'Académie des Inscriptions et Belles-Lettres*, 123/1 (1979), 70–86; Nicholas A. Wright, 'The *Tree of Battles* of Honoré Bouvet and the Laws of War', in *War, Literature, and Politics in the Late Middle Ages*, ed. by C. T. Allmand (Liverpool: Liverpool University Press, 1976), pp. 12–32; Blumenfeld-Kosinski, *Poets, Saints, and Visionaries*, pp. 133–40; Hanly, 'Philippe de Mézières and the Peace Movement', pp. 74, 79–80; n. 36 above.

65 The Duchess Valentina Visconti of Orleans, on whom see n. 62 above, was Deschamps's patroness and he dedicated several poems to her, see Eustache Deschamps, *Oeuvres complètes*, ed. by Auguste-Henri-Édouard Queux de Saint Hilaire and Gaston Raynaud, 11 vols. (Paris: Firmin-Didot, 1878–1903), III, no. CCCXCII, pp. 166–67, IV, no. DCCLXXI, pp. 269–70, VII, nos MCCCXLIV–MCCCXLV, pp. 122–25, VIII, no. MCCCCIX, pp. 24–26 and Noëlle-Laetitia Perret, *Les traductions françaises du De regimine principum de Gilles de Rome. Parcours matériel, culturel et intellectuel d'un discours sur l'éducation* (Leiden – Boston: Brill, 2011), pp. 158–59.

66 Eustache Deschamps, *Balades pour Machaut*, in *Oeuvres complètes*, I, nos CXXIII–CXXIV, pp. 243–46 (composed in 1377 just after Machaut's death); Philippe de Mézières, *Songe*, II, pp. 20, 223, cf. I, pp. 20, 26–27, 30 n. 1, 50 n. 1. See: Laura Kendrick, 'Rhetoric and the Rise of Public Poetry: The Career of Eustache Deschamps', *Studies in Philology*, 80/1 (1983), 1–13; Jean-Patrice Boudet and Hélène Millet (eds),

clearly adopts his mentors' worldview, built around the ideal knight and crusader who would bring peace to Europe and liberate the Holy Land, this man is not Peter. Significantly, Deschamps's *dixième preux* is Bertrand Du Guesclin,[67] while Cyprus is included amongst the countries where one finds the hideous practice of poisoning. This association, which clearly belongs to the negative literary *locus* tradition of Cyprus, might constitute an allusion to master Angel, a Cypriot doctor in the service of King Charles II of Navarre (1349–87), called the Bad; Angel was ordered by his lord to poison the King of France Charles VI, but apparently did not obey, a story mentioned in the *Grandes Chroniques de France*.[68] Deschamps's *marguerite* poems show no connection with the Cypriot king either[69] and, in fact, only occasionally does he speak of Cyprus, never mentioning Peter by name.

In his *Miroir de mariage*, a debate-poem on the advantages and disadvantages of marriage, probably written between 1381 and 1389, Deschamps vaguely speaks of a Cypriot king's murder that led to the island becoming tributary to the Genoese, thus clearly alluding to Peter; the central figure, Franc Vouloir, tells his friend Folie that she caused Cyprus to lose its king. A few verses later, the poet mistakenly attributes the feats of the capture of Alexandria and Antalya to 'le roy Jehan de Lezinan'.[70] In his *Balade pour conquerir de cuer la Terre Sainte*, probably composed in 1395, there is

---

Eustache Deschamps et son temps, Textes et Documents d'Histoire Médiévale, 1 (Paris: Publications de la Sorbonne, 1997); Deborah Sinnreich-Levi (ed.), *Eustache Deschamps, French Courtier-Poet: His Work and His World* (New York: AMS Press, 1998); Danielle Buschinger (ed.), *Autour d'Eustache Deschamps. Actes du colloque du Centre d'études médiévales de l'Université de Picardie – Jules Verne, Amiens, 5–8 novembre 1998*, Médiévales, 2 (Amiens: Presses du Centre d'études médiévales, 1999); Blumenfeld–Kosinski, *Poets, Saints, and Visionaries*, pp. 121–31; Thierry Lassabatère and Miren Lacassagne (eds), *Eustache Deschamps, témoin et modèle. Littérature et société politique (XIVe–XVIe siècles)* (Paris: PUPS, 2008); Thierry Lassabatère, *La cité des hommes: Eustache Deschamps, expression poétique et vision politique* (Paris: H. Champion, 2011); Hanly, 'Philippe de Mézières and the Peace Movement', pp. 66, 71–73.

67 Eustache Deschamps, *Balade (Sur le trépas de Bertrand du Gesclin)*, in *Oeuvres complètes*, II, no. CCVII, pp. 28–30, cf. nos CCVI, CCXXII, pp. 27–28, 48–49.
68 Eustache Deschamps, *Balad (Contre les empoisonneurs)*, in *Oeuvres complètes*, III, no. CCCCLXV, pp. 282–83. See Suzanne Duvergé, 'Un empoisonneur aux gages de Charles le Mauvais: Maître Angel', *Bulletin Hispanique*, 38 (1938), 369–73 and Maria Narbona Cárceles, 'La contribution d'Eustache Deschamps à la construction du mythe de Charles, dit "le Mauvais", à partir de la fiction du Lyon', in *Eustache Deschamps, témoin et modèle*, pp. 33–47 (42); n. 93 below for the *Grandes Chroniques de France*.
69 Eustache Deschamps, *Lay amoureux, Lay de Franchise, Éloge d'une dame du nom de Marguerite, Prière d'amour à sa dame*, and *Le Miroir de mariage*, in *Oeuvres complètes*, II, nos CCCVI–CCCVII, pp. 193–203, 203–14, III, nos DXXXIX–DXL, pp. 379–80, 381–82, and IX, pp. 64, 191 respectively. See Miren Lacassagne, 'Le *Lai de Franchise* d'Eustache Deschamps ou de l'autre côté du miroir', *Le Moyen Âge*, 116/3–4 (2010), 645–56.
70 Eustache Deschamps, *Le Miroir de mariage*, in *Oeuvres complètes*, IX, pp. 361–62, ll. 11226–54, esp. 11226–27 ('Resgarde a Chyppre a quel present | Tu luy fis de leur roy tuer!') and 11252–54; I have not been able to consult Monique Dufournaud-Engel, *'Le Miroir de mariage' d'Eustache Deschamps. Édition critique accompagnée d'une étude littéraire et linguistique*, 2 vols (unpublished doctoral thesis, McGill University, 1975). See generally: Monique Engel, 'Le *Miroir de mariage* d'Eustache Deschamps, sources et traditions', in *Seconda miscellanea di studi e ricerche sul quattrocento francese*, ed. by Franco Simone, J. Beck, and Gianni Mombello (Chambéry – Torino: Centre d'études franco-italien, 1981), pp. 143–67; Jeannine Quillet, 'Le *Miroir de mariage* d'Eustache Deschamps', in *Amour, mariage et transgressions au Moyen Âge. Actes du*

a reference to Cyprus within the context of liberating the Holy Land but again no direct mention of Peter; the poet appeals to the leaders of the Christian world (the Cypriot king, Janus at the time, mentioned with those of France, Spain, Aragon, England, Portugal, and Navarre as well as the pope, the emperor, the Genoese, the Venetians, and the Hospitallers of Rhodes) to stop fighting each other and follow the example of Godfrey of Bouillon, directing their bellicosity for the crusader cause.[71] On another two occasions he mentions luxury items from Cyprus, textiles embroidered in Cypriot gold thread ('de Chypre or fin') that should be included in a bride's trousseau and the 'oyseaulx de Chippre' (perfumes in bottles or perfumed pastes, both in the shape of birds) that should be used in the bridal room; similarly to Mézières, who mentions the 'precieux aromas d'oyseles de Chippre', he alludes to the prosperous economy of Cyprus in the middle of the fourteenth century and echoes the trend for Cypriot luxury products, probably promoted by Peter during his two journeys to the West, as Philippe Trélat suggests.[72]

In a *Brevis tractatus* he wrote in 1400, Mézières's compatriot Étienne de Conty (mid-fourteenth century-1413), a learned monk at the abbey of Saint-Pierre de Corbie, praises Peter's Alexandria campaign and deplores the advances of the Muslims ever since then, drawing special attention to the fact that the king spent a year in France at the time of the coronation of Charles V and that his chancellor was Mézières. Conty promotes the idea that only the king of France could claim to be the *rex christianissimus*, the one who always assisted the Holy Church against enemies like Emperor Frederick II (1220–50). Accordingly, of Christendom's seventeen kingdoms, the most richly endowed was that entrusted to the Most Christian King, whose constable was the brave Bertrand Du Guesclin, and, of the five kings in the West who were crowned and anointed (those of France, England, Scotland, Sicily and Apulia, and Jerusalem), only the French king's divine right to rule came directly from God without being mediated by the pope and only his subjects were pure Christians ('Sciendum est quod inter omnes reges christianos rex Francie dicitur esse major, potencior, nobilior, sanctior et rationabilior'). The Kingdom of Cyprus belonged to the fourth out of four groups in the order of precedence of kingdoms,[73] Conty

---

colloque d'Amiens (mars 1983), ed. by Danielle Buschinger and André Crépin (Göppingen: Kümmerle, 1984), pp. 457–64; Sylvia Huot, 'The *Miroir de mariage*: Deschamps responds to the *Roman de la Rose*', in Sinnreich-Levi, *Eustache Deschamps, French Courtier-Poet*, pp. 131–44.

71 Eustache Deschamps, *Balade (Exhortation à la croisade)*, in *Oeuvres complètes*, I, no. XLIX, pp. 138–39 (l. 27 for the reference to Cyprus), cf. nos VIII, LXIV–LCVIII, LXXXIV, CLXVIII, pp. 80–81, 159–66, 187–88, 300–01 and notes at pp. 329, 357, 395.

72 Eustache Deschamps, *Autre balade (Pour les nouveaulx mariez et de leur mesnage)* and *Le Miroir de mariage*, in *Oeuvres complètes*, VIII, no. MCCCCLI, pp. 137–38 and IX, p. 189, l. 5762 respectively; Philippe de Mézières, *Songe*, I, pp. 167, 339, *Oratio tragedica*, pp. 312–13, and *Le Livre de la Vertu*, p. 80. See: Philippe Trélat, 'Le goût pour Chypre. Objets d'art et tissus précieux importés de Chypre en Occident (xiiie–xve siècles)', *Cahiers du Centre d'Études Chypriotes*, 43 (2013), 455–72 (pp. 467–68); Nicolaou-Konnari, 'Women in Medieval Famagusta', pp. 624-25 with bibliography; n. 82 below.

73 Philippe Contamine, 'Une interpolation de la "Chronique Martinienne": le "Brevis Tractatus" d'Étienne de Conty, official de Corbie († 1413)', in *L'Historiographie en Occident du ve au xve siècle, Actes des congrès de la Société des historiens médiévistes de l'enseignement supérieur public, 8e congrès (Tours, 1977) = Annales*

ignoring the fact that its king was also titular king of Jerusalem and that the Cypriots had fought against the enemy of the Church Frederick II in 1229–33.[74]

Machaut's *dits* exerted a great influence on John Froissart, also a poet who turned historian, in a series of *flower* poems. The verse 'Comme elle [la marguerite] fait les biaus jardins d'Egipte', in Froissart's *Le Dit de la Marguerite* (c. 1364), echoes the verse from Machaut's homonymous poem and evokes the Cypriot king, although the *dit* was most probably not inspired by him, as Froissart did fall in love with a lady named Marguerite.[75] The poet, however, knew Peter personally. From 1361 to 1369, he resided in England at the court of Queen Philippa but travelled often to the Continent. He may have seen Peter during the king's visit to London in November 1363, was in Bologna in late June 1368, when Peter visited the town during his second European tour, and followed the king to Ferrara in July of the same year and probably to Venice. In *Le Joli Buisson de Jonece*, his last *dit amoureux* composed in 1373, Froissart speaks affectionately about his encounter with Peter, who received him honourably in Bologna and gave him forty ducats in Ferrara:[76]

Et c'est raisons que je renomme
De Cippre le noble roy Pere
Et que de ses bienfais me pere. [...]
Le quel me reçut à ce temps
Com cilz qui moult estoit sentans
D'onnour et d'amour grant partie [...]
Et me delivra à Ferrare [...]
Quarant ducas l'un sur l'aultre.

---

de Bretagne et des Pays de l'Ouest, 87/2 (1980), 367–86, esp. pp. 380, 381 ('subjectos regni Francie, qui sunt omnes christiani catholici secundum Deum'), 382 n. 70 ('et habebat quemdam militem nomine Philippum de Maceriis, natum de episcopatu Ambianensy, tunc cancellarium suum'), 383 (Cyprus said to have only five cities), 384–85 ('quemdam militem britonem conestabularium suum nomine Bertrandum de Claikin meliorem militem et audaciorem et fideliorem de tota Christianitate tunc temporis'), 385 (quotation). See Graeme Small, *Late Medieval France* (New York: Palgrave Macmillan, 2009), pp. 8–10.

74 Peter W. Edbury, *The Kingdom of Cyprus and the Crusades 1191–1374* (Cambridge: Cambridge University Press, 1991), pp. 51–70.

75 Jean Froissart, *Le Dit de la Marguerite*, in *'Dits' et 'Débats'*, pp. 46–52 (esp. 50), 147–53 (esp. 148 l. 21), 216–17. See: Bernard Ribémont, 'Froissart, le mythe et la marguerite', *Revue des langues romanes*, 94/1 (1990), 129–37; Spencer, *Dialogues of Love and Government*, pp. 97–103; Wollock, *Rethinking Chivalry and Courtly Love*, p. 163; n. 28 above.

76 Jean Froissart, *Le Trettie du Joli Buisson de Jonece*, in *Poésies de J. Froissart*, extraites de deux manuscrits de la Bibliothèque du Roi et publiées pour la première fois par Jean Alexandre Buchon (Paris: Verdière, 1829), pp. 326–512, esp. 16, 337–38; Jean Froissart, *Le Joli Buisson de Jonece*, ed. by Anthime Fourrier (Geneva: Droz, 1975), ll. 348–62. Froissart was in Italy for the marriage of Philippa's son, Lionel, Duke of Clarence (1338–68), to Yolanda/Violante Visconti (1354–86), sister of Giangaleazzo and niece of Bernabò, on whom see n. 62 above. For Froissart's encounters with Peter, see Jean Froissart, *Oeuvres de Froissart. Chroniques*, ed. by M. le baron Joseph-Bruno-Marie-Constantin Kervyn de Lettenhove, 26 vols (Bruxelles: Victor Devaux, 1870–77), I, pp. 152, 168–70, 233–34, 245, 419, 476; Jorga, *Philippe de Mézières*, pp. 378–79, who erroneously cites Froissart's *L'Espinette amoureuse* as the work in which the poet mentions his encounter with Peter in Bologna; Jean Froissart, *'Dits' et 'Débats'*, 'Introduction', p. 72.

As Renate Blumenfeld-Kosinski remarks, 'Unlike Philippe de Mézières and Honoré Bovet, Christine de Pisan [(c. 1364–c. 1430)] was not herself a politician or diplomat, nor did she receive a salary from any employer, as did Eustache Deschamps [...] as a nonnoble laywoman, her possibilities for any intervention in secular or religious politics were limited to her writings, which in turn were the only source of her income'.[77] Indeed, her many works deal with both the Hundred Years' War and the French civil war, her literary production climaxing after the assassination of Louis of Orleans, Charles VI's brother, in 1407. Both her *Livre du chemin de long estude* (1402–03) and *Livre des fais et bonnes meurs du sage roy Charles V* (1404) were intended to provide counsel to Charles VI, the first one also dedicated to him.[78] Christine was very well acquainted with the work of the French authors who wrote about Peter. She addressed a letter to Eustache Deschamps in 1403 and, for her *Livre des faits d'armes et de chevalerie* (c. 1410), written for the dauphin Louïs of Guyenne (1397–1415), she copied liberally from Bovet's *L'Arbre des batailles*. Most importantly, she knew personally and appreciated Mézières, through her father Thomas (c. 1310–c. 1387) and, perhaps, through Deschamps too, and sold property to him in 1392. She probably learned from him what she says about Peter in her *Livre de la Mutacion de Fortune*, completed in 1403, although she may have been influenced by Machaut too.[79] Dedicated to the Duke of

---

77 Blumenfeld-Kosinski, *Poets, Saints, and Visionaries*, p. 150.
78 Christine de Pisan, *Le Livre du chemin de long estude*, ed. by Robert Püschel (Paris: Le Soudier, 1881; Geneva: Slatkine Reprints, 1974); Christine de Pisan, *Le Livre des fais et bonnes meurs du sage roy Charles V*, ed. by Suzanne Solente, 2 vols (Paris: H. Champion, 1936–40) and ed. by Nathalie Desgrugillers-Billard (Clermont-Ferrand: Paleo, 2009). See indicatively from a huge bibliography: Joël Blanchard, 'Christine de Pizan et les raisons de l'histoire', *Le Moyen Âge*, 92 (1986), 417–36; Claire Le Ninan, 'L'idée de croisade dans deux œuvres de Christine de Pizan', *Cahiers de recherches médiévales*, 8 (2001), 251–61; Karen Green and Constant J. Mews (eds), *Healing the Body Politic: The Political Thought of Christine de Pizan*, Disputatio, 7 (Turnhout: Brepols, 2005); Delogu, *Theorizing the Ideal Sovereign*, chapter 3; Françoise Autrand, *Christine de Pizan: une femme en politique* (Paris: Fayard, 2009); Danielle Buschinger, Liliane Dulac, Claire Le Ninan, and Christine Reno (eds), *Christine de Pizan et son époque. Actes du Colloque international des 9, 10 et 11 décembre 2011 à Amiens*, Médiévales, 53 (Amiens: Presses du Centre d'études médiévales, Université de Picardie – Jules Verne, 2012); Tracy Adams, *Christine de Pizan and the Fight for France* (University Park: The Pennsylvania State University Press, 2014); n. 36 above.
79 Christine de Pisan, *Le Livre de la Mutacion de Fortune*, ed. Suzanne Solente, 4 vols (Paris: Picard, 1959–66), I, 'Introduction', p. xcviii; Christine de Pisan, *Une epistre a Eustace Morel*, ed. by Jean-François Kosta-Théfaine (Clermont-Ferrand: Paleo, 2010); Christine de Pisan, *The Book of Deeds of Arms and of Chivalry*, English trans. by Summer Willard and Charity Cannon Willard (University Park: The Pennsylvania State University Press, 1999); Philippe de Mézières, *Songe*, I, pp. 614–15 criticizes Thomas de Pizan for his abilities as a royal advisor and an astrologist. See: Marie-Josèphe Pinet, *Christine de Pisan (1364–1430). Étude biographique et littéraire* (Paris: H. Champion, 1927; repr. Geneva: Slatkine Reprints, 1974), pp. 107 n. 2, 405–06; Jean-Louis Picherit, 'De Philippe de Mézières à Christine de Pisan', *Le moyen français*, 13 (1983), 20–36; Claude Gauvard, 'Christine de Pizan et ses contemporains: l'engagement politique des écrivains dans le royaume de France aux XIVe et XVe siècles', in *Une femme de lettres au Moyen Âge. Études autour de Christine de Pizan*, ed. by Liliane Dulac and Bernard Ribémont, Medievalia, 16 (Orleans: Paradigme, 1995), pp. 105–28; Liliane Dulac, 'La représentation de la France chez Eustache Deschamps et chez Christine de Pizan', in *Autour d'Eustache Deschamps*, pp. 79–92; Miren Lacassagne, 'L'échange épistolaire de Christine de Pizan et Eustache Deschamps', in *Contexts and Continuities. Proceedings of the IVth International Colloquium on Christine de Pizan (Glasgow 21–27 July 2000) Published in Honour of Liliane Dulac*, ed. by Angus J. Kennedy, Rosalind Brown-Grant, James C. Laidlaw, and Catherine M.

Burgundy Philip the Bold, Charles VI's uncle, the leader of the Burgundian branch of the House of Valois, and Louis of Orleans's opponent, the book provides counsel to the duke soon after he lost the regency of France to Louis in 1402. The work recalls in many ways the allegorical structure and messages of the *Songe*; it is a vast universal history in seven parts, from the creation of the world down to the establishment of the Roman Empire, the first part being an account of the poetess's life and the epilogue considering contemporary European history. Christine assumes in this book and her other writings the task of reforming France and of healing the schism by uniting the Christian princes, a task that Mézières's works had been unable to accomplish. She considers the countless disasters in human history to have been caused by both the whims of Fortune and man's moral failings and her advice to her readers includes the strengthening of legitimate dynastic succession and the amendment of their faults.[80]

Christine alludes to Peter in the third part of her book, when she speaks of the ills that befell the land where Venus was born after the treacherous murder of its good king. In the last part of the book, in which she considers contemporary figures, Christine dedicates forty verses to Peter, 'le bon roy de Chipre', without naming him. He is presented as the ruler and knight *par excellence*, who was destroyed by family feuds; a good king, upon whom Fortune had bestowed all positive qualities and whom everybody loved; a knight, who jousted in France; a crusader, who travelled to Italy and France and visited the pope in an effort to recruit men for a Holy War and who triumphantly took Alexandria but could not keep it because of lack of men; a tragic man, whom Fortune abandoned and of whose kinsmen Envy took hold, his own brother taking his life. Christine also refers to Queen Joanna I of Naples (1324/26–82), whose two husbands died of violent death, but does not associate her with Peter, who visited the queen in 1367; this mention may constitute an allusion to the *Songe*, Mézières comparing the murders of Peter and Joanna's first husband, Andrew of Hungary (1327–45), both committed by their closest relatives and barons.[81] However, in her *Livre des Trois Vertus*, written in 1405, Christine disapproves

---

Müller, 2 vols (Glasgow: University of Glasgow Press, 2002), II, pp. 453–65; Lori J. Walters, 'The *Vieil Solitaire* and the *Seulette*: Contemplative Solitude as Political Theology in Philippe de Mézières, Christine de Pizan, and Jean Gerson', in *Philippe de Mézières and His Age*, pp. 119–44 (122–26).

80 Nadia Margolis, *The Poetics of History: An Analysis of Christine de Pizan's 'Livre de la mutacion de Fortune'* (unpublished doctoral thesis, Stanford University, 1977); Kevin Brownlee, 'The Image of History in Christine de Pizan's *Livre de la Mutacion de Fortune*', *Yale French Studies*, Special Issue: *Contexts: Style and Values in Medieval Art and Literature* (1991), 44–56; Miren Lacassagne, 'La figure de Fortune dans *Le livre de la mutacion de Fortune* de Christine de Pizan et la poésie d'Eustache Deschamps', in *Au champ des escriptures. III*[e] *Colloque international sur Christine de Pizan, Lausanne, 18–22 juillet 1998*, ed. by Eric Hicks, Diego Gonzalez, and Philippe Simon, Études christiniennes, 6 (Paris: H. Champion, 2000), pp. 219–30; Blumenfeld-Kosinski, *Poets, Saints, and Visionaries*, pp. 150–61, esp. 152–56; Miranda Griffin, 'Transforming Fortune: Reading and Chance in Christine de Pizan's "Mutacion de Fortune" and "Chemin de long estude"', *The Modern Language Review*, 104/1 (2009), 55–70; Walters, 'The *Vieil Solitaire* and the *Seulette*, pp. 128–30.

81 Christine de Pisan, *Le Livre de la Mutacion de Fortune*, II, pp. 13–14, ll. 4583–92, IV, pp. 69–70, ll. 23301–42, pp. 72–73, ll. 23392–418 (Joanna I of Naples), p. 74, ll. 23460–63 (possible allusion to Valentina and Anglesia Visconti in a reference to the excellent marriage alliances of Bernabò Visconti's children); Jorga, 'L'épître', p. 3 and Philippe de Mézières, *Epistre lamentable*, p. 102. Leontios Makhairas, Χρονικό

of the extravagantly decorated, with tapestries embroidered 'de fin or de chippre', bedchamber of a merchant's wife, using Cyprus as a negative exemplum in conformity with previous literary patterns, while in her *Ditié de Jehanne d'Arc*, written in 1429, she chooses as her *preuse* Joan of Arc.[82]

In the second part of the *Livre des fais du bon messire Jehan le Maingre, dit Bouciquaut*, an anonymous biography of John II Le Meingre, known as Boucicaut (1366–1421), which has been attributed to Christine de Pizan among others, there are a few references to 'le bon roy Petre' and his taking of Alexandria. A heroic prose biography completed in 1409, the work was intended to celebrate and defend Boucicaut, renowned for his military skill and chivalric prowess, a crusader at the battle of Nicopolis (1396), marshal of France, and French governor of Genoa, against his critics at the royal court. In his latter capacity, Boucicaut dealt with attempts orchestrated by King Janus of Lusignan with the help of Venice to recover Famagusta, taken by the Genoese in 1373–74 during the reign of Peter I's son, Peter II. The marshal travelled personally to Cyprus, arriving on the island in July 1403 and returning to Famagusta in August after raiding Syria; during his stay, a new treaty was signed with Janus, the terms of which were less harsh than those of the previous one and suggest that the Cypriot king, who had no choice anyway, somehow trusted the French governor. Despite the difficult circumstances of Boucicaut's relationship with Cyprus, in his encomiastic biography the wandering Cypriot king and ardent crusader is not denigrated and neither are the other Lusignan kings. In fact, Boucicaut's portrayal as the ideal knight bears many similarities to the way Peter is depicted in Machaut's *Prise*, even though in real life both men committed serious mistakes in the government of Genoa and Cyprus and failed in their crusading enterprises.[83]

της Κύπρου, p. 181 mentions Peter's visit to Joanna, see Nicolaou-Konnari, 'Apologists or Critics?', p. 394. Four centuries later, Joanna continued to attract the interest of French thinkers, albeit in a negative way, see Voltaire, *Essai sur les moeurs et l'esprit des nations (IV). Chapitres 68–102*, ed. by Bruno Bernard, John Renwick, Nicholas Cronk, and Janet Godden, Les oeuvres complètes de Voltaire, 24 (Oxford: Voltaire foundation, 2011), chapter LXIX. On the Visconti ladies, see n. 62 above.

82 Christine de Pizan, *Le Livre des Trois Vertus*, ed. by Charity Cannon Willard with the collaboration of Eric Hicks (Paris: H. Champion, 1989), chapter xlii, p. 116; Christine de Pizan, *Le Ditié de Jehanne d'Arc*, ed. and English trans. by Angus J. Kennedy and Kenneth Varty, Medium Ævum Monographs, new series, 9 (Oxford: Society for the Study of Mediaeval Languages and Literature, 1977), l. 199. See: Kevin Brownlee, 'Structures of Authority in Christine de Pizan's *Ditié de Jehanne d'Arc*', in *The Selected Writings of Christine de Pizan. A Norton Critical Edition*, ed. and trans. by Renate Blumenfeld-Kosinski and Kevin Brownlee (New York: Norton, 1997), pp. 371–90; Michèle Guéret-Laferté, 'Jeanne la Preuse, Jeanne la Sainte: la "Pucelle" dans le *Ditié de Jehanne d'Arc* de Christine de Pizan', in *De l'hérétique à la sainte. Les procès de Jeanne d'Arc revisités*, ed. by François Neveux (Caen: Presses universitaires de Caen, 2012), pp. 213–26; n. 72 above.

83 *Le Livre des fais du bon messire Jehan le Maingre, dit Bouciquaut, Mareschal de France et gouverneur de Jennes*, ed. by Denis Lalande (Geneva: Droz, 1985), pp. 207.18 ('le bon roy Petre') 225.44, 353.37–38. See: Jean-Louis Picherit, 'Christine de Pisan et le *Livre des faicts du bon messire Jean le Maingre, dit Boucicaut, mareschal de France et gouverneur de Gennes*', *Romania*, 103 (1982), 299–331; Denis Lalande, *Jean II le Meingre, dit Boucicaut (1366–1421): étude d'une biographie héroïque* (Geneva: Droz 1988); Guillaume de Machaut, *La Prise* d'Alixandre, 'Introduction', pp. 29–30; Craig Taylor, *A Virtuous Knight: Defending Marshal Boucicaut (Jean II Le Meingre, 1366–1421)* (Woodbridge: York Medieval Press, 2019). For his journey to Cyprus

In the second stanza of his *Ballade des seigneurs du temps jadis*, one of the three ballades *of times past* placed in the middle of his *Grand Testament* and probably composed in 1461, François Villon (1431/2–63?), who may have been influenced by Machaut, mentions 'le roy de Chippre de renon'.[84] John L. La Monte identified convincingly this unnamed king of Cyprus with Peter against other candidates (Guy or John II of Lusignan). In the ballade, Villon summons a number of celebrated (and not so celebrated) persons, most of whom had died relatively recently and had suffered ugly deaths, to participate in a *danse macabre* in order to demonstrate the ephemerality and vanity of power and greatness. The king of Cyprus is mentioned as the fitting companion of the likes of Pope Calixtus III, the kings of Aragon, Bohemia, France, Scotland, and Spain as well as the worthy Charlemagne and Du Guesclin.[85]

It is appropriate to close this review of the depiction of Peter I of Lusignan in French literature with John of Arras's (fl. late fourteenth century) *Mélusine ou la noble histoire de Lusignan*, a prose romance commissioned by Duke John of Berry and completed in August 1393 that borrows from all main medieval genres, the *roman d'aventure*, the courtly romance, and the *chanson de geste*.[86] The romance recounts the foundation legend of the Lusignan dynasty, tracing the family's history from its origins from the legendary Mélusine, an enigmatic fairy figure who transformed into a serpent and whose father was Élinas, the king of Albanie (Scotland) [Fig. 9], in the eponymous fortress/town through its glorious rise in Europe and the Crusader Kingdoms of the Eastern Mediterranean. The story of the shape-shifting fairy had

---

and the treaty, see now Catherine Otten-Froux, 'Famagouste sous la domination génoise (1374–1464)', in *Famagusta, Volume II, History and Society*, pp. 71-180 (esp. 73, 103-07, 116, 140, 168) with all the older bibliography.

84 François Villon, *Oeuvres de François Villon*, ed. by Louis Thuasne, 3 vols (Paris: Auguste Picard, 1923), I, *Le Grant Testament, Ballade des seigneurs du temps jadis*, pp. 191–92 (191 l. 369), the other two ballades being the *Ballade des dames du temps jadis* and the *Ballade en vieil langage Françoys*, pp. 189–90 and 192–98 respectively; François Villon, *Poésies*, ed. by Jean Dufournet (Paris: Imprimerie nationale, 1984; repr. Flammarion, 1992), *Testament, Ballade des seigneurs du temps jadis*, pp. 112–15. See generally: Glynnis M. Cropp, 'Les trois ballades du temps jadis dans le *Testament* de François Villon', *Académie Royale de Belgique: Bulletin de la Classe des Lettres et des Sciences morales et politiques*, 5ᵉ série, 57 (1971), 316–41; Jane H. M. Taylor, *The Poetry of François Villon: Text and Context* (Cambridge: Cambridge University Press, 2001), pp. 58–85; Jean Dufournet, *Dernières recherches sur Villon* (Paris: H. Champion, 2008); Jean Dufournet and Marcel Faure (eds), *Villon entre mythe et poésie: actes du colloque organisé les 15, 16 et 17 décembre 2006 à la Bibliothèque historique de la Ville de Paris par Michael Freeman, Jean Dérens et Jean Dufournet* (Paris: H. Champion, 2011).

85 John L. La Monte, 'The "Roy de Chippre" in François Villon's "Ballade des seigneurs du temps jadis"', *The Romanic Review*, 23/1 (1932), 49–53; Hill, *A History of Cyprus*, II, p. 368 n. 4; Jean Dufournet, 'Une ballade méconnue de Villon: La Ballade des seigneurs du temps jadis', in *Nouvelles recherches sur Villon* (Paris: H. Champion, 1980), pp. 29–46; Glynnis M. Cropp, 'La "Ballade des seigneurs" de François Villon et les chroniques', *Le Moyen Âge*, 100 (1994), 221–36; Michael Freeman, *François Villon in His Works: The Villain's Tale* (Amsterdam – Atlanta: Rodopi, 2000), pp. 160–63.

86 Robert J. Nolan, 'The Romance of Melusine: Evidence for an Early Missing Version', *Fabula*, 15/1 (1974), 53–58 (p. 57) and 'The Origin of the Romance of Melusine: A New Interpretation', *Fabula*, 15/1 (1974), 192–201, claims that Machaut authored an early version of the romance, but, as Gaullier-Bougassas, 'Le Chevalier au Cygne', p. 115, rightly remarks, Machaut does not mention the fairy origins of the Lusignan family from Mélusine and the authors of the romance seem to ignore Machaut's work.

been circulating in France for a long time, but it seems that it was associated with the foundation of the Lusignan fortress and lineage in the early 1340s.[87]

Although Peter is not explicitly mentioned in Arras's romance, the deeds of the first Lusignans in Cyprus against the Saracens bear a strong resemblance to Peter's exploits. Historically, the Cypriot episode is a rewriting of the Third Crusade and of the acquisition of the island by Guy of Lusignan. The unnamed king of Cyprus is described as a worthy and courageous prince who died heroically fighting the infidel; Mélusine's son Urien, who married the daughter of the king of Cyprus Hermine and inherited the kingdom, and his brother Guion (variant of Guy), who married the daughter of the king of Armenia Florie, are depicted as the valiant liberators of Cyprus from the siege of the infidel sultan of Damascus. Thus, the fictional first Lusignan king of Cyprus bears a name not attested in the family while the fictional first Lusignan king of Armenia is named after the historical first Lusignan lord of Cyprus. This historical revisionism is intended to celebrate the chivalric values of the Cypriot branch of the Lusignan family and their manifestation in the work's illustrious patron, John of Berry, thus promoting the legitimisation of his political claims to the Poitou region, especially the town of Lusignan, in the 1370s.[88] The clearest allusion to Peter is made at the very end of the romance, when the author traces the most recent apparitions of the fairy. The Poitevin 'Percheval de Coulongne', who had been the chamberlain of the 'bon roy de Chippre', is said to have told John of Berry that, when he was in Cyprus, the king was afraid because the serpent of Lusignan ('la serpente de Lusignen') had showed herself to him, thus foretelling a loss to him or to his son Perrin, 'for she appears when one of the heirs of Lusignan is about to die'; and, indeed, within three days the king died in the hard way that everyone knows and pities.[89]

---

87 Caroline Prud'Homme, 'Mermaid, Mother, Monster, and More: Portraits of the Fairy Woman in Fifteenth-and Sixteenth-Century Melusine Narratives', in *Melusine's Footprint: Tracing the Legacy of a Medieval Myth*, ed. by Misty Urban, Deva F. Kemmis, and Melissa Ridley Elmes (Leiden – Boston: Brill, 2017), pp. 52–73, esp. 61–62, where she notes the dissociation of the character of the fairy from Lusignan in the fifteenth- and sixteenth-century printed editions of the story, due perhaps to the demise of the Lusignan house both in Poitou and Cyprus.

88 Jean d'Arras, *Histoire de Mélusine* (Geneva: Adam Steinschaber, 1478; repr. Bern: Société Suisse des bibliophiles, 1923–24) and Jehan d'Arras, *Mélusine*, revised ed. of the 1478 one by Charles Brunet (Paris: P. Jannet, 1854), pp. 15–26 (Élinas), 128–202 (Cypriot episode). See: Emmanuèle Baumgartner, 'Fiction and History: The Cypriot Episode in Jean d'Arras's *Mélusine*', in *Melusine of Lusignan: Founding Fiction in Late Medieval France*, ed. by Donald Maddox and Sara Sturm-Maddox (Athens, Georgia: University of Georgia Press, 1996), pp. 185–200; Daisy Delogu, 'Jean d'Arras Makes History: Politicai Legitimacy and the *Roman de Mélusine*', *Dalhousie French Studies*, 80 (Fall 2007), pp. 15–28; Catherine Gaullier–Bougassas, 'La fée Présine: une figure maternelle ambigue aux origines de l'écriture romanesque', in *550 Jahre deutsche Melusine – Coudrette und Thüring von Ringoltingen / 550 ans de Mélusine allemande – Coudrette et Thüring von Ringoltingen*, ed. by André Schnyder and Jean-Claude Mühlethaler (Berlin: Peter Lang, 2008), pp. 111–28.

89 Jehan d'Arras, *Histoire de Mélusine*, pp. 423–24. Perceval is mentioned by Machaut, see Hardy, *Édition critique de la* Prise d'Alexandrie, pp. xc, cxx, 58–83, 192–96, 216, 221–23, ll. 1967–2837, 6677–6829, L 1, 7558–603 and Miriam Salzmann's chapter in this volume.

A few years later, Coudrette (fl. late fourteenth-early fifteenth century) rewrites the myth in verse in the romance *Le Roman de Mélusine ou histoire de* Lusignan; the work was completed in *c.* 1401 and was commissioned by William VII Larchevêque, lord of Parthenay, a descendant of the Lusignans and an English partisan. Like John of Arras, Coudrette weaves together history and fiction, with elements of myth and popular traditions fused with epic, crusader narrative, knightly romance, and Christian doctrine in order to praise his patrons. He links the myth to the historical claims of a contemporary lineage threatened by extinction, the Parthenays, making Thierry, penultimate son of the fairy, the legendary ancestor of Larchevêque.[90] The Cypriot episode follows closely the one is Arras's romance without any significant changes, with one notable exception: the first son of Urien and Ermine, who also conquered Morea, Jaffa, and Tripoli, is named 'Griffons' instead of 'Henry', a common name for the members of the Lusignan dynasty; the name *Griffon* allows room for speculation since it is widely used as an ethnic name for the Greeks, albeit in a derogatory way, from the twelfth until sometime in the second half of the fourteenth century. Coudrette, however, does not mention the story of the apparition of the serpent of Lusignan to Peter [Figs 10–12].[91]

Peter is also mentioned in a number of *national* French histories, recorded from a royalist perspective in prose and the vernacular (with the exception of three texts in Latin) by an author who witnessed most of the events he recounts during a critical period for the French monarchy. These narratives often take the form of a dynastic history, their writers being all attached to patrons, to whom they are very loyal and whose chivalric achievements they praise, legitimising their authority and patrimony through lineage. The best example of this kind of French history is the voluminous compilation the *Grandes chroniques de France* and its culmination John Froissart's *Chroniques*.[92] Contrary to the literary works discussed above, in these French narratives Peter's portrayal is prosaic and unemotional, adhering to the unembellished facts; nevertheless, despite the absence of an allegorical or mythological use of the

---

90 Coudrette, *Le Roman de Mélusine*, 'Introduction', pp. 13–104 ; Tania M. Colwell, 'Patronage of the poetic Mélusine romance: Guillaume l'Archevêque's confrontation with dynastic crisis', *Journal of Medieval History*, 37/2 (2011), 215–29; Pierre Courroux, 'Mélusine et les Larchevêque. Légende et historiographie dans le Poitou du xive siècle', *Cahiers de Recherches Médiévales et Humanistes*, 26 (2014), 309–25; Shana Thomson, 'The Lady of the Marshes: Place, Identity, and Coudrette's Mélusine in Late-Medieval Poitou', *Peregrinations: Journal of Medieval Art & Architecture*, 5/3 (Spring 2016), 67–130.

91 Jean d'Arras, *Histoire de Mélusine*, p. 196 (Henry); Coudrette, *Le Roman de Mélusine*, pp. 158–71, 299–300, ll. 1496–1880, 5784–95, 5821–24, esp. pp. 167, 168, ll. 1770, 1792–1804 (Griffons). See Angel Nicolaou-Konnari, 'Strategies of Distinction: The Construction of the Ethnic Name *Griffon* and the Western Perception of the Greeks (Twelfth – Fourteenth Centuries)', *Byzantinistica. Rivista di Studi Bizantini e Slavi*, 2nd Series, 4 (2002), 181–96.

92 Gabrielle M. Spiegel, *Romancing the Past. The Rise of Vernacular Prose Historiography in Thirteenth-Century France* (Berkeley – Los Angeles – London: University of California Press, 1993); *Encyclopedia of the Medieval Chronicle*, pp. 608, 671–72; Norbert Kersken, 'High and late Medieval National Historiography', Leah Shopkow, 'Dynastic History', and Peter F. Ainsworth, 'Contemporary and "Eyewitness" History"', in *Historiography in the Middle Ages*, ed. by Deborah Mauskopf Deliyiannis (Leiden – Boston: Brill, 2012), pp. 181–215, 217–48, and 249–76 respectively.

Lusignan king's person, one may discern a distinct effort on the part of the French historians to appropriate him as a model ruler for France and the French monarchy.

The *Grandes chroniques de France*, drafted mainly at Saint-Denis but continued at the court as the official chronicle under Charles V, assumed its final form in 1461. The marriage between Peter's first-born, half-brother Guy, Prince of Galilee (1315/16–43), and Maria of Bourbon in 1330 is said to have been sought by their father Hugh IV because 'he strongly wished his kingdom to be ennobled by the French seed' ('ledit roy avoit grant desir que le royaume de Chipre fust ennoblis de la semence de France'), a comment that acknowledges both the identity differentiation of the Cypriot royal dynasty from its French origins and the French concern to reassert these links. The text mentions Peter on several occasions without naming him and makes sure to enhance the importance of his actions by associating them with France: 'le roy de Chipre' captured Antalya in 1361 assisted by the Hospitallers and many others, including French knights; he took the cross in Avignon on 31 March 1363, Pope Urban V proclaiming the crusade and appointing King John II of France as its leader; the Cypriot king was present at John II's funeral in Paris on 5–6 May 1364; he attended Charles V's coronation in Reims in May 1364 and the ensuing festivities and jousting; in February 1367, the king of France received the false information that the king of Cyprus, with the help of many Christian princes, had taken Alexandria for a second time on 5 December 1366, not being able to keep it the first time because of lack men, but in fact he had only reached an agreement with the sultan. The text also tells the story already mentioned above of the unfortunate doctor 'maistre Angel, né du pays de Chippre', without blaming him: he was 'a young, handsome man and a good, able doctor' and was probably lost in the sea in order to avoid poisoning Charles VI.[93]

On the other hand, the *Chroniques* of John Froissart, a vast work written between 1369 and 1400 and covering the period 1327–1400, include only two passages that concern Peter, despite the great influence exerted by Machaut's epic poem on Froissart and the latter's possible acquaintance with the Cypriot king discussed above. For his account of the great dynastic conflict between the kings of England and France, Froissart uses earlier narratives and documents but mainly relies on the testimonies of eyewitnesses, travelling extensively in pursuit of informants. His text offers a remarkable insight into a society, the values of which were the prowess, honour, and

---

93 *Les grandes chroniques de France*, ed. by Jules Viard, 10 vols, Société de l'histoire de France (Paris: H. Champion, 1920–53), IX, *Charles IV le Bel, Philippe VI de Valois*, pp. 104–05, 106–07 (quotation at p. 105); *Les grandes chroniques de France. Chronique des règnes de Jean II et de Charles V*, ed. by Roland Delachenal, 4 vols, Société de l'histoire de France (Paris: Renouard, 1910–20), I, pp. 331, 335, 339, 342–44, II, pp. 2–4, 26–27, 295–96 ('bel homme et jeune, et très grant clerc et subtil, appele maistre Angel'). See: Roland Delachenal, *Histoire de Charles V*, 5 vols (Paris: Alphonse Picard & fils, 1909–31), I, p. 144, II, p. 184 n. 3, pp. 323–24, 345, 352, 355, III, pp. 19, 101, 245, 494–96; Gabrielle M. Spiegel, *The Chronicle Tradition of Saint-Denis. A Survey* (Brookline – Leiden, Classical Folio Editions, 1978); Bernard Guenée, 'Les *Grandes Chroniques de France*: le roman aux rois (1274–1518)', in *Les lieux de mémoire*, II, *La Nation*, ed. by Pierre Nora (Paris: Gallimard, 1986), pp. 189–214; *Encyclopedia of the Medieval Chronicle*, pp. 728–29; n. 68 above for Angel. For a comparison of the 'Cypriot episodes' included in the French chronicles discussed in this paper and in the chronicle of Makhairas and other texts, see Nicolaou-Konnari, 'A Neglected Relationship', pp. 124–27 and 143–45 (notes).

chivalric ethos of the monarchy, the aristocracy, and the knights. Froissart expresses his admiration of the chivalric values and his loyalty to the knightly ruling class, although himself a product of the middle class. At the same time, he is aware of social mutations caused by poorly governed citizens and, particularly, of the growing tension between hereditary kingship and legitimacy acquired on the battlefield or by way of class intermarriage. Most importantly, he narrates heroic deeds accomplished in the course of a conflict between two countries without showing favouritism towards French or English personalities.[94]

The person of the 'jentil roy de Cippre' fits perfectly well within Froissart's worldview. The first passage (Book I) is a detailed account of Peter's first journey to Europe, for which he may have obtained information from the king's entourage: he describes the splendid feasts and jousts that were given in Peter's honour at the papal court in Avignon and many other royal and princely courts; he explains that, thanks to the peace with the English, the king of France could now pursue his Christian goal and take the cross in order to honour his kingdom while the king of England wisely chose not to because of his old age and for the sake of maintaining the peace with France; he adds that the latter did give Peter a big vessel with the name *Katherine/ Catelinne*; and he mentions the presence of the Cypriot king at the funeral of King John II of France. The second passage (Book III) is a brief mention of the king's murder by his second brother James, then constable of Jerusalem; Froissart interprets the cause of the regicide in terms of Peter's crusading activities, claiming that the constable was bribed by the infidels [Fig. 13]![95]

There are significant similarities between the historical outlook of Froissart and of the anonymous author of the *Chronique des quatre premiers Valois*. Composed in the last quarter of the fourteenth century, the narrative covers the period 1327–93, expressing the interests and ideology of the aristocracy. It contains several

---

94 Peter F. Ainsworth, *Jean Froissart and the Fabric of History. Truth, Myth and Fiction in the 'Chroniques'* (Oxford: Clarendon Press, 1990); Donald Maddox and Sara Sturm-Maddox, (eds), *Froissart Across the Genres* (Gainesville, University Press of Florida, 1998); Michel Zink, *Froissart et le temps* (Paris: Presses universitaires de France, 1998); Chris Given-Wilson, *Chronicles: The Writing of History in Medieval England* (London: The Hambledon Press, 2004), chapters 3–6 passim; Odile Bombarde (ed.), *Froissart dans sa forge*, Actes du colloque réuni à Paris du 4 au 6 novembre 2004 à l'Académie des inscriptions et belles-lettres au au Collège de France par M. Michel Zink (Paris: Boccard, 2006); *Encyclopedia of the Medieval Chronicle*, pp. 642–55; David Whetham, *Just Wars and Moral Victories: Surprise, Deception and the Normative Framework of European War in the Later Middle Ages* (Leiden – Boston: Brill, 2009), chapter 6; Ainsworth, 'Contemporary and "Eyewitness' History"', pp. 264–75; Kevin Brownlee, 'The Languages of History in Philippe de Mézières and Jean Froissart, in *Philippe de Mézières et l'Europe*, pp. 221–26.

95 *Chroniques de J. Froissart*, VI, §§ 503–04, 506–08, 510 and pp. 280–84 (journey), XII, §§ 59–60 (murder); Jean Froissart, *Chroniques. Livre I. Le manuscrit d'Amiens, Bibliothèque municipale n° 486*, ed. by George T. Diller, 5 vols (Geneva: Droz, 1991–98), III, pp. 279–89 (journey, quotation at p. 286). I have not seen Jean Froissart, *Chroniques. Dernière rédaction du premier livre. Édition du manuscrit de Rome Reg. lat. 869*, ed. by George T. Diller (Geneva: Droz, 1972) or Jean Froissart, *Chroniques: Troisième Livre. MS 865 de la Bibliothèque municipale de Besançon*, ed. by Peter F. Ainsworth, codicological study by Godfried Croenen (Geneva: Droz, 2007). Also, see now the project *The Online Froissart. A Digital Edition of the Chronicles of Jean Froissart*, led by Peter Ainsworth and Godfried Croenen, which provides transcriptions of all the main manuscript recensions: <https://www.dhi.ac.uk/onlinefroissart/> [accessed 13 June 2020].

passages of Cypriot interest, the ones concerning Peter being more detailed than the respective ones in Froissart's text. As far as we can tell, the author never met the Cypriot king and his informants are French nobles who had participated in the army of 'Pierron le bon roy de Cyppre' or, perhaps, Cypriot knights fighting in France. The chronicle provides a long and detailed account of Peter's visit to the papal court of Avignon, various princely courts in France, and the royal court in Westminster during his first journey to Europe. Peter is presented as the ideal knight, duly showing his reverence to the king of France, participating in numerous feasts and joustings, and wisely choosing to ignore the English king's alleged claim for the return of the Kingdom of Cyprus, 'which my ancestor King Richard entrusted long ago to one of your predecessors', after the conquest of Jerusalem. The taking of Alexandria follows closely Mézières's account (and to a lesser degree Machaut's), albeit in an abridged form, and so does the account of the 1367 Cypriot attacks against the Syrian coast and, particularly, of the raid against Tripoli. Brief entries that mention Peter's murder comply with the overall way the regicide is presented in French literature: the events are said to have been orchestrated by his brother, Prince John of Antioch (1329/30–75), and the text also includes the dramatic narrative of the fratricide's assassination, staged by Peter's widow, Eleanor of Aragon (?–1417), in 1375.[96]

In the continuations of the chronicles of William of Nangis (d. 1300) and Richard Lescot (c. 1310–58), composed at Saint-Denis during the reigns of John II and Charles V in the tradition of the *Grandes chroniques de France* albeit in Latin, Peter's first European tour with its crusading aim is briefly mentioned; in Lescot's continuation, the taking of Antalya by 'the illustrious king of Cyprus', with the help of French knights amongst others, is equally presented in crusading terms, vaguely placed in 1361.[97] The *Chronographia regum Francorum*, another Latin text written between 1405 and 1429, uses material from the *Grandes chroniques de France* and Cuvelier's biography of Du Guesclin. The story of Peter's deeds probably derives from Machaut and is given in a very sober and precise way. The text explains how the island came into the hands of the Lusignans, mentions the taking of Antalya, which earns the Cypriot king a comparison with his namesake Peter the Hermit, and gives

---

96 *Chronique des quatre premiers Valois (1327–1393)*, ed. by Siméon Luce, Société de l'histoire de France (Paris: Mme Ve Jules Renouard, 1862), pp. 41 (Cypriot knight in France: 'monseigneur Amory, ung chevalier de Cypre lors cappitaine de Beauvaiz'), 126–28, 144, 148–49 (journey, quotation at p. 128: 'Quant vous l'aurez conquise [la Saincte Terre], vous devrez rendre le royaume de Cyppre que jadiz mon anceseur le roy Richart bailla à garder à vostre predecesseur'), 164–66 (Alexandria), 185–91 (1367 raids), 200 (Peter's murder), 251 (Genoese invasion), 260–61 (the prince's murder).

97 *Chronique latine de Guillaume de Nangis, de 1113 à 1300, avec les continuations de cette chronique, de 1300 à 1368*, ed. by Hercule Géraud, Société de l'histoire de France, 2 vols (Paris: Renouard, 1843), II, pp. 330–31, 339, 360; *Chronique de Richard Lescot, religieux de Saint-Denis (1328–1344), suivie de la continuation de cette chronique (1344–1364)*, ed. by Jean Lemoine, Société de l'histoire de France (Paris: Renouard – H. Laurens, 1896), pp. 150–51 ('Isto anno, famosa civitas Descallie capta fuit per inclitum regem Cypri, auxilio fratrum Sancti Johannis de Jerusalem ac plurium nobilium regni Francie et aliorum regnorum qui egressi fuerant passagium transmarinum'), 153–54. See Spiegel, *The Chronicle Tradition of Saint-Denis*, pp. 111–12 and *Encyclopedia of the Medieval Chronicle*, pp. 743–44, 1018.

an account of Peter's tour in European courts, the glorious Alexandria crusade, and his raids against the Syrian coast; it particularly refers to the fact that the pope and the king of France gave money to the Companies in order to encourage them to join Peter's crusade against the Muslims and to Du Guesclin's appointment as the person to lead them in 1365. The text also discusses the king's murder, acknowledging his excesses but adhering to the belief that his brothers were complicit in the regicide.[98] The *Chronique normande du xive siècle*, an anonymous text written *c.* 1369–74 from a perspective sympathetic to the Valois kings, probably by a Norman, bears many similarities with the *Chronographia*; it also mentions Peter's visit to the pope in Avignon and the agreement with the Companies, most of whom are said to have been English.[99]

The *Annales occitanes du Petit Thalamus de Montpellier*, an annalistic text that records the history of the town in Occitan from the ninth century to 1426, with brief later resumptions, includes short entries about the tour in Europe of 'mossen P. rey de Chipre [...] per far lo sant passatge otra mar', the taking of Alexandria, the king's murder, misplaced in Famagusta and attributed to 'M. Jo. Desur' (probably the Admiral John of Tyre, not mentioned by the sources as one of the murderers), and the involvement of his brother, 'Henrie' (sic), Prince of Antioch; the text also claims that King James of Cyprus was murdered by his angry people in 1388 because he had assassinated his nephew, heir to the throne, most probably confusing James with his brother John, killed in 1375.[100] The *Recueil des croniques et anchiennes istories de la Grant Bretaigne, a present nomme Engleterre*, a history of England written by the French chronicler John of Waurin or Wavrin (*c.* 1400–*c.* 1474) from an Anglo-Burgundian standpoint, mentions Peter's first European tour, as indicated by miniature illustrations of the king of Cyprus explaining to Edward the Black Prince (1330–76) his crusader intentions in two of the extant manuscripts containing the work [Figs 14–15]; the scene refers to Peter's visit of Plantagenet-controlled areas in western France in March-April 1364, in particular Angoulême, where he was entertained by Edward. Unfortunately, Book II,

---

98 *Chronographia regum Francorum*, ed. by Henri Moranvillé, 3 vols, Société de l'histoire de France (Paris: Renouard – H. Laurens, 1891–97), II, pp. 300 (the taking of Antalia placed on 24 August 1360), 298–303 (European tour and Alexandria expedition), 303–05 (Peter's murder, accession of Peter II to the throne, Genoese invasion, accession of James I to the throne), esp. 303 ('Postea idem rex regens regnum suum cum magna pace et prosperitate libidini operam dedit nimis lascive se habendo, fecitque multas injurias et extortiones populo suo; quapropter occisus est quodam mane in lecto suo in Nichosiensi, urbe sua, a duobus fratribus suis'), 384 (Companies). See *Encyclopedia of the Medieval Chronicle*, p. 456.

99 *Chronique normande du xive siècle*, ed. by Auguste and Émile Molinier, Société de l'histoire de France (Paris: Renouard – H. Laurens, 1882), pp. 156–57 ('Et en ce temps vint le roy de Chippre devers le pappe et devers les plus grans princes de chrestienté requerre secors et aide pour guerrier les Sarrasins et conquerre la Sainte terre de Jherusalem'), 178–79 ('grands compaignies, dont li plus estoient Englois'), 327 and 340–41 (notes). See *Encyclopedia of the Medieval Chronicle*, pp. 379–80.

100 *Thalamus parvus. Le Petit thalamus de Montpellier*, Société archéologique de Montpellier (Montpellier: Jean Martel ainé, 1840), pp. 362–63 (tour), 369 ('Item, a X doctobre, M. P. rey de Chipre pres la ciutat dAlixandria en Suria, e la tenc v jorns.'), 383 ('Item, a [...] jorns del mes de febrier, M. P. rey de Chipra fo aucit en sa cambra en la ciutat de Fmagosta, per M. Jo. Desur cavalier Chipres de conssentiment del pobol e de M. Henrie princep de Antiocha frayre del dich rey, e fo rey apres lui I filh sieu apelat M. P.'), 413 (James's murder). See *Encyclopedia of the Medieval Chronicle*, p. 411.

which deals with the reign of Edward III of England, remains unpublished and I have not been able to consult any of the manuscripts containing the work.[101]

Interestingly, the image of Peter of Lusignan in the near contemporary chronicle of Leontios Makhairas and in later Cypriot historiography is essentially different from that in these French works. Leontios often demonstrates his adherence to the chivalric ideal and his undisguised partiality for the Lusignans, but he writes from a Cypro-centric perspective, expressing the concern of a new generation of Cypriots about the survival of the Lusignan Kingdom after the Genoese and the Mamluk invasions, even though he does underline Peter's partiality for France in the Hundred Years' War and his special bond with the king of France. He thus draws a fuller and more complex picture of Peter, powerfully describing the king's decline and fall, not hesitating to add some powerfully unpleasant touches to his portrait, but carefully avoiding to openly admit his brothers' implication in his murder, whose descendant (King Janus) Leontios serves.[102] In other words, his is a realistic assessment of the king's works and days and not an idealized hagiography, although it is impossible to know how accurate this portrayal is.

Accordingly, the Mélusine myth would not find its way into medieval Cypriot literature and historiography until 1580 in the diaspora, when Étienne of Lusignan, living in Paris after the island's Ottoman conquest, published his *Description de toute l'isle de Cypre*, using 'romans' he found in the French capital.[103] In true Renaissance spirit, Étienne dismisses the fairy nature of Mélusine as ahistorical, medieval fiction, although he makes sure not to dissociate the Lusignans of Cyprus from their worthy Poitevin ancestors. He proudly reminds his readers that Giovanni Boccaccio dedicated his *Genealogia Deorum* to Hugh IV and declares that Peter deservedly earned the surname 'le Grand'; he also attempts to rectify the infamous picture of Cyprus and he even includes a French translation of a hymn of praise for the island from Ludovico Ariosto's (1474–1533) *Orlando Furioso*. Étienne would return to the Mélusine topic at length in 1587 in his *Genealogies de soixante et sept tres-nobles et tres-illustres maisons*,

---

101 John of Wavrin, *Chroniques d'Angleterre*, BnF, MSS Fr. 77, fol. 259^v and Fr. 87, fol. 212^v ('comment le roy de cippre parla au prince de galles sur l'estat de la croix [...]').
102 Leontios Makhairas, Χρονικό, p. 163 (bond with the French king). The chronicler expresses his admiration for the values of the French *culture courtoise* on at least two occasions, ibid., pp. 342–43 (all manuscripts), 376–77 (only in V234^v); nonetheless, direct influences of chivalric literature are difficult to trace with precision, see Nicolaou-Konnari, 'Apologists or Critics?'. See this author's introductory chapter to this volume for Cypriot sources.
103 The name, though, seems to have been given to Cypriot women in the sixteenth century, even to Greek serfs who apparently copied the naming vogue of their masters: women of the noble families Nores and Bustron were named 'Melusines' or 'en langage Cypriot Milisines', see Estienne de Lusignan, *Description de toute l'isle de Cypre* (Paris: Guillaume Chaudière, 1580; repr. Famagusta: L'Oiseau, 1968; repr. Nicosia: The Bank of Cyprus Cultural Foundation, 2004), chapter 18, fol. 80^r and Estienne de Lusignan, *Les Genealogies de soixante et sept tres-nobles et tres-illustres maisons*, [...] (Paris: Guillaume le Noir, 1587), chapter XXXV, fol. 58^r; in 1549, an eighteen-year-old Greek *parica* from the village of Milikouri in the area of Marathasa, daughter of 'Michalis Petru Nomicu', is named 'Melisina', see Marina Ilia, *Socioeconomic Aspects of Rural Life in Venetian Cyprus*, 2 vols (unpublished doctoral thesis, University of Cyprus, Nicosia, 2021), II, pp. 59, 119, 182, 275.

albeit in a milder manner, retracting some of his former positions. In both works, he claims that a number of women of the royal dynasties of Jerusalem and Cyprus bore the name *Mélusine*, but he seems to confuse the fairy's name with the name *Mélisende*.[104]

Contrary to the Cypriot historiographical tradition, the idealistic depiction of King Peter of Lusignan in late fourteenth- and early fifteenth-century French literature and historiography, regardless of genre, demonstrates the extent to which his life captured the imagination of French authors and how, endowed with legendary proportions, it served their vision for a better future for France and Europe. Under the impact of contemporary political circumstances, Peter was appropriated by France, even though his *Francity* is not particularly emphasized: his chivalric valour and his devotion to the crusader goal represented a ruler's ethos and not merely an individual's merit, the tyrannical aspects of his government were ignored before his glorified deeds, and his murder was not attributed to his failures or failings but to the jealousy of his brothers and lieges and made him a martyr. If, then, for Leontios Makhairas Peter was a fallen Cypriot hero, for the French writers he assumed the proportions of an international popular hero, serving as a model ruler for a reformed France, a reformed Christendom, and a reformed Church.

---

104 Estienne de Lusignan, *Description*, chapter 21, fols 144^r–148^r (Hugh and Peter), pp. x and chapter 22, fols 191^r–192^r (myth of Mélusine), chapter 22, fols 200^r and chapter 24, fols 203^v, 207^r (name *Mélusine*), chapter 29, fols 218v–220v (Cyprus image), [p. 16] (Ariosto); Estienne de Lusignan, *Les Genealogies*, chapters XXVIII–XXXV, fols 39^v–58^r (where he explains that Melusine's father was not from Albania but from Scotland, chapter XXXI, fols 46^v–47^r, and rejects as pure fiction the origin of the Lusignans of Cyprus from Melusine's son Urien, chapter XXXII, fol. 51^v), chapter XXXV, fols 56^r–58^r (name *Mélusine*). For Ariosto's extract, see Ludovico Ariosto, *Orlando furioso*, ed. Lanfranco Caretti, 2 vols (Turin: Einaudi, 1966), vol. I, canto 18, CXXVI–CXLII, pp. 517–19. Cf. Grivaud, *Entrelacs chiprois*, p. 72 and Michalis Pieris, 'Ο Στέφανος Λουζιανιανός και τα Κυπριακά Ερωτικά του 16^{ου} αιώνα', in *Μεσαιωνική Λευκωσία. Πρωτεύουσα ώσμωσης Ανατολής και Δύσης*, ed. by Demetra Papanikola-Bakirtzis (Nicosia: The Leventis Municipal Museum of Nicosia, 2020), pp. 213-39 (231-32).

Fig. 1: Jean Froissart, *Chroniques*, Paris, Bibliothèque nationale de France, MS Fr. 2643, fol. 284ᵛ, 'Couronnment de Charles V le sage'.

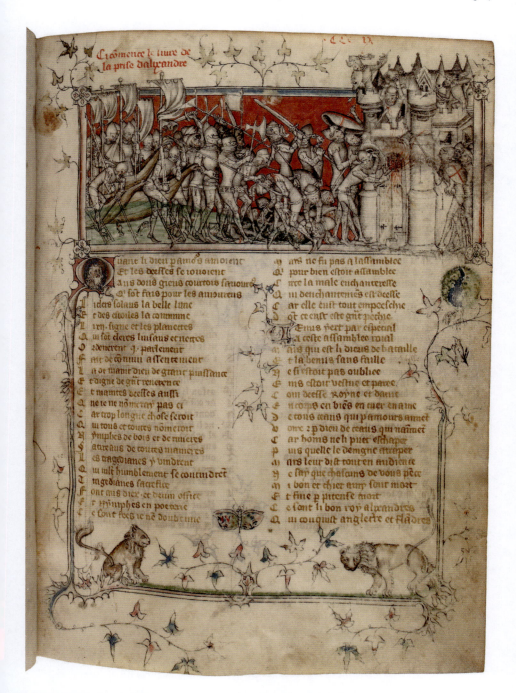

Fig. 2: Guillaume de Machaut, *Oeuvres*, Paris, Bibliothèque nationale de France, MS Fr. 1584, fol. 309ʳ, 'ci commence le livre de la prise d'alixandre' (La prise d'Alexandrie).

Fig. 3: Guillaume de Machaut, *Oeuvres narratives et lyriques*, Paris, Bibliothèque nationale de France, MS Fr. 9221, fol. 213ʳ, 'cy commance la prise d'alixandre' (naissance de Pierre I de Chypre).

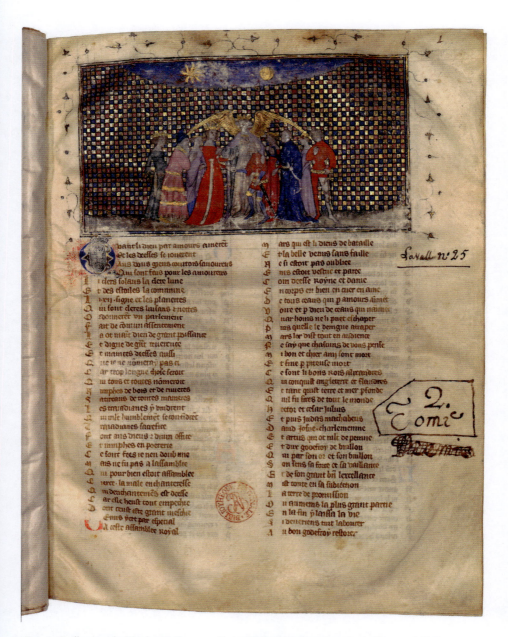

Fig. 4: Guillaume de Machaut, *Oeuvres*, Paris, Bibliothèque nationale de France, MS Fr. 22546, fol. 1ʳ, 'Pierre I de Chypre et les dieux'.

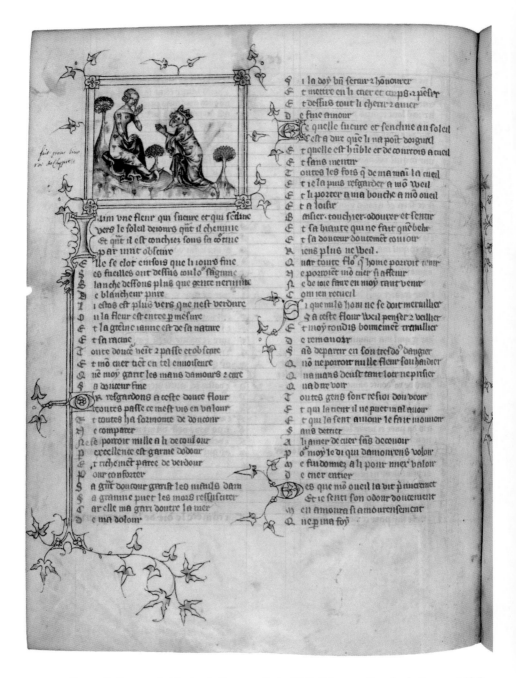

Fig. 5: Guillaume de Machaut, *Oeuvres*, Paris, Bibliothèque nationale de France, MS Fr. 1584, fol. 448[r], 'ci commence le dit de la marguerite' (Pierre I de Chypre et sa dame).

Fig. 6: Guillaume de Machaut, *Oeuvres narratives et lyriques*, Paris, Bibliothèque nationale de France, MS Fr. 9221, fol. 61ᵛ, 'le livre du lyon' (le narrateur guidé par le lion).

Fig. 7: *The Cartulary of the Holy Sepulchre*, Vatican City, Biblioteca Apostolica Vaticana, MS Vat. lat. 7241, feuille de garde, 'Iste liber est domini philippi de maseriis cancellarii regni cypri'.

Fig. 8: Gros of Peter I of Lusignan (obverse-reverse), Bank of Cyprus Cultural Foundation, Museum of the History of Cypriot Coinage (the Foundation's numismatic collection owns 11 coins issued by Peter I).

Fig. 9: Jean d'Arras, *Mélusine ou la noble histoire de Lusignan*, Paris, Bibliothèque nationale de France, Arsenal, MS 3353, fol. 22ᵛ, 'comment la noble forteresce de lusegnen en poictou fu fondee par melusigne'.

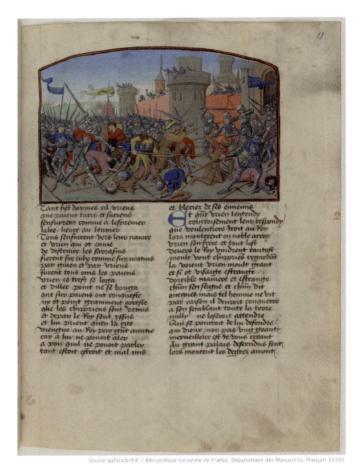

Fig. 10: Coudrette, *Le Roman de Mélusine ou l'histoire de Lusignan*, Paris, Bibliothèque nationale de France, MS Fr. 24383, fol. 13ʳ, Battle of Famagusta.

Fig. 11: Coudrette, *Le Roman de Mélusine ou l'histoire de Lusignan*, Paris, Bibliothèque nationale de France, MS Fr. 24383, fol. 14ʳ, Marriage of Urien and Hermine.

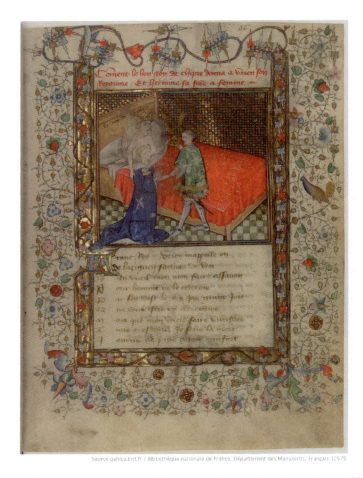

Fig. 12: Coudrette, *Le Roman de Mélusine ou l'histoire de Lusignan*, Paris, Bibliothèque nationale de France, MS Fr. 12572, fol. 36[r], Urien inherits Cyprus.

Fig. 13: Jean Froissart, *Chroniques*, Paris, Bibliothèque nationale de France, MS Fr. 2645, fol. 79ʳ, 'comment le roy de cippre fut tuez et murtri en son lit par l'enortement et corruption des mescreans et pour la bonte et hardiesse qui estoit au dit roy de cippre leur adversaire'.

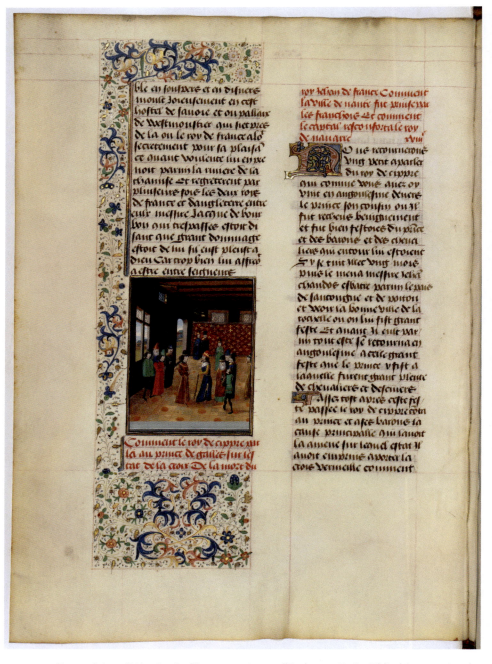

Fig. 14: John of Wavrin, *Anchiennes cronicques d'Engleterre*, Paris, Bibliothèque nationale de France, MS Fr. 77, fol. 259ᵛ, 'comment le roy de cippre parla au prince de galles sur l'estat de la croix' […].

Fig. 15: John of Wavrin, *Chronicques d'Engleterre*, Paris, Bibliothèque nationale de France, MS Fr. 87, fol. 212ᵛ, 'comment le roy de cippre parla au prince de galles sur l'estat de la croix' [...].

Part III

A Crusader Kingdom – Cypriot Society before and after Peter I

MIRIAM RACHEL SALZMANN

Stability or Chaos? Power Elites in Lusignan Cyprus between the 1360s and 1390s*

'And again, the devil was the father of yet more trouble'.[1] In this typical fashion, the Cypriot chronicler Leontios Makhairas commented on the upheavals in the Lusignan Kingdom of Cyprus in the second half of the fourteenth century, making a specific connection between the events leading up to King Peter I's violent death and Satan's influence. His perspective is understandable: in the turbulent years between 1365 and the 1380s, the 'sweet land of Cyprus', as he called it, experienced one upheaval after another. Following a long stable period under King Hugh IV (1324–59), which is usually seen as the heyday of Lusignan rule, King Peter I (1359–69) launched a number of great military campaigns against the Mamluks and the Turks. These expeditions were probably a reaction to the economic hardship resulting from the abolition of the papal trade embargo against the Muslim Levant in 1348. Although they brought Peter great fame, they also emptied the state treasury. The climax of these undertakings was Peter's crusade against Alexandria, a highly prestigious project that failed miserably. As a result, Cyprus found itself at war with the mighty Mamluk Sultanate; peace was only accomplished after some vassals and maybe even his brothers killed Peter I for violating the kingdom's customs and laws in early 1369. Shortly thereafter, in 1372, during the reign of the late king's son, Peter II, war broke out with the Genoese. It ended poorly for the Cypriots, with the loss of the important city of Famagusta and the exile of at least seventy nobles to Italy. Decades of recurring negotiations over

---

* This article is connected to research conducted for my PhD thesis *The Cypriot Aristocracy in the 15th Century: Social Structures, Social Mobility, and Identity Construction*, successfully defended at the Johannes Gutenberg-Universität Mainz in 2019. I would like to thank Ian Hathaway for his diligent proofreading and Angel Nicolaou-Konnari for her valuable comments.

[1] Quotation from the English translation of the text in Leontios Makhairas, *Recital concerning the Sweet Land of Cyprus entitled 'Chronicle'*, ed. and trans. by Richard M. Dawkins, 2 vols (Oxford: Clarendon Press, 1932), I, § 268. For what follows, however, the more recent diplomatic edition of all three extant manuscripts will be used, Leontios Makhairas, Χρονικό της Κύπρου. Παράλληλη διπλωματική έκδοση των χειρογράφων, ed. by Michalis Pieris and Angel Nicolaou-Konnari, Texts and Studies in the History of Cyprus, 48 (Nicosia: Cyprus Research Centre, 2003).

Miriam Rachel Salzmann • University of Mainz

the reparations to be paid to Genoa followed. When Peter II died without progeny in 1382, a rebellion of the nobility ensued because the interim governors of the island did not accept James, Peter I's brother and a hostage in the hands of the Genoese, as their next king. They feared that accepting James would have increased Genoese interference in the kingdom. James only managed to gain the throne later by bribing the most powerful Cypriot nobles with titles and estates.[2]

In view of the upheavals of the period, one might ask how these events influenced the balance of power in Cyprus. How stable were the Cypriot power elites in these troubled times? Can we trace significant changes in the distribution of power? How were sudden power vacuums dealt with? Were they conducive to social mobility in the highest governmental circles? Or, in other words, did the late fourteenth century offer many possibilities to Cypriot non-nobles to ascend the social ranks and take positions of power? These questions are of interest when discussing social mobility in Cypriot society between the fourteenth and fifteenth centuries more broadly. Many scholars have noted how large numbers of individuals of Greek or Oriental Christian descent, who had formerly been excluded from the highest echelons of the noble Frankish Lusignan society, managed to ascend and integrate into the governing circles between the 1370s and the end of Lusignan rule in 1474.[3] It is, however, unclear how far these processes had developed in the late fourteenth century. In order to answer these questions, I shall analyse the Cypriot power elites of the late fourteenth century from a largely prosopographical perspective. Who was in power at the time and, more importantly, who stayed in power and who did not?

As a basis for the analysis, we shall use John Haldon's definition of *power elite*, which he has recently put forth in an essay on Byzantine social elites and which is based on earlier work by Wright Mills. According to Haldon, 'a "power elite" or "ruling group" [means] a leading fraction of the economically dominant social strata, those who shared a situation in respect of access to political/ideological power and

---

2   For the island's history during the period in question, see: Peter W. Edbury, *The Kingdom of Cyprus and the Crusades, 1191–1374* (Cambridge: Cambridge University Press, 1991), pp. 141–211; Sir George Hill, *A History of Cyprus*, 4 vols (Cambridge: Cambridge University Press, 1940–52), II, pp. 380–446; Christopher Schabel, 'Like God from Heaven, but They Don't Call Him King. The Rebellion against James I of Cyprus', *Cahiers du Centre d'Études Chypriotes*, 43 (2013), 379–92.

3   Benjamin Arbel, 'The Cypriot Nobility from the Fourteenth to the Sixteenth Century. A New Interpretation', in *Latins and Greeks in the Eastern Mediterranean after 1204*, ed. by Benjamin Arbel, Bernard Hamilton, and David Jacoby (London: Frank Cass, 1989) [= *Mediterranean Historical Review*, 4/1 (1989)], 175–97; Peter W. Edbury, 'Cypriot Society under Lusignan Rule', in *Caterina Cornaro, Queen of Cyprus*, ed. by David Hunt (London: Trigraph Ltd, 1989), pp. 17–34 (21–22, 29–30, 33–34); Gilles Grivaud, *Entrelacs Chiprois. Essai sur les lettres et la vie intellectuelle dans le royaume de Chypre (1191–1570)* (Nicosia: Moufflon, 2009), pp. 28–33; Costas Kyrris, 'Cypriot Identity, Byzantium and the Latins, 1192–1489', *History of European Ideas*, 19 (1994), 563–73 (pp. 568–71); Jean Richard, 'Culture franque et culture grecque: Le royaume de Chypre au xvème siècle', *Byzantinische Forschungen*, 11 (1987), 399–415 (pp. 400, 404–07, 412–15); Wipertus H. Rudt de Collenberg, 'Δομὴ καὶ προέλευση τῆς τάξεως τῶν εὐγενῶν', in Ἱστορία τῆς Κύπρου, ed. by Theodoros Papadopoullos, 6 vols (Nicosia: Archbishop Makarios III Foundation, 1995–2011), IV, Μεσαιωνικὸν βασίλειον – Ἐνετοκρατία, pp. 785–862 (811–13).

influence [...].[4] Thus, the members of a power elite are those individuals who have access to actual power, in contrast to the more numerous members of a social elite. The social elite, according to Haldon, is a broader dominant social class with access to the means of economic production, which enables it to exercise political power in a general sense.[5] When focusing on the power elite, the question remains how power was wielded in the Lusignan Kingdom and, consequently, how the power elite can be discerned in the sources. Since the object of study is a monarchy, it is only reasonable to focus on those individuals who were close to the (theoretical) source and centre of power, the king or the regent, but also on men who executed crucial tasks, such as administering the kingdom's finances, leading military expeditions, etc. These criteria may or may not include all the men holding crown offices and titles. I will, therefore, examine who was part of the king's council of advisors[6] and who held important offices, who performed important tasks and functions, but also, when possible, who sat in the High Court, the highest state organ in the Lusignan Kingdom. Often, but not always, these circles overlapped.

The sources used for the analysis are various state documents as well as letters to state officials. These documents, such as peace treaties, privileges for the Italian maritime republics, or appointments of royal procurators, vary in structure, but they always mention the statesmen present to witness the document, either at the beginning or the end of the text. The witnesses are usually mentioned together with the date and the place of the issuing of the document (e.g., 'Datum et actum in Roma, anno Nativitatis Domini millesimo trecentesimo sexagesimo octavo, mense Maii, die vicesima, presentibus dilectis et fidelibus [...] consiliariis nostris, testibus ad premissa vocatis et specialiter congregatis').[7] Sometimes, as in the example mentioned, the underwriters are identified as the king's counsellors. State treaties from the 1390s (i.e., the second half of James I's reign), explicitly call these individuals the king's High Court, which was assembled according to Cypriot custom ('in presentia baronum altam curiam facientium secundum consuetudinem regni Cipri').[8] This identification is missing from earlier documents. All sources meticulously mention the witnesses' office and/or title, and therefore enable us to trace the careers of officials and their involvement in government matters. It is not entirely clear which protocol the order of the witnesses' names follows, although members of the royal family are usually mentioned first.[9] It seems that the most prestigious men would follow the royals. However, as these people held varied offices, we cannot be entirely sure that every document followed the same pattern nor can we be certain that the order mirrored the actual power balance. Thus, interpretations deriving from the order of names

---

4   John Haldon, 'Social Elites, Wealth, and Power', in *The Social History of Byzantium*, ed. by John Haldon (Chichester: Wiley-Blackwell Publishing, 2009), pp. 168–211 (172).
5   Haldon, 'Social Elites, Wealth, and Power', pp. 170–71.
6   Cf. also Gilles Grivaud's chapter in this volume.
7   Louis de Mas Latrie, *Histoire de l'île de Chypre sous le règne des princes de la maison de Lusignan*, 3 vols (Paris: Imprimerie impériale, 1852–61), II, pp. 307–08.
8   Mas Latrie, *Histoire de l'île de Chypre*, II, p. 420.
9   See, for example, Mas Latrie, *Histoire de l'île de Chypre*, II, pp. 289, 420, 428.

will have to be carried out with care. Nonetheless, examining the names of the men present in important acts will help us discern who belonged to the island's power elite. The documents mentioned above will be supplemented by less reliable information from the chronicles of the time, first of all the chronicles of Leontios Makhairas and Florio Bustron, but also William of Machaut's epic poem on Peter I's Alexandrian crusade. This text, despite being an epic, is so well informed about the men taking part in the events described that it can be used for our purposes, though one must take its tendentiousness into account.[10]

The easiest way to assess structures and changes in the power elites will be to follow the developments chronologically. I will focus on five crucial periods, beginning with the reign of Peter I. I will then concentrate on the aftermath of Peter's murder until about 1372 and on the war with the Genoese and the developments resulting from it. The last part of this essay will focus on the rebellion against James I and compare this period with the early 1390s, when James's position was firmly established.

Peter I's Reign

The first period of Peter I's reign is one of the most complicated in terms of power structures. Peter I was a very mobile king – he travelled to the West twice, between 1362 and 1365, and again in 1367–68. His mobility suggests that a twofold examination of power elites is necessary, concerning the statesmen accompanying Peter on his travels as well as those who stayed behind and administered the island during his absence. Unfortunately, very few sources shed light on the latter group since almost all of the extant sources were drawn up in Rome, Venice, or Genoa. Research on Peter I's reign often discusses his preference for foreign administrators and delves into their careers. While assessing the influence of this latter group, it is important to ask who these men were, where they joined the king, and for how long they served him.

The early years of Peter's reign, before his first journey to the West, offer rather few sources for our analysis:[11] Makhairas's list of persons honoured at Peter's coronation, a treaty renewing Venetian privileges, and the documentation of an embassy sent to Venice in 1361. According to Makhairas's chronicle, Peter I granted anew only the offices that were void at the time of his coronation – therefore, the list does not reflect the totality of office holders at the time. The chronicler records John and James of Lusignan, the king's brothers, whom Peter appointed constables of Cyprus and

---

10 For Machaut, I will use the most recent edition by Sophie Hardy, *Édition critique de la Prise d'Alixandrie de Guillaume de Machaut* (unpublished doctoral thesis, Université d'Orléans, 2011): <ftp://ftp.univ-orleans.fr/theses/sophie.hardy_1730.pdf>, and compare it with Guillaume de Machaut, *The Capture of Alexandria*, trans. by Janet Shirley, introduction and notes by Peter W. Edbury, Crusade Texts in Translation 8 (Aldershot: Ashgate, 2001). Reference to the old edition by Louis de Mas Latrie, *La Prise d'Alexandrie ou Chronique du roi Pierre Ier de Lusignan par Guillaume de Machaut* (Geneva: Jules-Guillaume Fick, 1877) will only be made where his comments are of interest.

11 For the few sources, also see Gilles Grivaud's chapter in this volume, n. 5.

Jerusalem respectively (John also became prince of Antioch).[12] Philip of Ibelin, who was a member of the second most important Cypriot noble family after the Lusignans and who had played a key role under Peter's father Hugh IV, became seneschal of Cyprus. Raymond Babin, also from an important noble family, was made butler,[13] while Hugh Ognibono/Ognibene/Ommebono, a physician from Mantua, became chancellor. Makhairas closes his list with Pietro Malocello, a merchant from Genoa, who had been active in the Eastern Mediterranean and had befriended Peter I. He was appointed chamberlain of Cyprus.[14]

Makhairas's list is not extensive. We can infer this thanks to the confirmation of privileges for the Venetian Republic signed on 16 August 1360.[15] The ratification of such an important treaty would surely have required the presence of notable members of the king's council. The document mentions John of Lusignan as first witness, describing him as '[presente] inclito et potenti barone domino Johanne de Lizignano fratre dicti domini regis, principe Anthioceno et conestabulo regni Cipri'.[16] Although he certainly owed the first place in the list of witnesses to being the king's brother, we know that he later served as regent in Cyprus during Peter's journeys to the West. Therefore, we may safely assume that he was the king's right-hand man.[17] Philip of Brunswick, whose name follows those of John of Lusignan and the bishop of Limassol Guy of Ibelin, was also an important man at the time. He was the son of Duke Henry II of Brunswick and seems to have come to Cyprus in the 1330s. He had married into one of the most important Cypriot families of the time, the Dampierres, who were closely connected to the royal family, and he is therefore called the king's cousin in some sources. Philip held the honorary title of the constable of Jerusalem, which probably did not involve any executive functions, but he accompanied Peter on his first journey to the West, and later even married his daughter Heloise to Peter's younger brother James. Before 1368, he remarried and wed Hugh IV's widow Alice of Ibelin. He was therefore connected to the royal family via multiple links.[18] Other witnesses of the treaty were John of Morphou, at that time marshal of Cyprus, the chamberlain Simon of Montolif, the *bailli* of the *Secrète* John Tenouri, and the chancellor

---

12 From 1268 on, the Lusignans also held the title of the king of Jerusalem and used to give out the Jerusalem crown offices well into the fifteenth century, long after the kingdom had been lost, see Edbury, *Kingdom of Cyprus*, p. 36.
13 Raymond was Peter's ambassador at the Roman curia in 1360, along with Jean de Caramayno, see *Bullarium Cyprium III: Lettres papales relatives à Chypre, 1316–1378*, ed. by Charles Perrat and Jean Richard, with the collaboration of Christopher Schabel, Sources et études de l'histoire de Chypre, 68 (Nicosia: Centre de Recherche Scientifique, 2012), nos u-230–39.
14 Leontios Makhairas, Χρονικό της Κύπρου, p. 117. For Malocello, see Leontios Makhairas, *Recital*, II, § 100, p. 94 n. 3 and cf. Mas Latrie, *Histoire de l'île de Chypre*, II, p. 425 n. 3.
15 Cf. Gilles Grivaud's chapter in this volume, n. 49, who also discusses the witnesses of the treaty.
16 Mas Latrie, *Histoire de l'île de Chypre*, II, p. 230.
17 Gilles Grivaud, in his chapter in this volume, n. 33–39, stresses John's central role as Peter's confident during his entire reign.
18 Mas Latrie, *Histoire de l'île de Chypre*, II, pp. 229–30, 248–49; Leontios Makhairas, Χρονικό της Κύπρου, p. 119; *Bullarium Cyprium III*, nos s-53, u-12, v-27, 121, 188.

Hugh Ognibono.[19] Unfortunately, the sources do not allow us to assess the relative strength of all these players and their influence on the king[20], with the exception perhaps of John of Lusignan and Philip of Brunswick mentioned above, who seem to have been most influential. But we can still make some important observations from both Makhairas's list and the treaty. All the members of the power elite came from old and established Cypriot noble families, apart from Pietro Malocello, who was Peter I's friend, Hugh Ognibono, who came from Mantua, and Philip of Brunswick. Raymond Babin, Philip of Brunswick, and John of Morphou, had been in power already under Hugh IV and were therefore experienced advisors.[21] James of Nores, turcopolier of Cyprus, and the admiral John of Tyre (d. 1368)[22] should probably be added to the circle, even if they are not visible in the sources. Both had also served under Hugh, and James of Nores would even play a role after Peter I's death.

The majority of the statesmen discussed above stayed in Cyprus when Peter set out on his first journey to the West late in 1362. The only member of the circle to accompany him was Philip of Brunswick. Instead, a different group of interesting men accompanied the king. When Peter confirmed the privileges of the Republic of Genoa during his stay there in March 1363, Philip of Brunswick was the first to be mentioned among his witnesses. His name is followed by those of Simon Tenouri, Guido da Bagnolo (the king's physician), Philip of Mézières (then the king's chancellor and therefore Hugh Ognibono's successor), and John of Ibelin (the seneschal of Jerusalem).[23] Four of these men (Philip of Mézières, Philip of Brunswick, Simon Tenouri, and John of Ibelin) were influential enough to present petitions for their

---

19 Mas Latrie, *Histoire de l'île de Chypre*, II, p. 230. A year later, we find John of Morphou as ambassador in Venice together with Thomas of Montolif, see Mas Latrie, *Histoire de l'île de Chypre II*, p. 233, Leontios Makhairas, Χρονικό της Κύπρου, p. 121, and *Bullarium Cyprium III*, no. u-281. It is not entirely clear whether Thomas had been active already under Hugh IV. In 1338, a Thomas of Montolif witnessed a treaty with the Genoese, but his office is not mentioned, see Mas Latrie, *Histoire de l'île de Chypre*, II, p. 179. In 1328, a man of the same name is mentioned as marshal, Mas Latrie, *Histoire de l'île de Chypre*, II, p. 141, but this Thomas had already died in 1360, *Bullarium Cyprium III*, no. u-241. It is, therefore, not clear which Thomas witnessed the 1338 treaty, and when the auditor Thomas started his career. There seems to have been a third Thomas around, as the 1369 *ordonnance* as well as the papal registers differentiate between an elder and a younger Thomas (the younger Thomas very probably being the auditor, the prosecutor of the state), see *Bullarium Cyprium III*, no. u-266 and Guillaume de Machaut, *The Capture of Alexandria*, pp. 205–06.

20 The holding of a certain office can only give clues about an individual's influence to a certain degree, as influence did not always directly coincide with the same office. The turcopolier James of Nores, for example, had a certain influence under Peter I, but he was by no means the most important statesman of his time, while John of Brie, who occupied the same office, was the first man after the king for a number of years and even acted as regent after Peter II's death, see below.

21 See, for example, Mas Latrie, *Histoire de l'île de Chypre*, II, pp. 178–79; cf. Gilles Grivaud's chapter in this volume, n. 47, who points to these advisors' importance for a smooth transition from Hugh IV's to Peter I's reign.

22 For detailed information on John of Tyre as admiral of Cyprus, see Nicholas Coureas, 'The Admirals of Lusignan Cyprus', *Crusades* 15 (2016), 117–34 (pp. 121–25).

23 Mas Latrie, *Histoire de l'île de Chypre*, II, pp. 248–49.

familiares to the Roman curia during Peter's stay in Rome in 1363.[24] It is noteworthy that two of these five men were foreigners. Only John of Ibelin came from an old Cypriot family. He was Peter's cousin and according to Makhairas had become seneschal of Jerusalem at Peter's coronation. The chronicle also records that he left Peter, probably during the journey through Europe, to go and fight together with the English against the French. Peter allegedly was enraged by this gesture, but forgave John when he returned to Cyprus in 1366. In the following years, John became one of the leading figures in the campaigns to protect Gorhigos and Adalia.[25] He was not, however, one of the most stable figures in Peter's retinue.

By contrast, Simon Tenouri stayed at Peter's side from 1363 until the end of his reign. Unfortunately, information on his family is scant. Simon's father, a certain John, was a statesman under Hugh IV (and probably the *bailli* of the *Secrète* mentioned above). However, the family name does not appear in other sources, such as the *Lignages d'Outremer*.[26] We do know some details about Simon himself, though. He was Simon of Montolif's nephew and therefore his aunt must have married into this well-known Cypriot family. Simon may have witnessed the signing of a treaty granted to the Venetian Republic in 1338, which allows us to set the beginning of his career during Hugh IV's reign. According to one version of Makhairas's chronicle, Simon accompanied John and Peter when, as young men, they ventured to the West against their father's will.[27] If this is true, we can assume that he had a close relationship with the royal family. Machaut mentions that Simon was also a friend of John of Morphou.[28] In any case, his career under Peter I is impressive. He accompanied the king on both his journeys to the West and played a leading role in all his campaigns. From at least 1365, he was marshal of Jerusalem.[29] Philip of Mézières even claims that

---

24 *Bullarium Cyprium III*, nos v-23, 26–28, 36. Guido da Bagnolo obtained only a canonry for himself later in 1363 and Philip of Mézières obtained privileges for his followers again in 1366, see *Bullarium Cyprium III*, nos v-42 and 164.

25 Leontios Makhairas, Χρονικό τῆς Κύπρου, pp. 119, 163, 165, 171.

26 Mas Latrie's editions of documents do not give any clues about the family, either. The tombstone of a certain 'Jean Tenouri', dating from 1341, is published in *Lacrimae Cypriae. Les larmes de Chypre ou Recueil des inscriptions lapidaires pour la plupart funéraires de la période franque et vénitienne de l'île de Chypre*, ed. by Brunehilde Imhaus, 2 vols (Nicosia: Department of Antiquities, 2004), I, no. 339. As another John witnessed the 1360 treaty (see above), either there were two men of the same name, or there must be a mistake in the reading of the tombstone. Sophie Hardy claims that 'Symon Thynoly' was an English knight, but it is unclear from where she takes this piece of information and, as she also considers John of Morphou (who was definitely a Cypriot) to be English, perhaps her source is wrong, see Hardy, *Édition critique de la* Prise d'Alixandrie, pp. 447, 441.

27 Mas Latrie, *Histoire de l'île de Chypre*, II, p. 179. For the adventure to the West, see Leontios Makhairas, Χρονικό τῆς Κύπρου, p. 108. The version is contained in Oxford, Bodleian Library, MS Selden, supra 14 (= O) and in Ravenna, Biblioteca Classense, MS gr. 187 (= R).

28 Hardy, *Édition critique de la* Prise d'Alixandrie, pp. 131–32, ll. 4552–56; Guillaume de Machaut, *The Capture of Alexandria*, p. 107.

29 Mas Latrie, *Histoire de l'île de Chypre*, II, pp. 249, 254, 291, 302, 308; Hardy, *Édition critique de la* Prise d'Alixandrie, p. 67, ll. 2277–79; Guillaume de Machaut, *The Capture of Alexandria*, pp. 63, 196 (a reference to an extract from an anonymous French chronicle, which also mentions him as naval commander in the 1367 campaigns); Leontios Makhairas, Χρονικό τῆς Κύπρου, pp. 153 (MSS O and R), 165, 168, 172, 180.

Simon fought in the wars of France under both John II and Charles V;[30] this could have happened between 1363 and 1365, when he was in Europe with Peter, although there is no other information on this issue. Be that as it may, Simon was one of the great winners of Peter's reign.

The two foreigners in Peter's retinue in 1363, Guido da Bagnolo and Philip of Mézières, are both well-known personalities and I shall not dwell upon them at length here. Their presence at Peter's side in 1363 is of interest for understanding the role of foreign power elites in this period. Guido da Bagnolo was a famous physician and humanist from Reggio Emilia in northern Italy. He is well known for his disputes with Petrarch. He had come to Cyprus in 1353 and probably served as physician under Hugh IV. He must have impressed Peter, because he served as his councillor for a long time, albeit with interruptions. He was one of Peter's important followers on his first journey, witnessing not only the Genoese treaty in March 1363, but also a contract with the Venetian Cornaro brothers concluded in Bruges in August of the same year. In 1365, Guido served as Peter's ambassador for a peace treaty with Genoa. But when Peter left for the East, Guido stayed in Venice. He only rejoined Peter on his second visit to Italy in 1368 and again he did not accompany him back to Cyprus, but remained in Italy where he died in 1370.[31] Philip of Mézières, on the other hand, seems to have come to Cyprus specifically to serve under Peter I once he had become king. The two had met in 1347, when Philip was returning from a pilgrimage to Jerusalem. In c. 1361 he became Peter's chancellor and accompanied him on his journey to Europe and his Alexandria campaign, only to be sent to Europe again in 1366 in order to gather support against the Turks. Philip was on his way back to Cyprus when he heard of Peter's murder and decided to stay in Venice, whence he then went to Paris, where he lived until his death in 1405.[32] Thus, both Philip and Guido were important advisors to Peter, despite not actually having spent much time on Cyprus.

Guido da Bagnolo and Philip of Mézières were not, however, the only foreigners who gathered around Peter during his journey through Europe. Papal letters as well as state treaties suggest that Peter accepted into his retinue a broad range of clerics and laymen from France and Italy, and later also from the German Empire and Spain. During his stay at the curia in early 1363, Peter submitted petitions for many clerics from different origins, counting them among his *familiares*.[33] Indeed, his retinue at the time was full of foreigners, at least at the clerical level: his confessor, for example,

---

30 Philippe de Mézières, *Songe du Viel Pelerin*, ed. by Joël Blanchard, 2 vols, Textes littéraires français, 633, (Geneva: Droz, 2015), II, p. 958.
31 Franco Bacchelli, 'Guido da Bagnolo', in *Dizionario Biografico degli Italiani* (Rome: Treccani): http://www.treccani.it/enciclopedia/guido-da-bagnolo_(Dizionario-Biografico)/ (accessed 16.01.2018); Mas Latrie, *Histoire Histoire de l'île de Chypre*, II, pp. 272, 291, 302; cf. Gilles Grivaud's chapter in this volume, n. 64.
32 Philippe de Mézières, *Songe*, I, pp. lviii, lx, lxvi–vii, lxix, lxxvi–vii; cf. Gilles Grivaud's chapter in this volume, n. 65–66.
33 *Bullarium Cyprium III*, nos v-20, 47. The same phenomenon also occurs later on, although to a lesser degree, see, for example, *Bullarium Cyprium III*, no. v-140.

was Antonio di Rivello, bishop of Melfi.[34] However, it was only in June 1364 that the pope recommended to the Cypriot king Peter Thomas, who was to accompany the crusade to Alexandria as papal legate and is one of the most well-known figures of Peter's time.[35] Of Peter's clerical retinue, Peter Thomas would be the only one to truly influence politics in the Eastern Mediterranean in the years to come, while most of Peter's other favourites seem to have been men of less importance. An exception is Adhémar de la Voulte from Southern France. Brother of Brémond de la Voulte, one of Peter's important foreign supporters during the crusade discussed below, he acted as Peter's ambassador in 1364 and was installed as bishop of Limassol in 1367, rising directly from the office of a simple subdeacon to the dignity of bishop.[36]

Thus, Peter's clerical entourage during his journey through Europe was extremely mixed, although this was perhaps a short-lived phenomenon. The same can be said of the laymen who accompanied him. While Philip of Mézières and Guido da Bagnolo had travelled with Peter from the beginning, others joined him during his journey, mostly in the hope of joining his crusade. Peter favoured some of these men well enough to let them witness the procuration for Guido da Bagnolo to negotiate a peace treaty with Genoa in 1365. The names that appear are those of a certain Bernardo Al and a Tierceles of Bare, a Flemish knight, who is designated as the king's *maître d'hôtel* (steward of the royal household).[37] Neither of them appears in any other historical event of note. We may thus suggest that, though Peter did gather around him various foreigners during his journey, only the already well-known figures such as Philip of Mézières and Guido da Bagnolo really played a lasting role in the king's political circle.

In contrast to the sources on Peter's retinue during his journey, the information on the situation in Cyprus is very scarce. We know that Peter's brother John acted as regent, as attested by a letter with instructions written to him in April 1363,[38] but otherwise we can only speculate. Many important men from the end of Hugh IV's and the beginning of Peter's reign were still active in 1365 and later during Peter's campaigns. We may assume that they ran the every-day business together with John of Lusignan during the king's long absence. This group of people would have included James of Nores, John of Morphou, Thomas of Montolif, and Raymond Babin, among others.

When Peter returned from the West and set out for his campaign against Alexandria (1365), he did bring many foreigners from the West with him. Some of them had already joined him during his journey, others only came for the crusade itself. If our only source were the French poet William of Machaut, we would believe that

---

34 *Bullarium Cyprium III*, no. v-45.
35 *Bullarium Cyprium III*, nos v-98–99.
36 *Bullarium Cyprium III*, nos v-103, 178, 181. On Adhémar, see *Lemesos. A History of Limassol in Cyprus from Antiquity to the Ottoman Conquest*, ed. by Angel Nicolaou-Konnari and Chris Schabel (Newcastle upon Tyne: Cambridge Scholars Publishing, 2015), pp. 276, 359.
37 Mas Latrie, *Histoire de l'île de Chypre*, II, p. 254.
38 Mas Latrie, *Histoire de l'île de Chypre*, II, p. 250: 'à nostre feel chier et amé frere Johan de Lezegnan, prince d'Anthioche, conestable, regent et gouvernour de nostre dit royaume de Chipre'.

those heroic battles were fought almost entirely by Westerners, such as the powerful Viscount of Turenne William Roger, or Guy de Baveux. In Machaut's poem, especially prominent as Peter's confidents are Perceval de Coulonges, an otherwise completely unknown knight from Poitou,[39] and the aforementioned Brémond de la Voulte, a knight from the Languedoc.[40] Peter Edbury has recently shown that the main aim of Machaut's poem must have been to praise the chivalric prowess of Peter's western followers, whose friends and relatives would have been his target audience.[41] However, Machaut also mentions some Cypriots as leaders of the campaign. Apart from John of Lusignan, he refers to John of Morphou, Simon Tenouri, James of Nores, and to a lesser degree to John of Ibelin.[42] John Moustri stands out for having led some of the smaller expeditions on his own.[43] Moreover, at one point, Machaut concedes that he simply does not know the names of all the Cypriot, Venetian, and Genoese knights taking part in the campaign.[44]

A comparison of Machaut's poem with Makhairas's chronicle puts Machaut's account into perspective.[45] Although Makhairas mentions the names of many foreign knights participating in the expeditions, he never refers to Perceval de Coulonges or Brémond de la Voulte in his chronicle. More importantly, many Cypriot men are mentioned as ship captains in his campaign lists. Although John of Lusignan and the legate Peter Thomas are attributed the most important roles, Makhairas mentions

---

39 Hardy, *Édition critique de la* Prise d'Alixandrie, pp. xc, cxx, 58–83, 192–96, 216, 221–23, ll. 1967–2837, 6677–829, L 1, 7558–603; Guillaume de Machaut, *The Capture of Alexandria*, pp. 57, 64, 72–73, 144, 147, 166.

40 Hardy, *Édition critique de la* Prise d'Alixandrie, pp. 69–159, 196, 215, ll. 2345–5525, 6813, L 1; Guillaume de Machaut, *The Capture of Alexandria*, pp. 7, 10, 64–67, 89–91, 109, 118, 120, 144, 147; Leontios Makhairas, *Recital*, II, § 187, p. 119 n. 2.

41 Peter Edbury, 'Machaut, Mézières, Makhairas and Amadi: Constructing the Reign of Peter I (1359–1369)', in *Philippe de Mézières and His Age. Piety and Politics in the Fourteenth Century*, ed. by Renate Blumenfeld-Kosinski and Kiril Petkov, The Medieval Mediterranean, 91 (Leiden: Brill 2012), pp. 349–58 (355, 357).

42 Hardy, *Édition critique de la* Prise d'Alixandrie, pp. 71, 129, 131, 132, 138, 139, 152, ll. 2415–16, 4475–81, 4552, 4557, 4781, 4813–18, 5269–74; Guillaume de Machaut, *The Capture of Alexandria*, pp. 63, 66, 67, 73, 105–07, 120, 128.

43 Hardy, *Édition critique de la* Prise d'Alixandrie, pp. 109, 132–50, 243, ll. 3774, 4586–5187, 8321; Guillaume de Machaut, *The Capture of Alexandria*, pp. 91, 94–95, 114–15. Machaut even mentions Moustri as the admiral of a fleet of twenty-five ships in 1366, but in other instances he is clearly only a captain, see the aforementioned passages and cf. Coureas, 'The Admirals', p. 125. Moreover, John of Tyre was the admiral during this period, but as he was absent in the West in 1366, Moustri may have been a stand-in admiral or just called admiral in the sense of commander of the ships. For John of Tyre and his exile, see Coureas, 'The Admirals', pp. 121–25.

44 Hardy, *Édition critique de la* Prise d'Alixandrie, pp. 134–35, ll. 4657–60; Guillaume de Machaut, *The Capture of Alexandria*, p. 109.

45 For a thematic comparison of the two works, see 'Appendix I' to Angel Nicolaou-Konnari's introductory chapter to this volume. I use the chronicle of Makhairas for the comparison, since it is the main Cypriot historiographical source. The sixteenth-century chronicle known as the *Chronique d'Amadi* gives a very similar account to that of Makhairas without providing additional information that is relevant to this article, apart from one detail, discussed in n. 58 below. I therefore do not usually cite the parallel passages in the *Chronique d'Amadi*.

all the Cypriots found in Machaut as well as Philip of Brunswick, Philip of Ibelin, Guy of Milmars, Raymond Babin, Henry of Giblet, John of Brie (all from old noble Cypriot families), the Byzantine John Laskaris Kalopheros, and many others.[46] Thus, though Westerners played important roles during the reign of Peter I, the Cypriot power elite still appears to have remained stable.[47] It was composed of the same statesmen as at the time of his father.

We can support this claim thanks to evidence from Peter's second journey to Europe in 1368, during which he was accompanied by the same group of powerful men who had been part of his inner circle for quite some time. The information on Peter's retinue comes chiefly from three documents drawn up in the course of two days in Rome, on 19 and 20 May 1368. The documents concern various affairs, such as the peace with the Mamluk sultan and Marie de Bourbon's dowry. They were witnessed by Simon Tenouri (by then marshal of Jerusalem), Hugh of Lusignan (Peter's nephew), Philip of Ibelin, Philip of Mézières, James of Nores, the chamberlain of Cyprus Pietro Malocello, and John Moustri, who functioned as the king's chamberlain at that time. Last but not least signed Guido da Bagnolo, who had, as mentioned above, stayed in Italy in the preceding years and now rejoined Peter's entourage in Rome.[48] As before, we do not have any information on the power elites staying in Cyprus other than the fact that John of Lusignan acted as regent and that, according to Makhairas, Peter had appointed a certain John Visconti to be in charge of his household during his absence.[49]

To conclude, Peter's reign was indeed characterized by the influence of various western foreigners. At the same time, however, there was a sizeable and stable group of Cypriots in power. It was men from this circle who decided, in early 1369, to kill the king whom they had served for so many years. The reasons for the murder have already been discussed,[50] and I shall not dwell on them here. Suffice it to say that Peter's foreign favourites perhaps gave his Cypriot subjects reason to worry about their influence; however, the sources do not show any Cypriots directly ousted from power in favour of foreigners, although this may be the result of the lack of documentation.

The Aftermath of Peter I's Murder

Regardless of who actually killed Peter I, it is clear from the events directly following his murder that the act had been planned and accepted by the larger circle of the king's own power elite. When the High Court assembled on the day of Peter's murder, they elected John as regent for the new king, Peter I's son Peter II, who was then

---

46 Leontios Makhairas, Χρονικό της Κύπρου, pp. 150–51, 152–53, 164–65, 171–72.
47 Gilles Grivaud, in his chapter in this volume, n. 74, comes to the same conclusion.
48 Mas Latrie, Histoire de l'île de Chypre, II, pp. 289–90, 292, 307–08.
49 Leontios Makhairas, Χρονικό της Κύπρου, p. 180.
50 See indicatively Jean Richard, 'La revolution de 1369 dans le royaume de Chypre', Bibliothèque de l'École des Chartes, 110 (1952), 108–23 and Peter W. Edbury, 'The Murder of King Peter I of Cyprus (1359–1369)', Journal of Medieval History, 6 (1980), 219–33.

still a minor. They also chose Philip of Ibelin to be the lieutenant of James, Peter I's second brother, who in his capacity as seneschal had gone immediately to Famagusta to secure the population's oath on behalf of the new king. James of Nores, upon his return to Nicosia, fulfilled the important function of spokesman for the community of liegemen.[51] Moreover, the High Court appointed a committee of sixteen members to revise and reconfirm the *assizes* as the kingdom's law, and this group included some of the most important statesmen of the previous years: as Peter Edbury has pointed out, almost all the king's murderers took part in it, with the addition of Raymond Babin, Thomas of Montolif, John of Morphou and Simon Tenouri.[52]

Thus, almost all the men traced in the sources during Peter's rule held on tightly to the reins of power during this transition period, all the men, that is, who were of Cypriot descent. The foreigners who had been Peter's favourites either did not return to Cyprus at all, as was the case of Philip of Mézières and Guido da Bagnolo, or were disempowered after the king's death. John Moustri had been arrested under the pretext of his affair with Philip of Ibelin's wife, and later died during an attempt to escape from prison.[53] Others, such as Brémond de la Voulte, had long before left Cyprus of their own will and their estates on the island were confiscated. John Laskaris Kalopheros, a Byzantine who had come to Cyprus under Peter I, was dispossessed of his estates and put in prison. Although this affair was not directly connected to Peter's death, John's enemies used the murder of his protector to act against him.[54] One of the few exceptions was Pietro Malocello, who was still acting as chamberlain of Cyprus in 1373.[55]

The men of John's inner circle seem to have been the true power holders on the island during the following years. For example, on 15 May 1372, after Peter II's coronation as king of Cyprus, the Pisans sent a congratulatory letter to the new king, requesting at the same time that their privileges be confirmed under the new government. Apart from the king, the recipients of the letter included the regent John, 'bailo insule Cipri, fratri et amico karissimo [*sic*]', as well as Philip of Ibelin, Raymond Babin, John of Morphou, and Thomas of Montolif. It was also addressed to a certain Jacchetto the marshal and to John of Montolif, the *bailli* of Famagusta.[56] This list shows clearly that the men in charge were mostly the same as three years before and, indeed, the same people who had already been in power at the beginning of Peter I's reign.

---

51 John of Ibelin, *Le Livre des Assises*, ed. by Peter Edbury, The Medieval Mediterranean: People, Economies and Cultures, 400–1500, 50 (Leiden – Boston: Brill, 2003), pp. 733–34.
52 Guillaume de Machaut, *The Capture of Alexandria*, pp. 205–06; John of Ibelin, *Le Livre des Assises*, pp. 734, 736–37.
53 Leontios Makhairas, Χρονικό της Κύπρου, pp. 158, 165, 223–24. For his position as chamberlain, see Mas Latrie, *Histoire de l'île de Chypre*, II, pp. 291, 308.
54 Edbury, 'The Murder of King Peter I of Cyprus', p. 229; David Jacoby, 'Jean Lascaris Calophéros, Chypre et la Morée', *Revue des Études byzantines*, 26 (1968), 189–228 (pp. 192–94).
55 Mas Latrie, *Histoire de l'île de Chypre*, II, p. 425.
56 Louis de Mas Latrie, Nouvelles preuves de l'histoire de Chypre *sous le règne des princes de la maison de Lusignan*, 2 vols (Paris: J. Baur et Détaille, 1873–74), II, pp. 87–88. I have not been able to identify Jacchetto.

The transition of power thus seems to have been smooth, apart from the murder itself of course. Nevertheless, John and his group were not unopposed. The chronicles tell us that, as early as 1370, supporters of Queen Eleanor, Peter I's widow, tried to secure help from the pope and other western rulers to oust John from power. Two years later, Eleanor is said to have written letters to her father, Peter of Aragon, and to the pope in this regard. On the occasion of Peter II's coronation as king of Jerusalem in October 1372, Makhairas mentions how Eleanor tried to induce her son to grant fiefs to her supporters. However, the High Court pressured the young king into relinquishing his ability to dole out fiefs until his twenty-fifth birthday, thus preventing him from giving freely to his mother's followers.[57] Peter Edbury has shown that at least a great part of Eleanor's supporters were foreigners, such as a Catalan named Alfonso Ferrand, the Byzantines John Laskaris Kalopheros and George Monomachos, the Lombard Giacomo di San Michele, Francis of Marin, a Genoese, and another Catalan named Francis Saturno.[58] Unlike John, Eleanor therefore did not enjoy the support of any of the Cypriot nobility. She did not have any success in the power struggle during these first years, and John and his group of supporters were firmly in power.

The War with Genoa and Its Consequences

The war with the Genoese changed this situation radically. At the beginning of the war, Makhairas's chronicle describes how prominent figures undertook important actions: John and James of Lusignan led military expeditions, John of Morphou acted as ambassador, and so on.[59] However, the occupation of Famagusta by the Genoese

---

57 Leontios Makhairas, Χρονικό της Κύπρου, pp. 239–41, 247–48, 261–62. Peter Edbury, The Feudal Nobility of Cyprus, 1192–1400 (unpublished doctoral thesis, University of St Andrews, 1974): <http://hdl.handle.net/10023/6449> [accessed April 2021], p. 224 has interpreted this episode as a milestone in the conflict between John and Eleanor, since John lost his official power as regent with Peter II's accession to the throne and Eleanor could finally attempt to exert some influence over her son. However, this influence was obviously directly curbed by John's followers in the High Court.
58 Edbury, Feudal Nobility of Cyprus, pp. 228229. Maria Teresa Ferrer i Mallol, 'La reina Leonor de Chipre y los Catalanes de su entorno', in Chemins d'outre-mer. Études d'histoire sur la Méditerranée médiévale offertes à Michel Balard, ed. by Damien Coulon et al., Byzantina Sorbonensia, 20 (Paris: Sorbonne 2004), pp. 311–32 (314–15, 318) shows that other Catalans, such as Luis and Ramón Resta as well as a certain Joan Desbosc, all belonged to the royal household at the time, although we do not know if they took the queen's side. Ferrer i Mallol also offers detailed information on other Catalan supporters of Queen Eleanor, though most of them only travelled to Cyprus intermittently, such as for example her procurators in Catalonia, Jaume Fiveller and Lleó Marc. The former fetched Eleanor from Rhodes, where she had been exiled by Peter II, and acted as her advocate at the Cypriot court, see Ferrer i Mallol, 'La reina Leonor de Chipre', pp. 312, 315, 317–20. During the war with the Genoese, the chronicle of Amadi also mentions Eleanor's confessor Glimin of Narbonne acting in her interests, see Chroniques d'Amadi et de Strambaldi, première partie: Chronique d'Amadi, ed. by René de Mas Latrie (Paris: Imprimérie nationale, 1891), p. 467; The Chronicle of Amadi, trans. by Nicholas Coureas and Peter Edbury, Texts and Studies in the History of Cyprus, 74 (Nicosia: Cyprus Research Centre, 2015), § 953.
59 Leontios Makhairas, Χρονικό της Κύπρου, pp. 275–76, 278, 281–82, 282–83, 311–12, 330–31, 358.

was not only the turning point of the war, but also heralded the breakdown of the power structures that had characterized the preceding years. First of all, the Genoese executed Henry of Giblet, John of Gaurelles, and even the powerful Philip of Ibelin for murdering King Peter I.[60] By the end of the war, many other power holders had been removed. The Genoese exiled James of Lusignan as well as Thomas of Montolif, who was by then marshal of the Kingdom of Cyprus.[61] Makhairas records John of Morphou and Raymond Babin as other prominent exiles, in this case to Chios.[62] We have no other confirmation for this, apart from the indirect evidence that neither of them appears in the sources after 1374.[63] The Turcopolier James of Nores, who by that time must have been an old man, is last heard of in 1372.[64] Other powerful men, who had not been part of the highest power circle before the conflict, but who had played major roles in military operations during the war, were also expelled from the island: Guy of Milmars, who was the Cypriot admiral, along with Peter of Cassi, and Montolive of Verny.[65] The only person to remain in power after the war was, quite surprisingly, John of Lusignan himself. However, John was soon killed too, in 1375, on Queen Eleanor' orders,[66] who was apparently left in triumphant control of the situation.

How was this power gap filled, we may ask? Did Eleanor try to place all her supporters into high positions? How strong was her influence on the young Peter II? Unfortunately, very few sources survive from the years immediately after the war. Even the chronicles are largely silent. The only episode recounted in detail is the rise and fall of Thibaut of Belfarage (from the Arabic Abu'l Faraj?), a Melkite burgess who had already been in Peter I's service.[67] Thibaut had risen to some prominence during the war with the Genoese and had provided numerous services to the king and his uncles. He is said to have gained permission to recruit men-at-arms in Venice in order to besiege Famagusta, which he did without success. But apparently, the king's favour was such that he knighted Thibaut and granted him various estates as fiefs. Indeed, Thibaut was a member of the High Court at a fief-granting session as early as 1374.[68] According to the chronicles, at this point Thibaut became overly greedy and desired to become lord of the castle of

---

60 Leontios Makhairas, Χρονικό της Κύπρου, p. 303.
61 In 1383, a Thomas of Montolif was *bailli* of the *Secrète* and marshal of Jerusalem, but whether this is the same man as the auditor is impossible to say, see Mas Latrie, *Histoire de l'île de Chypre*, II, p. 396.
62 Leontios Makhairas, Χρονικό της Κύπρου, p. 380.
63 For John of Morphou, cf. Hill, *A History of Cyprus*, II, p. 395.
64 Leontios Makhairas, Χρονικό της Κύπρου, p. 260.
65 Mas Latrie, *Nouvelles preuves de l'histoire de Chypre*, I, pp. 72–74. The Genoese had imposed the exile of both Peter of Cassi and Montolive of Verny as an explicit precondition for peace in the treaty of 1374, see Carlo Sperone, *Real grandezza della Serenissima Repubblica di Genova* (Genoa: Giovanni Battista Tiboldi, 1669), p. 105.
66 Leontios Makhairas, Χρονικό της Κύπρου, pp. 387–88.
67 *Bullarium Cyprium III*, no. v-200.
68 Catherine Otten-Froux, 'Fief et féodalité tardive dans le royaume de Chypre aux XIVe et XVe siècles: l'exemple des vassaux génois des Lusignans', in *Identity / Identities in Late Medieval Cyprus. Papers Given at the ICS Byzantine Colloquium (London, 13–14 June 2011)*, ed. by Tassos Papacostas and Guillaume Saint-Guillain (Nicosia: Centre for Hellenic Studies, King's College London – Cyprus Research Centre, 2014), pp. 67–101 (91).

Gorhigos. Peter II refused. Thibaut then took revenge on the king's confessor, who had advised Peter on the matter, killing both the confessor and the viscount of Nicosia, who happened to be accompanying him. Consequently, Thibaut was himself put to death, despite his claim that Queen Eleanor had orchestrated his downfall because he had refused her sexual advances.[69] Although we have no way of confirming the veracity of this account, the story of Thibaut's quick rise and fall hints at the fact that the power vacuum created by the war allowed room for newcomers to rise to the top.

Indeed, very gradually, we see a new group of nobles emerging to take up important positions, though the limited information at our disposal does not show if they were Eleanor's supporters. At least two, if not three, of these men were 'newcomers' like Belfarage. Thomas Barech witnessed the peace treaty with the Genoese in 1374. Makhairas calls him a Greek burgess, but his name suggests Oriental Christian, probably Melkite, origin. After Peter II's death, Thomas became one of the twelve regents who administered the kingdom until James I arrived in Cyprus.[70] John Gorab came from a new, probably also Oriental Christian, family, attested for the first time in 1350. He had been the *maître d'hôtel* under Peter I and became auditor (prosecutor of the state) of Cyprus in 1378 at the latest. He had already been a member of the High Court in 1374, when the Genoese Giacomo Grillo received a fief.[71] One Robert Moustazo witnessed both the peace treaty in 1374 and the treaty against Genoa in 1378.[72] Unfortunately, we know nothing else about him and he does not appear in later sources. Considering we have records of his family only from the 1350s onward, we might speculate that he, too, was one of the fortunate winners of the power struggle that followed the war.

The most important person who appears on the scene in the years after the war came from one of the oldest noble families on Cyprus: John of Brie, who had been one among several naval commanders under Peter I and is attested as turcopolier of Cyprus in the peace treaty between Venice, Milan and Cyprus in 1378. On that occasion, John swore on the Bible as Peter II's representative. Similarly to the previously mentioned John Gorab, John of Brie is attested as a member of the High Court at sessions discussing fief issues as early as 1374. After Peter II's death, he would be the first of the twelve regents of the kingdom, the other eleven acting as his advisors.[73] Also coming from an old Cypriot family, John of Nevilles was viscount of Nicosia perhaps as early as 1369 or, more likely, in the early 1370s. Together with the other men mentioned, he would play a leading role in the years to come.[74]

---

69 Leontios Makhairas, Χρονικό της Κύπρου, pp. 388–402.
70 Sperone, *Real grandezza*, p. 108 and Leontios Makhairas, Χρονικό της Κύπρου, p. 412. The fact that Makhairas describes him as Greek suggests that he may have been a Melkite and that the chronicler categorized Orthodox Syrians together with the Orthodox Greeks, as they were technically members of the same church.
71 Edbury, 'The Murder of King Peter I of Cyprus', pp. 220, 227; Mas Latrie, *Histoire de l'île de Chypre*, II, p. 372; Otten-Froux, 'Fief et féodalité tardive dans le royaume de Chypre', p. 91.
72 Sperone, *Real grandezza*, p. 108; Mas Latrie, *Histoire de l'île de Chypre*, II, p. 372.
73 Mas Latrie, *Histoire de l'île de Chypre*, II, pp. 372, 420, 428, 436; Leontios Makhairas, Χρονικό της Κύπρου, p. 412; Otten-Froux, 'Fief et féodalité tardive dans le royaume de Chypre', p. 92.
74 Florio Bustron, *Chronique de l'île de Chypre*, ed. René de Mas Latrie, Collection de documents inédits sur l'histoire de France, Mélanges historiques, 5 (Paris: Imprimerie nationale, 1886; repr. as *Historia overo Commentarii di Cipro*, Kypriologiki Vivliothiki, 8 (Nicosia: Archbishop Makarios III Foundation,

All these men, apart from Thomas Barech, had already started their careers under Peter I: John of Brie as naval commander, John Gorab as *maître d'hôtel*, John of Nevilles probably as viscount of Nicosia. Therefore, although they had newly risen to the highest power elite, they had been present in Cypriot politics for a considerable time. It is noteworthy that three of these men were newcomers. However, with John of Brie, the king's right-hand man was still the scion of an old Cypriot family. Whether these men were Queen Eleanor's supporters is unfortunately impossible to say. Only Belfarage may have been the queen's favourite but lost her favour in the end. One point stands against the assumption that these men were close to the queen: when Peter II emancipated himself from his mother and had her sent back to Aragon in 1380,[75] all the aforementioned men remained in place.

The Rebellion against James I

Just as his father, Peter II was more short-lived than his power base. When he died without heirs in 1382, all the aforementioned men were members of the regency council, which according to Makhairas consisted of thirteen knights headed by John of Brie. The composition of this group is rather interesting. Its members were John Gorab, John of Nevilles, Thomas Barech, and nine other men mostly from old families: Peter of Antioch, Thomas of Morphou, Hamerin of Plessie, Wilmot of Montolif, Perot of Montolif, Arnold of Montolif, Hugh of La Baume, and Guy of La Baume. The only council member not identifiable as a member of an old family is Renier Scolar.[76] It is striking how few families are represented in this group – the Montolifs play a great role with three representatives, Hugh and Guy of La Baume were brothers, and Thomas of Morphou and Hamerin of Plessie probably stemmed from different branches of the same family. Thus, it seems that after Peter's death, the island was in the hands of a rather small power elite that had either been in power for a long time or represented powerful old families. This fact is all the more conspicuous considering that this group chose to reject James of Lusignan as their new king.

According to Lusignan tradition, James was the rightful heir to the throne, since he was the deceased king's nearest relative. However, James was still a captive of the Genoese at the time of Peter II's death. The Cypriot chronicles relate that, although the council wanted to accept James as king, they worried about the concessions he would have to make to the Genoese to secure his release. The brothers Wilmot and

---

1998)), p. 277, says that he took over the office from Henry of Giblet, when Peter I quarrelled with him and had him put into prison; but he later (p. 345) wants him to have taken over the office only in 1376, after Thibaut of Belfarage had killed his (nameless) predecessor. In Leontios Makhairas, Χρονικό της Κύπρου, p. 312, he appears as viscount during the conflict with the Genoese in 1372.

75 Hill, *A History of Cyprus*, III, p. 426.
76 Renier's origins are very unclear. His family does not appear in the usual Cypriot sources, such as the *Lignages d'Outremer*, and there is only one other man with the same surname mentioned by Leontios Makhairas, Χρονικό της Κύπρου, § 563: Daniel Scolar was one of the knights who were not exiled from Cyprus after the Genoese war in 1374.

Perot of Montolif exploited these worries and convinced the council to let them handle negotiations with James. According to the deal they brokered, the council would accept James only if the Genoese released him without conditions. If this was not the case, Peter II's sister Margaret would succeed him and marry a Cypriot nobleman; according to Makhairas, Perot secretly hoped he would be the fortunate husband.[77] By studying the acts of the Genoese notary Giovanni Bardi, Catherine Otten-Froux and especially Chris Schabel have proven that James's rejection must have had a much broader base than what the chroniclers' narrative tells us.[78] Bardi accompanied the galleys that brought James to Cyprus in the summer of 1383, and he records that they were greeted by missiles when they tried to land in Paphos. At the same time, peasants in the countryside reported that the powerful in Paphos had threatened to hang them should they acclaim James as king.[79] Later on, Bardi relates that negotiations began between the 'gubernatores' (also called 'rebelles' or 'inimici' in other instances),[80] who were staying at Sivouri, and James and the Genoese. These negotiations failed. Unfortunately, the rebels are not further identified. The only names mentioned are those of Perot of Montolif and John of Tiberias, who were sent to James as ambassadors.[81] However, the whole situation illustrated by Bardi suggests that the so-called rebellion must have been supported by the majority of the Cypriot elite. Some of James's friends and supporters are occasionally mentioned in the sources, but these are fleeting references. The only exception was the commander of Kyrenia, Luke of Antiaume, who openly supported James.[82] The Genoese certainly estimated the support for King James to be quite feeble, as they soon decided not to release him and to take him back to Genoa.[83]

Nevertheless, a year later the situation had changed. The power elite decided to accept James as king and sent for him, despite the harsh terms he had agreed to: Cyprus would have to pay huge reparatory sums to Genoa for decades. Again, the chronicles present this as a direct decision of the knights who had repented for their actions, though Makhairas also mentions that James sent 'Ερνὰτ/Αρνὰτ τε Μιλὰ' (probably Arnold of Milmars) from Genoa to promise estates and money to those who would support him. It is therefore likely that he bought his kingdom from his future vassals as well as from the Genoese. The aspirant king surely chose to grant amnesty to all the rebel faction, except for Perot and Wilmot of Montolif and a small group of their supporters. These men, who are said to have staunchly refused to accept James, were eventually beheaded.[84]

---

77 Leontios Makhairas, Χρονικό της Κύπρου, pp. 412–17.
78 Catherine Otten-Froux, 'Le retour manqué de Jacques Ier en Chypre', in *Actes du colloque 'Les Lusignans et l'Outre Mer'*, ed. by Claude Mutafian (Poitiers: Université de Poitiers, 1994), pp. 228–40; Christopher Schabel, 'Like God from Heaven', esp. pp. 382–83, 386, 389.
79 *Actes de Giovanni Bardi*, in *Gênes et l'Outre-mer. Actes notariés de Famagouste et d'autres localités du Proche-Orient (XIVe–XVe s.)*, ed. by Michel Balard, Laura Balleto, and Chris Schabel, Sources et études de l'histoire de Chypre, 72 (Nicosia: Centre de Recherche Scientifique, 2013), Part 2, pp. 293–94.
80 *Actes de Giovanni Bardi*, pp. 262–64, 294.
81 *Actes de Giovanni Bardi*, p. 295.
82 *Actes de Giovanni Bardi*, pp. 263, 296–97.
83 *Actes de Giovanni Bardi*, p. 333.
84 Leontios Makhairas, Χρονικό της Κύπρου, pp. 414–17.

King James I's Reign

One may thus conclude that apart from a small group of rebels who probably served as scapegoats, the Cypriot power elite mostly survived King James's coronation unscathed. If we believe Makhairas, they became even richer than before, as James honoured them with fiefs and titles.[85] Drawing on these powerful and experienced men instead of opposing them was probably the easiest way for James to build his power base. The situation was to solidify in the long run and we find many of the 1382 council members in high offices or as members of the High Court even in the 1390s.

The situation between 1382 and the 1390s is mostly illustrated by five High Court documents as well as by the documents on the rebellion. The High Court surely made many more important decisions during this period, but the only extant documents of its proceedings concern the conclusion of a new treaty with the Republic of Venice on 2 October 1389, admiral Peter of Caffran's embassy to Genoa in 1390, where he negotiated new conditions for the payments due to the Genoese, the ratification of the new Cypriot-Genoese treaty on 12 November 1391, John of Lusignan's appointment as James I's procurator for foreign affairs on 16 August 1395, and the ratification of the 1396 treaty with Venice on 18 October 1397.[86] Thus, all these documents are related to important decisions concerning foreign policy, and we can assume that the attending members of the High Court represented the most important men in the kingdom. The High Court documents are complemented by a newly edited document from the Archive of Padua (*Perg. 5685 part. 7*), which contains protocols concerning King Janus's divorce dated to the year 1407.[87] Janus married Anglesia Visconti, a sister of the duchess of Milan, in 1400 but later wished to annul the marriage.[88] The Padua document contains the statements of the witnesses summoned to provide information on the preparatory proceedings for the marriage and therefore also mentions individuals who played important roles at the Cypriot court around the year 1399, just one year after James I's death.

First of all, the documents reveal that at least half of the regents who ruled in 1382 were still in power in the 1390s. Most importantly, John of Brie was still a member of the High Court in 1390, 1395, and 1397. According to the 1395 document, he had also become prince of Galilee as well as turcopolier, an office that he still held in 1397. Similarly, John Gorab and John of Nevilles attended the High Court in 1389 (Gorab) and 1390 (both), although Nevilles only served as witness. Gorab continued to be auditor and had also acquired the title of lord of Caesarea, while Nevilles is recorded now as lord of Arsur instead of viscount;[89] perhaps he had grown too old to fulfil the

---

85 Leontios Makhairas, Χρονικό τῆς Κύπρου, p. 420.
86 Mas Latrie, *Histoire de l'île de Chypre*, II, pp. 416–18, 420–21, 423, 428–29, 436 n. 3.
87 I would like to thank Christina Kaoulla, who edited the document as part of her doctoral thesis, for sharing her as yet unpublished work with me, Christina Kaoulla, *The Quest for a Royal Bride. The Marriage of King Janus of Cyprus and Anglesia Visconti of Milan* (unpublished doctoral thesis, University of Cyprus, 2016).
88 Kaoulla, *Quest for a Royal Bride*, p. 40 and §§ 171, 195.
89 Mas Latrie, *Histoire de l'île de Chypre*, II, pp. 420, 428, 436 and n. 3.

duties of the office, as he died on 11 January 1391.⁹⁰ Other members of the 1382 council continued to hold important positions. Renier Scolar served as ambassador in 1386 and was *bailli* of the *Secrète* and lord of Bethsan in 1390, while Hugh of La Baume and his brother Guy bore the honorary titles of constable and marshal of Jerusalem and sat at the High Court in 1395. Hugh was also a member of the group of courtiers who discussed King Janus's marriage plans to Anglesia Visconti in December 1399, though he does not seem to have been part of the very inner circle of power then.⁹¹

Apart from the former regents, others who had been involved in the 1382 events also acquired positions of power, seemingly without consideration for the different sides they had supported. Peter of Caffran, the admiral, who had been James's valuable advisor in 1382, went on embassies to Genoa twice (1387, 1390)⁹² and witnessed the new treaty with Venice in 1389. John of Tiberias, on the other hand, who had represented the rebels in 1382, was sent as ambassador to Genoa only a year before Caffran's first voyage, in 1386, and attended the High Court as marshal of Armenia in 1397. James I's nephew John of Lusignan, lord of Beirut, attended the High Court both in 1390 and 1391. He seems to have been an important advisor to James I and went on a crucial embassy to Western Europe on the king's behalf in 1395, among others things in order to find a bride for the crown prince Janus.⁹³ The testimonies given at Janus's divorce trial present him as the most influential figure at court in the first years of Janus's reign.⁹⁴

Contrary to the situation in the 1370s, all the men mentioned above came from old Cypriot families, except for two foreign officers, Antony of Bergamo and Hodrade Provane, who both came from the Piedmont and occupied the office of *camerarius*.⁹⁵

---

90 Mas Latrie, *Histoire de l'île de Chypre*, II, p. 398 fills a lacuna in a document concerning the viscount of Nicosia, dated 13 February 1391, with the name *Nevilles*, but this is not possible, because John of Nevilles died on 11th January 1390, see *Lacrimae Cypriae*, I, pp. 152–53.
91 Kaoulla, *Quest for a Royal Bride*, pp. 36–38.
92 Mas Latrie, *Histoire de l'île de Chypre*, II, pp. 413, 420.
93 For both men, see Mas Latrie, *Histoire de l'île de Chypre*, II, pp. 412, 423, 428, 436, 438–39.
94 See, for example, Kaoulla, *Quest for a Royal Bride*, § § 29–32, 132–34, 249, etc.
95 The office of *camerarius* or *cambellanus* (chamberlain) is rather ambiguous, as there were two posts for which the term was used. According to Emmanuel-Guillaume Rey in his edition of Charles du Fresne Du Cange, *Les Familles d'Outre-mer de Du Cange* (Paris: Imprimerie impériale, 1869), p. 629, the *cambellanus* and the *camerarius* were originally two distinct officers. However, it is not clear whether this is accurate. In any case, the chamberlain was one of the five crown officers; he cared for the king's personal chambers, introduced liegemen into the royal presence, and administered the act of homage, receiving a fee for this service, see John of Ibelin, *Le Livre des Assises*, pp. 563, 570, 577, 588–89 and Edbury, *Kingdom of Cyprus*, p. 183. Rey claims that the *camerarius* in turn was originally responsible for the treasury and the upkeep of the palace and that the functions of the two offices as well as their designations got confused in the Kingdom of Jerusalem. Be this as it may, in Cyprus, we find two distinct offices designated by both terms, although the functional distinction seems to have been clear, sometimes clarified by the additions *of the king* and *of the kingdom*, see, for example, Mas Latrie, *Histoire de l'île de Chypre*, II, p. 291, where both officers witness a document. In the second half of the fourteenth century, the chamberlain of the kingdom seems to have been responsible for affairs between the king and his vassals as well as for financial issues, see for example, Mas Latrie, *Histoire de l'île de Chypre*, II, p. 425. As the kingdom's chamberlain, Antony was responsible for the crown's finances, imposing heavy taxes on the population, see Leontios Makhairas, Χρονικό της Κύπρου, pp. 422–23. Hodrade is mentioned in 1395 as 'regni Cipri camerarius', Mas

Antony was a jurist, and probably followed the old tradition of foreign scholars taking up important positions in the Cypriot administration;[96] Provane followed in his footsteps and was also present at the court after James I's death.[97]

Some men are recorded only once as members of the High Court during this period. But this should not deceive us. They could be important politicians all the same, even more than others who appear more often. We know that some of them had important offices: Arnold of Soissons had obviously succeeded John Gorab as auditor by 1395 and Reynald of Milmars was marshal of Cyprus when they participated in the workings of the High Court in 1395. Both seem to have been exiled to Genoa in 1374.[98] Perhaps they belonged to the elite group who had returned to Cyprus with James I. John Babin, who had been Janus's guardian when the crown prince grew up in Genoa, appears as chamberlain of Armenia in 1395, an office that had only symbolic value. From 1399 onwards, he seems to have been one of King Janus's most trusted advisors and became admiral of Cyprus. However, his importance under the late King James I is unclear.[99] There is no information on the rest of the witnesses and members of the High Court. We can only say that they must have been prestigious enough to be asked to be present at those crucial sessions.[100] Finally, Luke of Antiaume, who had so openly supported James in 1383, does not appear in the later sources at all.

Latrie, *Histoire de l'île de Chypre*, II, p. 428, therefore we can assume that he, also, was responsible for the kingdom's finances. The duties of the king's chamberlain are, unfortunately, less clear. See also Miriam Salzmann, '(Re)constructing Aristocratic Religious Identities in 15th-Century Cyprus', in *Menschen, Bilder, Sprache, Dinge. Wege der Kommunikation zwischen Byzanz und dem Westen. 3: Fallstudien*, ed. by Falko Daim, Dominik Heher, Claudia Rapp (Mainz: Verlag des Römisch-Germanischen Zentralmuseums, 2018), pp. 337–50 (346 n. 97).

96 Louis de Mas Latrie suggested that Antony already served as Peter I's ambassador in 1366, based on the mention of a certain clerk with the same name by Machaut, see Guillaume de Machaut, *La Prise d'Alexandrie*, pp. 127 and 283 n. 34; this identification has been doubted by Peter W. Edbury, who argues that Antonio only appears on Cyprus at the end of the 1370s, see Guillaume de Machaut, *The Capture of Alexandria*, p. 99 and n. 14.

97 Brunehilde Imhaus, in *Lacrimae Cypriae*, p. 93, considers Hodrade Provane to be the son of a certain Balian Provane, who was supposed to have held the fief of Comi according to Jean Darrouzès, 'Notes pour servir à l'histoire de Chypre (deuxième article)', Κυπριακαὶ Σπουδαί, 20 (1956), 31–63 (pp. 50–51); but the manuscript cited by Darrouzès calls him 'Embalin' and very probably refers to Ibelin Provane, who lived in the fifteenth century and held the fief of Comi, see *Le Livre des remembrances de la Secrète du royaume de Chypre (1468–1469)*, ed. by Jean Richard (with Theodore Papadopoullos), Sources et études de l'histoire de Chypre, 10 (Nicosia: Centre de Recherche Scientifique, 1983), no. 174. For his origin from the Piedmont, see Wipertus H. Rudt de Collenberg, 'Études de prosopographie généalogique des Chypriotes mentionnés dans les registres du Vatican 1378–1471', Μελέται καὶ Ὑπομνήματα, 1 (1984), 523–678 (p. 558). For his presence at court around 1399 / 1400, see Kaoulla, *Quest for a Royal Bride*, pp. 36–38 and § 69.

98 A certain 'Renaut de Milmars', who was among the exiled to Genoa, see Mas Latrie, *Nouvelles preuves de l'histoire de Chypre*, I, p. 74, could be this Reynald. Would this also be the same person as Arnold of Milmars, who came to Cyprus on behalf of James in order to promise the nobles new estates?

99 Mas Latrie, *Histoire de l'île de Chypre*, II, p. 428; Kaoulla, *Quest for a Royal Bride*, pp. 17, 40 and §§ 131–248, esp. 132–35, 173.

100 James of Montgesard and William Forte are cases in point; see Mas Latrie, *Histoire de l'île de Chypre*, II, pp. 423 and 436 n. 3.

In conclusion, Cypriot politics between the 1360s and the 1390s was characterized by astonishingly stable power circles, although a rather noticeable break occurred during and after the Genoese war. A strong power elite, coming both from Cyprus and abroad, dominated politics under Peter I, but in the end the Cypriots effectively defended their rights against the foreigners arbitrarily incorporated into their ranks by Peter I. After collectively deciding to murder him, this same elite, led by Peter's brother John of Lusignan, held the reins of power for several years, until they were ousted by Queen Eleanor and the Genoese. Despite these events, the new power elite that emerged from the ashes of war consisted mostly of men already active under Peter I. Newcomers from Oriental Christian families (who had also been active under Peter I) rose especially at this time, and it seems that the power vacuum after the war was conducive to their acquisition of power. However, with the exception of John Gorab, this social mobility was short-lived and in the next decades no newcomers appear in government circles. On the contrary, the power elite under James I stands out for its stability. It was dominated by men from old noble Cypriot families, who had either been in power long before James I's reign or had accompanied James into exile and then acquired positions of power during his own rule. Social mobility seems minimal, perhaps a conservative reaction to the shooting–star careers of the 1370s. Be this as it may, it is noteworthy that many of the men in power at the beginning of James I's reign played crucial roles in Cypriot politics for many decades, even throughout periods of great political disruptions.

GILLES GRIVAUD

Le roi Pierre 1er et son conseil

Le souvenir laissé par les dix années de règne de Pierre 1er est amplement conditionné par les voyages du souverain en Occident, par ses expéditions contre les Turcs et les Mamelouks, ainsi que par son assassinat, au petit matin du mardi 16 janvier 1369. Ces événements ont généré une abondante littérature conférant à la figure du roi les traits d'une figure exaltée, d'un chevalier intrépide relevant sans arrêt l'étendard de la croisade contre les infidèles, ayant en perspective le rétablissement d'un pouvoir chrétien protecteur des Lieux saints.[1]

Dans la construction de ce mythe, on sait le rôle déterminant tenu par les élogieux propagandistes que furent Philippe de Mézières (1327–1405) et Guillaume de Machaut (c. 1300–1377).[2] On sait également que cette image, élaborée pour

---

1 Ainsi, l'avis de George Hill, *A History of Cyprus*, 4 vols (Cambridge : Cambridge University Press, 1940–1952), II, p. 368 : « Peter I was undoubtedly the most striking figure of all the kings of the Lusignan dynasty. Personally attractive, a spirit restless yet dominated by one ruling passion, the prosecution of war against the infidel in obedience to what he genuinely believed to be a divine call, lusty, sensual and hot-headed, he lost his balance in his last days and degenerated into something like a tyrannical brute ».
2 Guillaume de Machaut, *La Prise d'Alexandrie ou chronique du roi Pierre I*er *de Lusignan*, éd. Louis de Mas Latrie (Genève : Imprimerie Jules-Guillaume Fick, 1877), pp. xviij–xxvi ; Nicolas Jorga, *Philippe de Mézières 1327–1405 et la croisade au XIV*e *siècle*, Bibliothèque de l'École des Hautes Études, Sciences philologiques et historiques 110 (Paris : Librairie Émile Bouillon, 1896), pp. 102–394 ; Alphonse Dupront, *Le mythe de croisade*, 4 vols, Bibliothèque des histoires (Paris : Gallimard, 1997), I, pp. 87–103 ; Angela Hurworth, « Le corps remembré : historiographie et hagiographie dans *La Prise d'Alixandre* », dans *Guillaume de Machaut 1300–2000*, dir. Jacqueline Cerquiglini-Toulet et Nigel Wilkins (Paris : Presses de l'Université de Paris-Sorbonne, 2002), pp. 107–18 ; Bernard Ribémont, « Le Chroniqueur, l'hagiographe et la mer. À propos de *La Prise d'Alexandrie* de Guillaume de Machaut », *Le Moyen Âge*, 116/1 (2010), 123–38 ; Sophie Hardy, *Édition critique de la* Prise d'Alexandrie *de Guillaume de Machaut* (thèse doctorale de Lettres modernes, Université d'Orléans, 2011), pp. lxxxix–cii ; Kevin Brownlee, « The Figure of Peter I and the Status of Cyprus in *Le Songe du vieil pelerin* : Crusade Ideology, Salvation History, and Authorial Self-Representation », dans *Philippe de Mézières and His Age. Piety and Politics in the Fourteenth Century*, dir. Renate Blumenfeld-Kosinski et Kiril Petkov, The Medieval Mediterranean, 91 (Leyde – Boston : Brill, 2012), pp. 165–88 ; Peter W. Edbury, « Machaut, Mézières, Makhairas and Amadi : Constructing the Reign of Peter I (1359–1369) », dans le même volume, pp. 349–58 ; Angel Nicolaou-Konnari, « Apologists or Critics ? The Reign of Peter I of Lusignan (1359–1369) Viewed by Philippe de Mézières (1327–1405) and Leontios Makhairas (ca. 1360/80–after 1432) », dans le même volume, pp. 359–401.

Gilles Grivaud • Université de Rouen-Normandie/GRHis

interpeller la conscience des élites politiques et lettrées d'Occident, ne correspond pas à l'image tirée de la lecture de Léontios Machairas (c. 1360/80–après 1432) ; en effet, si le chroniqueur chypriote ne cache pas son admiration pour les entreprises d'un roi animé par le souci de restaurer l'ancien esprit de croisade, il n'hésite pas à développer des critiques envers le comportement du souverain, en particulier durant les derniers mois de son règne, lorsque Pierre 1er apparaît comme un monarque enfermé dans un exercice solitaire du pouvoir, dérivant vers une attitude paranoaïque proche de la folie.[3]

Assurément, les points de vue des différents témoins et historiens des événements des années 1360 recèlent des contradictions, qui ont déjà été mises en lumière par d'éminents spécialistes, tels Louis de Mas Latrie et Nicolae Iorga en leurs temps, mais aussi, plus récemment, par Jean Richard, Peter W. Edbury et Angel Nicolaou-Konnari. Les avis éclairés de ces historiens ont souligné les partis pris idéologiques des auteurs médiévaux, dont aucun récit ne saurait, à lui seul, restituer la complexité d'un règne aussi bref que dense.[4]

Tout en gardant en mémoire les acquis de ces recherches, on peut interroger le mode de gouvernance adopté par Pierre 1er lorsqu'il occupe le trône, en tentant, notamment, de repérer les formes institutionnelles prises par la monarchie franque durant une période charnière de son histoire. Plusieurs questions méritent un examen attentif, afin de déterminer si le roi incarne une phase originale dans l'histoire du royaume des Lusignan, par exemple en infléchissant les axes des relations diplomatiques. Est-il, dès son couronnement, le 24 novembre 1358, ce monarque qui conduit seul les affaires du royaume ? Comme le souverain s'absente souvent du pays, sur quels organes de gouvernement et sur quels individus s'appuie-t-il pour développer ses entreprises, que ce soit pendant les expéditions militaires qu'il mène contre les émirats turcs ou contre les Mamelouks, ou durant ses longs voyages auprès des cours d'Occident, qu'il sollicite pour obtenir des soutiens à ses projets ? Sur les quasi dix années que dure son règne, Pierre se trouve hors de Chypre pour ainsi dire la moitié du temps. Or cet éloignement ne provoque pas de rupture majeure dans la conduite des affaires

---

3 Léontios Machairas, Χρονικό τῆς Κύπρου. Παράλληλη διπλωματική ἔκδοση τῶν χειρογράφων, éd. Michalis Pieris et Angel Nicolaou-Konnari, Sources et études de l'histoire de Chypre, 47 (Nicosie : Centre de Recherche Scientifique, 2003), pp. 108–222 (citations données avec l'orthographe améliorée).

4 Louis de Mas Latrie, *Histoire de l'île de Chypre sous le règne des princes de la maison de Lusignan*, 3 vols (Paris : Imprimerie impériale, 1852–1861), II, pp. 342–45 ; Jorga, *Philippe de Mézières*, pp. 394–95 et n. 5 ; Jean Richard, « La révolution de 1369 dans le royaume de Chypre », *Bibliothèque de l'École des Chartes*, 110 (1952), 108–23 (réimpr. dans Jean Richard, *Orient et Occident au Moyen Age : contacts et relations (XIIe–XIVe siècles)* (Londres : Variorum Reprints, 1976), n° IX) ; Peter W. Edbury, « The Murder of King Peter I of Cyprus (1359–1369) », dans *Journal of Medieval History*, 6 (1980), 219–33 (réimpr. dans Peter W. Edbury, *Kingdom of the Crusaders. From Jerusalem to Cyprus* (Aldershot : Variorum Reprints, 1999), n° XIII) ; Peter W. Edbury, *The Kingdom of Cyprus and the Crusades, 1191–1374* (Cambridge : Cambridge University Press, 1991), pp. 172–79 ; Peter W. Edbury, « Ἡ πολιτικὴ ἱστορία τοῦ μεσαιωνικοῦ βασιλείου ἀπὸ τὴ βασιλεία τοῦ Οὔγου Δ΄ ἕως τὴ βασιλεία τοῦ Ἰανοῦ (1324–1432) », dans *Ἱστορία τῆς Κύπρου*, dir. Théodoros Papadopoullos, 6 vols (Nicosie : Fondation de l'archévêque Makarios III, 1995–2011), IV, *Μεσαιωνικὸν βασίλειον – Ἑνετοκρατία*, pp. 60–63, 72–87 ; Edbury, « Machaut, Mézières, Makhairas and Amadi » ; Nicolaou-Konnari, « Apologists or Critics ? ».

du royaume, tant au plan social que politique ou diplomatique ; cette constance et cette stabilité apparaissent comme une preuve de la solidité des institutions, malgré les faux pas qui se multiplient durant les ultimes mois de règne, et qui aboutissent au régicide.

Pour approcher le mode de gouvernance adopté par Pierre 1er, les actes de la pratique manquent cruellement. Les textes attestant les formes prises par le gouvernement royal se limitent au traité établi avec les Vénitiens, le 16 août 1360, puis à trois lettres envoyées à Venise, à Montpellier et à Florence, en 1360, 1361, 1362, enfin à une lettre adressée au doge Marco Cornaro, depuis Famagouste, le 23 novembre 1366.[5] Aucun ban ou aucune ordonnance de la monarchie ne peut être associée à Pierre 1er, alors qu'on en possède plusieurs datant du règne de son père, Hugues IV.[6] On peut compléter la documentation en étudiant les lettres que le roi expédie depuis Avignon, Londres, Venise ou Rome, qui permettent de reconnaître plusieurs membres de son entourage parmi les témoins, et, dans la même perspective, l'analyse peut être enrichie des traités négociés sous pression à Gênes, le 5 mars 1363, puis le 18 avril 1365.[7] Néanmoins, force est de constater que le règne de Pierre 1er laisse peu de traces matérielles issues de la chancellerie ou de la bureaucratie, alors que leurs productions durent être aussi abondantes que celles laissées par les offices de la monarchie, durant le XVe siècle.[8] En conséquence, les textes littéraires demeurent fondamentaux pour approcher la réalité de la gouvernance du souverain, ce qui soulève d'infinis problèmes ; les partis pris idéologiques des chroniqueurs constituent un premier handicap, déjà évoqué, mais plus encore le vocabulaire qu'ils utilisent. Qu'il s'agisse de la chronique de Léontios Machairas ou de celle attribuée à Amadi, aucune n'est contemporaine des faits qu'elle relate, et leurs auteurs peuvent projeter sur une période antérieure la réalité d'institutions qui s'affirment plus tard, au cours du XVe siècle.[9]

Cette remarque introductive prend tout son sens lorsqu'il s'agit de reconnaître l'existence d'un Conseil du roi parmi les institutions de gouvernement. De manière générale, dans le système politique des monarchies féodales des XIIIe–XIVe siècles, le prince peut demander conseil dans son entourage, auprès des puissants, qu'ils soient ecclésiastiques ou laïcs, et qui se trouvent ainsi associés à la délibération politique ; à l'occasion, le prince peut solliciter des personnages plus modestes, des familiers qui vivent à sa cour ou en son hôtel, voire de simples bourgeois reconnus pour leurs compétences. Ces conseillers interviennent de manière informelle, à la demande du souverain, étant souvent nommés spécialement pour une affaire donnée, *ad hoc*, puis le Conseil du roi s'institutionnalise progressivement à partir du milieu

---

5 Mas Latrie, *Histoire de l'île de Chypre*, II, pp. 229–36, 286–88.
6 *Bans et ordonnances des rois de Chypre*, dans *Recueil des historiens des Croisades, Lois. II. Assises de la cour des bourgeois*, éd. Auguste-Arthur Beugnot (Paris : Imprimerie royale, 1843), pp. 354–79.
7 Mas Latrie, *Histoire de l'île de Chypre*, II, pp. 248–50, 253–67, 291–308.
8 *Chypre sous les Lusignan. Documents chypriotes des archives du Vatican (XIVe et XVe siècles)*, éd. Jean Richard, Bibliothèque archéologique et historique, 73 (Paris : P. Geuthner, 1962) ; *Le Livre des remembrances de la Secrète du royaume de Chypre, 1468–1469*, éd. Jean Richard avec la collaboration de Théodore Papadopoullos, Sources et études de l'histoire de Chypre, 10 (Nicosie : Centre de Recherche Scientifique, 1983).
9 Edbury, « Machaut, Mézières, Makhairas and *Amadi* », passim.

du XIIe siècle, tout du moins dans la France capétienne ; il devient alors un organe de gouvernement siégeant de manière régulière pour traiter des affaires que le roi soumet à la discussion. Cette évolution caractérise en particulier les institutions de la monarchie des derniers Capétiens, où le Conseil joue un rôle essentiel dans la vie du royaume sous Philippe IV le Bel ou Philippe V le Long. Les membres du Conseil prêtent serment au roi, en reçoivent des gages, étant le plus souvent recrutés parmi les vassaux du souverain. Le Conseil du roi, quelles que soient les variations affectant son intitulé, devient un organe de gouvernement assistant le prince, au même titre que l'Hôtel du roi, la Chambre des comptes ou le Parlement.[10] Les Lusignan semblent s'inscrire dans cette évolution, bien que les mentions de Conseil demeurent sporadiques au cours du XIVe siècle, et plus régulières au XVe, comme l'ont déjà souligné Jean Richard et Peter W. Edbury.[11]

À Chypre, c'est-à-dire à l'écart des évolutions qui marquent les régimes monarchiques de l'Occident latin, les Lusignan élaborent des institutions qui leur permettent d'asseoir solidement leur pouvoir en puisant à d'autres traditions administratives et politiques ; aux Byzantins, les premiers Lusignan empruntent beaucoup, notamment la *Secrète*, qui devient le bureau administrant les domaines de la couronne, qui contrôle la circulation des fiefs et qui gère les finances du royaume. Sans entrer dans le détail de l'histoire de la *Secrète* et sur ses diverses attributions, cet organe de gestion bureaucratique suit les revenus de la couronne, et renforce la surveillance sur l'ensemble de la matière féodale insulaire ; de manière logique, les archives et le personnel de la *Secrète* sont installés à l'intérieur du palais royal de Nicosie.[12] La *Secrète* est dirigée par un bailli,

---

10   À l'étude ancienne de Noël Valois, *Étude historique sur le conseil du roi. Introduction à l'inventaire des arrêts du conseil d'État* (Paris : Imprimerie nationale, 1886), répondent les travaux de : Paul Lehugeur, *Histoire de Philippe le Long roi de France (1316–1322)*, II, *Le mécanisme du gouvernement* (Paris : Librairie du recueil Sirey, 1931 ; réimpr. Genève : Slatkine reprints, 1975), pp. 9–42 ; Bernard Guenée, « Le conseil du roi au Moyen Âge », *La revue administrative*, 52/3 (1999), 5–9 ; Éric Bournazel, « Réflexions sur l'institution du conseil aux premiers temps capétiens (XIIe–XIIIe siècles) », *Cahiers de recherches médiévales et humanistes*, 7 (2000), 7–22 ; Olivier Canteaut, *Philippe V et son Conseil : le gouvernement royal de 1316 à 1322* (thèse présentée à l'École des Chartes, Paris, 2000), positions en ligne : http://v2.enc-sorbonne.fr/fr/positions-these/philippe-v-son-conseil-gouvernement-royal-1316-1322 (consulté le 23 février 2018) ; Olivier Canteaut, « Le roi de France gouverne-t-il par conseil ? L'exemple de Philippe V », dans *Consulter, délibérer, décider : donner son avis au Moyen Âge (France-Espagne, VIIe–XVIe siècles)*, dir. Martine Charageat et Corinne Leveleux-Teixeira, Études médiévales ibériques (Toulouse : Éditions Méridiennes, 2010), pp. 157–76 ; Olivier Canteaut, « Hôtel et gouvernement sous les derniers Capétiens directs », *Bibliothèque de l'École des Chartes*, 168/2 (2010), 373–410.

11   Jean Richard, « Οἱ πολιτικοὶ καὶ κοινωνικοὶ θεσμοὶ τοῦ μεσαιωνικοῦ βασιλείου », dans Ἱστορία τῆς Κύπρου, IV, pp. 339–40 ; Edbury, *Kingdom of Cyprus*, p. 188.

12   *Le Livre des remembrances*, pp. vii–xvii ; Richard, « Οἱ πολιτικοὶ καὶ κοινωνικοὶ θεσμοί », pp. 352–53 ; Edbury, *Kingdom of Cyprus*, pp. 191–92 ; *Griechische Briefe und Urkunden aus dem Zypern der Kreuzfahrerzeit. Die Formularsammlung eines königlichen Sekretärs im Vaticanus Palatinus Graecus 367*, ed. Alexander Beihammer, Quellen und Studien zur Geschichte Zyperns, 57 (Nicosie : Zyprisches Forschungszentrum, 2007), pp. 104–17 ; Gilles Grivaud, *Grecs et Francs dans le royaume de Chypre (1191–1474) : les voies de l'acculturation* (mémoire présenté pour l'Habilitation à diriger des recherches, Université Paris I-Panthéon-Sorbonne, 2001), pp. 238–44 ; Gilles Grivaud, « Les Lusignan et leur gouvernance du royaume de Chypre (XIIe–XIVe siècle) », dans *Europäische Governance im Spätmittelalter. Heinrich VII. von Luxemburg und die großen Dynastien Europas / Gouvernance européenne au bas moyen âge. Henri VII de Luxembourg et l'Europe des*

un officier que le roi choisit parmi ses chevaliers, et qui exécute aveuglément les ordres de son seigneur, si l'on se fie au mémoire que l'infant Ferrand dresse à charge contre Hugues IV, au début des années 1340.[13] Thomas de Picquigny occupe la charge de bailli en septembre 1328, et il la conserve au moins dix ans ;[14] en mai 1357, le bailli est Simon de Montolif,[15] en août 1360 Jean Tenouri,[16] en 1362, Nicolas Catellus,[17] de juillet 1372 à mars 1383 Thomas de Montolif.[18]

Si la *Secrète* des Lusignan reconduit l'institution byzantine homonyme – avec des fonctions équivalentes à celles de la Chambre des comptes de la monarchie capétienne –, l'Hôtel du roi semble se former à une époque plus tardive, probablement au début du XIVe siècle, quand Henri II fait construire le nouveau palais de la monarchie dans la capitale, Nicosie.[19] Si l'on se fie aux données de l'état des comptes de 1412–1413, l'Hôtel du roi se préoccupe du service personnel du souverain et de sa famille ; il se trouve divisé en plusieurs offices qui se chargent du logement, du vêtement, de la chapelle, de la ménagerie ; d'autres offices sont consacrés aux services domestiques,

---

grandes dynasties. Actes des 15es Journées lotharingiennes, 14–17 octobre 2008, dir. Michel Pauly (en collaboration avec Martin Uhrmacher et Hérold Pettiau), Publications de la Section historique de l'Institut grand-ducal de Luxembourg 124 – Publications du CLUDEM, 27 (Luxembourg : Section historique de l'Institut grand-ducal, 2010), pp. 351–74 (366–67).

13 Mas Latrie, *Histoire de l'île de Chypre*, II, pp. 184, 189, 194, 198.

14 Mas Latrie, *Histoire de l'île de Chypre*, II, pp. 144, 150, 158, 162, 167 ; *Chronique d'Amadi*, dans *Chroniques d'Amadi et de Strambaldi*, éd. René de Mas Latrie, 2 vols (Paris : Imprimerie nationale, 1891–1893), I, p. 401 ; Thomas de Picquigny obtient le privilège de citoyenneté vénitienne, le 13 mars 1334 : *I libri commemoriali della republica di Venezia. Regesti*, éd. Riccardo Predelli, 8 vols, Monumenti storici publicati dalla Deputazione veneta di storia patria, Serie 1°, Documenti (Venise : a spese della società, 1876–1914 ; réimpr. Cambridge : Cambridge University Press, 2012), II, p. 54, n° 332 ; *Les familles d'Outre-Mer de Du Cange*, éd. Emmanuel-Guillaume Rey, Collection de documents inédits sur l'histoire de France (Paris : Imprimerie impériale, 1869), p. 667 ; Edbury, *Kingdom of Cyprus*, p. 192. Les *Bans et ordonnances*, p. 375, n° XV, mentionnent un « Thomas de Pinqueny, bailly de la Segrete », qui officie le 22 février 1300 ; il s'agit sans doute d'un membre homonyme de la même famille, puisque la charge de bailli de la *Secrète* est exercée par Hugues Béduin en 1314 et Jacques de Fleury en 1315 : Jesús Ernesto Martínez Ferrando, *Jaime II de Aragón. Su vida familiar*, 2 vols (Barcelone : Consejo superior de investigaciones científicas. Escuela de estudios medievales, 1948), II, pp. 101, 107 ; Louis de Mas Latrie, « Nouvelles preuves de l'histoire de Chypre », *Bibliothèque de l'École des Chartes*, 33–34 (1873), 47–87 (p. 64).

15 *Bullarium Cyprium III : Lettres papales relatives à Chypre, 1316–1378*, éd. Charles Perrat, Jean Richard, et Christopher Schabel, Sources et études de l'histoire de Chypre, 68 (Nicosie : Centre de Recherche Scientifique, 2012), n° u-150.

16 Mas Latrie, *Histoire de l'île de Chypre*, II, p. 230 ; *Les familles d'Outre-Mer*, p. 667 ; Edbury, *Kingdom of Cyprus*, p. 192.

17 Rifoldo Livi, « Guido da Bagnolo, medico del re di Cipro », *Atti e memorie della R. Deputazione di storia patria per le provincie modenesi*, ser. 5, 11 (1918), 45–91 (p. 54) ; Edbury, *Kingdom of Cyprus*, p. 192.

18 Mas Latrie, *Histoire de l'île de Chypre*, II, p. 396 ; *Bullarium Cyprium III*, n° w-129 ; *Les familles d'Outre-Mer*, p. 562 ; Edbury, *Kingdom of Cyprus*, p. 192.

19 Richard, « Οἱ πολιτικοὶ καὶ κοινωνικοὶ θεσμοί », pp. 340–41, observe l'existence de cet Hôtel du roi à partir de la seconde moitié du XIVe siècle ; il semble néanmoins plus logique d'associer son établissement à l'édification du nouveau palais par Henri II, au tournant du XIVe siècle : Nicos Coureas, Gilles Grivaud, et Chris Schabel, « The Capital of the Sweet Land of Cyprus. Frankish and Venetian Nicosia », dans *Historic Nicosia*, dir. Demetrios Michaïlidès (Nicosie : Rimal Publications, 2012), pp. 139–40.

tels la cuisine, la paneterie.[20] L'Hôtel est placé sous la responsabilité d'un officier, qui porte parfois le titre de maréchal de l'Hôtel du roi, comme Baudouin de Nores, désigné sous ce titre de mars 1328 à janvier 1330;[21] plus souvent, les sources le désignent sous le titre de bailli de la cour, dont les plus célèbres titulaires demeurent Jean Visconti et Jean Gorap, qui subissent, l'un après l'autre, la colère de Pierre 1er durant l'année 1368.[22] On notera que cet Hôtel du roi se substitue aux grands offices, qui auparavant avaient en charge les services de la maison des rois de Chypre,[23] grands offices sur lesquels on reviendra plus bas.

Parmi les organes de gouvernement des Lusignan au XIVe siècle figure encore la Haute Cour, qui rassemble les vassaux du roi, et qui est convoquée pour trancher des litiges sur la matière féodale;[24] en 1341, l'infant Ferrand rapporte ainsi que Hugues IV « fecit congregari totum consilium istius terre Chipri » afin de déclarer traître l'infortuné Ferrand, mais, heureusement pour lui, le « consilium non ascendit voluntate regis ».[25] Ce type de réunion semble exceptionnel, car les documents d'archives montrent que le roi arrête des décisions importantes sans prendre l'avis de la Haute Cour. Ainsi, afin d'élaborer un traité de paix avec Venise, le 4 septembre 1328, le roi fait appel à cinq membres de son entourage, qui sont qualifié de « milites et consiliarios prefati domini regis »; il s'agit de trois grands officiers: Thomas de Montolif, maréchal de Chypre, Simon de Montolif, bouteiller de Jérusalem, Hugues Béduin, amiral de Chypre; leurs sont associés le bailli de la *Secrète* royale, Thomas de Picquigny, et Justin de Justinis, un juriste toscan au service des Lusignan de 1311 à 1342. Dans le cas du traité de 1328, ces cinq personnages sont explicitement reconnus comme les auteurs du texte final; en toute logique, le traité est validé par leurs signatures et celles d'autres témoins, parmi lesquels on reconnaît des prélats et des religieux, ainsi que d'autres grands officiers, tels Oddon de Dampierre, connétable de Jérusalem, Jean Babin, maréchal de Jérusalem, Baudouin de Nores, maréchal de l'Hôtel du roi; sont également témoins des seigneurs privés de distinctions particulières, comme Balian d'Ibelin-Arsur et Jean Bordon.[26]

Ce traité de 1328 se révèle précieux par le fait qu'il dévoile le *modus operandi* d'une prise de décision intéressant les relations diplomatiques et les rapports commerciaux du royaume avec une puissance étrangère. L'intérêt collectif justifie le recours à

---

20 Gilles Grivaud, « Un état des comptes du royaume de Chypre en 1412–1413 », *Bulletin de Correspondance Hellénique*, 122/1 (1998), 377–401 (pp. 386–87, 398–401).
21 Mas Latrie, *Histoire de l'île de Chypre*, II, pp. 141, 144, 158, 162; *Les familles d'Outre-Mer*, p. 685.
22 Léontios Machairas, Χρονικὸ τῆς Κύπρου, pp. 180 (où Pierre 1er « ἀφῆκεν νὰ παίρνη σκοπὸν τὸ σπίτιν του ἕναν πολλὰ ἀντρειωμένον καβαλλάρην ὀνόματι σὶρ Τζουὰν Βισκούντην »), 222 (« ὁ σὶρ Τζουὰν Γκοράπ ὁ ἐμπαλῆς τῆς αὐλῆς »); *Chronique d'Amadi*, pp. 418 (où Pierre 1er nomme Jean Visconte « guardian de casa sua »), 425 (Jean Gorap est « balio della corte del re »); Richard, « La révolution de 1369 », p. 109; Edbury, « The Murder of King Peter I », p. 227.
23 Richard, « Οἱ πολιτικοὶ καὶ κοινωνικοὶ θεσμοί », pp. 339–40; Edbury, *Kingdom of Cyprus*, pp. 181–83.
24 Maurice Grandclaude, *Étude critique sur les livres des Assises de Jérusalem* (Paris: Jouve et Cie éditeurs, 1923), pp. 160–63; Richard, « La révolution de 1369 », p. 118; Richard, « Οἱ πολιτικοὶ καὶ κοινωνικοὶ θεσμοί », pp. 344–45; Edbury, *Kingdom of Cyprus*, pp. 186–88.
25 Mas Latrie, *Histoire de l'île de Chypre*, II, p. 194.
26 Mas Latrie, *Histoire de l'île de Chypre*, II, pp. 142–44.

la concertation des grands officiers, et le roi demeure extérieur à l'élaboration du texte définitif ; en d'autres termes, les conseillers agissent au nom du roi pour la sauvegarde des intérêts de la couronne et de ses sujets. Ce document suffit-il pour affirmer qu'un Conseil régulier composé de membres fixes détermine la politique du royaume à l'époque de Hugues IV ? Certainement pas, mais trois autres documents datés de 1329, 1330 et 1338 aident à mieux appréhender la connaissance des rouages du gouvernement royal.

Le traité négocié avec les Génois, à Nicosie, le 16 février 1329, présente de fortes similitudes avec celui passé avec Venise, l'année précédente. Les tractations sont menées par quatre des grands officiers auteurs de l'accord de 1328 ; manque cependant le bouteiller de Jérusalem, Simon de Montolif. Les témoins qui signent le texte final se révèlent plus nombreux qu'en 1328 : hormis quelques prélats et religieux, on découvre les noms de plusieurs grands officiers : trois ont élaboré le diplôme, à savoir Oddon de Dampierre, connétable de Jérusalem, Thomas de Picquigny, bailli de la *Secrète*, et Justin de Justinis, auxquels s'ajoutent Simon de Montolif, bouteiller de Jérusalem, Jean de Plessie, bailli des tailles, Baudouin de Nores, maréchal de l'Hôtel du roi, Élie l'Aleman, vicomte de Nicosie ; enfin, huit autres seigneurs et un juriste complètent la liste des témoins pour la partie chypriote. Aucun de ces personnages n'est qualifié de conseiller, mais on ne saurait priver de cette qualité les quatre « tractatores » à l'origine de la rédaction définitive.[27]

Pour le second traité négocié avec les Génois, acté à Nicosie, le 21 février 1338, le *modus operandi* suit le modèle observé en 1328 et en 1329, puisque le roi désigne quatre négociateurs : Marc, évêque de Famagouste, Thomas de Picquigny, bailli de la *Secrète*, Barthélémy de Montolif, camérier du royaume de Chypre, et Justin de Justinis, tous étant expressément qualifiés de conseillers du roi. L'acte est validé par les signatures des quatre « tractatores », auxquelles s'ajoutent celles d'autres grands officiers : Guy de Lusignan connétable de Chypre, Huon d'Ibelin, comte de Jaffa et sénéchal de Jérusalem ; complètent la liste des témoins des clercs, et 22 noms de chevaliers, qui pour la plupart, appartiennent aux familles notables du royaume franc : de Montolif, de Nores, Babin, Tenouri.[28]

Le dernier acte du règne de Hugues IV à considérer concerne la ratification du contrat de mariage entre le fils du roi Guy, prince de Galilée, et Marie de Bourbon, établie à Nicosie, le 14 janvier 1330. L'acte, qui reprend le dispositif d'un formulaire, est signé de prélats et de religieux, et de cinq grands officiers : Guy d'Ibelin, sénéchal de Chypre, Hugues Béduin, amiral de Chypre, Simon de Montolif, bouteiller de Jérusalem, Baudouin de Nores, maréchal de l'Hôtel du roi, et Thomas de Picquigny, le bailli de la *Secrète*, auxquels se joint Justin de Justinis. Dans ce document, aucun des signataires n'obtient la qualité de conseiller.[29]

Que retenir de la confrontation des quatre documents ? Hugues IV ne gouverne pas seul, il est assisté de conseillers qui agissent pour la sauvegarde des intérêts de la

---

27 Mas Latrie, *Histoire de l'île de Chypre*, II, pp. 150–58.
28 Mas Latrie, *Histoire de l'île de Chypre*, II, pp. 166–79.
29 Mas Latrie, *Histoire de l'île de Chypre*, II, pp. 161–62.

couronne, et qui garantissent la validité des accords établis. Pendant dix ans, de 1328 à 1338, le souverain confie l'élaboration de sa diplomatie à des personnages, choisis sans doute pour leurs compétences et leur fidélité, qui forment des Conseils resserrés, comprenant quatre ou cinq membres. Deux personnages sont systématiquement associés aux prises de décision, le bailli de la *Secrète*, Thomas de Picquigny, et le juriste Justin de Justinis, ce qui leur confère la qualité de conseillers permanents du roi, et le titre de conseiller accompagne effectivement le nom de Justin de Justinis dans tous les documents officiels, ce juriste étant présenté comme tel à la cour du roi Henri II, dès 1309.[30] Les autres membres du Conseil sont retenus parmi les grands officiers, qu'il s'agisse de Thomas, Barthélémy ou Simon de Montolif, Hugues Béduin, Guy d'Ibelin, Baudouin de Nores.

On constate ainsi que Hugues IV confie l'élaboration de sa politique à un Conseil, qui ne paraît pas acquérir une forme institutionnelle officielle, contrairement à l'usage établi dans la monarchie capétienne contemporaine. Rien n'indique, dans le cas chypriote, que le Conseil soit réuni de manière permanente, et qu'il soit composé d'un nombre fixe de membres ; il semble davantage convoqué pour des usages précis, *ad hoc*, autour d'un noyau formé du bailli de la *Secrète* et d'un juriste, auxquels s'agrègent divers grands officiers. Ce Conseil, aussi informel et souple soit-il, conduit les alliances diplomatiques du royaume, s'il reçoit l'aval d'autres grands officiers, prélats et seigneurs, qui entérinent ses propositions. En d'autres termes, le roi s'appuie sur les élites de la société franque en leur déléguant une part active dans l'élaboration de la politique du royaume, en les associant à l'exercice du pouvoir, sans qu'il soit fait mention de la Haute Cour. Même un souverain aussi acariâtre et exigeant que Hugues IV, dont le règne est présenté comme celui d'un monarque absolu, négocie le concours des grands officiers pour obtenir l'adhésion des puissants à l'élaboration de choix politiques engageant le royaume dans ses relations extérieures.

Comment fonctionne ce cadre institutionnel, à la fois informel, souple et contraignant, pendant le règne de Pierre 1er ? Il convient d'abord de remarquer que Hugues IV organise sa succession de son vivant. Ses fils, Pierre et Jean, sont associés à l'exercice de la vie officielle assez tôt, comme en témoigne un acte du 24 septembre 1346, révélant que le roi assiste à la consécration de l'évêque de Limassol en présence de

---

30 Mas Latrie, « Nouvelles preuves » (1873), p. 56 ; Mas Latrie, *Histoire de l'île de Chypre*, II, pp. 141–42, 144, 150, 158, 162, 167, 179, 202 et n. 4, 272. Justin de Justinis, originaire de Città di Castello, est mentionné conseiller du roi Henri II en juillet 1309, et il obtient très tôt le privilège de citoyenneté vénitienne, en 1311 : *Chronique d'Amadi*, p. 309, et *I libri commemoriali della republica di Venezia. Regesti*, I, n° 489, p. 111, II, p. 69 ; il est associé aux négociations liées au mariage de Marie de Lusignan à Jaime II d'Aragon, en mai 1314 : Mas Latrie, *Histoire de l'île de Chypre*, III, p. 705, et Martínez Ferrando, *Jaime II de Aragón*, II, n° 153, pp. 104–05, n° 226 pp. 160–63 ; sa carrière de conseiller semble s'achever au milieu des années 1340, puisqu'il reçoit une indulgence *in articulo mortis*, le 14 septembre 1342, et disparaît avant août 1347 : *Bullarium Cyprium III*, n[os] t-20, 279 ; sa pierre tumulaire est déposée dans la chapelle des Pins de la cathédrale Sainte-Sophie, fixant la date de son décès au mardi 12 août 134(7 ?) : *Lacrimae Cypriae. Les larmes de Chypre, ou recueil des inscriptions lapidaires pour la plupart funéraires de la période franque et vénitienne de l'île de Chypre*, dir. Brunehilde Imhaus, 2 vols (Nicosie : Département des Antiquités, 2004), fiche n° 21 (l'épitaphe rapportant qu'il fut « CONSEILLIOUR DE NOSTRE SEIGNOUR LE ROI ») ; sa carrière a déjà été retracée par Edbury, *Kingdom of Cyprus*, pp. 190–91.

Pierre, comte de Tripoli, et de Jean, prince d'Antioche.[31] À cette date, les deux frères ont atteint l'âge de la majorité, et les chroniqueurs nous apprennent qu'ils nouent une étroite complicité lorsqu'ils fuient ensemble en Occident, en 1349. Pourchassés par les officiers de leur père, ramenés de force à Chypre, ils partagent la captivité dans les geôles de Cérines, et le courroux de Hugues IV est suffisamment retentissant pour que Clément VI intervienne auprès du roi afin d'implorer sa clémence envers ses fils.[32]

Sans exagérer l'importance de cette expérience, elle semble déterminante par le fait que l'entente entre les deux frères se traduit ultérieurement par un exercice conjoint du pouvoir durant une dizaine d'années, très certainement selon la volonté de Hugues IV ; on observe, en effet, que les deux frères sont soumis à la même stratégie matrimoniale, réalisant, en premières noces, des unions avec des veuves nettement plus âgées qu'eux ; ainsi, Échive de Montfort est mariée à Pierre, en 1342, Constance d'Aragon à Jean, un an plus tard, et les deux alliances permettent d'accroître le domaine royal de douaires convoités.[33] En août 1354, Jean et Pierre sollicitent de concert Innocent VI pour qu'il accorde des canonicats à des clercs qui sont leurs familiers.[34] Par la suite, la répartition des responsabilités est établie du vivant de leur père, si l'on admet les assertions de la chronique de Machairas et de celle attribuée à Amadi ; probablement afin de contrôler sa propre succession – qui d'un point de vue légal devait échoir à Hugues, fils de Guy, l'aîné de Pierre et Jean décédé en 1343 –, Hugues IV transmet le trône, de son vivant, à Pierre, le 24 novembre 1358 ; il s'agit d'une occurrence unique dans l'histoire des pratiques de gouvernement des Lusignan, qui voit Pierre, âgé de 30 ans environ, régner un an dans l'ombre de son père.[35] Avec la disparition de Hugues IV, le 10 octobre 1359, Pierre devient seul titulaire des deux couronnes de Chypre et de Jérusalem, même si la gouvernance du royaume appartient *de facto* aux deux frères.[36]

---

31   Conrad Eubel, *Hierarchia catholica medii et recentioris aevi [...]*, 9 vols (Münster : sumptibus et typis librariae Regensbergianae, 1913–1978), I, p. 367, n. 7 ; rééd. par Chris Schabel, « Ab hac hora in antea. Oaths to the Roman Church in Frankish Cyprus (and Greece) », dans *Crusader Landscapes in the Medieval Levant: The Archaeology and History of the Latin East*, dir. Micaela Sinibaldi, Kevin J. Lewis, Balázs Major et Jennifer A. Thompson (Cardiff : University of Wales Press, 2016), pp. 370-71.

32   Léontios Machairas, Χρονικό της Κύπρου, pp. 108–10 ; *Chronique d'Amadi*, pp. 407–08 ; Hardy, *Édition critique de la Prise d'Alexandrie de Guillaume de Machaut*, v. 507–96 ; *Bullarium Cyprium III*, n[os] t-448, 519, 619 ; Jorga, *Philippe de Mézières*, pp. 88–89, 104 ; Hill, *A History of Cyprus*, II, pp. 302–04 ; Edbury, « The Murder of King Peter I », p. 219 ; Edbury, *Kingdom of Cyprus*, p. 147.

33   *Bullarium Cyprium III*, n[os] t-3 (dispense pour l'union d'Échive de Montfort avec Pierre de Lusignan, datée du 28 juin 1342), 33 (dispense pour l'union de Constance d'Aragon avec Jean de Lusignan, datée du 19 juin 1343) ; Wipertus Rudt de Collenberg, « Les dispenses matrimoniales accordées à l'Orient Latin selon les Registres du Vatican d'Honorius III à Clément VII (1283–1385) », *Mélanges de l'École française de Rome - Moyen Âge / Temps modernes*, 89/1 (1977), 11–93 (p. 53).

34   *Bullarium Cyprium III*, n[os] u-53, 55.

35   Léontios Machairas, Χρονικό της Κύπρου, p. 111 ; *Chronique d'Amadi*, p. 408 ; Wipertus H. Rudt de Collenberg, « Les Lusignan de Chypre », Επετηρίς Κέντρου Επιστημονικών Ερευνών (Κύπρου), 10 (1979–1980), 85–319 (pp. 124–25) ; Edbury, *Kingdom of Cyprus*, pp. 147–48.

36   La date exacte d'accession de Pierre au trône, comme celle du décès de Hugues IV, reste sujette à discussion si on s'en tient aux récits des chroniqueurs, comme le remarqua Mas Latrie, *Histoire de l'île de Chypre*, II, p. 224, n. 2 ; néanmoins, le décès de Hugues IV, le jeudi 10 octobre 1359, est certifié par

En effet, Jean, prince d'Antioche, assume la direction des affaires dans l'île pendant trois ans, lorsque Pierre 1er part en Occident, de la fin octobre 1362 à octobre 1365. Le prince, connétable de Chypre et gouverneur du royaume, informe Pierre des événements importants intéressant le royaume, et il prend les initiatives nécessaires au règlement des tensions avec les Génois à Famagouste ; il exécute les ordres reçus de son frère, notamment durant l'été 1365, lorsqu'il faut armer la flotte destinée à l'expédition d'Alexandrie. Jean, prince d'Antioche, retrouve sa fonction de gouverneur lors du second voyage de Pierre, de la fin de l'année 1367 à octobre 1368. Quand il ne remplace pas le roi, le prince d'Antioche le seconde lors de chaque campagne militaire, ainsi lors des expéditions de Satalie, en août 1361, de Gorigos, au printemps 1367, d'Alexandrie, en octobre 1365, où, selon Machairas, Jean est « καπιτάνος φυσικὸς τῆς ἀρμάδας ». Lors de l'attaque lancée contre Tripoli, en janvier 1367, le prince d'Antioche est de nouveau le second du roi, de même en mai 1367, lorsqu'est formée la flotte devant réprimer la mutinerie de la garnison de Satalie.[37] Par sa proximité avec le roi, en vertu de sa fonction de connétable, mentionnée à partir de 1358,[38] le prince d'Antioche agit au cœur du système de gouvernement de Pierre 1er. Au lendemain du régicide, du fait de l'expérience acquise du pouvoir, la corégence lui est confiée durant la minorité de Pierre II, de manière presque naturelle pourrait-on dire, puisque le prince d'Antioche s'est toujours conduit comme un fidèle défenseur de la couronne.[39]

Jean, prince d'Antioche, forme le pivot central de la structure dirigeante, mais il n'est pas le seul frère du roi investi de responsabilités. Ayant atteint l'âge de la majorité en octobre 1365, Jacques, le cadet, obtiendrait la sénéchaussée de Chypre au moment de son adoubement ; on peine cependant à préciser le rôle qu'il tient ensuite, cette discrétion pouvant être justifiée par son jeune âge. On sait cependant qu'il est aux côtés du prince d'Antioche, à la cour, durant les journées qui précèdent l'assassinat de Pierre 1er.[40] Enfin, il faut rappeler que Hugues, petit-fils de Hugues IV, revient

---

une notice marginale de manuscrit (*Paris. gr. 1589*) : Jean Darrouzès, « Notes pour servir à l'histoire de Chypre (premier article) », Κυπριακαί Σπουδαί, 17 (1953), 81–102 (pp. 84, 91) (réimpr. dans Jean Darrouzès, *Littérature et histoire des textes byzantins* (Londres : Variorum Reprints, 1972), n° XIV) ; néanmoins, les doutes demeurent sur l'enchaînement des dates et sur l'intention de Hugues IV, comme le remarquent Peter W. Edbury et Chris Schabel dans leur contribution à ce volume.

37 Léontios Machairas, *Χρονικό τῆς Κύπρου*, pp. 126, 133–35, 140–41, 149–50 (citation), 165, 171, 177, 180, 186 ; *Chronique d'Amadi*, pp. 414, 416, 418 ; Mas Latrie, *Histoire de l'île de Chypre*, II, p. 308 ; Hardy, *Édition critique de la* Prise d'Alexandrie *de Guillaume de Machaut*, v. 2791, 4475, 4813 ; Edbury, « The Murder of King Peter I », p. 225, considère Jean d'Antioche comme le bras droit du souverain (« it is no exaggeration to see him as his brother's right-hand man »).

38 Sur la foi de Léontios Machairas, *Χρονικό τῆς Κύπρου*, p. 111 (ms de Venise seulement), 191 (ms d'Oxford seulement) ; *Chronique d'Amadi*, p. 408 ; *Les familles d'Outre-Mer*, pp. 211, 680 ; Rudt de Collenberg, « Les Lusignan de Chypre », p. 130 ; Edbury, *Kingdom of Cyprus*, pp. 163–64, 166–67.

39 Léontios Machairas, *Χρονικό τῆς Κύπρου*, p. 223 ; *Chronique d'Amadi*, pp. 426–27 ; *Bullarium Cyprium III*, n°s v-223, 229, w-11 ; Edbury, *The Murder of King Peter I*, p. 225.

40 Léontios Machairas, *Χρονικό τῆς Κύπρου*, pp. 108, 111, 191, 212, avec des versions différentes quant aux titres accordés par Hugues IV à Jacques selon les manuscrits, qui le citent connétable de Jérusalem et / ou sénéchal à une date inconnue, mais à la p. 154, Jacques reçoit la sénéchaussée au moment de son adoubement, à Alexandrie : *Chronique d'Amadi*, p. 415 ; pour sa part, le *Bullarium Cyprium III*, n°s w-19

à Chypre, sur pressions de la papauté et du roi de France. Participant à l'expédition d'Alexandrie, Hugues reçoit le titre de prince de Galilée, et sert fidèlement son royal cousin par la suite ; en mai 1367, il commande une des galères envoyées à Satalie, puis accompagne le roi en Italie, en octobre 1368.[41] Certes, faute de sources abondantes, les positions occupées à la cour par Jacques et Hugues de Lusignan peinent à être appréciées, mais on peut gager que les cousins renforcent l'influence du roi et du prince d'Antioche au palais.

Dans la structure du gouvernement assistant le souverain, il convient aussi d'apprécier le rôle dévolu à cet organe de gouvernement reconnu comme le Conseil du roi, structure informelle dont on a observé les larges compétences en matière diplomatique, à l'époque de Hugues IV. Une première remarque tend à souligner la stabilité du personnel politique assurant la transition du règne de Hugues IV à celui de Pierre 1er. Parmi les grands officiers, on reconnaît Raymond Babin, bouteiller de Chypre de décembre 1359 à 1373,[42] Jacques de Nores, turcoplier de Chypre de 1345 à 1372,[43] Jean de Sur, amiral de Chypre de 1350 à sa mort en mai 1367,[44] Jean du Morf, maréchal de Chypre de 1359 à une date postérieure à août 1373,[45] Thomas de Montolif, auditeur de Chypre de 1355 à 1372,[46] Philippe de Mézières, chancelier du

---

cite le titre de sénéchal en mars 1371 ; les *Lignages d'Outremer*, éd. Marie-Adélaïde Nielen, Documents relatifs à l'histoire des croisades, XVIII (Paris : Académie des Inscriptions et Belles-Lettres, 2003), p. 169, précisent que Jacques abandonne le titre de sénéchal de Chypre pour prendre celui de connétable de Jérusalem, à l'avènement de Pierre II ; également : *Les familles d'Outre-Mer*, p. 688 ; Rudt de Collenberg, « Les Lusignan de Chypre », p. 132 ; Edbury, « The Murder of King Peter I », p. 225 ; Edbury, *Kingdom of Cyprus*, pp. 173–75.

41 Léontios Machairas, Χρονικό της Κύπρου, p. 180 ; Mas Latrie, *Histoire de l'île de Chypre*, II, p. 291 ; *Chronique d'Amadi*, pp. 418, 426 ; *Lignages d'Outremer*, p. 168 ; *Les familles d'Outre-Mer*, p. 465 ; Rudt de Collenberg, « Les Lusignan de Chypre », pp. 141–43 ; Edbury, *Kingdom of Cyprus*, pp. 149–50.

42 Léontios Machairas, Χρονικό της Κύπρου, pp. 117–18, 126, 150–51 ; *Bullarium Cyprium III*, n[os] u-231–34, 236–38, 240, w-210 ; Louis de Mas Latrie, « Nouvelles preuves de l'histoire de Chypre », *Bibliothèque de l'École des Chartes*, 35 (1874), 99–158 (p. 106) ; *Les familles d'Outre-Mer*, p. 514 ; Jorga, *Philippe de Mézières*, p. 103 ; Edbury, « The Murder of King Peter I », pp. 227–28 ; Edbury, *Kingdom of Cyprus*, p. 175.

43 Léontios Machairas, Χρονικό της Κύπρου, pp. 126, 128–30, 140, 151, 165, 167, 172, 180, 222 ; *Chronique d'Amadi*, pp. 411–12, 426, 437 ; Mas Latrie, *Histoire de l'île de Chypre*, II, pp. 165, 291, 302, 308 ; *Bullarium Cyprium III*, n[os] t-122, 254, 317, u-76, 216, 226 ; dans le récit de Guillaume de Machaut, Jacques de Nores est seulement désigné par son titre de « tricoplier » : Hardy, *Édition critique de la Prise d'Alexandrie de Guillaume de Machaut*, v. 4557, 4783, 5269 ; Jorga, *Philippe de Mézières*, pp. 125, 127, 256, 354, 356–57, 370 ; Edbury, « The Murder of King Peter I », p. 226.

44 Léontios Machairas, Χρονικό της Κύπρου, pp. 126, 130–32, 140, 150, 153, 155, 176–77, 185 ; *Chronique d'Amadi*, pp. 412, 415, 417, 419 ; *Bullarium Cyprium III*, n[os] t-539, v-44, 152, 159 ; Jorga, *Philippe de Mézières*, pp. 108, 127, 256, 264, 275, 282, 301, 305.

45 Léontios Machairas, Χρονικό της Κύπρου, pp. 121, 140 ; Mas Latrie, *Histoire de l'île de Chypre*, II, pp. 230, 233, III, p. 741 ; *Bullarium Cyprium III*, n[os] u-281, w-213 ; *Les familles d'Outre-Mer*, pp. 568, 685 ; Jorga, *Philippe de Mézières*, p. 253 ; Rudt de Collenberg, « Études de prosopographie généalogique des Chypriotes mentionnés dans les registres du Vatican 1378–1471 », Μελέται και Υπομνήματα, 1 (1984), 523–678 (pp. 572–73).

46 Léontios Machairas, Χρονικό της Κύπρου, pp. 109 (il est bailli de Famagouste en 1349), 121, 140 ; *Chronique d'Amadi*, pp. 410, 431 ; *Bans et ordonnances*, p. 377, n° XXXII ; *Bullarium Cyprium III*, n° u-281 ; Jorga, *Philippe de Mézières*, pp. 117, 256.

royaume de Chypre à partir de 1361.[47] Pour les charges dont on peut suivre la carrière des titulaires, on remarque, d'une part, la constance et la fidélité des personnages servant le trône, d'autre part, le maintien du cadre établi par Hugues IV, qui avait installé au moins quatre des grands officiers actifs pendant le règne de Pierre 1er. Aucune rupture ne peut être décelée dans le proche entourage du trône après 1359, pour des raisons qui tiennent autant au poids de l'héritage politique qu'aux contraintes démographiques. Cette observation s'applique évidemment au personnel de la cour, comme le révèle l'exemple de Jean du Bois, qui sert sans discontinuité Hugues IV et son fils, comme chapelain et / ou secrétaire, entre 1348 et 1363.[48]

La continuité qui s'incarne à travers les individus marque aussi les institutions de gouvernement, et le Conseil du roi. Les rares actes émis par la Chancellerie de Nicosie entre 1359 et 1368 ne fournissent pas de détails sur le *modus operandi* des négociations menant à la ratification des traités de paix ; celui conclu avec Venise, le 16 août 1360, reconduit les privilèges de 1328, et les nouvelles clauses ajoutées ne sont accessibles que dans la formule finale du traité conservé aux archives de Venise. On remarque néanmoins que les garants signant l'acte sont, comme en 1328, le bailli de la *Secrète*, Jean Tenouri, un juriste italien formé à Bologne, Domenico Rodulfi, qui sont associés à l'évêque de Limassol, Guy d'Ibelin, et à cinq grands officiers : le connétable de Chypre, Jean de Lusignan prince d'Antioche, le connétable de Jérusalem, Philippe de Brunswick, le maréchal de Chypre, Jean du Morf, le camérier de Chypre, Simon de Montolif, et le chancelier de Chypre, Ugo Ommebono / Ognibene de Mantoue.[49] Si aucun de ces signataires n'est qualifié de conseiller du roi, ceux-ci semblent agir selon les dispositions arrêtées précédemment dans les dispositifs des traités de Hugues IV.

Le fonctionnement du Conseil du roi sous l'autorité de Pierre est dévoilé par la chronique de Machairas, qui le mentionne à plusieurs reprises. Au lendemain de la prise de Satalie, le roi interroge ses archontes pour connaître leurs opinions (« ἀρώτησεν τοὺς ἄρχοντες τῆς βουλῆς του »), et il suit leur avis quant à l'investissement de la place.[50] Une attitude similaire est observée en octobre 1365, après la capture d'Alexandrie, quand le roi interroge le légat Pierre Thomas et ses chevaliers sur l'opportunité de conserver le port ; là encore, le roi admet leur point de vue et décide le repli de la flotte sur Limassol.[51] En juin 1366, quand les émissaires mamelouks sont reçus à Nicosie, « « ὁ ῥήγας ὥρισεν καὶ ἐκράξαν τοὺς ἄρχοντες τῆς βουλῆς », et, une fois encore, le roi admet l'avis des archontes qui décident de confier la négociation à des

---

47 Jorga, *Philippe de Mézières*, pp. 109, 128 n. 4, où Jorga affirme que Philippe est élevé à cette charge en 1361, après l'expédition contre Satalie ; malgré le manque de documents relatifs à cette nomination, cette proposition est adoptée sur la base d'une interprétation rétrospective des textes de Philippe de Mézières par Nicolaou-Konnari, « Apologists or Critics ? », pp. 363–65. La charge est toujours occupée par Ugo Ommebono / Ognibene de Mantoue, en août 1360 : Mas Latrie, *Histoire de l'île de Chypre*, II, p. 230.
48 *Bullarium Cyprium III*, nos u-230, v-35.
49 Mas Latrie, *Histoire de l'île de Chypre*, II, pp. 229–30.
50 Léontios Machairas, Χρονικό τῆς Κύπρου, pp. 127–28, où seule la version du manuscrit de Venise formule la sollicitation du Conseil des archontes.
51 Léontios Machairas, Χρονικό τῆς Κύπρου, p. 155.

intermédiaires catalans.⁵² Par la suite, en février 1367, lorsque Pierre reçoit les envoyés du sultan à Famagouste, perturbé par les réclamations portées par les Vénitiens, les Génois et les Catalans, le roi « ἐρώτησεν τοὺς ἄρχοντες τῆς βουλῆς του », archontes qui l'engagent à faire la paix avec le sultan. Pierre se range à leur avis et, promet d'engager des négociations.⁵³ Les quatre occurrences rapportées, qui concernent le champ des relations diplomatiques et militaires, confirment que Pierre 1ᵉʳ ne détermine pas seul les orientations décisives pour l'avenir du royaume ; il questionne ses archontes, pour reprendre l'expression utilisée par Machairas, terme qui désigne expressément les grands officiers de la cour.

L'action du Conseil se révèle tout aussi décisive durant la dernière année du règne de Pierre, dominée par les intrigues de palais, et la chronique de Machairas relate, semble-t-il, le protocole d'une séance de Conseil, liée à la résolution de la crise provoquée par l'adultère supposé de la reine.⁵⁴ Ébranlé par la lettre de Jean Visconti qui dénonce la relation d'Éléonore avec Jean du Morf, le roi « ἐζήτησεν τοὺς ἄρχοντες τῆς βουλῆς του ». De manière assez procédurière, Pierre interroge ses frères, en premier lieu, puis les barons, les liges et enfin ses conseillers (« συνβουλατόρους »). N'obtenant que des réponses évasives de leur part, Pierre engage un dialogue, et finit par formuler une alternative afin de savoir s'il doit renvoyer sa femme, ou se venger de Jean du Morf. Le roi interpelle directement les membres du Conseil pour qu'ils rendent un avis qu'il promet de suivre, fondant son argument sur l'expérience dont disposent les anciens (« ἔχετε ἀνθρώπους παλαιοὺς τῆς βουλῆς πειρασμένους καὶ ἀπὸ 'ξαυτῆς τους εὑρίσκεται ἡ ἀλήθεια »)⁵⁵. Le roi poursuit en usant de paraboles induisant une réponse claire et ferme, dont il respectera et appliquera les attendus.

Les membres du Conseil demandent alors au roi de se retirer pendant leurs délibérations, et Machairas rapporte les discussions internes, les avis divergents. Au terme des délibérations, on préfère sacrifier Jean Visconti plutôt qu'attirer le déshonneur sur Chypre en renvoyant la reine à Barcelone, et, selon Machairas, cette décision pleine de bon sens est adoptée de manière collective. Alors, le Conseil fait appeler le roi pour l'informer de la décision, qu'il reçoit en manifestant sa satisfaction. Il remet ensuite au Conseil la lettre accusatoire de Visconti, ce qui permet une condamnation officielle pour traîtrise. La nuit suivante, Visconti est jeté en prison à Cérines. Aussi partial soit-il, le récit de Machairas relate les étapes logiques d'une séance de consultation du Conseil par le souverain. La résolution de cette première intrigue montre que Pierre gouverne toujours avec le concours de son Conseil, et qu'il respecte l'esprit des *Assises*, puisque la condamnation de Visconti est prononcée avec l'assentiment des membres du Conseil.

Ce passage est précieux en ce qu'il éclaire les relations entre le roi, son Conseil et la Haute Cour, qui, on le sait, représente l'assemblée souveraine pour appliquer la loi des *Assises*. Si l'on se fie à Machairas, le roi interpelle son Conseil sur un sujet

---

52   Léontios Machairas, *Χρονικό τῆς Κύπρου*, p. 160.
53   Léontios Machairas, *Χρονικό τῆς Κύπρου*, p. 167.
54   Léontios Machairas, *Χρονικό τῆς Κύπρου*, pp. 200–04.
55   Léontios Machairas, *Χρονικό τῆς Κύπρου*, p. 201, formule qui appartient seulement à la version du manuscrit d'Oxford.

déterminé, prend son avis, puis fait appliquer la décision par la Haute Cour, sans qu'elle soit consultée mais qui demeure l'institution légitimante. Le Conseil du roi n'est pas l'émanation de la Haute Cour, il est constitué des barons, ceux que Machairas appelle les archontes, et qui comprennent un cercle limité de membres importants des familles franques, ceux qui tiennent les grands offices. Or, il importe de souligner à quel point ces personnages sont étroitement apparentés.

Ainsi, pour nous en tenir aux exemples les mieux documentés, Jean de Lusignan, prince d'Antioche, a épousé Alice d'Ibelin, fille du sénéchal de Chypre, Guy.[56] Le prince de Galilée, Hugues de Lusignan, est uni à Marie du Morf, fille de Jean, comte de Rochas et maréchal de Chypre.[57] Jacques de Lusignan, le dernier membre de la fratrie royale, promu sénéchal de Chypre en octobre 1365, prend la main d'Héloïse de Brunswick, filleule de Hugues IV et surtout fille de Philippe de Brunswick, connétable de Jérusalem, qui avait eu le projet d'épouser Marguerite, la sœur du roi Pierre, pour finalement convoler en seconde noce avec la mère du roi, Alice d'Ibelin, veuve de Hugues IV.[58] Pour sa part, le turcoplier de Chypre Jacques de Nores donne sa fille, Isabelle, à Thomas de Montolif, sans doute l'auditeur de Chypre.[59] Quant au bouteiller de Chypre, Raymond Babin, il est le mari de Marie de Montolif, dont on ne sait établir la parenté exacte avec Thomas de Montolif, l'auditeur, et avec Simon, le bailli de la *Secrète*.[60] Sans reconstituer l'intégralité des réseaux de parenté liant les grands officiers entre eux et à la famille des Lusignan, derrière le trône, le gouvernement appartient en réalité à un noyau de lignages apparentés, où les pratiques endogamiques deviennent une règle. Cette constatation n'a rien de surprenant, tant les rangs de l'aristocratie franque s'étiolent sous les coups des épidémies de peste, ce qui justifie les fréquentes dispenses matrimoniales accordées par les papes.[61]

Dans ce système de gouvernement verrouillé par les élites franques, la marge de manœuvre abandonnée au souverain se limite au choix de rares conseillers, souvent recrutés parmi des étrangers. Déjà, sous Hugues IV, la longue carrière de Justin de Justinis révèle le souci d'associer aux prises de décision un spécialiste en droit, formé dans un *studium* italien,[62] et Pierre 1er reconduit cet usage ; au moins un nom de juriste italien actif dans son entourage peut être cité, celui de Domenico Rodulfi de Bologne,

---

56 *Bullarium Cyprium III*, nos t-259, 457 (dispense accordée le 14 avril 1350), v-5, w-111, 113, 119 ; *Lignages d'Outremer*, pp. 168–69 ; *Les familles d'Outre-Mer*, pp. 211–12 ; Rudt de Collenberg, « Les Lusignan de Chypre », p. 131.
57 *Bullarium Cyprium III*, nos w-155, 170 ; *Lignages d'Outremer*, p. 168 (où Jean du Morf est appelée « Joan de Montforte ») ; *Les familles d'Outre-Mer*, pp. 311–12 ; Rudt de Collenberg, « Les Lusignan de Chypre », pp. 142–43 ; Rudt de Collenberg, « Études de prosopographie », p. 573.
58 *Bullarium Cyprium III*, no v-121 ; *Lignages d'Outremer*, pp. 167–68 ; Rudt de Collenberg, « Les Lusignan de Chypre », pp. 134–35.
59 *Bullarium Cyprium III*, nos u-196, 276 ; Isabelle n'apparaît pas dans le tableau généalogique de Rudt de Collenberg, « Études de prosopographie », p. 571.
60 *Bullarium Cyprium III*, no u-231 ; Rudt de Collenberg, « Études de prosopographie », p. 566 (où Marie est appelée Marguerite).
61 Comme l'avait remarqué Rudt de Collenberg, « Les dispenses matrimoniales », pp. 53–54 ; Rudt de Collenberg, « Δομὴ καὶ προέλευση τῆς τάξεως τῶν εὐγενῶν », dans Ἱστορία τῆς Κύπρου, IV, pp. 805–06.
62 Cf. supra n. 30.

qui signe le traité du 13 août 1360.[63] La présence de médecins, également passés par une université italienne, illustre une orientation similaire, et le cas de Guido da Bagnolo, au service des Lusignan une dizaine d'années, révèle un autre long parcours avant le retour en Italie, aux côtés de Pierre 1er, en septembre 1363 ; plusieurs documents attestent que Guido est considéré comme un conseiller, ainsi, lors la mission à Gênes, début avril 1365, en compagnie de Pierre Thomas, ou à Rome, en mai 1368.[64]

Dans l'entourage de Pierre 1er, peu de personnages paraissent en définitive avoir été promus à une charge honorifique ouvrant l'accès au Conseil ; Philippe de Mézières succède à Ugo Ommebono / Ognibene de Mantoue comme chancelier du royaume de Chypre,[65] sans doute au tournant de l'année 1361, mais il réside peu à Nicosie, puisqu'il suit Pierre en Occident à partir d'octobre 1362 et en revient, trois ans plus tard, pour rejoindre l'expédition d'Alexandrie (octobre 1365), avant de regagner l'Occident à partir de juin 1366 ; la résidence à Chypre, limitée à trois années environ, s'explique par le fait que Philippe accomplit plusieurs missions diplomatiques pour le compte du roi, dont il devient un conseiller privé, à la fois inspirateur et ambassadeur zélé, que ce soit à Gênes, Milan, Avignon et Venise, où il s'installe en 1368.[66] Le cas de Pietro Malocello, élevé à la fonction de chambellan par le roi vers le début de l'année 1368, montre un autre cas de promotion exceptionnelle, celle d'un marchand génois qui, pour le compte du souverain, arme des galères et accomplit plusieurs missions à Avignon, en novembre 1361, mars 1365, 1369.[67]

---

63   Mas Latrie, *Histoire de l'île de Chypre*, II, p. 230.
64   Léontios Machairas, Χρονικό τῆς Κύπρου, pp. 143–44 ; Mas Latrie, *Histoire de l'île de Chypre*, II, pp. 254, 255 (« Guido de Regio, consiliarius regius ac scientie medicinalis doctor eximius »), 267, 302, 308 ; *Bullarium Cyprium III*, n[os] v-42, 118 ; *I libri commemoriali della republica di Venezia. Regesti*, III, p. 72, n° 425 ; Jorga, *Philippe de Mézières*, pp. 145, 152, 261, 264, 324 ; Livi, « Guido da Bagnolo, medico del re di Cipro » ; Edbury, *Kingdom of Cyprus*, p. 188 ; Franco Bacchelli, « Guido da Bagnolo », in *Dizionario biografico degli Italiani*, 61 (Rome : Treccani, 2004), pp. 388–90 ; Gilles Grivaud, « Literature », dans *Cyprus Society and Culture 1191–1374*, dir. Angel Nicolaou-Konnari et Chris Schabel, The Medieval Mediterranean, 58 (Leyde : Brill, 2005), pp. 228, 234–36 ; Gilles Grivaud, *Entrelacs chiprois. Essai sur les lettres et la vie intellectuelle dans le royaume de Chypre 1191–1570* (Nicosie : Moufflon, 2009), pp. 81–82.
65   Léontios Machairas, Χρονικό τῆς Κύπρου, p. 191 ; Philippe de Mézières, *The Life of Saint Peter Thomas*, éd. Joaquín Smet, Textus et studia carmelitana, 2 (Rome : Institutum Carmelitanum, 1954), p. 37 ; Jorga, *Philippe de Mézières*, p. 103. Philippe de Mézières conserve son titre de chancelier bien après son départ de Chypre, la dernière occurrence étant rapportée au 1er mars 1376 ou 1377 : Mas Latrie, « Nouvelles preuves » (1873), pp. 66–69, 76–78 ; Jean Richard, « La diplomatique royale dans le royaume d'Arménie et de Chypre (xiie–xve siècles) », *Bibliothèque de l'École des Chartes*, 144 (1968), pp. 77–78 (réimpr. dans Jean Richard, *Croisades et États latins d'Orient* (Londres : Variorum Reprints, 1992), n° XIX) ; Edbury, *Kingdom of Cyprus*, pp. 189–90 ; Nicolaou-Konnari, « Apologists or Critics ? », pp. 364–65.
66   Léontios Machairas, Χρονικό τῆς Κύπρου, pp. 143–44 ; *Bullarium Cyprium III*, n[os] v-28, 128, w-102, 106, 107, 187, 318 ; Mas Latrie, *Histoire de l'île de Chypre*, II, pp. 248–49, 254, 302, 308 ; Jorga, *Philippe de Mézières*, pp. 109, 128–29, 142, 152, 159, 206, 214–16, 232–51, 261, 284, 301, 321, 324, 327, 347, 381 ; Philippe Contamine, « Entre Occident et Orient. Philippe de Mézières (vers 1327–1405) : itinéraires maritimes et spirituels », dans *Philippe de Mézières and His Age*, pp. 21–31.
67   Léontios Machairas, Χρονικό τῆς Κύπρου, pp. 117, 126 (Pietro serait neveu du pape), 165, 172, 191 ; *Chronique d'Amadi*, p. 428 ; *Bullarium Cyprium III*, n[os] u-271, v-116 ; Mas Latrie, *Histoire de l'île de Chypre*, II, pp. 291, 302, 308 ; *I libri commemoriali della republica di Venezia. Regesti*, III, p. 72, n° 425 ; Mézières, *The Life of Saint Peter Thomas*, p. 169 ; *Les familles d'Outre-Mer*, pp. 632, 672 ; Jorga, *Philippe de Mézières*, pp. 151, 313.

Sans vouloir réduire l'importance du rôle tenu par le chancelier Philippe de Mézières ou par le chambellan Pietro Malocello, les émissaires envoyés en Occident par le roi restent, le plus souvent, choisis parmi les grands officiers. En juin 1360, Raymond Babin, le bouteiller, conduit une mission à Avignon, en compagnie de Pierre de Nores et du chevalier génois Jean de Carmayno ;[68] quelques mois plus tard, Jean du Morf, le maréchal, et Thomas de Montolif, l'auditeur, accomplissent le voyage de Venise et d'Avignon ;[69] Jean de Sur, l'amiral, se rend à Gênes et à Avignon durant l'été 1366, puis de nouveau à Gênes, au printemps 1367.[70] En mars de la même année, le turcoplier Jacques de Nores conduit l'ambassade au Caire, avant d'accompagner son roi à Rome au printemps 1368.[71]

Sans doute faudrait-il analyser plus finement la composition de l'entourage du roi pour déterminer si les familiers demeurés à ses côtés après les expéditions de Gorighos, de Satalie, d'Alexandrie ou de Tripoli, ont pu s'immiscer dans la conduite des affaires.[72] Que Pierre 1er prenne à son service des conseillers personnels, rétribués par des rentes et des fiefs, est assuré dans le cas de Guido da Bagnolo et de Philippe de Mézières,[73] mais ces nouveaux venus ont-ils contrebalancé le poids du Conseil dans l'élaboration de la politique de Pierre 1er ?[74] Au vu de l'évidence documentaire sauvegardée, on peut en douter, ce qui soulève la question de savoir jusqu'à quel point Pierre 1er fut le véritable auteur des axes de la politique suivie durant son règne. Circonscrit par l'héritage paternel et l'environnement familial, encadré par de grands officiers incarnant la cohésion du régime franc, le roi a respecté les équilibres initiaux, en s'appuyant notamment sur son Conseil pour gouverner, à l'instar des autres monarques de son époque. Les errances des derniers mois de sa vie ne sauraient, en conséquence, masquer de profondes continuités institutionnelles dans l'exercice du pouvoir, ni occulter que le gouvernement du royaume appartenait à des élites étroitement apparentées, formant bloc.

---

68 Léontios Machairas, Χρονικό τῆς Κύπρου, p. 118 ; *Bullarium Cyprium III*, n[os] u-230, 23 1 ; Edbury, *Kingdom of Cyprus*, p. 148.

69 Léontios Machairas, Χρονικό τῆς Κύπρου, p. 121 ; *Chronique d'Amadi*, p. 410 ; *Bullarium Cyprium III*, n° u-281 ; Edbury, *Kingdom of Cyprus*, p. 147.

70 Léontios Machairas, Χρονικό τῆς Κύπρου, p. 155 ; *Chronique d'Amadi*, p. 417 ; *Bullarium Cyprium III*, n° v-159 ; Jorga, *Philippe de Mézières*, pp. 305, 324.

71 Léontios Machairas, Χρονικό τῆς Κύπρου, p. 167 ; *I libri commemoriali della republica di Venezia. Regesti*, III, p. 72, n° 425 ; Jorga, *Philippe de Mézières*, p. 356 ; Edbury, *Kingdom of Cyprus*, pp. 148–49.

72 Peu d'évidences à relever à partir des noms cités dans les listes de participants aux diverses expéditions : Jorga, *Philippe de Mézières*, pp. 120, 277–80 ; Hardy, *Édition critique de la* Prise d'Alexandrie *de Guillaume de Machaut*, pp. 427–49.

73 Livi, « Guido da Bagnolo, medico del re di Cipro » ; Nicolae Jorga, « Le testament de Philippe de Mézières », *Bulletin de l'Institut pour l'étude de l'Europe sud-orientale*, 8 (1921), 119–40 (pp. 120–26) ; Nicolaou-Konnari, « Apologists or Critics ? », p. 364.

74 Jorga, *Philippe de Mézières*, p. 386, n. 5 ; Richard, « La révolution de 1369 », pp. 112–14 ; Edbury, « The Murder of King Peter I », p. 229.

JOHANNES PAHLITZSCH

The *Suriani* in Lusignan Cyprus until Peter I (1369)

Terminology, Legal Status, and the Curia Surianorum

The murder of Peter I (1359–69) and the Cypriot-Genoese war that ended with the cessation of Famagusta to Genoa in 1374 brought about fundamental changes in Cypriot society. Peter I had already initiated this change when he permitted the *perpyriarioi*, the Greek burgesses, to buy their freedom from the poll tax, which contributed to their social advancement. However, the overthrow of Peter's regime and particularly the ensuing war created a power vacuum in the elite that especially facilitated the rise of a number of wealthy Oriental Christians of various religious affiliations to high positions of power.[1] Cypriot sources from the end of the fourteenth century onwards designate all these Oriental Christians as *Suriani* or, similarly as *Sirici* or *Suriens*, even if they had been living on Cyprus for more than a century, and the highest social risers among them had converted to the Latin Church. The fifteenth-century Cypriot historian Leontios Makhairas counted, for example, the wealthy Nestorian merchant Francis Lakha among the *Syrianoi* ('Συριάνοι').[2] Furthermore, it seems that also in Venetian documents from the fifteenth century, Miaphysite Syrian Orthodox such as the Audeth family were regarded as *Sirici*, since in Venetian eyes they had immigrated to Cyprus from Syria, a term which in the fifteenth century was used to designate all Mamluk territories.[3]

---

[1] For this development, see the paper by Miriam Salzmann in this volume, to whom I am indebted for her support and her numerous suggestions in writing this paper.
[2] Leontios Makhairas, *Recital concerning the Sweet Land of Cyprus entitled 'Chronicle'*, ed. and trans. by Richard M. Dawkins, 2 vols (Oxford: Clarendon Press, 1932), I, § 92. Makhairas uses *Syrianoi* mainly for the Melkites but also sometimes for all Oriental Christians, see Angel Nicolaou-Konnari, 'Η ονοματολογία στα χειρόγραφα του Χρονικού του Λεοντίου Μαχαιρά', in *Αναδρομικά και Προδρομικά. Approaches to Texts in Early Modern Greek*, Papers from the Conference *Neograeca Medii Aevi* V (Exeter College, University of Oxford, September 2000), ed. by Elizabeth Jeffreys and Michael Jeffreys (Oxford: Sub-faculty of Modern Greek, Faculty of Medieval and Modern Languages, University of Oxford, 2005), pp. 327–71 (333, 366, 371).
[3] According to a Venetian document from 1448, see Louis de Mas Latrie, *Nouvelles preuves de l'histoire de Chypre sous le règne des princes de la maison de Lusignan*, 2 vols (Paris: J. Baur et Détaille, 1873–1874), II, p. 58. Jean Richard, 'Une famille de Vénitiens blancs dans le royaume de Chypre au milieu du xv^e

Johannes Pahlitzsch • Johannes Gutenberg University Mainz

In the period before these social upheavals however, the term *Suriani* as well as its equivalent terms seem to have had a more specific meaning that comprised only the Melkites, who were Chalcedonian Orthodox Christians belonging to the Byzantine Church and its Oriental Patriarchates, i.e., Antioch, Jerusalem, and Alexandria, and had for the most part been Arabic speaking since the end of the eighth century. However, scholarship is by no means in agreement concerning this development.[4] Moreover, the *Suriani* are said to have possessed a better legal status than other non-Latins in Cyprus, but it is unclear if this was really true and who exactly would have benefited from such a status. This paper, therefore, examines the development of the term *Suriani* until the crucial Cypriot-Genoese war as well as their legal status, focusing in particular on the so-called *curia Surianorum*, the jurisdiction of which remains obscure to this day.

Terminology

The terms *Suriani* or *Syri* in twelfth- and thirteenth-century Latin chronicles and pilgrim reports from the Kingdom of Jerusalem designated quite unambiguously Melkites.[5] In Syria and especially in Palestine and on the Sinai, the Melkites were

---

siècle: les Audeth et la seigneurie du Marethasse', *Rivista di studi bizantini e slavi*, 1 (1981), 89–129 (p. 95), demonstrates that the Audeth family were White Venetians. The Cypriot chronicles usually designate the Mamluk territories including Egypt as Syria, see, for example, Leontios Makhairas, *Recital*, I, § 646 and Georgios Boustronios, Διήγησις κρονίκας Κύπρου, ed. by Giorgos Kehagioglou, Texts and Studies in the History of Cyprus, 27 (Nicosia: Cyprus Research Center, 1997), p. 152.

4 Older literature suggests that the name *Suriani* always had a more inclusive meaning, see Jean Richard, 'Le peuplement latin et syrien en Chypre au XIIIe siècle', *Byzantinische Forschungen*, 7 (1979), 157–74 (repr. in Jean Richard, *Croisés, missionnaires et voyageurs: les perspectives orientales du monde latin médiéval*, Variorum Collected Studies Series, 182 (London: Ashgate, 1983), no. VII); Jean Richard, 'La Cour des Syriens de Famagouste d'après un texte de 1448', *Byzantinische Forschungen*, 12 (1987), 383–98 (pp. 383–86) (repr. in Jean Richard, *Croisades et états latins d'Orient. Points de vue et documents*, Variorum Collected Studies Series, 383 (Aldershot: Ashgate, 1992), no. XVII); and also Gilles Grivaud, 'Les minorités orientales à Chypre (époque médiévale et moderne)', in *Chypre et la Méditerranée orientale: formations, identitaires: perspectives historiques et enjeux contemporains. Actes du colloque tenu à Lyon, 1997, Université Lumière-Lyon 2, Université de Chypre*, ed. by Yiannis I. Ioannou, Françoise Métral, and Marguerite Yon, Travaux de la Maison de l'Orient méditerranéen, 31 (Lyons: Maison de l'Orient et de la Méditerranée Jean Pouilloux, 2000), pp. 43–70 (51–53).

5 The oldest Latin reference known to me of the Melkites' designation as a group of their own can be found in Charlemagne's 808 report of the churches and monasteries in the Holy Land, the *commemoratorium de casis Dei*, which offers a list of the hermits on the Mount of Olives grouped according to their liturgical language, citing among them six 'Syriani' as well as one 'Syrus' at the entrance to the mountain and another one in Gethsemane, see Michael McCormick, *Charlemagne's Survey of the Holy Land. Wealth, Personnel, and Buildings of a Mediterranean Church between Antiquity and the Middle Ages* (Washington, D.C.: Dumbarton Oaks Research Library and Collection, 2011), pp. 206–07, l. 19, 21 and Anna-Dorothee van den Brincken, *Die 'Nationes christianorum orientalium' im Verständnis der lateinischen Historiographie von der Mitte des 12. bis in die zweite Hälfte des 14. Jahrhunderts*, Kölner historische Abhandlungen, 22 (Cologne – Vienna: Böhlau, 1973), pp. 81–82. For numerous references in Latin texts to *Suriani*, be they clerics, bishops, or monks, in Syria and Palestine after 1187, including the travel reports of Wilibrand of

called *Suryānī* also in Arabic. In this context, however, the term did not derive from the toponym 'Syria'. Rather, it referred to the Melkites' use of Syriac as liturgical language until the thirteenth century and beyond.[6] The Miaphysite Syrian Orthodox called themselves *Sūryāyē* in Syriac or *Suryānī* in Arabic for the same reason. The Latin sources from the Kingdom of Jerusalem nevertheless differentiate between these Syrian Orthodox, who are designated as Jacobites, and the Melkites. Fidentius of Padua, who was the vicar of the Franciscan province of the Holy Land in the 1260s, is the only author known to me that calls all indigenous Christians *Suriani*, dividing them into the followers of the *ritum Grecorum* and *Jacobitarum*.[7]

The question arises whether this terminology was also valid in Cyprus in the thirteenth and fourteenth centuries up to the reign of Peter I. In order to answer this

---

Oldenburg and Magister Thietmar, see Johannes Pahlitzsch, *Graeci und Suriani im Palästina der Kreuzfahrerzeit: Beiträge und Quellen zur Geschichte des griechisch-orthodoxen Patriarchats von Jerusalem*, Berliner Historische Studien, 33 (Berlin: Duncker & Humblot, 2001), pp. 242–52 and Johannes Pahlitzsch, 'The People of the Book', in *Ayyubid Jerusalem. The Holy City in Context*, ed. by Robert Hillenbrand and Sylvia Auld (London: Altajir Trust, 2009), pp. 435–40. Jacques of Vitry, archbishop of Acre from 1216 to 1225, gave a very detailed description of the *Suriani*, which he differentiated from the Greeks because of their language; however, both groups agreed concerning doctrine and rite, see his *Histoire orientale = Historia orientalis*, ed. and French trans. by Jean Donnadieu (Turnhout: Brepols, 2008), chapter 75, pp. 294–304. See also van den Brincken, *Die 'Nationes christianorum orientalium'*, pp. 86–89 and Ilse Schöndorfer, *Orient und Okzident nach den Hauptwerken des Jakob von Vitry*, Europäische Hochschulschriften III, 743 (Frankfurt am Main: Peter Lang, 1997), pp. 83–86.

6 In Palestine and on the Sinai, the Melkites developed their own Christian Palestinian Aramaic dialect. In a Christian Arabic manuscript of 1164 (MS Sinaiticus Arab. 391), the author claimed that *suryānī filasṭīnī*, i.e., Christian Palestinian Aramaic, had been the language God used when speaking to Adam and hence the first-ever language. In the context of the second half of the twelfth century under the rule of the Crusaders, this statement has to be seen as a reminder to retain the identity and solidarity of one's own community, see Johannes Pahlitzsch, 'Some Remarks on the Use of Garšūnī and other Allographic Writing Systems by the Melkites', *Intellectual History of the Islamicate World*, 7 (2019), 278–98 (p. 283). The term 'Syrian Orthodox' in modern scholarship is reserved for the Miaphysite West Syrian Church. Its use for the Melkites, by analogy to 'Greek Orthodox', is thus confusing, as in Nicolas Coureas, 'The Syrian Melkites of the Lusignan Kingdom of Cyprus (1192–1474)', *Chronos*, 40 (2019), 75–94 (p. 75), or in Christopher Schabel, 'The Ecclesiastical History of Lusignan and Genoese Famagusta', in *Famagusta, Volume II, History and Society*, ed. by Gilles Grivaud, Angel Nicolaou-Konnari, and Chris Schabel, Mediterranean Nexus 1110–1700. Conflict, Influence and Inspiration in the Mediterranean Area, 8 (Turnhout: Brepols, 2020), pp. 297–362 (I am indebted to the author for providing me with a copy of his paper before its publication). In Christopher Schabel, 'Religion', in *Cyprus. Society and Culture 1191–1374*, ed. by Angel Nicolaou-Konnari and Christopher Schabel, The Medieval Mediterranean, 58 (Leiden and Boston: Brill, 2005), pp. 157–219 (169 and 209), one finds 'Syrian Melkite', which would designate a Melkite specifically from Syria which is misleading as the term *Surianus* does not have a geographical meaning in this context, as mentioned above. See also below.

7 Fidentius of Padua, *Liber recuperationis Terre Sancte*, in: *Projets de croisade (v. 1290–v. 1330)*, ed. Jacques Paviot, Documents relatifs à l'histoire des croisades, 20 (Paris: Académie des Inscriptions et Belles-Lettres, 2008), pp. 53–169 (cap. 9, p. 64), written in 1290/91; van den Brincken, *'Nationes christianorum orientalium'*, pp. 76–103, 210–30, and especially 222. In the region of the Principality of Antioch in northern Syria, the Latin term may have had a broader meaning (just as in the work of Fidentius of Padua), probably because Miaphysite Syrian Orthodox consituted a great part of the population, a fact that differentiated this part of Syria from the Kingdom of Jerusalem.

question, it is necessary to examine Latin as well as Greek sources from Cyprus. Let us begin with Latin ecclesiastical sources.[8] A papal letter from 1222 is the first Latin document regarding Cyprus to mention the *Suriani* beside the Miaphysite Syrian Orthodox (*Iacobini*), East Syrian Christians (*Nestorini*), and others who do not obey the Roman Church but wander as if 'headless' (*acephali*), i.e., without a bishop of their own, supported by their ancient sects and errors.[9] While the *Suriani* are obviously regarded as a different group from the Miaphysite Syrian Orthodox and the East Syrians, it seems that the papacy ranked them among the non-Chalcedonians and accordingly perceived them as heretics. This, however, is the only textual evidence for this attitude, which we may therefore consider to be a mistake due to the lack of experience or information about the situation in Cyprus on the side of the papacy at this early stage of Latin rule.

All later Latin ecclesiastical texts, instead, clearly saw *Suriani* and Greeks as part of one group, mentioning them together constantly.[10] In 1237, for example, Pope Gregory IX complained about the appointment of Greek and *Suriani baillis* as administrators of crown lands and nobles' estates,[11] and Innocent IV reported in 1250 that envoys from the Greek Church of Cyprus had petitioned that the tithes of the free *Suriani* and

---

8   Schabel, 'Religion', pp. 161–70, provides an overview of the references to *Suriani*.
9   *The Cartulary of the Cathedral of Holy Wisdom of Nicosia*, ed. by Nicholas Coureas and Christopher Schabel, Texts and Studies in the History of Cyprus, 25 (Nicosia: Cyprus Research Centre, 1997), no. 35, pp. 123–24, with a 1332 rubric adding Maronites; a new edition can be found in *Bullarium Cyprium I: Papal Letters Concerning Cyprus 1196–1261*, ed. by Christopher Schabel, with an Introduction by Jean Richard, Texts and Studies in the History of Cyprus, 64/1 (Nicosia: Cyprus Research Centre, 2010), no. c–41, pp. 233–34 (English translation in *The Synodicum Nicosiense and Other Documents of the Latin Church of Cyprus, 1196–1373*, selected and trans. by Christopher Schabel, Texts and Studies in the History of Cyprus, 39 (Nicosia: Cyprus Research Centre, 2001), no. X.9, p. 292).
10 As already pointed out by van den Brincken, '*Nationes christianorum orientalium*', pp. 84–88, the Latin lists of the different *nationes* in the Holy Land mention the *Suriani* or *Syri* as their own *natio* that nevertheless concurred with the Greeks with regard to their faith, see the pilgrim report of the Anonymus V of c. 1180: 'Alii sunt Suriani [...] Grecis in fide et sacramentis per omnia concordantes', in *Itinera Hierosolymitana crucesignatorum (saec. XII–XIII)*, III, ed. by Sabino de Sandoli, Studium Biblicum Franciscanum. Collectio major, 24 (Jerusalem: Franciscan Printing Press, 1983), p. 34 or Jacques de Vitry, *Histoire orientale. Historia orientalis*, ed. and trans. by Jean Donnadieu, Sous la règle de Saint Augustin, 12 (Turnhout: Brepols, 2008), p. 298: 'Consuetudines autem et institutiones Grecorum in divinis officiis et in aliis spiritualibus Suriani penitus observant et eis tanquam superioribus suis obediunt'. See also below n. 22. A later reflection of this description of the *Suriani* as a distinct *natio* of Greek, i.e. Chalcedonian Orthodox faith in Cyprus, can be found in the documentation of the miracles performed by Peter Thomas from the 1360s, where a certain 'Georgius nomine, natione Syrus, de secta Graecorum' is mentioned as a witness, Philippe de Mézières, *The Life of Saint Peter Thomas*, ed. by Joachim Smet, Textus et studia historica Carmelitana, 2 (Rome: Institutum Carmelitanum, 1954), p. 180 (I am indebted to Christopher Schabel for this reference). For the Miaphysite Syrian Orthodox on Cyprus in the thirteenth century, see the recently published study of Alice Croq, 'From Amida to Famagusta via Cairo: The Syrian Scribe Yūsuf ibn Sbāṭ in His Eastern Mediterranean Context c. 1350–1360', *Al-Masāq*, 33:3, 235-256, DOI: 10.1080/09503110.2020.1778892 (accessed 22.10.2020).
11 Louis de Mas Latrie, *Histoire de l'île de Chypre sous le règne des princes de la maison de Lusignan*, 3 vols (Paris: Imprimerie impériale, 1852–61), III, p. 642: 'balivos quoque Grecos et Surianos' (= *Bullarium Cyprium I*, no. d-27, pp. 320–22, with corrections to Louis de Mas Latrie).

Greeks in the Kingdom of Cyprus be completely relinquished.[12] The *Bulla Cypria* of 1260, which established the modus vivendi of the Greek Church under Latin rule, specified that this agreement was to be extended to the *Syri*, who shared mores, rites and the 'judgement of a shared law' ('communisque iuris censuram)' with the Greeks since ancient times.[13] Since there is no evidence for a Melkite bishop on Cyprus, the Melkites were apparently part of the Byzantine Orthodox Church organization, and the provisions of the *Bulla Cypria* indeed seem to have acknowledged that they were under the jurisdiction of the Greek episcopacy.[14]

Several papal complaints from the 1260s confirm this affiliation of the *Suriani* to the Greek Church, mentioning that Greeks and *Suriani* together did not obey to the rules of the *Bulla Cypria*.[15] The rulings of a provincial council that took place in 1280 and at which Archbishop Ranulph presided, state that the sacrament of penance was improperly imposed by the 'nationem Graecorum et Syriorum'. They threatened all 'Graecis et Syriis', be they bishops, priests, or laymen, with excommunication if they did not follow the regulations. According to this ruling, Greeks and *Suriani* constituted one community (*nationem*) that was regarded as part of one Church defined by their common doctrine based on the ecumenical council of Chalcedon.[16] A long dispute between the Greek and Latin bishops about jurisdiction over the *Suriani* from the year 1310 onwards shows how this perception still prevailed in the fourteenth century, at least on the Greek side. The matter was still discussed in Famagusta in the 1360s and then again in 1373.[17] Moreover, Latin reports of different processions

---

12 *Acta Innocenti IV PP. (1243–1254)*, ed. by Theodosius Haluščynskyj, Pontificia commissio ad redigendum Codicem Iuris Canonici Orientalis, Fontes ser. 3, 4,1 (Rome: Typis Pont. Univ. Gregoriana, 1962), no. 74, p. 131 (= *Bullarium Cyprium I*, no. e-42, pp. 381–85, trans. in *Synodicum Nicosiense*, no. X.18, p. 303); Schabel, 'Religion', p. 169.

13 *Cartulary*, no. 78, p. 202 (= *Bullarium Cyprium I*, no. f-35, p. 513, trans. in *Synodicum Nicosiense*, no. X.25, p. 320). Also see Chrysovalantis Kyriacou, *Orthodox Cyprus under the Latins, 1191–1571. Society, Spirituality, and Identities* (Lenham – Boulder – New York – London: Lexington Books, 2018), p. 17.

14 Nicholas Coureas, *The Latin Church in Cyprus 1313–1378*, Texts and Studies in the History of Cyprus, 65 (Nicosia: Cyprus Research Centre, 2010), p. 429.

15 *Bullarium Cyprium II: Papal Letters Concerning Cyprus 1261–1314*, ed. by Christopher Schabel, Texts and Studies in the History of Cyprus, 64/2 (Nicosia: Cyprus Research Centre, 2010), no g-2, pp. 4–6 (*c.* Sept. 1261); *Cartulary*, no. 11, pp. 95–99 and no. 79, pp. 205–08 (both 1263) (= *Bullarium Cyprium II*, no. g-6, pp. 8–14 and no. g-7, pp. 14–18, trans. in *Synodicum Nicosiense*, no. X.26, pp. 320–23); *Cartulary*, no. 75 (1263), pp. 184–86 (= *Bullarium Cyprium II*, no. g-9, pp. 21–23, trans. in *Synodicum Nicosiense*, no. X.27, pp. 324–25); *Bullarium Cyprium II*, g-29, pp. 48–51 (*c.* late 1263/early 1264); *Cartulary*, no. 76, pp. 186–90 and no. 77, pp. 190–94 (both 1264) (= *Bullarium Cyprium II*, no. g-27, pp. 39–44 and no. g-28, pp. 44–47, trans. in *Synodicum Nicosiense*, no. X.28, pp. 325–28); *Cartulary*, no. 106 (1267), pp. 269–70 (trans. in *Synodicum Nicosiense*, nos X. 29, pp. 328–29).

16 *Synodicum Nicosiense*, no. B.7.a, pp. 126–29. The use of the term *natio* was obviously not consistent with regard to the *Suriani*, see above n. 10.

17 The issue of the jurisdiction over the *Suriani* was discussed several times in the fourteenth century and it seems that various papal legates decided in favour of the Latin bishops. At least in theory, therefore, the Greeks lost the jurisdiction over the Syrians in the course of the fourteenth century, although we know nothing about the actual legal practice. According to Schabel, 'The Ecclesiastical History of Lusignan and Genoese Famagusta', p. 323, 'the real issue was simply jurisdiction over the new Syrians [who arrived after 1260], which the Latins claimed *de iure* but which the Greeks held *de facto*', since they were not covered

and religious festivals from the fourteenth century may serve as an argument *ex negativo*. While Greeks, Armenians, 'Nestorians', 'Jacobites', and other Christians are regularly mentioned in these texts as participating in processions, the *Suriani* are absent.[18] Since it is not likely that they never took part in these events, it seems that Latin ecclesiastical authors by this time perceived the *Suriani* as members of the Greek community.[19]

Latin and French legal literature, too, seems to have used the term *Surianus* or *Suriens* for Melkites and connected them to the Greeks. To be precise, actual legal documents from the period under investigation, such as deeds or testaments, seldom mention *Suriani* at all and if so, they do not provide any information on their religious affiliation.[20] In contrast, the different collections of the laws of the Kingdom of Jerusalem, which were mostly written in the middle of the thirteenth century in Old

---

by the rulings of *the Bulla Cypria* according to the Latins. See also a letter from Pope John XXII to bishop Baldwin of Famagusta dated 1321, *Acta Ioannis XXII (1317–1334)*, Pontificia Commissio ad redigendum Codicem Iuris Canonici Orientalis, Fontes ser. 3, 7,2, ed. by Aloysius L. Tăutu (Rome: Typis Pont. Univ. Gregoriana, 1952), no. 37, p. 76, registered in *Bullarium Cyprium III: Lettres papales relatives à Chypre, 1316–1378*, ed. Charles Perrat and Jean Richard, with the collaboration of Christopher Schabel, Sources et études de l'histoire de Chypre, 68 (Nicosia: Centre de Recherche Scientifique, 2012) no. r-107, p. 59 (trans. in *Synodicum Nicosiense*, no. X.39, p. 348), in which John requests that Baldwin should admonish the Greeks and the *Syri* not to worship the Eucharistic bread and wine before its consecration; see Coureas, *The Latin Church in Cyprus 1313–1378*, p. 431. On the basis of the ecclesiastical texts, Schabel, 'Religion', p. 169, concludes: 'Syrian Melkites had been on Cyprus for a long time, were factors in the rural and urban economy, preserved a separate identity, and yet were united with the Greeks religiously'.

18 See for example Philip of Mézières's eyewitness account of the procession of 1362 that was conducted because of a wave of the plague: 'Certe ibi erant Graeci, Armeni, Nothorini (Nestorians), Jacobini, Georgiani, Nubiani, Indiani, Aethiopiani, et alii multi Christiani' who all had different rites and languages, Philippe de Mézières, *The Life of Saint Peter Thomas*, pp. 100 and 156 for a similar list of participants at the funeral of Peter Thomas. See Schabel, 'Religion', pp. 156–60 and Schabel, 'The Ecclesiastical History of Lusignan and Genoese Famagusta', pp. 314–15. James of Verona, who visited Nicosia in 1335, lists 'Greeks, Jacobites, Armenians, Georgians, Maronites, and Nestorians', Reinhold Röhricht, 'Le pèlerinage du moine Augustin Jacques de Vérone (1335)', *Revue de L'Orient latin*, 3 (1895), 155–302 (p. 178). See Grivaud, 'Les minorités orientales', pp. 49–50.

19 Coureas, 'The Syrian Melkites', p. 85, assumes erroneously that the reference in a 1365 letter addressed by Pope Urban V to 'Grecos, Syros seu Sorianos' must mean 'Greeks, Syrians, or Nestorians' as three separate groups; it rather indicates that both terms, 'Syrus' and 'Surianus', could be used interchangeably, see *Urbain V (1362–1370): Lettres communes analysées d'après les registres dits d'Avignon et du Vatican*, ed. by Marie-Hyacinthe Laurent, Michel Hayez, Mathieu Janine, and Anne-Marie Hayez, Bibliothèque des Écoles Françaises d'Athènes et de Rome, série 3, 12 vols (Paris: Boccard – Rome: École française, 1954–89), IV, no. 15019, p. 403 (also in *Acta Urbani PP. V (1362–1370)*, ed. by Aloysius L. Tăutu, Pontificia commissio ad redigendum Codicem Iuri Canonici Orientalis, Fontes ser. 3, 11 (Rome: Typis Pont. Univ. Gregoriana, 1964), no. 72, p. 119 and in *Bullarium Cyprium III*, no. v-112, p. 394). Schabel, *Synodicum Nicosiense*, no. X.58, p. 369, translates this passage accordingly, albeit in an abbreviated fashion, as 'Greek and Syrian'.

20 To complicate matters even more, sometimes Christian individuals mentioned in documents are referred to as *Suriani* by scholars solely on the basis of their Arabic name, as in the case of two bakers of Psimolophou in a document dated 1317, see Jean Richard, 'Le casal de Psimolofo et la vie rurale en Chypre au XIVᵉ siècle', *Mélanges d'Archéologie et d'Histoire publiés par l'École Française de Rome*, 59 (1947), 121–53 (pp. 135, 141) (repr. in Jean Richard, *Les relations entre l'Orient et l'Occident au Moyen Age*, Variorum Collected Studies Series, 69 (London: Ashgate, 1977), no. IV); see Richard, 'Le peuplement', p. 168.

French and were also applied in Cyprus, contain quite a few references to the *Suriens*.[21] John of Ibelin (c. 1216–66) wrote his *Livre des Assises* between 1265 and 1266. Like the ecclesiastical authors, he differentiated the Melkite *Suriens* from the Miaphysite Syrian Orthodox, the *Jacopins*.[22] The so-called *Cour de la Fonde*, the court of the market of Acre, heard cases concerning 'un Surien ou un Jude ou un Sarasin ou un Samaritan ou un Nestorin ou un Grifon ou un Jacopin ou un Ermine'.[23] Moreover, Philip of Novara in his *Livre de Forme de Plait*, written between 1249 and 1253 in Cyprus, distinguished Greeks and *Suriens* from all other non-Frankish Christians.[24] In the *Livre des Assises de la Cour des Bourgeois* that was probably written between 1229 and 1244 in the Kingdom of Jerusalem but also applied on Cyprus, we find several paragraphs discussing who could testify as bearer of warranty against whom. While one chapter stipulates that neither a Greek (*Grifon*) nor a *Suriens*[25] could testify against an Armenian (and the other way round), the following chapters do not mention the Greeks but rule that the *Suriens* could not be bearers of warranty against a *Nestourin, Jacobin, Samaratin*, a Muslim or a Jew. Moreover, there is no regulation providing that Greeks and *Suriens* are excluded from testifying against each other, so it is obvious that they are regarded as belonging to the same group before the law.[26]

It is true that these laws actually originated from the Kingdom of Jerusalem and it is not clear to what extent they reflect the situation in Cyprus.[27] They were, though, certainly used in the Lusignan Kingdom and their language shaped later texts. In a royal ban issued in Cyprus in 1299 or 1300, the viscount is ordered to summon every *Grifon* or *Surien* who claims to be a member of the clergy before the vicar of the Greeks ('vicaire des Grés') in order to pass judgment on him.[28] This text therefore confirms

---

21 For the Cypriot legal literature, see Gilles Grivaud, 'Literature', in *Cyprus. Society and Culture*, pp. 219–84 (246–57).
22 John of Ibelin, *Le Livre des Assises*, ed. by Peter. W. Edbury, The Medieval Mediterranean, 50 (Leiden: Brill, 2003), chapter 58, p. 167: The 'nacion qui ne sont obeissans a Rome: gres ne suriens ne ermins ne jacopins' could not be witnesses before the High Court.
23 *Livre des Assises de la Cour de Bourgeois*, ed. by Comte Auguste Beugnot, Recueil des historiens des croisades (hereafter RHC): Lois, II (Paris, 1843), pp. 4–226 (chapter 241, p. 171). The heading of chapter 243 (p. 178) should not be understood to mean that all Oriental Christians were *Suriens*, it rather shows the importance of language as an identity marker: 'Ici orrés où fu estably et coumandé […] où devent estre et maner en la cité les Grifons et les Suriens et les Jacobins et les Nestorins et les Mosserins et les Ermines et toutes autres langles Surienes'. It is unclear if Syriac or rather Arabic was meant by 'langles Surienes'.
24 'Mais encontre Gres et Suriens et tous autres Crestiens qui ne sont de la ley de Rome pevent porter garentie les gens de leur lei, […]', Philip of Novara, *Le Livre de Forme de Plait*, ed. and English trans. by Peter W. Edbury, Texts and Studies in the History of Cyprus, 61 (Nicosia: Cyprus Research Centre, 2009), chapter 28, p. 80 (translation at p. 237). This chapter was adopted with some changes in the *Livre contrefais* that was written at the beginning of the fourteenth century in Cyprus, see *Abrégé du Livre des Assises de la Cour des Bourgeois*, ed. by Comte Auguste Beugnot, in RHC: Lois, II, pp. 225–352 (chapter 24, p. 325; also see chapter 11, p. 306).
25 *Livre des Assises de la Cour de Bourgeois*, chapter 62, p. 54.
26 *Livre des Assises de la Cour de Bourgeois*, chapters 63–65, pp. 54–56; see Angel Nicolaou-Konnari, 'Greeks', in *Cyprus. Society and Culture*, pp. 13–62 (23).
27 Nicolaou-Konnari, 'Greeks', pp. 21–23.
28 *Bans et ordonnances des rois de Chypre*, in RHC: Lois, II, no. XIV.1, p. 364.

that Greeks and *Suriens* were seen as two groups that constituted one community with a common jurisdiction also in Cyprus.

Concerning the Greek usage of the term *Syrianoi*, a broader survey of its presence in Byzantine texts is appropriate here. *Syrianoi* or *Syroi* could have a wide variety of meanings in earlier Byzantine texts. According to Koray Durak's study of the terms Syria and Syrian in Byzantine writings from the eighth to the eleventh centuries, Syrian was in general a neutral term for people from Syria without any ethnic or religious connotation. It could, however, acquire a specific meaning in a certain context or when qualified with further explanations, such as in the case of the Miaphysite Syrian Orthodox.[29] Thus, Demetrios of Kyzikos reports in his tract on heretics (written between 1026 and 1028) that a schism emerged between the Syrians ('ἐν τοῖς Σύροις') because of the preaching of Jacob Baradaeus. Those who remained loyal to Orthodoxy 'were called *Melchitai* ('Μελχῖται'), i.e., the imperial ones ('βασιλικοί'), because the emperor (βασιλεύς) is called *Melchi* ('Μελχί') by the Hebrews and the Syrians ('Σύροις') [...] And those who believe in the monk Jacob, the Syrian, are named Jacobites ("Ἰακωβῖται")'.[30] While the reference to the Syrians seems to have primarily a geographical meaning but also, perhaps, a linguistic one, the term acquires a religious connotation by the designation of the Miaphysite Jacob Baradaeus as 'the Syrian'. This allusion is more evident in Theorianos's report on a religious disputation he had on behalf of Manuel I Komnenos in 1171 with the Armenians and the Syrian Orthodox. Among others, Theorianos conversed with a certain Theodoros, who was the representative 'of the Catholicos of the Jacobites, i.e., the Syrians' ('τοῦ Καθολικοῦ τῶν Ἰακωβιτῶν ἤτοι Σύρων').[31]

At the same time, Byzantine writings of the twelfth century usually designated Melkites as well as *Syroi* (Σύροι). The founder's *Typikon* of the Sabas Monastery near Jerusalem was most likely composed in its current form in the twelfth century for a monastery consisting of two groups, Greeks and *Syroi*, by which name the text clearly meant Melkites.[32] In the account of the attempt of the Greek patriarch of

---

29 Koray Durak, 'The Location of Syria in Byzantine Writing: One Question, Many Answers', *Journal of Turkish Studies*, 36 (2011), 45–55 (pp. 53–55).

30 Demetrios of Kyzikos, Περὶ αἱρέσεως τῶν Ἰακωβιτῶν καὶ τῶν Κατζιτζαρίων, in *Patrologiae cursus completus. Series Graeca* (hereafter *PG*), ed. by Jacques-Paul Migne, 161 vols (Paris: J.-P. Migne, 1857–66), CXXVII (1864), cols 880–902 (881); see Zachary Chitwood, 'The Patriarch Alexios Stoudites and the Reinterpretation of Justinianic Legislation against Heretics', *Greek, Roman and Byzantine Studies*, 54 (2014), 293–312 (pp. 300–01 and n. 22 for the authorship attributed to Demetrios of Kyzikos instead of Philippus Solitarius as stated in the edition).

31 Theorianos, 'Disputatio secunda cum Nersete patriarcha generali Armeniorum', in *PG*, CXXXIII (1864), cols 211–98 (277).

32 Eduard Kurtz, 'Τύπος καὶ παράδοσις καὶ νόμος τῆς σεβασμίας λαύρας τοῦ ἁγίου Σάββα', *Byzantinische Zeitschrift*, 3 (1894), 166–70 (pp. 168–70); English translation in *Byzantine Monastic Foundation Documents. A Complete Translation of the Surviving Founders' Typika and Testaments*, trans. by John Thomas and Angela Constantinides Hero, 5 vols (Washington, D.C.: Dumbarton Oaks Research Library and Collection, 2000), IV, no. 42, pp. 1311–18 (1312–13); Daniel Galadza, *Liturgy and Byzantinization in Jerusalem* (Oxford: Oxford University Press, 2018), pp. 97–98, suggests that the twelfth-century version of the *typikon* is based on a much older original text.

Jerusalem Leontios II (1176–85) to return to Jerusalem, the reason for Leontios' failure to establish himself permanently there was that, in the face of the strong resistance of the Latin Church, 'he considered it more profitable to sail away from there lest anything untoward be mischievously concocted because of him between the Orthodox Romans (i.e., Byzantines) and Syrians ('ὀρθοδοξούντων Ῥωμαίων καὶ Σύρων'), on the one hand, and the Latin rulers, on the other, [...]'.[33] The epithet *Orthodox* here expresses the contrast between the Byzantines and the Melkites, on the one hand, and the Latin Church, on the other.[34] At the end of the twelfth century, the Melkite Patriarch of Alexandria Markos asked the synod of Constantinople if the Orthodox Syrians ('ὀρθοδόξους Σύρους') could celebrate the liturgy in their own language or if they were forced to celebrate in Greek.[35] Markos obviously petitioned on behalf of his Melkite community in Egypt. The designation *Syroi*, qualified by the epithet *Orthodox*, had, therefore, no geographical connotation in this context.

Syros was also used in the sense of Melkite with reference to Cyprus. In his second letter to the Cypriots in 1229, Patriarch Germanos II of Constantinople addressed *Rhomaioi* and *Syroi*, both lovers of orthodoxy.[36] The official Greek translation of the *Bulla Cypria*, certified by a notary in 1287, translated the Latin 'ad Syros' as 'τοῖς Σύροις'.[37] Furthermore, in a note in the codex Vaticanus Palatinus graecus 367, datable to *c.* 1320, it is mentioned that a certain Syr Bertran died in 1320 and was buried in the church of the Theotokos *tōn Syrōn* ('τῶν Σύρων'), probably in Paphos.[38] And in an obituary of the Greek Orthodox Monastery of the Hiereon near Paphos, two *Syroi* were listed as members of the monastery: Thomas the *Syros*, a scribe (*grammatikos*) of Paphos ('Θωμᾶς ὁ γραμματικὸς τῆς Πάφου ὁ Σῦρος'), whose monastic name was

---

33 *The Life of Leontios, Patriarch of Jerusalem, Text, Translation, Commentary*, ed. by Dimitris Tsougarakis, The Medieval Mediterranean, 2 (Leiden – New York – Cologne: Brill, 1993), § 88, pp. 138–39, written by Theodosios Goudeles at the beginning of the thirteenth century (p. 18).

34 Accordingly, Theophanes Confessor, *Chronographia*, ed. Karl de Boor (Leipzig: Teubner, 1883), p. 452, qualifies the Miaphysite Syrian Orthodox as 'τοὺς αἱρετικοὺς Σύρους'.

35 Theodoros Balsamon, ''Ερωτήσεις κανονικαί', in Σύνταγμα τῶν θείων καὶ ἱερῶν κανόνων τῶν τε ἁγίων καὶ πανευφήμων ἀποστόλων καὶ τῶν ἱερῶν οἰκουμενικῶν καὶ τοπικῶν συνόδων, ed. by Georgios A. Rhalles and Michael Potles, 7 vols (Athens: G. Chartophylax, 1852–59; repr. 1966), IV, pp. 447–96 (452–53); English translation by Patrick D. Viscuso, *Guide for a Church under Islām* (Brookline: Holy Cross Orthodox Press, 2014), p. 74. See Johannes Pahlitzsch, 'Greek - Syriac - Arabic: The Relationship between Liturgical and Colloquial Languages in Melkite Palestine in the Twelfth and Thirteenth Centuries', in *Languages and Cultures of Eastern Christianity: Greek*, ed. by Scott F. Johnson, The Worlds of Eastern Christianity, 300–1500, 6, (Farnham: Ashgate, 2015), pp. 495–505 (503–04).

36 Germanos II of Constantinople, ''Επιστολὴ β'', in *Bibliotheca Graeca Medii Aevi*, ed. by Constantinos N. Sathas, 7 vols (Venice: Typois tou Chronou, 1872–73 – Paris: Maisonneuve et Cie: 1872–94; repr. Hildesheim: Olms Verlag, 1972), II, pp. 14–19 (14, 19).

37 Jean Darrouzès, 'Textes synodaux chypriotes', *Revue des études byzantines*, 37 (1979), 5–122 (p. 83); Georgios A. Ioannides, 'La *Constitutio o Bulla Cypria Alexandri Papae IV* del Barberinianus graecus 390', *Orientalia Christiana Periodica*, 66 (2000), 335–72 (p. 365).

38 *Griechische Briefe und Urkunden aus dem Zypern der Kreuzfahrerzeit*, ed. by Alexander D. Beihammer, Texts and Studies in the History of Cyprus, 57 (Nicosia: Zyprisches Forschungszentrum, 2007), no. 105.9, pp. 238, 310 (German translation). The editor also assumes that this Bertran was a Melkite because he obviously had a connection to the Greek Sekretikoi family to whom the manuscript can be attributed, ibid., 371 n. 214.

Theodosios and who died in 1294, and Isaias the *Syros*, who was the *metochiarios* of the monastery's metochion in Nicosia and died in 1308.[39]

The Greek *Syrianos*, which is obviously a transliteration of the Arabic *suryānī*, had a more specific meaning than the general term *Syros*, which could vary according to context. In a letter from the year 1232 to the cardinals of Rome, Patriarch Germanos II disputed the claim of the Church of Rome to be the 'mother of all Churches' by giving a list of the many 'peoples' ('ἔθνη') that were of the same mind as and in communion with the Greeks: the first in the East were the *Aithiopes*, then all the *Syrianoi*, farther in the north the Iberians (i.e., Georgians) but also others, such as the Goths, the Russians, or the Bulgarians. They all obeyed the Church of Constantinople like a mother, remaining unshaken in their orthodoxy.[40] It seems, therefore, that the term *Syrianoi* is chosen deliberately to distinguish the Melkites from the Miaphysite Syrian Orthodox. The same may hold true for two individuals called *ho Syrianos* ('ὁ Συριανός'): a certain priest Georgios the *Syrianos* witnessed a document from Patmos dated 1288,[41] and Ioannes the *Syrianos*, a member of the Greek upper class in Crete, was the recipient of a letter by Joseph Bryennios.[42] Even if *Syrianos* in these cases rather functions as a family name, it seems safe to assume that these families were of Melkite origin.

Legal Status

According to Leontios Makhairas, many *Syrianoi* from the Crusader States settled in Cyprus under the rule of Guy de Lusignan, who granted them the right to pay only half of the fees for buying and selling and none of the dues the indigenous population had to pay.[43] It is generally assumed that the Melkite settlers received these privileges because they enjoyed them already in the Crusader States.[44] It seems, though, far-fetched that all *Syrianoi* who settled on Cyprus later were treated in this way on the

---

39 Jean Darrouzès, 'Un obituaire chypriote: le Parisinus graecus 1588', Κυπριακαὶ Σπουδαί, 15 (1951), 23–62 (pp. 53, 31). See Erich Trapp, Rainer Walther, and Hans-Veit Beyer, *Prosopographisches Lexikon der Palaiologenzeit*, 12 vols, Addenda, Gesamtregister (Vienna: ÖAW Verlag, 1976–96) (hereafter PLP), XI, nos 27225–26.

40 Christos Arambatzes, 'Ἀνέκδοτη ἐπιστολὴ τοῦ Πατριάρχη Κωνσταντινουπόλεως Γερμανοῦ Β' πρὸς τοὺς Καρδιναλίους τῆς Ῥώμης (1232)', Ἐπετηρὶς Ἑταιρείας Βυζαντινῶν Σπουδῶν, 52 (2004–06), 363–78 (p. 377).

41 Maria Nystazopoulou-Pelekidou, Βυζαντινὰ ἔγγραφα τῆς μονῆς Πάτμου, 2. Δημοσίων λειτουργῶν, 2 vols (Athens: Institute of Byzantine Research, National Research Foundation, 1980), I, no. 75, p. 227 ('Γεώργιος ἱερεὺς ὁ Συριανὸς ὑπέγραψα').

42 Nikolaos B. Tomadakes, ''Ιωσὴφ μοναχοῦ τοῦ Βρυεννίου ἐπιστολαὶ Λ' καὶ αἱ πρὸς αὐτόν Γ'', Ἐπετηρὶς Ἑταιρείας Βυζαντινῶν Σπουδῶν, 46 (1983–86), 279–364 (p. 352); Raymond-Joseph Loenertz, 'Pour la chronologie des œuvres de Joseph Bryennios', *Revue des études byzantines*, 7 (1949), 12–32 (p. 23).

43 Leontios Makhairas, *Recital*, I, § 26: 'And also to the Syrians he granted that they should pay in all cases the half of the fees due for buying and selling, and whatever dues the natives paid they were not to pay'.

44 Jean Richard, 'Οἱ πολιτικοὶ καὶ κοινωνικοὶ θεσμοὶ τοῦ μεσαιωνικοῦ βασιλείου' and Giorgio Fedalto, ''Η Λατινικὴ Ἐκκλησία στὸ μεσαιωνικὸ βασίλειο', in Ἱστορία τῆς Κύπρου, ed. by Theodoros Papadopoullos, 6 vols (Nicosia: Archbishop Makarios III Foundation, 1995–2011), IV, Μεσαιωνικὸν βασίλειον - Ἐνετοκρατία, pp. 333–74 (360–62) and 667–732 (681–82) respectively.

basis of just this reference. Jean Richard even claimed that the *Syrianoi* on Cyprus had a different legal status than the Greek population because they did not have to pay the poll-tax and were thus regarded as free.[45] While it seems likely that the *Suriani*, just as other non-Latin Christians, never paid a poll-tax in the Kingdom of Jerusalem,[46] Richard's assumption for Cyprus is founded solely on Makhairas, who indeed speaks of the grant of freedoms and liberties of enfranchisement in the passage just mentioned, but with regard to Franks of lower rank and not to the *Syrianoi*, who are mentioned only in the next sentence.[47] Furthermore, we have to keep in mind that Makhairas wrote in the fifteenth century, and that, at least according to Grivaud, the version of the chronicle we have today may have taken shape only in the sixteenth century.[48] We should therefore be skeptical about the information conveyed here.

Similarly, Peter Edbury's interpretation of Philip of Novara's chapter on the procedure for establishing boundaries as an expression of 'a legal pecking-order determined by religion' is not satisfactory. This chapter rules that in cases where local inhabitants had to take an oath to determine the boundaries of a certain property, first a Frank should be asked. 'If they do not find a *Franc* of the *loi de Rome*, and they find a *Surien* whom they consider worthy of faith [...] they should follow him. If they do not find a *Surien* and they find a Greek, similarly'. If they do not find a Greek, other Christians and finally Muslims should be asked. Obviously, this procedure originated in the Kingdom of Jerusalem, where the indigenous Melkites were, at least in certain areas, a majority, and most likely had better local knowledge than Greek clerics or monks. It seems thus far fetched to build the argument for a general legal superiority of the *Suriens* over the Greeks in Cyprus on this quite specific case. And, actually, in the case of the compensation for an assault, *Suriens* and Greeks (as well as serfs) had the same status: they were all due half of the amount that had to be paid if the victim was a Frank.[49]

---

45 See Jean Richard's statement in his still influential paper 'La Cour des Syriens', p. 386, that 'les Syriens étaient considérés comme libres (*miamoun*)'; cf. n. 47 below.

46 Jonathan Riley-Smith, 'Government and the Indigenous in the Latin Kingdom of Jerusalem', in *Medieval Frontiers: Concepts and Practices*, ed. by David Abulafia and Nora Berend (Aldershot: Ashgate, 2002), pp. 121–31 (129), points out that there is at least no evidence that they ever did.

47 Leontios Makhairas, *Recital*, I, § 26, p. 24: 'Καὶ τοὺς πιὸν χαμηλοὺς ἐποῖκεν τους νὰ ἔχουν ἐλευθερίες μιαμουνάτα διὰ νὰ φριαντζιάζουν'. Interestingly, the whole § 26 and the beginning of § 27 of Makhairas's text, which deal with the measures taken by Guy de Lusignan to attract people to settle on Cyprus, are missing in manuscript Venet. Marc. Gr. VII, 16, 1080, which is regarded as the one closest to the original version of the chronicle; see Leontios Makhairas, *Χρονικό τῆς Κύπρου. Παράλληλη διπλωματική ἔκδοση τῶν χειρογράφων*, ed. by Michalis Pieris and Angel Nicolaou-Konnari, Texts and Studies in the History of Cyprus, 48 (Nicosia: Cyprus Research Centre, 2003), pp. 27–42, for the manuscript tradition of the text, and pp. 78–79, for the diplomatic edition of this passage according to the three manuscripts.

48 Gilles Grivaud, *Entrelacs chiprois: essai sur les lettres et la vie intellectuelle dans le royaume de Chypre, 1191–1570* (Nicosia: Moufflon Publications, 2009), p. 188.

49 Philip of Novara, *Le livre de forme de plait*, ed. and English trans. by Peter W. Edbury (Nicosia: Cyprus Research Centre, 2009), chapters 53, 60, pp. 132, 148, 267 (translation); Peter W. Edbury, 'Latins and Greeks on Crusader Cyprus', in *Medieval Frontiers*, pp. 133–42 (137). For case studies of the population distribution in the Kingdom of Jerusalem, see Ronnie Ellenblum, *Frankish Rural Settlement in the Latin Kingdom of Jerusalem* (Cambridge: Cambridge University Press, 1998), esp. pp. 119–44, 234–52, who,

In contrast, there is evidence that *Suriani* and Greeks in Cyprus were governed by the same ecclesiastical courts.[50] The *Bulla Cypria* made it quite clear that *Syri* and Greeks shared a law since ancient times ('communisque iuris censuram ab antiquo servantes'), as mentioned above.[51] The codex Vaticanus Palatinus graecus 367, in turn, contains a final judgement by the bishop of Solea/Nicosia Leontios on the marriage annulment between Theodora, the daughter of Konstantinos Sekretikos, and Thomas, son of Zakē (for Arabic Zakī) David who must have been a Melkite, since his family apparently belonged to the same religious community as Theodora's and was of Near Eastern origin. The procedure described in this document follows the manual of the Greek episcopal court of Paphos/Arsinoe in the codex Parisinus graecus 1391 from the beginning of the fourteenth century,[52] demonstrating that this manual was based on actual legal practice. Moreover, the case shows that the Greek episcopal court was also competent for cases involving Greeks and *Suriani*, in accordance with the ruling of the *Bulla Cypria*. Even the personnel involved in these cases may have consisted partly of *Suriani*: Thomas' representative was obviously a Melkite, namely the priest and *deutereuon* (i.e., the deputy of the *protopresbyteros*) of the Greek archiepiscopal Church Ioannes ʿAbd al-Masīḥ.[53] And maybe the above-mentioned *Syros* Thomas, the *grammatikos* of Paphos, was employed as scribe at the episcopal court of Paphos.[54]

In 1321, the Greek bishops of Solea/Nicosia and Lefkara filed a petition to pope John XXII that confirms the above observations. It concerned the already mentioned dispute on the jurisdiction over the *Suriani*. The two bishops maintained that, according to the ruling of the *Bulla Cypria*, the *Suriani* living in the kingdom were subject to the jurisdiction of the Greek bishops. The Greek bishops 'were to decide on the confirmation of the elections of the abbots of the Syrians' and were in possession of the right 'of hearing the marriage cases which would occasionally

---

however, misunderstands the term *Surianus* used in the property documents referred to in his study as encompassing all indigenous Oriental Christians, be they Chalcedonians or not. Regarding the legal status of the *Suriani*, recent scholarship is more cautious, see, for example, Nicolaou-Konnari, 'Greeks', p. 27.

50 In contrast to the opinion of Richard, 'La Cour des Syriens', p. 386, who claimed that the 'Syriens' had their own courts while being vague about who these 'Syriens' were.

51 *Cartulary*, no. 78, p. 202 (= *Bullarium Cyprium I*, no. f-35, p. 513, trans. in *Synodicum Nicosiense*, no. X.25, p. 320).

52 *Zyprische Prozessprogramme*, ed. by Dieter Simon (Munich: C. H. Beck, 1973); Christopher Schabel, 'The Status of the Greek Clergy in Early Frankish Cyprus', in *"Sweet Land ... " Lectures on the History and Culture of Cyprus*, ed. by Julian Chrysostomides and Charalambos Dendringos (Camberley: Porphyrogenitus, 2006), pp. 165–207 (196–97) (repr. in Christopher Schabel, *Greeks, Latins, and the Church in Early Frankish Cyprus*, Variorum Collected Studies, 949 (Farnham: Ashgate, 2010), no. I).

53 *Griechische Briefe und Urkunden*, no. 93, pp. 224–25 (German translation, pp. 299–300) and n. 161 at p. 361, where Beihammer convincingly argues that Thomas must have been a Melkite since also his representative Ioannes ʿAbd al-Masīḥ was a Melkite priest. See Schabel, 'Religion', p. 209 and Angel Nicolaou-Konnari, 'Women in Medieval Famagusta: Law, Family, and Society', in *Famagusta, Volume II, History and Society*, pp. 509–633 (528–30) (I am very grateful to the author for allowing me access to this important publication before its publication).

54 See n. 39 above.

arise among said Syrians or between them and the Greeks [...]'.[55] Concerning matters of canon law, Greeks and *Suriani* were evidently governed by the same Greek episcopal courts until the beginning of the fourteenth century. In the following years, the question of ecclesiastical jurisdiction was disputed but apparently still not resolved by 1373.[56]

The Cours des Suriens *in the Kingdom of Jerusalem and the Cypriot* curia Surianorum

According to the manual of the Parisinus graecus 1391, the Greek episcopal courts were competent also for secular matters of property transactions, loans, and other issues. They thus became 'a kind of arbitration tribunal for every kind of litigation between Greeks' according to Angel Nicolaou-Konnari.[57] But did these courts have jurisdiction also over the *Suriani* in matters of secular law? Louis de Mas Latrie assumed as early as the nineteenth century that the so-called *Cour des Suriens* was a separate court for *Suriens* civil law matters in Cyprus.[58] Jean Richard shared this opinion. He claimed that the *Suriens* followed their own customs in matters of private law and—just as in the Kingdom of Jerusalem—had their own courts for the application of these laws; in his view, these Syrian courts should not be confused with the Greek ones.[59]

It therefore seems worthwhile to reexamine the origins of the *Cour des Suriens* in the Crusader States. According to John of Ibelin's most likely legendary description, after the Frankish conquest of Jerusalem in 1099, the *Suriens* requested that Godfrey of Bouillon grant them their own court, which would regulate all of their internal disputes, with the exception of capital offences. This court designated as *Cour des Suriens* consisted of a chairman who, as John of Ibelin puts it, 'est apelé reys (i.e., *raʾīs*) en lor lenguage arabic', and of jurors.[60] The *Cour des Suriens* appears to be a general example for the maintenance of the autonomous jurisdiction that the indigenous populace had already enjoyed as *dhimmīs*, i.e., members of the protected non-Muslim

---

55 John XXII, *Acta*, no. 36, pp. 72–73, also in *Bullarium Cyprium III*, no. r-106, pp. 58–59 (trans. in *Synodicum Nicosiense*, no. X.38, p. 345).
56 See n. 17 above.
57 Nicolaou-Konnari, 'Greeks', p. 25.
58 Mas Latrie, *Histoire de l'île de Chypre*, I, p. 103, in his historical overview.
59 Richard, 'La Cour des Syriens', p. 386; Grivaud, 'Les minorités orientales', p. 52, follows Richard. The evidence given in n. 79, is however from the sixteenth century; *Lacrimae Cypriae. Les larmes de Chypre*, ed. by Brunehilde Imhaus, 2 vols (Nicosia: Département des Antiquités, 2004), I, p. 132 n. 2: 'L'on sait qu'en Chypre la communauté syrienne jouissait d'un statut privilégié, car elle avoit ses propres cours de justice'. Nicolaou-Konnari, 'Greeks', p. 24, seems also to imply that there was a separate court for the Syrians.
60 John of Ibelin, *Livre*, Prologue, pp. 54–55. The Arabic term *raʾīs* has the basic meaning of head of a community. For its different meanings in the Kingdom of Jerusalem, see Jonathan Riley-Smith, 'Some Lesser Officials in Latin Syria', *English Historical Review*, 87 (1972), 1–26 (pp. 5, 9–15); Jonathan Riley-Smith, *The Feudal Nobility and the Kingdom of Jerusalem, 1174–1277* (London: Macmillan, 1973), pp. 47–49, 90–91.

communities under Muslim rule.[61] And indeed, the Chalcedonian *Suriens* were not the only ones to have their own courts under crusader rule. There is also proof of a Muslim qāḍī in Jabala (Syria) for the 1170s and 1180s, as well as of the corresponding Rabbinic courts in Acre and Tyre.[62]

Before the crusades, the Greek patriarchs of Jerusalem headed the Melkite community in Palestine regarding spiritual as well as secular matters. The establishment of crusader rule, however, as well as the appointment of a Latin patriarch of Jerusalem caused the Greek patriarchs and members of the episcopate to go into exile in Constantinople.[63] This did not lead to a collapse of the patriarchate's court or a separation of Greek and Melkite jurisdiction. We know of at least one man who in 1122 held the secular offices of the *archōn*, i.e., a civil Byzantine administrative official, and of a judge (*kritēs*): the clergyman Georgios, who was also the *chartophylax* of the Anastasis, i.e., the representative of the exiled Greek patriarch of Jerusalem. As head of this community and responsible for secular as well as for religious tasks, he continued effectively the tradition of the time preceding the crusades. Most likely the same Georgios, apparently a Greek, is mentioned in two Latin records from Jerusalem dating from 1124/25, where he is called Georgius *rais* or *raicius*. It seems, therefore, that he presided over the *Cour des Suriens* described by John of Ibelin, which was thus identical with the court of the Greek patriarch.[64]

Concerning the Kingdom of Jerusalem, the term *Cour des Suriens* can thus be regarded as a solely Frankish designation for the episcopal courts of the Greek patriarchs of Jerusalem which continued to exist unchanged since the Islamic period. They were competent for Greeks and *Suriens* alike and covered accordingly both canon and civil law. This assumption is supported by an Arabic contract of purchase between a Melkite and the Georgian abbot of the monastery of the Holy Cross near Jerusalem, dated to 1169. The entirety of this text conforms to the usual form of Islamic contracts, which the Melkites had obviously adopted for their business before the establishment of the Crusader States. A certain Michael ibn Qurīl confirmed the

---

61 See in general Jonathan Riley-Smith, 'The Survival in Latin Palestine of Muslim Administration', in *Eastern Mediterranean Lands in the Period of the Crusades*, ed. by Peter M. Holt (Warminster: Aris & Phillips, 1977), pp. 9–22.

62 Benjamin Z. Kedar, 'The Subjected Muslims of the Frankish Levant', in *Muslims under Latin Rule, 1100–1300*, ed. by James M. Powell (Princeton: Princeton University 1990), pp. 135–74 (141–42); Joshua Prawer, *The History of the Jews in the Latin Kingdom of Jerusalem* (Oxford: Clarendon Press, 1988), pp. 54, 97. Nothing is known of courts for the non-Chalcedonian Christian communities, which, nevertheless, must have continued to exist in accordance with the situation before 1099.

63 Mathilde Boudier, 'L'Église melkite au IXe siècle à travers le conflit entre David de Damas et Siméon d'Antioche. Apports d'un dossier documentaire inédit', *Annales islamologiques*, 52 (2018), 45–80; Pahlitzsch, *Graeci und Suriani*; Johannes Pahlitzsch, 'The Greek Orthodox Church in the First Kingdom of Jerusalem (1099–1187)', in *Patterns of the Past, Prospects of the Future. The Christian Heritage in the Holy Land*, ed. by Thomas Hummel, Kevork Hintlian, and Ulf Carmesund (London: Melisende, 1999), pp. 195–212.

64 Johannes Pahlitzsch and Dorothea Weltecke, 'Konflikte zwischen den nicht-lateinischen Kirchen im Königreich Jerusalem', in *Jerusalem im Hoch- und Spätmittelalter: Konflikte und Konfliktbewältigung – Vorstellungen und Vergegenwärtigungen*, ed. by Dieter Bauer, Klaus Herbers, and Nikolas Jaspert, Campus Historische Studien, 29 (Frankfurt a. M. – New York: Campus-Verlag, 2001), pp. 119–45 (128–30).

validity of the document, while one of the witnesses is Gabriel, presbyter of the Anastasis, who signed the otherwise Arabic document in Greek.[65] Thus, a Melkite notary or scribe and a Greek cleric from the Orthodox patriarchate of Jerusalem were involved in this legal transaction. Even if the court of the patriarchate is not mentioned in the document, it nevertheless demonstrates how the different groups within the patriarchate of Jerusalem, be they Greeks, Melkites or Georgians, acted together independently of any Frankish laws and courts and followed their old legal customs from the pre-crusader period. The existence of a separate court for the Melkites is thus highly unlikely.[66]

In Lusignan Cyprus the term *Cour des Suriens* seems to have assumed a different meaning. Christopher Schabel discusses a document concerning a quarrel between the Franciscans of Nicosia and the chapter of Nicosia Cathedral dated to 1299 that mentions a certain Frankish nobleman and knight, 'Thomas of Finion, the *reeys Siriorum*, which is to say the viscount of the *Siriorum* in Cyprus or in the city of Nicosia', as witness. Schabel interprets this phrase to mean that he presided over a *Cour des Suriens* in Nicosia but had authority throughout Cyprus.[67] For the period up to 1374, two more individuals designated as *ra'īs* of the *Suriani* are known: Jean Ponsan, also a Frankish knight, is called 'rais des Suriens de Nicosie' on his tombstone dated 1356;[68] and a royal ban from 1355 refers to a 'rays de Famagoust'.[69] This is obviously not the same institution as the *Cour des Suriens* in the Kingdom of Jerusalem, which was a court presided over by a Chalcedonian Orthodox, either Greek or Melkite, and where this community's law was applied.

There was, nevertheless, an institution in the Kingdom of Jerusalem which dealt with cases involving *Suriani* under the presidency of a Frank, the so-called *Cour de la Fonde* of Acre. John of Ibelin added to his description of the origins of the *Cour des Suriens*: 'And in one place (i.e., Acre) in the kingdom there are jurats of the *cort de Suriens* and no *reys* (i.e., *ra'īs*); but the *bailli* of the *Fonde* of that place is like a *reys*. And the pleas of the *Suriens* concerning the aforesaid quarrels come before him (the

---

65 The document has been edited with German translation and commentary in Pahlitzsch, *Graeci und Suriani*, pp. 314–24.
66 Riley-Smith, 'Government and the Indigenous', p. 130, however, assumes that the Melkites had been given their own minor courts, 'that must have dealt with those "secular" cases which under Muslim rule would have been heard by their bishops'. Riley-Smith was not aware of the evidence presented here and in any case confirms that the creation of special secular courts for the Melkites would have been a Latin innovation; see also Riley-Smith, *Feudal Nobility*, pp. 89–90, and Riley-Smith, 'Some Lesser Officials', pp. 3–4, where it becomes clear that the idea of separate secular Melkite courts is problematic.
67 The document is published in Christopher Schabel, 'A Neglected Quarrel over a House in Cyprus in 1299: The Nicosia Franciscans vs. the Chapter of Nicosia Cathedral', *Crusades*, 8 (2009), 173–90 (pp. 180, 189): 'Thoma de Finion, reeys Siriorum (quod est dictu vicecomes Siriorum in Cipro seu civitate Nicossie)'. Already Richard, 'La Cour des Syriens', p. 388, assumed that there were two *Cours des Suriens*: one in Nicosia for the whole of Cyprus and another one especially for Famagusta. A *raicius* in Nicosia can be found in 1210, but he was most probably a seigneurial *bailli*, Nicolaou-Konnari, 'Greeks', p. 24.
68 *Lacrimae Cypriae*, I, fiche no. 258, p. 132 n. 2.
69 *Bans et ordonnances*, no. XXXII, p. 377: 'Seaus qui son dou dyossé de Famagoust voizent o bailly et au rays de Famagoust'; in n. a, the editor Beugnot says: 'nous apprenons ici qu'il existait un reïs et une juridiction syrienne à Famagouste.'

bailli) and are determined by the jurats of this court just as they are before the *reis*'.[70] The *Livre des Assises des Bourgeois* described the responsibilities and the procedure of the *Cour de la Fonde* in Acre in greater detail. A Frankish *bailli* presided over it and it involved four *Suriens* and two Franks as members of the jury. It was competent for cases of selling, purchasing, debt, pledges and other matters in which members of various non-Latin religious groups were involved.[71] Thus, Marwan Nader has called it a 'special small-claims court for inter-communal cases'.[72] It is unclear what is meant by the term *Suriens*, used for the four persons who served as jurors, i.e., whether these jurors actually had to be Melkites or whether non-Chalcedonians could serve as jurors as well. Maybe the designation *Suriens* was transferred from the *Cour des Suriens* to the *Cour de la Fonde*, as the two courts were somehow related according to John of Ibelin; in the process of this transfer, *Suriens* may have changed its meaning to become a rather generic term in the new context of the *Cour de la Fonde*.

The *Cour de la Fonde* took over the function of the non-Frankish courts in secular matters, since in Acre, the main commercial center of the kingdom, a separation of jurisdiction between the different groups constantly doing business together was no longer feasible.[73] But while the *Cour des Suriens* as well as the courts of the non-Chalcedonian Christian, Jewish, and Muslim communities proclaimed judgment according to their own customs, the *Cour de la Fonde* was to judge the indigenous population of the Kingdom of Jerusalem according to the laws laid down in the *Livre des Assises des Bourgeois*.[74] This market court would probably not have judged any cases pertaining to the sphere of religious law.

---

70 John of Ibelin, *Livre*, Prologue, p. 55: 'En aucun [according to Riley-Smith, 'Some Lesser Officials', p. 6 n. 10, this must be understood as a singular] leuc dou reiaume a jurés de la cort de Suriens et n'i a point de reys, mais le bailli de la fonde de cel leuc est come reys. Et les plais des Suriens des quereles avant dites vienent devant lui et sont determinés par les jurés de cele cort ausi con [read: come] devant le reis, […]'. Thus, John of Ibelin seems to regard the *Cour de la Fonde* as another kind of *Cour des Suriens*. Maybe it developed out of the *Cour des Suriens* of Acre.

71 *Livre des Assises de la Cour des Bourgeois*, chapter 241, pp. 171–73. See: Joshua Prawer, 'Social Classes in the Crusader States: the "Minorities"', in *A History of the Crusades, V: The Impact of the Crusades on the Near East*, ed. by Norman P. Zacour and Harry W. Hazard (Madison: University of Wisconsin Press, 1985), pp. 59–116 (104–06); Prawer, *The History of the Jews*, pp. 98–100.

72 Marwan Nader, *Burgesses and Burgess Law in the Latin Kingdoms of Jerusalem and Cyprus (1099–1325)* (Aldershot and Burlington: Ashgate, 2006), p. 160. Concerning the selection of witnesses, the *Livre des Assises de la Cour des Bourgeois*, chapter 241, pp. 172–73, rules with regard to the *Cour de la Fonde* that, in disputes between members of the same community, the witnesses' religious affiliation was not relevant. Obviously the *Cour de la Fonde* dealt also with intra-communal cases.

73 Prawer, 'Social Classes', p. 105; Marie-Luise Favreau-Lilie, '"Multikulturelle Gesellschaft" oder "Persecuting Society"? Franken und Einheimische im Königreich Jerusalem', in *Jerusalem im Hoch- und Spätmittelalter: Konflikte und Konfliktbewältigung*, pp. 55–93 (77–79); Riley-Smith, 'Government and the Indigenous', p. 130; Nader, *Burgesses and Burgess Law*, p. 160. However, the existence of such a court is only expressly known for Acre. Outside Acre, the regulation of cases in which members of different indigenous congregations were involved is less clear, see Riley-Smith, *Feudal Nobility*, p. 91. Probably, as the case was under Muslim rule, it was possible to agree on one of the courts of the parties involved or to address the judges of the ruling class.

74 *Livre des Assises de la Cour des Bourgeois*, chapter 241, p. 172. Marwan Nader, 'Urban Muslims, Latin Laws, and Legal Institutions in the Kingdom of Jerusalem', *Medieval Encounters*, 13 (2007), 243–70 (p. 250).

Maybe this model was introduced in Cyprus after the fall of Acre in 1291. In that case, the court presided by Thomas of Finion in 1299 was actually the Cypriot adoption of the *Cour de la Fonde* from Acre rather than of the Palestinian *Cour des Suriens*.[75] One indication supporting this hypothesis could be that Thomas was called 'reeys Siriorum quod est dictu vicecomes Siriorum in Cipro'. In John of Ibelin's account of the establishment of the *Cour de la Fonde*, we find the little noticed but very similar remark that its president, the *bailli*, 'may be called in this case viscount and he guides the *Suriens* of the said kingdom'.[76]

The sharp increase of immigrants to Cyprus from the mainland after the Mamluk conquest of the Crusader States in 1291 may have created a similar situation to that in Acre, resulting in the creation of an analogous court. Now as previously in Acre, the authorities had to cope with a very diverse group of people who were interconnected in many ways in a dynamic economic environment.[77] At the same time the Greek episcopal courts continued to be competent for Melkites in matters of canon law, which included family and inheritance law as demonstrated above, although their jurisdiction was soon to be disputed by the Latin Church, maybe specifically because of the introduction of the new court.

The little evidence we possess about the workings of this court comes from the archives of Venice and Genoa. On 16 August 1297, i.e., about the time when Thomas of Finion was the *reeys Siriorum*, the Genoese notary Lamberto di Sambuceto drew up a document in Nicosia. It states that the Genoese Thomas Bulla committed himself to manage the total amount of 450 white bezants on behalf of a certain Alis, the daughter of the deceased Obertus de Clavaro and his wife Florencia, both Genoese citizens as well. Thomas, however, received 250 white bezants of this sum from Maceo de Caiffa (i.e., from Haifa), who had obviously received this money from Alis's mother Florencia at an earlier time and had promised to return it as soon as Alis was married, functioning as her dowry ('patrimonio'). Thomas Bulla, on his part, promised to keep the money Maceo had passed on to him until the time of Alis's marriage. After her

---

75 Contrary to the common opinion as voiced, for example, most recently by Catherine Otten-Froux, 'Quelques aspects de la justice à Famagouste pendant la période génoise (1373–1464)', in Πρακτικά του Τρίτου Διεθνούς Κυπρολογικού Συνεδρίου (Λευκωσία, 16–20 Απριλίου 1996), II: Μεσαιωνικό Τμήμα, ed. by Athanasios Papageorgiou (Nicosia: Etaireia Kypriakon Spoudon, 2001), pp. 333–51 (339).

76 The first half of the sentence has already been quoted, see above n. 70. It reads in its entirety: 'Et les plais des Suriens des quereles avant dites vienent devant lui [i.e. the *bailli*] et sont determinés par les jurés de cele cort ausi con [read: come] devant le reis, qui vaut autant a dire en cest cas come visconte a mener les Suriens ou dit reiaume', John of Ibelin, *Livre*, Prologue, p. 55. The grammar of this sentence is quite loose but with regard to the context it seems that the subject of the final relative clause has to be the *bailli*, not the *reis*. It remains unclear what is meant by the phrase that the bailli of the *Cour de la Fonde* 'guides the *Suriens* of the said kingdom', since this court seems to have been competent only for Acre, see above n. 73.

77 David Jacoby, 'The Rise of a New Emporium in the Eastern Mediterranean: Famagusta in the Late Thirteenth Century', Μελέται καὶ Ὑπομνήματα, 1 (1984), 145–79 (repr. in David Jacoby, *Studies on the Crusader States and on Venetian Expansion*, Variorum Collected Studies Series, 301 (Northampton: Ashgate, 1989), no. VIII). While most of the immigrants probably settled in Famagusta, also other parts of the island must have been affected, especially Nicosia, where the first known *curia Sirianorum* in Cyprus could be found.

wedding, Alis would have to go with her new husband to the 'curia Sirianorum', verify that this was her husband and then exonerate ('quietare') the said Maceo. Only then would Thomas give her the 250 bezants he had obtained earlier from Maceo.[78] It seems that Maceo was an immigrant from Haifa, obviously not a Frank, because otherwise there was no reason to involve the *curia Sirianorum*. Although he had handed over the money he had promised to keep for Alis to a Genoese, he still had to be released from his obligation by the court of the *Sirianorum*, which was obviously competent for his business transactions even if they involved a Genoese party.[79]

The only other pre-1369 reference to a case involving the *curia Sirianorum* that I know of is to be found in the testament of a certain Fetus, the son of Feras Simiteculo, a rich Venetian citizen resident in Famagusta, which was issued on 3 April 1363 by Simeone, notary and priest of San Giacomo dell'Orio in Venice, during a temporary stay in Cyprus. Fetus desired to be buried in the Greek church of St Epiphanios in Famagusta and demanded that part of his money should be used for the enfranchisement of ten Greek clerics for the salvation of his soul. He was apparently a White Venetian, either of Greek or more likely of Melkite origin since the name of his father Feras seems to be Arabic, Firās.[80] Fetus's testament consists of a long list of legacies. Among other things, he bequeathed to his wife Maria the proceeds of the sale of a house that used to belong to his brother Teodorus to the Latin monastery of St Anthony, proceeds that were registered on his name in the *curia Surianorum* in Famagusta. Finally, Fetus stipulated that all his possessions should be sold by the *raise* and the jurors of the *curia Surianorum* at this same court and the revenues should be used by his fiduciaries to pay for all his bequests.[81] While Fetus registered his testament with a Venetian notary, nevertheless selling the house of his brother as well as selling his belongings after his death fell within the jurisdiction of the Court of the *Suriani*, even if one party was a Latin institution, as was the case with the monastery of St Anthony.

---

78   Lamberto di Sambuceto, *Notai Genovesi in Oltremare atti rogati a Cipro (11 Ottobre 1296–23 Giugno 1299)*, ed. by Michel Balard, Collana Storica di Fonti e Studie, 39 (Genoa: Universita di Genova, 1983), no. 60, pp. 74–75. See Nicolaou-Konnari, 'Women in Medieval Famagusta', pp. 530, 601–02, 603.
79   Marwan Nader, 'Courts of Non-Noble Jurisdiction and Laws of Roman Provenance in Fourteenth-Century Famagusta', *Crusades*, 15 (2016), 135–56 (p. 141 n. 46), refers to this document but interprets it incorrectly, saying that according to the deed 'this court recognised in law a marriage between a Genoese woman and a Syrian Christian'.
80   Catherine Otten-Froux, 'Un notaire vénitien à Famagouste au XIVe siècle. Les actes de Simeone, prêtre de San Giacomo dell'Orio (1362–1371)', Θησαυρίσματα, 33 (2003), 15–159 (p. 37). White Venetians or White Genoese were non-Latin Christians, including Greeks, but also Jews, of Venetian or Genoese citizenship, see David Jacoby, 'Citoyens, sujets et protégés de Venise et de Gênes en Chypre, du XIIIème au XVème siècle', *Byzantinische Forschungen*, 5 (1977), 159–88 (pp. 169–72). Various members of the Simiteculo family are mentioned in Venetian documents as doing business in Alexandria, Constantinople, Tyre, Crete, and Cyprus from 1179 onwards. Fetus's sister is called Uxira, which might be an Arabic name, Otten-Froux, 'Un notaire vénitien', no. 6, p. 45. See also Coureas, *The Latin Church in Cyprus 1313–1378*, p. 474 and Coureas, 'The Syrian Melkites', p. 83.
81   Otten-Froux, 'Un notaire vénitien', no. 6, pp. 44–47, gives a very detailed summary of the document. See Nicolaou-Konnari, 'Women in Medieval Famagusta', p. 559, cf. pp. 555, 557, 563, 594, 599.

In each of these two cases brought before the Court of the *Suriani*, a non-Latin Christian was involved. It is unknown if Maceo de Caiffa was a Melkite or a non-Chalcedonian Christian. Fetus was probably a Melkite but also a Venetian citizen. He could probably choose to bring his cases either to a Venetian court or to the *curia Surianorum*. Maceo did business with Genoese citizens, Fetus with a Latin monastery. Therefore, the only requirement for bringing a case before this court obviously was that the one most affected was a non-Latin. However, no case is documented that involved exclusively non-Latins. The Cypriot *curia Surianorum* differed from the *Cour de la Fonde* in this respect, as the court in Acre did not judge Latins at all.[82] It is due to the nature of the sources that in both cases discussed here Italians played a part. On the basis of just two documents it is impossible to establish which rules this court followed and to whom its jurisdiction extended. It seems, however, that the rules were quite flexible.[83]

But why were these courts in Cyprus called *curia Surianorum*? Despite the evidence presented above concerning the history of the term *Suriani* and its equivalents, it would be in contradiction to the actual function of this kind of court if it were competent only for the Melkites. Though, as far as we know, *Suriani*, *Syroi* or *Suriens* still had the exclusive meaning of Melkite in all other contexts until the reign of Peter I, the designation *curia Surianorum* in particular seems to have followed the model of the *Cour de la Fonde* of Acre and to have become a generic term for inter-communal courts as early as the end of the thirteenth century.[84]

---

82 At least at no point in the *Livre des Assise de la Cour des Bourgeois* is the suggestion made that Latin merchants were subject to the jurisdiction of the *Cour de la Fonde*, see Nader, *Burgesses and Burgess Law*, pp. 160–61.

83 Nicolaou-Konnari, 'Women in Medieval Famagusta', pp. 534–40, 542, 551, 553, has recently presented cases of women who decided to marry according to the Syrian custom instead of the Frankish custom, since the dowry regulations 'secundum morem et consuetudinem Sirie' were more favourable towards women, as the dowry contract between Manuel de Romania and his Genoese wife shows (Lamberto di Sambuceto, *Notai Genovesi in Oltremare atti rogati a Cipro (gennaio – agosto 1302)*, ed. by Romeo Pavoni, Collana Storica di Fonti e Studie, 49 (Genoa: Università di Genova, 1987), no. 236, p. 283). Nicolaou-Konnari suggests that these cases show how women could apply to the legal traditions most advantageous to them. However, though they followed the Syrian custom, documents such as the contract between Manuel de Romania (probably a Greek) and his wife, which was drawn up in a private house in Famagusta in 1302, and the 1361 contract between Andreas, son of the White Venetian Ioannis de Baruti (Beirut), and his future wife of Syrian descent Aylix, the sister of Philipus Mistehel from Famagusta *(Nicola de Boateriis, notaio in Famagosta e Venezia (1355–1365)*, ed. by Antonino Lombardo, Fonti per la storia di Venezia, sez. 3, archivi notarili (Venezia: Comitato per la pubblicazione delle fonti relative alla storia de Venezia, 1973), no. 70, pp. 73–75), make no reference to the *curia Surianorum*; the latter document (p. 74) mentions that, also in 1361, a similar contract between Andreas and Aylix was recorded in Arabic by the priest Jacob of the church of St Mary of Nazareth, see Jean Richard, 'Aspects du notariat public à Chypre sous les Lusignans', in *Diplomatics in the Eastern Mediterranean 1000–1500. Aspects of Cross-Cultural Communication*, ed. by Alexander Beihammer, Maria Parani, and Christopher Schabel, The Medieval Mediterranean, 74 (Leiden: Brill, 2008), pp. 207–21 (211–12). Moreover, in none of these cases do the documents specify if the Oriental Christians involved were Melkites or members of other Eastern Christian denominations.

84 See above pp. 17–18##.

Only after the Genoese takeover of Famagusta in 1374 can we garner more information on the *curia Surianorum* of Famagusta. The establishment of Genoese rule surely had an effect on the institutions in Famagusta,[85] and the term *Suriani* by this time included not only Melkites but all Oriental Christians, be they Chalcedonians or not.[86] Nevertheless, in consideration of the scarcity of sources it might be worthwhile to take a look at the evidence from that period. Catherine Otten-Froux enumerates several cases documented in the Archivio di Stato di Genova that attest to the activity of this court in Famagusta between 1374 and 1464. It seems that there was an ongoing conflict between the *capitaneus* and the *curia* of the *podestà*, on the one hand, and the *curia Surianorum*, on the other, over competence and the laws to apply.

In a register from 1389, the Genoese captain and *podestà* reminded 'le rais de li Sorianym' and his court to guard the property of the deceased Badin Musta, judging from his name maybe a *Surianus*, 'according to our customs and our order'.[87] On another occasion, the Genoese captain ordered the viscount and the jurors of the *curia Siriorum* to annul a document that was issued in their court for (again, judging from the name) the Greek Giorgio Chillax, who is listed as an interpreter in the register of the *massaria*, i.e., the treasury, for 1442.[88] In 1455, Chiriaco de Bardi, maybe a Greek, informed his debtor Domenico Semano via the Genoese court that he had to redeem the pledge for a house; the latter replied that the vicar who was responsible for the Genoese court in Famagusta was not competent for this case, which was still pending at the court of the Syrians.[89]

The report of a case of 7 December 1448 has been published by Jean Richard:[90] John Bibi, a Latin convert of a well-known family of White Genoese of Melkite origin,[91] died in Famagusta. He had been married to the daughter of Marcus Zebas (maybe for Arabic aṣ-Ṣabbāḥ) according to the customs of the Cypriots ('consuetudinem Ciprianorum'). The Zebas family was also of Near Eastern origin, although we do not know anything about their religious affiliation. Marcus addressed the 'curie Siriorum' asking its viscount, at this time Nicola de Spinola, to restore his daughter's dowry to the family according to the customs of this court. While the viscount was willing to support this claim, Thomas Bibi, John's brother, appealed to the Genoese captain Pietro de Marco, who set aside the viscount's judgement. Two representatives of the viscount, Laurentius de Neffino, whose family originated apparently from the area

---

85 Richard, 'La cour des Syriens', p. 388.
86 For the example of Leontios Makhairas, see n. 2 above and Leontios Makhairas, *Recital*, I, §§ 92, 111, 375, 411, 437, 654, 681, 685. See Mas Latrie, *Nouvelles Preuves*, II, pp. 58, 60. Later crusader sources also used the term for all Oriental Christians, see Richard, 'Le peuplement latin et syrien', p. 166.
87 Otten-Froux, 'Quelques aspects', p. 339.
88 Otten-Froux, 'Quelques aspects', pp. 340 (the date is not given but the event may be situtated in the 1440s), 336 (Giorgio Chillax as interpreter).
89 Otten-Froux, 'Quelques aspects', pp. 339–40.
90 In Richard, 'La cour des Syriens', pp. 397–98, as an appendix.
91 Recent scholarship usually connects the Bibi family with the Orthodox Pipēs ('Bibi') monastery, see Kyriacou, *Orthodox Cyprus*, p. xxix. Jean Richard suggests that the Bibi family actually did found the monastery, see *Le livre des remembrances de la Secrète du royaume de Chypre (1468–1469)*, ed. by Jean Richard and Theodoros Papadopoullos, Sources et Études de l'Histoire de Chypre, 10 (Nicosia: Centre de Recherches Scientifique, 1983), no. 217, p. 200 n. 2.

of Tripoli, and John Duca, whose family name indicates a Greek origin,[92] pressed charges against the captain because he interfered with a court 'to which in this city the *Siriani et Cypriani* (i.e., in this context probably the Greeks)[93] have always gone and still do so'.[94] This claim to an allegedly old tradition of Greeks and *Suriani* both having recourse to the *curia Surianorum* is in a sense supported by the proclamation of James II after his recovery of Famagusta in 1464 that 'the Greek burgesses should have their court of the *Suriani*'.[95] Though the two cases from 1297 and 1363 do not suggest any involvement of Greeks with the *curia Surianorum*, this proclamation could be interpreted as a confirmation of the hypothesis that, already in the period before 1374, the *curia Surianorum* served as a court for all kinds of inter-communal cases, just like the *Cour de la Fonde* of Acre.

The question of jurisdiction is also at the centre of the dispute concerning the dowry of Marcus Zebas' daughter. While the Bibi family were under Genoese jurisdiction, Marcus Zebas was subject to the *curia Surianorum*. But even in Genoese Famagusta, the documents are not very specific about the competence of this latter court, its jurisdiction and organization. Some of the known viscounts belonged to great Genoese families, and it appears that the court was subordinate to the *capitaneus*, who also seemed to be responsible for the execution of the court's penalties. Otten-Froux concludes that the *curia Surianorum* was quite active at the time of the Genoese rule in Famagusta and dealt with civil matters in cases where one party was either a *Surianus* or a Greek.[96] All in all, the fifteenth-century Genoese documents from Famagusta seem to reflect an older tradition, according to which these courts were competent for Greeks as well and followed their own customs. It is doubtful that the latter point was actually true in view of the fact that a Frank had to preside over the *curia Surianorum*, who certainly did not apply the laws of the non-Frankish population. It seems more plausible that these references are a distant echo of the twelfth and thirteenth centuries (both in Jerusalem and Cyprus as mentioned above), when Greeks and *Suriani* were indeed subject to the same autonomous jurisdiction in both religious and secular law.

---

[92] A Giovanni Ducha is listed for 1456 as an interpreter, see Otten-Froux, 'Quelques aspects', p. 336.

[93] Following Richard, 'La cour des Syriens', pp. 394–95, Michel Balard, 'La Massaria génoise de Famagouste', in *Diplomatics in the Eastern Mediterranean*, pp. 235–50 (243–44), interprets *Cypriani* as the subjects of the king of Cyprus.

[94] Richard, 'La cour des Syriens', p. 397: 'cum in hac civitate semper Siriani et Cypriani habuerent [sic] et habent recursum suum ad dictam curiam'.

[95] Florio Bustron, *Chronique de l'île de Chypre*, ed. by René de Mas Latrie, Collection de documents inédits sur l'histoire de France, Mélanges historiques, 5 (Paris: Imprimerie nationale, 1886; repr. as *Historia overo Commentarii di Cipro*, Kypriologike Bibliotheke, 8 (Nicosia: Archbishop Makarios III Foundation, 1998)), p. 412: 'Li borghesi greci haver debbono la loro corte de Suriani'. Certainly this meant that the Greeks should particpate in the *curia Surianorum*, not have their own special court. On the basis of his belief that the *Suriani* had a different legal status than the Greeks and their own courts, Richard, 'La cour des Syriens', p. 395, assumes that because the Greek *perpyriarioi* had been enfranchised by the fifteenth century and finally reached a status equal to the *Suriani*, they were then esteemed worthy of being judged by the same courts as the *Suriani*.

[96] Otten-Froux, 'Quelques aspects', p. 340.

In conclusion, the following should be noted: first, the term *Suriani* in its different forms quite unambiguously designated the Melkites in the period under consideration. Only in the context of the fundamental social upheavals after the murder of Peter I and the cession of Famagusta to Genoa did this term become more inclusive, since these events led to the rise of various families of Near Eastern origin independent of their original religious affiliation. Second, there is no evidence for a separate Melkite jurisdiction before the end of the thirteenth century. It is unclear if the Greek ecclesiastical courts, which definitely dealt with secular matters, also served the *Suriani* as their secular courts. At least, there is no proof for the contrary. The thirteenth-century Greek episcopal courts of Cyprus should therefore be regarded as the Cypriot version of the *Cours des Suriens* as it existed in the Kingdom of Jerusalem. Third, new courts competent for secular inter-communal cases developed at the end of the thirteenth century first in Nicosia and then also in Famagusta, probably because of the sharp rise in the numbers of immigrants from the region of the former Crusader States. These courts were called *curia Siriorum* or *Surianorum* but seem actually to be a continuation of the *Cour de la Fonde* with regard to their composition and function. The scarce evidence in the sources before the 1370s does not clarify whether, besides *Suriani* (including White Venetians) and Italian merchants, these Cypriot courts also dealt with Greeks, other non-Chalcedonian Christians, Jews, and Muslims, as had indeed been the case in Acre. But it seems very likely, which would give the term *curia Surianorum* a broader meaning. In general, it is characteristic of the *curia Surianorum* to operate in a grey area, lacking a clearly defined competence and jurisdiction. This situation opened up opportunities for non-Frankish groups, who could participate as jurors in the Frankish judicial system and were able, to a certain extent, to choose where their cases were to be heard.

PART IV

The Rise of a New Power – Muslim-Turkish Anatolia

RHOADS MURPHEY

The Long Prose 'Epic' of Sarı Saltuk Dede (fl. c. 1260 to 1298) as a Source for Understanding the Style and Context of Crusading Warfare in the Late Thirteenth-Century Near and Middle East*

The purpose of the present chapter is to examine the concept of knighthood and the mentality of the active participants in 'crusader warfare' as they are presented in a narrow group of sources which record the participants' own perceptions of events and can thus be regarded as genuine reflections of their military ethos and their self-defined behavioural norms. Despite the fact that the Balkans and Anatolia underwent a period of extreme political fragmentation in the late thirteenth century, which witnessed the effective retreat of the state and the structures and institutions of the state, the overwhelming majority of the indigenous sources that survive from the period reflect the perspective and biases of the state and its apologists. Judgmental attitudes towards the nomads and nomadic warriors are difficult to escape if one approaches their history exclusively from the point of view of contemporary court-based chroniclers. These writers were not only members of the intelligentsia and inclined to decry the nomads' lamentable lack of 'civilized' values, but were also at the same time serving bureaucrats and administrators. By instinct they regarded the tribes as 'fractious' and their 'rebellious' leaders as a chronic source of threat to the very existence of the state.

---

* Some aspects of this topic were touched on previously in a paper published online. See Rhoads Murphey, 'Gazi Ideology and the Ideal Virtues of the Gazi Warrior at the Time of the Founding of the Ottoman Empire', in Uluslararası Süleyman Paşa ve Kocaeli Tarihi Sempozyumu Bildirileri (Kocaeli: Kocaeli Büyükşehir Belediyesi, Kültür ve Sosyal İşleri Başkanlığı, 2017), I, pp. 35–44. [http://www.kocaelitarihisempozyumu.com/bildiriler3/Rhoads%20MURPHEY.pdf].

Rhoads Murphey • University of Birmingham

Crusading, Society, and Politics in the Eastern Mediterranean in the Age of King Peter I of Cyprus, ed. by Alexander Beihammer and Angel Nicolaou-Konnari, MEDNEX, 10 (Turnhout, 2022), pp. 385–415
© BREPOLS PUBLISHERS   10.1484/M.MEDNEX-EB.5.128472

In Anatolia, the period after the first Mongol invasion in 1243 is sometimes, rather euphemistically, dubbed the period of the Mongol 'Protectorate'.[1] During this period, the progressive diminution of the zone under the direct control of the Seljukid state of Rūm that resulted in its bipartite and, for a time between c. 1249 and 1254, even tripartite division into what amounted to mini-states or principalities, left the state impoverished, not just in terms of land and financial resources, but also in terms of its administrative cohesion. With the state lands divided into multiple territorial enclaves based at separate provincial capitals—all of which competed for the restoration of unitary control under a single sovereign ruler—, it was the nomads who, in spite of the sneering and judgmental attitude of the bureaucrat historians who recorded their activities, emerged as the main power brokers. In such periods of state dissolution, they could be co-opted into acting as agents representing the interests of an existing state or mini-state authority (i.e., in defence of the existing political order), but as large contingents of the Turkmen migrated westward and northward in the wake of the second Mongol invasion of Anatolia in 1256, opportunities also arose for them to act in a capacity as free agents, providing the power nucleus around which new state formations could be created.

The rapidity with which the Anatolian Seljukid state retreated from the apogee it had reached in terms of its military might and internal cohesion under the rule of Sultan 'Alā' al-Dīn Kaykubād I (1220–1237) could hardly be denied, even by such determined apologists of the regime and defenders of its imperial dignity as the historian Ibn Bībī, whose chronicle, the *Avāmir al-'Alā'iyya*, was completed in 1281.[2] It was clear even to the most impassioned supporters of the dynasty that, by the mid-century point, the centre of gravity in the state had shifted decisively away from the centre—and the previously exclusive locus of imperial authority based in the capital Konya—and was now multi-centred and distributed between zones of localized authority and control spread out along the margins and frontiers of the rapidly imploding Seljukid state of Rūm.[3] Throughout the state of civil war that persisted for the decade and

---

1   The term anachronistically applying a political form of the modern times to the political order of medieval Anatolia, gained particular currency after the publication (in 1968) of Claude Cahen's *Pre-Ottoman Turkey: A General Survey of the Material and Spiritual Culture and History, c. 1071–1330*, trans. from the French by J. Jones-Williams (New York: Taplinger Publishing Company, 1968).

2   The facsimile edition based on the Aya Sofya Library manuscript no. 2985, which was copied in 679 A.H./ 1280–81, i.e. the same year as the work's completion, provides the most reliable text of the *Avāmir al-'Alā'iyya*. See *El evamirü'l-Alaiyye fi'l-umuri'l-alaiyye*, ed. by Adnan Sadık Erzi (Ankara: Türk Tarih Kurumu, 1956).

3   The triangular dimensions of the power struggle within the Seljukid State of Rum in the years between 1246 and 1261 amongst the minor sons of Ghiyāth al-Dīn Kaykhusraw II (d. 1246) has been questioned in some accounts. See for example the 'Genealogical Table of Seljuk Sultans of Anatolia' in *The Seljuks of Anatolia: Court and Society in the Medieval Middle East*, ed. by Andrew Peacock, and Sara Yıldız (London: I.B. Tauris, 2012), p. 276, where the schematic outline of the complex wrangling for power between Kaykhusraw II's sons that is offered denies any real agency or political involvement to the third son 'Alā al-Dīn Kaykubād II (d. 1254). However, the fact that Kaykubād II was only seven years old at the time of his father's death in 1246 and himself only survived to the age of fifteen did not prevent him from

a half between the installation of 'Izz al-Dīn Kaykāwus II on the throne in Konya in 1246 and his eventual ouster and exile in 1261, the power dynamics and political fate of the state as well as its potential for revival and reunification rested firmly with the Turkmen tribes and their tribal leadership.

The Seljukid state was tributary to the Mongols from 1243 onwards and the state was further weakened by the internal squabbles and extended periods of contested succession referred to above. The troubled reign of 'Izz al-Dīn Kaykāwus II (1246–1261) marked the end of the territorial integrity of the Seljukid realm under a single ruler. Although he reigned between 1246 and 1248 as sole sovereign, from 1249 onwards the kingdom was divided and he ruled jointly, first with one brother then with two, until he was finally forced off the throne in 1261 and compelled to take up exile outside the kingdom where he died (in the Crimea) in 1279.[4] As a consequence of the fragmentation of the state that gained in pace and intensity after the second Mongol invasion of Anatolia in 1256, power, influence as well as military and fiscal control devolved to the regions throughout the 1260s and 1270s corresponding to the time frame in which the epic tale of Sarı Saltuk and his band of heroes unfolds.

Sarı Saltuk's tale was collected and compiled from oral sources in the 1470s by Ebu'l-Hayr Rūmī in the *Saltuk-name*. The tale is set in specific localities such as Dobruja and the Crimea that were situated at the contested crossroads of empires and far removed from the field of vision and sphere of interests of the Konya-based chroniclers of dynastic glory, such as Ibn Bībī.[5] Therefore, despite the fact that the oral account of the events themselves is removed by almost two centuries from the lifespan of the protagonist Sarı Saltuk, who died in 1297, they provide a reliable record of the underlying conditions in these frontier regions whose social, political, cultural and economic makeup and horizons were a closed book to the court chroniclers of the time.[6]

For the purpose of drawing an accurate portrait of the life and self-defined priorities of the frontier warriors who conducted 'crusading' activity along the northern Bulgarian and the southern Russian fronts during the second half of the thirteenth century, no other source comes close to the *Saltuk-name* in its evocative resonance

---

serving as the figurehead and champion of a faction at court that remained steadfastly determined, at this time of division and fracture within the Seljukid polity, to seize its share of the available power and assets of the state.

4 For more detail on the confused political conditions within the Seljukid polity at this time, see Osman Turan, *Selçuklular zamanında Türkiye* (Istanbul: Turan Neşriyat Yurdu, 1971), pp. 521–22, and on the flight of the Turkmen from central Anatolia under the pressure of Mongol occupation, pp. 523–74. See also, on the issue of divided sovereignty and the increased financial burden imposed by the tributary status of the Seljukid realm after the second Mongol invasion of Anatolia in 1256, Faruk Sümer's article 'Kaykavus II', in *Diyanet Vakfı Islam Ansiklopedisi*, 44 vols (Istanbul and Ankara: ISAM, 1988–2014), XXV (2002), pp. 355–57.

5 The empires, some old some newly formed, that contested for control over these borderland regions were: (a) the Byzantine empire, (b) the Second Bulgarian Empire and (c) the Jochid Ulus of the Golden Horde.

6 Ebu'l-Hayr-ı Rûmî, *Saltuk-name*, ed. Şükrü Halûk Akalın, Kültür ve Turizm Bakanlığı yayınları, Kaynak Eserler Dizisi 8, 11, 3 vols (Ankara: Kültür ve Turizm Bakanlığı yayınları, 1988–1990).

and narrative credibility. It is perhaps the most locally grounded of the relatively small corpus of rare surviving folk-based or tribe-based narratives written (recited) with the express purpose of extolling the virtues of the tribesmen and their way of life. The *Saltuk-name* also advocates for the preservation of this way of life. The nomads inhabited a world and cherished a thought-world that was distinct from the world of courtly traditions, etiquette, ceremony, rituals and intellectualized versions of kingly virtue and knighthood expressed in the chronicle record inscribed by Ibn Bībī.

For an understanding of locally-grounded contemporary attitudes towards the ideal attributes of the hero and the quality of heroism associated with *alp-erenlik* and *bahadurluk*, terms that can be taken as the rough Turkic equivalents of 'knightliness' and 'valourousness' in the western chivalric tradition, we must turn to the evocation of these virtues and values in popular and folk narrative as they were preserved in the collective memory of the tribe and communicated in the form of epic tales, stories and oral recitations about the exploits of warrior braves (*alps*, *bahadurs*) of the past. Such tales typically convey an embellished and embroidered version of the past that can, from time to time, verge on the fabulous or—in deference to their audiences' shared taste for the dramatic or the magical—even the fantastic. However, these recitals, centred around the theme of heroism and the celebration of its most notable exponents, give us an arguably more realistic and less filtered account of prevailing conditions in the frontier regions than that inscribed in the court-centred chronicle record.

However fanciful or chronologically confused the folk recitations seem to modern tastes and expectations, these tales relating the exploits of the legendary *alps* and *bahadurs* can be regarded as a more reliable reflection of the thought world (*weltanschauung*) and the life experience (*lebenswelt*) of participants in 'crusade' than the intellectualized, politicized and ideologically motivated literary compositions produced by state bureaucrats and court advisers. In their eagerness to provide a sequentially ordered analysis of cause and effect in 'real-time' historical perspective, it is to the court chronicles that modern historians mostly turn. The common outlook, shared experience and shared space or locality that defined the sense of community or tribal belonging in the frontier regions are aspects of individual identity that are much better sought in the spontaneous literary artefacts rooted in those same localities than in the judgmental musings of outsiders to those traditions.[7]

Paul Wittek was undoubtedly correct in his observation that the court-centred Historiographers Royal (whether based in Constantinople or in Konya as the case might be) cared little and knew less about events that were unfolding in the frontier regions and thus failed for the most part to record them in their histories.[8] The migration of significant numbers of Muslim nomadic groups from inner Anatolia

---

[7] On the close connection between identity and locality, see Maurice Halbwachs, *On Collective Memory*, trans. by Lewis Coser (Chicago: University of Chicago Press, 1992), p. 70 *et seq*.

[8] For the markedly similar blind spot in both Seljukid and Byzantine historiography, see Paul Wittek, 'Yazicioglu Ali on the Christian Turks of the Dobruja', *Bulletin of the School of Oriental and African Studies*, 14 (1952), 639–68 (pp. 654–55).

to the northern part of the Balkans in the mid-thirteenth century finds little trace in either the Byzantine or the Seljukid chronicle record. It is only thanks to the insertion of new material from oral sources and compilations of *destans* (epic tales) centred around the historical figure of 'Izz al-Dīn Kaykāwus II (d. 1279) still circulating in the early decades of the fifteenth century at the time when Yazıcıoğlu Ali was preparing his Turkish translation of the Persian original of Ibn Bībī's thirteenth-century history that the path taken by these historic migrations can be partially reconstructed.

Ebu'l-Hayr's compilations date from the late fifteenth century (1470s) and the earliest dateable manuscripts that survive were copied no earlier than the 1570s. Nevertheless, the *Saltuk-name* unquestionably remains an indispensable, though not yet fully or adequately exploited, source for capturing the essence of social relations, military conditions and political realities that prevailed along the extended Byzantine-Seljukid frontier at the time of 'Izz al-Dīn Kaykāwus II's European (later Trans-Danubian) exile during the 1260s and 1270s.

It is clear from the volume of the material dutifully collected by the original compiler/collator of the story cycle revolving around the life and exploits of Sarı Saltuk, and subsequently greatly amplified and expanded by copyists and compilers of later centuries, that the heroism and bravery exhibited by the legendary heroes celebrated in the tale still struck a deeply resonant chord at the heart of the tribal consciousness of the Turkmen who lived in the late sixteenth century. The Topkapı Palace manuscript of the *Saltuk-name* copied in the year 1000 A.H. (AD 1591) and consisting of 618 folios (1236 pages) is the only manuscript that contains all three volumes (books) of the epic tale. However, two further manuscripts that preserve fragmentary and partial versions of the text focusing on parts of the narrative that relate to events taking place in particular geographical regions, have been preserved in codices now housed in the National Library in Ankara. One of these is a complete version of Book One only (MS B-64), which focuses mostly on Europe and comprises 283 folios (566 pages). Although this codex is undated, it retains a number of linguistic features and archaisms that suggest reliance on an earlier prototype or stemma that is now lost. A second codex (MS 17,292) that was copied in 985 A.H. (AD 1577) contains the text of Books Two and Three, which together comprise 449 pages of text if one excludes the title page. Taken together, these codices (Book One comprised of 566 pages) and Books Two and Three (comprised of 449 pages) account for a total narrative prose tale consisting of more than one thousand pages of text in Arabic script.[9]

The gap of 300 years between the events of the 1270s and the copying of the first surviving manuscripts in the 1570s inevitably opened the way for various errors of fact and historical inaccuracies to enter into the text, but later accretions and additions to the tale did little harm to the creators' collective intent, which was to uphold tribal values and honour the memory of its heroes who lived in former times. Writers of court-based history would have had little sympathy for these values and traditions,

---

9 Since the Arabic script omits the vowel sounds in many words, it can be considered a form of short-hand form of transmitting the Turkish text.

nor much direct connection with the locations and conditions at the frontier which produced them, but oral history preserving the attitudes and life experiences of the direct and most active participants in frontier warfare fills an important gap in our understanding of the past and allows us, if only partially and 'through a glass darkly', to resurrect the context and condition of displacement, relocation, exile, migration, movement and search for a new 'homeland' experienced by tribal populations expelled from Anatolia, either by the political misfortune of an ally or overlord (such as 'Izz al-Dīn Kaykāwus II) or by the relentless pressure on available grazing and pasture land resulting from the inexorable westward advance of the Mongols beginning from the 1240s.

The self-told tale of Sarı Saltuk and the Oghuz tribesmen who followed him to Dobruja offer us a glimpse into real life conditions and dynamic movements at the margins of empire providing us with an alternative and much needed corrective to the rather static and narrowly focused perspective offered by state-centred history.

Before we embark on the task of mining the text of the *Saltuk-name* for evidence about the world view and life experience of the nomads it is appropriate that we should first offer some introductory remarks on two key topics relating to the investigation:

(1) Excursus on the Tribe: background information on the structure, character and organization of the Tribe.
(2) Excursus on the Text: background information on the structure, character and organization of the Text.

Excursus on the Tribe

During periods characterized by the retreat of the state, the focus of loyalty of the tribe was per force more inward looking and reliant on the self-governing structure of the tribe itself. Events such as the destruction of the Caliphate in 1258 and the lack of a coherent or stable political centre in Anatolia at the same time led to the localization of power and its concentration at levels below that of multi-clan tribal confederations, called *ulus*, in the service of established states. Smaller units of association such as the *obuk* (a kinship-based loyalty group) or even the *ayil* (a herding unit) composed of a few, not necessarily genealogically related, tents camped together for more efficient performance of tasks relating to management of the herd, provided the social context on which tribal life unfolded.[10] It is important to recognize that while all of the organizational units referred to above existed at every stage of state

---

10 For a discussion of these terms and their significance for the Mongol social system and social stratification and political organization in the Mongol and post-Mongol eras, see Shagdaryn Bira, 'The Mongols and Their State in the Twelfth and Thirteenth Centuries', in *History of The Civilizations of Central Asia*, ed. by Muhammad Seyfeydinovich Asimov and Clifford Edmund Bosworth, 6 vols [incomplete] (Paris: UNESCO, 1992–), IV, Part 1 (1998), pp. 243–59, and Christopher Atwood, 'The Administrative Origins of Mongolia's Tribal Vocabulary', *Eurasia: Statum et Legem*, le 1/4 (2015), 7–45. Bira makes the astute and highly pertinent observation that while some larger tribal groupings incorporating several *oymaks* (clans) might join together and form a confederation of tribes with a wider territorial base referred to

formation, integration and disintegration, the degree of their interconnectivity with the hierarchical structures imposed by the state varied considerably according to the various phases of the state's development.

As a general rule, historians tend to regard the dissociative phases of state-tribe relations in which links with wider structures were weak as problematic, and they regard any deviation from the ideal of unity and central control as constituting a pathological phase in the evolution of the state. Periods and places such the Balkans and Anatolia in the second half of the thirteenth century when and where the ideal of the unitary state seemed to become a progressively more elusive goal for both the Byzantine and the Seljukid empires are mostly regarded as abnormal and aberrant phases of imperial history. If the master narrative of the state dominates our understanding of the period, then we are forced to accept the conclusion that periods in which any weakening of associative linkages between clans, war bands and other self-governing nomadic groups operating at the local level, on the one hand, and the state, on the other, should be regarded, not just as abnormal, but wholly pathological. There is however an alternative viewpoint which insists that lack of state centralization and concentration of power within its own home-grown power networks and hierarchies was a far less 'normal' and normative state of affairs in the Middle Ages than the defenders of the state would have us believe. Centrifugal forces may have been in evidence, but the assumption that the regionalization and even localization of power and power networks could only have a destructive influence on the body politic is unproven.

Already in the 1930s and 1940s scholars with an interest in tribal organisation and its relationship to state power were debating the question concerning the healthiness or otherwise of the independence of the tribe from state-imposed authority structures in the historical past and reaching starkly diverging conclusions. Boris Vladimirtsov's pioneering work on Mongol social organization, published posthumously in 1934, took the view that tribes and tribalism were a primitive or pre-state evolutionary development and that internal structures within tribes were gradually subordinated to or even eliminated by the advanced hierarchical structures and mechanisms for central control developed by the state, a process which he believed had its beginnings even as early as the Ghengizid era.[11] On the other side of the debate, Owen Lattimore took the view that organizational structures of tribes followed their own developmental trajectory independent from the state and that the tribe managed to preserve its independence and co-exist with the state throughout the Middle Ages and persisted into the modern era.[12] Lattimore saw that in its essence the tribe was a self-governing

---

as *ulus*, these formations did not always or inevitably lead to state formation, but merely mimicked the state by displaying some 'state-like' features such as top-down authority structures developed to organize joint activities such as military campaigning more efficiently.

11 Boris Vladimirtsov, Общественный строй монголов: Монгольский кочевой феодализм (Leningrad, 1934); French edition: *Le régime social des Mongols: le féodalisme nomade*, trans. by Michel Carsow (Paris: Librairie d'Amerique et d'Orient, Adrien-Maisonneuve, 1948).

12 Owen Lattimore, *Inner Asian Frontiers of China* (New York: American Geographical Society, 1940, repr. Hong Kong, New York: Oxford University Press, 1988), see in particular, p. 56.

entity that could exist either in opposition to the state or in cooperation with it according to its own calculation of what best suited its interest.[13]

During periods of rapidly shifting political alliances and fluid territorial borders, the tribesmen themselves were subject to a process of splintering and re-affiliation arising from the necessities imposed by dislocation, forced migration and exile to new areas of occupation. A suitable new location with plentiful resources for grazing their herds might only be available at a considerable distance from the zone of seasonal transhumance that they had formerly occupied. The splitting up of the tribe into sub-clan and smaller groups dispersed over a wide territory was a traumatic event that created the need for recruiting new members of the tribe and win-over affiliates and allies to contribute their labour and take part in the collective pursuits of the new tribal formation. This was a usual event in steppe history and was accommodated by means of well-established tribal institutions developed to foster bonds of friendship, mutual support and common loyalty from elements drawn from diverse origins.

The institution known as *anda* (tally friendship) and a closely related form with a similar purpose known by the name *nöker* and *nöker*ship (comradeship, companionship) had a wide application among the Mongols. This type of alliance (whether an *anda* pact or a relationship between co-equal *nökers*) was strictly individual and personal and had no wider political meaning in the context of a federation of tribes or inter-territorial construct. A war band or raiding party composed of a few dozen fighters could be constructed (and equally readily disbanded) on the basis of such private covenants between diverse elements without the need for either common kinship or common clan affiliation to be eligible for membership. The sole criteria for membership were friendship and commitment to a shared project undertaken by mutual agreement in equal partnership.

The Turks of Inner Asia in the pre-Islamic era were known to operate on a similarly small-scale basis characterized by locally resident horizontal command structures as opposed to vertical chains of command linked to a remote authority figure. A company of thirty 'lads' (*oğlan*), i.e., warrior braves, could operate independently separated from their leader (captain) called *chur* by only one layer of 'rank', but since the captain was usually chosen (elected) amongst his comrades on a merit basis in recognition of his martial skills and proven record of bravery in battle, his position within the band was more that of *primus inter pares* than that of commanding officer. After the westward migration of the Turks into the Islamic world in Iran, the Caucasus and Asia Minor in later centuries when they were dispersed over a wide expanse of the Eurasian landmass, far removed from their original homeland in the Inner Asian

---

13 Atwood, 'Administrative Origins', p. 8, citing Lattimore's view that: 'territorially-based state structures could not really develop in truly nomadic conditions' lends support to the idea that rather than viewing state-tribe relations through the prism of mutual opposition or looking for evidence of one being subsumed by the other, it is more productive, as well as historically accurate, to view them as having existed side by side as parallel planetary universes whose orbits rarely intersected.

steppe, such localized forms of cooperative association and self-governance remained the norm in many parts of their adopted homeland in western Asia.[14]

The localism and egalitarianism of nomadic social structure made the nomads largely invisible (as well as unintelligible) to observers in contiguous settled societies except at those times the nomads were engaged in 'depredations' against their neighbours. However, when those 'depredations' took place on a remote frontier, such activity (often conducted on a small scale) still managed to pass beneath the radar of the historians who were after-all only responsible for recording large-scale events, which had a direct impact on the health and safety of the core territories of the empire. The inner dynamics that governed movement, migration, displacement and supplementing of the pastoral economy by the mounting of periodic raiding parties into contiguous zones, whether in the steppe or the settled world, remained an enigma the cracking of whose secret code was of little interest to such historians. However opaque it may be, the only really reliable evidence we really have to draw upon to understand this secret world is that provided in the self-declarations of the nomads found in long-prose epic tales such as the *Saltuk-name*.

A key aspect of the largely hidden sub-tribal, sub-clan highly localized formations such as the war band composed of voluntary recruits is the fact that they were made up of individuals who were social equals. The small scale of such formations removed the need for (and the desirability of) hierarchical authority structures being imposed from outside the self-selecting group. The 'title' assigned to the co-equal members of the group of warrior braves called *bagatur* (also *ba'adur/bahadur*) was used more in the sense of an honorific given in recognition of bravery shown in battle than it was to convey social status or 'rank' within the tribe. Such titles whose origin dates from the pre-Islamic era were morphed into Islamic equivalents such as *alp-eren* or *gazi* in later centuries, but it is important to recognize that they conveyed no broader political significance nor did they imply membership in a 'privileged' social status group recognized by broader society. In his pioneering study on the historical significance of the *alp* figure based largely on literary sources Fuad Köprülü made the questionable assumption that as a tradition (institution) *alphood* or *bahadurluk* could or should be likened to the same kind of infeudation and subordination to an overlord as that encountered in western feudalism. Köprülü even goes so far as to speculate about the existence of a nomadic 'nobility' (*göçebe asilzadeliği*) that was capable of being inherited.[15]

Despite the initial success of the conquests led by Ghengiz Khan and his immediate successors, far from succeeding in the imposition of a vertically integrated power structure over an extended territorial base, it is clear that throughout large parts of

---

14 For a discussion of the institutional and organizational basis on which the assembling of the 'bands of thirty' rested in the East among the eighth century Gök Turks and in the West among the tenth century Pechenegs and an investigation of the history and significance of the 'title' *chur*, see Otto J. Maenchen-Helfen, *The World of the Huns: Studies in their History and Culture* (Berkeley: University of California Press, 1973), pp. 393–400.

15 See Fuad Köprülü, 'Alp' in *Islam Ansiklopedisi*, 13 vols (Ankara: Milli Eğitim Bakanlığı, 1950–1988), I (1950), pp. 379–84.

western Asia in the middle to late Middle Ages large regions brought together under a shared imperial administration that was capable of exerting consistent local control from a single administrative centre or capital city was a relatively rarity. Tribesmen based in the regions engaged in wider alliances as and when they deemed it profitable or otherwise advantageous, but this happened only from time to time, and military partnerships entered into for short-term gain, were as rapidly dissolved as they had been formed.[16]

Our understanding of social stratification among the nomads of the western Eurasian steppe in the medieval era is most probably distorted by facile accounts of the Mongol imperium in the post-Ghengizid era that imagine a much more orderly universe under the direction and tutelage of the Great Khans of China than ever can have existed in reality. The presumption that effective centralized rule by stable dynasties represented a kind of norm from which other, more localized, forms and mechanisms of governance represent some kind of deviation, must be considered a serious distortion of the actual conditions that prevailed at the time. If there was no autocracy whose lifespan lasted more than one or two generations, then equally there was no opportunity for the development of a hereditary aristocracy or a favoured elite to whom power and administrative authority could be assigned and re-assigned by the state.

It is far more productive, in addition to being reflective of actual historical conditions, for us to imagine not a system with powers devolved to the regions which all the while retained their links to a single central authority, but rather one made up of multi-centred power structures that existed fully autonomously at the local level. These local power centres were perfectly capable of co-existing with other power centres in their region and since their leadership structures were all tribally based there was no great need for communication across a wider geographical space. Several such chieftaincies or commanderies could happily manage their sector of a wider frontier or region acting independently one from the other. Coordination of effort on a wider scale was rarely necessary and certainly not a permanent desideratum.

Under the conditions of tribal dispersion and self-governance described above, a typical unit of cohabitation consisted of the *oba*, or shared campsite, which typically corresponded to a clustering of 5–10 tents with a population (of all ages and genders) of up to about fifty people.[17]

By pooling their resources of young able-bodied males, one or two *obas* would be capable of assembling a small raiding party composed of twenty to thirty braves while a season's campaigning over a wider territory might require the mobilization of several hundred braves selected from ten to fifteen *obas*. Mention has already

---

16 On the transient character of such alliances in particular among the Kipchak tribes of the southern Russian steppe and the lower Volga region, see Reşit Rahmeti Arat, 'Kıpçak' in *Islam Ansiklopedisi*, VI, pp. 713–16, see in particular, p. 714: 'zaman zaman müşterek hareket için birleşmişlerdir. Garpta [...] Kıpçak grupları, ayrı ayrı çok müessir hamleler yapabilecek kudrette olmakla beraber, bir idare altında ve muayyen merkezler etrafında toplanmamışlardır'.
17 For this definition of *oba*, see *Tarama Sözlüğü*, 8 vols (Ankara:Türk Tarih Kurumu Basımevi, 1963–1977), V (1971), pp. 2903–2904.

been made of the compact size of smaller raiding parties consisting of thirty young lads (*oğlan, yiğit*).[18] From the testimony of the *Saltuk-name* we learn of the denser groupings required for operations over a more prolonged period or for a season of campaigning lasting several months. When the Turkmen accompanying Sarı Saltuk, or more precisely their protégée 'Izz al-Dīn Kaykāwus II, set out from Dobruja to the Crimea in 1264, we are told that their combined forces consisted of one thousand braves.[19] Of these 1000 braves, 300 were left behind in Dobruja to manage and defend their homestead in Babadag, located south of Tulcea near the modern-day border between Romania and Moldova. The remaining 700 made up the scouting party that set out for the Crimea to seek their fortune there.[20] Later on this group was further sub-divided for distribution across several fronts in southern and eastern Crimea.

The force assigned to one of the warrior chieftains named Kara Davud consisted of 400 braves charged with reconnaissance and raiding against the eastern portions of the frontier with Russia.[21] There are several other references in the text of the *Saltuk-name* to the gathering together of recruits (implied rather indiscriminately from multiple local sources) without much attention being paid to their ethnicity or religion.[22] It is highly significant that, in the case of the expeditions carried out by Kara Davud, it was not just the followers and rank-and-file soldiers who are described as a rag-tag assemblage drawn from diverse elements, but the leader himself was both an outsider and, at the same time, a recent convert to Islam. It is clear from the text that Kara Davud was by origin not a Turkmen, but a Tatar since, at his first introduction to the narrative, he is described as such:

> There was a *gazi* who hailed from the country around Caffa, a Tatar. They called him Kara Davud by name. Following his association with the Seyyid (i.e., Sarı Saltuk) he took part in numerous raids and accomplished many acts of manly valour.[23]

---

18 See above, note 12.
19 *Saltuk-name*, I, p. 153.
20 *Saltuk-name*, I, p. 154.
21 *Saltuk-name*, I, p. 174: *Kara Davud 400 yiğit uydurup, azm-i Rus etti*. The use of the verb *uydurmak* ('to cobble together, gather up from random ingredients ready to hand') is not accidental. It means that some of his forces were likely to have been local recruits gathered at locations close to the areas targeted for attack.
22 *Saltuk-name*, I, p. 174, which records the words of advice provided by a local ally to Kara Davud about the best strategy for troop recruitment on the eve of campaign. This advice is given verbatim in the closely clipped sentences presented in the form of simulated dialogue that was typical of this genre of oral literature: *Bir alay top olun*. The active meaning and sense of *top olmak* (to mass together, gather up in a group) is no longer used in modern Turkish. For the archaic form *top olmak*, see the *Tarama Sözlüğü*, V, p. 3824.
23 *Saltuk-name*, I, p. 161: 'Kefe diyarında bir gazi vardı. Tatar idi. Adına Kara Davud derlerdi. Seyyidden sonra çok gazalar ve erlikler eylemiştir'. On the participation of large numbers of Tatar 'freelancers' in raids against the Russian frontier in the last decades of the thirteenth century, see Istvan Vasary, *Cumans and Tatars: Oriental Military in the Pre-Ottoman Balkans, 1185–1365* (Cambridge: Cambridge University Press, 2005). In Vasary's opinion, for these volunteers, hunger for booty was a stronger motivation than the attraction of contributing to the success of 'Holy War'.

So far as the context of frontier warfare of the thirteenth century is concerned, *nöker-ship*, sometimes misleadingly translated as 'body guard' or member of an elite corps attached to imperial service, carried the less exalted, but still highly regarded, sense of fellow member of a military brotherhood or simply comrade-in-arms. *Nökers* pledged themselves to loyal service to their fellow warriors, not to a remote political authority and—while they were bound to obey the orders of the chiefs who led their collective ranks—the maintaining of group solidarity took precedence over other commitments. As an institution *nöker*ship can be compared to *comitatus* in the pre-Christian Germanic and Nordic traditions in which a shared code of ethics, traditions of honour and service obligation were accepted as binding on all; both set and monitored by members of the band in a self-imposed and self-regulating manner. In a sense thus, it was adherence to the code of practice and self-defined performance standards that determined a warrior's merit and not his position, rank or seniority within the association.

The designation *nöker* carried in origin a mostly honorific meaning as is clear from its use in describing Ghengiz Khan's rise to prominence in the pre-imperial phase of his career recorded in the anonymous *Secret History of the Mongols*. The strict dictionary meaning of *nöker* is 'friend' and its association with a process of vassalization, subordination, or loyalty to a supreme ruler within a system of imperial governance postdates the elevation of the warrior chief Temujin as ruler at the tribal council (*kurultai*) of 1206. It was only then that the title Ghengiz Khan was awarded to him.[24]

The self-governance and free agency associated with tribal life and near the frontiers of empires in dissolution and at times of political confusion or fluidity attending the emergence of new empires was accompanied and perhaps accentuated—in the case of the Byzantine-Bulgarian-Crimean-Russian borderlands in the late thirteenth century—by a surrounding frontier environment characterized by cultural syncretism which attended the arrival of new populations and nomadic migrations of significant scale, intensity and duration. A pluralistic religious environment, fluidity of religious identity and the competition between cultures regarding religious and sectarian identities had an indisputable, but scarcely definable, let alone measurable, impact on the forms of 'crusading' warfare that took shape in this frontier area. In any case, for our analysis of the *Saltuk-name* it is not the complexity of religious identity or the faith traditions of the participants that will form our principal focus, but more how far the text allows us to detect, sometimes faintly sometimes more distinctly, the principal elements of the military values and martial instincts as well as the

---

24 Confirmation of the basic meaning of the term stripped of its connotations as applied within a system of precedence or state affiliation is provided in a number of sources. See, for example, Bira, 'Mongols and Their State', p. 245: 'Nöker (*nüküd*) means "friend" and the term referred to a member of a group of warriors who freely [emphasis is mine] declared themselves to be the "men" of a chosen leader, irrespective of their origin or tribal affiliation'. See also Antoine Mostaert, *Dictionnaire Ordos*, 3 vols (Peking: Catholic University, 1941–1944), II (1942), p. 498: *nökör* – ami, *nökörlö* – nouer les relations d'amitié; *Mongolian-English Dictionary*, compiled by Ferdinand Lessing, Mattai Halfold and others (Berkeley: University of California Press, 1960), p. 593: *nøkyr* – friend, comrade, companion. *Türkiye'de Halk Ağzından Derleme Sözlüğü*, 12 vols (Ankara: Türk Dil Kurumu, 1963–1982), IX (1977), p. 3255: *nöger* – erkek arkadaş, *nögerlik etmek* – arkadaşlık, dostluk etmek.

behavioural norms that animated the main participants in the frontier warfare of this time and of this place, i.e., the nomads. The text unquestionably offers us an un-prevaricating self-portrait of the nomads; one unfiltered by the values, prejudices and authorial inclinations of those who saw themselves as the standard bearers of High (i.e., 'written' as opposed to 'oral') Culture.

Nomadic or steppe warfare practiced as a way of life and source of livelihood had its own traditions as well as an ancient pedigree that far predated the rise of Islam in the mid-seventh century AD. and its gradual spread amongst the Turks of Central Asia during the ninth and tenth centuries. The importance of booty raiding as a source of material wealth and sustenance for the tribe is given prominence in oral traditions associated with steppe warriors of the earlier, Inner Asian, phase of the history of the Oghuz Turks, in particular the *Oghuz-name* which honours the memory of their eponymous founder-figure Oghuz Khan.[25] The two well-springs of tribal pride, honour and boastfulness were, on the one hand, military prowess and the lust for reputation and glory within the tribe based on a warrior's excellence in horsemanship and his bravery and manliness in battle and, on the other hand, desire for and competiveness with other warrior braves over the accumulation of plunder, booty and loot.

The Islamicized term *ganimet*, applied to the acquisition of booty in later centuries, provided a polite veneer to cloak the 'primitive' origins of the practice, but could not fully disguise its essential purpose. In its sanitized form *ganimet* was a term used to indicate that spoils of war were a source of wealth that derived legitimately from the engagement by 'Holy Warriors' (*gazis*) in 'Holy War' (*gaza*) against the infidels. Other stripped-down terms unadorned with high moral overtones such as *çapul* ('sack'), *doyum* ('satiety deriving from surfeit of plunder') remained in use side by side with the more dignified Islamic term and both are encountered even in written sources chiefly intended for circulation in court circles and amongst members of the literary elite.[26]

For a better understanding of the ways in which booty, apart from its importance to the material well-being of the tribe, served as an indication of a warrior's bravery and merit as measured by his fellow tribesmen, the *Secret History of the Mongols*, completed *c.* 1240, a short time after the death of Ghengiz Khan in 1227, provides some useful clues. In a revealing passage, Ghengiz Khan upbraided his grandson Güyük—later (in 1246) himself elevated as *khan* but seemingly still in his teens at the time the rebuke was issued—for his insubordination and excessive pride in his own achievements. Ghengiz Khan's censure was delivered as follows:

> [During the campaign] you took one or two Orusut (Russian) | and Kibča'ut (Kipchak) [captive], but while you haven't yet acquired | as booty even the hoof

---

25 For purposes of our analysis in this chapter, we have made use of the text transcribed and translated by Balazs Danka. See footnote 28 below.
26 On customs associated with the accumulation of *ganimet* in the Islamic context and the expectation, indeed obligation on the part of members of the social elite, that a portion of these gains should be invested in charitable and socially beneficial projects, see Fuad Köprülü, 'Selçukiler zamanında Anadolu'da Türk Medeniyeti', *Milli Tetebbüler Mecmuası*, 2/5 (1331/1915), 193–223 (pp. 220–21). See also, Fuad Köprülü, 'Bahadur' in *Islam Ansiklopedisi*, II (1961), pp. 217–19.

of a kid, you make yourself into a hero; | having left home but once, you pretend that you alone have | accomplished everything.[27]

Another source which is useful in this regard is the epic tale and heroic story cycle devoted to the legendary figure of the eponymous founder of the Oghuz Turks in their original homeland in Inner Asia that circulated widely (in oral form) throughout western Asia in the thirteenth to fifteenth centuries among the newly converted and still incompletely acculturated Oghuz tribesmen who had migrated from Inner Asia in the wake of the Mongol invasions of the early thirteenth century. An early version of the epic tale (the *Oghuz-name*) was first copied down in Uyghur script and a codex, whose stemma is traceable to a date around 1300, is preserved in Paris in the Bibliothèque Nationale.[28] In the context of the pre-Islamic norms that prevailed in Inner and Central Asia before the westward migration of the Turks, which are transparently reflected in this codex, the only two types of booty to be distinguished are described, un-emotively, as 'dead booty' (i.e., moveable goods) and 'live booty' (i.e., human captives and livestock). Both forms of booty are seen as legitimate gain that fell to the soldiers' lot as the natural proceeds from battle, earned by their joint efforts and sweat and toil rather than as a compensation granted them by any outside authority for their participation in a 'just war'. For the participants, the spoils of war were not regarded as a reward vouchsafed, but simply what belonged by right to the victors, whose army proved itself more courageous and more valiant as tried in a contest of arms. In one passage from the Paris codex of the *Oghuz-name* the richness of the reward that fell to the victors is described as follows:

> After the fight, Oguz Kagan's army, bodyguards (i.e., comrades at arms, fellow warriors) and people (i.e., rank and file members of the tribe) gained so much [in the way of] inanimate goods (i.e., moveable property) that an insufficiency of beasts of burden (lit. horses, mules and oxen) turned out to load the goods and carry [them] away.[29]

---

27 *The Secret History of the Mongols: A Mongolian Epic Chronicle of the Thirteenth Century*, trans. by Igor de Rachewiltz, shorter version ed. by John C. Street, Madison Books and Monographs 4 (University of Wisconsin, 2015). http://cedar.wwu.edu/cedarbooks/4, paragraph 277, p. 196. Compare *The Secret History of the Mongols: for the first time done into English out of the original tongue and provided with an exegetical commentary*, trans. by Francis Cleaves (Cambridge, Mass.: Harvard University Press, 1982), paragraph 277, p. 218.

28 For a facsimile edition of the Paris MS Suppl. Turc 1001 with translation, see Balazs Danka, *The Pre-Islamic Oguz-nama: A philological and linguistic analysis* (unpublished doctoral thesis, University of Szeged, 2016) [URL: http://doktori.bibl.u-szeged.hu/3179/1/danka_disszertacio_06_20.pdf].

29 Balazs Danka, 'The Pre-Islamic Oguz-nama', pp. 99–101. For the distinction between *ölüg bargu* (inanimate or moveable booty) and *dirig bargu* (animate booty or captives) see Danka, p. 101 (ll. 7–9). For other passages referring to *bargu* (booty), see Danka, p. 77 (l. 9) and p. 79 (l. 1). In addition, see Gerard Clauson, *An Etymological Dictionary of Pre-Thirteenth Century Turkish* (Oxford: Oxford University Press, 1972), p. 142 (*ölüg bargu*) and p. 560 (*olüg bargu tüşdi*, 'large quantities of booty fell to the lot of the army'). For a related lexical variation in the form *bark* (*ba:r*) referring to moveable property and household goods, see Clauson, p. 359. The term used in a compound expression, joined together with the word for house/household (*ev*) survives in western Turkic dialect in the expression *ev bark*, 'a man's house, household and household effects'. See James Redhouse, *A Turkish and English Lexicon* (Istanbul: American Mission, 1890), p. 232.

In this passage, it is the martial skills and heroic virtues of the warriors themselves that are being showcased and celebrated and the same is true throughout the course of the narrative of the *Saltuk-name*, in which political causes and even the identity of rulers and political agents are mentioned only in passing and hardly given any prominence. Proper understanding of the main thrust of the narrative requires that we should dwell, however briefly, on some of the stylistic features of the text itself.

Excursus on the Text

The *Saltuk-name* represents something of an anomaly within the genre to which it is usually assigned, namely the *menakib-name* which typically relates the exploits/praiseworthy actions (sg. *mankaba*) of a particular individual, usually a spiritual leader or saintly figure, who remains the protagonist and central personage at the centre of the episodic reiterations of the tale, whose central purpose is to extoll his virtues.[30] Although it shares some common features with this genre, the text that has survived is neither a biographical nor a hagiographic account of Sarı Saltuk and his life and exploits, but rather a kind of stream of consciousness narrative relating the wanderings and exploits of the tribesmen who accompanied him during his missionary voyages. In the narrative, Sarı Saltuk makes frequent appearance—often in the form of a kind of *deus ex machina* presence or animating spiritual influence—but rarely takes a direct or active role in the proceedings. He is not described as an active participant in any of the battles, raids or campaigns, which form the main narrative thread of the tale. Those whose exploits (*mankaba*) are recited and invoked while at the same time being given recognition as the real 'heroes' of the tale are his lieutenants, the warrior braves. Commending the fighting spirit of these warriors persistently emerges as the abiding theme which links all the plots and subplots developed in the tale. The warrior brave as an ideal 'type', the qualities of true *prud'homme* who upholds the honourable traditions of the knightly profession are main themes to which the narrative repeatedly returns as the tale progresses.

The main purpose of the narrative in the *Saltuk-name* is not to relate the exploits of a single hero figure, but a series of heroic figures and to praise their shared virtues and their ability to perform commendable and often semi-miraculous feats of bravery. In essence thus, it is not the hero figure as an individual which is being celebrated in the text, so much as the quality of heroism itself. To reinforce the central message relating to the essence of heroism and heroic virtue, the narrators/reciters of the tale are not constrained to drawing their subject matter from a single historical era or place. The tale is constantly being added to and further elaborated by each new generation of tribesmen who have inherited a tradition that is centred on legendary heroes of the past, but it is also expandable and able to incorporate references to more recent events connected with the collective memory of the tribe. Because of the multiplicity of 'heroes' whose achievements are being recalled and celebrated, the narrative often

---

30 See Charles Pellat, 'Manāḳib', in *Encyclopaedia of Islam, Second Edition*, 12 volumes (Leiden: Brill, 1960–2005), VI (1991), pp. 349–57.

takes on a convoluted, fragmentary, disjointed as well as chronologically confused character. In segments of the tale that are juxtaposed as the narrative unfolds, heroes and villains from different centuries and different geographic locations appear side by side in the same episode as though they were fellow countrymen and contemporaries.

Alongside figures such as Hüsām al-Din Çoban, the Seljukid governor of Kastamonu in the 1220s, whose path might conceivably have crossed with Sarı Saltuk before his emigration to Dobruca in 1261, the text relates the exploits of Timur (Tamerlane), whose rise to prominence in Central Asia dated from the 1370s and whose first appearance in the eastern margins of Asia Minor was not before the mid-1390s. Such historical anomalies posed no problem so far as the tastes of the nomadic audiences gathered to be entertained by the recital of the epic feats of epic heroes were concerned. Poetic licence dictated that so long as the dramatic tension was maintained at high levels and the basic message concerning the heroism of their tribal ancestors was clearly delivered, the auditors (receptors) were not disposed to quibble over the lack of attention to accuracy in factual detail.

An important feature of the text that must be emphasized relates to its origin in oral transmission, repetition and recitation. It is this feature which explains the embroidering and enrichment of the text through the course of multiple performances and, only much later, woven into a rambling, errant and highly digressive tale, collected, collated and inscribed from the mouths and memories of multiple informants/reciters. In rural and nomadic settings, the habit and tradition of oral recitation of stories, epic tales and dramatizations of the historical past featuring select heroes and villains drew on an immense reserve retained in the collective memory of the tribe. The literary tastes, preferences and expectations of nomad/folk audiences changed little over time, and it is clear that it is in part due to the unchanging nature of their partiality for this type of story-telling – incorporating elements of the magical, the supernatural and the heroic – that these tales first recorded by Ebu'l-Hayr Rūmī in the 1470s retained their currency and popularity into the sixteenth and seventeenth centuries when the tales were copied down as text in the only manuscripts that have survived to our day.[31]

The insertion of marginal headings, rubrics and chapter divisions by scribes responsible for the transcribing of the surviving codices of the *Saltuk-name* reveals the manner in which the text was converted from oral recitations—often devoted exclusively to the recounting of exploits by one particular, regionally or locally remembered or renowned 'hero' figure—into self-contained segments or sub-plots. These individual segments might typically fill only a few folios of the thousand-page work.[32] An example of this

---

31 On the popularity of the *aşık* (troubadour) tradition in later centuries, see Fuad Köprülü, 'Türk edebiyatında aşık tarzının menşe ve tekamülü hakkında bir tecrübe', *Milli Tetebbüler Mecmuası*, 1/1 (1331/1915), 5–46; Pertev Nail Boratov, 'La littérature des aşıq' in *Philologiae Turcicae Fundamenta*, ed. by Alessio Bombaci, Louis Bazin, and others, 2 vols (Wiesbaden: Franz Steiner, 1959–1964), II, pp. 129–46. For a detailed study of the survival of oral histories, storytelling and folk history celebrating the career and exploits of Tiryaki Hasan Pasha, see Claire Norton, *Plural Pasts: Power, Identity and the Ottoman Sieges of Nagykanizsa Castle* (London: Routledge, 2017), see especially pp. 56–58, for her remarks on the survival and vitality of oral culture into the early 1600s in popular forms such as the *gazavat-name* (victory recital).

32 For an account of the length and inscription histories of the various surviving codices, see p. 387 above.

is found in the section of the text that recounts the exploits of several of the warrior braves who accompanied the tribal contingents who first sojourned into the Crimea in 1264. In one of the manuscripts,[33] the scribe responsible for the copying this part of the text has added a chapter heading by the insertion in the margin of the phrase: *matlab-i diyar-i Kefe* ('Investigation on the Region of Caffa/Crimea').[34] A few folios further on,[35] the narrative is once again sub-divided, by the scribe's intervention aimed at introducing 'order' into the rambling style typical of the long-prose epic tale, by means of another rubric added in the margin: *matlab-i Kara Davud ve Kemal Ata, ma Kızıl Elma*. By inserting such rubrics, the scribe draws the readers' attention—by means of a device which would have been superfluous for a 'listener' of the orally-recited tale—to the fact of a shift in narrative focus to a new sub-topic, namely the particular role in the conquest of the Crimea played by two particular celebrated heroes, i.e., Kara Davud and Kemal Ata and their quest for the legendary 'Golden Apple'.[36]

The text of the *Saltuk-name* which survives today is a work of compilation which took its original compiler Ebu'l-Hayr Rūmī seven years to complete from oral samples he collected and collated over the period 1473–1480.[37] In later centuries, further layers of interpretation, and sometimes also distortion, were introduced into the text by means of scribal intervention. Thus, the neatly transcribed presentation copy, the one with the most comprehensive contents that is today preserved in the Topkapı Palace library, shows evidence of considerable scribal tinkering with the text that amounts to an effective bowdlerization whereby the overtone and sectarian meaning in some passages has been altered to suit the political and religious sensitivities of the age in which it was copied. The date the copying of this codex was completed was 1000 A.H./ AD 1591. which coincided with a period of heightened tension after the recent conclusion of thirteen years of fighting during the Safavid-Ottoman War of 1578–1590 at which time oppositional sectarian politics had dominated interstate discourse between the Safavids and Ottomans.[38]

---

33 Ankara Milli Kütüphanesi, MS B-64, fol. 115a.
34 In addition to its standard dictionary meanings of investigation, quest or search, the term had a specialized meaning noted by Edward Lane, *An Arabic-English Lexicon*, One Volume in 8 parts (London and Edinburgh: Williams and Norgate, 1863–1893), I, p. 1865: 'a place or time of seeking [...] particularly applied to a place where anything remarkable is to be sought or looked for in a book'.
35 Ankara Milli Kütüphanesi, MS B-64, fol. 122b.
36 In Turkic myth and folk imagination, the focus of the symbolic quest for the 'Golden Apple' shifted in accordance with the path of tribal migration and conquest in particular periods from Byzantium (Constantinople) to Muscovy (Moscow) and in later centuries after the establishment of the Ottoman capital in Istanbul in 1453 to the capital of the Western Roman Empire (Rome). Its invocation by the scribe of this codex in the context of campaigns carried out against Russia in the pre-Ottoman age was a kind of deliberate antiquarianism being used to signal for his readers the genuine thirteenth-century origins of the tales being transmitted in the text.
37 *The Legend of Sarı Saltuk: Collected from Oral Tradition by Ebu'l-Ḥayr Rūmi*, ed. by Fahir Iz, 7 parts (Cambridge: Harvard University Printing Office, 1974–1984), I, editor's preface.
38 For remarks on the distortions, alternations and general censoring introduced into the codex copied in 1591, see Ahmed Yaşar Ocak, *Sarı Saltuk: Popüler Islam'ın Balkanlar'daki Destanı Öncüsü (XIII. Yüzyıl)*, revised 2nd ed. (Ankara: Türk Tarih Kurumu Basımevi, 2011), p. 7.

Another feature of orally transmitted long prose epics such as the *Saltuk-name* is their monumental length and overall tendency—despite the brevity, succinctness and simplicity of the narrative style and sentence structure in the particular segments that make up the tale—to a kind of narrative verboseness. This verboseness is related to the narrative's origin in speech and extemporaneous performance, which allows ample scope for diversion, digression and repetition. Scribes show their awareness of the danger that a reading (or even an inattentive 'listening') audience might struggle to follow the main plot of the story or become confused by the multiplicity of voices represented in the tale (recitation) by their use of standard rhetorical devices to break up the text and rally their audiences' flagging attention. One frequently employed device was interjection of phrases such as: 'raviler rivayet ederler ki [...]' ('the narrators [of tales] have related that [...]'), which serves to reassure the listener/readers concerning the authenticity of their source material in a reliable 'teller of tales' while at the same time signalling the shift to a new chapter, episode or sub-plot out of which the overall narrative has been constructed.[39]

The reliance on the testimony provided in orally transmitted accounts is not just a literary device employed by scribes; it reflected the preferences of contemporary folk audiences, who considered such testimony to provide a reliable, faithful and accurate form of preserving memories of past events that was less subject to falsification, alteration, or misrepresentation than the written word. The verbatim word of the bards carried greater authority for them than the pronouncements of the literati whose motives and sincerity they mistrusted.[40]

A final aspect relating to the oral character of the *Saltuk-name* narrative that deserves notice is the appearance in the text of mythical beasts, the slaying of dragons and reference to the use of magic, especially on the part of the main protagonist Sarı Saltuk, who is credited with an ability to be physically present in two different locations at the same time. All these hallmarks of folk storytelling appear unabashedly in the text, a fact that signals that this is a work that was unlikely to have appealed either to

---

39 A sense of how common this scribal device was can be gained from the frequency with which it was employed in a few sample pages drawn from the Crimea episode of the tale. See, for example, *Saltuk-name*, I, p. 153, where the phrase: 'raviler rivayet edip eyidürler kim' is used to mark the beginning of a new segment of the narrative, several pages later the phrase: 'Yazdılar. Bu zamana değin hikayet kaldı' (I, p. 155) is inserted to indicate the ending of that particular episode. On the same page (*Saltuk-name*, I, p. 155) the beginning of a new segment is set apart in the text with the insertion of the phrase: 've dahi nakildir ki', i.e., 'a[nother] narrator has related that' [...]. A short space later (*Saltuk-name*, I, p. 156) once again the phrase: 'raviler şöyle rivayet edip eyidürler kim' is used to mark the beginning of an extended digression relating to a different chronological age belonging to the time of Tamerlane, who lived until the early years of the fifteenth century, which takes up two pages of text (pp. 156–58). But, once this thematically linked, but chronologically disjointed, tale has been transmitted, the scribe indicates the need to 'get back to his sheep' by his use of the bridging expression (at the top of p. 159): 'Biz geldik yine Seyyid Sarı Saltuk hikayetine', which can be considered as the rough equivalent of the expression 'revenons à nos moutons'.

40 For the long afterlife of orality in the age of literacy and its preferability so far as the tastes of certain audiences were concerned, see Dennis Green, *Medieval Listening and Reading: The Primary Reception of German Literature, 800–1300* (Cambridge: Cambridge University Press, 1994), in particular the section of 'Oral Aspects of Reading', p. 147 *et seq.*

the tastes or literary preferences or to the faith practices of urban, literate mainstream Orthodox audiences. Thus, since it had its roots and origins in the countryside and was stamped with the literary and cultural approval of inhabitants of the countryside, the text can be trusted to provide us with an honest account of conditions in the frontier districts in which the nomads were operating. At the same time, it also offers a faithful and non-judgmental record of tribal custom, traditions and the general *modus vivendi* of the nomads, obtained directly from genuine native informants.

The text also displays features, in both form and content, that resonate closely with those found in other texts similarly devoted to the topic of extolling the virtues of the ideal warrior that were produced in Anatolia in the early fourteenth century. One of these accounts is a monumentally proportioned versified work, the *Garib-name*, which—although it is an authored work as opposed to a narrative tale passed down in story form by anonymous bards and troubadours—draws a largely consistent, though perhaps less visceral, portrait of the way of life and the value system adopted by the nomads living in frontier regions.[41] The *Garib-name* was completed by Âşık Paşa in 1330 just before his death in 1333. In form it is a mystical-didactic poem written in a more refined register than the *Saltuk-name*. The fact that it survives in multiple copies is an indication that the work had achieved considerable popularity starting soon after the author's death and retained its reputation and popularity in the centuries which followed. One portion of the poem, found in couplets 8493 to 8549, is devoted exclusively to the subject of the virtues and attributes of the *preux chevalier* and valorous knight in his account of the exemplary figure of the *alp* warrior.[42]

What is noticeable about the list of positive traits embodied in the ideal knight is any reference to the purity of his religious conviction and piety or any indication of an obligation to loyalty or obedience to an overlord or higher political authority. At the heart of Âşık Paşa's definition of the nine qualities/virtues incumbent on the gallant knight lies the concept of faithfulness and friendship to one's warrior comrades. Providing and reciprocating of friendship between faithful companions (*yar*) belonging to a band of stalwart warriors is found in the list—set out in ascending order of importance—in the place of pride as the final crowning or ninth attribute of the true knight.[43] The other eight qualities expected of the dedicated *alp* warrior were as follows:
(1) stout heart (*muhkem yürek*)
(2) physical prowess/bodily strength (*bazu'da kuvvet*)
(3) unwavering commitment (*gayret/hamiyyet*)
(4) a swift steed (*at*)
(5) a set full set of armour for the protection of self and mount in battle (*don*)

---

41 Âşık Paşa, *Garib-nâme*, ed. by Kemal Yavuz (Istanbul: Türk Dil Kurumu Yayınları, 2000). The definitive edition in 2 parts (part 1, pp. 1–288, part 2, pp. 293–534) contains 10,592 couplets.
42 Âşık Paşa, *Garib-nâme*, part 2, pp. 430–32.
43 Persian *yar* corresponds to Turkic *inağ* in eastern Turkic dialect as indicated in the authoritative dictionary compiled by Şeyh Süleyman al-Buhari, *Lugat-i Çagatay ve Türki-yi Osmani* (Istanbul: Mehran Matbaası, 1298/1882), p. 62: inağ = *yar-i sadık* (trustworthy friend); *hemrah-ı muvafık* (agreeable/reliable travelling companion). The same source (p. 290) provides the following equivalents for yar: *refik* (companion), *dost* (friend) and, by extension, *çeri* (mess mate, fellow soldier).

(6) a strong bow (*yay*)
(7) a keen sword (*kılıç*)
(8) a piercing lance (*süğü / süngü*).

The particular importance placed in Âşık Paşa's poem on friendship as an essential attribute of the good warrior tallies closely with the moral guidance and advice (*öğüt*) offered to the young warrior braves (*yiğit*) in the Sarı Saltuk legend. It is to the several revelatory passages of this narrative that we now turn in the final section of our contribution in this chapter on the theory and practice of knightliness and knightly valour among the nomadic Turks of the late thirteenth century.

Excerpts from the *Saltuk-name* Illustrating Concepts of Knightly Honour According to the Traditions of the Turkmen Alp Warrior[44]

Group 1: Excerpts Illustrating Notions of Bravery and its Manifestations in Battle Among the Alp Warriors

Ways of taunting or humiliating a defeated enemy included forms such as the planting of the captured battle-standard of a military adversary head-to-tail and buried in the ground.[45] Such practices are illustrated in the text in a passage relating the aftermath of the defeat of the Russian 'infidels' during the course of a skirmish. In response to the slight to his military reputation, the Russian ruler spoke of his intent to gain revenge by exclaiming:

> I swear that until such time as I take Kara Davud captive I will remain in the saddle and will not dismount [until I have gained my revenge on him]. So saying, he marched on until he reached the vicinity of the capital of the Sarmatian steppe.[46]

This passage reveals a set of shared values and recognized military attributes which honour the brave and steadfast and revile the weak and those who refuse a challenge or elect to withdraw from the fray without offering any resistance. There is no dishonour in defeat, but fleeing the field of battle before encountering the enemy is universally regarded as cowardly. Thus the notion that an enemy, regardless of his faith or political allegiance, can be noble if he adheres to the strictures of the shared military honour code is given clear expression in this passage. Moreover, the text as a whole speaks to a wide range of the chivalric virtues expected of the Muslim

---

44 In what follows the excerpts will be grouped in five main subject categories starting with passages relating to the martial skills and professionalism of the *alp* warriors and finishing with passages relating to forms of peaceful accommodation with former adversaries defeated in war.
45 *Saltuk-name*, I, p. 164: 'Han'a koştular sancağı baş aşağı diktiler'.
46 *Saltuk-name*, I, p. 174: 'Atımdan inmem dahı Kara Davudu ele getirmeyince' dedi. Dahı yürüdü, doğru taht-i Deşt üzere geldi'. The capital of the Sarmatian steppe refers to the city of Sarai (Saray) on the lower Volga that served as the court for the Jochid ulus of the Golden Horde.

warrior. These virtues have relatively little to do with the sanctity and justice of their cause and speak mostly to the definition of those personal character traits such, as comradeship, courage, reliability and perseverance, that set an example of perfection for fellow practitioners of the *gaza*.

Another passage which is revelatory of the chivalric virtues expected of the noble warrior consists of the professional and moral advice (*öğüt*) given by Sarı Saltuk himself to his followers concerning their behaviour on and off the battlefield:

> Comrades. Preserve your honour and reputation. Know that it is shameful to shrink from battle. Those who do so will lose face with their womenfolk. The genuinely brave man must persevere [in battle] to the death. It is preferable to die a hero's death a day earlier than to remain living while bearing the stain of cowardice. Let no one say that the Han's followers are effeminate.[47]

In another part of the tale Saltuk's successor Ece Halil, serving as leader of the clan and commander of the troops,[48] exhorted his lieutenant Ayas-i Rumi (Ilyas) and the braves fighting under his command, who had been backed into a corner by an advancing adversary, and urged them to fight fearlessly and with such bravery as to enter legend alongside other legendary fighters. Their reward will not be in Paradise, but consist in having gained the immortality of fame within the collective memory of the tribe. The text at this point, towards the end of the narrative and after the death of the main hero Sarı Saltuk in 1297, presents a simulated dialogue between the two commanders with these words:

> They camped. That same night, Ece Halil summoned his lieutenant to his side and addressed him so: 'My captain, you should know that we are confined to a place from which there can be no escape. To us no alternative remains but to accept martyrdom; an outcome that befits us given the risk associated with the practice of our trade and profession which is soldiering. Let us give ourselves heart and soul to the task of countering the enemy, [showing faithfulness to our traditions], and earn thereby an honourable place in legend and serve as an example to all the world'.[49]

The heroes of the *Saltuk-name* are repeatedly depicted in the text as vying with one another to achieve ever greater acts of valour and bravery. When the enemy hurled taunts, maledictions and curses (*nefrinler*) down on the Muslims below who were

---

47 *Saltuk-name*, I, p. 175: 'Ad ve san sakının kim gazadan kaçmak aybdur ki avratlarınız yanında yüzünüz kalmaz. Er olan gayret üzere ölmek gerektir. Dünyada muhannes adla diri olup, yürümekten bir gün evvel ölmek yeğrektir, ve dahı demesinler kim – 'Han uğruğı güni (kuni)dir', dedi'. The Han in this context would be Berke Khan ruler of the Jochid Ulus between 1257 and 1266.
48 Ece Halil's military activities in conjunction with the Catalans during their raids in Thrace in 1308–1309 are well documented in sources dating from the early fourteenth century. He died in 1312. See the article by Zerrin Günal in *Diyanet Vakfı Islam Aniklopedisi*, X (1994), pp. 379–80.
49 *Saltuk-name*, III, p. 308: 'Kondular. Ol gice [Ece Gazi] İlyas'ı katına davet edip eyitti: 'Server bilmiş ol bize gerü bu yerde yer kalmadı. Pes bize şehadetten gayrı pişe yoktur. Can u dilden baş ortaya koyup, bu kafirlerle bir ceng edelim ki alemlere dastan olsun' dedi'.

besieging their defensive walls, the hero Çoban Ata climbed up to high place towering over their ramparts and issued a challenge of his own:

> Look here you infidels, I have something I want to say to you' and so saying Çoban brought forth some mighty boulders and hurled them down on the church below. Upon witnessing this, the enemy forces were left with no other option but to flee [from their positions on the ramparts] and take refuge in the inner precincts of the church/monastery.[50]

Two other *gazi* heroes Kemal Ata and Kara Davud, the latter of whom had earlier joined the *gazis* on the Russian front with 400 of his braves (*yiğit*), witnessed Çoban in action and showed no hesitation in marvelling at his stalwart posture and in celebrating it for the benefit of the *gazis* whom we must imagine were gathered to hear the anonymous bard sing his praises and to take inspiration from his heroic example:

> The other warriors named Kemal and Davud witnessed the bravery and daring exhibited by their comrade Çoban, they cried out their praise and gave voice to a unanimous bravo [for what he had accomplished].[51]

A final vignette from the *Saltuk-name* that provides an evocative insight into the martial spirit that animated the *alp* warriors of the northern Balkans in the late thirteenth century relates to the rituals attending the burial of a hero who has fallen in battle. When a *gazi* died in combat, it was a point of honour and of self-regard that he should be buried with his shield. This was to prove that he died a hero's death and did not shrink from facing his opponents in battle. There are several references to this custom in the text of which I will offer here the example of the burial of the leader of the *gaza* Ilyas Gazi and his replacement in that role by Ayas Gazi. The occasion is related towards the end of book three of the *Saltuk-name*:

> That night the spirit of [their fallen comrade] Ilyas appeared to Ayas Baba in a dream. He was lying [dead] at the base of a mountain and he addressed Ayas saying: 'I have died in battle. Do me the honour of burying me here'. After that the gazis arrived at the appointed place and carried out a search

---

50 *Saltuk-name*, I, p. 164: 'Kafirler. Ben sizinle söylşem' deyü büyük büyük taşlar getirip kiliseye pertab eyledi. Kafirler kaçtılar, kilise içine girdiler'.
51 *Saltuk-name*, I, p. 164: 'Çoban'dan çün Kemal ve Davud [bu halı ve şecaat ve cüreti göricek] tahsinler ve aferinler ettiler'. The text as transcribed by Akalın follows the form provided in codex B-64, fol. 123a, l. 13 by omitting the phrase in brackets. The rephrased version is found in the Topkapı version on folio 102a, l. 11 (cf. *The legend of Sarı Saltuk*, ed. by Fahir İz, Pt. 2 [1974], p. 203). With the addition of *şecaat* (bravery) and *cüret* (boldness) the copyist has expanded the chosen idiom to underline even more forcefully for the audience of listener/readers of his own time, the comradely bond and unshakeable *esprit de corps* that animated the *gazi* warriors who presided over the frontier in an earlier (arguably more heroic) age than their own. These values had, or so the copyist seems to imply, gradually diminished over time such that by the time of copying (in the case of the Topkapı codex in the year 1600) there remained only a faint echo of the once fervent martial spirit that had resounded among the warrior heroes of the frontier in the thirteenth century.

whereupon they discovered where the body lay. They buried him there with his body armour in conformity to the wish he had always expressed: 'Bury me with my personal belongings, that is to say my soldier's dress'. Accordingly, they carried out his wishes and buried him with his full battle dress. They then observed obsequies to mourn his passing and cooked a communal meal which they consumed together as a charitable offering [and to commend his soul to his maker].[52]

Group 2: Excerpts Illustrating the Stigma that Attached to Warriors or Warrior Bands Considered to be in Breach of the Warriors' Honour Code

On the other side of the equation, acts which reflected shame (*ar*) or dishonour (*neng*) on the perpetrators were noted with disapproval and rightful indignation by the oral informants whose traditional values colour the text. At the head of the list of dishonourable acts, coming right after turning one's back on an adversary and fleeing the battlefield, consisted of initiating an attack against an enemy with whom peaceful relations had been previously established and solemnized by an oath. Such oath-breaking (*naks-i ahd*) was held by tradition to legitimize the use of force on the grounds that if the first blow is struck by the enemy, such aggression renders them legitimate targets of counter attack. On this subject, volume one of the *Saltuk-name* provides a telling example. In addressing the Russian fighters advancing against the Muslim camp he uses the following formula:

> Hey you infidels. Because it is you who have broken your oath (to observe the terms of peaceful relations) and have come forth against us, know that I have arrived on the scene. Make ready to give battle.[53]

In another part of the text in the context of skirmishes with the forces of the Wallachian beys the leader of the gazis uttered the following words to the envoy sent from the opposing camp:

> It is you who have broken the peace. What happened to your promise to respect the peace with him and with his entire tribe? Since it was you as oath-breaker who have initiated this act of hostility between us, it is now in the hands of God. He will decide [by judging who among us is just and who is unjust] the outcome of battle. We have never turned our faces away from the testing of our mettle in battle through

---

52 *Saltuk-name*, III, p. 309: 'Ol gece Ayas Baba düşünde gördü kim Ilyas-i Rumi bir dağ dibinde yatur. Eyitti: 'Ben şehid oldum, beni bunda defn edesiz. Pes vardılar ol yeri aradılar anda meyyitin buldular. Cebesiylebile defn eylediler. Zira vasiyeti daim ol idi kim: 'beni esbabımla yani libasumla defn edesiz' derdi. Hem öyle ettiler, mezarın yaptılar. [...] Pes ondan İlyas için gaziler gaza donun giydiler matem eylediler. Ruhı-y-çün taamlar pişirdiler sadakalar ettiler'. Muslim traditions regarding salvation revolved around the concept of *furkan* which denoted a separation (in God's eyes) between believers and unbelievers. The declaration that a deceased person was 'good' (in the eyes of his fellow men) formed an integral part of God's absolution.
53 *Saltuk-name*, I, p. 176: 'Ey kafirler. Çün ahdınızı sıdınz [ve] geldiniz üş[te] ben vardım. Hazır olun'.

wielding our swords, no matter what the odds and even if a world full of infidels stood against us'. So said the leader of the Muslim fighters to the envoy of the infidels.[54]

The sentiment of the final sentence and the spirit of boast and bravado in which it is delivered provide a typical expression of the *gazi* ethos and the ideals cherished by the *kahramanlık* cult of the warrior heroes who combined braggadocio concerning their military prowess with a sense that they behaved forthrightly and honourably in battle.

The need for a warrior brave to preserve his reputation is a central theme; one that is revisited constantly throughout the digressions which make up the meandering narrative of the *Saltuk-name*. A related theme, and one that also makes frequent reappearance in the narrative, is the nature of loyalty and the obligation of gratitude that was owed by a *gazi* warrior to a generous patron, benefactor or protector. Degrees of fidelity and infidelity also served as important ways of measuring merit in the value system adopted by the frontiersmen. A simulated conversation between the *server* (i.e., Sarı Saltuk, 'The Chief') and an unnamed *gazi* figure he encountered on the Danube frontier during the period of his return to Dobruja towards the end of his life reinforce this point.[55] During the conversation, philosophical questions such as the meaning of life and the reasons for its brevity are addressed by the *server* and the unnamed *gazi*. The exchange went as follows:

> The Chief said: 'Do you know what is cause of man's short life-span?' To this the gazi warrior replied: 'I have been informed by the legendary hero Battal Gazi that it comes from three main causes. The first of these is overeating, the second is from the maledictions of ill-wishers, while the third [and most important] is from ingratitude shown to a benefactor whose bread and salt one has shared'. To this the Chief responded: 'May the sustenance provided by the guardians and protectors of such ingrates stick in their craws [and fail to nourish] those who bruise the feelings of their guardians by their ingratitude. Heed these words my gazi devotees: Take good care always to acknowledge the help vouchsafed to you by your benefactors, lest some harm should befall you as the [deserved] result. May you be spared the destitution [that befalls those who are left bereft of a protector].[56]

While the first two sources of ill ease listed here can be regarded as trivial or obvious, the frontiersmen were keenly conscious of the third cardinal rule which consisted of the obligation of loyalty to a host or patron whose 'bread and salt' one has shared. In customary

---

54 *Saltuk-name*, III, p. 305: 'Çün siz sulhu bozdunuz kanı [yani hani] onunla ahdınız kim her giz ana ve anun kavmine düşman olmasanız gerek idi. Çünkim sizler sulhu bizden öndin bozdunuz, emr-i Hak ne ise kılıç olduğumuzda malum oluna. Varın. Biz gazadan yüz döndermezuz, eğer dünyada dolu kafir dahi olsa' dedi'.
55 The title *server* (chief) was used interchangeably with reference to both spiritual leaders such as Sarı Saltuk and representatives invested with temporal authority or those entrusted with military command.
56 *Saltuk-name*, II, p. 246: 'Server eyitti: 'Ömr kısalığı neden bilirsin?' dedi. Ol kişi eyitti: 'Seyyid Battal Gazi'den işittim ki üç nesnedendir. Biri çok yemekten, ikinci bed-duadan, üçüncü hakk-i nan ü nemeğe münkir olmaktan' dedi. Pes Server eyitti: 'ol kişinin ol nan ü nemek ki anun velisinin gönlü yıka. Ana aşık imdi gaziler, hakk-i nan u nemekten key sakının kim zarar erismeye, darlığa düşmeyesiz' dedi'.

belief and in terms of standard social practice, *nankörlük* or ingratitude created not just bad karma, but could be the direct cause of an individual's undoing. Togetherness and mutual cooperation created the social cement that held society together and were at the heart of the frontier *modus vivendi* which had to envisage and accommodate temporary truces and friendship pacts with former opponents; in particular the Christian neighbours across the frontier. This was a necessary precondition for stabilizing a shared frontier that would otherwise become unpredictable and dangerous for all.

Group 3: Excerpts Illustrating the Methods of Troop Recruitment Employed by the Warrior Bands Operating on the Frontier

The text of the *Saltuk-name* is full of examples of *gazis*, including members of the top leadership and close confederates of Sarı Saltuk himself such as İlyas-i Rumi (known formerly as El-Leon/Alyon), who had converted to the cause under the influence of Sarı Saltuk's eloquence and persuasiveness. Another convert, Ilgaz-i Rumi, was offered a leadership role in the *gaza* in exchange for his agreement to join forces with Sarı Saltuk:

> Ilgaz the Greek feigned conversion at first [in order to escape being put to death] but subsequently reverted to his Orthodox Christian faith. Later on, he was convinced to make an honest confession of faith and became a Muslim heart and soul. In recognition of his sincere conversion, the Chief (i.e., Sarı Saltuk) gave him a leadership position and made him a commander of troops. After so doing, he issued the call to battle saying: 'Let us go forth on campaign [against the non-Muslims].[57]

Another convert named Mervanik turned against his own kin (presumed to be his father or another close relative) in the context of a dynastic struggle in which the father had favoured the succession to his throne of another son who had thus become Mervanik's sworn enemy. The offer of assistance by Sarı Saltuk to ensure the success of Mervanik's cause in the internecine struggle for control of this minor city-state/petty kingdom is just the kind of historical circumstance that would have prompted side-switching or cross-border alliances, even if consolidating the relationship required a marriage alliance or even changing religions as a consequence. This situation is reflective of shared political culture found on both sides of the religious divide at a time and in a place (i.e., medieval Anatolia) in which might made right and where the claiming one's right often required resort to alliances and allegiances that might seem incongruous or out of place to the modern observer. The poignancy of the father's impassioned plea to his rebellious and wayward son Mervanik is telling of the harsh political realities of the time:

> Raston (Mervanik's overlord/father) said: 'May the Lord's punishment for ingratitude (*nankörlük*) [literally failure to 'see', i.e., acknowledge the bread

---

57 *Saltuk-name*, II, p. 217: 'Ilgaz-i I Rumi müdara kasdın edip, iman arza kıldı. Amma gine döndü [...] Sonra [...] parmak götürüp ıman arz kılıp [...] Müslüman oldu, can u dilinde. Server ona mukaddemlik verdi, askere baş eyleyip eyitti: 'Yürü gaza edelüm' dedi'.

and salt eaten at a patron/benefactor's table] result in your own blindness.[58] Am I not the descendant and son of your sworn overlord and destined to be your rightful overlord myself?' To Raston's exclamation Mervanik replied: 'Yes. What you say is true, but [during your time of authority] you refused to follow the people's advice and instead did as you yourself saw fit. As a consequence, you have allowed the people to be trampled underfoot [by the armies of the oppressors]. All that has befallen us is due to your ill-fated decisions and rightly resulted in the mantle of rule being lifted from your shoulders. You have heeded the advice of the sowers of disruption and now look at your fate. Because of your bad judgement you have given no thought to the wellbeing of the poor people of the country and neglected the protecting of their interests. Now that it is their turn to spare you a thought, they are disinclined to do so'. So saying, Mervanik came forth and brought Raston to the presence of the Chief Sarı Saltuk. Afterwards, Sarı Saltuk entrusted the governance of that country to Mervanik and said to him: 'You belong to the same lineage of this accursed one named Raston. Henceforth let rule over this country be passed on to you (by right of descent).[59]

Compromise political solutions and tributary relations as an alternative to regime change were often chosen as the preferred way of concluding the kind of casual campaigning and opportunistic raiding that took place along the Russian frontier in this period. Tribute payment as an alternative to direct rule by the Golden Horde was also a preferred option for those regions of the far western frontier that could not be properly monitored or controlled by the authorities based in Sarai (Saray) on the Lower Volga. Another example of continuity of rule in the same family after the defeat of an adversary by the *gazis* is provided in the case of a certain Hırakün who appears to have been a minor lord of Wallachian marches.[60] After the defeat of Hırakün, the disposition of his lands and possessions after defeat in battle is described as follows:

> The Chief Sarı Saltuk entered *Hırakün*'s palace and, seizing him by the hair, he chopped off his head. He then hung it on the rafters of the palace roof. When the people saw this, they came forward to offer their submission and agreed to pay tribute. The Chief then installed *Hırakün*'s son as the successor to his deposed

---

58 The expression 'gözünde dizinde durmak' is recorded by Ömer Asım Aksoy with this same meaning of blindness (as well as paralysis) being God's rightful punishment for ingrates. See Ömer Asım Aksoy, *Atasözleri ve Deyimler Sözlüğü*, 2 vols. (Ankara: Türk Dil Kurumu, 1965, 3rd repr. 1981), II, p. 689 (item No. 4863).

59 *Saltuk-name*, II, p. 239: 'Hey Mervanik, tüz etmeğim gözüne dursun. Ben senin beyin oğlu değilmiyem, ve dahi begin olam?' dedi. Mervanik: 'Evet öylesin, illa nasihat tutmadın ve kendi biline (bildiğin gibi) iş ettin. Bizi at ayağı altında ko[y]dun. Senin şumluğundan böyle olup, devlet başından gitti. Müfsidler sözüne uydun. Üş [işte] halın gördün. [...] Çün böyle eyledin il halin fakirler ahvalın anıp esirgemedin. Bu halk dahi seni esirgemez' deyip ileri geldi. [...]. Server ol dıyarı Mervanik'e verdi [ve] eyitti: 'Sen dahi bu lain soyundansın. Beylik senin olsun' dedi'.

60 *Saltuk-name*, III, pp. 212 *et seq.*

father's throne and [without tarrying further] the *Server* himself set out to return to his base at Babadag.⁶¹

The reason for handing the fortress over to a local figure was that, in addition to gaining the loyalty and gratitude of the local population, the representatives of prominent families who were left in charge were far more likely to cooperate with and show obedience to the overlords who had recognized their autonomy and local authority in this way. Through a combination of threat, intimidation and application of actual military force, on the one hand, and lenience and generosity to the vanquished in the aftermath of battle, on the other, the Turco-Mongol overlords were able to achieve the pacification of the territories they had taken by the sword.

The expectations from campaign on the part of the self-mobilizing and self-rewarding freelance booty raiders of the immediate frontier zone were set considerably lower than even this level of expectation of co-operation from the vanquished. A share in the proceeds deriving from the campaign itself was enough to satisfy their wants. The immediacy of this settling of the distribution of shares shows that no long-term political ambitions or competing agendas were allowed to complicate the process. A sense of this freewheeling nature of the campaigns and the ease with which they were wound up is provided in the text:

> They pressed on from there (i.e., the land of Moscovy) carrying out [extensive] raids throughout the territory as they went. The dedicated band of Saltuk's warriors were gladdened by the plentiful booty that entered their hands during the course of the campaign. After that, they carried out [more] sallies into the lands of the Russians.⁶²

Group 4: Excerpts Illustrating General Conditions of Warfare on the Frontier and Accommodation Between Communities Situated on Opposite Sides of the Border in Cross-Cultural Frontier Environments

With reference to their own traditions and military etiquette and gallantry citing in particular the example of ʿAlī ibn Abī Ṭālib, ('The Lion of God' and the nephew and son-in-law of the Prophet Muhammad), the *gazi*s gave prominence in their warrior code to the five rules of engagement the faithful observation of which they held to be binding on all the noble warriors who made up their ranks. These consisted of the following constraints placed on the participants in *gaza*:

1. Never kill those who have asked for quarter.
2. Don't pursue an enemy who is in retreat (both to be seen as generous and merciful in victory and to avoid being trapped by an enemy stratagem designed to catch them in an ambush).

---

61 *Saltuk-name*, III, p. 223: 'Server içeri girip, Hırakün'ı saçından tütüp, bastı. Başın kesti. Çıkıp saray damında astı. Kale halkı onu görüp, gelip haraca kesildiler, muti oldular. Andan Hırakün'ün oğlun beğ edip, Server gerü andan azm-i Baba edip gitti'.
62 *Saltuk-name*, II, p. 239: 'Andan dahi ol illere akınlar ettiler. Pes Seyyid'in kavmi vafir ganimet ellerine girdi, şad geldiler. Andan Rus diyarına akınlar ettiler'.

3. Don't turn your back on an advancing army or shrink from doing battle with them if they carry out a strike against you.
4. Don't kill an adversary until you engaged in battle and exchanged at least three blows.
5. Don't carry out pre-emptive strikes but wait until you can give legitimate response to one who has attacked you first.[63]

Another passage which specifies the moral code and the rules of engagement as practiced by *gazi* warriors is found in the second book of the *Saltuk-name* which describes conditions during the capture of Christian towns in northwest Anatolia around Kastamonu. After having defeated and made peace with his Byzantine adversaries Sarı Saltuk makes the following declaration to his *gazi* followers:

> Do not kill the priests of the infidels, the infirm or other innocents [who are incapable of defending themselves]. [If you kill them] you will have their innocent blood on your hands. Also refrain from killing those who, having refrained from fighting, have requested quarter lest you have the shedding of the blood of those innocents on your hands. By doing so you will become rebels against the word of God and will earn His wrath and merit the meting out of His punishment'. So saying Sarı Saltuk pronounced his interdiction and had it proclaimed by the public criers. He then reinforced the announced prohibition [against unprovoked violence] by saying: 'You should kill, as retribution for the unjustly murdered innocent victims, any person who fails to observe this interdiction.'[64]

Despite the general horror of war, certain civilities and restraints on unprovoked violence were to be observed, especially with respect to non-combatants and the general civilian population. This was a far cry from the modern concept of 'total war'.

As for the typical extent and duration of *gaza*, the text makes it clear that the raiding parties organized themselves for short incursions with limited strategic aims. An indication of this is given in a passage in which the leader of an incursion against the Russian frontier addresses the gazi rank-and-file in the following manner:

> Saying: 'It is now three months that we have be roving and roaming in enemy territory in search of [easy] targets. The time has come that we must return to base [to recoup our energy]'. After the sounding of the war horn summoning the troops, they then moved off from that place in the direction of their home base in the Sarmatian steppe.[65]

---

63 *Saltuk-name*, I, p. 166: 1. 'Cenkte aman diyene öldürme'; 2. 'Kaçanı kovma'; 3. 'Düşmandan yüz çevirme'; 4. 'Üç darb geçmeden garimin (hasım/düşman) öldürme'; 5. 'Evvel kimseye hamle kılma'.
64 *Saltuk-name*, II, p. 238: 'Kafirlerin papazların ve hastaların ve masumları öldürmen, kanlu olursuz. Ve amma ceng etmeyip aman diyenleri dahı öldürmen, kanlu olursuz ve asiler olup Hak Hazretinden hışm ve azaba uğrarsız' dedi. Nida ettirip yasak eyledi. 'Yasak tutmayanı onun yerine öldürün' dedi'.
65 *Saltuk-name*, I, p. 167: 'Üç aydır kafir ilindeyiz. Dönmek vaciptir' deyü heman nefir çalıp andan göçtüler, Deşt'e gittiler'.

When the results from pursuing the enemy promised little in the way of material benefit and profit (*ganimet*) for the *gazi*s, they showed no interest in pointless pursuit of a retreating adversary:

> The infidels avoided contact and engagement with the Muslim forces and routinely withdrew to places of greater safety. The Muslim forces paid no attention to this ruse and moved off [without pursuing them].[66]

Group 5: Excerpts from the Text Illustrating the Strategy of Accommodation With the Enemy (istimalet) as a Commonplace Component of Warfare in the Frontier Context[67]

That the condition of war on the frontier with the Christian world in the northern Balkans and along the borders with the Byzantine empire in northwest Anatolia accommodated periodic declarations of peace and mutual acceptance needs no repeating here. But how this worked in actual practice and the attitudes of mutual trust on which it was founded are not always well understood or accurately conveyed so long as one's sole source of reference is the polemics and apologetics recorded in the contradictory viewpoints of the opposing sides. That is why texts like the *Saltuk-name* that reflect of the folk perspective and are not evasive about the true nature of social reality as lived by the residents of the frontier are so important. Religious adversaries were characterized and compared in terms of their reliability versus unreliability in the observing of peace agreements. The greatest dishonour was deemed to consist, not so much of believing the wrong creed, as from reneging on one's promises given under oath. In this context, the deviousness of the 'Persians' is compared with the trustworthiness of the 'Greeks' when it came to the matter of honouring their commitments.

This is expressed in a passage found in volume one of the *Saltuk-name* where the text reads as follows:

> Until the Day of Judgment it is from the Persian kingdoms that sowers of mischief and corruption will continue to issue forth. They (the Persians) are not good people. As for the Greeks, they are a righteous people who hold to their agreements and are desirous of living in peace.[68]

Towards the end of Book Three of the *Saltuk-name* this need for peaceful coexistence and the preserving of an atmosphere of trust between allies, protégées, vassals, neighbours and their overlords is brought into clear relief in the context of the 'infidel prince' Şerban, who despite his confessional identity as a Christian was a loyal and

---

66 *Saltuk-name*, I, p. 167.: 'Kafir Müslümanlara gelmediler, kaçtılar. Pes [gaziler] onlara tınmadılar, geçtiler'.
67 This strategy consisted of three principal elements: voluntary surrender (aman) and indemnity payments (haraç) in the shorter term alongside attempts to encourage religious conversion on a voluntary basis in the mid to longer terms.
68 *Saltuk-name*, I, p. 181: 'Kıyamete değin müfsidler [...] Acem mülkünden geliserler. Hayırlu taife değildir. [...] Bu Rum sulh taifedir, sadıktur'.

reliable friend of the Muslims and studiously refrained from making common cause with his fellow Christian princes or joining forces with them on occasions when they amassed armies of invasion aimed against Muslim territories in the Balkans. The text is quite explicit on the importance attached to good neighbourly relations and mutual trust, which took precedence over religious identity and loyalties, at least in the mind of Prince Şerban (lit. 'The Serb'). The way his loyalties, actions and commitments are described and prioritized in the text is reflective of the type of historical relations that actually existed between Muslims and Christians at the birth of the Ottoman state in the Balkans a century later in the mid-fourteenth century. It is beyond dispute that it was in part due to their alliance with the Branković family and other regional power brokers of the Serbian borderlands that Murad I (1362–1389) and his successor Bayezid I (1389–1403) were able to achieve such striking and rapid success in promoting and furthering the *gaza* in the Danube region. The way this dynamic operated, as perceived and recorded in folk memory, is provided for us in a revealing passage in the final part of the narrative.

The narrators (folk bards) have related to us in their epic narrations that in that place (i.e., Wallachia) there was an infidel lord whose name was Şerban (i.e., The Serb). He was on friendly terms with His Honour (i.e., Sarı Saltuk). He saw that the infidels had advanced against the Muslims and straight away he summoned up his captains and said: 'Listen up men and hear what I have to say. You should know that it is said that the observing of good neighbourly relations is a most blessed state and a divinely enjoined virtue. If an enemy were to be advancing against us we could count on them [as good neighbours] to come to our aid. You should also be aware that the Turks are a fierce race. The Lord Almighty Creator of the World created them out of his fury to serve as a trial to the disciples of Jesus. Come let us be one with them. They are a strange and curious people and their ways and customs are beyond our ken. They are a curiously formidable adversary. For this long they have entertained friendly relations with us. What sense is there in making enemies of them now? What say you?' The confederates gathered there found Şerban's advice both sensible and practical so they came to the aid of the Muslims and made common cause with them.[69]

Under similar conditions of strong pressure from the Christian camp to join the anti-Ottoman coalition, the King of Hungary is portrayed in the text as having opted to remain neutral and deciding to honour the existing peace agreement with the Turks. One might argue that this was motivated in large part by fear of retribution on the part of the Turks in revenge for their waywardness, but it is presented in such a way that the reader/listener is inclined to accept that such inter-faith agreements

---

69 *Saltuk-name*, II, pp. 305–06: 'Raviler eyyitdir [ki] ol yerde bir kafir beği var idi, adına Şerban derlerdi. Seyyid'le dostluk ederdi. Gördü ki Müslümanlar üzere bu kafirler geldi, tiz tutup katına beğlerin getirdi. Eyitti: 'Kişiler, sizlere ne derem? Bilmiş olun kim konşu hakkı Tanrı hakkıdır derler. Bizim üstümüze bir düşman gelse anlar bize yardım ederlerdi. Ve bir dahı bu Türkler yavuz halktur. Halik-i cihan bunları kendü hışmından yaratmıştır. Isa kavmine bela olmak için. Gelin bunlara bir olalım, anlar yad halktur. Huyların ve hallerin bilmeziz ve yad yağıdır. Bunlar bunca demden beri bize dostluk ederler. Şimdi bun deminde düşmanlık vechi yoktur. Ne dersiz' dedi. Ol kavm ol sözü maslahat görüp, Müslümanlara yardıma geldiler, birlik oldular'.

THE LONG PROSE 'EPIC' OF SARI SALTUK DEDE (FL. C. 1260 TO 1298)   415

reached against the background of intra-faith divisions constituted a normal state of affairs in the borderlands between Islam and Christianity in the northern zone. In the response framed by Kaydafan, identified as the King of Hungary in the source, to an invitation by his fellow Christians to join the fray against the Turks he offers the following reason for his reluctance to take part:

> Declaring: 'I have a solemn covenant with Saltuk. I will not raise my sword against his followers', he sheathed his sword. After saying the words: 'You may go out and fight them. As for me, I intend to carry out my oath', he stood at the rear of the assembled troops.[70]

As can be seen from the several examples provided in the above and from many others of similar character scattered throughout all parts of the text, the practical realities associated with war and peace along the frontier are evoked in the *Saltuk-name* using a voice filled with neither religious zealotry nor rhetorical excess, but framed in simple straightforward terms and delivered in measured tones. What the text reveals most vividly is a sense of the professional pride and high standards of service exhibited by—or at least offered as a model to be emulated by—the warrior class whose business it was to carry out *gaza*.

---

70 *Saltuk-name*, III, p. 307: 'Ben Saltıh'la andluyam. Ben kılıç çekmezam anlara' deyü kılıçın mühürledi. 'Siz ceng edin. Ben andım yerine gelsin' deyip, leşkerin ardında durdu'.

ROMAIN THURIN

'Wolves and Sheep Drank and Grazed Together'

A Case Study on the Formation of the Anatolian Beyliks

It would be an understatement to suggest that there is little scholarship examining the so-called 'Anatolian beyliks'. To date, few monographs on individual beyliks have been published. The most developed scholarship has come from Turkey and is narrative driven. As for the limited articles and books outside of Turkish scholarship, those are, with a few exceptions, often restricted to sketching broad historical summaries of the era.[1]

The period running from the second invasion of Anatolia by Bāijū Noyan in 1256 to the Battle of Ankara in 1402 saw the rise, collapse, and resurgence of most of the beyliks. Studying this century and a half is fraught with considerable difficulties. Historians of the Seljuk period wrote few accounts. After the collapse of the Ilkhanate in 1335, the scarcity of sources becomes even more problematic until the rise of Ottoman historiography in the early fifteenth century. Besides the limited number of sources, Seljuk historians showed little enthusiasm for the Turkmen groups who made up the core of many of the beyliks. Historians such as Ibn Bībī or Aqsarāyī were more concerned with the depredations caused by the Turkmens than by their history, way of life, or modes of social organization. The later Ottoman sources are not always reliable because of both temporal distance from the events of the late thirteenth and early fourteenth century and Ottoman centrism. Except for the Karāmānids, to whom major historians of the Ottoman period devoted perhaps a page or two, Ottoman scholars never dealt extensively with the history of the beyliks.

---

1 See for example, Paul Wittek, *Das Fürstentum Mentesche: Studie zur Geschichte Westkleinasiens im 13.–15. Jahrhundert*, Istanbuler Mitteilungen, 2 (İstanbul: Archäologisches Institut des Deutschen Reiches, 1934; repr. Amsterdam: Oriental Press, 1967); Himmet Akın, *Aydın Oğulları Tarihi Hakkında bir Araştırma*, Ankara Üniversitesi Dil ve Tarih-Coğrafya Fakültesi Yayınları, 60 (Istanbul: Pulhan Matbaası, 1946); Mustafa Çetin Varlık, *Germiyanoğulları Tarihi*, Atatürk Üniversitesi Yayınları, Atatürk Üniversitesi, 288 (Ankara: Sevinç Matbaası, 1974); Elizabeth Zachariadou, *Trade and Crusade: Venetian Crete and the Emirates of Menteshe and Aydin (1300–1415)*, (Venice: Istituto ellenico di studi bizantini e postbizantini di Venezia, 1983); İsmail Hakkı Uzunçarşılı, *Anadolu Beylikleri ve Akkoyunlu, Karakoyunlu Devletleri*, Türk Tarih Kurumu Yayınları, 8 (Ankara: Türk Tarih Kurumu, 1969).

Romain Thurin • University of Notre Dame

The term 'beylik' itself is problematic. Despite recent interpretations by Jürgen Paul and others, the origin and initial meaning of the word 'beylik' is still understudied.[2] The purpose of this article is not to offer a new definition of 'beylik'. Hence, beylik is used here as a historiographical term designating the Turkmen polities or lordships that rose from the disintegration of the Seljuk sultanate of Rūm. The present paper, however, seeks to contribute to the scholarly discussion on the emergence of the beyliks. Because of insufficient space, the ambition is not to be exhaustive but to develop a few hypotheses to account for the rise of the beyliks in late thirteenth-century Anatolia. To achieve its aim, this article concentrates on two of the most prominent of the early beyliks, the Germiyānids and the Karāmānids. There is sufficient material about both of the beyliks to reconstruct their pre-history and highlight the factors behind their development into independent lordships. Using the two beyliks as case studies, this paper will show when and under what conditions the two entities took shape. It will assert that despite the 'all-encompassing' and somehow reductive nature of 'beylik' as a historiographical term, the core of what later became the Germiyānids and the Karāmānids resulted from different circumstances. Whereas the former can trace its roots back to the Seljuk conquests of the eleventh and twelfth centuries, the latter emerged during the Mongol period. Despite such different 'prehistories', the second Mongol invasion of Anatolia in 1256 proved pivotal in the development of the two beyliks. The chaos caused by Bāijū Noyan in Central Anatolia and the half decade of economic crisis that followed the invasion forced many of the Anatolian Turkmens to band together and form larger groups to withstand the rise of the Mongols. In short, the second Mongol invasion proved seminal in the formation of the Karāmānid beylik and the migration of the Germiyānids from Malatya to Kütahya in western Phrygia. Finally, this paper will show that some of the most powerful emirs in the Seljuk sultanate of Rūm tried to bribe the Karāmānids and the Germiyānids into submission in the aftermath of Bāijū's second invasion. By doing so, these emirs strengthened the grip of the two beyliks over their respective regions and allowed them to survive well into the thirteenth century and beyond.

Prehistory of the Beyliks: The Origins of the Germiyānids

Scholarship on the Germiyānids has shown only minimal interest in the prehistory of the beylik of Kütahya. Despite a distinct lack of scholarly engagement, the Germiyānid beylik, unlike its more famous Ottoman and Karāmānid counterparts, is perhaps the one whose prehistory can be written with the strongest degree of confidence.

It is customary for scholars to start the history of the Germiyānids with the first report of a group identifiable as 'Germiyān/Garmiān' or 'Turkmens of Germiyān' (Germiyān/atrāk-i Germiyān/Garmiān)[3] in Seljuk sources. Among the limited

---

2 See, among others, Jürgen Paul, 'Mongol Aristocrats and Beyliks in Anatolia: A Study of Astarābādī's Bazm va Razm', *Eurasian Studies*, 9 (2011), 105–58 (p. 105).
3 Ibn Bībī, *Al-Avāmir al-ʿAlāʾiyya, fī l-Umūr al-ʿAlāʾiyya*, ed. by Jaleh Mottahedin, (Tehran: Pizhūhishgāh-i ʿUlūm-i Insānī va Muṭālaʿāt-i Farhangī, 2011), p. 442.

corpus of Anatolian Seljuk sources, Ibn Bībī is the first to introduce the Turkmens of Germiyān, as a group dwelling near Malatya at the time of the Bābāʾī revolt of 1240. Around 1239–40, the Bābāʾī insurgents, strengthened by victories in southern Anatolia, marched towards Malatya. The commander (*sarlashkar*) of the city, Muẓaffar al-Dīn ibn ʿAlīshīr, encountered the Bābāʾī with his troops but was soon forced to retreat, overwhelmed by the might of his opponents. Muẓaffar al-Dīn ibn ʿAlīshīr refused to back down, gathered another army in Malatya, and prepared for the next battle. Ibn Bībī claims that the bulk of Muẓaffar al-Dīn's second army was composed of 'Kurds and Germiyāns' ('Kurdān wa Germiyān').[4] Once again, Muẓaffar al-Dīn and his host of Kurds and Germiyāns failed, being unable to overcome the zeal and determination of the Turkmens and Kurds forming the Bābāʾī armies. The fate of the Seljuk commander is unknown. According to the Syriac historian Bar Hebraeus, himself a native of Malatya, most of the troops raised by Muẓaffar al-Dīn fell on the battlefield.[5] The son of ʿAlīshīr, like his fellow soldiers, may not have lived to see another day.

For all the vividness of this account, Ibn Bībī never explains who these enigmatic 'Germiyāns' are. Ibn Bībī wrote with his contemporaries in mind. The historian assumed that his readers among the most educated circles of late thirteenth-century Rūm would know about the Germiyāns and thus never felt the need to add further explanation. Yet, Ibn Bībī often adds 'turkān' or 'atrāk', i.e., 'Turk', to Germiyān under the form 'atrāk-i Germiyān', i.e., 'Turks/Turkmens of Germiyān'.[6] This specification, although rather elusive, shows that the Germiyāns were a group of Turkmen nomads, but little more.

The preeminent Turkish historian Mehmet Fuat Köprülü once suggested that 'Germiyān' was the name of a Turkmen group hailing from eastern Iran. According to Köprülü the Germiyāns moved to Malatya in the thirteenth century along with the armies of the Khwārizmshāh. Köprülü founded his claim on the orthographical and phonological similarities between Germiyān, written 'Garmiān' or 'Karmiān' in the Perso-Arabic script, and the region of Kerman in eastern Iran.[7] Köprülü thus concluded that Germiyān referred to Kerman, the homeland of the Germiyānids. For Köprülü's contemporary, İsmail Hakkı Uzunçarşılı, and Mustafa Varlık, who wrote a generation later, Germiyān was originally a tribal name. Later, the name of the tribe became that of a beylik and a family.[8] Uzunçarşılı and Varlık did not, however, bring

---

4 Ibn Bībī, p. 442.
5 Bar Hebraeus, *The Chronography of Gregory Abû'l-Faraj 1225–1286, the Son of Aaron, the Hebrew Physician Commonly Known as Bar Hebraeus, Being the First Part of his Political History of the World*, I: *English Translation*, II: *Syriac Texts*, ed. by Ernest A. Wallis Budge (London, 1932, repr. Piscataway: Gorgias Press, 2003), p. 405.
6 Ibn Bībī, p. 598.
7 Mehmet Fuat Köprülü, *The Origins of the Ottoman Empire*, trans. by Gary Leiser, SUNY Series in the Social and Economic History of the Middle East (Albany: State University of New York Press, 1992), p. 37.
8 Mustafa Çetin Varlık, 'Germiyanoğulları', *Diyanet Vakfı İslam Ansiklopedisi*, 44 vols (Istanbul and Ankara: ISAM, 1988–2014), XIV (1996), pp. 33–35.

any evidence to substantiate their assumption. Irène Mélikoff, in an often-cited article in the Encyclopedia of Islam, popularized Uzunçarşılı and Varlık's thesis without further evidence.[9] With the exception of Varlık, these eminent scholars failed to notice a critical element: the existence of a territory called 'Garmian' (Կարմիան) in the immediate vicinity of Malatya.

Edouard Dulaurier, a nineteenth-century orientalist, and leading authority in medieval Armenian sources, found mentions of a region designated as Karmian or Garmian in the chronicle of Matthew of Edessa. The latter, who wrote 140 years before Ibn Bībī, mentioned the existence of a community of 'Turkmens of Germiyān/Garmiān' near Malatya.[10] According to the Armenian historian, around 1121 the Turkish emir Ilghāzī ibn Artuq Bey ruled, among other territories, over a region named Garmian. Like Ibn Bībī, Matthew of Edessa placed Garmian in the vicinity of Malatya.[11] Dulaurier concluded that Garmian must have been a name given during the Seljuk era to a region near Malatya. By analogy with the later Germiyānid beylik, Dulaurier assumed that Garmian was the name of a Turkmen bey.[12] Another orientalist, Charles Defremery suggested that Garmian be corrected into Garsian, the Armenian rendering of Χαρσιανόν, the name of the former Byzantine theme of Charsianon.[13]

Both hypotheses suffer from significant shortcomings. The first reference to Garmian in Muslim sources is in the account of Ibn Bībī, who wrote in the 1280s. Muslim historians, whether from the Seljuk realm or beyond, would not have failed to mention the existence of a Turkish emir powerful enough to posthumously give his name to an entire region. Likewise, the numerous references to Garmian in the Georgian Chronicle contradict the possibility of the name being an Armenian reading of Χαρσιανόν. There are, eventually, few reasons to doubt the Armenian and Georgian sources. As shown by Matthew of Edessa and the Georgian Chronicle, Garmian must have been the name given by locals to a region located north-east of Malatya at the junction between the ancient Roman provinces of Sophene and Cappadocia.[14]

This does not, however, demonstrate any connection between Ibn Bībī's 'Turkmens of Germiyān' and the Armenian/Georgian region of Garmian. To my knowledge, Claude Cahen was the first scholar who tried to establish a link between the Germiyānids

---

9   Irène Mélikoff, 'Germiyān-Oghullari', *Encyclopaedia of Islam, Second Edition*, 12 volumes (Leiden: Brill, 1960–2005), II (1965), pp. 989–90.
10 Edouard Dulaurier, *Bibliothèque historique arménienne, ou, choix des principaux historiens arméniens* (Paris: A. Durand, 1858), p. 459.
11 Charles Defrémery, 'Review of Récit de la première croisade, extrait de la chronique de Matthieu d'Edesse et traduit de l'arménien'', in *l'Athenaeum Français: Journal universel de la littérature, de la science et des beaux-arts*, 1 (1852), 24–25 (p. 25); Matthew of Edessa, *Chronicle*, trans. by Robert Bedrosian, (Long Branch, NJ: Sources of the Armenian Tradition, 2017), p. 126.
12 Dulaurier, *Bibliothèque historique arménienne*, p. 459.
13 Defrémery, 'Review', p. 25.
14 See *Kartlis Tskhovreba: Histoire de la Georgie*, trans. by Marie Félicité Brosset (St Petersburg: Académie impériale des Sciences de Russie, 1849), p. 387, n. 5.

and the region of Garmian. Yet, Cahen did not systematically examine all mentions of 'Turkmens of Garmian' in twelfth-century sources.[15]

Contemporary sources, whether in Arabic, Armenian, or Georgian, are clear: important communities of Turkmen lived in Garmian throughout the twelfth century. Matthew of Edessa claims that as early as 1119 a sizeable group, if not multiple significant groups, of Turkmens inhabited the region.[16] When exactly the Turkmens arrived in Garmian is not clear. The years 1119–21 and the campaigns of Ilghāzī ibn Artuq Bey in Syria, however, seem to have been a seminal period in the history of the Turkmens of Garmian.

In 1119, Ilghāzī, the Turkish emir of Mardin, mustered an important force of Turkmens intending to fight against the crusaders.[17] After the battles of Ager Sanguinis and Hab in 1119, Ilghāzī and his troops attacked the vicinity of 'Azāz in Syria.[18] The count of Edessa Joscelin I gathered his armies and forced Ilghāzī and his Turkmens to flee to the northwesternmost region of Ilghāzī's emirate, the territory known in Armenian and Georgian sources as 'Garmian'.[19]

In 1121, Ghāzī, the emir of Ganja (modern Azerbaijan), attacked the Kingdom of Georgia with a large host of Turkmens from the Caucasus.[20] King David IV of Georgia (1089–1125) defeated Ghāzī's armies. In the aftermath, the remnants of the Turkmen troops split up into two groups. One group fled to Garmian and asked Ilghāzī for support against the Georgians. As a response, Ilghāzī gathered an enormous army of nomads, among whom were a group of Turkmens from Garmian.[21] The details of the famous Battle of Didgori between the Muslim coalition and the Kingdom of Georgia are well known and need no recounting here. Suffice to say that the Georgians won and that many of Ilghāzī's Turkmens fell during the battle.

This brief sketch shows that sizeable groups of Turkmens had already settled in Garmian as early as 1119–21, and perhaps even before. Although it is uncertain that the remnants of Ilghāzī's armies were the first Turkmens to settle in Garmian, it is clear that Ilghāzī's group, at least, increased Turkmen presence in the area. A few years later, the remnants of Ghāzī's armies probably increased settlements in the region too.

The exact socio-political organization of the Turkmens of Garmian after 1121 is unclear. We know, however, from multiple sources, among them Matthew of Edessa, that the Turkmens of Garmian revered and obeyed Ilghāzī because of his lineage. The later Armenian author Smbat Sparapet (d. 1276) offers a more precise explanation.

---

15 Claude Cahen, 'Notes pour l'histoire des Turcomans d'Asie Mineure au XIIIe siècle', *Journal Asiatique*, 239 (1951), 335–54, (pp. 349–50).
16 Matthew of Edessa, p. 126.
17 Ibn al-Qalānisī, *Dhayl Tārīkh Dimashq: History of Damascus 365–555 a. h. by Ibn al-Qalânisî from the Bodleian Ms. Hunt. 125., being a continuation of the history of Hilâl al-Sâbi*, ed. by Henry Frederick Amedroz (Beirut: Catholic Press of Beirut, 1908), p. 198; English translation: *The Damascus Chronicle of the Crusades: Extracted and Translated from the Chronicle of Ibn Al-Qalanisi* trans. by Hamilton Alexander Rosskeen Gibb, (London: 1932, repr. London: Dover Publications, 2003), p. 160.
18 Matthew of Edessa, p. 126.
19 Matthew of Edessa, p. 126.
20 Matthew of Edessa, p. 126.
21 Matthew of Edessa, p. 126.

Without placing emphasis on the Turkmens of Garmian, Smbat Sparapet argues that various groups of Turkmens from eastern Anatolia and Syria obeyed Ilghāzī because of the prestige of his tribe among the Oghuz.[22] Smbat does not mention to which tribe Ilghāzī belonged. Yet, as Cahen and Sümer once noted, other sources show that Ilghāzī belonged to the Döger, one of the twenty-two (or twenty-four) Oghuz tribes.[23] It is not clear whether the Döger tribe, per se, had a leadership position among the Turkmens of Garmian. It is, however, certain that a prestigious family, perhaps a clan from the Döger, the Artuqids, led the confederation of the Turkmens of Garmian, at least during the first half of the twelfth century.[24]

Considering the existence of at least two waves of Turkmen migrations to Garmian, one may raise a few hypotheses about the prehistory of the Germiyānids. Rather than a tribe per se, as claimed by Mélikoff, Uzunçarşılı and Varlık, one may be tempted to describe the Turkmens of Garmian as a confederation. It is clear from the sources that multiple groups of Turkmens from various origins moved to Garmian in the early twelfth century. These groups seem to have gathered around and found supra-tribal leadership in the person of Ilghāzī and his successors. Had the Turkmens of Garmian all been the members of one of the Oghuz tribes, perhaps the Afshar, as claimed by Uzunçarşılı and Köprülü,[25] the connection between the Artuqids and the Döger would have been far less exceptional. That so many sources emphasize the origins of the Artuqids among the Döger as a major source of legitimacy among the Turkmens of eastern Anatolia and of Garmian is everything but a coincidence. For the eastern Anatolian Turkmens to be that impressed by the Döger means that the other tribes of Garmian must have considered their own groups less prestigious than the famous Oghuz tribe.

For the rest of the twelfth century, the Turkmens of Garmian kept making sporadic appearances in local sources. In 1161, they served the Shāh-Arman of Akhlāt during a campaign against King George III of Georgia (1156–84).[26] Around 1191, the Turkmens of Garmian once again raided Georgia.

It is difficult to precisely determine when the Turkmens of Garmian entered Seljuk service. A hiatus of fifty-one years separates the last mention of the Turkmens of Garmian in the Georgian Chronicle from Ibn Bībī's account of the Bābā'ī revolt. The solution to the problem may be found in the hagiography of John Lazaropoulos. Retelling a short-lived conflict between the Seljuks and the Empire of Trebizond in 1222–23, the hagiographer claims that the Seljuk Sultan 'Alā' al-Dīn Kayḳubād

---

22 Smbat Sparapet, *Chronicle*, trans. by Robert Bedrosian (Long Branch NJ: Sources of the Armenian Tradition, 2005), p. 67.
23 Faruk Sümer, *Oğuzlar (Türkmenler) Tarihleri – Boy Teşkilatı – Destanları*, 2nd edn (Ankara: Ankara Üniversitesi Yayınları, 1972), p. 206; Claude Cahen, 'Les tribus turques d'Asie Occidentale pendant la période seljukide", *Wiener Zeitschrift für die Kunde des Morgenlandes*, 51 (1948), 178–80 (p. 180).
24 Sümer, *Oğuzlar*, p. 206; Cahen, 'Les tribus turques', p. 180. On the Artukids, see also Carole Hillenbrand, *A Muslim Principality in Crusader Times: The Early Artuqid State*, (Leiden: Nederlands Historisch-Archaeologisch Instituut te Istanbul, 1990).
25 Uzunçarşılı, *Anadolu Beylikleri*, p. 39; Köprülü, *Origins*, p. 37.
26 *Kartlis Tskhovreba, Histoire de la Georgie*, p. 387.

(1220–37) exerted a strong authority among various group of Turkmens. Among such groups, Lazaropoulos mentions the Turks from the 'land of Garmian' ('χώραν τῶν Καρμιάνον').[27] Both Cahen and Peacock identified the 'Karmiānoi Turks' as the Germiyānids. Yet, whereas the former considered it a proof of the existence of the Germiyānids before 1240, the latter deemed it anachronistic. If taken at face value, Lazaropoulos's story means that the Turkmens of Garmian entered Seljuk service at an unknow date, between 1191 and 1223.

There is little doubt that the confederation of 'Turkmens of Garmian', mentioned in twelfth-century Armenian and Georgian sources are Ibn Bībī's 'Turkmens of Garmiān'. Germiyān or Garmian was not the name of a Turkmen leader, but the name of a region north-east of Malatya. The Turkmens who migrated to Garmian in the twelfth century, formed a confederation which came to be identified in the sources with the name of the region where they settled. In the second half of the thirteenth century, the Turkmens of Garmian, for reasons we shall soon examine, migrated to western Anatolia, and formed the core of the future Germiyānid beylik.

The Origins of the Karāmānids

If 'prehistory' is ill-suited to describe the 'pre-beylik' period of the Turkmens of Garmian, the term is adequate for the study of the Karāmānids. Unlike their counterparts who later settled in Kütahya, the 'origin story' of the Karāmānids is akin to that of the Ottomans, shrouded in a veil of mystery and speculations. Around 1261, the founding father of the dynasty, Karīm al-Dīn Karāmān, more often referred to as Karāmān bey, burst out on the political scene of the Seljuk sultanate.[28] The two foremost contemporary witnesses, the Seljuk historian Ibn Bībī and the Armenian Smbat Sparapet, were left bewildered by the sudden appearance of a threatening host of ten thousand Turkmens under Karāmān's leadership. Ibn Bībī, whose account shows complete and utter disdain for the Karāmānids, knew almost nothing about Karīm al-Dīn and his ancestors. As an 'origin story', the Seljuk historian merely states that before 1256 Karāmān bey sold charcoal to the city of Larenda for a living.[29] After Bāijū Noyan's second invasion of Anatolia, Karāmān and his brothers took advantage of the chaos to become bandits.[30]

Smbat, unlike Ibn Bībī, does not talk about a modest origin. The Armenian historian makes Karīm al-Dīn Karāmān a powerful emir and the leader of large groups of Turkmens from the Taurus.[31] The differences between the two accounts can be easily explained by considering the background and interests of the two

---

27 John Lazaropoulos, *Synopsis, The Hagiographic Dossier of St Eugenios of Trebizond in Codex Athous Dionysiou 154: A Critical Edition with Introduction, Translation, and Commentary* ed. and trans. by Jan Olof Rosenqvist (London: Coronet Books, 1996), p. 332.
28 Ibn Bībī, p. 589.
29 Ibn Bībī, p. 589.
30 Ibn Bībī, p. 589.
31 Smbat Sparapet, p. 113.

authors. The Seljuk historian Ibn Bībī framed the Karāmānid Turkmens as a disease, an incontrollable plague, responsible for the collapse of the Seljuk sultanate. Smbat, instead, extolled Karāmān Bey as a major threat, a 'second Saladin' in order to further praise King Hethum I's (1226–70) victory over the Turkmens.[32]

Essentially, contemporary accounts knew nothing about the prehistory of the Karāmānids except one fact: Karāmān bey was a Turkmen from the Taurus Mountain, who may have sold charcoal for a living before Bāijū's invasion of 1256. In view of such a lack of details, the modern historian, left in complete obscurity, can only share his predecessors' bewilderment.

Later historians of the Ottoman period knew more about the origins of the Karāmānids than their thirteenth-century forerunners. These historians, unlike their counterparts from the Seljuk era, had access to documents unknown to Ibn Bībī and relied upon oral traditions gathered during the apex and after the fall of the Karāmānid dynasty. The first to write a somehow complete account of Karāmānid prehistory was Mehmet Neshrī. Neshrī, who dedicated his work to the Ottoman sultan Bayezid II (1481–1512), devoted a rather extensive chapter to the early Karāmānids in his Kitab-i Cihān-Nümā, a universal history of the world. It is not clear why Neshrī, unlike other Ottoman historians, dedicated so much space to the early Karāmānids. Victor Ménage suggested that Neshrī grew up in Karāmān to explain the historian's interest in the local beylik. As of late, Menage's claim is still considered controversial and awaits further debates.[33]

In contrast to the Turkmens of Garmian, Neshrī shows that the ancestors of the Karāmānids did not move to Anatolia in the wake of the eleventh-century Seljuk conquests. Rather, Neshrī views the proto-Karāmānids as a group of Turkmens who settled in Iran at an unknown date.[34] The author's lack of precise chronological and geographic data shows that details surrounding the prehistory of the Karāmānids may have already been forgotten by the fifteenth century. Neshrī considers the rise of the Mongols as a turning point in the history of the proto-Karāmānids.[35] The invasions led by Chinggis Khan's generals forced the proto-Karāmānids to leave Iran at an unspecified date. Neshrī claims that the ancestors of the Karāmānids arrived in Anatolia during the reign of 'Alā' al-Dīn Kaykubād.[36] The timeframe provided by Neshrī is vague and too broad to allow a safe conclusion concerning the migration date and point of departure of the proto-Karāmānids. Other documents about which more will be soon said can, however, further illuminate the discussion.

---

32 Smbat Sparapet, p. 113.
33 Victor L. Ménage, *Neshrî's History of the Ottomans: The Sources and Development of the Text* (London: Oxford University Press, 1964).
34 Neshrī, *Mehmed Neşrî, Kitâb-ı Cihan-Nümâ: Neşrî Tarihi*, ed. by Faik Reşit Unat and Mehmet Altay Köymen, 2 vols, Türk Tarih Kurumu Yayınlarından III. Seri, 2 (Ankara: Türk Tarih Kurumu, 1949), I, p. 43.
35 Neshrī, I, p. 43.
36 Neshrī, I, p. 45.

Under the leadership of a certain Nūre Sūfī, described as a 'Sufi saint' (*pīr*),[37] the ancestors of the Karāmānids settled in the Taurus Mountains near Ermenek.[38] No contemporary account provides information about Nūre Sūfī, the mysterious ancestor of the Karāmānids. Nūre Sūfī, like his Ottoman counterpart Ertoghrul, is absent from Ibn Bībī's history. His existence is however confirmed by two documents. The first is an inscription dating from the early 14th century. This inscription, engraved on the mausoleum of Karīm al-Dīn Karāmān, Nūre Sūfī's son, in the village of Balkusan near Ermenek reads: 'This is the tomb of […] Karīm al-Dīn Karāmān, son of Nūre/ Nūra' ('al-turba […] Karīm al-Dīn Qarāmān bin Nūre/Nūra').[39] The other is a waqf document from the fifteenth century, which locates the tomb of Nūre Sūfī in the former hamlet of Afsharviran near modern Mersin. The document confirms that Nūre Sūfī was the forefather of the Karāmānids and reads: 'Vakf-i türbe-i Nūre Sofi cedd-i A'lā-yi âl-i Karāmān türbenin binası taştan'.[40]

The only source providing further details on the life of Nūre is the Karāmān-nāme of Shikārī. Written in the sixteenth century by an otherwise hardly identifiable author known under the nom de plume Shikārī, the Karāmān-nāme is plagued by many issues, among which a strong tendency to mix historical facts with oral history and traditions of dubious origin.[41] Like Neshrī, Shikārī argues that the ancestors of the Karāmānids led by Nūre, who is called Nūreddin, left their homeland during the reign of Sultan 'Alā' al-Dīn.[42] Unlike Neshrī's vague mention of 'Iran' as motherland of the ancestors of the Karāmānids, Shikārī specifies that the proto-Karāmānids have lived in Shirvān for five generations. Later in the text, Shikārī becomes more precise and claims that the proto-Karāmānids inhabited the foothills of the Alborz Mountains.[43] Thus, if one takes Shikārī at face value, the ancestors of the Karāmānids, like many Turkmen communities past and present, must have lived between their winter pastures in Shirvān and their summer pastures on the cooler flanks of the Alborz.[44]

If one considers a generation to be thirty years[45] and assumes that Nūre Sūfī was a mature man during the reign of Sultan 'Alā' al-Dīn Kaykubād, five generations

---

37 For the exact meaning of the term in the context of Turkish Islam, see Safi Arpaguş, 'Pîr', *Diyanet Vakfı Islam Ansiklopedisi*, 44 vols (Istanbul and Ankara: ISAM, 1988–2014), XXXIV (2007), pp. 272–73.
38 Neshrī, p. 43.
39 *Thesaurus d'Epigraphie Islamique, XI–XIIe livraisons*, 2013, n. 2115 <http://www.epigraphie-islamique.org/epi/login.html> [accessed 29 May 2020].
40 Tapu ve Kadastro Genel Müdürlüğü, Tapu Arşiv Dairesi Başkanlığı, Tapu Tahrir Defterleri, Konya Evkaf Defteri H.881 (M.1476) and H.906 (M.1500), İçil Evkaf Defteri H.976.
41 Shikārī, *Şikârî Karamannâme [Zamanın kahramanı Karamanîler'in tarihi]*, ed. by Metin Sözen and Necdet Sakaoğlu (Karaman: Karaman Valiliği, 2011).
42 Shikārī, p. 103.
43 Shikārī, p. 124.
44 On nomadism in the Alborz Mountains, see for example, Bernard Hourcade, 'Les nomades du Lâr face à l'expansion de Téhéran', *Revue Géographique de l'Est*, 17 (1977), 37–51; Hasan Talaei, Ali Norallahy, and Bahman Firouzmandi Shireh-jin, 'Ethnoarchaeology of Nomadism and Tribe Ways in the West of Central Zagros' (In Persian), *Social Sciences*, 6.2 (2014), 163–95.
45 On the subject, see for example Bennett M. Berger, 'How Long Is a Generation?', *The British Journal of Sociology*, 11.1 (1960), 10–23 (p. 10).

would mean that the first ancestor of the Karāmānids to settle in Shirvān arrived in the 1070s. Whilst such estimates should be taken simply as an approximate calculation, it is important to note that sizeable communities of Turkmens settled in Shirvān during the reign of the first Great Seljuks.[46] These communities kept living in Shirvān throughout the twelfth century. The fate of the Turkmens of Shirvān and Mughan in the thirteenth century is well documented in many contemporary sources. According to Zakarīyā Qazwīnī, many, if not most, of the Turkmen communities left Shirvān in the wake of the Mongol invasions.[47] In sum, Neshrī and Shikārī's claims are very plausible, despite not being easily verified.

Nevertheless, the Mongols are absent from Shikārī's introductory chapters on the early Karāmānids. The only mention of an enemy who forced the proto-Karāmānids to leave their homeland occurs later in the text, but Shikārī remains vague and never specifies the identity of this mysterious enemy ('düşmen').[48] This should not be surprising considering the encomiastic nature of the Karāmān-nāme. Rather than a historical work in the strict sense, Shikārī's work is a romance eulogizing the forefathers of the deceased Karāmānid dynasty as a band of ghāzī fighting the holy war against various infidels. Considering the aim of the Karāmān-nāme, it would have been unacceptable for Shikārī to start his account with his champions of jihad defeated and broken by the power of Mongol infidels.

In Anatolia, according to Shikārī, the proto-Karāmānids lived for some time around Sivas. Later, they moved to the Cilician border at the instigation of 'Alā' al-Dīn Kaykubād. A certain vizier by the name of Süleyman Pasha advised 'Alā' al-Dīn to move Nūre's tribe to Cilicia to have him fight against the 'infidels of Ermenek' ('Ermenek kafirleri').[49] This part has often been considered an invention. There is little doubt that Ibn Bībī, who served in the Seljuk chancery, would have provided a much more detailed account on the origins of the Karāmānids had the Turkmens of Nūre served Kaykubād in the 1230s. The absence of Ibn Bībī's drawing connections between 'Alā' al-Dīn Kaykubād and Nūre Sūfī suggests that it is unlikely that there was such a relationship. Simply if Nūre Sūfī moved to the Cilician border at the behest of 'Alā' al-Dīn Kaykubād, this would have provided a ripe opportunity for Ibn Bībī to add further detail to his spiteful account of the Karāmānids and position them as a band of ungrateful and traitorous Turkmens. Just like the absence of the Mongols in the earliest parts of the text, the official appointment by the Seljuk sultan needs to be understood as a literary device aimed at legitimizing the Karāmānids.

At any rate, it is safe to assume that these two accounts contain a kernel of truth, albeit distorted by the time distance and the authors' intentions. The ancestors of the Karāmānids may have moved to Anatolia along with the Khwārizmian armies.

---

46 See, for instance, *Tārīkh al-Bāb wa Sharwān, A History of Sharwān and Darband in the 10th -11th centuries*, trans. by Vladimir Minorsky (Cambridge: Heffer, 1958), p. 35; Claude Cahen and Vladimir Minorsky, 'Le Recueil transcaucasien de Masûd b. Nâmdâr, début du VIe/XIIe siècle', *Journal Asiatique*, 237 (1949), 93–142 (p. 126).
47 Zakarīyā al-Qazwīnī, *Āthār al-bilād wa-akhbār al-'ibād*, ed. by n. n. (Beirut: Dar Sader, 1960), p. 564.
48 Shikārī, p. 124: 'vilâyetimiz düşmen tâlân eyledi. Cümle kabilemi alub Rum'a çıkdım'.
49 Shikārī, p. 106.

Between 1225 and 1230, the Khwārizmshāh Jalāl al-Dīn Mingburnu (1220–31), who tried to build an army powerful enough to oppose the Mongols, recruited many of the Turkmen of Mughan and Shirvān.[50] Until the battle of Yashijemen in 1230, in which Mingburnu fought against 'Alā' al-Dīn Kaykubād, the nomadic element of the Khwārizmian armies were headquartered in the Mughan steppe, where the pastures proved ideal for the nomads. After Yashijemen, the remnants of the Khwārizmian forces wandered about for some time before entering the service of 'Alā' al-Dīn Kaykubād. The sultan of Rūm divided the Khwārizmian army into four parts. In addition, 'Alā' al-Dīn bestowed upon four of the Khwārizmian chiefs land grants ('iqṭā'') in frontier regions.[51] Two of the Khwārizmian leaders, Kuchlu Sengum and Yilan Bogha, moved their armies to their *iqṭā'*-land in Larenda and Niğde. Both cities are very close to Ermenek, where the Karāmānids settled, according to Ottoman sources between 1220 and 1237.[52]

The migration of parts of the Khwārizmian armies from the Mughan steppe to Cilicia under Mongol pressure resembles the accounts of Neshrī and Shikārī. It is thus possible, albeit conjectural, that the Ottoman accounts contain a faint echo of historical truth. 'Alā' al-Dīn Kaykubād may not have settled the proto-Karāmānids specifically on the Cilician border but a larger group of nomads, the Khwārizmians, among them the forces led by Nūre. By the time of Shikārī, the names of the Khwārizmian chiefs Kuchlu Sengum and Yilan Bogha may have fallen into oblivion. From this faint echo of the past, only one piece of convenient memory remained, that of the ancestors of the Karāmānids being settled by 'Alā' al-Dīn Kaykubād near the Armenian frontier as part of a larger force. Alternatively, Shikārī may have been tempted to temper the truth and replace the Khwārizmian leaders with Nūre Sūfī, the ancestor of his champions.

In sum, the accounts given by Ottoman historians about the origins of the Karāmānids are plausible, albeit impossible to verify. Until 1256, the date at which the Karāmānids are mentioned for the first time in contemporary sources, the proto-Karāmānids were a petty group of nomads. Both their military power and political ambitions remained limited. The Germiyānids, unlike the Karāmānids, were a well-organized and powerful confederation of Turkmen tribes. After 1256, however, the military power of the Karāmānids caught up with that of their counterparts from Malatya. In 1277 the two groups fought against each other for the first time during the conflict ensuing the Mamluk sultan Baybars's invasion of Anatolia. The once unknown Karāmānids proved a massive challenge and eventually defeated an army from the powerful Turkmen confederation. Something had altered the socio-political organization of many smaller Turkmen groups, between 1243 and 1256; the Mongols. Affected by the destruction caused by the Mongols, smaller groups of nomads, among them the Karāmānids, banded together to resist the threat of rival groups and other invaders.

---

50 Al-Nasawī, *Sīrat al-Sulṭān Jalāl al-Dīn Mankubirtī*, ed. by Ḥāfiẓ Aḥmad Ḥamdī, (Cairo: Dār al-Fikr al-'Arabī, 1853), p. 362.
51 Ibn Bībī, p. 388.
52 Ibn Bībī, p. 388.

The Years of Bāijū Noyan: The First Mongol Invasion

The title, which may come to the reader as dramatic, did not spring from this author's fertile imagination. These are the words of Qāḍī Aḥmad of Niğde, a fourteenth-century scholar of the Seljuk period. Recounting the Seljuk defeat of Köse Dağ against the Mongols with a certain melancholy, the historian claims that the people of Anatolia remembered the events of 1243 as 'the year of Bāijū' ('sāl-i Bāijū').[53] In other words, the Mongol invasions had traumatized the inhabitants of Anatolia to such an extent that its memory was still alive in the fourteenth century.

The scholarly analysis of the 'year of Bāijū' is often limited to acknowledging that the Mongols pushed many Turkmens westward. The details of the Turkmen migrations to the Byzantine borders are often overlooked. Likewise, considering the Byzantine- and Ottoman-centric nature of modern scholarship, the fate of the Turkmens who moved south to the Cilician borders is too often ignored due to this scholastic silo. Finally, the impact of the Mongol invasions in Anatolia is usually studied through a long-term perspective. Charles Melville, for example, argues that 'although not accompanied by the physical destruction that they brought to parts of north-eastern Iran and Transoxiana, the Mongol invasions of Anatolia introduced a period of considerable change, even if not necessarily of economic decline'.[54] Over the long run, Melville's comment on economic decline holds true. The Mongol conquest of Anatolia did not lead to permanent destructions of the magnitude of what happened, for instance, in Merv. Yet, considering a shorter period (1243–61), Melville's argument is contradicted by contemporary sources. Between 1243 and 1261, the Mongol conquests led to a sharp economic decline in Anatolia and beyond. Despite the economic recovery that took place between 1265 and 1276/77, the crisis of 1243–65 had drastic consequences for the lives of the people in Anatolia, both sedentary and nomads. To make a parallel with our contemporary world, one may argue that on the long run, the global economy recovered from the 1973 oil crisis. Yet, one cannot ignore that the crisis of 1973 had profound, short-term economic consequences. The same holds true for the impact of the Mongol invasions on the economy of Anatolia. As Osman Turan once argued, when analysing the consequences of Mongol presence in Anatolia one must distinguish long-term consequences from short-term results.[55]

At first, the Great Khan Ögedeï (1229–41) sent Bāijū to lead reconnaissance raids in Anatolia.[56] Bāijū adopted a cautious policy vis-à-vis the Seljuks of Rūm. For about a decade, the Mongols launched sporadic attacks on the Seljuk frontier but

---

53 Ahmad of Niğde, *Niğdeli Kadı Ahmed'in El-Veledü'ş-Şefîk Ve'l-Hâfidü'l-Halîk'ı (Anadolu Selçuklularına Dair Bir Kaynak)*, I: İnceleme – Tercüme, II: Farsça Metin, ed. by Ali Ertuğrul, Türk Tarih Kurumu Yayınları, III-2. Dizi, 10ᵃ (Ankara: Türk Tarih Kurumu, 2015), II, p. 365.

54 Charles Melville, 'Anatolia under the Mongols', in *The Cambridge History of Turkey*, I: *Byzantium to Turkey, 1071–1453*, ed. by Kate Fleet (Cambridge: Cambridge University Press, 2008), pp. 51–101 (p. 101).

55 Osman Turan, *Selçuklular Zamanında Türkiye: Siyâsi Tarih Alp Arslan'dan Osman Gazi'ye (1071–1318)* (Istanbul: İstanbul Matbaası, 1971, repr. Istanbul: Ötüken Neşriyat, 2010), p. 523.

56 Het'um the Armenian, *History of the Tartars [The Flower of Histories of the East]*, trans. by Robert Bedrosian (Long Branch: Sources of the Armenian Tradition, 2004), G.39 (chapter 18).

never engaged the forces of the sultan into pitched battles.[57] The friar and diplomat, Simon of Saint Quentin, regards the Bābā'ī revolt of 1239/40 as a turning point in the history of the Seljuks. Seeing how the Bābā'ī movement had brought the Seljuks to their knees, Simon claims that by 1243 the Mongols considered the time to be ripe for an invasion.[58] Bāijū defeated the Seljuks at Köse Dağ, a defile near Erzincan, in 1243.[59] In the aftermath, the debacle and cowardice of Ghiyāth al-Dīn Kaykhusraw II (1237–46), who left the battlefield to hide in the palace of Kubādābād, opened the gates of Anatolia to Mongol raids.[60]

Many contemporary sources describe Bāijū Noyan as a bloodthirsty man, a savage with a taste for pillage, a cruel man among a cruel people.[61] Although contemporary sources may have amplified the most sinister aspects of the Mongol commander's personality, Bāijū's actions honoured his reputation. The noyan attacked the most prosperous Anatolian cities with ferocity. Erzurum, one of the great cities of eastern Anatolia first fell to the Mongols in 1243. Erzurum's inhabitants barricaded themselves behind the walls of the city. For over twenty days, people showed tenacity and resisted the Mongol assaults. When it became clear that no relief would come from Kaykhusraw II's armies, the inhabitants of Erzurum offered to surrender for their lives. Bāijū accepted the deal. Yet, the Mongol commander soon showed his colours and renounced his oath. Upon entering the city, the Mongols massacred most of its inhabitants and enslaved the survivors.[62]

Next, Bāijū turned to another major city, Erzincan. Once more, the Mongols massacred the inhabitants of the city.[63] Kayseri fell after Erzincan. This time, the sources deal more extensively with the extent of the massacre. Simon of Saint Quentin claims that, according to two of his informants, the Mongols killed between 100,000 and 300,000 ('C. Milia - CCC. Milia') people in Kayseri.[64] As usual, one must be very cautious in taking medieval numbers at face value. Other sources, without showing the same level of precision as Simon of Saint Quentin, confirm the damages caused by Bāijū. Ibn Bībī, among others, claims that the Mongols first burnt the surroundings of Kayseri before killing most of its inhabitants and destroying all the houses in the

---

57 Het'um the Armenian, G.39 (chapter 18).
58 Simon of Saint Quentin, *Historia Tartarorum*, ed. by Jean Richard, (Paris: P. Geuthner, 1965), p. 65: 'Tandem audientes quod Paparoissole tali modo et cum tam paucis quasi cepisset victoriam de Turcis obtinere, animati quamplurimum ex debilitate Turcorum, in anno sequenti Turquiam integre invasere'.
59 Ibn Bībī, p. 461; Ibn al-ʿAmīd, ed. by Claude Cahen, 'La Chronique des Ayyoubides d'al-Makīn b. al-ʿAmīd, *Bulletin d'études orientales*, 15 (1955–57), p. 154; Ibn Wāṣil, *Mufarrij al-kurūb fī akhbār Banī Ayyūb*, ed. by Gamal al-Din al-Sayyal, Hasanayn Muhammad Rabi, and Umar Abd al-Salam Tadmuri, 6 vols (Cairo: Maṭbaʿat Jāmiʿat Fuʾād al-Awwal and Beirut: 1953–2004), V, pp. 326–27; Aḥmad of Niğde, p. 364; Baybars al-Manṣūrī, *Zubdat al-fikra fī tārīkh al-hijra*, ed. by Donald S. Richards (Berlin: Das arabische Buch, 1998), p. 21.
60 Bar Hebraeus, p. 407.
61 Ibn al-ʿAmīd, p. 154; Simon of Saint Quentin, p. 66 ('anima ferocitatem').
62 Simon of Saint Quentin, p. 75; Vardan Arewelts'i, *Compilation of History*, trans. by Robert Bedrosian, (Long Branch NJ: Sources of the Armenian Tradition, 2007), p. 88.
63 Simon of Saint Quentin, p. 75.
64 Simon of Saint Quentin, p. 76.

city.⁶⁵ Vardan Arveltsi's account is similar, but further adds that the Mongols showed no mercy to their prisoners, who were gruesomely executed.⁶⁶ Sivas fell last, during the 'year of Bāijū'. Since the inhabitants surrendered before the Mongol assault, Bāijū promised to spare them. Yet, the Mongol commander once again partially renounced his oath, looted many houses, and enslaved countless women and young girls.⁶⁷

A year later, in 1244, another noyan, Yasawur, attacked Malatya on his way back from a raid in Syria. Adopting a strategy similar to that of Bāijū, Yasawur burnt all the crops and vineyards near the city.⁶⁸ The governor of Malatya proved able to bribe the Mongols away and collected an immense tribute of gold coins and other jewels from the inhabitants. Malatya, like the other major cities of Anatolia payed a hefty price. After Yasawur's departure, the region stood ruined. A plague soon broke out, and the inhabitants of Malatya suffered from a terrible famine.⁶⁹ Bar Hebraeus describes the pitiful state of his hometown after the departure of Yasawur with graphic detail and dismay. The plague proved so severe that the inhabitants of Malatya died *en masse* from sickness. Among the surviving adults, many, unable to provide their children with sustenance, sold them on slave markets at a miserable price.⁷⁰

The consequences were dramatic for many of the inhabitants of Anatolia. The destruction of Erzincan, Erzinjan, Malatya and Sivas forced many among the survivors to abandon their lands. Ibn Bībī states that some of the richest and most influential people of Kayseri and Malatya proved able to flee and reach Aleppo.⁷¹ The Byzantine historian Nikephoros Gregoras stresses the fate of many commoners among Kaykhusraw II's subjects, who, penniless, abandoned their houses and fled for their lives in the wake of Bāijū's invasion. Flocks of desperate people flooded Byzantine markets and paid for basic sustenance with gold and silver.⁷² Hence Gregoras's account suggests that famines like that of Malatya occurred in various parts of Anatolia.

Considering the destructions caused by the Mongols in Anatolia, to call 1243 'the year of Bāijū' seems warranted. As regards the consequences for the Turkmens of Anatolia, the sources for 1243 are quite scanty, something that in part may be because of a lack of interest of sedentary historians in their Turkmen neighbours. It is clear, however, that amidst the chaos a few organized groups of Turkmens revolted against the sultan. In southern Anatolia, in the ancient region of Isauria, a Turkmen leader, who was known as Aḥmad in Ibn Bībī's account and Coterinus according to Simon of Saint Quentin (Quṭb al-Dīn Aḥmad?), revolted against Kaykhusraw II. Quṭb al-Dīn Aḥmad claimed to be the son of the former sultan 'Alā' al-Dīn Kaykubād and justified

---

65   Ibn Bībī, p. 463; Ibn al-'Amīd, p. 154.
66   Vardan Arewelts'i, p. 88.
67   Simon of Saint Quentin, p. 75; Vardan Arewelts'i, p. 88.
68   Bar Hebraeus, p. 411.
69   Bar Hebraeus, p. 411.
70   Bar Hebraeus, p. 411.
71   Ibn al-'Adīm, *Zubdat al-Halab min Tārīkh Ḥalab*, ed. by Khalīl 'Umrān al-Manṣūr, 2 vols (Beirut: Dār al-Kutub al-'Ilmīyah, 1996), II, p. 515.
72   Nikephoros Gregoras, *Byzantina Historia*, ed. by Ludwig Schopen, Corpus Scriptorum Historiae Byzantinae, 38–39, 2 vols (Bonn: Weber, 1829–1830), II, pp. 42–43 (book VI, chapter 3).

his uprising through characterizing Kaykhusraw as incompetent and effeminate ('iners ac muliebris est nec dignus terram tenere').[73] For three months, Quṭb al-Dīn Aḥmad and his Turkmens ransacked farms in the vicinity of Konya.[74] The revolt came to an end when the Armenian lord Constantin of Lampron later stopped the Turkmens of Quṭb al-Dīn near Alanya and executed their leader.[75]

The causes of the uprising are unclear. Simon claims that Quṭb al-Dīn's revolt started at the instigation of Seljuk emirs but does not specify who they were and under what circumstances they took action.[76] Cahen interpreted the events as an attempt by a group of Turkmen to rid themselves of the Seljuks. Such an interpretation has two shortcomings. First, Quṭb al-Dīn according to the sources fought not to build his own independent emirate but to replace his alleged brother, the incapable sultan Kaykhusraw II. Second, considering that the Turkmens of Quṭb al-Dīn focused on looting farmlands, it is clear that scarcity of resources must have, at least in part, motivated their actions.

This seems to be corroborated by the behaviour of another group of Turkmen, the Germiyānids, in the aftermath of Köse Dağ. Details are limited, but Ibn Bībī claims that the Germiyānids started cutting the roads between Malatya and Aleppo after Kaykhusraw's defeat against the Mongols.[77] This account is confirmed by the historian Ibn al-ʿAdīm, a native of Aleppo who, without explicitly mentioning the Germiyānids, asserts that important groups of Turkmens from southern Rūm fell upon the people fleeing Anatolia for Aleppo.[78] The behaviour of the Germiyānids resembles that of the Turkmens of Quṭb al-Dīn. Considering the dreadful famine that hit Malatya after the Mongols burnt the crops of the region, it is very plausible that the Germiyānids embraced banditry, not for pleasure, but to ensure the survival of their group.

From these multiple examples it becomes clear that the first Mongol invasion of Anatolia proved highly destructive. The Mongols pillaged some of the most prosperous cities of the sultanate and condemned many people, both sedentary and nomads, to a life in poverty. Calm was restored, however, once the Mongols and the Seljuks signed a peace treaty. Kaykhusraw II's death in 1246 triggered a conflict among his heirs, but a group of influential emirs led by Qaratay proved able to keep order for a few years in the sultanate of the Seljuks. The situation however took a dire turn in 1256 during the second Mongol invasion of Anatolia, the second 'year of Bāijū Noyan'.

The Second Mongol Invasion and the Rise of the Beyliks

The first 'year of Bāijū' proved a turning point in the history of the sultanate of Rūm. The once powerful kingdom of Sultan ʿAlāʾ al-Dīn Kaykubād was reduced to being yet another vassal state of the Mongol empire. Yet, despite the high death

---

73 Simon of Saint Quentin, p. 81; Ibn Wāṣil, p. 327.
74 Simon of Saint Quentin, p. 81.
75 Simon of Saint Quentin, p. 81.
76 Simon of Saint Quentin, p. 81.
77 Ibn Bībī, p. 472.
78 Ibn al-ʿAdīm, p. 515.

toll, the immediate consequences of the first Mongol invasion remained confined to turning the sultanate into a vassal state. Once Bāijū departed and Kaykhusraw II had quelled the few Turkmen revolts, life returned to the pre-Mongol state of affairs. Thirteen years later, however, Bāijū once again invaded Anatolia and fought against Kaykhusraw's son, 'Izz al-Dīn Kaykāwūs II (1246–57). All over the Near East, contemporary historians of various origins, the same people who had analysed the outcome of Bāijū's first invasion, came to a rare consensus: the second Mongol invasion of Anatolia forever altered the socio-political landscape of the region and gave way to the emergence of the beyliks.

What happened? In 1256, the Mongols resumed their campaigns in the Islamic world. Hūlāgū, who used the Mughan steppe previously occupied by Bāijū as a base for his armies, sent the Mongol commander to Rūm, where his forces could use the pastures of central Anatolia.[79] Sultan Kaykāwūs II refused to allow the Mongol army to settle in the heart of his realm. A battle between Kaykāwūs and Bāijū soon ensued. After suffering a defeat, Kaykāwūs was forced to flee to Nicaea. During that very year, most sources agree, large groups of Turkmens banded together to resist the Mongols. Among these Turkmens, a certain Karīm al-Dīn Karāmān formed a powerful force in the Cilician Mountains. Four years later, out of nowhere, the Turkmens of Karāmān Bey were able to meddle in Seljuk politics.

As mentioned, Ibn Bībī's account of the rise of the Karāmānids is rather laconic. As an explanation for the sudden appearance of a force of 10,000 rebellious Turkmen in 1261, Ibn Bībī argues that Karāmān Bey and his men took advantage of the chaos caused by Bāijū to become bandits.[80] Yet, Ibn Bībī also claims that Karāmān Bey was a mere charcoal dealer. How could a petty bandit and simple trader from the Taurus region, a man of little power and influence, grow powerful enough within a mere four years to threaten the Seljuk sultanate? Ibn Bībī's account is missing some crucial elements. Unfortunately, as mentioned, the other contemporary witness, Smbat Sparapet, is just as elusive as Ibn Bībī. The Armenian historian claims that Karāmān Bey was a Turkmen lord who exerted influence over the nomads of the region, but fails to explain where Karāmān's influence came from.[81] Something must have happened between 1256 and 1261 for an unknown Turkmen to become a powerful warlord, able to threaten both the Seljuk sultanate and the Armenian kingdom of Cilicia.

Fortunately, other sources, among which Byzantine historians add some illuminating details to the accounts of Ibn Bībī and Smbat Sparapet. George Akropolites, an influential Byzantine aristocrat, diplomat, and historian of the period, witnessed Bāijū's second invasion of Anatolia. Whereas Ibn Bībī emphasizes that Karāmān Bey took advantage of Bāijū's invasion, Akropolites underlines the disruptions which the Mongols caused among the Turkmen communities of Anatolia. Because of the

---

79 Bar Hebraeus, *Tārīkh mukhtaṣar al-duwal*, ed. by Khalīl al-Manṣūr (Beirut: Dār al-Kutub al-'Ilmīyah, 1997), p. 231.
80 Ibn Bībī, pp. 590–91.
81 Smbat Sparapet, p. 113.

turmoil ignited by the Mongols, the Turkmens of Anatolia made more frequent raids on Byzantine merchants.[82]

Akropolites does not expatiate on the nature of the disruptions caused by Bāijū, but his disciple, George Pachymeres, complements the account of his predecessor. He argues that after Kaykāwūs's defeat against Bāijū many of the Turkmens refused to submit to the Mongols. To defend themselves against the invaders, sizeable groups of Turkmens fled to the mountains. From the mountains, these Turkmens launched raids against the sedentary inhabitants of Anatolia. Other groups, Pachymeres continues, focused on capturing Byzantine fortresses in order to defend themselves against the Mongols.[83]

Hence, the three accounts make plain that Bāijū's invasion was a serious threat to the security and perhaps to the way of life of the Anatolian Turkmens. The imminent danger caused them to form larger units and prey upon weaker targets to ensure their survival. Yet, the accounts of the three historians lack precision and do not explain in what way the Mongol invasion proved threatening to the Anatolian Turkmens and why the Turkmens refused to submit to the Mongols.

It is worth noting that after the disaster of Köse Dağ and the death of Kaykhusraw II most of Kaykāwūs II's military power depended on Turkmen groups from southern and central Anatolia. During the succession conflict with his brother Kılıç Arslan IV (1248–65), Kaykāwūs II had defeated his rival with the help of various Turkmen groups but also Kurdish and Arab nomads. During Bāijū's second invasion, Kaykāwūs II once again gathered his Turkmen forces to oppose the Mongols.[84] Among the Turkmens who responded to Kaykāwūs's call were the famous 'Turkmens of the uj' and some unidentifiable groups from regions in southern Anatolia, such as the Bozkır, Gülnar, and Bulgar Mountains. The presence of the Germiyānids among Kaykāwūs's loyalists is not directly confirmed but plausible because of the presence of their leader, Karīm al-Dīn 'Alīshīr, among Kaykāwūs supporters.[85]

On 14 October 1256, Bāijū defeated Kaykāwūs II and his Turkmen troops. The Mongol commander freed Kaykāwūs's brother and rival Kılıç Arslan IV and established him as the new sultan of Rūm.[86] Following Kılıç Arslan's enthronement, Bāijū and his tumen occupied the central Anatolian steppes.[87] It is likely, and has been frequently pointed out by scholars, that this caused many of the Turkmens of the central Anatolian steppes to look for pastures elsewhere. Most of the Turkmens loyal to Kaykāwūs II came from mountainous regions in southern Anatolia. Given

---

82   George Akropolites, *The History*, trans. by Ruth Macrides, Oxford Studies in Byzantium (Oxford: Oxford University Press, 2007), p. 315.
83   George Pachymeres, *Relations historiques*, livres I–VI, ed. by Albert Failler, trans. by Vitalien Laurent, Corpus Fontium Historiae Byzantinae, 24/1–2, 2 vols (Paris: Belles Lettres, 1984), livres I–VI, ed. and trans. by Albert Failler, Corpus Fontium Historiae Byzantinae, 24/3–5, 3 vols (Paris: Institut Français d'Études Byzantines, 1999–2000), I, pp. 32–33 (book I, chapter 5–6); pp. 184–85 (book II, chapter 24).
84   Ibn Bībī, p. 532.
85   Ibn Bībī, p. 555.
86   Bar Hebraeus, *Tārīkh*, p. 231; Ibn Bībī, p. 554.
87   Bar Hebraeus, p. 425.

that the battle took place in the early autumn the Turkmens of the Bozkır, Gülnar, and Bulgar Mountains must have been ready to move with their beasts to the central Anatolian plains to spend the winter season under milder climatic conditions. Bāijū's sudden migration to their area of choice must have 'locked' the Turkmens out of their winter pastures and forced them to look for less suitable alternatives.

Soon thereafter, the Mongols launched a campaign against the remnants of Kaykāwūs's forces.[88] The key source for the events, Bar Hebraeus, does not state who the remnants of Kaykāwūs's partisans opposing Bāijū were. Yet, considering that most of Kaykāwūs's forces consisted of Turkmens, there is little doubt that the loyalists hunted down by Bāijū were the 'Turkmens who refused to submit to the Mongols and fled to the mountains' mentioned by Pachymeres and Akropolites.

This explains why many of the Anatolian Turkmens according to Pachymeres showed very little sympathy for the Mongols. Yet, Bāijū's occupation of the best pastures in central Anatolia and subsequent campaigns against the remnants of Kaykāwūs's forces only partly explain why so many Turkmens embraced a life of banditry. Here, it is necessary to factor in the general economic consequences of Bāijū's second invasion. The Mongol commander acted in 1256 as he had done in 1243. This time, Bāijū's destructions may have been ever more widespread than in the aftermath of Köse Dağ. The Mamluk historian Baybars al-Manṣūrī, among many others, argues that the magnitude of Bāijū's second invasion was unprecedented. According to another contemporary witness, Kyrakos of Ganja, Bāijū's 1256 campaign was similar to that of 1243. Hence, the Mongols once again ravaged the lands between Erzurum and Aksaray but this time added Elbistan and the vicinities of Konya to their list of victims.[89] A year later, Malatya, too, once again was seriously affected by the conflicts between the Seljuks and the Mongols in addition to the many raids led by the Aghacheri Turkmens.[90] Like in 1243, a famine broke out and the inhabitants of Malatya and Erzincan had to battle for their survival.[91] In a case of traumatic *deja-vu*, in Malatya, desperate people sold their children, again as slaves, to the Aghacheri Turkmens and resorted to cannibalism to ensure their survival.[92]

In 1258, the Mongols took Baghdad. The 'Abbāsid capital had long lost its status as the wealthiest city of the Islamic world but remained an economic powerhouse and a major trade hub in the Near East.[93] The fall of Baghdad in 1258, a mere year after Bāijū's devastations in Rūm, was the nail in the coffin for the populations of the Islamic East. Most contemporary witnesses agree that the events of 1256–58 had a dramatic impact on the region's living conditions. By early 1258, famine struck

---

88 Bar Hebraeus, p. 426.
89 Aqsarā'ī, *Müsâmeret ül-ahbâr: Mogollar zamanında Türkiye Selçukluları Tarihi*, Aksaraylı Mehmed oğlu Kerîmüddin Mahmud, ed. by Osman Turan, Türk Tarih Kurumu Yayınlarından III. Seri, 1 (Ankara: Türk Tarih Kurumu, 1944), p. 41; Kyrakos of Ganja, *History of the Armenians*, trans. by Robert Bedrosian, (New York: Sources of the Armenian Tradition, 1986), p. 311; Bar Hebraeus, p. 426.
90 Bar Hebraeus, p. 427.
91 Bar Hebraeus, p. 427.
92 Bar Hebraeus, p. 427.
93 Wilhelm Heyd, *Histoire du Commerce du Levant au Moyen Age*, (Leipzig: O. Harrassowitz, 1885), p. 107.

the Islamic Near East. Before long, a great plague broke out. Finally, in addition to famine and plague, a severe crisis of inflation took over most areas from Anatolia to Egypt.[94] The crisis lasted at least until 1260. At this date, Rashīd al-Dīn describes the Islamic central lands from Baghdad to Anatolia as still 'in ruins, devoid of farmers and seeds'.[95] The economic crisis, which affected the sedentary population of Anatolia, no doubt affected the nomadic people as well. As historical anthropologists have demonstrated countless times, Turkmen nomads did not live in autarchy. Rather, pastoral nomads depended on their sedentary neighbours to complete their diets with necessary staples such as grain.[96] In time of peace, nomads bought or bartered for such staples. In 1256–58, Anatolia was in ruins and many of its crops reduced to ashes. Likewise, the famine which struck most of the Near East must have further prevented the Turkmens, already weakened by Bāijū's seizure of the central Anatolian steppes, from buying grain and other necessity goods.

In short, the years 1256–58 proved seminal in the history of Anatolia. It is during this period that many of the Turkmens of Anatolia, among them the Karāmānids and the Turkmens of Lādik, gathered and formed larger groups; the embryo of the future beyliks. The period 1256–58, however, proved more significant for the Turkmens of Anatolia than 1243. Unlike in 1243 when the Mongol forces retreated to Mughan, in 1256 Bāijū's tumen occupied the central Anatolian plains. Bāijū's occupation deprived large Turkmen groups from their mode of production. The campaigns led by Bāijū against the remnants of Kaykāwūs's armies consisting mostly of Turkmens made the situation even more dire and forced many of them to flee to remote and mountainous regions.

Harassed by the Mongols, threatened by starvation, the Turkmens, who needed to defend themselves and secure their pastures, rallied to charismatic leaders, and started to form larger groups.[97] Among the earliest Turkmen leaders to emerge from the crisis was Karīm al-Dīn Karāmān, who suddenly surfaced at the head of a powerful coalitions of nomads. Confronted with food scarcity and insecurity, these Turkmen groups embraced a life of banditry. Rather than fighting against the invincible Mongols, they preyed upon some of their weaker neighbours, among them Armenian and Byzantine merchants and settlements. By 1261, Karāmān Bey, the once impoverished charcoal dealer, attacked Konya in the name of the Seljuk sultan in exile, Kaykāwūs II. The new sultan Kılıç Arslan IV proved able to bribe the Turkmen leader away by granting him an *iqṭāʿ* in Ermenek. A year later, the ambitious Karāmān attacked the Armenian kingdom of Cilicia. Despite some initial successes, the conquests did not last, and King Hethum I defeated and killed the Turkmen leader on the battlefield. Karāmān's brother Bunsuz, along with Karāmān's sons, were

---

94 Bar Hebraeus, p. 431.
95 Rashīd al-Dīn, *Jāmiʿal-Tawārīkh*, trans. by Wheeler Thackston (Cambridge MA: Harvard University, Dept. of Near Eastern Languages and Civilizations, 1998), p. 504.
96 See for example Anatoly M. Khazanov, *Nomads and the Outside World* (Madison: University of Wisconsin Press, 1994).
97 Pachymeres, I, pp. 32–33 (book I, chapter 5–6).

soon put in jail by Kılıç Arslan IV and his vizier Mu'īn al-Dīn Sulayman Pervāneh (d. 1277). The young Karāmānid beylik was beheaded.

A year later, in 1264, another Karīm al-Dīn, 'Alīshīr of the Germiyānids, was also executed in Konya, among a host of significant emirs. Sultan Kılıç Arslan and his Mongol overlords accused Karīm al-Dīn 'Alīshīr of supporting Kaykāwūs II during Bāijū's second invasion. Two of the most powerful Turkmen groups of the period were left leaderless. Yet, a mere 15 years later, in 1278, the Germiyānids and the Karāmānids fought against each other, this time supporting two different sides during the Mamluk sultan Baybars's (1260–77) invasions of Anatolia. By 1278, the two Turkmen groups, seemingly leaderless in 1264 stood as powerful as ever.

Gazi Warriors in the West: The Germiyānids after 1261

What happened to the Germiyānids between the enthronement of Kılıç Arslan IV as sultan and the Karāmānid revolt of 1276–78 is obscured by the dearth of sources. Ibn Bībī makes no reference to the Germiyānids in the time between their raiding activities in 1243 and their fight against the Karāmānids in 1277. Yet, whereas the Germiyānids in 1243 still settled in eastern Anatolia, by 1277 they had relocated to the west, near the Byzantine border. What happened to them in the intervening period is still unclear. Claude Cahen once contended that the Seljuks moved the Germiyānids from Malatya to western Anatolia in 1276–77 to fight against the Karāmānids.[98] Such a hypothesis is questionable. In 1277, when the Seljuk vizier Fakhr al-Dīn 'Ālī summoned the Germiyānids to fight against the Karāmānids, Ibn Bībī claims that the Turkmens set off not from Malatya, but from their base somewhere near Degirmençayı near modern Sivrihisar.[99] Ibn Bībī's assertions thus contradicts Cahen's interpretation and show that the Germiyānids had already settled in Western Anatolia before 1277. Contrary to Cahen, Sümer argued that the Germiyānids left Malatya in 1260 under Mongol pressure.[100] Considering contemporary sources, Sümer's hypothesis appears more plausible than Cahen's. Yet, Mongol pressure does not seem to have been the chief reason behind the migration of the Germiyānids.

A first hint can be found in a later source, the Kitāb-i Diyārbakriyya, a history of the Aq-Qoyunlu written in the fifteenth century by Abū Bakr al-Tehrānī. In the first chapters, al-Tehrānī outlines the life of Pahlavān Bey, a forefather of Tūr 'Ālī, the first Aq-Qoyunlu leader. Al-Tehrānī explains that after fleeing Azerbaijan from the Mongols, Pahlavān Bey entered the service of the Seljuks. The latter sent him along with the 'sons of 'Ajamshir' to the Seljuk-Byzantine frontier.[101] There, near Bursa ('hudūd-i Būrsā') Pahlavān Bey and the sons of 'Ajamshir fought the holy war for the

---

98 Claude Cahen, 'Notes pour l'histoire', p. 353.
99 Ibn Bībī, p. 598.
100 Sümer, Oğuzlar, p. 162.
101 Al-Ṭihrānī, Abū Bakr-i Ṭihrānī, Kitāb-i Diyārbakriyya, Ak-Koyunlar Tarihi, ed. by Necati Lugal and Faruk Sümer, Türk Tarih Kurumu Yayınları, III. Dizi, 7, 2 vols (Ankara: Türk Tarih Kurumu, 1993), p. 15.

Seljuks against Byzantine infidels.¹⁰² Considering that most thirteenth-century sources identify the ruling Germiyānid dynasty as 'sons of 'Alīshīr', the 'sons of 'Ajamshir' mentioned in the Kitāb-i Diyārbakriyya must be no one else than the Germiyānid leaders. Al-Tehrānī places these developments during the reigns of Kılıç Arslan IV and Ghiyāth al-Dīn Khaykhusraw III (1265–1284), in other words, between 1261 and 1277–78, the date at which the Germiyānids are mentioned around Degirmençayı in contemporary sources.¹⁰³ Yet, Kılıç Arslan IV died in 1265. Therefore, if one takes the Kitāb-i Diyārbakriyya at face value, the Germiyānids moved near Degirmençayı before 1265. Such claim can however be further refined with the use of contemporary sources.

In 1257, upon coming back to Konya from Nicaea, Kaykāwūs II, who still feared Bāijū, sent his men to Malatya to recruit troops from the Turkmens, Arabs, and Kurds of the region.¹⁰⁴ Later that year, another of Kaykāwūs's generals, 'Alī Bahādur, went to Malatya to muster an army. Bahādur first fought against the Aghacheri Turkmens of the region, imprisoned their commander, Jūtī Bey, and took control of one of their groups.¹⁰⁵ Later, 'Alī Bahādur, who realized the staggering might of the Mongol armies, returned to Kaykāwūs. At this point, no evidence proves that 'Alī Bahādur recruited soldiers from among the Germiyānids. Yet, later events hint such a possibility.

In 1261, Kaykāwūs II, put under pressure by his brother and his Mongol allies, once again fled to Nicaea.¹⁰⁶ Bahādur determined to fight for the sultan, recruited troops from Sivrihisar near Degirmençayı, where the Germiyānids lived in 1277. Bahādur failed and was forced to flee. What happened in the aftermath is most interesting. Pervāneh and the Mongols, infuriated by Kaykāwūs II's constant resistance, gathered a lengthy list of emirs and leaders who had been loyal to Kaykāwūs's during the civil war.¹⁰⁷ The Mongols then executed these emirs one by one. Among them was Karīm al-Dīn 'Alīshīr, the forefather of the ruling dynasty of the Germiyānids. Cahen was not sure whether the Karīm al-Dīn 'Alīshīr executed in 1261 was the same as the eponymous progenitor of the Germiyānid dynasty.¹⁰⁸ Yet, the later account of the fifteenth-century Ottoman historian Yazıcıoğlu calls the same person 'Karīm al-Dīn 'Alīshīr Germiyānoğlu'.¹⁰⁹ In addition, Ibn Bībī's history often refers to the descendants of 'Alīshīr as 'awlād-i 'Alīshīr Germiyānii', which comes very close to the designation used by Yazıcıoğlu and suggests that the Karīm al-Dīn 'Alīshīr killed in 1261 was indeed the progenitor of the 'Alīshīrid dynasty. It is not known how and in what way Karīm al-Dīn 'Alīshīr supported Kaykāwūs II. Likewise, there is no evidence suggesting that any of the Turkmens recruited in Malatya in 1258 belonged to the

---

102   Al-Ṭihrānī, p. 15.
103   Al-Ṭihrānī, p. 15.
104   Bar Hebraeus, *Tārīkh*, p. 233.
105   Bar Hebraeus, p. 426; Bar Hebraeus, *Tārīkh*, p. 233.
106   Ibn Bībī, p. 551; Bar Hebraeus, p. 445. On Kaykāwūs II's life in Constantinople, see Rustam Shukurov, *The Byzantine Turks, 1204–1461*, The Medieval Mediterranean, 105 (Leiden: Brill, 2016), pp. 101–05.
107   Ibn Bībī, p. 555.
108   Cahen, 'Notes pour l'histoire', p. 352.
109   Ali Yazıcıoğlu, *Tevârîh-i Âl-i Selcuk [Oguznâme-Selcuklu Tarihi]*, ed. by Abdullah Bakır (Istanbul: Çamlıca Basım Yayın, 2017), p. 776.

Germiyānids. Yet, the mention of troops from Sivrihisar serving ʿAlī Bahadur in 1261 and the execution of Karīm al-Dīn ʿAlīshīr in the aftermath is perplexing. If not the entire confederation, at least some people among the ruling strata of the Germiyānids supported Kaykāwūs II against Kılıç Arslan IV and the Mongols.

Finally, Smbat Sparapet claims without going into further details that the Mongols 'took Malatya in 1266–67'.[110] Considering the abundance of lush pastureland around Malatya, there is no doubt that the Mongols would have wanted to keep it for their own armies to the detriment of the local Turkmens, among them the Germiyānids. Although Smbat's account does not confirm that the Germiyānids moved west at this date, 1266–67 may be the latest date that the Germiyānids could have left Malatya for Degirmençayı.

In sum, based on the limited amount of contemporary evidence one can draw the following conclusions: 1) The Germiyānids left Malatya for a region near Degirmençayı/Sivrihisar not in 1277 as Cahen once suggested but before 1265. 2) Sümer was probably right to consider that the Germiyānids left Malatya around 1260. However, considering the execution of ʿAlīshīr in 1261, it seems that the Germiyānids set forth not because of Mongol pressure but in order to fight for Kaykāwūs II during the Seljuk civil war between 1258 and 1261. 3) If Pahlavān Bey did in fact move to western Anatolia under Kılıç Arslan IV's command, not with ʿAlīshīr himself, but with ʿAlīshīr's sons, it is a reasonable inference that the leadership of the Germiyānids decided to serve Kılıç Arslan IV after the death of ʿAlīshīr in 1261.

What happened to the Germiyānids between 1261 and 1277 is however subject to speculation. The Kitāb-i Diyārbakriyya is a fifteenth-century source and may contain later traditions. Likewise, none of the thirteenth-century Seljuk historians mention the Germiyānids fighting the holy war for Kılıç Arslan IV on the Seljuk-Byzantine frontier. Yet, the Kitāb-i Diyārbakriyya may contain a kernel of truth. According to Ibn Shaddād, after the battle of Elbistan in 1277, in which the Mamluks fought against a coalition of Seljuk and Mongol forces, Sultan Baybars' troops had a Seljuk emir among their prisoners, who was called Shihāb al-Dīn Ghāzī b. ʿAlīshīr al-Turkumānī.[111] The use of *ghāzī* as a *laqab* ('honorific') for Shihāb al-Dīn, son of Alīshīr the Turkmen, seems to indicate that the Turkmen emir did in fact fight the holy war for the Seljuks as mentioned in the Kitāb-i Diyārbakriyya.

Nevertheless, encouraging the Germiyānids and other loyal Turkmen groups to raid Byzantium would have proved advantageous for the Seljuks who could have ensured that the nomads fought not against the subjects of the sultans but against the Byzantine Christians. It is also possible that Kılıç Arslan IV and the Pervāneh may have wanted to punish the Byzantines for offering shelter and troops to the disgraced Kaykāwūs II by planting a powerful Turkmen group near the Byzantine border.[112]

---

110 Smbat Sparapet, p. 652.
111 Ibn Shaddād, *Tārīkh al-Malik al-Ẓāhir*, ed. by Ahmat Hutait, Bibliotheca Islamica (Wiesbaden: Franz Steiner Verlag, 1983), p. 173.
112 According to Aqsarāʾī, p. 49, Theodore II Laskaris lent three thousand soldiers to support Kaykāwūs II's campaign to reclaim the Seljuk throne.

Finally, Kılıç Arslan IV and the Pervāneh may have wanted to bribe the Germiyānids into obedience rather than destroy their group once and for all. During the civil war between the two brothers Kaykāwūs II and Kılıç Arslan IV, the former had always proved able to best his brother with the help of the many groups of Turkmens into his service. Kılıç Arslan and the Pervāneh, whose armies were limited in size by the Mongols, must have hoped to use the Germiyānid Turkmens as a source of manpower for regional conflicts and perhaps even against the Mongols themselves. Such is what happened in 1277–78, when the Seljuk vizier Fakhr al-Dīn ʿAlī subdued the false Seljuk prince supported by the Karāmānids thanks to the help of the Germiyānids and their leaders. Such a policy, although successful at first, backfired in the early 1280s, when amidst the chaos caused by the Seljuk and Mongol civil wars the Germiyānids achieved their independence from their overlords, once and for all.

A Phoenix from the Taurus: The Karāmānids after 1263

The history of the Karāmānids during the thirteen years separating the death of Karīm al-Dīn Karāmān in 1263 from the Karāmānid revolt of 1276–78 is as obscure as that of their Germiyānid counterparts. Kılıç Arslan IV and the Pervāneh feared the Turkmen force led by Karāmān Bey, that much is clear from the sources. Just like in the case of the Germiyānids, the Seljuks were eager to avoid a confrontation with the Karāmānids and sought to bribe the Turkmens of Ermenek into submission. To buy Karīm al-Dīn Karāmān's loyalty, Kılıç Arslan and Pervāneh gave the city of Ermenek to the Turkmen leader as an *iqṭāʿ*. Bunsuz, Karāmān's brother, also benefited from the generosity of the Seljuk government and was appointed *amīr jāndār*.[113] Ibn Bībī, whose contempt for the Karāmānids has few limits, emphasizes the greed and arrogance of the new emir of Ermenek. Karāmān Bey is described from the onset as a man harbouring seditious ambitions against the Seljuks but ultimately as too powerful to be brought to justice.[114]

The death of Karāmān Bey in a battle against the Armenians of Cilicia in 1263 assuaged the fears of the Seljuks. When news of Karāmān's death reached Konya, Kılıç Arslan immediately moved against Bunsuz. The sultan put the Karāmānid emir into jail. Before long, Karāmān's sons were put under house arrest too. Ibn Bībī recalls the events with great bitterness. The Seljuk historian refers to the sons of Karāmān Bey as 'snake children' (*mārbachegān*). With the benefit of hindsight, Ibn Bībī adds that these children grew up to become dragons and later brought grief to the kingdom of the Seljuks.[115]

If our records are correct, by 1263 most, if not all, of Karāmān's presumptive heirs languished in prison or were under house arrest. The time was ripe for the Seljuks to eliminate all Turkmen troublemakers once and for all. In all likelihood, the broken

---

13 Ibn Bībī, p. 591.
14 Ibn Bībī, p. 591.
15 Ibn Bībī, p. 591.

Karāmānid dynasty was doomed to eclipse along with its founders. For a yet unknown reason, however, Kılıç Arslan and Pervāneh did not kill the sons of Karāmān Bey. At first, Pervāneh kept them under house arrest in the castle of Kavāle.[116] After the murder of Kılıç Arslan IV in 1265, Pervāneh's behaviour goes from puzzling to outright incomprehensible. In a Hitchcockian twist, Pervāneh, freed the sons of Karāmān from their prison.[117] Back to their base near Ermenek, the sons of Karāmān soon regained leadership among their father's Turkmens.

Let us briefly recall that, as emphasized by most historians of the period, the rise of Karāmān Bey and his Turkmen made Pervāneh and Kılıç Arslan shiver in fear and liberally distribute prestigious titles and territories. Why would the politically astute Pervāneh free the sons and potential heirs of a meddlesome enemy? The sources do not provide any satisfactory answer to this question. One may however surmise a few explanations. It is tempting to see Pervāneh's behaviour as an attempt to impose direct control on the Turkmens of Ermenek. As the most powerful man in the Seljuk administration, Pervāneh must have been aware of Karāmān's rise to leadership among the Turkmens of Ermenek. With the vacuum created by Karāmān's death and the imprisonment of most of his potential successors, the Turkmens of Ermenek were theoretically left leaderless. Rather than waiting to witness the rise of another Karāmān, Pervāneh may have been tempted to free his sons and place them under his power. The Seljuk vizier may have hoped that by freeing Mehmet Bey ibn Karāmān and his sons the potential leader of the Turkmens of Ermenek would remain grateful and obedient to his person. Furthermore, Pervāneh may have seen in the followers of the Karāmānids a potential source of manpower. Perhaps Pervāneh sought to emulate Kaykāwūs II so as to use the Anatolian Turkmens against the Mongols one day.

A few possible hints may be adduced in support of such an idea. An anonymous Seljuk chronicle starts the subsection of his history dealing with Pervāneh's rise to power with a brief discussion of the Karāmānids. The author thus shows that one of Pervāneh's first decisions as a vizier of Kılıç Arslan was to appease the Karāmānids.[118] With such an appeasement policy, Pervāneh tried to keep the Turkmens under control and prevent them from causing troubles in the southern Taurus region. His report is very brief, but the anonymous historian concludes his account on Pervāneh and the early Karāmānids with an ominous sentence claiming that 'in the time of the Pervāneh, wolves and sheep drank and grazed together.'[119]

This statement may refer to the revolt of Sharaf al-Dīn Mas'ūd ibn Khatir. The latter was originally one of Pervāneh's closest allies and a powerful emir. Between 1261 and 1277, Sharaf al-Dīn Mas'ūd ruled over the rich city of Niğde. Before the revolt of Baybars, Ibn Khatir colluded with the Karāmānids. His involvement with both the

---

116 Ibn Bībī, p. 591.
117 Ibn Bībī, p. 591.
118 Anonymous author, *Tārīkh-i Āl-i Saljūq*, ed. by Nādara Jalalī (Tehran: Daftar-e Nasher-e Miras Maktoob, 1958), p. 63.
119 Anonymous *Tārīkh-i Āl-i Saljūq*, p. 63.

Karāmānids and Baybars contributed to the revolt of 1276–78. In the aftermath, the Mongols took direct control of Anatolia and de facto ended centuries of Seljuk rule. Sharaf al-Dīn Masʿūd's collusion with the Karāmānids shows that some of the most influential emirs in Rūm had carefully considered collaborating with the Turkmens against the Mongols. In the end, both the appeasement policy of Pervāneh and Sharaf al-Dīn Masʿūd's conspiracy severely backfired.[120] Free to rebuild their power in the southern Taurus, the sons of Karāmān Bey emerged more powerful than ever. With the help of the mysterious Jimrī, who impersonated one of Kaykāwūs's sons, the Karāmānids managed to take over Konya and appoint their own 'Seljuk' prince as sultan. Once again, the triumph of the Karāmānids proved short-lived. The Mongols, supported by the loyal emir Fakhr al-Dīn ʿAlī and the Germiyānids, defeated Mehmet Bey and Jimrī and partially restored order in Anatolia. This time however, some of Mehmet Bey's relatives survived the onslaught and retreated to the Taurus Mountain. For the next fifty-five years, the Mongols never proved able to dislodge the Karāmānids from their fortresses in the mountains.

Conclusions

In sum, this paper has reconstructed the formative period of two of the most prominent Turkmen beyliks and brought to the forefront numerous differences between the Germiyānids and the Karāmānids. Whereas the former emerged as a significant force in the twelfth century, amidst the conquest of the Great Seljuks, the latter rose to significance only a century and a half later. Such differences may be explained by the unique circumstances of eastern Anatolia and the Caucasus during the twelfth century. Whereas the ancestors of the Germiyānids lived in a contested zone characterized by frequent conflicts, the ancestors of the Karāmānids dwelled in a more remote region dominated after the 1120s by Georgian hegemony.

The Mongol invasions however shattered the socio-political landscape of early thirteenth century Anatolia and the Caucasus. At first, the rise of the Mongols forced the ancestors of the Karāmānids to abandon their homeland for Anatolia. Later, the events of 1256 forced many Turkmens of Anatolia, among them the Karāmānids, to form larger confederations to withstand the loss of pasturelands and the temporary collapse of the economic system of the Islamic Near East. The Germiyānids, supported by their better organization, and perhaps greater military might seem to have been able to better withstand the Mongol invasions of Anatolia. Their role during the 'second year of Baiju' remains mysterious. However, as exemplified by the support offered by Karīm al-Dīn ʿAlīshīr to the 'anti-Mongol' party led by Kaykāwūs II, the Germiyānids seem to have sided against the Mongols. The old Turkmen confederation, or at least some of its leaders, probably foreshadowed the danger posed by a larger and more powerful group of pastoral nomads. Finally, this paper illuminated the role of Seljuk emirs in allowing the early Germiyānid and Karāmānid beyliks to survive. The death

---

20 On the revolt of Ibn Khatir, see Aqsarāʾī, pp. 100–04.

of Abaqa Khan in 1282 and the decade of chaos which ensued in the Ilkhanate gave the Germiyānids and the Karāmānids enough freedom to survive and consolidate their power in their respective bases of central and southern Anatolia. Over the following decades, the Germiyānids and the Karāmānids benefited from the decline of Mongol authority in Anatolia. The former acquired Ankara in 1299 and became a threat for the Byzantine Empire. The latter repeatedly preyed upon their Armenian neighbours and proved a constant thorn in the side of the Mongols. In 1327-28, the Karāmānids seized Konya and continued their expansion northward. The era of the beyliks had started.

DANIELE BAGLIONI

Italian Vernaculars as Diplomatic Languages in the Medieval Levant

In 1992, the French Tunisian linguist Claude Hagège published a book that was soon to become a best-seller in both France and abroad, through its immediate translation into several languages. The book had an inspiring title, *Le souffle de la langue* (*The Breath of Language*), and was entirely devoted to an issue that was extremely topical in the last decade of the twentieth century: 'Which common language for a united Europe?'.[1] Hagège examined all possible candidates, English, German, French, Spanish, Latin, Esperanto, and Italian, briefly tracing the history of each language in search of its international appeal or, in Hagège's words, its 'vocation fédératrice'.[2] The solution proposed by the author was to preserve European multilingualism as a resource, assigning, however, a leading role to English, German and, above all, French.

Neither Hagège's personal convictions on the linguistic policy of the European Union nor his somewhat clumsy attempts to promote French as a language 'more international than the others', thanks to its alleged versatility or 'vocation multiple' ('multiple inclination'), are pertinent to the present study.[3] Still, it is worth noting how Hagège depicts the diffusion of Italian out of Italy, which in his opinion before the nineteenth century was limited to the influence of the financial power of the Italian maritime republics in the Eastern Mediterranean. According to Hagège, this influence left some traces in the vocabulary of the Balkan languages, which nevertheless was not sufficient to give Italian a real international status, because of the episodic and regional character of its diffusion.[4]

This view, which can be summarized with the formula 'Italian vernaculars as spoken languages for trade in the Mediterranean', was certainly not new. The important research of Benedetto Vidos and the Kahanes in the first half of the last century and, later, of Manlio Cortelazzo repeatedly emphasized the role of Italian

---

1 Claude Hagège, *Le souffle de la langue: voies et destins des parlers d'Europe* (Paris: Odile Jacob, 1992).
2 Hagège, *Le souffle de la langue*, pp. 13–14.
3 Hagège, *Le souffle de la langue*, Chapter 4, «Le français et la vocation multiple», pp. 91–121.
4 Hagège, *Le souffle de la langue*, pp. 28–30.

Daniele Baglioni • Università Ca' Foscari Venezia

as a Mediterranean common language for trading and seafaring, thus stressing the vehicular and oral character of its circulation.[5] More recent studies by historians and linguists have shown, however, that in the Early Modern Levant and, more precisely, in Constantinople and in several provinces of the Ottoman Empire, from the Middle East to North Africa, Italian was also used for written communication, not only in documents concerning trade, but also in international treaties involving non-Italian states, as for instance in Anglo-Ottoman or even in Ottoman-Polish and Ottoman-Russian relations.[6]

This diffusion of written Italian 'as a diplomatic and commercial lingua franca', in the words of Bernard Lewis,[7] that is, as a language by which not only the Italians but also the English and other Westerners were able to communicate with the Ottomans and their subjects, gives rise to a significant historiographical problem: if one maintains that in the Middle Ages the international use of Italian was restricted to its spoken circulation for trading purposes, the spread of the same language for high diplomacy, already attested just a few decades after the Fall of Constantinople, seems to come out of the blue.[8] Of course, one may point out that Italian vernaculars did

---

5   See especially Benedetto E. Vidos, *Storia delle parole marinaresche italiane passate in francese* (Firenze: Olschki, 1939); Henry Kahane, Renée Kahane, and Andreas Tietze, *The Lingua Franca in the Levant. Turkish Nautical Terms of Italian and Greek Origin* (Urbana: University of Illinois Press, 1958); Manlio Cortelazzo, *Venezia, il Levante e il mare* (Pisa: Pacini, 1989).

6   Linguistic studies on Italian as an international language in the Eastern Mediterranean were inaugurated by Francesco Bruni, 'Lingua d'oltremare: sulle tracce del "Levant Italian" in età preunitaria', *Lingua Nostra*, 60 (1999), 65–79 (repr. in Francesco Bruni, *L'italiano fuori d'Italia* (Firenze: Cesati, 2013), pp. 135–62), a book that includes several other essays on the same topic. Further contributions specifically focusing on the diffusion of Italian in the Ottoman Empire have been made by Laura Minervini, 'L'italiano nell'impero ottomano', in *Lo spazio linguistico italiano e le 'lingue esotiche': rapporti e reciproci influssi. Atti del XXXIX congresso internazionale di studi della Società di Linguistica Italiana (Milano, 22–24 settembre 2005)*, ed. by Emanuele Banfi and Gabriele Iannàccaro (Rome: Bulzoni, 2006), pp. 49–66, and Daniele Baglioni, 'Lettere dall'impero ottomano alla corte di Toscana (1577–1640). Un contributo alla conoscenza dell'italiano nel Levante', *Lingua e Stile*, 46 (2011), 3–70; Daniele Baglioni, 'Il veneziano dopo Venezia: sondaggi sulle varietà italiane(ggianti) dell'Impero Ottomano', in *Il veneziano «de là da mar». Contesti, testi, dinamiche del contatto linguistico e culturale*, ed. by Daniele Baglioni (Berlin: de Gruyter, 2019), pp. 201–22; see also the chapter devoted to the Early Modern Levant in Emanuele Banfi, *Lingue d'Italia fuori d'Italia. Europa, Mediterraneo e Levante dal Medioevo all'età moderna* (Bologna: il Mulino, 2014), pp. 213–52. Finally, the particular context of the seventeeth-century Maghreb, where Italian served as a language for intermediation between Westerners, Turks, and Moors, notably for slave ransoms and commercial transactions, has been described by Joe Cremona in several essays, recapitulated in Joseph Cremona, 'Histoire linguistique externe de l'italien au Maghreb', in *Romanische Sprachgeschichte. Histoire linguistique de la Romania*, ed. by Gerhard Ernst, Martin-Dietrich Gleßgen, Christian Schmitt, and Wolfgang Schweickard, 3 vols (Berlin: De Gruyter, 2003–10), I, pp. 961–66; a selection of documents in Italian from sixteenth- and seventeenth-century Tunis has been edited with commentary by Daniele Baglioni, *L'italiano delle cancellerie tunisine (1590–1703). Edizione e commento linguistico delle 'carte Cremona'* (Rome: Scienze e Lettere, 2010).

7   Bernard Lewis, *From Babel to Dragoman: Interpreting the Middle East* (London: Weidenfeld & Nicholson, 2004), p. 24.

8   One of the first Ottoman documents in Italian is the letter that Mehmet II the Conqueror sent to the Venetian Doge Cristoforo Moro in 1471, edited by Victor Ménage, 'Seven Ottoman Documents from the Reign of Meḥemmed II', in *Documents from Islamic Chancelleries. First Series*, ed. by Samuel M. Stern (Oxford: Cassirer, 1965), pp. 81–118 (82–87).

serve as administrative languages in the Venetian and Genoese colonies and that their bureaucratic uses likely influenced the writing practices of the Ottoman dragomans, who were mostly recruited among the Greeks of the islands, i.e. among the most Italianized of the Greeks. This is certainly part of the truth, but the recurrence of a well-established diplomatic vocabulary already in the first treaties and capitulations drafted in Italian or translated into Italian by the Ottoman Porte clearly indicates that the practice of diplomatic writing in Italian existed before 1453 and that this practice increased but did not originate under Ottoman rule.

The aim of the present contribution is to investigate the origins of this practice, on the basis of the relatively few extant diplomatic documents in Italian written in the Eastern and Southern Mediterranean in the period from 1100 to 1453. First, a brief survey of the documents available in modern editions and of the contexts of their production will be presented, with particular attention paid to the multilingual 'institutional patterns of communication' recently studied by David Jacoby for the Latin Empire of Constantinople and other Frankish territories.[9] Second, the language of the documents will be analyzed, especially for what concerns loanwords and terms regarding institutions of the Eastern Mediterranean states. This part of the vocabulary is extremely interesting, since all documents are translations of diplomas written in either French or Oriental languages, often by non-Italian interpreters, and consequently need to be examined in a multiliteracy context. Finally, the possible relations between these documents and diplomatic writing in Italian in the Ottoman Levant from the sixteenth century onwards will be indicated, on the basis of some of the translators' choices concerning honorific titles and formulas, which anticipate the uses of Ottoman dragomans.

The Documents

In the medieval Mediterranean, Italian vernaculars were generally used in written form within the Italian communities, that is, in the administration of the Italian colonies and in their relations with their respective motherlands, whereas for international

---

9 David Jacoby, 'Multilingualism and Institutional Patterns of Communication in Latin Romania (Thirteenth-Fourteenth Centuries)', in *Diplomatics in the Eastern Mediterranean 1000–1500. Aspects of Cross–Cultural Communication*, ed. by Alexander D. Beihammer, Maria G. Parani, and Christopher Schabel (Leiden: Brill, 2008), 27–48. For Cyprus in particular, see: Alexander Beihammer, 'Byzantine Chancery Traditions in Frankish Cyprus: The Case of the Vatican MS *Palatinus Graecus 367*', in *Identités croisées en un milieu méditerranéen: le cas de Chypre (Antiquité - Moyen Age)*, ed. by Sabine Fourrier and Gilles Grivaud (Mont Saint-Aignan: Presses universitaires de Rouen et du Havre, 2006), pp. 301–15; Angel Nicolaou-Konnari, 'Diplomatics and Historiography: The Use of Documents in the Chronicle of Leontios Makhairas', in *Diplomatics in the Eastern Mediterranean*, pp. 293–323; Alexander Beihammer, 'Multilingual Literacy', *Byzantine and Modern Greek Studies*, 35/2 (2011), 149–69; Angel Nicolaou-Konnari, 'Συνέχειες και ασυνέχειες στη δουλοπαροικιακή πολιτική της βενετικής διοίκησης στην Κύπρο', in *Κοινωνίες της υπαίθρου στην ελληνοβενετική Ανατολή (13ος–18ος αι.)*, ed. by Kostas E. Lambrinos (Athens: Athens Academy, 2018), pp. 51–91 (57–63).

communication other languages were preferred.[10] Indeed, Venetian and the other Italian dialects could not compete either with Latin or with French. This explains why for the whole medieval period there are no diplomatic documents whose original versions were drafted in any variety of Italian. Even later, in the Ottoman Empire, Italian continued to be employed mostly for translations, although there are a few pertinent exceptions, such as the Ottoman-Polish capitulations of 1502 and 1519 and the Franco-Ottoman capitulations of 1536, all of which were originally drafted in Italian.[11]

The number of Italian translations is not high (I was able to count c. fifty edited texts for the period considered) and varies according to the century, the subjects involved and the original languages.[12] The practice of translating treaties and diplomatic letters is not attested in the twelfth century (the only document dating from this period, a letter sent from a lieutenant of Saladin to the Pisans, was translated into Italian more than two centuries later)[13] and is still extremely rare in the thirteenth century. It becomes more and more frequent from the second half of the fourteenth century onwards, especially as concerns documents in which Venice was involved. Venetian is by far the most frequently employed Italian vernacular, followed by Pisan, which was mostly used in relations between Pisa and the Arab states of North Africa, and Genoese, whose attestations in diplomatic documents are extremely rare (I could only find two documents, the two translations of the pact between Genoa and the Tatar khan of Crimea of the years 1380–81, both edited by Cornelio Desimoni).[14] Moreover, it is important to distinguish between, on the one hand, agreements with the Crusader States and other Frankish political entities (as, for instance, the Hospitallers of Rhodes), which were generally not translated, since Latin and French were easily readable by Italians, and, on the other, peace treaties with Muslim powers (such as the Ayyubid Emirate of Aleppo, the Khanate of the Golden Horde in Crimea, the Mamluk Sultanate of Cairo, the Ilkhanate of Persia, the Hafsid Emirate of Tunis

---

10   Laura Minervini, 'Veneziano e francese nell'Oriente latino', in *Il veneziano 'de là da mar'. Contesti, testi, dinamiche del contatto linguistico e culturale*, ed. by Daniele Baglioni, Beihefte zur Zeitschrift für romanische Philologie, 421 (Berlin: de Gruyter, 2019), pp. 177–99.
11   See respectively Dariusz Kołodziejczyk, *Ottoman–Polish Diplomatic Relations (15th–18th Century). An Annotated Edition of* Ahdnames *and Other Documents*, The Ottoman Empire and its Heritage, 18 (Leiden: Brill, 2000), pp. 210–12 and 218–21; *Négociations de la France dans le Levant […]*, ed. by Ernest Charrière, 4 vols (Paris: Imprimerie nationale, 1848–60), I, pp. 283–94.
12   The great majority of the documents concern Venice and may be found in *Diplomatarium Veneto-levantinum, sive acta et diplomata res venetas graecas atque levantis illustrantia*, ed. by Georg Martin Thomas and others, Monumenti storici dalla R. Deputazione veneta di storia patria, serie prima, Documenti, V, IX (Venice: Typis Marci Vicentini, 1880–99), I: *1300–1350* (henceforth DVL I), II: *1351–1454* (henceforth DVL II). For those documents that have been re-edited in the publications of the series *Pacta Veneta* by Marco Pozza (Rome: Viella), reference has been made to the more recent edition.
13   *I diplomi arabi del R. Archivio fiorentino*, ed. by Michele Amari (Florence: Le Monnier, 1873), pp. 265–66.
14   Cornelio Desimoni, 'Trattato dei Genovesi col khan dei Tartari nel 1380–1381 scritto in lingua volgare', *Archivio Storico Italiano*, 20 (1887), 161–65. On these documents see also Fiorenzo Toso, 'Documenti del genovese nel Levante', in Fiorenzo Toso, *Il mondo grande. Rotte interlinguistiche e presenze comunitarie del genovese d'oltremare. Dal Mediterraneo al Mar Nero, dall'Atlantico al Pacifico* (Alessandria: Edizioni dell'Orso, 2020), pp. 29–42 (34–35).

and the early Ottoman state), which necessarily had to be rendered into a western language and thus allowed the use of, besides Latin, the Italian vernaculars as well.

The translations were generally made on the spot by interpreters regularly or occasionally at the service of the Italian republics, who delivered them to the ambassadors together with the original instruments. This is explicitly stated in the Venetian version of the pact between Venice and the Emir of Tunis of 1438, re-edited by Francesca Girardi[15]. The text is entirely in the vernacular of Venice, but at the end of the treaty the following note in Latin was added:

> Nota quod per trucimanum ex arabica lingua in latinam hec pax translata fuit et in manibus nobilis viri ser Blanchi Delfino consulis Tunisii originarium in arabico remansit (Note that this treaty has been translated by an interpreter from the Arabic language into Romance [evidently *latina* here indicates a Romance vernacular] and the original in Arabic remained in the hands of the nobleman sir Blanco Delfino, consul of Tunis).

Once the ambassadors had brought or sent back the documents to Italy, both the original and the translation were preserved in the archives of the local chancelleries and eventually copied into registers, such as the Venetian *Libri Pactorum* and *Libri Commemoriali*.

The interpreters were sometimes Italians, such as the Bonaiunta de Cascina who in 1264 is reported to have translated the peace treaty between the Pisans and the emir of Tunis 'de lingua arabica in latina [*sic!*]' (i.e. Pisan),[16] or the Zoane Rizo, 'torciman de Caffa', who is mentioned as a witness in one of the aforesaid versions of the pact between Genoa and the Tatar khan of Crimea.[17] Furthermore, a Pisan, probably Ciolo di Anastasio Bofeti, was responsible for the Italian translation of the letter that the Ilkhan of Persia Öljeitü sent to the French King Philip le Bel in 1305.[18] More frequently, however, the interpreters were recruited from among the local population, as in the case of Sabadin Catip (that is, *kātip* 'scribe'), who in 1358 translated for the Venetians two treaties with the Tatar khan Berdibeg and whose name might reveal a Jewish origin,[19] and of the many anonymous translations whose language betrays a non-native writer.

In one document, the translation of the privileges that the Mamluk Sultan Bursbey granted to the Venetians in 1422, an interesting collaboration between Westerners and locals is attested. The privileges are said to have been translated into Latin (i.e.

---

15   *Venezia e il regno di Tunisi. Gli accordi diplomatici conclusi fra il 1231 e il 1456*, ed. by Francesca Girardi, Pacta Veneta. Materiali, 1 (Roma: Viella, 2006), pp. 67–73.
16   Arrigo Castellani, *La prosa italiana delle Origini. I. Testi toscani di carattere pratico*, 2 vols (Bologna: Pàtron, 1982), I, pp. 383–94 (394).
17   Desimoni, 'Trattato dei Genovesi col khan dei Tartari', p. 164.
18   Valeria Bertolucci Pizzorusso, 'Traduzione in volgare pisano di una lettera dell'Ilkhan di Persia al re di Francia Filippo il Bello (1305)', in Valeria Bertolucci Pizzorusso, *Scritture di viaggio. Relazioni di viaggiatori e altre testimonianze letterarie e documentarie* (Rome: Aracne, 2011), pp. 260–90 (arguments in favour of the attribution to Ciolo di Pisa are at pp. 287–89).
19   *DVL* II, doc. 24, pp. 47–51 and doc. 26, p. 52.

Venetian) by Sain, chief interpreter of the sultan, in collaboration with a certain Zanon Saimben, probably a renegade, as one may infer by the fact that his name is apparently Italian (Venetian) and that he is reported to be a Muslim; finally, the whole work was supervised by the Venetian ambassador Lorenzo Capello, who is said to have been very competent in the Arabic language.[20]

Collaborations such as the one described in detail in the privileges of 1422 may not have been exceptional, especially as regards the practice of the 'two-tier translation', that is, 'translation through an intermediate language', according to the terminology introduced by Lewis for Ottoman diplomatic writing.[21] For example, the reply of the Armenian King of Cilicia Leo II to the Venetian ambassador Tommaso Bondumier, probably dating from the seventies of the thirteenth century as hypothesized by its more recent editor,[22] must have been originally drafted in Armenian, according to the general practice of the local chancellery.[23] Unfortunately, only the Italian translation has been preserved, but the recurrence in the Italian version of several French loanwords, such as *damaço* 'damage', *querre* 'to seek for, to enquire', and *feo* 'fief', seems to indicate that the text was translated not directly from Armenian, but from an intermediate French version. This may also be the case with the translations of the two pacts between Venice and the emir of Aleppo of 1208 and 1225, which are the oldest examples of the use of an Italian vernacular in the diplomatic relations with Eastern Mediterranean states and also the earliest attestations of the use of Venetian in official documents.[24] The two texts show a certain influence of French for vis-à-vis both the vocabulary (*avenanteça* 'convenience', *tener* 'fief, territory', *plusor* 'many') and the spelling (*baigno, centenairo*). Nevertheless, it is not clear whether the influence of French is to be attributed to the existence of a previous French translation or to the familiarity of the anonymous translator, certainly a local, with the administrative language of the crusaders.[25]

Diplomatic instruments delivered by the ambassadors only in the original versions and later translated in Italy are much more rarely attested. Five Arabic documents

---

20 DVL II, doc. 174, pp. 320–27 (327): 'Translactada in latin per trucimanno Sain, grando trucimanno del soldan, e Zanon Saimben, scriptor de la fe sarainescha, presente a tutte cose i segnori ambassatori, e specialmente misser Lorenzo Capello predicto, de la lingua arabica peritissimo et molto experto' ('Translated into Latin (i.e. Venetian) by the interpreter Sain, chief interpreter of the sultan, and Zanon Saimben, scrivener of Muslim faith, in the presence of the lord ambassadors, especially the aforesaid Lorenzo Capello, who is very skilled and expert in the Arabic language').

21 Lewis, *From Babel to Dragoman*, p. 24.

22 *I trattati con il regno armeno di Cilicia 1201–1333*, ed. by Alessio Sopracasa, Pacta Veneta, 8 (Rome: Viella, 2001), pp. 53–56.

23 Jean Richard, 'La diplomatique royale dans les royaumes d'Arménie et de Chypre (XIIe–XVe siècles)', *Bibliothèque de l'École des chartes*, 144 (1986), 69–86.

24 *I trattati con Aleppo 1207–1254*, ed. by Marco Pozza (Venice: Il cardo, 1990), pp. 25–33 and 34–43. An edition of the earliest treaty with a linguistic and philological commentary is provided by Gino Belloni and Marco Pozza, 'Il più antico documento in veneziano. Proposta di edizione', in *Guida ai dialetti veneti*, XII, ed. by Manlio Cortelazzo (Padua: Cleup, 1990), pp. 5–23.

25 The same observation can be made with respect to one of the two extant versions in Venetian of a brief letter sent from Aleppo in 1300 by the Ilkhan Ghazan to the Doge Pietro Gradenigo, in which even French plural forms, such as *letres* and *ros* (ie. *rois* 'kings') are to be found; both versions were recently edited by

concerning Pisa, three of which date from the twelfth and thirteenth centuries and the other two from 1422, constitute an interesting case. These documents were translated into Italian in the first half of the fifteenth century by a Cypriot, Tommaso di Ramondo Cardus, who had been appointed for this task by the seigniory of Florence (Pisa had been conquered by Florence in 1406). According to Michele Amari, who published the texts in his collection of the Arabic diplomas of the Archives of Florence,[26] Tommaso was a very bad interpreter, who made frequent mistakes and misunderstood much of what he read.[27] What is relevant, however, is the fact that the seigniory of Florence had to recruit a Cypriot in order to have the documents translated, evidently because in fifteenth-century Tuscany interpreters from Arabic were completely lacking.

The solution found in 1366 for the translation of a letter by which the emir of Bona and Bugia ('Annāba and Biğāya, on the Algerian coast) granted commercial privileges to the Pisans is even more interesting. The translation of the Arabic original into Pisan was probably done in Pisa, as is suggested by the material characteristics of the document.[28] Nevertheless, the Italian vernacular was written not in the Latin alphabet, but in Arabic letters (as far as I know, it is the only example of this practice in the history of the Italian language). Since it is highly plausible that in fourteenth-century Pisan chancelleries nobody could read either Arabic or Italian in Arabic characters, one is led to suppose that the interpreter, probably a North African who knew Pisan but not the Latin alphabet, wrote the text for himself as a personal note and read it aloud before Doge Giovanni Dell'Agnello.[29] Of course, this is a very exceptional case, but it demonstrates how problematic translating from Eastern and Southern Mediterranean languages was in Italy and, more generally, in Western Europe, thus accounting for the rarity of this practice for the whole medieval period and also for the Early Modern Era.

Vittorio Formentin, *Prime manifestazioni del volgare a Venezia. Dieci avventure d'archivio* (Roma: Edizioni di Storia e Letteratura, 2018), 'Notizie da Aleppo. Una lettera dell'ilkhan Ghazan al doge di Venezia', pp. 285–309.

26 *I diplomi arabi del R. Archivio fiorentino*, pp. 265–66 (Second Series, doc. XI), p. 282 (Second Series, doc. XXI), pp. 288–89 (Second Series, doc. XXV), pp. 295–302 (Second Series, doc. XXIX), pp. 309–12 (Second Series, doc. XXXI). The pact with the emir of Tunis (1264) has been re-edited by Castellani (see n. 16 above). On these documents see also Livio Petrucci, 'Il volgare nei carteggi tra Pisa e i paesi arabi', in *Studi offerti a Luigi Blasucci dai colleghi e dagli allievi pisani*, ed. by Lucio Lugnani, Marco Santagata, and Alfredo Stussi (Lucca: Pacini Fazzi, 1996), pp. 413–26; Livio Petrucci, 'Documenti in volgare nei carteggi tra Pisa e i paesi arabi', in *Pisa crocevia di uomini, lingue e culture: L'età medievale. Atti del Convegno (Pisa, 25–27 ottobre 2007)*, ed. by Lucia Battaglia Ricci and Roberta Cella (Rome: Aracne, 2009), pp. 207–16.

27 *I diplomi arabi del R. Archivio fiorentino*, p. LXXI: '[…] un Tommaso di Ramondo Cardus da Nicosia in Cipro, il quale leggea male l'arabico, lo capiva peggio, fieramente storpiava l'italiano, e non ebbe tanto cervello da accorgersi dell'ordine in cui andavan presi i versi d'un testo scritto, credo io, a due colonne' ('a certain Tommaso di Ramondo Cardus from Nicosia, in Cyprus, who badly read Arabic, understood it worse, fiercely mangled Italian, and did not have enough brain to notice the order of the verses in a text written – as I suppose – in two columns').

28 Petrucci, 'Il volgare nei carteggi tra Pisa e i volgari arabi', p. 425.

29 *I diplomi arabi del R. Archivio fiorentino*, pp. 119–22 (First Series, doc. XXXIII). A linguistic analysis of the text has been recently provided by Daniele Baglioni, 'Italoromanzo in caratteri arabi in un diploma magrebino del Trecento', in *Contatti di lingue - contatti di scritture. Plurilinguismo e plurigrafismo dall'Antichità all'Età moderna*, ed. by Daniele Baglioni and Olga Tribulato (Venice: Edizioni Ca' Foscari, 2015), pp. 177–96.

The Language

The linguistic form of the texts generally corresponds to the vernacular of the Italian republic involved, that is, of the political subject that commissioned the translation. Thus, treaties with Venice are in Venetian, pacts with Pisa are in Pisan, and agreements with Genoa are in Genoese. The only partial exception is found in the privileges that King Henry II of Cyprus granted to the Pisans in 1291, edited by Giuseppe Müller,[30] in which, besides characteristics of the Pisan vernacular, northern-Italian features are also to be found, as for instance the lenition of the intervocalic plosive in *amado* 'loved' and the present participle *staghante* 'staying'. This coexistence of different linguistic varieties is due to the fact that the translation, by an unknown interpreter probably working in Cyprus, was later transcribed in Pisa by a notary from the surrounding countryside, Piero di ser Bartolomeo da Pontedera.[31] Therefore, it is reasonable to suppose that the original translation made by the Cypriot interpreter was in a northern-Italian vernacular (either Genoese or Venetian) and that the Pisan notary Tuscanized the language, though inadvertently leaving traces of the previous draft.

The remainder of the documents, albeit regionally more homogeneous, often display an interesting mixture of archaic features, as is the norm in colonial varieties, and, conversely, recent phenomena, which might reveal frequent or constant contacts between the interpreters and the Italian cities. For example, in the agreements with Venice dating from the late fourteenth and fifteenth centuries, mostly edited by Georg Martin Thomas in *DVL* I and II, one observes, on the one hand, the recurrence of the article *lo*, which in Venice by that time had been replaced by the form *el*, and, on the other, the almost systematic occurrence of the diphthong *uo* (*fuora*, *luogo*, *nuoxer*, *tuor*) and the prevalence of the subject pronoun *mi* (*me*) over the earlier form *io* (*I*), both being innovations of Late Medieval Venetian generally absent from the legal and administrative documents written in the colonies.[32] Nevertheless, since most of the

---

30   *Documenti sulle relazioni delle città toscane coll'Oriente cristiano e coi Turchi fino all'anno MDXXXI*, ed. by Giuseppe Müller (Florence: Cellini, 1879), doc. LXXIII, pp. 108–09.

31   See the note at the end of the document, *Documenti sulle relazioni delle città toscane coll'Oriente cristiano e coi Turchi*, p. 109: 'Que quidem omnia singula et suprascripta scripta fuerunt in presenti libro et carta per me Pierum ser Bartholomei notarii de Ponte Here, notarium et scribam publicum dicte Curie maris, prout in quadam privata copia inveni, de verbo ad verbum' ('Indeed each and every one of the above-written words was written in this book and page by me, Piero di ser Bartolomeo notary of Pontedera, notary and public scrivener of the aforesaid Curia maris, exactly as I found it in a private copy, word-for-word').

32   On the chronology of the diphthongization of [ɔ] to [wɔ] in Venetian, see Daniele Baglioni, 'Sulle sorti di [ɔ] in veneziano', in *Actes du XXVIIe Congrès international de linguistique et philologie romanes (Nancy, 15–20 juillet 2013)*, ed. by Eva Buchi, Jean-Paul Chauveau, and Jean-Marie Pierrel, 3 vols (Strasbourg: Société de linguistique romane / EliPhi, 2016), I, pp. 353–65. On the diffusion of *mi* in the northern Italian vernaculars, see Laura Vanelli, *I dialetti italiani settentrionali nel panorama romanzo. Studi di sintassi e morfologia* (Rome: Bulzoni, 1998), 'I pronomi soggetto nei dialetti italiani settentrionali', pp. 51–89. An overall description of the main linguistic changes from Early Venetian to Modern and Contemporary Venetian is provided by Ronnie Ferguson, *A Linguistic History of Venice* (Florence: Olschki, 2007).

translations have survived in transcriptions copied in Venice in the *Libri Pactorum* and *Libri Commemoriali*, the possibility of a linguistic updating of the texts by the Italian scribes cannot be excluded.

As already mentioned, the most interesting aspect of the language of the texts lies in the vocabulary, especially as regards the large quantity of loanwords. Most of these are designations of institutions, taxes, and generally *realia* characteristic of the Eastern Mediterranean states, for which no corresponding terms were at hand in Italian. This typology is very frequent in the agreements with the Tatar khans of Crimea, where words of Tatar (i.e. Kipchak), Persian, Arabic, Mongolian, and even Chinese origin are to be found, as for instance *aylocho* and *carezo*, both names of taxes,[33] *tamoga*, a seal and metonymically also customs duty,[34] *paysam*, originally a metallic tablet of authority in use in China and Mongolia, which in our texts indicates a safe-conduct,[35] and finally *Rabimuol* and *Siual*, both names of months of the Islamic calendar.[36] Unsurprisingly, the Arabic names of the months also occur in the translations of the documents issued by other Muslim states, besides offices like *chady/cadi* < *qāḍī* 'Islamic judge',[37] *aciebo/azebo* < *ḥāǧib* 'chamberlain',[38] *naybo* <*nāyb* 'deputy',[39] and *nadro* <*nāẓir* 'inspector'[40] in the treaties with the Mamluk sultans, *scecha* <*šayḫ* 'elder' and *moscèrufo* <*mušārif* 'customs inspector' in the pacts of the Pisans with the emir of Tunis,[41] and *subassi* <*subaşı* and *zalabi/zelebi* <*çelebi*, both Ottoman titles,[42] in the agreements with the Turks. Analogously, in the Venetian versions of the chrysobulls of the Komnenoi of Trebizond one encounters the titles *(megas) primichirio* <μέγας πριμικήριος, *prothosevastos* <πρωτοσέβαστος, and *chier* <κῦρ.[43]

On the basis of their high frequency, it is possible to suppose that these terms were well known and probably also commonly used by the Italian ambassadors and merchants whose activities were based in the Levant, and that for this reason they were left untranslated by the interpreters. In some cases the word morphology provides clear evidence for this hypothesis: for example, in the pact between the Venetians and the Ilkhan Abū Saʿīd Bahādur (incorrectly transcribed as Monsait) of 1320, besides *tomaga* (i.e. *tamoga*, customs duty) and *tomagazi* (i.e. *tamogacı* ʻa

---

33 DVL II, doc. 14, p. 24, doc. 15, p. 24; doc. 25, p. 51. Respectively from Turkish *aylık* (monthly (tax)) and *ḫarāc*, from Ar. *ḫarāǧ* (lit. 'exit'); on the latter word as a loan in Early Modern Italian, see Giorgio Raimondo Cardona, 'Caraccio, caracciaro', *Lingua nostra*, 31 (1970), 20–21.

34 DVL II, doc. 15, pp. 25–26; see also the metathetic variant *tomaga*, DVL I, doc. 85, p. 173. From Turkish *tamġa* (seal), see Gerhard Doerfer, *Türkische und mongolische Elemente im Neupersischen*, 3 vols (Wiesbaden: Franz Steiner, 1965), II, pp. 554–65.

35 DVL II, doc. 24, pp. 48 and 54. From Chinese *p'ai-tzu* 'silver or bronze tablet'.

36 DVL II, doc. 15, p. 26; doc. 24, p. 51 and doc. 25, p. 52. Respectively from Ar. *rabīʿu-l-awwal* and *šawwāl*, the third and the tenth month of the Islamic calendar.

37 DVL II, doc. 100, p. 169, doc. 194, p. 362, doc. 203, p. 371.

38 DVL II, doc. 100, p. 107, doc. 168, p. 311, doc. 174, p. 323.

39 DVL II, doc. 100, pp. 169–71 doc. 168, p. 311 doc. 205, p. 375; plural *naybi* in doc. 174, p. 321.

40 DVL II, doc. 194, p. 362.

41 Castellani, *La prosa italiana delle Origini*, pp. 393 and 391.

42 DVL II, doc. 203, p. 371; doc. 134, p. 223, doc. 159, p. 290, doc. 164, p. 302.

43 DVL II, doc. 98, pp. 166–67; doc. 98, pp. 166–67; doc. 78, p. 127, doc. 199, p. 367.

customs officer'), the hybrid verb *tomagar* also occurs, formed by the Turkish word *tomaga* + the Italian infinitive ending *-ar(e)* and meaning 'to pay customs duty'.[44] This blend must obviously have originated in the spoken varieties of Italian used by the merchants travelling to the Ilkhanate of Persia, thus showing how vital the word *tamoga* was in their conversations. This case is similar to that of the Byzantine word *komerkion*, often found in documents from both the Black Sea and Asia Minor, from which the nomen agentis *comercler* 'customs officer' was derived by adding to the word the Venetian suffix *-er*.[45]

Other foreign words must have had a more limited circulation, at least in Western Europe, as is shown by the fact that they are followed in the translations by explanatory glosses. An interesting example is the Greek word χρυσόβουλ(λ)ον, which is glossed in the translations of the chrysobulls in favour of the Venetians issued by the Trapezuntine emperors Alexios III (1357) and Manuel III (1396). In the chrysobull of Manuel, the interpreter privileges the etymology, thus literally translating *chrisofolo, zoè bolla d'oro* ('chrysobull, that is to say golden bull').[46] The translator of the chrysobull of Alexios shows a more functional approach and glosses *crusovolo, se intende la concession de lo imperador* ('chrysobull, by which the emperor's concession is meant').[47] Alternatively to glossing, a frequent strategy of the interpreters is to establish, within the same text, a synonymic correspondence between a foreign word designating a local object or honorific title and a more generic Italian term, which is in this way resemantized. For example, in the pacts with the khans of Crimea concerning both Venice and Genoa, the Tatar word *khan* is sometimes left untranslated (or, better, adapted as *can(e)*, plural *can(n)i*) and sometimes translated as *baroni* 'barons', a word that circulated both in Italy and in the Levant, but mostly with reference to Christian noblemen, either Westerners or Byzantines, and whose application to Muslim dignitaries is therefore unexpected.[48]

The Formulas

An analysis of the vocabulary of the Italian translations of Levantine diplomatic texts must consider not only single words, but also formulaic expressions, especially those with which the sovereign affirms his power (*legitimatio*) and recognizes the authority of his addressee (*inscriptio*). These are extremely frequent in the documents issued

---

44 DVL I, doc. 85, pp. 173–76 (173): 'Item, che nessuna citade o luogo del nostro Imperio li nostri Veneciani no possa esser constreti a tomagar' ('Also, that in none of the cities and regions of our Empire are our Venetians to be forced to pay customs duty').
45 The word is attested four times in the treaty between Venice and the Tatar Khan Berdibeg of 1358, DVL II, doc. 24, pp. 47–51.
46 DVL II, doc. 145, pp. 250–51 (250).
47 DVL II, doc. 98, pp. 164–67 (167).
48 Desimoni, 'Trattato dei Genovesi col khan dei Tartari', pp. 161–65. In the aforementioned Italian translation of the letter of the Ilkhan Öljeitü to Philip the Fair, 'baroni' refers exclusively to the Franks, Bertolucci Pizzorusso, 'Traduzione in volgare pisano di una lettera dell'Ilkhan di Persia al re di Francia', pp. 278–79.

by the Muslim states and, subsequently, in their Italian translations, although the texts vary considerably according to the writer and to the degree of sophistication of the chancellery to which he belongs. For example, the formulaic repertory of the diplomas of the Mamluk sultans is extremely rich and includes self-qualifications like 'king of the two seas' (*regnador de li do mari*, corresponding to the Ar. *Maliku-l-baḥrayn*) and 'shadow of God on earth' (*ombria de Dio in la soa terra*, corresponding to the Ar. *ḍill-u-llāhi fī-l-'arḍ*).[49] On the contrary, the contemporary diplomas issued by the Ilkhans of Persia are much rougher, the self-qualification of the sovereign being limited to the very basic formula *imperador de Turis* ('emperor of Tabriz').[50] What is interesting is that many of these formulas will later be inherited by the Ottoman sultans and, subsequently, reflected in the Italian translations of their documents. Thus, for instance, in the Ottoman-Polish capitulations of 1533, which have only survived in the Italian translation, Süleyman the Magnificent qualifies himself as *sopra la tera [...] la onbra di Dio* and boasts that he reigns over the Black Sea and the White Sea (i.e. Ottoman Turkish *aqdeŋiz*, the Mediterranean), thus reinterpreting the Coranic formula *al-baḥrāni* 'the two seas' with a concrete reference to the extension of his empire.[51]

In order to give an example of the origin and the gradual fixation of these celebrative formulas, the case of the locution *Gran Signor* can be considered. As is well known, in Renaissance Italian and also in other contemporary European languages *Gran Signor* (or, in French, *Grand Seigneur*) commonly designated the Ottoman sultan. Bernard Lewis hypothesized that the Italian expression is a calque on the Greek μέγας αὐθέντης, meaning 'the great lord' – just as *Gran Signor* – which left a visible trace in the vocabulary of Turkish, since the Turkish common word for *lord* or *sir*, *effendi*, is a local adaptation of the Greek αὐθέντης.[52]

The data contained in the Italian documents confirm Lewis' hypothesis. Indeed, the earliest attestation of *Gran Signor* occurs in the translation of a Greek text, a letter that Alexios III Komnenos sent in 1373 to the Venetian Doge Andrea Contarini. Strangely enough, in this document the honorific title applies not to Alexios, but to his addressee.[53] This is quite an exceptional case, however, since in all other documents *gran signor* refers to the writing sovereign and, more precisely, to a Muslim sultan. This can be observed already in 1375, when the Mamluk Sultan al-Ashraf Shaʿbān qualifies himself as the *grando signor*.[54] Finally, from 1390 onwards, the title becomes

---

49 Both formulas can be read in the *legitimatio* of the Italian translation of the letter sent in 1366 by the Sultan al-Ashraf Shaʿbān to the Venetian Doge Marco Cornaro, DVL II, doc. 68, pp. 113–15 (113).
50 The formula occurs three times in the Italian version of the letter sent in 1372–73 by the Ilkhan Uways khan to the Venetian *bailo* in Trebizond, DVL II, doc. 97, p. 163.
51 Kołodziejczyk, *Ottoman-Polish Diplomatic Relations*, pp. 230–31.
52 Bernard Lewis, *The Muslim Discovery of Europe* (New York: Norton, 1982), p. 84.
53 DVL II, doc. 98, p. 165: 'Serenissimo et excellentissimo domino Andree Contareno, Dei gratia Duci Venetiarum, etc., [...] gran signor et presiado per tuti, Duca de Veniexia' ('Most serene and excellent sir Andrea Contarini, by the grace of God Doge of Venice, etc., [...] great lord praised by all, Doge of Venice').
54 DVL II, doc. 100, p. 168.

a prerogative of the Ottoman sultan, who systematically introduces himself as the 'great lord' and the 'great admiral', from Bayezid I to Mehmet II and also later.[55]

A quick look at the Greek documents drafted by the Ottoman chancelleries allows to see that, in the same period, the Greek locution μέγας αὐθέντης begins to designate exclusively the Sultan. For example, in his letter to the inhabitants of Ioannina of 1431 the Grand Vizier Sinan Pasha declares that he has been sent by the 'great lord' ('μᾶς ἔστειλεν ὁ μέγας αὐθέντης'), without feeling the need for any further specification.[56] And later, in 1450, in the letter sent from Mehmet II to the Hospitallers of Rhodes, the Sultan qualifies himself as the μέγας αὐθέντης 'great lord' and the μέγας ἀμηρᾶς ('great admiral'), a combination that has already been observed in the documents in Italian and that is evidently at the origin of the Italian formulas.[57] Therefore, in conclusion, it is interesting to see how a Greek generic title, which originally could apply to Christian sovereigns as well, the Byzantine ones excepted, gradually became specialized to indicate the Ottoman sultan, thus influencing Italian and, through Italian, all other Western European languages, although it left no traces in Ottoman Turkish, in which apparently no similar expression ever existed.

This brief survey of the extant diplomatic documents in Italian regarding the Levant in the period 1100–1453 has shown that Italian vernaculars did serve as diplomatic languages already in the Middle Ages. By this period Italian had not yet reached the importance it would eventually achieve in the sixteenth and seventeenth centuries, when it was commonly used as the main European language for diplomatic communications between the Ottomans and the western countries. Nevertheless, Italian vernaculars played a relevant role as translation languages and were written not only by Italians, but also by non-native interpreters. The role of non-Italian interpreters seems to have been particularly crucial in the fourteenth and fifteenth centuries, especially in Veneto-Levantine relations, for which an abundant documentation is available. The translations of Arabic and Turkish diplomas, mostly made by Greeks, have transmitted loanwords, calques, and formulaic expressions from the Oriental languages into Italian, thus paving the way for the great diffusion of Italian as a diplomatic language after the fall of Constantinople.

---

55 *DVL* II, doc. 134, pp. 222–23 ('gram signor et grando armiraio Bayssit signor'), pp. 303–04 ('gran signor, gran amirà Mussibei', 'gran signor e gran amirà Mussibey'), doc. 172, p. 318 ('el gran signor e grande amirà soltan Mahametbei, fio del gran signor et grande amirà Condochicij de Basaithbei'), doc. 198, pp. 366–67, doc. 199, p. 369, and doc. 201, p. 370 ('gran signor et gran admirà soltan Maometh bey / Morathbey').

56 *Acta et diplomata graeca Medii Aevii sacra et profana*, ed. by Franciscus Miklosich and Iosephus Müller, 6 vols (Wien: Carl Gerold, 1860–90), III, p. 282.

57 *Acta et diplomata graeca*, III, p. 286.

Part V

The Schismatic Ally – Byzantium between Islam and Unionism

ALEXANDER D. BEIHAMMER

Crusade, Civil Strife, and Byzantine-Turkish Coalitions in the Time of Emperor John VI Kantakouzenos (1341–54)

Byzantium's involvement in fourteenth-century crusading projects in the Aegean and the Eastern Mediterranean was rather shadowy and insignificant.[1] At times, Constantinople agreed to support Christian leagues and naval campaigns and, especially after John V's rise to power in 1354, serious efforts were made to resume negotiations about the union of the Churches. Yet, various factors, such as the Byzantine civil wars, military weakness, tensions with the Italian maritime states and other Latin powers, as well as the dogmatic differences with the papacy, can be held responsible for preventing Byzantium from becoming fully integrated in Christian coalitions and from assuming a substantial role in Christian initiatives to fight the Muslim foe. At first sight, this reluctance to join the struggle for a common cause may appear irrational and almost self-destructive, given that Byzantium was one of the main victims of the expansionist thrust that swept over western Anatolia in the wake of the Mongol invasion and the decay of the Seljuk sultanate of Rum. The near-contemporary historians George Pachymeres and Nikephoros Gregoras vividly describe the rapid onslaught of Turkish warrior groups from the western fringes of the Anatolian plateau to the Aegean coastland.[2] What for one-and-a-half centuries formed a relatively stable borderland started crumbling in the 1260s and within a few decades the heartland of Byzantine Asia Minor turned into a contested war zone dominated

---

1 For a similar observation, see Deno Geanakoplos, 'Byzantium and the Crusades, 1261–1354', in *A History of the Crusades*, III: *The Fourteenth and Fifteenth Centuries*, ed. by Kenneth M. Setton and Harry W. Hazard (Madison: University of Wisconsin Press, 1975), pp. 27–68 (31): 'Byzantium was, to be sure, not directly involved in all these expeditions, and never really responded positively to appeals for a crusade, although a change in the situation had effected a partial alteration of the Byzantine attitude'.
2 See, for instance, George Pachymeres, *Relations historiques, livres I–VI*, ed. by Albert Failler, trans. by Vitalien Laurent, Corpus Fontium Historiae Byzantinae, 24/1–2, 2 vols (Paris: Belles Lettres, 1984), *livres VII–XIII*, ed. and trans. by Albert Failler, Corpus Fontium Historiae Byzantinae, 24/3–5, 3 vols (Paris: Institut Français d'Études Byzantines, 1999–2000), I, 288–93 (book III, chapter 21–22); Nikephoros Gregoras, *Byzantina Historia*, ed. by Ludwig Schopen, Corpus Scriptorum Historiae Byzantinae, 38–39,

Alexander D. Beihammer • University of Notre Dame

Crusading, Society, and Politics in the Eastern Mediterranean in the Age of King Peter I of Cyprus, ed. by Alexander Beihammer and Angel Nicolaou-Konnari, MEDNEX, 10 (Turnhout, 2022), pp. 457–488
© BREPOLS PUBLISHERS 10.1484/M.MEDNEX-EB.5.128475

by a number of Turkish lordships (*beyliks*) along with some isolated Byzantine and Genoese enclaves.[3] The gradual loss of territories in Asia Minor prepared the ground for the turning point of 1354, in which the Ottoman Turks under the leadership of Emir Orhan's son Süleyman took hold of the city of Gallipoli and thus ushered in a new phase of expansion over the Balkan Peninsula.[4] Although modern historians, with the benefit of hindsight, tend to regard this development either as the beginning of Byzantium's irremediable downfall or as a major step towards the Ottomans' rise to predominance, it would be an impermissible oversimplification to explain the events of 1354 in a deterministic manner as the inevitable outcome of a linear historical process. The conquest of the Gallipoli Peninsula can hardly be understood without factoring in the peculiar situation of the preceding years since the early 1340s. While the Turkish-Christian hostilities in the Aegean culminated in the crusade of Smyrna in 1344, Byzantium, after the premature death of Andronikos III in June 1341, was dragged into a new civil war between the partisans of the late emperor's intimate friend and army commander John Kantakouzenos and the Constantinopolitan loyalist party represented by the empress dowager Anna of Savoy, Patriarch John XIV Kalekas, and Alexios Apokaukos.[5] In the years of this conflict (1341–47) the Byzantine warring factions were unable to lend any efficient support to the Christian allies in the Aegean, but they were in desperate need of manpower, which Turkish emirs in western Asia Minor were happy to provide. Inevitably, this caused a significant increase of Turkish raids and attacks in the provinces of Thrace and Macedonia. The disastrous demographic and economic results of the civil war and the disintegration of the central administration could not be reversed during John VI Kantakouzenos's sole reign as senior emperor of the Palaiologan house until 1354. On the contrary, the aggressive expansionist policy of the Serbian king Stephan Dušan (1331–55) and new wars with Venice and Genoa further weakened the remnants of Byzantium's political and military power.[6]

---

2 vols (Bonn: Weber, 1829–30), I, 195 (book VI, chapter 8): Turkish raids in the towns beyond the Maeander River, which formed the border of the Byzantine territories; I, 214–15 (book VII, chapter 1): Turkish raids and conquests in the western coastland of Asia Minor.

3 For a brief survey of major events, see Donald M. Nicol, *The Last Centuries of Byzantium, 1261–1453* (Cambridge: Cambridge University Press, 1993), pp. 80–87, 122–30, 138–47, 169–75. For more details and bibliography, see below, p. 460 with n. 13.

4 For this event, see Colin Imber, *The Ottoman Empire, 1300–1481* (Istanbul: Isis Press, 1990), pp. 23–25; Nicol, *Last Centuries*, pp. 241–42, 244–45; Georgios Vogiatzis, Η πρώϊμη Οθωμανοκρατία στη Θράκη: άμεσες δημογραφικές συνέπειες (Thessalonica: Herodotos 1998); for the viewpoint of traditional Turkish historiography, see İsmail Hakkı Uzunçarşılı, *Osmanlı Tarihi*, I: *Anadolu Selçukluları ve Anadolu Beylikleri hakkında bir mukaddime ile Osmanlı Devleti'nin kuruluşundan İstanbul'un fethine kadar*, Türk Tarih Kurumu Yayınları XIII. Dizi, 16^{a10} (Ankara: Türk Tarih Kurumu, 1947), pp. 155–58.

5 For a brief summary of major events, see Nicol, *Last Centuries*, pp. 185–208, and Donald M. Nicol, *The Reluctant Emperor: A Biography of John Cantacuzene, Byzantine Emperor and Monk, c. 1295–1383* (Cambridge: Cambridge University Press, 1996), pp. 45–83. The most detailed analysis of political forces in the time of the second civil war is still Klaus-Peter Matschke, *Fortschritt und Reaktion in Byzanz im 14. Jh.: Konstantinopel in der Bürgerkriegsperiode von 1341 bis 1354*, Berliner Byzantinistische Arbeiten, 42 (Berlin: Akademie Verlag, 1971).

6 Nicol, *Last Centuries*, pp. 209–50; Nicol, *Reluctant Emperor*, pp. 84–133.

No doubt, both prior to and during the period in question numerous members of the Byzantine ruling elite were involved in conflicts and peaceful interactions with the Turks of Asia Minor. It was John Kantakouzenos, however, who in Donald Nicol's words was 'the first emperor who came face to face with the leaders of the Osmanlis or Ottoman people'.[7] His personal friendship with Umur Beg of Aydın, the alliance with the Ottoman ruler Orhan, and—from a symbolical point of view even more shocking—the wedding of his daughter Theodora to the Ottoman chief convey the impression of a statesman and military leader who constantly sought the backing of Turkish warriors to promote his ambitions at the expense of his compatriots and the Byzantine state.[8] While the Latin powers in the Aegean were exposed to Turkish assaults and the Byzantine subjects in the provinces suffered the fatal consequences of raids and depredations, he and his partisans were accused of betraying the Christian cause and pursuing their aims without any moral restraints. Kantakouzenos's *Histories*, a work combining characteristics of apologetic historiography and memoirs, which covers the period 1320–56 with a special focus on the time of the second civil war and the protagonist's sole reign, clearly reflects the harsh critique that political opponents within and without the empire vociferously articulated against the author's attitudes towards the Turks. Among a broad range of arguments explaining and justifying his course of action in matters of dynastic legitimacy, political decision-making, and warfare, his alliances, collaborations, and personal relations with Turkish rulers constitute a recurring theme that is frequently commented upon in speeches put into his own or his supporters' mouth.[9] This apologetic tendency has a strong impact on modern scholarship, which tends to judge and interpret Kantakouzenos's personality and his responsibilities for political developments up to the Ottoman conquest of Gallipoli along the same criteria.[10] The resulting narrative not only adopts biased

---

7   Nicol, *Reluctant Emperor*, p. 3.
8   Nicol, *Last Centuries*, pp. 174–75, 188, 198–200, 202–04; Nicol, *Reluctant Emperor*, pp. 34–36, 67, 68–69, 71, 74, 76–77; for the marriage of Theodora to Orhan, see Anthony A. M. Bryer, 'Greek Historians on the Turks: the Case of the First Byzantine-Ottoman Marriage', in *The Writing of History in the Middle Ages: Essays Presented to R. W. Southern*, ed. by Ralph H. C. Davis and John M. Wallace-Hadrill (Oxford: Clarendon Press, 1981), pp. 471–93, reprinted in Anthony Bryer, *Peoples and Settlement in Anatolia and the Caucasus, 900–1900*, Variorum Reprint, CS274 (London: Ashgate, 1988), no. IV.
9   John Kantakouzenos, *Historiarum libri IV*, ed. Ludwig Schopen, Corpus Scriptorum Historiae Byzantinae, 23–25, 3 vols (Bonn, 1828–32). For a summary of scholarship on Kantakouzenos's *Histories* and useful bibliographical references, see Savvas Kyriakidis, 'Accounts of Military Operations in the Histories of the Byzantine Emperor John VI Kantakouzenos (1347–1354): Critical Remarks', *Journal of Early Christian History*, 5 (2015), 76–93.
10 Ursula V. Bosch, *Kaiser Andronikos III. Palaiologos: Versuch einer Darstellung der byzantinischen Geschichte in den Jahren 1321–1341* (Amsterdam: A. M. Hakkert, 1965), pp. 176–93, 195, describes Kantakouzenos as 'von Machtgier besessen' who fought 'ohne Rücksicht auf die Interessen des Reiches, für die Legitimität seiner Herrschaft.' From a Marxist point of view, E. Frances, 'La féodalité byzantine et la conquête turque', *Studia et Acta Orientalia*, 4 (1962), 69–90, pointing to the feudal aristocracy's propensity to defect to the Turks, suggests the existence of a deliberate plan of founding a 'Byzantine-Turkish empire' as an attempt of the feudal aristocracy to rescue its interests by betraying the fatherland to the Turks. Ernst Werner, 'Johannes Kantakuzenos, Umur Paša und Orchan', *Byzantinoslavica*, 26 (1965), 255–76, rejects this interpretation by pointing out that many behavioural patterns in Kantakouzenos's relations with

views, be they positive or negative, of Kantakouzenos as the principal initiator of these alliances but is also influenced by the decay paradigm that pervades almost all levels of scholarly discussions on the late Byzantine period. Hence, Kantakouzenos's image is unavoidably tinged by our knowledge of the final outcome and projects post-1354 experiences back to earlier periods.

In this essay I shall examine Byzantine-Turkish relations in the time of John Kantakouzenos from a different angle. The *ex post eventu* question as to who is to blame for the Turkish expansion has been sufficiently answered, though in different ways. Perhaps more important is to understand how, under what circumstances, and on the basis of what principles did Byzantine-Turkish coalitions work during this period. This would allow us to go beyond the pro-Latin vs. pro-Turkish dichotomy that dominates scholarly discussions and view political attitudes of the Byzantine elite more comprehensively. As has already been indicated, the *Histories* by John Kantakouzenos provide the most detailed information about Byzantine perceptions of the Turks of Asia Minor as a political and military power. Additional insights into the nature of Byzantine-Turkish coalitions can be gained from Nikephoros Gregoras's *Roman History*, the second contemporary source of the period in question, and Enverī's *Düstūrnāme*, a versified Turkish account of the life and deeds of Umur Beg of

---

the Turks reflect well-established practices and an attempt to rule according to his ideals. Byzantium's tragedy lies in the fact that the internal crisis and struggle for centralization coincided with the Turkish westward migration and thus facilitated their way to Europe. George Ostrogorsky, *History of the Byzantine State*, trans. by Joan Hussey (New Brunswick: Rutgers University Press, revised ed. 1969), p. 520, bewails the overall decay of the empire's political power, which in his view is reflected in Theodora's marriage to Orhan: 'The times had indeed changed: once the greatest rulers in Christendom had not been considered worthy of the hand of a Byzantine princess, and now a Byzantine princess was to grace the harem of a Turkish sultan'. Klaus-Peter Todt, *Kaiser Johannes VI. Kantakuzenos und der Islam: Politische Realität und theologische Polemik im palaiologenzeitlichen Byzanz*, Religionswissenschaftliche Studien, 16 (Würzburg: Oros Verlag, 1991), pp. 43–46, 50–51, 52–54, accepts the arguments brought forward by Kantakouzenos against the accusation of having stirred up the barbarians against his compatriots. All sides involved were at pains to win over Turkish allies but Kantakouzenos was more successful because of his personal relations. Devastation and looting were usual practices of warfare and it was only the Turks' interest in slaves that brought a further exacerbation. His opponents' relentlessness along with the loss of lands and resources left him no other choice, but his opponents equally contributed to the empire's downfall. Nicol, *Reluctant Emperor*, pp. 172–78, admits that Kantakouzenos because of his military experience knew 'it was too late to stem the Turkish tide in Asia Minor' but nevertheless considers him 'undoubtedly naive in his relationships with his Turkish allies'. Under the influence of his friend Gregory Palamas, he may have hoped 'for some kind of peaceful co-existence', but, in conclusion, 'there can be no doubt that Cantacuzene's dealings with the Turks [...] contributed more than any other factor to his political downfall'. Nicol, *Last Centuries*, pp. 203–04, expresses a much more positive opinion, rejecting the 'pious disapproval of historians' by underlining the Turkish emirates' significance as 'a valuable source of manpower' and Kantakouzenos's 'excellent personal relationships with their leaders'. He appreciated them as intelligent leaders but was also aware of the Turks' being barbarians and ghazis of holy war. Theodora's marriage points to fallen standards but things were still better than in Trebizond. Imber, *Empire*, pp. 22–25: 'service in the pay of John Kantakouzenos [...] was undoubtedly a factor in the subsequent Ottoman conquest of the region'; Colin Imber, *The Ottoman Empire, 1300–1650: The Structure of Power* (New York: Palgrave Macmillan, 2002), p. 9: Orhan achieved a bridgehead in Europe by exploiting the civil war in Byzantium and Kantakouzenos's seeking of allies.

Aydın (1309/10–48), which was written in 1465 and dedicated to Mehmed II's grand vizier Mahmud Pasha but relies on sources reaching back to the fourteenth century.[11]

Many of Kantakouzenos's views and attitudes are at odds with the ideas originating from pro-Latin circles within the Byzantine ruling elite. The Frankish-Turkish conflicts in the Aegean and the revival of the crusading spirit in the Latin East prompted Venice, the papacy, and other western powers to make overtures to the Byzantines about joining an anti-Turkish league and started new initiatives for negotiations about the ecclesiastical union. After 1354 pro-Latin attitudes gained further momentum as a result of John V's policy of rapprochement to the papacy and the preparations of a new crusade led by King Peter I of Cyprus. The two surviving advisory speeches by Demetrios Kydones epitomize these ideas. They argue in favour of Byzantine support to Amadeus VI of Savoy's crusading forces, which in August of 1366 recaptured Gallipoli from the Turks, and forthrightly reject proposals about the city's surrender to Sultan Murād I some years later.[12] Hence, there were opposing opinions about what survival strategy Byzantium had to adopt. Their proponents agreed in the diagnosis of the problem regarding the deadly menace posed by the Turks' unrestrained expansion, but they had very different ideas about how the imperial government should tackle this challenge. John Kantakouzenos articulated the views of those who through the experiences of war, diplomacy, and informal interaction had become familiar with the Turks. They were certainly aware of the dangers but also appreciated the advantages

---

11 The edition of the books I–XXIX by Ludwig Schopen (see above, n. 2) was supplemented by a separate edition of the final part: Nikephoros Gregoras, *Historiae Byzantinae libri postremi*, ed. by Immanuel Bekker, Corpus Scriptorum Historiae Byzantinae, 48 (Bonn: Weber, 1855). For a complete German translation with detailed comments, see Nikephoros Gregoras, *Rhomäische Geschichte, Historia Rhomaïke*, trans. by Jan Louis van Dieten, Bibliothek der Griechischen Literatur, 4, 8, 24, 39, 59, 5 vols (Stuttgart: A. Hiersemann, 1973–2003), *sechster Teil (Kapitel XXX–XXXVII), in Fortsetzung der Arbeit von Jan Louis van Dieten* trans. by Franz Tinnefeld, Bibliothek der Griechischen Literatur, 66 (Stuttgart: A. Hiersemann, 2007). For a discussion of the author's life and work, see the introductions to van Dieten's translation, I, pp. 1–41, II, pp. 1–20. The first part of the *Roman History* (books I–XI on the period 1204–1341) was written in 1347, the final version of the continuation between 1349–51, the concluding section (books XXXVI–XXXVII on the period 1355–58) contemporarily with the events described up to the author's death. For Enverī, see Paul Lemerle, *L'émirat d'Aydin, Byzance et l'Occident: recherches sur la "Geste d'Umur pacha"* (Paris: Presses Universitaires de France, 1957); edition and translation: Enverī, *Le destān d'Umūr Pacha (Düstūrnāme-i Enverī)*, ed. and trans. by Irène Mélikoff-Sayar, Bibliothèque byzantine, 2 (Paris: Presses Universitaires de France, 1954).

12 Demetrios Kydones, 'Oratio pro subsidio Latinorum, Ῥωμαίοις συμβουλευτικός, ἐγράφη δὲ ἀποδημήσαντος ἐν Ῥώμῃ τοῦ κυροῦ Ἰωάννου τοῦ Παλαιολόγου ἐπὶ τῆς πατριαρχίας τοῦ κυροῦ Φιλοθέου', in *Patrologia Graeca* 154, ed. by Jacques Paul Migne (Paris, 1866), coll. 961–1003; Demetrios Kydones, '*Oratio de non reddenda Callipoli*, Συμβουλευτικὸς ἕτερος περὶ Καλλιπόλεως αἰτήσαντος τοῦ Μουράτου', in *Patrologia Graeca* 154, ed. by Jacques Paul Migne (Paris, 1866), coll. 1009–36. For a recent analysis of these speeches, see Judith R. Ryder, *The Career and Writings of Demetrios Kydones: A Study of Fourteenth-Century Byzantine Politics, Religion and Society*, The Medieval Mediterranean, 85 (Leiden: Brill, 2010), pp. 57–81. The older scholarly literature dates *De non reddenda Callipoli* to the summer of 1371 or alternatively to the reign of Andronikos IV, i.e., 1376 or 1377. Recently, arguments for the summer of 1375 have been brought forward: Raúl Estangüi Gómez, *Byzance face aux Ottomans: Exercice du pouvoir et contrôle du territoire sous les derniers Paléologues (milieu XIV*ᵉ*–milieu XV*ᵉ *siècle)*, Byzantina Sorbonensia, 28 (Paris: Publications de la Sorbonne, 2014), pp. 257–62.

they could achieve by collaborating with them and thus hoped for viable agreements securing a modus vivendi and peaceful coexistence. Thus, it is also important to understand communication strategies, diplomatic tools, and ceremonial aspects employed in Byzantine-Turkish encounters.

When John Kantakouzenos in the 1320s made his first appearance on the stage of Byzantine dynastic rivalries, the political structures of western Asia Minor had already undergone a profound transformation. The Ottoman Turks were about to consolidate their rule in Bithynia and prepared themselves to seize the region's urban centres, such as Bursa, Nicomedia, and Nicaea. The Menteşe Turks, who in 1282 had entrenched themselves in the Maeander (Menderes) estuary, were in control of the port city of Miletus/Balat as well as large parts of Caria and the Maeander hinterland. The Germiyānid principality centred in Kütahya had developed under Yaʿqūb ibn ʿAlīshīr (1300–40) into an influential regional power. Initially subordinate commanders of the Germiyānids, such as Mehmed ibn Aydın and Saruhan Beg, had succeeded in carving out their own independent principalities. Hence, the Aydınids ruled over the coastal cities of Ayasuluk/Ephesus and Smyrna as well as the Kaystros (Küçük Menderes) valley while the Saruhanids held sway over Magnesia and Nymphaion (Nif) along with the Hermos (Gediz) valley. Likewise, in the years 1302–06, the Karasi Turks established themselves in Balıkesir, Pergamon, and the coastland of Mysia.[13] After Andronikos III's victory over his grandfather, the imperial government of Constantinople adopted new diplomatic approaches to these Turkish rulers. Between 1328 and 1335, Andronikos III had a number of face-to-face meetings and entered intense negotiations with the Karasi Turks, the Ottomans, as well as the emirs of Aydın and Saruhan, which included lavish gift exchanges, ritual acts of subordination on the part of the Turkish rulers, payments, and agreements on military alliances, which in part were directed against Byzantium's Genoese adversaries.[14] Through these contacts and treaties, the imperial government proceeded to a *de facto* acknowledgement of the Turkish lordships' legitimacy and political authority on the soil of its former provinces.

Thus, from early onwards the Byzantine experiences of and approaches to the Turkish presence differed quite sharply from those of the Latin powers in the

---

13 For these developments, see Paul Wittek, *Das Fürstentum Mentesche. Studie zur Geschichte Westkleinasiens im 13.–15. Jh.*, Istanbuler Mitteilungen, 2 (Istanbul, 1934), pp. 15–57; Lemerle, *L'émirat d'Aydin*, pp. 19–26, 63–64; Elisabeth Zachariadou, *Trade and Crusade: Venetian Crete and the Emirates of Menteshe and Aydin (1300–1415)*, Bibliothèque de l'Institut hellénique d'études byzantines et post-byzantines de Venise, 11 (Venice: Istituto ellenico, 1983), pp. 1–12; Elisabeth Zachariadou, 'The Emirate of Karasi and That of the Ottomans: Two Rival States', in *The Ottoman Emirate (1300–1389): Halcyon Days in Crete I, A Symposium Held in Rethymnon, 11–13 January 1991*, ed. by Elisabeth Zachariadou (Rethymnon: Crete University Press, 1993), pp. 225–36 (225–26); Mustafa Çetin Varlık, 'Germiyanoğulları' in *Türkiye Diyanet Vakfı İslam Ansiklopedisi*, 44 vols (Istanbul and Ankara: ISAM, 1988–2014), XIV (1996), pp. 33–35; for an extensive discussion of the origins of the Germiyānid beylik, see the chapter of Romain Thurin in this volume.

14 Franz Dölger, *Regesten der Kaiserurkunden des oströmischen Reiches von 565–1453*, IV: *Regesten von 1282–1341* (Munich: C. H. Beck, 1960), no. 2727 (meeting with the Karasi lord Demirhan, son of Yahşi, in 1328), no. 2762–63 (treaty with the Ottoman ruler Orhan, autumn of 1330), nos 2820–21; Nicol, *Last Centuries*, pp. 174–75 (meetings with Saruhan Beg as well as the sons of Mehmed ibn Aydın, Hızır, Süleymanshāh and Umur in 1335; four-day meeting between Umur and John Kantakouzenos at Karaburun).

area. Kantakouzenos's course of action in the following decades was by no means unprecedented or merely driven by the peculiarities of the civil war and the personal choices of this man. Rather, it formed part of a newly established political culture. Byzantium and the Aegean world in the fourteenth century were highly fragmented and conflict-ridden. Political options were contingent upon an intricate interplay between a few supra-regional western powers and numerous small- or medium-size local lordships. Political constellations were constantly changing, and coalitions were shifting according to the exigencies of the moment. Internal strife, decreasing resources in terms of money and manpower, social unrest, and a lack of naval forces in the decades after 1284 further exacerbated the predicaments of the Byzantine ruling elite and pushed it towards developing its own survival strategy based on the simultaneous maintenance of multiple channels of communication and coalitions with both Christian and Muslim powers. Byzantine decision makers and court officials were able to make ample use of a long tradition of diplomatic techniques, multi-linguistic communication skills, and treaty making procedures with the Muslim world. Various forms of Byzantine-Turkish interaction ever since the 1260s, which after a period of limited low-level contacts between local representatives and Turkish chieftains gradually intensified and culminated in the agreements with Emir Orhan and Umur Beg in the 1330s, brought about a further strengthening of these capacities and increased the wealth of experiences in dealing with each other. Generally speaking, Byzantium's policy operated on two different levels: on the one hand, the imperial government was willing to support western crusading plans, and there were many voices articulating the vision of a united Christian league rescuing Byzantium from its Muslim foes. On the other hand, the ruling elite in Constantinople kept working towards coming to terms with the Turks. When the civil war eventually turned things upside down in Byzantium and both camps were in a sudden need for manpower, forging coalitions with the Turks was but a logical choice in this situation.

Turkish Involvement in the Civil War, 1341–47

The involvement of troops from the western Anatolian beyliks in the Byzantine civil war of the years 1341–47 was closely linked with the course of hostilities in Thrace and Macedonia, the frequently changing power relations between the warring parties, and the contest between their leaders for gaining the manpower resources of foreign lords. While Kantakouzenos's friend and ally Umur Beg of Smyrna and the Ottoman chief Orhan were certainly the main players in the region, the emirates of Karasi and Saruhan also contributed significantly to the crossing of Turkish troops to Europe. In some cases, Turkish warrior groups mentioned in the sources cannot be identified with certainty. Apparently, the overall instability in the areas affected by the hostilities attracted not only allies of the warring parties but also numerous adventurers and raiders, who tried their luck in making booty and captives. The radius of action of Turkish warrior groups extended over the entire war zone from Berrhoia at the southwestern fringes of the Macedonian plain and the ports of the Thermaic Gulf as far as the Rhodope Mountains, the Propontis coastland, and the suburbs of

Constantinople in eastern Thrace. Within this region, Turkish hosts usually coordinated their movements with those of the Byzantine warring parties, while Kantakouzenos's headquarters in Didymoteichon and other strongholds in the Maritsa valley played a crucial role as rallying points and places of refuge for military units. All in all, one can distinguish two distinct phases of Turkish involvement: The first one is marked by the predominance of Umur Beg, who between late 1342 and June 1345 undertook three expeditions in support of Kantakouzenos's cause. The second one between the summer of 1345 and early 1347 is characterized by Kantakouzenos's advance to eastern Thrace and the Gallipoli Peninsula, as well as the increasing efforts of the warring factions to secure Turkish support by diplomatic means.

The unexpected demise of Emperor Andronikos III seems to have caused the emirs in western Asia Minor to temporarily ignore the treaties they had reached with Byzantium during the 1330s and to prepare for naval raids across the Hellespont straits. In the months between late June and August 1341, in which John Kantakouzenos sought to secure the support of the Thracian aristocracy for a campaign against the Bulgarians, the Turks of Saruhan, Karasi, and Aydın set out to threaten or even to invade the mainland of Thrace.[15] The Ottomans are not explicitly mentioned as participating in these acts of aggression, but Kantakouzenos is said to have sent an embassy to Orhan to renew the peace treaty and thus to forestall a potential conflict.[16] We have no information about the reasons for this unexpected turn to hostilities against Byzantium, but Gregoras describes Umur's expedition as being driven by the latter's wish to defend Kantakouzenos against his internal opponents in the Byzantine senate.[17] Irrespective of Gregoras's emphasis on Umur's loyalty, this allows us to assume that the Turkish emirs tried to take advantage of the internal tensions that emerged in Byzantium in the wake of the emperor's death. While Umur is said to have been dissuaded from his attack by a message of Kantakouzenos, Yahşi of Karasi actually mounted an attack with his fleet on the coastland of the Thracian Peninsula, where he was twice repelled by Byzantine troops before he agreed to come to terms with Kantakouzenos.[18]

Umur Beg next appeared on the scene in late 1342 in an especially precarious moment, in which John Kantakouzenos had taken refuge with the Serbian king Stephan Dušan while his wife Irene and according to Enverī the *Esen tekfūr*, who may be identified with one of her brothers, John or Manuel Asan,[19] held firm in Didymoteichon against the pressure of the Bulgarian troops of Ivan Alexander. After arriving with a large fleet in the mouth of the Maritsa River he brought some relief to the besieged and seems to have gained the support of Süleyman of Saruhan,[20] but

---

15 Kantakouzenos, II, 65–66 (book III, chapter 9), 69–70 (book III, chapter 10); Gregoras, II, 596–99 (book XII, chapter 7), for Umur's expedition; for the chronology, see the comments to van Dieten's translation, III, 241–42 (n. 27), 253–54 (n. 65).
16 Kantakouzenos, II, 66 (book III, chapter 9).
17 Gregoras, II, 598–99 (book XII, chapter 7).
18 Kantakouzenos, II, 69–70 (book III, chapter 10).
19 Enverī, v. 1371–72; for the identification, see Lemerle, *L'émirat d'Aydin*, p. 163.
20 Enverī, v. 1391–92.

due to the military superiority of the Bulgarians and the harsh weather conditions of the winter period he failed to reach Kantakouzenos.[21] At the same time, the Constantinopolitan faction seems to have gained the support of another Turkish emirate, most probably that of Karasi. For Alexios Apokaukos, who in the spring of 1343 arrived with his fleet in Thessalonica, reportedly was accompanied by 32 'Persian ships'.[22] The warriors carried on these ships joined the campaign of the *megas kontostaulos* Monomachos against the city of Berrhoia, which along with the lord of Thessaly had sided with Kantakouzenos, and they ransacked and looted its surroundings.[23]

While Apokaukos and his troops entrenched themselves in Thessalonica and exerted increasing pressure on Kantakouzenos in Berrhoia, Umur Beg, in response to his ally's call for help, set off from Smyrna for a second naval expedition. In the fall of 1343, he advanced along with about 200 ships via Euboea to various ports in the Thermaic Gulf. The environs of Thessalonica were ransacked, Berrhoia was secured for Kantakouzenos's rule, and Apokaukos was forced to withdraw, but despite these achievements the seizure of Thessalonica proved impossible after the zealots killed and tortured Kantakouzenos's partisans in the city.[24] Kantakouzenos and Umur moved to Thrace to put siege to Peritheorion near the mouth of the Nestos River. The besiegers achieved some minor successes, such as the submission of nearby Abdera and the capture of its governor, Empress Anna's cupbearer Goudeles, and they sent an embassy consisting of a Byzantine and Turkish representative for negotiations to Constantinople. Yet both diplomatic and military efforts were doomed to failure, and Kantakouzenos and Umur in January 1344 withdrew to Didymoteichon.[25]

Over the following months, Kantakouzenos's and Umur's troops established a new camp at the destroyed city of Traianoupolis near the mouth of the Maritsa River. Thence they mounted attacks on the province of Morrha and the cities of Stenimachos and Koutzaina in the Rhodope Mountains. The cities of Koumoutzena and smaller places in the vicinity submitted voluntarily.[26] Kantakouzenos thus significantly extended

---

21 Kantakouzenos, II, 344–48 (book III, chapter 56); Gregoras, II, 648–52 (book XIII, chapter 4), Enverī, v. 1365–99; Lemerle, pp. 160–64 (who dates Umur's first expedition between December 1342 and February 1343); Nicol, *Last Centuries*, pp. 197–98.
22 Kantakouzenos, II, 357–58 (book III, chapter 58); Gregoras, II, 671 (book XIII, chapter 9); Nicol, *Last Centuries*, p. 199.
23 Kantakouzenos, II, 381 (book III, chapter 62).
24 Kantakouzenos, II, 383–94 (book III, chapters 63–64); Gregoras, II, 673–74 (book XIII, chapter 10); Enverī, v. 1400–1502 (who omits Umur's return to Smyrna and inserts a fictitious episode about the arrival and coronation of 'Qaloyan tekfürun oğlı' [= John V] in Thessalonica); Lemerle, *L'émirat d'Aydin*, pp. 164–66; Nicol, *Last Centuries*, p. 199.
25 Kantakouzenos, II, 394–404 (book III, chapters 64–66); for additional details see Gregoras, II, 676–77 (book XIII, chapter 10) (in the late fall of 1344 Umur followed Kantakouzenos with 6,000 elite troops over the pass of Christoupolis while the fleet was sailing along the Thracian coast), II, 692–93 (book XIV, chapter 1).
26 Kantakouzenos, II, 404–06, 415–19 (book III, chapters 66–68); Enverī, v. 1503–1644 (who mentions Siroz/Serres, Hiristo/Christoupolis, Zihna/Zichna, Eksya/Xanthi, Buru/Peritheorion, İğrican/Gratianoupolis as having surrendered to Kantakouzenos's army); Lemerle, *L'émirat d'Aydin*, pp. 166–75.

his sphere of influence, but this success prompted his adversaries in Constantinople to seek an understanding with Ivan Alexander of Bulgaria. The latter was willing to invade the recently occupied territories only if the Turks withdrew from Thrace. Constantinople, therefore, set into motion a plot to cause discontent among Umur's troops and to force him to abandon the campaign.[27] The departure of his Turkish allies in the late spring of 1344 (Umur may have arrived in Smyrna in about June 1344) not only diminished Kantakouzenos's manpower but also encouraged his enemies to mount new attacks. Stephan Dušan advanced to Zichna, Ivan Alexander joined Constantinopolitan troops at Stilbnos, and the Bulgarian local ruler Momitzilos, who had been appointed governor of the Merope region by Kantakouzenos, was instigated to switch sides.[28]

The overall turmoil encouraged Turkish hosts to take advantage of the situation by raiding and ransacking regions affected by the hostilities. Kantakouzenos encountered one of those groups on his way to Koumoutzena.[29] Latin ships heading eastwards to participate in the Holy League's expedition against Smyrna fell upon a Turkish naval contingent near Pallene in the Kassandra Peninsula.[30] The surviving Turks, while marching overland back to the Hellespont straits, defeated a strong Serbian host, forcing Dušan to retreat, and offered their services to Kantakouzenos, who was besieging Gratianoupolis at that time.[31] This brought a temporary respite and enabled him for all the manifold menaces to seize the city in June 1344 and to reach a peace treaty with Ivan Alexander.[32]

The later part of 1344 and first half of 1345 saw the hostilities and devastations spread to regions of eastern Thrace, the Gallipoli Peninsula, and the suburbs of Constantinople.[33] Despite some new negotiations between the warring parties and

---

27 Kantakouzenos, II, 407–10 (book III, chapters 66–67); Gregoras, II, 693–94 (book XIV, chapter 1); Enverī, v. 1645–76, 1839–66 (who also talks about Umur Beg's return on ships sent by Qaloyan Beg [i.e., John V, the government of Constantinople] but without mentioning the preceding negotiations); Lemerle, L'émirat d'Aydin, pp. 176–79.
28 Kantakouzenos, II, 420–22 (book III, chapter 68); Gregoras, II, 708 (book XIV, chapter 5). For Momitzilos fighting on Kantakouzenos's side, see also Enverī, v. 1569–80: bir bahâdır Sırf ilinde var idi | Mumcila adı katı cebbâr idi; Lemerle, L'émirat d'Aydin, pp. 168–69.
29 Kantakouzenos, II, 415–18 (book III, chapter 68).
30 Kantakouzenos, II, 422–23 (book III, chapter 68).
31 Kantakouzenos, II, 423–25 (book III, chapter 69).
32 Kantakouzenos, II, 425–27 (book III, chapter 69).
33 Kantakouzenos, II, 474–76 (book III, chapters 75–76) (conquest of Garella, Karya, Polyboton, Teristasin), 477–78 (book III, chapter 77) (Chora), 479 (book III, chapter 77) (Charioupolis, Apra), 482–83 (book III, chapter 77) (advance from Daphnidion to the environs of Constantinople and the Propontis, all cities surrendered except Ainos, Hexamilion, Gallipoli), 484 (book III, chapter 78) (after the subjugation of Lower Thrace, advance to Adrianople, Bizye, and the Pontus region), 489–91 (book III, chapter 79) (conquest of Bizye and other towns), 492 (book III, chapter 80) (from Charioupolis attacks on other cities), 498 (book III, chapter 81) (attacks on Pontus cities except Sozopolis), 502 (book III, chapter 82) (camp outside Constantinople), 518 (book III, chapter 84) (conquest of Region, Athyra, Damokraneia, Selymbria, Empyrites, city of Derke Lake, fortification of Apameia), 519 (book III, chapter 84) (devastations left the surroundings of Constantinople uninhabited), 525–26 (book III, chapter 85) (surrender of Adrianople and surrounding castles, Tzermanianou, Hierax).

an initiative of the Genoese of Galata to mediate a peace agreement, the military operations dragged on with undiminished intensity and the living conditions of the population further deteriorated.[34] Meanwhile, Momitzilos, who in late 1344 attacked and partly destroyed ships of Umur anchored in the harbour of Abdera, excelled as one of the most powerful allies of the Constantinopolitan government.[35] Turkish auxiliary forces continued to support Kantakouzenos's operations in 1344 and 1345 and wrought havoc to places that refused to surrender.[36] After Umur's retreat, however, they were deprived of a strong leadership and seem to have been recruited from different parts of Asia Minor, which made it more difficult to control their movements and to contain their raiding activities. At the same time, Empress Anna and the Constantinopolitan court made increasing efforts to create a counterweight by winning over more Turkish allies. Süleyman of Karasi crossed over to the Gallipoli Peninsula to fight on the empress's side, but after a face-to-face meeting with Kantakouzenos he returned home.[37] A Constantinopolitan embassy to the Ottoman chief was outstripped by Kantakouzenos's diplomatic skills so that Orhan entered an alliance with the latter. This enabled Kantakouzenos's troops to extend their attacks to the Pontus region and the suburbs of Constantinople with Turkish troops ravaging and pillaging.[38]

In the spring of 1345, Umur Beg set out for his last expedition in support of Kantakouzenos. After losing the port of Smyrna and the greatest part of his fleet as a result of the Holy League's attack in October 1344, he was no longer able to reach the Byzantine territories by sea and thus had to make a deal with the emir of Saruhan so as to obtain permission to cross the latter's territories on the land route to the Dardanelles straits.[39] After joining Kantakouzenos in Didymoteichon, the allies jointly attacked Momitzilos, who had been promoted to the rank of *despotes* by Empress Anna and continued to show hostility to Kantakouzenos on his domains in the region between Merope and Xanthi.[40] Despite the peace treaty with Ivan Alexander, the Turks pillaged Bulgarian territories, and the united Byzantine-Turkish army defeated and killed Momitzilos in a battle near Peritheorion on 7 July 1345.[41] Meanwhile, the Turkish presence in the

---

34 Kantakouzenos, II, 434–35 (book III, chapter 71), 437–68 (book III, chapters 72–74), 474–75 (book III, chapter 76), 502–22 (book III, chapters 82–84), 519–20 (book III, chapter 84), 524–25 (book III, chapter 85); for devastations, see the list in n. 33.
35 Kantakouzenos, II, 428 (book III, chapter 70).
36 Kantakouzenos, II, 482–83 (book III, chapter 77), 519 (book III, chapter 84).
37 Kantakouzenos, II, 476 (book III, chapter 76), 507–08 (book III, chapter 82).
38 Kantakouzenos, II, 498–99 (book III, chapter 81).
39 Kantakouzenos, II, 529–30 (book III, chapter 81); Gregoras, II, 726 (XIV. 9); Enverī, v. 2276–88 (according to his version it was Süleyman, the son of Saruhan, who instigated Umur to give up the siege of the castle of Izmir and to go on gaza again), v. 2295–96 (Süleyman of Karasi also met Umur or even joined the campaign); Lemerle, *L'émirat d'Aydin*, pp. 212–13. For the Frankish conquest of Smyrna, see Enverī, v. 1867–1992; Lemerle, *L'émirat d'Aydin*, pp. 180–90.
40 Kantakouzenos, II, 428–31, 436–37 (book III, chapters 70–71).
41 Kantakouzenos, II, 530–34 (book III, chapter 86); Gregoras, II, 727–29 (book XIV, chapters 9–10); Enverī, v. 2321–26 (Umur Beg is presented as the one who killed Mumcila); Lemerle, *L'émirat d'Aydin*, pp. 210–11, 213–15.

region had become so intense that Stephan Dušan in fear of an attack withdrew from Pherai, which for many months had endured the siege of the Serbian army.[42]

The murder of Alexios Apokaukos on 11 July 1345 eliminated Kantakouzenos's worst enemy and gave reason to hope for a quick takeover in Constantinople, but eventually the prisoner revolt was quelled and failed to bring the downfall of Empress Anna's regime.[43] On the instigation of his allies Umur and Süleyman of Saruhan, Kantakouzenos rather than securing the possession of Pherai, as he originally intended, moved forth with his army to Constantinople. It quickly became clear, however, that the city was well defended and Empress Anna was in full control of the situation.[44] In the recently re-fortified castle of Apameia, where the army had pitched camp to march against Pherai and other recalcitrant cities of Macedonia, Süleyman suddenly died of a fever and Umur was forced to return to Smyrna to appease the lord of Saruhan, as rumours accusing Umur of being responsible for the son's death began to spread.[45] This event marked both the end of Umur's direct involvement in the civil war and the victory of Stephan Dušan, who took Pherai and other cities of Macedonia and proclaimed himself *basileus* of the Serbs and Romans.[46]

In the civil war's final phase from the fall of 1345 onwards, Stephan Dušan turned out to be the real winner in this internecine struggle by gaining large swathes of land in Macedonia and Thessaly on expense of the Byzantine Empire. The Turks of Asia Minor thus remained the last source of manpower the warring parties could resort to. Constantinople sent the *panhypersebastos* Isaac Asanes and another court dignitary holding the title of *parakoimomenos* to persuade Süleyman of Karasi to enter a new alliance, but both attempts failed.[47] John Vatatzes, a partisan of Kantakouzenos, who had been appointed governor of cities in Thrace, threw in his lot with the empress's faction and won the support of the Saruhan emirate. While Kantakouzenos claims that the Turks in Vatatzes's service refused to follow him further when they realized that they were attacking territories loyal to him, Gregoras holds that because of Kantakouzenos's rescuing crops and livestock the Turks ran short of booty and began starving.[48] In a new attempt, Empress Anna sent George Tagaris to negotiate an alliance with the Saruhan Turks. After crossing over to Thrace, men of Umur, who had mingled with their ranks under the pretext of joining the campaign, persuaded the Turkish soldiers to switch sides. This turn of events proved especially profitable for the Turks, for not only did they receive the promised gifts and stipends from the Constantinopolitan government, but they also made large amounts of booty and

---

42 Kantakouzenos, II, 468–69 (book III, chapter 75), 546–47 (book III, chapter 89).
43 Kantakouzenos, II, 541–46 (book III, chapter 88); Enverī, v. 2321–40; Lemerle, *L'émirat d'Aydin*, p. 215.
44 Kantakouzenos, II, 546–50 (book III, chapter 89); Gregoras II, 726–27 (book XIV, chapter 9); Enverī, v. 2341–42, 2359–62 (speaks about a fictitious surrender of Istanbul and the submission of its inhabitants); Lemerle, *L'émirat d'Aydin*, pp. 216–17.
45 Kantakouzenos, II, 550–51 (book III, chapter 89); Enverī, v. 2341–58 (who mentions Süleyman's illness and death and Umur's escorting the coffin back home); Lemerle, *L'émirat d'Aydin*, pp. 216–17.
46 Kantakouzenos, II, 551–52 (book III, chapter 89).
47 Kantakouzenos, II, 507 (book III, chapter 82).
48 Kantakouzenos, II, 552–56 (book III, chapter 90); Gregoras, II, 741–43 (book XIV, chapter 11).

captives while making their way to Kantakouzenos in Selymbria and ransacking Bulgarian territory.[49]

Kantakouzenos's greatest success in solidifying his network of supporters was the wedding of his daughter Theodora to Emir Orhan. By solemnizing this marriage in June 1346 in Selymbria, the emperor ideologically and dynastically consolidated his coalition with the Ottomans while the Ottoman ruler as the emperor's son-in-law became a member of the imperial family's extended kin group. This step automatically foiled any further attempt of the other side to approach the Ottomans.[50] A few months later, on 7 February 1347, John Kantakouzenos was uncontested lord of Constantinople.

Views and Attitudes towards Byzantine-Turkish Alliances, 1341–47

Undoubtedly, the Turkish allies not only fuelled the Byzantine war machinery by providing significant resources of manpower but also exacerbated the disastrous situation of the war-ridden regions in Thrace and Macedonia. Their primary incentives for fighting in this conflict were the gifts and stipends granted by their Byzantine allies, as well as the prospects of acquiring rich booty and captives. This made their actions hardly controllable. They constantly menaced the local population and caused extensive devastation to crops, livestock, and rural areas.[51] The Byzantine ruling elite was aware of the dangers posed by unruly hosts of raiders and many voices forthrightly condemned these coalitions.[52] Yet, the warring parties were ready to

---

49 Kantakouzenos, II, 591–96 (book III, chapter 96), for Tagaris, see below, n. 115–16.
50 Kantakouzenos, II, 585–89 (book III, chapter 95); Gregoras, II, 762–63 (book XV, chapter 5).
51 From among a number of similar descriptions see, for instance, Kantakouzenos, II, 381 (book III, chapter 62): 'τὸ Περσικὸν δὲ διεσκέδαστο ἐπὶ λεηλασίαν καὶ ἐν ἡμέρᾳ μιᾷ τὴν περὶ Βέρροιαν ἅπασαν ἐπῆλθε γῆν καὶ τὰ μέγιστα ἐκάκωσεν. ἀνθρώπους τε γὰρ ἠνδραπόδισαντο καὶ ἀπέκτειναν πολλοὺς καὶ βοσκημάτων ἤλασαν ἀγέλας καὶ οἰκίας ἐνέπρησαν τὰς ἐπὶ τὰς κώμας καὶ τῶν ἄλλων, ὅσα προσήκει πολεμίους, οὐδενὸς ἠμέλουν'. Kantakouzenos, II, 391 (book III, chapter 64): 'Τὸ μὲν οὖν Περσικὸν αὐτίκα, ἐπεὶ ἐπύθοντο τὸν μέγαν δοῦκα ἀποπεπλευκέναι εἰς Βυζάντιον, τὰ περὶ Θεσσαλονίκην ἅπαντα ἐπιδραμόντες χωρία ἐληΐζοντο καὶ ἠνδραπόδισαν οὐκ ὀλίγους'. Kantakouzenos, II, 595 (book III, chapter 96): 'ἐκεῖνοι δὲ ζημίαν οὐ μικρὰν ἡγούμενοι τὸ κεναῖς ἀναχωρεῖν χερσὶν ἐπεστράτευσαν Μυσοῖς, καὶ ἀπέκτειναν πολλοὺς κατὰ τὴν ἔφοδον ἐκείνην καὶ ἠνδραπόδισαντο, καὶ βοσκημάτων ἐκράτησαν παμπόλλων, καὶ, εἴπερ ποτὲ, ἐκάκωσαν Μυσίαν'. For a similar statement, see Gregoras, II, 747–48 (book XV, chapter 1): 'Περσικαὶ δὲ δυνάμεις, ἐξ Ἀσίας δι' Ἑλλησπόντου πᾶσαν ὥραν διαπεραιούμενοι, καθάπερ ἐξ οἰκείων ἐς οἰκείας νομάς καὶ ἐπαύλεις, συχνὰς ἐποιοῦντο νύκτωρ καὶ μεθ' ἡμέραν τὰς θηριώδεις ἐφόδους κατὰ τῶν Θρακικῶν πόλεων [...] οὔτε γὰρ ὑποζυγίων, οὔτε ποιμνίων οὐδὲν τοῖς ταλαιπώροις Θραξὶν ἐλέλειπτο, οὔτε βοῶν ἀροτήρων οὐδείς [...]'. Enverī, v. 1387–94: 'yağı olan yeri vîrân etdiler | her ki tapmadısa giryân etdiler | ol ilün mâl ü esîrin aldılar | toptolu Dimetokayı kıldılar | [...] | iki ay ol ili târâc etdiler | kaçanın habbeye muhtac etdiler' ('they laid waist the lands that were hostile | they plunged into grief whoever did not submit | they took the goods and captives of this land | they filled Didymoteichon entirely | [...] | they pillaged this land for two months | the refugees were in need of grain').
52 Kantakouzenos, II, 396 (book III, chapter 64), rendering the words of the emissary Jacob Broulas, who was sent to Constantinople to conduct peace negotiations: 'βάρβαροι γὰρ ἤδη εἶναι Πέρσαι οἱ τὸν πρὸς Ῥωμαίους ἐπιτετραμμένοι πόλεμον κἀκείνῳ συμμαχήσοντες, οἷς τὸ φονεύειν τρυφή καὶ τὸ ἐξανδραποδίζεσθαι καὶ ἀποδίδοσθαι ἐπὶ δουλείᾳ κέρδους ἥδιον παντός, καὶ οἶκτος οὐδὲ εἷς, οὐδὲ ἔλεος τῶν ἀτυχούντων, οἷα δὴ φύσει πολεμίων ὄντων διὰ τὴν περὶ τὸ σέβας ἀκροτάτην ἐναντιότητα'.

accept these damages because of the significant advantages they had to gain from their allies. This accounts for Kantakouzenos's repeated efforts to present himself as being forced to do so because of the behaviour of his internal opponents and the external threats posed by the Serbs and the Bulgarians.[53] He argues that his foes in Constantinople were just as eager to gain the Turks' support and to secure fresh troops. Although Kantakouzenos starkly underlines the sincere feelings of loyalty and devotion his allies cherished for him,[54] our sources clearly show that the Turks readily negotiated with both warring parties and supported whoever was willing to meet their demands.[55] Suffering from a constant lack of money and troops, the Byzantine chiefs had no choice other than to customize their own military goals to the expectations of the Turkish auxiliary forces and to let them a free hand in optimizing their gains. Given that for a long time neither side was able to prevail, not surprisingly, a vicious circle of violence and destruction was set into motion.

On the occasion of a joint raid of Byzantine and Turkish forces on towns in Thrace and the Rhodope Mountains in early 1344, Kantakouzenos characteristically states in his third-person account:

> The emperor was unbearably distressed about that, but there was no remedy for this evil. Neither did the cities side with him so that the barbarians desisted from attacking them, nor did he possess sufficient forces from the Romans against the enemies so that the Persians could be dismissed, and he would be able to go to this war with his Roman supporters.[56]

In a similar vein, Kantakouzenos maintained that his opponents had handed over cities and lands to the Serbs and Bulgarians in order to make them allies, whom they were ready to use against him. He would not have been able to put up resistance with the Byzantine troops he had as his disposal. He had no other choice than to forge his own alliance in order to repel and destroy his enemies. Such an alliance

---

53 Kantakouzenos, II, 506–07 (book III, chapter 82): 'τῆς τε βαρβαρικῆς πρὸς τοὺς ὁμοφύλους, ἔφασκεν, ἐπαγωγῆς οὐκ ἐκεῖνον ἦρχθαι, ἀλλ' αὐτούς, πρώτους ἐπ' αὐτὸν ἐπενεγκόντας, καὶ οὐ μόνον τούτου ἕνεκα, ἀλλὰ καὶ τρόποις ἑτέροις χρῆσθαι τοῖς βαρβάροις καταναγκάζοντας· χρήματα γὰρ ἐκεῖνοι παρεχόμενοι καὶ πόλεις προϊέμενοι καὶ τὴν Ῥωμαίων ἡγεμονίαν μεγάλων καὶ θαυμασίων τινῶν ἀποστεροῦντες, οὐ Κράλην μόνον ἔπεισαν τὸν Τριβαλῶν δυνάστην, ἀλλὰ καὶ Ἀλέξανδρον τὸν βασιλέα Μυσῶν αὐτῷ πολεμίους εἶναι, [...], ὑφ' ὧν πρὸς ἀνάγκην καὶ αὐτὸν συνελαυνόμενον, τῇ συμμαχίᾳ χρῆσθαι τῇ βαρβαρικῇ'.
54 See, for instance, Kantakouzenos, II, 386–87 (book III, chapter 63) (Umur haranguing his soldiers in Euboea): 'τὸ μὲν ὑπὲρ ἐκείνου κινδυνεύειν, ὡς ῥᾳστώνης πάσης ἥδιον καὶ πολλὴν ἡμῖν οἴσει τὴν εὐδοξίαν καὶ τὸ θαυμάζεσθαι παρὰ πάντων [...] οὐ γὰρ ὥσπερ οἱ πολλοὶ τὸ βασιλέως φίλος προσαγορεύεσθαι εἱλόμην μόνον, ἀλλ' οὕτως αὐτῷ συντέτηκα, ὥστ' εἰ συμβαίη τῶν ἀνηκέστων ἐκεῖνόν τι παθεῖν, ἀβίωτον ἡγησόμενος τὸν βίον καὶ αὐτός'.
55 Kantakouzenos's statements are partly corroborated by Gregoras, II, 763 (book XV, chapter 5): 'ἡ βασιλὶς Ἄννα [...] ἐφ' ἑτέρας ἐτρέπετο· καὶ δῶρα τὴν ταχίστην δαψιλέστερα πέμψασα τοῖς περὶ Φιλαδέλφειαν σατράπαις Κάρας καὶ Λυδοὺς συνήθροισε, καὶ Ἴωνας, καὶ ὅσοι τῶν ἱππέων ἦσαν ἐκεῖθεν ἐπίλεκτοι Περσῶν'.
56 Kantakouzenos, II, 404 (book III, chapter 66): 'βασιλεὺς δὲ ἠνιᾶτο μὲν πρὸς τὰ τοιαῦτα οὐκ ἀνεκτῶς, θεραπεία δὲ τοῦ κακοῦ οὐδεμία ἐξευρίσκετο. οὔτε γὰρ αἱ πόλεις προσεχώρουν, ὥστε αὐτῶν ἀποσχέσθαι τοὺς βαρβάρους, οὔτε ἀποχρῶσαν πρὸς τοὺς πολεμίους εἶχε δύναμιν ἐκ Ῥωμαίων, ὥστε ἀποπέμπεσθαι τοὺς Πέρσας, ὡς ἅμα τοῖς συνοῦσι Ῥωμαίοις τὸν πόλεμον διοίσων'.

could be found nowhere else than among the Persians in Asia.[57] Despite the author's optimism about the Turks' military efficiency he had also to admit that the agreements with the Turks were highly fragile. Turkish troops could be easily infiltrated by hostile agents and inveigled to switch sides or abandon the campaign.[58] The commanders had to be very circumspect in maintaining the loyalty of their soldiers and alert to the slightest signs of discontent from among their ranks.[59] Sufficient supplies and a steady stream of gifts and booty were necessary for keeping up the discipline and fighting morale of the soldiers.[60] This was an additional factor that made it difficult to contain their looting and pillaging and explains why the boundaries between hostile territories and regions affected by military operations were so blurred. The Byzantine chiefs made attempts to channel the Turks' greed for ransacking towards specific directions or to divert them from certain areas and their inhabitants.[61] At times, they announced the arrival of Turkish warriors so as to warn the local population of imminent attacks.[62] As these attempts were not always successful, the warring parties harshly accused one another of having taken insufficient measures to afford protection to the non-combatant people. A case in point is a disastrous raid on the Thracian suburbs of Constantinople, in which many people came to death while the Turks made huge profits.[63] Kantakouzenos accuses his archenemy Alexios Apokaukos of this disaster, who is said to have been too confident in his forces to take any appropriate measures or to warn the inhabitants of the region.[64] The Constantinopolitan government, in turn, blamed Kantakouzenos for having given permission to his allies to devastate Bulgarian territory as a reward for their support. Kantakouzenos characterized this accusation

---

57 Kantakouzenos, II, 467 (book III, chapter 74): 'ἐκεῖνοι μὲν γὰρ Μυσοῖς καὶ Τριβαλοῖς πόλεις καὶ χώρας καταπροϊέμενοι συμμάχους ἐποιήσαντο, οἷς ἐπ᾽ ἐμὲ διανοοῦνται χρῆσθαι [...] αὕτη δὲ οὐδαμόθεν ἀνθίστασθαι οὐκ ἂν ἄλλοθεν παρέσται, ἢ ἐξ Ἀσίας Περσική'.
58 Kantakouzenos, II, 407–10 (book III, chapter 66) (Mavrommates, a man from Philadelphia, persuaded Umur's men to urge for departure), II, 591–95 (book III, chapter 96) (Umur's soldiers persuade the troops of Saruhan to switch to Kantakouzenos's camp).
59 Kantakouzenos, II, 409 (book III, chapter 66): 'ἐπὶ πεντεκαίδεκα μὲν οὖν ἡμέραις ὁ Ἀμοὺρ τοῖς Πέρσαις διετέλεσε διαλεγόμενος καὶ πείθειν ἐπιχειρῶν μὴ ἀπαίρειν εἰς Ἀσίαν'.
60 Kantakouzenos, II, 593 (book III, chapter 96): 'ἀλλ᾽ ἀπελθόντας εἰς Βυζάντιον πρὸς βασιλίδα καὶ δῶρα δεξαμένους καὶ τὰ ἐπηγγελμένα χρήματα τῷ σφῶν σατράπῃ ἐπανήκειν πρὸς αὐτόν, καὶ πάντα τὰ κελευόμενα ποιεῖν'.
61 Kantakouzenos, II, 477–78 (book III, chapter 77), esp. 478: 'καὶ τῶν Περσῶν τοὺς ὑπολειπομένους ἀνδραποδίζειν ἐπιχειρούντων, ἐκώλυσεν ὁ βασιλεὺς ἐλθὼν καὶ περιέσωσε τὴν πολίχνην' (i.e., the city of Chora in Thrace, the inhabitants of which only surrendered after an earthquake did serious damage to their walls and houses).
62 Kantakouzenos, II, 595 (book III, chapter 96): 'μᾶλλον μὲν οὖν καὶ πρόνοιαν ἐποιεῖτο πλείστην τοῖς Μυσοῖς τὴν τῶν βαρβάρων ἔφοδον ἀεὶ μηνύειν'.
63 Kantakouzenos II, 482 (book III, chapter 77): 'ἡ λοιπὴ δὲ στρατιὰ μετὰ τῆς Περσικῆς τὰ περὶ Βυζάντιον κατέδραμον πάντα ἄχρι Προποντίδος καὶ ἐκάκωσαν ἐς τὰ μάλιστα. ἀπέκτεινάν τε γὰρ οἱ βάρβαροι πλείστους καὶ ἠνδραποδίσαντο'.
64 Kantakouzenos, II, 482–83 (book III, chapter 77): 'καίτοι δυνάμενος τὴν προσήκουσαν περὶ τὴν χώραν πρόνοιαν ποιεῖσθαι τὴν ἔφοδον ἀπαγγέλλων, ὁ δ᾽ οὐδὲν ἐποίει τῶν δεόντων'.

as a shameless lie, but he readily admitted that his troops were simply too weak to bring the Turks to heel.[65]

Another factor is the increasing exhaustion of the territories affected by the civil war. The impoverished population and the devastated agricultural areas no longer yielded the amount of goods needed to meet the Turks' demands. This led to a further extension of Turkish raiding activities into adjacent regions.[66] Kantakouzenos asserts that he made every effort to alert non-combatant people and to persuade his allies to release their captives,[67] but this statement hardly conceals the alarming extent Turkish looting and ransacking had reached.

The involvement of Turkish allies in the Byzantine civil war was not only an internal matter but was also discussed in diplomatic contacts with western powers. This is exemplified by an embassy sent by John Kantakouzenos to Pope Clement VI (1342–52) in September 1347, i.e., a few months after his takeover in Constantinople.[68] Building an atmosphere of mutual confidence was a precondition for improving relations with the leaders of Latin Christendom and resuming the negotiations about the union of the churches. The Byzantine envoys dispatched to Avignon, namely the *protovestiarites* George Spanopoulos, the *praitor tou demou* Nicolas Sigeros and a group of Frankish dignitaries, were instructed to explain the reasons for the emperor's alliances with the Turks. The peculiar circumstances of the civil war, the argument goes, forced the emperor to do so, but by no means does this imply that he accepted community with the infidel barbarians. He declared himself ready to participate in the crusade the pope and secular rulers in Italy and the West were preparing against the barbarians. He would be pleased to contribute the utmost to their destruction not only by providing safe transport to Asia Minor but also by fighting in person with his army. He would happily cede all privileges to his predecessors save the eagerness to do good things and the desire to see the barbarians suffer reprisals for what they had done to the Christians for such a long time.[69]

In the ensuing negotiations with Pope Clement VI, Kantakouzenos was keen to appear as a staunch supporter of the common Christian struggle against the Turks and as a ruler fully committed to the restoration of the ecclesiastical union. He starkly emphasized, however, the great significance a careful preparation of such an enterprise had for its successful outcome and insisted that this issue could only be resolved in the framework of an ecumenical council, which would have to be convened at one of the coastal cities reachable by both the papal and the Byzantine delegations.

---

65 Kantakouzenos, II, 595 (book III, chapter 96): 'ἐλέγετο δὲ, ὡς βασιλεὺς αὐτοῖς ἐπιτρέψειε τὴν ἔφοδον ἀμειβόμενος τῆς συμμαχίας· ἐψεύδοντο δὲ ἀκράτως οἱ λογοποιοῦντες'.
66 Kantakouzenos, II, 595 (book III, chapter 96): 'ἀλλὰ πλείους ὄντες, ἢ ὥστε ἄγεσθαι ὑπὸ Ῥωμαίων, ἀφ' ἑαυτῶν αὐτοὶ ἐπήεσαν κέρδους ἕνεκα. Λαμβάνειν γὰρ παρὰ Ῥωμαίων οὐδὲν ἐξῆν, τῶν μὲν ἤδη διεφθαρμένων, τῶν ὑπολοίπων δὲ τελούντων ὑπὸ βασιλέα'.
67 Kantakouzenos, II, 595 (book III, chapter 96): 'οὐ μὴν ἀλλὰ καὶ πρὸς τοὺς φίλους ἀεὶ πολύν τινα λόγον ἐποιεῖτο περὶ Ῥωμαίων τῶν ἐξανδραποδιζομένων ἀγανακτῶν [...]'.
68 Franz Dölger, *Regesten der Kaiserurkunden des oströmischen Reiches von 565–1453*, V: *Regesten von 1341–1453*, unter verantwortlicher Mitarbeit von Peter Wirth (Munich: C. H. Beck, 1965), no. 2930 (22 September 1347).
69 Kantakouzenos, III, 53–54 (book IV, chapter 9).

Kantakouzenos constantly highlights the pope's favourable attitude towards his person as the new head of the Palaiologan house and guardian of the young emperor John V, as well as the pope's enthusiasm for the idea of an ecumenical council.[70] Besides the author's overall tendency to whitewash his actions, this account clearly reflects the emperor's need to cleanse himself from the stigma of his unholy coalitions with the barbarians by pointing to the moral support of the pope as the highest spiritual authority in Christendom outside the Byzantine church. In response to the rumours about his detestable relations with the enemies of Christ, he had to project the image of a true Christian ruler striving for Christian unity and victory.

Yet the statements referring to the time after the end of the civil war do not necessarily mirror his diachronic attitudes towards western crusading plans and Byzantine-Latin relations. In his brief report about the conquest of Smyrna by the Holy League in October 1344, Kantakouzenos notes with a sigh of relief that Umur Beg had been forced to abandon the campaign in Thrace before the Frankish attack occurred. In his eyes, this was a sign of divine favour, for 'the emperor used to say that if the conquest of Smyrna had happened while Umur was still in Thrace, not only he himself but everybody would have thought that Umur had lost the city because of his favour for the emperor. But now, as he was there along with his army, he cannot be blamed for this conquest.'[71] In other words, Kantakouzenos considered it a propitious twist of fate that he was in no way involved in the fall of Smyrna. A shrewd politician struggling for his throne and prevalence, he had to manoeuvre his way through the opposing claims and aims of western crusader chiefs and his Turkish allies. While paying lip-service to the idea of crusading and the common Christian cause of fighting the infidel, he knew well that these activities ran counter to his own goals and the best thing he might hope for in such a quandary was to opt for pragmatism and to keep a position of neutrality. The emperor was fully aware of the prowess of western armies in the Eastern Mediterranean and the papacy's pivotal role in shaping Latin attitudes towards Byzantium, but he was also cognizant that securing and expanding his own sphere of influence was largely contingent upon good relations and, if need be, profitable coalitions with his Turkish neighbours in western Asia Minor. This was not only the lesson he had learned during the civil war but formed part of a Byzantine collective experience going back to the 1260s and was practiced by numerous other political players in the Aegean world.

Byzantine-Turkish alliances continued to be an important tool of policy making beyond the end of the civil war and were causally linked with the power struggle among the main players in the Balkan Peninsula. In a diplomatic exchange in January 1351 with the Bulgarian tsar Ivan Alexander, who complained about Turkish attacks on his territories, John Kantakouzenos claimed that it was not him who had turned the

---

70 Kantakouzenos, III, 54–62 (book IV, chapter 9); Dölger, *Regesten*, V, no. 2937 (spring of 1348).
71 Kantakouzenos, II, 419–20 (book III, chapter 68): Ἔλεγε δὲ ὁ βασιλεὺς, ὡς, εἰ συνέβαινεν Ἀμοὺρ κατὰ τὴν Θράκην διατρίβοντος ἁλῶναι Σμύρναν, οὐκ αὐτὸς μόνον, ἀλλὰ καὶ πάντες ἄνθρωποι τῆς εἰς βασιλέα ἕνεκα εὐνοίας τὴν πόλιν Ἀμοὺρ ἀπολωλεκέναι ἂν ὑπώπτευσαν. νυνὶ δὲ ἐκείνου μετὰ τῆς στρατιᾶς ἐκεῖ παρόντος, μηδεμίαν πρὸς αὐτὸν αἰτίαν εἶναι τῆς ἁλώσεως'.

Ottoman Turks against the tsar's territories, but he was forced to collaborate with them in order to restore his rule over imperial territories. For all his oaths, the Serbian king refused to revert cities he had seized from the empire. The emperor, therefore, advised Ivan Alexander to support him in preventing the Turks from crossing over to Thrace by providing money for the construction of galleys. The emperor himself would give as much as possible for the maintenance of his own naval force and thus they could position galleys in the Hellespont to fend off the barbarians. Should the Serbian king not be willing to do justice to both of them, they could bring new barbarians across the straits to attack him. The Bulgarian king initially agreed to this plan but backed down under Serbian pressure.[72] In short, Serbian expansionism under Stephan Dušan exacerbated the struggle for territorial control in the southern Balkans and foiled the attempts to forge Christian alliances in the time after the end of the civil war. Serbia, Bulgaria, and Byzantium pursued individual goals, which they would not abandon for the sake of a common strategy. Moreover, effective defensive efforts and military activities required huge amounts of money. In the short run, it was much cheaper to make agreements with Turkish warlords, who drew much of their profit from pillaging and ransacking and thus constituted a much smaller burden to the state treasury.

Diplomacy, Communication, and Cross-Cultural Interaction

The exigencies of the civil war, military advantages of the warring parties, and bright prospects of material gains constituted incentives for both Byzantines and Turks to make agreements and to forge alliances. However, in order to better understand the positive results of these endeavours and the reasons for their viability, one has also to factor in other aspects, such as communication strategies and mechanisms of mutual approach, which were provided by well-established diplomatic practices and the accumulated experience of long-term coexistence. John Kantakouzenos and, to a lesser extent, Nikephoros Gregoras refer to these matters from the Byzantine point of view, presenting them as an essential part of the negotiation procedures. Enverī reflects the vantage point of Umur Beg and the Turkish beyliks through the lens of a fifteenth-century Ottoman re-interpretation. Inevitably, this brings some anachronistic distortion, but the claims, expectations, and diplomatic strategy of the Turkish side are still recognizable.

Enverī's account about Umur Beg's involvement in the civil war starts off with a letter by John Kantakouzenos calling on Umur's support and ends with a fictitious presentation of Umur as being formally recognized by the people of Istanbul as their lord before he returned to Smyrna.[73] It is not always possible to draw a distinction

---

72 Kantakouzenos, III, 162–64 (book IV, chapter 22); Dölger, *Regesten*, V, no. 2969; for the treaty with Serbia and the doubtful authenticity of the pertinent information, see Dölger, *Regesten*, V, no. 2967 (December 1350).
73 Enverī, v. 1339–58, v. 2359–62.

between the original core of fourteenth-century material and later additions reflecting tendencies of the time of Sultan Mehmed II. Be that as it may, using the coalitions with the Byzantine court as a means of underpinning concepts of authority and ascendancy and elevating his prestige certainly was an important component of Umur's strategy. Kantakouzenos's letter calls the late emperor Andronikos III Umur's brother (*kardaş*) and implies that the two rulers are on an equal footing. The former's demise makes Umur the heir of the emperor's rank so that he becomes 'sultan of the surface of earth and khan of land and sea'. These titles, which draw on both Seljuk and Ottoman chancery practices, express a concept of universal rule that according to the letter emanates from Umur's personal relation with the Byzantine emperor. Enverī links this concept with the notion of a lord-vassal relationship regarding Umur's Byzantine allies: 'Should God allow us to see your face', Kantakouzenos explains, 'I will sacrifice my life and head on your way. This entire land will be yours, majesty. We, your servants, implore you to accept our homage, with all our soul and heart we turn to your gate'.[74] Hence, the alliance is tantamount to a submission to Umur's sovereignty. In this section, Enervī certainly projects fifteenth-century realities of Ottoman sultanic rule back to the formation period of the Aydınid beylik, yet the core of the original situation is still recognizable. The military support for the *domestikos*—the title designating Kantakouzenos in the Düstūrnāme—, whom the lord of Aydın acknowledged as Andronikos III's lawful regent, secured the former a significant rise in rank and prestige. This included links of spiritual kinship with the imperial family and some influence on Byzantine affairs.

The titles and epithets used for Umur all emphasize the idea of a sovereign encompassing jihad traditions and elements of Muslim-Persian kingship. While the text by default attaches the Ottoman military title of *paşa* to Umur, it also uses a number of Persian royal titles, such as *şehriyâr*, 'great king' (v. 1712, 1769), *pâdişâh*, 'supreme king' (v. 1356, 1673, 1792), *şâh-i civân*, 'young shah' (v. 1343), and even *hüdâvend-i cihân*, 'lord of the world' (v. 1761). His capacity as champion of Islam and virtuous warlord is highlighted in the honorifics *şâh-i guzât*, 'king of the ghazi warriors' (v. 1440) and *bahâdır lâ-nazir*, 'unmatched hero' (v. 1694). The notions of hegemonial authority and ghazi tradition articulated by these title elements underpin Umur's image as a Muslim model ruler, who is depicted along the lines of Ottoman forms of self-representation. Accordingly, formal submissions of local commanders and townspeople are a constantly recurring pattern in Enverī's account. These events consist of welcome ceremonies and official encounters, gift offerings, and gestures of devotion at a performative level: 'The emissaries [of Thessalonica] came and their faces touched the ground, some of them bowed their knees and some remained upright'.[75] Momitzilos is said to have kissed the hand of both the paşa and Kantakouzenos when he entered their service.[76] After

---

74 Enverī, v. 1354–58: 'cân u başı yoluna kılam fidâ | cümle bu ildür senün ey pâdişâ | kullarunuz yalvaruruz tapuna | cân ü dilden yüz sürerüz kapuna'.
75 Enverī, v. 1465–66.
76 Enverī, v. 1571–72.

the surrender of a host of Greek soldiers, 'each of them came before the pasha and kissed the ground'.[77] The townspeople of Eksya/Xanthi came out wailing and paid homage to the paşa, kissing the ground and offering gifts.[78] Similar submission ceremonies are described with respect to Serres, Zihna, and Christoupolis.[79] More elaborate is a largely fictitious report describing an alleged surrender of the people of Thessalonica. It mentions the arrival of Kantakouzenos along with *Qaloyan tekfürun oğlı*, i.e., John V. They were well received by Umur and his 30,000 Turks on foot and horseback. Kantakouzenos kissed the paşas's knees while he and John submitted to him. In exchange, Umur put a crown on the son's head and acclaimed him, and the city of Thessalonica was handed over to them.[80] Despite the purely fictitious character of this account, it is an interesting document illustrating early Ottoman perceptions of the transition from Byzantine to Muslim rule. By way of supporting Kantakouzenos, Umur gained control over the Byzantine imperial family and the succession procedures therein. The fact that Umur took an active part in the negotiations with the Constantinopolitan faction, as Kantakouzenos asserts, might be the origin of this assumption.

Unlike Enverī's *Düstūrnāme*, Ottoman dynastic chronicles show a tendency to depict Ottoman forms of interaction with the Christians exclusively in the light of Islamic law regarding jihad and Muslim rule over non-Muslim communities. Modern scholars largely adopt this view in order to explain Ottoman methods of conquest and dealings with Christian lords.[81] The emphasis on conflict and subjugation, however, conceals features of cultural and ideological interaction resulting from a shared set of values and political concepts. This goes a long way towards explaining why these coalitions could actually materialize and persevere for quite a long time. As we have seen above, Kantakouzenos justifies his collaboration with the Turks primarily as an inevitable necessity.[82] Moreover, both he and Nikephoros Gregoras place much emphasis on sentiments of esteem, loyalty, and even affection when describing his relations with Umur Beg and Emir Orhan. We may think of encomiastic features aiming at highlighting Kantakouzenos's ascendancy as an emperor who was acknowledged by both Greeks and Turks. In order to be persuasive, however, these statements had to be more than eulogizing rhetoric and refer to factual circumstances. In Gregoras's words, Umur Beg 'a long time ago had become a very fervent devotee and had promised to voluntarily hold up his friendship with him and his children and successors for his entire life. And he actually kept this friendship until the end, the

---

77 Enverī, v. 1637–38.
78 Enverī, v. 1543–46.
79 Enverī, v. 1510, 1514–15, 1525–26.
80 Enverī, v. 1491–1502.
81 The standard study on this topic is still Halil İnalcik, 'Ottoman Methods of Conquest', *Studia Islamica*, 2 (1954), 104–29, reprint in Halil İnalcik, *The Ottoman Empire: Conquest, Organization, and Economy, Collected Studies* (London: Ashgate, 1978), no. 1; the same approach shapes the argument in Halil İnalcik, 'The Rise of the Turcoman Maritime Principalities in Anatolia, Byzantium, and the Crusades', *Byzantinische Forschungen*, 9 (1985), 179–217.
82 See above, n. 56.

like of which I think never ever occurred anywhere else'.[83] In a similar vein, Umur's naval attack of 1341 is described as being motivated by the emir's 'wrath and fury' caused by attempts of members of the senate to demote Kantakouzenos. Umur showed full obedience to his ally, for when Kantakouzenos sent him word to stop his advance, 'the lord gave his command more easily than to a slave'.[84] The Turkish ally thus appears as a close companion replete with affection and compassion for his friend's fate, blindly fulfilling his wishes. Gregoras further expatiates on the motif of a friend's emotional involvement in his report of Umur's first arrival outside Didymoteichon. The Turkish emir is described as being deeply distressed by the emperor's absence and the uncertainties of his fate in foreign lands. His sadness forbade him to accept the empress's invitations: 'I would most probably break down seeing her present fate, as well as the tragedies and calamities afflicting the imperial house'.[85] Gregoras interprets the alliance between the two rulers as an affectionate relationship between people of different cultural, religious, and linguistic background. Despite these gaps, the geographical distance, and the fact that Umur Beg numbered among Byzantium's enemies, Gregoras readily admits that the Turkish chief was a man of gentle behaviour and fully adhered to Greek education. Rather than common origin, Gregoras argues, it is the convergence in mind that creates harmony and kinship of soul. The historian thus combines the classical notion of friendship with one of the key principles of Byzantine diplomacy, namely that political alliances go hand in hand with the adoption of Byzantine cultural and moral values.

Descriptions of emotions have to be seen in connection with sophisticated communication strategies, which enabled the interlocutors to build confidence, forge ideological links, and cement their personal ties. This presupposed linguistic skills, a high degree of familiarity with the other's mentality, and a capability to bridge cultural and ideological gaps on the basis of shared principles and values. Such qualities are frequently mentioned as outstanding characteristics of successful envoys and go-betweens who managed to bring these coalitions to fruition. Most intriguingly, Kantakouzenos mentions representatives of Umur participating in negotiations with his opponents in Constantinople. Umur, thus, rather than a mere provider of auxiliary forces, is described as an active supporter and spokesman of Kantakouzenos's policy, who stood up for the emperor's goals and ambitions vis-à-vis his own people and in negotiations with the enemies. Being trapped with his fleet in stormy weather at the coast of Euboea, Umur reportedly harangued his soldiers, highlighting not only the great glory they obtained by fighting for the emperor but also his profound feelings of friendship, which would make his life unworthy should something fatal happen to his friend.[86] During the same campaign, Umur sent his envoys to Thessalonica in a bid to persuade the city chiefs to side with the emperor

---

83 Gregoras, II, 597–98 (book XII, chapter 7): 'Οὗτος οὖν ἐκ πολλοῦ [...] ἐραστὴς ἐγεγόνει πάνυ τοι σφόδρα διάπυρος, καὶ φιλίαν τηρήσειν αὐθαίρετον ἐπηγγείλατο διὰ βίου παντὸς αὐτῷ τε καὶ παισὶ διαδόχοις αὐτοῦ [...]'.
84 Gregoras, II, 598 (book XII, chapter 7).
85 Gregoras, II, 648–50 (book XIII, chapter 4).
86 Kantakouzenos, II, 386–87 (book III, chapter 63).

and to surrender the city.[87] Likewise, in another diplomatic contact with Empress Anna, the embassy to Constantinople consisted of Kantakouzenos's emissary Jacob Broulas and a representative of Umur called Salatin (Salāḥ al-Dīn).[88]

Both in Kantakouzenos's entourage and in Constantinople there was a group of Byzantine aristocrats, who had a rich experience of long-term interaction with the Turks and maintained strong personal bonds with some of their leaders. They can be aptly described as a group of cultural go-betweens and mediators who by virtue of their linguistic skills, personal networks, and acquaintance with the other side successfully prepared the ground for agreements and coalitions. Mavrommates,[89] a partisan of Kantakouzenos, was bribed by Alexios Apokaukos to instigate Umur's soldiers to abandon the campaign and to return home. Loukas Georgios was sent to Umur to negotiate with him about his departure on ships provided by Empress Anna.[90] The *megas stratopedarches* John Vatatzes undertook a mission on behalf of Empress Anna to the Saruhan Turks in order to win them over for an alliance against Kantakuzenos.[91] His successor in the office of *megas stratopedarches*, George Tagaris,[92] embarked on another mission to the Saruhan emirate to gain their military support. The four individuals stood all out for their acquaintance with the Turks, be it because of their origins from Asia Minor (Mavrommates and Tagaris hailed from Philadelphia) or their network of friends and relatives (Tagaris's father Manuel [d. 1342] was governor of Philadelphia and maintained friendly relations with Saruhan; one of Vatatzes's daughters was married to Süleyman of Karasi).[93] Loukas Georgios and Vatatzes were also known as well-versed diplomats with a long experience in embassies and negotiations.[94] As for Vatatzes, it is explicitly stated that he mastered

---

87 Kantakouzenos, II, 393 (book III, chapter 64).
88 Erich Trapp, Rainer Walther, and Hans-Veit Beyer, *Prosopographisches Lexikon der Palaiologenzeit*, 12 vols, Addenda, Gesamtregister (Vienna: ÖAW Verlag, 1976-966) (hereafter PLP), no. 24737; Kantakouzenos, II, 398–99 (book III, chapter 65).
89 PLP, no. 17462; Kantakouzenos, II, 407–08 (book III, chapter 66).
90 PLP, no. 15143; Kantakouzenos II, 414–15 (book III, chapter 68).
91 Matschke, *Fortschritt*, p. 169; PLP, no. 2518 (he was *apographeus* [1333-41] and later governor of Thessalonica [1343] and held the position of *megas stratopedarches* in the time of the civil war [1343–45]); Kantakouzenos, II, 552–53 (book III, chapter 90).
92 PLP, no. 27399; Kantakouzenos, II, 591–92 (book III, chapter 96).
93 For Tagaris, see Kantakouzenos, II, 591 (book III, chapter 96): 'ἦν γὰρ αὐτῷ [i.e., Sarchanes] καὶ συνήθης πρότερον ἐπὶ Φιλαδέλφειαν πολὺν χρόνον τῷ πατρὶ συνδιατρίψαντι'. George's father Manuel was [PLP, no. 27400] *megas stratopedarches* [1321–29] and governor of Philadelphia, defending the city successfully on various occasions against the Turks. George was *megas stratopedarches* in the years 1346–55. For Vatatzes, see Kantakouzenos, II, 552 (book III, chapter 90): 'ἦν γὰρ πρός τινας τῶν σατραπῶν φιλίαν ἔχων τῷ τε τὴν φωνὴν αὐτῶν εἰδέναι καὶ διαλέγεσθαι Περσιστί, ἄλλως θ' ὅτι καὶ βασιλεὺς παρὰ τὸν τοῦ πολέμου χρόνον διὰ ταύτην τὴν αἰτίαν τοῖς Πέρσαις ἐκέλευεν ἀεὶ συνεῖναι· ἐξ ὧν ἐγίνετο ἐν συνηθείᾳ πρὸς αὐτούς'. Gregoras, II, 741 (book XIV, chapter 11): 'ἅτε δύναμιν ἔχων συχνὴν ἐξ Ἀσίας, ἣν ἐκ Τροίας ἐζητηκότι πέπομφεν ὁ σατράπης Σουλυμᾶν, γαμβρὸς ἐπὶ θυγατρὶ πρὸ βραχέος αὐτῷ καταστάς'. Vatatzes (PLP, no. 2518) had one son married to a daughter of Patriarch John Kalekas and two daughters married to the son of Alexios Apokaukos and Süleyman of Karasi.
94 Loukas Georgios had served Andronikos III in diplomatic missions and on behalf of Empress Anna negotiated the extradition of Kantakouzenos from Stephan Dušan (PLP, no. 15143); Kantakouzenos, II, 414 (book III, chapter 60): 'εὐφυῶς τε ἔχοντα πρὸς τὰς πρεσβείας καὶ ἄλλως ἐπιτήδειον ὄντα τῷ σατράπῃ'.

'the Persian language',[95] which most probably means the Turkish vernacular used in the western Anatolian emirates rather than the learned idiom of the written Persian language, which was widely used in the former territories of the Seljuk sultanate of Rūm and the Mongol-held regions of Asia Minor as a literary and administrative language. Similar characteristics may have applied to the *panhypersebastos* Isaac Asanes, who in 1345 had a leading position in the state affairs of Constantinople as *mesazon* and highest representative of the senatorial aristocracy.[96] He was married to Arachantloun Theodora, the daughter of the Ilkhānid ruler Abaqa (1265–82), and Maria Palaiologina, the so-called *Despoina ton Mougoulion*, an illegitimate daughter of Emperor Michael VIII.[97] We may assume that this relation earned him some familiarity with the customs and habits of the Persian-Mongol world, something that qualified him for leading another embassy to Süleyman of Karasi.[98] Other important aspects were long-standing loyalty or bonds of kinship to the leading figures of the ruling house. Loukas Georgios served both Andronikos III and Empress Anna as skilful ambassador for many years. John Vatatzes had an in-law relationship with Patriarch John XIV Kalekas on account of his son's wedding to the patriarch's daughter. These personal ties not only recommended them to the leaders they were representing in their missions but also increased the esteem the Turkish emirs cherished for them as members of the imperial court's innermost circle, as is articulated, for instance, in a statement put into Umur's mouth.[99] In summary, a certain acquaintance with Turkish customs, proficiency in the Turkish language, and personal links with Byzantine and Turkish elites were the ingredients that made an excellent negotiator, even if the desired goals could not always be achieved. We possess only very few snaps of information about their Turkish peers: A eunuch called Chatzes is mentioned as emissary of Orhan,[100] who was sent to ratify a peace treaty with Kantakouzenos. In contrast to the Byzantine envoys, who held all high ranks and offices at the imperial court, the Ottoman ruler seems to have preferred well-educated household slaves. Probably, the eunuch in question was a slave of Greek origin and thus was able to communicate with his Byzantine counterparts and to draw up treaty documents.

Apart from experienced ambassadors, Byzantine-Turkish diplomacy also relied on a broad spectrum of ceremonies and ritual acts advancing all sorts of messages in words, symbols, and gestures. The exchange of gifts is one of the most crucial moments in diplomatic contacts and serves a variety of purposes:[101] It signals good

---

95 Kantakouzenos II, 552 (book III, chapter 90): 'τῷ τε τὴν φωνὴν αὐτῶν εἰδέναι καὶ διαλέγεσθαι Περσιστί'.
96 PLP, no. 1494; Matschke, *Fortschritt*, p. 154.
97 PLP, nos 1141, 21395.
98 Kantakouzenos, II, 507 (book III, chapter 82).
99 Kantakouzenos, II, 415 (book III, chapter 68): 'βασιλίδι τε χάριν πολλὴν κατατιθέμενος ἐν τούτῳ καὶ αὐτῷ, ὄντι τῶν ἐπιτηδείων' ('showing much gratitude for this to the empress and to himself [Loukas Georgios], who was one of his friends').
100 PLP, no. 30717; Kantakouzenos, II, 498 (book III, chapter 81).
101 Anthony Cutler, 'Significant Gifts: Patterns of Exchange in Late Antique, Byzantine, and Early Islamic Diplomacy', *Journal of Medieval and Early Modern Studies*, 38 (2008), 80–101; Cecily J. Hilsdale, *Byzantine Art and Diplomacy in an Age of Decline* (Cambridge: Cambridge University Press, 2014).

will, respect, and gratitude, projects wealth and power, helps enticing potential allies into accepting envisioned agreements, and rewards an ally's allegiance. Moreover, a gift's nature and value express common ideological attitudes, which underpin a sense of cohesion and unity and help determine the hierarchical relation between givers and recipients. A high gift value was a clear sign of superiority in terms of power and influence. It could signal the recipient's inferior status vis-à-vis the giver but also numerous advantages the former was to gain on the basis of this status. The success or failure of gift exchanges, therefore, was a crucial moment in the process of approaching each other and of affirming or defying pre-existing relations.

In a bid to win him over, Alexios Apokaukos offered gifts and sums of money to Umur Beg, promising to reward him even more lavishly should he cease to support Kantakouzenos. Umur rejected the offer because he was unwilling to come to terms with Apokaukos. Accepting gifts would have created a moral obligation Umur sought to avoid: 'When the emissaries asked him to accept the gifts, he refused to take them, stating that it was characteristic of an unworthy man and slave of money one day to pretend to take gifts for friendship's sake and after a short while to wage war'.[102] The giving side, too, may have put its position at risk and it had to carefully weigh costs and benefits. On occasion of the negotiations about Umur's retreat in 1344, Gregoras points out that excessive gifts might eventually drain the giver's resources and cause more problems than advantages. Kantakouzenos is said to have stated that a sum of more than 10,000 gold coins spent to inveigle the Turks into departure would be a great damage for the Constantinopolitan faction and weaken its military power whereas he and his supporters would grow much stronger.[103]

In contrast, a successful gift exchange served to reaffirm previous bonds of friendship between the two sides and increased the prospects of a positive outcome while the negotiations were going on. When Süleyman of Karasi met with John Kantakouzenos at a place in the Gallipoli Peninsula, the emir confirmed his alliance with the emperor by giving horses and weapons while Kantakouzenos offered him his own presents in return.[104] In a similar vein, when in the weeks before his abdication in December 1354, John Kantakouzenos received a last embassy of Orhan and his son Süleyman regarding the surrender of Gallipoli and other cities in Thrace, the emperor expressed his gratitude for their good will and rewarded the Ottoman emissaries generously with gifts, fixing a period in which the Turkish garrisons would start withdrawing from the occupied strongholds.[105]

Yet the contest between the Byzantine factions enabled the Turks to maximize their profits by violating their commitments and making lucrative deals with both sides. The Saruhan Turks, for instance, in the summer of 1346 switched sides to Kantakouzenos's camp. Through an embassy, they pledged loyalty to him but on condition that they first take the gifts and money Empress Anna had promised them. The Saruhan chiefs

---

102   Kantakouzenos, II, 384 (book III, chapter 63).
103   Gregoras, II, 693–94 (book XIV, chapter 1).
104   Kantakouzenos, II, 476 (book III, chapter 76): 'Σουλιμάν, τῶν κατὰ τὴν Ἀσίαν σατραπῶν εἷς'.
105   Kantakouzenos, III, 284 (book IV, chapter 39).

were granted an audience at the imperial court, in which they prostrated themselves before the empress and took lavish presents in return. They even agreed to another joint action with the military commanders in Constantinople in order to seize the city of Selymbria.[106] The increasing predominance of Kantakouzenos's troops enabled the Turks to make the most of their double-dealing with the Byzantine factions and to neglect all rules of fair game.

Owing to their multi-layered symbolic value, horses played a crucial role in diplomatic gift exchanges. They loomed large as a means of transport and battle techniques and constituted an exquisite symbol of rank and prestige for both Byzantine and Turkish noblemen. The available reports suggest that Umur Beg's soldiers had only a very small number of horses at their disposal during their naval raids. This explains why horses were given great significance in discussions about the cohesion and internal hierarchy in Umur's army. While on campaign in late 1342, Umur Beg marched with his troops from the city of Bera at the mouth of the Maritsa River to Didymoteichon.[107] The figures given by Kantakouzenos—29,000 soldiers, among them 2,000 *logades*, i.e., 'chiefs', on 380 ships[108]—are certainly exaggerated, but they reflect the structure of Umur's army, which apart from the rank and file soldiers seems to have included a large group of clan leaders and subordinate chiefs commanding their retinue and followers. This is corroborated by Enverī, who with respect to the same event speaks of 15,000 foot-soldiers and 100 horsemen.[109] One may think of a perpetuation of nomadic organizational patterns consisting of tribal subunits and kin groups knit together by a common sense of loyalty to the ruling beylik chiefs.[110]

Enverī provides more specific insights into the structure of Umur's warrior elite. He mentions a group of outstanding ghazi fighters by name, who had a leading position in the command structures, were especially loyal, and fought at the forefront, namely Ilyās Beg, Dündar Beg, Uğurlu Beg, Old Pişrev, and Ehad Subaşı. We do not have more information about their kinship relations and family background, but we may assume that they formed the core of Umur's entourage of warlords and ghazi champions.[111] There were also some additional forces which stood under the command of his brothers and were affiliated to other cities in the Aydın emirate. They did not fight constantly on Umur's side but joined forces if need arose in large-scale campaigns. On occasion of the Frankish attack on Smyrna, Enverī mentions people from Tire und Ayasuluk, Umur's brothers Hızır Beg, Süleymanshāh, and İsa Beg, some of their close companions, such as Arslan, the vizier of Hızır Beg, his son Toğan, as well as the sons of Hwāce Hasen, Bedreddin and Ali Mardān, and other kinsmen of the paşa.[112]

---

106 Kantakouzenos, II, 597 (book III, chapter 96): 'καὶ οἱ στρατηγοὶ πρὸς βασιλίδα εἰσελθόντες προσεκύνουν τε καὶ ἐδέχοντο δῶρα παρ' ἐκείνης φιλοτίμως, συνέβαινόν τε οἱ τῶν Βυζαντίων ἄρχοντες τοῖς Πέρσαις [...]'.
107 Kantakouzenos, II, 344–46 (book III, chapter 56).
108 Kantakouzenos, II, 344–45 (book III, chapter 56).
109 Enverī, v. 1375–76.
110 See the discussion in the chapter of Rhoads Murphey in this volume.
111 Enverī, v. 1441–44.
112 Enverī, v. 1933–1934 (Tire und Ayasuluk), v. 1993–94 (Umur's brothers), v. 2057–60, 2061–64 (companions and kinsmen).

On receiving messages about Umur's arrival, Empress Irene dispatched soldiers, officials, and 100 horses to give a warm welcome and to express her appreciation for the ally and his troops. Umur was invited to continue his way on horseback and to distribute all other horses among his most noble chiefs. The empress's envoys also apologized for being unable to offer more horses because of the ongoing hostilities. As the number of horses was much smaller than that of the chieftains, only the eldest and most outstanding commanders received one. Umur himself, in a show of solidarity with his horseless *logades*, ostentatiously refused to mount a horse: 'It was better that he walked, for by tiring himself along with them he would make the hardships of the trip easier and more bearable.'[113] The episode clearly illustrates the emir's efforts to outbalance internal tensions arising from the contention about wealth and prestige. Enverī also stresses the significance of horses as diplomatic gifts in his report about the negotiations with the people of Thessalonica in the fall of 1343. As always, Umur appears as the protagonist, who received the Greek emissaries and discussed the termination of hostilities with them. The envoys reportedly invited him to switch sides. As a reward they would pay him a sum of 200,000 florins and make him *tekfûr* and *şâh* of the entire country. In order to highlight Umur's ascendancy, Enverī depicts the envoys as prostrating themselves before him and showering him and his companions with gifts, among them three horses.[114] Despite the diametrically opposed viewpoints of the Byzantine and the Turkish accounts they agree that horses constitute a crucial element in Byzantine-Turkish gift exchange as an especially prestigious symbol of military power and aristocratic status.

The symbolism inherent in riding on horseback played a crucial role in the public meeting between John Kantakouzenos and Umur Beg outside the walls of Thessalonica:[115] Umur approached the emperor with a small number of chiefs on horseback but dismounted and prostrated himself while drawing near. While continuing his way on foot, the emperor sent him order to mount again and he did so. We are dealing with a whole sequence of gestures through which the emir publicly demonstrated his loyalty and devotion to his overlord. In response, the emperor expressed his gratitude and esteem by allowing him to face him on an equal footing. Interestingly, Kantakouzenos notes that the procedure was extensively discussed beforehand,[116] which suggests that the meeting was carefully stage-managed as a ritualized show of gestures manifesting the emperor's relationship with his allies. It may well be that the messages projected in this meeting were designed to persuade other potential allies to seek an agreement. Again, 200 eminent magnates were given

---

113 Kantakouzenos, II, 346 (book III, chapter 56): 'βέλτιον πεζεύειν καὶ αὐτόν, ἐν τῷ συμπονεῖν αὐτοῖς ῥᾴω καὶ φορητοτέραν τὴν ἐκ τῆς ὁδοῦ ποιοῦντα ταλαιπωρίαν'.
114 Enverī, v. 1463-86, esp. 1474-76: 'sen iki yüz bin filuri bizden al | biz seni tekfur edelüm ko anı cümle ile şâh edelüm biz seni, v. 1483-84: yine elçi getürdi üç at | armağanun haddı yok toydı guzât'.
115 Kantakouzenos, II, 392-93 (book III, chapter 64): 'αὐτὸς μὲν ἔφιππος μετὰ ὀλίγων τῶν ἀρίστων [...] εἰς ὑπάντησιν τοῦ βασιλέως ᾔεσαν [...] τοῦ ἵππου ἀποβὰς ὁ Ἀμοὺρ, προσεκύνει τε τὸν βασιλέα καὶ ἐβάδιζε πρὸς αὐτὸν πεζός'.
116 Kantakouzenos, II, 393 (book III, chapter 64): 'πολλὰ πρότερον περὶ τοῦ πεζὸς ἐλθεῖν φιλονεικήσας'.

horses,[117] an act of generosity, which apparently was to highlight the bright prospects of gains the emperor's allies obtained.

Publicly performed gestures of grief and displays of emotions were employed to showcase sentiments of friendship and devotion between Byzantine and Turkish lords. When Umur was informed outside Didymoteichon about the hardships Kantakouzenos had to endure on his flight to the Serbian King in 1342 'he groaned and burst into tears out of compassion.'[118] In a similar vein, on receiving the Byzantine emissary Pringyps, Umur 'poured dust on his head and wholeheartedly thanked God',[119] for Apokaukos had spread rumours about Kantakouzenos's death during his sojourn in Serbia. Another aspect of Umur's emotional attachment to the emperor is exhibited by an episode in which Umur is described as protecting the emperor's reputation from insults and defamation. After Salatin's return from his mission to Constantinople, Umur refused to open the sealed letter addressed to him by the Constantinopolitan court and handed it over to Kantakouzenos lest the insults and slander it might contain come to the knowledge of other people.[120] The described course of action is used to illustrate profound loyalty and a serious concern about Kantakouzenos's wellbeing and success.

This set of positive gestures and emotions contrasts with an entire arsenal of verbal and non-verbal signs of refusal, abjection, humiliation, and disrespect. The spectrum of behavioural patterns ranged from moderate expressions of discontent and contempt to serious corporal abuse. Under the pressure of his subordinate commanders, Umur was forced to come to an agreement with the government of Constantinople about his departure from Thrace. Personally, he would have preferred to stay and ensured Kantakouzenos of his loyalty. Hence, for a long time he refused to see the ambassador Loukas Georgios and met him only after many requests. Likewise, Süleyman of Karasi refused to look at an emissary who had been sent from Constantinople for negotiations.[121] During the negotiations about the surrender of Gallipoli in 1354, Orhan's son Süleyman expressed his indignation about the Byzantine overtures by addressing the emperor in his reply letter simply with his name instead of his title, which in turn caused a harsh reaction by the imperial court.[122] Apparently, in this way Süleyman articulated his refusal to recognize Kantakouzenos as his overlord. Later he apologized for this diplomatic gaffe and blamed his scribe for this blunder, but there is no doubt that he had intentionally addressed the emperor in such an offensive way in order to articulate his defiance for the emperor's authority.

A very harsh way to manifest one's unwillingness to come to terms with an opponent was to corporally abuse the latter's emissary and representative. Alexios Apokaukos

---

17 Kantakouzenos, II, 394 (book III, chapter 64).
18 Kantakouzenos, II, 345 (book III, chapter 56): 'πολλὰ στενάζων καὶ δάκρυα τῶν ὀφθαλμῶν ὑπὸ συμπαθείας ἀφιείς'.
19 Kantakouzenos, II, 384 (book III, chapter 63): 'κόνιν μὲν κατεχέατο τῆς κεφαλῆς καὶ θεῷ πολλὰς ὡμολόγει χάριτας τῆς ἀγγελίας'.
20 Kantakouzenos, II, 400–01 (book III, chapter 65).
21 Kantakouzenos, II, 507 (book III, chapter 82).
22 Kantakouzenos, III, 266, 268–69 (book IV, chapter 36).

granted an honourable reception to Umur's emissary Salatin and dismissed him with lavish gifts. Jacob Broulas, instead, faced harsh treatment: Apokaukos's men shaved his beard, tonsured his head, broke his nose and legs, rubbed his face with soot, and dragged him bloodstained across the marketplace. Upon these acts of abuse, he was incarcerated in the prison of the Great Palace.[123] Apokaukos thus kept the lines of communication with Umur open apparently in the hope for a future agreement. At the same time, he forthrightly rejected all possibilities for a peaceful settlement with Kantakouzenos.

An especially splendid form of official contacts consisted of public face-to-face meetings between Byzantine and Turkish rulers. We already mentioned Umur's arrival at Didymoteichon and his meeting with Kantakouzenos outside the walls of Thessalonica.[124] Kantakouzenos also recorded other meetings he had with Süleyman of Karasi in the Gallipoli Peninsula and with the emir of Saruhan in Didymoteichon.[125] We are not told many details about the ceremonial setting of these encounters but we may safely assume that both sides used them as a setting to project the political and ideological parameters of their mutual relations. The best-documented event of this kind was the celebration of the wedding between the emperor's daughter Theodora and the Ottoman ruler Orhan, which took place in 1346 on a plain outside the walls of Selymbria.[126] Anthony Bryer has carefully examined all historiographical traditions about this marriage, its ceremonial aspects, the customs of paying dowries and bride prices, the legal status of the bride, and related statements of canon law.[127] He views this marriage as a turning point in Byzantine-Turkish relations, which signalled the beginning of the collaboration with the Ottomans and was one of the first steps towards the empire's downfall.[128] In retrospect we all know that this turned out to be true but in the mid-1340s such a twist of fate was not yet foreseeable.

After Umur's setback resulting from the Latin conquest of the port of Smyrna and the loss of his fleet, Kantakouzenos sought to continue his hitherto successful policy of alliances by turning to another powerful ruler in western Asia Minor. The conquest of the Bithynian cities and the incorporation of the Karasi emirate in Mysia had made the Ottomans the predominant entity in the region and their main strongholds were situated at a relatively short distance from Constantinople and the Byzantine territories. Previous experiences had taught him that Turkish allies were hardly controllable, but in a time when the greatest menace to the empire's territorial integrity emanated from Stephan Dušan's Serbia one could hardly foresee permanent Turkish conquests on European soil. Irrespective of whether it was the Byzantine or, if we believe Kantakouzenos and Gregoras, the Ottoman side that took the initiative for the marriage proposal,[129] such an endeavour, unprecedented though

---

123 Kantakouzenos, II, 398–99 (book III, chapter 65).
124 Kantakouzenos, II, 345–46 (book III, chapter 56), 392–93 (book III, chapter 64).
125 Kantakouzenos, II, 476 (book III, chapter 76), 530 (book III, chapter 86).
126 Kantakouzenos, II, 585–89 (book III, chapter 95); Gregoras, II, 762–63 (book XV, chapter 5).
127 Bryer, 'Marriage', pp. 471–93.
128 Bryer, 'Marriage', pp. 473, 476.
129 Kantakouzenos, II, 585 (book III, chapter 95): 'Ορχάνης πρὸς Καντακουζηνὸν τὸν βασιλέα πρεσβείαν πέμψας ἠξίου ἐκδοῦναί οἱ πρὸς γάμον τὴν θυγατέρα'.

at the level of dynastic matrimonial ties, clearly tallied with traditional strategies of establishing interpersonal bonds and was able to furnish favourable results to both sides. According to Gregoras, Orhan exerted a great amount of pressure to reach his goal. There is no way to check the reliability of his report, but some of the arguments mentioned fit well to the situation in 1346. There were prospects of military aid but also the menace of an Ottoman agreement with Empress Anna. The outstanding wealth and power of the Ottoman state made an agreement especially desirable.[130] As for Orhan, marriages were an effective means of expanding his rule and consolidating his dynasty.[131] Kantakouzenos further profited from this liaison by formally making Orhan his son-in-law.[132] According to Byzantine dynastic concepts, this created a spiritual father-son relationship, which underlined the emperor's ascendancy and, at the same time, tightened the bonds between the two rulers. The relation with Orhan was to reach a similar level of intimacy to that with Umur Beg.[133]

Kantakouzenos describes both the negotiation procedure and the ceremonial elements of the marriage in great detail. Apparently, he and his entourage perceived the marriage as an event of crucial political and ideological significance. The celebrations were an outstanding opportunity for Kantakouzenos to present his family as claimant to dynastic legitimacy as against the rival court of Empress Anna in Constantinople and to project his new relationship with the Ottoman court to dignitaries of both sides.[134] The Ottoman ruler, in turn, did not attend the event in person and thus was not compromised in his rank by performing any act of subordination.[135] The centrepiece of the family's public appearance was a *prokypsis* ceremony, during which the imperial bride was standing on a wooden platform surrounded by precious curtains and illuminated by torches held by kneeling eunuchs. The emperor positioned himself nearby sitting on horseback while the empress along with her other two daughters stayed back in the imperial tent.[136] In this way, John Kantakouzenos harked back on a longstanding tradition of *prokypsis* ceremonies, which seem to have replaced the emperor's appearances in the Hippodrome during the Comnenian period and according to the mid-fourteenth-century descriptions of Pseudo-Kodinos were regularly performed on great feast days such as Christmas and Epiphany. Through its combination of splendid garments and artificial illumination, the ceremony recalled the sunrays metaphor as a central feature of Byzantine imperial ideology. By situating it into the wedding festivities of Selymbria, Kantakouzenos manifested both his

---

130 Gregoras, II, 762–63 (book XV, chapter 5).
131 Juliette Dumas, 'Des esclaves pour époux ... stratégies matrimoniales dans la dynastie ottomane (mi-XIVe – début XVIe siècle)', *Clio*, 34 (2011), 255–75.
132 Kantakouzenos, II, 585 (book III, chapter 95): 'οὐκέτι γὰρ ἔσεσθαι σύμμαχον καὶ φίλον, ἀλλὰ υἱὸν, καὶ προθύμως δουλεύσειν αὐτόν τε καὶ τὴν σύμπασαν στρατιάν'.
133 Kantakouzenos, II, 586 (book III, chapter 95): 'μάλιστα γὰρ αὐτῷ λυσιτελεῖν τὴν φιλίαν καὶ τὴν οἰκειότητα τοῦ βαρβάρου'.
134 Kantakouzenos, II, 587 (book III, chapter 95): 'οὕτω γὰρ ἔθος εἶναι τοῖς βασιλεῦσι ποιεῖν ταῖς θυγατράσι πρὸς γάμον ἀγομέναις'.
135 Kantakouzenos, II, 587 (book III, chapter 95): 'καὶ στρατιὰν ἐκέλευε πέμπειν, ἥτις ἄξει τὴν γυναῖκα πρὸς αὐτόν'.
136 Kantakouzenos, II, 588 (book III, chapter 96).

claims to the imperial city and his desire to grant the Ottoman emir a paramount position in his system of alliances.[137]

At the same time, Kantakouzenos sought to emphasize his unwavering commitment to the emperor's traditional role as protector of the Orthodox faith. Marrying a Byzantine princess off to a Muslim lord had been occasionally discussed, and there had been some matrimonial links of members of the imperial court with Turkish and Mongol rulers. In c. 1087, the Seljuk sultan Malikshāh proposed a marriage with a daughter of Alexios I, but the Byzantine side spurned the proposal.[138] In 1197, the sultan of Konya, Ghiyāth al-Dīn Kaykhusrau, after taking refuge with the court of Alexios III was baptized and married a Byzantine princess.[139] Michael VIII Palaiologos married his illegitimate daughter Maria to the Ilkhānid ruler Abaqa.[140] None of these examples, however, constitutes a precedent for Theodora's marriage to Orhan, which goes a decisive step further both with respect to the bride's status as the emperor's legitimate daughter and Orhan's Muslim identity. Most probably, Kantakouzenos had to respond to critique of this kind uttered by people of his environment and the broader ruling elite. He justified his decision by referring to a letter exchange with Umur Beg, who reportedly advised him to seek a coalition and establish matrimonial bonds with Orhan because of his outstanding prowess and his proximity to the Byzantine territories.[141] Umur Beg thus served in Kantakouzenos's narrative as an outside authority, whose word had special weight because of his close relations with the emperor and his role as a mediator between the Byzantine and Turkish spheres. Kantakouzenos also stresses that Theodora throughout her time at the Ottoman court stayed a good Christian, granting shelter to Christian slaves and leading people who had converted to Islam back to the true faith.[142] The marriage was to be presented as something more than a political deal serving military purposes. It was also to the benefit of the Christians in Asia Minor, as Theodora increased Christian influence at the Ottoman court and afforded protection to Christian subjects. It is doubtful,

---

137 Otto Treitinger, *Die oströmische Kaiser und Reichsidee nach ihrer Gestaltung im höfischen Zeremoniell* (Darmstadt: Wissenschaftliche Buchgesellschaft, 1956), pp. 112–20; Michael Jeffreys, 'The Comnenian Prokypsis', *Parergon*, 5 (1987), 38–53; Ruth Macrides, 'Ceremonies and the City: The Court in Fourteenth-Century Constantinople', in *Royal Courts in Dynastic States and Empire*, ed. by Jeroen Duindam, Tülay Artan, Metin Kunt (Leiden: Brill, 2011), pp. 217–35 (233–35); for the Pseudo-Kodinos descriptions, see Ruth Macrides, Joseph A. Munitiz, and Dimiter Angelov, *Pseudo-Kodinos and the Constantinopolitan Court: Offices and Ceremonies*, Birmingham Byzantine and Ottoman Studies, 15 (Farnham: Ashgate, 2013), pp. 132–35.
138 Anna Komnene, *Alexias*, ed. by Diether R. Reinsch and Athanasios Kambylis, Corpus Fontium Historiae Byzantinae 40/1–2 (Berlin: W. de Gruyter, 2001), p. 195 (book VI, chapter 12.3).
139 Dmitri Korobeinikov, 'A sultan in Constantinople: the feasts of Ghiyāth al-Dīn Kay-Khusrau I', in *Eat, Drink, and Be Merry (Luke 12:19): Food and Wine in Byzantium, Paper of the 37th Annual Spring Symposium of Byzantine Studies in Honour of Professor A. A. M. Bryer*, ed. by Leslie Brubaker and Kalliroe Linardou (Aldershot: Ashgate, 2003), pp. 94–108 (100–01).
140 PLP, nos 1141, 21395.
141 Kantakouzenos, II, 586–87 (book III, chapter 95).
142 Kantakouzenos, II, 588 (book III, chapter 95): '[Theodora] παρεβλάβη κατὰ τὴν πίστην οὐδὲν [...] ἀλλὰ καὶ πολλοὺς τῶν πρὸς τὴν ἀσέβειαν ὑπαχθέντων ἀνεκαλέσατο λόγοις πείθουσα πρὸς τὴν αἵρεσιν τῆς ἀληθείας'.

however, whether she would have been able to convert people to Christianity. When Kantakouzenos eventually gained the throne of Constantinople, Orhan confirmed the newly established ties with the emperor by way of a face-to-face meeting in Skoutarion (Üsküdar), in which he formally congratulated the emperor for gaining the throne.[143] This meeting also provided a good opportunity to publicly display the bonds of kinship between the two dynasties. Orhan, therefore, made his appearance along with the four sons he had obtained from different women and a number of dignitaries from his entourage. A program of festivities and amusements framed by hunting excursions and lavish banquets highlighted the cordial relations between the two families. These activities culminated in a visit to Constantinople: The emir's sons and other family members entered the imperial city accompanying Theodora and the emperor and were showered with gifts. Orhan himself, however, stayed back in the camp, most probably in order to avoid any signs or gestures of inferiority and subordination. Being received at his father-in-law's residence may have made him appear as a petitioner seeking the emperor's protection.

Conclusions

Returning to the initial question as to why fourteenth-century Byzantium so reluctantly joined Christian crusading leagues while pursuing its own policy towards the Turks, we are now able to pinpoint various factors explaining the peculiarities of Byzantine attitudes. The Turkish penetration of western Asia Minor, besides warfare, brought about a significant intensification of contacts between the highly fragmented Byzantine-Frankish world of the Aegean and the Muslim-Turkish entities in western Anatolia. In an atmosphere marked by incessant conflicts and violence, many of the powers involved in local affairs developed successful strategies of accommodation, which allowed them to reach temporary peace agreements and commercial treaties with the Turkish emirates. After massive losses of territories and ill-fated attempts to stop the Turkish advance, the Byzantine imperial government in the 1330s stabilized its relations with both the Ottomans and the Aydın Turks. The civil war resulting from the premature death of Andronikos III, however, created a sudden demand for allies and manpower, to which the Turks of Asia Minor responded much more efficiently than the neighbouring Serbs and Bulgarians. The warring factions were aware of the devastating consequences the involvement of Turkish troops had for the local population, but for a lack of alternatives and owing to the short-term advantages they gained they kept pursuing these alliances. In retrospect, the historical discourse of John Kantakouzenos and Nikephoros Gregoras countered the criticism contemporary observers uttered against this practice. At the same time, both Byzantine and Muslim chronicles refer extensively to the sophisticated communication strategies the two sides developed with the support of skilled

---

143 Kantakouzenos, III, 28 (book IV, chapter 4): "Ὀρχάνης δὲ ὁ βασιλέως γαμβρὸς [...] πανοικησίᾳ ἦλθε πρὸς τοῦ Βυζαντίου τὴν περαίαν, ὃ Σκουτάριον ἐγχωρίως ὀνομάζεται, συνησθησόμενος ἐπὶ τῇ νίκῃ".

go-betweens on account of their linguistic and cultural competences and by way of diplomacy, gift exchange, ceremonies, ideological concepts, and close interpersonal relations. The image of John Kantakouzenos as a corrupt politician, who for his personal ambitions forsook his subjects and the empire, ignores these aspects. He rather stood for a broader historical experience which taught the Byzantine ruling elite to see the collaboration with the Turks as a successful means of political survival and consolidation. It was only after the Ottoman conquest of the Gallipoli Peninsula in 1354 that the pro-Latin faction in Constantinople came to the foreground, but this occurred under different circumstances, in which the Turks had fully emancipated from Byzantine influence and the crumbling Serbian empire gradually gave way to Ottoman expansion over Thrace and Macedonia. The Byzantine-Ottoman alliance corroborated by the matrimonial bonds of 1346 had established close dynastic links between the two families. The events of 1354 were hardly foreseeable. Rather than the result of Kantakouzenos's alliance strategy, they should be seen as the outcome of internal tensions at the Ottoman court, in which Orhan's son Süleyman sought to build up an independent base of power in the lands opposite the Karasi province and thus from raiding switched to colonizing the territories in the Thracian Peninsula.

SEBASTIAN KOLDITZ

John V Palaiologos in Rome

Rethinking an Imperial Visit and 'Conversion'

In mid-October 1364, Pope Urban V for the first time addressed a letter to John Palaiologos, 'imperatori Graecorum illustri'. The supreme pontiff had just received John's message, delivered to him by the Genoese Michael Malaspina.[1] The emperor's letter, which has not come down to us, seems to have been full of joy over the pope's recent proclamation of the *passagium generale* against the infidels—and John had even promised to join the forces of the Latins.[2] The pope praised the emperor for his intention: the 'Christi fideles, in prefato profecturi passagio' would soon come 'ad partes tui imperii' and abstain from any offence against the emperor and his subjects. The impression of harmony is, however, treacherous. The *basileus* had taken his initiative against the background of the continuous advances Ottoman forces made in the Thracian hinterland of Constantinople.[3] His *mesazon* Demetrios Kydones informs us in a private letter of the same year that John V had deliberately abstained from sending an official diplomatic mission to the Curia, disappointed as he was about the usual rumors and promises of a crusade against the Turks that never

---

1 See *Lettres secrètes et curiales du pape Urbain V (1362–1370) se rapportant à la France extraites des registres d'Avignon et du Vatican*, ed. by Paul Lecacheux and Guillaume Mollat, Bibliothèque des Écoles Françaises d'Athènes et de Rome, 3 Série (Paris: De Boccard, 1902–55), no. 1305. Previously, the letter had been published in *Caesaris S. R. E. Card. Baronii, Odorici Raynaldi et Jacobi Laderchii Annales Ecclesiastici*, 37 vols (Bar-le-Duc: Guerin, 1864–1883), XXVI, p. 103 (1364, no. 27); it is curiously absent from *Acta Urbani PP. V (1362–1370)*, ed. by Aloysius L. Tăutu, Pontificia commissio ad redigendum codicem iuris canonici orientalis, Fontes, Series III, 11 (Rome: Pontificia Universitas Gregoriana, 1964).
2 Urban V, *Lettres secrètes et curiales*, no. 1305: 'admodumque gratum redditur nostris affectibus quod tua letetur sublimitas quod ad recuperationem Terre Sancte ac impugnationem hostium superborum sacratissime fidei [...] indiximus passagium generale, quodque in tanto nostri Salvatoris obsequio [...] nobiscum et cum orthodoxis principibus aliisque Christi fidelibus ingenti, prout tua indicabat epistola, devotione concurras, ad hoc tua et tuorum subditorum auxilia prompta liberalique magnificentia offerendo'.
3 The critical situation of Byzantium in the 1360s has been outlined by Vasilike Nerantze-Varmaze, 'Κωνσταντινούπολη 1360–1370. Μιὰ περίοδος ἀποθάρρυνσης', *Byzantina*, 13/2 (1985), 923–35.

Sebastian Kolditz • University of Heidelberg

materialized.[4] The Byzantine court was quite aware that King Peter of Cyprus had not yet obtained tangible results while travelling the Occident in search of support for his crusading venture.[5]

The pope, in turn, had still another message to convey to John V. He hoped to reunite him and his people to the body of the Holy Catholic and Apostolic Church from which they had split, thereby incurring misery and injury as lost sheep that should be brought back to the Lord's flock.[6]

Once again, we encounter the well-known link between the two concerns of church union and military help so characteristic of late Byzantium,[7] but John V did not choose to play the role of the humble supplicant. Instead, he sought to enflame the crusading spirit among the Latin princes by offering his own assistance to such a venture. Perhaps his letter explicitly mentioned Peter of Cyprus, but this king is strikingly absent in Urban's reply – in contrast to the late King John II of France, who once had been designated leader of the pope's projected crusade.[8]

When in April 1365 the pope wrote again to the *basileus* informing him that the 'passagium occidentis christianorum' could not take place 'ex certis impedimentis',[9] Peter was mentioned in passing. The purpose of this letter, which perhaps had been

---

4 Demetrios Kydones, *Correspondance*, ed. by Raymond-Joseph Loenertz, Studi e testi 186, 208, 2 vols (Vatican: Biblioteca Apostolica, 1956), I, no. 93, pp. 125–28, cf. Franz Tinnefeld, *Demetrios Kydones, Briefe*, I/2, Bibliothek der griechischen Literatur, 16 (Stuttgart: Hiersemann, 1982), no. 59, pp. 353–60. The letter was addressed to Simon Atumano, recently promoted to an Italian bishopric by the pope. Earlier, he had stayed in Constantinople and had, seemingly in vain, tried to get involved in the political relations with the West.

5 Cydonès, Correspondance, I, p. 127, ll. 60–65: 'ἠξίουν δὲ ἀφορᾶν καὶ πρὸς τὸν ῥῆγα τῆς Κύπρου, ὅς, οὐχὶ διὰ πρέσβεων δεηθείς, ἀλλ' αὐτὸς δι' ἑαυτοῦ τὴν συμμαχίαν αἰτήσας τῇ τε κοινωνίᾳ τῆς πίστεως καὶ τοῦ γένους καὶ τῷ τοσαῦτ' ἀναλῶσαι εἰκότως ἂν οὐδενὸς ἀτυχῆσαι πιστεύσας, κινδυνεύει λοιπὸν αὐτῷ τῶν ἐλπίδων μεμφόμενος ἀναστρέφειν, οὐδὲν ἕτερον ἐκ τῆς ἀποδημίας κερδάνας ἢ τὸ δόξαι μόνον ἀναλωτικός τις καὶ μεγαλόψυχος εἶναι'. Cf. Tinnefeld, *Demetrios Kydones, Briefe*, I/2, p. 355, ll. 60–66. For Peter's journey in the Occident and particularly his visit to Avignon see Aziz Suryal Atiya, *The Crusade in the Later Middle Ages* (London: Methuen, 1938), p. 331; Peter Edbury, *The Kingdom of Cyprus and the Crusades, 1191–1374* (Cambridge: Cambridge University Press, 1991), p. 164; Peter Edbury, 'The Crusading Policy of King Peter I of Cyprus, 1359–1369', in *The Eastern Mediterranean Lands in the Period of the Crusades*, ed. by Peter M. Holt (Warminster: Aris and Phillips, 1977), pp. 90–105 (92) (repr. in Peter Edbury, *Kingdoms of the Crusaders: From Jerusalem to Cyprus*, Variorum Collected Studies, 653 (Aldershot: Ashgate, 1999), no. XII). See also the contributions by Peter Edbury and Christopher Schabel in this volume.

6 Urban V, *Lettres secrètes et curiales*, no. 1305, p. 211.

7 See inter alia Donald M. Nicol, 'Byzantine Requests for an Oecumenical Council in the Fourteenth Century', *Annuarium Historiae Conciliorum*, 1 (1969), 69–95.

8 For the role given to John in the projected crusade and its possible reasons, see Atiya, *Crusade*, pp. 332–34; Edbury, *Kingdom of Cyprus*, pp. 162–63; Kenneth M. Setton, *The Papacy and the Levant (1204–1571)*, 4 vols (Philadelphia: American Philosophical Society 1976–84), I, pp. 244–45; Norman Housley, *The Later Crusades: From Lyons to Alcazar, 1274–1580* (Oxford: Oxford University Press, 1992), p. 40; Maurice Prou, *Étude sur les relations politiques du pape Urbain V avec les rois de France Jean II et Charles V (1362–1370)* (Paris: Vieweg, 1888), pp. 23–29.

9 Urban V, *Lettres secrètes et curiales*, no. 1703, p. 292; see also Urban V, *Acta*, no. 74, pp. 122–23, and *Annales Ecclesiastici*, XXVI, pp. 120–21 (1365, no. 22, wrongly dated to 18 June).

occasioned by the visit of a Byzantine émigré, John Laskaris Kalopheros, at the Curia,[10] was not to secure Byzantine military cooperation, but to make the emperor reflect that the Greeks had to face calamities due to their separation from the Universal Church. John V is exhorted to visit the Apostolic See in person.[11] The Cypriot crusading initiative thus indirectly contributed to the resumption of contacts between Avignon and Constantinople after a phase of silence. The current crusading projects allowed the *basileus* to launch his own initiative—a clever step according to Oskar Halecki.[12]

Based exhaustively on archival and narrative sources, Halecki's seminal book is still the basic guide for any effort to reconsider the question of Byzantine-Western relations during the reign of John V,[13] which culminated in John's personal profession of faith in Rome in October 1369. It would be useless to give a more detailed outline of what happened in the course of these years. For the most part they were characterized by intense political and diplomatic relations among numerous actors – including the Byzantine court, the Greek Patriarchate of Constantinople, the Curia, first residing at Avignon and later, from July 1367 onwards, again on Italian soil,[14] and the court of Hungary, visited by John V early in 1366.[15] At that time, in January 1366, Pope

---

10 Ambrosius K. Eszer, *Das abenteuerliche Leben des Johannes Laskaris Kalopheros*, Schriften zur Geistesgeschichte des östlichen Europa, 3 (Wiesbaden: Harrassowitz, 1969), pp. 25–27, 123. The presence of regular Byzantine envoys ('ambaxiatoribus imperatoris Grecorum') at the Curia at this time is ascertained by financial notes regarding the gifts they received: Karl Heinrich Schäfer, *Die Ausgaben der apostolischen Kammer unter den Päpsten Urban V. und Gregor XI. (1362–1378)*, Vatikanische Quellen zur Geschichte der päpstlichen Hof- und Finanzverwaltung, 6 (Paderborn: Schöningh, 1937), p. 108 [14 April 1365].
11 Urban V, *Lettres secrètes et curiales*, no. 1703, p. 292: 'Et si pro hoc, ut te optare percepimus, ad apostolicam Sedem accederes, quod utinam facto perficias, tantumque bonum et gaudium sit ad nostra tempora reservatum, letificabis profecto ecclesiam universam [...]'.
12 Oskar Halecki, *Un empereur de Byzance à Rome. Vingt ans de travail pour l'union des églises et pour la défense de l'empire d'Orient 1355–1375*, Travaux historiques de la société des sciences et des lettres de Varsovie, 8 (Warsaw: Wydane z Zasiłku Wydziału Nauki, 1930; repr. London: Variorum, 1972), p. 86.
13 For the reign of John V in general see Radivoj Radić, *Vreme Jovana V Paleologa (1332–1391)* (Belgrade: Vizantološki Institut SANU, 1993). Byzantine-Western relations in the first half of his reign have been analyzed by Vasilike Nerantze-Varmaze, *Τὸ Βυζάντιο καὶ ἡ δύση (1354–1369). Συμβολὴ στὴν ἱστορία τῶν πρώτων χρόνων τῆς μονοκρατορίας τοῦ Ἰωάννη Ε΄ Παλαιολόγου* (Thessalonike: Aristoteleio Panepistemio, 1982).
14 For the genesis and motivation of Urban's project to bring the Curia back to Rome, see Josep Trenchs Odena, 'Albornoz, Roma y Urbano V', in *Genèse et débuts du Grand Schisme d'occident (1362–1394). Colloque 25–28 Septembre 1978* (Paris: Éditions du CNRS, 1980), pp. 95–106 (102–05); Antoine de Rosny, 'Urbain V, Pétrarque et la question romaine', in *La papauté à la Renaissance*, ed. by Florence Alazard and Frank La Brasca (Paris: Honoré Champion, 2007), pp. 135–52; Ludwig Vones, *Urban V. (1362–1370). Kirchenreform zwischen Kardinalkollegium, Kurie und Klientel*, Päpste und Papsttum, 28 (Stuttgart: Hiersemann, 1998), pp. 446–51. For the logistics, see Johann Peter Kirsch, *Die Rückkehr der Päpste Urban V. und Gregor XI. von Avignon nach Rom: Auszüge aus den Kameralregistern des vatikanischen Archivs* (Paderborn: Schöningh, 1898), esp. pp. ix–xvi.
15 The most detailed treatment of John's visit with King Louis of Hungary—besides Halecki, *Empereur*, pp. 111–37—is Nerantze-Varmaze, *Βυζάντιο*, pp. 77–124. See also Setton, *Papacy*, I, pp. 288–89; Radić, *Vreme Jovana V Paleologa*, pp. 307–12; Polymnia Katsone, *Μία επταετία κρισίμων γεγονότων. Το Βυζάντιο στα έτη 1366/1373 (η διαμάχη Ανδρονίκου και Ιωάννη Ε΄ των Παλαιολόγων)*, Byzantina Keimena kai meletai, 33 (Thessalonike: Kentro Byzantinon Ereunon, 2002), pp. 21–28; Gerald Schwedler, *Herrschertreffen des Spätmittelalters. Formen –Rituale – Wirkungen*, Mittelalter-Forschungen, 21 (Ostfildern: Thorbecke, 2008),

Urban again sent a letter to John announcing the joint campaign against the Turks that would be led by the kings Louis of Hungary and Peter of Cyprus together with the 'Green' Count Amadeus VI of Savoy, the letter's bearer.[16] Independently of this message, the Palaiologan visit to Buda culminated in a joint diplomatic effort by the emperor and King Louis at the Curia. The pope's reply to the emperor (1 July 1366) consisted in a profession of faith John V had to accept.[17] Consequently, King Louis now likewise gave priority to the *reductio Graecorum* as a precondition for his military intervention.[18]

Meanwhile, Amadeus of Savoy had departed on his crusading venture in the spring of 1366 and had succeeded in re-conquering the Ottoman stronghold of Gallipoli.[19] Afterwards the count turned his forces against the Bulgarian tsar since the latter prevented John V from returning from Hungary to his capital via Bulgarian territory.[20] In return for his successful intervention,[21] Amadeus urged the emperor to undertake to travel in person to the pope in order to profess the catholic faith and thus to set an example for the Greeks to return to the bosom of the Roman

---

pp. 349–50, 451; John Meyendorff, 'Projets de concile oecuménique en 1367: Un dialogue inédit entre Jean Cantacuzène et le légat Paul', *Dumbarton Oaks Papers*, 14 (1960), 147–77 (pp. 153–56); Elisabeth Malamut, 'Byzance, Serbie, Angevins de 1308 à 1366 et le bouleversement de l'échiquier géopolitique dans l'Orient chrétien', in *La diplomatie des états angevins aux XIIIe et XIVe siècles*, ed. by Zoltán Kordé and István Petrovics (Rome: Accademia d'Ungheria in Roma, 2010), pp. 141–53 (150–52).

16 See Urban V, *Acta*, no. 90, pp. 148–49, and *Annales Ecclesiastici*, XXVI, p. 122 (1366, nos 1–2), dated 25 January 1366. For Amadeus's crusading plans and preparations, see Eugene L. Cox, *The Green Count of Savoy: Amadeus VI and Transalpine Savoy in the Fourteenth Century* (Princeton NJ: Princeton University Press, 1967), pp. 204–09; Setton, *Papacy*, I, pp. 285–86. Recently, the question whether Amadeus's campaign should be classified as a crusade has been taken up by Matteo Magnani, 'The Crusade of Amadeus VI of Savoy between History and Historiography', in *Italy and Europe's Eastern Border (1204–1669)*, ed. by Iulian Mihai Damiani, Ioan-Aurel Pop, Mihailo S. Popović and Alexandru Simon (Frankfurt am Main: Peter Lang, 2012), pp. 215–36 (233–36).

17 See infra, n. 100.

18 Nerantze-Varmaze, *Βυζάντιο*, pp. 115–20, has argued that Louis' attitude towards John's request of help hardened when the pope's letters arrived at Buda.

19 Cox, *The Green Count*, pp. 219–20; Setton, *Papacy*, I, pp. 298–300; Nerantze-Varmaze, *Βυζάντιο*, pp. 133–34; Donald M. Nicol, *The Last Centuries of Byzantium, 1261–1453*, 2nd edn (Cambridge: Cambridge University Press, 1993), pp. 265–66.

20 This prohibition of transit resulted from the previous military conflicts between Hungary and Bulgaria in 1365 (Hungarian annexation of Vidin) and Bulgaria and Byzantium in 1364 (victory of John V): see Meyendorff, 'Projets de concile oecuménique', § 11, pp. 153–54 and 173; Vassil Gjuzelev, 'Der letzte bulgarisch-byzantinische Krieg (1364)', in *Geschichte und Kultur der Palaiologenzeit*, ed. by Werner Seibt, Österreichische Akademie der Wissenschaften, Denkschriften, 241 (Vienna: Verlag der ÖAW, 1996), pp. 29–34; John Fine, *The Late Medieval Balkans. A Critical Survey from the Late Twelfth Century to the Ottoman Conquest* (Ann Arbor: University of Michigan Press, 1994), p. 367.

21 See Setton, *Papacy*, I, pp. 301–06; Halecki, *Empereur*, pp. 147–48; Nerantze-Varmaze, *Βυζάντιο*, pp. 139–44; Radić, *Vreme Jovana V Paleologa*, pp. 318–22; *Die byzantinischen Kleinchroniken*, ed. and trans. by Peter Schreiner, Corpus Fontium Historiae Byzantinae, 12/1–3, 3 vols (Vienna: Verlag der ÖAW, 1975–79), II (1977), pp. 295–97. The most detailed source for the course of the Savoyard venture, the account book of Amadeus's paymaster Antonio Barberi, unfortunately does not outline the military events, see *Illustrazioni della spedizione in Oriente di Amedeo VI (il Conte Verde)*, ed. by Federico Bollati di Saint-Pierre (Torino: Fratelli Bocca, 1900).

Church.[22] At the same time negotiations were held in the Byzantine capital, which opened further prospects for the church union. During a long discussion with the intellectually versed ex-emperor and monk John-Joasaph Kantakouzenos in early June 1367,[23] the Latin Patriarch of Constantinople, Paul,[24] who had accompanied the Green Count on his campaign, made concessions to the Byzantine request for an ecumenical council,[25] which was to discuss matters of separation between the two churches in the course of its deliberations. This prospect opened a realistic chance to come to terms with the Roman See.[26]

Pope Urban V, however, soon rejected these ideas, when he received the Green Count, Patriarch Paul, and their entourage together with a Byzantine delegation that included ecclesiastical officials at Viterbo in October 1367.[27] Among the numerous

---

22 The exact terms of the accord between John and Amadeus did not come down to us. Some aspects can be deduced from a papal letter concerning the restitution of a pledge John V had to depose at Pera, see Halecki, *Empereur*, pp. 149–50 and 380–81 (no. 15). The Count of Savoy arrived at Constantinople shortly before or on 9 April 1367, see *Illustrazioni della spedizione*, p. 120 (no. 450). Later Savoyard historiography turned the memory of his stay there into a fictitious story of conflicts between the virtuous Amadeus and a devious emperor called 'Alexios', who sought to circumvent his engagements towards the Church of Rome: see Jean Servion's 'Chronique de Savoye' (late fifteenth century) in *Historiae patriae monumenta*, III: *Scriptores I*, ed. by Carlo Baudi di Vesme et al. (Torino: Royal Typography, 1840), colls. 314–19; cf. Daniel Chaubet, *L'historiographie savoyarde*, 2 vols, Cahiers de civilisation alpine, 12–13 (Torino: Slatkine, 1994–96), I, pp. 65–98.
23 See Meyendorff, 'Projets de concile oecuménique', pp. 156–59, 164–77: edition and translation of the Greek text of the *dialexis*. For a synopsis of such discussions, see Claudine Delacroix-Besnier, 'Rencontres entre théologiens grecs et latins et échanges culturels sous les règnes de Jean VI Cantacuzène et de Jean V Paléologue', in *Italy and Europe's Eastern Border (1204–1669)*, ed. by Iulian Mihai Damiani, Ioan-Aurel Pop, Mihailo S. Popović and Alexandru Simon (Frankfurt am Main: Peter Lang, 2012), pp. 95–108.
24 For Paul, the former archbishop of Smyrna, who in 1366 succeeded to Peter Thomas as Latin patriarch of Constantinople, see Halecki, *Empereur*, pp. 36–38; Meyendorff, 'Projets de concile oecuménique', pp. 152–53, 157; Dan Ioan Mureșan, 'Le patriarcat latin de Constantinople comme paradoxe ecclésiologique', in *Réduire le scisme? Ecclésiologies et politiques de l'union entre Orient et Occident (XIIIe–XVIIIe siècle)*, ed. by Marie-Hélène Blanchet and Frédéric Gabriel, Centre de recherche d'histoire et civilisation de Byzance, Monographies, 39 (Paris: Association des amis du Centre d'histoire et civilisation de Byzance, 2013), pp. 277–302 (294).
25 For this fundamental conception and its continuous rejection by the Avignon papacy, see inter alia Nicol, 'Byzantine requests'; Wilhelm de Vries, 'Die Päpste von Avignon und der christliche Osten', *Orientalia Christiana Periodica*, 30 (1964), 85–128 (pp. 106–09); Katherine Walsh, 'Zwischen Mission und Dialog. Zu den Bemühungen um Aussöhnung mit den Ostkirchen im Vorfeld des Konzils von Ferrara-Florenz', in *Toleranz im Mittelalter*, ed. by Alexander Patschovsky and Harald Zimmermann, Vorträge und Forschungen, 45 (Sigmaringen: Thorbecke, 1998), pp. 297–34 (318–20).
26 Cf. Meyendorff, 'Projets de concile oecuménique', pp. 159–60.
27 Amadeus, the Patriarch Paul and the Greek delegates left Constantinople on 9 June 1367, see *Illustrazioni della spedizione*, p. 146 (no. 612): 'vsque ad diem nonam mensis iunii, qua die Dominus vltima vice recessit de Pera, veniendo apud Venecias'. For the meeting with the pope at Viterbo and Rome, see Halecki, *Empereur*, pp. 163–66; Nerantze-Varmaze, Βυζάντιο, pp. 155–57. A Greek bishop who was invited to dine with the pope in the Apostolic Palace on 15 November 1367 certainly belonged to the delegation, see Schäfer, *Die Ausgaben*, p. 211: 'pro dono speciali facto per papam cuidam episcopo Greco et quibusdam suis complicibus de Grecia, qui ista die cum papa comederunt in palacio Apost. Rome 150 fl'.

letters Urban finally sent to various Byzantine recipients on 6 November 1367,[28] one was addressed to three eastern patriarchs – namely Philotheos Kokkinos of Constantinople, Niphon of Alexandria, and Lazaros of Jerusalem – but it did not even mention the plan of convening an ecumenical council. Instead, the pope praised the intention of the hierarchs 'super reductione Graecorum ad sacrosanctae Romanae ac universalis Ecclesiae unitatem' and exhorted them to persist in this attitude, which would result in an immeasurable spiritual benefit for the Greeks.[29] Urban apparently avoided making any concession to the Greek church leaders, who should instead come to the Apostolic See.[30] Kantakouzenos, whose usefulness for the progress of union the pope clearly recognized, was called upon to exhort the emperor, the clergy and the people 'ad faciendam unionem praefatam'.[31] This Roman attitude effectively snubbed the Eastern Church hierarchy and rendered the subsequent negotiations of the Latin Patriarch Paul in Constantinople awkward and inconclusive,[32] though we unfortunately do not know which reactions the papal responses actually provoked in Constantinople when they were publicly read at the Hippodrome on 24 September 1368.[33]

In need of effective aid from the Latins, John V, however, kept his promise to visit the Holy See. Most likely already in 1368, as has recently been shown,[34] he went on the journey. Arriving at Naples, he was magnificently received by Queen Joanna and her entourage on 9 August 1369.[35] Continuing his maritime journey

---

28 Urban V, *Acta*, nos 124–31d, pp. 201–13.
29 Urban V, *Acta*, no. 126, pp. 204–05.
30 Urban V, *Acta*, no. 126, p. 205: 'Ceterum valde gratum habebimus, quod cum magnifico viro Ioanne Palaeologo imperatore Graecorum illustri et cum aliis multis viris litteratis et authenticis de clero et populo Graecorum ad sanctam Sedem Apostolicam, matrem et magistram cunctorum fidelium, ad quam idem imperator venturum se obtulit, veniatis, ubi vos libenter videbimus et condignis honoribus prosequemur ac [...] tollentur schismata [...]'.
31 Urban V, *Acta*, no. 130, p. 209, addressed 'Prudenti viro Catacusino, Ordinis Sancti Basilii, olim imperatori Graecorum'.
32 This can only be deduced from Pope Urban's short answer to a seemingly discouraging report Paul had sent from Constantinople in 1368, see Halecki, *Empereur*, p. 370 (no. 11).
33 *Die byzantinischen Kleinchroniken*, I, p. 94 (no. 9/22); for comments, see II, p. 300: Schreiner is certainly right in suggesting that it was above all the pope's letter addressed to the people of the capital (Urban V, *Acta*, no. 125, pp. 202–03) which was read out. The event has also been interpreted as a deliberate measure of Philotheos Kokkinos to arouse a popular anti-Latin movement: E. M. Lomize, 'Proekt unii 1367 g. v kontekste politiki Konstantinopol'skogo Patriarchata na Balkanach vtoroj poloviny XIV v.', in *Slavjane i ich sosedi III: Katolicizm i pravoslavie v srednie veka* (Moscow: Akademija Nauk, 1991), pp. 29–40 (35–36).
34 Raúl Estangüi Gómez, *Byzance face aux Ottomans. Exercice du pouvoir et contrôle du territoire sous les derniers Paléologues (milieu XIVe–milieu XVe siècle)*, Byzantina Sorbonensia, 28 (Paris: Publications de la Sorbonne, 2014), pp. 364–66.
35 Cf. *Cronicon Siculum incerti auctoris ab anno 340 ad annum 1396*, ed. by Josephus de Blasiis (Naples: Giannini, 1887), p. 22: 'Anno domini millesimo CCCLXVIIII die VII augusti Imperator Constantinopolitanus grecus intravit cum quatuor galeis apud castrum Maris, quem domina regina satis honorifice recepit, et deinde die nono eiusdem in die sancti Laurentii dictus imperator intravit Neapolim'. See also Alexander A. Vasiliev, 'Il viaggio dell'imperatore bizantino Giovanni V Paleologo in Italia (1369–1371) e l'unione di Roma del 1369', *Studi Bizantini e Neoellenici*, 3 (1931), 151–93 (pp. 177–78).

to Rome still in the same month,[36] the emperor arrived there when the pope still resided in the region of Viterbo as he usually did during the summer months of his sojourn in Italy. By means of an embassy comprising John's distinguished *mesazon* Demetrios Kydones[37] the following steps were arranged: the pope nominated a small committee of four cardinals, which received the emperor's profession of the catholic faith – as held by the Roman and universal Church – and had it written down. This being done, the pope himself would receive John V with all honors due to a catholic prince.[38] Consequently, two acts, which took place on 18 and 21 October 1369 respectively, constituted the so-called 'conversion' of John V, who stayed at Rome until March 1370.[39]

The course of the main events is easily outlined – its bearing and significance, however, is more difficult to grasp: While contemporaries, especially the pope himself, held high expectations with regard to the impact that the emperor's conversion would have on the Greek population and Church,[40] modern scholars

---

36 *Cronicon Siculum*, p. 22; Halecki, *Empereur*, p. 190. News of John's arrival in Italy soon reached Venice where the Senate decided on 6 October to send an embassy to the *basileus* in Rome, see Setton, *Papacy*, I, p. 312, n. 193.

37 For the role Kydones had played in Byzantine relations with the papacy before 1369 and for his view of the Latins, see Frances Kianka, 'Byzantine-Papal Diplomacy: The Role of Demetrius Cydones', *The International History Review*, 7/2 (1985), 175–213 (esp. pp. 190–94); Judith R. Ryder, *The Career and Writings of Demetrius Kydones. A Study of Fourteenth-Century Byzantine Politics, Religion and Society*, The Medieval Mediterranean, 85 (Leiden and Boston: Brill, 2010), pp. 70–81; *Demetrios Kydones, Briefe*, I/1, trans. by Franz Tinnefeld, Bibliothek der griechischen Literatur, 12 (Stuttgart: Hiersemann, 1981), pp. 4–52 (15–20) ('Das Leben des Demetrios Kydones').

38 The sequence is explicitly mentioned in the *instrumentum publicum* Urban V issued at Viterbo for the nomination of the committee. This instrument became a part of the charter containing John's profession, see Luca Pieralli, 'Un imperatore di Bisanzio a Roma: La professione di fede di Giovanni V Paleologo', in *L'union à l'épreuve du formulaire*, ed. by Marie-Hélène Blanchet and Frédéric Gabriel, Centre de recherche d'histoire et civilisation de Byzance, Monographies, 51 (Leuven-Paris: Peeters, 2016), pp. 97–143 (121–22): 'nos volentes eundem imperatorem, in prima eius visione ac receptione, tamquam catholicum principem et alios Grecos, tam clericos et religiosos, quam etiam prelatos, et laicos existentes cum eo, qui ad eiusdem Ecclesie venire voluerint unitatem, professione dicte fidei ac iuramento et abiuratione [...] premissis, ad pacis osculum et alias decenter et licite recipere, et congrue honorificationis impendiis honorare'.

39 See Halecki, *Empereur*, p. 227; Vasiliev, 'Il viaggio', p. 187. For John's subsequent stay at Venice and the question of his treatment by the Venetian authorities, see Katsone, Μία επταετία, pp. 68–87; Raymond-Joseph Loenertz, 'Jean V Paléologue à Venise (1370–1371)', *Revue des Études Byzantines*, 16 (1958), 217–32; Julian Chrysostomides, 'John V Palaeologus in Venice (1370–1371) and the Chronicle of Caroldo: a re-interpretation', *Orientalia Christiana Periodica*, 31 (1965), 76–84; Radić, *Vreme Jovana V Paleologa*, pp. 350–55; Peter Schreiner, 'Gli imperatori bizantini nella cronachistica veneziana', in *The Byzantine-Ottoman Transition in Venetian Chronicles*, ed. by Sebastian Kolditz and Markus Koller, Venetiana 19 (Rome: Viella, 2018), pp. 109–23 (117–19).

40 See, for instance, a letter Urban addressed 'universis christifidelibus', announcing his joy over John's obedience and profession (13 November 1369): Urban V, *Acta*, no. 170, p. 292: 'Nos enim speramus, quod idem imperator, prout ipse Nobis fuit pollicitus, gratia Dei vestrisque favoribus communitus, circa conversionem et reductionem aliorum in huiusmodi schismate persistentium talem sollicitudinem adhibebit [...]'; the pope's expectations were even higher in his letter to the Doge of Venice (29 January 1370), Urban V, *Acta*, no. 182, pp. 309–10: 'speratur quod sicut quondam Constantini imperatoris conversio

usually agree on the assumption that John's conversion was a purely personal, private act without any relevance for the further course of discussions on church union.[41] Such an understanding is based on the notion of individual affiliation to a religious community, which has changed by an act of conversion.[42] Nevertheless, the case of a *basileus* of the Romans, who as a private person was following his conscience[43] in confessing the faith of the Roman Church while he apparently continued to exercise the prerogatives his status implied in the Eastern Church,[44] seems to me a rather anachronistic construction.

It is the aim of the present paper to discuss some aspects that might shed some new light on the nature of the act of 1369 and, more generally, on John V's ecclesiastical policy. These aspects include a closer look at the symbolic dimension of the events taking place during John's stay in Rome – as compared to another imperial visit in the preceding year. Secondly, we shall distinguish the public from the non-public elements in the act of 'conversion' and, thirdly, take into consideration the perspective of the 1350s, when John V had launched the first project of ecclesiastical reunification and supposedly had already 'converted' for the first time. Finally, the consequences of the emperor's turn towards Rome on the Byzantine stage will be discussed.

---

fuit causativa conversionis innumerabilium populorum, sic eiusdem Ioannis imperatoris exemplo et opere, gratia favente divina, infiniti populi schisma et errores Graecorum sectantes, ad caulam Domini reducentur'.

41 Inter alia Joseph Gill, *Byzantium and the Papacy, 1198–1400* (New Brunswick, NJ: Rutgers University Press, 1979), p. 221; Nicol, *Last Centuries*, p. 271 ('a purely personal matter'); Halecki, *Empereur*, p. 205 ('la conversion de l'empereur, qui restait une conversion purement individuelle au catholicisme du rite latin'); Kianka, 'Byzantine-Papal Diplomacy', p. 195; Katsone, Μία επταετία, p. 67.

42 The term 'conversion' *in nuce* contains the idea of an inwardly, necessarily individual 'return' (ἐπιστροφή) to God, see Peter Gerlitz, 'Konversion (I. Religonsgeschichtlich)', in *Theologische Realenzyklopädie*, vol. 19 (Berlin-New York: de Gruyter, 1990), pp. 559–63; see also the terminological and phenomenological discussions by Helmut Zander, *"Europäische" Religionsgeschichte: religiöse Zugehörigkeit durch Entscheidung – Konsequenzen im interkulturellen Vergleich* (Berlin-Boston: De Gruyter, 2016), pp. 222–33; Kim Siebenhüner, 'Glaubenswechsel jenseits des Eurozentrismus. Überlegungen zum Konversionsbegriff und zur Differenzierung frühneuzeitlicher Konversionsphänomene', in *Religiöse Grenzüberschreitungen. Studien zu Bekehrung, Konfessions- und Religionswechsel*, ed. by Christine Lienemann-Perrin and Wolfgang Lienemann (Wiesbaden: Harrassowitz, 2012), pp. 251–69 (251–55), and Moisés Mayordomo, '"Conversion" in Antiquity and Early Christianity: Some Critical Remarks', in ibidem, pp. 211–26.

43 Thus Nicol, *Last Centuries*, p. 271: 'But as a private individual he could follow his own conscience'. The individualistic notion of conscience, however, is an anachronistic concept for the later Middle Ages.

44 These prerogatives were fixed during the later reign of John V, see Vitalien Laurent, 'Les droits de l'empereur en matière ecclésiastique. L'accord de 1380/82', *Revue des Études Byzantines*, 13 (1955), 5–20. According to Petre Guran, 'Patriarche hésychaste et empereur latinophrone. L'accord de 1380 sur les droits impériaux en matière ecclésiastique', *Revue des Études Sud-Est Européennes*, 39 (2001), 53–62 (esp. pp. 54, 62), it was by means of this accord that John V resumed his role as *orthodoxos basileus* he had 'resigned' by his conversion. The text itself, however, does not contain any allusion to such a previous change of status.

The Symbolic Dimension of Two Imperial Visits to Rome

There is no contemporary Greek account of the visit John V paid to Rome in 1369. Even the so-called Short Chronicle no. 9, which, among other events, mentions John V's stay at Buda, the sojourn of Amadeus VI in Constantinople and the public reading of the papal letters in 1368,[45] only refers to the emperor's return in October 1371 and to the imprisonment of some aristocrats suspected of a conspiracy in December.[46] About a century later, the Greek classizising historian Laonikos Chalkokondyles provides us with a highly confused account of the emperor's travel to Venice, France, the *basileus tôn Keltôn* (in this case England), and back to Venice where the emperor was finally detained for reasons of debt.[47] Some elements of this story probably refer to Manuel II's voyage to the West in 1400–02.[48] Nevertheless, it had considerable influence on modern 'reconstructions' of John V's travel until Vasiliev's thoughtful analysis from 1931 separated facts from myth.[49] Chalkokondyles, however, talked neither about a sojourn of John V in Rome nor about an act of conversion on this occasion.[50]

We thus entirely depend on Latin sources, above all on three accounts produced in the milieu of the Curia: the so-called First Life of Urban V[51] contained in an anonymous collection of papal lives that form a continuation of Bernard Gui's *Flores chronicorum* and were presumably produced by an author of French origin under Benedict XIII;[52] the Second Life[53] written by the Apostolic *scriptor* and secretary Werner of Bonn (or

---

45 *Die byzantinischen Kleinchroniken*, I, p. 94 (nos 9/18–22).
46 *Die byzantinischen Kleinchroniken*, I, p. 94 (no. 9/23): ἔτει ͵ϛωπ΄, ὀκτωβρίῳ κη΄, ἔφθασεν στὴ Πόλη βασιλεὺς Ἰωάννης, καὶ δεκεβρίῳ ε΄ ἐκράτησαν τοὺς ἄρχοντας Γλαβᾶν, Ἰωάννην Ἀσάνην, Μανουὴλ Βρυένη, τὸν πανυπερσέβαστον τὸν Τζαμπλάκον καὶ τὸν Ἀγάλον'. Cf. Radić, *Vreme Jovana V Paleologa*, pp. 360–62.
47 Laonikos Chalkokondyles, *The Histories*, ed. and trans. by Anthony Kaldellis, Dumbarton Oaks Medieval Library, 33, 2 vols (Cambridge, Mass.: Harvard University Press, 2014), I, pp. 78–80 (book I).
48 See John W. Barker, *Manuel II Palaeologus (1391–1425): A Study in Late Byzantine Statesmanship* (New Brunswick, NJ: Rutgers University Press, 1969), pp. 167–99; for Venice, cf. Niccolo Zorzi, 'Der Empfang byzantinischer Kaiser in Venedig in palaiologischer Zeit (Johannes V., Manuel II., Johannes VIII.): Nachlese aus venezianischen und byzantinischen Quellen', in *Venedig als Bühne: Organisation, Inszenierung und Wahrnehmung europäischer Herrscherbesuche*, ed. by Romedio Schmitz-Esser, Knut Görich and Jochen Johrendt (Regensburg: Schnell & Steiner, 2017), pp. 163–84 (170–72).
49 Vasiliev, 'Il viaggio', pp. 168–76, based on a nearly exhaustive review of earlier historiography from Gibbon to the early twentieth century.
50 The only other Byzantine historian to treat the later fourteenth century, albeit very briefly, Doukas, completely ignores John V's trip to Rome. Instead, he assumes that John had made a journey of two years to Italy and Germany in his youth as co-emperor of John Kantakouzenos in order to collect funds for the defense of Constantinople. This is completely fictitious. See Ducas, *Historia Turcobyzantina (1341–1462)*, ed. by Vasile Grecu (Bucarest: Editura Academiei, 1958), p. 67 (chapter XI, 1–2).
51 *Vitae paparum Avenionensium*, ed. by Stéphane Baluze, new ed. by Guillaume Mollat, 4 vols (Paris: Letouzey et Ané, 1914–1927), I, pp. 349–82.
52 For the manuscripts of the collection, see *Vitae paparum Avenionensium*, I, pp. 570–75; for the character of these *vitae*, see Guillaume Mollat, *Étude critique sur les Vitae paparum Avenionensium d'Étienne Baluze* (Paris: Letouzay et Ané, 1917), pp. 58–82. As Mollat has clearly shown, the *Life of Urban V* in this collection essentially depends on Werner's *Second Life*, ibid., pp. 64–65.
53 *Vitae paparum Avenionensium*, I, pp. 383–93.

Hasselbecke),[54] whose history of the popes runs from Martin IV to Urban V, and finally the so-called *Iter Italicum Urbani V*,[55] transmitted in a manuscript written by the Occitan Bertrand Boysset at Arles in the fifteenth century but going back to an eye-witness, a certain Garoscus de Ulmoisca.[56]

The First Life usually provides detailed information on visits to the papal court, but it is very succinct with regard to John V: the emperor was honorably received and 'reductus ad romane Ecclesie unitatem', he swore obedience to the pope and had a bull issued confirming this act.[57] Finally, the emperor returned after a short while ('paulo post').[58]

Werner of Hasselbecke goes into more detail: according to his account, it was the emperor who expected the pope's arrival in Rome before he could make his profession on 18 October 1369. Werner also refers in some detail to the chrysobull the emperor issued on that occasion.[59] He then succinctly describes the encounter between the emperor and the pope on the following Sunday: the pope received John V at St Peter's; after the latter ascended the stairs,[60] they entered the basilica together, and Urban celebrated mass in the emperor's presence. The rest of the emperor's sojourn is passed over in silence. Werner merely tells us that John V departed in March (1370).[61]

Boysset's text is the most elaborate one: according to him, the Greek emperor made his profession in a church of the Holy Spirit. It lists the cardinals attending the event but fails to mention the emperor's written document.[62] Above all, the *Iter*

---

54 For Werner see Ludwig Schmitz, 'Wer ist Werner von Lüttich?' *Neues Archiv der Gesellschaft für ältere deutsche Geschichtskunde*, 22 (1897), 771–75; *Repertorium Fontium Medii Aevi*, 11 vols (Rome: Istituto Storico Italiano per il Medio Evo, 1962–2007), XI, p. 445; Mollat, *Étude critique sur les Vitae paparum*, pp. 48–58; for the manuscripts, see *Vitae paparum Avenionensium*, I, pp. 576, 581.
55 *Vitae paparum Avenionensium*, IV, pp. 131–37.
56 See Franz Ehrle, 'Die Chronik des Garoscus de Ulmoisca Veteri und Bertrand Boysset (1365–1415)', *Archiv für Literatur- und Kirchengeschichte des Mittelalters*, 7 (1900), 311–420 (pp. 313–17, 404–14).
57 *Vitae paparum Avenionensium*, I, p. 372: 'Anno etiam prenotato, scilicet [MCCC]LXVIIIJ, ad dictum Urbanum papam Rome existentem venit Johannes Paleologus, imperator Grecorum; fuitque receptus honorifice ac tractatus per dictum papam et cardinales paulo minus quemadmodum si fuisset imperator Romanorum. Qui demum fuit reductus ad romane Ecclesie unitatem, juravitque eidem perpetuo obedire ac fidem ipsius servare in futurum. Super quo certam bullam grece et latine conscripsit, et sua bulla aurea sigillavit, quam in archivis Ecclesie conservandam dicto pape assignavit'.
58 In fact, John V stayed in Rome until March 1370 (cf. Halecki, *Empereur*, p. 227).
59 *Vitae paparum Avenionensium*, I, p. 391: 'Eodem anno, die XIIJ octobris, dominus papa venit ad Urbem, ubi jam dominus imperator Grecorum, nomine Johannes Paleologus, expectabat eum; qui in die sancti Luche in domo Sancti Spiritus de Urbe, professionem fecit in presentia quinque cardinalium et duorum prothonotariorum, et juravit se perpetuo servaturum. Postea subscripsit manu propria cum sanguine conchilii et bulla aurea sigillavit cartam scriptam grece et latine, repositam in archiviis Ecclesie'.
60 *Vitae paparum Avenionensium*, I, p. 391: 'dominica XXJ dicti mensis, dominus papa veniens ad gradus Sancti Petri, eumdem imperatorem obvium ascendentem excepit; et simul euntes ad ecclesiam, dominus papa in ejus presentia celebravit'.
61 *Vitae paparum Avenionensium*, I, p. 392.
62 *Vitae paparum Avenionensium*, IV, p. 135: 'Item XVIIJ die mensis octobris [...] dominus inperator Grecorum, alias de Constantinnoble, fuit in una ecclesia vocata Sancti Spiritus prope Sanctum Petrum Rome. Et illa die confessus est in eadem ecclesia fidem catholicam [...] et errores Grecorum reprobavit'.

gives a vivid description of the reception at St Peter's: the pope left his residence and went to the church 'super scalam', where his cathedra had been set up. There he took seat surrounded by his cardinals. On his arrival, John V bowed his knees thrice and, drawing near, he kissed the pope's feet, hands and mouth. Thereafter, the pope rose up, took the emperor by his hand, and began chanting *Te Deum* while they made their entry into the church.[63] A large number of Greeks were attending when the pope celebrated the mass. The same day, the emperor had lunch with the pope and the cardinals.[64] Once again, the text is silent about the following months. There is only a hagiographical source from the late fourteenth century, written in order to promote the canonization of Urban V, which suggests that John V frequently sought the presence of the pope during these months, dining together with him and spending time in familiar conversation.[65] The more official Roman accounts have a clear focus on the sphere of symbolic communication and public ritual.

This also applies to another imperial visit to Rome that had taken place exactly one year before the ceremonial encounter between the pope and the basileus. On Saturday, 21 October 1368, according to the *Vita Secunda*, Urban V had encountered the Western Emperor Charles IV[66] at one of the city's northern gates, the Porta

---

[63] *Vitae paparum Avenionensium*, IV, p. 135: 'Item die XXIJ [sic!] mensis octobris, que fuit die dominica, dominus noster papa Urbanus quintus exivit de palatio suo Rome et ivit coram ecclesia Sancti Petri super scalam ; et ibi erat una cathedra bene parata pro eo cum omnibus cardinalibus et prelatis indutis cum eo. Et papa sedebat in cathedra solus in pontificalibus. Et statim venit inperator Grecorum, alias de Constantinnoble, ad eum. Et tam cito quod vidit papam flexit genua tribus vicibus. Isto facto, venit ad papam et osculavit pedes ejus, manus et os. Et postea surrexit, et accepit dictum dominum inperatorem per manum, et incepit dicere Te Deum laudamus etc. Et intraverunt in ecclesiam Sancti Petri insimul'.

[64] *Vitae paparum Avenionensium*, IV, pp. 135–36: 'Et ibi erat presens dictus inperator cum multa congregatione Grecorum. Et eadem die dominus inperator pransus fuit cum papa et etiam omnes cardinales'. A shorter French version of the itinerary preserved in the abbey of St Victor at Marseille provides no additional information, see Franz X. Glassschröder, 'Notizen über Urbans V. Romreise 1367–70 aus dem Klosterarchiv von S. Victor', *Römische Quartalschrift für christliche Altertumskunde und Kirchengeschichte*, 3 (1889), 299–302 (pp. 301–02). For the ceremony see Radić, *Vreme Jovana V Paleologa*, pp. 346–47.

[65] 'Liber de vita et miraculis beati Urbani papae quinti. Prima pars', in Joseph-Hyacinthe Albanès and Ulysse Chevalier, *Actes anciens et documents concernant le bienheureux Urbain V pape, sa famille, sa personne, son pontificat, ses miracles et son culte* (Paris: Picard, 1897), pp. 375–430, p. 392 (cap. 51): '[the Emperor of Constantinople] summo pontifici adhesit et devote obedivit, ipsum devotissime venerando, et in tantum quod propter devotionem quam dictus imperator Constantinopolitanus ad ipsum et mores suos habebat, ipsum sepissime visitabat et jocalia sibi devota tribuebat, et sepius ipso domino Urbano ignorante, dictus imperator non invitatus ad ejus prandium veniebat, et ambo simul, diversis tamen mensis paratis et ornatis more pontificali et imperiali, sua capiebant cibaria pro solo domino Urbano preparata [...]; et dictus imperator dicebat se in tali refectione melius refici in corpore et anima, quam cum tumultu et alias solemnissime sibi prandium pararetur'. Cf. Halecki, *Empereur*, p. 199.

[66] On Charles IV's second Italian campaign (1368/69), see Gustav Pirchan, *Italien und Kaiser Karl IV. in der Zeit seiner zweiten Romfahrt*, Quellen und Forschungen aus dem Gebiet der Geschichte, 6, 2 vols (Prague: Kraus, 1930); Ellen Widder, *Itinerar und Politik. Studien zur Reiseherrschaft Karls IV. südlich der Alpen*, Forschungen zur Kaiser- und Papstgeschichte des Mittelalters, 10 (Cologne: Böhlau, 1993), pp. 266–357, 442–72.

Collina.[67] This time, however, it was the pope who entered the city from outside,[68] while Charles, who had arrived ahead of the pope, welcomed him, took his horse's reins, and guided him all the way to St Peter's, thus acting 'vice stratoris', as Werner explicitly says.[69] This distribution of roles continued inside the church, where Charles led the pope to the altar.[70]

The two instances of papal-imperial encounter in 1368 and 1369 clearly show one similarity: it is always the emperor who demonstrates humility towards the successor of Peter. But at the same time there is an inversion of roles: in 1368 the emperor took the active part by introducing the pope into the city; whereas in 1369 John V, of whom no ceremonial entry is recorded, was led into St Peter's by the hand of the pope. The ceremonial arrangements for Charles IV emphasized the emperor's humility, but they also displayed his imperial rights and presented him bringing the pope back to Rome as a strong supporter of the main project of Urban's pontificate.[71] John V instead appeared as a poor stranger in Rome, who had to seek papal guidance regardless of his imperial rank.

In fact, we should not overemphasize the importance of the *basileus*'s visit in the eyes of the Latins. Curiously, neither his 'conversion' nor his solemnly staged encounter with the pope evoked an echo in narrative sources beyond the immediate sphere of the Curia. For example, there is no allusion in the letters of Coluccio Salutati who enthusiastically commented on Urban's Roman renewal in a letter to Petrarch[72] and called the pope 'non solum reparatorem Urbis, sed totius Italie, et, si fata patiantur, etiam orbis'. He also drew a vivid picture of Urban's entry led by Charles IV as the meeting of the two supreme and universal monarchs of the

---

67 Customarily, the emperors entered Rome through Porta Collina, see Achim Thomas Hack, *Das Empfangszeremoniell bei mittelalterlichen Papst-Kaiser-Treffen*, Forschungen zur Kaiser- und Papstgeschichte des Mittelalters, 18 (Cologne: Böhlau, 1999), pp. 136–39, 319.
68 The situation had been carefully arranged during a first meeting between Urban and Charles at Viterbo, see Martin Bauch, *Divina favente clemencia. Auserwählung, Frömmigkeit und Heilsvermittlung in der Herrschaftspraxis Kaiser Karls IV.*, Forschungen zur Kaiser- und Papstgeschichte des Mittelalters, 36 (Cologne: Böhlau, 2015), p. 156; Widder, *Itinerar und Politik*, p. 323. Several payments to papal *cursores* sent to the emperor in September/October 1368 suggest further negotiations: Schäfer, *Die Ausgaben*, pp. 220–21.
69 *Vitae paparum Avenionensium*, I, pp. 389–90: 'Die sabbati XXJ dicti mensis, dominus papa venit Romam; quem idem imperator, vice stratoris, addextravit a porta Colina, que est prope castrum Sancti Angeli, usque ad basilicam Sancti Petri, pedester eundo et tenendo frenum equi'. Similar details are mentioned in the *Iter: Vitae paparum Avenionensium*, IV, p. 134: 'Et ivit dictus inperator de dicta ecclesia [S. Maria Maddalena] Romam pedester, tenens frenum domini nostri pape'. Cf. Pirchan, *Italien und Kaiser Karl IV.*, pp. 298–300; Widder, *Itinerar und Politik*, pp. 324–25.
70 *Vitae paparum Avenionensium*, I, p. 390 (Vita II): 'Deinde, descendente domino papa, idem imperator ipsum deduxit usque ad altare'.
71 Urban's return of his own accord in fact foiled the emperor's ambition to become the main agent in a project to repatriate the pope to the Eternal City, see Bauch, *Divina favente clemencia*, p. 155.
72 Coluccio Salutati, *Epistolario*, vol. 1, ed. by Francesco Novati, Fonti per la Storia d'Italia, 15 (Roma: Istituto Storico Italiano per il Medioevo, 1891), libro II, no. 11, pp. 80–84 (81).

world[73] in a letter to Boccaccio. Similarly, regional Italian chronicles from Bologna,[74] Orvieto,[75] or the court of the Malatesta[76] registered many moments of the pope's Roman years (1367–70) and followed Charles IV on his way to the city and back again in 1369. But the presence of the Byzantine emperor in Italy goes completely unnoticed by them. This is still true for Bartolomeo Sacchi, called Platina, who compiled his lives of the Roman popes in the 1470s. He admitted that he lacked reliable information about a visit Charles IV had paid to Rome in Urban's pontificate – obviously misled by the date of Charles' imperial coronation in 1355.[77] In contrast to this blurred memory, however, the sojourn of John V was completely forgotten at Platina's time.

The Public and the Non-public Sphere

In the near-contemporary Lives of Urban V, the two stages of the Byzantine emperor's 'conversion' are differently treated. The *Vitae* convey detailed descriptions of the public ritual that took place on 21 October, but they ignore any details about the procedure of John's profession of faith three days earlier. The reason for this discrepancy seems obvious: John's profession did not belong to the well-staged sphere of public acts the authors of the Lives pursued so diligently; it did not even take place in a church, as Boysset makes us believe, but in the private chamber of Nicolas de Besse, cardinal deacon of Santa Maria in Via Lata (who died only some weeks later),[78] situated at the hospital of Santo Spirito in Sassia close to the Vatican.[79]

---

73 Coluccio Salutati, *Epistolario*, libro II, no. 12, pp. 85–88 (86): 'Deinde venit letissima dies qua Christi vicarius, stratore augusto, Romam intravit. Ihesu bone, quod illud spectaculum fuit, quando duo totius orbis maximi principes, imo singulares monarche, tanta pace, tanta concordia [...] insimul convenere; quando Urbanus, pontificali apparatu candido equo impositus, frenum cesare baiulante, Urbem invectus est!'.
74 *Corpus Chronicorum Bononiensium*, ed. by Albano Sorbelli, Rerum Italicarum Scriptores: Nuova edizione, 18/1 (Città di Castello: S. Lapi, 1939), III, p. 240 (Cronaca A): 'A questo tempo lo imperadore s'era partito de Thoschana, et era andato a Roma a fare lo dicto parlamento cum lo papa. [...] anzi se disse che lo imperadore gli andò incontra et aspectò alla porta et menò le redame al papa de fino a Sam Piero'.
75 *Ephemerides Urbevetanae dal Codice Vaticano Urbinate 1745*, ed. by Luigi Fumi, Rerum Italicarum Scriptores: Nuova edizione, 15/5 (Città di Castello: Lapi, 1920), I, p. 93.
76 'Cronaca Malatestiana del secolo XIV', in *Cronache Malatestiane dei secoli XIV e XV*, ed. by Aldo Francesco Massèra, Rerum Italicarum Scriptores: Nuova edizione, 15/2 (Bologna: N. Zanichelli, 1924), pp. 31–32. The emperor's stay in Rome receives very little attention, see p. 32, l. 21–23: 'Poi se partì, et andò a Roma e stette cum lo papa tuto verno, sì che non intrò mai in lo terreno de quello da Millano'.
77 *Platynae Historici Liber de vita Christi ac omnium pontificum*, ed. by Giacinto Gaida, Rerum Italicarum Scriptores: Nuova edizione, 3/1 (Città di Castello: S. Lapi, 1932), p. 279: 'At vero cum Karolus imperator intellexisset Urbanum Romam profectum, eo et ipse quoque cum uxore et liberis statim advolans, in itinere Lucam Pisanis, Miniate oppidum Florentinis adimit, sibique vendicat. Profectus ne sit Romam, haud satis constat, cum ab Innocentio Sexto pontifice Romano coronam imperii accepisse dicatur [...]'.
78 Conrad Eubel, *Hierarchia catholica medii aevi*, 2 vols, 2nd ed. (Münster: Regensberger, 1913–14), I, p. 18. He died on 5 November 1369.
79 For the accomodation of cardinals there, see Gisela Drossbach, *Christliche caritas als Rechtsinstitut. Hospital und Orden von Santo Spirito in Sassia (1198–1378)* (Paderborn: Schöningh, 2005), pp. 109–10.

The original document of John V's profession signed and sealed by the emperor is very precise in this respect.[80] The charter itself[81] uniquely combines two distinct documents on one parchment: the first of them is a bilingual imperial chrysobull, written in two columns, the Greek text on the left side and its Latin equivalent on the right, the other document is a notarial act (*publicum instrumentum*) written below the imperial signature and drafted according to the usual rules by a Roman notary, assisted by two apostolic chamber clerics.[82] The notarial act precisely attests to the procedure that had been followed:

First of all, the four cardinals, nominated for this purpose by the pope when he was still in Viterbo on 7 October 1369, commissioned three bilingual clerics, among them the Latin Patriarch Paul, to act as interpreters. Then John's profession was read out first in Greek by his *chancellor* ('cancellarius') Demetrios Kydones, then in Latin by the notary Niccolo di Checcoli. When those able to do so[83] had asserted that both versions were in perfect congruence, the emperor swore his oath and the notarial act was officially commissioned. At the end of the document, we find the list of witnesses present at this short ceremony. One archbishop, three bishops and four other *curiales* appear on the Latin side.[84] In contrast, there are only three Byzantine witnesses: Francesco Gattilusi, the ruler of Lesbos,[85]

---

80 Pieralli, 'Un imperatore', p. 123: 'in domo hospitalis Sancti Spiritus in Saxia, quam reverendissimus in Christo pater dominus Nicolaus [...] habitabat, videlicet in eius camera superiori'.
81 The original is preserved in the Vatican Archives, A.A. Arm. I-XVIII, no. 401. It had first been edited by Spyridon Lampros, 'Αὐτοκρατόρων τοῦ Βυζαντίου χρυσόβουλλα καὶ χρυσᾶ γράμματα ἀναφερόμενα εἰς τὴν ἕνωσιν τῶν ἐκκλησιῶν', *Neos Hellenomnemon*, 11 (1914), 94–128 and 241–54, nos 10–12, pp. 241–53. This reference as well as Urban V, *Acta*, nos 167–68, pp. 283–90 (Latin profession + *instrumentum publicum*) have now been replaced by Pieralli's rigorous diplomatic edition: Pieralli, 'Un imperatore', pp. 111–24 and the photographs pp. 139–41. See also Franz Dölger, *Regesten der Kaiserurkunden des Oströmischen Reiches von 565–1453*, V: *Regesten von 1341–1453*, unter verantwortlicher Mitarbeit von Peter Wirth (Munich and Berlin: C. H. Beck, 1965), no. 3122. Pieralli, 'Un imperatore', pp. 106–10, clarified the provenance of a second, partially different version of the profession, which is of no value for understanding the act of 1369 but has repeatedly been edited, inter alia in *Monumenta spectantia ad unionem ecclesiarum graecae et romanae*, ed. by Augustin Theiner and Franz Miklosich (Vienna: Wilhelm Braumüller, 1872), no. 9, pp. 37–43. *Annales Ecclesiastici*, XXVI, pp. 162–64 contains the Latin text of the emperor's profession with only few modifications; the list of witnesses is copied from the *instrumentum*.
82 The *publicum instrumentum* was issued by the Roman notary Nicolaus quondam Checcoli de Romanis de Auximo and two apostolic notaries and clerics of the papal chamber: Eblo de Mederio and Petrus de Albiartz, see Pieralli, 'Un imperatore', p. 124; cf. Schäfer, *Die Ausgaben*, p. 779, sv de Mederio, p. 714, sv de Albiartz.
83 Cf. Pieralli, 'Un imperatore', pp. 122–23: 'et prout dicti domini patriarcha et episcopus Drenopolitanus et frater Antonius, et dominus Demitrius asseruerunt in virtute prestiti iuramenti per eos retulerunt eidem domino imperatori, in lingua greca ut dixerunt, quod dicta professio scripta in latina gramatica concordabat in effectu cum dicta professione seu scriptura greca lecta per prefatum dominum Demitrium [...]'.
84 Pieralli, 'Un imperatore', p. 123. The archbishop was Arnold of Auch (1357–1371), *camerarius pape*, assisted by the bishops of Fréjus, Arezzo and Marsi; for the papal chaplain Gauselinus de Pradallo see Schäfer, *Die Ausgaben*, p. 797, s.v. de Pradallo.
85 For his role in union politics see Christopher Wright, *The Gattilusio Lordships and the Aegean World 1355–1462*, The Medieval Mediterranean, 100 (Leiden and Boston: Brill, 2014), pp. 345–46, 348–49.

and two persons whose ability to understand both Greek and Latin is explicitly referred to: the *miles* Michael Strongylos[86] and Philip Tzykandyles,[87] 'domicellus Constantinopolitanus'.[88]

At first sight, their linguistic skills sufficiently explain why these witnesses were chosen. But during the strictly bilingual ceremony anybody knowing only Greek would have been an equally good witness as the numerous Latins who did not understand Greek. Linguistic competence thus hardly explains that the Greek side nominated so few and, above all, so low-ranking witnesses. The contrast becomes evident through comparison to another important document John V issued during his stay in Rome: the renewal of the Byzantine *treugua* with Venice, dated 1 February 1370. This document[89] was written by Tzykandyles in both Greek and Latin, but the list of witnesses neither includes his own name nor that of Strongylos, but four high-ranking dignitaries in the imperial retinue: the emperor's uncle and *megas domestikos* Demetrios Palaiologos,[90] the *epi tu kanikleiu* Manuel Angelos,[91]

---

86 Not mentioned in Erich Trapp, Rainer Walther and Hans-Veit Beyer, *Prosopographisches Lexikon der Palaiologenzeit*, 12 vols, Addenda, Gesamtregister (Vienna: ÖAW Verlag, 1976-96) (hereafter PLP), but among the other bearers of that name (PLP, nos 26942–55) none was a high-ranking dignitary. Strongylos seems to have been close to the emperor in whose name he made payments to Amadeus of Savoy during the latter's crusade (*Illustrazioni della spedizione*, p. 6). He was considered a proponent of church union in a papal letter (November 1367), see Halecki, *Empereur*, p. 368 (no. 9).

87 PLP, no. 28131. Tzykandyles seemingly entered the scene in the emperor's retinue in 1369. In 1371 he received a papal letter of recommendation for the court of Cyprus (Halecki, *Empereur*, p. 249) while in 1374 he was to act as an intermediary at the imperial court for the embassy sent by Pope Gregory XI (Halecki, *Empereur*, p. 294) but was at the same time sent to the Curia by the *basileus* (Halecki, *Empereur*, p. 305). Tzykandyles can thus be seen as an important diplomatic agent in the time of John V. For a general tableau of diplomats see Sophia Mergiali-Sahas, 'A Byzantine ambassador to the West and his office during the fourteenth and fifteenth centuries: a profile', *Byzantinische Zeitschrift*, 94 (2001), 588–604 (pp. 593–98). I assume that Michael was related to Manuel Tzykandyles, the famous scribe in the service of ex-Emperor John Kantakouzenos and Demetrios Kydones, see PLP, no. 28129; Brigitte Mondrain, 'L'ancien empereur Jean VI Cantacuzène et ses copistes', in *Gregorio Palamas e oltre. Studi e documenti sulle controversie teologiche del XIV secolo bizantino*, ed. by Antonio Rigo (Florence: Olschki, 2004), pp. 249–96 (esp. pp. 250–58), but their relationship is not known.

88 Dölger, *Regesten*, V, no. 3122, is clearly wrong in mentioning further witnesses: they are erroneously transposed from no. 3127 (the treaty with Venice, 1 February 1370). Radić, *Vreme Jovana V Paleologa*, p. 346 argues that all the witnesses were already adherents of the Latin faith.

89 *Diplomatarium Veneto-Levantinum*, ed. by Georg Martin Thomas and Riccardo Predelli, 2 vols (Venice: Deputazione Veneta di storia patria, 1880–99), II, no. 89, pp. 151–56, the list of witnesses p. 156: 'presentibus auunculis carissimis nostris megadomestico domino Dimitrio Paleologo epi tu canicliu domini Manueli Angeli et domini Andronici Paleologi, ac mega etheriharca domino Alexio Listari'. See also Dölger, *Regesten*, V, no. 3127. In 1390, it was again Tzykandyles who wrote the Latin [!] text of the treaty with Venice (*Diplomatarium Veneto-Levantinum*, II, no. 135, p. 229).

90 PLP, no. 21455, a short biography in Tinnefeld, *Demetrios Kydones, Briefe*, I/2, pp. 426–30.

91 Cf. PLP, no. 91040 and Tinnefeld, *Demetrios Kydones, Briefe*, I/1, p. 195. While his identification with a homonymous *epi tou kanikleiou* active in 1354 is rather plausible, it seems to me far less obvious to identify this imperial dignitary with the *civis Thessalonicensis* praised for his adoption of the Catholic faith in a papal letter from 1365 (Halecki, *Empereur*, p. 364 [no. 5]). This identification is taken for granted by Claudine Delacroix-Besnier, 'Conversions constantinopolitaines au XIVe siècle', *Mélanges de l'École française de Rome, Moyen Age*, 105 (1993), 715–61 (pp. 739–40).

Andronikos Palaiologos[92] and Alexios Laskaris (Listari), *megas hetaireiarches*.[93] This was a truly imperial list of witnesses comparable to those of other treaties with the Serenissima.[94] We may assume that the group of Byzantine witnesses attending the emperor's profession of faith had deliberately been confined to a small number of people whose distinctive feature did not consist in rank but perhaps in a certain degree of intimacy and confidentiality with the emperor, or even more so with Demetrios Kydones, the actual *spiritus rector* of the ceremony. It was Kydones, the document tells us, who had translated the Latin original of the profession – the oath the pope had sent to the emperor in advance, not the Latin text of John's *professio* – into Greek.[95] The small circle of witnesses, all of whom favored the faith of the Latins, certainly underlines the strictly non-public character of the act of profession.

In the Greek text the profession is called a *horkômotikón mystikón grámma*. There is no Byzantine 'type' of legal document thus designated.[96] The term *horkômotikón* was regularly used for the emperor's treaties with Venice because they contained the emperor's oath.[97] More remarkable is the term *mystikón*, which is to be translated

---

92 He was fallaciously identified with the emperor's homonymous son by Halecki, *Empereur*, p. 192; corrected by Peter Charanis, 'The Strife among the Palaeologi and the Ottoman Turks, 1370–1402', Byzantion, 16 (1942/43), 286–14 (p. 291). The witness of 1370 is perhaps identifiable with an *exadelphos* of Andronikos III, cf. PLP, no. 21434.

93 PLP, no. 14526. He has been identified with Alexios Laskaris Hyaleas, present at Thessalonike in March 1368, by Estangüi Gómez, *Byzance face aux Ottomans*, p. 365 and n. 14.

94 For these treaties Sebastian Kolditz, 'Fides Graecorum et Venetorum. Absicherung und Nichterfüllung vertraglicher Bestimmungen als Faktor in den venezianisch-griechischen Beziehungen des 13. bis 15. Jahrhunderts', in *Der Bruch des Vertrages. Die Verbindlichkeit spätmittelalterlicher Diplomatie und ihre Grenzen*, ed. by Georg Jostkleigrewe and Gesa Wilangowski, Zeitschrift für Historische Forschung, Beihefte, 55 (Berlin: Duncker & Humblot, 2018), pp. 203–44. During the reigns of Manuel II and John VIII, the lists of Byzantine witnesses in these treaties usually include the names of the two *mesazontes* in hierarchical order, see the detailed discussion by Thierry Ganchou, 'Nikolaos Notaras, mésengyos tôn Ausonôn, et le mésastikion à Byzance au XVe siècle', *Bizantinistica*, 14 (2012), 151–81 (pp. 168–74). As far as I see, a systematic analysis of the names included in these lists does not yet exist for the earlier Palaeologan period.

95 Pieralli, 'Un imperatore', p. 123: 'professione [...] quam ipse dominus Demitrius ex ipsa scriptura latina in grecam litteram se asseruit transtulisse.'

96 Franz Dölger and Johannes Karayannopulos, *Byzantinische Urkundenlehre. Die Kaiserurkunden*, Byzantinisches Handbuch, III, 1.1 (Munich: C. H. Beck, 1968), pp. 100–04, tend to identify the term *horkômotikón* with a diplomatic treaty (after 1261), but the only *horkômotikón mystikón grámma* they mention is John's profession of faith (p. 49). For references to other documents termed *horkômotikón* see Lexikon zur byzantinischen Gräzität, vol. 2, fasc. 5 (Vienna: Verlag der ÖAW, 2005), s.v. ὀρκωμοτικός. The self-designation of the imperial document is given in the *corroboratio*-clause, see Pieralli, 'Un imperatore', p. 120: 'εἰς δήλωσιν τοίνυν τῶν εἰρημένων καὶ ἀσφάλειαν μείζονα τὸ παρὸν ὀρκωμοτικὸν μυστικὸν ἐξεθέμην γράμμα'; for the Latin translation of this phrase which tries to imitate the position of the words in the Greek text and therefore is necessarily secondary to the Greek text, see ibid., p. 117.

97 For the imperial oath in Palaiologan times, see Renaud Rochette, 'Empereurs et serment sous les Paléologues', in *Oralité et lien social au Moyen Age (Occident, Byzance, Islam)*, ed. by Marie-France Auzépy and Guillaume Saint-Guillain (Paris: Association des amis du Centre d'histoire et civilisation de Byzance, 2008), pp. 157–67, where several instances of oaths taken by the emperors are discussed. For the regular recurrence of imperial oath-taking in Byzantine-Venetian treaties, see Kolditz, 'Fides Graecorum et Venetorum', p. 209.

as 'private', if not 'secret', and is in explicit contrast to 'public'. In the Latin text, the document's designation is rendered quite innocently as 'iuramentum misticum instrumentum', thus avoiding an actual translation. Taken together, these observations suggest that the circumstances under which John V swore his acceptance of the Roman faith had deliberately been orchestrated in advance, most probably in the course of the negotiations Kydones had conducted at the Curia early in September 1369 when he was sent there to announce John's arrival. We thus understand why the profession was made in the absence of both the pope and the cardinals, although Urban V had already returned to Rome some days earlier.[98] The rules of rank would have compelled the emperor to bring all his high dignitaries with him to an official meeting with the pope, which necessarily would have turned the profession into a public event. It seems, however, that John Palaiologos consciously sought to ensure that the profession would not become notorious, especially not among the Greeks. The Roman sources do not purport that the profession was publicly read during the mass John V attended on October 21. What became manifest to all, instead, was the honorable appearance of the *basileus* at the stairs of St Peter, not as a gesture of humiliation[99] but of reverence to the supreme pontiff.

The text of John's profession of faith is of limited value for understanding the nature of his 'conversion', as it did not emanate from the situation itself but literally follows the formulae sent by the pope in July 1366.[100] These, in turn, can be traced back to the profession of faith Michael VIII had accepted in his negotiations with the papacy.[101] Following these precedents Urban V demanded that John V furthermore swear a *iuramentum* as well as the *abiuratio schismatis*,[102] both of which were nearly identical oaths except for the initial phrase 'omne schisma prorsus abiuro' contained

---

[98] According to the '*Iter*', Urban had arrived in Rome on 13 October 1369, see *Vitae paparum Avenionensium*, IV, p. 135; similarly, the *Vita Secunda*, see above n. 59.

[99] This is suggested by Stephen W. Reinert, 'Fragmentation (1204–1453)', in *The Oxford History of Byzantium*, ed. by Cyril Mango (Oxford: Oxford University Press, 2002), pp. 248–83 (269): 'No other Byzantine emperor had abased himself so profoundly to the papacy, which *ipso facto* reveals the extent of John V's despair over the future of his realm'.

[100] See Urban V, *Acta*, no. 107, pp. 170–75; cf. *Annales Ecclesiastici*, XXVI, pp. 123–24 [1366, nos 4–6]). Besides an extended version of the Creed the text contains passages on the sacraments, especially the Eucharist and matrimony, and on Roman primacy.

[101] For a more detailed evaluation, also with respect to the differences between the three ratifications of Michael VIII's profession (1274, 1277 and 1279), see now Pieralli, 'Un imperatore', pp. 103–06.

[102] Urban V, *Acta*, no. 108, p. 175: 'Et quia ad soliditatem et firmitatem eiusdem negotii expedit, quod tu aliique Graeci post professionem eamdem praestetis debitum iuramentum et abiuretis omne schisma, formas huiusmodi iuramenti et abiurationis, olim per clarae memoriae Michaelem Palaeologum, imperatorem Graecorum praedecessorem tuum, in simili reconciliatione praestiti ac factae [...] fecimus praesentibus annotari'. The two, originally alternative versions of the oath originated in the context of the Second Council of Lyons, see Burkard Roberg, '*Omne schisma abiuro*... Zur Eidesleistung der byzantinischen Delegation auf dem Lugdunense II von 1274', in *Aus Archiven und Bibliotheken. Festschrift für Raymund Kottje zum 65. Geburtstag*, ed. by Hubert Mordek (Frankfurt: Peter Lang, 1992), pp. 373–90. The *abiuratio* as a personal oath of the emperor later appears in Michael VIII's letter to Pope John XXI, sent in April 1277, see Luca Pieralli, *La corrispondenza diplomatica*, no. 20, pp. 321–22.

in the *abiuratio*.¹⁰³ John's profession, however, omits the *abiuratio*. Instead, a short phrase is inserted in the *iuramentum* before the statement on papal primacy: 'et abrenuntio omni scismati'.¹⁰⁴ We do not know whether the change from 'abjure' to 'renounce' reflects a deliberate decision. Another aspect is perhaps more important: Although the profession contains doctrines unacceptable to the Greek Church such as the *filioque*,¹⁰⁵ the text neither refers to 'errors' of the Greeks nor does it anathematize the eastern christians or demand a rejection of the Greek Church. It merely contained an abjuration of schism, that is, the pitiful state of ecclesiastical separation. Therefore, the question arises whether the act the Byzantine emperor performed at Rome can really be understood as an act of 'conversion', definitions of which usually include the rejection of at least those elements of a former religious belief considered irreconcilable with the new religious adherence.¹⁰⁶ In order to discuss this question, we have to look back to the time before 1369.

John V's First Rapprochement to the Papacy and Its Background

John V had already sought a rapprochement with the papacy in late 1355, when he drafted an ambitious project for a future church union and forwarded it to Urban's predecessor Innocent VI.¹⁰⁷ I do not intend to go into the details of that well-known plan, such as the emperor's promises to send his son Manuel to Avignon, to support a plenipotentiary papal legate in his attempts to bring the Greeks to Roman obedience and to found Latin schools for the education of the Byzantine elite.¹⁰⁸ These proposals have been

---

103 The *iuramentum* formula in Urban V, *Acta*, no. 108, pp. 175–76, is nearly litterally reproduced in the emperor's profession: Pieralli, 'Un imperatore', p. 117, inc: 'Unde suprascriptam fidei veritatem', des.: 'canonum subiacere'. The second formula (no. 108, p. 176, inc.: 'Ego Ioannes, etc., omne schisma prorsus abiuro et suprascriptam'), instead, does not occur.
104 See Pieralli, 'Un imperatore', p. 117; cf. ibid., p. 120 (in Greek): 'καὶ παντὶ σχίσματι παντελῶς ἀποτάσσομαι'.
105 Pieralli, 'Un imperatore', p. 116 (Latin): 'Credo etiam spiritum sanctum plenum et perfectum, verumque Deum ex patre et filio procedentem [...]' and p. 118 (Greek): '"Ετι πιστεύω τὸ πνεῦμα τὸ ἅγιον ἐντελῆ καὶ τέλειον καὶ ἀληθῆ Θεόν, ἐκ πατρὸς καὶ υἱοῦ ἐκπορευόμενον [...]'.
106 See the discussion by Tia M. Kolbaba, 'Conversion from Greek Orthodoxy to Roman Catholicism in the Fourteenth Century', *Byzantine and Modern Greek Studies*, 19 (1995), 120–34 (pp. 122–23), who argues that acceptance (of the *filioque*, etc.) and renunciation (of Greek doctrines) constituted the act of conversion. Cf. the nearly contemporary cases of conversion to the Greek Church mentioned in the register of the patriarchate, infra n. 161.
107 The text of John's promise is transmitted in a collection of letters and documents regarding church union, missionary activities among the Mongols, and the affairs of Romania compiled in the Vatican register 62: This collection, written in 1367, was commissioned by Urban V prior to his journey to Rome: Karl Borchardt, 'Reg. Vat. 62: Ein päpstliches Dossier zur Politik gegenüber Ungläubigen und Schismatikern aus dem Jahre 1369', *Quellen und Forschungen aus italienischen Archiven und Bibliotheken*, 76 (1996), 147–218 (pp. 156–60). It is thus highly probable that Urban V was fully aware of the existence of John's earlier promise (ibid., p. 206 [no. 177]) when he received the emperor in Rome in 1369, but the register does not contain any document concerning the relations between John V and the papacy after 1355.
108 For a detailed discussion see Halecki, *Empereur*, pp. 31–42; Gill, *Papacy*, pp. 208–10; Nerantze-Varmaze, Βυζάντιο, pp. 58–60.

regarded either as completely unrealistic[109] or as a sign of profound Latin conviction that might have originated from the influence exerted by his mother Anna of Savoy.[110]

We should, however, be cautious regarding the terminology. The emperor's promise consisted in being loyal, obedient, and reverent towards the pope and the universal Church of Rome and to receive the papal legates with due reverence.[111] The union of churches was alluded to as an aim of the emperor's policy, but the central concepts are obedience and reverence, while matters of faith remain virtually absent. Nor did the emperor make an unconditional offer. He expected military aid against his enemies in return,[112] particularly against the infidels, and he demanded that the Curia bear the expenses of a joint Christian campaign under John's personal command.[113]

Previously, another ruler, namely the Serbian tsar Stephan Dušan, had made almost the same demand on the pope, as Halecki noticed.[114] This becomes clear from Innocent's reply to Dušan in December 1354.[115] And it is very likely that the papal

---

109 According to Gill, *Papacy*, p. 209, the chrysobull was 'at the same time fantastic and realistic. Fantastic in implying that the Greeks at large would accept union within six months [...] realistic in that it did not start off demanding a world-crusade'.

110 It is often assumed that Anna's Latin background conditioned her son's positive attitude towards the Roman Church, cf. Halecki, *Empereur*, p. 204; de Vries, 'Die Päpste von Avignon', pp. 88–89. In fact, we lack any evidence of a pro-Latin tendency in John's education or of such an influence on his early policy. The religious dimension of Anna's marriage to Andronikos III is discussed by Sandra Origone, *Giovanna di Savoia alias Anna Paleologina. Latina a Bisanzio (c. 1306 –c. 1365)* (Milan: Jaca, 1999), pp. 46–49. In the 1350s, the empress dowager rather embraced Palamism instead of returning to Latin beliefs, ibid., pp. 148–49, but the Franciscan influence on her is stressed by Walsh, 'Zwischen Mission und Dialog', pp. 324–26. Anna died as an Orthodox nun and was remembered in the Synodicon of Orthodoxy: Jean Gouillard, 'Le synodikon de l'Orthodoxie: édition et commentaire', *Travaux et Mémoires*, 2 (1967), 1–316 (pp. 101–03).

111 *Monumenta spectantia ad unionem ecclesiarum graecae et romanae*, no. 8, pp. 29–37 (p. 34, in Latin): 'quod ero fidelis, obediens, reuerens et deuotus beatissimo patri et domino domino Innocentio [...] et eius successoribus, et obseruabo et percomplebo debitam obedientiam et reuerentiam ad ipsum sanctissimum papam et eius successores, et recipiam legatos et nuntios suos cum omni reuerentia et deuotione', (p. 29, in Greek): 'ἵνα ὦ πιστὸς καὶ ὑπήκοος εἰς σέβας τε καὶ εὐμένειαν τῷ μακαριωτάτῳ πατρὶ καὶ δεσπότῃ κυρῷ Ἰννοκεντίῳ ... καὶ τοῖς αὐτοῦ διαδόχοις, καὶ διατηρῶ καὶ ἐκπληρῶ τὴν ὀφειλομένην ὑπακοήν τε καὶ τὸ σέβας πρός τε αὐτὸν τὸν ἁγιώτατον δεσπότην τὸν πάπαν καὶ τοὺς αὐτοῦ διαδόχους, καὶ δέχωμαι τοὺς δελεγάτους αὐτοῦ καὶ ἀποκρισιαρίους μετὰ παντὸς σεβάσματος καὶ εὐμενείας'. For similar oath formulas, see Christopher Schabel, 'Ab hac hora in antea: Oaths to the Roman Church in Frankish Cyprus (and Greece)', in *Crusader landscapes in the medieval Levant. The archaeology and history of the Latin East*, ed. by Micaela Sinibaldi et al. (Cardiff: University of Wales Press, 2016), pp. 361–71. The absence of matters of faith in the oath is thus not surprising. I express my sincere thanks to Christopher Schabel for clarifying this point and for his further valuable comments on this study.

112 *Monumenta*, no. 8, p. 36: 'quod dictus dominus papa me adiuuet contra omnes inimicos meos et maxime infideles cum maiori exercitu et multitudine Cristianorum'.

113 *Monumenta*, no. 8, p. 36: 'quod dominus noster papa provideat nobis de expensis fiendis et de stipendijs erogandis pro aliqua parte exercitus. [...] Item quod ego sim principalis capitaneus, signifer et vexillarius sancte matris ecclesie'.

114 See Halecki, *Empereur*, pp. 41–42.

115 *Acta Innocentii PP. VI (1352–1362)*, ed. Aloysius L. Taŭtu, Pontificia commissio ad redigendum codicem iuris canonici orientalis, Fontes III, 10 (Rome: Pontificia Universitas Gregoriana, 1961), no. 28, pp. 50–55 (the date is to be corrected to 24 December 1354), p. 52: inter alia Stephan had demanded 'contra Turchos ipsos capitaneus ordinari, ut ipsius Ecclesiae spirituali adiutus auxilio et directus consilio [...] populum de luporum eorundem, scilicet Turchorum, faucibus potenter erueres [...]'.

embassy sent to the Serbian court, which included Peter Thomas, the future legate of great renown, was still engaged in difficult and ultimately futile negotiations[116] when John sent his offer to Avignon – a few days before Dušan died. The fanciful project developed by the young Palaiologos should thus be read against the background of a precarious power constellation in the region: the powerful 'tsar of the Serbs and the Greeks'[117] obviously was the most dangerous rival of John V, who in turn had managed to forge ties of friendship and peace with other regional powers in the first year of his undivided sovereignty and continued to do so, even with the Ottomans.[118] At the same time, the two imperial rivals in the southern Balkans also dispatched their respective envoys to the newly-crowned Western Emperor Charles IV, and both of them received friendly responses from him.[119] Eventually, Palaiologan prestige prevailed: Stephan was merely addressed as *rex Rassie* in the response issued by Charles's chancery. In contrast, John's imperial title was unconditionally acknowledged by his western counterpart.[120]

The political nature of John V's proposal in 1355 is thus evident. It did not imply an imminent religious conversion although Pope Innocent VI gave it exactly this interpretation in a message he sent to the unnamed 'patriarch of the Greeks' (at that date Kallistos I) in August 1356: illuminated by the Holy Spirit, John

---

116 These negotiations are treated in detail in: *The Life of Saint Peter Thomas by Philippe de Mézières*, ed. by Joachim Smet (Rome: Institutum Carmelitanum, 1954), chapters 20–22: Dušan is depicted as the prototype of a despotic ruler in this hagiographic account. See Frederick J. Boehlke, *Pierre de Thomas: Scholar, Diplomat, and Crusader* (Philadelphia: University of Pennsylvania Press, 1966), pp. 83–100; Renate Blumenfeld-Kosinski, 'Philippe de Mézières's Life of Saint Pierre de Thomas at the Crossroads of Late Medieval Hagiography and Crusading Ideology', *Viator*, 40/1 (2009), 223–48 (pp. 238–39). For the duration of Peter's stay in Serbia from March 1355 to spring 1356 see Boehlke, *Pierre de Thomas*, p. 98.

117 The Greek version of Dušan's imperial title (assumed at the end of 1345) emphasized territorial connotations ('βασιλεὺς καὶ αὐτοκράτωρ Σερβίας καὶ Ῥωμανίας') and differed from the ethnocentric Slavic form *car Srbljem i Grkom*. Both versions, however, contained at least an implicit claim to replace Byzantium. For the background of the title, see George Christos Soulis, *The Serbs and Byzantium during the reign of Tsar Stephan Dušan (1331–1355) and his Successors* (Washington: Dumbarton Oaks, 1984), pp. 27–31; Ljubomir Maksimovic, 'L'empire de Stefan Dušan: Genèse et caractère', *Travaux et mémoires*, 14 (2002), 415–28 (pp. 423–28).

118 In the course of 1355, John V concluded a treaty with the rival emperor Matthew Kantakouzenos (Dölger, *Regesten*, V, no. 3039), similarly with the Bulgarian tsar Ivan Alexander (Dölger, *Regesten*, V, no. 3047). The emperor granted privileges to his supporter Francesco Gattilusio on Lesbos (Dölger, *Regesten*, V, no. 3043) and intervened in the affairs of the Russian church (ibid., no. 3045). In the following years he also obtained a temporary alliance with the Ottoman Emir Orḫan, see now Thierry Ganchou, 'Les chroniques vénitiennes et les unions ottomanes des filles de l'empereur byzantin Jean V Palaiologos, Eirènè et Maria (1358 et 1376)', in *The Byzantine-Ottoman Transition in Venetian Chronicles*, ed. by Sebastian Kolditz and Markus Koller, Venetiana, 19 (Rome: Viella, 2018), pp. 163–96 (172–79). For a critical discussion of the assumption that Dušan died on a campaign against Byzantium see Fine, *Late Medieval Balkans*, p. 335.

119 *Collectarius perpetuarum formarum Johannis de Geylnhusen*, ed. by Hans Kaiser (Innsbruck: Wagner, 1900), no. 179 and 180, pp. 167–70.

120 See *Collectarius*, no. 179, p. 167: 'Illustri principi domino Stephano Rassie regi, fratri nostro in Christo karissimo'; *Collectarius*, no. 180, p. 169: 'Johanni Paliologo, imperatori Constantinopolis, consanguineo et amico nostro carissimo'. Cf. Bernd-Ulrich Hergemöller, *Cogor adversum te. Drei Studien zum literarisch-theologischen Profil Karls IV. und seiner Kanzlei* (Warendorf: Fahlbusch, 1999), pp. 357–61.

Palaiologos had abjured schism and errors and had converted ('conversus') to the bosom and faith of the Roman and universal Church whose absolute primacy he acknowledged.[121] Did the pope indeed believe, as he wrote, that the patriarch had been 'operis promotor' and that he would continue his efforts for the 'conversion of the multitude of the Greeks'?[122] John V also received a papal letter exhorting him to persist in his religious zeal. This message was full of rhetorical praise and void of political or military commitment,[123] but it did not allude to the notion of conversion. We might therefore conclude that the idea of conversion played a certain role in contemporary interpretations of John's project, but it did not correspond to the emperor's intention.

A scenario of conversion is, however, closely related to the subsequent mission of Peter Thomas, the papal envoy who visited John V in 1356/57. This encounter is only recorded in Peter's Life written by Philip of Mézières.[124] According to his account the envoy found the emperor campaigning and, being honorably received,[125] started to preach and discuss the catholic faith with the Greeks ('semper de fide Catholica cum Graecis disputante') in the hope of gaining them for the true light of the Roman Church.[126] In the end, the emperor 'factus est verus Catholicus et obediens ecclesiae Romanae articulos fidei sigillatim confitendo'.[127] He took an oath to the envoy, promised to depose the 'perfidious' patriarch and to have a 'Catholic one' elected in his place.[128] John also received the Eucharist at Peter's hands. Philip of Mézières's hagiographic account cannot be influenced by John's later Roman

---

121 Innocent VI, *Acta*, no. 91, p. 171: 'quod imperator idem schismate et erroribus, quibus antea tenebatur implicitus, abiuratis, ad sanctae Romanae, catholicae atque apostolicae et universalis Ecclesiae gremium ac ad unam et indivisibilem fidem eiusdem Ecclesiae, extra quam, teste Apostolo, nulli est gratia, nulli salus, usus consilio meliori, conversus, Ecclesiam ipsam in suam et universorum christifidelium dominam [...] firmiter et simpliciter recognovit'.
122 Innocent VI, *Acta*, pp. 171–72: the pope considers the patriarch the emperor's main adviser and 'principalem salutaris huiusmodi operis promotorem' though he wonders that he had not received any patriarchal letter; nevertheless he exhorts the patriarch 'quatenus prudenter considerans, quantis illa civium supernorum anima gaudiis exultabunt, in tua et ipsius imperatoris ac numerosae multitudinis Graecorum conversione, quam, Deo propitio, consequi credimus et speramus [...] huiusmodi salutare opus, praestante Deo, feliciter inchoatum, usque ad eius felicem exitum, quod pius et misericors dignetur ipse concedere, operosis et efficacibus assidue studiis prosequaris'.
123 Innocent VI, *Acta*, no. 84a, pp. 155–58, dated 21 July 1356.
124 *Life of Saint Peter Thomas*, pp. 74–75; see Boehlke, *Pierre de Thomas*, pp. 141–50; brief allusions in Blumenfeld-Kosinski, 'Philippe de Mézières's Life of Saint Pierre de Thomas', p. 239.
125 *Life of Saint Peter Thomas*, p. 74: 'Postea in quodam exercitu ubi imperator erat venit, ibique ab imperatore et suis baronibus cum magnis laudibus et honoribus receptus fuit'.
126 *Life of Saint Peter Thomas*, p. 75: Peter Thomas hoped 'ut ad verum lumen ecclesiae Romanae caecitatem Graecorum reducere valeret'. For the role of preaching in the Life of Peter Thomas, see Nicholas Coureas, 'Philippe de Mézières' portrait of Peter Thomas as a preacher', *Carmelus*, 57/1 (2010), 63–80.
127 *Life of Saint Peter Thomas*, p. 75.
128 *Life of Saint Peter Thomas*, p. 75: 'hoc in manibus ipsius Domini Fratris Petri tactis manibus ad sancta Dei evangelia iuravit, omnia etiam promittens observare et facere observari pro posse quae ad sanctam ecclesiam Romanam pertinent, necnon patriarcham Graecum perfidum et unitatis ecclesiae inimicum promisit deponi, et unum alium Catholicum eligi debere'.

'conversion' since the Life was already written in 1366.[129] Though the author was not an eyewitness of these events, he inserted a document into his work which corroborates his narrative and displays all characteristics of authenticity.[130] In this letter to the pope, dated 7 November 1357, John V narrated that Peter had asked him whether he would confess the doctrines of the Roman Church. After consulting his dignitaries, John replied in a sophisticated manner: he would continue to work for the union of the two churches and he repeated his promise to be obedient to the pope.[131] Furthermore John took the oath to abide personally in the faith of the Roman Church and in his obedience to the pope.[132] Once again the concept of obedience played a dominant role, but John V was ready to make further personal advances to the papal demand of a profession of faith. With regard to his people and the Greek Church, however, he declared that he was unable to make all of his subjects share his obedience. Only if a papal legate arrived with galleys and auxiliary troops could the emperor win the people over. Nevertheless, optimism prevailed: John attributed his recent successes, such as the defeat of his rival Matthew Kantakouzenos, to the pope's blessings[133] and reassured the pope that he would depose the patriarch.[134] Such far-ranging prospects, however, were deferred to the future. They do not mitigate the impression of a rather balanced, if not reluctant, response John gave to the pope. Probably, the Curia considered this insufficient. At this point the exchange of letters was effectively interrupted for some years.

It is difficult to answer the question as to whether John V had for the first time converted long before 1369.[135] Undoubtedly, the *basileus* had assured his obedience to Rome and even professed his acceptance of 'anything held by the Roman Church'. But this does not mean that he had turned away from the Byzantine Church, over which he continued to preside. The papacy's position is equally inconsistent. In 1359, Innocent VI addressed the *basileus* in a manner appropriate for a catholic prince, but his successor Urban V stopped doing so.[136]

---

129 For the date of composition of the *Vita* immediately after the death of Peter Thomas early in 1366, see Nicolae Jorga, *Philippe de Mézières (1327–1405) et la croisade au XIVe siècle* (Paris: 1896, repr. London: Variorum, 1973), pp. 343–45; Blumenfeld-Kosinski, 'Philippe de Mézières's Life of Saint Pierre de Thomas', p. 236.

130 The letter is inserted in *Life of Saint Peter Thomas*, pp. 76–79; It has also been edited in Innocent VI, *Acta*, no. 109, pp. 200–03; see furthermore Dölger, *Regesten*, V, no. 3071; Boehlke, *Pierre de Thomas*, pp. 147–48.

131 *Life of Saint Peter Thomas*, p. 77: 'Et cum consilio et deliberatione baronum nostrorum dicto Fratri Domino Petro respondimus quod, sicut promisimus ita volumus, ut simus obedientes et fideles ac devoti Romanae ecclesiae, immo et promittimus et iuramus'.

132 *Life of Saint Peter Thomas*, pp. 77–78: 'et firmiter ego promitto et teneo omnia integre quae sancta Romana ecclesia tenet'. The switching from 'we' to 'I' might corroborate the personal character of the subsequent profession.

133 *Life of Saint Peter Thomas*, p. 78. Matthew Kantakouzenos had been defeated by the Serbian *kaisar* Vojihna and handed over to John V in 1357, see Estangüi Gómez, *Byzance face aux Ottomans*, pp. 125–26.

134 *Life of Saint Peter Thomas*, p. 79.

135 In favour of this assumption: Boehlke, *Pierre de Thomas*, p. 149.

136 Boehlke, *Pierre de Thomas*, p. 164, who also refers to the military aid Innocent mobilized for the East in 1359, again via his legate Peter Thomas (ibid., pp. 166–68). For the later address formula and its implications see Delacroix-Besnier, 'Conversions constantinopolitaines', pp. 727, 731–32.

Our difficulty in understanding the emperor's position is primarily due to (early) modern binary concepts of exclusive belonging to one church or another,[137] which is also implied by theoretical models of conversion. Accordingly, professing either the 'Latin faith' or the 'Greek' one would necessarily mean belonging exclusively to the Latin Church or the Greek Church, respectively. But perhaps, these boundaries did not seem as rigid for John himself: he might either have had a rather blurred conception of them, or he blurred them intentionally as far as possible. Probably his personal life did not change substantially in the wake of his profession in 1357. Did the Roman 'conversion' of 1369 really have a stronger effect? Did it affect the emperor's status or his memory? And how did it influence the general dynamics of 'conversion' so markedly visible at Constantinople[138] in the second half of the fourteenth century? We can only make some short remarks on these issues.

Traces of the Imperial 'Conversion' in the Aftermath of 1369?

First of all, it appears to me that John V Palaiologos remained the 'Orthodox emperor of the Romans' after 1369. Admittedly, the last twenty years of his long reign were characterized by frequent dynastic troubles,[139] but it seems rather improbable that the emperor's legitimacy as an Orthodox ruler was at stake during these conflicts, at least in the 1370s.[140] Although John had been accorded a portable altar[141] and the right to

---

137 Phenomena of multiple religious belonging including the Christian faith have only recently come into the focus of systematic studies, cf. inter alia *Many Mansions? Multiple Religious Belonging and Christian Identity*, ed. by Catherine Cornille (New York: Orbis, 2002); *Many yet one? Multiple religious belonging*, ed. by Peniel J. R. Rajkumar and Joseph Prabhakar Dayam (Geneva: World Council of Churches Publications, 2016). These studies, however, concentrate on adherence to various religious traditions, not on pluri-confessional Christian identities.
138 For a general outline see Delacroix-Besnier, 'Conversions constantinopolitaines'.
139 Cf. Charanis, 'Strife among the Palaeologi', pp. 287–300; Barker, *Manuel II Palaeologus*, pp. 18–36; Jonathan Harris, *The End of Byzantium* (New Haven: Yale University Press, 2010), pp. 47–50, 54–55; Thierry Ganchou, 'Autour de Jean VII: Luttes dynastiques, interventions étrangères et résistance orthodoxe à Byzance (1373–1409)', in *Coloniser au Moyen Âge*, ed. by Michel Balard and Alain Ducellier (Paris: Armand Colin, 1995), pp. 367–85 (esp. pp. 368–69, 373–74); Katsone, Μία επταετία, pp. 91–162.
140 In the long run, religious affiliations might have played a certain role in the formation of 'parties', especially around Andronikos IV and his son John VII who enjoyed a particularly Orthodox renown: see Ganchou, 'Autour de Jean VII', pp. 375–77. But there is no explicit evidence for immediate repercussions of John V's 'conversion'. When Ganchou, p. 375, assumes 'il restait l'idée choquante que le protecteur et le défenseur naturel de l'Église orthodoxe eût «latinisé»', it remains unclear which voices declared themselves shocked about the emperor's 'latinismos'. Recently, Estangüi Gómez, *Byzance face aux Ottomans*, pp. 201–69, has convincingly stressed the political and economic achievements of John V in the early 1370s, particularly in Macedonia, tolerated by the Ottomans. This led to the formation of a 'turkophile' aristocratic faction around Andronikos IV which primarily opposed the political, not the religious, rapprochement between John V and Rome.
141 See *Urbain V (1362–1370): Lettres communes analysées d'après les registres dits d'Avignon et du Vatican*, ed. by Marie-Hyacinthe Laurent, Michel Hayez, Mathieu Janine, Anne-Marie Hayez, Bibliothèque des Écoles Françaises d'Athènes et de Rome, 12 vols (Paris: De Boccard, and Rome: École française, 1954–1989), IX (1983), no. 26466, p. 201; the object of this concession (13 February 1370) is omitted in the partial edition in Urban V, *Acta*, no. 183, pp. 310–11.

privately attend mass according to the Latin rite at his palace early in the morning[142] by Pope Urban V, the Greek palace clergy continued to serve the imperial family. This is evident from the famous trial of the protopapas Konstantinos Kabasilas, who was repeatedly tried for various dogmatic deviations by the patriarchal synod between 1383 and 1385.[143] In the course of the trial the emperor repeatedly intervened in favour of this cleric.[144] An even more striking argument concerns the emperor's lasting memory: he was unqualifiedly commemorated among the Orthodox emperors in the diptychs that were included in the Synodicon of Orthodoxy.[145] Although he is not praised like his father-in-law John Kantakouzenos, who fought against the heresies of Barlaam and Akindynos,[146] the formula used to commemorate John V does not differ from that for other emperors. An emperor of questionable orthodoxy, such as the unionist Michael VIII, would of course have been erased from the diptychs.[147] Obviously, John V did not belong to that category in the eyes of his contemporaries and in the official memory of the Greek Church. This observation corresponds to what has been stated above, that John V's 'conversion' is not mentioned in the works of late Byzantine historiography. Even Silvestros Syropulos did not refer to it in his monumental history of the Council of Florence, at least not in those parts that have come down to us. The contents of the missing first book cannot be reconstructed,[148]

---

142 Urban V, *Lettres communes*, IX, no. 26547, p. 222: 'conceditur ut sibi per proprium vel alium sacerdotem latinum duntaxat et alias idoneum, juxta ritum quem eadem Romana servat Ecclesia, antequam illucescat dies missam celebrari facere valeat'.

143 See Christof Kraus, 'Der Fall des Priesters Konstantinos Kabasilas. Historische Bemerkungen zu einem Urkundenkomplex im Patriarchatsregister von Konstantinopel aus den Jahren 1383–1385', in *Wiener Byzantinistik und Neogräzistik*, ed. by Wolfram Hörandner, Johannes Koder, Maria A. Stassinopoulou (Vienna: Verlag der ÖAW, 2004), pp. 248–63.

144 Kabasilas held the office of protopapas at the Blachernai Church and protopapas of the *basilikos klêros*. Due to the lack of sources, the structure and prosopography of the imperial clergy in late Byzantium cannot be reconstructed in detail, see Christof Kraus, *Kleriker im späten Byzanz. Anagnosten, Hypodiakone, Diakone und Priester 1261–1453*, Mainzer Veröffentlichungen zur Byzantinistik, 9 (Wiesbaden: Harrassowitz, 2007), pp. 427–33. For the emperor's interventions in favour of Kabasilas, see Kraus, 'Der Fall des Priesters Konstantinos Kabasilas', pp. 250–51, 254, arguing for a strong personal relationship between the emperor and Kabasilas.

145 'Le synodikon de l'Orthodoxie', p. 99: "Ἰωάννου τοῦ ἐν εὐσεβεῖ τῇ μνήμῃ γενομένου ἀοιδίμου βασιλέως ἡμῶν τοῦ Παλαιολόγου αἰωνία ἡ μνήμη' (for the formulas ibid., p. 97).

146 'Le synodikon de l'Orthodoxie', p. 99. Kantakouzenos is praised as 'τοῦ στερρῶς ὑπὲρ τῆς ἐκκλησίας Χριστοῦ καὶ τῶν ὀρθῶν αὐτῆς δογμάτων καὶ λόγοις καὶ πράγμασι καὶ διαλέξεσι καὶ συγγράμμασι ὅλῃ ψυχῇ διὰ βίου ἀγωνισαμένου [...]'.

147 'Le synodikon de l'Orthodoxie', p. 97: Theodore (II Laskaris) Dukas is immediately followed by Michael the Younger ('τοῦ νέου'), i.e., Michael IX, who precedes his father Andronikos II in memory due to his earlier death. The disambiguating attribute makes unmistakebly clear that Michael VIII was omitted. For his *damnatio memoriae*, burial and the Orthodox confession of Empress Theodora after his death, see Ekaterini Mitsiou, 'Regaining the true faith: The confession of faith of Theodora Palaiologina', in *L'union à l'épreuve du formulaire*, ed. by Marie-Hélène Blanchet and Frédéric Gabriel, Centre de recherche d'histoire et civilisation de Byzance, Monographies, 51 (Leuven-Paris: Peeters, 2016), pp. 77–96.

148 For this loss due to missing folia in the manuscript Cod. Paris. gr. 427, see Laurent's remarks in *Les « Mémoires » du Grand Ecclésiarque de l'Église de Constantinople Sylvestre Syropoulos sur le concile de Florence*, ed. by Vitalien Laurent, Concilium Florentinum Documenta et scriptores, 9 (Paris: Éditions du CNRS, 1971), pp. 49, 62.

but to judge from the surviving text, Syropulos nowhere alluded to John V as predecessor of his grandson's unionist policy.[149] It rather seems that the confession of 1369 had passed almost unnoticed in contemporary Byzantium.

Consequently, it did not impact the dynamics of 'conversion' to the Latin faith in a way Pope Urban V had hoped when he announced the emperor's step to the eastern clergy.[150] Instead, other forces played a major role in initiating conversion movements among the Byzantine elite, such as the activities of the Dominican friars at Pera,[151] the missionary zeal of Peter Thomas in the 1350s, or the formation of a close network of Latinophile intellectuals around Demetrios Kydones in the later decades of his life.[152] The case of Kydones furthermore shows that the Palamite controversy played a fundamental role in alienating numerous Byzantine intellectuals from the new official theology of the Byzantine Church. Opposition networks existed in Constantinopolitan monasteries.[153] Nevertheless, anti-Palamite and Latinophile positions should not be equated. The position of the emperors themselves clearly contradicts such assumptions. John V did not hinder the enforcement of Palamism, nor did he effectively mitigate the patriarchs' strife against leading anti-Palamite intellectuals, which reached a first climax shortly before the emperor's journey to Rome.[154] On the other hand, John Kantakouzenos, the main proponent of Palamas, maintained close

---

149 Cf. Les « Mémoires » du Grand Ecclésiarque [...] Sylvestre Syropoulos, p. 687 (index, where no entry for John V can be found).
150 Urban V, Acta, no. 184, pp. 311–13. In this letter, John V is compared to Constantine the Great, but the nature of his Roman 'conversion' is only allusively circumscribed ('ad maternum accessit gremium'). In a similar vein, the Greek clerics were called to abandon the state of schism and return to the obedience of the Church of Rome. The letter was certainly handed over to John V himself on his way back to Constantinople. Thus, it was left to him whether he had it proclaimed or not.
151 Cf. Raymond-Joseph Loenertz, 'Fr. Philippe de Bindo Incontri O.P. du couvent de Péra, inquisiteur en Orient', in Raymond-Joseph Loenertz, Byzantina et Franco-Graeca, 2 vols (Rome: Edizioni di Storia e Letteratura, 1978), II, pp. 19–38; Claudine Delacroix-Besnier, Les Dominicains et la chrétienté grecque aux XIVe et XVe siècles, Collection de l'École française de Rome, 237 (Rome: École française de Rome, 1997), pp. 185–97.
152 See inter alia Delacroix-Besnier, 'Conversions constantinopolitaines', pp. 741–48; Frances Kianka, Demetrius Cydones (c. 1324–c. 1397): Intellectual and diplomatic relations between Byzantium and the West in the Fourteenth Century (New York: Fordham University, 1981), pp. 211–16; Tinnefeld, 'Das Leben des Demetrios Kydones', pp. 42–48, 51.
153 See Raúl Estangüi Gómez, 'Saint-Sauveur de Chôra. Un monastère catholique à Constantinople dans le troisième quart du XIVe siècle', Estudios bizantinos, 1 (2013), 140–97. This study clearly profiles Chora as a center of opposition to Palamism in the 1360's, but I am not sure whether the brilliant case-studies indeed support the interpretation that the monastery was a place of 'Catholicism' in Constantinople.
154 For the patriarch's action against Prochoros Kydones in 1368, see the succinct outline by Tinnefeld in Demetrios Kydones, Briefe, I/1, pp. 237–44; and the detailed study by Antonio Rigo, 'Il monte Athos e la controversia palamitica dal concilio del 1351 al Tomo sinodale del 1368. Giacomo Trikanas, Procoro Cidone e Filoteo Kokkinos', in Gregorio Palamas e oltre, pp. 1–51. The climate of persecution in these years is illustrated by Estangüi Gómez, 'Saint-Sauveur de Chôra', pp. 162–66. We cannot agree with Nerantze-Varmaze, Βυζάντιο, pp. 159–60, that the patriarch's measures actually aimed at Prochoros's brother Demetrios Kydones and at the proponents of unionist attitudes.

relations to Avignon throughout his reign[155] and remained an influential interlocutor in the eyes of the Curia even after his retreat from the political scene.

Besides such ambiguities of positioning in the religious field, numerous individual cases of conversion to the Latin Church are only documented if the converts sought a position in the Latin clerical hierarchy and thus opted for a complete integration.[156] Even in these cases, however, the actual procedure of 'conversion' usually remains unknown to us. The notion of 'conversion' is even more problematic if this act did not lead to a disaffiliation from 'Byzantine Orthodox' society. The most prominent of these cases is Demetrios Kydones himself, who openly embraced Latin Thomistic theology and was soon considered a 'conversus ad fidem' by his Dominican friends, yet we do not know of any formal act of conversion – if it ever happened.[157] His 'Apology' rather shows him concerned about correcting unfounded prejudices of his Greek fellows against the Latins. His complex religious and intellectual identity defies a simple classification as a 'Latin' or a 'Catholic'[158] – or even as a 'catholic cleric' as Urban V did when he granted Kydones a canon's benefice in the Chapter of Patras in recognition of his role in the act of 1369.[159]

The Avignon papacy considered the Greeks schismatics, who lived in self-imposed separation from the Universal Church.[160] But besides demanding the abjuration of schism, the Latin side did not name dogmatic 'errors' of Greek theology a 'convert' had to distance himself from in order to become a Catholic. In this respect conversion from the Latin to the Greek Church gives a different impression. When a growing number of Latins living in Constantinople decided to profess the Orthodox faith after 1360 due to various reasons, they had to make their confessions at the patriarchal

---

155 See Gill, *Papacy*, pp. 205–08; Raymond-Joseph Loenertz, 'Ambassadeurs grecs auprès du pape Clément VI 1348', *Orientalia Christiana Periodica*, 19 (1953), 178–96; Nicol, 'Byzantine requests', pp. 82–86.

156 To mention only two cases from the pontificate of Urban V, we may single out the Constantinopolitan monk 'Petrus qd. Condi Stephani' (Kontostephanos?), who after his confession was examined for his aptitude to administer a monastery belonging to the diocese of Rethymno, see Urban V, *Lettres communes*, VII (1981), no. 22173, p. 309; and the priest Manuel Laskaris – 'olim de scismate Grecorum ad fidem catholicam cum tota sua familia conversus' – who also aspired after a benefice on Crete, probably supported by John Laskaris Kalopheros, see Urban V, *Lettres communes*, VIII (1982), no. 23372, p. 80; Eszer, *Das abenteuerliche Leben*, p. 63.

157 The evidence is dicussed by Tinnefeld, 'Das Leben des Demetrios Kydones', pp. 15–16; Kianka, 'Byzantine-Papal Diplomacy', pp. 178–81; Ryder, *Career and Writings*, pp. 188–91.

158 See the meticulous discussion by Judith R. Ryder, "Catholics" in the Byzantine Political Elite: The Case of Demetrius Kydones', in *Languages of Love and Hate. Conflict, Communication and Identity in the Medieval Mediterranean*, ed. by Sarah Lambert and Helen Nicholson (Turnhout: Brepols, 2012), pp. 159–74, who rightly argues against a binary pattern of belonging either to the Latin or Greek ecclesiastical sphere.

159 Urban V, *Acta*, nos 187 and 187a, pp. 316–19, addressed 'Dilecto filio Demitrio Chidoni, clerico Constantinopolitano'. These documents neither refer to Kydones's position at the imperial court nor to his supposed conversion. Kydones himself assumed a critical attitude to these papal remunerations, as he believed they should retain him at the Curia, see his letter to Prochoros: Demetrios Kydones, *Correspondance*, I, p. 73 (no. 39), ll. 29–36 (Tinnefeld, *Demetrios Kydones, Briefe*, I/2, no. 71, p. 413).

160 Cf. de Vries, 'Die Päpste von Avignon', pp. 90–109.

synod, and these acts were recorded in the patriarchal register.[161] One of the main elements these confessions contained was the formal condemnation of the *filioque* and its insertion into the Creed as well as of the religious customs and way of life (*ethima, politeia, diagôgê*) of the Latins.[162] In contrast to the formula the *basileus* had sworn in Rome, the explicit dissociation from a former religious affiliation stood at the center of these acts of conversion. They thus point to mechanisms characterizing conversions in the age of confessionalism[163] in contrast to the diffuse Latinophile attitudes among the late Byzantine elite.

Be that as it may, the dynamization of religious affiliations in late Byzantium[164] deserves attention, also in a comparative and systematic perspective.[165] Recent studies on contemporary phenomena of conversion propose flexible concepts such as multiple religious belonging or conversional biographies of several stages.[166] Probably, John V Palaiologos, whose inward religious convictions naturally remain inaccessible to us, was a worthy precursor to this kind of religious modernity. Apparently, he was commemorated as an Orthodox prince in Byzantium, while modern researchers, aware of what happened in Rome in 1369, often considered him a 'true' Catholic. It

---

161 See Johannes Preiser-Kapeller and Ekaterini Mitsiou, 'Übertritte zur byzantinisch-orthodoxen Kirche in den Urkunden des Patriarchatsregisters von Konstantinopel' in *Sylloge diplomatico-palaeographica I. Studien zur byzantinischen Diplomatik und Paläographie*, ed. by Christian Gastgeber and Otto Kresten, Österreichische Akademie der Wissenschaften, Denkschriften, 392 (Vienna: Verlag der ÖAW, 2010), pp. 233–88; Christian Gastgeber, 'Der Umgang des Patriarchats von Konstantinopel mit der lateinischen Kirche im 14. Jahrhundert. Opposition im Patriarchat(sregister) von Konstantinopel', in *Byzanz und das Abendland: Begegnungen zwischen Ost und West*, ed. by Erika Juhász (Budapest: Eötvös-József-Collegium, 2013), pp. 131–59 (142–54); Christian Gastgeber, '*Confessiones fidei* im Patriarchatsregister von Konstantinopel (14. Jahrhundert)', in *L'union à l'épreuve du formulaire*, ed. by Marie-Hélène Blanchet and Frédéric Gabriel, Centre de recherche d'histoire et civilisation de Byzance, Monographies, 51 (Leuven-Paris: Peeters, 2016), pp. 145–89; most recently with a focus on the converts' motives Ekaterini Mitsiou, '»I believe what the Great Church believes«. Latin Christians and their Confessions of Faith in fourteenth-Century Byzantium', in *Menschen, Bilder, Sprache, Dinge: Wege der Kommunikation zwischen Byzanz und dem Westen*, ed. by Falko Daim, Dominik Heher, and Claudia Rapp, Byzanz zwischen Orient und Okzident, 9/1–2, 2 vols (Mainz: Verlag des RGZM, 2018), II, pp. 311–22.

162 See Preiser-Kapeller and Mitsiou, 'Übertritte zur byzantinisch-orthodoxen Kirche', pp. 234–38. Based on the observation of a temporal coincidence between some of these conversion records in the register and imperial journeys to the West, Gastgeber, 'Der Umgang', pp. 155–57, suggests that the activities of the patriarchate could be understood as a specific form of opposition to the emperors' policy.

163 *Konversion und Konfession in der Frühen Neuzeit*, ed. by Ute Lotz-Heumann, Jan-Friedrich Mißfelder and Matthias Pohlig, Schriften des Vereins für Reformationsgeschichte, 205 (Gütersloh: Gütersloher Verlagshaus, 2007).

164 Interconfessional fluidity as a characteristic feature of Pera-Constantinople has been stressed by Mitsiou, 'I believe what the Great Church believes', p. 311.

165 For a nuanced view on models of individual conversion in early modern Christianity, see Siebenhüner, 'Glaubenswechsel jenseits des Eurozentrismus', pp. 261–68. The classic study by Kurt Aland, *Über den Glaubenswechsel in der Geschichte des Christentums* (Berlin: Töpelmann, 1961), ignores Byzantium and postulates that inner-Christian conversion became an important phenomenon only because of the Reformation (p. 75).

166 For the concept of 'conversion career' see Henri Gooren, *Religious Conversion and Disaffiliation. Tracing Patterns of Change in Faith Practices* (New York: Palgrave, 2010), p. 3.

seems to me that this ambiguity could only arise because John V managed to keep his profession of the faith of the Roman Church out of the Byzantine public sphere, thanks to the way his *mesazon* Demetrios Kydones had staged the non-public and public elements of this unique act of 'conversion'.[167]

---

167 We should not pass over the different explanation given by Ryder, '"Catholics" in in the Byzantine Political Elite', pp. 173–74. According to her, Kydones's political theory, which emphasized the common bonds between the Latin and the Greek world instead of polarization, helped a majority in Byzantium to accept the emperor's step. But it seems to me that neither the majority nor even a substantial minority of Byzantines actually knew what had happened in Rome. They probably knew no more than that the *basileus* had journeyed to the West in search for military aid against the Turks. Coming back to Constantinople, he might even have brought some soldiers with him, see Setton, *Papacy*, I, p. 315.

CHARLES C. YOST

Anti-Palamism, Unionism, and the 'Crisis of Faith' of the Fourteenth Century*

The defeat of Latin valour by Turkish arms at Nicopolis in September of 1396 was among the crown of evils consummating Barbara Tuchman's gripping—if dated—account of the 1300s as the 'calamitous century'.[1] If the French knights who died at Nikopolis were among the last, ill-starred generation of a century that has been presented in classic scholarship as decaying, moribund, or convulsed by various crises,[2] their Byzantine contemporaries, the Greek Christians whom those knights ostensibly came to save, have fared little better in classic political histories of 'the Byzantine state'.[3] Despite the inherent lure of 'sickness unto death' narratives of 'late' Byzantium wracked by

---

* I thank Alexander Beihammer, Chris Schabel, and the anonymous reviewer for their helpful suggestions for improving this article.
1 Barbara Tuchman, *A Distant Mirror: The Calamitous Fourteenth Century* (New York: Alfred A. Knopf, 1978). On the battle of Nikopolis specifically, see pp. 567–94.
2 See, besides Tuchman, *A Distant Mirror*, above all, John Huizinga, *The Autumn of the Middle Ages*, trans. Rodney J. Payton and Ulrich Mammitzsch (Chicago: The University of Chicago Press, 1996). For contributions that consider these historiographical conventions critically and broadly, see Howard Kaminsky, 'From Lateness to Waning to Crisis: The Burden of the Later Middle Ages', *Journal of Early Modern History*, 4 (2000), 85–125 and Donald Sullivan, 'The End of the Middle Ages: Decline, Crisis, or Transformation?' *The History Teacher*, 14 (1981), 551–65. For studies testing these conventions by considering the validity of their application to particular aspects of late medieval society, see William J. Courtenay, 'Huizinga's Heirs: Interpreting the Late Middle Ages,' in *Herbst des Mittelalters? Fragen zur Bewertung des 14. und 15. Jahrhunderts*, ed. by Jan M. Aertsen and Martin Pickavé, Miscellanea Mediaevalia, 31 (Berlin: W. de Gruyter, 2004), pp. 26–36; James L. Goldsmith, 'The Crisis of the Late Middle Ages: The Case of France', *French History*, 9 (195), 417–50; Guy Bois, 'On the Crisis of the Late Middle Ages', *The Medieval History Journal*, 1 (1998), 311–21; Michael Bailey, 'A Late-Medieval Crisis of Superstition', *Speculum*, 84 (2009), 633–61.
3 Edward Gibbon, *The Decline and Fall of the Roman Empire*, VI (1788), chapters LIX–LXVIII, see esp. chapter LXIII ('Civil Wars and the Ruin of the Greek Empire') and, regarding the Battle of Nikopolis, see chapter LXIV ('Moguls, Ottoman Turks'), part 4 and chapter LXVI ('Union of the Greek and Latin Churches'), part 1; George Ostrogorsky, *A History of the Byzantine State*, trans. Joan Hussey, 3rd rev. edn (New Brunswick: Rutgers University Press, 1969), esp. pp. 491–509; Steven Runciman, *The Fall of Constantinople, 1453* (Cambridge: Cambridge University Press, 1965); Donald M. Nicol, *The Last Centuries of Byzantium, 1261–1453*, 2nd edn (Cambridge: Cambridge University Press, 1993); Paul Lemerle, *Histoire de Byzance* (Paris: Presses Universitaires de France, 1969), p. 125, this latter cited in Aristeides

Charles C. Yost • University of Notre Dame

Crusading, Society, and Politics in the Eastern Mediterranean in the Age of King Peter I of Cyprus, ed. by Alexander Beihammer and Angel Nicolaou-Konnari, MEDNEX, 10 (Turnhout, 2022), pp. 517–549
© BREPOLS ⚜ PUBLISHERS   10.1484/M.MEDNEX-EB.5.128477

its own share of plague and fratricidal warfare,[4] scholars of intellectual history and Greek theology have long seen in this precise period a golden age of the spirit.[5]

For instance, the re-capture of Constantinople from the Latins in 1261 has been presented as the dawn of a century of intellectual ferment consisting in the re-invigoration of institutions of learning and study of the classical tradition. The Byzantine intellectuals of this so-called 'Palaiologan Renaissance' not only evinced new esteem for ancient Greek eloquence, but, particularly in the later stages of this movement, new openness to intellectual currents originating in the Latin West, both ancient and medieval.[6] This new Byzantine enthusiasm for the intellectual culture of their western contemporaries is palpable in the writings of the statesman and intellectual Demetrios Kydones (c. 1324–98), who memorably described his first bewitching encounter with the writings of St Thomas Aquinas as 'tasting the lotus'.[7] This new enthusiasm for Latin intellectual culture and theology—an awareness which was

---

Papadakis and John Meyendorff, *The Christian East and the Rise of the Papacy: The Church AD 1071–1453*, The Church in History, 4 (Crestwood: St Vladimir's Press, 1994), p. 275, who apparently agrees with Lemerle's judgment, see also pp. 309–10.

4 But note: Nicol, *Last Centuries*, e.g., p. xiii: 'If I have described this experience in terms of the failing strength and mortal illness of an invalid, it is with reference to the institution rather than to its people'; see also the title of chapter 7: 'Symptoms and causes of decline' and of 'Part III The mortal illness of Byzantium: the age of civil wars – 1321–54'. Also, Angeliki E. Laiou, 'The Palaiologoi and the World Around Them (1261–1400)', in *The Cambridge History of the Byzantine Empire, c. 500–1492*, ed. by Jonathan Shepard (Cambridge: Cambridge University Press, 2008), pp. 803–33 (822–24, on 'Social tensions, civil wars', and 832, where she refers to the changes endured by 'the Byzantine state [...] through the crises of the fourteenth century').

5 Within the entry on 'Byzantium, History of' in *The Oxford Dictionary of Byzantium*, ed. by Alexander Kazhdan, 3 vols (Oxford: Oxford University Press, 1991), I, pp. 345–62, see the subsection by Alice-Mary Talbot, '"Empire of the Straits" (1261–1453)', pp. 358–62, who remarks on both aspects––i.e., the intellectual and spiritual renewals––of the positive evaluation of the politically and economically declining Palaiologan Empire, both of which aspects will be considered in greater detail below.

6 See, especially, Edmund Fryde, *The Early Palaeologan Renaissance (1261–c. 1360)*, The Medieval Mediterranean, 27 (Leiden: Brill, 2000); Ihor Ševčenko, 'The Palaeologan Renaissance', in *Renaissances Before the Renaissance: Cultural Revivals of Late Antiquity and the Middle Ages*, ed. by Warren T. Treadgold (Stanford, 1984), pp. 144–223; *Art et société à Byzance sous les Paléologues. Actes du Colloque organisé par l'Association international des études byzantines à Venise en septembre 1968*, ed. by Association international des études byzantines, Bibliothèque de l'Institut hellénique d'études byzantines et post-byzantines de Venise, 4 (Venice: Stamperia di Venezia, 1971), e.g., contributions by D. A. Zakythinos, 'États-Sociétés-Cultures. En guise d'introduction,' pp. 1–12, Ihor Ševčenko, 'Théodore Métochites, Chora et les courants intellectuels de l'époque,' pp. 15–39, and Hans-Georg Beck, 'Besonderheiten der Literatur in der Palaiologenzeit,' pp. 43–52. Regarding greater openness of Palaiologan society to intellectual currents from the Latin West, see, besides the article of Beck, Marcus Plested, *Orthodox Readings of Aquinas: Changing Paradigms in Historical and Systematic Theology* (Oxford: Oxford University Press, 2012), pp. 29–107, 115–36. See also Michael Angold, 'Byzantine "Nationalism" and the Nicaean Empire', *Byzantine and Modern Greek Studies*, 1 (1975), 49–70, who stresses the crucial contribution of the pre-1261 period of exile to the intellectual flowering of the Palaiologan era.

7 Demetrios Kydones, *Apologie della propria fede: 1. Ai Greci Ortodossi*, ed. by Giovanni Mercati in *Notizie di Procoro e Demetrio Cidone, Manuele Caleca e Teodoro Meliteniota ed altri appunti per la storia della teologia della letteratura bizantina del secolo XIV*, Studi e Testi, 56 (Vatican City: Biblioteca Apostolica Vaticana, 1931), p. 363: Λωτοῦ δὴ γευσάμενος οὐχ οἷός τ' ἦν λοιπὸν κρατεῖν ἐμαυτοῦ [...]; see also Plested, *Orthodox Readings*, pp. 63–72.

owed in no little part to the intensified presence of Latins in the Greek East, itself a byproduct of the western incursions and conquests of the late twelfth and thirteenth centuries—was a contributing factor to a new sympathy for the Latin West among certain late Byzantine intellectuals. Some of them, such as Demetrios Kydones himself, even entered the communion of the Roman Church.[8]

But for scholars of Byzantine theology and religious history, and particularly those of an Eastern Orthodox bent, late Byzantium's high reputation rests upon the achievement of its 'hesychast' theologians, chief among whom St Gregory Palamas (c. 1296–1359).[9] The principal pioneer in this field was Father John Meyendorff, whose 1959 study of Gregory Palamas broke fecund ground in its presentation of late Byzantine theology as consisting in innovative fidelity to the legacy of the fathers of the Greek Church.[10] The positive reappraisal of the theological and spiritual legacy of the Palaiologan-era Byzantines was further elaborated by his student, Aristeides Papadakis, and is taken for granted today by many young researchers of Greek theology and related fields. A golden age of the 'Byzantine spirit', indeed.[11]

---

8 Regarding Kydones particularly, see Frances Kianka, 'The Apology of Demetrius Cydones: A Fourteenth-Century Autobiographical Source', *Byzantine Studies*, 7 (1980), 57–71; Judith R. Ryder, *The Career and Writings of Demetrius Kydones: A Study of Fourteenth-Century Byzantine Politics, Religion and Society*, The Medieval Mediterranean, 85 (Leiden: Brill, 2010); Frances Kianka, 'Divided Loyalties? The Career and Writings of Demetrius Kydones', in *Greeks, Latins, and Intellectual History 1204–1500*, ed. by Martin Hinterberger and Chris Schabel, Bibliotheca, 11 (Leuven: Peeters, 2011), pp. 243–62. On greater sympathy for Latin theology among certain Byzantine intellectuals see, again e.g., Beck, 'Besonderheiten der Literatur', pp. 43–52 and Plested, *Orthodox Readings*, pp. 29–107, 115–36. Regarding Byzantines who 'entered communion with the Roman Church', see Claudine Delacroix-Besnier, 'Conversions constantinopolitaines au XIVe siècle', in *Mélanges de l'École française de Rome: Moyen-Age, Temps modernes*, 105.2 (1993), 715–61; Tia M. Kolbaba 'Conversions from Greek Orthodoxy to Roman Catholicism in the Fourteenth Century', *Byzantine and Modern Greek Studies*, 19 (1995), 120–34; John Meyendorff, *Byzantine Theology: Historical Trends and Doctrinal Themes* (New York: Fordham University Press, 1979), pp. 105–07; Papadakis and Meyendorff, *Christian East*, pp. 317–19 (though the view of Kydones and others presented here is ultimately negative. Papadakis is possessed of an extreme Orthodox confessional bias). For other items relevant to the issue of greater openneness to the West and on Byzantines embracing union with Rome, see below.
9 Aristeides Papadakis, 'Palamas, Gregory' in *Oxford Dictionary of Byzantium*, III, 1560.
10 Jean Meyendorff, *Introduction à l'étude de Grégoire Palamas*, Patristica Sorbonensia, 3 (Paris: Éditions du Seuil, 1959). English translation: *A Study of Gregory Palamas*, trans. George Lawrence (London: Faith Press, 1964, repr.1974).
11 Aristeides Papadakis, *Crisis in Byzantium: The Filioque Controversy in the Patriarchate of Gregory II of Cyprus (1283–1289)* (Crestwood: St Vladimir's Seminary Press, 1997); Papadakis and Meyendorff, *Christian East*, pp. 293–317; Jaroslav Pelikan, *The Christian Tradition: A History of the Development of Doctrine*, II: *The Spirit of Eastern Christendom (600–1700)* (Chicago: The University of Chicago Press, 1974), pp. 252–98 (chapter 6: 'The Last Flowering of Byzantine Orthodoxy'), on p. 252, Pelikan writes: 'In many ways the period from the twelfth to the fifteenth century may be identified as the time when Byzantine orthodoxy reached its flowering'; on Palamas particularly, see pp. 261–70; see also Meyendorff, *Byzantine Theology*, pp. 76–78, 103–14; Kallistos Ware, 'The Jesus Prayer in St Gregory of Sinai', *Eastern Churches Review*, 4.1 (1972), 21–22, on St Gregory of Sinai as the leader of a [spiritual] renaissance—a rebirth and revival' in early-fourteenth century Byzantium that came to fruition in Palamas's day. And see Meyendorff, *Grégoire Palamas*, p. 65, in which he typifies these intellectual and spiritual trends as considered above in the dynamic opposition between the 'Monks' and the 'Humanists', on which heuristic see further below.

Certainly, the scholars who forged or deepened the study of these intellectual and spiritual trends in fourteenth-century Byzantium were not unaware of the military, social, and political 'crises' that convulsed the late empire and constituted the essential contexts of those developments.[12] But 'crisis' is not merely a matter of civil strife, military defeat, the loss of territory or even life.[13] In this paper, I propose that this heady mixture of intellectual discovery and yearning for the divine, of which submission to the Roman Church and the Palamite dogma were the archetypal results, produced a crisis in the late-fourteenth century Greek East. This spiritual crisis, which resulted from the synthesis of revulsion toward the 'innovations' of Gregory Palamas, on the one hand, and the acceptance of a particular (almost certainly Latin-influenced) ecclesiological outlook, on the other, may be observed in the writings of one prominent Greek theologian: Manuel Kalekas (c. 1360–1410).[14] As a result of this synthesis, Kalekas endured a 'crisis of faith', or, perhaps better, a crisis of confidence in his ancestral Church of Constantinople. Through this process, opposition toward Palamas and advocacy of union with the Roman Church—previously, distinct theological positions that could, in spite of their distinctiveness, coincide in the life of one Greek thinker[15]—became welded together into a unified whole, wherein the election of the Roman Church became, at the same time, a conscious denial that his own ancestral Church of Constantinople could be the one, true Church of Jesus Christ. For Kalekas this was not merely an academic discussion. It was an anxiety-ridden matter of salvation or damnation: A true crisis of the fourteenth century.

In order to elaborate this crisis mentality, this paper must scrutinize more closely the relationship between opposition to the theology of Palamas, or anti-Palamism, and the phenomenon of Byzantines united to the Roman Church, or unionism. Of course, it is nothing new to posit a relationship of deep sympathy, even considerable overlap, between anti-Palamism and unionism as theological positions. In fact, it may be considered as a worn convention in standard histories of Byzantine ecclesiastical history or theology. Meyendorff articulated a dichotomy between 'Monks' and 'Humanists' as a fundamental dynamic driving controversies in Byzantium.[16] This 'Monks' vs. 'Humanists' heuristic, *mutatis mutandis*, has been subsequently deployed by scholars of

---

12 E.g., Alice-Mary Talbot, '"Empire of the Straits" (1204–61)', in *Oxford Dictionary of Byzantium*, I, 358–62.
13 Indeed, Aristeides Papadakis recognized this very clearly as is seen in the title of his monograph, cited above, *Crisis in Byzantium*, which deals with a 'crisis' of a theological character; also see, Papadakis and Meyendorff, *Christian East*, pp. 275–76, where he speaks of the Palamite controversy as a 'fourteenth century crisis'.
14 Alice-Mary Talbot, 'Kalekas, Manuel', in *Oxford Dictionary of Byzantium*, II, 1092; Raymond-Joseph Loenertz, 'Manuel Calécas, sa vie et ses oeuvres d'après ses lettres et ses apologies inédites', *Archivum Fratrum Praedicatorum*, 17 (1947), p. 199. For further bibliography on Kalekas, see below.
15 Plested, *Orthodox Readings*, pp. 58–60, makes this important point about how these positions (and their opposites, i.e., Palamism and anti-unionism/Latinism) are distinct and possibly (but not necessarily) coinciding in a given figure (for more on this, see below).
16 Meyendorff, *Grégoire Palamas*, pp. 42–43, 324–25, and 65 (where he writes): 'Comme on l'a souvent constaté, l'histoire de la pensée byzantine est tout entière marquée, depuis le IXe siècle, par l'opposition, plus ou moins ouverte suivant les époques, entre les promoteurs de l'humanisme profane et les moines'; Meyendorff, *Byzantine Theology*, pp. 54–65.

Byzantine intellectual and religious history.[17] According to this view, whether the debates have to do with Palamite theology or union with Rome, the antagonists were inspired by essentially irreconcilable views about God, man, revelation, philosophy, and their mutual relations. Palamas's opponents, the Humanists, struggled against his theology because it was essentially at odds with their own views of the exalted place of human reason and the philosophical heritage of ancient Greece—views that at the same time made them sympathetic to Latin scholasticism. From the perspective granted by this heuristic of 'Monks vs. Humanists', there is no need to explain any 'connection' between anti-Palamism and unionism, since the internal unity between them is taken for granted.[18]

In his 2013 monograph *Orthodox Readings of Aquinas*, Marcus Plested challenges the assumption of a necessary linkage between opposition to Palamas and union with Rome. After all, Nikephoros Gregoras, Palamas's last major opponent, exhibited hostile attitudes toward the Latin West. Prochoros Kydones, who was deposed from the priesthood in 1368 for his opposition to Palamism, never seems to have joined his famous brother Demetrios in entering communion with Rome. Even in the case of Barlaam the Calabrian, who following his condemnation in 1341 became a bishop under papal authority in Southern Italy, Plested reminds us that it was his attack on the Latin *Filioque* that was the occasion for his first dispute with Palamas.[19]

What, then, do we make of the coincidence of anti-Palamism and unionism in a particular thinker, or that the passage of Byzantines from rebellion against the Palamism of Constantinople to Roman communion became an increasingly common phenomenon in the course of the fourteenth century? In the case of anti-Palamites who submitted to Rome, Plested wishes to avoid conflating what he sees as two distinct doctrinal positions. To the extent that a relationship did develop between these positions, Plested sees it as accidental and the result of external pressures: 'over the latter half of the fourteenth century, anti-Palamism became an increasingly untenable position for a member of the Orthodox Church, leaving some with no option but to jump ship altogether'.[20] In its basic contours, this appraisal seems to echo that of George-Gennadios Scholarios, the first patriarch of Constantinople following the Turkish conquest in 1453, who had this to say about two of the best-known instances of unionist anti-Palamites of the fourteenth century:

> Since it is clear to all that [Demetrios] Kydones and his disciple [Manuel] Kalekas were driven out from the sacred precincts [of the Church] on account of other

---

17 e.g., Papadakis and Meyendorff, *Christian East*, pp. 317–19; Jane Baun, 'Church', essay no. 7 in *Palgrave Advances in Byzantine History*, ed. by Jonathan Harris (Houndmills: Palgrave Macmillan, 2005), pp. 116–18, see esp. p. 117 (with some critical qualification). On the victory of Palamas and his followers in the Greek Church as the victory of monastic 'fundamentalism' over rationality, see Dirk Krausmüller, 'The Rise of Hesychasm', in *The Cambridge History of Christianity*, V: *Eastern Christianity*, ed. by Michael Angold (Cambridge: Cambridge University Press, 2006), pp. 101–26.

18 For another articulation of the natural agreement between, on the one hand, the anti-Palamite and unionist parties, and, on the other, the pro-Palamas and anti-union parties, see Basileios L. Dentakes, Ἰωάννης Κυπαρισσιώτης ὁ σοφὸς καὶ φιλόσοφος, Ἡσυχαστικαὶ καὶ φιλοσοφικαὶ μελέται, 3 (Athens, 1965), pp. 31–32.

19 Plested, *Orthodox Readings*, pp. 58–60.

20 Plested, *Orthodox Readings*, pp. 221–22 (direct quotation is from p. 222), see also pp. 115, 118–20.

heterodoxies, for they happened to be followers of the heresy of Akindynos and Barlaam; they fled to the Roman Church and on account of this they provided, as payment to the Church that had received them, the defense [of the *Filioque*] against their own Mother [Church] through some sophistical arguments, while, at the same time, they were eager to present their change as something reasonable for themselves and to inform everyone that they did not prefer that [Roman] Church by necessity since they had nowhere else to flee to, but because they had found that Church in all things thinking better than the one that had nurtured them.[21]

Although Scholarios sees Kydones and Kalekas as having both broken with Constantinople and united with Rome, only their break with their native church is a true expression of their convictions, which are anti-Palamite convictions. Their union with Rome was forced upon them by their expulsion from their Mother Church—'since they had nowhere else to flee to'—it was not heartfelt. This view, obviously biased, prods us to scrutinize the relationship between anti-Palamism and unionism in the minds of two of the most distinguished theologians of the fourteenth century. By investigating the ecclesiological content of their beliefs, and while keeping an eye on the changing historical context, we shall begin to grasp the nature of this fourteenth-century crisis of confidence in the Church of Constantinople.

I shall first give an overview of the thought of a 'pre-crisis' anti-Palamite, John Kyparissiotes (*c*. 1310–78),[22] who will provide a foil serving to throw into stronger relief the 'crisis' mentality as this is seen in the thought of Manuel Kalekas (*c*. 1360–1410). As Plested would insist, historical context is important here, and thus should be kept in mind.[23] Because the later course of the fourteenth century marked the steady progress of the establishment of Palamism as orthodoxy in the magisterium of the Constantinopolitan Church,[24] it is natural that the outlook of the later-born Kalekas, who would have had no recollection of a *status ante Palamam* in the Greek Church, would have differed from that of the older Kyparissiotes. The influence upon the full elaboration of the crisis mentality stemming from anti-Palamites' potentially differing perceptions of how far wrong things had gone—differing as a result of their distinct experiences and historical contexts—should not be overlooked.

The criterion for judging whether this crisis mentality has manifested is, above all, ecclesiological: did the men here under consideration deny that the Church of Constantinople, on account of the errors of her hierarchs, was the 'true Church'? An

---

21 George Gennadios Scholarios, *Oeuvres complètes*, ed. by Martin Jugie, Louis Petit, and Xénophon A. Sidéridès, 8 vols (Paris: Maison de la bonne presse, 1928–36), III, p. 94: "Ἔπειτα σαφές ἐστι πᾶσιν, ὅτι καὶ Κυδώνης καὶ ὁ μαθητὴς ἐκείνου Καλέκας ἐξηλαύνοντο μὲν τῶν ἱερῶν περιβόλων δι' ἄλλας κακοδοξίας· τῆς γὰρ Ἀκινδύνου καὶ Βαρλαὰμ αἱρέσεως ἐτύγχανον θιασῶται· ἐπὶ δὲ τὴν ῥωμαϊκὴν ἐκκλησίαν κατέφευγον, καὶ διὰ τοῦτο μισθὸν παρέσχον τῇ δεξαμένῃ σφᾶς ἐκκλησίᾳ τὴν κατὰ τῆς μητρὸς αὐτῶν συνηγορίαν ἐν τοῖς σοφιστικοῖς λόγοις ἐκείνοις, ἅμα δὲ ἠβουλήθησαν καὶ ἑαυτοῖς εὔλογον ἐπιδεῖξαι τὴν μετάθεσιν καὶ πληροφορῆσαι πάντας, ὡς οὐχ ὑπ' ἀνάγκης εἵλοντο τὴν ἐκκλησίαν ἐκείνην, οὐκ ἔχοντες ἄλλοθί που καταφυγεῖν, ἀλλὰ διότι τὴν ἐκκλησίαν ἐκείνην εὕρισκον καὶ ἐν πᾶσιν ἄλλοις φρονοῦσαν ἄμεινον τῆς θρεψαμένης αὐτούς".
22 Alice-Mary Talbot, 'Kyparissiotes, John', in *Oxford Dictionary of Byzantium*, II, p. 1162.
23 See discussion above and n. 20.
24 Regarding these developments, see below.

affirmative answer indicates the manifestation of the 'crisis of confidence' because of which a Greek Christian would feel compelled to abandon the church of his ancestors and, as a necessary corollary, embrace the communion of a foreign church. Thus, the onset of this crisis also inaugurates a new era of 'Byzantine unionism', in which election of Rome and rejection of Constantinople become two sides of the same coin.

Indeed, as we shall see, besides alternative histories and troubling memories of the traumatic events on the path to the consummation of Constantinople's embrace of Palamite theology, ecclesiological considerations of a particular character were significant for a Greek such as Manuel Kalekas in his doubts and ultimate denial that his native church was the 'true Church' of Jesus Christ. The content of these considerations will be spelled out more clearly below. Finally, it is also my hope that this paper will convey some sense of the anxiety and consternation characterizing this crisis mentality, the anxiety of a Greek gripped by ruminations that the church in which he had been 'born and raised' might be false.

The Pre-Crisis Mentality: John Kyparissiotes (c. 1310–78)

Though persecuted and long-suffering, the understudied John Kyparissiotes (c. 1310–78) was unafflicted by the crisis mentality.[25] In the summer of 1371, Demetrios Kydones addressed a letter to Kyparissiotes, then an exile in the Kingdom of Cyprus, as to a man of many sorrows. As though forced exile and its accompanying conditions of poverty and friendlessness were not bad enough, Kydones considers that now 'the abominable ones' will justify themselves at Kyparissiotes's expense, and consider his misfortunes as 'the recompense of blasphemy'.[26] Although Kydones does not specify who these 'abominable ones' are, or what they supposed his addressee's 'blasphemy' was, reading between the lines we see the ongoing conflagration of controversy over Palamas as the firestorm that drove the hapless Kyparissiotes to Cyprus. By the time Kydones wrote, the Palamites had dominated the Great Church for approximately twenty-four years. This was the culmination of a historical process with which Kyparissiotes himself was intensely concerned, and of which he wrote a detailed account that differs from the conventional and familiar narrative of the Palamite controversy as this has been told by modern Eastern Orthodox scholars such John Meyendorff and Aristeides Papadakis.[27]

---

25 For what follows on Kyparissiotes's life, see Alice-Mary Talbot, 'Kyparissiotes, John' in *Oxford Dictionary of Byzantium*, II, p. 1162, and especially the monograph of Dentakes, Ἰωάννης Κυπαρισσιώτης, esp. pp. 11–34, to date the sole monograph dedicated to John Kyparissiotes.

26 See Demetrios Kydones, *Correspondance*, ed. by Raymond-Joseph Loenertz, Studi e testi, 186, 2 vols (Vatican City: Biblioteca Apostolica Vaticana, 1956–60), I, no. 35, pp. 67–68, and in particular ll. 11–12: 'ὁ δὲ τῶν κακῶν κολοφών, ὅτι καὶ βλασφημίας δίκας ἀπαιτεῖσθαι δόξεις τοῖς μιαροῖς'.

27 See, above all, Meyendorff, *Grégoire Palamas*, pp. 65–170; Meyendorff, *Byzantine Theology*, pp. 76–77; Gregory Palamas, *The Triads*, ed. by John Meyendorff, trans. by Nicholas Gendle, The Classics of Western Spirituality (London: SPCK, 1983), pp. 5–8 (from the introduction); Papadakis and Meyendorff, *The Christian East*, pp. 287–93 (esp. pp. 290–93); Aristeides Papadakis, 'Constantinople, Councils of', 'Local

The conventional narrative of the Palamite controversy has it like this. In the 1330s began the famous quarrel between the philosopher Barlaam the Calabrian (c. 1290–1348)[28] and the Athonite monk Gregory Palamas, a quarrel ultimately dealing with the question of a distinction in God between His knowable, immanent energies and His unknowable, transcendent essence, as well as the hesychastic method of prayer. In 1341, Barlaam was condemned by a council presided over by Emperor Andronikos III (r. 1328–41),[29] which also (according to Papadakis and Meyendorff)[30] vindicated Palamas's distinction between the energies and essence.

Council of 1341', 'Local Council of 1347', and 'Local Council of 1351', in *Oxford Dictionary of Byzantium*, I, pp. 515–16. Also, more recently, see Robert J. Sinkewicz, 'Gregory Palamas' in *La Théologie byzantine et sa tradition*, II: *XIIIe–XIXe s.*, ed. by Carmello Giuseppe Conticello and Vassa Contoumas-Conticello (Turnhout: Brepols, 2002), pp. 131–37. I have relied heavily on Sinkewicz's sketch of the outbreak of the Palamite controversy in my own recounting of it in the following paragraph. In the main Sinkewicz's account does not differ greatly from that of Meyendorff or Papadakis, except in one major point: Sinkewicz, unlike Papadakis and Meyendorff, *The Christian East*, p. 290, does not claim that the synod of 1341 explicitly approved of Palamas's distinction between God's essence and energy (see Sinkewicz, 'Gregory Palamas', p. 134). Also see Joan M. Hussey, *The Orthodox Church in the Byzantine Empire*, Oxford History of the Christian Church (Oxford: Oxford University Press, 1986; repr. 2010), pp. 257–60, who, on p. 258, merely indicates that the first, June session of the 1341 synod condemned Barlaam, and that 'subsequent synodal sessions [i.e., presumably, after the death of Andronikos III] that year confirmed the Palamite position'.

28 Alice-Mary Talbot, 'Barlaam of Calabria', in *Oxford Dictionary of Byzantium*, I, p. 257.
29 Alice-Mary Talbot, 'Andronikos III Palaiologos', in *Oxford Dictionary of Byzantium*, I, p. 95.
30 Meyendorff, *Grégoire Palamas*, pp. 80–84; Papadakis and Meyendorff, *The Christian East*, p. 290 (cf. Sinkewicz, 'Gregory Palamas', p. 134 and Hussey, *Orthodox Church*, p. 258). Now is not the place to undertake a thorough-going examination of the position, maintained by Meyendorff and Papadakis, but openly disputed or rejected by other scholars (such as Martin Jugie, *Theologia dogmatica christianorum orientalium ab ecclesia catholica dissidentium*, I: *Theologiae dogmaticae Graeco-russorum: Origo, historia, fontes* (Paris: Letouzey et Ané, 1926), p. 436), that the first synod dealing with the controversy between Barlaam and Palamas and gathered on June 10, 1341 explicitly endorsed Palamas's distinction between the energies and essence (see Meyendorff, *Grégoire Palamas*, pp. 80–81). First, Meyendorff's direct evidence in favor of this position, i.e., statements in the document allegedly representing the conclusions of that synod (i.e., the *Tome of 1341* in *Das Register des Patriarchats von Konstantinopel*, 2. Teil: *Edition und Übersetzung der Urkunden aus den Jahren 1337–1350*, ed. and trans. by Herbert Hunger, Otto Kresten, Ewald Kislinger, and Carolina Cupane, Corpus Fontium Historiae Byzantinae, 19/2 (Vienna: Österreichische Akademie der Wissenschaften, 1995), no. 132, pp. 206–56, see Meyendorff, *Grégoire Palamas*, p. 405), is slight (i.e., two statements) and not entirely unambiguous (see esp. Meyendorff, *Grégoire Palamas*, p. 83, n. 78 and n. 79; for indirect evidence marshalled by Meyendorff, in the form of testimonies from roughly contemporary writers, see p. 81 and ns 65, 66, and 67). The *Tome of 1341* itself does not contain a ringing endorsement of the Palamite distinction — certainly not in the way one might expect of a document thus characterized by Meyendorff and Papadakis as enshrining the victory of Palamite theology. Although Meyendorff does list a number of MS witnesses of this *Tome* (see Meyendorff, *Grégoire Palamas*, pp. 405–06), as can be seen from his discussion of the direct evidence for his interpretation of this text (p. 83, nos 78–79), he seems to be relying on the Patrologia Graeca edition, hence not a critical edition. But we must consider the possibility that the Patrologia Graeca version may represent a later version of the *Tome* that had been interpolated by Palamites in order to shore up their control over the Great Church after the victory of Kantakouzenos by means of fabricating an endorsement of their theology by an ecumenical council presided over by the deceased, indisputably legitimate, emperor Andronikos III. (Of the MSS that Meyendorff lists on pp. 405–06, the only one he dates precisely is dated 1369; another four are dated simply to the fourteenth century, with another dated to the turn of the fourteenth and

Following the death of the emperor in that same year, the succession of a regency government led by the late emperor's wife Anna of Savoy (c. 1306–65)[31] and the Patriarch John XIV Kalekas (r. 1334–47),[32] and the challenge to that regency government mounted by John Kantakouzenos (c. 1295–1383),[33] the fortunes of Palamas seemed to plummet and he himself was excommunicated on November 4 of 1344.[34] These actions against Palamas have been presented as political in their motivation, taken by Patriarch John Kalekas against a man whom he saw as a dangerous spiritual sponsor of Kantakouzenos and thus a threat to his own political ambitions.[35] The victorious entry of Kantakouzenos into Constantinople in 1347 resulted in another reversal of fate, this time for Kalekas, who was himself deposed in that year and succeeded by Isidore I (r. 1347–50), the first in a line of solidly Palamite patriarchs.[36] The approbation of the theology of Palamas that had—according to the conventional narrative—already happened at the June session of the synod of 1341 was merely confirmed at subsequent synods.[37]

Of course, as the case of John Kyparissiotes itself shows, 1351 was not the end of opposition to Palamas. Later developments in the crystallization of the Palamite victory include the patriarchal synod's pursuit of suspected anti-Palamites among the ranks of the bishops and monastics,[38] the canonization of Gregory Palamas in

---

fifteenth centuries; the remaining ten are fifteenth century and later). Further inquiry must be deferred to another time. (A critical edition of the *Tome* is a great *desideratum*). For the present purpose, it is important to note merely that in the conventional historiography of the controversy (i.e., according to Meyendorff and Papadakis) the first synod of 1341 vindicated Palamite theology. As we shall see in this paper, not all Byzantines who were near contemporaries of the synod shared this view.

31 Alice-Mary Talbot and Anthony Cutler, 'Anna of Savoy', in *Oxford Dictionary of Byzantium*, I, p. 105.
32 Alice-Mary Talbot, 'John XIV Kalekas', in *Oxford Dictionary of Byzantium*, II, pp. 1055–56.
33 Alice-Mary Talbot, 'John VI Kantakouzenos', in *Oxford Dictionary of Byzantium*, II, pp. 1050–51.
34 Meyendorff, *Grégoire Palamas*, pp. 110–12.
35 Meyendorff, *Grégoire Palamas*, p. 13; Papadakis and Meyendorff, *Christian East*, pp. 290–91; Talbot, 'Palamas, Gregory', in *Oxford Dictionary of Byzantium*, III, p. 1560.
36 Alice-Mary Talbot, 'Isidore I Boucheiras', in *Oxford Dictionary of Byzantium*, II, p. 1015, who refers to him as a 'Palamite patriarch of Constantinople'; Papadakis and Meyendorff, *Christian East*, pp. 291–92. At his elevation, Isidore made a profession of faith including a clause explicitly rejecting Barlaam, Akindynos, John Kalekas, and their followers; see Jean Darrouzès, *Les regestes des actes du patriarcat de Constantinople I: Les actes des patriarches, V: Les regestes de 1310 à 1376* (Paris: Institut Français d'études byzantines, 1977), no. 2276. Isidore's immediate successor was Kallistos I (on whom, see Alice-Mary Talbot and Anthony Cutler, 'Kallistos I', in *Oxford Dictionary of Byzantium*, II, p. 1095), whose reign saw great strides in the consolidation of the Palamite victory. See also Hussey, *Orthodox Church*, pp. 258–59, and p. xxvii for the relevant section of her list of patriarchs of Constantinople, and see Talbot, 'Palamas, Gregory', in *Oxford Dictionary of Byzantium*, III, 1560.
37 See above items cited above in n. 27.
38 For examples of this, see various acta of the patriarchal synod: *Das Register des Patriarchats von Konstantinopel, 3. Teil: Edition und Übersetzung der Urkunden aus den Jahren 1350–1363*, ed. and trans. by Johannes Koder, Martin Hinterberger, and Otto Kresten, Corpus fontium historiae byzantinae, 19/3 (Vienna: Österreichische Akademie der Wissenschaften), nos 245–51, pp. 424–71, and Darrouzès, *Regestes*, V, nos 2469 and 2470; no. 2415; no. 2419; no. 2315. For the text of the solemn rejection of the errors of Akindynos by Maximos Kalopheros in 1350, see *Acta et diplomata Graeca medii aevi sacra et profana*, I: *Acta patriarchatus Constantinopolitani, MCCCXV–MCCCII, tomus prior*, ed. By Franz Miklosich and Joseph Müller (Vienna: C. Gerold, 1860), p. 295 and for a similar solemn rejection made by the priest Joasaph

1368,[39] the updating of the *Synodikon of Orthodoxy*, a liturgical text commemorating the historical 'triumph of orthodoxy' over heresy, to include the names of principal opponents of Palamas in the list of anathematized heretics,[40] and, of course, the flight of anti-Palamites like our Kyparissiotes to Cyprus and elsewhere.[41] As to when he fled Constantinople, Basileios Dentakes suggested that Kyparissiotes' silence on the subject of the condemnation of Prochoros Kydones, brother of Demetrios, Athonite monk, and anti-Palamite, by a synod of 1368, provides some basis for thinking that he had left Constantinople prior to this development.[42] Along the same lines of this reasoning, a more specific chronological window for Kyparissiotes's flight from Constantinople might be suggested by his awareness of the Palamites' harsh treatment of the corpse of Nikephoros Gregoras after his death in 1359/60.[43] Thus, perhaps, Kyparissiotes left Constantinople sometime between 1359 or 1360 and 1368, eventually to arrive on Cyprus, where he planned his next move. This 'next move' brings us to the question of Kyparissiotes's union with Rome, since, as Kydones's letter informs us, he was thinking of going to Italy.[44] Among the reasons given by Dentakes for considering Kyparissiotes's 'conversion to Roman Catholicism' 'exceedingly

in 1397, see *Acta et diplomata Graeca medii aevi sacra et profana*, II: *Acta patriarchatus Constantinopolitani, MCCCXV–MCCCCII, tomus posterior*, ed. by Franz Miklosich and Joseph Müller (Vienna: C. Gerold, 1862), pp. 295–96.

39 Talbot, 'Palamas, Gregory', in *Oxford Dictionary of Byzantium*, III, 1560.
40 Alexander Kazhdan, 'Synodikon of Orthodoxy', in *Oxford Dictionary of Byzantium*, III, 1994; Jean Gouillard, 'Le synodikon de l'Orthodoxie: edition et commentaire', *Travaux et memoires*, 2 (1967), pp. 1–3, 29–31. Athonite monks would send a request that anathemas against Barlaam and Akindynos be sent to the Holy Mountain so as to be inscribed in their own synodikon: see, Darrouzès, *Regestes*, V, no. 2509.
41 On Cyprus as refuge for anti-Palamites, see Chris Schabel, 'Religion', in *Cyprus: Society and Culture 1191–1374*, ed. by Angel Nicolaou-Konnari and Chris Schabel, The Medieval Mediterranean, 58 (Leiden: Brill, 2005), p. 211; two examples of anti-Palamites seeking asylum elsewhere besides Cyprus are Manuel Kalekas (see esp. Manuel Kalekas, *Correspondance*, ed. by Raymond-Joseph Loenertz, Studi e Testi, 152 [Vatican City: Biblioteca Apostolica Vaticana, 1950], pp. 23–46, and Loenertz, 'Manuel Calécas', and below) and Demetrios Kydones (see items cited above, n. 8). On these men and their acquaintances as exiles from Constantinople, see also Claudine Delacroix-Besnier, 'Manuel Calécas et les Frères Chrysobergès, grecs et prêcheurs', in *Actes de congrès de la Société des historiens médiévistes de l'enseignement supérieur public, 32nd Congress* (Dunkerque, 2001), esp. pp. 157–60, and Thierry Ganchou, 'Dèmètrios Kydônès, les frères Chrysobergès et la Crète (1397–1401): De nouveaux documents', in *Bisanzio, Venezia e il mondo franco-greco (XIII–XV secolo)* (= Βυζάντιο, Βενετία και ο ελληνοφραγκικός κόσμος ($13^{ος}$–$15^{ος}$ αιώνας): Πρακτικά του διεθνούς συνεδρίου που οργανώθηκε με την ευκαιρία της εκατονταετηρίδας από τη γέννηση του Raymond-Joseph Loenertz O.P. Venetia, 1–2 Δεκεμβρίου 2000), ed. by Chrysa A. Maltezou and Peter Schreiner (Venice: Istituto Ellenico, 2002), pp. 435–93.
42 Dentakes, *Ἰωάννης Κυπαρισσιώτης*, pp. 20–21. Regarding Prochoros and his sufferings, see Alice-Mary Talbot, 'Kydones, Prochoros', in *Oxford Dictionary of Byzantium*, II, 1161–62; Plested, *Orthodox Readings*, pp. 73–84. Prochoros was compelled to read the anathemas against the anti-Palamites that had been inserted, by request of Athonite monks, into their synodikon and to append his signature (see Darrouzès, *Regestes*, V, no. 2509; *Tome against Prochoros Kydones*, in Patrologia Graeca 151, ed. by Jacques-Paul Migne [Paris, 1865], col. 696A. For Prochoros's later condemnation as a heretic by the Patriarchal Synod, see the entry for the 'Condamnation synodale' in Darrouzès, *Regestes*, V, no. 2541, dated 'Avril 1368').
43 See John Kyparissiotes, *First Book of the Palamite Transgressions*, in Patrologia Graeca 152, ed. by Jacques-Paul Migne (Paris, 1866), cols 733D–36A.
44 Demetrios Kydones, *Correspondence*, I, p. 68.

probable', the most substantial is that he is recorded between November 1376 and December 1377 as a member of the retinue of Pope Gregory XI, from whom he even received a stipend.[45]

So, Kyparissiotes was an anti-Palamite and, likely, united to the Roman Church. But let us suspend judgment on this coincidence until we have a better sense of Kyparissiotes' thought. Hopefully, this will allow us to determine the relationship between Kyparissiotes' anti-Palamism and his unionism. The question here is whether any election of the Roman Church on Kyparissiotes's part followed as a necessary and logical consequence of his objection to the Palamite doctrine approved by Constantinople or whether it was, in fact, predicated upon something extraneous to his thought, such as opportunism or worldly desperation.[46]

The text of John Kyparissiotes under present consideration constitutes but a small part of his massive and still mostly unedited polemical *opus* against the Palamites: the *Four Books of the Palamite Transgressions*, the first part of which he wrote after the death of Gregoras *c.* 1360 (which, again, Kyparissiotes references) and before he had fled from Constantinople, that is before 1368.[47] Let us consider the 'Fourth Discourse' of the 'First Book' of this work.[48] It bears this title: 'That the Church of the Palamites was assembled contrary to every Christian order, concerning which ten questions are asked'.[49] This title obviously anticipates Kyparissiotes's negative assessment of the so-called 'Church of the Palamites', whose innovations, Kyparissiotes thinks, have rendered Christians 'doubtful' or 'uncertain' (ἀμφιβόλους) about the true faith.[50] The prepositional phrase 'παρὰ Χριστιανικὴν κατάστασιν' may be interpreted as conveying Kyparissiotes's view of the illegality of the establishment of this 'Church'.

---

45 For the information in this paragraph, see esp. Dentakes, Ἰωάννης Κυπαρισσιώτης, pp. 11–34 (regarding John Kyparissiotes's so-called 'conversion', and for the direct quotations presented above, see pp. 31–33); Talbot, 'Kyparissiotes, John', in *Oxford Dictionary of Byzantium*, II, 1162.
46 See above, for the perspectives of Marcus Plested and George Gennadios Scholarios. On Kyparissiotes and the Roman Church, see the essay of Sebastian Kolditz in this volume.
47 John Kyparissiotes, *Palamite Transgressions*, cols 663–738 (only a partial edition. See the next note). Regarding this work (including its title, as given above) and its structure, see Jugie, *Theologia dogmatica*, p. 481; Talbot, 'Kyparissiotes, John' in *Oxford Dictionary of Byzantium*, II, 1162; and see the 'Notitia' at Patrologia Graeca 152, cols 661–64, which Migne here indicates has been copied from 'Fabric[ii], *Biblioth[eca] Gr[aeca]* ed. Harles, t. XI'. Regarding the dating of this text, see Dentakes, Ἰωάννης Κυπαρισσιώτης, p. 18, who suggests that he wrote this text before leaving Constantinople; the *terminus post quem* is based on John Kyparissiotes's mention of the treatment of the corpse of Gregoras (see again the 'Notitia', cols 661–64). Regarding the date of Gregoras's death, Alice-Mary Talbot, 'Gregoras, Nicephorus', in *Oxford Dictionary of Byzantium*, II, pp. 874–75, writes that he 'died … between 1358 and 1361', and cf. 'Notitia', cols 663–64, which indicates the year of death as 1360. For John Kyparissiotes's mention of the dead Gregoras, see *Palamite Transgressions*, cols 733D–36A, and also see the next footnote.
48 Despite what the 'Notitia' in Migne (at cols 661–64) seems to suggest, on the basis of Jugie and Talbot (cited above), it seems that the Patrologia Graeca reproduces only two 'discourses' ('λόγοι') of the 'first book' of Kyparissiotes' much larger work against the Palamites. The 'Fourth Sermon' runs from cols 699–738B.
49 Kyparissiotes, *Palamite Transgressions*, cols 699–700: "Ὅτι παρὰ πᾶσαν Χριστιανικὴν κατάστασιν ἡ τῶν Παλαμιτῶν Ἐκκλησία συνέστη· περὶ ὃ ζητεῖται ιʹ".
50 Kyparissiotes, *Palamite Transgressions*, col. 663B. 'Ambiguity' or 'doubt' (ἀμφίβολον and its variants) regarding the Orthodox faith is a key concern for Manuel Kalekas, as we shall see below.

In the first subsection of this discourse, Kyparissiotes gives a highly condensed history of the Palamite controversy, or rather, of how the followers of Palamas came to power in the Church. His historical narrative jars considerably with that which has been told by Meyendorff and other modern scholars and has become 'conventional'. Kyparissiotes begins with Palamas himself, surrounded by 'three or four disciples' on Mount Athos. Palamas lures over more disciples and eventually 'overturns the entire monastic order'. Armed with the *Hagioretic Tome* (an exposition of the Palamite doctrine signed by Athonite monks, which Kyparissiotes refers to as 'that tome fabricated against piety, which [Palamas] evidently named for the place [of Mount Athos]'), this crew descends upon Constantinople, where Palamas eventually wins influence over 'some of the powerful people' who take Palamas and his like as their 'teachers'. By 'some of the powerful people', Kyparissiotes is presumably referring to John Kantakouzenos and other notables whose successful seizure of power assisted Palamas and his followers in accessing the upper echelons of the Church. According to John Kyparissiotes, 'these powerful people […] after they had won their victories established the teachers that they had thus acquired for themselves in the Church, and [they] named this ('ταύτην') 'of God', and they drove everyone into worship, proclaiming the Church teaches these things'. So much for Kyparissiotes's historical preface to his discourse 'showing how the affairs of this Church proceeded, and that it is not justly, nor sacredly called by this name'—that is, the Palamites should not be dignified by the name of 'church' at all.[51]

In contrast to the pseudo-ecclesial Palamite gang, Kyparissiotes offers a series of positive definitions of the true 'Church of God': 'according to the divinely-handed down oracles, the Holy Church of God is a sacred gathering not necessarily constituted by a crowd of holy men, but even by a very few […] for the Holy Word somewhere said, "Where two or three are gathered in my name, there I am in their midst"'.[52] The value

---

51 Kyparissiotes, *Palamite Transgressions*, cols 700C–01A: 'Μετὰ τοσούτων τοίνυν τῶν αἱρέσεων καὶ τοιαύτης τῆς ἀποστάσεως εἰσπηδήσας ὁ Παλαμᾶς, καὶ τὸ μὲν πρῶτον τρεῖς ἢ τέτταρας ἑαυτῷ μαθητεύσας, ἐνίους δὲ καὶ τῶν ἐν τῷ Ἱερῷ ὄρει παρυποκλέψας, ἐπιβοώμενος ὡς ἄρα Βαρλαὰμ τὰς ἑκασταχοῦ θεοφανείας, καὶ τὰς ἄλλοτ' ἄλλας πραγματευθείσας τοῖς πώποτε μακαρίοις ἐλλάμψεις, διασύρει, καὶ πᾶσαν ἀνατρέπει μοναχικὴν κατάστασιν· καὶ τούτους διὰ τούτων ὑποσύρας, καὶ ὑποσημῆναι δι' ἁπλότητα παρασκευάσας τὸν σχεδιασθέντα κατὰ τῆς εὐσεβείας Τόμον ἐκεῖνον, ὃν καὶ ἐκ τοῦ τόπου ἐπωνυμίας σαφῶς ἠξίωσεν· ἔπειτα καὶ ἐπὶ τὴν Μεγάλην πόλιν ἐλάσας, καὶ τί μὲν ὑποδεικνὺς τὸ τῆς ἀσεβείας ὁμοῦ καὶ ἀπάτης γραμματεῖον, τί δὲ τοὺς ἠκολουθηκότας ἀναιδείας ὑπέκκαυμα καὶ ἀδολεσχίας παριστῶν, ἐκεῖνο περιφανῶς πρὸς ἐνίους τῶν δυνατῶν ἐξήνυσεν, ὃ φησιν ὁ μέγας Ἀπόστολος· «Ἔσται καιρὸς, ὅτε τῆς ὑγιαινούσης διδασκαλίας οὐκ ἀνέξονται, ἀλλὰ κατὰ τὰς ἰδίας ἐπιθυμίας ἑαυτοῖς ἐπισωρεύσουσι διδασκάλους, κνηθόμενοι τὴν ἀκοήν. Καὶ ἀπὸ μὲν τῆς ἀληθείας τὴν ἀκοὴν ἀποτρέψουσι· ἐπὶ δὲ τοὺς μύθους ἐκτραπήσονται.» Καὶ οὐδὲ τούτους ἁπλῶς καὶ ὡς ἔτυχεν, ἀλλ' ὡς ἂν ἡμῖν ῥηθείη, πόνοις προτέροις μακροῖς καὶ πᾶσι τοῖς ἀρέσκουσι πρὸς τὴν τῆς ἀρχῆς κλοπὴν καὶ περιποίησιν. Τοὺς οὖν οὕτως ἐπισωρευθέντας ἑαυτοῖς διδασκάλους, τῶν τροπαίων διηνυσμένων, εἰς Ἐκκλησίαν καταστήσαντες, καὶ ταύτην τοῦ Θεοῦ ὀνομάσαντες, πάντας ἐλαύνουσιν ἐπὶ τὴν θρησκείαν· «Ἡ Ἐκκλησία ταῦτα πρεσβεύει», κεκραγότες. Δι' ἅπερ καὶ ἡμεῖς τὸν παρόντα συνεστησάμεθα λόγον, παριστῶντες τὰ τῆς Ἐκκλησίας ταύτης ὅπως προέβη, καὶ ὡς οὐ δικαίως, οὐδ' ὁσίως τῷ προσρήματι τούτῳ λέγεται.' The *Hagioretic Tome* (with an introduction) is found in Gregory Palamas, Συγγράμματα, II: Πραγματεῖαι καὶ ἐπιστολαὶ γραφεῖσαι κατὰ τὰ ἔτη 1340–1346, ed. by Panagiotis K. Chrestou and others (Thessaloniki: Kyromanos, 1994), pp. 563–78.

52 Kyparissiotes, *Palamite Transgressions*, col. 701D: 'Ὡς ἂν δὲ πρότερον τὸν τῆς Ἐκκλησίας τοῦ Θεοῦ γνῶμεν ὅρον, ἁγία τοῦ Θεοῦ Ἐκκλησία ἐστὶ κατὰ τὰ θεοπαράδοτα λόγια σύναξις ἱερὰ οὐ μόνον ἐκ πλειόνων καὶ μακαρίων ἀνδρῶν, ἀλλὰ καὶ ἐξ ἐλαττόνων, ἐπὶ τῷ ὀνόματι τοῦ ἀληθινοῦ φωτὸς τοῦ φωτίζοντος πάντα

of this definition, which allows the Church to be identified with an extreme minority, would have been of obvious value to anti-Palamites such as Kyparissiotes who found themselves increasingly marginalized in the face of the entrenchment of Palamites in the hierarchy of the Constantinopolitan Church and the establishment of Palamism as orthodoxy in the late 1340s, 1350s, and 1360s.[53] Supplementary descriptions of the Church likewise serve Kyparissiotes's particular theological outlook. The Church is 'founded upon the rock of the apostolic and patristic traditions' and never innovates theologically. 'The Holy Church of God is the teacher of divine and human things; and, according to the saying of the Apostle, "she takes prisoner every thought to Christ"—that is, in accordance with the common conceptions of God; on the basis of these, as the divine Basil says, she begins her inquiry into everything, and back to them she strives to restore [this inquiry] again [...] in nothing does she transgress the boundaries that have already been established, or the tradition of the fathers [...]. Moreover, the holy Church of God is the whole, fully limbed ('ὁλομέλεια') Body of Christ, referring to one Head'. The true 'Church of God' is known by 'the fruit of the Spirit, which is, according to the divine Apostle: charity, joy, peace, patience, kindness, goodness, faith, mildness, temperance'.[54]

So much for Kyparissiotes's definition of the true 'Church of God'. It comes as no surprise that Kyparissiotes's idealized 'Church of God' is completely incompatible with the 'Church of the Palamites', given the manner of the establishment of this 'Church' and the behavior of her adherents—a point he proceeds to demonstrate throughout this discourse.[55] For instance, Kyparissiotes argues that the Palamites had been earlier anathematized by the legitimate ecclesiastical authority: 'Thus the confessor John [Kalekas], blessed and great among the patriarchs, in his many and

---

ἄνθρωπον ἐρχόμενον εἰς τὸν κόσμον συνελθοῦσα. Ὁ γὰρ ἱερὸς ἔφησέ που λόγος, «Ὅπου εἰσὶ δύο ἢ τρεῖς συνηγμένοι εἰς τὸ ἐμὸν ὄνομα, ἐκεῖ εἰμι ἐν μέσῳ αὐτῶν»'.

53 Again, see Plested, *Orthodox Readings*, pp. 221–22, also pp. 115, 118–20, and above.

54 Kyparissiotes, *Palamite Transgressions*, cols 701D–04C: "Ἔτι ἁγία τοῦ Θεοῦ ἐστιν Ἐκκλησία θίασος ἱερός, σχοίνισμα κληρονομίας Χριστοῦ· Βασίλειον ἱεράτευμα, λαὸς περιούσιος Θεοῦ, ἐπὶ τῇ πέτρᾳ τῶν ἀποστολικῶν καὶ πατρικῶν παραδόσεων τεθεμελιωμένη, καὶ μηδέν τι καινοφανὲς ἐπ' ἀναιρέσει τῶν ἐξαρχῆς παραδεχομένη δογμάτων. Τὸ μὲν γὰρ ὁ σωτήριος προησφαλίσατο Λόγος, «Διδάσκοντες αὐτοὺς.» φησί, «τηρεῖν πάντα, ὅσα ἐντειλάμην ὑμῖν·» τὸ δ' ὁ θεῖος Ἀπόστολος, «Τὰς βεβήλους καινοφωνίας περιίστασο.» Καὶ πάλιν, «Κἂν ἄγγελος ἐξ οὐρανοῦ εὐαγγελίσηται παρ' ὃ παρελάβετε, κἂν ἐγὼ Παῦλος, ἀνάθεμα ἔστω.» Ἔτι ἁγία τοῦ Θεοῦ ἐστιν Ἐκκλησία διδάσκαλος θείων καὶ ἀνθρωπίνων πραγμάτων· καὶ κατὰ τὸν μὲν Ἀπόστολον, «αἰχμαλωτίζουσα πᾶν νόημα εἰς Χριστόν·» τουτέστι πρὸς τὰς κοινὰς περὶ Θεοῦ ἐννοίας· κἀκ τούτων, ὡς ὁ θεῖος φησὶ Βασίλειος, ἀρχομένη πάντα ζητεῖν, καὶ πρὸς αὐτὰς πάλιν ἀποκαθιστᾶν πειρᾶται· κἂν γραφικὸν ἐμπέσῃ τι ῥῆμα, ὡς ἡ ἐν Χαλκηδόνι ἁγία καὶ οἰκουμενικὴ διωρίσατο σύνοδος, μὴ ἄλλως ἑρμηνεύουσα τοῦτο, ἢ ὡς οἱ τῆς Ἐκκλησίας φωστῆρες καὶ διδάσκαλοι διὰ τῶν οἰκείων συγγραμμάτων παρέθεντο· ἐν οὐδενὶ παραβαίνουσα τοὺς ἤδη τεθέντας ὅρους, ἢ τὴν ἐκ τῶν Πατέρων παράδοσιν. Ἔτι, ἁγία τοῦ Θεοῦ ἐστιν Ἐκκλησία σώματος ὁλομέλεια τοῦ Χριστοῦ, ἐπὶ μίαν ἀναγομένη κεφαλήν, κατὰ τὸ εἰρημένον ὑπὸ τοῦ Κυρίου, «Καὶ γενήσεται μία ποίμνη, εἷς ποιμήν.» Ἔπεται δὲ ἐξ ἀνάγκης τῇ καλῶς ἐκ τῶν θεουργῶν ὁρισθείσῃ λογίων ἁγίᾳ τοῦ Θεοῦ Ἐκκλησίᾳ ὁ καρπὸς τοῦ Πνεύματος. Ὁ δέ ἐστι, κατὰ τὸν θεῖον Ἀπόστολον, ἀγάπη, χαρά, εἰρήνη, μακροθυμία, χρηστότης, ἀγαθωσύνη, πίστις, πραότης, ἐγκράτεια'.

55 See, e.g., Kyparissiotes, *Palamite Transgressions*, cols 705B–08B (ch. 3: Εἰ ἁγία τοῦ Θεοῦ Ἐκκλησία ἡ διὰ σύγχυσιν καὶ μισθὸν προδοσίας τὴν ἀρχὴν συστᾶσα).

diverse synodical *acta*, declared Palamas to be cast out of the sacred precincts, along with his followers'.[56]

In the final subchapter of this discourse, the ultimate proof of the failure of the Palamite sect to satisfy the criteria of the true Church is the outrageous treatment that the Palamites mete out to the corpses of their enemies, whom Kyparissiotes calls 'saints'. Some corpses are exhumed from their graves, others are left to rot unburied. Kyparissiotes gives the example of Nikephoros Gregoras, the last anti-Palamite to withstand Palamas to his face. The Palamites went on abusing the corpse of Nikephoros as though the 'insults, abuse, and imprisonments' that he had suffered at their hands were not enough. Clearly, according to Kyparissiotes the Palamites cannot be the 'true Church of Christ'.[57] That is not surprising at all, but something remains unclear: how does the Church of Constantinople fit into all of this? Is she the true Church of Christ?

This question can be answered by another: does Kyparissiotes identify the Church of Constantinople and the Palamite Church? Obviously, the church, in a specific and institutional sense, over which the Palamites gained power, as described by Kyparissiotes in his condensed history, is the Church of Constantinople. According to Kyparissiotes, Kantakouzenos and his associates successfully ensconced Palamas and his followers in the leadership of the Church of Constantinople, which they used as a platform for presenting themselves as the 'Church of God' and their doctrines as orthodoxy. Thus, the connection between the Palamites and the Constantinopolitan See is undeniable. But it is also qualified. Following this history, Kyparissiotes specifies that his indictment is against 'not everyone constituting *this* (ταύτην), but only those first establishing this Palamite pseudo-Church 'from the beginning'. Naturally, when referring to those who 'first established' this Church, Kyparissiotes has in mind Palamas and his original collaborators and handlers specifically. Kyparissiotes is denying that they could be the Church of God. Does the generality of believers that now constitute this 'Church', and that does not incur Kyparissiotes's indictment, therefore refer only to to rank-and-file Greek Christians belonging to Constantinople specifically or to the faithful of the universal Church beyond Constantinople? Though, again, context would seem to support the first interpretation, Kyparissiotes does not feel the need to be altogether clear on this point and even in this lack of specificity, as we shall see, he demonstrated that he was not beholden to a crisis mentality.[58]

---

56 Kyparissiotes, *Palamite Transgressions*, col. 708C: 'Ὁ μὲν οὖν μακαρίτης καὶ μέγας ἐν πατριάρχαις ὁ ὁμολογητὴς Ἰωάννης ἐν πολλαῖς μὲν καὶ διαφόροις αὐτοῦ συνοδικοῖς πράξεσιν ἀποκήρυκτον θείων περιβόλων ἀπεφήνατο Παλαμᾶν, καὶ τοὺς συμφρονοῦντας αὐτῷ [...]'.

57 Kyparissiotes, *Palamite Transgressions*, cols 733D–37B, esp. cols 733D–36A: 'Πρὸς τούτοις δὲ καὶ τὸ θαυμαστὸν ἐκεῖνο σῶμα τοῦ μεγάλου τῆς ἀληθείας κήρυκος παιζόμενόν τε καὶ περιφερόμενον ἐφ' ἱκανόν· καὶ τοῦτο μὲν ἐν φιλοσόφοις ὄντος, οἷος οὐδεὶς ἐν αὐτοῖς θαυμασιώτερος· τοῦτο δ' ἐν ἀσκηταῖς, οἷος οὐδεὶς ἕτερος σπουδαιότερος· τοῦτο δ' ἐν τοῖς ὑπὲρ εὐσεβείας ἀγῶσι καὶ τοῖς ἀπὸ τῶν πειρατῶν προπηλακισμοῖς καὶ λοιδορίαις καὶ καθείρξεσιν οἷος οὐδεὶς ἄλλος ἐν ἅπασι καρτερικώτερος· Νικηφόρου, φημὶ, τοῦ θαυμαστοῦ Γρηγορᾶ [...]'. And see Dentakes, *Ἰωάννης Κυπαρισσιώτης*, pp. 19–20, where he cites relevant passages from Kyparissiotes, *Palamite Transgressions*.

58 Kyparissiotes, *Palamite Transgressions*, col. 701CD: '[...] Προσέχειν δ' ἄξιον, ὡς οὐ κατὰ πάντων ἡμῖν ὁ λόγος προῆκται τῶν νῦν ταύτην συμπληρούντων, ἀλλὰ περὶ μόνων τούτων ταύτην τὴν ἀρχὴν συστησαμένων, εὐαριθμήτων τινῶν ὄντων, καὶ σχεδὸν αὐτῶν τῶν ἡμῖν ἐπὶ μαρτυρίᾳ μνημονευομένων. Οὔτε γὰρ περὶ τῶν

ANTI-PALAMISM, UNIONISM, AND THE 'CRISIS OF FAITH'   531

The crucial role of this distinction between the original establishers of the Palamite dogma and those constituting the Church at present in Kyparissiotes's thought becomes evident in a later passage where he claims that 'it is proper for every Christian to consider who he should call the holy Church of God and even what manner of men are eminent in this [Church], but he *ought not consider* to be the holy Church of God whoever should happen 'to seize the [patriarchal] throne, establishing a sect of those like-minded to them'.[59]

Kyparissiotes is urging that the 'Church of God' not be blindly identified with the hierarchy, otherwise 'it would seem that even from the beginning the synagogue of Arians is the holy Church of God; and the synagogue of the Monothelites, and of the Iconoclasts; for many and divers such as these seized the [patriarchal throne]'. His point is that this would obviously be absurd. Kyparissiotes goes on to say that, 'in accordance with the account of the holy Church of God, it is necessary that he who presides over this both think and teach Orthodox doctrines'. Otherwise, despite any appearances to the contrary, 'the holy Church of God is not with him'. A hierarch must be Orthodox if he is to be rightly considered the hierarch of the 'holy Church of God'. But Kyparissiotes clearly sees no guarantee that hierarchs *will be* Orthodox.[60] The distinction between the fallible hierarchy and the true 'Church of God' is crucial in Kyparissiotes's thought. Despite heresy at the highest level of the institutional church, this 'Church of God' could persist below the hierarchy even in the faith of 'two or three' orthodox Christians.[61]

Faced with the errors of the hierarchs of Constantinople, did John Kyparissiotes, in the final analysis, deny that his ancestral church was the 'true Church'? Not really, except in the most qualified sense: he merely maintained that those men who had established Palamism as 'orthodoxy', including the hierarchs currently dominating Constantinople, cannot constitute the true Church; he explicitly stated that his condemnation does not apply to the generality of believers.[62] It is essentially Kyparissiotes's distinction between the Palamite heretics themselves and the Church *per se*, a heuristic of specification applicable to past heresies, that

---

τὸν ἀριθμὸν μόνον συμπληρούντων ἀνάγκη λέγειν, οὔτε τινὸς τῶν ἐν ἀξιώμασι διαπρεπόντων, τοῦ καιροῦ τοῦτο καὶ τῆς συνηθείας καταναγκάσαντος· οὔτε μὴν τῶν δημοτικῶν ἀνδρῶν, ἔργον τὸν βίον, καὶ οὐ τὴν τῶν δογμάτων πρόνοιαν ποιουμένων'.

59 Kyparissiotes, *Palamite Transgressions*, col. 704CD: 'Τούτων διορισθέντων, σκοπεῖν προσήκει πάντα Χριστιανόν, τίνα τε δεῖ καλεῖν ἁγίαν τοῦ Θεοῦ Ἐκκλησίαν, καὶ ὁποίους τοὺς ἐν αὐτῇ διαλάμποντας, καὶ μὴ ὅτι τις ὑπελάβετο τοῦ θρόνου, φατρίαν τῶν ὁμογνωμονούντων συστησάμενος, τάδε ἢ τάδε πρότερον φρονεῖν ἀναπείσας, τοὺς τοιούτους εἶναι νομίζειν ἁγίαν τοῦ Θεοῦ Ἐκκλησία [...]'.
60 Kyparissiotes, *Palamite Transgressions*, cols 704D–06B, chapter 2: 'Εἰ διὰ τὸν δεῖνα καὶ τὸν δεῖνα πατριαρχεύοντα ἁγία τοῦ Θεοῦ Ἐκκλησία λέγεται): [...] Εἰ γὰρ τοῦτ' ἦν, ἐξαρχῆς ἐδόκει ἂν καὶ ἡ τῶν Ἀρειανῶν συναγωγὴ ἁγία τοῦ Θεοῦ Ἐκκλησία· καὶ ἡ τῶν Μονοθελητῶν, καὶ ἡ τῶν Εἰκονομάχων· πολλῶν μὲν τοιούτων καὶ διαφόρων ἐπειλημμένων τοῦ θρόνου [...]. Ἔτι, κατὰ τὸν δοθέντα τῆς ἁγίας τοῦ Θεοῦ Ἐκκλησίας λόγον δεῖ τὸν ταύτης προϊστάμενον καὶ φρονεῖν καὶ διδάσκειν ὀρθά. Ἂν δὲ τοῖς τεθεῖσιν ἀντιπολιτεύηται, οὐδὲ τοῖς ὁρισθεῖσι περικλείεται, καὶ οὕτω τὸ κατ' αὐτὸν οὐκ ἔστιν ἁγία τοῦ Θεοῦ Ἐκκλησία. Οὔκουν γε οὐδ' ὁ τοιοῦτος προσηκόντως ἂν διακούσειε τῆς ἱερᾶς ταύτης κλήσεως· δοκεῖ δὲ μόνον μὴ τοιοῦτος ὤν'.
61 Kyparissiotes, *Palamite Transgressions*, col. 701D.
62 Kyparissiotes, *Palamite Transgressions*, col. 701CD, and see above.

preempts the conclusion that the Church of Constantinople as such cannot be the true Church—the conclusion that is at the center of the crisis mentality. Based on what we now know of his ecclesiology and historical understanding, the heresy of the Palamites need not have forced him, as a logical consequence, to forswear his ancestral church and seek the one true Church elsewhere. He might have been content to be one of the 'two or three' Greek Christians gathered in the Lord's name in His one true Church of the Orthodox few, awaiting the eventual restoration of an Orthodox hierarchy in Constantinople, just as Constantinople had recovered from periods of rule by heretical hierarchs in times bygone.[63] After all, Kyparissiotes himself, born in the early fourteenth century, could well remember a time before Palamas. If he did enter Roman communion—which seems likely—then this, it is feared, was the result of something more crass than theological convictions.[64] As Scholarios would say, 'because he had nowhere else to go to' ...[65]

The Crisis Mentality: Manuel Kalekas (c. 1360–1410)

The public life of Manuel Kalekas, apparently a native of Constantinople, is bookended by events through which we can see clearly the anti-Palamite and unionist aspects of his theological profile respectively. In 1396, he was plucked out of historical obscurity when he was summoned before the Patriarchal Synod in Constantinople to answer for his allegedly dissident views regarding the theology of Palamas. In 1410, Manuel died on the island of Lesbos dressed in the habit of a Dominican friar.[66] Certain

---

63   Kyparissiotes, *Palamite Transgressions*, col. 701D and col. 704D on the true Church as potentially persisting in the few true Christians (rather than in the hierarchy or the many), and cols 672B–73B regarding the eventual recovery of the Church (Dentakes, Ἰωάννης Κυπαρισσιώτης, pp. 19–20, cites a relevant passage from col. 673AB).
64   On the likelihood of Kyparissiotes's entrance into Roman communion, see Dentakes, Ἰωάννης Κυπαρισσιώτης, pp. 30–33 and Talbot, 'Kyparissiotes, John', in *Oxford Dictionary of Byzantium*, II, p. 1162, who indicate that Kyparissiotes became a stipendiary of the pope, thus revealing one possible 'crass' motive.
65   But cf. Dentakes, Ἰωάννης Κυπαρισσιώτης, pp. 32–33.
66   On Manuel Kalekas see, above all, works by Raymond-Joseph Loenertz, 'Manuel Calécas, sa vie et ses oeuvres d'après ses lettres et ses apologies inédites', *Archivum Fratrum Praedicatorum*, 17 (1947), 195–207 and Manuel Kalekas, *Correspondance*, ed. by Raymond-Joseph Loenertz, Studi e Testi, 152 (Vatican City: Biblioteca Apostolica Vaticana, 1950), pp. 16–45. See also Jugie, *Theologia dogmatica*, pp. 482–83; Jean Gouillard, 'Les influences latines dans l'oeuvre théologique de Manuel Calécas', *Échos d'Orient*, 37 (1938), 35–52; Jean Gouillard, 'Calécas (Manuel)', in *Dictionnaire d'histoire et de géographie ecclésiastiques*, ed. by Alfred Braudillart, Albert de Meyer, and Étienne van Cauwenbergh, 31 vols (Paris: Libraire Letouzey et Ané and Turnhout: Brepols, 1912–2015), XI (1949), pp. 380–84; Agostino Pertusi, 'Gli studi latini di Manuele Caleca e la traduzione del De Trinitate di Boezio', in *Miscellanea Giovanni Galbiati, Archeologia storia, filologia classica e bizantina, Filologia orientale e semitica glottologia, letteratura medioevale paleografia arte*, Fontes ambrosiani 25–27, 3 vols (Milan: U. Hoepli, 1951), III, pp. 283–312; Hans-Georg Beck, *Kirche und theologische Literatur im Byzantinischen Reich*, Byzantinisches Handbuch im Rahmen des Handbuchs der Altertumwissenschaft, 2.1 (Munich: C. H. Beck, 1959), pp. 740–41; Erich Trapp, Rainer Walther, and Hans-Veit Beyer, *Prosopographisches Lexikon der Palaiologenzeit*, 12 vols, Addenda, Gesamtregister (Vienna: Österreichische Akademie der Wissenschaften, 1976-96), no. 10289; Alice-Mary Talbot, 'Kalekas, Manuel', in *Oxford Dictionary of Byzantium*, II, 1092; Claudine Delacroix-Besnier, *Les dominicains et*

passages of Manuel's various writings against Palamas or in favour of ecclesiastical union yield insight into his views about the nature of the Church established by Christ and her relationship to Constantinople and Rome.

Although it is not certain that Manuel himself had entered communion with Rome around the time he was summoned by the Patriarchal Synod, evidence suggests that he was at least on his way there. By the time he came under synodal scrutiny, he had already established contacts with 'Latinophiles' such as Demetrios Kydones and Maximos Chrysoberges, and through them with Fr Elias Petit, a former vicar general of the Dominicans operating in territories of the Greek East under Genoese rule. Moreover, after he had come under scrutiny by the patriarchal synod, Manuel fled to Pera, the Genoese-controlled suburb separated from Constantinople by the Golden Horn, where he seems to have found asylum among the Dominicans.[67]

From exile in Pera, Manuel composed a number of *apologiae* defending his own integrity and orthodoxy and attacking his ecclesiastical adversaries. Manuel addressed one of these *apologiae* to his namesake the emperor Manuel II Palaiologos,[68] in which he informed his sovereign about the circumstances that had set him upon this path of exile—specifically, his confrontation with the officers of the Great Church—and pleaded with him to intervene as an 'impartial judge' between him and his Palamite adversaries.[69] After excusing himself for bothering the emperor about his own misfortunes, Manuel asserts the importance of truth above all, particularly theological truth, upon which depends eternal salvation.[70] With this in mind, Manuel reports to the emperor his perception of the disturbing 'contradiction' between the 'ancient and new [teachers]' of the Church. After undertaking an investigation—not a little annoying to some in the Church who had 'their office as their only proof'—Manuel determined that the doctrines of the Palamites were obscurantist and unhinged from 'the most common notions concerning God and the principles of faith' and 'the decrees of the fathers'. The results of his investigation into the matter were not

---

la chretienté grecque aux XIVe et XVe siècles, Collection de l'école française de Rome, 237 (Rome: École française de Rome, 1997), pp. 267–71; Christos Triantafyllopoulos, *Conversions from Orthodoxy to Roman Catholicism in Fourteenth-Century Byzantium: The Case of Manuel Calecas and His Apologias* (unpublished MA thesis, University of London, 2000); Claudine-Delacroix-Besnier, 'A propos du manuscrit FX 28 de la Bibliothèque communale de Sienne', *Mélanges de l'École française de Rome*, 113.2 (2001), pp. 735–66; Delacroix-Besnier, 'Manuel Calécas', pp. 151–64; Plested, *Orthodox Readings*, pp. 115–19.

67 See entries mentioned above in nn. 14 and 67, but esp. Manuel Kalekas, *Correspondance*, pp. 16–31; Loenertz, 'Manuel Calécas', pp. 199–203. Relevant to the question of when Manuel embraced communion with the Latin Church, George Dennis, editor and translator of the letters of Emperor Manuel II, convincingly asserts that one letter in which the emperor describes an unnamed, disgruntled Greek who has embraced Latin religious rites with gusto refers to Manuel Kalekas: *The Letters of Manuel II Palaeologus: Text, Translation, and Notes*, ed. and trans. by George T. Dennis, Corpus Fontium Historiae Byzantinae, 8 (Washington, DC: Dumbarton Oaks Center for Byzantine Studies, 1977), no. 30, pp. 74–79 and see p. 78 n. 1.

68 For this *apologia*, see Manuel Kalekas, *Correspondance*, 'Appendix,' no. 1, pp. 156–57 (French summary), pp. 308–18 (Greek text).

69 Regarding Manuel's request for imperial intervention specifically, see Manuel Kalekas, *Correspondance*, 'App.' no. 1. 5, p. 156 ('Rien n'égale les maux qui dérivent de l'absence d'un juge impartial'), pp. 311–12.

70 Kalekas, *Correspondance*, 'App.' no. 1. 1–3, p. 156; pp. 308–10.

only the conclusion that the Palamites interpreted the fathers in a prejudicial and piecemeal fashion, but that the Palamite doctrine of the distinction between God's energies and essence was absolutely at odds with the Orthodox faith.[71]

The other result of Manuel's investigation was his arraignment before a tribunal of the Great Church.[72] Called upon to answer for himself—after all, the Palamite Distinction had been the established doctrine of the Church for decades—Manuel replied that he was quite eager to make his profession of unswerving fidelity to the ancient doctrines of the Church. But his inquisitors were not interested in his belief in those doctrines. They were only concerned with Manuel's belief (or lack thereof) in the distinction between the divine energies and essence.[73]

'And so it is,' continues Manuel who proceeds to the heart of the problem, which is an ecclesial problem, a defect of his ancestral church: 'If she, from the time she was established, never decreed falsehood, but always obtained the truth in all things, then it would hold true that no one would be in any doubt ('ἀμφιβάλλειν') whatsoever concerning the things she speaks. But, if she has pronounced many things that are not true and has often been afflicted by heresies, with the result that (on the one hand) [today] she subjects those who were in agreement with her in the past to insoluble curses while (on the other hand) she now admires as great men those who opposed her [in the past],' can anyone today be so sure that any 'newer' doctrine pronounced by the Church of Constantinople is 'truth' rather than 'falsehood', is orthodoxy rather than heresy? Doubts gnaw the faithful, 'since there is no teaching ('διδασκαλία') leading the way and showing what is true and what is false'. The feelings of anxiety resulting from this situation are aggravated by the fact that the inconstancy of Constantinople is not merely a matter of ancient history, but a recent phenomenon, for Constantinople 'has decreed contrary things concerning the topic now proposed [i.e., the Palamite doctrine], with the result that it has been placed in doubt ('ἐν ἀμφιβόλῳ') by which of the two [contrary] decrees [that she has made] it is necessary to abide. For it is absurd that she who otherwise proclaims

---

71 Kalekas, *Correspondance*, 'App.' no. 1. 4, p. 311: 'Τοῦτο δὴ βουληθεὶς καὶ περὶ τῶν νῦν λεγομένων ἔχειν, καὶ τοσούτῳ μᾶλλον ὅσῳ καὶ πολλοὺς τοὺς ἀντιλέγοντας εὕρισκον παλαιούς τε καὶ νέους, ἵνα κατὰ τῶν ἐναντίων ἱστάμενος τῇ τε ἀληθείᾳ καὶ τοῖς οἰκείοις χαρίζομαι – τοὺς τοίνυν ἑκατέρωθεν λόγους ἀκριβῶς διελθὼν οὐκ ἄνευ πάντως τῆς τῶν εὐχῶν συμμαχίας, ἀνερευνῶν δὲ καὶ τοὺς ὑπὲρ τῆς ὑποθέσεως ζῶντας, εἴ τι καὶ λέγειν ἔχοιεν τῶν γεγραμμένων καινότερον, καὶ τοὺς μὲν ὁρῶν πρὸς ἔπος λέγοντας οὐδέν, ἀξιοῦντας δὲ τὰ παρ' ἑαυτῶν οὕτως ἔχειν οἷον ἄν τις ἐν Ἀθήναις ἠξίωσε τοὺς τοῦ Σόλωνος νόμους, καὶ τοὺς λόγον τινὰ περὶ τούτων προθυμουμένους ἀκούειν περιέργους εἶναι [ἡγουμένους] καὶ τῶν ἐπαράτων ἐγγύς, ἀπόδειξιν δὲ μόνην τὸ ἑαυτῶν προβαλλομένους ἀξίωμα, εἰ δὲ καί τι προΐσχοιντο, ποτὲ μὲν ἐπὶ τὰ ἀφανῆ καταφεύγοντας, καὶ τὴν πεῖραν καὶ τὰς αἰσθήσεις μηδὲν μηδαμῇ τῶν περὶ θεοῦ κοινοτάτων ἐννοιῶν καὶ τῶν τῆς πίστεως ἀρχῶν ἐπιστρεφομένους, μήτε μὴν τῶν διδασκαλικῶν ἀποφάσεων [...]'.

72 Jean Darrouzès, *Les regestes des actes du patriarcat de Constantinople I: Les actes des patriarches*, VI: *Les regestes de 1377 à 1410* (Paris: Institut français d'études byzantines, 1979), no. 3022, who cobbles together Manuel's so-called 'procès synodal' on the basis of various sources by Manuel Kalekas himself (above all, the *apologiae* in Manuel Kalekas, *Correspondance*, 'App.' nos 1–3, pp. 308–23). Manuel was by no means the only Greek to undergo this sort of scrutiny by the Patriarchal Synod, see Darrouzès, *Regestes*, V, nos 2414, 2470, 2469, 2415, 2419.

73 Kalekas, *Correspondance*, 'App.' no. 1. 6, pp. 312–13.

herself to preside over the whole world (οἰκουμένη) as teacher ('διδάσκαλον') does not want to apply her teaching within her own jurisdiction, as though begrudging her own [adherents]'.[74] Constantinople's historical lapses, no less than her current maddening unclarity regarding the doctrinal controversy du jour demonstrate the defect of her magisterium: it is fallible. In Manuel's view, a disqualifying defect.

In no uncertain terms, Manuel spells out from what it is that this defect disqualifies Constantinople in the prologue to a treatise on the Palamite controversy that he authored around this time, his *On Essence and Energy*.[75] In the passage in question, and with greater historical concreteness than in his letter to the emperor, Manuel refers to Constantinople's alleged self-contradiction on the question of the Palamite Distinction and from this 'flip-flopping' he derives an explicit ecclesial assessment of his Mother See:

> […] Since there was a time when the church herself, prior to this [later] decree [of 1351], published another contradictory [decree]; and those who still live and were present then in that synod under the Emperor Andronikos bear witness [to this], as do the synodical acta that were produced regarding these things, as well as that which has been recorded concerning them; so that there is doubt (ἀμφίβολον) about which of these decrees has truth on its side; for contradictory propositions cannot both be true at the same time, and because *it is impossible that she who judges and maintains absolutely contradictory things about these important matters of faith—sometimes this way, sometimes the opposite—and freely issues forth [contradictory] declarations through letters and acta be called and believed to be the catholic Church. For the catholic Church must always speak the truth; since even the Lord decreed that the one disobeying her is a heathen and a publican*.[76]

---

74 Kalekas, *Correspondance*, 'App.' no. 1. 7, p. 313: '"Ἔχει γὰρ οὑτωσί. εἰ μὲν ἐξ οὗπερ αὕτη συνέστη τὸ ψεῦδος οὐκ ἐψηφίσατο, ἀλλ' ἀεὶ τῆς ἀληθείας ἐν πᾶσιν ἐτύγχανε, καλῶς ἂν ἔχοι περὶ ὧν λέγοι μηδένα μηδ' ὁπωσοῦν ἀμφιβάλλειν. εἰ δὲ πολλὰ καὶ τῶν μὴ ὄντων ἐξεῖπε καὶ ταῖς αἱρέσεσι συνεσχέθη πολλάκις, ὥστε καὶ τοὺς [μὲν] αὐτῇ τηνικαῦτα συμφωνήσαντας ἀραῖς ἀλύτοις ὑπάγειν, τοὺς δ' ἀντειπόντας νῦν ὡς μεγάλους θαυμάζειν, πῶς ἄν τις τὸ τῇ ἐκκλησίᾳ ταύτῃ νεώτερόν τι δοκεῖν ὥς τι τῶν ἀναγκαίων εἰς ἀπόδειξιν προβαλεῖται, μὴ προηγουμένης διδασκαλίας καὶ δεικνύσης τί μὲν ἀλήθεια τί δὲ ψεῦδος, καὶ τί μὲν ἀναιρεῖται τῶν ὁμολογουμένων τοῦδέ τινος ὑποτεθειμένου, τί δὲ συμβαίνει; καὶ τοσούτῳ τοῦτο μᾶλλον εἰκὸς ὅσῳ καὶ περὶ τῆς προκειμένης νῦν ὑποθέσεως ἐψηφίσατο τἀναντία, ὥστε νῦν ἐν ἀμφιβόλῳ κεῖσθαι ποτέρα τῶν ἀποφάσεων τίθεσθαι δεῖ. ἄτοπον δὲ καὶ ἄλλως τῆς μὲν οἰκουμένης ἁπάσης διδάσκαλον ἑαυτὴν ἐπαγγέλλεσθαι προκαθῆσθαι, εἴσω δὲ ἑαυτῆς ὥσπερ τοῖς οἰκείοις φθονοῦσαν μὴ βούλεσθαι τὴν διδασκαλίαν ἐκτείνειν […].'

75 Kalekas, *Correspondance*, pp. 27–30. For this text, see Patrologia Graeca 152, ed. by Jacques-Paul Migne (Paris, 1866), cols 283–428.

76 Kalekas, *On Essence and Energy*, col. 285A: '[…] ὡς ἦν καιρός, ὅτε ἡ Ἐκκλησία αὕτη τῆς ἀποφάσεως ταύτης πρότερον ἑτέραν ἐναντίαν ἐξήνεγκε· καὶ μαρτυροῦσιν οἱ καὶ νῦν ἔτι ζῶντες τῇ συνόδῳ τότε παραγενόμενοι, καὶ αἱ προβᾶσαι συνοδικαὶ πράξεις ἐπὶ τούτοις, βασιλεύοντος Ἀνδρονίκου, καὶ τὰ ἱστορούμενα περὶ τούτων· ὥστ' ἀμφίβολον εἶναι ποτέρα τῶν ἀποφάσεων τούτων τἀληθὲς μεθ' ἑαυτῆς ἔχει· τὴν γὰρ ἀντίφασιν μὴ δύνασθαι συναληθεύειν, καὶ ὅτι ἀδύνατον τὴν λεγομένην καὶ πιστευομένην καθολικὴν Ἐκκλησίαν αὐτὴν εἶναι, τὴν περὶ τῶν αὐτῶν τῆς πίστεως κεφαλαίων νῦν μὲν οὕτως, νῦν δ' ἐκείνως τἀναντιώτατα κρίνουσαν καὶ κρατοῦσαν, καὶ παρρησίᾳ γράμμασι καὶ πράγμασιν ἀποφαινομένην. Δεῖ γὰρ τὴν καθολικὴν Ἐκκλησίαν ἀληθεύειν ἀεί· ἐπεὶ καὶ τὸν παρακούοντα ταύτης ἐθνικὸν καὶ τελώνην ὁ Κύριος εἶναι διωρίσατο'.

In the first place, we observe that Manuel, like John Kyparissiotes, adheres to a narrative on the Palamite controversy running contrary to the conventional story told by modern scholars.[77] Like Kyparissiotes, Manuel believes that the Distinction had been previously condemned. The site of this condemnation was a council during the reign of an 'Andronikos', clearly Andronikos III (1328–41) who presided over a synod convened in June of 1341 just before he died and soon after which the civil war began.[78] Though Manuel says nothing about the condemnation of Barlaam by this council, he is convinced that through this council the Church of Constantinople formally condemned the energies/essence distinction that she would later validate in 1351.[79] But Manuel's naming of the emperor who reigned during the synod does more than provide historical context for the synodal condemnation. By this information, Manuel may have intended to emphasize the authority of a synod gathered under the auspices of a legitimate emperor. Whereas the legitimacy of Andronikos III was beyond question, subsequent synodal gatherings related to the Palamite question (in August of 1341, in 1347, and 1351) were gathered under the aegis of the 'usurper' John Kantakouzenos, who either had not yet seized the imperial dignity (as in 1341), or the legitimacy of whose imperial status might have been questioned, thus casting doubt on the authority of the subsequent synods over which he presided.[80]

---

77   For this 'conventional story', see above.
78   Talbot, 'Andronikos III Palaiologos', in *Oxford Dictionary of Byzantium*, I, p. 95; Papadakis, 'Constantinople, Councils of', 'Local Council of 1341', in *Oxford Dictionary of Byzantium*, I, p. 515, who indicates 'The council was convoked (10 June) under the presidency of Emperor Andronikos III to resolve the dispute between Gregory Palamas and Barlaam of Calabria'; Sinkewicz, 'Gregory Palamas', p. 135.
79   Obviously, this runs counter to the narrative of Meyendorff and Papadakis: cf. e.g., Papadakis, 'Constantinople, Councils of', 'Local Council of 1341', in *Oxford Dictionary of Byzantium*, I, p. 515; Meyendorff, *Grégoire Palamas*, pp. 80–84 (and see discussion above and nn. 27–30).
80   On the synodal gatherings in question, see Papadakis, 'Constantinople, Councils of', 'Local Council of 1341', 'Local Council of 1347', 'Local Council of 1351', in *Oxford Dictionary of Byzantium*, I, pp. 515–16; Sinkewicz, 'Gregory Palamas', pp. 135–37; Meyendorff, *Byzantine Theology*, p. 77; Meyendorff, *Grégoire Palamas*, pp. 80–83, 86–88, 129–30, 141–53, although Kantakouzenos was not physically present there, on the conciliar session of February 2, 1347 deposing Patriarch John Kalekas, see pp. 119–20. According to Meyendorff (and Papadakis), the 'Tome' published after the conciliar session of February 8, 1347, presided over by the empress-mother and regent Anna of Savoy and John Kantakouzenos (and at which the young John V was apparently present), essentially reiterated the decision that had been reached by a previous session of February 2, 1347 'présidé par Anne'; moreover, the decision of the session of February 8 was reiterated once more '[q]uelques semaines plus tard' at another session, in St Sophia, in the presence of Anna, John V, and John Kantakouzenos—according to Meyendorff, then, '[t]rois synodes en tout se tinrent donc à Constantinople, en quelques semains, pour confirmer le palamisme' (see Meyendorff, *Grégoire Palamas*, p. 129; Papadakis, 'Local Council of 1347', in *Oxford Dictionary of Byzantium*, I, pp. 515–16). I doubt that Manuel Kalekas shared this same finely-parsed understanding of the order of the discrete conciliar sessions of 1347, and I am uncertain whether he would have viewed a council presided over by an empress-regent and an emperor in his minority (John V, born 1332, would have been about 15 years old, see Alice-Mary Talbot and Anthony Cutler, "John V Palaiologos," in *Oxford Dictionary of Byzantium*, II, p. 1050), let alone an empress-regent, a minor and a figure potentially seen as a usurper (i.e., John Kantakouzenos), as authoritative. (On Anna and the regency, see Alice-Mary Talbot and Anthony Cutler, 'Anna of Savoy', in *Oxford Dictionary of Byzantium*, I, p. 105). It is plausible that in Manuel's view these sessions might lack the authority of a synod presided over by the undisputed emperor Andronikos III. Anyway, at the end of the day, the significant point, as far as Manuel Kalekas

We also see that Manuel, like John Kyparissiotes, claims that the teaching of the Palamites, who now constituted the magisterium of the Church of Constantinople specifically, had sewn doubts in the minds of the faithful.[81] It is, in fact, such doubts, or rather the nature of the magisterium responsible for them, that leads Manuel to claim what he so boldly (or scandalously) has claimed in this passage. He has claimed nothing less than that the Church that has issued decrees regarding the Palamite Question—that is the Church of Constantinople—*cannot* be identified as the 'catholic Church'. Why? Because the catholic Church *must* be perfectly inerrant ('For the catholic Church must always speak the truth'). Manuel sees this quality of infallibility as implicit in Christ's alleged statement that 'that the one disobeying her [i.e., the Church] is a heathen and a publican'. Manuel's prooftext supposedly drawn from words of Christ is actually a paraphrase of Christ's words on the settlement of quarrels among brethren found in the Gospel according to Matthew 18. 15–17: 'But if thy brother shall offend against thee, go, and rebuke him between thee and him alone. If he shall hear thee, thou shalt gain thy brother. And if he will not hear thee, take with thee one or two more: that in the mouth of two or three witnesses every word may stand. And if he will not hear them: tell the church. And if he will not hear the church, let him be to thee as the heathen and publican.'[82] In Manuel's exegesis, the

---

is concerned, is that the Church of Constantinople has contradicted herself and espoused error. The question of the relative authoritative weight of the supposed councils in question is of comparatively less importance. In other words, even if we take for granted the 'authoritative status' of the discrete sessions of 1341, 1347, 1351 as Meyendorff, Papadakis, cited above, and others do, Manuel Kalekas's point—given his own belief regarding the nature of the synodal session of 1341 presided over by Andronikos III—about the contradiction and error of the Constantinopolitan Church still stands. In fact, in a later work Manuel Kalekas will deny the authority of any council or conciliar decree that does not have papal consent—see *Four Books against the Errors of the Greeks*, trans. Ambrogio Traversari, Patrologia Graeca 152, ed. by Jacques-Paul Migne (Paris, 1866), col. 201C—on the dating of this work, see Manuel Kalekas, *Correspondance*, ed. Loenertz, pp. 45–46 and notes 92–93 below. As to the synod of 1351, according to Papadakis, 'Local Council of 1351' in *Oxford Dictionary of Byzantium*, I, p. 516: 'Emp[eror] John VI convened the synod in Blachernai (28 May) to reaffirm the decisions of 1341 and 1347. Gregory Palamas, Patr[iarch] Kallistos I, and the opposition were all present [...]. The synodal Tomos produced by this synod 'was signed in Aug. in Hagia Sophia [...] [Emperor] John V Palaiologos, who was not in Constantinople then, signed in Feb. or Mar. 1352'. On the ambiguous role of the Byzantine emperor in the ecclesiastical synod, see Aristeides Papadakis and Anthony Cutler, 'Councils', in *Oxford Dictionary of Byzantium*, I, pp. 540–43.
81 Kyparissiotes, *The Palamite Transgressions*, col. 663B: '[...] τὸ μέγα τῆς εἰρήνης [οἱ Παλαμῖται] διέλυσαν χρῆμα· καὶ τοσαύτην ἐνέθηκαν ταῖς ἁπάντων ψυχαῖς τὴν ἀκαιρίαν, ὡς μὴ μόνον τῶν γνησιωτάτων ἀποστῆσαι σπουδάσαι δογμάτων, καὶ μηδὲν τῶν εἰς Χριστιανοὺς ἐξαρχῆς ἀνηκόντων ἀκίνητον ἐᾶσαι φιλονεικῆσαι, ἀλλ' ἀμφιβόλους καὶ ἡμᾶς αὐτοὺς ἐν τοῖς περὶ αὐτῶν καταστῆσαι λόγοις [...]'. For Kyparissiotes's account of how the Palamites worked their way into a position of authority in the church—and his account, as the story of the hesychast controversy and the revolt of Kantakouzenos, obviously has to do with the Constantinopolitan Church specifically, even if he himself is not explicit on that point—see above. Manuel's identification of the Palamites and the officials of the Constantinopolitan Church should by now be clear (e.g., see his *apologia* addressed to the emperor considered above), even if he does not always *completely* spell out this identification.
82 *The Greek New Testament*, ed. Kurt Aland, Matthew Black, Carlo M. Martini, Bruce M. Metzger, Allen Wikren, with the Institute for New Testament Textual Research, 2nd ed. (Stuttgart: Württemberg Bible Society, 1966; 1968), p. 69: ''Εὰν δὲ ἁμαρτήσῃ [εἰς σὲ] ὁ ἀδελφός σου, ὕπαγε ἔλεγξον αὐτὸν μεταξὺ σοῦ καὶ αὐτοῦ μόνου. ἐὰν σου ἀκούσῃ, ἐκέρδησας τὸν ἀδελφόν σου· ἐὰν δὲ μὴ ἀκούσῃ, παράλαβε μετὰ σοῦ ἔτι ἕνα ἢ

quarrels that Christ foresees as arising among brethren are doctrinal quarrels, disputes about true faith. In the procedure Christ outlines for settling these quarrels, Manuel sees the elaboration of a system of adjudication that has the Church herself as the final tribunal. But if at this final stage of the quarrel one of the disputants disregards the decision of the Church, then that disputant is to be treated 'as the heathen and publican'. In this, Manuel understands Christ as not only saying that the decree of the Church is the 'final word' on doctrinal ambiguities and controversies, such that individual Christians can put their confidence in her judgment, but that the Church herself *is* the very criterion of the true faith, such that the orthodoxy of an individual is determined on the basis of whether he obeys the Church or not. But this status requires magisterial inerrancy. There should be no question of the Church's erring; the only question is whether a Christian obeys the Church.

But this theoretically true condition of the Church does not apply to the reality of Constantinople. Christ may have established the catholic Church as the final tribunal at which all questions regarding the faith, and the troubled conscience of every Christian in good faith, come to rest, but the adherent of vacillating Constantinople is in a state of anxious 'doubt,' not rest. Since Constantinople has decreed two contrary judgments regarding the Palamite Question, then in one of those instances she must have erred. Therefore, the Church of Constantinople cannot be that 'church' of which Jesus Christ spoke in the Gospel according to St Matthew and which Manuel qualifies as 'catholic'.

Thus, we have two distinct ecclesial concepts—the Church of Constantinople and the catholic Church—that are being explicitly disassociated on the grounds of magisterial infallibility. Implicit to this claim is the idea that these two concepts could be, or should be, associated but, given the reality of Constantinople's fallibility, cannot be. In short, Constantinople is deficient as a church: a Christian should be able to trust the judgment of the Church, but a Christian cannot trust Constantinople. The starkness of Manuel's denial that his ancestral church could be the Church to which Christ in the Gospel had referred should not be missed. This determination could mean nothing other than a true parting of ways between Manuel and the church of his fathers. But what can a Christian make of a pure denial? If the Church of which Christ had spoken had vanished from the earth, then the Christian can only despair of his faith.[83] If not Constantinople, then, what or where is that 'true Church'?

For such a Church as that—infallible teacher and sacred measure of orthodoxy—a man would rightly wander over the earth Odysseus-like until he found her, wherever she is, and embrace her with her whole heart. So Manuel wrote in a letter to an unnamed acquaintance dwelling in Constantinople.[84] Some seven years had passed

---

δύο, ἵνα ἐπὶ στόματος δύο μαρτύρων ἢ τριῶν σταθῇ πᾶν ῥῆμα· ἐὰν δὲ παρακούσῃ αὐτῶν, εἰπὲ τῇ ἐκκλησίᾳ· ἐὰν δὲ καὶ τῆς ἐκκλησίας παρακούσῃ, ἔστω σοι ὥσπερ ὁ ἐθνικὸς καὶ ὁ τελώνης'. The English translations of Bible passages, except in cases when they are presented as dependent clauses within larger quotations from Manuel Kalekas, are taken from the Douay-Rheims Bible.

83 Cf. Manuel Kalekas, *Against the Errors of the Greeks*, cols 245CD, 248AB; Kalekas, *Correspondance*, no. 83, p. 290, lines 121–26.
84 Kalekas, *Correspondance*, no. 83, pp. 287–92 (esp. 83. 7, p. 290).

since Manuel had fled his Mother City under duress and audaciously declared that the church of his fathers was not the Church of Christ. Since then, Manuel himself had become a stranger to his own. Even now he addressed these words to his friend from the island of Mitylene, under Genoese lordship, where he was to live out the rest of his days dressed in the habit of a Dominican friar.[85] Despite the hard facts of exile, Manuel endeavored to convince his friend that he had achieved that long-desired harbour of salvation and refuge from the storms of doctrinal controversy and ambiguity wracking the Greek Church.[86] For how long the haven of the Roman Church had formally sheltered this Greek dissident is uncertain, though it seems likely that Manuel had embraced her communion already in 1396, in fact around the time that he had broken with Constantinople.[87] As we shall see, this duality of affirmation of Rome and denial of Constantinople as explicit propositions integrally linked to each other is the feature of Manuel's thought that distinguishes him from John Kyparissiotes.

In his letter, Manuel endeavored to convince his friend that in embracing the Church of the foreigners he had found his way home, even as he suffered terribly from nostalgia. With an intensity that he confessed to his friend, he yearned for the sights and sounds of familiar things. But Manuel feared these longings like a siren-song, lest ensnared by them he abandon the true Church—that pearl he had purchased at the fearsome price of the hatred of his countrymen—and return to the 'crumbs' of the Greeks.[88]

As for those Greeks, whom Manuel excoriates for introducing in the Palamite Distinction a doctrine subversive of the monotheistic foundation of Christianity, Manuel wonders 'who is so stupid to call [them] … the apostolic and catholic Church?' After all, Manuel says, the Church must be inerrant, lest her adherents be troubled by anxious 'doubts' ('ἀμφιβόλοις') as to whether the faith she professes and the sacraments she offers truly save. For this reason, Christ himself, 'who founded her on the rock, prophesied that the gates of hell (the contradictions of the heretics) would not prevail, and he allotted the one not heeding her to be ranked among the pagans and the publicans'—utterances only meaningful if they represented perpetual guarantees about the Church. Indeed, Manuel understood that guarantee

---

85 Kalekas, *Correspondance*, pp. 27–46, although Loenertz, p. 148, specifies that he wrote letter no. 83 'avant sa prise d'habit' of the Dominicans. On Mitylene under the Genoese, see in particular Christopher Wright, *The Gattilusio Lordships and the Aegean World, 1355–1462*, The Medieval Mediterranean, 100 (Leiden: Brill, 2014).
86 See esp. Kalekas, *Correspondance*, no. 83. pp. 287–92 (above all, see paragraph 9, pp. 291–92, and see below).
87 Especially if George Dennis is right about the identity of the disgruntled Greek described in a letter of Emperor Manuel II (see Manuel II, *Letters*, n. 30, pp. 74–79, esp. p. 78, n. 1, and see my n. 68 above). When I began to consider that Manuel's embrace of Roman communion had happened even prior to 1396, I took my considerations to my colleague, Joshua Robinson, now librarian at Dumbarton Oaks. I am grateful to Dr Robinson for patiently hearing me explain the evidence of the sources, for confirming me in my suspicions, and encouraging me to follow in the direction suggested by the evidence and my instincts.
88 Kalekas, *Correspondance*, no. 83. esp. 1–4, pp. 287–89.

to be Christ himself, who gave his assurance that 'I am with you all days, unto the consummation of the age.'[89]

We have already heard this—specifically Manuel's denial that the Church of Constantinople could be the *true* Church, the 'apostolic and catholic Church,' established by Christ as inerrant. But in this letter he goes further. He identifies this 'Church of Christ' with the 'Church of the West'. Although Manuel is unwilling to concede that the only argument he has for this identification is a *negative* one—i.e., that the Greek Church is not the 'Church of Christ'—this is essentially what he is does at this point in the letter 'because even this shows the true teachings of this [Latin] Church concerning everything. For otherwise the Church of Christ would be nowhere on earth before the consummation of the world, which is rejected as absurd and entirely contrary to the faith.'[90]

Manuel makes his strongest case for the Western Church being, and his ancestral church not being, the catholic Church established by Christ in his *magnum opus* in defense of the orthodoxy of the Latins: his so-called *Four Books Against the Errors of the Greeks*, a massive *apologia* for the *Filioque* and other elements of Latin religious culture that he composed sometime in the last decade of his life. The only complete printed edition of this work is the fifteenth century translation made by Ambrogio Traversari and found in the Patrologia Graeca.[91] Internal evidence suggests that Manuel wrote this

---

89 Kalekas, *Correspondance*, no. 83. 7, pp. 289–90: 'Τίς δὲ τοσοῦτον ἀλόγιστος τοὺς ἀνέδην οὕτω τὰς ἀξιολόγους ἀναιροῦντας καὶ κοινοτάτους περὶ θεοῦ ὑπολήψεις καὶ οἷς φασι τοῖς τῆς κοινῆς πίστεως διδασκάλοις φανερῶς μαχομένους, ἀποστολικὴν καὶ καθολικὴν ἐκκλησίαν ἀναγορεύειν; εἰ γὰρ τὸ μίαν ἁγίαν καὶ ὅσα περὶ ταύτης ἑξῆς ὁμολογεῖν ὡς ἀναγκαῖον ἐν τῷ συμβόλῳ τῆς πίστεως περιέχεται (ἐν ταύτῃ γὰρ μόνῃ τὴν πίστιν ἐνεργεῖσθαι δι' ἀγάπης ἐστιν) εἰ μέλλοιμεν τῶν ἀπ' αὐτῆς καὶ τῶν κατ' αὐτὴν μυστηρίων τὴν ὠφέλειαν ἔχειν, τὴν δ' ἀνάγκη διὰ παντὸς ἐν ταῖς τῆς πίστεως ἀποφάσεσιν ἀληθεύειν (ἄλλως γὰρ ἐν ἀμφιβόλοις ἂν ἦμεν ὁπότε τῆς ἀληθείας ἐν τοῖς περὶ θεοῦ λόγοις τυγχάνοι καὶ μή), ἧς διὰ τοῦτο καὶ πύλας Ἅιδου (τὰς τῶν αἱρετικῶν ἀντιλογίας) οὐ κατισχύσειν ὁ ταύτην οἰκοδομήσας ἐπὶ τῇ πέτρᾳ προέφη, καὶ τὸν αὐτῆς παρακούσαντα τοῖς ἐθνικοῖς καὶ τελώναις συντάττειν προσέταξεν, (ἃ δὴ φανερῶς ἀεὶ τὴν ἐκκλησίαν ἀληθεύειν προϋποτίθησι) καὶ ἅμα «μεθ' ὑμῶν εἰμι πάσας τὰς ἡμέρας ἕως τῆς συντελείας τοῦ αἰῶνος» προσέθηκε. Cf. Kalekas, *Against the Errors of the Greeks*, cols 245C–D, 248A–C.

90 Kalekas, *Correspondance*, no. 83. 7, p. 290: 'καὶ ταῦτά φημι οὐχ ὅτι διὰ τὴν εἰρημένην καινοτομίαν ἀποροῦντας ἐπὶ τὴν τῆς Δύσεως ἐκκλησίαν καταφευκτέον, ἀλλ' ὅτι καὶ τοῦτο τὴν περὶ πάντα τῶν δογμάτων ἀλήθειαν τῆς ἐκκλησίας ταύτης συναποδείκνυσιν. ἄλλως γὰρ οὐδαμοῦ τῆς γῆς ἂν ἦν πρὸ τῆς συντελείας ἡ τοῦ Χριστοῦ ἐκκλησία, ὅπερ ὡς ἄτοπον καὶ τὴν πίστιν παντελῶς ἀνειρῶν ἀπερρίφθω'. In no. 83. 9, p. 149; pp. 291–92, Manuel does not so much provide an *argument* for the inerrancy of the Western Church or her identification with the Church of Christ but expatiates on her virtues.

91 Kalekas, *Against the Errors of the Greeks*, cols 11–258. On the approximate time in which this work was written, see Kalekas, *Correspondance*, pp. 45–46. This text has only ever been printed in full in the Latin translation made by Ambrogio Traversari, although the small sections of the Greek text edited by Leon Allatios in his various works have been reproduced in Migne's edition (see the 'Notitia' at Patrologia Graeca 152, cols 9–10, which Migne indicates is copied from 'Fabric[ii]…etc.', as in n. 47 above). Especially because Traversari's *ad verbum* translation poses many difficulties, at many points I have also consulted the photographic reproduction of a Greek MS of this text that is currently located at the Universitätsbibliothek in Basel, MS B VI 20 (henceforth: MS B). In my transcriptions of this MS as presented in the following notes, I have endeavored to supply (tacitly) aspirations, accents, and sensible punctuation where they seemed to be lacking in the MS. For a couple of studies which concern this text see Gouillard, 'Les influences latines', pp. 36–52; Delacroix-Besnier, *Les dominicains*, pp. 267–71.

work—or at least completed its final stages—before the attempted resolution of the Western Schism at the Council of Pisa in 1409 by the election of Pope Alexander V.[92]

The two pillars upon which Manuel establishes his arguments for the Western Church and against the Eastern Church are Scripture and history. As always, ecclesial inerrancy remains the lynchpin of the argument. As far as Scripture is concerned, Manuel reprises a couple of old favorites. First, the passage regarding dispute settlement from Matthew 18 ('if he will not hear the church, let him be to thee as the heathen and publican'), in order to prove that Christ established the Church as an absolutely trustworthy arbiter of doctrinal disputes (something for which inerrancy is a prerequisite). Without this institutional insurance against error, the 'common multitude of Christians' would be incapable of knowing which side is the Orthodox side in a doctrinal dispute, since 'both sides might seem to offer true reasons'. In that case, they would be inculpably ignorant, 'yielding themselves to every spirit, unless the ecclesiastical authority is open and manifest to the faithful'. Otherwise, demanding that the rank-and-file have the capacity to judge between heresy and orthodoxy in subtle matters of faith is to ask the impossible, and God would never ask that—hence the divine institution of an inerrant Church.[93] And so, we have come full circle to the problem Manuel had raised years ago in his *apologia* to the emperor: the ambiguity and doubt that have arisen from the lack of a trustworthy magisterium in the Church of Constantinople.[94] Second, Manuel refers once more to Christ's valediction in Matthew 28. 20 ('and behold I am with you all days, even to the consummation of the world'), in order to argue for the permanence of Christ's disposition.[95] Then there are the well-known Petrine passages providing obvious grist to the pro-papal mill: 'Thou art Peter; and upon this rock I will build my church, and the gates of hell shall not prevail against it' (Matt. 16. 18); the three-fold command of the Risen Christ to Peter of 'Feed my lambs [...] Feed my sheep' (Jo. 21. 15–17); Christ's prayer for Peter that his 'faith fail not' and his exhortation to Peter that 'thou, being once converted, confirm thy brethren' (Luke 22. 31–32).[96] Finally, Manuel offers a remarkable interpretation of the already remarkable story in Matthew in which Christ directs Peter to pay the tribute with a coin that he would find in the mouth of a fish. In Christ's instruction that the same one coin will satisfy the tribute for both himself and Peter, Manuel understands Christ as intending that the Christian faithful render to Peter (and his successors) reverence equivalent to that which is owed to Christ himself.[97]

---

92 For evidence for the *terminus ante quem*, see Kalekas, *Against the Errors of the Greeks*, col. 238C, where Manuel refers to the problem of the Great Western Schism as between two popes and makes no mention of the solution attempted at Pisa through the election of Alexander (on the Council of Pisa and the Western Schism, see Antony Black, 'Popes and Councils', in *The New Cambridge Medieval History*, VII: *c. 1415–c. 1500*, ed. by Christopher Allmand (Cambridge: Cambridge University Press, 1998), pp. 65–66. For Manuel's treatment of the problem posed by the Western Schism, see below.
93 Kalekas, *Against the Errors of the Greeks*, cols 248D–49C.
94 See above.
95 Kalekas, *Against the Errors of the Greeks*, col. 248BC = MS B, fol. 138ʳ.
96 Kalekas, *Against the Errors of the Greeks*, cols 240D–41A, 246D, 247BC = MS B, fols 133ᵛ, 137ᵛ, 138ʳ.
97 Kalekas, *Against the Errors of the Greeks*, col. 241B = MS B, fol. 133ᵛ. See Matt. 17. 23–26.

All of this Scripture provides the idealized image of the 'true' Church that matches the historic profile of Rome but not Constantinople. Inerrancy is at the center of this image. No heretic or his doctrines have ever held sway over 'the Church of Peter in Rome', Manuel insists.[98] In making this case, Manuel is compelled to offer a defense of the orthodoxy of Pope Honorius I (625–638) 'accused' of heresy because of his behaviour during the Monothelite controversy.[99] Manuel adduces testimony of St Maximos the Confessor in behalf of Honorius's orthodoxy.[100] He also has recourse to the canonical legal principle that a heretic cannot, by definition, be pope (and a heretic on the papal throne would be immediately and *ipso facto*, deposed).[101] On the other hand, Manuel asserts that every other church, for more or less time, has gone astray into heresy.[102]

Manuel's references to Patriarchs Nestorius and Pyrrhus, the iconoclasts, and other patristic-era heresy is reminiscent of John Kyparissiotes's own catalog of heresies considered above. But Manuel's presentation of the historic course of heresies differs remarkably from Kyparissiotes. Whereas Kyparissiotes presents the heresies as having afflicted, simply, 'the Church,' in an unspecified sense, Manuel explicitly links them to Constantinople or the Eastern Church *in particular*. If Kyparissiotes raised the problem of heresiarchs appearing as legitimate hierarchs, Manuel ruminated upon its implications: it may be clear in hindsight that Nestorius or Pyrrhus were heretics, but in their own day they presented themselves as the 'true Church' and accordingly demanded the obedience of their Christian subjects—among whom, it can be

---

98   Manuel asserts the inerrancy of the Roman Church multiple times, e.g., Kalekas, *Against the Errors of the Greeks*, cols 240D, 245CD, 246D–248C = MS B, fol. 133^{r-v}, 137^v–138^r. (See, e.g., fol. 138^r: 'τῆς δὲ τοῦ Πέτρου κατὰ τὴν Ῥώμην ἐκκλησίας').

99   Regarding Honorius and Monothelitism: for Honorius's correspondence with Patriarch Sergios of Constantinople, which has occasioned speculation about Honorius's orthodoxy, see Philippus Jaffé, *Regesta pontificum Romanorum ab condita ecclesia ad annum post Christum natum MCXCVIII*, I.2: *Ab anno DXC usque ad annum DCCCLXXXII*, ed. Paul Ewald, 2nd ed. (Leipzig: Veit, 1885), esp. no. 2018, pp. 224–25, and also see no. 2024, pp. 225–26. For a view on Honorius very different from that of Manuel, see Steven Runciman, *The Eastern Schism: A Study of the Papacy and the Eastern Churches during the XIth and XIIth Centuries* (Oxford University Press, 1955; repr. Eugene: Wipf and Stock Publishers, 2005), pp. 17, 162. On these subjects, see also Pelikan, *The Christian Tradition*, pp. 62, 67–68, 150–53; Hussey, *Orthodox Church*, pp. 13–24; John Norman Davdison Kelly, *The Oxford Dictionary of Popes*, Oxford Paperback Reference (Oxford and New York: Oxford University Press, 1986; repr. 1989), pp. 70–71; Friedhelm Winkelmann, *Der monenergetisch-monotheletische Streit*, Berliner Byzantinistische Studien, 6 (Frankfurt am Main: Peter Lang, 2001). For a more recent and comprehensive visitation of the problem of Monothelitism, see especially Jack Tannous, 'In Search of Monotheletism', *Dumbarton Oaks Papers*, 68 (2014), pp. 29–67. I thank Fr Alexis Torrance for this last reference.

100   Kalekas, *Against the Errors of the Greeks*, cols 245D–46A. And see Andrew Louth, *Greek East and Latin West: The Church AD 681–1071*, The Church in History, 3 (Crestwood: St Vladimir's Seminary Press, 2007), pp. 14–15 (while Louth writes on p. 14 that 'Honorius [...] suggested the idea that Christ had a single will, the heresy known as monotheletism', the same author indicates in n. 3 below that 'St Maximos the Confessor, however, always defended [Honorius] against the charge of heresy'). But against Louth (and others who would present Honorius as the originator of Monothelitism), see Tannous, passim and esp. p. 31 and n. 7.

101   Kalekas, *Against the Errors of the Greeks*, col. 245D.

102   Kalekas, *Against the Errors of the Greeks*, col. 246CD = MS B, fol. 137^v.

imagined, were many simple folk. But not for their simplicity, nor for their good intentions in obeying hierarchs they thought lawful, were they spared later on from the terrible anathema of the universal Church. Accordingly, whereas Kyparissiotes simply sees the Church as having recovered from these various heresies in the course of time and by the merciful disposition of God, Manuel believes that a trustworthy criterion of truth must be rooted in one certain place to which people in doubt can have recourse, and this he proclaims to be the Western Church led by Rome, whence shone the salvation of Eastern Christianity when it was adrift in heresy.[103]

In Manuel's view, it was the Western Church under Rome, as to an unfailing beacon of orthodoxy, that the Byzantine confessors looked time and again for assistance against the heresies gripping their ancestral church and countrymen. But, left to themselves, the Greek saints who constituted this minority party of orthodoxy within Byzantium remained insufficient from an ecclesiological standpoint. 'Even if in the midst of heresies', Manuel writes, 'there were always others acknowledging the true faith, they were [but] a remnant—as it were a little spark of truth. Truly, they did not have enough strength either to call a council nor did they dare otherwise to resist, since they were a small party and often hidden'.[104] The inability to call a council—not simply because they are so few and so hidden, but because in their fewness or hiddenness they could not obtain the single condition of a true ecumenical council: papal approval[105]—rendered them 'ecclesiologically inert', in themselves incapable of providing a solution to heresy and therefore not a 'true Church' but a mere 'remnant'. How different from Kyparissiotes, who reckoned that the Church of Jesus Christ would survive in but 'two or three' Orthodox Christians gathered in his name!

Manuel's ecclesiology demands union with the Western Church—even at the price of division from Constantinople—as the solution to the recurrent lapses of Constantinople into heresy. This is not merely a matter of 'ancient history'—all of it has a very timely application to—if, indeed, it is not grounded (at least partially) in—Manuel's personal experience of the Palamite controversy. Indeed, Manuel sees himself as the latest of the band of Greek mavericks such as Athanasius, Gregory Nazianzen, and Maximos the Confessor, who, left to themselves a mere 'remnant', were united to the Western Church against their own countrymen enthralled by diverse heresies.[106]

---

103 Kalekas, Kalekas, *Against the Errors of the Greeks*, cols 244CD–45A, 246B, 250C; Kyparissiotes, *The Palamite Transgressions*, cols 703D–06B.
104 Kalekas, *Against the Errors of the Greeks*, cols 244CD–45A, esp. 244D: '[...] Etsi enim semper inter haereses aliqui vera de fide sentientes, reliqui erant, veluti quaedam scintilla veritatis: verum, non tantum habebant roboris, ut vel synodum cogere, aliasque obsistere auderent, cum ipsi minima pars essent, ac saepius occulerentur [...]'.
105 Kalekas, *Against the Errors of the Greeks*, cols 244D–45A.
106 See, e.g., Kalekas, *Correspondance*, 83. 5–8 (esp. 8), pp. 289–91 (particularly p. 291), also see 'App.' no. 5, p. 160; p. 325 (a Greek excerpt from Kalekas's *Against the Errors of the Greeks*, ed. by Loenertz from the MS Vaticanus graecus 1112, see Loenertz's note at Kalekas, *Correspondance*, p. 325, n. 5); Kalekas, *Against the Errors of the Greeks*, cols 244CD–45A, 254BC. Also relevant to Manuel's implicit connection between the struggles against Constantinople of the Greek saints bygone and the present situation: col. 250D in

In his spokesmanship for the Western Church against the East, Manuel Kalekas might be suspected of hypocrisy. After all, was not the Western Church, currently riven by papal schism, hopelessly divided between pro-Avignon and pro-Roman allegiances? Manuel is forced to address this problem explicitly—which he claims is not a problem at all. In the first place, the Western Schism—unlike the Palamite Controversy in the East—has nothing to do with doctrinal questions, but purely questions of who the true successor of St Peter is. Both claimants to this title share one and the same Orthodox faith. There is no theological difference here, and so the faithful are not in a state of doubt about what the true faith is.[107] Manuel's continued mentions of the 'Church in' or 'according to Rome' shows that the schism had not harmed his belief in Roman primacy and that, moreover, his concept of 'Western Church' can more or less be identified with the 'Roman Church'—even if there is some question of which pope is the *true* Roman pontiff, for Manuel there is no question that the Roman Church is the *true* head of the Church. Needless to say, the Western Schism posed a potential roadblock to Manuel's vindication of the Western Church over Constantinople and his own brief attempt to downplay this problem may well have involved the glossing over of anxieties gripping at least some of the Latin faithful as to who was in fact the true heir to Peter—a question that would naturally have serious implications as to the validity of sacraments.[108]

This is all something very different than we found in John Kyparissiotes. The key difference is that Manuel specifically identifies or specifically distinguishes between the idealized 'Church' and particular, historic 'churches'. While Kyparissiotes did single out the professed Palamites from the body of the Church and deny that the former could be considered as the 'true Church', that very concept of 'true Church' remains for Kyparissiotes vague and unspecified. According to Manuel, the Western Church headed by Rome reifies the 'true Church', at least in a privileged way, whereas he denies that the Eastern Church headed by Constantinople can be this 'true Church'.[109] Magisterial inerrancy is the decisive criterion in Manuel's binary judgment in favour of Rome and against Constantinople. Whereas Kyparissiotes was satisfied with a

---

comparison with MS B, fol. 139^v (there remains some question regarding the proper interpretation of these passages—as can be seen from the Latin translation in the Patrologia Graeca, Ambrogio Traversari himself may have been somewhat unclear about Manuel's intended meaning). Regarding this 'remnant' language, cf. Kyparissiotes, *Palamite Transgressions*, pp. 703–04D.

107   Kalekas, *Against the Errors of the Greeks*, cols 238B–C = MS B, fol. 132^r.
108   If there is only one true pope, and it is unclear who this is, then there must at least be some question of the efficacy of sacraments—specifically, the absolution of sins—offered by priests committed to one of the two allegiances. Scholars have debated about whether the Western Schism should truly be considered a 'crisis' troubling the lives of the faithful. On the 'crisis' side, see: Renate Blumenfeld-Kosinski, *Poets, Saints, and Visionaries of the Great Schism, 1378–1417* (University Park: Pennsylvania State University Press, 2006). On the other side, see Howard Kaminsky, 'The Great Schism,' in *The New Cambridge Medieval History*, VI: *c. 1300–1415*, ed. by Michael Jones (Cambridge: Cambridge University Press, 2000), pp. 674–96, who sees little evidence that the Schism stirred up spiritual anguish among the peoples of Europe.
109   See, e.g., Kalekas, *Against the Errors of the Greeks*, cols 246C–48D = MS B, fol. 137^r–38^r; see also cols 250D–51A, 240D.

faith that would never fail entirely, even if that faith lived on only in a few individuals at odds with the heresiarchs visibly running the church, Manuel emphasized the need for a clear and identifiable ecclesiastical magisterium—that is, within the hierarchy—that must, above all, be perfectly inerrant as teacher—a conviction not only formed by, probably, the influence of Latin ecclesiology, but undoubtedly by his own anxiety-provoking experience of the vacillating inconstancy of his ancestral church (at least in his perception) on the Palamite Question.

Two premises distinguish Manuel's mentality as that of 'crisis'. First, Manuel's assumption that the 'true Church' *must* be identified with a particular, historic church. This assumption is implicit in Manuel's other beliefs about the Church—that Christ intended her to be the final and trustworthy tribunal of doctrinal questions, and hence necessarily infallible—and is based in practical need. 'For the Lord presupposed', writes Manuel, 'that the Church'—thus intended by Christ as the final judge of theological questions—'should be some defined thing', otherwise believers 'could not know where' to turn in order to find the authoritative teacher they need to show them the difference between truth and falsehood in controversies regarding the faith, especially when of the two sides engaged in the controversy 'both seem to offer true reasons. Truly, the common multitude of Christians, as well as human infirmity, would not be able to discern, and it would seem that confusion and fighting would break out in ecclesiastical affairs, unless that presupposed Church discerns discretely regarding each thing'. Interestingly, Manuel asserts that, 'unless there is an ecclesiastical authority that is clear and manifest to the faithful', the people would be 'without fault' in their confusion since God does not demand the impossible—and for most, subtle theologizing is impossible.[110]

---

110 Kalekas, *Against the Errors of the Greeks*, cols 248D–49C: '[...] Praesupponit enim Dominus, Ecclesiam definitam esse aliquam rem, et hanc semper veracem, aliis quae sunt utilia et necessaria annuntiare, atque agere. Neque enim nisi semper verax essent futura, indefiniter per omne tempus ad hanc fideles mitteret, de rebus ambiguis decernentem adituros. Neque si indefinitum ejus, apud fideles definitum esset, scire possent quo se conferre deberent, vel sua omnia referre, ut obtemperantes quidem securi jam et tuti esse possent: non obtemperantes autem, cum ethnicis se et infidelibus statuendos scirent. Se neque tamen nisi ea, ad quam mitterentur, Ecclesia, vera semper de omnibus dictare praesupponeretur, scire possent, quando renuere, quando obtemperare deberent, cum qui ab invicem different, veras ambo rationes proferre viderentur: communis vero Christianorum multitudo, simulque infirmitas humana discernere non possent, confusioque ac pugna ecclesiasticis in rebus pullulatura videretur: nisi subjecta Ecclesia, definite singula decerneret. Sed et sine culpa omnino essent, omni spiritui se permittentes, nisi aperta et manifesta fidelibus essent ecclesiastica autoritas: Deo quidem possibilia a cunctis exigente, illis vero obscura non valentibus dignoscere: sive omnes omnino oportebat divinarum rerum scientiam jugiter adeptos in tanta confusione rerum, et ipsos ambiguae fidei veritatem dignoscere: at id in multitudine contigere, possibile non est'. Cf. MS B, fol. 138ᵛ: '[...] ὑποτίθησι γὰρ ὁ Κύριος ὡρισμένον τι πρᾶγμα τὴν ἐκκλησίαν, καὶ ταύτην διαπαντὸς ἀληθεύουσαν τοῖς ἄλλοις τὰ συμφέροντα καὶ παραινεῖν καὶ πράττειν. Οὔτε γὰρ, ἂν εἰ μὴ διαπαντὸς ἀληθεύειν ἔμελλεν ἀπροσδιορίστως κατὰ πάντα καιρὸν, τοὺς πιστοὺς ἐπὶ ταύτην παρέπεμπε περὶ τῶν ἀμφιβαλλομένων ἀκουσομένους, οὔτε τοῦ κατ' αὐτὴν παρὰ τοῖς πιστοῖς ἀορίστου ὡρισμένου καθεστηκότος, ὅπου δέον ᾔδεισαν ἂν τὰ ἑαυτῶν ἀναφέρειν [...]'. My interpretation and translation of this challenging passage is based upon the readings found in both the PG (only the Latin text of Traversari is represented) and the MS.

The second premise is that there are only really two churches in the world, and hence only two ecclesial candidates for identification as the one true Church: The Western Church ruled by Rome and the Eastern Church ruled by Constantinople. Manuel expresses this 'reductionistic' ecclesiology in his treatise *Against the Errors of the Greeks* in a different context. While urging the acceptance of the *Filioque* as Orthodox, Manuel writes: 'who deny that belief, it is clear, venerate neither [church]; however, I do not know of a third church to have, but separated from both, they wage war against both'.[111] For Manuel, when it comes to ecclesial membership, there is no 'third way'. Given this premise, it becomes clear how—in spite of his reluctance to concede that his embrace of Roman communion was predicated merely upon his rejection of fallible Constantinople—an argument *against* Constantinople being the true Church was in fact an argument *for* Rome, as Manuel himself acknowledged.[112] The only other option was to conclude that Christ's promises to the faithful, as contained in Scripture (e.g., Matthew 28. 20, 16. 18, Luke 22. 31–38) were false and this conclusion, so monstrous and 'absurd', Manuel would never allow.[113]

Conclusion

The question of whether a 'crisis of faith' or a 'crisis of confidence' in the Church of Constantinople afflicted certain Byzantine thinkers of the fourteenth century is the search for a new understanding, on their part, of contemporary developments contributing to the turbulence of their times. The Great Church of Constantinople's acceptance of the theology of Gregory Palamas and the persistent claims put forth by the Roman Church amidst ongoing schism, in themselves distinct challenges, became joined together in one seamless theological perspective that I have described by the term 'crisis', an admittedly 'loaded word' in late medieval and Byzantine historiography.[114] But, in a way, that label may be misleading. Because the understanding achieved by a Greek such as Manuel Kalekas—that the Roman Church, and not the Church of Constantinople, is the one, true Church established by Jesus Christ—was not itself the 'crisis', but the *solution* of the crisis.

---

111 Kalekas, *Against the Errors of the Greeks*, cols 202D–03A: 'Enimvero quoniam communis utriusque Ecclesiae sententia, Spiritum sanctum a Patre, et Filio procedere, verum esse promulgatum est, aliterque sentientes, maledictioni addicti sunt: constat profecto, quia, qui modo istud confitentur, digni sunt, qui asseverentur, et nostras diligere Ecclesias, illarumque sententiam, quasi unius confessionem complecti, atque continere; qui vero illam sententiam negant, neutram venerari perspicuum est; tertiam autem, nescio quam aliam Ecclesiam habere, ab utraque separatam, ambabusque bellum indicentem'.
112 See above.
113 Regarding these Scriptural loci, the need of inerrancy, etc., see above and, e.g., Kalekas, *Correspondance*, p. 290.
114 See, e.g., Tuchman, *Distant Mirror*; Papadakis, *Crisis in Byzantium*, and other relevant items cited in the notes and the historiographical discussion in the introduction of this essay.

We approach nearer to 'crisis' when we refer to the belief that would have precipitated in a sincere anti-Palamite anxiety and 'doubts'[115] about Constantinople, doubts that, given the existence of certain other premises, would have forced the solution, inexorable as a syllogism, that Rome, and not Constantinople, is the true Church. This belief, upon which Manuel Kalekas is most explicit, is that the true Church established by Jesus Christ must be perfectly inerrant. This belief, while fomenting anxieties and doubts about the magisterium of Constantinople, was itself a product of a kindred sense of uncertainty—Manuel's complaints about common Greek Christians being bereft of the institutional assurance that they need in order to know that what they believe is in fact the saving faith were rooted in his own experience. At the same time, the ideal of magisterial inerrancy was derived from a particular understanding of Scripture. However, this belief in and of itself was not sufficient to deepen the crisis into a fully conscious denial that Constantinople was the true Church. This requires another belief, also expressed by Manuel, namely that the idealized, true Church of Jesus Christ *must* be identified with a particular, institutional, hierarchical church.[116]

After all, although John Kyparissiotes might have agreed that the Church of Jesus Christ must be inerrant, he did not believe that this ideal *must* be incarnated in a particular, institutional see. Though he acknowledged, like Manuel, that the Church of Constantinople had erred many times and, under the sway of Palamism, was erring again, he merely attributed the error to the hierarchy as opposed to the Church *per se* and this distinction preempted the wholesale and explicit denial that the Church of Constantinople is the true Church as this is expressed in the writings of Manuel Kalekas. Indeed, any apparent clarity offered by Kyparissiotes's distinction between false shepherds and the Sheepfold as such is, from another perspective, bedeviled by vagueness arising from a lack of distinction between the idealized Church established by Christ (or 'THE Church') and the institutional, particularized church (or 'a church')—when Kyparissiotes refers to individual pseudo-Christians (i.e., Gregory Palamas and his followers), he presumably included in that condemnation most of the the hierarchy of Constantinople (at least at its highest levels), although he is not so explicit about it. But is that body of the Church, from which Kyparissiotes desires to distinguish the malignant hierarchy, the body of Constantinople specifically or of the Church in a more universal sense? He does not feel the need to specify.

So different is Manuel, whose rejection of his ancestral church and embrace of the Roman Church was predicated upon a conceptual distinction between particular institutions and the idealized Church whose quality of inerrancy is enshrined in Scripture and demanded by the earnest, fallible, and doubt-ridden Christian conscience. This conceptual distinction gave Manuel the critical distance necessary to measure Rome and Constantinople against this idealized profile. A particular

---

115 ἀμφίβολον in its variant forms, as we have seen, appears in the writings of Kyparissiotes and Kalekas both, for the latter of whom it has a special significance.
116 See esp. Kalekas, *Against the Errors of the Greeks*, cols 248D–49C and MS B, fol. 138ᵛ, although the interpretation of the passages in question is a rather difficult.

interpretation of Scripture, history, as well as his own experience, provided Manuel more than enough reason to identify Rome with this idealized Church. No, not simply 'enough reason to identify'—as though Rome better fit the outline of the idealized Church—Manuel's premises and observations absolutely *forced* the conclusion that Rome *must be* and Constantinople *cannot be* the one true Church established by Jesus Christ. For, as if the positive case for Rome as being the one true Church were not enough to convince—and Manuel believed that it was enough[117]—there is yet another, third belief consummating Manuel's peculiar mentality, which forged the anxieties and doubts into an unbridled impulse toward union with Rome. This belief, which Manuel expresses without reflection and is entirely lacking in John Kyprissiotes, is that the only particular, institutional, and hierarchical churches that are candidates for identification with this true Church are the 'Western Church' and the 'Eastern Church'. In Manuel's thought, these two churches, thus geographically designated, may be ultimately reduced to the Roman and Constantinopolitan sees.[118] Therefore, if Constantinople is not the true Church, then Rome must be the true Church. Otherwise, as Manuel himself reflects, this true Church has vanished from the face of the earth contrary to God's own promise.[119]

Having reviewed the premises of this 'crisis mentality', and how they inhere in Manuel Kalekas but not John Kyparissiotes, and drawing near the end of this essay, I offer a suggestion for possible trajectories for future research, particularly in view of the (admitted) shortcoming of this article. After all, it might be alleged that from the outset I overstated the case. That I had seemed to refer to a crisis of broader proportions than the scruples of one Greek. My major task in this paper was the explication of the 'crisis mentality', for which Manuel Kalekas served as an ideal case, since he documented aspects of that peculiar perspective in his voluminous writings. Indeed, considering the space dedicated in this essay to the elaboration of this mentality of crisis as seen (or not seen) in the writings of Kyparissiotes and Kalekas, it would scarcely be reasonable to consider its manifestation in yet other texts. I still hope that my efforts here will be considered worthwhile, since the significance of the breadth (or not) of this so-called 'crisis' could scarcely be appreciated if the mentality behind it were not understood. Nevertheless, the broader manifestation of this mentality of crisis has yet to be demonstrated. I do not believe, however, that Manuel Kalekas was the only Greek who doubted whether the church of Gregory Palamas could be the Church of Jesus Christ. Like Manuel, John Kyparissiotes referred to doubts afflicting his fellow Greeks,[120] even if he lacked the other premises constituent of

---

117 See, e.g., Kalekas, *Correspondance*, no. 83. 7, 9, pp. 289–90, 291–92.
118 See Kalekas, *Against the Errors of the Greeks*, cols 202D–03A. Manuel identifies the two particular churches in these rather broad geographical terms (see, e.g., Kalekas, *Correspondance*, p. 290; Kalekas, *Against the Errors of the Greeks*, col. 197D), but he also denominates them by reference to Rome or Constantinople specifically (see, Kalekas, *Against the Errors of the Greeks*, col. 250D = MS B, fol. 139^v). It important to note that when Manuel was writing, the Western Papal Schism was ongoing, and for his treatment of that problem, see see above.
119 See, e.g., Kalekas, *Correspondance*, no. 83. 7, p. 290, and n. 84 above in this paper.
120 Kyparissiotes, *Palamite Transgressions*, col. 663B. For Kalekas, see, e.g., his *On Essence and Energy*, col. 285A.

the mentality that would force him to reject Constantinople and embrace Rome in the same way as Manuel did—as the result of ecclesiological convictions.[121] Indeed, I venture that close study of the correspondence of Manuel Kalekas and Demetrios Kydones,[122] and other texts related to the men in their circle,[123] will reveal evidence of a crisis of greater proportions than has been erstwhile suspected.

---

[121] At the beginning of this essay, I referred to 'the acceptance of a particular (almost certainly Latin-influenced) ecclesiological outlook'. I am convinced that Latin (including Thomist) ecclesiology exerted a crucial influence over Manuel's outlook, and thus constitutes a key component of the crisis mentality. But rather than (vainly) try to treat the extent and nature of Manuel's borrowings from Latin (and Thomist) ecclesiology in a satisfactory way here, I shall defer treatment of this issue to a subsequent contribution. In the meantime, however, I trust that readers will draw their own conclusions about Kalekas's use of western ecclesiology based upon the foregoing exposition of his thought, and at least credit the great probability of this definite influence in view of Manuel's contacts with Kydones and Dominicans (and his own eventual entrance into the Dominican Order) as well as his own engagement with the thought of St Thomas Aquinas. For relevant bibliography, see above nn. 14 and 67, (esp., e.g., the contributions by Loenertz and Delacroix-Besnier) and for Manuel's engagement with Aquinas in particular, see esp. Plested, *Orthodox Readings*, pp. 115–18, which focuses primarily on Manuel's engagement with Aquinas in his (i.e., Manuel Kalekas') *On the Faith and on the Principles of the Catholic Faith* (in Patrologia Graeca 152, ed. by Jacques-Paul Migne [Paris, 1866], cols 429–662)—though Plested says nothing about Manuel's ecclesiology, let alone its relationship to that of Aquinas.

[122] Kalekas, *Correspondance*; Demetrios Kydones, *Correspondance*.

[123] Particularly promising is an unedited text contained in Vaticanus Graecus 579, of which Loenertz, *Correspondance*, pp. 80–83, provides a partial overview and translation, but which deserves greater study. I have consulted this manuscript *in situ* and via photographic reproduction, and I plan to publish on this text in the future.

ALEXIS TORRANCE

Cyprus in the Late Byzantine Theological Landscape, with Special Reference to the Palamite Controversy*

Late Byzantine Theology and Cyprus

In terms of the direct and active role of Cyprus in late Byzantine theology, several figures, documents, and events have been emphasized in secondary scholarship.[1] Given the popular perception of the status of the island as a crusader kingdom from 1192–1489, an overarching theme is, unsurprisingly, East-West relations. Most examples serve as a commentary of one kind or another on this larger question. There is the famous and rather unique incident of the thirteen monks of Kantara martyred as heretics by the Latins in 1231, an event which unsurprisingly fuelled animosity at the time, and in recent history has resurfaced to help bolster a negative theological stance among the Cypriot Orthodox vis-à-vis Roman Catholicism.[2] Conversely, we find, for instance, the treatise by George Lapithes (whose name

---

* I am most grateful to Alexander Beihammer for initially inviting me to contribute to this project, and to Christopher Schabel for many precious and helpful comments and suggestions. I am likewise grateful to the editors of *Analogia: The Pemptousia Journal for Theological Studies* for allowing me to reproduce in what follows the core of the following article: Alexis Torrance, 'Receiving Palamas: The Case of Cyprus, 1345–1371', *Analogia*, 4:1 (2018), 67–85.

[1] See, for instance, Harry J. Magoulias, 'A Study in Roman Catholic and Greek Orthodox Relations on the Island of Cyprus between the Years AD 1196 and 1360', *The Greek Orthodox Theological Review*, 10/1 (1964), 75–106; Benedict Englezakis, *Studies on the History of the Church of Cyprus, 4th–20th Centuries* (Aldershot: Ashgate, 1995), esp. pp. 213–20; Christopher Schabel, 'Religion', in *Cyprus: Society and Culture 1191–1374*, ed. by Angel Nicolaou-Konnari and Christopher Schabel, The Medieval Mediterranean, 58 (Leiden: Brill, 2005), pp. 157–218.

[2] This episode is discussed in Christopher D. Schabel, 'The Greek Bishops of Cyprus, 1260–1340, and the Synodikon Kyprion', *Kypriakai Spoudai*, 64–65 (2000–2001), 217–34 (repr. in Christopher D. Schabel, *Greeks, Latins, and the Church in Early Frankish Cyprus*, Variorum Collected Studies Series, 949 (Farnham: Ashgate, 2010), no. III).

Alexis Torrance • University of Notre Dame

will emerge again below) on the seven sacraments. This treatise, influenced by the Latin enumeration and explanation of the sacraments, became popular in the Byzantine theological world into the early modern period.[3] By contrast to the incident of the thirteen monks, here we find a counter example from a more peaceful period for those who would rather emphasize the shared theological and (to some extent) liturgical heritage of East and West. Another would be the importing of the feast of the Presentation of the Virgin from the Byzantine rite via Cyprus to the West.

Beyond the incident of the thirteen martyrs and a few curiosities of liturgical history, the theological place of Cyprus in the late Byzantine period is rarely discussed.[4] An exception to this is the life and work of Neophytos the Recluse residing near Paphos, who died in 1214. His fame and writings were disseminated beyond Cyprus, and the unique iconographic program in his enclosure (*enkleistra*) continues to be of tremendous interest to Byzantine art historians.[5] Further into the thirteenth century, the figure of George/Gregory II of Cyprus (1241–90), patriarch of Constantinople from 1283–89, is of no little significance. Famous as the anti-unionist patriarch who rejected the Union of Lyons (and whose thought was taken up by several Palamites), his ties to the Kingdom of Cyprus, where he was born, raised, and initially educated, remain understudied.[6] One wonders, for example, what role his connection to Cyprus may have played during the period of his initial support for Michael VIII's plans to unite with Rome.

Another person to mention as we approach the Palamite Controversy is a figure who becomes a hero of the Hesychast movement, namely Gregory of Sinai (died 1346). His link to Cyprus is small yet intriguing. In his vita composed by the Palamite Patriarch Kallistos I (1350–53; 1355–63), he recounts how Gregory, after having been ransomed from captivity at Laodikeia in Syria, sails to Cyprus and becomes the apprentice of a seasoned ascetic there, becoming a rasophore (novice) monk on the island of Cyprus. He does not stay long and settles into monastic life not on Cyprus, but at Sinai.[7] This would be near the end of the thirteenth century. However, Kallistos records a detail here worth pondering, namely that a certain 'Leo the Cypriot', a

---

3 On which, see Englezakis, *Church of Cyprus*, p. 218.
4 Cyprus's place in the theological landscape of the West has received greater treatment: on this see especially Schabel, *Greeks, Latins, and the Church*.
5 See Cyril A. Mango and Ernest J. W. Hawkins, 'The Hermitage of St Neophytos and Its Wall Paintings', *Dumbarton Oaks Papers*, 20 (1966), 119–206; Englezakis, *Church of Cyprus*, pp. 97–211; and Catia Galatoriotou, *The Making of a Saint: The Life, Times and Sanctification of Neophytos the Recluse* (Cambridge: Cambridge University Press, 1991).
6 For more on Gregory of Cyprus, see Aristeides Papadakis, *Crisis in Byzantium: The Filioque Controversy in the Patriarchate of Gregory II of Cyprus (1283–1289)* (Crestwood, NY: St Vladimir's Seminary Press, 1997), esp. pp. 37–61 and *La vie et l'oeuvre théologique de Georges/Grégoire II de Chypre (1241–1290), patriarche de Constantinople*, ed. by Jean-Claude Larchet (Paris: Cerf, 2012), esp. pp. 13–45.
7 For more on the life of Gregory of Sinai, see David Balfour, 'Saint Gregory of Sinai's Life Story and Spiritual Profile', *Theologia*, 53/1 (1982), 30–62 and David Balfour, 'Was St Gregory Palamas St Gregory the Sinaite's Pupil?', *St Vladimir's Theological Quarterly*, 28 (1984), 115–30.

learned ascetic who had emigrated to Constantinople, had written glowingly about Gregory's piety and sweet nature.[8]

There is a significance here that begins to open onto the issue of the role of Cyprus in the Palamite Controversy. In a letter written in the summer of 1346 to the Cypriot George Lapithes, the anti-Palamite Gregory Akindynos urges him to send out more treatises against Palamas, explaining that Lapithes could safely do so via his Cypriot compatriots who reside in Constantinople, who are all treated as fervent anti-Palamites.[9] Cyprus is considered by Akindynos to be a bastion against Palamism, and he perceives it as a base from which anti-Palamite thought can easily be copied and disseminated across the region. What is interesting, however, is that one of the Cypriots at Constantinople that Akindynos assumes is part of the anti-Palamite network is a certain 'Leo'. Is the Leo mentioned by Kallistos the same as the Leo mentioned by Akindynos? The *Prosopographisches Lexikon der Palaiologenzeit* (PLP) equates these two otherwise unknown Cypriot Leos, and there seems little reason not to do so.[10] However, it raises an interesting hermeneutical question. If these two Leos are one and the same, what is the relationship of Leo the Cypriot to the Palamite question? On the one hand, he is recorded as having written a glowing description of Gregory of Sinai, an ardent practitioner and teacher of Hesychast principles, and on the other as being a safe recipient for the anti-Palamite discourses of George Lapithes. Is there a contradiction here? Perhaps in 1346 Leo the Cypriot was undecided regarding the Palamite affair, or perhaps (like Akindynos) he dissociated the monastic practices and experiences of the Hesychasts from Palamas's teaching on the divine energies, accepting the first but rejecting the second. Or perhaps Akindynos was assuming that Leo's Cypriot background was enough to make an ally of someone who was not an ally after all. We can only conjecture, although by 1351 Nikephoros Gregoras tells Lependrinos on Cyprus that he no longer wishes to correspond with Leo as their friendship had cooled, perhaps indicating that by then Leo had definitively sided with the pro-Palamas camp.[11] In any case, whatever we are seeing in the case of Leo the Cypriot, it gives us insight into the kind of problems of interpretation that face any scholar of the Hesychast and/or Palamite Controversy, to which we turn.

Gregory Palamas: The Initial Controversy

Before engaging more directly with a number of texts related to Cyprus itself, it might be worth offering by way of context a brief summary of the issues at stake in the

---

8   See the entry for 'Leo the Cypriot' in Erich Trapp, Rainer Walther, and Hans-Veit Beyer, *Prosopographisches Lexikon der Palaiologenzeit*, 12 vols, Addenda, Gesamtregister (Vienna: ÖAW Verlag, 1976-96) (hereafter PLP), no. 14772. For the reference from Kallistos, see Kallistos I, *Vita Gregorii Sinaitae* 5 (ed. Beyer).
9   Gregory Akindynos, *Letters*, ed. by Angela Constantinides Hero, Corpus Fontium Historiae Byzantinae, 21 = Dumbarton Oaks Texts, 7 (Washington, DC: Dumbarton Oaks, 1983), no. 60, pp. 242–47.
10 PLP, no. 14772.
11 Nikephoros Gregoras, *Epistulae*, ed. by Pietro L. M. Leone, 2 vols (Matino: Tipografia di Matino, 1982–83), II, no. 44, p. 155.

Hesychast debates. As Sinkewicz pointed out some time ago, the initial theological issue that sparked the controversy in the late 1330s was not monastic practice, or theories regarding the light of the Transfiguration, still less Greek versus Latin thought, but the concept of the knowledge of God, which escalated rapidly to the concept of sanctification.[12] Barlaam of Calabria and Gregory Palamas had both written against the Latin doctrine of *Filioque*, but Palamas was dissatisfied with the basis on which Barlaam had rejected it, namely an extreme form of apophaticism that ruled out any positive knowledge of God. From this spark the debate escalated to matters of monastic practice and experience: Barlaam equated the Athonite spirituality of his day with Messalianism and mocked the alleged visions of divine light experienced by the ascetics. The debate was now to be dominated by the question of sanctification.

Palamas served as a key representative of the Athonite cause, arguing that Barlaam was attacking the very foundations of Christian belief and practice. He maintained that the sanctification experienced by Christian ascetics was God himself present to the believer through his own uncreated activity or energy ('ἐνέργεια'). Its end result was the deification (θέωσις) of the human being to an equality with God by grace. This uncreated energy of God that rendered human beings divine was not identical, argued Palamas, with the imparticipable divine essence ('οὐσία') itself, even if it was properly inseparable from the divine essence and thus could be termed 'natural' or 'essential'. This deifying energy was identical to the glory and light of God, made manifest through the person of Christ to the disciples at the Transfiguration on Tabor, and subsequently to the saints down the ages.

This is the bare bones of Palamas's position, spelled out in detail early on in his *Triads* (1338–40), the *Tomos of the Holy Mountain* (1340), and then throughout his career until his death in 1359. What is important to emphasize is that his thought hinges on the possibility and meaning of sanctification and specifically deification, and it is on this basis that the essence-energy distinction is elaborated.[13]

Gregory Akindynos's Correspondence with George Lapithes

Let us turn now to Cyprus and its role in the controversy. The documents of chief concern for our enquiry are the correspondence from the anti-Palamite Gregory Akindynos to the Cypriot anti-Palamite George Lapithes (dated by Hero to 1345–48);[14] the letter of the pro-Palamite Joseph Kalothetos to certain monks of Cyprus who had petitioned for information regarding the controversy (dated by Tsames to 1346–47);[15] a synodal letter of Patriarch Kallistos from 1361/62 to Cypriot

---

12   Robert Sinkewicz, 'The Doctrine of the Knowledge of God in the Early Writings of Barlaam the Calabrian', *Medieval Studies*, 44 (1982), 181–242.
13   For more on the importance of this emphasis, see Alexis Torrance, 'Precedents for Palamas' Essence-Energies Theology in the Cappadocian Fathers', *Vigiliae Christianae*, 63 (2009), 47–70.
14   Gregory Akindynos, *Letters*, no. 42, pp. 174–87; nos 46–47, pp. 194–203; no. 60, pp. 242–47.
15   Joseph Kalothetos, Letter no. 4 in Ἰωσὴφ Καλοθέτου συγγράμματα, ed. by Demetrios G. Tsames (Thessalonica: Centre for Byzantine Research, 1980), pp. 385–94. Unless otherwise stated, translations are my own.

clergy and nobles;[16] and the letter of John VI Kantakouzenos (then monk Joasaph) to bishop John of Karpasia dated by Darrouzès to 1370/71.[17]

We begin with the letter penned by the anti-Palamite Gregory Akindynos (c. 1300–48), who was at first a mediator between Barlaam and Palamas, but later an enemy of both.[18] His extant correspondence is an extremely valuable source both for the controversy and the figures involved. One such figure, the Cypriot George Lapithes (mentioned above for his treatise on the seven sacraments), was the recipient of several letters between 1345–48, though none of his replies to Akindynos or his other anti-Palamite works have survived.[19] What is clear from this correspondence is that Lapithes is perceived as a leader among the anti-Palamites, even an organizing force. He has not only reproached the 'great minds' of Constantinople for not speaking out against Palamas (he is thinking primarily of Nikephoros Gregoras, who will eventually take on the mantle for the anti-Palamites), but even Akindynos himself for speaking too feebly in opposition. There is evidently frustration in Lapithes's mind that Cyprus is not in a closer orbit of ecclesiastical influence.

We glimpse in the letters of 1345–46, a moment of excited opportunity for Akindynos and his sympathizers. He has finally won the support of Patriarch John Kalekas and is counting up his allies, although his sense of victory will be short lived. He indulges in an interesting rhetoric of widespread anti-Palamism, boasting amongst others in the support of Cyprus (most particularly in the person of the philosopher Lapithes). Interestingly, in a letter to Nikephoros Gregoras at this time he praises Lapithes as a bastion against both Palamism and 'Latin profane new-fangled talk'.[20] Akindynos remained anti-Latin in the midst of his anti-Palamite diatribes, and seems to have known Lapithes to be likeminded.

It is hard to make any firm judgments on the reception of Palamas on the island of Cyprus at this point, except that treatises and correspondence regarding the controversy were flowing back and forth from a relatively early stage and, as mentioned above, it was at least assumed by Akindynos to be a haven for anti-Palamism. The intellectual exchange between Cyprus and Constantinople, particularly via elusive

---

16   See Jean Darrouzès, *Les regestes des actes du patriarcat de Constantinople I: Les actes des patriarches*, V: *Les regestes de 1310 à 1376* (Paris: Institut Français d'Études Byzantines, 1977), no. 2443, pp. 370–72. The text of the letter remains, to my knowledge, unedited, but I am grateful to the Patriarchal Institute for Patristic Studies and its director Professor Symeon Paschalidis for kindly giving me access to the microfilm copy of Mount Athos, Stavronikita Monastery, MS 62, fols 295–98, in which the letter is found.
17   In Jean Darrouzès, 'Lettre inédite de Jean Cantacuzène relative à la controverse palamite', *Revue des Études Byzantines*, 17 (1959), 7–27 (Greek text of letter at pp. 15–21).
18   For detailed sympathetic discussion of Akindynos, see Juan Nadal Cañellas, *La résistance d'Akindynos à Grégoire Palamas: enquête historique, avec traduction et commentaire de quatre traités édités recemment*, I: *Traduction des quatre traités de la 'Refutation du dialogue entre un Orthodoxe et un Barlaamite' de Gregoire Palamas*, II: *Commentaire historique* (Leuven: Peeters, 2006) and Juan Nadal Cañellas, 'Le rôle de Grégoire Akindynos dans la controverse hésychaste du XIVe siècle à Byzance', in Eastern Crossroads: Essays on Medieval Christian Legacy, ed. by Juan Pedro Monferrer-Sala (Piscataway, NJ: Gorgias Press, 2007), pp. 31–58.
19   Gregory Akindynos, *Letters*, no. 42, pp. 174–87; no. 46–47, pp. 194–203; no. 60, pp. 242–47.
20   Gregory Akindynos, *Letters*, no. 44, ll. 56–69, pp. 190–93.

learned Cypriots living in the capital, such as Leo the Cypriot discussed earlier (and Akindynos also mentions a Bartholomew, a Kosmas, and a Blassios[21]) is intriguing. Another figure among Akindynos's supporters is the Cypriot Hyakinthos, an anti-Palamite elected metropolitan of Thessalonica in 1345, the predecessor to the see of none other than Gregory Palamas himself.[22] Are there firm grounds to elaborate a type of anti-Palamite theological network among Cypriot intellectuals by the mid 1340s? This is at least the impression Akindynos wants to make, though to establish it beyond doubt would require further work.

However we deal with the patchy history to be gleaned from Akindynos, Cyprus itself was supplied with a resident anti-Palamite spokesperson, George Lapithes. What was the theological content of his anti-Palamism? One can only assume that his major arguments are similar to those of Akindynos, outlined briefly in *Letter* 42 to Lapithes and in an accompanying anti-Palamite treatise.[23] The main and recurring charge of the anti-Palamites was that the single and undivided Godhead had been cut up into a multitude of countless 'divinities' ('θεότητες') via the doctrine of divine energies. This was perceived as a new polytheism, or a species of ditheism (Akindynos also added, like Barlaam before him, the charge of Messalianism to Palamas and his followers). The language of 'higher' ('τὸ ὑπερκείμενον') and 'lower' ('τὸ ὑφείμενον') in God on any level was repeatedly attacked as execrable.[24] By contrast, for Akindynos the divine energies, such as divine life, wisdom, goodness, were either simply identical with the one divine essence, or in the context of sanctification, they appear as identical to the Son and/or Holy Spirit (never, that is, a *tertium quid*). Deification, in other words, seems to have a place in his thought, even if, in my opinion, it is rather muted and undeveloped (if not confused). He likewise has a concept of created grace (linked especially to the sacraments), which prepares for, but is not the same as, the deification given by the Son and Holy Spirit.[25]

Without imputing all of Akindynos's views to Lapithes, we can nevertheless be confident that the basic thrust of their anti-Palamism was similar, and revolved

---

21 Gregory Akindynos, *Letters*, no. 60, pp. 244–45.

22 For more on the figure of the anti-Palamite Hyakinthos of Thessalonica, see Kostas P. Kyrres, 'Ὁ Κύπριος Ἀρχιεπίσκοπος Θεσσαλονίκης Ὑάκινθος καὶ ὁ ρόλος του εἰς τὸν ἀντιπαλαμιτικὸν ἀγῶνα ['The Cypriot Archbishop of Thessaloniki Hyakinthos and his Role in the Anti-Palamite Struggle'], *Kypriakai Spoudai*, 25 (1961), 89–122. See also Kostas P. Kyrres, 'Ἡ Κύπρος καὶ τὸ Ἡσυχαστικὸν ζήτημα κατὰ τὸν XIV αἰῶνα' ['Cyprus and the Hesychast Question in the fourteenth century'], *Kypriakai Spoudai*, 26 (1962), 19–32.

23 Gregory Akindynos, *Letters*, no. 42, pp. 174–87. We do not know which of his anti-Palamite treatises Akindynos sent to Lapithes.

24 One could almost call it Akindynos' hobby-horse. In a letter to Akindynos early on in the controversy, Palamas had made reference to the idea of lower and higher divinity in a relative manner with regard to divine energy (participable and thus 'lower') and essence (imparticipable and thus 'higher'). Akindynos refused to interpret this reference as anything other than a thoroughgoing polytheism or ditheism. For the epistle and discussion, see Juan Nadal Cañellas, 'La rédaction première de la *Troisième lettre de Palamas à Akindynos*', *Orientalia Christiana Periodica*, 40 (1974), 233–85.

25 The issue of sanctification and deification in the thought of Akindynos is briefly discussed in Juan Nadal Cañellas, 'Gregorio Akíndinos', in *La théologie byzantine et sa tradition*, II: *XIIIe–XIXe s.*, ed. by Carmelo Giuseppe Conticello and Vassa Conticello (Turnhout: Brepols, 2002), pp. 189–314 (241–50).

around the concern that Palamas was 'cutting up' the one deity into innumerable 'divinities'. Akindynos clearly saw Cyprus as a bastion for his cause, and even appears to be making plans to flee there if the going gets too tough for him in the capital.[26] Not all the Cypriots, however, were necessarily on his side.

Joseph Kalothetos's Letter to Certain Monks of Cyprus

If an alliance of sorts among Cypriot intellectuals had developed in favour of Akindynos and against Palamas, this was not the end of the story. According to the dating of Tsames, in 1346 or 1347 the ardently pro-Palamite monk Joseph Kalothetos was approached by some monks of Cyprus and asked to give a concise account of Palamite doctrine.[27] Kalothetos was a disciple of Palamas and had become a monk first at Esphigmenou monastery on Mount Athos before eventually becoming the superior of a monastery in Constantinople. His interlocutors from Cyprus were evidently confused by the debate, having no doubt heard the kinds of arguments reflected in Akindynos's correspondence with Lapithes. They wanted to hear the other side, and Kalothetos obliged with what Tsames describes as the 'most beautiful' letter of the collection.[28]

The letter begins with an appeal to following the saints, and argues that if these were to be followed with a rigorous, pious, and upright life, then the issue at hand (namely, the teaching on the divine energies) would be known to us quickly. He will speak to them, he goes on, regarding the natural and essential energies of God ('τῶν φυσικῶν […] καὶ οὐσιωδῶν ἐνεργειῶν') and similarly 'about the divine light that shone forth on Mount Tabor'.[29]

He argues that one must revere the three divine and uncreated persons, the divine and uncreated essence, and the common divine and uncreated energy of the uncreated essence, such as wisdom, goodness, power, providence, and foreknowledge.[30] As a faithful disciple of Palamas, he introduces the doctrine of the two wills and energies in Christ (divine and human) promulgated at the sixth ecumenical council. He does so both to reinforce a sense of patristic precedence and to argue that the divine energies must be uncreated: 'for all that is of the divinity is uncreated, and all that is of the humanity is created'.[31]

He turns briefly to the light of Tabor, emphasizing that this divine light can neither be an essence nor a creature. Rather, the saints called this light 'a natural glory of God, effulgence, grace, energy, Holy Spirit, chrism, seal, divinity, unapproachable light and diverse other names'.[32] He then continues on to address the anti-Palamites more directly and attempts to call them out on their own ambiguous and imprecise

---

26 Gregory Akindynos, *Letters*, no. 42, ll. 182–86, pp. 184–85.
27 Joseph Kalothetos, *Letter* 4, pp. 385–94. It is discussed in Tsames, Ἰωσὴφ Καλοθέτου, pp. 354–56.
28 Tsames, Ἰωσὴφ Καλοθέτου, p. 354.
29 Joseph Kalothetos, *Letter* 4. 4, p. 386.
30 Joseph Kalothetos, *Letter* 4. 5, p. 386.
31 Joseph Kalothetos, *Letter* 4. 6, p. 387.
32 Joseph Kalothetos, *Letter* 4. 7, p. 387.

positions. His opponents state that they only glorify the Holy Trinity and its uncreated essence, whereas any divine energy (including the light of Tabor) is created.[33] But when confronted with the divine energies as uncreated in Scripture, such as divine power and wisdom, they say that the essence and energy are identical, not 'divided undividedly' or 'united dividedly' (Palamas's position), but simply completely the same.[34]

Kalothetos is in fact playing on the conflicts within anti-Palamite thought to bolster his case. Once they are 'stuffed full' of the testimonies of the saints regarding the distinction between the unnameable and transcendent divine essence and the nameable divine energies, they will say that the Son and the Holy Spirit are energies, which is absurd, or they will propose that the pure partake of the essence of God. When in turn the 'voices of the theologians' crowd them out on this point, they will argue that the saints participate in a creature. Notice that it is the concept of deification that serves as the hinge for Kalothetos's argument. Rather than offer a clear doctrine of sanctification and deification, the anti-Palamites are ultimately happy, he says, to shift from one argument to another, because their goal is not to articulate truth but 'by treachery to deceive the simple'.[35] In juxtaposing entangled intellectuals and the simplicity of the saints, he is composing a tune that all sides would play, but especially the Palamites.

Having extolled the straightforward and universal witness of the Fathers, and before supplying the standard florilegium of patristic quotations to back up his position, Kalothetos moves on to a more involved theological argument, in paragraphs 9 and 10. This is perhaps the most interesting section because he wholeheartedly uses several terms that constantly triggered the anti-Palamites. In particular, he defends the use of the terms higher/superior ('τὸ ὑπερκείμενον') and lower/inferior ('τὸ ὑφείμενον') with regard to God:

The essence of God is said to be "higher", his energy what is "lower" […] The essence is 'higher' according to the principle of cause, of being imparticipable, unnameable, having existence of itself. Again, the energy is said to be "lower" as what is caused, participable, nameable, as not having existence of itself but existing in the essence. The energy is rightly called "divinity" ('θεότης') by the saints […]. The essence is also called divinity, but inexactly and not in a proper sense ('καταχρηστικῶς καὶ οὐ κυρίως').[36]

He continues in paragraph 10 with even stronger language:

There is, in short, the lower principle and the higher principle and both are named divinities ('καὶ τῶν δύο λεγομένων θεοτήτων'). While two divinities are named homonymously, yet there is one divinity, insofar as they are united, both the essence and the energy, and [the distinction between higher and lower is maintained] because the natural energy is from the essence, not the essence from the energy.[37]

---

33 This is Barlaam's position.
34 Joseph Kalothetos, *Letter* 4. 8, p. 387.
35 Joseph Kalothetos, *Letter* 4. 8, p. 388.
36 Joseph Kalothetos, *Letter* 4. 9, p. 388.
37 Joseph Kalothetos, *Letter* 4. 10, p. 388.

Kalothetos is living dangerously here. On the one hand, by using the language of higher, lower, and even 'divinities' (or 'Godheads') in the plural in a positive manner, he was supplying fuel to the anti-Palamite fire. On the other hand, he evidently perceives a real need to address the charges regarding these terms that were no doubt being leveled as a constant refrain against Palamas on Cyprus. The fact remains, however, that even Gregory Palamas tended to be more guarded in his language.[38] Whether Kalothetos's explanation for the use of such terms would satisfy his audience is unclear. He clearly interprets the terms in a manner that precludes, to his mind, any ditheistic or polytheistic implications. Divine energy is by definition not a 'substance' with independent existence, but it is thereby also undividedly distinguishable from substance or essence. The divine essence is 'higher' than the energy in the sense of being the unnameable 'cause' of nameable energy. The word 'divinity' or 'Godhead' itself, being a divine name, must properly speaking refer to energy rather than the unnameable essence,[39] even if Kalothetos then awkwardly introduces the language of two 'divinities' or 'Godheads', before pulling back to apply the term 'one divinity/Godhead' to the whole (essence and energy). One can assume that the mere use of these terms would be considered sufficiently damning in the eyes of Akindynos's sympathizers such as Lapithes. While indeed providing, as he had promised, a succinct and useful summary of the Palamite position, Kalothetos's occasional exuberance of theological expression doubtless played into anti-Palamite hands.

Kallistos I and John Kantakouzenos

Our knowledge regarding the relationship between Cyprus and the Palamite Controversy after the unexpected death of Akindynos in 1347–1348 is rather scant. What is clear is that Cyprus continued to serve as a haven for anti-Palamite intellectuals and churchmen in the decades that followed. Patriarch Ignatios of Antioch, Metropolitan Cyril of Side, and Metropolitan Arsenios of Tyre all take refuge there in the midst of questions regarding their fidelity to the Palamite cause. We cannot, however, precisely reconstruct their theological positions. The clearest anti-Palamite text attributed to one of these, a letter purportedly sent by Metropolitan Cyril to his *chartophylax* at Side, is recorded in the patriarchal register of Constantinople in 1359/1360.[40] However, under the patriarchate of Philotheos

---

38 A direct response by Palamas to the charge of propagating a theory of two 'higher' and 'lower' divinities/Godheads via the essence-energy distinction can be found in his *Antirrhetics against Akindynos*, ed. by L. Kontogiannes and B. Phanourgakes in Γρηγορίου τοῦ Παλαμᾶ συγγράμματα, ed. by Panagiotis K. Chrestou, 5 vols (Thessalonica: Kyromanos, 1962–1992), pp. 220–23 (book III, chapter 3.19).
39 This was already a key argument made by Gregory of Nyssa against the Eunomians, on which see Torrance, 'Precedents', pp. 64–65.
40 *Das Register des Patriarchats von Konstantinopel*, III: *Edition und Übersetzung der Urkunden aus den Jahren 1350–1363*, ed. by Johannes Koder, Martin Hinterberger, Otto Kresten, Corpus Fontium Historiae Byzantinae, 19/3 (Vienna, 2001), no. 248, pp. 446–50.

Kokkinos, this text is declared a forgery by the synod and Cyril is posthumously rehabilitated in 1364/1365.[41] That said, there is a rather consistent unease on the part of the patriarchate regarding the anti-Palamite potential of refugee bishops on Cyprus.

An important example of this is the letter of Kallistos I (died 1363) to the Cypriot clergy and nobility.[42] It was written in late 1361 or early 1362, and concerns at once the efforts of the papal legate Peter Thomas (soon to become Latin patriarch of Constantinople) to win the Greeks of the island over to obedience to the Roman Church, as well as the arrival on the island of the anti-Palamite Metropolitan Arsenios of Tyre. It is an illuminating instance of the intertwining of anti-Latin and anti-Palamite sentiments among the Palamites. The chief sentiment of the letter is anti-Latin, but it moves easily to an attack on Barlaam and Akindynos, with a warning against welcoming Metropolitan Arsenios of Tyre who had fled for refuge to Cyprus on being condemned by the synod as an Akindynist. The Barlaamites and Akindynists are sharers in the doctrines of the Latins, says Kallistos, and he further claims that all their members in Constantinople had colluded with the papal legate when he was there. The episode with Arsenios of Tyre evidently gave the patriarchate the perception that Cyprus had become a dangerous sanctuary for anti-Palamites. Whether he also had in mind the anti-Palamite Patriarch Ignatios of Antioch, who had resided on Cyprus during the reign of Hugh IV, is unclear, but there is no direct record of animosity between Kallistos and Ignatios.[43]

That Cyprus served as an intellectual outpost for anti-Palamites from the 1340s until at least the 1370s, if not the early 1400s, is clear, though what that meant for theology 'on the ground' is far harder to reconstruct. Continuing anxieties regarding the dissemination of anti-Palamite thought on Cyprus was enough for the former emperor John Kantakouzenos (c. 1292–1383), by then monk Joasaph, to send a dogmatic letter and copies of his pro-Palamite Antirrhetics against Prochoros Kydones to bishop John of Karpasia in around 1370/71.[44] By now, Palamas's legacy had been liturgically enshrined at Constantinople (his official glorification or canonization took place in 1368), but the ideological battle evidently still continued. Kantakouzenos's letter can almost be considered a 'pre-emptive strike' since his main order of business is

---

41 *Register des Patriarchats*, no. 247, pp. 442–46.
42 Darrouzès, *Regestes*, no. 2443, pp. 370–72.
43 See Gilles Grivaud, 'Literature', in *Cyprus: Society and Culture 1191–1374*, ed. by Angel Nicolaou-Konnari and Christopher Schabel (Leiden: Brill, 2005), pp. 219–84 (233).
44 The Greek text of Kantakouzenos' letter can be found in Darrouzès, 'Lettre inédite de Jean Cantacuzène', pp. 15–21. John of Karpasia appears to surface only here in the Greek sources and is thus said by Darrouzès and others to be otherwise unknown. However, Schabel mentions him in passing as having lost a case in the early 1360s to the Latin bishop Leodegar of Famagusta regarding the pastoral care of Syrian (Melkite) Christians in his diocese, with Peter Thomas arbitrating: Schabel, 'Religion', p. 170. I am grateful to Schabel for further pointing out to me that it appears that John was bishop by 1354 and died in 1371, citing as primary evidence *Acta Urbani V*, no. 72; *Synodicum Nicosiense*, no. X.58; and *Bullarium Cyprium III*, no. t-326. Perhaps bishop John of Karpasia's biography is worth revisiting on the basis of both the Latin and Greek sources.

to refute a set of theses written by the anti-Palamites that have, he has heard, been copied and sent to Cyprus.[45]

Kantakouzenos's letter begins with a historical summary of the Palamite controversy from Kantakouzenos's perspective, mentioning several more anti-Palamites who had fled to Cyprus.[46] He utilizes a classic Palamite comparison between the anti-Palamites and the Arians of old: just as the latter accused Basil the Great and Gregory the Theologian of tritheism for worshipping the Holy Trinity, so too the former 'accuse and charge us as polytheists for saying that just as the nature of God is uncreated and uncircumscribed, so also the energy of this blessed essence is uncreated and uncircumscribed'.[47] He goes on to address a series of nineteen specific accusations against the Palamites.

His approach is particularly interesting given what we have seen in Kalothetos's letter to Cypriot monks. Whereas Kalothetos unabashedly uses the language that anti-Palamites found so problematic (divinities, higher and lower in God, as well as divine 'energies' in the plural), Kantakouzenos avoids all these. He talks exclusively of God's 'ἐνέργεια' in the singular: there is 'one nature, one power, one energy, one divinity'.[48] He repeatedly anathematizes anti-Palamite slurs like 'lower/inferior divinities' ('ὑφείμεναι θεότητες'), but does not make any effort in doing so to appropriate or explain the Palamite use of some of the underlying terms (which, of course, were never used in this combination even by Kalothetos). Kantakouzenos is content with disowning the slurs and repeatedly affirming the inseparability of the divine essence and energy. This diplomatic approach extends even to offering no Palamite alternative to the accusation that God's energy is self-subsistent as visible light. He simply anathematizes this position without discussing the Palamite view of the light of Tabor. His careful language gave Jugie the impression of a softened or even modified Palamism here.[49] Darrouzès disagrees and views the letter, as a whole, a work more of diplomatics than theology.[50] Both, in other words, wish to distance us from the idea that the contents of the letter might be understood as a true reflection of Palamite theology.

---

45 From Demetrios Kydones's correspondence (*Epistle* 35), we can add that the anti-Palamite John Kyparissiotes is on Cyprus at this time, having fled there following the condemnation of Prochoros Kydones in 1368. This could be another important piece of the puzzle, but its significance cannot be determined with any certainty.
46 They are Antouemes the Koubouklarios, Anthony of Tyre (who had briefly become patriarch of Antioch before being deposed) and, at the time of writing, a certain monk named Anthony Kolybas: Darrouzès, 'Lettre inédite de Jean Cantacuzène', p. 17.
47 Darrouzès, 'Lettre inédite de Jean Cantacuzène', p. 17.
48 Darrouzès, 'Lettre inédite de Jean Cantacuzène', p. 18 (anathema 8). For Palamas's own discussion of the issue of singular and plural for the divine energy, an issue to which he was sensitive, see his *One Hundred and Fifty Chapters*, ed. and trans. by Robert E. Sinkewicz, Pontifical Institute of Mediaeval Studies, Studies and Texts 83 (Toronto: Pontifical Institute of Mediaeval Studies, 1988), 68, pp. 162–63.
49 Martin Jugie, 'Palamite (controverse)', in *Dictionnaire de théologie catholique*, ed. by Jean Michel Alfred Vacant, Eugène Mangenot, Émile Amann, 30 vols (Paris: Letouzey et Ané, 1902–50), XI (1931), col. 1796.
50 Darrouzès, 'Lettre inédite de Jean Cantacuzène', p. 14.

If anything, however, I would contend that such assessments reflect the 'divide and conquer' mentality among certain scholars who, through a form of hyper-contextualization of the sources, end up proposing nearly as many forms of Palamite theology as there are Palamites. Differences in modes of expression or emphasis need not imply differences in underlying theology, though of course they may. Let us consider a selection from Kantakouzenos's nineteen anathemas to get a better impression of this.

1. For they say that we actually glorify two divinities in God, one essence and another non-essence, to which I say, let anyone who thinks this be anathema. Rather we glorify one divinity: Father, Son, and Holy Spirit.

2. Again they say that together with the persons (*hypostaseis*) of the Holy Trinity, we worship other divinities, to which I say, let anyone who thinks this be anathema. Rather we worship one divinity in three persons, Father, Son, and Holy Spirit.[51]

In these two anathemas Kantakouzenos disowns the language of 'divinities'. But even Kalothetos's brief foray into this territory is not necessarily at odds with the monk-emperor's position. Let us not forget that Kalothetos, in the passage cited above, ends his argument with a clarificatory emphasis that 'there is one divinity', and he certainly never suggests that Christians worship multiple divinities. Kantakouzenos's language here is not, in other words, a 'modification' of the theology of the Palamites. He goes on:

4. Again they say that we worship uncreated gods of infinite number, inferior ('ὑφείμενοι') and issuing ('προϊόντας') from the essence of God, which we properly call gods and divinities: and I say, let anyone who thinks this be anathema. Rather we believe in one God: Father, Son, and Holy Spirit.

6. Again they say that we glorify the visible, natural energy of God, subsisting of itself as light: let anyone who thinks this be anathema. Rather we glorify the natural energy of God that does not subsist of itself, but is inseparable from the essence of God, uncreated and uncircumscribed.

7. Again they say that we call the uncreated and natural energy of God a different nature ('ἑτεροφυής') and unlike and lower to an infinitely infinite degree, anhypostatic and non-existent, being to the nature what the Son is to the Father and the Holy Spirit: and I say, let anyone who thinks this be anathema. Rather we say that the uncreated natural energy of God exists inseparably in the nature and that wherever there is the nature, there also is the energy, and wherever the energy, there also the nature.[52]

As before, Kantakouzenos is disowning the specific use of certain terms, usages that are in fact universally rejected by the Palamites. Kalothetos's particular theological use of the terms 'inferior' and 'divinities', as we saw above, is not put to the service of calling the divine energies 'inferior gods or divinities' that are independently subsistent and worshipped in themselves. In anathema seven, Kantakouzenos is deploying the logic of the sixth ecumenical council, something that is again common to all the Palamites. Consider two further anathemas, each conveying a classic Palamite concern:

---

51 Darrouzès, 'Lettre inédite de Jean Cantacuzène', p. 17.
52 Darrouzès, 'Lettre inédite de Jean Cantacuzène', p. 18.

14. Again they say that we call effects ('ἀποτελέσματα') uncreated: let anyone who thinks this be anathema. Rather we say that the effects are creatures ('κτίσματα'), receiving a beginning to their existence: but the power that works these effects is uncreated ('ἡ δὲ δύναμις ἡ ταῦτα ποιήσασά ἐστιν ἄναρχος').

15. Again they say that we consider the deified body of the Lord—the partaking of which renders us even now communicants of the divine nature—not to be sanctified and deified by that same divinity which sanctified the body nailed to the cross, but by some other non-essential and lower divinity. I say to those who think thus: anathema. Rather we say that that same divine power and divinity which sanctified the body taken from the Virgin, which is forever found to be holy, the same is that which sanctifies the blessed bread and the blessed cup and changes the bread into the same body of the Lord and the fruit of the vine into his same precious blood: and we believe that these things are the precious body and blood of Christ and not another; and whoever is not born again of water and spirit, that is the Holy Spirit, and whoever does not eat of the body of our Lord Jesus Christ and drink his blood, is unable to inherit the kingdom of God.[53]

The distinction between uncreated divine energy or power and its created effects is nothing novel from a Palamite perspective. Kantakouzenos's words are taken practically verbatim from Palamas himself.[54] Similarly, the sacramental backdrop of Palamite spirituality is not out of the ordinary.[55]

The last 'anathema' I wish to consider is perhaps the most interesting in that Kantakouzenos does not actually anathematize the position in question. It reads:

17. Again they say that we consider that which is prepared by God for the saints to be uncreated. In fact, though liars in all things, they have spoken truly on this point, for this is indeed our thinking. They are undone by their own words, however, since in accusing us of this they profess to find satisfaction in some creature. For us, because we have been taught and learned from Christ that he himself is the inheritance of the elect, and of the apostle Paul, that the saints become inheritors of God and co-inheritors of Christ, it follows necessarily that the inheritance of the elect is uncreated. Thus, the blasphemy falls on their own head.[56]

The fact that Kantakouzenos gladly takes ownership of this position on behalf of the Palamites tells us something of its centrality to the overall cause. It should come as

---

53 Darrouzès, 'Lettre inédite de Jean Cantacuzène', pp. 19–20.
54 Gregory Palamas, *One Hundred and Fifty Chapters*, 140, pp. 244–45. It is important to clarify here that both Palamas and Kantakouzenos are referring to the created effects of God's activity/energy in a general way. When speaking specifically of deification, there was a limited way in which the 'ἀποτέλεσμα' or 'effect' of God's deifying grace could be understood by Palamas to be uncreated ('ἄκτιστος'), inasmuch as the deified saints can rightly be said to become uncreated by grace: see Gregory Palamas, *Epistle 3 to Akindynos* [*Letter 5*], ed. by John Meyendorff in *Γρηγορίου τοῦ Παλαμᾶ συγγράμματα*, ed. by Panagiotis K. Chrestou, 5 vols (Thessalonica: Kyromanos, 1962–92), I, 308. On the whole, however, this particular argument regarding the term ἀποτέλεσμα is rare in Palamas' writings.
55 On the sacramental dimension of Gregory Palamas' thought, see Georgios Mantzaridis, *The Deification of Man: St Gregory Palamas and the Orthodox Tradition* (Crestwood, NY: St Vladimir's Seminary Press, 1997).
56 Darrouzès, 'Lettre inédite de Jean Cantacuzène', p. 20.

no surprise that it involves the themes of sanctification and ultimately of deification, themes with which the whole controversy had opened. The monk-emperor might indeed be considered diplomatic and sensitive with regard to certain of his formulations, scrupulously avoiding terms and concepts that would require further elaboration, such as divine 'energies' in the plural, the nature of the light of Tabor, higher and lower in God, and the use of the term 'divinities'. This is to be expected given the text's genre. Yet there was still something that remained utterly non-negotiable: the eschatological promise of deification, which, by definition, involved for the Palamites a real sharing and communion in the uncreated divine life.[57]

Conclusion

From these few texts directed to the island of Cyprus during the Palamite Controversy we are given a glimpse, perhaps even a microcosm, of the larger intellectual tug-of-war that was taking place in the Byzantine theological world in the fourteenth century. In the correspondence of Akindynos with George Lapithes we were served the essential theological arguments as well as the larger political ambitions of the anti-Palamites: Cyprus and Cypriot intellectuals residing in the Empire were a significant part of these ambitions. The letter of Joseph Kalothetos gave to the Cypriot monks a spirited defence of Palamas's thought, one which at certain points could, on the level of terminology rather than theology, play into anti-Palamite hands. Neither, incidentally, had combined anti-Palamism with pro-Latin sentiments in their texts. This was to occur in the letter of Kallistos I, who was incensed by reports of the papal legate Peter Thomas's conduct towards the Greek clergy on the island. He readily combined anti-Latin sentiment with pro-Palamite thought in his exhortation to the Cypriots, seeing the Latins and anti-Palamites as practically co-conspirators. Finally, we discussed John Kantakouzenos's letter to John of Karpasia, which offered a more irenic and terminologically sensitive defence of Palamas's thought, even while holding fast to strong Palamite language of deification by uncreated grace. Reflective of his more diplomatic mould generally, there is no explicit link made in this text between anti-Palamite thought and pro-Latin sympathies.

While we cannot learn in detail from these texts what the Palamite Controversy looked like in the daily religious life of Cypriots at the time, we can at least witness some of the upheaval it caused. Despite the promise Cyprus held in the eyes of Akindynos as an anti-Palamite bastion, an island which, on the surface, boasted seemingly ideal conditions for the incubation and propagation of anti-Palamite thought (including for John Kyparrisiotes, a figure discussed in this volume by Charles Yost), our scant evidence indicates that contrary to what we might expect, it was the likes of Kalothetos, Kallistos I, and Kantakouzenos who would eventually win the minds and hearts of the island's Greeks. A series of letters at the end of the fourteenth/beginning of the

---

57 Kantakouzenos mentions deification again in the ninth anathema where the pure, united to God, become gods by grace: Darrouzès, 'Lettre inédite de Jean Cantacuzène', p. 18.

fifteenth century between the Greek Dominican Manuel Kalekas and the Cypriot intellectual Manuel Raoul, both ardent anti-Palamites, indicate as much.[58] That said, on the level of the intellectual 'safety' of being vocally anti-Palamite among Greek speakers, Cyprus was clearly an important place of refuge for some time.

Our primary concern has not, however, been to give an in-depth view of ecclesiastical life on Cyprus during this period, merely to bring together several texts of the Palamite controversy that pertain to the island. In doing so, I suggest that we are faced with an interesting microcosm of the larger question of Gregory Palamas's theological reception in late Byzantium and beyond. The tidy dichotomy of hesychast monk vs intellectual/humanist, or the easy elision of anti-Palamite and pro-Latin (issues discussed further in Yost's chapter in this volume), are certainly called into question by what we have examined, but not entirely so. While scholars such as Meyendorff may have taken such characterizations too far, they are nevertheless part of the 'climate' of the debate from its early days and not simply a 'neo-Palamite' invention of the twentieth century. Cyprus of the fourteenth century may not have been a theological powerhouse for the late Byzantines, but its unique social, political, and ecclesiastical landscape nonetheless played an important role in helping to clarify and negotiate the intricacies of the central issues at stake in the Palamite Controversy. It also contributed to the shaping of Byzantine perceptions regarding the apparent co-inherence of anti-Palamism, intellectual pursuit, and Latin theology, perceptions that continue to mark the reception of Palamas.

---

58 Especially Manuel Kalekas, *Correspondance*, ed. Raymond-Joseph Loenertz, Studi e testi, 152 (Vatican: Biblioteca apostolica Vaticana, 1950), no. 77, pp. 275–78, where he laments that the common people on Cyprus have embraced the thought of Palamas.

The maps were designed by Angel Nicolaou-Konnari and created by Romain Thurin using either in part or in entirety ArcGIS® software by Esri. ArcGIS®, ArcMap™, and Arcgis Pro™ are the intellectual property of Esri and are used herein under licence.

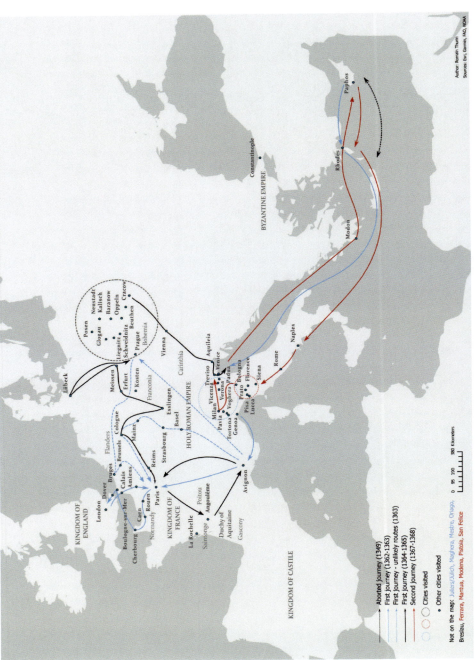

Map 1: The Travels of Peter I of Lusignan

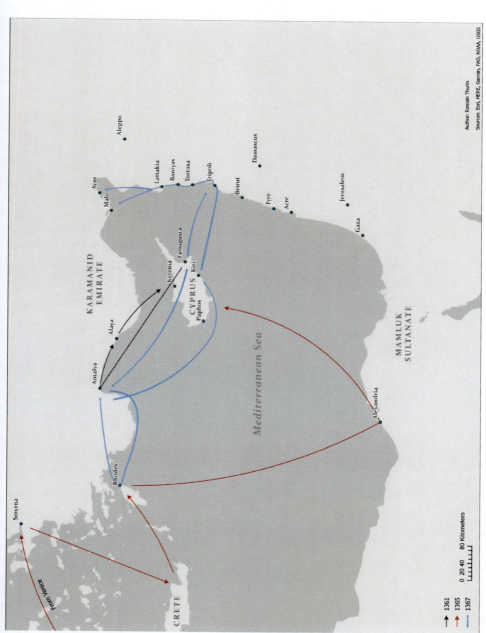

Map 2: The Military Expeditions of Peter I of Lusignan

List of Figures

ANGEL NICOLAOU-KONNARI, Peter I of Lusignan (1329–69, 1359) in Historical Sources and Modern Popular Culture

Fig. 1: Conrad Grünemberg, *Beschreibung der Reise von Konstanz nach Jerusalem*, Karlsruhe, Badische Landesbibliothek, Cod. St. Peter pap. 32, fol. 27ʳ, View of Famagusta. 63

Fig. 2: Guillaume de Machaut, *Oeuvres narratives et lyriques*, Paris, Bibliothèque nationale de France, MS Fr. 9221, fol. 235ᵛ, 'comment l'acort fu du roy de chyppre et de lesparre'. 64

Fig. 3: Albert Chevallier Tayler, *The Entertainment of the Five Kings by the Vintners' Company* (1903). From: Sir Harry C. Luke, *A Portrait and an Appreciation. Cyprus* (London: Harrap, 1965²), p. 65. 65

Fig. 4: Panos Ioannides, Πέτρος ο Πρώτος, televised series, director Andreas Constantinides (Cyprus Broadcasting Corporation, 1994). 66

Figs 5a-b: Michalis Pieris, dramatic adaptation of the chronicle of Leontios Makhairas (TH.E.PA.K., Nicosia, 1998). 67

Figs 6a-b: Hambis Tsangaris, engravings inspired by the tragic story of Arodaphnoussa. 68

JOHANNES PREISER-KAPELLER, A Climate for Crusading? Environmental Factors in the History of the Eastern Mediterranean during the Life and Reign of Peter I of Cyprus (1329–69)

Fig. 1: Reconstruction of summer wetness and dryness across the Eastern Mediterranean for the year 1330; the colour scale from red to green shows the Palmer Drought Severity index, ranging from -4 or less (extreme drought) to +4 or above (extremely moist) (data: Cook and others, 'Old World Megadroughts'; map: J. Preiser-Kapeller, 2017). 147

Fig. 2: Reconstruction of summer wetness and dryness in Cyprus for the years 1250–1450 (Palmer Drought Severity index) (data: Cook and others, 'Old World Megadroughts'; graph: J. Preiser-Kapeller, 2017). 148

LIST OF FIGURES

Fig. 3: Reconstruction of summer wetness and dryness across Europe and the Mediterranean for the year 1330; the colour scale from red to green shows the Palmer Drought Severity index, ranging from -4 or less (extreme drought) to +4 or above (extremely moist) (data: Cook and others, 'Old World Megadroughts') and network of trade connections of Famagusta according to Pegolotti, *La pratica della mercatura*; map: J. Preiser-Kapeller, 2017). 149

Fig. 4: Map of important cities and centres of sugar production on fourteenth century Cyprus (data: Ouerfelli, *Le Sucre*) and sites of tree ring data (cf. https://www.ncdc.noaa.gov/data-access/paleoclimatology-data/datasets/tree-ring; map: J. Preiser-Kapeller, 2017). 150

Fig. 5: Nile flood maxima data for the years 1270 to 1439 (data: Popper, *The Cairo Nilometer*; al-Maqrīzī, *Mamluk Economics*; graph: J. Preiser-Kapeller, 2017). 151

Fig. 6: Differences in wheat prices in Egypt across a year with a sufficient Nile flood level and a year with an insufficient Nile flood level in the fourteenth century (data: Borsch, *The Black Death*; graph: J. Preiser-Kapeller, 2017). 152

Fig. 7: Reconstruction of summer wetness and dryness across the Eastern Mediterranean for the year 1362; the colour scale from red to green shows the Palmer Drought Severity index, ranging from -4 or less (extreme drought) to +4 or above (extremely moist) (data: Cook and others, 'Old World Megadroughts'; map: J. Preiser-Kapeller, 2017). 153

Fig. 8: Reconstruction of summer wetness and dryness for the area of Antalya for the years 1250–1450 (Palmer Drought Severity index) (data: Cook and others, 'Old World Megadroughts'; graph: J. Preiser-Kapeller, 2017). 154

Fig. 9: Reconstruction of summer wetness and dryness for the area of Konya for the years 1250–1450 (Palmer Drought Severity index) (data: Cook and others, 'Old World Megadroughts'; graph: J. Preiser-Kapeller, 2017). 155

Fig. 10: Reconstruction of summer wetness and dryness for the area of Lebanon for the years 1250–1450 (Palmer Drought Severity index) (data: Cook and others, 'Old World Megadroughts'; graph: J. Preiser-Kapeller, 2017). 156

Michalis Olympios, Angevin and Lusignan Visual Claims to the Crown of Jerusalem: Parallel Lives?

Fig. 1: Simone Martini, *St Louis of Toulouse crowning Robert I of Anjou*, c. 1317–19 (Museo di Capodimonte, Naples). Photo: Reproduced with the permission of the Ministero per i Beni e le Attività Culturali / Alinari Archives, Florence. 168

Fig. 2: Simone Martini, *St Louis of Toulouse crowning Robert I of Anjou*, detail. 169

Fig. 3: Cristoforo Orimina, *Angevin Genealogy*, in the Anjou Bible, fol. 4r (frontispiece), 1340s. Photo: Reproduced with the permission of KU Leuven, Maurits Sabbe Library.   170

Fig. 4: Giovanni Bertini and Pacio Bertini, Tomb of Robert I of Anjou, 1343–46 (Santa Chiara, Naples). Photo: Alinari Archives, Florence.   171

Fig. 5: Bellapais Abbey, tympanum and lintel of main refectory portal, 1340s/50s. Photo: Michalis Olympios.   172

Fig. 6: Famagusta, Ss Peter and Paul of the Nestorians, view of the east end, third quarter of fourteenth century. Photo: Michalis Olympios.   173

ANGEL NICOLAOU-KONNARI, 'Le roy de Chippre de renon': The Depiction of Peter I of Lusignan in French Literature

Fig. 1: Jean Froissart, *Chroniques*, Paris, Bibliothèque nationale de France, MS Fr. 2643, fol. 284ᵛ, 'Couronnment de Charles V le sage'.   306

Fig. 2: Guillaume de Machaut, *Oeuvres*, Paris, Bibliothèque nationale de France, MS Fr. 1584, fol. 309ʳ, 'ci commence le livre de la prise d'alixandre' (La prise d'Alexandrie).   307

Fig. 3: Guillaume de Machaut, *Oeuvres narratives et lyriques*, Paris, Bibliothèque nationale de France, MS Fr. 9221, fol. 213ʳ, 'cy commance la prise d'alixandre' (naissance de Pierre I de Chypre).   308

Fig. 4: Guillaume de Machaut, *Oeuvres*, Paris, Bibliothèque nationale de France, MS Fr. 22546, fol. 1ʳ, 'Pierre I de Chypre et les dieux'.   309

Fig. 5: Guillaume de Machaut, *Oeuvres*, Paris, Bibliothèque nationale de France, MS Fr. 1584, fol. 448ʳ, 'ci commence le dit de la marguerite' (Pierre I de Chypre et sa dame).   310

Fig. 6: Guillaume de Machaut, *Oeuvres narratives et lyriques*, Paris, Bibliothèque nationale de France, MS Fr. 9221, fol. 61ᵛ, 'le livre du lyon' (le narrateur guidé par le lion).   311

Fig. 7: *The Cartulary of the Holy Sepulchre*, Vatican City, Biblioteca Apostolica Vaticana, MS Vat. lat. 7241, feuille de garde, 'Iste liber est domini philippi de maseriis cancellarii regni cypri'.   312

Fig. 8: Gros of Peter I of Lusignan (obverse-reverse), Bank of Cyprus Cultural Foundation, Museum of the History of Cypriot Coinage (the Foundation's numismatic collection owns 11 coins issued by Peter I).   312

Fig. 9: Jean d'Arras, *Mélusine ou la noble histoire de Lusignan*, Paris, Bibliothèque nationale de France, Arsenal, MS 3353, fol. 22ᵛ, 'comment la noble forteresce de lusegnen en poictou fu fondee par melusigne'.   313

Fig. 10: Coudrette, *Le Roman de Mélusine ou l'histoire de Lusignan*, Paris, Bibliothèque nationale de France, MS Fr. 24383, fol. 13ʳ, Battle of Famagusta. 314

Fig. 11: Coudrette, *Le Roman de Mélusine ou l'histoire de Lusignan*, Paris, Bibliothèque nationale de France, MS Fr. 24383, fol. 14ʳ, Marriage of Urien and Hermine. 315

Fig. 12: Coudrette, *Le Roman de Mélusine ou l'histoire de Lusignan*, Paris, Bibliothèque nationale de France, MS Fr. 12575, fol. 36ʳ, Urien inherits Cyprus. 316

Fig. 13: Jean Froissart, *Chroniques*, Paris, Bibliothèque nationale de France, MS Fr. 2645, fol. 79ʳ, 'comment le roy de cippre fut tuez et murtri en son lit par l'enortement et corruption des mescreans et pour la bonte et hardiesse qui estoit au dit roy de cippre leur adversaire'. 317

Fig. 14: John of Wavrin, *Anchiennes cronicques d'Engleterre*, Paris, Bibliothèque nationale de France, MS Fr. 77, fol. 259ᵛ, 'comment le roy de cippre parla au prince de galles sur l'estat de la croix' [...]. 318

Fig. 15: John of Wavrin, *Chronicques d'Engleterre*, Paris, Bibliothèque nationale de France, MS Fr. 87, fol. 212ᵛ, 'comment le roy de cippre parla au prince de galles sur l'estat de la croix' [...]. 319

Index

Abaqa Khan, Ilkhānid ruler   442,
   479, 486; *see also* Arachantloun
   Theodora (Abaqa's daughter); Isaac
   Asanes (Abaqa's son-in-law); Maria
   Palaiologina, *Despoina ton Mougoulion*
   (Abaqa's wife); Michael VIII
   Palaiologos (Abaqa's father-in-law)
'Abbāsids, dynasty/caliphate   434
Abdera, city, Thrace   465, 467
Abel, biblical figure, brother of Cain, the
   younger son of Adam and Eve   38
Abū Bakr al-Tehrānī, author of Kitāb-i
   Diyārbakriyya   436
Abu'l Faraj, *see* Thibaut of Belfarage
Abu Qir, lake, Nile Delta   144
Abū Saʿīd Bahādur, Ilkhānid (incorrectly
   transcribed as Monsait)   451
Acem, *see* Persian
Achaea, principality of,
   Peloponnese   87, 89-90, 246
Acre, port city, Latin Kingdom of
   Jerusalem   77, 79, 85, 89, 97, 107, 109-
   110, 112, 142n, 157, 159, 165, 167, 247, 253,
   363n, 367, 374-377, 379, 381-382
Adalia, *see* Antalya
Adam, biblical figure   363
Adhémar de la Voulte, ambassador and
   bishop of Limassol   331; *see also*
   Brémond de la Voulte (Adhémar's
   brother)
Adramyttion, city, western Asia
   Minor   94-95
   - Gulf of Adramyttion   115
Adrianople, city in Thrace   466n
Aegean Sea   78-80, 82, 86, 90, 94-98,
   100-101, 109, 113-119, 122-123, 125, 133,
   189, 191, 457-459, 461, 463, 473, 487

Africa   143
   - North Africa   95, 444, 446, 449
Afshar, Oghuz tribe   422
Afsharviran, hamlet, Cilicia   425
Agalos, Byzantine nobleman   497n
Agareni, *see* Hagarenes, Turks
Agathangelos, semi-fictional character
   for Nikephoros Gregoras's
   student   102, 103n; *see also*
   Nikephoros Gregoras (teacher of
   'Agathangelos')
Ager Sanguinis, battle of   421
Aghacheri Turkmen tribe   434, 437; *see
   also* Turkmens
Aigues Mortes, port city, southern
   France   187
Aimery of Lusignan, brother of King
   Henry II of Lusignan and Amaury,
   lord of Tyre   180
Ain Jalut, city/battle of, Palestine   247
Ainos, city, Thrace   466
Ajamshir, the sons of; *see* Germiyānids
Akhlāt, city, eastern Anatolia   422
Akindynist   560; *see also* Gregory
   Akindynos
Aksaray, city, central Anatolia   434
ʿAlā' al-Dīn Kaykubād I, Seljuk sultan of
   Konya   386, 422, 424-427, 430-431
ʿAlā al-Dīn Kaykubād II, Seljuk sultan of
   Konya   386n
ʿAlā'iyya, *see* Alaya
Alanya, *see* Alaya
Alaya/ʿAlā'iyya/Candelore (modern
   Alanya), city and emirate, southern
   Anatolia   18, 23, 97, 111, 116, 386, 431
Albania   89, 305; *see also* Scotland
   (Albanie)

INDEX

Albert Chevallier Tayler, artist   60, 65, 571
Alborz, mountain range, northern Iran   425
Aleppo, city, northern Syria   255-256, 430-431, 446, 448
Alessio Corner, member of the Senate and the *sapientes* of Crete   125n, 127n
Alexander V, pope   540
Alexander the Great, king, one of the pagan Worthies   277
Alexander, king of Mysians   470n
Alexandria, city, Egypt   11, 13-15, 22-24, 26, 33, 37-40, 43, 49, 55, 61n, 69, 71, 77, 80-81, 82n, 84, 105, 107, 111, 119, 142n, 144, 175, 178, 186, 188, 200-202, 204, 235, 242, 246-248, 251-252, 255-256, 258n, 259-269, 276, 284-286, 287-288, 291-292, 295-296, 300, 302-303, 307-308, 323, 330-331, 354-356, 359-360, 362, 369, 378n, 494, 573
Alexandrians   11, 37, 81, 84, 105, 175, 251, 256, 259, 261-262, 263n, 265-267, 269, 270n, 326
Alexios I Komnenos, Byzantine emperor   486
Alexios III Angelos, Byzantine emperor   486
Alexios III, emperor of Trebizond   452-453
Alexios, fictitious emperor in Savoyard historiography   493n
Alexios Apokaukos, Byzantine statesman   458, 465, 468, 471, 478, 480, 483-484
Alexios Laskaris (Hyaleas), *megas hetaireiarches*   503n, 504
Alexios Philanthropenos, Byzantine nobleman and general   93
Alfonso Fadrique, vicar general of the Catalan Duchy of Athens   94
Alfonso Ferrand, Catalan supporter of Queen Eleanor of Aragon   335
'Alī Bahadur, Seljuk commander   437-438
'Alī ibn Abī Ṭālib, nephew and son-in-law of the Prophet Muhammad   411

Ali Mardān, Aydınid commander   481; *see also* Bedreddin (Ali Mardān's brother); Hwāce Hasen (Ali Mardān's father)
Alice of/d' Ibelin, second wife of King Hugh IV of Lusignan   15, 49, 90, 181, 279, 327, 358; *see also* Eschiva (Alice's daughter); John of Antioch (Alice's son); Margaret (Alice's daughter); King Peter I of Lusignan (Alice's son); Philip of Brunswick (Alice's second husband)
Alice of/d' Ibelin, second wife of John of Antioch   358; see also Guy d'Ibelin, seneschal of Cyprus (Alice's father)
Alice of Majorca, niece of King Peter I of Lusignan   49, 203, 204n; *see also* Eschiva (Alice's mother); Ferrand of Majorca (Alice's father); King Hugh IV of Lusignan (Alice's maternal grandfather); Peter of Campofregoso (Alice's lover); Philip of Ibelin (Alice's husband)
Alis, Genoese, daughter of Obertus de Clavaro   377-378; *see also* Florencia (Alis's mother)
'Alīshīr Germiyānī, see Karīm al-Dīn 'Alīshīr
'Alīshīr the Turkmen, father of Shihāb al-Dīn   438
'Alīshīrids, dynasty   437
All Saints Day   42, 45, 212
Alyon, *see* İlyas-i Rumi
Amadeus VI, (Green) Count of Savoy, son of a half-brother of Empress Anna of Savoy   21, 23, 36n, 104-105, 194, 195, 224, 461, 492-493, 497, 503; *see also* Anna of Savoy (Amadeus's aunt); Emperor John V Palaiologos (Amadeus's cousin); Paul, Latin Patriarch of Constantinople (Amadeus's co-ambassador)
Amadi, Francesco, chronicle attributed to   35, 50, 142, 178-180, 184, 332n, 335n, 347, 353

INDEX 577

Amaury, lord of Tyre   89, 112, 118, 164, 180; *see also* Aimery of Lusignan (Amaury's brother); King Henry II of Lusignan (Amaury's brother)
Ambianensy, bishopric of, Philip of Mézières's place of birth   293
Ambrogio Traversari, monk and theologian   540, 544n
Amedeo of Savoy, *see* Amadeus VI, count of Savoy
Amiens, city, France   21
Amorgos, island, Aegean Sea   129
Amory de Beauvaiz, Cypriot knight, captain of Beauvaiz   302
Anamur/Anemourion, city, southern Anatolia   97
Anatolia   19, 71, 78-79, 82-83, 86-87, 92, 95, 97, 109-110, 113-114, 118-119, 145, 191, 245-247, 249, 254, 257, 263n, 283, 383, 385-388, 390-391, 403, 409, 412-413, 417-419, 422-424, 426-436, 438, 440-442, 457, 479, 487; *see also* Asia Minor
 - Anatolian beyliks   83, 87, 91, 106, 109, 247, 249, 417, 463
Andrea Contarini/Contareno, doge of Venice   453
Andrea Navagero, official historian of Venice   38
Andrea Zane, podestà of Treviso   39, 45; *see also* Loredan *palazzo* (owned by Andrea Zane)
Andreas, son of the White Venetian Ioannis de Baruti   379n; *see also* Aylix, sister of Philipus Mistehel (Andreas's wife)
Andrew of Hungary   161-162, 295; *see also* Joanna I, queen of Naples (Andrew's wife)
Andronikos II Palaiologos, Byzantine emperor   93-94, 98-99, 101, 142, 512n; *see also* Andronikos III Palaiologos (Andronikos II's grandson); Michael IX Palaiologos (Andronikos II's son); Michael VIII Palaiologos (Andronikos II's father);

Yolanda-Eirene of Montferrat (Andronikos II's second wife)
Andronikos III Palaiologos, Byzantine emperor   99-101, 105, 458, 462, 464, 475, 478n, 479, 487, 504n, 507n, 524, 535-536, 537n; *see also* Andronikos Palaiologos (Andronikos III's cousin); Andronikos II Palaiologos (Andronikos III's grandfather); Anna of Savoy (Andronikos III's second wife); Emperor John V Palaiologos (Andronikos III's son)
Andronikos IV Palaiologos, Byzantine emperor   461n, 511n; *see also* John VII Palaiologos (Andronikos IV's son)
Andronikos Palaiologos, perhaps Andronikos III Palaiologos's cousin   503n, 504
Anemourion, *see* Anamur
Angady, *see* Engadi
Angel, Cypriot doctor in the service of King Charles II of Navarre   291, 300
Angelo of Lucca/Angelus de Luca, soldier   179, 208-209
Angelo Michiel, Venetian nobleman   134n
Angelus, *see* Sancti Angeli, castle
Angevins   51, 80, 82, 85, 87-90, 94, 98, 157-164, 166-167, 170, 181, 183, 185
Anglesia Visconti, wife of King Janus of Lusignan   289n, 295n, 340-341; *see also* Bernabò Visconti, lord of Milan (Anglesia's father); Valentina Visconti (Anglesia's sister)
Anglo-Burgundians   303; *see also* Burgundians
Anglo-French   248-249, 279, 284
Anglo-Ottomans   444
Angoulême, city, France   21, 303
Anjou, county of, France   98, 158-159, 163, 167-169, 171, 181, 572-573; *see also* Angevins; Cristoforo Orimina; Niccolò Alunno d'Alife
 - Anjou or Mechelen Bible   89, 161-164, 171, 573

Ankara, city, central Anatolia   389, 417, 442
Anna of Savoy, Byzantine empress   101, 105, 458, 465, 467-468, 470n, 478-480, 485, 507, 525, 536n; *see also* Amadeus VI, count of Savoy (son of a half-brother of Anna); Emperor Andronikos III Palaiologos (Anna's husband); Emperor John V Palaiologos (Anna's son)
'Annāba, *see* Bona
Anonimo Romano, chronicler   113
Antalya/Adalia/Antalia/Descallie/Satalia/Satalie, city and emirate, southern Anatolia   18, 20, 24, 43-44, 49, 55, 70-71, 97, 116, 119, 145, 154, 180, 186, 191-194, 201, 203, 214, 220, 223-224, 246, 283, 288, 291, 300, 302-303, 329, 354-356, 360; *see also* Takka/Tekke, emir of
Anthony Kolybas, anti-Palamite monk   561n
Anthony of Tyre, patriarch of Antioch   561n
Anthony, St, Latin monastery, Famagusta   378
Antibarum (Antivari/Bar), Montenegro   215, 225
Antioch, city, northern Syria, principality of   16, 24, 27, 44n, 46, 88, 140, 157, 158, 164, 165, 183, 187, 268, 270, 278, 302-303, 327, 331n, 338, 353-356, 358, 362, 363, 374n, 559, 560-561
Antonio Barberi, paymaster of Count Amadeus VI of Savoy   492n
Antonio García Gutiérrez, Spanish dramatist   59
Antonio di Rivello, bishop of Melfi, confessor of King Peter I of Lusignan   223, 331
Antonius, Latin monk   502
Antony of Bergamo, Piedmontese jurist, chamberlain and ambassador of King Peter I of Lusignan   341-342
Antony, clerk   342n

Antouemes the Koubouklarios, anti-Palamite   561
Apameia, city, western Anatolia   466n, 468
Apra, city, Thrace   466n
Apulia, region, Italy   141n, 292
Aq-Qoyunlu, Turkmen tribal confederation   436
Aqsarāyī/Aqsarā'ī, Seljuk historian   417, 438n
Aquileia, city, northern Italy   22, 193, 215, 221-222, 225
Aquitaine, duchy of   21
Arabia   254
Arabic/Arabs   31, 32 37, 72, 87, 110, 141n, 245, 251, 252, 254, 257, 261, 262, 266n, 268, 270-271, 274, 336, 362-363, 366n, 367n, 370, 372-375, 378, 379n, 380, 389, 419, 421, 433, 437, 446-449, 451, 454
Arachantloun Theodora, daughter of the Ilkhānid ruler Abaqa   479; *see also* Isaac Asanes (Arachantloun Theodora's husband); Maria Palaiologina, Michael VIII Palaiologos's illegitimate daughter (Arachantloun Theodora's mother)
Aragon, kingdom of   16-17, 20, 25, 56, 57, 60, 70, 72, 80, 87-90, 138, 159, 162, 163, 292, 297, 302, 335, 338, 352n, 353
Aramaic, language   363
Archipelago/Greek Archipelago   285; *see also* Aegean Sea
Arezzo, city, Italy   15
- bishop of   502n
Arians   531, 561
Arles, city, France   498
Armenia   72, 111-112, 115, 118, 140, 194, 201, 254, 298, 341-342
-Cilician Armenia   26, 78, 80, 85-86, 97, 110-111, 114
Armenian/s   42, 86, 92, 246, 366, 367, 368, 420, 421, 423, 427, 431-432, 435, 439, 442, 448
- language   448

Arnaldus Bernardieberardi, preceptor of the Hospital 230
Arnemuiden, town/battle of, Netherlands 243
Arnold of Milmars, Cypriot ambassador to Genoa 339, 342n; *see also* Renaut de Milmars (could be the same person); Reynald of Milmars (could be the same person)
Arnold of Montolif, member of the regency council of Cyprus 338
Arnold of Soissons, auditor of Cyprus 342
Arnold, archbishop of Auch 502n
Arodaphnoussa, popular song and fictitious character in the homonymous work 59, 60-61, 68, 571
Arsenios, metropolitan of Tyre 559-560, 561n
Arsenite, faction in Byzantium 99
Arsinoe, Greek bishopric of 372
Arslan, vizier of Hızır Beg 481; *see also* Toğan (Arslan's son)
Arsur/Azoto, Latin Kingdom of Jerusalem 27, 48, 185, 203, 238, 340, 350
Arthur of Connaught, prince 62
Arthur, legendary British king, one of the Christian Worthies 53, 277
Artuqids, clan and dynasty from the Döger tribe 422
Asandamur, Mamluk emir 261, 264-267
al-Ashraf Sha'bān, Mamluk sultan of Egypt 83, 143n, 251, 253, 255, 258, 260-261, 266, 268-269, 453
Asia 78, 80, 392, 394 469n, 471, 478n, 480n
 - Inner Asia 392, 397-398
 - Western Asia 393-394, 398
 - Central Asia 397-398, 400
Asia Minor 53, 78-79, 83-85, 87, 91-94, 97-102, 104-105, 111, 113-115, 121-124, 145, 192-194, 264, 392, 400, 452, 457-460, 462, 464, 467-468, 472-473, 478-479, 484, 486-487
Âşık Paşa, poet 403-404
Athanasius, St, theologian 543
Athens/Athènes, duchy of, Greece 87-88, 94, 177, 215, 225, 534
Athonite 102, 524, 526, 528, 554
Athos, *see* Mount Athos
Athyra, city, Propontis coast 466
At Wierzynek's, restaurant in Cracow 62; *see also* Mikołaj Wierzynek
Audeth, Cypriot family of White Venetians 361, 362n
Austria 20, 51, 135n, 192
Auximo (Osimo), town, Italy 502
Avignon, city/seat of the papacy, Provence 14, 19, 21, 23, 38, 40-41, 43, 48, 52, 70, 85, 87, 90-91, 96, 99, 100n, 177, 179-180, 185-188, 190-191, 193, 195, 198-200, 204, 206, 208-211, 212-213, 219, 221-223, 229, 230-233, 235-239, 284, 300-303, 347, 359-360, 372, 390n, 391, 393n, 506, 508, 514, 544
Ayas Gazi/Baba, leader of *gaza* 406, 407n; *see also* Ilyas Gazi (Ayas Gazi's predecessor as a *gaza* leader)
Ayas, port city, Cilicia 25, 43, 72, 80, 86, 256-257, 265
Ayas-i Rumi (Ilyas/İlyas), lieutenant of Ece Halil 405
Ayasuluk, *see* Ephesus
Aydın, emirate, western Anatolia 79, 92, 94-96, 100-102, 113, 115, 117, 459, 461-462, 464, 475, 481, 487
Aylix, sister of Philipus Mistehel 379; *see also* Andreas, son of Ioannis de Baruti (Aylix's husband)
al-'Aynī/Badr al-Dīn al-'Aynī, Mamluk historian 37, 252
Ayyubids, dynasty in Egypt and Syria 253, 446
'Azāz, city, northern Syria 421
Azerbaijan/Ganja 421, 434, 436
Azoto, *see* Arsur

INDEX

Babadag, town, south-eastern Romania   395, 411
Bābā'ī/Paparoissole, revolt of   419, 422, 429
Babin, Cypriot noble family   351; see also John Babin; Jean Babin; Raymond Babin
Babylon (Egypt), sultan of   142n, 200-221, 235
Badin Musta, maybe a *Surianus*   380
Baghdad, capital of 'Abbāsid Caliphate   434
Bahā' al-Dīn ibn al-Mufassar, Mamluk commander   258
Baḥrī, Mamluk military unit and ruling elite   247
Bāijū Noyan, Mongol commander   417-418, 423-424, 428-437, 441
bailli of the *Secrète* of Cyprus   327, 329, 334, 336n, 341, 348-352, 356, 358
Baktamur, *sharīf* and Alexandria's governor   255
Balat, see Miletus/Palatia
Baldassarre Bonaiuti, chronicler   39
Baldwin, bishop of Famagusta   366n
Balian d'Ibelin-Arsur, Cypriot nobleman   350
Balian Provane   342n; see also Embalin Provane (perhaps the same with Balian and Ibelin); Hodrade Provane (Balian's son); Ibelin Provane (perhaps the same with Balian and Embalin)
Balıkesir, city, western Asia Minor   93
Balkans   192, 202, 385, 389, 391, 406, 413-414, 443, 458, 473, 474, 508
Bāniyās/Valania, city, Syria   25, 72, 259
Bannockburn, battle of, Scotland   243
Bapheus, site/battle of, north-western Asia Minor   93
Bar Hebraeus, Syriac historian   419, 430, 434
Baranow, city, Poland   22
Barcelona, city, Catalonia   16, 357

Bardi, noble family, see Chiriaco de Bardi, Giovanni Bardi
Barlaam of Calabria, bishop under papal authority in southern Italy, theologian   101, 512, 521-522, 524, 525n-526n, 528n, 536, 554-556, 558n, 560; see also Gregory Akindynos; Gregory Palamas
Barlaamites   560; see also Barlaam of Calabria
Barqūq, Mamluk sultan   254n
Barsbāy, Mamluk sultan   258, 270
Barthélémy de Montolif, chamberlain of Cyprus   351, 352
Bartholomew the Apostle, see Corpus Christi, church, Nicosia
Bartholomew, a Cypriot living in Constantinople   556
Bartolomeo Ghisi, lord of Tenos and Mykonos   95
Bartolomeo Sacchi, called Platina, author   501
Basel, city, Switzerland   20, 540n
Basil of Caesarea, the Great   494n, 529, 561
Battal Gazi, legendary hero   408
Baudouin de Nores, maréchal de l'Hôtel du Roi de Chypre   350-352
Bavaria, region, Germany   20, 192
Baybars al-Manṣūrī, Mamluk historian   434
Baybars, Mamluk sultan   253, 256, 258, 427, 436, 438, 440-441
Baydamur, emir   238
Bayezid I, Ottoman sultan   414, 454
Bayezid II, Ottoman sultan   424
Bayramoğlu, village, north-western Anatolia   99
Beatrice of Provence   162; see also Charles I of Anjou (Beatrice's husband); Charles II, king of Naples (Beatrice's son)
Bedreddin   481; see also Ali Mardān (Bedreddin's brother); Hwāce Hasen (Bedreddin's father)

INDEX 581

Beirut, city, Lebanon   23, 80, 166, 182, 256-258, 260, 265, 341, 379
Belgium   51
Bellapais Abbey, Cyprus   89, 166, 167n, 172, 573
Benedetto II Zaccaria, Genoese ruler of Chios   79n
Benedict XII, pope   15, 56, 86, 101, 115-116, 182, 497
Benedict of Cumae, Dominican friar   99
Benedictines   289
Bentivegna Traversario, notary   132
Bera, city, southern Thrace   481
Berdibeg, Tatar khan   447, 452n
Berke Khan, ruler of the Jochid Ulus   405n
Bernabò Visconti, lord of Milan   19-21, 40, 190, 192, 289, 293n, 295n; *see also* Anglesia Visconti (Bernabò's daughter); Galeazzo II Visconti (Bernabò's brother); Giangaleazzo Visconti (Bernabò's nephew); Valentina Visconti (Bernabò's daughter); Yolanda/Violante Visconti (Bernabò's niece)
Bernard Gui, historian   497
Bernardo Al, knight   331
Bernardus de Marcrinio, dominus de Planis   230
Berrhoia, city, Macedonia   463, 465, 469n
Berry, duke of   51
Bertini, Florentine family, *see* Giovanni Bertini; Pacio Bertini
Bertran, *see* Syr Bertran
Bertrand Boysset, Occitan historian   498
Bertrand Du Guesclin/de Claikin, Breton knight   21, 287-288, 291-292, 293n, 297, 302-303
Bertrand, archbishop of Naples   209
Bethsan, city, Palestine   341
Beuthen, city, Silesia   22
Bibi, Cypriot family   380n 381; *see also* John Bibi; Thomas Bibi; Pipēs ('Bibi') monastery

Biğāya, *see* Bugia
Bira, Shagdaryn   390n
Birgi, *see* Pyrgion
Bithynia, region, northwest Anatolia   93, 100, 462, 484
Bizye, city, eastern Thrace
Blachernai, church of/synod in, Constantinople   512n, 537
Black Death   16, 83, 96, 118, 139, 143, 146, 152, 247, 254, 572
Black Prince, *see* Edward the Black Prince
Black Sea   43, 111, 118, 452-453
Blanco Delfino, Venetian consul in Tunis   447
Blassios, Cypriot living in Constantinople   556
Boccaccio, *see* Giovanni Boccaccio
Boethian   277
Bohemia, kingdom of   22, 43, 51, 70, 297
Bollati di Saint-Pierre, Federico Emanuele   224
Bologna, city, Lombardy   21, 26, 293, 501
Bona/'Annāba, Algerian coast   449
Bonaiunta de Cascina, interpréter   447
Boucicaut/Bouciquaut, *see* John II Le Meingre
Boulogne-sur-Mer, port city, northern France   21, 45
Bourbon, duchy of/house of   51, 90, 181-185, 246, 300, 333, 351; *see also* Louis of Clermont, duke of Bourbon; Maria of Bourbon
Bozkır, region, southern Anatolia   433-434
Brabant, duchy of   14, 20
Brémond de la Voulte, knight from the Languedoc   332, 334; *see also* Adhémar de la Voulte (Brémond's brother)
Breslau, city, Silesia   22
Brétigny, France   247-248
Bretons   49
British   62, 141

Brittany, duchy of   45
Bruges, city, Flanders   14, 20, 330
Brunswick, duchy/house of, see Heloise/Héloïse de Brunswick; Henry II, duke of Brunswick; Philip of Brunswick
Brussels/Bruxelles, city, Brabant   14, 20
Bucentaur, the state barge of the doges of Venice   39
Buda, city, Hungary   492, 497
Bugia/Biğāya, port city, Algeria   449
Buḫtur, Arab dynasty in Lebanon   257
Būlāq, river port, Cairo   259
Bulgar Mountains, southern Anatolia   433-434
Bulgaria   466, 474, 492n
Bulgarians   370, 387, 396, 464-465, 466, 467, 469-471, 473-474, 487, 492, 508n
Bulla Cypria   13-14, 32, 177, 179-180, 191n, 198, 201n-204n, 206, 208-209, 211, 213-214, 219, 222-224, 230-233, 235-238, 365, 366n, 369, 372
Bunsuz, Turkmen leader   435, 439; see also Karīm al-Dīn Karāmān (Bunsuz's brother)
Burdegala (Bordeaux), Aquitaine   230
Burdur, city, central Anatolia   97n
Burgundians   295; see also Anglo-Burgundians
Burgundy, duchy of   280, 287, 295
Bursa, city, northwestern Anatolia   99, 436, 462
Bursbey, Mamluk sultan   447
Buru, see Peritheorion
Bustron, Florio, Cypriot chronicler   35, 326
Bustron, Cypriot noble family   304n; see also Bustron, Florio
Buṭrus, Arabic name for *Petros* (King Peter I of Lusignan)   255
Byzantine Empire/Byzantium   82, 84, 86-87, 95, 97-99, 101-102, 105-106, 135n, 202, 244, 387n, 401, 413, 438, 442, 455, 457-458, 460-464, 468, 469n, 471n, 473-474, 477, 481n, 487, 489n, 490, 492n, 508n, 512n, 513, 515, 516n, 517, 519-520, 543, 565
Byzantines   79, 100, 110, 112-113, 115, 142, 335, 369, 438, 452, 460-461, 468, 469n, 470, 472n, 474, 496, 498-499, 508n, 516n, 519-521, 522n, 525n, 565; see also Roman/s

Ca' Corner, palace in San Luca, Venice   39; see also Corner Piscopia – Loredan *palazzo*, Venice
Caen, city, Normandy   40
Caesarea, city, Palestine   340
Caffa/Kefe, port city, Crimea   192, 215, 219, 225, 395, 401, 447
Caiffa, see Haifa
Cain, biblical figure   286
Cairo, Egypt   23-24, 36-37, 77, 83, 87, 98, 143-144, 151, 247, 252, 255, 258-266, 268-269, 446, 572
Calabria, region, southern Italy   36, 101, 162, 521, 254, 554
Calais, port city, northern France   20, 193-194
Calixtus III, pope   297
Caltabellotta, town, Sicily   88
Camporegio, street in Siena, Tuscany   39
Candelore, see Alaya
Candia, capital city, Crete   94-96, 122, 124-126, 128n, 129-130, 132
Capetians, French royal dynasty   89, 161, 163
Cappadocia, region, eastern Anatolia   420
Caria, region, southwestern Anatolia   92, 462, 470n
Carinthia, duchy of   22
Carlo Zeno   38; see also Iacopo Zeno
Carmelites, order   104
Carobert, son of Charles Martel   161
Caroldo, Gian Giacomo, Venetian historian   39
- *Historie venete dal principio della citta fino all'anno*   1382 39

Carolingians 241
Casimir III the Great, king of
   Poland 22, 43, 54
Cassan Cigala/Qāzān, Genoese
   ambassador 266, 267n, 269
Castellani, Arrigo 449n
Castello, see Città di Castello
Catalans 23-24, 70, 79n, 80, 83, 88, 94,
   258, 262-266, 335, 357, 405
   - Grand Catalan Company 84, 89,
   93, 98, 244
Catalonia 264, 335n
Caterina Cornaro, queen of Cyprus 59
Catherine, St, church, Nicosia 44
Catherine, St, monastery, Mount
   Sinai 269
Catholic faith 87, 104, 110, 207, 210-211,
   214, 220, 224, 227, 283n, 285, 293n,
   368, 490, 492, 495, 496n, 498n, 503n,
   509-510, 513n, 514-515, 516n, 526, 535,
   537-540, 551
Cattaneo, Genoese family 100; see also
   Domenico Cattaneo
Caucasus 392, 421, 441
Celts 497
Cérines, see Kyrenia
Chalcedon, city, Bithynia 365, 529n
   - Council of Chalcedon 365, 529n
Chalcedonians 362, 364, 372, 374-376,
   379, 380, 382
Chalkidike, peninsula, northern
   Greece 117
Chamout Raïs, Turkish captain 146n
Champagne, principality of 164
Chania, city, Crete 129
Charioupolis, city, eastern
   Thrace 466n
Charlemagne, Holy Roman Emperor,
   one of the Christian Worthies 41,
   277, 297, 362n
Charles I, count of Anjou 88-89,
   98, 158-159, 162-163, 166-167; see also
   Beatrice of Provence (Charles I's
   wife); Charles II, king of Naples
   (Charles I's son); Louis IX, king of
   France/St Louis (Charles I's brother);
   Philip of Anjou (Charles I's son)
Charles II, king of Naples and count of
   Anjou 88-90, 159, 161-164, 181; see
   also Beatrice of Provence (Charles II's
   mother); Charles Martel (Charles II's
   firstborn son); Charles I, count of
   Anjou (Charles II's father); Louis of
   Toulouse (Charles II's son); Mary of
   Hungary (Charles II's wife); Philip
   of Taranto (Charles II's son); Robert
   I, king of Naples (Charles II's son);
   Robert of Taranto (Charles II's
   grandson)
Charles II, the Bad, king of
   Navarre 291
Charles IV of Luxembourg Holy Roman
   Emperor and King of Bohemia 20,
   22, 26, 43, 46, 52, 54, 60, 96, 192, 278-
   279, 499-501, 508; see also Elizabeth of
   Pomerania (Charles IV's fourth wife);
   Karlstein/Karlštejn, castle
Charles IV, king of France 41n, 86,
   114; see also Philip VI, king of France
   (Charles IV's successor)
Charles V, duke of Normandy and later
   king of France 14, 20-21, 52, 99, 202,
   276, 279, 280, 288, 290, 292, 294, 300,
   302, 306, 330, 573; see also John II, king
   of France (Charles V's father); John
   of Berry (Charles V's brother); Philip
   the Bold (Charles V's brother)
Charles VI, dauphin and later king
   of France 282, 284-285, 288-291,
   294-295, 300; see also Louis I, duke of
   Orleans (Charles VI' brother); Philip
   the Bold (Charles VI's uncle)
Charles Martel, firstborn son of Charles
   II, king of Naples 161-162; see also
   Carobert (Martel's son); Louis of
   Toulouse (Martel's brother); Mary
   of Hungary (Martel's mother);
   Philip of Taranto (Martel's brother);
   Robert I, king of Naples (Martel's
   brother)

Charles of Parma, fiancé of Margaret, daughter of King Peter I of Lusignan and Eleanor of Aragon   289n
Charles, duke of Calabria   162; *see also* Maria and Joanna I, queen of Naples (Charles's daughters); Mary of Valois (Charles's wife); Robert I, king of Naples (Charles's father); Yolande of Aragon (Charles's mother)
Charsianon/Garsian, Byzantine theme   420
Chatzes, eunuch and emissary   479
Cherbourg, city, Normandy   20
Chiara, Santa, *see* Santa Chiara
China   138, 249, 394, 451
Chios, island, Aegean Sea   79n, 94, 100, 113-114, 118, 336
Chiriaco de Bardi, maybe a Greek   380; *see also* Domenico Semano (Chiriaco's debtor)
Chora Monastery, Constantinople   513n
Chora, city, Thrace   466n, 471n
Christianity   50, 85, 199, 214, 220, 224, 235-236, 266, 269, 293n, 415, 487, 515n, 539, 543
Christian/s   15, 21-22, 27, 34, 36-37, 40, 51, 56, 69, 77-78, 80-81, 85, 87, 89, 91, 93-94, 97-98, 104, 110, 113-114, 116, 119, 133, 135, 140n, 142, 146, 157, 165, 167, 189, 190, 191-192, 194, 196-197, 189, 192, 194, 196-197, 201, 207, 210-211, 214-215, 220, 224-225, 227, 231-232, 234, 238, 245-248, 251-252, 263, 265-270, 277-278, 281-285, 287-289, 292, 293n, 295, 299-300, 301, 345, 361-364, 366-367, 371, 372n, 374, 378n, 379, 380, 382, 396, 409, 412-415, 438, 452, 454, 457-459, 463, 472-474, 476, 486-487, 490, 506-507, 511n, 515, 517, 523, 527, 530-532, 537n, 538, 541, 542-543, 545, 547, 554, 560n, 562
- Christian Commonwealth/Christendom   36, 40, 43, 58, 79, 110, 157, 165, 282, 285, 292, 305, 460n, 472, 473
- Christian-Mongol, *see* Mongols
- Christian-Muslim, *see* Muslims
- Oriental Christians, *see* Oriental
- Syrian (Melkite) Christians   364, 378n, 560n; *see also* Melkites; Syrians
Christine de Pizan, French author   33, 277, 280n, 282n, 294-296; *see also* Thomas de Pizan (Christine's father)
Christopher the Martyr, St   140n
Christoupolis/Hiristo (modern Kavala), city, eastern Macedonia   465n, 476
Cilicia   80, 92, 140, 246, 247, 426, 427-428, 432, 435 439, 448; *see also* Armenia (Cilician Armenia)
Ciolo di Anastasio Bofeti, Pisan translator   447
Città di Castello, city, Italy   352n
Clare, St, Latin convent in Nicosia   26
Clarissan, order   161
Clement V, pope (born Raymond Bertrand de Got)   84-85, 98, 112
Clement VI, pope (born Pierre Roger, served as archbishop of Rouen)   15, 16, 48, 50, 56, 80, 96, 101, 102, 115-116, 119, 182, 190, 211, 353, 472
Çoban Ata, hero   406; *see also* Saltukname (epic tale)
Collina/Colina, porta, Rome   500
Collocensi (Kalosca, Hungary), archdiocese of   195n
Collocensi dicta Rodo (Rhodes), diocese of   215, 225; *see also* Rhodes/Rodo
Cologne, city/cathedral, Germany   14, 20, 22, 46n
Coluccio Salutati, chancellor of Florence   500
Combe, Étienne   251
Comi, fief, Cyprus   342n
Comnenian dynasty   451, 485; *see also* Alexios I Komnenos; Manuel I Komnenos
Connaught, ancient kingdom, Ireland   62

Conrad Grünemberg, German pilgrim   44n, 63, 571
Conradin, last Hohenstaufen king of Jerusalem   158
Constance d'Aragon, see Constance of Sicily
Constance of Sicily/Constance d'Aragon, daughter of Frederick III, king of Sicily   89-90, 353; see also King Henry II of Lusignan (Constance's first husband); John of Antioch (Constance's second husband)
Constantine I the Great, Roman emperor   135, 513n
Constantine V, king of Cilician Armenia   97
Constantin of Lampron, Armenian lord   431
Constantinides, Andreas, director   61, 66, 571
Constantinople   17, 19, 22-23, 26, 36, 48, 82, 87-88, 93-94, 98-99, 100n, 101-105, 112, 140n, 179, 181, 185, 195, 197, 206, 209, 213, 215, 219, 225, 233, 235-237, 274, 282, 369-370, 374, 378n, 388, 401n, 437n, 444-445, 454, 457-458, 462-472, 474, 476-481, 483-485, 487-489, 490n, 491, 493-494, 497-499, 502n, 503, 508n, 511, 513-514, 515n, 516n, 518, 520-523, 525-544, 546-549, 552-553, 555, 557, 559-560
Coran   453
Corfu, island, Ionian Sea   215, 225
Corinth, city, Peloponnese   215, 225
Cornaro, Venetian family   55n, 330; see also Caterina Cornaro; Marco Cornaro
Corner Piscopia – Loredan *palazzo*, palace in Venice, see Loredan *palazzo*; see also Ca' Corner, palace in San Luca
Corner, Venetian family   45, 140-141; see also Alessio Corner
Corpus Christi, church, Nicosia, also dedicated to Bartholomew the Apostle and Sancti Sabastiani martiris   25, 44
Corycus, see Gorhigos
Coterinus, see Quṭb al-Dīn Aḥmad
Coudrette, French author   299, 314-316, 574; see also William VII Larchevêque
Council of Vienne   85
Courtrai, battle of/city, west Flanders   243
Cracow, capital city, Poland   14, 22, 43, 54-55, 62, 70
Crécy, battle of, northern France   54, 243
Cretans/Cretenses   38, 96, 121, 124-125, 126-131
Crete, island   20-21, 23, 38, 51, 70, 83, 86, 94-96, 121-134, 141n, 185, 192, 194, 215, 225, 282, 370, 378n, 514n
- Cretan Senate   96, 124-125, 126n, 128, 131, 132n-133n, 134
- Cretan Great Council   122n, 133
Crimea, peninsula, Black Sea   95, 387, 395-396, 401, 402n, 446-447, 451, 452
Cristoforo Moro, doge of Venice   444n
Cristoforo Orimina, Italian illuminator   162, 170, 573; see also Anjou (Anjou or Mechelen Bible); Niccolò Alunno d'Alife
Cross, see True Cross
- Cross of the Good Thief   15, 277
- Cross of the Good Thief, church, Famagusta   50
Crusader States   85, 87, 109, 110, 166-167, 253, 256, 270, 273-274, 377, 382, 446
Cuvelier, French author/trouvère   33, 287-288, 302
Cyclades, group of Greek islands, Aegean Sea   94n
Cypriots, 22-23, 35, 55-56, 60-61, 82, 84, 97, 111, 114, 196-197, 199, 100n, 245, 247, 254-255, 258-259, 262-265, 268-269, 270n, 284, 293, 304, 323, 332-333, 343, 369, 380, 553, 556-557, 564, 563
- Frankish Cypriots   61
- Greek Cypriots   32, 60-61
- Latin Cypriots   55

Cyprus   11, 14-24, 26-27, 31-32, 34, 36-37, 38n, 39, 41-43, 46n, 47-50, 52, 54-56, 59-62, 69-72, 75, 77, 78, 80-91, 95-96, 102, 106 109-119, 121, 133n, 134-146, 148, 150, 157-158, 164-167, 177-188, 190, 192-206, 208-211, 213-214, 219, 221-224, 230-238, 241-243, 245-249, 251, 253-255, 257-259, 261-265, 267, 268n, 269-271, 273, 275n-276n, 278-286, 288-289, 291-292, 293, 295-298, 300-305, 316-319, 323-324, 326-331, 333-334, 335n, 336-337, 339-340, 341-343, 346, 350, 361-365, 366n, 367-368, 370-373, 375, 377-379, 381-382, 445n, 449n, 450, 461, 490, 492, 503n, 523, 526, 551-557, 559-561, 564-565, 571, 571-572, 574
Cyril, metropolitan of Side   559-560
Czechs   60, 62
Damanhūr, city, Delta of Nile   263n, 265,
Damascus, city, Syria   37, 252, 255-257, 269, 298
Damokraneia, city, eastern Thrace   466n
Dampierre, Cypriot family   327; see also Eschiva of Dampierre; Oddon de Dampierre
Daniel Scolar, Cypriot knight   338n
Danube, river   389, 408, 414
Daphnidion, city, eastern Thrace   466n
Dardanelles   100n, 467, 469n
David II, king of Scotland   53
David IV, king of Georgia   421
David, king of Israel, one of the Jewish Worthies   277
Değirmençayı, small village near modern Sivrihisar, central Anatolia   92, 436-438
Delfino, Venetian family, see Blanco Delfino; Giovanni Delfino
Demetrios Kydones, *mesazon* and chancellor of Emperor John V Palaiologos   36, 105-106, 368n, 461, 489, 495, 502, 503n, 504, 513-514, 516, 518-519, 521-523, 526, 533, 549, 561n; see also Prochoros Kydones (Demetrios's brother)

Demetrios of Kyzikos, author   368
Demetrios Palaiologos, *megas domestikos*   503
Demirhan, lord of Karasi/Demirhan of Karasi   100, 462n; see also Yahşi of Karasi (Demirhan's father)
Denis, St   15, 21, 182
Denizli, see Laodikeia
Denmark, kingdom of   20, 43, 53-54, 60
Denores, see Nores, de
Derke, lake, eastern Thrace   466n
Descallie, see Antalya
Desimoni, Cornelio   446
Didgori, battle of   421
Didymoteichon/Dimetoka, city, western Thrace   464-465, 467, 469n, 477, 481, 483-484
Dimetoka, see Didymoteichon
Dobruca/Dobruja, region, Danube Delta   387, 390, 395, 400, 408
Döger, Oghuz tribe   422
Domenico Cattaneo, Genoese governor of Phocaea   101
Domenico Querini, Venetian consul in Palatia   131
Domenico Rodulfi, Italian jurist   356, 358
Domenico Semano   380; see also Chiriaco de Bardi
Domenico, see San Domenico
Dominicans   45-46, 99, 100n, 101, 103-104, 164, 513, 514, 532, 533, 539, 549n, 565
Donato Bossi, Milanese author/scribe   38
Donato di Neri, chronicler   39
Douay-Rheims Bible   538n
Doukas, Byzantine historian   497, 580n
Dover, port city, England   20
Drenopolitanus, bishop of (Nicholas of Drenopolis)   502
Dündar Beg, ghazi fighter   481

Eblo de Mederio, apostolic notary and cleric of the papal chamber   502n
Ebu'l-Hayr Rūmī, author/compiler   387, 389, 400-401

INDEX

Ece Halil/Ece Gazi, military commander 405; *see also* Ayas-i Rumi (Ece Halil's lieutenant); Sarı Saltuk (Ece Halil's predecessor)
Échive de Montfort, *see* Eschiva of Montfort
Edessa, crusader county of 420-421
Edward I, king of England 139
Edward III, king of England 20, 42, 45, 53-54, 86, 244, 248-249, 276, 304; *see also* Edward the Black Prince (Edward III's son); *Katherine/Catelinne* (the ship Edward III gave to King Peter I of Lusignan); Lionel, duke of Clarence (Edward III's son); Philippa of Hainault (Edward III's wife)
Edward the Black Prince, son of King Edward III of England 21, 51, 303
Eğridir, city, central Anatolia 97n
Egypt/Egipte/Egypte 24-25, 41, 56n, 71, 77, 80-83, 98, 106, 109-111, 119, 142-144, 152, 194, 203, 247, 249, 251, 253, 255, 258, 263-264, 266-268, 280, 293, 362n, 369, 435, 572
Ehad Subaşı, ghazi fighter 481
Eksya, *see* Xanthi
Elbistan, city, eastern Anatolia 434, 438
Eleanor of Aragon/Éléonore d'Aragon, queen of Cyprus, second wife of King Peter I of Lusignan 16-17, 20, 25, 35, 56-57, 60-61, 70, 72-73, 90, 302, 335-338, 343, 357; *see also* John of Morphou (Eleanor's lover); Margaret (Eleanor's daughter); Peter II of Lusignan (Eleanor's son); Peter of Ribargoza (Eleanor's father)
Eleazarus, Biblical priest 283n
Éléonore d'Aragon, *see* Eleanor of Aragon
Elias Petit, Fr, vicar general of the Dominicans 533
Élie l'Aleman, viscount of Nicosia 351
Élinas, king of Albanie (Scotland), mythical figure 297, 298n; *see also* Mélusine
Elizabeth of Pomerania, fourth wife of Charles IV of Luxembourg, Holy Roman Emperor 43, 60; *see also* Casimir III the Great, king of Poland (Elizabeth's grandfather)
El-Leon, *see* İlyas-i Rumi
Embalin Provane 342n; *see also* Balian Provane (perhaps the same with Embalin and Ibelin); Hodrade Provane (Balian's son); Ibelin Provane (perhaps the same with Balian and Embalin)
Emona, Roman town, part of modern Ljubljana 215, 225
Empyrites, city, Thrace 466
Engadi/Angady, vineyards of 283n
England/*Engleterre/Grant Bretaigne* 20, 24, 26, 42, 45, 51, 53-54, 60, 70, 86, 90, 113, 139, 143, 192, 242-244, 276, 287, 292-293, 300-301, 303-304, 497
Englishmen/*Englois* 195, 243-244, 249, 279, 284, 287, 289, 301, 303, 329, 444
Enverī, Turkish poet-chronicler 113, 117, 460, 464, 467n, 474-476, 481-482
Ephesus/Ayasuluk/Theologo, western Asia Minor 71, 92, 96, 113, 117, 121, 123, 127-129, 130-131, 132n, 134, 462, 481
Epiphanios, St, church, Famagusta 378
Epirus, despotate of 87, 98
Erfurt, city, Germany 22
Ermenek, city, southeastern Anatolia 92, 425-427, 435, 439-440
Ermine/Ermines, order 367
Ermine, mythical figure 299; *see also* Hermine
Ermolao Minotto, Venetian consul in Theologo 131
Ertoghrul, Ottoman chief 425
Erzincan, city, north-eastern Anatolia 429-430, 434
Erzurum, city, north-eastern Anatolia 429-430, 434

588 INDEX

Eschiva of/de Scandelion, mistress of King Peter I of Lusignan   25, 57, 72
Eschiva of Dampierre   203n; *see also* Hugh IV of Lusignan (Eschiva's uncle); Philip of Ibelin, lord of Arsur (Eschiva's husband)
Eschiva of Montfort/Échive de Montfort, first wife (and cousin) of King Peter I of Lusignan   15-16, 56, 182-183, 353; *see also* Hugh IV of Lusignan (Eschiva's uncle)
Eschiva, daughter of King Hugh IV of Lusignan   47, 90; *see also* Alice of Ibelin (Eschiva's mother); Alice of Majorca (Eschiva's daughter); Ferrand of Majorca (Eschiva's husband)
Eschiva, daughter of King Peter I of Lusignan   56; *see also* Eschiva of Montfort (Eschiva's mother)
Esphigmenou, monastery, Mount Athos   557
Esslingen, city, Germany   22
Ethiopians (Aithiopes/Aethiopiani)   366n, 370
Étienne de Conty, author   33, 292
Euboea, island, Aegean Sea   465, 470n, 477
Eunomians, followers of Eunomius, bishop of Cyzicus   559n
Euphrates, river   91
 - Upper Euphrates   91
Europe/Europeans   18, 25, 31-34, 38, 40, 45, 49-53, 55, 57, 62, 70, 78-82, 84, 87, 89, 91, 106, 110-112, 118, 137, 140, 146, 149, 158, 203, 241-245, 247, 249, 254, 263, 268, 270, 274, 276, 279, 281-282, 284-285, 287, 290, 291, 293, 295, 297, 301-303, 305, 329-331, 333, 341, 389, 443, 449, 452-454, 460n, 463, 484, 544n, 572
Eustache Deschamps, courtier and author   33, 280, 290-291, 294
Eustorgius, St, basilica in Milan   48
Evagoras I, king of Salamis   31

Fakhr al-Dīn 'Alī, Seljuk vizier   436, 439, 441
Famagusta, port city, Cyprus   15, 17-18, 22-25, 27, 44, 49, 50, 54, 63, 70-72, 80-82, 88-89, 138, 149, 165-167, 173, 178, 185, 197-198, 245-247, 273n, 278, 296, 303, 314, 323, 334-336, 361, 365, 375n, 377n, 378, 379n, 380-382, 560n, 571-574
Fazio degli Uberti, Florentine poet   41
Feast of the Five Kings   20, 53, 55, 60, 62, 65, 571; *see also* Picard, Sir Henry (allegedly arranged the feast); Vintners' Company/Worshipful Company of Vintners (host of the feast); Vintners' Company's Swan feast
Federico Franconi, Dominican preacher   164
Feras Simiteculo (in Arabic Firās), White Venetian, resident of Famagusta   378; *see also* Fetus Simeteculo (Feras's son); Teodorus Simiteculo (Feras's son); Uxira (Feras's daughter)
Ferrand of Majorca   47, 49, 89-90, 183, 349-350; *see also* Alice of Majorca (Ferrand's daughter); Eschiva, daughter of Hugh IV and Alice of Ibelin (Ferrand's wife); Ferrand, younger son of James I of Majorca (Ferrand's father); King Hugh IV of Lusignan (Ferrand's father-in-law); Isabella of Ibelin (Ferrand's mother)
Ferrand, younger son of James I of Majorca, former commandant of the Catalan Grand Company in Greece   89-90; *see also* Ferrand of Majorca (Ferrand's son); Isabella of Ibelin (Ferrand's wife)
Ferrara, city, Italy   26, 293
Fetus Simiteculo, White Venetian, resident of Famagusta, either of Greek or more likely of Melkite origin   378-379; *see also* Feras Simiteculo (Fetus's father); Maria Simiteculo (Fetus's wife); Teodorus Simiteculo (Fetus's brother); Uxira (Fetus's sister)

INDEX 589

Fidentius of Padua, vicar of the Franciscan province of the Holy Land 263
Filippo de Varesio, Genoese provost (*prepositum*) 197, 233
Filippo Villani, Florentine humanist and historian 52-53
Firās, *see* Feras Simiteculo
Flanders 14, 20, 70, 280, 331
Florence, city, Tuscany 18, 26, 39, 41, 45, 52, 72, 115, 138, 162, 168, 171, 189, 193, 347, 349, 572-573
- Council of Florence 512
Florencia, Genoese citizen, wife of Obertus de Clavaro 377; *see also* Alis (Florencia's daughter)
Florie, mythical figure 298; *see also* Guion (Florie's husband)
Florimond of Lesparre, Gascon lord in the service of King Peter I of Lusignan 24-25, 49-50, 64, 71-72, 204, 264n
Folie, literary figure, friend of Franc Vouloir 291
Franc Vouloir, literary figure 291
France, kingdom of 13-14, 19-21, 24, 26, 33, 35, 40, 41n, 42, 48-53, 60, 69-70, 80, 85-86, 90, 109, 112-115, 117, 138, 146n, 158, 163, 179, 181, 187, 189-198, 202, 214-215, 220-222, 224-225, 242-243, 249, 253, 276, 278-279, 282, 284-285, 287-289, 291-292, 293n, 295-305, 330-331, 348, 351, 355, 443, 490, 497
Francesco Gattilusi/Gattilusio, Genoese ruler of Lesbos 105, 502, 508n
Francesco Landini, Italian blind composer and organist 52
Francesco Marcello, member of the Senate and the *sapientes* of Crete 127n
Francesco Pegolotti, Florentine merchant and politician 137, 149, 572
Francesco Petrarca/Petrarch, scholar, poet, and diplomat 40, 41n, 56, 275, 330, 500

Francis of Arezzo, bishop of Limassol 15
Francis Lakha, Nestorian merchant of Famagusta 361
Francis of Marin, Genoese supporter of Queen Eleanor of Aragon 335
Francis Saturno, Catalan supporter of Queen Eleanor of Aragon 335
Franciscans, order 47, 159, 160-161, 163, 363, 375, 507n
François Villon, French poet 33, 277, 297
Franconia, region, Germany 22
Franks 55-56, 60-61, 79, 83-84, 87-88, 94, 110, 113-114, 157, 189, 241, 244, 253, 256-257, 259, 261, 263n, 265-269-271, 273, 285, 302, 324, 351, 367, 371, 373-376, 379n, 381-382, 445-446, 452n, 461, 467n, 472-473, 481, 487
Frederick II, Holy Roman Emperor 292
Frederick III, king of Sicily 88-89; *see also* Constance of Sicily (Frederick III's daughter); James II, king of Majorca (Frederick III's brother); Peter III, king of Aragon (Frederick III's father)
Free Companies 20, 84, 192, 244-245, 288, 303
Fréjus, bishop of 502n
Frenchmen/Français 19-20, 32-35, 37, 40-43, 48-49, 54, 59, 61n, 79-88, 90-91, 98-99, 114-115, 117, 140, 161, 163, 166, 177, 187, 190-191, 194n, 204, 245n, 247-249, 255n, 268n, 273-277, 279-280, 282, 284-285, 287, 289, 292, 294, 296, 297, 299-305, 329, 331, 366-367, 443, 445-448, 453, 497, 499n, 517, 533n
Fulk de Villaret, Hospitaller Grand Master 111

Gabriel Adorno/Adurno, doge of Genoa 196-197, 230-234, 236-237
Gabriel, presbyter of the Anastasis 375
Gabriele D'Annunzio, Italian author 59

Galata, suburb of Constantinople 467
Galeazzo II Visconti, lord of Milan 19; *also see* Bernabò Visconti (Galeazzo's brother); Giangaleazzo Visconti (Galeazzo's son)
Galicia, Spain 50n
Galilee, principality of 41, 70, 88, 183, 300, 340, 351, 355, 358
Gallipoli, city, eastern Thrace 96, 102, 105, 458-459, 461, 464, 466-467, 480, 483-484, 488, 492
Ganja (modern Azerbaijan), *see* Azerbaijan
Garella, town, eastern Thrace 466
Garmiān/Karmian, territory in the vicinity of Malatya 91, 418-424
Garoscus de Ulmoisca, chronicler 498
Garsian, *see* Charsianon
Gascony, duchy of 21, 49, 70, 274n
Gasparino Barzizza, author 41
Gauselinus de Pradallo, papal chaplain 502n
Gebze, city, northwestern Anatolia 99
Gediz, river, *see* Hermos
Genoa, city/maritime republic 19, 20, 22, 24, 26, 38, 51, 55, 59, 70-71, 80-81, 83, 95-96, 109, 124, 132, 192, 196-201, 231-233, 237, 262-264, 266, 268-269, 270n, 271, 296, 324, 326-328, 330-331, 335-337, 339-342, 347, 359, 360-361, 377, 382, 446-447, 450, 452, 458
Genoese 19, 22-23, 25-26, 38-39, 49, 56, 71-72, 79n, 82, 85n, 86, 89, 93-94, 96, 111-113, 121, 123, 165, 187n, 190, 196-201, 203, 230-234, 236-237, 252, 259, 261-264, 266-267, 269, 270n, 285, 289, 291-292, 296, 302n-303n, 304, 323-324, 326, 328n, 330, 332, 335-340, 343, 351, 354, 357, 359, 360-362, 377-381, 445-446, 450, 458, 462, 467, 489, 533, 539
- White Genoese 378n, 380; *see also* John Bibi, White Genoese of Melkite origin; Marcus Zebas (John Bibi's father-in-law); Thomas Bibi (John Bibi's brother)

Geoffrey Chaucer, English poet 42, 275, 277, 287n, 289n
George/Gregory II of Cyprus, patriarch of Constantinople 552
George III, king of Georgia 422
George Akropolites, Byzantine historian 432-434
George of the Halfcastes, St, church, Nicosia 137n
George Lapithes, Cypriot writer and scholar, opponent of Gregory Palamas 551, 553-557, 559, 564; *see also* Gregory Akindynos
George Monomachos, Byzantine supporter of Queen Eleanor of Aragon 335, 465
George Pachymeres, Byzantine historian 93n, 99, 433-434, 457
George/Gennadios Scholarios, patriarch of Constantinople 521-522, 527, 532
George Spanopoulos, *protovestiarites* 472
George Tagaris, *megas stratopedarches* and negotiator 468, 469n, 478; *see also* Manuel Tagaris, governor of Philadelphia (George Tagaris's father)
Georgia, kingdom of 421-422
Georgians/Iberians 88, 366n, 370, 374-375, 420-423, 441
Georgios Boustronios, Cypriot chronicler 103n, 362n
Georgios the *Syrianos*, Orthodox priest 370
Georgios/Georgius, Byzantine administrative official (*archōn*), judge (*kritēs*), *rais* of the *Cour des Suriens*, and *chartophylax* of the Anastasis 374
Georgius (Syrus), witness of Peter Thomas's miracles 364n
Gerace, city, Calabria 36
Germanos II, patriarch of Constantinople 369-370
Germans 54, 70, 87, 284, 330, 396

INDEX 591

Germany 14, 20, 22, 51, 70, 198, 200, 234, 249, 330, 497n
Germiyānid emirate 92, 418-420, 423, 437, 439, 441, 462
Germiyānids/Karmiānoi/Germiyāns, Turkish dynasty 91, 92-93, 418-420, 422-423, 427, 431, 433, 436-439, 441-442, 462
Geronimo Cavatorta, Venetian councillor of Crete 126
Gerusalemme, *see* Jerusalem
Gethsemane, Jerusalem 362
Gharb, city, Mount Lebanon 257
Ghāzī, the emir of Ganja (modern Azerbaijan) 421
Ghazza, city, Palestine 256n
Ghengiz Khan (born Temujin), founder of the Mongol Empire 393, 396-397; *see also* Güyük (Ghengiz Khan's grandson)
Ghengizids, Mongol dynasty 391-392
Ghiyāth al-Dīn Kaykāwūs II, Seljuk sultan of Konya 92
Ghiyāth al-Dīn Kaykhusraw I, Seljuk sultan of Konya 486
Ghiyāth al-Dīn Kaykhusraw II, Seljuk sultan of Konya 386n, 429-433
Ghiyāth al-Dīn Khaykhusraw III, Seljuk sultan of Konya 437
Giacomo Grillo/Jacopo Grillo, Genoese merchant, fief holder in Cyprus 55n, 337
Giacomo Mudazzo, member of the Senate and the *sapientes* of Crete 125n, 126, 127n
Giacomo dei Rossi, Lombard knight 40
Giacomo di San Michele, Lombard supporter of Queen Eleanor of Aragon 335
Giangaleazzo Visconti, first duke of Milan 289n, 293n; *see also* Bernabò Visconti (Giangaleazzo's uncle); Galeazzo II Visconti (Giangaleazzo's father); Valentina Visconti, duchess of Orleans (Giangaleazzo's daughter); Yolanda/Violante Visconti (Giangaleazzo's sister)
Gibelet/Jubail, cathedral of/city/lordship of, County of Tripoli 166, 256-257
Giblet, Cypriot noble family 57, 278; *see also* Henry Giblet; Maria of Giblet
Gil Álvarez de Albornoz, cardinal of Santa Sabina 192
Giorgio Chillax, Greek interpreter 380
Giorgio da Molin, one of the *sapientes* of Crete 125n
Giorgio de Nores/Denores, Cypriot nobleman 36
Giorgio Stella, Genoese historian 38
Giovanni Bardi, Genoese notary 339
Giovanni Bertini, Florentine sculptor 162, 171, 573
Giovanni Boccaccio, author 40-41, 113, 274n-275n, 304, 501
Giovanni Dell'Agnello, doge of Pisa 449
Giovanni Delfino, doge of Venice 129n
Giovanni Ducha, interpreter 381n; *see also* John Duca, representative of the viscount Nicola de Spinola
Giovanni Moro, Venetian consul in Theologo 129, 131n
Giovanni Morosini, Venetian nobleman 41
Giovanni Mudazzo, Venetian consul in Theologo 131n
Giovanni Sanudo, duke of Crete 129
Giovanni Villani, chronicler 113, 115
Giuliano Zeno, Venetian ambassador to Miletus/Palatia 124
Giuseppe Montanelli, Italian statesman and author 59
Giuseppe Verdi, Italian opera composer 59
Glabas, Byzantine aristocrat 497n
Glimin of Narbonne, confessor of Queen Eleanor of Aragon 335
Glogau, duchy of, Silesia 22

Gloucester, duke of   62
Godfrey of Bouillon, king of Jerusalem, one of the Christian Worthies   277, 292, 373
Godfrey, bishop Hebron   139
Goffredo Morosini, duke of Crete   125
Golden Horde, khanate   249, 254, 387n, 404, 410, 446; see also Jochid Ulus
Golden Horn, natural harbor, Bosporus   533
Gorhigos/Gorigos/Korikos/Korykos/Corycus, coastal city, Cilicia   17, 24, 70-71, 97, 119, 145, 245-246, 264, 329, 337, 354, 360
Gothic, style   44, 89, 163, 166
Goths   370
Goudeles, cupbearer of Empress Anna of Savoy   465
Gradenigo, Venetian family, see Leonardo Gradenigo; Pietro Gradenigo
Grado, city/diocese of, north-east Adriatic Sea   193
Graeci, see Greeks
Grand Canal, Venice   39
Grand Karaman, Turkish ruler of Karamania   24; see also Karāmān
Grant Bretaigne, see England
Gratianoupolis/İğrican, city, Thrace   465n, 466
Great Famine   113, 135n
Great Schism   33
Greece   60, 88-89, 98, 101, 113-114, 189, 244, 521
Greeks/*Graeci*/*Grés*/*Gres*/*Grkom*   14, 17, 41, 55, 56n, 57, 61, 70, 82, 85, 102-103, 106, 201, 246n, 255n, 299, 304n, 324n, 337, 361, 363, 364-376, 378-379, 380-382, 413, 445, 476, 489, 491-492, 493n, 494-495, 496n, 497-499, 505-506, 507n, 508-509, 512, 514, 517, 520, 523, 530, 532, 533n-534n, 539-540, 543, 546-548, 560, 564-565
- Greek Cypriot dialect   32, 34, 60
- *Grif(f)ons*   367

- Medieval Greek language   32, 94, 364, 368-369, 375, 452, 497, 502-504, 508n, 533n, 540n, 555n, 560n, 565, 567
- Orthodox Greeks, see Orthodox
- Vernacular   34
Green Count, see Amadeus VI of Savoy
Gregory II of Cyprus, see George II of Cyprus
Gregory IX, pope   364
Gregory XI, pope   103, 503n, 527
Gregory Akindynos, Byzantine theologian   512, 522, 525n, 526n, 553-557, 560, 564; see also Barlaam of Calabria; George Lapithes; Gregory Palamas
Gregory Nazianzen, Byzantine theologian and saint   543
Gregory of Nyssa, Byzantine theologian and saint   92, 559n
Gregory Palamas, Byzantine theologian, Athonite monk   102, 460n, 513, 519-521, 523-526, 528, 530, 532-533, 536n, 537n, 546-548, 553-560, 561n, 563-565; see also Barlaam of Calabria; George Lapithes; Gregory Akindynos; Gregory of Sinai, St
Gregory of Sinai, St, representative of the Hesychast movement   103, 519, 552-553; see also Gregory Palamas
Griffon, mythical figure   299
Grif(f)ons, see Greeks
Grimante, family of, see John of Grimante; Peter of Grimante
Grkom, see Greeks
Guido da Bagnolo/de Regio, physician, councillor, and ambassador of King Peter I of Lusignan   40, 328, 329n, 330-331, 333-334, 359-360
Guildhall, library   54
Guillaume de Machaut, see William of Machaut
Guion (variant of Guy), mythical figure, Mélusine's son   298; see also Florie (Guion's wife); Urien (Guion's brother); Thierry (Guion's brother)

Gülnar, region, southern Anatolia   433-434
Guy de Baveux, Westerner in the service of King Peter I of Lusignan   332
Guy of/d'Ibelin, bishop of Limassol   17, 185, 327, 356; *see also* Philip of Ibelin (Guy's brother)
Guy of Ibelin, constable of Cyprus   203n
Guy d'Ibelin, seneschal of Cyprus   351, 352, 358; *see also* Alice of Ibelin (Guy's daughter, wife of John of Antioch)
Guy of La Baume, member of the regency council of Cyprus, marshal of Jerusalem   338, 341; *see also* Hugh of La Baume (Guy's brother)
Guy of Lusignan, father of Hugh IV of Lusignan   353
Guy of/de Lusignan, lord of Cyprus, founder of the dynasty, and ex-king of Jerusalem   274, 297-298, 370-371
Guy of/de Lusignan/Guido de Lisignano, Prince of Galilee, first-born son of King Hugh IV of Lusignan, constable of Cyprus   15, 17, 47, 48, 90, 179, 181, 183, 206, 208, 300, 351; *see also* Hugh of Lusignan (Guy's son); Maria of Bourbon (Guy's wife); Maria of Ibelin (Guy's mother)
Guy of Milmars, admiral of Cyprus   333, 336
Güyük, Ghengiz Khan's grandson   397
Güzelhisar, *see* Tralleis

Hab, battle of   421
Habsburg, dynasty   249
Hades   540n
Hafsid, dynasty/emirate   446
Hagarenes/Agareni   191-192, 214, 220, 224-225
Hagia Sophia/St Sophia, church, Constantinople   537n
Haifa/Caiffa, city, Palestine   377, 379
Hainaut, county of   14, 20
Halmyros, battle of, central Greece   243

Hamāh, city, central Syria   256-257
Hamerin of Plessie, member of the regency council of Cyprus   338
Ḥāmid, emirate, southern Anatolia   97, 109, 116
Hebrew, language   164
Hebrews   368
Hebron, city, Palestine   139
Hector, one of the pagan Worthies   277
Hejaz (western Arabia)   254
Helen, St, mother of Emperor Constantine I   135, 278n
Hélie de Talleyrand, cardinal and apostolic legate   19, 22, 197
Hellespont   464, 466, 474
Heloise/Héloïse de Brunswick   327, 358; *see also* King Hugh IV of Lusignan (Heloise's godfather); James I of Lusignan (Heloise's husband); Philip of Brunswick (Heloise's father)
Henrie, princep de Antiocha, wrong name for John of Antioch   303
Henry II of Lusignan, king of Cyprus   88-90, 111, 112, 118, 164, 180, 189, 273n, 349, 352, 450; *see also* Aimery of Lusignan (Henry II's brother); Amaury, lord of Tyre (Henry II's brother); Constance of Sicily (Henry II's wife); Hugh IV of Lusignan (Henry II's nephew and successor); Maria (Henry II's sister)
Henry II, duke of Brunswick   327; *see also* Philip of Brunswick (Henry II's son)
Henry II, king of England   243
Henry VI, king of Germany, Holy Roman Emperor   87
Henry of Giblet, Cypriot nobleman   27, 73, 333, 336, 338
Henry Knighton, chronicler   42
Henry of Mosa, cantor of King Peter I of Lusignan, organist of the diocese of Liège   52

Henry, Prince of Galilee   41; *see also* Janus of Lusignan (Henry's brother)

Hermine/Ermine, mythical figure, daughter of the king of Cyprus   298-299, 315, 574; *see also* Griffons (Hermine's son); Urien (Hermine's husband)

Hermos (Gediz), river, Anatolia   93, 113, 462

Hesychasm   102, 104, 552

Hesychasts   82, 102-103, 519, 524, 537, 552-554, 565

Hethum I, king of Armenia   424, 435

Hexamilion, city, eastern Thrace   466n

Hierax, castle, eastern Thrace   466n

Hiereon, Greek Orthodox monastery near Paphos, with a metochion in Nicosia   369; *see also* Isaias the *Syros*

Hırakün, Wallachian lord   410, 411n

Hiristo, *see* Christoupolis

Hızır Beg of Ephesus   96, 101, 113, 462n, 481; *see also* İsa Beg (Hızır's brother); Mehmed Beg ibn Aydın (Hızır's father); Süleymanshâh (Hızır's brother); Umur Pasha (Hızır's brother)

Hodrade Provane, *camerarius* of King James I of Lusignan from the Piedmont   341, 342n; *see also* Balian Provane (Hodrade's father); Embalin Provane (perhaps the same with Balian and Ibelin); Ibelin Provane (perhaps the same with Balian and Embalin)

Hohenstaufen, German noble family/dynasty   88, 158, 161, 167; *see also* Conradin

Holy Church   34, 192, 292, 528-529, 531

Holy Cross, *see* True Cross

Holy Land   20, 38, 53, 56n, 78, 79, 81, 85-86, 109, 110-115, 119, 139, 142, 157-158, 165-166, 188-189, 190-192, 195n, 281, 285, 287, 291-292, 362n, 363, 364n

- Saincte Terre/Sainte terre/Terra Sancta/Terre Sancte   198, 214-217, 215, 220, 222, 224-225, 227-228, 291, 302n, 303n, 363, 489

Holy League   90, 95-96, 100-101, 104, 121-122, 124, 126, 132-133, 466-467, 473

Holy Sepulchre   16, 194, 263, 267, 269, 281n, 312, 573

Honorat Bovet, Provençal Benedictine monk and author   33, 287, 289-290, 294

Honorius I, pope   542

Hospital/Hospitallers, order/knights   21, 23-24, 77-78, 79n, 84-85, 87, 94-96, 109, 111-118, 126, 133n, 140-141, 143, 195-196, 199, 201-203, 212, 226-227, 230, 292, 300, 446, 454, 501, 502n; *see also* St John of Jerusalem

Hospitalis Santi Johannis Jerosolimitani, *see* St John of Jerusalem

Hugh II of Lusignan, king of Cyprus   59, 158, 273n

Hugh III of Lusignan, king of Cyprus, also known as Hugh of Antioch-Lusignan   158, 164; *see also* Maria of Antioch (Hugh's aunt)

Hugh IV of Lusignan/Hugues IV, king of Cyprus/*Hugo rex Cipri*   13, 14-16, 44, 47-48, 50, 56, 69, 89-90, 95-96, 102, 109, 114-119, 140n, 165-167, 177, 179-186, 203, 204n, 206, 208, 210, 242, 246, 249, 255n, 274, 300, 304, 305n, 323, 327-331, 347, 349-356, 358, 560; *see also* Alice of Ibelin (Hugh IV's second wife); Alice of Majorca (Hugh IV's granddaughter); Eschiva (Hugh IV's daughter); Eschiva of Dampierre (Hugh IV's niece); Ferrand of Majorca (Hugh IV's son-in-law); Guy of Lusignan, Prince of Galilee (Hugh IV's first-born son); Guy of Lusignan (Hugh IV's father); Heloise, of Brunswick (Hugh IV's goddaughter); Henry II of Lusignan (Hugh IV's uncle and predecessor); Hugh of Lusignan (Hugh IV's grandson); James I of Lusignan (Hugh IV's son); John of

Antioch (Hugh IV's son); Margaret (Hugh IV's daughter); Maria of Bourbon (Hugh IV's daughter-in-law); Maria of Ibelin (Hugh IV's first wife); Peter I of Lusignan (Hugh IV's son)
Hugh of Antioch-Lusignan, see Hugh III of Lusignan
Hugh of La Baume, member of the regency council of Cyprus, constable of Jerusalem   338, 341; see also Guy of La Baume (Hugh's brother)
Hugh of Lusignan/Hugues de Lusignan/Hugo de Lisignano, prince of Galilee, son Guy of Lusignan and Maria of Bourbon, grandson of King Hugh IV of Lusignan   14, 17, 18, 19, 47-48, 50, 70, 90-91, 177n, 178-189, 191, 204n, 205-210, 213, 245, 333, 354-355, 358; see also Marie du Morf, daughter of John of Morphou, Count of Roucha (Hugh's wife); King Peter I of Lusignan (Hugh's uncle); Robert of Taranto (Hugh's stepfather)
Hugh Ognibono/Ognibene/Ommebono/Ugo Ommebono, physician from Mantua and chancellor of the Kingdom of Cyprus   327-328, 356, 359
Hugh, count of Jaffa   183
Hugo de Lisignano, see Hugh of Lusignan, Prince of Galilee
Hugues IV, see Hugh IV of Lusignan
Hugues Béduin, *bailli* of the *Secrète* and admiral of Cyprus   349n, 350-351, 352
Hugues de Lusignan, see Hugh of Lusignan, prince of Galilee
Hūlāgū, khan, Mongol ruler   432
Humbert II, Dauphin of Viennois   95, 117, 202
Hundred Years' War   33, 243-244, 247, 274-275, 290, 294, 304
Hungarian   89, 161, 492n
Hungary, kingdom of   20, 22, 43, 46n, 54, 105, 161-163, 192-193, 195n, 202, 221-223, 295, 414, 415, 491-492

Huon d'Ibelin, count of Jaffa and seneschal of Jerusalem   351
Hüsām al-Din Çoban, Seljuk governor of Kastamonu   400
Hwāce Hasen, father of Bedreddin and Ali Mardān   481
Hyakinthos, Cypriot anti-Palamite metropolitan/archbishop of Thessalonica   556
Hyaleas, see Alexios Laskaris

Iacobini, see Jacobites
Iacopo Zeno, bishop of Padua   38; see also Carlo Zeno
Ibelin Provane, holder of the fief of Comi   342n; see also Balian Provane (perhaps the same with Embalin and Ibelin); Embalin Provane (perhaps the same with Balian and Ibelin); Hodrade Provane (Balian's son)
Ibelin, family/castle in the Latin Kingdom of Jerusalem   203; see also Alice of Ibelin (second wife of King Hugh IV of Lusignan); Alice of Ibelin (second wife of John of Antioch); Balian d'Ibelin-Arsur; Guy d'Ibelin; Huon d'Ibelin; John of Ibelin; Maria of Ibelin (first wife of King Hugh IV of Lusignan); Philip of Ibelin
Iberian Peninsula   88
Iberians, see Georgians
Ibn al-'Adīm, Arab historian from Aleppo   431
Ibn 'Arrām, prefect and viceroy of Alexandria   256, 263n
Ibn Bībī, Seljuk chronicler   386-389, 417, 419-420, 422-426, 429-432, 436-437, 439
Ibn Qāḍī Šuhba/Ibn Qāḍī Shuhba, Syrian historian   37, 252, 258, 261, 263, 264n
Ibn Shaddād, Arab chronicler   438
Ibn Taghrī Birdī, Egyptian historian   264n

Ibrāhīm al-Tāzī, captain of the Alexandrian arsenal   259, 266
Iconoclasts   531, 542
Ierapetra, city, Crete   127
Ierusalem, *see* Jerusalem
Ignatios II, patriarch of Antioch   140, 559-560
Iğrican, *see* Gratianoupolis
Île de la Cité   21
Ilgaz-i Rumi/Ilgaz-i I Rumi/Ilgaz, *gaza* leader   409
Ilghāzī ibn Artuḳ Bey, Turkish emir of Mardin   420-422
Ilkhān Ghazan, Ilkhānid ruler   253, 448n
Ilkhanate   417, 442, 446, 452
Ilkhānids/Ilkhāns   78, 85, 111, 253, 479, 486
Ilyās Beg, ghazi fighter   481
Ilyas Gazi/İlyas-i Rumi' (known formerly as El-Leon/Alyon), ghazi fighter   406, 407n, 409; *see also* Ayas Gazi (Ilyas Gazi's successor)
Imbros, island, northern Aegean   117
Indian Ocean   143
Indiani   366
Innocent IV, pope   364
Innocent VI, pope   16-18, 32, 48, 50n, 90, 96, 102, 104, 177, 179, 180n, 181, 184-188, 190, 205-206, 208-209, 211, 213, 353, 501n, 506-508, 510
Ioannes ʿAbd al-Masīḥ, priest   372
Ioannes the *Syrianos*, member of the Greek upper class in Crete   370
Ioannides, Panos   61, 66, 571
Ioannis de Baruti, White Venetian, father of Andreas (husband of Aylix)   379
Ionia   101n
Ionian Sea   87, 89
Ionians   470n
Iran (Persia)   80, 85, 95, 249, 253, 392, 419, 424-425, 428 446-447, 452-453
Irene, Byzantine Empress, John VI Kantakouzenos's wife   464, 482; *see also* John Asan (Irene's brother); Manuel Asan (Irene's brother)

İsa Beg, Umur Pasha's brother   481; *see also* Hızır Beg of Ephesus (İsa Beg's brother); Mehmed Beg ibn Aydın (İsa Beg's father); Süleymanshâh (İsa Beg's brother)
Isaac Asanes, *mesazon, panhypersebastos,* and diplomat   468, 479; *see also* Abaqa, Ilkhānid ruler (Isaac Asanes's father-in-law); Arachantloun Theodora (Isaac Asanes's wife); Maria Palaiologina (Isaac Asanes's mother-in-law)
Isabella of Ibelin, daughter of Philip of Ibelin, seneschal of Cyprus   89-90; *see also* Ferrand, son of James I of Majorca (Isabella's husband); Ferrand of Majorca (Isaella's son)
Isabella/Margaret/Maria of Morea, despotissa   26
Isabelle, daughter of James of Nores/ Norès   358; *see also* Thomas of Montolif, auditor of Cyprus (Isabelle's husband)
Isaias the *Syros*, *metochiarios* of the Hiereon monastery's metochion in Nicosia   370; *see also* Hiereon monastery
Isauria, region, south-western Anatolia   430
Isidore I Boucheiras, patriarch of Constantinople   525
Islam   77, 79n, 94, 253, 374, 392-393, 395, 397-398, 415, 420, 425n, 432-435, 441, 451, 455, 475-476, 486; *see also* Muslims
İsparta, city, central Anatolia   97n
Israelites   285
Istanbul, *see* Constantinople
Italians   40, 87, 94, 100-101, 113, 202, 254, 265-266, 269, 274, 379, 382, 444, 446-447, 451, 454
Italy   37, 40, 51, 84, 87, 88-89, 112, 117, 158, 166, 181, 188, 190-191, 195, 198, 244-245, 274, 293n, 295, 323, 330, 333, 443, 447-449, 452, 457, 495, 497n, 501, 521, 526

INDEX   597

Ivan Alexander, tsar of Bulgaria   464, 466-467, 473-474, 508n
Izmir, *see* Smyrna
'Izz al-Dīn Kaykāwus II, Seljuk sultan of Konya   387, 389, 390, 395, 432-441; *see also* Ghiyāth al-Dīn Kaykhusraw II ('Izz al-Dīn Kaykāwus II's father); Kılıç Arslan IV ('Izz al-Dīn Kaykāwus II's brother)

Jabala, city, Syria   374
Jacchetto, marshal of Cyprus   334
Jacob Baradaeus (the Syrian), Miaphysite preacher   368
Jacob Broulas, John Kantakouzenos's emissary   469n, 478, 484
Jacob, priest of the church of St Mary of Nazareth   379n
Jacobites/*Iacobini*/*Jacobini*/Jacobins/ Jacopins   363-364, 366-368
Jacopo Grillo, *see* Giacomo Grillo
Jacques de Fleury, *bailli* of the *Secrète* of Cyprus   349n
Jacques de Lusignan, *see* James I of Lusignan
Jacques de Nores, *see* James of Nores/ Norès
Jacques of Vitry, archbishop of Acre   363
Jadra (Zadar/Zara), city, Dalmatia   215, 225, 229
Jaffa, city, Israel   25, 88, 180, 183, 299, 351
Jaime II d'Aragon, *see* James II, king of Majorca
Jalā'irid, sultanate   254
Jalāl al-Dīn Mingburnu, Khwārizmshāh   419, 427
James I of Lusignan/Jacques de Lusignan, king of Cyprus, constable of Jerusalem, seneschal of Cyprus, brother of King Peter I of Lusignan and father of King Janus of Lusignan   35, 39, 56, 70, 184, 204, 289-290, 301, 303, 324-326, 334-343, 358; *see also* Heloise daughter of Philip of Brunswick (James I's wife); Hugh IV of Lusignan (James I's father); John of Lusignan, lord of Beirut (James I's nephew); John of Antioch (James I's brother)
James II of Lusignan, king of Cyprus   381
James III of Lusignan, king of Cyprus   146
James II, brother of Peter III, king of Aragon   88; *see also* James II, king of Majorca (James II's nephew)
James I, of Majorca   89-90; *see also* Ferrand, former commandant of the Catalan Grand Company (James I's younger son); Ferrand of Majorca (James I's grandson)
James II, king of Majorca/Jaime II d'Aragon, son of Peter III, king of Aragon   88-90, 352n; *see also* James II, brother of Peter III, king of Aragon (James II's uncle); Maria/Marie de Lusignan, sister of King Henry II of Lusignan (James II's wife); Peter of Ribargoza (James II's fourth son)
James of Compostela, St   16, 50n
James of Cyprus/Lusignan, *see* James I of Lusignan
James of Montgesard, member of the High Court of Cyprus   342n
James of/de Nores/Norès/Jacques de Nores, Cypriot baron, ambassador, turcopolier of Cyprus   27, 58, 185, 264, 265n, 328, 331-334, 336, 355, 358, 360; *see also* Isabelle (James's daughter); Thomas of Montolif, auditor of Cyprus (James's son-in-law)
James de Nores, *see* James of Nores/ Norès
James of Verona, monk who visited Nicosia in   1335 366n
Jan Długosz, Polish chronicler   43
Janghara, emir   256
Janko of Czarnków, Polish chronicler, diplomat, crown deputy chancellor of the Treasury of Poland   43

598 INDEX

Janus of Lusignan, king of Cyprus, son of James I of Lusignan, king of Cyprus   35-36, 41, 289n, 292, 296, 304, 340-342; *see also* Anglesia Visconti (Janus's first wife); Henry, prince of Galilee (Janus's brother); John Babin (Janus's guardian)
Jaume Fiveller, procurator of Queen Eleanor of Aragon in Catalonia   335n; *see also* Lleó Marc
Jean d'Antioche, *see* John of Antioch
Jean Babin, marshal of Jerusalem   350
Jean du Bois, Cypriot nobleman, chaplain and/or secretary   356
Jean Bordon, Cypriot nobleman   350
Jean de Caramayno/Carmayno, *see* John Carmain
Jean Froissart, *see* John Froissart
Jean Gorap, *see* John Gorap
Jean de Lusignan, *see* John of Antioch
Jean du Morf, *see* John of Morphou
Jean de Morphou, *see* John of Morphou
Jean de Plessie, Cypriot nobleman, *bailli des tailles*   351
Jean Ponsan, Cypriot knight   375
Jean de Sur, *see* John of Tyre
Jean Tenouri; *see* John Tenouri
Jean Visconti/Visconte, *see* John Visconti
Jehan de Lezinan, king of Cyprus in Eustache Deschamps's *Miroir de marriage*   291
Jehan le Maingre, *see* John II Le Meingre
Jehanne d'Arc, *see* Joan of Arc
Jerusalem, city/kingdom of   16, 17, 18, 27, 36, 41-42, 50-51, 53-54, 56, 63, 70, 77, 79, 86-90, 95, 98, 110, 112, 114, 157-167, 178, 181, 183-186, 189, 201-202, 212, 226-227, 230, 247, 263, 267-268, 274, 281-285, 292, 293, 301-302, 303n, 305, 327-330, 333, 335, 336n, 341, 350-351, 353, 354n, 355n, 356, 358, 362-364, 366-369, 371, 373-376, 381-282, 283n, 394, 571-572
Jews   263n, 277, 367, 376, 378n, 382, 447

Jimrī, rebel and impersonator of one of ʿIzz al-Dīn Kaykāwus's sons   441
Jirjī, Syrian emir   257
Jo. Desur, *see* John of Tyre
Joan de Montforte, *see* John of Morphou
Joan Desbosc, Catalan member of the Cypriot royal household   335n
Joan of Arc   296
Joanna I, queen of Naples, Sicily, and Jerusalem   25, 57, 117, 159, 162, 185, 205, 295, 296n, 494; *see also* Andrew of Hungary (Joanna's first husband); Charles, duke of Calabria (Joanna's father); Louis of Taranto (Joanna's second husband); Maria, daughter of Charles, duke of Calabria (Joanna's sister); Mary of Valois (Joanna's mother); Robert I, king of Naples (Joanna's grandfather)
- Golden Rose, award given by the pope   57, 205
Joanna L'Aleman, mistress of King Peter I of Lusignan   24-26, 57, 60, 72
Joasaph Kantakouzenos, *see* John Kantakouzenos
Joasaph, Byzantine priest   526n
Jochid Ulus   387n, 404n, 405n; *see also* Golden Horde
Johan de Lezegnan, *see* John of Antioch
Johanne de Lizignano, *see* John of Antioch
Johannes Paleologus, *see* John V Palaiologos, emperor
Johannis de Jerusalem/Hospitalis Johannis Jerosolimitani, Sancti, *see* St John of Jerusalem
John II Le Meingre/Jehan le Maingre, known as Boucicaut/Bouciquaut, French marshal   296; *see also* Christine de Pizan's *Livre des fais du bon messire Jehan le Maingre, dit Bouciquaut*
John II of Lusignan, king of Cyprus   297
John II, king of France/Johannes rex Francie   19-21, 48, 53, 86, 181, 189-191,

194-195, 197-198, 214-215, 220-222, 224-225, 278, 300-301, 330, 490; *see also* Charles V, duke of Normandy and later king of France (John II's son); John of Berry (John II's son); Philip the Bold (John II's son)

John V Palaiologos/Qaloyan Beg, Byzantine emperor   22-23, 36n, 101-102, 104-106, 198, 201-202, 457, 461, 465n-466n, 473, 476, 489-492, 493n, 494-503, 505-506, 508-513, 515-516, 536n-537n; *see also* Amadeus VI of Savoy (John V's cousin); Andronikos III Palaiologos (John V's father); Anna of Savoy (John V's mother); Manuel II Palaiologos (John V's son)

John VII Palaiologos, Byzantine emperor   511n; *see also* Andronikos IV Palaiologos (John VII's father)

John VIII Palaiologos, Byzantine emperor   504n

John XI Bekkos, patriarch of Constantinople   98

John XIV Kalekas, patriarch of Constantinople   458, 478n, 479, 525, 529, 530n, 536n, 543n, 555

John XXI, pope   505n

John XXII, pope   86, 99, 100n-101n, 114, 118, 366n, 372

John of Antioch/Jean d'Antioche/ John of Lusignan/Jean de Lusignan/ Jean/Johan de Lezegnan/Johanne de Lizignano, constable of Cyprus and prince of Antioch, brother of King Peter I of Lusignan   16, 24, 27, 44, 46-48, 56, 69, 183, 187, 242, 268, 270, 278, 291, 302-303, 326-329, 331-336, 343, 352-354, 356, 358; *see also* Alice of Ibelin (John's mother); Alice of Ibelin (John's second wife, daughter of Guy, seneschal of Cyprus); Constance of Sicily/ Constance d'Aragon (John's first wife); King Hugh IV of Lusignan (John's father); King James I of Lusignan (John's brother); Jehan de Lezinan (king in the poem *Miroir de marriage*)

John of Arras, French author   297-299, 313, 573; *see also* John of Berry (commissioned *Mélusine ou la noble histoire de Lusignan*); *Mélusine* (myth/ romance)

- *Mélusine ou la noble histoire de Lusignan*   297, 331, 573

John Asan, brother of Irene, John VI Kantakouzenos's wife   464, 497n; *see also* Manuel Asan (John Asan's brother)

John Babin/Jean Babin, admiral of Cyprus, chamberlain of Armenia, Janus of Lusignan's guardian   342, 350

John the Baptist/Johannes Baptiste, St   118, 212

John of Berry, duke, commissioned John of Arras's *Mélusine ou la noble histoire de Lusignan*   276n, 288, 297-298; *see also* Charles V, duke of Normandy and later king of France (John's brother); John II, king of France (John V's father); John of Arras; *Mélusine* (myth/romance); Philip the Bold (John's brother)

John Bibi, White Genoese of Melkite origin   380; *see also* Marcus Zebas (John Bibi's father-in-law); Thomas Bibi (John's brother)

John of Brie, prince of Galilee, turcopolier, head of (and member) of the regency council of Cyprus   328, 333, 337-338, 340

John Carmain/Jean de Caramayno/Jean de Carmayno/Johannes de Carmayno, Genoese knight   178-179, 210, 327, 360; *see also* Pierre de Nores (John Carmain's co-ambassador); Raymond Babin (John Carmain's co-ambassador)

John Duca, representative of Nicola de Spinola, viscount of the *curia Surianorum*   381; *see also* Giovanni Ducha, interpreter

John/Jean Froissart, French chronicler   13-14, 26, 33, 39, 42, 44, 54, 58n, 276, 280, 288, 289n, 293, 299-302, 306, 317, 573-574; *see also* Marguerite, a lady with whom John Froissart fell in love

John of Gaurelle/Gaurelles, Cypriot baron   27, 336

John Gorab/John Gorap/Jean Gorap/, Cypriot baron, *bailli* of the *Secrète, maître d'hôtel*, auditor, member of the High Court and of the regency council of Cyprus, lord of Caesarea   27, 350, 337-338, 340, 342-343

John of Grimante, naval captain in the service of King Peter I of Lusignan   259, 261; *see also* Peter of Grimante (John's brother)

John Hawkwood, mercenary leader in Italy   195

John of Ibelin, jurist, author of a legal treatise   14-15, 34, 186, 367, 373-377

John of Ibelin, seneschal of Jerusalem, cousin of King Peter I Lusignan, 328-329, 332

John of Jerusalem, St, order/knights of   199, 201n, 211-212, 215, 220, 222, 225-227, 230 302n; *see also* Hospital/Hospitallers

John-Joasaph Kantakouzenos, *see* John Kantakouzenos

John Kantakouzenos/Cantacuzene, *megas domestikos*, later John VI Kantakouzenos, Byzantine emperor, also known as ex-emperor and monk John-Joasaph Kantakouzenos   99, 101-103, 105, 117, 457-488, 493-494, 497n, 503n, 512-513, 524n, 525, 528, 530, 536, 537n, 555, 599-564; *see also* Irene (John VI Kantakouzenos's wife)

John Kyparissiotes, anti-Palamite Byzantine theologian   103, 522-523, 525-532, 536-537, 539, 542-544, 547-548, 561n

John Laskaris Kalopheros, Byzantine man-at-arms in the service of King Peter I of Lusignan   333-335, 491, 514n

John Lazaropoulos, hagiographer   422-423

John of Lusignan, *see* John of Antioch

John of Lusignan, lord of Beirut   340-341; *see also* James I of Lusignan (John's uncle)

John of Montolif, *bailli* of Famagusta   334

John of Morphou/Jean de Morphou/Jean du Morf/Joan de Montforte, count of Roucha/Rouchas/Rochas, Cypriot baron, lover of Eleanor of Aragon, ambassador, marshal, and chamberlain of Cyprus   26, 35, 57, 72, 179, 180, 186-189, 255, 327-329, 331-332, 334-336, 355-358, 360; *see also* Marie du Morf (John's daughter)

John Moustri/John of Moustry, Cypriot leader of the campaign against Alexandria, (stand-in) admiral   49, 332-334

John of Moustry, *see* John Moustri

John of Nevilles, lord of Arsur, viscount of Nicosia, member of the regency council of Cyprus   337-338, 340, 341

John Palaiologos, despot   93; *see also* Emperor Michael VIII Palaiologos (John's brother)

John of Reading, English chronicler   42

John of Rochefort, Breton lord in the service of King Peter I of Lusignan   24-25, 49

John Stow, English chronicler   54
- *Annales of England*   54

John Tenouri/Jean Tenouri, *bailli* of the *Secrete* of Cyprus   327, 329, 349, 356; *see also* John, Simon Tenouri's father (perhaps the same person)

John of Tiberias, Cypriot nobleman   339, 341

John of Tyre/Jean de Sur/Jo. Desur, admiral of Cyprus 18, 303, 328, 332n, 355, 360
John Vatatzes, *megas stratopedarches*, governor of cities in Thrace 468, 478-479; *see also* Süleyman of Karasi (John Vatatzes's son-in-law)
John Visconti/Jean Visconti/Jean Visconte, Cypriot nobleman 72, 279, 333, 350, 357
John of Verona, man-at-arms in the service of King Peter I of Lusignan 245
John of Waurin/Wavrin, French chronicler 303, 318-319, 574
John, bishop of Karpasia 103, 555, 560, 564
John, Simon Tenouri's father 329; *see also* John Tenouri, *bailli* of the Secrète of Cyprus (perhaps the same person)
Jonathas, Biblical figure 283
Joscelin I, count of Edessa 421
Joseph Bryennios, Byzantine monk 370
Joseph Kalothetos, pro-Palamite Byzantine monk 103, 554, 557-559, 561-562, 564
Josephite, faction 99
Joshua, one of the Jewish Worthies 277
Jubail, *see* Gibelet
Judas Maccabeus/Judas Machabeus, one of the Jewish Worthies 277, 283n
Julian, calendar 251n
Juliers, duchy of 14, 20
Julius Caesar, one of the pagan Worthies 277
Justin de Justinis, Tuscan jurist in the service of the Lusignans 350-352, 358
Justinopolis (Capo d'Istria), diocese of 215, 225
Jūtī Bey, Turkmen commander 437

Kaimakli, suburb of Nicosia, Cyprus 61n
Kallistos I, patriarch of Constantinople 103, 508, 525n, 537n, 552-554, 559-560, 564
Kalopheros, Byzantine family, *see* John Laskaris Kalopheros; Maximos Kalopheros
Kantara, village and castle, Cyprus 551
Karaburun, peninsula, Gulf of Smyrna 101, 462n
Kara Davud, Tatar *gazi* chieftain 395, 401, 404, 406
Karāmān bey, *see* Karīm al-Dīn Karāmān
Karāmān, Turkish emirate of 97, 109, 114n, 116, 145, 418, 424, 436, 441; *see also* Grand Karaman
Karāmānids 91-92, 113-114, 119, 264, 417-418, 423-427, 432, 435-436, 439-442
Karasi, emirate of 93, 95, 100, 115, 462-465, 467, 468, 478-480, 483-484, 488
Karīm al-Dīn ʿAlīshīr of the Germiyānids, founder of the Germiyānid emirate 433, 436-438, 441; *see also* Shihāb al-Dīn
Karīm al-Dīn Karāmān, Nūre Sūfī's son 92, 423-425, 432, 435, 439-441; *see also* Bunsuz (Karīm al-Dīn Karāmān's brother)
Karlstein/Karlštejn, castle in Prague 46, 60, 62
- Virgin Mary, *capella regia* in the castle's Minor Tower 46
Karmiānoi 423; *see also* Germiyānids; Germiyāns
Karpasia, peninsula/village, Cyprus 103, 555, 560, 564; *see also* John, bishop of Karpasia
Karpathos, island, Aegean Sea 94
Karya, city, Thrace 466n
Kasrawān, region, northern Lebanon Mountain 257
Kassandra, peninsula, northern Greece 466

Kastamonu, city, northern central Anatolia   400, 412
Katherine/Catelinne, King Peter I of Lusignan's ship, a gift from King Edward III of England   20, 54, 301
Kaydafan, king of Hungary in *Saltukname*   415
Kayseri, city, central Anatolia   429-430
Kaystros/Küçük Menderes, river   92, 462
Kefe, see Caffa
Keltôn, see Celts
Kemal Ata, a ghāzī fighter   401, 406
Kemalpaşa, *see* Nymphaion
Kent, duke of   62
Kerak, fortress, Jordan   256
Kerman, region, eastern Iran   419
Kerynia, *see* Kyrenia
Khalīl, Mamluk sultan   253, 262
Khwārizmians   426-427; *see also* Jalāl al-Dīn Mingburn
Kibča'ut, *see* Kipchak
Kılıç Arslan IV, Seljuk sultan of Konya   92, 433, 435-440; *see also* Izz al-Dīn Kaykāwus II (Kılıç Arslan IV's brother)
Kipchak/Kibča'ut, Turkic tribes   253, 394n, 397, 451
Kiti, port city, Cyprus   24-25
Komnenoi, *see* Comnenian dynasty
Konstantinos Kabasilas, *protopapas* at the Blachernai Church   512
Konstantinos Sekretikos, father of Theodora   372
Kontostephanos, *see* Petrus qd. Condi Stephani
Konya, city, central Anatolia   94, 145, 155, 386-388, 425n, 431, 434-437, 439, 441-442, 486, 572
Korikos/Korykos, *see* Gorhigos
Köse Dağ, battle of   428-429, 431, 433-434
Kosmas, Cypriot living in Constantinople   556
Kosten, city, Poland   22

Koumoutzena, fortresss, Thrace   465-466
Kouris, river, Cyprus   140-141
Koutzaina, city, Rhodope Mountains   465
Kubādābād, palace, southern Anatolia   429
Kuchlu Sengum, Khwārizmian chief   427
Küçük Menderes, *see* Kaystros
Kurds/Kurdān   254, 419, 433, 437
Kütahya, city, western Anatolia   92, 418, 423, 462
Kyrakos of Ganja, Armenian historian   434
Kyrenia/Kerynia/Cérines, port city, Cyprus   17-18, 166, 339, 353, 357
- Kyrenia/Kerynia, castle   48, 180
Kyzikos, city, northwestern Anatolia   93, 368

La Fenice, theatre, Venice   59
La Rochelle, port city, west coast of France   21
Lādik, *see* Laodikeia
Lakha, brothers, Nestorian merchants in Famagusta   54, 70
- Lakha, Francis   361
Lamberto Baldwin della Cecca, bishop of Limassol   116
Lamberto di Sambuceto, Genoese notary   377
Lampsakos, port city, Asian shore of the Hellespont   104
Languedoc, region, southern France   332
Laodikeia (Denizli)/Lādik, city near the modern city of Denizli, western Asia Minor   92, 435
Laodikeia/Latakia/Lattakia, port city in Syria   72, 256-257
Laonikos Chalkokondyles, Byzantine historian   497
Larenda, city, southeastern Anatolia   423, 427

Larnaca, city, Cyprus   60
Latakia/Lattakia, see Laodikeia
Lateran Church   106
Latin   32, 36, 41, 51, 55, 77-79, 82, 84-87, 90, 94, 96n, 98-99, 102-106, 109-110, 113-114, 116-118, 140, 157-159, 161, 163, 165-167, 186, 253, 275, 282, 285, 287, 289-299, 302, 348, 362-366, 369, 371, 374, 375n, 376-380, 443, 446-447, 448n, 449, 457, 459, 460, 461-462, 466, 472-473, 484, 488, 489-490, 493-494, 495n-496n, 497, 498n, 500, 502-507, 511-513, 515, 516n, 517-521, 533n, 540, 544-545, 549n, 551-552, 554-555, 560, 564-565; see also Romance, language/vernacular
- Latin Church   82, 98-99, 102, 361, 369, 377, 511, 514, 517n, 533n, 540
- Latin Empire of Constantinople   82, 87-88, 98, 445
- Latinism   511n, 520n
- Latinization   104, 511n
- Latinophile   36, 104-105, 513, 515, 533
Laupen, battle of   243
Laurencius Celsi, see Lorenzo Celsi
Laurentius de Neffino, representative of Nicola de Spinola, viscount of the curia Surianorum   380
Laurentius (Lawrence), St   494
Lazaros, patriarch of Jerusalem   494
Lebanon   37, 145, 156, 252, 257-259, 572
Lebanon Mountain   257-258
Lecto/Lecco (Muslim Principality of Asia Minor? Lithuania?), king of   53
Lefkara, village, Cyprus   372
Leo II, Armenian King of Cilicia   448
Leo the Cypriot, a learned ascetic who emigrated to Constantinople   552-553, 556
Leo Marmaras, owner of a griparia   124-126, 128
Leodegar, Latin bishop of Famagusta   560
Leon Allatios, Greek scholar and theologian   540
Leonardo Giustiniani, translator   41

Leonardo Gradenigo, sopracomito of Crete   133n
Leontios II, Greek patriarch of Jerusalem   369
Leontios Makhairas, Cypriot chronicler   13-14, 34-35, 37, 46-50, 54, 57-60, 61n, 62, 67, 69, 76n, 135, 137, 139-140, 145, 178-179, 184, 186-188, 203-204, 245-247, 252-254, 258n, 261, 263, 264n, 268, 278, 279n, 280, 286, 304-305, 323, 326-329, 332-333, 335-340, 346-347, 353-354, 356-358, 361, 370-371, 571
Lependrinos, a correspondent of Nikephoros Gregoras   553
Lesbos, island, Aegean Sea   100-101, 103-105, 115, 502, 508n, 532
Leuven, city, Flanders   162, 170, 573
Lezegnan/Lezinan, see Lusignan/Lusignans
Lido, island, Venetian Lagoon   39
- San Nicolò, monastery   39
Liège, diocese of   52
Liegnitz, city, Silesia   22
Limassol, port city, Cyprus   15, 17, 62, 116, 183, 185, 212, 327, 331, 352, 356; see also Nimocium
Linora, female name popular in Cyprus   57n
Lionel, duke of Clarence, son of King Edward III of England   293n; see also Philippa of Hainault, queen of England (Lionel's mother); Yolanda/Violante Visconti (Lionel's wife)
Listari, see Alexios Laskaris
Lizignano, see Lusignan/Lusignans
Lleó Marc, procurator of Queen Eleanor of Aragon   335n; see also Jaume Fiveller
Lombardy   18, 40, 85n, 192, 245, 335
London/Londres, capital city, England   20-21, 42, 53, 54n, 55, 60, 62, 69, 293, 347
- Corporation of London Records   62n
- London Metropolitan Archives   54n, 60n, 62n

604 INDEX

Longos, harbour, Chalkidike peninsula   117
Loredan, Venetian family   45n
Loredan *palazzo*/Corner Piscopia *palazzo*/Corner Piscopia – Loredan *palazzo*, palace in Venice   39n, 44-45; *see also* Andrea Zane (one of its owners); Corner family (one of its owners); Ca' Corner, palace in San Luca
Lorenzo Capello, Venetian ambassador   448
Lorenzo Celsi/Laurencius Celsi, doge of Venice   39, 40, 198, 234
Lorenzo de Monacis, Venetian diplomat and chancellor of Crete   38, 55
Lorenzo Zane, Venetian councillor of Crete   126-127
Lorenzo, San Maggiore, *see* San Lorenzo Maggiore, church
Louis I the Great, king of Hungary   22, 43, 46n, 54, 105, 202, 291n, 292, 491n, 492
Louis I, duke of Orleans   289n, 294, 295; *see also* Charles VI, dauphin and king of France (Louis I's brother); Valentina Visconti, duchess of Orleans (Louis I's wife)
Louis IX, king of France/St Louis   81n, 158, 181, 247, 253; *see also* Charles I of Anjou (Louis IX's brother); Louis of Clermont, duke of Bourbon (Louis IX's grandson); Maria of Bourbon (Louis IX's great granddaughter)
Louis of Clermont, duke of Bourbon   90, 181; *see also* Maria of Bourbon (Louis's daughter); King Louis IX of France (Louis's grandfather)
Louis of Guyenne, dauphin of Viennois and duke of Guyenne   294
Louis of Hungary, *see* Louis I the Great
Louis of Taranto   159n; *see also* Joanna I, queen of Naples (Louis's wife)
Louis of Toulouse, St, bishop of Toulouse and second son of King Charles II of Naples   160-163, 168, 169, 572; *see also* Charles Martel (Louis's brother); Mary of Hungary (Louis's mother); Philip of Taranto (Louis's brother); Robert I, king of Naples (Louis's brother)
Louis, St, *see* Louis IX, king of France
Loukas Georgios, Byzantine ambassador   478-479, 483
Lübeck, city, Baltic coast of Saxony   22
Luca, St, *see* San Luca   39
Lucca, city, Tuscany   26, 179, 208-209, 501n
Ludovico I Gonzaga, ruler of Mantua   46n
Ludovico Ariosto, poet   304, 305n
Luis Resta, Catalan member of the Cypriot royal household   335n; *see also* Ramón Resta
Luke of Antiaume, commander of Kyrenia   339, 342
Luke, St/*die sancti Luche*   498n
Lusignan/Lusignans, dynasty/family/kingdom, 13, 32, 35-36, 41, 45, 51, 80, 84, 87-90, 106, 109-112, 133, 140-141, 157-158, 164-167, 181, 185, 246n, 247, 259, 274, 283, 288, 289n, 297-299, 302, 304, 305n, 313-316, 323, 325, 327, 345n, 363n, 367, 573-574; *see also* Aimery of Lusignan (King Henry II's brother); Amaury, lord of Tyre (King Henry II's brother); Eschiva (King Hugh IV's daughter); Étienne of/de Lusignan; Guy of Lusignan (King Hugh IV's father); Guy of Lusignan (lord of Cyprus, ex-king of Jerusalem); Guy of Lusignan, prince of Galilee (son of King Hugh IV, constable of Cyprus); King Henry II; King Hugh II; King Hugh III; King Hugh IV; Hugh of Lusignan (son of Guy of Lusignan, prince of Galilee); King James I; King James II; King James III; King Janus; John of Antioch

(King Hugh IV's son); King John II;
Margaret (King Peter I's daughter);
Margaret/Marguerite (King Hugh
    IV's daughter); Maria/Marie de
    Lusignan (King Henry II's sister);
    King Peter I; King Peter II; Robert of
    Lusa (perhaps Lusignan)
  - Lezegnan/Lezinan/Lizignano/
    Lusignen   291, 298, 331n, 327
Lusignan, Étienne of/de, historian   35,
    46, 56n, 58n, 304
Luxembourg   20, 22, 43, 192, 278
Lycia, region, southern Anatolia   97
Lydians   470n
Lykos, valley, southwestern
    Anatolia   92
Lyons/Lyon, city, France   283n
  - Second Council of   98, 505n
  - Union of   552

Maccabees, Old Testament   277, 283
Macedonia, region, southern
    Balkans   98, 458, 463, 468-469, 488, 511
Maceo de Caiffa, businessman in
    Famagusta   377-379
Maeander/Menderes, river,
    southwestern Anatolia   92, 113, 458n,
    462
Maghreb   258-259, 270n, 444n
Magnesia/Manisa, city, western
    Anatolia   41, 93, 462
Mahametbei, see Mehmed II
Mahmud Pasha, Mehmed II's grand
    vizier   461
Mainz, city, Germany   14, 20
Mājid ibn al-Qazwīna, Mamluk
    vizier   258
Majorca/Mallorca, city/kingdom
    of   47, 49, 88-89, 90, 159, 163, 183, 203;
    see also Alice of Majorca; Ferrand of
    Majorca; James I of Majorca; James II
    of Majorca; Sancia of Mallorca
Malatesta, family, rulers of Rimini   501
Malatya, city, eastern Anatolia   91, 418-
    420, 423, 427, 430-431, 434, 436-438

Malikshāh, Seljuk sultan   486
Mallorca, see Majorca
Malo, port city, Cilicia   25, 72
Mamluks   23, 31, 37, 77-83, 85-87, 95,
    97-98, 106, 109-111, 114, 118-119, 140,
    144-145, 157, 159, 167, 202, 203, 242-249,
    251-271, 284, 304, 323, 333, 345-346, 356
    361, 362n, 377, 427, 434, 436, 438, 446-
    447, 451, 453
Manisa, see Magnesia
al-Manṣūra, city/battle of, Egypt   253
Mantua, city, Lombardy   356, 359
Manuel III, emperor of Trebizond   452
Manuel Angelos, epi tu kanikleiu   503
Manuel Asan, brother of Irene, John VI
    Kantakouzenos's wife   464; see also
    John Asan (Manuel Asan's brother)
Manuel Bryennes, Byzantine
    aristocrat   497n
Manuel Kalekas, Byzantine monk and
    theologian   103-104, 478n, 520-523,
    526n-527n, 532-549, 565
Manuel I Komnenos, Byzantine
    emperor   368
Manuel Laskaris, Byzantine priest   514
Manuel II Palaiologos, Byzantine
    emperor   504n, 506, 533, 539n; see
    also John V Palaiologos (Manuel II's
    father)
Manuel Raoul, Cypriot
    intellectual   565
Manuel de Romania, probably a
    Greek   379n
Manuel Tagaris, governor of
    Philadelphia   478; see also George
    Tagaris (Manuel's son)
Manuel Tzykandyles, Byzantine
    scribe   503n
Manuel Zaccaria, Genoese
    nobleman   111
Maometh bey, see Mehmed II
al-Maqrīzī, Mamluk historian   37,
    142-144, 151, 252, 258n, 259n, 264n,
    266n, 572
Marathasa, valley, Cyprus   304n

Marc, bishop of Famagusta   351
Marcantonio Coccio Sabellico, Venetian historian   39
Marco Borgognono, member of the Senate and the *sapientes* of Crete   127n
Marco Cornaro, doge of Venice   347, 453n
Marco Fradello, one of the *sapientes* of Crete   125n
Marco, San/Mark, St, *see* San Marco
Marcus Zebas (aṣ-Ṣabbāḥ?)   380-381; *see also* John Bibi (Marcus's father-in-law)
Mardin, city, southeastern Anatolia   421
Mareotis, lake, Egypt   144
Margaret III of Flanders   280
Margaret of Morea, *see* Isabella of Morea
Margaret/Marguerite, daughter of King Hugh IV of Lusignan and sister of King Peter I of Lusignan   280, 281n, 339, 358
Margaret, daughter of King Peter I of Lusignan   17, 280, 281n, 289n; *see also* Charles of Parma (Margaret's fiancé); Peter II of Lusignan (Margaret's brother)
Margarita, prison, Nicosia   27, 44, 281
Marghera, city, Italy   19
Marguerite, female name/a poem/ French lady associated with Peter I (?)   279-280, 287, 291, 293, 310, 573; *see also* Margaret (daughter of King Peter I of Lusignan)
Marguerite, a lady with whom John Froissart fell in love   293
Marguerite, *see* Marie de Montolif, Raymond Babin's wife
Marguerite, *see* Margaret/Marguerite, daughter of King Hugh IV of Lusignan
Maria of Antioch, aunt of Hugh of Antioch-Lusignan   158, 164

Maria of Bourbon/Marie de Bourbon, of Achaea and Morea, titular Latin Empress of Constantinople, daughter-in-law of King Hugh IV of Lusignan   17, 19, 26, 47-48, 90, 179, 181-185, 206, 208-209, 213, 246, 300, 333, 351; *see also* Guy of Lusignan (Maria's first husband); Hugh of Lusignan (Maria's son); Louis of Clermont, duke of Bourbon (Maria's father); Louis IX, king of France (Maria's great grandfather); Philip VI, king of France (Maria's second cousin); Robert of Taranto (Maria's second husband)
Maria Donnaregina, Santa, *see* Santa Maria Donnaregina
Maria of Giblet, Cypriot noblewoman   73, 278
Maria of Ibelin, King Hugh IV of Lusignan's first wife   180; *see also* Guy of Lusignan, prince of Galilee (Maria's son); Philip, count of Jaffa (Maria's brother)
Maria of Lusignan/Marie de Lusignan, sister of King Henry II of Lusignan, wife of James II of Majorca   352n
Maria of Morea, *see* Isabella of Morea
Maria Palaiologina, *Despoina ton Mougoulion*, illegitimate daughter of Emperor Michael VIII Palaiologos   479; *see also* Abaqa, Ilkhānid ruler (Maria Palaiologina's husband); Arachantloun Theodora (Maria Palaiologina's daughter); Isaac Asanes (Maria Palaiologina's son-in-law)
Maria, Fetus Simiteculo's wife   378
Maria, sister of Joanna I, queen of Naples   162; *see also* Charles, duke of Calabria (Maria's father); Mary of Valois (Maria's mother); Robert I, king of Naples (Maria's grandfather)
Marie de Bourbon, *see* Maria of Bourbon

Marie de Montolif/Marguerite, Raymond Babin's wife 358
Marie du Morf, daughter of John of Morphou, count of Roucha 358; see also Hugh of Lusignan, grandson of Hugh IV of Lusignan (Marie's husband)
Marino Morosini, Venetian consul in Theologo 131n
Marino Sanudo Torsello, Venetian statesman and author 79, 111, 115, 140, 142
Maritsa/Marica, valley/river 102, 464-465, 481
Mark's basilica, see San Marco
Markos, Melkite patriarch of Alexandria 369
Maronites 364n
Mars, ancient Greek God of war 277
Marseille, port city, southern France 499n
Marsi, bishop of Fréjus 502n
Martin IV, pope 498
Martin, St 42, 46n
Martino Zaccaria, leader, lord of Chios 79n
Mary of Hungary, wife of Charles II, king of Naples 161-163; see also Charles Martel (Mary's son); Louis of Toulouse (Mary's son); Philip of Taranto (Mary's son); Robert I, king of Naples (Mary's son); Santa Maria Donnaregina, church (where Mary was buried)
Mary of Nazareth, St, church 379n; see also Jacob, priest of St Mary
Mary of Valois, wife of Charles, duke of Calabria 162; see also Maria (Mary's daughter); Joanna I, queen of Naples (Mary's daughter)
Matteo Mudazzo, sopracomito of Crete 133n
Matthew of Edessa 420-421
Matthew Kantakouzenos, son of John Kantakouzenos 508n, 510

Matthew, Evangelist 537-538, 541, 546
Matuška, Waldemar, Czech singer 62
Mavrommates, man from Philadelphia 471n, 478
Maximos Chrysoberges, Byzantine theologian 533
Maximos Kalopheros, Byzantine author 525n
Maximos the Confessor, St 542-543
Mechelen 89, 162
- Anjou or Mechelen Bible 89, 161-164, 171, 573; see also Cristoforo Orimina; Niccolò Alunno d'Alife
Mediterranean/White Sea 11, 15, 51, 77-83, 85, 86n, 87, 91, 96-97, 106, 109-114, 118, 121-122, 132-133, 135-138, 141n, 144, 146-147, 179, 153, 157-158, 167, 205, 241-244, 246, 251-252, 274, 281, 297, 327, 331, 443-445, 448-449, 451, 453, 457, 473, 571-572
Mehmed Beg ibn Aydın, founder of Aydın dynasty 92, 95, 97n, 101, 113, 462; see also Hızır of Ephesus (Mehmed's son); İsa Beg (Mehmed's son); Süleymanshâh (Mehmed's son); Umur Pasha (Mehmed's son)
Mehmed II, Ottoman sultan 444n, 454, 461, 475
Mehmed Neshrī, Ottoman historian 424-427
Meissen, city, Saxony 22
Melchi, the Byzantine emperor for Hebrews and Syrians 368
Melchitai, see Melkites
Melfi, city, Basilicata, Italy 223, 331; see also Antonio di Rivello, bishop of Melfi
Mélisende, see Mélusine
Melisina, Greek parica from the village of Milikouri, Cyprus 304n; see also Mélusine; Michalis Petru Nomicu (Melisina's father)
Melkites/Melchitai 56, 336-337, 361n, 362-372, 374-380, 382, 560n

Mélusine, myth/romance   297, 299, 304-305, 313-316, 573-574; *see also* John of Arras (author of *Mélusine ou la noble histoire de Lusignan*); John of Berry (commissioned *Mélusine ou la noble histoire de Lusignan*); Coudrette (author of *Le Roman de Mélusine ou histoire de Lusignan*); William VII Larchevêque (commissioned *Le Roman de Mélusine ou histoire de Lusignan*)

Mélusine/Melusine/Mélisende, mythical figure   297-298, 304-305; *see also* Élinas, the king of Albanie (Mélusine's father); Guion (Mélusine's son); Melisina (Greek *parica* from Milikouri); *Mélusine* (myth/romance); Thierry (Mélusine's son); Urien (Mélusine's son)

Menemen, plain, western Anatolia north of Smyrna   93

Menteşe, emirate, southwestern Anatolia   23, 85, 92, 94-96, 121-129, 131n-132n, 134n
- Menteşe Turks   85, 92, 94 462

Merope, region, Thrace   466-467

Mersin, port city, southern Anatolia   425

Merv, city, eastern Iran   428

Mervanik, convert to Islam, *gazi* leader   409-410; *see also* Raston (Mervanik's overlord/father)

Mesopotamia   254

Mesothynia, region, Asian side of the Bosporus   100

Messalianism, Christian sect   554, 556

Messina/Messanensi, city/diocese of, Sicily   215, 225

Mestre, city, Veneto   19, 22

Miaphysites/Monophysites   87, 361, 363-364, 367-368, 369n, 370

Michael IX Palaiologos, Byzantine emperor   93, 412n; *see also* Andronikos II Palaiologos (Michael IX's father)

Michael VIII Palaiologos, Byzantine emperor   78, 93, 97-99, 479, 486, 505, 512, 552; *see also* Abaqa, Ilkhānid ruler (Michael VIII's son-in-law); Andronikos II Palaiologos (Michael VIII's son); John Palaiologos, despot (Michael VIII's brother); Maria Palaiologina (Michael VIII's illegitimate daughter); Theodora Palaiologina (Michael VIII's wife)

Michael ibn Qurīl, witness in a document   374

Michael Loulloudes, scribe   92n

Michael Malaspina, Genoese ambassador   489

Michael Strongylos, witness of John V Palaiologos's profession of faith   503

Michael the Younger, *see* Michael IX Palaiologos, emperor

Michalis Petru Nomicu, father of Melisina (Greek *parica* from Milikouri)   304n

Mikołaj Wierzynek, a wealthy burgess of Cracow   55, 62

Mikuláš Wurmser, court painter of Emperor Charles IV   46

Milan, city/duchy of, Lombardy   19-21, 26, 38, 40, 48, 72, 289n, 337, 340, 359

Miletus/Palatia, port city, western Anatolia   71, 96, 121, 123-129, 130n, 131n-132, 462

Milikouri, village, Cyprus   304n

Milmars, Cypriot noble family, *see* Arnold of Milmars; Guy of Milmars; Renaut de Milmars; Reynald of Milmars

Ming, dynasty, China   249

Miniate, *see* San Miniato

Misericordia, church, Nicosia   27, 44

Mitylene, island, Aegean Sea   101n, 539

Modena, city, northern Italy   26

Modon, harbour, Peloponnese   26

Moldova   395

Momitzilos/Mumcila, Bulgarian local ruler, governor of the Merope region   466-467, 475

INDEX 609

Mongols 77-78, 85, 92, 94, 111-113, 138, 243, 247, 249, 253, 262, 386-387, 390-392, 394, 396-398, 411, 418, 424, 426-442, 451, 457, 479, 486, 506n
- Christian-Mongols 85
Monophysites, see Miaphysites
Monothelites 531, 542
Monovgat, port city, southern Anatolia 97
Monreale/Montisregalis, diocese of, Sicily 161, 215, 225
Monsait, see Abū Saʿīd Bahādur
Montferrat/Montisferrati, Italian noble family 101, 201; see also Yolanda-Eirene of Montferrat (Emperor Andronikos II's second wife)
Montfort, Cypriot noble family 15-16, 56, 182-183, 353; see aslo Eschiva of Montfort (first wife and cousin of Peter I)
Montisregalis, see Monreale
Montolif of/de, Cypriot noble family 351; see also Arnold of Montolif; Barthélémy de Montolif; John of Montolif; Marie/Marguerite de Montolif; Perot of Montolif; Simon of/de Montolif, *bailli* of the *Secrète*, chamberlain, and marshal of Cyprus; Simon de Montolif, butler/*bouteiller* of Jerusalem; Thomas of/de Montolif, marshal of Cyprus; Thomas of/de Montolif, auditor of Cyprus; Thomas of Montolif, the elder; Thomas of Montolif, the younger; Wilmot of Montolif
Montolive of Verny, admiral of Cyprus 336
Montpellier, city, Languedoc 19, 23, 40, 303, 347
Mont-Sainte-Catherine-lès-Provins, convent/church, Champagne 164
Moravia, marquis of 20, 192
Morea, principality of 26, 246, 299
Morf, see Morphou
Morgarten, battle of 243

Morosini, Venetian family; see Giovanni Morosini; Goffredo Morosini; Marino Morosini; Nicola/Nicolo Morosini
Morphou/Morf, Cypriot noble family; see also John of Morphou; Marie du Morf; Thomas of Morphou
Morrha, province, eastern Rhodope 465
Moscow/Muscovy/Moscovy, Grand Duchy of 401n, 411
Moses, Biblical figure 285
Mosserins, Eastern Christians of various denominations from Upper Mesopotamia 367
Mount Athos, peninsula, northern Greece 513, 528, 555, 557; see also Esphigmenou, monastery; Stavronikita, monastery
Mount of Olives, Jerusalem 362
Mount Pagos, hill/castle, near Smyrna 95
Mount Sinai, Sinai Peninsula 103, 269, 362, 363n, 519n, 552-553
Mount Sipylus, western Anatolia, near Manisa 93
Mount Tabor, Lower Galilee 554, 557-558, 561, 564
Mount Zion, Jerusalem 159
Mudazzo, Venetian family, see Giacomo Mudazzo; Giovanni Mudazzo; Matteo Mudazzo
Muʿīn al-Dīn Sulayman Pervāneh, Seljuk vizier 92, 436-441
Mübāriz al-Dīn Mehmed Bey, emir of Tekke 97
Mughan steppe, northwestern Iran 426-427, 432, 435
Muhammad, prophet 411
Mumcila, see Momitzilos
Murād I, Ottoman sultan 105, 414, 461
Muslims 23, 36, 50, 53, 77-80, 82-85, 94-95, 97-99, 104-105, 109, 118, 121, 132, 146, 188-189, 192, 199, 202, 247, 251, 253, 256-257, 259, 263-264, 266, 269-270, 282-283,

285, 289, 292, 303, 323, 367, 371, 373-374, 375n, 376, 382-383, 388, 404-405, 407-409, 413, 414, 420-421, 446, 448, 451-453, 457, 463, 475-476, 486-487
Muẓaffar al-Dīn ibn ʿAlīshīr, commander of Malatya   419
Mykonos, island, Aegean Sea   95
Myra, coastal city, southern Anatolia   18, 70
Mysia, region, northwestern Anatolia   93, 462, 484, 470n

Naples/Neapolis, city/kingdom of/archdiocese of   17-18, 25, 57, 72, 80, 85, 88-89, 90, 157, 161-163, 167-168, 171, 181, 184, 205, 209, 295, 494, 572-573; see also Bertrand, archbishop of Naples
Nāṣir al-Dīn Muḥammad ibn Qarājā al-Sharīfī, Mamluk emir   264-265
al-Nāṣir Ḥasan, Mamluk sultan of Egypt   83, 260; see also al-Nāṣir Muḥammad (al-Nāṣir Ḥasan's father)
al-Nāṣir Muḥammad, Mamluk sultan of Egypt   144, 260; see also al-Nāṣir Ḥasan (al-Nāṣir Muḥammad's son)
Navarre, kingdom of   164, 192n, 291-292
Naxos, island, Aegean Sea   79, 94-95
Nazareth, city, Palestine   379n
Neapolis, see Naples
Neapolitans   51, 160, 162-165, 181, 189, 209, 494n
Negroponte, island, Aegean Sea   79, 94-96, 113
Neopatrensi/Neopat<r>ensi (Neopatras), archdiocese of   215, 225
Neophytos the Recluse, St   552
Nestorians/Nestorins/Nestorini/Nestourins/Nothorini   44, 166, 173, 361, 364, 366-367, 573; see also Soriani
Nestorius, patriarch of Constantinople   542
Nestos, river, Thrace   465
Neustadt Kalisch, city, Bohemia   22
Nicaea, city, northwestern Anatolia   100, 432, 437, 462

Nicaean Empire   78
Niccolò Acciaiuoli, grand seneschal of the Kingdom of Naples   17-18, 184n, 189
Niccolò Alunno d'Alife, royal secretary and notary of the Kingdom of Naples   162
Niccolo di Checcoli/Nicolaus Checcoli de Romanis de Auximo, Roman notary   502
Niccolò di Poggibonsi, traveller   181
Niccolò Sanudo, duke of Naxos   95
Nicholas IV, pope   85, 110
Nicholas the Confessor, St, Latin cathedral of Famagusta   165
Nicola de Spinola, viscount of the curia Surianorum   380
Nicola Giustiniani, Venetian ambassador   266
Nicola Mazamurdi, boat owner   125-126
Nicola Morosini/Nicolo Morosini, Venetian consul in Theologo   131n, 134n
Nicola Zorzi, Venetian consul in Theologo   131n
Nicolas de Besse/dominus Nicolaus, cardinal deacon of Santa Maria in Via Lata   501, 502n; see also Santo Spirito in Sassia, church
Nicolas Catellus, bailli of the Secrète of Cyprus   349
Nicolas Sigeros, praitor tou demou   472
Nicolaus Checcoli de Romanis de Auximo, see Niccolo di Checcoli
Nicolaus, dominus, see Nicolas de Besse
Nicolo Morosini, see Nicola Morosini
Nicolo Pisani, Venetian consul in Palatia   131
Nicolò di Scacchi, Veronese poet   41
Nicolò, St, see San Nicolò
Nicomedia, city/gulf of, Sea of Marmara   93, 99-100, 462
Nicopolis, city/battle of, northern Bulgaria   249, 282-283, 296, 517

INDEX 611

Nicosia, capital city/archdiocese of,
  Cyprus 15-17, 23-25, 27, 35, 44, 46, 49,
  57, 69, 83, 87-88, 112, 137, 166, 185, 204,
  211, 215, 219, 225, 238, 273n, 281, 303n,
  334, 337-338, 341n, 348-349, 351, 356,
  359, 366n, 370, 372, 375, 377, 382, 449n
Nif, see Nymphaion
Niğde, city, southcentral Anatolia 427-
  428, 440
Nikephoros Gregoras, Byzantine
  historian 37, 102, 103n, 430, 457, 460,
  464, 468, 474, 476-477, 480, 484, 485,
  487, 521, 526-527, 530, 553, 555; see also
  Agathangelos (semi-fictional character
  for Gregoras's student); Lependrinos
  (Gregoras's correspondent)
Nile, river, Africa 84, 142-144, 151-152,
  258-259, 260-261, 572
  - Canopic branch of the Nile 144
  - Delta 265
  - Nilometer 143, 151, 572
Nimocium, diocese of; see Limassol
Niphon, patriarch of Alexandria 494
Nores, de/Denores, Cypriot noble
  family 304n, 351; see also Baudouin
  de Nores; Giorgio Denores/de
  Nores; Jacques de Nores; James de
  Nores; Isabelle, daughter of James de
  Nores; Pierre de Nores
Normans 161, 303-302
Normandy 20-21
Nothorini, see Nestorians
Notre-Dame, church, Boulogne-sur-
  Mer 45
Nubians 366n
Nūre Sūfī, leader and 'Sufi saint'
  (pīr), father of Karīm al-Dīn
  Karāmān 425-427
al-Nuwayrī/Nuwairī, Mamluk polymath
  and historian 37, 142, 144, 251, 254,
  255n, 256, 258n, 259, 261-262, 268n, 270
Nymphaion/Nif/Kemalpaşa, city,
  western Asia Minor 93, 462
Nyssa (Sultanhisar), city,
  Cappadocia 92

Obertus de Clavaro, Genoese citizen,
  husband of Florencia and father of
  Alis 377
Occitan, language 32, 275
Occitanie, region, southern
  France 303, 498
Oddon de Dampierre, constable of
  Jerusalem 350-351
Odysseus, hero of Homer's
  Odyssey 538
Ögedeï, Mongol Great Khan 428
Oghuz Khan 397-398
Oghuz, Turkish tribe 390, 397, 398,
  422
Ognibene de Mantoue, see Hugh
  Ognibono
Old Pişrev, ghazi fighter 481
Old Testament 283
Öljeitü, Ilkhān of Persia 447, 452n
Oppeln, city, Silesia 22
Orhan, emir of Menteşe 95
Orhan, Ottoman emir 96, 100,
  458-459, 460n, 462-464, 467, 469,
  476, 479-480, 483-488, 508n; see also
  Süleyman (Orhan's son); Theodora
  Kantakouzene (Orhan's wife)
Oriago, town, Veneto 19
Oriental 46, 79, 214-215, 220, 222, 224-
  225, 284, 286, 362, 420, 445, 454
  - Oriental Christians 56, 324, 337,
    343, 361, 367, 372n, 379-380
Orleans, city, France 51, 287, 289n,
  290n, 294-295
Orthodox Christians 94, 106, 192, 214,
  220, 224, 337, 362, 364n, 365, 368-370,
  375, 403, 409, 486, 489, 496n, 507n,
  511-512, 514-515, 519, 521-523, 526, 527n,
  529-534, 538, 540-544, 546, 551
  - Miaphysite Syrian Orthodox, see
    Miaphysites; see also Syrians
  - Orthodox Greeks 85, 337n, 363n,
    364n, 365, 369; see also Greeks
  - Orthodox Syrians 337n, 365, 369;
    see also Syrians
  - Syrian Orthodox, see Syrians

Orusut, *see* Russian
Orvieto, city, Umbria   501
Osmanlis, *see* Ottomans
Ottomans   36, 93, 96, 99-100, 102, 105, 113, 121, 123, 141, 249, 258-259, 304, 401, 414, 417-418, 423-425, 428, 437, 444-448, 451, 453-454, 458-459, 460, 462-464, 467, 469, 474-476, 479-480, 484-489, 492, 508
- Ottoman Empire   95, 444, 446

Pacio Bertini, Florentine sculptor   162, 171, 573
Padua, city, Veneto   19, 38, 340, 363
Pahlavān Bey, Aq-Qoyunlu chief   436, 438
Palaiologos, Byzantine dynasty   87, 458, 473, 492, 504n, 508, 518-519; *see also* Andronikos II Palaiologos; Andronikos III Palaiologos; Andronikos IV Palaiologos; Andronikos Palaiologos (perhaps Andronikos III's cousin); Demetrios Palaiologos; John V Palaiologos; John VII Palaiologos; John VIII Palaiologos; John Palaiologos (despot); Manuel II Palaiologos; Maria Palaiologina, *Despoina ton Mougoulion*; Michael VIII Palaiologos; Michael IX Palaiologos; Theodora Palaiologina
Palamas, Costis, Greek poet   61
Palamism/anti-Palamism   103, 507n, 513, 517, 520-522, 527, 529, 531, 536n, 547, 553, 555-556, 561, 564-565
Palamites/anti-Palamites   37, 102-104, 513, 520-539, 543-545, 547, 551-565
Palatia, *see* Miletus/Palatia
Palentina, *see* Parentina
Palermo/Panormitana, city, Sicily   161, 215, 225
Palestine   77, 194, 362, 363n, 374
Palestinians   77, 166, 363n, 377
Pallene, location in Kassandra Peninsula   466

Palokythro, village, Cyprus   140
Panormitana, *see* Palermo
Paparoissole, *see* Bābā'ī
Paphos, port city, Cyprus   17-18, 25, 52, 140, 339, 369, 372, 552
Parentina/Palentina (Poreč), diocese of, Istria   215, 225
Paris, city, France   20-21, 70, 99, 187, 276, 288, 300, 304, 330, 372, 373, 398
Parthenays, French noble family   299; *see also* William VII Larchevêque, lord of Parthenay
Passion of Christ, order   281n, 283
Patmos, island, Aegean Sea   370
Patras, city/archdiocese of, Peloponnese   215, 225, 229
- Chapter of Patras   514
Paul, archbishop of Smyrna   104
Paul, Latin patriarch of Constantinople, former archbishop of Smyrna   493-494, 502; *see also* Amadeus VI of Savoy (Paul's co-ambassador)
Paul, St, St Paul the Apostle/Paulus   528n, 529n, 563
Pavia, town, southwestern Lombardy   19
Pease, Lorenzo Warriner, American missionary   138n
Pechenegs, semi-nomadic people   393
Pediaios, river, Cyprus   184
Pegai, city, Propontis coast   93
Pelekanon, battle of, Gulf of Nicomedia   99
Peloponnese, peninsula, southern Greece   114
Pentagia, village, Cyprus   146
Pera, city opposite Constantinople   225, 493n, 513, 515n, 533
Perceval de Coulonges/Percheval de Coulongne, Poitevin knight   71, 298, 332
Pergamon, city, northwestern Asia Minor   93, 462
Peritheorion/Buru, city/battle of, western Thrace   465, 467

Perot of Montolif, member of the regency council of Cyprus 338-339; *see also* Wilmot of Montolif (Perot's brother)
Perrin, fictitious character standing for King Peter II of Lusignan 298
Persia, *see* Iran
Persian/Persians 92n, 94n, 389, 403n, 413, 419, 425n, 451, 465, 469n, 470-471, 475, 478n, 479, 481n
Pedena, city/diocese of, Istria 215, 255
Peter I of Lusignan, king of Cyprus, king of Jerusalem, king of Cilician Armenia, and count of Tripoli, 11, 13-15, 17, 20-21, 23-24, 31-62, 69-73, 75, 77, 80-84, 86-91, 97, 105-106, 109, 117, 119, 121, 135-137, 138n, 139-140, 144-146, 165-167, 175, 177-180, 182-206, 208-209, 211, 213-214, 219, 222-224, 230-234, 236-238, 241-249, 251-256, 261, 263-265, 267-269, 273-305, 312, 321, 323-338, 342n, 343, 345-347, 350, 352-353, 355-361, 363, 379, 382, 461, 490, 492, 508n, 509, 568-569, 571, 573; *see also* Alice of Ibelin (Peter I's mother); Alice of Majorca (Peter I's niece); Eleanor of Aragon (Peter I's second wife); Eschiva of Montfort (Peter I's first wife and cousin); Eschiva of/de Scandelion (Peter I's mistress); Eschiva (Peter I's daughter); King Hugh IV of Lusignan (Peter I's father); James I of Lusignan (Peter I's brother); Joanna L'Aleman (Peter I's mistress); John of Antioch (Peter I's brother); Margaret (Peter I's daughter); Margaret/Marguerite (Peter I's sister); Peter II of Lusignan (Peter I's son)
- Order of the Sword 15, 17, 44-45, 50, 53, 69, 283
Peter II of Lusignan, king of Cyprus, son of Peter I of Lusignan and Eleanor of Aragon 16, 20, 25, 27, 34n, 57, 73, 289, 296, 303n, 323-324, 328n, 333-339, 354, 355n; *see also* John of Antioch (Peter II's uncle); Margaret (Peter II's sister) and Eleanor; Valentina Visconti (Peter II's wife)
Peter III, king of Aragon 88; *see also* Frederick III, king of Sicily (Peter III's son); James II (Peter III's brother); James II, king of Majorca (Peter III's son)
Peter of Antioch, member of the regency council of Cyprus 338
Peter the Apostle, St 501n, 541-542, 544
Peter of Caffran, admiral and ambassador of Cyprus 340-341
Peter of Campofregoso, Genoese admiral 49; *see also* Alice of Majorca (Peter's lover)
Peter of Cassi, Cypriot nobleman 336
Peter of Grimante, naval captain in the service of King Peter I of Lusignan 259, 261; *see also* John of Grimante (Peter's brother)
Peter of Herentals, monk and author 37
Peter the Hermit 302
Peter Martyr, St, tomb of 48
Peter and Paul, Ss, Nestorian church, Famagusta 44, 173, 212, 221-222, 226, 573
Peter of Pleine Chassagne, apostolic legate 85
Peter of Ribargoza, father of Eleanor of Aragon, queen of Cyprus 90; *see also* James II, king of Majorca (Peter of Ribargoza's father)
Peter Thomas, apostolic legate, Carmelite friar, apostolic legate, Archbishop of Crete, Latin Patriarch of Constantinople 13-14, 17, 18, 20-23, 70, 81, 90, 104, 185, 187, 197-200, 233, 235-236, 276, 282, 286, 331-332, 356, 359, 364n, 366n, 493n, 508-509, 510n, 513, 560, 564
Peter, St, basilica in Rome 25, 498-500, 505

Petrarch, *see* Francesco Petrarca
Petrus de Albiartz, apostolic notary and cleric of the papal chamber   502n
Petrus qd. Condi Stephani (Kontostephanos?), Constantinopolitan monk   514n
Petrus Demandi, archdeacon of Limassol   212
Pherai, city, Macedonia   468
Philadelphia, city, western Asia Minor   470n-471n, 478
Philip IV/Philip the Fair/Philip le Bel, king of France   85-86, 112, 348, 447, 452
Philip V, king of France   86, 348
Philip VI, king of France   41n, 86, 95, 115-116, 181; *see also* Charles IV, king of France (Philip VI's predecessor); Maria of Bourbon (Philip VI's second cousin)
Philip of Anjou, son of Charles I, count of Anjou   159n
Philip the Bold, duke of Burgundy   21, 280, 295; *see also* Charles V, duke of Normandy and later king of France (Philip's brother); Charles VI, dauphin and king of France (Philip's nephew); John II, king of France (Philip's father); John of Berry (Philip's brother)
Philip of Brunswick, constable of Jerusalem   49, 185n, 327-328, 333, 356, 358; *see also* Alice of Ibelin (Philip's wife); Heloise de Brunswick (Philip's daughter); Henry II of Brunswick (Philip's father)
Philip the Fair, *see* Philip IV of France
Philip of Ibelin, lord of Arsur, seneschal of Cyprus   27, 48-49, 89 185, 203-204, 238-239, 327, 333-334, 336; *see also* Isabella of Ibelin (Philip's daughter); Alice of Majorca (Philip's second wife); Eschiva of Dampierre (Philip's first wife); Guy of Ibelin, bishop of Limassol (Philip's brother); King Peter I of Lusignan (Philip's third cousin)

Philip of Mézières, chancellor of Cyprus and author   13-16, 18, 20, 22-23, 25, 33, 40, 46-47, 50-53, 55, 58, 81, 146, 185, 188, 189n, 275-276, 277n, 278, 281-286, 287-288, 290, 292, 294-295, 302, 312, 328-331, 333-334, 345, 355, 356n, 359-360, 366n, 509, 573
Philip of Novara, Latin Eastern historian   367, 371
Philip of Taranto, son of Charles II, king of Naples, and Mary of Hungary   161; *see also* Charles Martel (Philip's brother); Louis of Toulouse (Philip's brother); Robert I, king of Naples (Philip's brother)
Philip Tzykandyles, witness of John V Palaiologos's profession of faith   503
Philip, count of Jaffa   180; *see also* Maria of Ibelin (Philip's sister)
Philippa of Hainault, queen of England   276, 293; *see also* Edward III, king of England (Philippa's husband); Edward the Black Prince (Philippa's son); Lionel, duke of Clarence (Philippa's son)
Philippe II, king of Spain   136
Philippus Solitarius, author   368n
Philipus Mistehel, Famagustan of Syrian descent, brother of Aylix (wife of Andreas, son of Ioannis de Baruti)   379
Philotheos Kokkinos, patriarch of Constantinople   494, 559-560
Phocaea, Genoese colony, western Asia Minor   79, 94, 100, 101
Phrygia, region, central Anatolia   92, 100n, 418
Piave, Francesco Maria, Italian librettist   59
Picard, Sir Henry, vintner and Lord Mayor of London   20, 53, 54n
Piedmont, region, northwest Italy   341, 342n
Piero di ser Bartolomeo da Pontedera, notary   450

INDEX 615

Pierre de Nores, Cypriot nobleman, royal ambassador 360; *see also* John Carmain (Pierre's co-ambassador); Raymond Babin (Pierre's co-ambassador)
Pierre Roger, archbishop of Rouen and future pope, *see* Clement VI
Pietro de Marco, Genoese captain 380
Pietro Gradenigo, doge of Venice 448n
Pietro Grimani, *sopracomito* of Crete 133
Pietro Lando, member of the Senate and the *sapientes* of Crete 127n
Pietro Malocello, Genoese nobleman, apostolic nuncio, chamberlain of Cyprus 38, 200n, 327, 328, 333-334, 359-360
Pietro Querini, one of the *sapientes* of Crete 126
Pins, chapel of 352n; *see also* Sainte-Sophie, cathedral
Pipēs ('Bibi'), Orthodox monastery in Nicosia 380; *see also* Bibi, family
Pisa, city/maritime republic, Tuscany 26, 39, 95, 446, 447n, 449, 450, 501n, 541n
- Council of Pisa 541
Pisans 39, 131, 294, 334, 446-447, 449, 450-451, 501n
Pistoia, city, Tuscany 26, 117
Pizan, Italo-French family, *see* Christine de Pizan; Thomas de Pizan
Planis, dominus de, *see* Bernardus de Marcrinio
Plantagenet, house of 21, 303
Platina, *see* Bartolomeo Sacchi
Plessie, Cypriot noble family, *see* Hamerin of Plessie; Jean de Plessie
Plested, Marcus 521-522, 527n, 549n
Plutarch, Greek philosopher and author 41
Podskalský, Zdeněk, Czech film director 62
Poitevins 274, 298, 304

Poitiers, city, Poitou 54, 85
Poitou, region, west-central France 21, 288, 298, 332
Poland 22, 43, 51, 54, 55n, 62, 249, 444, 446, 453
Pola, city/diocese, Istria 215, 225
Polyboton, city, Thrace 466n
Pontedera, city, Tuscany 450
Pontus, region, Black Sea coastland 466n, 467
Portugal 292
Posen, region, Greater Poland 22
Prague, city, Bohemia 14, 20, 22, 46, 52, 54, 60, 70, 278
Prato, city, Tuscany 26
Premonstratensians, order 166
Pringyps, Byzantine emissary 483
Prochoros Kydones, Byzantine monk and theologian 513n-514n, 521, 526, 560, 561n; *see also* Demetrios Kydones (Prochoros's brother)
Propontis (Sea of Marmara) 93n, 463, 466, 471n
Provane, Piedmontese family, *see* Balian Provane; Embalin Provane (perhaps the same with Balian and Ibelin); Hodrade Provane (Balian's son); Ibelin Provane (perhaps the same with Balian and Embalin)
Provençal, language 41, 162, 289
Provins, town, Champagne 164
Pseudo-Kodinos, Byzantine author 485, 486n
Psimolophou, village, Cyprus 184, 366n
Pyrgion/Birgi, town, western Asia Minor 92
Pyrrhus, patriarch of Constantinople 542

Qāḍī Aḥmad of Niǧde, Seljuk scholar 428
Qalawūn, Mamluk sultan 97, 144, 253
Qaloyan, *see* John V Palaiologos
al-Qalqashandī, Mamluk polymath 252n

Qaratay, Seljuk emir   431
Qāzān, *see* Cassan Cigala
Quṭb al-Dīn Aḥmad/Coterinus, Turkmen leader   430-431
Quṭlūbughā al-Manṣūrī, Mamluk amir   525

Rabbinic courts   374
Rabimuol, month of the Islamic calendar   451
Ragusa, diocese and city, Dalmatia   215, 219, 225
Ramon Muntaner, Catalan mercenary and writer   244n
Ramón Resta, Catalan member of the Cypriot royal household   335n; *see also* Luis Resta
Ranulph Higden, chronicler   42
Ranulph, archbishop of Nicosia   365
Rashīd al-Dīn, Persian historian   435
Raston, Mervanik's overlord/father   409-410
Raymond Babin, Cypriot knight and ambassador, butler of Cyprus   178-179, 185-186, 203, 210, 327-328, 331, 333-334, 336, 355, 358, 360; *see also* John Carmain (Raymond Babin's co-ambassador); Marie de Montolif (Raymond Babin's wife); Pierre de Nores (Raymond Babin's co-ambassador)
Raymond Bertrand de Got, future pope, *see* Clement V, pope
Raymond, archbishop of Nicosia   238
Reggio Emilia, region, northern Italy   330
Region, town, eastern Thrace   466n
Reims, city, France   21, 276, 300
Renaut de Milmars, Cypriot nobleman   342n; *see also* Arnold of Milmars (could be the same person); Reynald of Milmars (could be the same person)
Renier Scolar, lord of Bethsan, ambassador, *bailli* of the *Secrète*, and member of the regency council of Cyprus   338, 341
Resta, Catalan family, *see* Luis Resta; Ramón Resta
Rethymno, city, Crete   129, 514n
Reynald of Milmars, marshal of Cyprus   342; *see also* Arnold of Milmars (could be the same person); Renaut de Milmars (could be the same person)
Rhodes/Rodo, island, Aegean Sea   18, 21, 23-25, 49, 51, 70-72, 78, 79n, 83, 85, 87, 94-95, 112-116, 128, 132n, 133n, 142, 195, 201, 215, 225, 230, 247-248, 269, 292, 335n, 446, 454; *see also* Collocensi dicta Rodo, diocese of
Rhodope Mountains   463, 465, 470
Richard I the Lionheart, king of England   54, 59, 243, 302n
Richard Lescot, French chronicler   302
Robert I, king of Naples, also known as Robert the Wise   89, 159-164, 166-169, 171, 572-573; *see also* Andrew of Hungary (husband of Joanna I, queen of Naples); Charles II, king of Naples (Robert I's father); Charles Martel (Robert I's brother); Charles, duke of Calabria (Robert I's son); Joanna I, queen of Naples (Robert I's granddaughter); Louis of Toulouse (Robert I's brother); Mary of Hungary (Robert I's mother); Philip of Taranto (Robert I's brother); Sancia of Mallorca (Robert I's second wife); Yolande of Aragon (Robert I's first wife)
Robert Moustazo, witness of treaties   337
Robert of Lusa (perhaps Lusignan), English knight   245
Robert of Taranto, prince of Achaea and titular Latin emperor of Constantinople   17, 90, 181, 184n; *see also* Maria of Bourbon (Robert's wife); Hugh of Lusignan (Robert's

stepson); Charles II, king of Naples (Robert's grandfather)
Rochefort, city, Aquitaine   24-25, 49
Rodo, see Collocensi dicta Rodo, diocese of; see also Rhodes
Roger Bacon, English philosopher   243
Roger de Flor, leader of the Catalan Grand Company   93
Roger de Pins, master of the Hospital   195, 199 230; see also Sainte-Sophie, chapel of the Pins
Roger of Wendover, English historian   42
Roman/s   100n, 142n, 211, 226, 233, 244, 327n, 329, 369, 420, 460, 461n, 468, 469n, 470, 472n, 493, 494, 496, 498-499, 500-502, 505-506, 508n, 509, 511, 513n, 521, 532, 539n, 544, 546, 548, 551; see also Byzantines
- Holy Roman Emperor   43, 54
- Roman Church   86, 142, 192, 207, 210, 212, 214, 220, 224, 226-227, 235, 364, 492-496, 498, 509-510, 512n-513n, 516, 519-520, 522, 526-527, 539, 542n, 544, 546-547, 560
- (Western) Roman Empire   295, 401n
- Roman Pontiff   36, 544
Romance (latina), language/vernacular   447; see also Latin
Romania   88, 94, 141n, 190, 193-194, 211, 221-222, 379n, 395, 506
Rome, city, Italy   11, 16, 25-26, 36, 48-49, 57, 58n, 72, 99, 102, 104, 106, 135n, 177, 187, 289, 326, 329, 333, 347, 359-360, 367n, 370-371, 489, 491, 493, 495-501, 503, 505-507, 510, 511n, 513, 515, 516n, 519n, 521-523, 526, 533, 539, 542-544, 546-549, 552
Roucha/Rochas/Rouchas, count of, see John of Morphou
Rouen, city, Normandy   20, 115-116
Rudolf, duke of Vienna   22
Ruggiero Querini, one of the *sapientes* of Crete   125n

Rum, Seljuk sultanate of Konya   78, 94, 386, 413n, 418-419, 427-428, 431-434, 441, 457, 479
Rus (Russia/Russians)   249, 395n, 411n
Russia   43, 80, 387, 394n, 395-396, 401, 406; see also Rus
Russians/Orusut   370, 397, 404, 406, 407, 410-412, 444, 508; see also Rus

Sabadin Catip, translator   447
Sabas Monastery, near Jerusalem   368
al-Ṣabbāḥ, see Marcus Zebas
Safavids, Iranian dynasty   401
Safed, city, Palestine   256
Sayda/Sidon, city, Palestine   25, 72, 257, 261-262
Sain, Turcoman chief interpreter   448
Saint-Denis, basilica, France   300, 302
Saint-Pierre de Corbie, abbey, northern France   292
Sainte-Sophie, Latin cathedral, Nicosia   352n
- chapel of the Pins   352n
Saintonge, region, western France   21
Saladin, sultan, founder of the Ayyubid dynasty   253, 256n, 424, 446
Salāḥ al-Dīn, see Salatin
Salamis, ancient city, Cyprus   31
Salatin/Salāḥ al-Dīn, representative of Umur Pasha   478, 483-484
al-Ṣāliḥ Ayyūb, Ayyubid sultan   253; see also Tūrān Shāh (al-Ṣāliḥ Ayyūb's son)
Ṣāliḥ ibn Yaḥyā, member of the Buḥtur dynasty and author   37, 252, 257, 258n, 260
Saltıh, see Sarı Saltuk
Saltuk-nāme, epic tale   91, 387-390, 393, 395-396, 399-409, 412-413; see also Sarı Saltuk
Salzburg, city and diocese, Austria   193, 215, 221-222, 225
Samaritans   367
Samos, island, Aegean Sea   94
San Domenico, convent in Camporegio   39

San Felice, city, Lombardy   26
San Giacomo dell'Orio, church,
    Venice   378; see also Simeone, priest of
San Lorenzo Maggiore, Franciscan
    church, Naples   160
San Luca, parish in Venice   39; see also
    Ca' Corner, palace in San Luca
San Marco, ducal chapel, Venice
    (St Mark's basilica)   39
San Miniato, town, Tuscany   501n; see
    also Miniate
San Nicolò, monastery, Lido,
    Venice   39
Sancia of Mallorca, wife of Robert I,
    king of Naples   159, 161-163
Sancta Unio, naval league   113, 115n
Sancti Angeli, castle of   500n
Sancti Sabastiani martiris, see Corpus
    Christi, church, Nicosia
Sancti Spiritus de Urbe/in Saxia, see
    Santo Spirito in Sassia
Sandwich, harbour   54
Sanudo, Venetian family, see Giovanni
    Sanudo; Marino Sanudo Torsello;
    Niccolò Sanudo
Santa Chiara, church, Naples   89, 161-
    162, 164, 171, 573
Santa Maria Donnaregina, church,
    Naples   163; see also Mary of
    Hungary (her burial place)
Santa Maria Novella, Dominican
    convent, Florence   45
Santa Maria in Via Lata, church,
    Rome   501
Santo Spirito in Sassia, church/hospital,
    Rome   498, 501, 502n
Saracens   23, 34n, 42, 142, 165n, 269n,
    279n, 284, 287-288, 298, 303n, 367
Ṣarafand, village, Palestine   262
Sarai (Saray), city on the lower
    Volga   404n, 410,
Sarasin, see Saracens
Saray, see Sarai
Sarchanes, see Saruhan Beg
Sardinia, kingdom of   88

Sarı Saltuk Dede, hero of Turkish
    epic tale   91, 385, 387, 389-390, 395,
    399-400, 402, 404-405, 408-412, 414,
    415; see also Ece Halil (Sarı Saltuk's
    successor); Ilgaz-i Rumi (Sarı
    Saltuk's ally); Ilyas Gazi (Sarı Saltuk's
    confederate); Saltuk-nāme (epic tale)
Sarmatian, steppe   404, 412
Saruhan Beg, Turkish chief, founder of
    the Saruhan emirate   92, 101, 462,
    478n; see also Süleyman (Saruhan's
    son)
Saruhan, emirate of/beylik of   94, 115,
    117, 462-464, 467-468, 471, 478, 480,
    484
Saruhanids   462
Sasa Beg, subordinate commander of
    the Menteşe Turks   92
Satalia/Satalie, see Antalya
Savoy, county of   14, 20, 21, 23, 36n, 101,
    105, 194, 195n, 224, 458, 461, 492, 493n,
    503n, 507, 525, 536n
Savoyards   492n-493n
Saxony   20, 22, 192
Sayf al-Dīn al-Jūbānī, Mamluk
    commander   265
Schweidnitz, city, Silesia   22
Sclavonia, region, Croatia   193, 221-222
Scotland, kingdom of   42, 53, 60, 244,
    249, 292, 297, 305
Sekretikoi, Cypriot family   369n;
    see also Konstantinos Sekretikos;
    Theodora (Konstantinos Sekretikos's
    daughter)
Seljuks   78, 91-92, 94, 97, 113, 123, 386-
    387, 388n, 389, 391, 400, 417-420, 422-
    424, 426, 428-429, 431-432, 434-441,
    457, 475, 479, 486
Selymbria, city, eastern Thrace   466,
    469, 481, 484-485
Seneschal's Bridge, Nicosia   137n
Şerban ('The Serb'), prince   413-414
Serbia   98, 474, 483-484, 488, 508n
Serbs/Srbljem   98, 414, 458, 464, 466,
    468, 470, 474, 483, 487-488, 507-508, 510

Serenissima, see Venice
Serres/Siroz, city, Macedonia 465n, 476
Seyyid, *see* Sarı Saltuk
Shāh-Arman of Akhlāt 422
Sharaf al-Dīn Masʿūd ibn Khatir, Mamluk emir 440-441
Shihāb al-Dīn Ghāzī b. ʿAlīshīr al-Turkumānī, Turkish chief, son of ʿAlīshīr the Turkmen 258n, 438; *see also* Karīm al-Dīn ʿAlīshīr
Shikārī, author 425-427
Shirvān, region, eastern Caucasus 425-427
Sicilian Vespers 88
Sicilians 185
Sicily, island, kingdom of 83, 87-88, 90, 117, 141n, 142, 158-159, 161, 167, 181, 185n, 189, 192-193, 221-222, 292
Side, city, southern Anatolia 559
Sidon, *see* Sayda
Siena, city, Tuscany 26, 39, 160
Silesia, region, Central Europe 22, 54
Silvestros Syropulos, Byzantine official 512-513
Simeone, notary and priest of San Giacomo dell'Orio in Venice 378
Simiteculo, Cypriot family of Syrian descent 378n; *see also* Feras Simiteculo; Fetus Simiteculo (Ferus's son); Maria (Fetus's wife); Teodorus Simiteculo (Ferus's son); Uxira (Ferus's daughter)
Simon Atumano, bishop of Gerace in Calabria 36, 490n
Simón Bocanegra, drama 59; *see also* Antonio García Gutiérrez
Simon Boccanegra, doge of Genoa 19, 38; *see also Simón Bocanegra*, drama; *Simon Boccanegra*, opera
Simon Boccanegra, opera 59; *see also* Giuseppe Verdi
Simon of/de Montolif, *bailli* of the Secrète and chamberlain of Cyprus, marshal of Jerusalem 327, 329, 349, 352, 356, 358; *see also* Simon de Montolif, butler of Jerusalem; Simon Tenouri (Simon of Montolif's nephew)
Simon de Montolif, butler of Jerusalem 350-351; *see also* Simon of Montolif, *bailli* of the Secrète and chamberlain of Cyprus, marshal of Jerusalem
Simon of Saint Quentin, friar, diplomat, and historian 429, 430
Simon Tenouri, marshal of Jerusalem 328-330, 332-334; *see also* John (Simon's father); Simon of Montolif (Simon's uncle); Symon Thynoly (perhaps the same person)
Simone Martini, Sienese painter 160, 168-169, 572
Sinai, peninsula, Egypt; *see also* Mount Sinai 362, 363n
Sinan Pasha, Ottoman grand vizier 454
Siroz, *see* Serres
Sitia, city, Crete 125, 127-129
Siual, month of the Islamic calendar 451
Sivas, city, eastern Anatolia 426, 430
Sivouri, village, Cyprus 339
Sivrihisar, city, central Anatolia 92, 436, 437, 438
Skoutarion/Üsküdar, city, Anatolian shore of the Bosporus 487
Slavic, language 508n
Smbat Sparapet, Armenian author 421-424, 432, 438
Smithfield/Smethfeld, district in central London 45
Smyrna/Izmir, gulf of/ port city, Aegean coast of Asia Minor 15, 23, 86, 93-96, 100, 102, 104, 113, 117-118, 133n, 186, 190, 192, 194, 201, 202, 211-212, 458, 462-463, 465-468, 473-474, 481, 484, 493n
Solea, valley and region, Cyprus 372
Solomon, Old Testament king of Israel 164, 283

Solon, Athenian politician and lawmaker 534
Sophene, Roman province 420
Sozopolis, coastal city, Thrace 466
Spain, kingdom of 26, 292, 297, 230, 443
Split, diocese and city, Croatia 215, 225
Spyridon, St 135
Srbljem, see Serbs
Stavronikita, monastery on Mount Athos 555n
Stavrovouni, monastery in Cyprus 50n, 278
Stenimachos, city, Rhodope Mountains 465
Stephan Dandolo, Venetian envoy 101
Stephan Dušan, Serbian tsar 98, 458, 464, 466, 468, 474, 478n, 484, 507
Stilbnos, city, central Bulgaria 466
Strambali, Diomedes, Cypriot owner of the manuscript containing the Italian translation of Leontios Makhairas's chronicle and/or translator 246n
Strasbourg, city, Alsace 14, 20
Strigoniensi (Esztergom), city/diocese of, Hungary 215, 225
Süleyman of Karasi, Turkish chief 467-468, 478-480, 483-484; see also John Vatatzes (Süleyman of Karasi's father-in-law)
Süleyman the Magnificent, Ottoman sultan 453
Süleyman Pasha, Seljuk vizier 426
Süleyman of Saruhan, Turkish chief, son of Saruhan Beg 464, 467n, 468, 471
Süleyman, Ottoman chief, son of Emir Orhan 96, 458, 480, 483, 488
Süleymanshāh 101, 462n, 481; see also Mehmed Beg ibn Aydın (Süleymanshāh's father); Umur Pasha (Süleymanshāh's brother); Hızır of Ephesus/Hızır Beg (Süleymanshāh's brother); İsa Beg (Süleymanshāh's brother)
Sultanhisar, see Nyssa
Svoboda, Karel, composer 62

Swan feast, see Feast of the Five Kings
Swiss 138
Switzerland 51
Symon Thynoly, knight, perhaps member of the Tenouri family 329n
Syr Bertran, perhaps a Melkite, buried in the church of the Theotokos tōn Syrōn 369
Syria 56, 77, 80-81, 83, 85, 109-111, 140, 142, 144-145, 157, 166, 245, 247, 253, 254n, 256, 261-262, 264, 268, 270n, 303n, 361-363, 368, 374, 421-422, 430, 552
Syriac, language 363, 367n, 419
Syrianoi, family of Melkite descent 361, 362n, 368, 370-371; see also Georgios the *Syrianos*; Ioannes the *Syrianos*
Syrians 24, 37, 55, 81, 114, 165, 167, 245, 252-253, 256, 258-263, 265, 268n, 302-303, 337, 364, 365n-366n, 368-369, 370n, 372-373, 375n, 378n-379n, 380
- *curia Siriorum/Surianorum* 373n, 377-378, 381
- Miaphysite Syrian Orthodox, see Miaphysite; see also Orthodox
- Orthodox Syrians 337n, 365, 369; see also Orthodox
- Syrian (Melkite) Christians, see Christians; see also Melkites; Syrians
- Syrian Melkites; see Melkites
- Syrian Orthodox 337n, 363, 365, 368-369; see also Orthodox

Tabor, see Mount Tabor
Tabriz/Turis, city, Persia 453
Tagaris, Byzantine noble family, see George Tagaris; Manuel Tagaris
Takka/Tekke, emir of 70, 97; see also Antalya
Tamerlane/Timur, Turco-Mongol military leader 254, 262, 270n, 400, 402n
Ṭaqbughā Khāzindār al-ʿAlāʾī, Mamluk emir and ambassador 269, 270

Taranto, city, Apulia   17, 90, 159n, 161, 181, 184; *see also* Louis of Taranto; Philip of Taranto; Robert of Taranto
Tarasios, St, patriarch of Constantinople   140
Tartūs/Tortosa, city, Syria   25, 72, 165, 259
Tatars   395, 446-447, 451-452
Taurus, mountains/region   92, 423-425, 432, 439-441
Ṭaybughā al-Ṭawīl, Mamluk emir   258, 260
Tekke, *see* Takka
Templars, order/knights   85, 87, 112
Temujin, *see* Ghengiz Khan
Tenos, island, Aegean Sea   95
Tenouri, Cypriot noble family   329n, 351; *see also* John Tenouri, *bailli* of the *Secrète* of Cyprus; John, Simon Tenouri's father; Simon Tenouri; Symon Thynoly
Teodorus Simiteculo, resident of Famagusta   378; *see also* Feras Simiteculo (Teodorus's father); Fetus Simiteculo (Teodorus's brother); Uxira (Teodorus's sister)
Tergestina (Trieste), city/diocese, northern Adriatic   215, 225
Teristasin, fort, Thrace   466n
Terra Sancta, *see* Holy Land
Teutonic Order/Teutons   53n, 249
Thebes, city/diocese of, Boeotia   215, 219, 225
Theobald V, king of Navarre and count of Champagne   164
Theodora Kantakouzene, daughter of John VI Kantakouzenos   459, 460n, 469n, 484, 486-487; *see also* Orhan, Ottoman emir (Theodora's husband)
Theodora Palaiologina, Byzantine empress   512n; *see also* Michael VIII Palaiologos (Theodora's husband)
Theodora, daughter of Konstantinos Sekretikos   372; *see also* Thomas, son of Zakē David (Theodora's husband)

Theodore II Dukas Laskaris, emperor of Nicaea   438n, 512n
Theodore Metochites, Byzantine statesman, Grand Logothete   99
Theodoros, representative of the Catholicos of the Jacobites   368
Theodosios Goudeles, Byzantine author   369n
Theodosios, monk, *see* Thomas the *Syros*
Theologo/Theologus, *see* Ephesus
Theophanes Confessor, Byzantine chronicler   369n
Theorianos, Byzantine diplomat   368
Theotokos *tōn Syrōn*   369, church, Paphos; *see also* Syr Bertran
Thermaic, gulf of Thessalonica   463, 465
Thessalonica/Thessalonike, city/diocese of, Macedonia   465, 469n, 475-477, 478n, 482, 484, 503n-504n, 556, 556n
Thessaly, region, Greece   98
Thibaut of Belfarage (in Arabic Abu'l Faraj), Cypriot knight of Melkite burgess descent   336-337, 338n
Thierry, mythical figure, Mélusine's son   299; *see also* Guion (Thierry's brother); Urien (Thierry's brother)
Thietmar, magister, German pilgrim   363n
Thomas Aquinas, St, theologian and philosopher   273n, 518, 521, 549n; *see also* Thomist
Thomas Barech, member of the regency council of Cyprus   337-338
Thomas Bibi, John Bibi's brother   380
Thomas Bulla, Genoese citizen   377
Thomas of Finion, Cypriot nobleman, *reeys Siriorum*   375, 377
Thomas de Montolif, *see* Thomas of Montolif
Thomas of/de Montolif, auditor, marshal, and *bailli* of the *Secrète* of Cyprus, ambassador to the pope (probably the same person

with Thomas of Montolif, the younger)   179, 186, 188-189, 328n, 331, 334, 336, 349, 355, 358, 360; *see also* Isabelle, daughter of James of Nores (Thomas's wife); James of Nores (Thomas's father-in-law); Thomas of Montolif, the elder; Thomas of/de Montolif, marshal of Cyprus
Thomas of Montolif, the elder   328; *see also* Thomas of Montolif, the younger; Thomas of/de Montolif, auditor of Cyprus; Thomas of/de Montolif, marshal of Cyprus
Thomas of/de Montolif, marshal of Cyprus   328n, 350; *see also* Thomas of Montolif, the elder; Thomas of Montolif, the younger; Thomas of/de Montolif, auditor of Cyprus
Thomas of Montolif, the younger (probably the same person with Thomas of/de Montolif, auditor of Cyprus)   328n; *see also* Thomas of Montolif, the elder; Thomas of/de Montolif, marshal of Cyprus
Thomas of Morphou, member of the regency council of Cyprus   338
Thomas de Picquigny/Pinqueny, *bailli* of the *Secrète* of Cyprus   349-352
Thomas de Pizan   294n; *see also* Christine de Pizan (Thomas's daughter)
Thomas the *Syros*, a scribe, the *grammatikos* of Paphos, whose monastic name was Theodosios   369-370, 372
Thomas Walsingham, English chronicler   42
Thomas, son of Zakē David   372; *see also* Theodora, daughter of Konstantinos Sekretikos (Thomas's wife)
Thomist, theology/ecclesiology   514, 549n; *see also* Thomas Aquinas, St
Thrace, peninsula/region of   96, 102, 105, 405n, 458, 463-465, 468-470, 471n, 473-474, 480, 483, 488-489

Thuringia, region, central Germany   22
Thyraion (Tire), city, western Asia Minor   92, 481
Tierceles of Bare, Flemish knight   331
Timur, *see* Tamerlane
Timurid, empire   254
Tire, *see* Thyraion
Tiryaki Hasan Pasha, Ottoman military commander   400n
Titus, St, revolt of   20-21, 38, 96, 121, 123, 131, 133-134
Toğan, son of Arslan (vizier of Hızır Beg)   481
Tommaso Bondumier, Venetian ambassador   448
Tommaso di Ramondo Cardus, Cypriot translator   449
Topkapı Palace, Istanbul   389, 401, 406n
Tortona, city in Piemonte, Italy   19
Tortosa, *see* Tartūs
Toulouse, city/county of, France   89, 160-161, 163, 168-169, 572
Traianoupolis, city, Thrace   465
Tralleis (Güzelhisar), ancient city, western Asia Minor   92
Trani, cathedral of, Apulia   159n
Transoxiana, historical region of Turkistan   428
Trebizond, empire of   422, 451, 453n, 460n
Tréguier, cathedral of, Brittany   45
Treviso, city, Veneto   45
Tripoli/Tripolis, count of/county of, Lebanon   15, 24-25, 71-72, 88, 137n, 157, 165, 183, 248, 256-257, 262, 264-265, 282, 299, 302, 353-354, 360, 381
Troodos Mountains, Cyprus   140n
Troy, Homeric city   478n
True Cross/Holy Cross   19, 45-46, 53, 264, 267, 278n, 374, 563
Truth, queen, fictive character in Philip of Mézières's *Songe du Vieux Pèlerin*   51, 285
Tryphon the Martyr, St   140
Tulcea, city, southeastern Romania   395

INDEX 623

Tunis, city, Tunisia   158, 443, 444n, 446-447, 449n, 451
Tūr ʿĀlī, Aq-Qoyunlu leader   436
Tūrān Shāh, last sultan of the Ayyubid dynasty   253; *see also* al-Ṣāliḥ Ayyūb (Tūrān Shāh's father)
Turcopoles   185, 245-246, 264, 328, 336-337, 340, 355n
Turenne, Viscounty of   254, 332
Turis, *see* Tabriz
Turkey   21, 71, 116, 145, 146n, 200, 246, 417, 429
Turkmen/Turkmens   78, 91-92, 114n, 254, 257-259, 386-387, 389, 395, 404, 417-428, 430-441; *see also* Aghacheri Turkmens
Turks   19, 22, 24, 34n, 41, 50, 79, 82-84, 90-91, 94-95, 100-102, 105-106, 109, 113-119, 191, 122-123, 134n, 145, 146n, 165n, 185, 190-194, 195n, 201-202, 211-212, 214, 219-220, 223-225, 245-246, 345, 279n, 283, 323, 330, 388, 392, 393n, 397-398, 401n, 403n, 404, 414-415, 419, 423, 429, 444n, 450n, 451, 459-464, 466-468, 469n, 470-474, 476, 478, 480-481, 487-489, 492, 507, 516n
 - Anatolian Turks/Turks of Anatolia   79, 86, 109-110, 113, 118, 191, 249, 283
 - Aydın Turks/Turks of Aydın   79, 94-95, 100, 102, 117, 487
 - Germiyān Turks   418-419, 423
 - Karaman Turks   110, 114, 116, 118
 - Karasi Turks/Turks of Karasi   93, 462
 - Menteşe Turks/Turks of Menteşe   85, 92, 94, 462
 - Oghuz Turks   397-398
 - Ottoman Turks   93, 96, 99, 453-454, 458, 462, 474
Tuscany, region, Italian peninsula   41, 449, 450, 501n
Tyre, port city/lordship/archdiocese of, Lebanon   18, 89, 158, 164, 180, 303, 328, 332n, 374, 378n, 559-560, 561

Tzamplakos, Byzantine aristocrat   497n
Tzermanianou, castle, eastern Thrace   466n
Tzykandyles, Byzantine family, *see* Manuel Tzykandyles; Philip Tzykandyles

Ugo Ommebono, *see* Hugh Ognibono
Uğurlu Beg, ghazi fighter   481
Uljay, Mamluk emir   261
Umur Pasha/Umur Beg of Aydın Smyrna   95, 101, 113, 117, 459-461, 462n, 463-468, 470n-471n, 473-486; *see also* Hızır of Ephesus/Hızır Beg (Umur Pasha's brother); İsa Beg (Umur Pasha's brother); Mehmed Beg ibn Aydın (Umur Pasha's father); Süleymanshâh (Umur Pasha's brother)
Urban V, pope   19-27, 32, 36n, 37, 45, 48-49, 50, 52, 55, 57, 86, 90, 104, 106, 177-178, 185, 187-188, 190-205, 211, 213-214, 219, 222, 223-224, 230-233, 235-238, 289, 300, 366n, 489-490, 491n, 492-494, 495n, 497-501, 505-506, 510, 512-514
Urien, mythical figure, Mélusine's son   298-299, 305n, 315-316, 574; *see also* Griffons (Urien's son); Guion (Urien's brother) Hermine (Urien's wife); Thierry (Urien's brother)
Üsküdar, *see* Skoutarion
Uways, Ilkhānid ruler   453n
Uxira, daughter of Feras Simiteculo   378; *see also* Fetus Simeteculo (Uxira's brother); Teodorus Simiteculo (Uxira's brother)
Uyghurs   398

Valania, *see* Bāniyās
Valentina Visconti, first wife of King Peter II of Lusignan   289n, 295n; *see also* Anglesia Visconti (Valentina's sister); Bernabò Visconti (Valentina's father)

Valentina Visconti, duchess of
    Orleans   289n, 290n; *see also*
    Giangaleazzo Visconti (Valentina's
    father); Louis I, duke of Orleans
    (Valentina's husband)
Valois, kings/house of   295, 301, 303;
    see also Mary of Valois
Vardan Arveltsi   430
Vatican   179, 196, 312, 369, 372, 501,
    502n, 506n, 549n, 573
Vegetius, late Roman writer   244
Venetians   17, 20, 22-23, 25-26, 38-39,
    41, 46, 72, 79n, 82-84, 86, 94-96, 101,
    109, 113, 115-117, 121-134, 140-141, 183,
    188, 193-194, 200, 202-203, 234, 252,
    261, 263-267, 269, 270n, 292, 326-327,
    329-330, 332, 347, 349n, 352n, 357, 361,
    378, 379, 444n, 445-448, 450-454,
    495n, 504n
    - White Venetians   362n, 378,
      379n, 382; *see also* Andreas, son
      of the White Venetian Ioannis de
      Baruti; Audeth (Cypriot family
      of White Venetians); Aylix (wife
      of Andreas, son of the White
      Venetian Ioannis de Baruti); Feras
      Simiteculo (father of the White
      Venetian Fetus Simiteculo); Fetus
      Simiteculo (White Venetian,
      either of Greek or more likely of
      Melkite origin); Ioannis de Baruti;
      Maria Simiteculo (Fetus's wife);
      Teodorus Simiteculo (Fetus's
      brother); Uxira (Fetus's sister)
Venice, city/maritime republic   13-14,
    19-20, 22, 24-26, 38, 39-41, 44-45, 51-53,
    59, 70-72, 80-81, 83, 94-96, 98, 100, 109,
    115-118, 121-124, 126-127, 129, 131-134,
    184, 188, 192-194, 198-200, 202-203,
    234, 237-238, 247, 262-264, 268-269,
    271, 276n, 286, 293, 296, 326, 328n, 330,
    336-337, 340-341, 347, 350-351, 354n,
    356, 359, 360, 377-378, 446-448, 450-
    452, 453n, 454, 458, 461, 493n, 495n,
    497, 503-504

Venus, ancient Greek goddess of
    love   273, 277, 295
Verona, city, Veneto   19, 245, 366n
Vicenza, city, Veneto   19
Victor, St, abbey in Marseille   499
Vidin, city and fortress, Serbia   105,
    492n
Vienna, city, Austria   22, 70
Villani, Italian family, *see* Filippo Villani;
    Giovanni Villani
Villeneuve-lès-Avignon/Villanova,
    town, France   206, 208-210
Vintners' Company/Worshipful
    Company of Vintners   53, 54n, 60,
    62, 65, 571; *see also* Feast of the Five
    Kings
    - Vintners' Company's Swan
      feast   62
Violante Visconti, *see* Yolanda/Violante
    Visconti
Virgin Mary   34, 552, 563
    - Chapel of Virgin Mary, *see*
      Karlstein/Karlštejn, castle
Visconti family   38, 289n, 296n; *see also*
    Anglesia Visconti; Bernabò/Barnabò
    Visconti; Giangaleazzo/Galeazzo
    Visconti; Valentina Visconti, Peter II's
    wife; Valentina Visconti, duchess of
    Orleans; Yolanda/Violante Visconti
Viterbo, city, central Italy   493, 495,
    500n
Vittore Trevisan, Venetian councillor of
    Crete   125
Voghera, city, Lombardy   19
Vojihna, Serbian kaisar   510n
Volga, river, Russia   394n, 404n, 410
Voulte, de la, noble family, *see* Adhémar
    de la Voulte; Brémond de la Voulte
Vrchlický, Jaroslav, Czech writer   60, 62

Waldemar IV, king of Denmark   43,
    53-54
Wales   62
Wallachia   414
Wallachians   407, 410

INDEX

Werner of Bonn/Werner of Hasselbecke, Apostolic scriptor and secretary   497-498, 500
Werner of Hasselbecke, *see* Werner of Bonn
Westminster Abbey, London   54
Westminster, palace, London   53, 302
White Company, English mercenary company in Italy   195
White Genoese, *see* Genoese
White Sea, *see* Mediterranean
White Venetians, *see* Venetians
Wilibrand of Oldenburg, pilgrim   362n-363n
William VII Larchevêque, lord of Parthenay, commissioned *Le Roman de Mélusine ou histoire de Lusignan*   299; *see also* Coudrette (author of *Le Roman de Mélusine ou histoire de Lusignan*); *Mélusine* (myth/romance)
William of Adam, Dominican writer   142
William Conti, Dominican, papal legate   104
William of Felton, seneschal of Poitou   21, 288
William Forte, member of the High Court of Cyprus   342n
William Galioti, cantor of Paphos   52
William of Machaut, French poet and chronicler   13-15, 21-22, 33-35, 37, 43-44, 46-55, 57-58, 64, 69, 76n, 81, 182, 188, 252, 254, 257, 259, 261, 263-264, 265n, 275-281, 284, 287-288, 290, 293-294, 296-297, 298n, 300, 302, 307-311, 326, 329, 331-333, 342n, 345, 355n, 571, 573
Wilmot of Montolif, member of the regency council of Cyprus   338-339; *see also* Perot of Montolif (Wilmot's brother)
William of Nangis, French chronicler   33, 302
William of Ras, Cypriot nobleman   263
William Roger, viscount of Turenne   332
Worshipful Company of Vintners, *see* Vintners' Company

Xanthi/Eksya, city, Thrace   465n, 467, 476

Ya'qūb ibn 'Alīshīr, Germiyānid ruler   92, 462
Ya'qūb, a Jew   263n
Yahşi, lord of Karasi   100n, 462n, 464; *see also* Demirhan, lord of Karasi (Yahşi's son)
Yalak Ova, area of, northwestern Asia Minor   93n
Yalbughā al-Khāṣṣakī, *Atābak* and later emir of Sultan al-Nāṣir Ḥasan   83, 257-266
Yasawur, Mongol military commander   430
Yashijemen, battle of   427
Yazıcıoğlu Ali, Ottoman historian   389, 437
Yilan Bogha, Khwārizmian leader   427
Yolande of Aragon, wife of Robert I, king of Naples   163; *see also* Charles, duke of Calabria (Yolande's son)
Yolande-Eirene of Montferrat, second wife of Emperor Andronikos II Palaiologos   101
Yolanda/Violante Visconti, wife of Lionel, duke of Clarence   293n; *see also* Bernabò Visconti (Yolanda's uncle); Giangaleazzo Visconti (Yolanda/Violante's brother)
York, duke of   62
Yuan, Mongol dynasty in China   138

Zaccaria, Genoese family   94, 100, 113-114, 118; *see also* Benedetto II Zaccaria; Manuel Zaccaria; Martino Zaccaria
Zakarīyā Qazwīnī, Persian historian   426

Zakē (for Arabic Zakī) David   372; *see also* Thomas (Zakē's son)
Zanon Saimben, scrivener of Muslim Faith of the Mamluk sultan of Egypt   448
Zebas, family   380; *see also* Marcus Zebas
Zeno, Venetian family, *see* Carlo Zeno; Giuliano Zeno; Iacopo Zeno
Zichna/Zihna, city, Macedonia   465n, 466, 476
Zoane Rizo, 'torciman de Caffa'   447

List of Contributors

DANIELE BAGLIONI is Full Professor in Italian Linguistics at the University Ca' Foscari in Venice. His research interests lie primarily in the diffusion of the Italian language in the Medieval and Early Modern Mediterranean and in contact phenomena between Italian, Greek, Turkish, and the Semitic languages, especially as far as lexical loanwords and allographic traditions are concerned. His publications include two books, notably *La scripta italoromanza del regno di Cipro. Edizione e commento di testi di scriventi ciprioti del Quattrocento* (2006), several articles in international peer-reviewed journals, and chapters in reference books.

ALEXANDER BEIHAMMER is Heiden Family Professor of Byzantine History at the University of Notre Dame. His research focuses on Byzantine diplomacy and cross-cultural relations, in particular with the Muslim world, and the transformation of Asia Minor from Byzantine to Ottoman times. His most recent book is *Byzantium and the Emergence of Muslim-Turkish Anatolia, ca. 1040–1130* (2017).

MIKE CARR is lecturer in Late Medieval History at the University of Edinburgh. His research focuses on the history of the Mediterranean during the period 1000-1500, especially the interactions between Latin, Greek, and Islamic cultures, boundaries, merchants, and the crusades. Besides journal articles and book chapters, he has published *Merchant Crusaders in the Aegean, 1291-1352* (2015).

JOHN FRANCE is Professor Emeritus at Swansea University. His main academic interests focus on the fields of crusading and warfare. His main publications include the monographs *Hattin* (Oxford University Press, 2015), *Perilous Glory: Understanding Western Warfare (BC3000-Gulf Wars)* (Yale University Press, 2011), *The Crusades and the Expansion of Catholic Christendom 1000-1714* (Routledge, 2005), *Western Warfare in the Age of the Crusades 1000-1300* (UCL Press, 1999), and *Victory in the East: a Military History of the First Crusade* (Cambridge University Press, 1994).

PETER EDBURY is Professor Emeritus at Cardiff University. He has written widely on the history of Cyprus and the Latin East, including *The Kingdom of Cyprus and the Crusades 1191-1374* (1991; Greek translation 2003) and the critical editions of John of Ibelin's *Le Livre des Assises* (2003) and Philip of Novara's *Le Livre de Forme de Plait* (2009). Since his retirement in 2013, he, together with Massimiliano Gaggero of the Università degli Studi di Milano, has been preparing an edition of the *Chronicle of Ernoul* and the *Old French Continuation of William of Tyre*. 2015 saw the appearance of another collaborative work: Nicholas Coureas and Peter Edbury, *The Chronicle of Amadi translated from the Italian*.

CHARALAMBOS GASPARIS is Research Director at the Institute of Historical Research of the National Hellenic Research Foundation in Athens. He is a specialist in the history of Greek territories under Venetian rule during the Late Middle Ages. He has published books and articles on rural society and city life, economy and commerce in Crete and in other Venetian colonies in the Aegean. He has also edited Latin sources concerning Venetian Crete from the thirteenth to the fifteenth century, notably the *catastici* for the regions of Dorsoduro (2004) and Chanea (2008).

GILLES GRIVAUD, ancien membre de l'École française d'Athènes, est professeur d'histoire médiévale à l'Université de Rouen-Normandie/GRHis. Ses recherches portent sur le royaume de Chypre aux époques franque et vénitienne, ainsi que sur l'historiographie grecque moderne et contemporaine. Il a codirigé avec Alexandre Popovic l'ouvrage collectif *Les conversions à l'islam en Asie Mineure et dans les Balkans aux époques seldjoukide et ottomane. Bibliographie raisonnée, 1800-2000* (2011); il est l'auteur d'*Entrelacs chiprois. Essai sur les lettres et la vie intellectuelle dans le royaume de Chypre, 1191-1570* (2009) et de *Venice and the defence of the Regno di Cipro: Giulio Savorgnan's Unpublished Cyprus Correspondence, 1557-1570* (2016); et il a récemment coédité, avec Angel Nicolaou-Konnari et Chris Schabel, *Famagusta, Vol. II, History and Society* (2020)

SEBASTIAN KOLDITZ is research associate ('Akademischer Rat') at the Chair of Medieval History at the University of Heidelberg. His research interests include Byzantine-Western relations, the Ecumenical Councils, maritime history and space structures in the Mediterranean, as well as the prosopography and networks of commercial and political actors between Italy and the late Byzantium. Besides numerous journal articles, book chapters, and edited volumes, he is the author of the monograph *Johannes VIII. Palaiologos und das Konzil von Ferrara-Florenz (1438/39). Das byzantinische Kaisertum im Dialog mit dem Westen* (2013-2014).

ANGEL NICOLAOU-KONNARI is Associate Professor of the History of Hellenism under Latin Rule at the University of Cyprus. Her research interests focus on the Latin-ruled Greek world, particularly the history of Lusignan and Venetian Cyprus. Her main publications include a diplomatic edition of the *Chronicle* of Leontios Makhairas (with Michalis Pieris, 2003) and the collective volumes *Famagusta, Volume II, History and Society* (ed. with Gilles Grivaud and Chris Schabel, 2020), *Lemesos: A History of Limassol in Cyprus from Antiquity to the Ottoman Conquest* (ed. with Chris Schabel, 2015), and *Cyprus. Society and Culture 1191-1374* (ed. with Chris Schabel, 2005).

KAKIA NIKOLAOU is a Consultant Psychiatrist. She was Head of the Addictions' Department 'IANOS' at the Psychiatric Hospital of Thessaloniki from 2008 to 2021. She received her medical degree from Universität zu Köln and specialised in Psychiatry at the Psychiatric Hospital of Attica in Athens. She is also a holder of a MSc in Clinical and Public Health Aspects of Addiction from the Institute of Psychiatry, National

Addiction Centre, Maudsley Hospital, King's College, University of London (1999) and of a PhD from the Laboratory of Forensic Medicine and Toxicology, School of Medicine, Aristotle University of Thessaloniki (2017). She is trained in Systemic Family Therapy and in Motivational Interviewing and is a member of the Motivational Interviewing Network of Trainers (MINT) and member of the MINT Trainer Certification Raters' Group.

MICHALIS OLYMPIOS is Associate Professor in the History of Western Art at the University of Cyprus. His research interests revolve around the study of medieval art and architecture in Europe and the Latin East. He has published widely on Gothic architecture and sculpture in Northern France, Lusignan/Venetian Cyprus, and other places in the late medieval and early modern Eastern Mediterranean. He is the co-founder and current co-editor (with Chris Schabel) of *Frankokratia: A Journal for the Study of Greek Lands under Latin Rule* (published by Brill since 2020).

CLÉMENT ONIMUS is Maître de Conference for the history of the Arab world at Université Paris 8 (Vincennes-Saint Denis). His research focuses on the political and social history of the medieval Near East as well as on historiography and writing in the Middle Ages, especially in the Mamluk period. Apart from journal articles, he has published a monograph entitled *Les maîtres du jeu. Pouvoir et violence politique à l'aube du sultanat mamlouk circassien (784-815/1382-1412)* (2019).

JOHANNES PAHLITZSCH is Professor of Byzantine Studies at the Johannes Gutenberg-Universität Mainz, Germany. He wrote a monograph on the history of the Greek Orthodox Patriarchate of Jerusalem in the crusader period, is co-editor of *Christian-Muslim Relations. A Historical Bibliography (600-1500)*, and edited the Arabic translation of the Byzantine law book *Procheiros Nomos*. He is the author of numerous articles on the situation of Oriental Christians under Muslim rule in the Middle Ages and the relations between Byzantium and the Islamic world. He is member of the board of the Leibniz Science Campus Mainz 'Byzantium between Orient and Occident'.

JOHANNES PREISER-KAPELLER is Senior Research Associate at the Institute of Medieval Research, Division of Byzantine Research, at the Austrian Academy of Sciences and team leader of the research group 'Byzantium and Beyond'. His research interests include Byzantium and the medieval world, social and spatial network analysis, environmental and climate history, and the socioeconomic, ecclesiastical, and diplomatic history of Byzantium as well as the relations between Byzantium and the Caucasus. His most recent monograph is *Die erste Ernte und der große Hunger. Klima, Pandemien und der Wandel der Alten Welt bis 500 n. Chr.* (2021).

MIRIAM RACHEL SALZMANN is Academic Assistant at the Chair of Byzantine History at Johannes Gutenberg University Mainz. Her research focuses on cultural contacts between Late Byzantium and the Latin world, the social and cultural history of medieval Cyprus, and late medieval translations. She has recently published her dissertation under the title *Negotiating Power and Identities. Latin, Greek and Syrian Élites in Fifteenth-Century Cyprus* (2021) and is currently working on a fifteenth-century Venetian translation of the Doukas chronicle.

CHRIS SCHABEL is Professor of Medieval History at the University of Cyprus. Co-editor of *Frankokratia* (with Michalis Olympios), his recent publications include *Pierre Ceffons et le déterminisme radical au temps de la peste noire* (Paris 2019), the co-edited volumes (with Monica Brînzei) *The Cistercian James of Eltville* and *Philosophical Psychology in Late-Medieval Commentaries on Peter Lombard's Sentences* (Brepols 2018 and 2020), and the co-authored volumes (with William Duba) *Bullarium Hellenicum* and *Principia on the Sentences: The Rise of a New Genre of Scholastic Debate* (Brepols 2015 and forthcoming).

ROMAIN THURIN is PhD candidate at the Medieval Institute of the University of Notre Dame. His research interests focus on the political and social history of the Islamic World in the later Middle Ages, especially the history of Anatolia under the Seljuks, Mongols, and the bezliks as well as Central and Inner Asian pastoral nomads. His most recent publication is 'China and the Two Romes. The 1081 and 1091 "Fulin" Embassies to the Song Empire', *Journal of the Economic and Social History of the Orient*, 64 (2021), 55–92.

ALEXIS TORRANCE is Archbishop Demetrios Associate Professor of Byzantine Theology at the University of Notre Dame. His research interests include Greek Patristic, Byzantine, and Orthodox Theology, in particular Christology, ascetic thought, and theological anthropology. His numerous publications include the two monographs *Repentance in Late Antiquity: Eastern Asceticism and the Framing of the Christian Life, ca. 400–650* (2013) and *Human Perfection in Byzantine Theology: Attaining the Fullness of Christ* (2020).

CHARLES YOST is Assistant Professor of Medieval History at Hillsdale College. His research interests focus on Medieval and Byzantine intellectual and religious history and, in particular, on the relations between the Churches of Rome and Constantinople and Byzantine unionists and anti-unionists. One of his recent publications is 'Neither Greek nor Latin, but "Catholic": Aspects of the Theology of Union of John Plousiadenos', *Journal of Orthodox Christian Studies*, 1 (2018), 43–59.